To our wives, Tina, Debbie,
and Suzie, children, Kary, Katy, Kelly, Christa, Kimberly,
Jack, and Meg, and grandchildren, Rachel and Jack,
for their supportive entrepreneurial spirit

ABOUT THE AUTHORS

ROBERT D. HISRICH

Robert D. Hisrich is the Garvin Professor of Global Entrepreneurship and Director for the Center for Global Entrepreneurship at Thunderbird. He holds an MBA and a doctorate from the University of Cincinnati.

Professor Hisrich's research pursuits are focused on entrepreneurship and venture creation: entrepreneurial ethics, intrapreneurship, women and minority entrepreneurs, venture financing, and global venture creation. He teaches courses and seminars in these areas, as well as in marketing management and product planning and development. His interest in global management and entrepreneurship resulted in two Fulbright Fellowships in Budapest, Hungary, honorary degrees from universities in Russia and Hungary, and being a visiting faculty member in universities in Austria, Australia, Ireland, and Slovenia. Professor Hisrich serves on the editorial boards of several prominent journals in entrepreneurial scholarship, is on several boards of directors, and is author or coauthor of over 250 research articles appearing in such journals as *Journal of Marketing, Journal of Marketing Research, Journal of Business Venturing, Journal of Small Business Finance, Small Business Economics, Journal of Developmental Entrepreneurship,* and *Entrepreneurship Theory and Practice.* Professor Hisrich has authored or coauthored 13 books, including *Marketing: A Practical Management Approach* and the recently published *How to Fix and Prevent the 13 Biggest Problems That Derail Business.*

MICHAEL P. PETERS

Michael P. Peters is Professor Emeritus of the Marketing Department at the Carroll School of Management, Boston College. He has his PhD from the University of Massachusetts, Amherst, and his MBA and BS from Northeastern University. Recently retired from full-time teaching, Professor Peters has been a visiting professor at the American College of Greece in Athens, Greece, where he has been developing an entrepreneurship and business planning component in its new MBA program. In addition he continues to write, lecture, serve on numerous boards, and assist in the management of a family business. Besides his passion for assisting entrepreneurs in new ventures he has consulted and conducted seminars and workshops worldwide related to entrepreneurship, international and domestic decision making for new product development, market planning, and marketing strategy. He has published over 30 articles in such journals as the *Journal of Business Research, Journal of Marketing, Journal of Marketing Research, Journal of International Business Studies, Columbia Journal of World Business, Journal of Business Venturing,* and the *Sloan Management Review.* Professor Peters has coauthored three texts: *Marketing a New Product: Its Planning, Development and Control, Marketing Decisions for New and Mature Products,* and *Entrepreneurship,* now in its seventh edition. He was Department Chair and Director of the Small Business Institute at Boston College for more than 16 years. He loves photography, tennis, golf, and kayaking on Cape Cod Bay.

ENTREPRENEURSHIP

SEVENTH EDITION

ROBERT D. HISRICH, PH.D.

Garvin Professor of Global Entrepreneurship
Director, Center for Global Entrepreneurship
Thunderbird

MICHAEL P. PETERS, PH.D.

Professor Emeritus
Carroll School of Management
Boston College

DEAN A. SHEPHERD, PH.D.

Research Fellow and Associate Professor
Kelley School of Business
Indiana University

Boston Burr Ridge, IL Dubuque, IA Madison, WI New York San Francisco St. Louis
Bangkok Bogotá Caracas Kuala Lumpur Lisbon London Madrid Mexico City
Milan Montreal New Delhi Santiago Seoul Singapore Sydney Taipei Toronto

The McGraw-Hill Companies

ENTREPRENEURSHIP
International Edition 2008

10 09 08 07 06 05 04
20 09 08
CTF ANL

When ordering this title, use ISBN: 978-007-125952-1 or MHID: 007-125952-X

Printed in Singapore

www.mhhe.com

DEAN A. SHEPHERD

Dean A. Shepherd is the Dean's Research Fellow and Associate Professor of Entrepreneurship and Strategy at the Kelley School of Business, Indiana University. Dean received his doctorate and MBA from Bond University (Australia) and a Bachelor of Applied Science from the Royal Melbourne Institute of Technology. His research interests include the decision making of entrepreneurs, new venture strategy, venture capital, growth, and opportunity. Dean is also an associate editor for the *Journal of Business Venturing* and on the review board for numerous entrepreneurship and management journals.

PREFACE

Starting and operating a new business involves considerable risk and effort to overcome the inertia against creating something new. In creating and growing a new venture, the entrepreneur assumes the responsibility and risks for its development and survival and enjoys the corresponding rewards. The fact that consumers, businesspeople, and government officials are interested in entrepreneurship is evident from the increasing research on the subject, the large number of college courses and seminars on the topic, the more than two million new enterprises started each year (despite a 70 percent failure rate), the significant coverage and focus by the media, and the realization that this is an important topic for industrialized, developing, and once-controlled economies.

Who is the focus of all this attention—who is willing to accept all the risks and put forth the effort necessary to create a new venture? It may be a man or a woman, someone from an upper-class or lower-class background, a technologist or someone lacking technologic sophistication, a college graduate or a high school dropout. The person may be an inventor, manager, nurse, salesperson, engineer, student, teacher, homemaker, or retiree. It is someone able to juggle work, family, and civic responsibilities while meeting payroll.

To provide an understanding of this person and the process of creating and growing a new venture, this seventh edition of *Entrepreneurship* is divided into four major sections.

Part 1—The Entrepreneurial Perspective introduces the entrepreneur and the entrepreneurial process from both a historical and a research perspective. The role and nature of entrepreneurship as a mechanism for creating new ventures and affecting economic development are presented, along with career aspects and the future direction of entrepreneurship. The characteristics and background of entrepreneurs are discussed, as well as some methods for individual self-assessment and various aspects of international entrepreneurship.

Part 2—Creating and Starting the Venture focuses on all the elements in the entrepreneurial process that are a part of creating a new venture. After a discussion of creativity and obtaining the right business area, the legal issues—such as intellectual property protection and product safety and liability—are addressed. Important aspects of the business plan are then presented, with a chapter being devoted to each of the major components of the business plan: the marketing plan, the organizational plan, and the financial plan.

Part 3—Financing the New Venture focuses on one of the most difficult aspects of creating and establishing a new venture. After a discussion of the alternative sources of capital, specific attention is given to three primary financing mechanisms: informal risk capital, venture capital, and going public.

Part 4—Managing, Growing, and Ending the New Venture presents material related to establishing, developing, and ending the venture. Particular attention is paid to developing an entrepreneurial strategy, establishing strategies for growth, managing the new venture during growth, early operations, expansion, and accessing external resources for growth. Managerial skills that are important to the successful performance and growth of a new venture are included in this section. This part also addresses going global—selecting and entering a market outside the company's national boundaries—as well as methods for ending the venture. Specific topics examined include mergers and acquisitions, franchising, joint ventures, and human and financial resources needed for growth.

To make *Entrepreneurship* as meaningful as possible, each chapter begins with a profile of an entrepreneur whose career is especially relevant to the chapter material. Chapter objectives follow, and numerous examples occur throughout. Important Web sites to assist the reader in getting started, as well as articles from *Entrepreneur* magazine and Ethics boxes, are also included in this seventh edition. Each chapter concludes with research tasks, class discussion questions, and selected readings for further information.

Many people—students, business executives, entrepreneurs, professors, and publishing staff—have made this book possible. Of great assistance were the detailed and thoughtful comments of our reviewers: Kenneth M. Becker (University of Vermont), Karen Bishop (University of Louisville), Joseph Coombs (University of Richmond), Teresa A. Daniel (Kaplan University), Mike Ewald (North Central University), Lyle L. Holscher (Alexandria Technical College), Susan Losapio (Southern New Hampshire University), Pedro David Perez (Cornell University), Richard L. Smith (Iowa State University), Ethne Swartz (Fairleigh Dickinson University), and Mary D. Torma (Lorain County Community College). Particular thanks go to Nick Papantonis for help and ideas in Chapter 7, "The Business Plan"; to Bill Wetzel and Lynn Moore for helpful comments on Chapter 12, "Informal Risk Capital, Venture Capital, and Going Public"; and to Greg Stoller for reviewing specific chapter material. Special thanks are given to Carol Pacelli for preparing the manuscript so competently and to Lakesh Dasari and Julie Lutz for providing research material, editorial assistance, and case development for this edition. Also thanks to our editors—Allison Belda, editorial coordinator, and Ryan Blankenship, sponsoring editor—for their guidance and demanding writing schedule, and to our supplement providers—Susan D. Peters (California State University—Pomona), for her wonderful work on the Instructor's Manual, and Sun Tech Data Systems, for its work on the Test Bank and PowerPoint slides.

We are deeply indebted to our spouses, Tina, Debbie, and Suzie, whose support and understanding helped bring this effort to fruition. It is to future entrepreneurs—our children Kary, Katy, Kelly, Christa, Kimberly, Jack, and Meg and grandchildren Rachel and Jack—and the generation they represent—that this book is particularly dedicated. May you always beg forgiveness rather than ask permission.

Robert D. Hisrich
Michael P. Peters
Dean A. Shepherd

CONTENTS IN BRIEF

CONTENTS

1

THE ENTREPRENEURIAL PERSPECTIVE

1

THE NATURE AND IMPORTANCE OF ENTREPRENEURSHIP

LEARNING OBJECTIVES

1
To introduce the concept of entrepreneurship and its historical development.

2
To explain the entrepreneurial process.

3
To identify the basic types of start-up ventures.

4
To explain the role of entrepreneurship in economic development.

5
To discuss ethics and entrepreneurship.

OPENING PROFILE

OPRAH WINFREY

Born in Kosciusko, Mississippi, in 1954, Oprah Winfrey spent her early years in a house without electricity and running water. Education and books helped Oprah to realize that this was not all that there was in life. As a result of her hard work and dedication, at the age of 19, while still in high school, she landed her first broadcasting job as a reporter for radio station WVOL in Nashville and simultaneously enrolled in Tennessee State University to study speech and performing arts. During her sophomore year oprah became the first African American anchor at Nashville's WTVF-TV. In 1977 she moved to Baltimore to coanchor the six o'clock news, where she was also recruited to cohost Baltimore's local talk show *People Are Talking*. In 1984 Oprah relocated to Chicago to host WLS-TV's half-hour morning talk show, *AM Chicago*. The new show ran opposite Phil Donahue's show, which had been the dominant TV talk show in Chicago for more than a decade. Within a month, Oprah was beating Donahue in ratings, and in less than a year, the show expanded to one hour and was renamed *The Oprah Winfrey Show*. This was the beginning of Oprah's career and the foundation for her future success as an entrepreneur and a businesswoman.

www.oprah.com

In 1984, already a very successful talk show host, Oprah met with Jeff Jacobs, looking for help with a new contract. Jeff, at that time a known entertainment lawyer, convinced Oprah to establish her own company instead of being simply a talk show host hired by someone else. As a result, Harpo, Inc., was established in 1986, with Jeff Jacobs eventually joining as president. Oprah and Jeff, although not agreeing on everything, were able to create an effective alliance in which Oprah's creativity and intuition were well complemented by Jeff's business acumen and ability to effectively navigate through the ambiguities of the entertainment industry, particularly on the issues of intellectual property. Harpo, Inc., enjoyed substantial savings on agents and managers, especially during the first years of the company's operation.

Early in the company's existence, Harpo, Inc., operated as a true entrepreneurial venture with no formal structure and a hectic, high-pressured work environment. As the company grew and the show became more and more popular, Oprah realized that she needed help building the true corporate foundation for her company. She hired her former boss, a TV station executive, as chief operating officer (COO) to build corporate departments—accounting, legal, and human resources—and to make Harpo, Inc., run like a true corporation. Even with the rapid growth of her company, Oprah did not change her approach to dealing with employees and business partners. Her choice of people to work with was based on only one criterion: trust.

The Oprah show became the core of the business, contributing a large share of revenue each year. In 2001 nearly $300 million of Harpo's revenue came from the show. It airs in 107 countries and has held a No.1 position in U.S. daytime talk shows for 16 years, despite at least 50 other rivals. However, Oprah did not stop there. During the first years of the company's existence Oprah entered into two alliances—with TV syndicator King World to distribute her show and with ABC to air her TV movies. In the past few years she has made a few more deals. In November 1998, Oprah invested in Oxygen Media LLC, which was controlled by Geraldine Laybourne and Carsey-Werner-Mandabach (CWM LLC). Oxygen Media LLC includes a women's cable network for which Oprah produces and stars in the show called *Use Your Life*. The Harpo, Inc., movie division produces films like *Tuesdays with Morrie* and contributes about $4 million a year in revenue.

In 2000 Oprah launched *O, The Oprah Magazine,* which serves as a personal growth guide in the new century. It is credited as being the most successful start-up magazine in the industry. One year after its launch it reached a paid circulation of 2.5 million and earned $140 million in revenue. This is an incredible achievement, given that successful magazines usually take five years to turn a profit. Oprah also created a motivational "Live Your Best Life" tour that was attended by 8,500 women in four cities. With all her success and despite the many requests, Oprah is reluctant to license her name because she is not only the chief content creator but also the chief content itself. This is probably the most unique aspect of all Oprah's businesses: She is able to successfully leverage herself into various entertainment categories.

Today Oprah is an owner and the chair of Harpo, Inc.; Harpo Productions; Harpo Studios, Inc.; Harpo Films, Inc.; Harpo Print LLC; and Harpo Video, Inc., with a total net worth of over $1 billion. The organization has grown to include 221 people, of whom 68 percent are women, and has a modest turnover of 10 to 15 percent. In 2002, the first international edition of *O, The Oprah Magazine* was launched in South Africa. *The Oprah Winfrey Show* continues to impress the industry with an average of 7.2 million viewers per episode, beating the second-ranked show by 35 percent. Jeff Jacobs, the president of Harpo, Inc., has 10 percent of the ownership of that company, with Oprah still holding 90 percent. At this time, she is not willing to go public with any of her ventures.

Having come from poverty, Oprah is one of the largest philanthropists of our time. She donates at least 10 percent of her annual income to charity, most of it anonymously. Oprah's main focus is on women, children, and education. She established an Oprah Winfrey foundation and a Scholars Program that provides grants toward education for women, children, and families, as well as scholarships for students in the United States and abroad who plan to use their education to give something back to their communities. Oprah's commitments extended to her initiation of the National Child Protection Act in 1991 by testifying before the U.S. Senate Judiciary Committee to establish a national database of convicted child abusers. As a result, in 1993 President Clinton signed the national "Oprah Bill." In 1997, Oprah created Oprah's Angel Network, a campaign encouraging people to help others in need, which has already raised $12 million from viewer donations, sponsors, and celebrity contributions. The funds are used to grant scholarships and to build homes and schools in developing countries. As a result of Oprah's contributions to television, social awareness, education, film, and music, in 1998 she was named one of the 100 most influential people of the 20th century by Time magazine.

Although Oprah readily admits that she cannot read a balance sheet and doesn't think of herself as a businesswoman, in fact she is. While she might not know all the business terminology and nuances, she has a true entrepreneurial spirit that helps her focus on her vision and gives her the energy to continue coming up with new creative ideas. As a true entrepreneurial woman, she was able to clearly identify her areas of weakness and create an executive team capable of successfully running the media and entertainment giant that she created. This is what often distinguishes a great from a good entrepreneur—the ability to spot an idea with the right emotional and strategic fit and to identify the resources necessary to take advantage of the opportunity.

The saga of Oprah Winfrey reflects the story of many entrepreneurs in a variety of industries and various-sized companies. The historical aspect of entrepreneurship, as well as the decision that Oprah Winfrey and others have made to become entrepreneurs, is reflected in the following remarks of two successful entrepreneurs:

> Being an entrepreneur and creating a new business venture is analogous to raising children—it takes more time and effort than you ever imagine and it is extremely difficult and painful to get out of the situation. Thank goodness you cannot easily divorce yourself from either situation.
>
> When people ask me if I like being in business, I usually respond: On days when there are more sales than problems, I love it; on days when there are more problems than sales, I wonder why I do it. Basically, I am in business because it gives me a good feeling about myself. You learn a lot about your capabilities by putting yourself on the line. Running a successful business is not only a financial risk, it is an emotional risk as well. I get a lot of satisfaction from having dared it—done it—and been successful.

Do the above quotes and the profile of Oprah Winfrey fit your perception of the career of an entrepreneur? Entrepreneurship is an exciting field of study. Research indicates that individuals who study entrepreneurship are three to four times more likely to start their own business, and that they will earn 20 to 30 percent more than students studying in other fields. To understand the field better, it is important to learn about the nature and development of entrepreneurship, the entrepreneurial process, and the role of entrepreneurship in the economic development of a country.

NATURE AND DEVELOPMENT OF ENTREPRENEURSHIP

Who is an entrepreneur? What is entrepreneurship? What is an entrepreneurial process? These frequently asked questions reflect the increased national and international interest in entrepreneurs by individuals, university professors and students, and government officials.

entrepreneur Individual who takes risks and starts something new

In spite of all this interest, a concise, universally accepted definition has not yet emerged. The development of the theory of entrepreneurship parallels to a great extent the development of the term itself. The word *entrepreneur* is French and, literally translated, means "between-taker" or "go-between."

Earliest Period

An example of the earliest definition of an entrepreneur as a go-between is Marco Polo, who attempted to establish trade routes to the Far East. As a go-between, Marco Polo would sign a contract with a money person (forerunner of today's venture capitalist) to sell his goods. A common contract during this time provided a loan to the merchant–adventurer at a 22.5 percent rate, including insurance. While the capitalist was a passive risk bearer, the merchant–adventurer took the active role in trading, bearing all the physical and emotional risks. When the merchant–adventurer successfully sold the goods and completed the trip, the profits were divided, with the capitalist taking most of them (up to 75 percent), and the merchant–adventurer settling for the remaining 25 percent.

Middle Ages

In the Middle Ages, the term *entrepreneur* was used to describe both an actor and a person who managed large production projects. In such large production projects, this individual did not take any risks, but merely managed the project using the resources provided, usually by the government of the country. A typical entrepreneur in the Middle Ages was the cleric—the person in charge of great architectural works, such as castles and fortifications, public buildings, abbeys, and cathedrals.

17th Century

The reemergent connection of risk with entrepreneurship developed in the 17th century, with an entrepreneur being a person who entered into a contractual arrangement with the government to perform a service or to supply stipulated products. Since the contract price was fixed, any resulting profits or losses were the entrepreneur's. One entrepreneur in this period was John Law, a Frenchman, who was allowed to establish a royal bank. The bank eventually evolved into an exclusive franchise to form a trading company in the New World—the Mississippi Company. Unfortunately, this monopoly on French trade led to Law's downfall when he attempted to push the company's stock price higher than the value of its assets, leading to the collapse of the company.

Richard Cantillon, a noted economist and author in the 1700s, understood Law's mistake. Cantillon developed one of the early theories of the entrepreneur and is regarded by some as the founder of the term. He viewed the entrepreneur as a risk taker, observing that merchants, farmers, craftsmen, and other sole proprietors "buy at a certain price and sell at an uncertain price, therefore operating at a risk."[1]

18th Century

In the 18th century, the person with capital was differentiated from the one who needed capital. In other words, the entrepreneur was distinguished from the capital provider (the present-day venture capitalist). One reason for this differentiation was the industrialization occurring throughout the world. Many of the inventions developed during this time were reactions to the changing world, as was the case with the inventions of Eli Whitney and Thomas Edison. Both Whitney and Edison were developing new technologies and were unable to finance their inventions themselves. Whereas Whitney financed his cotton gin with expropriated British crown property, Edison raised capital from private sources to develop and experiment in the fields of electricity and chemistry. Both Edison and Whitney were capital users (entrepreneurs), not providers (venture capitalists). A venture capitalist is a professional money manager who makes risk investments from a pool of equity capital to obtain a high rate of return on the investments.

19th and 20th Centuries

In the late 19th and early 20th centuries, entrepreneurs were frequently not distinguished from managers and were viewed mostly from an economic perspective:

> Briefly stated, the entrepreneur organizes and operates an enterprise for personal gain. He pays current prices for the materials consumed in the business, for the use of the land, for the personal services he employs, and for the capital he requires. He contributes his own initiative, skill, and ingenuity in planning, organizing, and administering the enterprise. He also assumes the chance of loss and gain consequent to unforeseen and uncontrollable circumstances. The net residue of the annual receipts of the enterprise after all costs have been paid, he retains for himself.[2]

Andrew Carnegie is one of the best examples of this definition. Carnegie invented nothing, but rather adapted and developed new technology in the creation of products to achieve economic vitality. Carnegie, who descended from a poor Scottish family, made the American steel industry one of the wonders of the industrial world, primarily through his unremitting competitiveness rather than his inventiveness or creativity.

entrepreneur as an innovator An individual developing something unique

In the middle of the 20th century, the notion of an *entrepreneur as an innovator* was established:

> The function of the entrepreneur is to reform or revolutionize the pattern of production by exploiting an invention or, more generally, an untried technological method of producing a new commodity or producing an old one in a new way, opening a new source of supply of materials or a new outlet for products, by organizing a new industry.[3]

The concept of innovation and newness is an integral part of entrepreneurship in this definition. Indeed, innovation, the act of introducing something new, is one of the most difficult tasks for the entrepreneur. It takes not only the ability to create and conceptualize but also the ability to understand all the forces at work in the environment. The newness can consist of anything from a new product to a new distribution system to a method for developing a new organizational structure. Edward Harriman, who reorganized the Ontario and Southern railroad through the Northern Pacific Trust, and John Pierpont Morgan, who developed his large banking house by reorganizing and financing the nation's industries, are examples of entrepreneurs fitting this definition. These organizational innovations are frequently as difficult to develop successfully as the more traditional technological innovations (transistors, computers, lasers) that are usually associated with being an entrepreneur.

This ability to innovate can be observed throughout history, from the Egyptians who designed and built great pyramids out of stone blocks weighing many tons each, to the Apollo lunar module, to laser surgery, to wireless communication. Although the tools have changed with advances in science and technology, the ability to innovate has been present in every civilization.

DEFINITION OF ENTREPRENEUR TODAY

The concept of an entrepreneur is further refined when principles and terms from a business, managerial, and personal perspective are considered. In particular, the concept of entrepreneurship from a personal perspective has been thoroughly explored in this century. This exploration is reflected in the following three definitions of an entrepreneur:

> In almost all of the definitions of entrepreneurship, there is agreement that we are talking about a kind of behavior that includes: (1) initiative taking, (2) the organizing and reorganizing of social and economic mechanisms to turn resources and situations to practical account, (3) the acceptance of risk or failure.[4]
>
> To an economist, an entrepreneur is one who brings resources, labor, materials, and other assets into combinations that make their value greater than before, and also one who introduces changes, innovations, and a new order. To a psychologist, such a person is typically driven by certain forces—the need to obtain or attain something, to experiment, to accomplish, or perhaps to escape the authority of others. To one businessman, an entrepreneur appears as a threat, an aggressive competitor, whereas to another businessman the same entrepreneur may be an ally, a source of supply, a customer, or someone who creates wealth for others, as well as finds better ways to utilize resources, reduce waste, and produce jobs others are glad to get.[5]
>
> Entrepreneurship is the dynamic process of creating incremental wealth. The wealth is created by individuals who assume the major risks in terms of equity, time, and/or career commitment or provide value for some product or service. The product or service may or may not be new or unique, but value must somehow be infused by the entrepreneur by receiving and locating the necessary skills and resources.[6]

Although each of these definitions views the entrepreneur from a slightly different perspective, they all contain similar notions, such as newness, organizing, creating, wealth, and risk taking. Yet each definition is somewhat restrictive, since entrepreneurs are found in all professions—education, medicine, research, law, architecture, engineering, social work, distribution, and the government. To include all types of entrepreneurial behavior, the following definition of entrepreneurship will be the foundation of this book:

entrepreneurship Process of creating something new and assuming the risks and rewards

> *Entrepreneurship* is the process of creating something new with value by devoting the necessary time and effort, assuming the accompanying financial, psychic, and social risks, and receiving the resulting rewards of monetary and personal satisfaction and independence.[7]

This definition stresses four basic aspects of being an entrepreneur. First, entrepreneurship involves the creation process—creating something new of value. The creation has to have value to the entrepreneur and value to the audience for which it is developed. This audience can be (1) the market of organizational buyers for business innovation, (2) the hospital's administration for a new admitting procedure and software, (3) prospective students for a new course or even college of entrepreneurship, or (4) the constituency for a new service provided by a nonprofit agency. Second, entrepreneurship requires the devotion of the necessary time and effort. Only those going through the entrepreneurial process appreciate the significant amount of time and effort it takes to create something new and make it operational. As one new entrepreneur so succinctly stated, "While I may have worked as many hours in the office while I was in industry, as an entrepreneur I never stopped thinking about the business."

The third part of the definition involves the rewards of being an entrepreneur. The most important of these rewards is independence, followed by personal satisfaction. For profit entrepreneurs, the monetary reward also comes into play. For some profit entrepreneurs, money becomes the indicator of the degree of success achieved. Assuming the necessary risks is the final aspect of entrepreneurship. Because action takes place over time, and the future is unknowable, action is inherently uncertain.[8] This uncertainty is further enhanced by the novelty intrinsic to entrepreneurial actions, such as the creation of new products, new services, new ventures, and so on.[9] Entrepreneurs must decide to act even in the face of uncertainty over the outcome of that action. Therefore, *entrepreneurs* respond to, and create, change through their entrepreneurial actions, where *entrepreneurial action* refers to behavior in response to a judgmental decision under uncertainty about a possible opportunity for profit.[10] We now offer a process perspective of entrepreneurial action.

entrepreneurial action Refers to behavior in response to a judgmental decision under uncertainty about a possible opportunity for profit

ENTREPRENEURS VERSUS INVENTORS

inventor An individual who creates something new

There is a great deal of confusion about the nature of an entrepreneur versus an inventor. An *inventor,* an individual who creates something for the first time, is a highly driven individual motivated by his or her own work and personal ideas. Besides being highly creative, an inventor tends to be well educated, with college or, most often, postgraduate degrees; has family, education, and occupational experiences that contribute to creative development and free thinking; is a problem solver able to reduce complex problems to simple ones; has a very high level of self-confidence; is willing to take risks; and has the ability to tolerate ambiguity and uncertainty.[11] A typical inventor places a high premium on being an achiever and measures achievement by the number of inventions developed and the number of patents granted. An inventor is not likely to view monetary benefits as a measure of success.

As indicated in this profile, an inventor differs considerably from an entrepreneur. Whereas an entrepreneur falls in love with the organization (the new venture) and will do almost anything to ensure its survival and growth, an inventor falls in love with the invention and will only reluctantly modify the invention to make it more commercially feasible. The development of a new venture based on an inventor's work often requires the expertise of an entrepreneur and a team approach, as many inventors are unable to focus on just one invention long enough to commercialize it. Inventors really enjoy the process of inventing, not implementing.

THE ENTREPRENEURIAL PROCESS

entrepreneurial process The process of pursuing a new venture, whether it be new products into existing markets, existing products into new markets, and/or the creation of a new organization[12]

The process of pursuing a new venture is embodied in the *entrepreneurial process,* which involves more than just problem solving in a typical management position.[13] An entrepreneur must find, evaluate, and develop an opportunity by overcoming the forces that resist the creation of something new. The process has four distinct phases: (1) identification and evaluation of the opportunity, (2) development of the business plan, (3) determination of the required resources, and (4) management of the resulting enterprise (see Table 1.1). Although these phases proceed progressively, no one stage is dealt with in isolation or is totally completed before work on other phases occurs. For example, to successfully identify and evaluate an opportunity (phase 1), an entrepreneur must have in mind the type of business desired (phase 4).

Identify and Evaluate the Opportunity

opportunity identification The process by which an entrepreneur comes up with the opportunity for a new venture

Opportunity identification and evaluation is a very difficult task. Most good business opportunities do not suddenly appear, but rather result from an entrepreneur's alertness to possibilities or, in some cases, the establishment of mechanisms that identify potential opportunities. For example, one entrepreneur asks at every cocktail party whether anyone is using a product that does not adequately fulfill its intended purpose. This person is constantly looking for a need and an opportunity to create a better product. Another

AS SEEN IN *ENTREPRENEUR* MAGAZINE

CHANGES IN THE ENVIRONMENT

This year promises to be a big one for anniversaries . . . spelling challenges and opportunities for entrepreneurs:

1. *DVD becomes ubiquitous:* DVD players crossed a threshold in 2002: They're now in 33 percent of U.S. homes. That's caused several movie studios to stop distributing films on VHS tape. But most DVD players lack VHS' prime benefit: recording. DVD recordables are still $800-plus products, says Tara Dunion, director of the Consumer Electronics Association. That means there's a short-term opportunity providing a service to convert treasured tapes to DVD format (think wedding and baby videos). Whenever a new device gains a wide following, says Dunion, an aftermarket is sure to follow. That can mean everything from DVD carrying cases (say, one with a licensed SpongeBob Squarepants design on the cover for the kids' minivan movies) to cigarette-lighter chargers for portable DVD players. Already run a video store? Time to accelerate your DVD transition, and think about renting DVD players to accommodate VHS clients who desire DVD-only releases.
2. *HIPAA regulations take effect:* On April 14, 2003, the federal government institutes new health care privacy regulations based on the Health Insurance Portability and Accountability Act of 1996 (HIPAA). Entrepreneurial firms such as NaviMedix Inc. will profit from the deadline. NaviMedix provides a Web-based repository of medical offices' information. In addition to making it possible to check patients' eligibility under their health plans, the company also acts as a vault for records, customizing features to adhere to the privacy procedures of individual medical practices. There's non-tech opportunity as well. "A lot of offices are still fairly paper-based," says Lynne Dunbrack, NaviMedix's director of HIPAA compliance. That means each practice's "gatekeeper" needs training in what information can be given to whom, and procedures such as verifying identities when accessing paper files. The same training will go on at insurance companies and their

TABLE 1.1 Aspects of the Entrepreneurial Process

Identify and Evaluate the Opportunity	Develop Business Plan	Resources Required	Manage the Enterprise
• Opportunity assessment • Creation and length of opportunity • Real and perceived value of opportunity • Risk and returns of opportunity • Opportunity versus personal skills and goals • Competitive environment	• Title page • Table of Contents • Executive Summary • Major Section 1. Description of Business 2. Description of Industry 3. Technology Plan 4. Marketing Plan 5. Financial Plan 6. Production Plan 7. Organization Plan 8. Operational Plan 9. Summary • Appendixes (Exhibits)	• Determine resources needed • Determine existing resources • Identify resource gaps and available suppliers • Develop access to needed resources	• Develop management style • Understand key variables for success • Identify problems and potential problems • Implement control systems • Develop growth strategy

partners, including software providers like NaviMedix itself. But doctors' offices are a golden opportunity because turnover is high, and regulations require existing staff to take refresher courses.

3. *Video-on-demand becomes reality:* Video-on-demand has been heralded as the next big thing for more than a decade. This time it's for real. Really. By midyear 2003 cable companies will be running large-scale trials. Still dubious? "The industry itself was skeptical," says Steve Fredrick of Novak Biddle Venture Partners. "There were a lot of things that needed to come together, but by all measures, we've met critical mass." (Translation: The cable companies have spent so much money that it has to succeed.) Other than the cable, says Fredrick, almost every component in the video food chain is wide open. Among the areas ripe for activity: technologies to distribute multiple video streams over digital cable, new content providers, and new advertising models. One reason for optimism is the rocket-like takeoff of video recorders like TiVo. "Video-on-demand deploys that functionality, but the hardware is in the network," says Fredrick. "It will do for video and movies what the Web did for static text."
4. *Fuel-cell technology takes off:* The media have fawned over fuel cells for years, but usually for cars. (Fuel cells convert fuel to electricity with minimal pollution.) But the initial consumer application of the technology may come in a smaller format: handheld computers. MTI MicroFuel Cells Inc. of Albany, New York, completed three technology prototypes last year. This year, the company is launching product prototypes with an eye toward a 2004 rollout. Competitors are trying to beat it to the punch.
5. *Fuel cells outlast lithium ion batteries, today's portable power champ:* "Electronics are going to a 24/7 mode of operation," says Bill Acker, MicroFuel's president and CEO. Fuel cell PDAs and mobile phones won't conk out before your day ends. The extra juice is also enabling such combinations as digital cameras that link to mobile phones. Applying fuel cells to other devices will also open new opportunities. Think of wireless speakers. Rather than substituting a dangling power cord for dangling speaker wire, build a fuel cell and wireless connection into the speakers—and, suddenly, they can be anywhere in a living room.

ADVICE TO AN ENTREPRENEUR

1. What is it about these "anniversaries" that provides entrepreneurs opportunities?
2. Which "anniversary" above do you believe provides the greatest opportunity for you to form a management team and enter the industry?
3. Does an analysis of trends like this provide ideas about possible entrepreneurial opportunities or is it like trying to drive a car by looking in the rearview mirror?
4. What advice would you give an entrepreneur who says, "I want to create a company and enter the fuel cell industry not because I think there is a lot of money to be made there, but I want to do some good, I want to help the environment"?

Source: Reprinted with permission of Entrepreneur Media, Inc., "Remember When: These Are the Milestones You'll Remember 2003 By. Hope You Take Advantage," by Chris Sundlund, January 2003, *Entrepreneur* magazine: www.entrepreneur.com.

entrepreneur always monitors the play habits and toys of her nieces and nephews. This is her way of looking for any unique toy product niche for a new venture.

Although most entrepreneurs do not have formal mechanisms for identifying business opportunities, some sources are often fruitful: consumers and business associates, members of the distribution system, and technical people. Often, consumers are the best source of ideas for a new venture. How many times have you heard someone comment, "If only there was a product that would . . ." This comment can result in the creation of a new business. One entrepreneur's evaluation of why so many business executives were complaining about the lack of good technical writing and word-processing services resulted in the creation of her own business venture to fill this need. Her technical writing service grew to 10 employees in two years.

Due to their close contact with the end user, channel members in the distribution system also see product needs. One entrepreneur started a college bookstore after hearing all the students complain about the high cost of books and the lack of service provided by the only bookstore on campus. Many other entrepreneurs have identified business opportunities through a discussion with a retailer, wholesaler, or manufacturer's representative. Finally, technically oriented individuals often conceptualize business opportunities when working on other projects. One entrepreneur's business resulted from seeing the application of a plastic resin compound in developing and manufacturing a new type of pallet while developing the resin application in another totally unrelated area—casket moldings.

Whether the opportunity is identified by using input from consumers, business associates, channel members, or technical people, each opportunity must be carefully screened and evaluated. This evaluation of the opportunity is perhaps the most critical element of the entrepreneurial process, as it allows the entrepreneur to assess whether the specific product or service has the returns needed compared to the resources required. As indicated in Table 1.1, this evaluation process involves looking at the length of the opportunity, its real and perceived value, its risks and returns, its fit with the personal skills and goals of the entrepreneur, and its uniqueness or differential advantage in its competitive environment.

window of opportunity The time period available for creating the new venture

The market size and the length of the *window of opportunity* are the primary bases for determining the risks and rewards. The risks reflect the market, competition, technology, and amount of capital involved. The amount of capital needed provides the basis for the return and rewards. The methodology for evaluating risks and rewards, the focus of Chapters 7 and 9, frequently indicates that an opportunity offers neither a financial nor a personal reward commensurate with the risks involved. One company that delivered bark mulch to residential and commercial users for decoration around the base of trees and shrubs added loam and shells to its product line. These products were sold to the same customer base using the same distribution (delivery) system. Follow-on products are important for a company expanding or diversifying in a particular channel. A distribution channel member such as Kmart, Service Merchandise, or Target prefers to do business with multiproduct, rather than single-product, firms.

Finally, the opportunity must fit the personal skills and goals of the entrepreneur. It is particularly important that the entrepreneur be able to put forth the necessary time and effort required to make the venture succeed. Although many entrepreneurs feel that the desire can be developed along with the venture, typically it does not materialize. An entrepreneur must believe in the opportunity so much that he or she will make the necessary sacrifices to develop the opportunity and manage the resulting organization.

Opportunity analysis, or what is frequently called an opportunity assessment plan, is one method for evaluating an opportunity. It is not a business plan. Compared to a business plan, it should be shorter; focus on the opportunity, not the entire venture; and provide the basis for making the decision of whether or not to act on the opportunity.

An opportunity assessment plan includes the following: a description of the product or service, an assessment of the opportunity, an assessment of the entrepreneur and the team, specifications of all the activities and resources needed to translate the opportunity into a viable business venture, and the source of capital to finance the initial venture as well as its growth. The assessment of the opportunity requires answering the following questions:

- What market need does it fill?
- What personal observations have you experienced or recorded with regard to that market need?
- What social condition underlies this market need?
- What market research data can be marshaled to describe this market need?
- What patents might be available to fulfill this need?

- What competition exists in this market? How would you describe the behavior of this competition?
- What does the international market look like?
- What does the international competition look like?
- Where is the money to be made in this activity?

Develop a Business Plan

business plan The description of the future direction of the business

A good *business plan* must be developed in order to exploit the defined opportunity. This is a very time-consuming phase of the entrepreneurial process. An entrepreneur usually has not prepared a business plan before and does not have the resources available to do a good job. Although the preparation of the business plan is the focus of Chapter 7, it is important to understand the basic issues involved as well as the three major sections of the plan (see Table 1.1). A good business plan is essential to developing the opportunity and determining the resources required, obtaining those resources, and successfully managing the resulting venture.

Determine the Resources Required

The entrepreneur must determine the resources needed for addressing the opportunity. This process starts with an appraisal of the entrepreneur's present resources. Any resources that are critical need to be differentiated from those that are just helpful. Care must be taken not to underestimate the amount and variety of resources needed. The entrepreneur should also assess the downside risks associated with insufficient or inappropriate resources.

The next step in the entrepreneurial process is acquiring the needed resources in a timely manner while giving up as little control as possible. An entrepreneur should strive to maintain as large an ownership position as possible, particularly in the start-up stage. As the business develops, more funds will probably be needed to finance the growth of the venture, requiring more ownership to be relinquished. The entrepreneur also needs to identify alternative suppliers of these resources, the focus of Chapter 11, along with their needs and desires. By understanding resource supplier needs, the entrepreneur can structure a deal that enables the resources to be acquired at the lowest possible cost and with the least loss of control.

Manage the Enterprise

After resources are acquired, the entrepreneur must use them to implement the business plan. The operational problems of the growing enterprise must also be examined. This involves implementing a management style and structure, as well as determining the key variables for success. A control system must be established, so that any problem areas can be quickly identified and resolved. Some entrepreneurs have difficulty managing and growing the venture they created.

Types of Start-Ups

lifestyle firm A small venture that supports the owners and usually does not grow

What types of start-ups result from this entrepreneurial decision process? One very useful classification system divides start-ups into three categories: lifestyle firms, foundation companies, and high-potential ventures. A *lifestyle firm* is privately held and usually achieves only modest growth due to the nature of the business, the objectives of the entrepreneur, and the limited money devoted to research and development. This type of firm may grow after several years to 30 or 40 employees and have annual revenue of about

$2 million. A lifestyle firm exists primarily to support the owners and usually has little opportunity for significant growth and expansion.

foundation company A type of company formed from research and development that usually does not go public

high-potential venture A venture that has high growth potential and therefore receives great investor interest

gazelles Very high growth ventures

The second type of start-up—the *foundation company*—is created from research and development and lays the foundation for a new business area. This firm can grow in 5 to 10 years from 40 to 400 employees and from $10 million to $20 million in yearly revenue. Since this type of start-up rarely goes public, it usually draws the interest of private investors only, not the venture-capital community.

The final type of start-up—the *high-potential venture*—is the one that receives the greatest investment interest and publicity. While the company may start out like a foundation company, its growth is far more rapid. After 5 to 10 years, the company could employ around 500 employees, with $20 million to $30 million in revenue. These firms are also called *gazelles* and are integral to the economic development of an area.

Given that the results of the decision-making process need to be perceived as desirable and possible for an individual to change from a present lifestyle to a radically new one, it is not surprising that the type and number of new business formations vary greatly throughout the world as well as throughout the United States. Some regions in the United States have more support infrastructure and a more positive attitude toward new business creation.

ROLE OF ENTREPRENEURSHIP IN ECONOMIC DEVELOPMENT

The role of entrepreneurship in economic development involves more than just increasing per capita output and income; it involves initiating and constituting change in the structure of business and society. This change is accompanied by growth and increased output, which allows more wealth to be divided by the various participants. What in an area facilitates the needed change and development? One theory of economic growth depicts innovation as the key, not only in developing new products (or services) for the market but also in stimulating investment interest in the new ventures being created. This new investment works on both the demand and the supply sides of the growth equation; the new capital created expands the capacity for growth (supply side), and the resultant new spending utilizes the new capacity and output (demand side).

product-evolution process Process for developing and commercializing an innovation

In spite of the importance of investment and innovation in the economic development of an area, there is still a lack of understanding of the *product-evolution process*. This is the process through which innovation is developed and commercialized through entrepreneurial activity, which in turn stimulates economic growth.

iterative synthesis The intersection of knowledge and social need that starts the product development process

The product-evolution process, illustrated in Figure 1.1 as a cornucopia, the traditional symbol of abundance, begins with knowledge in the base technology and science—such as thermodynamics, fluid mechanics, or electronics—and ends with products or services available for purchase in the marketplace.[14] The critical point in the product-evolution process is the intersection of knowledge and a recognized social need, which begins the product development phase. This point, called *iterative synthesis,* often fails to evolve into a marketable innovation and is where the entrepreneur needs to concentrate his or her efforts. The lack of expertise in this area—matching the technology with the appropriate market and making the needed adjustments—is an underlying problem in any technology transfer.

ordinary innovations New products with little technological change

technological innovations New products with significant technological advancement

breakthrough innovations New products with some technological change

The innovation can, of course, be of varying degrees of uniqueness. Most innovations introduced to the market are *ordinary innovations,* that is, with little uniqueness or technology. As expected, there are fewer *technological innovations* and *breakthrough innovations,* with the number of actual innovations decreasing as the technology involved increases. Regardless of its level of uniqueness or technology, each innovation (particularly the latter two types) evolves into and develops toward commercialization through

FIGURE 1.1 Product Evolution

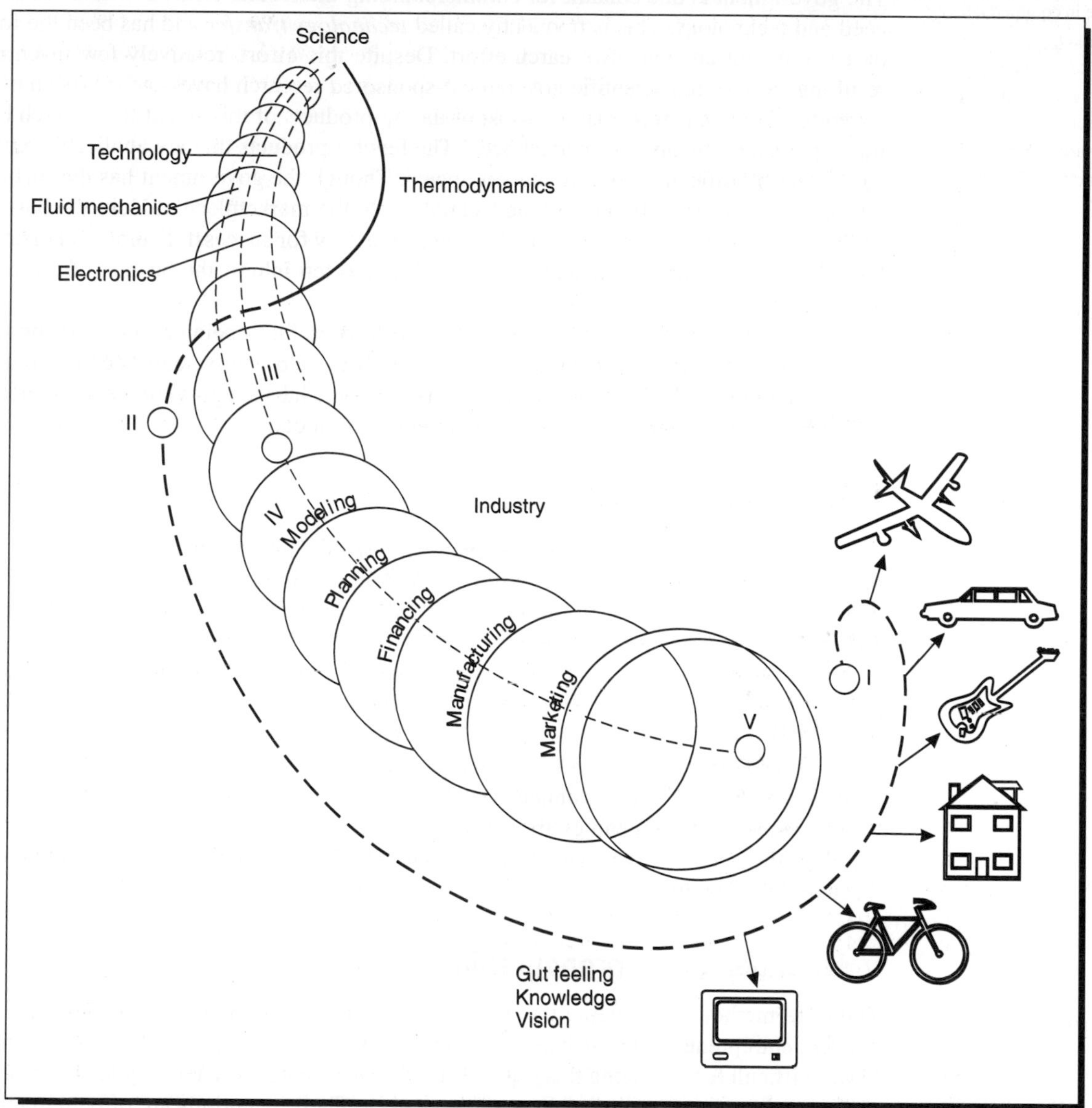

I Recognition of social need
II Initiation of technological innovation
III Iterative synthesis leading to invention (pressing toward invention)
IV Development phase
V Industrial phase

one of three mechanisms: the government, corporate entrepreneurship, or independent entrepreneurship.

Entrepreneurship has assisted in revitalizing areas of the inner city. Individuals in inner-city areas can relate to the concept and see it as a possibility for changing their present situation. One model project in New York City changed a depressed area into one that now has many small entrepreneurial companies.

government as an innovator A government active in commercializing technology

technology transfer Commercializing the technology in the laboratories into new products

Government as an Innovator

The government is one conduit for commercializing the results of the synthesis of social need and technology. This is frequently called *technology transfer* and has been the focus of a significant amount of research effort. Despite this effort, relatively few inventions resulting from sound scientific government-sponsored research have reached (been transferred to) the commercial market. Most of the by-products of this scientific research have little application to any commercial need. The few by-products that are applicable require significant modification to have market appeal. Though the government has the financial resources to successfully transfer the technology to the marketplace, it lacks the business skills, particularly marketing and distribution, necessary for successful commercialization. In addition, government bureaucracy and red tape often inhibit the business from being formed in a timely manner.

Recently, this problem has been addressed with federal labs being required to commercialize some of their technology each year. In order to help their scientists commercialize their technology and think more entrepreneurially, some labs are providing entrepreneurial training and are working with university entrepreneurial centers.

Corporate Entrepreneurship

Corporate entrepreneurship (entrepreneurship within an existing business) can also bridge the gap between science and the marketplace. Existing businesses have the financial resources, business skills, and frequently the marketing and distribution systems to commercialize innovation successfully. Yet, too often the bureaucratic structure, the emphasis on short-term profits, and a highly structured organization inhibit creativity and prevent new products and businesses from being developed. Corporations recognizing these inhibiting factors and the need for creativity and innovation have attempted to establish an entrepreneurial spirit in their organizations. In the present era of hypercompetition, the need for new products and the entrepreneurial spirit have become so great that more and more companies are developing an entrepreneurial corporate environment, often in the form of strategic business units (SBUs). Corporate entrepreneurship is discussed in Chapter 3.

Independent Entrepreneurship

The third method for bridging the gap between science and the marketplace is via independent entrepreneurship, such as the creation of a new organization. Many entrepreneurs have a difficult time bridging this gap and creating new ventures. They may lack managerial skills, marketing capability, or financial resources. Their inventions are often unrealistic, requiring significant modification to be marketable. In addition, entrepreneurs frequently do not know how to interface with all the necessary entities, such as banks, suppliers, customers, venture capitalists, distributors, and advertising agencies.

Yet, in spite of all these difficulties, entrepreneurship is presently the most effective method for bridging the gap between science and the marketplace, creating new enterprises, and bringing new products and services to the market. These entrepreneurial activities significantly affect the economy of an area by building the economic base and providing jobs. In some areas, entrepreneurship accounts for the majority of new products and net new employment. Given its impact on both the overall economy and the employment of an area, it is surprising that entrepreneurship has not become even more of a focal point in economic development.

ETHICS AND SOCIAL RESPONSIBILITY OF ENTREPRENEURS

The life of the entrepreneur is not easy. An entrepreneur must take risks with his or her own capital in order to sell and deliver products and services while expending greater energy than the average businessperson in order to innovate. In the face of daily stressful situations and other difficulties, the possibility exists that the entrepreneur will establish a balance between ethical exigencies, economic expediency, and social responsibility, a balance that differs from the point where the general business manager takes his or her moral stance.[15]

A manager's attitudes concerning corporate responsibility are related to the organizational climate perceived to be supportive of laws and professional codes of ethics. On the other hand, entrepreneurs with a relatively new company who have few role models usually develop an internal ethical code. Entrepreneurs tend to depend on their own personal value systems much more than other managers when determining ethically appropriate courses of action.

Although drawing more on their own value system, entrepreneurs have been shown to be particularly sensitive to peer pressure and general social norms in the community, as well as pressures from their competitors. The differences between entrepreneurs in different types of communities and in different countries reflect, to some extent, the general norms and values of the communities and countries involved. This is clearly the case for metropolitan as opposed to nonmetropolitan locations within a single country. Internationally, there is evidence to this effect about managers in general. U.S. managers seem to have more individualistic and less communitarian values than their German and Austrian counterparts.

The significant increase in the number of internationally oriented businesses has impacted the increased interest in the similarities and differences in business attitudes and practices in different countries. This area has been explored to some extent within the context of culture and is now beginning to be explored within the more individualized concept of ethics. The concepts of culture and ethics are somewhat related. Whereas ethics refers to the *"study of whatever is right and good for humans," business ethics* concerns itself with the investigation of business practices in light of human values. Ethics is the broad field of study exploring the general nature of morals and the specific moral choices to be made by the individual in his relationship with others. While business ethics has emerged as an important topic within popular and academic publications in the past few decades, to date it has been treated ahistorically and with an orientation dominated by the U.S. perspective.

business ethics The study of behavior and morals in a business situation

Although the English word *ethics* is generally recognized as stemming from the Greek *êthos,* meaning "custom and usage," it is more properly identified as originating from *swĕdhêthos,* in which the concepts of individual morality and behavioral habits are related and identified as an essential quality of existence.

Most Western authors credit the Greek philosophers Socrates (469–399 B.C.), Plato (427–347 B.C.), and Aristotle (384–322 B.C.) as providing the earliest writings upon which currently held ethical conceptions are based. Much earlier writings pertaining to moral codes and laws, however, can be found within both Judaism (1800 B.C.) and Hinduism (1500 B.C.). American attitudes on ethics result from three principal influences: the Judeo-Christian heritage, a belief in individualism, and opportunities based upon ability rather than social status. The United States was formed by immigrants from other countries, frequently fleeing oppression in their homelands, dedicated to creating a society where their future and fortunes would be determined by their abilities and dedication to work.

ETHICS

Morris Housen is a busy guy. The founder and CEO of Birch Point Paper Products—a five-year-old company in Shirley, Massachusetts, that makes customized napkins, cups, plates, and place mats—he is also the chief operating officer at Irving Industries, a business started by his grandfather and great-uncle that produces 120 tons of tissue paper each day and does about $85 million in annual sales. And besides his two day jobs, Housen does extensive volunteer work for the Anti-Defamation League.

But several times each month, Housen finds the time to sit down in front of his laptop at his home in Acton, Massachusetts, and write carefully crafted messages to his two children, Molly and Ethan. That would be wholly unremarkable if not for the fact that neither of Housen's children, ages 3 and 5, yet knows how to read. But that doesn't matter, since Housen, 37, doesn't intend to show his children what he's written for years—not until they are embarking on their own adulthoods.

Housen is one of a growing number of entrepreneurs who are choosing to create a legacy statement, or an ethical will. While traditional wills deal with the disposition of property and possessions, these documents are a creative way of passing on a business owner's experiences, family history, values, and work ethic to the next generation. As an estate-planning tool they can take various forms, from a single letter to a series of essays. (The only difference between legacy statements and ethical wills is that a legacy statement is presented to heirs when a business owner is still alive, while an ethical will is bequeathed after he is deceased.)

Housen sees his legacy statement as a way to explain to his children why he often spends long hours away from his family building his business. He also wants them to understand values such as teamwork and honesty, points he illustrates by relating stories about his business in his legacy statement. "For me, a written document is more powerful, precise, and thought-out than a conversation could ever be," Housen says.

To illustrate the value of teamwork, for instance, Housen writes about his experience developing a successful marketing campaign for Birch Point Paper. The campaign—which echoed the milk lobby's famous "Got milk?" advertisements—depicted such messy situations as coffee spilled on a $1 million check, followed by the tag line "Got napkins?" The idea for the campaign was the result of a collective effort among his staff, the kind of interdependency Housen wants his kids to appreciate.

Source: From Jeremy Kahn, "Where There's an (Ethical) Will, There's a Way," *Fortune Small Business* 11, no. 8.

A central question in business ethics is, "For whose benefit and at whose expense should the firm be managed?"[16] In addressing this question we focus on the means of ensuring that resources are deployed fairly between the firm and its stakeholders—the people who have a vested interest in the firm, including employees, customers, suppliers, and society itself. If resource deployment is not fair, then a stakeholder is being exploited by the firm.

Entrepreneurship can play a role in the fair deployment of resources to alleviate the exploitation of certain stakeholders. Most of us can think of examples of firms that have benefited financially because their managers have exploited certain stakeholders—receiving more value from them than they supply in return. This exploitation of a stakeholder group can represent an opportunity for an entrepreneur to more fairly and efficiently redeploy the resources of the exploited stakeholder. Simply stated, where current prices do not reflect the value of a stakeholder's resources, an entrepreneur who discovers the discrepancy can enter the market to capture profit. In this way the entrepreneurial process acts as a mechanism to ensure a fair and efficient system for redeploying the resources of a "victimized" stakeholder to a use where value supplied and received is equilibrated.[17]

Therefore, while there is evidence that some use the entrepreneurial process to exploit others for profit, it is important to understand that the entrepreneurial process can be an important means of helping exploited stakeholders and at the same time setting up a viable business. Think of the entrepreneurial process as a tool that can be used effectively to achieve outcomes for the benefit of others (and the entrepreneur) rather than to the detriment of others. Some aspects of business ethics are indicated in the Ethics box in each chapter. Ethics is not only a general topic for conversation but a deep concern of businesspeople.

THE FUTURE OF ENTREPRENEURSHIP

As evidenced by the many different definitions, the term *entrepreneurship* means different things to different people and can be viewed from different conceptual perspectives. However, in spite of the differences, there are some common aspects: risk taking, creativity, independence, and rewards. These commonalities will continue to be the driving force behind the notion of entrepreneurship in the future. One thing is clear: The future for entrepreneurship appears to be very bright. We are living in the age of the entrepreneur, with entrepreneurship endorsed by educational institutions, governmental units, society, and corporations. Entrepreneurial education has never been so important in terms of courses and academic research. The number of universities and colleges offering at least one course in entrepreneurship increases each year. The number of faculty teaching entrepreneurship as well as the number of endowed chairs increases regularly. There are some unique entrepreneurial programs as well, such as master's programs in entrepreneurial science and technology entrepreneurship, and MBA with a concentration in bioscience.

Entrepreneurship education throughout the world is also growing. Many universities in Europe have well-established programs in entrepreneurship. Most universities and associations do research on entrepreneurship, followed by training courses and then education courses—courses for which degree credit is given. Very few universities are yet involved in the actual enterprise creation process where the university, faculty, and/or students share in the sales and profits of the new venture.

This increase in course offerings has been accompanied by an increase in academic research, endowed chairs in the area, entrepreneurship concentrations and majors, and centers of entrepreneurial activity. This trend will continue, supported by an increase in PhD activity, which will in turn provide the needed faculty and research effort to support the future increases in course offerings, endowed positions, centers, and other research efforts.

Various governments are taking an increased interest in promoting the growth of entrepreneurship. Individuals are encouraged to form new businesses and are provided such government support as tax incentives, buildings, roads, and a communication system to facilitate this creation process. Encouragement by the federal and local governments should continue in the future as more lawmakers understand that new enterprises create jobs and increase economic output in the area. Some state governments in the United States are developing their own innovative industrial strategies for fostering entrepreneurial activity and the timely development of the technology of the area. The impact of this strategy is seen in the venture-capital industry, which is always sensitive to government regulations and policies. Many states now have their own state-sponsored venture funds, where a percentage of the fund has to be invested in ventures in the state.

Society's support of entrepreneurship will also continue. This support is critical in providing both motivation and public support. Never before have entrepreneurs been so revered by the general populace. Entrepreneurial endeavors in the United States are considered honorable and even, in many cases, prestigious pursuits. A major factor in the development of this societal approval is the media. The media have played, and will continue to play, a powerful and constructive role by reporting on the general entrepreneurial spirit in the United States and highlighting specific success cases of this spirit in operation. Major articles in such newspapers as *The New York Times, The Wall Street Journal,* and the *Washington Post* have focused on the pioneer spirit of today's entrepreneurs, describing how this spirit benefits society by keeping the United States in the lead in technology. General business magazines such as *Barron's, BusinessWeek, Forbes,* and *Fortune* have provided similar coverage by adding special columns on entrepreneurship and venturing. Magazines such as *Black Enterprise, Entrepreneur, and Inc.*—which focus on specific issues of the entrepreneurial process, starting new ventures, and small, growing businesses—have built solid and increasing circulation rates. Television on both a national and a local level has highlighted entrepreneurship by featuring specific individuals and issues involved in the entrepreneurial process. Not only have local stations covered regional occurrences, but nationally syndicated shows such as *The Today Show, Good Morning America,* and *20/20* have had special segments devoted to this phenomenon. This media coverage uplifts the image of the entrepreneur and growth companies and focuses on their contributions to society.

Finally, large companies will continue to have an interest in their special form of entrepreneurship—corporate entrepreneurship—in the future. These companies will be increasingly interested in capitalizing on their research and development (R&D) in today's hypercompetitive business environment. The largest 15 companies in the United States account for over 20 percent of the total U.S. R&D and over 40 percent of private-sector R&D. General Electric, for example, has created several $1 billion businesses internally in the last 15 years and has moved all its lighting research and development to Hungary to its joint venture, Tungstram. Other companies will want to create more new businesses through corporate entrepreneurship in the future, particularly in light of the hypercompetition and the need for globalization.

IN REVIEW

SUMMARY

The definition of an entrepreneur has evolved over time as the world's economic structure has changed and become more complex. Since its beginnings in the Middle Ages, when it was used in relation to specific occupations, the notion of the entrepreneur has been refined and broadened to include concepts that are related to the person rather than the occupation. Risk taking, innovation, and creation of wealth are examples of the criteria that have been developed as the study of new business creations has evolved. In this text, entrepreneurship is defined as the process of creating something new with value by devoting the necessary time and effort; assuming the accompanying financial, psychological, and social risks; and receiving the resultant rewards of monetary and personal satisfaction and independence.

The entrepreneur then goes through the entrepreneurial process, which involves finding, evaluating, and developing opportunities for creating a new venture. Each step is essential to the eventual success of the new firm and is closely related to the other steps. Before the opportunity identification stage can result in a meaningful search, the potential entrepreneur must have a general idea about the type of company desired. There are both formal and informal mechanisms for identifying business opportunities. Although formal mechanisms are generally found within a more established company, most entrepreneurs use informal sources for their ideas, such as being sensitive to the complaints and chance comments of friends and associates. Once the opportunity is identified, the evaluation process begins. Basic to the screening process is understanding the factors that create the opportunity: technology, market changes, competition, or changes in government regulations. From this base, the market size and time dimension associated with the idea can be estimated. It is important that the idea fit the personal skills and goals of the entrepreneur, and that the entrepreneur have a strong desire to see the opportunity brought to fruition. In the process of evaluating an opportunity, the required resources should be clearly defined and obtained at the lowest possible cost.

The decision to start an entrepreneurial venture consists of several sequential steps: (1) the decision to leave a present career or lifestyle, (2) the decision that an entrepreneurial venture is desirable, and (3) the decision that both external and internal factors make new venture creation possible. Although the decision-making process is applicable to each of the three types of start-up companies, the emphasis in each one is certainly different. Because of their differing natures, foundation companies and high-potential ventures require a more conscious effort to reach a defensible decision on these points than do lifestyle firms.

The study of entrepreneurship has relevance today, not only because it helps entrepreneurs better fulfill their personal needs but because of the economic contribution of the new ventures. More than increasing national income by creating new jobs, entrepreneurship acts as a positive force in economic growth by serving as the bridge between innovation and the marketplace. Although the government gives great support to basic and applied research, it has not had great success in translating the technological innovations to products or services. Although corporate entrepreneurship offers the promise of a marriage of those research capabilities and business skills that one expects from a large corporation, the results so far in many companies have not been spectacular. This leaves the entrepreneur, who frequently lacks both technical and business skills, to serve as the major link in the process of innovation development and economic growth and revitalization. The study of entrepreneurship and the education of potential entrepreneurs are essential parts of any attempt to strengthen this link so essential to a country's economic well-being.

RESEARCH TASKS

1. Ask five entrepreneurs what the term entrepreneurship means to them. Be prepared to present the commonalities and differences of these definitions to the class. Can differences in the definitions be explained by the "type" of entrepreneur interviewed?
2. What impact does entrepreneurship have on your local, state (or province), and national economies? Use data to back up your arguments.
3. Research the policy statements of your local, state (or province), and national governments for their goals and objectives regarding the importance of entrepreneurship and means of encouraging it.
4. Speak to people from five different countries and ask what entrepreneurship means to them and how their national culture helps and/or hinders entrepreneurship.

CLASS DISCUSSION

1. List the content that you believe is necessary for an entrepreneurship course. Be prepared to justify your answer.
2. Do you believe that ethics and social responsibility should be part of an entrepreneurship course or did the textbook authors just include a section on it to be "politically correct"?

3. What is the role of government in entrepreneurship? To what extent should it help protect people from entrepreneurship? Should it simply get out of the way and leave the market to reward or punish inappropriate behavior? Given your answers to the above questions, what specific steps should the government take or what steps has it taken that should be reversed?
4. What excites you about being an entrepreneur? What are your major concerns?

SELECTED READINGS

Aldrich, Howard E.; and Martha Argelia Martinez. (Summer 2001). Many Are Called, but Few Are Chosen: An Evolutionary Perspective for the Study of Entrepreneurship. *Entrepreneurial Theory and Practice*, pp. 41–56.

More than a decade ago, three elements indispensable to an understanding of entrepreneurial success were identified: process, context, and outcomes. Although the knowledge of entrepreneurial activities has increased dramatically, we still have much to learn about how process and context interact to shape the outcome of entrepreneurial efforts.

Ardichvili, Alexander; Richard Cardozo; and Sourav Ray. (2003). A Theory of Entrepreneurial Opportunity Identification and Development. *Journal of Business Venturing*, vol. 18, pp. 105–123.

This paper builds on existing theoretical and empirical studies in the area of entrepreneurial opportunity *identification and development. It utilizes Dubin's theory building framework to propose a theory of the* opportunity *identification process. It identifies the entrepreneur's personality traits, social networks, and prior knowledge as antecedents of entrepreneurial alertness to* business opportunities. *Entrepreneurial alertness, in its turn, is a necessary condition for the success of the* opportunity *identification triad: recognition, development, and* evaluation.

Brouwer, Maria T. (2002). Weber, Schumpeter and Knight on Entrepreneurship and Economic Development. *Journal of Evolutionary Economics*, vol. 12, pp. 83–105.

This paper interprets the discussion on entrepreneurship and economic development that was started by Weber, Schumpeter, and Knight. The paper demonstrates how these three authors influenced each other on the topics of importance of innovation and entrepreneurship, uncertainty, and perceptiveness and hidden qualities of people.

Drayton, William. (2002). The Citizen Sector: Becoming as Entrepreneurial and Competitive as Business. *California Management Review*, vol. 44, no. 3, pp. 120–32.

This article explores the aspects that have driven the entrepreneurial transformation of the social half of society that has taken place over the last two and a half decades, identifies three management challenges made urgent by this shift, and describes its impact on the rest of society.

Fiet, James; Alexandre Piskounov; and Pankaj Patel. (2005). Still Searching (Systematically) for Entrepreneurial Discoveries. *Small Business Economics*, vol. 25, pp. 489–504.

In this article the authors examine how entrepreneurs can search deliberately for discoveries. They use consideration sets to impose constraints on how and where they search. A consideration set is a promising set of information channels, which entrepreneurs can select and search based on prior knowledge. To decide how to search the channels in a consideration set, they apply existing mathematical formalism to illustrate a maximal search sequence. Because there is some probability that a search sequence could continue indefinitely, they determine stopping rules. They argue that entrepreneurial search is more feasible within a consideration set than it is in the rest of the world.

Gifford, Sharon. (1998). Limited Entrepreneurial Attention and Economic Development. *Small Business Economics*, vol. 10, no. 1, pp. 17–30.

Economic development depends on the allocation of entrepreneurial resources to efforts to discover new profit opportunities. Limited entrepreneurial attention is allocated between maintaining current activities and starting new activities. The problem of allocating limited entrepreneurial attention in a variety of contexts is addressed.

Hayton, James C.; Gerard George; and Shaker A. Zahra. (Summer 2002). National Culture and Entrepreneurship: A Review of Behavioral Research. *Entrepreneurial Theory and Practice*, pp. 33–52.

The article reviews and synthesizes the findings of 21 empirical studies that examine the association between national cultural characteristics and aggregate measures of entrepreneurship, individual characteristics of entrepreneurs, and aspects of corporate entrepreneurship.

Keh, Hean; Maw Der Foo; and Boon Chong Lim. (2002). Opportunity Evaluation under Risky Conditions: The Cognitive Processes of Entrepreneurs. *Entrepreneurship: Theory & Practice*, vol. 27, pp. 125–48.

This study uses a cognitive approach to examine opportunity evaluation, *as the perception of* opportunity *is essentially a cognitive phenomenon. The authors present a model that consists of four independent variables (overconfidence, belief in the law of small numbers, planning fallacy, and illusion of control), a mediating variable (risk perception), two control variables (demographics and risk propensity), and the dependent variable* (opportunity evaluation). *They find that illusion of control and belief in the law of small numbers are related to how entrepreneurs evaluate opportunities. Their results also indicate that risk perception mediates* opportunity evaluation.

Laukkanen, Mauri. (2000). Exploring Alternative Approaches in High-Level Entrepreneurship Education: Creating Micro-Mechanisms for Endogenous Regional Growth. *Entrepreneurship & Regional Development*, vol. 12, pp. 25–47.

The paper argues that there is a downside related to conceptual and efficacy notions of entrepreneurship and education, breeding unreasonable and unpredictable expectations. This paper explores alternative strategies in university-based entrepreneurial education describing the dominant pattern of education, based on an individual-centered mind-set.

McMullen, Jeffrey; and Dean Shepherd. (2006). Entrepreneurial Action and the Role of Uncertainty in the Theory of the Entrepreneur. *Academy of Management Review*, vol. 31, pp. 132–52.

By considering the amount of uncertainty perceived and the willingness to bear uncertainty concomitantly, the authors provide a conceptual model of entrepreneurial action that allows for examination of entrepreneurial action at the individual level of analysis while remaining consistent with a rich legacy of system-level theories of the entrepreneur. This model not only exposes limitations of existing theories of entrepreneurial action but also contributes to a deeper understanding of important conceptual issues, such as the nature of opportunity and the potential for philosophical reconciliation among entrepreneurship scholars.

Office of Advocacy, U.S. Small Business Administration. (2000). The Third Millennium Small Business and Entrepreneurship in the 21st Century.

This report is an update of the report published for the 1995 White House Conference on Small Business. The new edition discusses rapid changes in the small business sector; the heterogeneity, diversity, and complexity of the small-business environment; barriers to entry and inhibitors to growth that small business will continue to face; and the overall small-business and entrepreneurial sectors' future growth.

Osborne, Stephen W.; Thomas W. Falcone; and Prashanth B. Nagendra. (2000). From Unemployed to Entrepreneur: A Case Study in Intervention. *Journal of Developmental Entrepreneurship,* vol. 5, no. 2, pp. 115–36.

A summary of the entrepreneurial potential, training, and success of a group of recently unemployed workers from a wide spectrum of previous occupations and industries.

Wennekers, Sander; and Roy Thurik. (1999). Linking Entrepreneurship and Economic Growth. *Small Business Economics*, vol. 13, no. 1, pp. 27–55.

The concept of entrepreneurship is discussed, with the aim of explaining entrepreneurship's role in the process of economic growth. By considering three levels on which entrepreneurship can be analyzed (individual, firm, and aggregate level), the relationship between entrepeneurship and economic growth is examined.

END NOTES

1. Robert F. Herbert and Albert H. Link, *The Entrepreneur—Mainstream Views and Radical Critiques* (New York: Praeger Publishers, 1982), p. 17.
2. Richard T. Ely and Ralph H. Hess, *Outlines of Economics,* 6th ed. (New York: Macmillan, 1937), p. 488.
3. Joseph Schumpeter, *Can Capitalism Survive?* (New York: Harper & Row, 1952), p. 72.
4. Albert Shapero, *Entrepreneurship and Economic Development* (Wisconsin: Project ISEED, LTD, The Center for Venture Management, Summer 1975), p. 187.
5. Karl Vesper, *New Venture Strategies* (Englewood Cliffs, NJ: Prentice Hall, 1980), p. 2.
6. Robert C. Ronstadt, *Entrepreneurship* (Dover, MA: Lord Publishing Co., 1984), p. 28.
7. This definition is modified from the definition first developed for the woman entrepreneur. See Robert D. Hisrich and Candida G. Brush, *The Woman Entrepreneur: Starting, Financing, and Managing a Successful New Business* (Lexington, MA: Lexington Books, 1985), p. 18.
8. L. V. Mises, *Human Action: A Treatise on Economics,* 4th rev. ed. (San Francisco, CA: Fox & Wilkes, 1949).
9. See T. M. Amabile, "Entrepreneurial Creativity through Motivational Synergy," *Journal of Creative Behavior* 31 (1997), pp. 18–26; J. A. Schumpeter, *The Theory of Economic Development* (New Brunswick: Transaction Publishers, 1934); W. B. Gartner, "What Are We Talking about When We Talk about Entrepreneurship?" *Journal of Business Venturing* 5 (1990), pp. 15–29.
10. J. S. McMullen, and D. A. Shepherd, "Toward a Theory of Entrepreneurial Action: Detecting and Evaluating Opportunities," *Academy of Management Review* 31 (2006), pp. 132–52.
11. This and other information on inventors and the invention process can be found in Robert D. Hisrich, "The Inventor: A Potential Source for New Products," *The Mid-Atlantic Journal of Business* 24 (Winter 1985–86), pp. 67–80.
12. G. T. Lumpkin, and G. G. Dess, "Clarifying the Entrepreneurial Orientation Construct and Linking It to Performance, " *Academy of Management Review* 21 (1996), pp. 135–72.
13. A version of this process can be found in Howard H. Stevenson, Michael J. Roberts, and H. Irving Grousbeck, *New Business Ventures and the Entrepreneur* (Burr Ridge, IL: Richard D. Irwin, 1985), pp. 16–23.
14. This process is discussed in Yao Tzu Li, David G. Jansson, and Ernest G. Cravelho, *Technological Innovation in Education and Industry* (New York: Van Nostrand Reinhold, 1980), pp. 6–12.

15. For summary of the research on ethics in entrepreneurship, see the papers published as part of the Ruffin Lecture Series of 2002 by the Business Ethics Society of The Darden School, University of Virginia.
16. E. R. Freeman, "A Stakeholder Theory of the Modern Corporation." In T. C. Beauchamp and N. E. Bowie (eds.), *Ethical Theory and Business* (Englewood Cliffs, NJ: Prentice Hall, 1994), pp. 66–76 (quote from p. 67).
17. S. Venkataraman, "Stakeholder Value Equilibration and the Entrepreneurial Process." In R. E. Freeman and S. Venkataraman (eds.), *Ethics and Entrepreneurship—The Ruffin Series,* Volume 3 (2002).

2

THE ENTREPRENEURIAL MIND-SET

LEARNING OBJECTIVES

1
To introduce effectuation as a way that expert entrepreneurs think.

2
To develop the notion that entrepreneurs learn to be cognitively adaptable.

3
To acknowledge that some entrepreneurs experience failure and to recognize the process by which they maximize their ability to learn from that experience.

4
To move beyond individual entrepreneurs to distinguish between entrepreneurially managed firms and more traditionally managed firms.

5
To provide some scales for capturing the extent to which entrepreneurs and their firms reflect entrepreneurial thinking.

OPENING PROFILE

EWING MARION KAUFFMAN

Born on a farm in Garden City, Missouri, Ewing Marion Kauffman moved to Kansas City with his family when he was eight years old. A critical event in his life occurred several years later when Kauffman was diagnosed with a leakage of the heart. His prescription was one year of complete bed rest; he was not even allowed to sit up. Kauffman's mother, a college graduate, came up with a solution to keep the active 11-year-old boy lying in bed—reading. According to Kauffman, he "sure read! Because nothing else would do, I read as many as 40 to 50 books every month. When you read that much, you read anything. So I read the biographies of all the presidents, the frontiersmen, and I read the Bible twice and that's pretty rough reading."

www.kauffman.org

Another important early childhood experience centered on door-to-door sales. Since his family did not have a lot of money, Kauffman would sell 36 dozen eggs collected from the farm, or fish he and his father had caught, cleaned, and dressed. His mother was very encouraging during these formative school years, telling young Ewing each day, "There may be some who have more money in their pockets, but Ewing, there is nobody better than you."

During his youth, Kauffman worked as a laundry delivery person and was a Boy Scout. In addition to passing all the requirements to become an Eagle Scout and a Sea Scout, he sold twice as many tickets to the Boy Scout Roundup as anyone else in Kansas City, an accomplishment that enabled him to attend, for free, a two-week scout summer camp that his parents would not otherwise have been able to afford. According to Kauffman, "This experience gave me some of the sales techniques which came into play when subsequently I went into the pharmaceutical business."

Kauffman went to junior college from 8 to 12 in the morning, then walked two miles to the laundry where he worked until 7 p.m. Upon graduation, he went to work at the laundry full time for Mr. R. A. Long, who would eventually become one of his role models. His job as route foreman involved managing 18 to 20 route drivers, where he would set up sales contests, such as challenging the other drivers to get more customers on a particular route than he could obtain. Ewing says, "I got practice in selling and that proved to be beneficial later in life." R. A. Long made money not only at the laundry business but also on patents, one of which was a form fit for the collar of a shirt that would hold the shape of the shirt. He showed his young protégé that one could make money with brains as well as brawn. Kauffman commented, "He was quite a man and had quite an influence on my life."

Kauffman's sales ability was also useful during his stint in the Navy, which he joined shortly after Pearl Harbor on January 11, 1942. When designated as an apprentice seaman, a position that paid $21 per month, he responded, "I'm better than an apprentice seaman, because I have been a sea scout. I've sailed ships and I've ridden in whale boats." His selling ability convinced the Navy that he should instead start as a seaman first class, with a $54 monthly salary. Kauffman was assigned to the admiral's staff, where he became an outstanding signalman (a seaman who transmitted messages from ship to ship), in part because he was able to read messages better than anyone else due to his previous intensive reading. With his admiral's encouragement, Kauffman took a correspondence navigator's course and was given a deck commission and made a navigation officer.

After the war was over in 1947, Ewing Kauffman began his career as a pharmaceutical salesperson after performing better on an aptitude test than 50 other applicants. The job involved selling supplies of vitamin and liver shots to doctors. Working on straight commission, without expenses or benefits, he was earning pay higher than the president's salary by the end of the second year; the president promptly cut the commission. Eventually, when Kauffman was made Midwest sales manager, he made 3 percent of everything his salespeople sold and continued to make more money than the president. When his territory was cut, he eventually quit and in 1950 started his own company—Marion Laboratories. (Marion is his middle name.)

When reflecting on founding the new company, Ewing Kauffman commented, "It was easier than it sounds because I had doctors whom I had been selling office supplies to for several years. Before I made the break, I went to three of them and said, 'I'm thinking of starting my own company. May I count on you to give me your orders if I can give you the same quality and service?' These three were my biggest accounts and each one of them agreed because they liked me and were happy to do business with me."

Marion Laboratories started by marketing injectable products that were manufactured by another company under Marion's label. The company expanded to other accounts and other products, and then developed its first prescription item, Vicam, a vitamin product. The second pharmaceutical product it developed, oyster shell calcium, also sold well.

In order to expand the company, Kauffman borrowed $5,000 from the Commerce Trust Company. He repaid the loan, and the company continued to grow. After several years, outside investors could buy $1,000 worth of common stock if they loaned the company $1,000 to be paid back in five years at $1,250, without any intermittent interest. This initial $1,000 investment, if held until 1993, would have been worth $21 million.

Marion Laboratories continued to grow and reached over $1 billion per year in sales, due primarily to the relationship between Ewing Kauffman and the people in the company, who were called associates, not employees. "They are all stockholders, they build this company, and they mean so much to us," said Kauffman. The concept of associates was also a part of the two basic philosophies of the company: Those who produce should share in the results or profits, and treat others as you would like to be treated.

The company went public through Smith Barney on August 16, 1965, at $21 per share. The stock jumped to $28 per share immediately and has never dropped below that level, sometimes selling at a 50 to 60 price/earnings multiple. The associates of the company were offered a profit sharing plan, where each could own stock in the company. In 1968 Kauffman brought Major League Baseball back to Kansas City by purchasing the Kansas City Royals. This boosted the city's economic base, community profile, and civic pride. When Marion Laboratories merged with Merrill Dow in 1989, there were 3,400 associates, 300 of whom became millionaires as a result of the merger. The new company, Marion Merrill Dow, Inc., grew to 9,000 associates and sales of $4 billion in 1998 when it was acquired by Hoechst, a European pharmaceutical company. Hoechst Marion Roussel became a world leader in pharmaceutical-based health care involved in the discovery, development, manufacture, and sale of pharmaceutical products. In late 1999 the company was again merged with Aventis Pharma, a global pharmaceutical company focusing on human medicines (prescription pharmaceuticals and vaccines) and animal health. In 2002, Aventis's sales reached $16.634 billion, an increase of 11.6 percent from 2001, while earnings per share grew 27 percent from the previous year.

Ewing Marion Kauffman was an entrepreneur, a Major League Baseball team owner, and a philanthropist who believed his success was a direct result of one fundamental philosophy: Treat others as you would like to be treated. "It is the happiest principle by which to live and the most intelligent principle by which to do business and make money," he said.

Ewing Marion Kauffman's philosophies of associates, rewarding those who produce, and allowing decision making throughout the organization are the fundamental concepts underlying what is now called *corporate entrepreneurship* in a company. He went even further and illustrated his belief in entrepreneurship and the spirit of giving back when he established the Kauffman Foundation, which supports programs in two areas: youth development and entrepreneurship. Truly a remarkable entrepreneur, Mr. K, as he was affectionately called by his employees, will now produce many more successful "associate entrepreneurs."

Like Ewing Marion Kauffman, many other entrepreneurs and future entrepreneurs frequently ask themselves, "Am I really an entrepreneur? Do I have what it takes to be a success? Do I have sufficient background and experience to start and manage a new venture?" As enticing as the thought of starting and owning a business may be, the problems and pitfalls inherent to the process are as legendary as the success stories. The fact remains that more new business ventures fail than succeed. To be one of the few successful entrepreneurs requires more than just hard work and luck. It requires the ability to think in an environment of high uncertainty, be flexible, and learn from one's failures.

HOW ENTREPRENEURS THINK

Entrepreneurs think differently than nonentrepreneurs. Moreover, an entrepreneur in a particular situation may think differently when faced with a different task or decision environment. Entrepreneurs must often make decisions in highly uncertain environments where the stakes are high, time pressures are immense, and there is considerable emotional investment. We think differently in these environments than we do when the nature of a problem is well understood and we have time and rational procedures at hand to solve it. Given the nature of an entrepreneur's decision-making environment, she must sometimes (1) effectuate, (2) be cognitively adaptable, and (3) learn from failure. We now discuss the thought process behind each of these requirements.

Effectuation

As potential business leaders you are trained to think rationally and perhaps admonished if you do not. This admonishment might be appropriate given the nature of the task but it appears that there is an alternate way of thinking that entrepreneurs sometimes use, especially when thinking about opportunities. Professor Saras Sarasvathy (from Darden, University of Virginia) has found that entrepreneurs do not always think through a problem in a way that starts with a desired outcome and focuses on the means to generate that outcome. Such a process is referred to as *causation*. Our description of the entrepreneurial process in Chapter 1 reflects a causal explanation. Rather, entrepreneurs sometimes use an *effectuation process,* which means they take what they have (who they are, what they know, and whom they know) and select among possible outcomes. Professor Saras is a great cook, so it is not surprising that her examples of these thought processes revolve around cooking.

causal process A process that starts with a desired outcome and focuses on the means to generate that outcome

effectuation process A process that starts with what one has (who they are, what they know, and whom they know) and selects among possible outcomes

> Imagine a chef assigned the task of cooking dinner. There are two ways the task can be organized. In the first, the host or client picks out a menu in advance. All the chef needs to do is list the ingredients needed, shop for them, and then actually cook the meal. This is a process of causation. It begins with a given menu and focuses on selecting between effective ways to prepare the meal.
>
> In the second case, the host asks the chef to look through the cupboards in the kitchen for possible ingredients and utensils and then cook a meal. Here, the chef has to imagine possible menus based on the given ingredients and utensils, select the menu, and then prepare the meal. This is a process of effectuation. It begins with given ingredients and utensils and focuses on preparing one of many possible desirable meals with them.[1]

Sarasvathy's Thought Experiment #1: Curry in a Hurry

> In this example I [Sarasvathy] trace the process for building an imaginary Indian restaurant, "Curry in a Hurry." Two cases, one using causation and the other effectuation, are examined. For the purposes of this illustration, the example chosen is a typical causation process that underlies many economic theories today—theories in which it is argued that artifacts such as firms are inevitable outcomes, given the preference orderings of economic actors and certain simple assumptions of rationality (implying causal reasoning) in their choice behavior. The causation process used in the example here is typified by and embodied in the procedures stated by Philip Kotler in his *Marketing Management* (1991: 63, 263), a book that in its many editions is considered a classic and is widely used as a textbook in MBA programs around the world.
>
> Kotler defines a market as follows: "A market consists of all the potential customers sharing a particular need or want who might be willing and able to engage in exchange to satisfy

that need or want" (1991: 63). Given a product or a service, Kotler suggests the following procedure for bringing the product/service to market (note that Kotler assumes the market exists):

1. Analyze long-run opportunities in the market.
2. Research and select target markets.
3. Identify segmentation variables and segment the market.
4. Develop profiles of resulting segments.
5. Evaluate the attractiveness of each segment.
6. Select the target segment(s).
7. Identify possible positioning concepts for each target segment.
8. Select, develop, and communicate the chosen positioning concept.
9. Design marketing strategies.
10. Plan marketing programs.
11. Organize, implement, and control marketing effort.

This process is commonly known in marketing as the STP—segmentation, targeting, and positioning—process.

Curry in a Hurry is a restaurant with a new twist—say, an Indian restaurant with a fast food section. The current paradigm using causation processes indicates that, to implement this idea, the entrepreneur should start with a universe of all potential customers. Let us imagine that she wants to build her restaurant in Pittsburgh, Pennsylvania, USA, which will then become the initial universe or market for Curry in a Hurry. Assuming that the percentage of the population of Pittsburgh that totally abhors Indian food is negligible, the entrepreneur can start the STP process.

Several relevant segmentation variables, such as demographics, residential neighborhoods, ethnic origin, marital status, income level, and patterns of eating out, could be used. On the basis of these, the entrepreneur could send out questionnaires to selected neighborhoods and organize focus groups at, say, the two major universities in Pittsburgh. Analyzing responses to the questionnaires and focus groups, she could arrive at a target segment—for example, wealthy families, both Indian and others, who eat out at least twice a week. That would help her determine her menu choices, decor, hours, and other operational details. She could then design marketing and sales campaigns to induce her target segment to try her restaurant. She could also visit other Indian and fast food restaurants and find some method of surveying them and then develop plausible demand forecasts for her planned restaurant.

In any case, the process would involve considerable amounts of time and analytical effort. It would also require resources both for research and, thereafter, for implementing the marketing strategies. In summary, the current paradigm suggests that we proceed inward to specifics from a larger, general universe—that is, to an optimal target segment from a predetermined market. In terms of Curry in a Hurry, this could mean something like a progression from the entire city of Pittsburgh to Fox Chapel (an affluent residential neighborhood) to the Joneses (specific customer profile of a wealthy family), as it were.

Instead, if our imaginary entrepreneur were to use processes of effectuation to build her restaurant, she would have to proceed in the opposite direction (note that effectuation is suggested here as a viable and descriptively valid alternative to the STP process—not as a normatively superior one). For example, instead of starting with the assumption of an existing market and investing money and other resources to design the best possible restaurant for the given market, she would begin by examining the particular set of means or causes available to her. Assuming she has extremely limited monetary resources—say $20,000—she should think creatively to bring the idea to market with as close to zero resources as possible. She could do this by convincing an established restaurateur to become a strategic partner or by doing just enough market research to convince a financier to invest the money needed to start the restaurant. Another method of effectuation would be to convince a local Indian restaurant or a local fast food restaurant to allow her to put up a counter where she would actually sell a selection of Indian fast food. Selecting a menu

> and honing other such details would be seat-of-the-pants and tentative, perhaps a process of satisficing.[2]
>
> Several other courses of effectuation can be imagined. Perhaps the course the entrepreneur actually pursues is to contact one or two of her friends or relatives who work downtown and bring them and their office colleagues some of her food to taste. If the people in the office like her food, she might get a lunch delivery service going. Over time, she might develop enough of a customer base to start a restaurant or else, after a few weeks of trying to build the lunch business, she might discover that the people who said they enjoyed her food did not really enjoy it so much as they did her quirky personality and conversation, particularly her rather unusual life perceptions. Our imaginary entrepreneur might now decide to give up the lunch business and start writing a book, going on the lecture circuit and eventually building a business in the motivational consulting industry!
>
> Given the exact same starting point—but with a different set of contingencies—the entrepreneur might end up building one of a variety of businesses. To take a quick tour of some possibilities, consider the following: Whoever first buys the food from our imaginary Curry in a Hurry entrepreneur becomes, by definition, the first target customer. By continually listening to the customer and building an ever-increasing network of customers and strategic partners, the entrepreneur can then identify a workable segment profile. For example, if the first customers who actually buy the food and come back for more are working women of varied ethnic origin, this becomes her target segment. Depending on what the first customer really wants, she can start defining her market. If the customer is really interested in the food, the entrepreneur can start targeting all working women in the geographic location, or she can think in terms of locating more outlets in areas with working women of similar profiles—a "Women in a Hurry" franchise?
>
> Or, if the customer is interested primarily in the idea of ethnic or exotic entertainment, rather than merely in food, the entrepreneur might develop other products, such as catering services, party planning, and so on—"Curry Favors"? Perhaps, if the customers buy food from her because they actually enjoy learning about new cultures, she might offer lectures and classes, maybe beginning with Indian cooking and moving on to cultural aspects, including concerts and ancient history and philosophy, and the profound idea that food is a vehicle of cultural exploration—"School of Curry"? Or maybe what really interests them is theme tours and other travel options to India and the Far East—"Curryland Travels"?
>
> In a nutshell, in using effectuation processes to build her firm, the entrepreneur can build several different types of firms in completely disparate industries. This means that the original idea (or set of causes) does not imply any one single strategic universe for the firm (or effect). Instead, the process of effectuation allows the entrepreneur to create one or more several possible effects irrespective of the generalized end goal with which she started. The process not only enables the realization of several possible effects (although generally one or only a few are actually realized in the implementation) but it also allows a decision maker to change his or her goals and even to shape and construct them over time, making use of contingencies as they arise.[3]

Our use of direct quotes from Sarasvathy on effectuation is not to make the case that it is superior to thought processes that involve causation; rather, it represents a way that entrepreneurs sometimes think. Sarasvathy clearly describes the implications of effectuation for the entrepreneur in terms of five basic principles.[4]

patchwork quilt principle Means-driven action that emphasizes the creation of something new with existing means rather than discovering new ways to achieve given goals

1. *The patchwork quilt principle*. This is a principle of means-driven (as opposed to goal-driven) action. The emphasis here is on creating something new with existing means rather than discovering new ways to achieve given goals. The "patches" are the means—the "who I am," "what I know," and "whom I know" (which represent "what I have")—and these patches are combined to form something new and unique (the effectual quilt). As noted by Sarasvathy, "It is not the particular patches that are important; it is what the entrepreneur does with them."

affordable loss principle Prescribes committing in advance to what one is willing to lose rather than investing in calculations about expected returns to the project

2. *The affordable loss principle.* This principle prescribes committing in advance to what one is willing to lose rather than investing in calculations about expected returns to the project. This calculation of what one is willing to lose is not dependent upon guessing correctly in a highly uncertain environment but depends on the entrepreneur's current financial condition and psychological willingness to bear a specified loss. Using this principle, entrepreneurs can experiment with a new venture in an uncertain environment with a known maximum loss if things don't work out.

bird-in-hand principle Involves negotiating with any and all stakeholders who are willing to make actual commitments to the project; determines the goals of the enterprise

3. *The bird-in-hand principle.* This principle involves negotiating with any and all stakeholders who are willing to make actual commitments to the project, without worrying about opportunity costs or carrying out elaborate competitive analyses. Furthermore, who comes on board determines the goals of the enterprise. Not vice versa. Here effectuation emphasizes the inputs from stakeholders who actually make commitments to and therefore help to shape the new venture—without regard for the opportunity costs of satisfying these existing stakeholders at the expense of other possible stakeholders. As the saying goes, "A bird in the hand is worth two in the bush."

lemonade principle Prescribes leveraging surprises for benefits rather than trying to avoid them, overcome them, or adapt to them

4. *The lemonade principle.* This principle suggests acknowledging and appropriating contingency by leveraging surprises rather than trying to avoid them, overcome them, or adapt to them. Rather than coping with unexpected events, in thinking effectually entrepreneurs treat these unexpected events as an opportunity to "run with" an emerging situation—to turn the unexpected into the valuable and profitable. Consistent with this principle, it is possible to look at the flip side of most threats to find or generate opportunities.

pilot-in-the-plane principle Urges relying on and working with people as the prime driver of opportunity and not limiting entrepreneurial efforts to exploiting factors external to the individual

5. *The pilot-in-the-plane principle.* This principle urges relying on and working with people as the prime driver of opportunity and not limiting entrepreneurial efforts to exploiting factors external to the individual, such as technological trajectories and socioeconomic trends. This principle builds on the notion that when the future is truly unknown, focusing on better ways to predict the future will not be useful. Rather, entrepreneurs thinking effectually focus on aspects of the future they can control by their own actions; in doing so, they do not need to predict the future.

All of the above principles enable entrepreneurs to put themselves in control of their new ventures (not rely on some preprogrammed flight plan) so they can not only navigate the environment but also shape it and exploit unexpected events.

These principles of effectuation help entrepreneurs think in an environment of high uncertainty. Indeed organizations today operate in complex and dynamic environments that are increasingly characterized by rapid, substantial, and discontinuous change.[5] Given the nature of this type of environment, most managers of firms need to take on an entrepreneurial mind-set so that their firms can successfully adapt to environmental changes.[6] This entrepreneurial mind-set involves the ability to rapidly sense, act, and mobilize, even under uncertain conditions.[7] In developing an *entrepreneurial mind-set,* individuals must attempt to make sense of opportunities in the context of changing goals, constantly questioning one's "dominant logic" in the context of a changing environment, and revisiting "deceptively simple questions" about what we think to be true about markets and the firm. For example, effective entrepreneurs are thought to continuously "rethink current strategic actions, organization structure, communications systems, corporate culture, asset deployment, investment strategies, in short every aspect of a firm's operation and long-term health."[8]

entrepreneurial mind-set Involves the ability to rapidly sense, act, and mobilize, even under uncertain conditions

To be good at these tasks individuals must develop a *cognitive adaptability.* Mike Haynie, a retired major of the U.S. Air Force and now professor at Syracuse University, has developed a number of models of cognitive adaptability and a survey for capturing it, to which we now turn.[9]

The financial scandals of 2002 have already led to increased action by legislators and associations, and many companies are beginning to develop a code of ethics for all employees.

There are a number of advantages to implementing a code of ethics. The more your employees are aware of proper conduct, the more likely they are to do the right thing. They'll better understand their responsibilities and expectations and assume the appropriate level of accountability when identifying and managing business risks. A code of ethics is more than just a formal document outlining related policies. It's about integrating positive values throughout an organization. Here are some key components to an effective program:

Leaders Set the Example: Employees often model their own behavior after executives, managers, and others who've succeeded in the company. Therefore, everyone at every level must adhere to the firm's guidelines. What seems like a small action—discussing confidential financial information with a colleague, for instance—can have a ripple effect throughout all staff. If the members of senior management do not follow the highest ethical standards at all times, they shouldn't be surprised when those who report to them fail to do so.

Ethics Is a Core Value: Companies known for their ethical business practices make ethics a key element of their corporate culture. Conducting yourself with integrity is considered as important as bottom-line results. Ethical standards are applied anytime a decision is made or an action is taken, not just during controversial situations. A recent survey by our company found that more organizations are taking ethics into account when hiring employees. Fifty-eight percent of chief financial officers polled said the qualities that impress them most about applicants, aside from ability and willingness to do the job, are honesty and integrity. That's a substantial increase from only 32 percent in 1997.

Employees Feel Safe to Share Concerns: The work environment must be one in which people feel they can deliver bad news to management without fear of repercussions. In an ethics-driven company, staff members can report any type of wrongdoing—whether it is false information on an expense report or major financial fraud—and feel confident they will not suffer negative career consequences. Once supervisors are made aware of a potential problem, they need to take immediate action. Failure to follow through on even minor issues can undermine the success of an ethics program.

Having a code of ethics will not prevent every crisis, but it will ensure that staff members have a clear understanding of expectations. Collaborate with employees on defining the rules, and make sure everyone is aware of the requirements. Then take steps to instill core values throughout the organization. With regular reinforcement, ethics will guide every decision your team makes and become a central element in the way your company conducts business.

Source: From Max Messmer, "Does Your Company Have a Code of Ethics?" *Strategic Finance,* April 2003. Excerpted with permission from Strategic Finance published by the Institute of Management Accountants, Montvale, NJ. For more information about reprints from Strategic Finance, contact PARS International Corp. at 212/221-9595.

Cognitive Adaptability

cognitive adaptability Describes the extent to which entrepreneurs are dynamic, flexible, self-regulating, and engaged in the process of generating multiple decision frameworks focused on sensing and processing changes in their environments and then acting on them

Cognitive adaptability describes the extent to which entrepreneurs are dynamic, flexible, self-regulating, and *engaged* in the process of generating multiple decision frameworks focused on sensing and processing changes in their environments and then acting on them. Decision frameworks are organized prior knowledge about people and situations that are used to help someone make sense of what is going on.[10] Cognitive adaptability is reflected in an entrepreneur's metacognitive awareness, that is, the ability to reflect upon, understand, and control one's thinking and learning.[11] Specifically, metacognition describes a higher-order cognitive process that serves to organize what individuals know and recognize about themselves, tasks, situations, and their environments in order to promote effective and *adaptable* cognitive functioning in the face of feedback from complex and dynamic environments.[12]

How cognitively adaptable are you? Try the survey in Table 2.1 and compare yourself to some of your classmates. A higher score means that you are more metacognitively aware

TABLE 2.1 Mike Haynie's "Generalized Measure of Adaptive Cognition"

How Cognitively Flexible Are You? On a scale of 1 to 10, where 1 is "not very much like me," and 10 is "very much like me," how do you rate yourself on the following statements?

Goal Orientation	
I often define goals for myself.	**Not very much like me—1 2 3 4 5 6 7 8 9 10—Very much like me**
I understand how accomplishment of a task relates to my goals.	**Not very much like me—1 2 3 4 5 6 7 8 9 10—Very much like me**
I set specific goals before I begin a task.	**Not very much like me—1 2 3 4 5 6 7 8 9 10—Very much like me**
I ask myself how well I've accomplished my goals once I've finished.	**Not very much like me—1 2 3 4 5 6 7 8 9 10—Very much like me**
When performing a task, I frequently assess my progress against my objectives.	**Not very much like me—1 2 3 4 5 6 7 8 9 10—Very much like me**
Metacognitive Knowledge	
I think of several ways to solve a problem and choose the best one.	**Not very much like me—1 2 3 4 5 6 7 8 9 10—Very much like me**
I challenge my own assumptions about a task before I begin.	**Not very much like me—1 2 3 4 5 6 7 8 9 10—Very much like me**
I think about how others may react to my actions.	**Not very much like me—1 2 3 4 5 6 7 8 9 10—Very much like me**
I find myself automatically employing strategies that have worked in the past.	**Not very much like me—1 2 3 4 5 6 7 8 9 10—Very much like me**
I perform best when I already have knowledge of the task.	**Not very much like me—1 2 3 4 5 6 7 8 9 10—Very much like me**
I create my own examples to make information more meaningful.	**Not very much like me—1 2 3 4 5 6 7 8 9 10—Very much like me**
I try to use strategies that have worked in the past.	**Not very much like me—1 2 3 4 5 6 7 8 9 10—Very much like me**
I ask myself questions about the task before I begin.	**Not very much like me—1 2 3 4 5 6 7 8 9 10—Very much like me**
I try to translate new information into my own words.	**Not very much like me—1 2 3 4 5 6 7 8 9 10—Very much like me**
I try to break problems down into smaller components.	**Not very much like me—1 2 3 4 5 6 7 8 9 10—Very much like me**
I focus on the meaning and significance of new information.	**Not very much like me—1 2 3 4 5 6 7 8 9 10—Very much like me**
Metacognitive Experience	
I think about what I really need to accomplish before I begin a task.	**Not very much like me—1 2 3 4 5 6 7 8 9 10—Very much like me**
I use different strategies depending on the situation.	**Not very much like me—1 2 3 4 5 6 7 8 9 10—Very much like me**
I organize my time to best accomplish my goals.	**Not very much like me—1 2 3 4 5 6 7 8 9 10—Very much like me**

I am good at organizing information.	**Not very much like me—1 2 3 4 5 6 7 8 9 10—Very much like me**
I know what kind of information is most important to consider when faced with a problem.	**Not very much like me—1 2 3 4 5 6 7 8 9 10—Very much like me**
I consciously focus my attention on important information.	**Not very much like me—1 2 3 4 5 6 7 8 9 10—Very much like me**
My "gut" tells me when a given strategy I use will be most effective.	**Not very much like me—1 2 3 4 5 6 7 8 9 10—Very much like me**
I depend on my intuition to help me formulate strategies.	**Not very much like me—1 2 3 4 5 6 7 8 9 10—Very much like me**
Metacognitive Choice	
I ask myself if I have considered all the options when solving a problem.	**Not very much like me—1 2 3 4 5 6 7 8 9 10—Very much like me**
I ask myself if there was an easier way to do things after I finish a task.	**Not very much like me—1 2 3 4 5 6 7 8 9 10—Very much like me**
I ask myself if I have considered all the options after I solve a problem.	**Not very much like me—1 2 3 4 5 6 7 8 9 10—Very much like me**
I re-evaluate my assumptions when I get confused.	**Not very much like me—1 2 3 4 5 6 7 8 9 10—Very much like me**
I ask myself if I have learned as much as I could have after I finish the task.	**Not very much like me—1 2 3 4 5 6 7 8 9 10—Very much like me**
Monitoring	
I periodically review to help me understand important relationships.	**Not very much like me—1 2 3 4 5 6 7 8 9 10—Very much like me**
I stop and go back over information that is not clear.	**Not very much like me—1 2 3 4 5 6 7 8 9 10—Very much like me**
I am aware of what strategies I use when engaged in a given task.	**Not very much like me—1 2 3 4 5 6 7 8 9 10—Very much like me**
I find myself analyzing the usefulness of a given strategy while engaged in a given task.	**Not very much like me—1 2 3 4 5 6 7 8 9 10—Very much like me**
I find myself pausing regularly to check my comprehension of the problem or situation at hand.	**Not very much like me—1 2 3 4 5 6 7 8 9 10—Very much like me**
I ask myself questions about how well I am doing while I am performing a novel task. I stop and re-read when I get confused.	**Not very much like me—1 2 3 4 5 6 7 8 9 10—Very much like me**

Result—A higher score means that you are more aware of the way that you think about how you make decisions and are therefore more likely to be cognitively flexible.

Source: M. Haynie and D. Shepherd (working paper), "A General Measure of Adaptive Cognition: A Metacognitive Perspective for Capturing the Entrepreneurial Mindset."

and this in turn helps provide cognitive adaptability. Regardless of your score, the good news is that you can learn to be more cognitively adaptable. This ability will serve you well in most new tasks, but particularly when pursuing a new entry and managing a firm in an uncertain environment. Put simply, it requires us to "think about thinking which requires, and helps provide, knowledge and control over our thinking and learning activities—it requires us to be self-aware, to think aloud, to reflect, to be strategic, to plan, to have a plan in mind, to know what to know, to self-monitor.[13] We can achieve this by asking ourselves a series of questions that relate to (1) comprehension, (2) connection, (3) strategy, and (4) reflection.[14]

comprehension questions Questions designed to increase entrepreneurs' understanding of the nature of the environment

1. *Comprehension questions* are designed to increase entrepreneurs' understanding of the nature of the environment before they begin to address an entrepreneurial challenge, whether it be a change in the environment or the assessment of a potential opportunity. Understanding arises from recognition that a problem or opportunity exists, the nature of that situation, and its implications. In general, the questions that stimulate individuals to think about comprehension include: What is the problem all about? What is the question? What are the meanings of the key concepts? Specific to entrepreneurs, the questions are more likely to include: What is this market all about? What is this technology all about? What do we want to achieve by creating this new firm? What are the key elements to effectively pursuing this opportunity?

connection tasks Tasks designed to stimulate entrepreneurs to think about the current situation in terms of similarities and differences with situations previously faced and solved

2. *Connection tasks* are designed to stimulate entrepreneurs to think about the current situation in terms of similarities and differences with situations previously faced and solved. In other words, these tasks prompt the entrepreneur to tap into his or her knowledge and experience without overgeneralizing. Generally, connection tasks focus on questions like: How is this problem similar to problems I have already solved? Why? How is this problem different from what I have already solved? Why? Specific to entrepreneurs, the questions are more likely to include: How is this new environment similar to others in which I have operated? How is it different? How is this new organization similar to the established organizations I have managed? How is it different?

strategic tasks Tasks designed to stimulate entrepreneurs to think about which strategies are appropriate for solving the problem (and why) or pursuing the opportunity (and how)

3. *Strategic tasks* are designed to stimulate entrepreneurs to think about which strategies are appropriate for solving the problem (and why) or pursuing the opportunity (and how). These tasks prompt them to think about the what, why, and how of their approach to the situation. Generally, these questions include: What strategy/tactic/principle can I use to solve this problem? Why is this strategy/tactic/principle the most appropriate one? How can I organize the information to solve the problem? How can I implement the plan? Specific to entrepreneurs, the questions are likely to include: What changes to strategic position, organizational structure, and culture will help us manage our newness? How can the implementation of this strategy be made feasible?

reflection tasks Tasks designed to stimulate entrepreneurs to think about their understanding and feelings as they progress through the entrepreneurial process

4. *Reflection tasks* are designed to stimulate entrepreneurs to think about their understanding and feelings as they progress through the entrepreneurial process. These tasks prompt entrepreneurs to generate their own feedback (create a feedback loop in their solution process) to provide the opportunity to change. Generally, reflection questions include: What am I doing? Does it make sense? What difficulties am I facing? How do I feel? How can I verify the solution? Can I use another approach for solving the task? Specific to the entrepreneurial context, entrepreneurs might ask: What difficulties will we have in convincing our stakeholders? Is there a better way to implement our strategy? How will we know success if we see it?

Entrepreneurs who are able to increase cognitive adaptability have an improved ability to (1) adapt to new situations—i.e., it provides a basis by which a person's prior experience and knowledge affect learning or problem solving in a new situation; (2) be creative—i.e., it can lead to original and adaptive ideas, solutions, or insights; and (3) communicate one's reasoning behind a particular response.[15] We hope that this section of the book has not only provided you a deeper understanding of how entrepreneurs can think and act with great flexibility, but also an awareness of some techniques for incorporating cognitive adaptability in your life.

We have discussed how entrepreneurs make decisions in uncertain environments and how one might develop an ability to be more cognitively flexible. It is important to note that entrepreneurs operate in such uncertain environments because that is where the opportunities for new entry are to be found and/or generated. There is the possibility that opportunities exist in more stable environments, but even in this situation the entrepreneur's new entry may create industry instability and uncertainty. Given the inherent uncertainty in entrepreneurial action, there is the possibility that an entrepreneur will experience failure. Failure can be valuable if the entrepreneur is able to learn from it. We now investigate the process of learning from business failure.

Learning from Business Failure[16]

Businesses fail. In 2004, a total of 9,186 U.S. firms filed for Chapter 11 bankruptcy (Chapter 11 provides for a business to continue operations while formulating a plan to repay its creditors) and 20,192 U.S. firms filed for Chapter 7 bankruptcy (Chapter 7 is designed to allow individuals to keep certain exempt property while the remaining property is sold to repay creditors) (www.uscourts.gov). Business failure occurs when a fall in revenue and/or a rise in expense is of such magnitude that the firm becomes insolvent and is unable to attract new debt or equity funding; consequently, it cannot continue to operate under the current ownership and management. Failure is particularly common among entrepreneurial firms because the newness that is the source of an opportunity is also a source of uncertainty and changing conditions.

Although there are many causes of business failure, the most common is insufficient experience. That is, entrepreneurs who have more experience will possess the knowledge to perform more effectively the roles and tasks necessary for success. This experience need not come solely from success. In fact, it appears that we may learn more from our failures than our successes.[17]

A leading entrepreneurship scholar, Rita McGrath, has argued that because entrepreneurs typically seek success and try to avoid failure their projects, errors are introduced that can not only inhibit the learning and interpretation processes but also make project failure more likely or expensive than necessary. She proposes that there are benefits to be gained from the pursuit of risky opportunities, even if that pursuit increases the potential for failure. This entrepreneurial process of experimentation generates improvements in technologies.[18] Although Professor McGrath focuses on the failure of projects within a firm, it appears that the process of learning from failure also benefits society through the application of that knowledge to subsequent businesses. Other businesses can learn from an entrepreneur's mistake and that learning can help our economy.

But what about the entrepreneur who is the owner/manager of a business that fails? Is this an opportunity to learn? Perhaps, but it would seem that the issue is more complex. The motivation for managing one's own business is typically not simply one of personal profit but also loyalty to a product, loyalty to a market and customers, personal growth, and the need to prove oneself.[19] Some entrepreneurs use their business to "create a product that flows from their own internal desires and needs. They create primarily to express subjective conceptions of beauty, emotion, or some aesthetic ideal."[20] For members of a family business, the firm may not only be a source of income but also a context for family activity and the embodiment of family pride and identity. This suggests that the loss of a business is likely to generate a negative emotional response from the entrepreneur; this negative emotional response is referred to as *grief*.[21]

grief A negative emotional response a person feels from the loss of something important

Although we normally think of grief as occurring in the context of the death of a loved one, a broadly similar reaction can occur when a close relationship is ended through separation, or when a person is forced to give up some aspect of life deemed to be important.[22] One entrepreneur that I know exhibited a number of worrying emotions when his family business failed. There was numbness and disbelief that this business he had created 20-odd years ago was no longer alive. There was some anger toward the economy, competitors, and debtors. A stronger emotion than anger was that of guilt and self-blame. He felt guilty that he had caused the failure of the business, that it could no longer be passed on to his children, and that as a result he had failed not only as a businessperson but also as a father. These feelings caused him distress and anxiety. He felt the situation was hopeless, became withdrawn, and at times depressed. These are all symptoms of grief. After the failure of their business, it is likely that most entrepreneurs feel grief—a negative emotional response to the loss of their business, capable of triggering behavioral, psychological, and physiological symptoms.

This grief can interfere with entrepreneurs' ability to learn from the failure and quite possibly their motivation to try again. For entrepreneurs, learning from business failure occurs when they can use the information available about why the business failed (*feedback information*) to revise their existing knowledge of how to manage their own business effectively (*entrepreneurial knowledge*)—that is, revise assumptions about the consequences of previous assessments, decisions, actions, and inactions. For example, Ravi Kalakota has learned a number of lessons from the loss of his business, Hsupply.com, such as, "Don't let venture capitalists hijack your vision," "Don't rapidly burn through capital to achieve short-term growth," and "Don't underestimate the speed others will imitate your products and services."[23]

Grief is a negative emotional response, and negative emotion(s) have been found to interfere with individuals' allocation of attention in the processing of information. Such interference negatively impacts an individual's ability to learn from that negative event.[24] For the entrepreneur, this could mean focusing attention on the day that the business closed (i.e., dwelling on announcements to employees, buyers, and suppliers, as well as handing over the office keys to a liquidator), rather than allocating sufficient attention on feedback information, such as previous actions and/or inactions that caused the deterioration in business performance and ultimately the loss of the business.

Grief Recovery Process An individual has recovered from grief when thoughts about the events surrounding, and leading up to, the loss of the business no longer generate a negative emotional response. Those that feel grief over the loss of a business will eventually recover from grief or will suffer chronic grief requiring professional psychological assistance (which is beyond the scope of this book). The two primary descriptions of the process of recovering from grief are classifiable as either loss-oriented or restoration-oriented.

loss-orientation An approach to grief recovery that involves working through, and processing, some aspect of the loss experience and, as a result of this process, breaking emotional bonds to the object lost

restoration-orientation An approach to grief recovery based on both avoidance and a proactiveness toward secondary sources of stress arising from a major loss

Loss-orientation refers to working through, and processing, some aspect of the loss experience and, as a result of this process, breaking emotional bonds to the object lost. This process of constructing a series of accounts about the loss gradually provides the loss with meaning and eventually produces a changed viewpoint of the self and the world. Changing the way that an event is interpreted can allow an individual to regulate emotions so that thoughts of the event no longer generate negative emotions. Entrepreneurs with a loss-orientation might seek out friends, family, or psychologists to talk about their grief. But they may also focus their thoughts on the time spent in creating and nurturing the business and may ruminate about the circumstances and events surrounding the loss of the business. It appears that such thoughts could evoke a sense of yearning for the way things used to be or foster a sense of relief that the events surrounding the loss (e.g., arguing with creditors, explaining to employees, family, and friends the business has failed) are finally over. While these feelings of relief and pain wax and wane over time, in the early periods of grief, painful memories are likely to dominate.[25]

Restoration-orientation is based on both avoidance and a proactiveness toward secondary sources of stress arising from the loss of the business. For avoidance, it is possible that entrepreneurs can distract themselves from thinking about the loss of the business to speed recovery from grief. For the entrepreneur, founding a new business might enhance recovery from grief over the loss of a previous business (although there is the possibility that the same mistakes will be replicated because these individuals have not sufficiently learned from the loss).

A restoration-orientation is not simply about avoidance, however; it also involves the way that a person attends to other aspects of his or her life (e.g., coping with daily life, learning new tasks). It refers to being proactive toward secondary sources of stress instead of being concerned with the loss itself. Such activities enable individuals to distract themselves from thinking about the loss while simultaneously maintaining essential activities necessary for restructuring aspects of their lives. This may apply to the entrepreneur, for whom the loss of the business itself generates a negative emotional response while causing the loss of income, social status, and positive perceptions of self. For example, an entrepreneur must reorganize his life to cope without the business. It might be necessary to apply for jobs, join the unemployment line, and/or sell the house and move to a less expensive neighborhood (requiring the children to change schools). There might also be other stressors, such as responding to questions such as: "What do you do for a living?" or "How is your business going?" In addressing these secondary sources of stress, the entrepreneur is able to eventually reduce the negative emotions associated with thoughts of the events surrounding the loss of the business.

A Dual Process for Grief Which process of grief recovery is most effective? It is not an "either/or" choice between the two orientations. Both loss-oriented and restoration-oriented coping styles are likely to have different costs. A loss-orientation involves confrontation, which is physically and mentally exhausting, whereas a restoration-orientation involves suppression, which requires mental effort and presents potentially adverse consequences for health. Oscillation between the two grief orientations enables a person to obtain the benefits of each and to minimize the costs of maintaining one for too long—this *dual process* speeds the recovery process.[26] Speeding the recovery process is important because it more quickly reduces the emotional interference with learning.

dual process for grief Involves oscillation between the two grief recovery approaches (loss-orientation and restoration-orientation)

For example, starting with a loss-orientation provides an individual the ability to first focus on aspects of the loss experience and begin processing information about the business loss as well as breaking the emotional bonds to the business. When one's attention begins to shift from the event to aspects of the grief itself then learning is likely reduced by emotional interference and the individual should switch to a restoration-orientation. Switching to a restoration-orientation encourages individuals to think about other aspects of their life. It also breaks the cycle of continually thinking about the symptoms of grief; such thoughts can increase feelings of grief.[27] This restoration-orientation also provides the opportunity to address secondary causes of stress, which may reduce the emotional significance of the loss of the business. When information processing capacity is no longer focused on the symptoms associated with grief, the individual can shift back to a loss-orientation and use his/her information processing capacity to generate further meaning from the loss experience and also further reduce the emotional significance of the loss of the business. Oscillation should continue until the self-employed individual has recovered from grief.

Bill Lewis represents an example of someone who has experienced grief and recovered from it. He had founded eight businesses and been through two bankruptcies when he was interviewed by *Inc.* magazine.[28] He stated:

> [The business is] a child. . . . [Losing the business] was devastating. . . . The things that were going on in my life—I'd lost my company, lost my home, lost everything. I couldn't handle it. . . . There was a time . . . when I sat in my office and cried, and then put a gun to my head. . . . When I finally got over all that [pain and anger associated with the loss of the

business] was when I quit blaming other people. . . . It was my fault because I didn't plan far enough ahead. It was stupid as hell of me to sit there exposed like that. . . . Listen, this lesson was extremely expensive. I paid dearly, my family paid dearly. . . . Yeah, I learned a lot. . . . I'd be an incredible CEO for some company. I'm the best.

The dual process of grief recovery has a number of practical implications. First, knowledge that the feelings and reactions being experienced by the entrepreneur are normal for someone dealing with such a loss may help to reduce feelings of shame and embarrassment. This in turn might encourage the entrepreneur to articulate her feelings of grief, possibly speeding the recovery process. Second, there are psychological and physiological outcomes caused by the feelings of loss associated with grief. Realizing that these are "symptoms" of grief can reduce secondary sources of stress and may also assist with the choice of treatment. Third, there is a process of recovery from grief, which offers entrepreneurs some comfort that their current feelings of loss, sadness, and helplessness will eventually diminish. Fourth, the recovery and learning process can be enhanced by some degree of oscillation between a loss- and a restoration-orientation. Finally, recovery from loss offers an opportunity to increase one's knowledge of entrepreneurship. This provides benefits to the individual and to society.

MANAGERIAL VERSUS ENTREPRENEURIAL DECISION MAKING

Although we normally think of entrepreneurship in terms of individuals creating new organizations, Chapter 1 indicated that firms (as well as individuals) can be entrepreneurial. Howard Stevenson, a professor at Harvard University, believes that entrepreneurship represents a mode of managing an existing firm that is distinct from the way existing firms are traditionally managed. Entrepreneurial management is distinct from traditional management in terms of eight dimensions: (1) strategic orientation, (2) commitment to opportunity, (3) commitment of resources, (4) control of resources, (5) management structure, (6) reward philosophy, (7) growth orientation, and (8) entrepreneurial culture.[29] The nature of the differences among these dimensions in represented in Table 2.2 and described in greater detail below.[30]

TABLE 2.2 Distinguishing Entrepreneurially from Traditionally Managed Firms

Entrepreneurial Focus	Conceptual Dimension	Administrative Focus
Driven by perception of opportunity	Strategic orientation	Driven by controlled resources
Revolutionary with short duration	Commitment to opportunity	Evolutionary with long duration
Many stages with minimal exposure	Commitment of resources	A single stage with complete commitment out of decision
Episodic use or rent of required resources	Control of resources	Ownership or employment of required resources
Flat with multiple informal networks	Management structure	Hierarchy
Based on value creation	Reward philosophy	Based on responsibility and seniority
Rapid growth is top priority; risk accepted to achieve growth	Growth orientation	Safe, slow, and steady
Promoting broad search for opportunities	Entrepreneurial culture	Opportunity search restricted by controlled resources; failure punished

Source: This table is taken from T. Brown, P. Davidsson, and J. Wiklund, "An Operationalization of Stevenson's Conceptualization of Entrepreneurship as Opportunity-Based Firm Behavior," *Strategic Management Journal* 22 (2001), p. 955.

AS SEEN IN *ENTREPRENEUR* MAGAZINE

WHAT ME WORRY? HOW SMART ENTREPRENEURS HARNESS THE POWER OF PARANOIA

Depending on who you're talking to, paranoia is: (1) a psychotic disorder characterized by delusions of persecution, (2) an irrational distrust of others, or (3) a key trait in entrepreneurial success.

Sound crazy? Not according to Andrew S. Grove, president and CEO of Intel Corp. in Santa Clara, California, and author of *Only the Paranoid Survive* (Doubleday/Currency). The title of Grove's book comes from an oft-repeated quote that has become the mantra of the chip king's rise to the top of the technology business.

"I have no idea when I first said this," Grove writes, "but the fact remains that, when it comes to business, I believe in the value of paranoia." To those who suffer from clinical delusions of persecution, of course, paranoia is neither a joke nor a help. However, in a business context, the practice of voluntarily being highly concerned about potential threats to your company has something of a following.

"If you're not a little bit paranoid, you're complacent," says Dave Lakhani, an entrepreneur in Boise, Idaho, who offers marketing consulting to small businesses. "And complacency is what leads people into missed opportunities and business failure."

PICK YOUR PARANOIA

Being paranoid, according to Grove, is a matter of remembering that others want the success you have, paying attention to the details of your business, and watching for the trouble that inevitably awaits. That basically means he is paranoid about everything. "I worry about products getting screwed up, and I worry about products getting introduced prematurely," Grove writes. "I worry about factories not performing well, and I worry about having too many factories."

For Grove, as for most advocates of paranoia, being paranoid primarily consists of two things. The first is not resting on your laurels. Grove calls it a "guardian attitude" that he attempts to nurture in himself and in Intel's employees to fend off threats from outside the company. Paranoia in business is also typically defined as paying very close attention to the fine points. "You need to be detail-oriented about the most important things in your business," says Lakhani. "That means not only making sure you're working in your business but that you're there every day, paying attention to your customers."

As an example of paranoia's value in practice, Lakhani recalls when sales began slowly slumping at a retail store he once owned. He could have dismissed it as a mere blip. Instead, he worried and watched until he spotted a concrete cause. "It turned out one of my employees had developed a negative attitude, and it was affecting my business," Lakhani says. "As soon as I let him go, sales went back up."

The main focuses of most entrepreneurs' paranoia, however, are not so much everyday internal details as major competitive threats and missed opportunities. Situations in which competition and opportunity are both at high levels are called "strategic inflection points" by Grove, and it is during these times, typically when technology is changing, that his paranoia is sharpest.

Paranoia is frequently a welcome presence at major client presentations for Katharine Paine, founder and CEO of The Delahaye Group Inc. In the past, twinges of seemingly unfounded worry have caused Paine to personally attend sales pitches where she learned of serious problems with the way her firm was doing business, she says. The head of the 50-person Portsmouth, New Hampshire, marketing evaluation research firm traces her paranoid style to childhood days spent pretending to be an Indian tracking quarry through the forest. When she makes mental checklists about things that could go wrong or opportunities that could be missed, she's always keeping an eye out for the business equivalent of a bent twig. "If you are paranoid enough, if you're good enough at picking up all those clues, you don't have to just react," says Paine, "you get to proact and be slightly ahead of the curve."

Strategic Orientation and Commitment to Opportunity

The first two factors that help distinguish more entrepreneurially managed firms from those that are more traditionally managed relate to strategic issues—strategic orientation and commitment to opportunity. An emphasis on strategy in developing a deeper understanding of

PARANOID PARAMETERS

There is, of course, such a thing as being too paranoid. "There are times when it doesn't make any sense," acknowledges Lakhani. Focusing on details to the point of spending $500 in accounting fees to find a $5 error is one example of misplaced paranoia. Worrying obsessively about what every competitor is doing or what every potential customer is thinking is also a warning sign, he says. Lack of balance with interests outside the business may be another. "If your whole life is focused around your work, and that's the only thing you're thinking about 24 hours a day, that becomes detrimental," Lakhani says.

For Paine, failing to act is a sign that you're going past beneficial paranoia and into hurtful fear. "Fear for most of us results in inaction—absolute death for an entrepreneur," she says. "If we feared the loss of a paycheck or feared entering a new market, none of our businesses would have gotten off the ground."

All this may be especially true for small-business owners. While paranoia may be appropriate for heads of far-flung enterprises, some say entrepreneurs are already too paranoid. It's all too easy for entrepreneurs to take their desire for independence and self-determination and turn it into trouble, says Robert Barbato, director of the Small Business Institute at the Rochester Institute of Technology in Rochester, New York. Typically, entrepreneurs take the attitude that "nobody cares as much about this business as I do" and exaggerate it to the point of hurtful paranoia toward employees and even customers, he says. "They're seeing ghosts where ghosts don't exist," warns Barbato.

That's especially risky when it comes to dealing with employees. Most people—not just entrepreneurs—do their work for the sense of accomplishment, not because they are plotting to steal their employer's success, Barbato says. He acknowledges this may be a difficult concept for competition-crazed entrepreneurs—especially those who have never themselves been employees—to understand. "People who own their own business are not necessarily used to moving up the ranks," Barbato notes. Entrepreneurs must learn to trust and delegate if their businesses are to grow.

PRACTICAL PARANOIA

No matter how useful it is, paranoia may be too loaded a label for some entrepreneurs. If so, critical evaluation or critical analysis are the preferred terms of Stephen Markowitz, director of governmental and political relations of the Small Business Association of Delaware Valley, a 5,000-member trade group. The distinction is more than name-deep. "When I say 'critically evaluate,' that means look at everything," Markowitz explains. "If you're totally paranoid, the danger is not being able to critically evaluate everything."

For example, Markowitz says a small retailer threatened by the impending arrival of a superstore in the market would be better served by critically evaluating the potential for benefit as well as harm, instead of merely worrying about it. "If you're paranoid," he says, "you're not going to critically evaluate how it might help you."

Whatever name it goes by, few entrepreneurs are likely to stop worrying anytime soon. In fact, experience tends to make them more confirmed in their paranoia as they go along. Paine recalls the time a formless fear led her to insist on going to a client meeting where no trouble was expected. She lost the account anyway. "The good news is, my paranoia kicked in," she says. "The bad news is, it was too late. That made me much more paranoid in the future."

ADVICE TO AN ENTREPRENEUR

A friend who has just become an entrepreneur has read the above article and comes to you for advice:

1. I worry about my business, does that mean that I am paranoid?
2. What are the benefits of paranoia and what are the costs?
3. How do I know I have the right level of paranoia to effectively run the business and not put me in the hospital with a stomach ulcer?
4. Won't forcing myself to be more paranoid take the fun out of being an entrepreneur?

Source: Reprinted with permission of Entrepreneur Media, Inc., "How Smart Entrepreneurs Harness the Power of Paranioa," by Mark Henricks, March, 1997, *Entrepreneur* magazine: www.entrepreneur.com.

entrepreneurship at the firm level is not surprising because both entrepreneurship and strategy have important implications for the performance of the firm.

Strategic orientation refers to those factors that are inputs into the formulation of the firm's strategy. We can think of it as the philosophy of the firm that drives its decision about strategy; the way that it looks at the world and the way it looks at itself and these perceptions are the driving factors behind the firm's strategy. The strategy of entrepreneurial management is driven by the presence or generation of opportunities for new entry and is less concerned about the resources that may be required to pursue such opportunities. Acquiring and marshaling the necessary resources represents a secondary step for the entrepreneurially managed firm and perhaps part of the thinking about the implementation of discovered opportunities. Resources do not constrain the strategic thinking of an entrepreneurially managed firm. In contrast, the strategy of traditional management is to use the resources of the firm efficiently. Therefore the type and the amount of resources that the firm has (or knows it can readily access) represent a key starting point for thinking strategically about the future of the firm. Only those opportunities that can be pursued effectively using existing resources are considered the appropriate domain of further strategic thinking.

Both entrepreneurship and strategy are more than simply thinking about the future of the firm, they are also concerned with the firm taking action. It is through its actions that a firm is judged, often by analysis of its financial and competitive performance. Entrepreneurially and traditionally managed firms can be distinguished in terms of their commitment to opportunity. More entrepreneurially managed firms are commited to taking action on potential opportunities and therefore can pursue opportunities rapidly, making the most of windows of opportunity. They also are able to withdraw their resources from a particular opportunity and do so rapidly, such that if initial feedback from the pursuit of an opportunity provides information suggesting that it might not be the right opportunity for the firm, then management can "pull the plug," minimizing losses from the initial pursuit. In contrast, traditionally managed firms tend to place considerable emphasis on information; information is derived from data collection and analysis of that information to determine, say, the return on resources to be deployed. If the traditionally managed firm chooses to pursue the given opportunity, it would be with a much larger initial investment and the intention of remaining in that line of business for a considerable time.

Commitment of Resources and Control of Resources

It is important to note that entrepreneurs still care about the resources they must commit to the pursuit of an opportunity, but the opportunity is central to their thinking. Thoughts of resources turn more to how the firm can minimize the resources that would be required in the pursuit of a particular opportunity. By minimizing the resources that the firm must invest in order to initially pursue an opportunity, the amount of resources at risk if the opportunity does not "pan out" is also minimized. For example, entrepreneurially managed firms may "test the waters" by committing small amounts of resources in a multistep manner with minimal (risk) exposure at each step. This small and incremental process of resource commitment provides the firm the flexibility to change direction rapidly as new information about the opportunity or the environment comes to light. Psychologically, these smaller sunk costs help stop entrepreneurially managed firms from becoming entrenched with a particular course of action, especially if that course of action turns out to be a losing one. In contrast, when traditionally managed firms decide to commit resources to an opportunity, they do so on a large scale. That is, rather than put a toe in to test the water, they make calculations based on the ambient temperature over the last week, the density of the water, and whether a pool cover has been used or not. If, based on that calculation, the water is theoretically deemed to be sufficiently warm, the traditional manager commits to that assessment with a full swan dive. Having made a large commitment of resources the firm often feels compelled to justify the initial decision to commit and so the initial commitment gains momentum that maintains the status quo of continual resource commitment. Therefore, a traditionally managed firm uses in-depth analysis of available information to go for it or not—and if they do go for it, then the investment of resources is not easily reversed.

Over and above the commitment of resources, entrepreneurially and traditionally managed firms differ in their control of resources. Entrepreneurially managed firms are less concerned about the ownership of resources and more concerned about having access to others' resources, including financial capital, intellectual capital, skills, competencies, and so on. Entrepreneurially managed firms operate from the standpoint, "Why do I need to control resources if I can access them from others?" Access to resources is possible to the extent that the opportunity allows the firm to effectively deploy others' resources for the benefit of the entrepreneurial firm *and* the owner of the invested resources. In contrast, traditionally managed firms focus on the ownership of resources and the accumulation of further resources. They believe that if they control their own resources then they are self-contained. For these firms, the control that comes with ownership means that resources can be deployed more effectively for the benefit of the firm.

Management Structure and Reward Philosophy

The management structure of the entrepreneurially managed firm is organic. That is, the organizational structure has few layers of bureaucracy between top management and the customer and typically has multiple informal networks. In this way, entrepreneurially managed firms are able to capture and communicate more information from the external environment and are sufficiently "fluid" to be able to take quick action based on that information.

In addition, entrepreneurially managed firms are more structured to make use of both their internal networks (for example, through informal communication channels at work) and external networks (with buyers, suppliers, and financial institutions), which provide information and other resources important in the discovery/generation and exploitation of opportunities. In contrast, the traditionally managed firm has a structure well suited for the internal efficiencies of allocating controlled resources. There is a formalized hierarchy with clear roles and responsibilities, highly routinized work, and layers of middle management to "manage" employees' use of the firm's resources. Traditionally managed firms have structures that are typically inwardly focused on efficiency rather than on detecting and rapidly acting on changes in the external environment.

Firms are organized not only by their structures but also by their reward philosophy. The entrepreneurially managed firm is focused on pursuing opportunities for new entry that represent new value for the firm (and hopefully for others, including society as a whole). It is not surprising then that entrepreneurially managed firms have a philosophy toward rewards that compensates employees based on their contribution toward the discovery/generation and exploitation of opportunity. Given the organic structure described above, employees often have the freedom to experiment with potential opportunities and are rewarded accordingly. The traditionally managed firm rewards management and employees based on their responsibilities, where responsibilities are typically determined by the amount of resources (assets and/or people) that this manager or employee controls. Promotion is a reward and provides that manager control of even more resources and therefore further scope for rewards.

Growth Orientation and Entrepreneurial Culture

In an entrepreneurially managed firm there is a great desire to grow the firm and do so at a rapid pace. Although traditionally managed firms may also desire to grow, they prefer growth to be slow and at a steady pace. That is, they prefer a pace of growth that is more "manageable" in that it does not "unsettle the firm" by putting at risk the resources that the firm controls and thus does not put at risk the jobs and power of top management.

Culture also distinguishes entrepreneurially and traditionally managed firms. Entrepreneurially managed firms provide an organizational culture that encourages employees to generate ideas, experiment, and engage in other tasks that might produce creative output. Such

TABLE 2.3 Scale to Capture How Entrepreneurially a Firm Is Managed

	Strategic Orientation	
As we define our strategies, our major concern is how to best utilize the sources we control.	1 2 3 4 5 6 7 8 9 10	We are not constrained by the resources at (or not at) hand.
We limit the opportunities we pursue on the basis of our current resources.	1 2 3 4 5 6 7 8 9 10	Our fundamental task is to pursue opportunities we perceive as valuable and then to acquire the resources to exploit them.
The resources we have significantly influence our business strategies.	1 2 3 4 5 6 7 8 9 10	Opportunities control our business strategies.
	Resource Orientation	
Since our objective is to use our resources, we will usually invest heavily and rapidly.	1 2 3 4 5 6 7 8 9 10	Since we do not need resources to commence the pursuit of an opportunity, our commitment of resources may be in stages.
We prefer to totally control and own the resources we use.	1 2 3 4 5 6 7 8 9 10	All we need from resources is the ability to use them.
We prefer to use only our own resources in our ventures.	1 2 3 4 5 6 7 8 9 10	We like to employ resources that we borrow or rent.
In exploiting opportunities, access to money is more important than just having the idea.	1 2 3 4 5 6 7 8 9 10	In exploiting opportunities, having the idea is more important than just having the money.
	Management Structure	
We prefer tight control of funds and operations by means of sophisticated control and information systems.	1 2 3 4 5 6 7 8 9 10	We prefer loose, informal control. There is a dependence on informal relations.
We strongly emphasize getting things done by following formal processes and procedures.	1 2 3 4 5 6 7 8 9 10	We strongly emphasize getting things done even if this means disregarding formal procedures.
We strongly emphasize holding to tried and true management principles and industry norms.	1 2 3 4 5 6 7 8 9 10	We strongly emphasize adapting freely to changing circumstances without much concern for past practices.
There is a strong insistence on a uniform management style throughout the firm.	1 2 3 4 5 6 7 8 9 10	Managers' operating styles are allowed to range freely from very formal to very informal.

output is highly valued by entrepreneurial management because it is often the source of opportunities for new entries. Opportunities are the focus of the entrepreneurially managed firm.

In contrast, the traditionally managed firm begins with an assessment of the resources that it controls and this is reflected in its organizational culture. So while a traditionally managed firm is still interested in ideas, it is only interested in ideas that revolve around currently controlled resources. With only ideas considered that relate to currently controlled resources, the scope of opportunities discovered and generated by a traditionally managed firm is limited. Entrepreneurial culture is discussed in greater detail in Chapter 3.

It is unlikely that there are many firms that are "purely" entrepreneurially managed or purely traditionally managed; most firms fall somewhere in between. Table 2.3 presents a scale for determining how entrepreneurially managed a particular firm is. The higher the score, the more entrepreneurially managed the firm is.

There is a strong emphasis on getting line and staff personnel to adhere closely to their formal job descriptions.	1 2 3 4 5 6 7 8 9 10	There is a strong tendency to let the requirements of the situation and the personality of the individual dictate proper job behavior.
	Reward Philosophy	
Our employees are evaluated and compensated based on their responsibilities.	1 2 3 4 5 6 7 8 9 10	Our employees are evaluated and compensated based on the value they add to the firm.
Our employees are usually rewarded by promotion and annual raises.	1 2 3 4 5 6 7 8 9 10	We try to compensate our employees by devising ways that they can benefit from the increased value of the firm.
An employee's standing is based on the amount of responsibility s/he has.	1 2 3 4 5 6 7 8 9 10	An employee's standing is based on the value s/he adds.
	Growth Orientation	
Growth is not necessarily our top objective. Long-term survival may be at least as important.	1 2 3 4 5 6 7 8 9 10	It is generally known throughout the firm that growth is our top objective.
It is generally known throughout the firm that steady and sure growth is the best way to expand.	1 2 3 4 5 6 7 8 9 10	It is generally known throughout the firm that our intention is to grow as big and as fast as possible.
	Entrepreneurial Culture	
It is difficult to find a sufficient number of promising ideas to utilize all of our resources.	1 2 3 4 5 6 7 8 9 10	We have many more promising ideas than we have time and resources to pursue.
Changes in the society-at-large seldom lead to commercially promising ideas for our firm.	1 2 3 4 5 6 7 8 9 10	Changes in the society-at-large often give us ideas for new products and services.
It is difficult for our firm to find ideas that can be converted into profitable products/services.	1 2 3 4 5 6 7 8 9 10	We never experience a lack of ideas that we can convert into profitable products/services.

Source: This table is taken from T. Brown, P. Davidsson, and J. Wiklund, "An Operationalization of Stevenson's Conceptualization of Entrepreneurship as Opportunity-Based Firm Behavior," *Strategic Management Journal* 22 (2001), Appendix.

IN REVIEW

SUMMARY

In this chapter we focused on the mind-set of entrepreneurs and entrepreneurial firms. We started with the concept of effectuation, which challenges traditional notions of the way that entrepreneurs think about their tasks. Although entrepreneurs think about some tasks in a causal way, they also are likely to think about some tasks effectually (and some entrepreneurs more so than other entrepreneurs). Rather than starting with the desired outcome in mind and then focusing on the means to achieving that outcome, entrepreneurs sometimes approach tasks by looking at what they have—their means—and selecting among possible outcomes. Who is to say whether the "causal chef" that starts with a menu or the "effectual chef" that starts with what is in the cupboard produces the best meal? But we can say that expert entrepreneurs think effectually about opportunities. The notion of effectuation leads to five principles: (1) the patchwork quilt principle, (2) the affordable loss principle, (3) the bird-in-the-hand principle, (4) the lemonade principle, and (5) the pilot-in-the-plane principle.

These principles help entrepreneurs make decisions in uncertain environments. When dealing with uncertainty, entrepreneurs must remain flexible in the way that they think and in their actions. In this chapter we introduced the notion of cognitive flexibility and emphasized that it is something that can be measured and learned. By asking questions related to comprehension, connection, strategy, and reflection, entrepreneurs can maintain an awareness of their thought process and in doing so develop greater cognitive adaptability.

Despite the way that he thinks (causally or effectually) and despite being cognitively flexible, an entrepreneur's firm may still fail. Failure represents an opportunity to learn but that learning is typically not automatic or instantaneous. Rather, learning from failure is difficult because business failure is a major loss to the entrepreneur. Most are likely to feel grief, which interferes with the learning process. Entrepreneurs who are able to recover from grief more quickly will be in a better position to learn from the experience. The good news is that there is something that entrepreneurs can do to enhance their grief recovery process. By using a dual process of grief recovery that oscillates between a loss- and a restoration-orientation, entrepreneurs can maximize their processing of information and minimize the emotional interference to that process. Obviously, grief is more complicated than we have presented here, but there are benefits to be gained in simply knowing that it is natural to feel grief when something important is lost, that most people recover, and that there is a process that can enhance that recovery (which may involve professional psychological counseling).

The focus of this chapter is on the way that individual entrepreneurs think, but at the end of the chapter we do acknowledge that firms themselves can have an entrepreneurial mind-set. To demonstrate this entrepreneurial mind-set, we contrasted entrepreneurially managed firms with traditionally managed firms on eight dimensions: (1) strategic orientation, (2) commitment to opportunity, (3) commitment of resources, (4) control of resources, (5) management structure, (6) reward philosophy, (7) growth orientation, and (8) entrepreneurial culture. Fortunately, a scale has been developed by three leading Swedish researchers that enables us to assess firms in terms of where they fall on the scale between entrepreneurial and traditional management.

In the next chapter we discuss the intentions of individuals to become entrepreneurs by creating a new organization. We then turn to entrepreneurship within existing firms and look at how these firms can encourage organization members to be more entrepreneurial.

RESEARCH TASKS

1. Ask an entrepreneur about his business today and ask him to describe the decisions and series of events that led the business from start-up to its current form. Would you classify this process as causal, effectual, or both?
2. Ask two entrepreneurs and five students (not in this class) to fill out Mike Haynie's "Generalized Measure of Adaptive Cognition" (see Table 2.1). How do you rate relative to the entrepreneurs? Relative to your fellow students?
3. Request the participation of managers from two companies and then ask them to fill out an "entrepreneurial management" scale (see Table 2.3). Based on the scale,

which firm is more entrepreneurially managed? Does this coincide with your "gut feel" about the businesses?

4. When conducting a homework exercise for another class (especially a case analysis), ask yourself compression questions, connection questions, strategy questions, and reflection questions. What impact did this have on the outcome of the task?

CLASS DISCUSSION

1. Do you really think that entrepreneurs think effectually? What about yourself, do you sometimes think effectually? In what ways is it good? Then why are we taught in business classes to always think causally? Are there particular problems or tasks in which thinking causally is likely to be superior to effectuation? When might effectuation be superior to causal thinking?
2. To be cognitively flexible seems to require that the entrepreneur continually question himself or herself. Doesn't that create doubt that can be seen by employees and financiers such that success actually becomes more difficult to achieve? Besides, although flexibility is a good thing, if the firm keeps changing based on minor changes in the environment, the buyers are going to become confused about the nature of the firm. Is adaptation always a good thing?
3. Individuals think because they have a brain, but do firms really think? Do they have a personality and philosophy? Can they learn and retain knowledge? Are these things simply held in the brains of individuals and therefore not really a firm-related phenomenon?
4. Great care must be taken in discussing the following topic—perhaps it is best achieved in small groups and perhaps a group of one where we each reflect on the answers. When you have lost something important, did you predominantly use a loss- or a restoration-orientation? Were you able to oscillate between the two? If you did oscillate, do you believe that this helped you emotionally overcome the loss? Did you learn from the experience—in the end, did it make some sense?

SELECTED READINGS

Audia, Pino; Edward Locke; and Ken Smith. (2000). The Paradox of Success: An Archival and a Laboratory Study of Strategic Persistence Following Radical Environmental Change. *Academy of Management Journal*, vol. 43, pp. 837–53.

In this archival study of the airline and trucking industries over a 10-year period and a laboratory study, the authors reveal that greater past success led to greater strategic persistence after a radical environmental change, and that such persistence induced performance declines.

Baron, Robert. (1998). Cognitive Mechanisms in Entrepreneurship: Why and When Entrepreneurs Think Differently than Other People. *Journal of Business Venturing*, vol. 13(4), pp. 275–95.

In this conceptual article, the author presents information on a study which examined the possible differences in the thinking of entrepreneurs and other people. This paper offers a number of implications of a cognitive perspective for entrepreneurship research.

Brown, Terence; Per Davidsson; and Johan Wiklund. (2001). An Operationalization of Stevenson's Conceptualization of Entrepreneurship as Opportunity-Based Firm Behavior. *Strategic Management Journal*, vol. 22, pp. 953–69.

This article describes a new instrument that was developed specifically for operationalizing Stevenson's conceptualization of entrepreneurial management. The instrument should open up opportunities for researchers to further evaluate entrepreneurship in existing firms.

Busenitz, Lowell; and Jay Barney. (1997). Differences between Entrepreneurs and Managers in Large Organizations: Biases and Heuristics in Strategic Decision Making. *Journal of Business Venturing*, vol. 12(1), pp. 9–30.

In this article the authors explore the differences in the decision-making processes between entrepreneurs and managers in large organizations. In particular they focus on a number of biases, such as the overconfidence bias, but also point out some benefits from the use of biases and heuristics.

Covin, Jeffery; and Dennis Slevin. (1988). The Influence of Organization Structure on the Utility of an Entrepreneurial Top Management Style. *Journal of Management Studies*, vol. 25, pp. 217–34.

This study examines the influence of organization structure on the relationship between top management's entrepreneurial orientation and financial performance. The authors find that an entrepreneurial top management style has a positive effect on the performance of organically structured firms and a negative effect on the performance of mechanistically structured firms.

Covin, Jeffery; and Dennis Slevin. (1989). Strategic Management of Small Firms in Hostile and Benign Environments. *Strategic Management Journal*, vol. 10, pp. 75–87.

The article reports the results of a study in which the overall strategic orientation, the competitive tactics, and the organizational attributes of small manufacturing firms in hostile and benign environments are examined. Findings indicate that performance among small firms in hostile environments is positively related to an organic structure, an entrepreneurial strategic posture, and a competitive profile characterized by a long-term orientation, high product prices, and a concern for predicting industry trends. In benign environments, on the other hand, performance is positively related to a mechanistic structure, a conservative strategic posture, and a competitive profile characterized by conservative financial management and a short-term financial orientation, an emphasis on product refinement, and a willingness to rely heavily on single customers.

Gaglio, Connie-Marrie; and Jerome Katz. (2001). The Psychological Basis of Opportunity Identification: Entrepreneurial Alertness. *Journal of Small Business Economics*, vol. 16, pp. 95–111.

In this article the authors describe a model of entrepreneurial alertness and propose a research agenda for understanding opportunity identification. They investigate the origin of the entrepreneurial alertness concept and the notion of the psychological schema of alertness.

Hitt, Michael; Barbara Keats; and Samuel DeMarie. (1998). Navigating in the New Competitive Landscape: Building Strategic Flexibility and Competitive Advantage in the 21st Century. *Academy of Management Executive*, vol. 12, pp. 22–43.

The article cites the importance of building strategic flexibility and a competitive advantage for organizations to survive in the face of emerging technical revolution and increasing globalization. The nature of the forces in the new competitive landscape requires a continuous rethinking of current strategic actions, organization structure, communication systems, corporate culture, asset deployment, and investment strategies—in short, every aspect of a firm's operation and long-term health.

Ireland, R. Duane; and Michael Hitt. (1999). Achieving and Maintaining Strategic Competitiveness in the 21st Century: The Role of Strategic Leadership. *Academy of Management Executive*, vol. 13, pp. 43–55.

In this article the authors acknowledge that effective strategic leadership practices can help firms enhance performance while competing in turbulent and unpredictable environments. They then describe six components of effective strategic leadership. When the activities called for by these components are completed successfully, the firm's strategic leadership practices can become a source of competitive advantage. In turn, use of this advantage can contribute significantly to achieving strategic competitiveness and earning above-average returns in the next century.

Kreiser, Patrick; Louis Marino; and K. Mark Weaver. (2002). Assessing the Psychometric Properties of the Entrepreneurial Orientation Scale: A Multi-Country Analysis. *Entrepreneurship: Theory & Practice*, vol. 26(4), pp. 71–95.

This study supports modeling entrepreneurial orientation (EO) with three subdimensions—innovation, proactiveness, and risk taking—and find that the three subdimensions of EO are able to vary independently of one another in many situations. This study also provides strong support for the cross-cultural validity of the Covin and Slevin EO scale.

McGrath, Rita. (1999). Falling Forward: Real Options Reasoning and Entrepreneurial Failure. *Academy of Management Review*, vol. 24,: pp. 13–30.

Although failure in entrepreneurship is pervasive, theory often reflects an equally pervasive antifailure bias. Here, the author uses real options reasoning to develop a more balanced perspective of the role of entrepreneurial failure in wealth creation, which emphasizes managing uncertainty by pursuing high-variance outcomes but investing only if conditions are favorable. This can increase profit potential while containing costs. The author also offers propositions that suggest how gains from entrepreneurship may be maximized and losses mitigated.

McGrath, Rita; and Ian MacMillan. (2000). *The Entrepreneurial Mindset: Strategies for Continuously Creating Opportunity in an Age of Uncertainty*. Harvard Business School Press, Cambridge, MA.

In this book the authors provide tips on how to achieve an entrepreneurial mind-set. For example, they discuss the need to focus beyond incremental improvements to entrepreneurial actions, assess a business's current performance to establish the entrepreneurial framework, and formulate challenging goals by using the components of the entrepreneurial framework.

Mitchell, Ron; Lowell Busenitz; Theresa Lant; Patricia McDougall; Eric Morse; and Brock Smith. (2002). Toward a Theory of Entrepreneurial Cognition: Rethinking the People Side of Entrepreneurship Research. *Entrepreneurship: Theory & Practice*, vol. 27(2), pp. 93–105.

In this article the authors reexamine "the people side of entrepreneurship" by summarizing the state of play within the entrepreneurial cognition research stream, and by integrating the five articles accepted for publication in a special issue focusing on this ongoing narrative. The authors propose that the constructs, variables, and proposed relationships under development within the cognitive perspective offer research concepts and techniques that are well suited to the analysis of problems that require better explanations of the distinctly human contributions to entrepreneurship.

Sarasvathy, Saras. (2001). Causation and Effectuation: Toward a Theoretical Shift from Economic Inevitability to Entrepreneurial Contingency. *Academy of Management Review*, vol. 26(2), pp. 243–64.

In this article, the author argues that an explanation for the creation of artifacts such as firms/organizations and markets requires the notion of effectuation. Causation rests on a logic of prediction, effectuation on the logic of control. The author illustrates effectuation through business examples and realistic thought experiments, examines its connections with existing theories and empirical evidence, and offers a list of testable propositions for future empirical work.

Sarasvathy, Saras. (2006). *Effectuation: Elements of Entrepreneurial Expertise*. Edward Elgar Publishers.

A book that gives the history of the development of effectuation and provides provocative new applications and future research directions.

Sarasvathy Saras. *www.effectuation.org.*

Up-to-date collection of works on effectuation.

Shepherd, Dean. (2003). Learning from Business Failure: Propositions about the Grief Recovery Process for the Self-Employed. *Academy of Management Review,* vol. 28, pp. 318–29.

In this paper the author uses the psychological literature on grief to explore the emotion of business failure, suggesting that the loss of a business from failure can cause the self-employed to feel grief—a negative emotional response that interferes with the ability to learn from the events surrounding that loss. The author discusses how a dual process of grief recovery maximizes the learning from business failure.

Shepherd, Dean. (2004). Educating Entrepreneurship Students about Emotion and Learning from Failure. *Academy of Management Learning & Education,* vol. 3, pp. 274–288.

In this article the author offers suggested changes to pedagogy to help students manage the emotions of learning from failure and discusses some of the challenges associated with measuring the implications of these proposed changes. The author then expands his scope to explore the possibility of educating students on how to manage their emotions to avoid failure and, more generally, improve their emotional intelligence, and how organizations can improve their ability to help individuals regulate their emotions.

Stevenson, Howard; and J. Carlos Jarillo. (1990). A Paradigm of Entrepreneurship: Entrepreneurial Management. *Strategic Management Journal*, vol. 11 (Special Issue), pp. 17–27.

In this article the authors propose that the very concept of corporate entrepreneurship sounds to many entrepreneurship scholars as something of an oxymoron. They point out that there is no doubt that, of late, entrepreneurship in general has gained its status as a legitimate scholarly research subject, enjoying in addition much public interest. The authors offer a discussion of the concept of entrepreneurship within established firms.

END NOTES

1. S. Sarasvathy, "Causation and Effectuation: Toward a Theoretical Shift from Economic Inevitability to Entrepreneurial Contingency," *Academy of Management Review* 26 (2001), p. 245.
2. (Simon, 1959).
3. Sarasvathy, "Causation and Effectuation," pp. 245–47.
4. S. Sarasvathy, *Effectuation: Elements of Entrepreneurial Expertise* (Edward Elgar Publishers, 2006).
5. M. A. Hitt, "The New Frontier: Transformation of Management for the New Millennium," *Organizational Dynamics* 28, no. 3 (2000), pp. 7–17.
6. R. D. Ireland, M. A. Hitt, and D. G. Sirmon, "A Model of Strategic Entrepreneurship: The Construct and Its Dimensions,"*Journal of Management* 29 (2003), pp. 963–990. And Rita McGrath, and Ian MacMillan, *The Entrepreneurial Mindset: Strategies for Continuously Creating Opportunity in an Age of Uncertainty* (Harvard Business School Press, Cambridge, MA, 2000).
7. Ireland, Hitt, and Sirmon, "A Model of Strategic Entrepreneurship."
8. M. A. Hitt, B. W. Keats, and S. M. DeMarie, "Navigating in the New Competitive Landscape: Building Strategic Flexibility and Competitive Advantage in the 21st Century," *Academy of Management Executive* 12 (1998), pp. 22–43 (from page 26).
9. M. Haynie, E. Mosakowski, D. Shepherd, and C. Earley, (working paper). "Metacognition and the Entrepreneurial Mindset." And M. Haynie, and D. Shepherd, (working paper), "A General Measure of Adaptive Cognition: A Metacognitive Perspective for Capturing the Entrepreneurial Mindset."

10. Haynie and Shepherd (working paper).
11. G. Schraw, and R. Dennison, "Assessing Metacognitive Awareness," *Contemporary Educational Psychology* 19 (1994), pp. 460–75.
12. A. Brown, "Metacognition and Other Mechanisms," in F. E. Weinert and R. H. Kluwe (eds.), *Metacognition, Motivation, and Understanding* (Lawrence Erlbaum Associates, Hillsdale, NJ, 1987).
13. E. Guterman, "Toward a Dynamic Assessment of Reading: Applying Metacognitive Awareness Guiding to Reading Assessment Tasks," *Journal of Research in Reading* 25, no. 3 (2002), pp. 283–98.
14. Z. R. Mevarech, and B. Kramarski, "The Effects of Metacognitive Training versus Worked-out Examples on Students' Mathematical Reasoning," *British Journal of Educational Psychology* 73, no. 4 (2003), pp. 449–71. And D. Shepherd, M. Haynie, and J. McMullen, (working paper). "Teaching Management Students Metacognitive Awareness: Enhancing Inductive Teaching Methods and Developing Cognitive Adaptability."
15. Mevarech and Kramarski, "The Effects of Metacognitive Training."
16. Based on D. Shepherd, "Learning from Business Failure: Propositions about the Grief Recovery Process for the Self-Employed, *Academy of Management Review* 28 (2003) pp. 318–29.
17. S. B. Sitkin, "Learning through Failure: The Strategy of Small Losses," *Research in Organizational Behavior* 14 (1992), pp. 231–66.
18. R. McGrath, "Falling Forward: Real Options Reasoning and Entrepreneurial Failure," *Academy of Management Review* 24 (1999) pp. 13–30.
19. A. V. Bruno, E. F. McQuarrie, and C. G. Torgrimson, "The Evolution of New Technology Ventures over 20 Years: Patterns of Failure, Merger, and Survival," *Journal of Business Venturing* 7 (1992), pp. 291–302.
20. B. Cova, and C. Svanfeldt, "Societal Innovations and the Postmodern Aestheticization of Everyday Life," *International Journal of Research in Marketing* 10 (1993), pp. 297–310 (quote from page 297).
21. Interviews with employees of organizations that have died reveal negative emotions such as those associated with grief. See S. G. Harris, and R. I. Sutton, "Functions of Parting Ceremonies in Dying Organizations," *Academy of Management Journal* 29 (1986), pp. 5–30.
22. J. Archer, *The Nature of Grief: The Evolution and Psychology of Reactions to Loss* (New York: Routledge, 1999).
23. A. Gilbert, "Lessons Learned from Failure," *Information Week* 817 (2000), p. 111.
24. G. H. Bower, "How Might Emotions Affect Learning?" In S. Christianson (ed.) *The Handbook of Emotion and Memory: Research and Theory* (1992), pp. 3–31 (Lawrence Erlbaum: Hillsdale, NJ.) And A. Wells, and G. Matthews, *Attention and Emotion: A Clinical Perspective* (Hove, UK: Lawrence Erlbaum Associates Ltd., 1994).
25. M. S. Stroebe, and H. Schut, "The Dual Process of Coping with Bereavement: Rationale and Description," *Death Studies* 23 (1999), pp. 197–224.
26. Stroebe and Schut, "The Dual Process of Coping."
27. S. Nolen-Hoeksema, "Responses to Depression and Their Effects on the Duration of the Depressive Episode," *Journal of Abnormal Psychology* 100 (1991), pp. 569–82.
28. T. Richman, "The Lessons of Bankruptcy," *Inc. Magazine* (December 1990), http://inc.com/incmagazine.
29. H. H. Stevenson, and D. Gumpert, "The Heart of Entrepreneurship," *Harvard Business Review* 63 no. 2 (1985), pp. 85–94.
30. Based on T. Brown, P. Davidsson, and J. Wiklund. "An Operationalization of Stevenson's Conceptualization of Entrepreneurship as Opportunity-Based Firm Behavior," *Strategic Management Journal* 22 (2001), pp. 953–69 (table on page 955).

3

ENTREPRENEURIAL INTENTIONS AND CORPORATE ENTREPRENEURSHIP

LEARNING OBJECTIVES

1
To introduce the importance of perception of feasibility and desirability in explaining entrepreneurial intentions.

2
To understand the role of individuals' background characteristics in explaining entrepreneurial intentions.

3
To acknowledge the differences between male and female entrepreneurs and minority and nonminority entrepreneurs.

4
To demonstrate that management can influence the intentions of those within established organizations.

5
To discuss how established firms can develop an entrepreneurial culture.

OPENING PROFILE

ROBERT MONDAVI

Robert G. Mondavi, the son of poor Italian immigrants, began making wine in California in 1943 when his family purchased the Charles Krug Winery in Napa Valley, where he served as a general manager. In 1966, at the age of 54, after a severe dispute over control of the family-owned winery, Robert Mondavi used his personal savings and loans from friends to start the flagship Robert Mondavi Winery in Napa Valley with his eldest son, Michael Mondavi. Robert's vision was to create wines in California that could successfully compete with the greatest wines of the world. As a result, Robert Mondavi Winery became the first in California to produce and market premium wines that were expected to compete with premium wines from France, Spain, Italy, and Germany.

www.mondavi.com

In order to achieve this objective Robert believed that he needed to build a Robert Mondavi brand in the premium wine market segment. This resulted in the initial production of a limited quantity of premium wines using the best grapes, which brought the highest prices in the market and had the highest profit margins per bottle. However, he soon realized that this strategy, while establishing the brand, did not allow the company to generate enough cash flow to expand the business. In order to solve this problem Robert decided to produce less expensive wines that he could sell in higher volumes. He dedicated time and effort to finding the best vineyards in Napa Valley for the company's production of grapes. In addition, he signed long-term contracts with growers in Napa Valley and worked closely with each grower to improve grape quality.

Robert Mondavi built a state-of-the-art winery that became a premium wine-making facility as well as conveying a unique sense of Mondavi wines to the visitors. Soon the new winery became a place where the best practices in the production of premium wines were developed, eventually establishing the standard in the wine industry. Robert Mondavi was the first wine maker to assemble experts with various backgrounds in the fields of viticulture and wine-making to give advice on the new wines. He also developed new technology that allowed special handling of grapes and the cold fermentation of white wines. Furthermore, Mondavi's company created process innovations, such as steel fermentation tanks, vacuum corking of bottles, and aging of wines in new French oak barrels. Dedicated to growing vines naturally, Robert Mondavi introduced a natural farming and conservation program that allowed enhanced grape quality, environmental protection, and worker health. Moreover, from the very beginning, the company promoted the presentation of wine as part of a sociable way of everyday living. Robert Mondavi Winery was one of the first wineries to present concerts, art exhibitions, and culinary programs. In his book, Robert Mondavi describes his search for innovation:

> From the outset, I wanted my winery to draw inspiration and methods from the traditional Old World chateaux of France and Italy, but I also wanted to become a model of state-of-the-art technology, a pioneer in research and a gathering place for the finest minds in our industry. I wanted our winery to be a haven of creativity, innovation, excitement, and that unbelievable energy you find in a start-up venture when everyone is committed, heart and soul, to a common cause and a common quest.

In 1972 Mondavi's hard work and dedication to his venture were formally recognized when the Los Angeles Times Vintners Tasting Event selected the 1969 Robert Mondavi Winery Cabernet Sauvignon as the top wine produced in California.

Despite Robert Mondavi's relentless efforts, things did not always go smoothly. A noticeable improvement in the quality and reputation of the Robert Mondavi wines during the 1970s did not spark the interest of reputable five-star restaurants and top wine shops across the country. So, for over a decade, Mondavi traveled throughout the country and abroad, promoting Napa Valley wines and the Robert Mondavi brand name. Often, while dining alone on business trips, Mondavi offered restaurant employees the opportunity to taste his wine. Slowly, Mondavi got his wines on the wine lists of the top five-star restaurants in the United States. By the end of the 1970s, restaurant owners, famous wine connoisseurs, and industry critics were eager to be introduced to Robert Mondavi products. Recognizing the increased popularity of his wines, Mondavi began slowly raising the prices of his wines to the price level of comparable French wines. Subsequently, the company expanded its capacity to produce 500,000 cases of premium wines annually.

About this time Robert Mondavi started building a portfolio of premium wine brands to satisfy the needs of consumers in various price and quality segments of the domestic wine market. As a result, from the late 1970s until the 1980s Robert Mondavi diversified its portfolio through acquisition and further growth of the Woodbridge, Bryon, and Coastal brands of California wine. Most of these acquisitions were financed through long-term debt.

In the early 1990s Robert Mondavi faced financial difficulties as a result of the rapid expansion; the increased competition; and a *phylloxera* infestation of several of the company's vineyards, which necessitated replanting. After contemplating the matter for several years, Robert Mondavi decided to raise enough capital to continue expansion of his company while maintaining family control of the company. On June 10, 1993, Robert Mondavi issued 3.7 million shares of stock at $13.50 a share and began trading on the NASDAQ as MOND. The initial public offering (IPO) raised approximately $49.95 million, bringing the company's market capitalization to $213.3 million.

The IPO was structured with two classes of stock: Class A common stock issued to the Mondavi family, and Class B common stock offered to the public. Class A shares carried 10 votes per share, and Class B shares carried one vote per share. This structure allowed the Mondavi family to retain 90 percent ownership of the company and, subsequently, to preserve control over the company's destiny. Robert Mondavi stock was trading at $8 a share a few days after the initial offering and at $6.50 a share six months later, slashing the company's value, and the Mondavi family's wealth, by half.

One factor affecting the price decrease in the stock was the difficulty that the investment community and analysts had in valuing Robert Mondavi due to a lack of information on the wine industry. There were only two other publicly traded wine companies, both in low-end wine categories. To help solve this problem, Robert Mondavi began educating investors, trying to convince them that it is possible to build a strong globally recognized business selling premium wines. As part of his knowledge-building and awareness-creation campaign, Robert sent teams to New York, Boston, and Chicago, who brought wine presentations, receptions, and tastings to the investors. According to Robert Mondavi, "Well, we had to mount an effective campaign and take it right to them, and not just explain our approach but put our wines right in their hands! Let them taste, in their own mouths, our expertise and commitment to excellence."

At the same time the company was continuing its innovating efforts, creating in 1994 a revolutionary, capsule-free, flange-top bottle design, which became widely accepted in the industry.

In the mid-1990s, the company started engaging in various multinational partnerships on a 50 : 50 basis: Its partnership with the Baron Philippe de Rothschild of Chateau Mouton Rothschild in Bordeaux, France, resulted in the creation of *Opus One* wine in 1979; with the Frescobaldi family of Tuscany, Italy, Mondavi launched *Luce, Lucente,* and *Danzante* wines in 1995; with the Eduardo Chadwick family of Chile, it introduced *Caliterra* wines in 1996; and with Australia's largest premium producer, Southcorp, it began producing and marketing new wines from Australia and California in 2001.

Today, the company continues to pursue its goals around the world with its unique cultural and innovative spirit and its consistent growth strategy, reaching revenue of over $441 million in 2002. The company produces 20 unique and separate labels representing more than 80 individual wines from California, Italy, Chile, and France and sells its wines in more than 80 countries. Some of the popular Robert Mondavi fine wine labels such as Robert Mondavi Winery, Robert Mondavi Coastal Private Selection, and Woodbridge Winery have gained enormous popularity among wine lovers in the United States as well as the rest of the world. The company remains a close family business.

Recognized as the global representative of California wines, Robert Mondavi has been a major force in leading the U.S. wine industry into the modern era and has devoted his life to creating a fine wine culture in America. Through hard work and a constant striving for excellence, he has achieved his goal of causing California wines to be viewed as some of the great wines of the world.

THE INTENTION TO ACT ENTREPRENEURIALLY

Entrepreneurial action is most often intentional. Entrepreneurs intend to pursue certain opportunities, enter new markets, and offer new products—and this is rarely the process of unintentional behavior. Intentions capture the motivational factors that influence a behavior; they are indications of how hard people are willing to try, of how much of an effort they are planning to exert in order to perform the behavior. As a general rule, the stronger the intention to engage in a behavior, the more likely should be its performance.[1] Individuals have stronger intentions to act when taking action is perceived to be *feasible* and *desirable*. *Entrepreneurial intentions* can be explained in the same way.

entrepreneurial intentions The motivational factors that influence individuals to pursue entrepreneurial outcomes

entrepreneurial self-efficacy The conviction that one can successfully execute the entrepreneurial process

The perception of feasibility has much to do with an entrepreneur's self-efficacy. *Self-efficacy* refers to the conviction that one can successfully execute the behavior required; people who believe they have the capacity to perform (high self-efficacy) tend to perform well. Thus, it reflects the perception of a personal capability to do a particular job or set of tasks. High self-efficacy leads to increased initiative and persistence and thus improved performance; low self-efficacy reduces effort and thus performance. Indeed, people with high self-efficacy think differently and behave differently than people with low self-efficacy.[2] It appears that self-efficacy affects the person's choice of action and the amount of effort exerted. Entrepreneurship scholars have found that self-efficacy is positively associated with the creation of a new independent organization.[3]

perceived desirability The degree to which an individual has a favorable or unfavorable evaluation of the potential entrepreneurial outcomes

Not only must an individual perceive entrepreneurial action as feasible for entrepreneurial intention to be high, the individual must also perceive this course of action as desirable. *Perceived desirability* refers to an individual's attitude toward entrepreneurial action—the degree to which she has a favorable or unfavorable evaluation of the potential entrepreneurial outcomes.[4] For example, creative actions are not likely to emerge unless they produce personal rewards that are perceived as relatively more desirable than more familiar behaviors.[5]

Therefore, the higher the perceived desirability and feasibility, the stronger the intention to act entrepreneurially. We next investigate the background characteristics of entrepreneurs to understand why some individuals are more likely to engage in entrepreneurship than other individuals. That is, we examine how background characteristics provide an indication of whether certain individuals are more or less likely to perceive entrepreneurial action as feasible and/or desirable and therefore whether they are more or less likely to intend to be entrepreneurs.

ENTREPRENEUR BACKGROUND AND CHARACTERISTICS

Education

The educational level of the entrepreneur has received significant research attention. Although some may feel that entrepreneurs are less educated than the general population, research findings indicate that this is clearly not the case. Education is important in the upbringing of the entrepreneur. Its importance is reflected not only in the level of education obtained but also in the fact that it continues to play a major role in helping entrepreneurs cope with the problems they confront. Although a formal education is not necessary for starting a new business—as is reflected in the success of such high school dropouts as Andrew Carnegie, William Durant, Henry Ford, and William Lear—it does provide a good background, particularly when it is related to the field of the venture. Although nearly 70 percent of all women entrepreneurs have a college degree, with many having graduate degrees, the most popular college majors are English, psychology, education, and sociology, with fewer having degrees in engineering, science, or math. Both male and female entrepreneurs have cited an educational need in the areas of finance, strategic planning, marketing (particularly distribution), and management. The ability to communicate clearly with both the written and the spoken word is also important in any entrepreneurial activity.

Even general education is valuable because it facilitates the integration and accumulation of new knowledge, providing individuals with a larger opportunity set (i.e., a broader base of knowledge casts a wider net for the discovery or generation of potential opportunities) and assists entrepreneurs in adapting to new situations.[6] The general human capital of an entrepreneur can provide knowledge, skills, and problem-solving abilities that are transferable across many different situations. Indeed, it has been found that while education has a positive influence on the chance that a person will discover new opportunities, it does not necessarily determine whether he will create a new business to exploit the discovered opportunity.[7] To the extent that individuals believe that their education has made entrepreneurial action more feasible, they are more likely to become entrepreneurs.

Personal Values

Although there have been many studies indicating that personal values are important for entrepreneurs, frequently these studies fail to indicate that entrepreneurs can be differentiated from managers, unsuccessful entrepreneurs, or even the general populace with regard to these values. For example, although entrepreneurs tend to be effective leaders, this does not distinguish them from successful managers. Studies have shown that the entrepreneur has a different set of attitudes about the nature of the management process and business in general. The nature of the enterprise, opportunism, the institution, and the individuality of the entrepreneur diverge significantly from the bureaucratic organization and the planning, rationality, and predictability of its managers.

In one study, five consensus characteristics found across consumer and leadership groups included superior product quality; quality service to customers; flexibility, or the ability to adapt to changes in the marketplace; high-caliber management; and honesty and ethics in business practices.[8] Another aspect of personal values that is very important to entrepreneurs is ethics and the ethical behavior of the entrepreneur. Entrepreneurs do differ from managers on some aspects of ethics, as is discussed in the article in the Ethics box.

Age

The relationship of age to the entrepreneurial career process also has been carefully researched.[9] In evaluating these results, it is important to differentiate between entrepreneurial age (the age of the entrepreneur reflected in his or her experience) and chronological age. As discussed in the next section, entrepreneurial experience is one of the best predictors of success, particularly when the new venture is in the same field as the previous business experience.

In terms of chronological age, most entrepreneurs initiate their entrepreneurial careers between the ages of 22 and 45. A career can be initiated before or after these ages, as long as the entrepreneur has the necessary experience and financial support, and the high energy level needed to launch and manage a new venture successfully. Also, there are milestone ages every five years (25, 30, 35, 40, and 45) when an individual is more inclined to start an entrepreneurial career. As one entrepreneur succinctly stated, "I felt it was now or never in terms of starting a new venture when I approached 30." Generally, male entrepreneurs tend to start their first significant venture in their early 30s, while women entrepreneurs tend to do so in their middle 30s.

ETHICS

Understanding the factors that contribute to and influence the ethical conduct of managers and entrepreneurs is important for the future of the U.S. economic system as well as the economic system of the world. The significance of these factors becomes all the more salient when operating in a hypercompetitive global economy. In such an environment, competitors aggressively disrupt the status quo and seek to change the rules of competition. While current businesses impact the ethical standards used in present business dealings, emerging entrepreneurial companies set the ethical tone for the future economic system of the world.

Although the U.S. has strong laws, such as the Foreign Corrupt Practices Act of 1977, and promotes ethical behavior on the part of managers and entrepreneurs, the ethical attitudes of these groups are not well understood. How will managers and entrepreneurs react in certain situations? Will they have high ethical standards in their internal and external dealings? Will managers, because of their more bureaucratic environment, have higher ethical standards than entrepreneurs? Or, will entrepreneurs, because their business practices more closely reflect their personal values, have higher ethical attitudes than managers?

In one study, 165 entrepreneurs and 128 managers were surveyed using a detached measuring instrument containing binary, response questions, scenarios, and comprehensive demographic information.

Generally, entrepreneurs and managers differed only slightly in their views regarding the ethics of various activities and their ethical perceptions regarding others. There were few differences in the two groups regarding their evaluation of the ethical nature of 12 circumstances and 7 scenarios. The similarities in ethical attitudes between the two groups of decision makers seem to be one of the important findings, which can be explained by similar legal, cultural, and educational factors that affect the ethical attitudes of both groups. Some significant differences consistently indicate that entrepreneurs are more prone to hold ethical attitudes.

The findings indicate that managers need to sacrifice their personal values to those of the company more than entrepreneurs. Also, entrepreneurs consistently demonstrate higher ethical attitudes in the internal dealings of the company, such as not taking longer than necessary for a job and not using company resources for personal use. These findings are consistent with the theory of property where we would expect someone to be more ethical in dealing with his/her own property. This finding suggests that, through increased ownership, managers might be motivated to have more ethical dealings with their company's assets. Profit-sharing companies (managers and other key employees) can therefore perhaps reduce the possibilities of moral hazard and opportunistic behavior within the company through some type of managerial ownership. Likewise, long-term relationships with customers and the community in general have to be reflected in the property of the company through philanthropic acts and different liability accounts.

Source: From Branko Bucar and Robert Hisrich, "Ethics of Business Managers vs. Entrepreneurs," *Journal of Developmental Entrepreneurship* 6, no. 1. Reprinted with permission of The Journal of Developmental Entrepreneurship.

Work History

work history The past work experience of an individual

Work history not only can be a negative displacement in the decision to launch a new entrepreneurial venture, but it also plays a role in the growth and eventual success of the new venture. While dissatisfaction with various aspects of one's job—such as a lack of challenge or promotional opportunities, as well as frustration and boredom—often motivates the launching of a new venture, previous technical and industry experience is important once the decision to launch has been made. Experience in the following areas is particularly important: financing, product or service development, manufacturing, development of distribution channels, and preparation of a marketing plan.

As the venture becomes established and starts growing, managerial experience and skills become increasingly important. Although most ventures start with few (if any) employees, as the number of employees increases, the entrepreneur's managerial skills come more and more into play. In addition to managerial experience, entrepreneurial experience is also important. Most entrepreneurs indicate that their most significant venture was not their first one. Throughout their entrepreneurial careers, they are being exposed to many new venture opportunities and gathering ideas for many more new ventures.

Finally, previous start-up experience can provide entrepreneurs with expertise in running an independent business as well as benchmarks for judging the relevance of information, which can lead to an understanding of the "real" value of new entry opportunities, speed up the business creation process, and enhance performance.[10] Previous start-up experience is a relatively good predictor of starting subsequent businesses.[11] To the extent that start-up experience provides entrepreneurs with a greater belief in their ability to successfully achieve entrepreneurial outcomes, this increased perceived feasibility will strengthen entrepreneurial intentions.

ROLE MODELS AND SUPPORT SYSTEMS

role models Individuals influencing an entrepreneur's career choice and style

One of the most important factors influencing entrepreneurs in their career path is their choice of a *role model*.[12] Role models can be parents, brothers or sisters, other relatives, or other entrepreneurs. Successful entrepreneurs are viewed frequently as catalysts by potential entrepreneurs. As one entrepreneur succinctly stated, "After evaluating Ted and his success as an entrepreneur, I knew I was much smarter and could do a better job. So I started my own business." In this way, role models can provide important signals that entrepreneurship is feasible for them.

Role models can also serve in a supportive capacity as mentors during and after the launch of a new venture. An entrepreneur needs a strong support and advisory system in every phase of the new venture. This support system is perhaps most crucial during the start-up phase, as it provides information, advice, and guidance on such matters as organizational structure, obtaining needed financial resources, and marketing. Since entrepreneurship is a social role embedded in a social context, it is important that an entrepreneur establish connections and eventually networks early in the new venture formation process.

As initial contacts and connections expand, they form a network with similar properties prevalent in a social network—density (the extensiveness of ties between the two individuals) and centrality (the total distance of the entrepreneur to all other individuals and the total number of individuals in the network). The strength of the ties between the entrepreneur and any individual in the network is dependent upon the frequency, level, and reciprocity of the relationship. The more frequent, in-depth, and mutually beneficial a relationship, the stronger and more durable the network between the entrepreneur and the individual.[13] Although most networks are not formally organized, an informal network for moral and professional support still greatly benefits the entrepreneur.

Moral-Support Network

moral-support network Individuals who give psychological support to an entrepreneur

It is important for each entrepreneur to establish a *moral-support network* of family and friends—a cheering squad. This cheering squad plays a critical role during the many difficult and lonely times that occur throughout the entrepreneurial process. Most entrepreneurs indicate that their spouses are their biggest supporters and allow them to devote the excessive amounts of time necessary to the new venture.

Friends also play key roles in a moral-support network. Not only can friends provide advice that is often more honest than that received from other sources, but they also provide encouragement, understanding, and even assistance. Entrepreneurs can confide in friends without fear of criticism. Finally, relatives (children, parents, grandparents, aunts, and uncles) also can be strong sources of moral support, particularly if they are also entrepreneurs.

As one entrepreneur stated, "The total family support I received was the key to my success. Having an understanding cheering squad giving me encouragement allowed me to persist through the many difficulties and problems."

Professional-Support Network

In addition to encouragement, the entrepreneur needs advice and counsel throughout the establishment of the new venture. This advice can be obtained from a mentor, business associates, trade associations, or personal affiliations—all members of a *professional-support network.*

professional-support network Individuals who help the entrepreneur in business activities

Most entrepreneurs indicate that they have mentors. How does one find a mentor? This task sounds much more difficult than it really is. Since a mentor is a coach, a sounding board, and an advocate—someone with whom the entrepreneur can share both problems and successes—the individual selected needs to be an expert in the field. An entrepreneur can start the "mentor-finding process" by preparing a list of experts in various fields—such as in the fundamental business activities of finance, marketing, accounting, law, or management—who can provide the practical "how-to" advice needed. From this list, an individual who can offer the most assistance should be identified and contacted. If the selected individual is willing to act as a mentor, he or she should be periodically apprised of the progress of the business so that a relationship can gradually develop.

Another good source of advice can be cultivated by establishing a network of business associates. This group can be composed of self-employed individuals who have experienced starting a business; clients or buyers of the venture's product or service; experts such as consultants, lawyers, or accountants; and the venture's suppliers. Clients or buyers are a particularly important group to cultivate. This group represents the source of revenue to the venture and is the best provider of word-of-mouth advertising. There is nothing better than word-of-mouth advertising from satisfied customers to help establish a winning business reputation and promote goodwill.

Suppliers are another important component in a professional-support network. A new venture needs to establish a solid track record with suppliers in order to build a good relationship and to ensure the adequate availability of materials and other supplies. Suppliers also can provide good information on the nature of trends, as well as competition, in the industry.

In addition to mentors and business associates, trade associations can offer an excellent professional-support network. Trade association members can help keep the new venture competitive. Trade associations keep up with new developments and can provide overall industry data.

Finally, personal affiliations of the entrepreneur also can be a valuable part of a professional-support network. Affiliations developed with individuals through shared hobbies, participation in sporting events, clubs, civic involvements, and school alumni groups are excellent potential sources of referrals, advice, and information. Each entrepreneur needs to establish both moral- and professional-support networks. These contacts provide confidence, support, advice, and information. As one entrepreneur stated, "In your own business, you are all alone. There is a definite need to establish support groups to share problems with and to obtain information and overall support for the new venture."

Therefore it is important to recognize that entrepreneurial activity is embedded in networks of interpersonal relationships. These networks are defined by a set of actors (individuals and organizations) and a set of linkages between them, and they provide individuals access to a variety of resources necessary for entrepreneurial outcomes.[14] These resources may assist in efforts to discover and exploit opportunities, as well as in the creation of new independent organizations.[15] The trust embedded in some of these

AS SEEN IN *ENTREPRENEUR* MAGAZINE

HOT OR NOT?

DO YOU BELIEVE THIS DIGITAL FRIDGE TECHNOLOGY REPRESENTS AN OPPORTUNITY?

Why, oh why, must employees stop working just because they're having lunch or stoking up on caffeine? They won't if your lunchroom is equipped with the Multi-Media Refrigerator ($8,000) from LG Electronics (www.lgappliances.com). A 25.5-cubic-foot refrigerator with an Internet connection and built-in LCD, the digital fridge lets workers keep researching Web projects and reading e-mail while they munch. The fridge has a built-in TV, camera, and Web radio so you can stretch videoconferences through coffee breaks. Here's a morale booster: Alternate photos of your office manager with those pencil requisition training videos on its LCD.[a]

DO YOU BELIEVE THIS "SMALL WORLD" TECHNOLOGY REPRESENTS AN OPPORTUNITY?

Rick Snyder, CEO of Ardesta, a holding firm in Ann Arbor, Michigan, has a mantra: "Smaller, faster, better, cheaper." He's talking about "small tech," a term that describes nanotechnology, microtechnology, and micro-electromechanical systems (MEMS). Nanotechnology in particular has gotten a lot of coverage as big companies like Hewlett-Packard and Intel have begun to introduce nano into computing. It's hard to pinpoint exactly what small tech is because it has so many wide-ranging applications. "I would call it more of a revolution than an evolution," says Snyder. Nanotechnology, for example, deals with matter at an atomic and molecular level—that is, with matter often described as being less than the width of a human hair in size. It's appearing in everything from stainproof coating for fabrics to scratch-resistant coating for eyeglasses to miniscule computer chip circuits from HP Labs.

Research funding for small tech is enormous. Ardesta is devoted to investing in and helping launch various small tech ventures with an ultimate goal of bringing actual products to market. Many businesses in this fledgling technological area are small entrepreneurial start-ups and spinoffs from research institutions. Life sciences and materials manufacturing are two industries that will really feel the early effects of the growing small tech market. Eventually, though, small tech will touch just about everything. Snyder calls it pervasive and transparent.

Some applications are out already and operating in your business right under your nose. Microtech is built into inkjet cartridges and portable projectors. At SmallTimes.com, a clearinghouse for information on small technology, the section devoted to applications is an eye-opener: A recent visit to the site brought up articles on nanotech use in products such as tennis rackets and LCD monitors, among others.

There are a million microscopic reasons to get excited, but it's important to keep them all in perspective. Snyder sees an accelerating growth curve over the next five years as small tech makes its way into real-life markets. But you shouldn't expect companies to shout "nano" or "MEMS" in their product advertising. The way you'll know small tech has touched your business is when Snyder's mantra comes into play: "Smaller, faster, better, cheaper."[b]

[a]Source: Mike Hogan, "Employees Can Munch and Work on the Web at the Same Time with This Time-Saver," *Entrepreneur* (February 2003), pp. 18–22.

[b]Source: Reprinted with permission of Entrepreneur Media, Inc., "Nanotechnology Will Soon Mean Big Changes in the Way You Do Business," by Amanda C. Kooser, March 2003, *Entrepreneur* magazine: www.entrepreneur.com.

networks provides potential entrepreneurs the opportunity to access highly valuable resources. For example, business networks are composed of independent firms linked by common interests, friendship, and trust and are particularly important in facilitating the transfer of difficult-to-codify, knowledge-intensive skills that are expensive to obtain in other ways.[16] These networks also create opportunities for exchanging goods and services that are difficult to enforce through contractual arrangements, which facilitates the pursuit of opportunities.[17] To the extent that a network provides an individual greater belief in his or her ability to access resources critical to the successful achievement of entrepreneurial outcomes, this increased perceived feasibility will strengthen entrepreneurial intentions.

MALE VERSUS FEMALE ENTREPRENEURS

Another individual characteristic among entrepreneurs that has been studied is gender. There has been significant growth in female self-employment, with women now starting new ventures at a higher rate than men. In fact, women are starting businesses in the United States at twice the rate of all businesses and are staying in business longer. According to the latest data from the Census Bureau and the Small Business Administration's (SBA) Office of Advocacy, 28 percent of all private companies are women-owned businesses. The Census Bureau's 2002 survey of business owners found that 6.5 million companies had female owners, 13.2 million had male owners, and 2.7 million were equally owned by males and females. Women-owned businesses grew at twice that national rate for all private companies from 1997 to 2002. Nearly one-third of women-owned businesses are connected with health care and social services. Much is known about the characteristics of entrepreneurs, their motivations, backgrounds, families, educational backgrounds, occupational experiences, and the problems of both female and male entrepreneurs.

Although the characteristics of male and female entrepreneurs are generally very similar, female entrepreneurs differ in terms of motivation, business skills, and occupational backgrounds. Factors in the start-up process of a business for male and female entrepreneurs are also different, especially in such areas as support systems, sources of funds, and problems.[18] The major differences between male and female entrepreneurs are summarized in Table 3.1. As indicated, men are often motivated by the drive to control their own destinies, to make things happen. This drive often stems from disagreements with their bosses or a feeling that they can run things better. In contrast, women tend to be more motivated by the need for achievement arising from job frustration in not being allowed to perform and grow in their previous job situation.

departure points The activities occurring when the venture is started

Departure points and reasons for starting the business are similar for both men and women. Both generally have a strong interest and experience in the area of their venture. However, for men, the transition from a past occupation to the new venture is often facilitated when the new venture is an outgrowth of a present job. Women, on the other hand, often leave a previous occupation with a high level of job frustration as well as enthusiasm for the new venture rather than practical experience, thereby making the transition somewhat more difficult. Sometimes what ends up as a business venture for women begins as a personal search. Such was the case for Kimberly Porrazzo, who planned to return to her previous job after her pregnancy. Frustrated in her search for a good nanny, she decided to create The Nanny Kit and also start the Southern California Nanny Center, a source of advice that houses an informational database maintained and updated by Porrazzo.

Start-up financing is another area where male and female entrepreneurs differ (see Table 3.1). Whereas men often list investors, bank loans, or personal loans in addition to personal funds as sources of start-up capital, women usually rely solely on personal assets or savings. This is a major problem for many women entrepreneurs—obtaining financing and lines of credit.

Occupationally, there are also vast differences between men and women entrepreneurs. Although both groups tend to have experience in the field of their ventures, men more often have experience in manufacturing, finance, or technical areas. Most women, in contrast, usually have administrative experience that is limited to the middle-management level, often in service-related areas.

In terms of personality, there are strong similarities between men and women entrepreneurs. Both tend to be energetic, goal-oriented, and independent. However, men are often more confident and less flexible and tolerant than women, which can result in very different management styles.

TABLE 3.1 Comparison of Male and Female Entrepreneurs

Characteristic	Male Entrepreneurs	Female Entrepreneurs
Motivation	Achievement—strive to make things happen Personal independence—self-image as it relates to status through their role in the corporation is unimportant Job satisfaction arising from the desire to be in control	Achievement—accomplishment of a goal Independence—to do it alone
Departure point	Dissatisfaction with present job Sideline in college, sideline to present job, or outgrowth of present job Discharge or layoff Opportunity for acquisition	Job frustration Interest in and recognition of opportunity in the area Change in personal circumstances
Sources of funds	Personal assets and savings Bank financing Investors Loans from friends and family	Personal assets and savings Personal loans
Occupational background	Experience in line of work Recognized specialist or one who has gained a high level of achievement in the field Competent in a variety of business functions	Experience in area of business Middle-management or administrative-level experience in the field Service-related occupational background
Personality characteristics	Opinionated and persuasive Goal-oriented Innovative and idealistic High level of self-confidence Enthusiastic and energetic Must be own boss	Flexible and tolerant Goal-oriented Creative and realistic Medium level of self-confidence Enthusiastic and energetic Ability to deal with the social and economic environment
Background	Age when starting venture: 25–35 Father was self-employed College educated—degree in business or technical area (usually engineering) Firstborn child	Age when starting venture: 35–45 Father was self-employed College educated—degree in liberal arts Firstborn child
Support groups	Friends, professional acquaintances (lawyers, accountants) Business associates Spouse	Close friends Spouse Family Women's professional groups Trade associations
Type of business started	Manufacturing or construction	Service related—educational services, consulting, or public relations

AS SEEN IN *ENTREPRENEUR* MAGAZINE

PROVIDE ADVICE TO AN ENTREPRENEUR ABOUT IMPROVING A BUSINESS THROUGH CERTIFICATION AS A WOMAN-OWNED BUSINESS

Is becoming a certified Women's Business Enterprise (WBE) really beneficial? We spoke with women entrepreneurs from a variety of industries to find out. Being certified as a Women's Business Enterprise (WBE) means a third-party certifying entity has confirmed that a business is at least 51 percent owned, managed, and controlled by a woman or women. The leading certifier is the Women's Business Enterprise National Council (WBENC), which certifies to a national standard and has 14 partner organizations across the country.

WHAT'S IN IT FOR YOU?

One of WBENC's goals is to achieve equal procurement opportunities for women. As a WBE, a business is recognized by more than 500 major U.S. corporations and eligible to apply for their supplier diversity programs. WBENC provides members access to databases of information, including contact information for programs and procurement executives and listings of sourcing opportunities. Members also are listed in the WBENC database that corporations and government agencies use to find WBEs.

BUT GETTING CERTIFIED IS ONLY STEP ONE

"Although [my company] had been certified through the City of Charlotte, North Carolina, for several years, we hadn't been able to convert that into actual contracts," says Beverly Green, 32, owner of Change-Ad Letter Co., a $2 million–plus manufacturer of electrical sign components. Further research showed she had been missing out on many opportunities. "I'd previously thought the value of certification was gaining local and regional government work, and that can be true." But Green's target market was corporations. Once she accessed WBENC's data on corporate purchasing practices, she was able to use this information to win major corporate accounts. Julie Rodriguez, 44, is president and CEO of Epic Cos., a $12 million–plus Harvey, Louisiana, supplier of commercial divers and utility vessels to the oil and gas industry. "Like everything else in life, you get out of [WBE] what you put in," she says. "The program has more to offer than just certification."

GETTING CERTIFIED

Applications and instructions for certification are available at www.wbenc.org; you can either complete the application online or print it and mail it in. Fees range from free to about $200, depending on the certifying entity and scope (local, regional, or national), and must be renewed annually. "The process is time-consuming, and the paperwork can be overwhelming, though this varies depending on the level of certification," says Green. "My national certification took about six months." National applications can require more than 100 pages of documentation. Women business owners say getting certified is worth the effort. Says Green, "Networking with other women-owned businesses and getting involved in organizations such as WBENC can lead to many opportunities and help open doors you would never have thought of."

ADVICE TO AN ENTREPRENEUR

A successful woman entrepreneur has read the above article and comes to you for advice:

> In the corporate world I hit the glass ceiling, and that is the reason why I became an entrepreneur. As an entrepreneur you are rewarded for good products and a good business, and gender has not really been an issue to date. Do you think that I should get certified as a "woman-owned" business? Is it worth filling out all that paperwork? Is it fair that I increase my access to possible government contracts by being certified as a woman-owned business? Or should I think about it more as a competitive advantage because every entrepreneur tries to best their competitive advantage into profits?

Source: Reprinted with permission of Entrepreneur Media, Inc., "Proof Positive. Want the Full Benefits of a Woman-Owned Business? Get Your Company Certified," by Aliza Pilar Sherman, February 2003, *Entrepreneur* magazine: www.entrepreneur.com.

The backgrounds of men and women entrepreneurs tend to be similar, except that most women are a little older when they embark on their ventures (35 to 40 versus 25 to 35), and their educational backgrounds are different. Men often have studied in technical or business-related areas, whereas women frequently have a liberal arts education.

Support groups also provide a point of contrast between the two gender groups. Men usually list outside advisors (lawyers, accountants) as their most important supporters, with the spouse being second. Women list their spouses first, close friends second, and business associates third. Moreover, women usually rely heavily on a variety of sources for support and information, such as trade associations and women's groups, whereas men are not as likely to have as many outside supporters.

Finally, businesses started by men and women entrepreneurs differ in terms of the nature of the venture. Whereas women are more likely to start a business in a service-related area such as retail, public relations, or educational services, men are likely to enter manufacturing, construction, or high-technology fields. The result is often smaller women-owned businesses with lower net earnings.

MINORITY ENTREPRENEURSHIP

Research on entrepreneurs defined by ethnicity or race has been sporadic. The problem is understanding the differences in the behavior of various ethnic groups in the context of the environment and the economic opportunities (or lack thereof) available in the societal context.

Most of the sparse literature dealing with minority entrepreneurship has focused on the characteristics of the group under study. Several studies have looked at the ownership rates and trends among minority groups. In terms of ownership, one study found the lowest participation rate for African Americans, the second highest but fastest growing participation rate for Hispanics, and the highest rate of ownership participation for Asians.[19] One of the earliest studies comparing African American and white business owners found more similarities than differences and found that white owners were less likely to be separated or divorced, more likely to have graduated from college, and likely to have been in business longer.[20] Another study found that minority business owners tended to be younger or better educated but otherwise were from family backgrounds similar to those of white business owners.[21] A study of minority and nonminority women entrepreneurs found significant differences on six of nine personality measures. Also, the typical minority woman was married, older, started her business at an older age, and was less likely to be a college graduate.[22] Exploring just minority business owners, one study found that the typical minority business owner was the oldest child in a blue-collar family; was married; had children; had a college degree and related business experience; and was primarily motivated by achievement, opportunity, and job satisfaction.[23]

The study of ethnic entrepreneurship has revealed differences among ethnic groups and instances where some ethnic entrepreneurs have access to established community resources. In order to truly understand the nature and role of this aspect of entrepreneurship, future research needs to focus on the overall process used by ethnic entrepreneurs in developing and maintaining an enterprise. In spite of this lack of research, there has been a significant increase in the number of Asian, African American, Hispanic, and Native American firms. Of U.S. businesses, 5.8 percent were owned by Hispanic Americans, 4.4 percent by Asian Americans, 4 percent by African Americans, and about 1 percent by American Indians. This 15.8 percent minority share of U.S. businesses is an increase from the 6.8 percent share in 1982, 9.3 percent share in 1987, 12.5 percent share in 1992, and 14.6 percent share in 1997. With an increase in the encouragement of entrepreneurship among minority groups, particularly in their formative high school years, and the increase in the number of role models, more minorities are likely to select entrepreneurship as a viable career option. Indeed, from 1982 to 2002 there has been a ten-fold increase in the number of businesses owned by American Indians/Alaskan natives and businesses owned by Hispanics has quadrupled.

ENTREPRENEURIAL INTENTIONS WITHIN EXISTING ORGANIZATIONS

Recently we have gained a greater understanding of the environmental conditions that motivate individuals within the organization to act entrepreneurially. The underlying assumption is that acting entrepreneurially is something that people choose to do and the top management of an organization can influence that choice by the corporate environment that it creates. This is consistent with the view that perceiving and acting upon opportunities is based, at least in part, on intentional behavior. As discussed earlier in this chapter, the general rule is that the stronger the intention to engage in entrepreneurial action, the more likely it will happen.

entrepreneurially fostering environment An environment that enhances organizational members' perceptions of entrepreneurial action as both feasible and desirable

A common theme across studies focusing on entrepreneurial intentions within existing organizations is that organizations differ in the extent to which they offer an environment that fosters entrepreneurial activity. Such "fostering" environments have been characterized by, for example, appropriate reward systems and top management support, explicit goals, and appropriate organizational values, to name three widely recognized characteristics.[24] A "fostering" environment is one that enhances organizational members' perceptions of entrepreneurial action as both feasible and desirable.[25]

Causes for Interest in Corporate Entrepreneurship

In Chapter 2 we acknowledged that established firms can be considered entrepreneurial and we highlighted some of the differences between firms that are more entrepreneurially managed and those that are more traditionally managed. This interest in entrepreneurship within established businesses has intensified due to a variety of events occurring on social, cultural, and business levels. On a social level, there is an increasing interest in "doing your own thing" and doing it on one's own terms. Individuals who believe strongly in their own talents frequently desire to create something of their own. They want responsibility and have a strong need for individual expression and freedom in their work environment. When this freedom is not there, frustration can cause that individual to become less productive or even leave the organization to achieve self-actualization elsewhere. This new search for meaning, and the impatience involved, has recently caused more discontent in structured organizations than ever before. When meaning is not provided within the organization, individuals often search for an institution that will provide it.

Corporate entrepreneurship is one method of stimulating, and then capitalizing on, individuals in an organization who think that something can be done differently and better. Most people think of Xerox as a large bureaucratic Fortune 100 company. Although, in part, this may be true of the $15 billion giant company, Xerox has done something unique in trying to ensure that its creative employees do not leave like Steve Jobs did to form Apple Computer, Inc. In 1989, Xerox set up Xerox Technology Ventures (XTV) for the purpose of generating profits by investing in the promising technologies of the company, many of which would have otherwise been overlooked.[26] Xerox wanted to avoid mistakes of the past by having "a system to prevent technology from leaking out of the company," according to Robert V. Adams, president of XTV.

The fund has supported numerous start-ups thus far, similar to Quad Mark, the brainchild of Dennis Stemmle, a Xerox employee of 25 years. Stemmle's idea was to make a battery operated, plain paper copier that would fit in a briefcase along with a laptop computer. While for 10 years, the idea was not approved by Xerox's operating committee, the idea was finally funded by XTV and Taiwan's Advanced Scientific Corporation. As is the case with all the companies funded by XTV, 20 percent of each company is owned by the founder and key employees. This provides an incentive for employees like Dennis Stemmle to take the risk, leave Xerox, and form a technology-based venture.

XTV provides both financial and nonfinancial benefits to its parent, Xerox. The funded companies provide profits to the parent company as well as the founders and employees, and now Xerox managers pay closer attention to employees' ideas as well as internal technologies. Is XTV a success? Apparently so, if replication is any indication. The XTV concept contains an element of risk in that Xerox employees forming new ventures are not guaranteed a management position if the new venture fails. This makes XTV different from most entrepreurial ventures in companies. This aspect of risk and no guaranteed employment is the basis for AT&T Ventures, a fund modeled on XTV.

What Xerox recognized is what hundreds of executives in other organizations are also becoming aware of: It is important to keep, or instill, the entrepreneurial spirit in an organization in order to innovate and grow. This realization has revolutionized management thinking. In a large organization, problems often occur that thwart creativity and innovation, particularly in activities not directly related to the organization's main mission. The growth and diversification that can result from flexibility and creativity are particularly critical since large, vertically integrated, diversified corporations are often more efficient in a competitive market than smaller firms.

The resistance against flexibility, growth, and diversification can, in part, be overcome by developing a spirit of entrepreneurship within the existing organization, called *corporate entrepreneurship*. An increase in corporate entrepreneurship reflects an increase in social, cultural, and business pressures. Hypercompetition has forced companies to have an increased interest in such areas as new product development, diversification, increased productivity, and decreasing costs by methods such as reducing the company's labor force.

Corporate entrepreneurship is most strongly reflected in entrepreneurial activities as well as in top management orientations in organizations. These entrepreneurial endeavors consist of the following four key elements: new business venturing, innovativeness, self-renewal, and proactiveness.[27]

New business venturing (sometimes called corporate venturing) refers to the creation of a new business within an existing organization. These entrepreneurial activities consist of creating something new of value either by redefining the company's current products or services, developing new markets, or forming more formally autonomous or semiautonomous units or firms. Formations of new corporate ventures are the most salient manifestations of corporate entrepreneurship. Organizational innovativeness refers to product and service innovation, with an emphasis on development and innovation in technology. It includes new product development, product improvements, and new production methods and procedures.

Self-renewal is the transformation of an organization through the renewal of the key ideas on which it is built. It has strategic and organizational change connotations and includes a redefinition of the business concept, reorganization, and the introduction of systemwide changes to increase innovation. Proactiveness includes initiative and risk taking, as well as competitive aggressiveness and boldness, which are particularly reflected in the orientations and activities of top management. A proactive organization tends to take risks by conducting experiments; it also takes initiative and is bold and aggressive in pursuing opportunities. Organizations with this proactive spirit attempt to lead rather than follow competitors in such key business areas as the introduction of new products or services, operating technologies, and administrative techniques.

Traditional Corporate Culture versus Entrepreneurial Culture

Business and sociological conditions have given rise to a new era in business: the era of the entrepreneur. For some established corporations, the positive media exposure and success of entrepreneurs are threatening as these smaller, aggressive, entrepreneurially driven firms are developing more new products and becoming major factors in select markets. Recognizing the results obtained by other large corporations when employees catch the "entrepreneurial fever," many companies are now attempting to create the same spirit, culture, challenges, and rewards of entrepreneurship in their organizations. Although in Chapter 2 we acknowledged that culture and reward philosophy distinguish entrepreneurially managed firms from those more traditionally managed, it is worth considering in greater detail what constitutes an entrepreneurial culture within an established firm.

corporate culture The environment of a particular organization

The typical *corporate culture* has a climate and a reward system that favor conservative decision making. Emphasis is on gathering large amounts of data as the basis for a rational decision and then using the data to justify the decision should the intended results not occur. Risky decisions are often postponed until enough hard facts can be gathered or a consultant hired to "illuminate the unknown." Frequently, there are so many sign-offs and approvals required for a large-scale project that no individual feels personally responsible.

entrepreneurial culture The environment of an entrepreneurial-oriented firm

The traditional corporate culture differs significantly from an *entrepreneurial culture*. The guiding directives in a traditional corporate culture are: Adhere to the instructions given, do not make any mistakes, do not fail, do not take the initiative but wait for instructions, stay within your turf, and protect your backside. This restrictive environment is, of course, not conducive to creativity, flexibility, independence, ownership, or risk taking—the guiding principles of corporate entrepreneurs. The goals of an entrepreneurial culture are quite different: to develop visions, goals, and action plans; to be rewarded for actions taken; to suggest, try, and experiment; to create and develop regardless of the area; and to take responsibility and ownership.

There are also differences in the shared values and norms of the two cultures. The traditional corporation is hierarchical in nature, with established procedures, reporting systems, lines of authority and responsibility, instructions, and control mechanisms. These support the present corporate culture and do not encourage new product, service, or venture creation. The culture of an entrepreneurial firm is in stark contrast to this model. Instead of a hierarchical structure, an entrepreneurial climate has a flat organizational structure with networking, teamwork, sponsors, and mentors abounding. Close working relationships help establish an atmosphere of trust that facilitates the accomplishment of visions and objectives. Tasks are viewed as fun events, not chores, with participants gladly putting in the number of hours necessary to get the job done. Instead of building barriers to protect turfs, individuals make suggestions within and across functional areas and divisions, resulting in a cross-fertilization of ideas.

traditional managers Managers in a non-entrepreneurial-oriented organization

As would be expected, these two cultures produce different types of individuals and management styles. A comparison of traditional managers, independent entrepreneurs (a.k.a., entrepreneurs), and corporate entrepreneurs (a.k.a., intrapreneurs) reveals several differences (see Table 3.2). While *traditional managers* are motivated primarily by promotion and typical corporate rewards, independent entrepreneurs and corporate entrepreneurs thrive on independence and the ability to create. The corporate entrepreneurs expect their performance to be suitably rewarded.

TABLE 3.2 Comparison of Independent Entrepreneurs, Corporate Entrepreneurs, and Traditional Managers

	Traditional Managers	Independent Entrepreneurs	Corporate Entrepreneurs
Primary motives	Promotion and other traditional corporate rewards, such as office, staff, and power	Independence, opportunity to create, and money	Independence and ability to advance in terms of corporate rewards
Time orientation	Short term—meeting quotas and budgets, weekly, monthly, quarterly, and the annual planning horizon	Survival and achieving 5- to 10-year growth of business	Between independent entrepreneurs and traditional managers, depending on urgency to meet self-imposed and corporate timetable
Activity	Delegates and supervises more than direct involvement	Direct involvement	Direct involvement more than delegation
Risk	Careful	Moderate risk taker	Moderate risk taker
Status	Concerned about status symbols	Not concerned about status symbols	Not concerned about traditional status symbols—desires independence
Failure and mistakes	Tries to avoid mistakes and surprises	Deals with mistakes and failures	Attempts to hide risky projects from view until ready
Decisions	Usually agrees with those in upper management positions	Follows dream with decisions	Able to get others to agree to help achieve dream
Who serves	Others	Self and customers	Self, customers, and sponsors
Family history	Family members worked for large organizations	Entrepreneurial small-business, professional, or farm background	Entrepreneurial small-business, professional, or farm background
Relationship with others	Hierarchy as basic relationship	Transactions and deal making as basic relationship	Transactions within hierarchy

Source: An extensively modified version of a table in G. Pinchot, *Intrapreneuring* (New York: Harper & Row, 1985), pp. 54–56.

There is a different time orientation in the three groups, with managers emphasizing the short run, independent entrepreneurs the long run, and corporate entrepreneurs somewhere in between. Similarly, the primary mode of activity of corporate entrepreneurs falls between the delegation activity of managers and the direct involvement of independent entrepreneurs. Whereas corporate entrepreneurs and independent entrepreneurs are moderate risk takers, managers are much more cautious about taking any risks.

Climate for Corporate Entrepreneurship

How can the climate for corporate entrepreneurship be established in an organization? In establishing an entrepreneurial environment within an established organization, certain factors and leadership characteristics need to be present.[28] The overall characteristics of a good entrepreneurial environment are summarized in Table 3.3. The first of these is that the organization operates on the frontiers of technology. Since research and development are key sources for successful new product ideas, the firm must operate on the cutting edge of the industry's technology, encouraging and supporting new ideas instead of discouraging them, as frequently occurs in firms that require a rapid return on investment and a high sales volume.

TABLE 3.3 Characteristics of an Entrepreneurial Environment

- Organization operates on frontiers of technology
- New ideas encouraged
- Trial and error encouraged
- Failures allowed
- No opportunity parameters
- Resources available and accessible
- Multidiscipline teamwork approach
- Long time horizon
- Volunteer program
- Appropriate reward system
- Sponsors and champions available
- Support of top management

Second, experimentation—trial and error—is encouraged. Successful new products or services usually do not appear fully developed; instead, they evolve. It took time and some product failures before the first marketable computer appeared. A company wanting to establish an entrepreneurial spirit has to establish an environment that allows mistakes and failures in developing new and innovative products. This is in direct opposition to the established career and promotion system of the traditional organization. Yet without the opportunity to fail in an organization, few, if any, corporate entrepreneurial ventures will be developed. Almost every entrepreneur has experienced at least one failure in establishing a successful venture. The importance and the difficulty of learning from the experience are discussed in Chapter 2.

opportunity parameters Barriers to new product creation and development

Third, an organization should make sure that there are no initial *opportunity parameters* inhibiting creativity in new product development. Frequently in an organization, various "turfs" are protected, frustrating attempts by potential entrepreneurs to establish new ventures. In one Fortune 500 company, an attempt to establish an entrepreneurial environment ran into problems and eventually failed when the potential entrepreneurs were informed that a proposed new product and venture was not possible because it was in the domain of another division.

Fourth, the resources of the firm need to be available and easily accessible. As one corporate entrepreneur stated, "If my company really wants me to take the time, effort, and career risks to establish a new venture, then it needs to put money and people resources on the line." Often, insufficient funds are allocated not to creating something new, but instead to solving problems that have an immediate effect on the bottom line. Some companies—like Xerox, 3M, and AT&T—have recognized this problem and have established separate venture-capital areas for funding new internal as well as external ventures. Even when resources are available, all too often the reporting requirements become obstacles to obtaining them.

Fifth, a multidisciplined team approach needs to be encouraged. This open approach, with participation by needed individuals regardless of area, is the antithesis of the typical corporate organizational structure. An evaluation of successful cases of corporate entrepreneurship indicated that one key to success was the existence of "skunkworks" involving relevant people. Developing the needed teamwork for a new venture is further complicated by the fact that a team member's promotion and overall career within the corporation are based on his or her job performance in the current position, not on his or her contribution to the new venture being created.

Besides encouraging teamwork, the corporate environment must establish a long time horizon for evaluating the success of the overall program as well as the success of each individual venture. If a company is not willing to invest money without a guarantee of return for 5 to 10 years, it should not attempt to create an entrepreneurial environment. This patient attitude toward money in the corporate setting is no different from the investment/return time horizon used by venture capitalists and others when they invest in an entrepreneurial effort.

Sixth, the spirit of corporate entrepreneurship cannot be forced upon individuals; it must be on a volunteer basis. There is a difference between corporate thinking and entrepreneurial thinking (discussed in Chapter 2), with certain individuals performing much better on one side of the continuum or the other. Most managers in a corporation are not capable of being successful corporate entrepreneurs. Those who do emerge from this self-selection process must be allowed the latitude to carry a project through to completion. This is not consistent with most corporate procedures for new product development, where different departments and individuals are involved in each stage of the development process. An individual willing to spend the excess hours and effort to create a new venture needs the opportunity and the accompanying reward of completing the project. A corporate entrepreneur falls in love with the newly created internal venture and will do almost anything to help ensure its success.

The seventh characteristic of a good entrepreneurial environment is a *reward system*. The corporate entrepreneur needs to be appropriately rewarded for all the energy, effort, and risk taking expended in the creation of the new venture. Rewards should be based on the attainment of established performance goals. An equity position in the new venture is one of the best rewards for motivating and eliciting the amount of activity and effort needed for success.

Eighth, a corporate environment favorable for corporate entrepreneurship has sponsors and champions throughout the organization who not only support the creative activity but also have the planning flexibility to establish new objectives and directions as needed. As one corporate entrepreneur stated, "For a new business venture to succeed, the corporate entrepreneur needs to be able to alter plans at will and not be concerned about how close they come to achieving the previously stated objectives." Corporate structures frequently measure managers on their ability to come close to objectives, regardless of the quality of performance reflected in this accomplishment.

Finally, and perhaps most important, the entrepreneurial activity must be wholeheartedly supported and embraced by top management, both by their physical presence and by making sure that the necessary personnel and financial resources are available. Without top management support, a successful entrepreneurial environment cannot be created.

Leadership Characteristics of Corporate Entrepreneurs

Within this overall corporate environment, certain individual characteristics have been identified that constitute a successful corporate entrepreneur. As summarized in Table 3.4, these include understanding the environment, being visionary and flexible, creating management options, encouraging teamwork, encouraging open discussion, building a coalition of supporters, and being persistent.

TABLE 3.4 Leadership Characteristics of a Corporate Entrepreneur

- Understands the environment
- Is visionary and flexible
- Creates management options
- Encourages teamwork
- Encourages open discussion
- Builds a coalition of supporters
- Persists

An entrepreneur needs to understand all aspects of the environment. Part of this ability is reflected in the individual's level of creativity, which generally decreases with age and education in most individuals. To establish a successful corporate venture, the individual must be creative and have a broad understanding of the internal and external environments of the corporation.

The person who is going to establish a successful new venture within the firm must also be a visionary leader—a person who dreams great dreams. Although there are many definitions of leadership, the one that best describes what is needed for corporate entrepreneurship is: "A leader is like a gardener. When you want a tomato, you take a seed, put it in fertile soil, and carefully water under tender care. You don't manufacture tomatoes; you grow them." Another good definition is that "leadership is the ability to dream great things and communicate these in such a way that people say yes to being a part of the dream." Martin Luther King, Jr., said "I have a dream" and articulated that dream in such a way that thousands followed him in his efforts, in spite of overwhelming obstacles. To establish a successful new venture, the corporate entrepreneur must have a dream and overcome all the obstacles in achieving it by selling the dream to others.

The third necessary leadership characteristic is that the corporate entrepreneur must be flexible and create management options. A corporate entrepreneur does not "mind the store," but rather is open to and even encourages change. By challenging the beliefs and assumptions of the corporation, a corporate entrepreneur has the opportunity to create something new in the organizational structure.

The corporate entrepreneur needs a fourth characteristic: the ability to encourage teamwork and use a multidisciplined approach. This also violates the organizational practices and structures taught in most business schools that are apparent in established organizational structures. In forming a new venture, putting together a variety of skills requires crossing established departmental structure and reporting systems. To minimize disruption, the corporate entrepreneur must be a good diplomat.

Open discussion must be encouraged in order to develop a good team for creating something new. Many corporate managers have forgotten the frank, open discussions and disagreements that were a part of their educational process. Instead, they spend time building protective barriers and insulating themselves in their corporate empires. A successful new venture within an established firm can be formed only when the team involved feels free to disagree and to critique an idea to reach the best solution. The degree of openness among the team members depends on the degree of openness of the corporate entrepreneur.

Openness leads also to the establishment of a strong coalition of supporters and encouragers. The corporate entrepreneur must encourage and affirm each team member, particularly during difficult times. This encouragement is very important, as the usual motivators of career paths and job security are not operational in establishing a new corporate venture. A good corporate entrepreneur makes everyone a hero.

Last, but not least, is persistence. Throughout the establishment of any new venture, frustration and obstacles will occur. Only through the corporate entrepreneur's persistence will a new venture be created and successful commercialization result.

ESTABLISHING CORPORATE ENTREPRENEURSHIP IN THE ORGANIZATION

An organization desiring to establish an entrepreneurial environment must implement a procedure for its creation. Although this can be done internally, frequently it is easier to use someone outside to facilitate the process. This is particularly true when the organization's environment is very traditional and has a record of little change and few new products being introduced.

top management commitment Managers in an organization strongly supporting corporate entrepreneurship

The first step in this process is to secure a commitment to corporate entrepreneurship in the organization by top, upper, and middle management levels. Without *top management commitment,* the organization will never be able to go through all the cultural changes necessary for implementation. Once the top management of the organization has been committed to corporate entrepreneurship for a sufficient period of time (at least three years), the concept can be introduced throughout the organization. This is accomplished most effectively through seminars, where the aspects of corporate entrepreneurship are introduced and strategies are developed to transform the organizational culture into an entrepreneurial one. General guidelines need to be established for corporate venture development. Once the initial framework is established and the concept embraced, corporate entrepreneurs need to be identified, selected, and trained. This training needs to focus on identifying viable opportunities and their markets and developing the appropriate business plan.

Second, ideas and general areas that top management is interested in supporting should be identified, along with the amount of risk money that is available to develop the concept further. Overall program expectations and the target results of each corporate venture should be established. As much as possible, these should specify the time frame, volume, and profitability requirements for the new venture, as well as the impact of the organization. Along with entrepreneurial training, a mentor/sponsor system needs to be established. Without sponsors or champions, there is little hope that the culture of the organization can be transformed into an entrepreneurial one.

Third, a company needs to use technology to make itself more flexible. Technology has been used successfully for the past decade by small companies that behave like big ones.[29] How else could a small firm like Value Quest Ltd. compete against very large money management firms, except through a state-of-the-art personal computer and access to large data banks? Similarly, large companies can use technology to make themselves responsive and flexible like smaller firms.

Fourth, the organization should be a group of interested managers who will train employees as well as share their experiences. The training sessions should be conducted one day per month for a specified period of time. Informational items about corporate entrepreneurship in general—and about the specifics of the company's activities in developing ideas into marketable products or services that are the basis of new business venture units—should be well publicized. This will require the entrepreneurial team to develop a business plan, obtain customer reaction and some initial intentions to buy, and learn how to coexist within the organizational structure.

Fifth, the organization needs to develop ways to get closer to its customers. This can be done by tapping the database, hiring from smaller rivals, and helping the retailer.

Sixth, an organization that wants to become more entrepreneurial must learn to be more productive with fewer resources. This has already occurred in many companies that have downsized. Top-heavy organizations are out of date in today's hypercompetitive environment. To accommodate the large cutbacks in middle management, much more control has to be given to subordinates at all levels in the organization. Not surprisingly, the span of control may become as high as 30-to-1 in divisions of such companies. The concept of "lean and mean" needs to exist if corporate entrepreneurship is to prevail.

Seventh, the organization needs to establish a strong support structure for corporate entrepreneurship. This is particularly important since corporate entrepreneurship is usually a secondary activity in the organization. Since entrepreneurial activities do not immediately affect the bottom line, they can be easily overlooked and may receive little funding and support. To be successful, these ventures require flexible, innovative behavior, with the corporate entrepreneurs having total authority over expenditures and access to sufficient funds. When the corporate entrepreneur has to justify expenses on a daily basis, it is really not a new internal venture but merely an operational extension of the funding source.

Eighth, support also must involve tying the rewards to the performance of the entrepreneurial unit. This encourages the team members to work harder and compete more effectively since they will benefit directly from their efforts. Because the corporate venture is a part of the larger organization and not a totally independent unit, the equity portion of the compensation is particularly difficult to handle.

Finally, the organization needs to implement an evaluation system that allows successful entrepreneurial units to expand and unsuccessful ones to be eliminated. The organization can establish constraints to ensure that this expansion does not run contrary to the corporate mission statement. Similarly, corporate ventures that fail to show sufficient viability should not be allowed to exist just because of vested interests.

Problems and Successful Efforts

Corporate entrepreneurship is not without its problems. One study found that new ventures started within a corporation performed worse than those started independently by entrepreneurs.[30] The reasons cited were the corporation's difficulty in maintaining a long-term commitment, a lack of freedom to make autonomous decisions, and a constrained environment. Generally, independent, venture-capital-based start-ups by entrepreneurs tend to outperform corporate start-ups significantly. On average, not only did the independents become profitable twice as fast, but they ended up twice as profitable.[31]

These findings should not deter organizations from starting the process. There are numerous examples of companies that, having understood the environmental and entrepreneurial characteristics necessary, have adopted their own version of the implementation process to launch new ventures successfully. One of the best known of these firms is Minnesota Mining and Manufacturing (3M). Having had many entrepreneurial successes, 3M, in effect, allows employees to devote a percentage of their time to independent projects. This enables the divisions of the company to meet an important goal: to generate a significant percent of sales from new products introduced within the last five years. One of the most successful of these entrepreneurial activities was the development of Post-it Notes by entrepreneur Arthur Fry. This effort developed out of Fry's annoyance that pieces of paper marking his church hymnal constantly fell out while he was singing. As a 3M chemical engineer, Fry knew about the discovery by a scientist, Spencer Silver, of a very-low-sticking-power adhesive, which to the company was a poor product characteristic. However, this characteristic was perfect for Fry's problem; a marker with a light sticking adhesive that would be easy to remove provided a good solution. Obtaining approval to commercialize the idea proved to be a monumental task until the samples distributed to secretaries within 3M, as well as to other companies, created such a demand that the company eventually began selling the product under the name Post-it.

Another firm committed to the concept of corporate entrepreneurship is Hewlett-Packard (HP). After failing to recognize the potential of Steven Wozniak's proposal for a personal computer (which was the basis for Apple Computer Inc.), Hewlett-Packard has taken steps to ensure that it will be recognized as a leader in innovation and not miss future opportunities. However, the entrepreneurial road at HP is not an easy one. Such was the case for Charles House, an engineer who went far beyond his entrepreneurial duty when he ignored an order from David Packard to stop working on a high-quality video monitor. The monitor, once developed, was used in NASA's manned moon landings and in heart transplants. Although projected to achieve sales of no more than 30 units, these large-screen displays have obtained good sales and profits.

IBM also decided that corporate entrepreneurship would help spur corporate growth. The company developed the independent business unit concept, in which each unit is a separate organization with its own mini-board of directors and autonomous decision-making authority on many manufacturing and marketing issues. The business units have developed such products as the automatic teller machine for banks, industrial robots, and the IBM personal computer. The latter business unit was given a blank check with a mandate to get IBM into the personal computer market. Corporate entrepreneur Philip Estridge led his group to develop and market the PCs, through both IBM's sales force and the retail market, breaking some of the most binding operational rules of IBM at that time.

These and other success stories indicate that the problems of corporate entrepreneurship are not insurmountable and that implementing corporate entrepreneurship can lead to new products, growth, and the development of an entirely new corporate environment and culture.

IN REVIEW

SUMMARY

Individuals become entrepreneurs because they intend to do so. The stronger the intention to be an entrepreneur, the more likely it is that it will happen. Intentions become stronger as individuals perceive an entrepreneurial career as feasible and desirable. These perceptions of feasibility and desirability are influenced by one's background and characteristics, such as education, personal values, age and work history, role models and support systems, and networks. Gender and race are also characteristics of individuals that help us understand the entrepreneurial phenomenon. Established firms can create environmental conditions to motivate individuals within their organizations to act entrepreneurially, that is, that allow organizational members to perceive entrepreneurial outcomes as feasible and desirable. Within existing corporate structures, this entrepreneurial spirit and effort is called *corporate entrepreneurship*.

To develop successful innovation, a corporation should establish a conducive organizational climate. Traditional managers tend to adhere more strictly to established hierarchical structures, to be less risk oriented, and to emphasize short-term results, all of which inhibit the creativity, flexibility, and risk taking required for new ventures. Organizations desiring an entrepreneurial climate need to encourage new ideas and experimental efforts, eliminate opportunity parameters, make resources available, promote a teamwork approach and voluntary corporate entrepreneurship, and enlist top management's support.

The corporate entrepreneur also must have appropriate leadership characteristics. In addition to being creative, flexible, and visionary, the corporate entrepreneur must be able to work within the corporate structure. Corporate entrepreneurs need to encourage teamwork and work diplomatically across established structures. Open discussion and strong support of team members are also required. Finally, the corporate entrepreneur must be persistent in order to overcome the inevitable obstacles.

The process of establishing corporate entrepreneurship within an existing organization requires the commitment of management, particularly top management. The organization must carefully choose leaders, develop general guidelines for ventures, and delineate expectations before the entrepreneurial program begins. Training sessions are an important part of the process. As role models and entrepreneurial ventures are introduced, the organization must establish a strong organizational support system, along with a system of incentives and rewards to encourage team members. Finally, the organization should establish a system to expand successful ventures and eliminate unsuccessful ones.

RESEARCH TASKS

1. Speak to three entrepreneurs and find out what motivated them to become entrepreneurs. Also find one person who, at one time, considered becoming an entrepreneur but did not do so. Find out why.
2. Interview two women entrepreneurs and find out whether they believe that the tasks of being an entrepreneur are different for them than for their male counterparts. What are the advantages of being a female entrepreneur? What are the disadvantages of being a female entrepreneur? Are these differences substantial or minor?
3. Interview three individuals employed within the research and development (R&D) departments of large, well-established companies. From the interview, gain an understanding of what the company does to foster corporate entrepreneurship, what it does to inhibit corporate entrepreneurship, and what it could be doing better toward further enhancing entrepreneurship throughout the whole organization
4. Search the Internet for four accounts of successful corporate entrepreneurship. What key factors for success are common across all of these accounts? Which are unique? If one company can foster an entrepreneurial climate within an existing firm, what stops another company from copying its process and taking away the initial advantage?

CLASS DISCUSSION

1. We know that people with high IQ scores, or even high SAT or high GMAT scores, do not necessarily do any better than others in school. How predictive do you believe personality tests are in predicting success as an entrepreneur? What are the dangers of classifying people using personality tests as "not very entrepreneurial" or "very entrepreneurial"? What are the potential benefits?
2. Why do role models have an impact on a person's decision to become an entrepreneur? Do you think that a person whose parent was an entrepreneur of a

failed business is more or less likely to start his or her own business than a person whose parents were managers of large, established companies?

3. To what extent do men and women differ as entrepreneurs in terms of the types of companies they create and manage, the industries in which they operate, the challenges they face, and their sources of competitive advantage? Are these differences greater or less than they were five years ago? Are we going to soon find that there are no differences between women and men entrepreneurs?
4. Isn't "corporate entrepreneurship" an oxymoron? Do the characteristics of an established organization, such as its routines and structure, increase efficiency but at the same time kill any entrepreneurial spirit? Is there any way that a company can have the best of both worlds?
5. Is increasing the entrepreneurial orientation of a firm *always* a good thing? Or are there circumstances or environments in which the further pursuit of opportunities can diminish firm performance?

SELECTED READINGS

Baron, Robert A.; and Gideon D. Markman. (2000). Beyond Social Capital: How Social Skills Can Enhance Entrepreneurs' Success. *Academy of Management Executive,* vol. 14, no. 1, pp. 106–16.

This article suggests that entrepreneurs' social skills—specific competencies that help them interact effectively with others—may play a role in their success. A high level of social capital, built on a favorable reputation, relevant previous experience, and direct personal contacts, often assists entrepreneurs in gaining access to venture capitalists, potential customers, and others.

Boden, Richard J.; and Brian Headd. (October 2002). Race and Gender Differences in Business Ownership and Business Turnover. *Business Economics,* pp. 61–72.

This article describes a study that uses a novel longitudinal Bureau of the Census employer data series to examine the survival prospects of new employer businesses for four different, mutually exclusive classifications of ownership: white non-Hispanics; white Hispanics; blacks; and Asians and other minorities.

Coleman, Susan. (2002). Constraints Faced by Women Small Business Owners: Evidence from the Data. *Journal of Developmental Entrepreneurship,* vol. 7, no. 2, pp. 151–74.

This article explores some of the possible constraints faced by women business owners. Although results do not demonstrate evidence of noneconomic discrimination against women-owned firms, they do reveal that certain characteristics typical of many women-owned firms, including small size, limited prospects for growth and profitability, and failure to provide collateral or guarantee, reduce the likelihood of obtaining debt capital.

Davidsson, Per; and Benson Honig. (2003). The Role of Social and Human Capital among Nascent Entrepreneurs. *Journal of Business Venturing,* vol. 18, pp. 301–31.

This study examines nascent entrepreneurship by comparing individuals engaged in nascent activities with a control group and finds that social capital is a robust predictor for nascent entrepreneurs, *as well as for advancing through the start-up process. With regard to outcomes like first sale or showing a profit, only one aspect of social capital, viz., being a member of a* business network, *had a statistically significant positive effect. The study supports* human capital *in predicting entry into nascent entrepreneurship, but only weakly for carrying the start-up process toward successful completion.*

Dess, Gregory; R. Duane Ireland; Shaker Zahra; Steven Floyd; Jay Janney; and Peter Lane. (2003). Emerging Issues in Corporate Entrepreneurship. *Journal of Management,* vol. 29, pp. 351–78.

In this article, the authors identify four major issues scholars can pursue to further our understanding about corporate entrepreneurship (CE). The issues explored include various forms of CE and their implications for organizational learning; the role of leadership and social exchange in the CE process; and key research opportunities relevant to CE in an international context. Throughout the article, the authors use the organizational learning theory as a means of integrating our discussion and highlighting the potential contributions of CE to knowledge creation and effective exploitation.

Dyer, Linda M.; and Christopher A. Ross. (April 2000). Ethnic Enterprises and Their Clientele. *Journal of Small Business Management,* pp. 48–66.

The goal of this article is to examine the relationships between ethnic-minority businesses and their co-ethnic customers. A theoretical framework emerges, which highlights three dimensions: (1) the coincident roles of business owner/manager and co-ethnic individual, (2) the easy flow of communication among co-ethnics, and (3) the symbolic aspects of ethnicity. These dimensions are causes of the ambivalent relations that exist between many businesses and their co-ethnic clients.

Hmieleski, Keith; and Andrew Corbett. (2006). Proclivity for Improvisation as a Predictor of Entrepreneurial Intentions. *Journal of Small Business Management,* vol. 44, pp. 45–63.

This study examines the relationship between improvisation and entrepreneurial intentions *and finds that* entrepreneurial intentions *are associated with measures of personality, motivation, cognitive style, social models, and improvisation. The strongest relationship is found between* entrepreneurial intentions *and improvisation.*

Jack, Sarah; and Alistair Anderson. (2002). The Effects of Embeddedness on the Entrepreneurial Process. *Journal of Business Venturing,* vol. 17, pp. 467–87.

In this study the authors examine the use of Gidden's theory of structuration to develop the conception of entrepreneurship as an embedded socioeconomic process. In particular they focus on the role of embeddedness in shaping and sustaining business, in recognizing and realizing opportunities, and in the effect of social structure on entrepreneurship.

Krueger, Norris. (2000). The Cognitive Infrastructure of Opportunity Emergence: *Entrepreneurship: Theory and Practice,* vol. 24, pp. 5–23.

In this article the author argues that seeing a prospective course of action as a credible opportunity reflects an intentions-driven *process driven by known critical antecedents. On the basis of well-developed theory and robust empirical evidence, he proposes an* intentions-based *model of the cognitive infrastructure that supports or inhibits how individuals perceive opportunities. The author also shows the practical diagnostic power this model offers to managers.*

Kuratko, Donald; R. Duane Ireland; Jeffrey Covin; and Jeffrey Hornsby. (2005). A Model of Middle-Level Managers' Entrepreneurial Behavior. *Entrepreneurship: Theory & Practice,* vol. 29, pp. 699–716.

In this article, the authors integrate knowledge about corporate entrepreneurship *and middle-level managers' behaviors to develop and explore a conceptual model. The model depicts the organizational antecedents of middle-level managers' entrepreneurial behavior, the entrepreneurial actions describing that behavior, and outcomes of that behavior, as well as factors influencing its continuance.*

Kuemmerle, Walter. (May 2002). A Test for the Fainthearted. *Harvard Business Review,* pp. 122–27.

Starting a business is rarely a dignified affair. The article discusses what really makes an entrepreneur; what characteristics set successful entrepreneurs apart, enabling them to start ventures against all odds and keep them alive even in the worst of times; and finally, whether, if you don't possess those characteristics, they can be developed.

Lerner, Miri; Candida Brush; and Robert Hisrich. (1997). Israeli Women Entrepreneurs: An Examination of Factors Affecting Performance. *Journal of Business Venturing,* vol. 12, no. 4, pp. 315–39.

This study analyzes the relationship between individual factors and the business performance of 220 Israeli women entrepreneurs. The applicability of five theoretical perspectives—motivations and goals, social learning, network affiliation, human capital, and environmental factors—is examined in terms of business performance. Findings indicate that network affiliation, human capital, and motivation theories have greater explanatory power than social learning or environmental perspectives.

Perry, Stephen C. (2002). A Comparison of Failed and Non-Failed Small Businesses in the United States: Do Men and Women Use Different Planning and Decision Making Strategies? *Journal of Developmental Entrepreneurship,* vol. 7, no. 4, pp. 415–28.

This article describes a study that investigates the influence of gender in U.S. small business failures. The main conclusion is that gender does not appear to be related to the failure of small businesses in the United States. Gender differences of both failed and nonfailed firms are also investigated for contextual variables and for variables having to do with planning and strategy problems.

Robb, Alicia M. (2002). Entrepreneurial Performance by Women and Minorities: The Case of New Firms. *Journal of Developmental Entrepreneurship,* vol. 7, no. 4, pp. 383–97.

The primary objective of this paper is to compare how business survival varies between men- and women- owned business start-ups and between minority- and nonminority-owned business start-ups. The results indicate that some of the differences in observed survival rates for new firms are driven by factors other than owner race and gender. However, preliminary evidence indicates that some groups may face greater obstacles in starting successful business ventures.

Shepherd, Dean; and Norris Krueger. (2002). An Intentions-Based Model of Entrepreneurial Teams' Social Cognition. *Entrepreneurship: Theory and Practice,* vol. 27, pp. 167–85.

In this article the authors present an intentions-based *model of how to promote entrepreneurial thinking in the domain of corporate entrepreneurship. They emphasize the importance of perceptions of desirability and feasibility and that these perceptions are from the team as well as the individual perspective.*

END NOTES

1. J. Ajzen, "The Theory of Planned Behavior," *Organizational Behavior and Human Decision Processes* 50 (1991), pp. 179–211.
2. A. Bandura, "*Self-Efficacy: The Exercise of Control* (New York: W.H. Freeman and Company, 1997). And D. A. Shepherd, and N. Krueger, "An Intentions-Based Model of Entrepreneurial Teams' Social Cognition," Special Issue on Cognition and Information Processing, *Entrepreneurship Theory and Practice* 27 (2002), pp. 167–85.
3. N. F. J. Krueger, and D. V. Brazael, "Entrepreneurial Potential and Potential Entrepreneurs." *Entrepreneurship Theory and Practice* 18 (1994), pp. 91–104.

4. Shepherd and Krueger, "An Intentions Based Model."
5. C. M. Ford, and D. A. Gioia, *Creativity in Organizations: Ivory Tower Visions and Real World Voices* (Newbury Park, CA: Sage, 1995).
6. See J. Gimeno, T. Folta, A. Cooper, and C. Woo, "Survival of the Fittest? Entrepreneurial Human Capital and the Persistence of Underperforming Firms," *Admininstrative Science Quarterly* 42 (1997), pp. 750–83.
7. P. Davidsson, and B. Honig, "The Role of Social and Human Capital among Nascent Entrepreneurs," *Journal of Business Venturing* 18 (2003), pp. 301–31.
8. For a summary of the results of this study, see "To the Winners Belong the Spoils," *Marketing News* 20 (October 10, 1986), pp. 1, 13.
9. Much of this information is based on research findings in Robert C. Ronstadt, "Initial Venture Goals, Age, and the Decision to Start an Entrepreneurial Career," *Proceedings* of the 43rd Annual Meeting of the Academy of Management (August 1983), p. 472; and Robert C. Ronstadt, "The Decision Not to Become an Entrepreneur," *Proceedings,* 1983 Conference on Entrepreneurship (April 1983), pp. 192–212.
10. A. C. Cooper, T. B. Folta, and C. Woo, "Entrepreneurial Information Search," *Journal of Business Venturing* 10 (1995), pp. 107–20. And M. Wright, K. Robbie, and C. Ennew, "Venture Capitalists and Serial Entrepreneurs," *Journal of Business Venturing* 12(3) (1997), pp. 227–249.
11. Davidsson and Honig, "The Role of Social and Human Capital."
12. The influence of role models on career choice is discussed in E. Almquist and S. Angust, "Role Model Influences on College Women's Career Aspirations," *Merrill-Palmer Quarterly* 17 (July 1971), pp. 263–97; J. Strake and C. Granger, "Same-Sex and Opposite-Sex Teacher Model Influences on Science Career Commitment among High School Students," *Journal of Educational Psychology* 70 (April 1978), pp. 180–86; Alan L. Carsud, Connie Marie Gaglio, and Kenneth W. Olm, "Entrepreneurs-Mentors, Networks, and Successful New Venture Development: An Exploratory Study," *Proceedings,* 1986 Conference on Entrepreneurship (April 1986), pp. 29–35; and Howard Aldrich, Ben Rosen, and William Woodward, "The Impact of Social Networks on Business Foundings and Profit: A Longitudinal Study," *Proceedings,* 1987 Conference on Entrepreneurship (April 1987), pp. 154–68.
13. A thoughtful development of the network concept can be found in Howard Aldrich and Catherine Zimmer, "Entrepreneurship through Social Networks." In *The Art and Science of Entrepreneurship* (Cambridge, MA: Ballinger, 1986), pp. 3–24.
14. H. Hoang, and B. Antoncic, "Network-Based Research in Entrepreneurship: A Critical Review," *Journal of Business Venturing* 18 (2003), pp. 165–88.
15. S. Birley, "The Role of Networks in the Entrepreneurial Process," *Journal of Business Venturing* 1 (1985), pp. 107–17; A. Cooper, and W. Dunkelberg, "Entrepreneurship and Paths to Business Ownership," *Strategic Management Journal* 7 (1986), pp. 53–68. B. Johannisson, *Networking and Entrepreneurial Growth*. In D. Sexton and H. Landström (eds.), *The Blackwell Handbook of Entrepreneurship* (Oxford, MA: Blackwell, 2000), pp. 26–44.
16. A. Larson, "Network Dyads in Entrepreneurial Settings: A Study of the Governance of Exchange Relationships," *Administrative Science Quarterly* 37 (1992), pp. 76–104; W. Powell, "Neither Market nor Hierarchy: Network Forms of Organization." In B. Staw and L. Cummings (eds.), *Research in Organizational Behavior* (Greenwich, CT: JAI Press (1990); B. Uzzi, "The Sources and Consequences of Embeddedness for the Economic Performance of Organization: The Network Effect," *American Sociological Review* 61 (1996), pp. 674–98.
17. Uzzi, "The Sources and Consequences of Embeddedness."

18. This material is also discussed in Robert D. Hisrich and Candida G. Brush, *The Woman Entrepreneur: Starting, Financing, and Managing a Successful New Business* (Lexington, MA: Lexington Books, 1986).
19. See B. A. Kirchhoff, R. L. Stevens, and N. I. Hurwitz, "Factors Underlying Increases in Minority Entrepreneurship: 1972–1977." In *Frontiers of Entrepreneurship Research,* ed. K. H. Vesper (Wellesley, MA: Babson College Center for Entrepreneurial Studies, 1982).
20. See J. A. Hornaday and J. Aboud, "The Characteristics of Successful Entrepreneurs," *Personnel Psychology* 24 (1971), pp. 141–53.
21. See E. Gomolka, "Characteristics of Minority Entrepreneurs and Small Business Enterprises," *American Journal of Small Business* 2, no. 1 (1977), pp. 12–21.
22. See J. F. DeCarlo and P. R. Lyons, "A Comparison of Selected Personal Characteristics of Minority and Non-Minority Female Entrepreneurs," *Journal of Small Business Management* 17 (1979), pp. 222–29.
23. See R. D. Hisrich and C. Brush, "Characteristics of the Minority Entrepreneur," *Journal of Small Business Management* 24 (1986), pp. 1–8.
24. (Hornsby et al., 1993; Kuratko et al., 1993; Zahra, 1991) "An Intentions-Based Model of Entrepreneurs Teams' Social Cognition. "Special Issue on Cognition and Information Processing, *Entrepreneurship; Theory and Practices* 27(2) 167–85.
25. Shepherd and Krueger, "An Intentions-Based Model."
26. For a discussion of XTV, see Larry Armstrong, "Nurturing an Employee's Brainchild," *BusinessWeek/Enterprise* (1993), p. 196.
27. For a discussion of corporate entrepreneurship elements and their measures, see G. T. Lumpkin and G. G. Dess, "Clarifying the Entrepreneurial Orientation Construct and Linking It to Performance," *Academy of Management Review* 12, no. 1 (1996), pp. 135–72; and B. Antoncic and R. D. Hisrich, "Intrapreneurship: Construct Refinement and Cross-Cultural Validation," *Journal of Business Venturing* 16, no. 61 (September. 2001), pp. 495–527.
28. For a thorough discussion of the factors important in corporate entrepreneurship, see R. M. Kanter, *The Change Masters* (New York: Simon & Schuster, 1983); and G. Pinchot III, *Intrapreneuring* (New York: Harper & Row, 1985).
29. For a discussion of this aspect, see Peter Coy, "Start with Some High-Tech Magic . . . ," *BusinessWeek/Enterprise* 1993, pp. 24–25, 28, 32.
30. N. Fast, "Pitfalls of Corporate Venturing," *Research Management* (March 1981), pp. 21–24.
31. For complete information on the relative performance, see R. Biggadike, "The Risky Business of Diversification," *Harvard Business Review* (May–June 1979), pp. 103–11; L. E. Weiss, "Start-Up Business: A Comparison of Performances," *Sloan Management Review* (Fall 1981), pp. 37–53; and N. D. Fast and S. E. Pratt, "Individual Entrepreneurship and the Large Corporation," *Proceedings,* Babson Research Conference (April 1984), pp. 443–50.

4

INTERNATIONAL ENTREPRENEURSHIP OPPORTUNITIES

LEARNING OBJECTIVES

1
To identify the aspects and importance of international entrepreneurship.

2
To identify the important strategic issues in international entrepreneurship.

3
To understand the factors affecting successful international entrepreneurship.

4
To present the problems and barriers to international entrepreneurship.

OPENING PROFILE

A. MALACHI MIXON III

Creativity, risk taking, and innovation in entrepreneurship are essential not only to the inception of new products and ventures, but also to a firm's successful transition into global markets. The case of Mal Mixon's notable revitalization of tiny Invacare Corporation exemplifies this connection.

www.invacare.com

Invacare traces its existence to the 1895 beginnings of the Worthington Company, a small Elyria, Ohio, firm that manufactured a line of vehicles especially designed for the physically challenged. Having undergone numerous changes due to mergers and acquisitions, the Worthington Company's small wheelchair business was sold to local investors, but on the basis of traditional business evaluation measures, there was not much to buy. Sales in 1979 were $19 million with 350 employees; the principal products were unwieldy, clunky steel manual wheelchairs, and no new products were on the drawing boards. The 1979 pro forma earnings statement that followed a Mixon-led leveraged buyout (LBO) indicated net earnings of only $100,000. Everest & Jennings, a public competitor more than seven times Invacare's size, controlled 80 percent of the domestic wheelchair market.

Mal Mixon, then vice president of marketing for the CT scanner products division of Johnson & Johnson's Technicare subsidiary, saw beyond manual wheelchairs and focused instead on the potential for home medical products. Assembling a group of local investors, he spearheaded a leveraged acquisition funded with $1.5 million of equity and $6.3 million in debt. The influence of Mixon's nurturing father, coupled with the effects of his upbringing in the small Oklahoma farming town of Spiro, instilled Mixon with confidence and a strong sense of purpose and determination. Intellectually curious, he learned to dream of the possibilities in life, to question everything, to take intelligent risks, to be persistent, and to become a fierce competitor. After he graduated from Harvard College, these traits were reinforced and supplemented with leadership skills acquired through four years of service in the Marine Corps, where he also learned how to deal with adversity. "You are taught to reach your objective no matter what . . . you never have an excuse for failure," says Mixon. Returning from the Marine Corps in 1966, Mal went back to Harvard for his MBA, graduating with distinction. He initially worked as a salesman, then became sales manager, and later was director of marketing for the Cleveland-based Harris Corporation. He moved to Ohio Nuclear, a subsidiary of Technicare, where he rose to vice president of sales and marketing of the CT scanner division. Mal was 39 years old when Johnson & Johnson divested Invacare.

Investing $10,000 of his own funds, $40,000 borrowed from friends, and a $100,000 note from Invacare, Mal took control of the company on January 2, 1980, retaining a 15 percent share. With a fierce tenacity reminiscent of the Marine Corps's "bulldog" mascot, Mixon's restructuring of Invacare was immediate and total. He soon replaced 16 of the 18 direct sales staff—"They didn't have fire in their bellies, and they didn't have the necessary talent"—and, more importantly, began working with the company's engineers to produce new products, believing that without a good product, nothing else matters. He initiated "one-stop shopping" by expanding the home health care line and cajoling, pleading, and offering volume discounts to skeptical customers in order to increase business. The three-pronged attack of revitalization, product/-service development, and aggressive competitive orientation proved effective, and soon Invacare was capturing market share from Everest & Jennings. In the process, Invacare reduced the weight of its standard wheelchairs from 68 to 15 pounds, introduced microprocessor electronic control systems for power wheelchairs, and offered "30 different crazy colors," while dramatically reducing lead times. Everest & Jennings watched its wheelchair market share erode from 80 to 5 percent today.

Sales and earnings accelerated through the early 1980s and by the end of 1983, Invacare had $70 million in sales and $2.8 million in net earnings. In 1984, the company went public to obtain operating capital and to pay down the short-term debt that helped fund the company's growth during the 1980s. The initial public offering ($11 adjusted to two stock splits, or $2.75/share on NASDAQ) raised $15 million.

A major challenge presented itself in 1986 when a Taiwanese competitor began selling in the United States at 20 percent below prevailing prices. Aided by the facilities consolidations and plan reconfigurations that were launched in 1985, Invacare relocated some of its manufacturing to Mexico. This further improved its overall cost structure and competitive position. Invacare attacked the competition, meeting the imports head-on in price, with a superior product and a more extensive distribution and service capability. Due to Invacare's aggressive response, the Taiwanese imports failed to gain a foothold and ceased to be a major market factor by 1987. Sales, product lines, and earnings have increased steadily since. Invacare posted $100 million in sales in 1986, surpassed $200 million in 1990, $600 million in 1996, and $1 billion in 2001.

Product lines now include manual and powered wheelchairs; home respirator devices for oxygen, aerosol, and sleep therapy; home care beds; assistive aids; replacement parts; disposables; and electronic control systems. From a tenuous and ambitious beginning ($19 million in sales and a 10 percent market share in standard wheelchairs), Invacare, headquartered in Elyria, Ohio, has manufacturing plants in the United States, Australia, Canada, Denmark, Germany, France, Mexico, New Zealand, Portugal, Sweden, Switzerland, and the United Kingdom, and has 6,100 employees worldwide. The company conducts business in more than 80 countries around the world and has the largest distribution network in the industry. In 2005, Invacare had revenue of $1.6 billion, experiencing a 19 percent (from $19 million in 1979 to $1.6 billion in 2005) annual compounded average sales growth. Net income was $62.21 million, a 28 percent (from $100,000 in 1979 to $62.21 million in 2005) annual compounded growth in net income. Invacare's stock price is around $33. It has had an 18 percent (from $1.66 year-end 1987 to around $33 in 2005) compounded annual growth in share price for the past 18 years.

Mal Mixon continues to adapt and successfully manage a rapidly expanding company on a global level. Mixon is also recognized as a visionary leader. As stated by a friend and business acquaintance, "He's able to develop a vision faster than most people can pick up the telephone." The ability to develop and articulate a sound vision, plan and execute an appropriate strategy for the enterprise, and maintain sound values are important elements of leadership, according to Mixon. Frequently, however, it is difficult for an entrepreneur to bridge the gap, or to manage and expand a venture, as evidenced by Steve Jobs and the turbulent growth of Apple Computer. As a new venture grows, there can be a need for more and more administration. It appears that this has been attended to in Invacare, as Mal has built a strong management team. Also, at times, a new infusion of the entrepreneurial spirit that has formed the venture is needed. Balancing entrepreneurship with administration becomes the challenge. As Mal puts it, "Entrepreneurship is creating business as opposed to administering business and having extensive personal capital at risk as opposed to compensation for a job."

INTRODUCTION

Unlike Mal Mixon, many entrepreneurs find it difficult to both manage and expand the venture they created, especially in terms of the global marketplace. In order to expand a venture, an entrepreneur needs to access his or her abilities in the management area to identify methods for domestic and even international expansion, as well as to determine when it may be necessary to turn the reins over to someone else. The latter is especially true in the case of international branches or plants that, by virtue of geography, limit the founding entrepreneur's control over operations. As a new venture grows and matures, a need can develop for more administration as well as for a new infusion of entrepreneurial spirit (intrapreneurship), as discussed in Chapter 2. Some entrepreneurs tend to forget a basic axiom in business: The only constant is change. Entrepreneurs like Mal Mixon, who understand this axiom, will effectively manage change by continually adapting organizational culture, structure, procedures, strategic direction, and products in both a domestic and an international orientation. Entrepreneurs in developed countries like the United States, Japan, Great Britain, and Germany must sell their products in a variety of new and different market areas early on in the development of their firms or, as in the case of Mal Mixon's Invacare, determine how to expand into and prosper in international markets.

Never before in the history of the world have there been such interesting and exciting international business opportunities. The opening of the once-controlled economies of Eastern and Central Europe, the former U.S.S.R., and the People's Republic of China to market-oriented enterprise and the advancement of the Pacific Rim provide a myriad of possibilities for entrepreneurs wanting to launch businesses in a foreign market as well as for existing entrepreneurial firms desiring to expand their businesses.

As more and more countries become market oriented and developed, the distinction between foreign and domestic markets is becoming less pronounced. What was once only produced domestically is now produced internationally. For example, Yamaha pianos are now manufactured in the United States. Nestlé's chocolate is made in Europe. This blurring of national identities will continue to accelerate as more and more products are introduced outside domestic boundaries earlier in the life of entrepreneurial firms.

In the past decade, organizations have been attempting to redefine themselves as truly global organizations. The pressure to internationalize is being felt in virtually every organization: nonprofit and for-profit, public and private, large and small. This need to internationalize is accelerating due to the self-interest of the organizations themselves as well as the impact of a variety of external events and forces. Who would have believed a decade ago that today seven-eighths of the markets of the world would be under some form of market economics? Even as late as August 1989, few would have predicted the rapid collapse of communism and the fall of the Berlin Wall, which presented astoundingly large new market opportunities and potentially more significant competition in the form of a unified Germany and the European Union. Who would have ever imagined that a trading agreement would emerge between Canada, Mexico, and the United States, creating one of the world's largest and most prosperous trading blocs? Or who would have imagined the rise of economic opportunities and power in China?

These changes are well recognized by organizations, which are investing trillions of dollars in a world economy that features emerging markets as the vehicles of future growth. About 85 percent of the world's population lives in developing countries, most of which are in dire need of major investment in infrastructure development. Just ask the potato farmers in the Chuvash Republic of Russia, who saw 26 percent of their crop rot because of inadequate distribution and warehousing, whether there is a need for such investment in infrastructure. Or, ask the economics professor in the Czech Republic, who has to leave the university to find other employment in order to live due to the low university wages, whether massive investment is needed. Clearly, these developing countries need training and education in order to develop an infrastructure that will support them in the next century.

The need for physical and technological infrastructure is no more apparent than in one of the fastest growing markets of this decade—the Pacific Rim. This area offers economically viable locations for manufacturing and trade. Over half of the world's population lives in Asia, and China contains 20 percent of the world's population. India alone is twice the size of Latin America. And then there is Japan, with its modern world economy, ranking third in the world in exporting and importing, surpassed only by the United States and Germany. Who will forget the shock when Japanese automobile companies voluntarily reduced their exports to the United States market after having successfully competed with the U.S. companies—Chrysler, Ford, and General Motors? Or, how many experienced shock when Japanese financiers bought a hallmark of American business tradition—Rockefeller Center?

There are also new market opportunities in Latin and South America, Africa, China, Vietnam, Iraq, and countries throughout the world in transition. These areas are becoming major attractions to multinational companies that want to grow and obtain a strong market position as the economies change and go through privatization and deregulation.

The internationalization of entrepreneurship and business creates wealth and employment that benefits individuals and nations throughout the world. International entrepreneurship is exciting as it combines the many aspects of domestic entrepreneurship with such other disciplines as anthropology, economics, geography, history, jurisprudence, and language. In today's hypercompetitive world with rapidly changing technology, it is essential for an entrepreneur to at least consider entering the global market.

International markets offer entrepreneurial companies new market opportunities. Since 1950, the growth of international trade and investment has been generally larger than the growth of domestic economies—even those of the United States and China. A combination of domestic and international sales offers the entrepreneur an opportunity for expansion and growth that is not available in the domestic market alone. Using today's rapidly changing technology, an entrepreneur can increase the reach of his marketing efforts and have an even brighter growth potential in the future.

THE NATURE OF INTERNATIONAL ENTREPRENEURSHIP

international entrepreneurship An entrepreneur doing business across his or her national boundary

Simply stated, *international entrepreneurship* is the process of an entrepreneur conducting business activities across national boundaries. It may consist of exporting, licensing, opening a sales office in another country, or something as simple as placing a classified advertisement in the Paris edition of the *International Herald Tribune*. The activities necessary for ascertaining and satisfying the needs and wants of target consumers often take place in more than one country. When an entrepreneur executes his or her business model in more than one country, international entrepreneurship is occurring.

With a commercial history of only 300 years, the United States is a relative newcomer to the international business arena. As soon as settlements were established in the New World, American businesses began an active international trade with Europe. Foreign investors helped build much of the early industrial trade with Europe as well as much of the early industrial base of the United States. The future commercial strength of the United States will similarly depend on the ability of U.S. entrepreneurs and established U.S. companies to take advantage of markets outside the country.

THE IMPORTANCE OF INTERNATIONAL BUSINESS TO THE FIRM

International business has become increasingly important to firms of all sizes—particularly today, when every firm is competing in a hypercompetitive global economy. There can be little doubt that today's entrepreneur must be able to move in the world of international business. The successful entrepreneur will be someone who fully understands how international business differs from purely domestic business and is able to respond accordingly. An entrepreneur entering the international market should address the following questions:

1. How is managing international business different from managing domestic business?
2. What are the strategic issues to be resolved in going global?
3. What are the options available for engaging in international business?
4. How should one assess the decision to enter into an international market?

The many different aspects of global entrepreneurship can be easily understood through the following formula:

$$GE = C_1 + PL + E + DC + C_2 + C_3$$

Where

GE = Global entrepreneurship

C_1 = Culture

PL = Politics and legal environment

E = Economy and economic integration

DC = Distribution channels

C_2 = Change

C_3 = Communication

This formula indicates the important aspects surrounding global entrepreneurship as well as the things that must happen in order for an entrepreneurial firm to truly be global. Culture, the political and legal environment, the economy, and the available distribution channels vary significantly from one country to the next, so each must be taken into account when deciding to go global, as discussed below. Change and communication also are important aspects of operating in a global environment, as are market selection and entry. These topics are discussed in Chapter 15, "Going Global."

INTERNATIONAL VERSUS DOMESTIC ENTREPRENEURSHIP

Although international and domestic entrepreneurs alike are concerned with sales, costs, and profits, what differentiates domestic from international entrepreneurship is the variation in the relative importance of the factors affecting each decision. International entrepreneurial decisions are more complex due to such uncontrollable factors as economics, politics, culture, and technology (see Table 4.1).

Economics

In a domestic business strategy, a single country at a specified level of economic development is the focus of the firm's entrepreneurial efforts. The entire country is almost always organized under a single economic system and has the same currency. Creating a business strategy for a multicountry area means dealing with differences in: levels of economic development; currency valuations; government regulations; and banking, venture capital, marketing, and distribution systems. These differences manifest themselves in each aspect of the entrepreneur's international business plan and methods of doing business.

One of the biggest problems entrepreneurs have is raising capital. The amount of private equity capital investment varies greatly by the area of the world, and the amount available is significantly less elsewhere than in the United States, as discussed in Chapters 11 and 12. European private equity capital investments grew from 5,546 million euros in 1995 to 25,116 million euros in 1999 and 34,986 million euros in 2000.

TABLE 4.1 International versus Domestic Business

- Economics
- State of economic development
- Balance of payments; balance of trade
- Type of economic system
- Political-legal environment
- Cultural environment
- Technological environment

Stage of Economic Development

The United States is an industrially developed nation with regional variances of relative income. While needing to adjust the business plan according to regional differences, an entrepreneur doing business only in the United States does not have to worry about a significant lack of such fundamental infrastructures as roads, electricity, communication systems, banking facilities and systems, adequate educational systems, a well-developed legal system, and established business ethics and norms. These factors vary greatly in other countries, from those industrialized to those in the process of developing, and they significantly impact a firm's ability to successfully engage in international business.

Balance of Payments

balance of payments The trade status between countries

With the present system of flexible exchange rates, a country's *balance of payments* (the difference between the value of a country's imports and exports over time) affects the valuation of its currency. The valuation of one country's currency affects business transactions between countries. At one time, Italy's chronic balance of payments deficit led to a radical depreciation in the value of the lira, the currency of Italy. Fiat responded by offering significant rebates on cars sold in the United States. These rebates cost Fiat very little because fewer dollars purchased many more lira due to the decreased value of the lira. Similar exchange rate divergences have occurred for Japanese automobile manufacturers and many products produced by Chinese firms, including steel and steel alloys.

Type of System

Pepsi-Cola began considering the possibility of marketing in the former U.S.S.R. as early as 1959, following the visit of U.S. Vice President Richard Nixon. When Premier Nikita Khrushchev expressed his approval of Pepsi's taste, the slow wheels of East–West trade began moving, with Pepsi entering the former U.S.S.R. 13 years later. Instead of using its traditional type of franchise bottler in this entry, Pepsi used a barter-type arrangement that satisfied both the socialized system of the former U.S.S.R. and the U.S. capitalist system. In return for receiving technology and syrup from Pepsi, the former U.S.S.R. provided the company with Soviet vodka and the right to distribute it in the United States. Many such *barter* or *third-party arrangements* have been used to increase the amount of business activity with the former U.S.S.R. and Eastern and Central European countries, as well as other countries in various stages of development and transition.

barter A method of payment using nonmoney items

third-party arrangements Paying for goods indirectly through another source

There are many difficulties in doing business in economies that are developing or in transition. These problems reflect gaps in these countries' basic knowledge of the Western system regarding business plans, product promotion, marketing, and profits; widely variable rates of return; nonconvertibility of the currency, which necessitates finding a barter item; differences between accounting systems; and nightmarish communications.

Political-Legal Environment

The multiplicity of political and legal environments in the international market creates vastly different business problems, opening some market opportunities for entrepreneurs and eliminating others. For example, U.S. environmental standards have eliminated the possibility of entrepreneurs establishing ventures to import several models of European cars. Another significant event in the political-legal environment involves the price fluctuations and significant increases in oil and other energy products in the last few years.

Each element of the business strategy of an international entrepreneur has the potential to be affected by the multiplicity of legal environments. Pricing decisions in a country that has a value-added tax will differ from pricing decisions made by the same entrepreneur in a country with no value-added tax. Advertising strategy is affected by variations in what can be said in the copy or in the support needed for advertising claims in different countries. Product decisions are affected by legal requirements with respect to labeling, ingredients, and packaging. Types of ownership and organizational forms vary widely throughout the world. The laws governing business arrangements also vary greatly, with over 150 different legal systems and national laws.

Clearly, the legal and political systems confronting the global entrepreneur vary significantly around the world. Overall, the political system (the government system of a country or other economic unit) needs to be analyzed according to its degree of collectivism versus individualism and the degree of democracy versus totalitarianism. While related (i.e., a system emphasizing collectivism tends to be totalitarian), there are some gray areas, as some democratic societies emphasize a mixture of collectivism and individualism.

In collectivism, a system stressing the primacy of collective goals, the needs of a society as a whole are viewed as being more important than individual freedom. Therefore, an individual may not have the right to do something if it is counter to the good of society. Socialism and Marxism are two examples of collectivism. Individualism, the opposite of collectivism, is a system in which the individual has the freedom to pursue his economic and political pursuits. In this case, the interests of the individual take precedent over the interests of society (state). Similarly, democracy and totalitarianism are opposites on the political spectrum. While democracy is a political system in which government is by the people, either exercised directly or through elected representatives, totalitarianism is a system of government where one person or political party exercises absolute control over everything and no opposing political parties are allowed.

political risk analysis Prior to entering into business in another country, an assessment of that country's political policies and its stability

While global entrepreneurs generally prefer to do business in stable and freely governed countries, good business opportunities often occur in different conditions. It is important to assess each country's policies as well as its stability. This assessment is referred to as *political risk analysis*. While there is some political risk in every country, the range from country to country varies significantly, and even in a country with a history of stability and consistency, these conditions could change. There are three major types of political risks that might be present: operating risk (risk of interference with the operations of the venture); transfer risk (risk in attempting to shift assets or other funds out of the country); and—the biggest risk of all—ownership risk (risk where the country takes over the venture's property and employees). Of course, conflict and changes in the solvency of the country are major risks to a global entrepreneur in a particular country. This can take such forms as guerilla warfare, civil disturbances, and even terrorism where the global entrepreneur's company and employees are the target. As evidenced by the September 11 attacks on the World Trade Center and the Pentagon, international terrorists can target U.S. interests both in and out of the country.

The legal system of a country also affects the global entrepreneur. A country's legal system is composed of the rules and laws that are used to regulate behavior as well as the processes by which the laws are enforced. The laws of a country regulate the business practices in a country, the manner in which business transactions are executed, and the rights and obligations involved in any business transaction between parties.

The global entrepreneur should have an overall sense of the legal system of a country but needs legal counsel when it comes to specifics. Ideally this legal counsel would have its headquarters in the United States, with an office in the target country. Several areas are critical to some extent for every global entrepreneur: (1) property rights, (2) contract law, (3) product safety, and (4) product liability.

Countries vary significantly in the degree to which their legal system protects the property rights of the individual and the business. The property rights of a business are the resources owned and the use of these resources and the income earned from this use. Besides buildings, equipment, and land, the protection of intellectual property is a very great concern, particularly for technology global entrepreneurs. Intellectual property—such as a book, computer software, a score of music, a video, a formula for a new chemical or drug, or some other protected idea—is very important to a firm and needs to be protected when going outside the United States. The three major forms of legal protection in the U.S. will be elaborated on in Chapter 6, "Intellectual Property and Other Legal Issues for the Entrepreneur." Few countries have laws and court procedures protecting intellectual property such as those in the United States. You probably have heard how videos can be purchased in China at 10 percent of the cost in the United States—sometimes even before being officially released. Even this book—which has legal editions in several languages, including Arabic, Chinese, Hungarian, Russian, Slovenian, and Spanish—has an illegal edition in the Iranian language, as Iran does not recognize world corporate laws. Before entering a country, the global entrepreneur needs to assess that country's protection of the intellectual property of her venture and the costs if these are copied illegally.

Another area of legal concern is the contract law of the country *and* how it is enforced. A contract specifies the conditions for an exchange and the rights and duties of the parties involved in this exchange. Contract law varies significantly from country to country, in part reflecting the two types of legal tradition—common law and civil law. Countries operating under common law include the United Kingdom, the United States, and most countries of the former British colonies. Countries operating under civil law include France, Germany, Japan, and Russia. Common law tends to be relatively nonspecific, so contracts under this law are longer and more detailed, with all the contingencies spelled out. Since civil law is much more detailed, contracts under it are much shorter.

In addition to the law itself, the global entrepreneur needs to understand how the law might be enforced and the judicial system securing this enforcement. If the legal system of the country does not have a good track record of enforcement, the contract can contain an agreement that any contract disputes will be heard in the courts of another country. Since each company might have some advantage in its home country, usually another country is selected. This aspect is very important for global entrepreneurs operating in developing economies with little or even a bad history of enforcement and other antibusiness countries. One company exporting Hungarian wine into Russia made sure any disputes in its Russian contracts would be heard in the Finnish court system rather than the Russian one.

The final overall area of legal concern pertains to the laws of the country regarding product safety and liability. Again, these laws vary significantly between countries, from very high liability and damage awards in the United States to very low levels in Russia. These laws also raise an ethical issue for the global entrepreneur, particularly one from the United States. When doing business in a country where the liability and product safety laws are much lower than one's home country, should you follow the more relaxed local standards or adhere to the stricter standards of your home country and risk not being competitive and losing the business? Each global entrepreneur must answer this question in one way or the other when doing business in a particular country.

Cultural Environment

The impact of culture on entrepreneurs and strategies is also significant. Entrepreneurs must make sure that each element in the business plan has some degree of congruence with

TABLE 4.2 Lost in Translation

Even the best-laid business plans can be botched by a careless translator. Here's how some of America's biggest companies have managed to mess things up:

Kentucky Fried Chicken	English: "Finger lickin' good."	Chinese: "Eat your fingers off."
Adolph Coors Co.	English: "Turn it loose."	Spanish: "Drink Coors and get diarrhea."
Otis Engineering Corp.	English: "Complete equipment."	Russian: "Equipment for orgasms."
Parker Pen Co.	English: "Avoid embarrassment."	Spanish: "Avoid pregnancy."
Perdue Farms Inc.	English: "It takes a tough man to make a tender chicken."	Spanish: "It takes a sexually excited man to make a chick affectionate."

Source: From "Speaking in Tongues," *Inc. Magazine,* June 2003. Reprinted with permission of *Inc. Magazine.*

the local culture. For example, in some countries, point-of-purchase displays are not allowed in retail stores as they are in the United States.

An increasingly important aspect of the cultural environment in some countries concerns bribes and corruption. How should an entrepreneur deal with these situations when it may mean losing the business? Such ethical issues are explored in the nearby Ethics box.

Sometimes one of the biggest problems for the international entrepreneur is finding a translator. As indicated in Table 4.2, significant problems can occur when careless translation occurs. To avoid such errors, care should be taken to hire a translator whose native tongue is the target language and whose expertise matches that of the original authors. Other more specific aspects related to culture that the global entrepreneur should consider are discussed later in this chapter.

Technological Environment

Technology, like culture, varies significantly across countries. The variation and availability of technology are often surprising, particularly to an entrepreneur from a developed country like the United States. While U.S. firms produce mostly standardized, relatively uniform products that can be sorted to meet industry standards, this is not the case in many countries, making it more difficult to achieve a consistent level of quality.

New products in a country are created based on the conditions and infrastructure operating in that country. For example, U.S. car designers can assume wider roads and less expensive gasoline than European designers. When these same designers work on transportation vehicles for other parts of the world, their assumptions need to be significantly altered.

CULTURE

Probably the single most important aspect that the global entrepreneur must consider is the crossing of cultures. While culture has been defined in many different ways, the term generally refers to common ways of thinking and behaving that are passed on from parents to children or transmitted by social organizations, developed, and then reinforced through social pressure. Culture is learned behavior and the identity of an individual and society.

Culture encompasses a wide variety of elements, including language, social situations, religion, political philosophy, economic philosophy, education, and manners and customs

The following is taken from an article written by Xiaohe Lu, regarding some of the ethical implications of international entrepreneurship in China:

It is pointed out that some international high technology firms see only a big market with huge needs for high technology products and well-trained but cheap technicians in China; for this reason, they invest in factories or establish centers for R&D in China. As soon as the new technology has been developed in China, those firms take it abroad in order to "package it," then sell it as imported high technology back to China. This is a particular form of exploiting China's resource technology.

Often the headquarters of corporations are located in their home countries, but the real corporate body is in China. The corporations usually pay qualified Chinese employees only 10 percent of what an employee in the USA is paid. In a competitive global economy, a country's intellectual capital is the most important resource of its development. Can such a "brain drain" be criticized or justified morally as well as economically? How should we be on our guard against it? Would such measures be beneficial to China or to the world?

Foreign brands are forcibly occupying China's markets. On the one hand, they bring some new technology, management, and life-style to China, and on the other hand, these foreign corporations have colonized and partitioned nearly every field of our daily lives. The space for national industries is increasingly narrowed; nearly all national brands are lost. Thus, China risks becoming a colony of developed countries.

The complexity and ubiquity of these issues present a challenge to international business ethics to keep pace. Whether willing or not, we are involved in an era during which the use and production of knowledge are becoming increasingly important points in economy. We are faced with new ethical difficulties and challenges. Business ethics should follow a process of discovery, studying new ethical issues, considering proper ethical guidelines for dealing with these issues, and promoting the knowledge economy. The framework of business ethics needs to adapt to the micro, meso, and macro level. Ethical issues about the technology basis of the knowledge economy should be added to the framework, such as issues about the justification and protection of intellectual property, plundering and protecting knowledge resources, and the role played by government in the protection of intellectual property. At a macro level, international competition is becoming more bitter and raises many new issues such as the issues of human rights, a country's sovereignty, and the gap between rich and poor countries.

Source: Excerpt from Xiaohe Lu, "Ethical Issues in the Globalization of the Knowledge Economy," *Business Ethics: A European Review* 10, no. 2 (2001). Reprinted with permission of Blackwell Publishing.

(see Figure 4.1). Language, sometimes thought of as the mirror of culture, is composed of verbal and nonverbal components. Messages and ideas are transmitted by the spoken words used, the voice tone, and nonverbal actions such as body position, eye contact, and gestures. An entrepreneur or someone on her team must have command of the language in the country in which business is being done. Not only is it important for information-gathering and evaluation but it is essential for communication among those involved as well as eventually in the advertising campaign developed and used. Even though English has generally become the accepted language of business, dealing with language almost always requires local assistance, whether in the form of a local translator, a local market research firm, or a local advertising agency.

One U.S. entrepreneur was having a difficult time negotiating an agreement on importing a new high tech microscope from a small entrepreneurial firm in St. Petersburg, Russia. The problems were resolved when the entrepreneur realized that the translations were not being done correctly and hired a new translator.

Equally important to the verbal language is the nonverbal or hidden language of the culture. This can be thought of in terms of several components—time, space, and business relationships. In most parts of the world, time is much more flexible than it is in the United States. For example, due to the variability in traffic and the possibility of significant congestion, it is difficult to set exact appointment times in Beijing or Hong Kong. Irish time means that a meeting usually starts anywhere from 15 to 30 minutes after the established posted time—which one U.S. professor at an Irish university found out when he was in the meeting room at the appointed starting time and no one showed up until 10 minutes later. The meeting started 15 minutes after that.

The second key aspect of nonverbal language is space—in particular, how much room exists between individuals when they talk. While Germans prefer more space than

FIGURE 4.1 Cultural Determinants

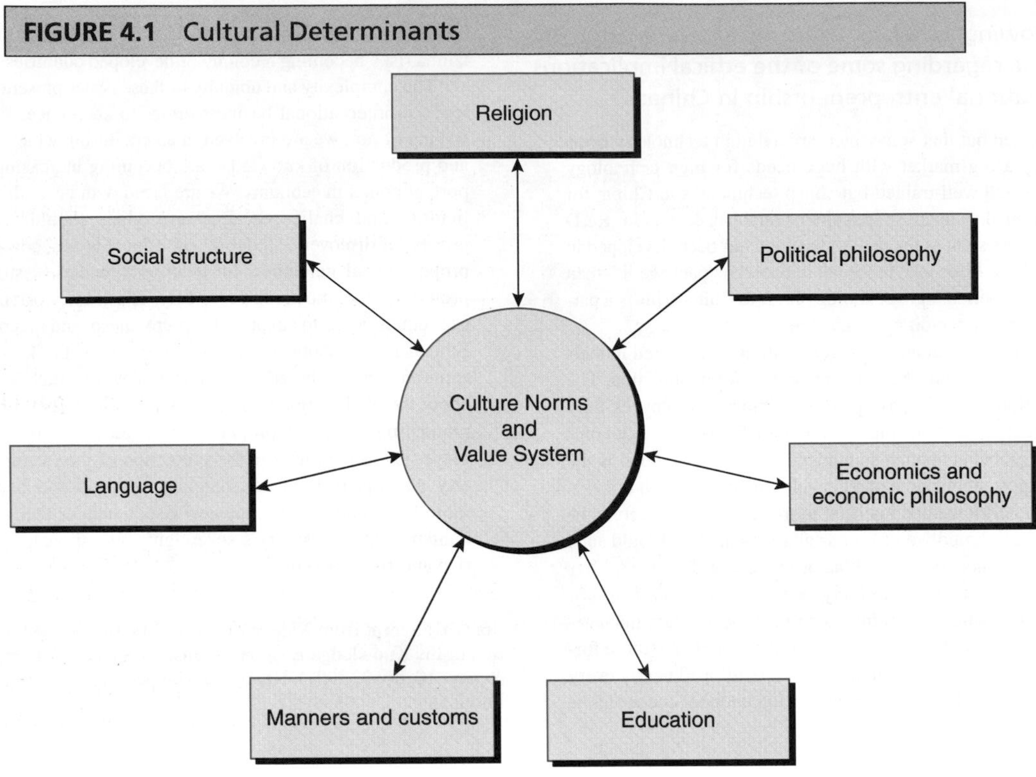

Americans, Arabic and Latin Americans like to stand closer when talking to people. Also, some cultures, like Hungarian, Russian, and Slavic, hug and even kiss when greeting a known business partner.

The final aspect of nonverbal language, business relationships, is also critical for the global entrepreneur to understand. In most countries, it is far more important to understand a potential business partner on a personal level before any transactions occur or even before business is discussed. One global entrepreneur in Australia met the president, the management team, and the family each on a different social occasion before any business between the two companies was discussed.

Social Structure

Social structure and institutions are also aspects of the culture facing the global entrepreneur. While the family unit in the United States usually consists of parent(s) and children, in many cultures it is extended to include grandparents and other relatives. This, of course, radically affects lifestyles, living standards, and consumption patterns.

Social stratification can be very strong in some cultures, significantly affecting the way people in one social strata behave and purchase. India, for example, is known for its hierarchical and relatively rigid social class system.

Reference groups in any culture provide values and attitudes that influence behavior. Besides providing overall socialization, reference groups develop a person's concept of self and provide a base line for compliance with group norms. As such, they significantly impact an individual's behavior and buying habits.

The global entrepreneur also needs to recognize that the social structure and institutions of a culture will impact the roles of manager and subordinate and how the two relate. In some cultures, cooperation between managers and subordinates is elicited through equality, while in other cultures, the two groups are separated explicitly and implicitly.

Religion

Religion in a culture defines the ideas for life that are reflected in the values and attitudes of individuals and the overall society. The impact of religion on entrepreneurship, consumption, and business in general will vary depending on the strength of the dominant religious tenets and those tenets' impact on the values and attitudes of the culture. Religion also provides the basis for some degree of transcultural similarity under shared beliefs and attitudes, as seen in some of the dominant religions of the world—Christianity, Islam, Hinduism, Buddhism, and Judaism, for example. In a similar way, the tenets of nonreligious or secularist societies such as Marxism–Leninism can also prove to be a powerful force affecting behavior.

Political Philosophy

The political philosophy of an area also impacts its culture. Since this topic will be treated separately later in this chapter, suffice it to say here that the rules and regulations of a country significantly impact the global entrepreneur and the way he conducts business. For example, embargoes or trade sanctions, export controls, and other business regulations may preclude a global entrepreneur from doing business in a particular culture or at the very least will impact the attitudes and behaviors of people in that culture when business is transacted.

Economics and Economic Philosophy

The economics and economic philosophy of a country impact its culture and the global entrepreneur. Whether the country overall is in favor of trade or trade restrictions, its attitudes toward balance of payments and balance of trade, its convertible or nonconvertible currency, and its overall trading policy all affect not only whether it is advantageous to do business in a certain market, but the types and efficiency of any transactions occurring. Some countries use import duties, tariffs, subsidization of exports, and the restriction on the importation of certain products to protect the country's own industry and maximize the gain of more exports than imports. Think how difficult it would be to do business in a country that restricted the exportation of the profits of an international entrepreneurial company. Or consider how much more difficult it would be to do business in a culture that was antimaterialism and very equalitarianist.

Education

Both formal and informal education affects the culture and the way the culture is passed on. A global entrepreneur not only needs to be aware of the education level, as indicated by the literacy rate of a culture, but also the degree of emphasis on particular skills or career paths. China, Japan, and India, for example, emphasize the sciences and engineering more so than many Western cultures.

The technology level of the firm's products may be too sophisticated depending on the educational level of the culture. This also influences whether customers are able to use the good or service properly and whether they are able to understand the firm's advertising or other promotional messages.

AS SEEN IN *ENTREPRENEUR* MAGAZINE

PROVIDE ADVICE TO AN ENTREPRENEUR ABOUT OUTSOURCING TO FOREIGN COMPANIES

Big companies do it all the time—outsource back-office processes offshore. According to IDC, the global IT outsourcing industry will grow from $56 billion in 2000 to an estimated $100 billion in 2005. But can smaller companies take advantage of the benefits of offshore outsourcing? "They can and they are," says Howard Lackow, senior vice president and director of outsourcing services with the Outsourcing Institute in Jericho, New York. "But depending on where [small businesses] are in the lifecycle of their business, it might not be the best alternative." Lackow notes that even though a business might be saving money by outsourcing offshore, the outsourcing relationship still takes a lot of structure and management time.

Outsourcing can be good for manning call centers or developing new computer applications—offshore, you can typically hire more labor for the same amount of money. Generally, outsourcing doesn't work well for companies that are in a high-growth mode (because they require faster turnaround) or that are closely managed; overseas outsourcing requires being more flexible and less hands-on, says Lackow. And then there's the very real ethical question—should you transfer jobs overseas, thus taking them out of the U.S. job market? "Don't look for either/or answers," says Randy Pennington, president of Pennington Performance Group, a Dallas-based business leadership consulting and training firm. Instead, he suggests coming up with creative ways to satisfy your employees, customers, and your business's needs. "You might say, 'We're going to keep existing operations here but grow [our customer service center] through overseas outsourcing,'" says Pennington.

If you find yourself in an all-or-nothing situation—for example, if outsourcing makes the difference between going bankrupt, or laying off 15 versus 50 employees—the thought process is key. Ask yourself: If every business outsourced offshore, would that be OK? What would the person I most respect do in this situation? How would I feel if my family and friends read about my decision in the newspaper? When keeping business in the United States is right, "what is more right? You have to decide," says Pennington. "Remember, not every ethical decision is a popular decision." Consider your goals and objectives. "Determine if the economics of [offshore outsourcing] are worth it," says Lackow. "Just know that it's not for everybody, and proceed with caution."

ADVICE TO AN ENTREPRENEUR

An entrepreneur who is growing so fast that she is finding it difficult to keep up with demand has read the above article and comes to you for advice.

"I understand their point that outsourcing overseas may actually save jobs here," she says, "but I need to assess the risks of slowing growth against the risk of growing by outsourcing some of my work to a company in a foreign country."

1. What are the risks of outsourcing? Why not acquire a manufacturing plant in a foreign country? Or why not enter into a joint venture with a foreign manufacturer?
2. What are the additional risks of pursuing any of these growth mechanisms in a foreign market (i.e., what are the risks associated with international business)?

Source: Reprinted with permission of Entrepreneur Media, Inc., "Take It Outside. Should You Outsource the Business Processes You Can't Handle to Another Country?" by Nichole L. Torres, February 2003, *Entrepreneur* magazine: www.entrepreneur.com.

Manners and Customs

Manners and customs, the final aspect of an area's culture, need to be carefully dealt with and monitored. Understanding manners and customs is particularly important for the global entrepreneur in negotiations and gift giving. In negotiations, unless care is taken, the global entrepreneur can come to an incorrect conclusion because her interpretations are based on her frame of reference—not the frame of reference of the culture. For example, the silence of the Chinese and Japanese has been used effectively in negotiating with American entrepreneurs who interpret this (incorrectly) as a negative sign. Agreements in these countries, as well as other countries in Asia and the Middle East, may take much longer because there is a desire to talk about unrelated issues. Aggressively demanding last-minute changes is a mannerism used by Russian negotiators.

Probably the area that requires the most sensitivity is gift giving. Gifts can be an important part of developing relationships in a culture but great care must be taken to ascertain whether it is appropriate to give a gift, what type of gift to give, how to wrap the gift, and the manner in which the gift should be given. For example, in China a gift is given with two hands and is usually not opened at that time but rather in the privacy of the recipient.

ECONOMIC SYSTEM AND DEVELOPMENT

Generally there are four broad categories of economic systems—market economy, command economy, mixed economy, and state-directed economy. The primary characteristic of a market economy is that all (or at least most) productive activities are privately owned rather than state (government) owned and the goods and services produced (the output of the economy) are not planned. Production and sales are determined by the interactions of supply and demand, which in turn determine price. For a market economy to work, there needs to be no restrictions on supply (no market monopolized by a single firm) and rigorous competition. This competition between privately owned firms produces economic efficiency, the lowest prices for consumers, and economic growth and development.

In a command economy, the type and quantity of the goods and services produced in a country and their selling prices are planned by the government. All businesses are state (government) owned and resources of the country are allocated for the "good of society." Mainly found in communist countries, the number of command economies has fallen significantly in the last three decades with the demise of communism. One high-ranking Chinese government official indicated that China was "moving from a command economy so [it] could compete with the West." Efficiency and low prices do not result in a command economy, as state-owned enterprises with little or no competition have little incentive to be efficient and control costs since they are supported by the government and cannot go out of business unless decided by the government.

A mixed economy has aspects of both a market and command economy, as some parts of the economy have private ownership while other sectors of the economy have significant state ownership and government planning. Mixed economies are relatively common in some countries in the European Union such as France, Italy, and Sweden. In the best interests of society, one sector usually under government control is health care.

In the final type of economy—a state-directed economy—the government plays a significant role in the investment activities of private enterprise through an established industrial policy. A state-directed economy is different from a mixed economy in that the state usually does not take public ownership of private enterprise but directs the investments of these private firms to support the goals of the industrial policy. Two of the best known state-directed economies are Japan and Korea.

The economic, political, and legal systems of a country impact its economic development and growth, making it more or less attractive to the global entrepreneur. Measures useful for determining and comparing the economic development of a country with other countries are the country's gross national product per head of population (GNP) and the purchasing power parity (PPP). GNP measures the total value of the goods and services produced annually by a country. PPP adjusts this GNP figure by the cost of living in the country and as such allows for a better direct comparison of countries for the global entrepreneur.

One of the most interesting trends since the late 1980s—and one that is providing opportunities for the global entrepreneur—is the increase in market-based economies paralleling the spread of democracy. This transformation from centrally planned command economies to market-based ones has opened up new and exciting markets unavailable before this time. Over 30 countries that were once a part of the former Soviet Union in the Eastern European bloc are moving or have moved to market-based economies. Similar trends have occurred in Asia, in countries such as China and Vietnam, as well as in Africa, in countries such as Angola, Ethiopia, and Mozambique. Also, many countries in Asia, Latin America, and Western Europe have privatized—sold former state-owned companies to private investors. This transformation has occurred because better economic results have been achieved under market-based economic systems than under command and mixed economic systems.

AVAILABLE DISTRIBUTION SYSTEMS

While the global entrepreneur need not be concerned about worldwide logistics today, due to state-of-the-art transportation methods and the ensuing cost reductions, one of the entrepreneur's biggest challenges concerns the distribution channels in the target country. Distribution channels vary significantly from one country to another, and it should quickly become apparent that the channel of distribution in any country is in a very powerful, strategic position that can affect the success of the global company.

In determining the best channel of distribution system for a country, the global entrepreneur needs to consider several factors: (1) the overall sales potential; (2) the amount and type of competition; (3) the cost of the product; (4) the geographical size and density of the country; (5) the investment policies of the country; (6) exchange rates and any controls; (7) the level of political risk; and (8) the overall marketing plan. Each of these factors affects the choice of the distribution system that will yield the greatest sales and profit results in the country.

BARRIERS TO INTERNATIONAL TRADE

There are varying attitudes throughout the world concerning trade. Starting around 1947 with the development of general trade agreements and the reduction of tariffs and other trade barriers, there has been an overall positive atmosphere concerning trade between countries.

General Agreement on Tariffs and Trade (GATT)

One of the longest-lasting agreements on trade is the General Agreement on Tariffs and Trade (GATT), which was established in 1947 under U.S. leadership. GATT is a multilateral agreement with the objective of liberalizing trade by eliminating or reducing tariffs, subsidies, and import quotas. GATT membership includes over 100 nations and has had eight rounds of tariff reductions, the most recent being the Uruguay Round that lasted from 1986 to 1993. In each round, mutual tariff reductions are negotiated between member nations and monitored by a mutually-agreed-upon system. If a member country feels that a violation has occurred, it can ask for an investigation by the Geneva-based administrators of GATT. If the investigation uncovers a violation, member countries can be asked to pressure the violating country to change its policy and conform to the agreed-upon tariffs and agreements. Sometimes this pressure has not been sufficient to get an offending country to change. While GATT has assisted in developing more unrestricted trade, its voluntary membership gives it little authority to ensure that this type of trade will occur.

Increasing Protectionist Attitudes

The support of GATT goes up and down. Although down in the 1970s, the support increased in the 1980s due to the rise in protectionist pressures in many industrialized countries. The renewed support reflected three events. First, the world trading system was strained by the persistent trade deficit of the United States, the world's largest economy, a situation that caused adjustments in such industries as automobiles, semiconductors, steel, and textiles. Second, the economic success of countries perceived as not playing by the rules (e.g., Japan and then China) also strained the world's trading system. The success of Japan and China as the world's large traders and the perception that their internal markets are, in effect, closed to imports and foreign investment have caused problems. Finally, in response to these pressures, many countries have established bilateral voluntary export restraints to circumvent GATT. The economic prosperity of the 1990s has lessened the interest in GATT.

Trade Blocs and Free Trade Areas

Around the world, groups of nations are banding together to increase trade and investment between nations in the group and exclude those nations outside the group. One little-known agreement between the United States and Israel, signed in 1985, establishes a Free Trade Area (FTA) between the two nations. All tariffs and quotas except on certain agricultural products were phased out over a 10-year period. In 1989, an FTA went into effect between Canada and the United States that phased out tariffs and quotas between the two countries, which are each other's largest trading partners.

Many trading alliances have evolved in the Americas. In 1991, the United States signed a framework trade agreement with Argentina, Brazil, Paraguay, and Uruguay to support the development of more liberal trade relations. The United States has also signed bilateral trade agreements with Bolivia, Chile, Colombia, Costa Rica, Ecuador, El Salvador, Honduras, Peru, and Venezuela. The North American Free Trade Agreement (NAFTA) among the United States, Canada, and Mexico is a much publicized agreement to reduce trade barriers and quotas and encourage investment among the three countries. Similarly, the Americas, Argentina, Brazil, Paraguay, and Uruguay operate under the Treaty of Asunción, which created the Mercosur trade zone, a free trade zone among the countries.

Another important trading bloc has been developed by the European Community (EC). Unlike GATT or NAFTA, the EC is founded on the principle of supranationality, with member nations not being able to enter into trade agreements on their own that are inconsistent with EC regulations. As nations are added, the EC trading bloc becomes an increasingly important factor for entrepreneurs doing international business.

Entrepreneur's Strategy and Trade Barriers

trade barriers Hindrances to doing international business

Clearly, *trade barriers* pose problems for the entrepreneur who wants to become involved in international business. First, trade barriers increase an entrepreneur's costs of exporting products or semifinished products to a country. If the increased cost puts the entrepreneur at a competitive disadvantage with respect to indigenous competitive products, it may be more economical to establish production facilities in the country. Second, voluntary export restraints may limit an entrepreneur's ability to sell products in a country from production facilities outside the country, which may also warrant establishing production facilities in the country in order to compete. Finally, an entrepreneur may have to locate assembly or production facilities in a country to conform to the local content regulations of the country.

IMPLICATIONS FOR THE GLOBAL ENTREPRENEUR

The cultural, political, economic, and distribution systems of a country clearly influence its attractiveness as a potential market and potential investment opportunity. Generally, the costs and political risks are lower in those market-oriented countries that are more advanced economically and politically. However, the long-run benefits to a global entrepreneur are the country's future growth and expansion. This opportunity may indeed occur in less developed and less stable countries. The global entrepreneur must carefully analyze the countries to determine the best one(s) (if any) to enter and then develop an appropriate entry strategy. This topic is discussed at greater length in Chapter 15, "Going Global."

IN REVIEW

SUMMARY

International business is becoming increasingly important to more and more entrepreneurs and to their countries' economies. International entrepreneurship—the conducting of business activities by an entrepreneur across national boundaries—is occurring much earlier in the growth of new ventures as opportunities open up in the hypercompetitive global arena. Several factors (economics, stage of economic development, balance of payments, type of system, political-legal environment, cultural environment, and technological environment) make decisions regarding international entrepreneurship more complex than those regarding domestic entrepreneurship.

RESEARCH TASKS

1. Interview three managers of multinational businesses to ascertain the benefits generated from engaging in international business as well as some of the challenges (problems).
2. Choose a country. Research and be prepared to report on that country's (a) stage of economic development, (b) political-legal environment, (c) cultural environment, and (d) technological environment. If you were advising an entrepreneur who was considering entering this country to sell his or her products, what would you say were the major strategic issues? (Be specific to the country chosen.)
3. Choose a transition economy. Research that country and its recent economic progress. Do you believe its economy will flourish or stagnate? Why? What can that country's government do (if anything) to "help" the economy flourish?

CLASS DISCUSSION

1. Make sure there is one foreign student in each small group. The group needs to discuss, and then report back to class on, the nature of business and entrepreneurship in the foreign student's home country. Such a discussion should include the country's (a) stage of economic development, (b) political-legal environment, (c) cultural environment, and (d) technological environment. Also explore how entrepreneurship and business failure are perceived in this country.
2. We typically focus on firms from well-developed economies entering markets of less developed economies. Do firms from less developed economies have a chance of success if they enter developed markets, such as the United States? What competitive advantage could a firm from a less developed economy rely on in entering developed markets? What would likely be the best entry mode?

SELECTED READINGS

Bliss, Richard T.; and Nichole L. Garratt. (October 2001). Supporting Women Entrepreneurs in Transitioning Economies. *Journal of Small Business Management,* vol. 39, no. 4, pp. 336–44.

This article discusses the need for an established support organization for women entrepreneurs in Poland. The authors discuss the framework for the Polish Association of Women Entrepreneurs (PAWE); the paradox of socialism's impact on women; changes in the perceived role of women in society; and problems encountered by women entrepreneurs in transitioning economies.

Coviello, Nicole E.; and Marian V. Jones. (July 2004). Methodological Issues in International Entrepreneurship Research. *Journal of Business Venturing,* vol. 19, no. 4, p. 485.

The article presents implications for developing a unifying methodological direction in the field and the evolution of a truly multidisciplinary approach. The paper also outlines the need for dynamic research designs that integrate positivist with interpretive methodologies and incorporate time as a key dimension. Finally, the paper discusses the need for better international entrepreneurship sampling frames and calls for more effort in establishing and reporting equivalence in cross-national studies.

Danis, Wade M.; and Andrew V. Shipilov. (2002). A Comparison of Entrepreneurship Development in Two Post-Communist Countries: The Cases of Hungary and Ukraine. *Journal of Developmental Entrepreneurship,* vol. 7, no. 1, pp. 67–94.

The paper describes the influence of systemic, historical, cultural, economic, and societal factors and government policies on the development of entrepreneurial ventures in Hungary and Ukraine. An attempt is made to better understand the reasons underlying difficulties in developing local entrepreneurial ventures.

Davis, Peter S.; and Paula D. Harveston. (2000). Internationalization and Organizational Growth: The Impact of Internet Usage and Technology Involvement among Entrepreneur-Led Family Business. *Family Business Review,* vol. 13, no. 2, pp. 107–20.

Using data from a U.S. survey of entrepreneur-led family businesses, this paper examines the extent to which certain entrepreneurial characteristics, Internet usage, and investments in information technology influence internationalization and organizational growth.

De Clercq, Dirk; Harry Sapienza; and Hans Crijns. (May 2005). The Internationalization of Small and Medium-Sized Firms. *Small Business Economics,* vol. 24, no. 4, pp. 409–419.

This paper contributes to the existing research by integrating the notions of organizational learning and entrepreneurial orientation into the body of international entrepreneurship. The research results suggest (1) that intensive knowledge renewal and exploitation regarding foreign markets and the internationalization process itself may increase internationalization by affecting the perceptions of opportunities offered by further international expansion, and (2) that firms with an entrepreneurial mind-set may be more likely to develop a long-term, substantial presence in the international arena, compared to firms that are more reactive or conservative.

Di Gregorio, Dante. (April 2005). Re-Thinking Country Risk: Insights from Entrepreneurship Theory. *International Business Review,* vol. 14, no. 2, pp. 209–26.

This article proposes an alternative perspective from which to approach country risk. By focusing on both the downside and upside elements of country risk, strategies may be devised to harvest upside volatility while containing downside volatility. Rather than being something to always avoid, country risk becomes an opportunity to profit from uncertainty.

George, Gerard; Johan Wiklund; and Shaker A. Zahra. (April 2005). Ownership and the Internationalization of Small Firms. *Journal of Management,* vol. 31, no. 2, pp. 210–33.

This article argues that the ownership structures of small and medium-sized enterprises influence their proclivity to take risks and expand the scale and scope of their internationalization efforts. The article provides interesting insights into the behavioral change of executives regarding the scale and scope of internationalization in the presence of external ownership.

Ghauri, Pervez; and Tony Fang. (2001). Negotiating with the Chinese: A Socio-Cultural Analysis. *Journal of World Business,* vol. 36, no. 3, pp. 303–25.

This paper analyzes the process of negotiation with China from a sociocultural perspective. Based on real cases and literature, a model is developed and some conclusions are drawn. Managerial implications are presented as four Ps (Priority, Patience, Price, and People), which sum up the essence of the Chinese business negotiation process.

Izyumov, Alexei; and Irina Razumnova. (April 2000). Women Entrepreneurs in Russia: Learning to Survive the Market. *Journal of Developmental Entrepreneurship,* vol. 5, no. 1, p. 1.

This article examines the status of women-owned businesses in Moscow, Russia. The authors discuss the advantages of home-based businesses to female entrepreneurs; the prevalence of unemployment and the increase in economic discrimination against Russian women; the development of entrepreneurial education programs for Russian women; and public organizations promoting women entrepreneurship.

Ling-yee, Li; and Gabriel O. Ogunmokun. (2001). Effect of Export Financing Resources and Supply-Chain Skills on Export Competitive Advantages: Implications for Superior Export Performance. *Journal of World Business,* vol. 36, no. 3, pp. 260–79.

This paper utilizes the resource-based theory of the firm to conceptualize export competitive advantages as the outcome of how management conceptualizes the firm's resource base and how management leverages the firm's core competencies to grow over time.

McMillan, John; and Christopher Woodruff. (Summer 2002). The Central Role of Entrepreneurs in Transition Economies. *Journal of Economic Perspectives,* vol. 16, no. 3, pp. 153–70.

This article summarizes the entrepreneurial patterns in transition economies, particularly those in China, Poland, Russia, and Vietnam. The importance of entrepreneurs in the transition economies is a reminder that the task of economic transition is not just a matter of government officials enacting certain policies or setting certain rules of operation for the new economy.

Mueller, Stephen L.; and Srecko Goic. (2002). Entrepreneurial Potential in Transition Economies: A View from Tomorrow's Leaders. *Journal of Developmental Entrepreneurship,* vol. 7, no. 4, pp. 399–414.

Based on the results of a 17-country study of business students' attitudes and perceptions about entrepreneurship, this article analyzes and compares the potential for entrepreneurship in six transition countries. The findings suggest that differences in entrepreneurial potential are best explained by the current level of economic development rather than by culture and previous experience with a market economy.

Oetzel, Jennifer M.; Richard A. Bettis; and Marc Zenner. (2001). Country Risk Measures: How Risky Are They? *Journal of World Business,* vol. 36, no. 2, pp. 128–45.

As global competition drives corporations into distant, unfamiliar markets, managers are searching for ways to minimize their uncertainty, frequently relying on country risk analysis. This paper investigates the extent to which country risk measures can predict periods of intense instability. Results indicate that commercial risk measures are very poor at predicting actual realized risk.

Oviatt, Benjamin M.; and Patricia P. McDougall. (September 2005). Defining International Entrepreneurship and Modeling the Speed of Internationalization. *Entrepreneurship: Theory & Practice,* vol. 29, no. 5, pp. 537–53.

This article provides a reformulated definition of international entrepreneurship. This model begins with an entrepreneurial opportunity and depicts the enabling forces of technology, the motivating forces of competition, the mediating perceptions of entrepreneurs, and the moderating forces of knowledge and networks, which collectively determine the speed of internationalization.

Pope, Ralph A. (2002). Why Small Firms Export: Another Look. *Journal of Small Business Management,* vol. 40, no. 1, pp. 17–26.

This article examines what factors motivate small firms to export. The results suggest that firms with 25 or fewer employees export for two main reasons: The firm has a unique product, and it has a technological advantage over competitors. Firms with more than 25 employees export for the above two reasons, plus to achieve economies of scale and to avoid losing out on foreign opportunities.

Ufuk, Hatun; and Özlen Özgen. (December 2001). The Profile of Women Entrepreneurs: A Sample from Turkey. *International Journal of Consumer Studies,* vol. 25, no. 4, pp. 299–308.

This article discusses research that was carried out among 220 married women in business in Ankara. The study examined working status, reasons for being in business, and the types of businesses involved among women entrepreneurs. It also examined the difficulties experienced in starting up and maintaining the businesses, the risks involved, earnings, the characteristics of the entrepreneurs, and future planning.

Zahra, Shaker A. (January 2005). A Theory of International New Ventures: A Decade of Research. *Journal of International Business Studies,* vol. 36, no. 1, pp. 20–28.

This paper reviews Oviatt and McDougall's original propositions, highlighting their important contributions to the field. The paper also highlights the progress made in research using Oviatt and McDougall's framework, the major debates that persist about the nature and role of international new ventures, the source of their competitive advantages, and the key issues to be explored in future research.

Zahra, Shaker A.; Juha Santeri Korri; and JiFeng Yu. (April 2005). Cognition and International Entrepreneurship: Implications for Research on International Opportunity Recognition and Exploitation. *International Business Review,* vol. 14 no. 2, pp. 129–46.

This article highlights the benefits to be gained from and the challenges associated with using a cognitive approach to international entrepreneurship research. Focusing on early internationalization, the authors propose that a significant shift can occur in international entrepreneurship research by applying a cognitive perspective and examining how entrepreneurs recognize and exploit opportunities in international markets.

CASES FOR PART 1

CASE 1A
TURNER TEST PREP CO.

INTRODUCTION

In the Spring of 2003, Jessica Turner felt that she had come to a crossroads with her business. As the founder and CEO of Turner Test Prep, a California company specializing in preparing people for the Certified Public Accountant (CPA) exam, she felt that she was not achieving market share and growing in the right direction. After three years of providing prep classes to both students and professionals, Turner had about 10 percent of the market and was facing fierce competition from her primary rival, National Testing Services. Uncertain with which growth direction to take, Jessica contemplated several options.

BACKGROUND

Jessica Turner started Turner Test Prep in the summer of 1997 after graduating from Case Western Reserve University's Weatherhead School of Management with a master's degree in accounting. She passed the CPA exam and began applying to Big Six accounting firms. Frustrated after receiving several rejections, Jessica began to consider other employment options. Her undergraduate degree was in business, and after graduation, Jessica worked for several years in the business office of a small test prep company based in San Francisco. The company prepared students who wanted to take primarily the SAT, GRE, GMAT, MCAT, and LSAT. Although her job was to manage the company's business affairs, she also began teaching math to students several nights a week. Jessica received training from the company in teaching basic testing skills, and she applied those skills toward teaching the math portion of the exams. She received positive feedback from her students as a conscientious and innovative teacher.

Jessica felt that her experience as a teacher for the test prep company helped her when she began studying for the CPA exam. She knew how to study efficiently, how to organize her notes, and how to practice for the various sections. Jessica was one of the 25 percent of students who passed all sections of the CPA exam on the first try.[1]

When contemplating what to do next, Jessica was struck by the fact that so many of her colleagues were unable to pass the exam. Convinced that she was not only skilled in the accounting and finance principles but also in knowing how to study effectively, she decided to start her own test prep business teaching specifically to the CPA exam. She was confident that students and professionals wishing to become CPAs would benefit from a full-service program that gave students full classes and individualized attention so that they could pass the exam.

Jessica returned to California, put together a business plan, and secured financing from a local venture capital firm specializing in small start-ups. She decided to focus her business and marketing efforts in the San Francisco Bay area. On the basis of her research and the Bay area's concentration of different types of businesses, Jessica estimated that there was a market of about 1,000 students a year.

THE CPA EXAM

Although people with undergraduate or graduate degrees in accounting or business may do accounting work for a company, becoming a CPA provides an additional certification that employers prefer. Becoming a CPA can increase an accountant's salary by 10 to 15 percent[2] and is typically necessary to secure upper-level positions. In order to be certified to become a CPA, people must fulfill the following requirements:

- Have a college or master's degree with 24 semester units dedicated to business-related subjects, and at least 24 credits in accounting (a minimum of three credits), auditing (a minimum of three credits), business law, finance, and tax subjects;
- Pass the CPA exam;
- Have two years of work experience with a bachelor's degree or one year of work experience with 150 course credits.[3]

The exam is offered two times a year, in May and November. It is a grueling two-day, 15-hour event comprised of multiple choice, essay questions, and problem sets. The subjects tested are: Business Law and Professional Responsibility, Auditing, Accounting and Reporting, and Financial Accounting and Reporting.

CPA EXAM PREP SERVICES

The CPA exam varies only slightly from state to state. In order to study for the exam, people typically purchase books, software, or an online course to help them prepare. The materials usually provide an overview of the tested material, study guides, and practice questions. The online tutorials often provide more practice questions and give students timed exams so that they can simulate actual testing conditions. Due to the amount of material covered on the exam as well as its level of difficulty, students are advised to give themselves four months to study.

In the San Francisco Bay area, several community colleges offer one-week review classes to help students prepare. These classes give students a starting point, after which they could use supplemental materials to study on their own.

NATIONAL TESTING SERVICES

National Testing Centers (NTC) is Turner's primary competition. NTC is a national test preparation company that has been in existence since 1962. The company focuses on virtually every standardized test that is offered and has programs for high school students taking the SAT, undergraduate students taking graduate school entrance tests (such as the GMAT, LSAT, GRE, and MCAT), and graduate students taking certification tests like the bar and CPA exams. In addition, the company has a program designed for international students taking the Test of English as a Foreign Language (TOEFL) exam.

NTC is a full-service program that offers a variety of options for students taking any of these exams. Most courses offer the opportunity to have classroom lectures, home-study videotapes, books, software, online tests, or a combination of any of these options.

The CPA course does not offer live classroom sessions but gives students the option of books, software, and online testing for one or all of the areas covered on the exam. Students also have a toll-free number that they can call if they have questions as well as online chats with NTC instructors to answer questions. NTC offers students a free repeat course if they do not pass the CPA exam and boasts a 75 percent pass rate. The course is priced from $1,000 to $1,500, depending on which of the services the student choose. Many of NTC's students are repeaters who initially chose to study on their own and use a book or software package. Such students are dedicated to passing the second time they take the exam and want the structure that the courses provide. NTC provides a study schedule, study techniques, and information about how to take the exam that, it boasts, can not be found in any other course on the market.

Many of NTC's students have also taken an NTC course for a previous entrance exam. NTC boasts a higher overall pass rate for all its courses than any other test prep center in the country. People who had taken a course for the GMAT and had passed, for example, felt confident that they would be equally prepared for passing the CPA exam. In a survey of undergraduate students who had taken NTC for the SAT, 85 percent said they would take another NTC course to prepare them for a graduate school entrance exam.

THE TURNER TESTING ADVANTAGE

Despite NTC's success, Jessica knew that with a pass rate of only 25 percent for first-time takers, there was a need to provide a comprehensive program to students so that they could pass on their first try. She devised a full-service program that lasted for six weeks and was three to six hours per day. She worked with accounting, finance, and law professors to design a curriculum to give students a comprehensive approach to studying for the exam. She hired the professors to give three live, one-hour lectures per day, and she taught the test-taking techniques and organizing skills necessary to easily assimilate the mountains of information that students needed to know. Jessica also provided audiotapes for students so that they could review the lectures at home and suggested that they listen to them in their cars to maximize the use of their time. The course also included several timed minitests for each topic and four practice essay questions, which Jessica and her professors graded. The responses to essays included many comments and much feedback to give students guidance on areas to improve.

Jessica also made herself completely available to her students. She felt that one-on-one attention was critical to their success, and she held bi-weekly meetings with each student to gauge progress and answer questions. In addition to the meetings, students could call Jessica or e-mail her with questions, and she promised to get back to them within 24 hours.

Jessica held two sessions a year in March and September, three months prior to the exams, allowing students to continue to study on their own before the exams. She also made herself available to students after the course to answer their questions and help them in any way she could. Pricing her course at $1,100 per student, she felt that she was providing her students with more of an advantage and better preparation than any of the NTC options. She also offered a guarantee, allowing students to repeat the course if they did not pass the exam.

Jessica had taken a year to develop the materials and create a marketing plan for her company. She decided to place ads in Bay area business schools to attract students contemplating taking the exam after graduation. She also created flyers to be placed in the schools and asked the school administrations if she could place them in students' mailboxes. She introduced herself to local businesses and tried to alert them to her program so that up-and-coming accountants would be encouraged to take her class if they wanted to take the CPA exam.

The first year that she ran the program she had 10 students. Despite the small class size, students felt that they had been well prepared for the exam and appreciated the individual attention they received. All students passed the exam. The second course had 45 students, 70 percent of whom passed. The last session that she held had 105 students and 80 percent of those students passed. Jessica did not feel comfortable advertising her pass rate, however, because many of her students had taken the CPA exam one or two times before and failed. She wasn't sure whether they passed after taking her course because of the quality of the program or because they were bound to pass it at some point.

EXHIBIT 1 Operating Costs for Turner Testing Services

Professor salaries (about 1,200 hours per year)	$75 per hour
Office space	$2,000 per month
Utilities and insurance	$1,000 per month
Materials	$600 per student
Printing	$500 per month
Marketing	$400 per month
Travel	$200 per month

SPRING 2003

By the spring of 2003, Jessica had finished teaching the course for the May exam and was looking forward to the September class. Although she was pleased that the number of students in each session was rising, she felt concerned that she was not making enough of an impact in the market. With only 10 percent of the market tapped, Jessica wanted to know how to improve her marketing and gain market share. She also wondered if she needed to format the course differently to attract students who did not want to attend live lectures. She had initially believed that students would benefit from a structured program that kept them on track, but now she was not so sure. Many times students did not come to class but opted to listen to the tapes at home. Finally, Jessica realized that in her zeal to get her business up and running she had neglected to calculate her break-even point. How many students did Jessica need to break even, and at what point could she recognize a profit? She realized that these were all critical questions that needed answers to ensure the future success of her business.

CASE 1B
A. MONROE LOCK AND SECURITY SYSTEMS

Ray Monroe was sitting back in his chair in his home office trying to understand why the new venture had not made him the rich man he thought he would be. A. Monroe Lock and Security Systems (AMLSS) had been established about two years ago and offered locksmithing services to residential and commercial customers as well as automobile owners in the greater

EXHIBIT 1 Demographic Profile of Present Market

Demographics	Newton	Needham	Wellesley
Total population	83,829	28,911	26,613
Total number of households	31,201	19,612	8,594
Percent family	66.7	73.3	76.0
Percent nonfamily	34.3	26.8	24.0
Total number of families	20,486	7,782	6,537
Number of married-couple families	17,209	6,887	5,772
Number of female householder families	2,500	728	607
Average household income	$86,025	$88,079	$113,686
Education			
Percent high school educated	94.5	96.4	97.6%
Percent college or higher educated	68.0	64.9	75.9%
Labor force			
Percent total population employed	66.1	64.9	63.0%
Percent female population employed	62.4	56.4	53.9%
Disability			
Percent with mobility or self-care disability (21–64)	10.4	9.0	6.4%
Percent with mobility or self-care disability (65+)	31.5	28.8	21.8%
Total number of housing units	32,112	10,846	8,861
Median number of rooms	6.4	6.9	7.6
Total number of owner-occupied housing units	21,692	8,587	7,139
Total number of renter-occupied housing units	9,509	2,025	1,455
Retail industry—number of establishments (2000)	595	168	187
Service industry—number of establishments (2000)	1,077	336	1,580

Boston area. These services included lock rekeying, lock and deadbolt installation and repair, master key systems, emergency residential lockouts, foreign and domestic automobile lockouts, and window security locks. In addition, AMLSS was certified by the Commonwealth of Massachusetts to perform alarm installation and offered a full range of alarm products.

Financial results have been relatively poor, with losses of $6,500 in the first year and a profit of only about $3,500 in year 2. Currently, AMLSS's target market is three local communities in the Boston area with similar demographics (see Exhibit 1).

BACKGROUND

Ray Monroe is the only child of parents who were both successful entrepreneurs. His parents are now deceased, and Monroe received a substantial inheritance that would satisfy any of his financial needs for the rest of his life. Ray had been educated at a local private high school and then at a small liberal arts college in Vermont. He was not a great student but always seemed to get by. His summers were usually spent at the college, taking summer courses.

Upon graduation, his father had helped him get a job with a friend who owned a security and alarm manufacturing business in the western part of the state. Ray worked in various areas of the business learning a great deal about alarms and locks. After two years there, Ray decided that he'd prefer to be his own boss and, using some of his inheritance, entered a special program to learn more about the locksmith business. His intent upon completion of the program was to start his own lock and security business. He felt from his experience and education that this market offered tremendous opportunities. Increased crime and residential house sales that often required new locks offered many opportunities to succeed in this business.

Ray did not want to offer alarm installations as part of his new venture since he felt that they were bothersome to install. He also knew that there were many large competitors already in the alarm market that would be able to offer products and service at much lower prices.

INDUSTRY STRUCTURE/COMPETITION

The locksmith industry was dominated by small operators, 60 percent of which consisted of an owner and one employee. Only about 20 percent of these firms had five or more employees.

Because of the low entry barriers, the number of small operators had grown dramatically in the past few years. These businesses were often operated out of the home with no storefront and concentrated mainly on the residential market. There were also a large number of family-owned businesses that usually had a retail store serving their communities for several generations of family members. The larger operators were the most sophisticated in terms of service and products and relied primarily on commercial accounts.

The Boston area was densely populated, with 160 locksmiths all advertising in the area yellow pages. In the three communities on which AMLSS concentrated, there were 37 other locksmiths.

PRESENT STRATEGY

Excluding alarms, Ray offered just about every locksmith service. His company van was used to store these products and any necessary tools for servicing his clients. This company van was 10 years old with a few minor dents, but it ran quite well.

Ray had a beeper system and a cellular phone in order to respond to customer requests. After 5 p.m., however, Ray turned off the system and refused to take calls. During his operating hours he was able to respond to all requests fairly quickly even if he was not in the office, primarily because of the beeper and cellular phone. He had tried using an answering machine, but it did not allow him to respond to a customer fast enough, especially if he was at a job that kept him out of the office for a number of hours. He also knew that many job requests were emergencies and required a quick response.

During the past year, Ray had decided to advertise in the yellow pages. He felt that with all the locksmiths listed in the yellow pages he needed to be at the top of the list, so he decided to use his middle name initial (for Arthur) to form A. Monroe Locksmith and Security Systems. The yellow pages ad seemed to help business and contributed to the $4,000 profit (see Exhibits 2 and 3 for billing and expenses).

Ray spent a lot of his time in the office thinking of ways to increase his business, yet to this point nothing had been very successful. His understanding was that many of his competitors had found that the yellow pages were the most likely place for customers to find a locksmith. His ad identified the three communities, the services he offered, and a telephone number. In addition, he included that he was bonded and insured and a

EXHIBIT 2 A. Monroe Monthly Billings for Year Two

January	$ 1,200.01
February	2,260.85
March	2,777.26
April	1,748.62
May	922.20
June	1,414.12
July	1,595.18
August	1,652.37
September	2,264.64
October	2,602.19
November	4,087.37
December	1,905.80
Total	$24,430.61

EXHIBIT 3 Year Two Expenses

Business expenses	
Selling expenses	$ 9,454
Memberships (chambers of commerce and Associated Locksmiths of America)	2,490
Telephone (includes beeper and cellular)	1,920
Office expenses (materials/supplies)	1,775
Yellow pages	4,200
Other promotional expenses	600
Total expenses	$20,439

member of the Massachusetts Locksmith Association. Competitors typically stressed products and services, 24-hour emergency service, follow-up guarantee service, being bonded and insured, and membership in the locksmith association.

Time was running out for Ray, and he was trying to think of other businesses that he could start up. He would often question his decision to enter the locksmith business, but then he would quickly decide that since he didn't really need the money, it wasn't a big deal. However, at some point he felt he should try to establish himself so he could settle down to a more routine life.

CASE 1C
BEIJING SAMMIES

When Sam Goodman opened a new Sammies café in Beijing's Motorola Building, he cut prices by 50 percent for the first three months in order to attract customers. The initial period was very successful but when he returned prices to normal, sales dropped dramatically and fell short of targets. The local store manager, when presenting the figures, suggested that Goodman simply lower the sales targets. Goodman was frustrated; the manager had failed to address any of the issues that were keeping customers from returning. There were countless orders that went out with missing utensils, in the wrong bag, or [with items] simply left out. Delivery orders were being sent hours late or to the wrong location. This typified Goodman's early experience; the market was showing interest in Beijing Sammies's products but he knew that without exceptional service, good food would not be enough. Goodman questioned whether he could find employees who were thinkers and problem solvers and he wondered how to improve upon the business in order to turn Beijing Sammies into a sustainable and profitable enterprise.

Source: This case was prepared by Christopher Ferrarone under the supervision of Boston College Professor Gregory L. Stoller as the basis for class discussion rather than to illustrate either effective or ineffective handling of an administrative situation.

According to Goodman, face and money were the two most important subjects. With experience as a student and businessman in China, he knew one must observe the cultural beliefs:

> Face is a huge issue here, and as the economy develops, so is money. If one is not relevant, the other is. Once you recognize this is crucial, it was not hard to learn. The difficult part is incorporating it into the business.We need to offer a superior experience in order for customers to justify paying more. This means providing a quality product with excellent service. It sounds easy, but in China the concept of service is not the same as in the West. I just can't seem to get my employees to understand that there is a way to serve the customer while also keeping the company's interest at heart. It is an, "all for us" or "all for them" mentality here.

Throughout the company's initial years Goodman sought to teach a service-oriented approach to his employees. In doing so, he ironically learned that face was as much of an important issue for Beijing Sammies's customers as it was for its employees.

BEIJING SAMMIES

Canadian native, Sam Goodman, started Beijing Sammies[4] in 1997. Aside from producing food for the everyday, walk-in customer, Sammies provided fare for company meetings, presentations, picnics, and gifts. Sammies was open for breakfast, lunch, and dinner and delivered all products to its customers. The menu included a selection of sandwiches, salads, bagels, brownies, cookies, coffee, soda, and tea (Exhibit 1).

Goodman started the company with personal savings and money borrowed from family. He opened his first café at the Beijing Language and Culture University with the goal of providing people with a place to "hang out" and enjoy homemade western food.

By 2003 Beijing Sammies had five outlets [composed] of four "deli-style" cafés and one kiosk. The stores were traditional in terms of layout and size for fast food restaurants. Two Sammies cafés were 1,200 square feet and the other two were roughly 800 square feet each, while the kiosk was a stand-alone structure with open seating inside the lobby of a corporate building. All of the café locations had enclosed seating that was maximized, as there was no need for self-contained kitchens.

EXHIBIT 1

Ordering Information

Min Order:
PEAK HOURS: 100rmb (Mon-Fri:10:30-13:30)
OTHER HOURS: 50rmb

Orders under 50 rmb: add 20 rmb service charge

Free delivery within Chao Yang CBD

Delivery takes 30-45 minutes during rush hours

For large orders or special time deliveries
please call 1 day in advance

Save Your Company Time & Money

Sammies Corporate Accounts

Convenience & Flexibility in
Payment, Ordering & Delivery

Sammies is a healthy alternative for your

Meetings ○ Seminars ○ Training Sessions

We provide menu suggestions.

For more information, special requests or
comments please call Customer Service:
English and Chinese service

6506 8838

www.beijingsammies.com

All prices subject to change.
Ingredients may change due to availability and freshness

Where East Eats West

CORPORATE DELIVERY

Monday - Friday: 8:00 a.m.-9:00 p.m.
Saturday - Sunday: 9:00 a.m.-7:00 p.m.

TEL: 6506 8838 FAX: 6503 2688

Online Ordering: www.beijingsammies.com

Breakfast & Lunch Meetings ○ Training Sessions

Where East Eats West

(*Continued*)

EXHIBIT 1 *Continued*

Sammie Packs

When ease and efficiency are the names of the game, these packs hit the spot. No need to ask everyone what they want, variety will take care of that. Sammies are cut into 1/4's for convenience,

GOOD FOR 6~8 PERSONS, EACH PACK COMES WITH VEGGIES N' DIP.

Predator Pack
For meat lovers with healthy appetites! Dante's Inferno, Classic Grilled Chicken and Frankenstein. (2 of each) 160

Classic Favorites
Deliciously simple and filling! Classic Turkey, Ham n' Cheese and Poseidon's Pleasure. (2 of each) 160

The Conglomerate
An assortment to suit all! Classic Roast Beef, Funky Chicken, Turkey Shoot, Homestead, Poseidon's Pleasure, Garden Special 160

Vegetarian
Healthy and loaded with taste! Poseidon's Pleasure, Early Bird, and Veggies n' Cheese (2 of each) 150

Bakery Bundles

Sammies selection of freshly baked goods, great for any occasion; meetings, boosting staff morale, customer gifts, picnics or parties. Guaranteed to bring a smile to anyone's face.

Muffin Madness A satisfying breakfast or afternoon treat! Includes all 6 varieties of Sammies' original recipe muffins. 18 small 55

Cookie Monster Sammies' freshly baked, original recipe cookies! Includes Chocolate Chunk, Double Chocolate and Oatmeal Raisin. 18 regular 55

The Bagel Bag Baked fresh everyday. Plain, Sesame & Cinnamon Raisin (2 of each) whole or cut in half, served with cream cheese (140g), strawberry preserves (70g) and butter 40

W.O.F.E (Warm Oven Fresh Eats) For meetings, after lunch, or anytime of the day, this box suits all tastes! Includes 2 Brownies(cut into 1/4), 8 mini-muffins, 6 regular cookies and 2 Biscottis 65

Box Lunches

Great for meetings, bus tours, travelling, picnics and parties !

Classic Box 40
Your choice of sammie
Potato Chips
Lg. Chocolate Chunk Cookie

Health Box 40
Your choice of sammie
Veggies & Dip
Lg. Oatmeal Raisin Cookie

The Central Kitchen

Goodman found that revenues of the first café were driven as much by corporate delivery orders as they were by the local walk-in customers. This motivated Goodman to open more cafés and a centralized kitchen in 1998. Located in Beijing's Chao Yang District, the kitchen ran from 10 p.m. to 5:30 a.m. each day making the sandwiches and baked goods for all of Sammies's locations. Between 5:30 and 6 a.m., trucks delivered the goods from the kitchen to each Sammies outlet. No cooking was done at any of the Sammies locations. Every sandwich, cookie, and muffin was prepared, baked, and packaged centrally. Only coffee and smoothies were prepared onsite at individual retail cafés.

While the central kitchen created a number of efficiencies for Beijing Sammies, what Goodman liked even more was the quality control that it provided:

> It is much easier for me to teach the kitchen staff how to make the food correctly than it is to teach all of the employees at each location. At the kitchen I can make sure that the product going out to all of the stores is consistent. In the end that's what I am striving for, to offer a consistently great product with superior service. Only having one kitchen to manage makes this task much easier.

The central kitchen not only provided Beijing Sammies with efficiencies with ingredients, machines, and manpower, but also allowed for larger customer capacity at each café location and enabled the employees to uniquely focus on customer service.

THE SAMMIE

The idea behind Beijing Sammies originated from Goodman. Moving to Hong Kong after college and subsequently moving to Beijing to attend Beijing Language and Culture University, Goodman yearned for a place to hang out and eat a traditional sandwich or "sammie" that reminded him of home. Three years later Beijing Sammies was named Beijing's #1 western food delivery service by City Weekend magazine.

Modeled after Goodman's version of a New York deli, Beijing Sammies's staple is the "sammie." Each sammie started with homemade bread made every night at Sammies's kitchen. Customers could order from a menu of standard sammies or could create their own. Goodman found the pre-set menu best for the local customers while many foreigners frequently customized their sandwich:

> Having a menu of pre-crafted sandwiches is a necessity. Many of the Chinese customers simply do not know how to order. They do not understand the notion of selecting different types of deli meats and condiments for a sandwich. I didn't even think about this at first. Personally, I know exactly what goes with roast beef and what goes with turkey.
>
> When we opened our first location many people came in and left without ordering. They didn't know how, and did not want to look foolish ordering something inappropriate. Many times, and this still happens, people come in and just order whatever the person in front of them ordered. Putting complete sandwiches together allows the inexperienced customer to come in and feel more comfortable about ordering.

Creating pre-made selections of sandwiches worked so well for Sammies that Goodman put together an "Ordering Tips" section on the menu. The section not only suggested what types of products to order for breakfast and what products to buy for lunch, but also provided a guide for corporate clients to ensure correct portions and variety for meetings. In addition, Sammies trained sales clerks to act as customer service representatives who could assist both the walk-in client and growing base of corporate delivery clients with their orders.

Corporate Clients and Sammies Rewards

As Beijing Sammies realized a growing corporate delivery base, Goodman adapted the model to provide the business client with as much flexibility and customization as possible. Sammies set up corporate accounts, online ordering, flexible payment options, and a rewards program.

Corporate customers who registered with Beijing Sammies could choose weekly or monthly payment terms whereby Beijing Sammies would send out itemized statements and invoices. Clients could choose to set up a debit account as well. Under the debit account, clients prepaid a certain amount (usually a minimum of rmb1000*) that was credited to an account and deducted each time an order was placed.

*Note: Conversion rate is: RMB8.3 = $1.

EXHIBIT 2 Beijing Sammies Introductory E-mail

OUR NEW SILK ALLEY SAMMIES CAFE IS ALSO OPEN!

Drop on by to enjoy some of your Sammies favorites . . . and more!

- Enjoy our wider breakfast selection
- Choose from café beverages and goodies
- Select from smoothies, espresso, cappuccinos, and our selection of baked goods
- Warm, inviting café atmosphere—whether you're networking, on a date, getting a meal-to-go or getting social, Sammies Xiu Shui Jie café is the place to be!

Located at the Silk Alley/Xiu Shui Jie south entrance on Chang An Jie, in the Chaoyang District; open every day from 07:30 to 24:00.

****WHERE EAST EATS WEST****

***THANKS FOR REGISTERING! NOW YOU CAN ORDER ALL YOUR SAMMIES FAVORITES THROUGH THE WEB!**

Browse online and order our delicious Sammies sandwiches, salads, baked goods including muffins, cookies, brownies, biscotti, and bagels. Great for business meetings, social events, breakfast, lunch, or dinner! Registration allows you to enjoy the following:

*****SAVE TIME*****

One-time registration of delivery information—no need to re-explain your contact info at every order. Just log in, order, and then submit for successful delivery every time you come to the Web site.

*****SAVE MONEY*****

Bonus points for future discounts—sign up and receive bonus points based on every RMB you order, which you can redeem for future discounts and Sammies products.

*****IMPROVED EFFICIENCY*****

Online ordering and delivery—order directly from our Web site menu and we'll deliver to you!

*****CUSTOM-MADE ORDERS*****

Customize your Sammies, and track your orders with our new menu and online ordering interface.

*****RE-ORDER YOUR FAVORITES*****

Quick ordering of your favorite Sammies items—registered users can re-order from a recorded list of past favorite orders.

*****ORDER 24 HOURS A DAY*****

Order hours or days in advance.

Questions? Please e-mail our helpful customer service staff at beijingsammies @yahoo.com. Tell a friend to visit us at www.beijingsammies.com.

Along with the flexible payment options, corporate customers could become enrolled in the Bonus Points program, which offered credits based on the frequency and size of orders. Customers who spent between rmb500 and 750 receive a rmb50 credit, orders between rmb750 and 1000 a rmb75 credit, and orders over rmb1000 are given a rmb100 credit. Furthermore, each time a client cumulatively spent over rmb5000 they were rewarded with a rmb500 credit. All of this could be done over the Beijing Sammies Web site, www.beijingsammies.com, where customers could log in and manage their account (Exhibit 2).

The Bonus Points program was offered to the walk-in customer as well. Customers who registered with Beijing Sammies online could become enrolled in the program. Every registered customer received a point for each rmb they spent. Every 10 points could be redeemed for 1 rmb off the next order. Extra points could be received

EXHIBIT 3 Corporate Clients

- Nokia China Investment
- U.S.A. Embassy
- Canada Embassy
- Intel PRC, Corp.
- Boeing
- AEA SOS
- American Chamber of Commerce
- Agilent
- Andersen Consulting
- Australia Embassy
- APCO Associates Inc.
- Benz
- Ford Foundation
- Henkel
- Hewlett-Packard
- IBM China Ltd.
- Motorola China Electronics, Ltd.
- Western Academy of Beijing
- Reuters

for filling out surveys, referring new customers, or attending selected special events. The point system was well received by Beijing Sammies's customers and contributed to a solid base of returning foreign clients (Exhibit 3).

Charity Sponsorship

Beijing Sammies served large numbers of foreigners and consequently, Goodman felt a strong responsibility to sponsor charity, youth, and community events focused around the Ex-pat community in Beijing:

> The Canadian community in Beijing and around China in general is pretty strong. As a foreign student here I really appreciated the sense of kinship that I felt even though I was far away from home. In addition, the foreign businesses and tourists have been very supporting of Beijing Sammies so I really enjoy and feel compelled to participate in the community's events.

Along with providing snacks and food, Beijing Sammies helped certain organizations by allowing promotional and ticket sale efforts to be staged from Sammies's locations. Sammies's sponsorship events included:

- Special Olympics
- Canadian Day and Independence Day
- Sporting and school events held by the Western Academy of Beijing and The International School of Beijing
- Annual Terry Fox Run for Cancer
- ACBC Baseball Events

SAMMIES'S EVOLUTION

Starting out with $25,000 borrowed from friends and family back in Canada, Goodman opened Beijing's first sandwich shop. In order to more easily get past the bureaucracy involved with opening the café, Goodman located a Chinese partner. After an initial four months of business, Beijing Sammies was a hit. The store was so successful that the new partner attempted to strong-arm Goodman out of the company by locking him out. In response, Goodman rallied some friends and broke into the shop one night and removed the appliances and supplies. The partner agreed to be bought out.

Soon after Goodman regained control, his landlord disappeared. The government demanded the tenants cover his back taxes. When they could not, it demolished the whole row and left the tenants with the bricks. Goodman was able to sell them for $25.

Goodman responded by opening a café at the Beijing Language and Culture University. Again, Sammies opened to a steady stream of customers, particularly from foreign students and local corporations.

In 1998, after realizing success with the first café in its newfound location, Goodman found another business partner. Together they planned to invest $350,000 more into Beijing Sammies. The next step was to build a centralized kitchen and add more café locations. Soon after construction started, however, the funds supposedly coming from the newfound business partner quickly dried up and Goodman was left financing the new kitchen on his own.

At the end of 1998, Sammies had a central kitchen with great capacity but no new store locations to deliver to. Goodman was able to generate yet another round of financing. With some western investment and all of the profits from his previous two years in business, Goodman was able to put $150,000 together and open three new cafés.

EXHIBIT 4

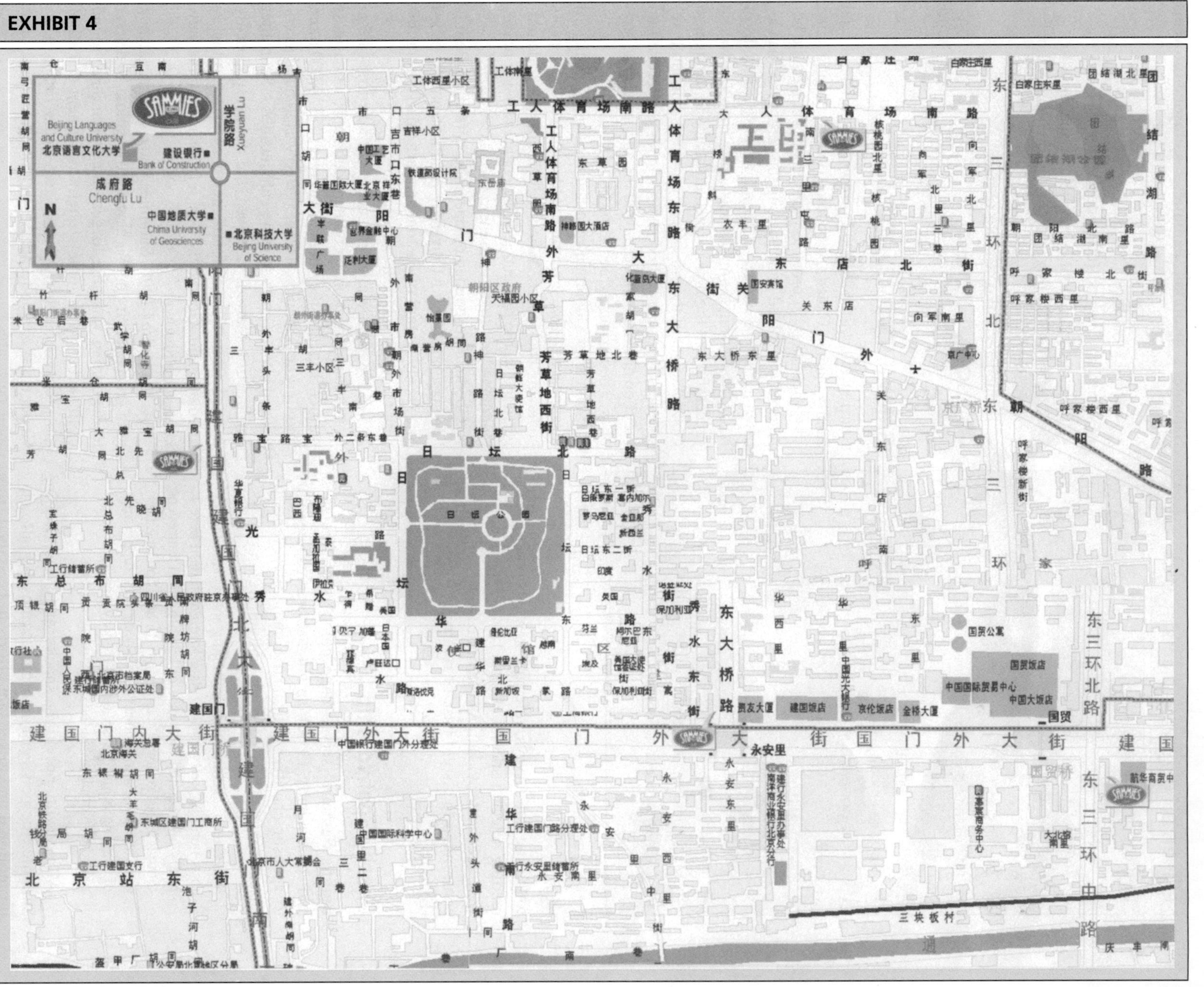
SAMMIES
Beijing Languages and Culture University
北京语言文化大学
建设银行
Bank of Construction
学院路
Xueyuan Lu
成府路
Chengfu Lu
N
中国地质大学
China University of Geosciences
北京科技大学
Beijing University of Science
工人体育场南路
建国门内大街
建国门外大街
东三环北路
朝阳门外大街
东大桥路
北京站东街
国贸饭店
中国国际贸易中心
中国大饭店
国贸公寓

In addition to the first café located at Beijing Language and Culture University, Sammies cafés were opened between 1998 and 2001 at the Silk Alley Market, 1/F Exchange Beijing, and The Motorola Building. A Sammies kiosk was also opened at the China Resource Building (Exhibit 4). The expansion allowed Goodman to more adequately serve the Beijing area while also firmly establishing Beijing Sammies in an increasingly competitive environment:

> Overall, I see the expansion into multiple cafés as a success. Two of the cafés are doing well while the two others have not met sales targets yet. The kiosk, because of less rent, is doing moderately well but is still not as busy as I'd like it to be. 2002 looks to be our best year to date with a revenue increase of 54%, and an operating profit of $20,000. However, due to the fact that the central kitchen is its own cost center, we will record a $24,000 loss (including depreciation). 2003 should show our first profits.

By the end of 2001, Beijing Sammies was recording monthly revenues over rmb500,000 and by 2003, the company had recorded positive net income in certain months (Exhibit 5).

COMPETITION

The economic expansion of the late 1990s dramatically changed dining in Beijing. Private establishments that catered to China's emerging middle class replaced old state-run restaurants. Most traditional meals were under $5 per person. Peking duck and other local specialties were the most popular, but new restaurants opened that offered regional tastes from all around Asia. Additionally, the number of western-style restaurants targeting tourists, expatriates, and younger, trendy Chinese customers increased.

Sam Goodman viewed all restaurants physically close to Sammies as competitors:

> As far as I'm concerned, everyone in Beijing who orders lunch is a potential customer and every restaurant serving it is a competitor. There are those who stick to the traditional Chinese meal, but who is to say that they will never try Sammies?
>
> I do not want to restrict Sammies to serving just western businesses or students. We are delivering not only to western businesses but to traditional Chinese companies as well. While we rely on western students for our walk-in business, we do have Chinese customers who come to Sammies every day. There are others who only come once in a while. These people go to the Chinese restaurants when they don't come here, so I must think broadly in terms of whom my customers are and who my competition is. Of course the western restaurants like McDonald's, Subway, Schlotzskys, and Starbucks are the most obvious competitors. Competition in this business is day-to-day as people rarely eat lunch at the same location each afternoon.

Like most major cities, Beijing had an array of restaurant choices ranging from traditional Chinese to Mexican, German, Scandinavian, Italian, Swiss, and English Continental.

THE GREAT WALL OF CHINA

As Beijing Sammies adapted to the competitive environment, Goodman increasingly turned to the delivery business for revenue. But the model did not work as planned, due to the lack of experience Goodman had in delivery logistics. Corporate clients were more demanding and lunch delivery complicated. Goodman states:

> We started out delivering from a central source. At first, things did not go as planned. Quite frankly, I was an inexperienced manager and made quite a few mistakes. The delivery model here in China is very different from the West. Clients have no understanding of what goes on behind the scenes, and they do not understand that it is nearly impossible for us to take a large delivery order for a corporate luncheon and bring it to them ten minutes later. I didn't plan for all of the possible problems that a different culture would bring. I should have put more effort and time into educating the customer about the product. This definitely had a negative impact on the business at first.

In addition to overcoming the existing perceptions and expectations of the customer, Goodman learned about the prevailing attitude of the employees. One of his biggest challenges was not securing the hard-to-come-by ingredients, dealing with the local government, or raising capital, but rather teaching his employees the concept of service. For many of Beijing Sammies's employees, service was little more than opening the store in the morning and closing it at night. To Goodman, service was much more. It was what he believed would differentiate Beijing Sammies from the other western food establishments, and what would cause the traditional Chinese consumer to pay more money for lunch. Service was not only delivering the product on time,

EXHIBIT 5 Income Statement

Beijing Sammies	Kitchen Office	Kitchen Production	Kitchen Delivery	Kitchen Café
Revenue			2,007,921.19	
Cost of Goods Sold	17,886.73		641,106.51	
Gross Profit	−17,886.73		1,366,814.68	
Gross Margin			68.07%	
Taxes	8,983.00		99,884.24	
Salary	583,260.12	308,911.56	267,225.53	
Insurance	57,067.01	24,131.97		
Rent Related	185,246.10	102,917.10	82,331.60	41,165.80
Utilities	38,075.39	41,237.04	22,891.23	2,531.10
Office Expenses	131,989.31	445.38	5,750.55	
Marketing/Advertising	29,687.74		25,129.00	
Transportation	37,798.57	256.75	20,545.85	
Maintenance	68,965.65	6,357.00	1,560.00	
Entertainment	16,660.54	1,033.50	2,388.10	
Law & Other Expenses	47,623.29			
Bank Charges	−91.60			
Others	1,238.08	5,987.22	10,414.69	
HR	8,580.00			
Legal/Gov't Charge	33,566.00			
Low Cost and Short-Lived Articles	14,581.58	21,594.56	4,869.28	
CK Service Fee	−327,302.43		100,396.06	
Total Expenses	935,928.34	512,872.07	643,386.13	43,696.90
Gross Income	−953,815.07	−512,872.07	723,428.55	−43,696.90
Amortization Pre-Operating Costs	154,683.52			
Amortization-Renovations	71,500.00			
Depreciation Expense	49,392.72	144,283.10	2,296.71	
Total	275,576.24	144,283.10	2,296.71	0.00
Net Income	−1,229,391.31	−657,155.17	721,131.84	−43,696.90

*Note: Exhibit 5 amounts are in Chinese Renminbi.

with the correct number of forks and knives, but was also helping the customer to understand the product. According to Goodman:

> For most of my employees it doesn't matter "how" you get things done—it just matters that you get the end result. The concept of face for them manifests itself with the feeling that appearance is much more important than the service or quality of the product. While for the customer, the service provided by us is part of the final product.

Just as the client base did not understand the wait for a delivery, the employee did not understand the product that Beijing Sammies was trying to sell:

> The staff does not understand the urgency needed in running a service-oriented business. The whole concept

By Café	SA Café	CR Café	EB Café	2002YTD		
				RMB	USD	
					0.120479942	conversion factor
1,562,707.90	2,413,590.26	253,667.83	308,161.39	6,546,048.56	788,667.55	
458,643.00	660,387.10	85,284.58	116,182.07	1,979,489.98	238,488.84	
1,104,064.90	1,753,203.15	168,383.25	191,979.32	4,566,558.58	550,178.71	
70.65%	72.64%	66.38%	62.30%	69.76%	69.76%	
26,129.18	126,258.34	8,716.06	15,408.20	285,379.02	34,382.45	
295,125.60	280,945.80	43,670.25	90,302.94	1,869,441.80	225,230.24	
12,160.29	6,641.12	2,151.96	0.00	102,152.34	12,307.31	
104,000.00	585,000.00	28,199.80	85,322.84	1,214,183.23	146,284.73	
45,492.79	7,103.90	7,587.91	6,598.31	171,517.66	20,664.44	
4,298.84	14,296.32	3,451.76	17,737.90	177,970.07	21,441.82	
18,306.60	41,151.07	17,203.88	43,155.50	174,633.78	21,039.87	
4,286.23	743.60	0.00	237.90	63,868.90	7,694.92	
12,139.01	21,128.90	1,843.40	1,625.00	113,618.96	13,688.81	
6,477.25	1,123.20	0.00	789.10	28,471.69	3,430.27	
	0.00	0.00	0.00	47,623.29	5,737.65	
	−103.48	7.15	39.00	−148.93	−17.94	
6,236.88	4,112.19	250.76	43.63	28,283.44	3,407.59	
	0.00	0.00	0.00	8,580.00	1,033.72	
	533.00	0.00	0.00	34,099.00	4,108.25	
5,411.90	2,859.58	0.00	13,277.94	62,594.84	7,541.42	
78,135.40	120,679.51	12,683.40	15,408.07	0.00	0.00	
618,199.96	1,212,473.04	125,766.30	289,946.32	4,382,269.07	527,975.52	
485,864.94	540,730.11	42,616.95	−97,967.00	184,289.51	22,203.19	
			15,468.34	154,683.36	18,636.24	
			16,300.87	92,852.02	11,186.81	
16,088.84	10,502.70	11,881.35	24,125.41	241,254.13	29,066.28	
16,088.84	10,502.70	11,881.35	55,894.62	488,789.51	58,889.33	
469,776.10	530,227.41	30,735.60	−153,861.62	−304,500.00	−36,686.14	

of service is new in China. The business traditions are very strong here. I don't know if it's because of the issue of face and pride, the political history, or something else, but our employees have a very difficult time understanding how we need to deliver service as much as we need to deliver a sandwich.

For Sam Goodman, the initial years of operations proved that Beijing Sammies could hold a niche. While he was pleased to see Beijing Sammies growing toward profitability, he was concerned about whether it could ever become cash-flow positive, and if so, whether he could sustain it. In addition, Goodman was no closer to finding the type of employee who would adopt his concept of service than he was when he started, and wondered if the answer lay in increased automation, training, or somewhere else.

EXHIBIT 5 Income Statement *(Continued)*

Beijing Sammies	Jan-02	Feb-02	Mar-02	Apr-02	May-02	Jun-02
Revenue	474,490.19	340,345.07	633,584.38	636,305.41	714,801.13	768,954.55
Cost of Goods Sold	116,310.43	112,891.03	209,662.56	221,218.57	185,420.17	221,374.62
Gross Profit	358,179.76	227,454.05	423,921.82	415,086.84	529,380.96	547,579.93
Gross Margin	75.49%	66.83%	66.91%	65.23%	74.06%	71.21%
Taxes	21,449.26	15,003.20	21,514.52	21,744.06	31,754.91	24,373.65
Salary	195,127.49	200,044.95	179,709.69	197,527.25	172,055.86	208,886.93
Insurance	9,027.64	8,697.01	10,910.74	10,991.92	7,642.39	10,484.72
Rent Related	118,045.59	118,045.53	118,045.66	118,045.92	118,046.11	112,665.80
Utilities	14,993.68	20,974.36	13,872.64	13,989.55	14,436.11	18,413.58
Office Expenses	7,002.19	9,775.81	10,184.63	15,715.78	23,112.66	15,346.73
Marketing/Advertising	2,080.00	8,476.00	5,473.00	7,670.00	17,500.60	24,986.00
Transportation	3,458.00	1,738.10	4,951.70	3,695.64	4,497.74	11,303.50
Maintenance	7,800.00	5,281.25	309.40	4,564.30	6,630.00	38,958.40
Entertainment	3,216.20	6,073.60	3,313.70	2,471.30	852.80	4,378.14
Law & Other Expenses	1,798.33	1,798.33	6,998.33	1,798.33	14,798.33	1,798.33
Bank Charges	104.00	78.00	−379.54	−13.17	163.15	−425.63
Others	845.00	234.00	7,179.64	4,312.10	0.00	3,208.14
HR	650.00	975.00	4,615.00	0.00	975.00	0.00
Legal/Gov't Charge	1,950.00	1,950.00	16,016.00	1,950.00	1,950.00	2,483.00
Low Cost and Short-Lived Articles	2,171.00	1,295.84	3,055.00	10,031.27	10,522.07	5,995.31
Total Expenses	389,718.38	400,440.96	405,770.11	414,494.24	424,937.72	482,856.60
Gross Income	−31,538.62	−172,986.92	18,151.72	592.60	104,443.24	64,723.33
Amortization Pre-Operating Costs	15,468.34	15,468.34	15,468.34	15,468.34	15,468.34	15,468.34
Amortization-Renovations	7,150.00	7,150.00	7,150.00	7,150.00	7,150.00	7,150.00
Depreciation Expense	24,125.41	24,125.41	24,125.41	24,125.41	24,125.41	24,125.41
Total	46,743.75	46,743.75	46,743.75	46,743.75	46,743.75	46,743.75
Net Income	−78,282.37	−219,730.67	−28,592.03	−46,151.14	57,699.49	17,979.58
Cumulative Net Income	−78,282.37	−298,013.04	−326,605.07	−372,756.22	−315,056.73	−297,077.14

Jul-02	Aug-02	Sep-02	Oct-02	2002YTD		
				RMB	USD	
					0.120479942	conversion factor
819,787.15	743,912.26	659,126.31	754,742.12	6,546,048.56	788,667.55	
271,224.40	216,298.58	210,682.54	214,407.10	1,979,489.98	238,488.84	
548,562.76	527,613.68	448,443.78	540,335.02	4,566,558.58	550,178.71	
66.92%	70.92%	68.04%	71.59%	69.76%	69.76%	
42,118.17	32,275.32	25,169.18	49,976.76	285,379.02	34,382.45	
151,037.11	172,597.30	181,573.80	210,881.44	1,869,441.80	225,230.24	
12,577.94	10,606.44	10,606.44	10,607.09	102,152.34	12,307.31	
99,665.80	124,581.20	142,870.82	144,170.82	1,214,183.23	146,284.73	
16,504.80	14,210.99	19,398.47	24,723.49	171,517.66	20,664.44	
21,650.58	29,671.43	33,736.55	11,773.71	177,970.07	21,441.82	
23,403.09	33,382.75	24,166.45	27,495.88	174,633.78	21,039.87	
5,270.98	18,112.15	5,557.37	5,283.72	63,868.90	7,694.92	
26,887.90	9,034.61	7,272.20	6,880.90	113,618.96	13,688.81	
546.00	461.50	4,406.35	2,752.10	28,471.69	3,430.27	
8,038.33	6,998.33	1,798.33	1,798.33	47,623.29	5,737.65	
176.80	117.00	9.36	21.10	−148.93	−17.94	
3,867.12	3,606.10	1,757.47	3,273.87	28,283.44	3,407.59	
0.00	0.00	0.00	1,365.00	8,580.00	1,033.72	
1,950.00	1,950.00	1,950.00	1,950.00	34,099.00	4,108.25	
3,622.32	20,954.62	3,919.89	1,027.00	62,594.32	7,541.36	
417,316.94	478,559.73	464,192.68	503,981.21	4,382,268.55	527,975.46	
131,245.82	49,053.95	−15,748.90	36,353.61	184,290.03	22,203.25	
15,468.34	15,468.34	15,468.34	15,468.34	154,683.36	18,636.24	
7,150.00	16,300.87	13,250.58	13,250.58	92,852.02	11,186.81	
24,125.41	24,125.41	24,125.41	24,125.41	241,254.13	29,066.28	
46,743.75	55,894.62	52,844.32	52,844.32	488,789.51	58,889.33	
84,502.07	−6,840.67	−68,593.23	−16,490.51	−304,499.48	−36,686.08	
−212,575.08	−219,415.74	−288,008.97	−304,499.48			

EXHIBIT 5 Income Statement *(Continued)*

2001–2002 Comparison

Beijing Sammies		Jan	Feb	Mar	Apr	May	Jun	Jul	Aug	Sep
Revenues-Total										
	2002	474,490	340,345	633,584	636,305	714,801	768,955	819,787	743,912	659,126
	2001	195,360	221,729	273,194	322,826	360,585	487,627	485,567	479,232	495,706
Revenues-CD										
	2002	125,663	101,290	209,557	173,213	226,170	269,890	360,783	338,797	92,303
	2001	118,331	167,267	157,382	190,320	164,654	161,971	153,994	142,709	136,926
Revenues-BY										
	2002	150,800	55,375	173,870	202,190	213,181	245,040	86,393	20,944	191,542
	2001	77,029	54,462	115,812	132,506	122,457	161,166	130,244	112,095	136,210
Revenues-SA										
	2002	171,306	166,733	221,391	231,774	255,840	229,739	286,696	260,326	273,640
	2001	0	0	0	0	73,473	164,492	172,101	197,597	197,532
Revenues-CR										
	2002	26,722	16,949	28,768	29,128	19,612	24,287	28,860	26,354	27,414
	2001	0	0	0	0	0	0	29,229	26,832	23,036
Gross Profit										
	2002	358,180	227,454	423,922	415,087	529,381	547,580	548,563	527,614	448,444
	2001	136,161	155,046	181,279	216,507	243,420	334,135	340,288	353,393	340,074
Total Expenses										
	2002	389,718	400,442	405,770	414,495	424,938	482,856	415,874	478,560	439,563
	2001	199,170	212,702	203,262	204,741	292,468	293,136	271,625	318,711	367,199
Salary										
	2002	195,127	200,045	179,710	197,527	172,056	208,887	151,037	172,597	181,574
	2001	130,803	135,100	123,547	123,572	136,526	141,993	143,111	165,208	161,795
Rent Related										
	2002	118,046	118,046	118,046	118,046	118,046	112,666	99,666	124,581	142,871
	2001	36,833	36,833	36,833	36,833	93,180	93,180	71,500	71,500	112,666
Insurance										
	2002	9,028	8,697	10,911	10,992	7,642	10,485	12,578	10,606	10,606
	2001	0	0	0	260	0	3,894	5,203	6,003	4,694
Utilities										
	2002	14,994	20,974	13,873	13,990	14,436	18,414	16,505	14,211	19,398
	2001	11,239	13,459	7,232	8,932	11,063	11,041	13,607	16,717	24,505
Office Expenses										
	2002	7,002	9,776	10,185	15,716	23,113	15,347	21,651	29,671	33,737
	2001	5,437	4,486	5,652	7,899	9,877	9,994	8,281	12,463	9,611
Marketing/Advertising										
	2002	2,080	8,476	5,473	7,670	17,501	24,986	23,403	33,383	24,166
	2001	1,950	7,150	2,842	3,900	19,682	17,508	6,838	14,598	9,460
Transportation										
	2002	3,458	1,738	4,952	3,696	4,498	11,304	5,271	18,112	5,557
	2001	1,158	1,131	2,298	2,662	2,989	1,219	2,428	2,522	2,510
Maintenance										
	2002	7,800	5,281	309	4,564	6,630	38,958	26,888	9,035	7,272
	2001	735	371	3,785	1,707	98	1,110	1,365	1,754	1,252
Entertainment										
	2002	3,216	6,074	3,314	2,471	853	4,378	546	462	4,406
	2001	0	520	4,976	5,881	2,896	0	1,123	255	12,332
Law & Other Expenses										
	2002	3,748	3,748	23,014	3,748	16,748	4,281	9,988	8,948	3,748
	2001	3,613	6,500	6,500	2,665	3,848	0	867	4,767	6,136
Taxes										
	2002	21,384	15,003	21,515	21,744	31,755	24,374	42,119	32,275	25,169
	2001	6,871	5,950	8,639	8,813	6,360	6,163	13,657	15,219	16,592

Oct	Nov	Dec	Total	Average	%	Total USD	Average USD
							0.12048 conversion factor
754,742	0	0	6,546,049	654,605	32.94%	788,668	78,867
501,579	565,923	534,743	4,924,071	410,339		593,252	49,438
110,257	0	0	2,007,923	200,792	12.52%	241,914	24,191
111,007	146,241	131,628	1,784,429	148,702		214,988	17,916
223,374	0	0	1,562,708	156,271	1.18%	188,275	18,827
155,964	173,991	172,487	1,544,423	128,702		186,072	15,506
316,147	0	0	2,413,592	241,359	66.65%	290,789	29,079
216,702	221,035	205,347	1,448,279	193,104		174,489	23,265
25,579	0	0	253,672	25,367	72.63%	30,562	3,056
17,908	24,656	25,284	146,944	24,491		17,704	2,951
540,335	0	0	4,566,559	456,656	33.45%	550,179	55,018
360,762	406,459	354,387	3,421,909	285,159		412,271	34,356
503,981	0	0	4,356,196	435,620	25.44%	524,834	52,483
358,769	367,961	383,097	3,472,840	289,403		418,408	34,567
210,881	0	0	1,869,442	186,944	5.67%	225,230	22,523
163,081	169,485	174,984	1,769,204	147,434		213,154	17,763
144,171	0	0	1,214,183	121,418	28.69%	146,285	14,628
118,045	118,048	118,047	943,497	78,625		113,672	9,473
10,507	0	0	102,152	10,215	174.55%	12,307	1,231
6,516	5,049	5,589	37,207	3,101		4,483	374
24,723	0	0	171,518	17,152	−0.10%	20,664	2,066
18,764	17,195	17,936	171,690	14,307		20,685	1,724
11,774	0	0	177,970	17,797	63.35%	21,442	2,144
10,245	10,773	14,229	108,948	9,079		13,126	1,094
27,496	0	0	174,634	17,463	42.87%	21,040	2,104
9,494	17,076	11,736	122,234	10,186		14,727	1,227
5,284	0	0	63,869	6,387	149.15%	7,695	769
2,626	1,651	2,439	25,635	2,136		3,088	257
6,881	0	0	113,619	11,362	588.67%	13,689	1,369
1,273	681	2,366	16,498	1,375		1,988	166
2,752	0	0	28,472	2,847	−13.33%	3,430	343
372	759	3,738	32,852	2,738		3,958	330
3,748	0	0	81,718	8,172	123.09%	9,845	985
867	867	0	36,630	3,053		4,413	368
49,977	0	0	285,315	28,531	83.43%	34,375	3,437
25,346	16,892	25,046	155,546	12,962		18,740	1,562

EXHIBIT 5 Income Statement *(Continued)*

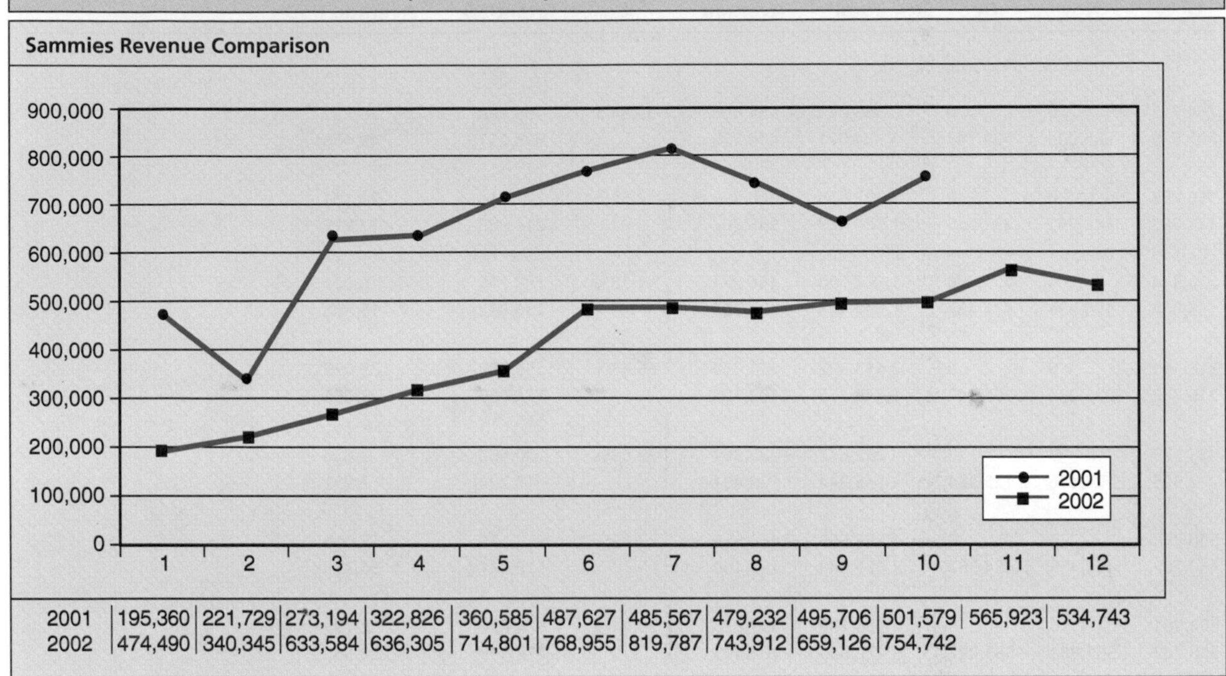

	1	2	3	4	5	6	7	8	9	10	11	12
2001	195,360	221,729	273,194	322,826	360,585	487,627	485,567	479,232	495,706	501,579	565,923	534,743
2002	474,490	340,345	633,584	636,305	714,801	768,955	819,787	743,912	659,126	754,742		

CASE 1D

"MAMMA MIA!" THE LITTLE SHOW THAT COULD!*

In the spring of 1988, Björn Ulvaeus, Benny Andersson, and Judy Craymer agreed that poor Broadway reviews marked the beginning of the end for "Chess." As the executive producer of the musical, Judy Craymer reflected on the recent failure and wondered what factors, other than the reviews, had contributed to "Chess's" Broadway failure. More immediate however was the question of how she was going to resurrect her career. As she left the project behind in search of new work, Craymer was convinced that there was a musical to be created out of the ABBA songs.

Almost a decade later, and after numerous attempts, Craymer finally received the approval of ABBA's Ulvaeus and Andersson to plan a musical based around their songs. By 2001, Craymer had flourishing productions of "Mamma Mia!" running in London, Toronto, and on tour across the United States. But even with this success, both Craymer and Ulvaeus were anxious about the show's fate once they decided to bring "Mamma Mia!" to Broadway in the fall of 2001. After all, bad reviews in New York 13 years earlier had caused their production of "Chess" to close after only 68 shows. Moreover, ABBA's music was more than 20 years old and consumer tastes in theater had undoubtedly changed in the new millennium. Another Broadway flop would likely wipe out the momentum behind the productions in Canada and on the road while also bringing 15 years of Craymer's hard work to an end. Was the idea of a show, surrounded and hyped by already existing songs, a solid business proposition? Would theatergoing audiences find merit in such a creation? Was risking the success of the other "Mamma Mia!" productions a sound decision?

The initial fears quickly subsided when "Mamma Mia!" tallied over $27 million in advance ticket sales prior to the October 18th opening, the second highest

Source: This case was prepared by Christopher Ferrarone under the supervision of Boston College Professor Gregory L. Stoller as the basis for class discussion rather than to illustrate either effective or ineffective handling of an administrative situation. This case was prepared entirely from existing, publicly available sources.

*Note: The phrase "The Little Show That Could" was coined by a member of the Las Vegas company.

advance sale ever on Broadway.[5] But even as ticket sales continued to break records, Craymer and Ulvaeus could not help but wonder why "Mamma Mia!" was having such great success while "Chess" had done so poorly. Moreover, as Craymer began to win awards and achieve recognition for the production, she wondered to what extent it mattered that she had not created anything "new." She questioned whether it was ABBA or she who deserved the accolades and whether the production would ever be considered on the same level as more traditional works such as "Les Miserables" or "Cats," the show that "Mamma Mia!" had just replaced at the Winter Garden Theater.[6]

ABBA

The ABBA history began in 1966 when Björn Ulvaeus and Benny Andersson first met. The two were singers in different bands; Björn in a musical group named the Hootenanny Singers and Benny in a group called the Hepstars. After the two became more acquainted with one another they began co-writing songs. As the decade progressed, they increased their collaborative efforts.

Three years later, in the spring of 1969, Björn and Benny met Agnetha Fältskog and Anni-Frid Lyngstad. At the time both women were mildly successful solo singers in Sweden. Eventually, Benny would marry Fältskog and Björn would marry Lyngstad and the quartet would become ABBA, an acronym of their first names.

In the early 1970s the group performed together as a cabaret act called "Festfolk." Mostly, the four covered a combination of existing music and humorous acts. It was quickly evident that audiences did not particularly enjoy the covered material; however, they did react positively to one of the group's original songs, "Hej gamle man." The team quickly put their efforts into creating a routine made up of their own material. In the spring of 1972 they recorded a song called "People Need Love," which was regarded as moderate hit.

In 1974, the group changed their name to ABBA and entered the Eurovision Song Contest with their song "Waterloo." The group won the contest and "Waterloo" consequently reached number one on the music charts across Europe, and attained a spot on the U.S. Top Ten.

Soon thereafter the group released the album entitled *Waterloo,* which became a huge hit in Sweden. From there, the group continued to work on their music, releasing numerous albums. However, it took nearly a year and a half before they obtained another worldwide hit. It ended up being the song, "SOS," taken off their third album, entitled *ABBA*. After "SOS," the group produced many hit singles throughout the 1970s:

Waterloo	No. 1 in April 1974
Ring Ring	No. 32 in July 1974
I Do I Do I Do I Do I Do	No. 38 in July 1975
SOS	No. 6 in September 1975
Mama Mia	No. 1 in December 1975
Fernando	No. 1 in March 1976
Dancing Queen	No. 1 in August 1976
Money Money Money	No. 3 in November 1976
Knowing Me Knowing You	No. 1 in February 1977
The Name of the Game	No. 1 in October 1977
Take a Chance on Me	No. 1 in February 1978
Summer Night City	No. 5 in September 1978
Chiquita	No. 2 in February 1979
Does Your Mother Know	No. 4 in May 1979
Angel Eyes/Voulez-Vous	No. 3 in July 1979
Gimme Gimme Gimme	No. 3 in October 1979
I Have a Dream	No. 2 in December 1979
The Winner Takes It All	No. 1 in August 1980
Super Trouper	No. 1 in November 1980

"Mamma Mia,"[i] also taken from the album *ABBA,* gave the group a number one spot on the British hit list, a feat that they were able to accomplish nine times between 1974 and 1980 (behind only The Beatles and Elvis). "Mamma Mia" was also a number one hit in Australia in 1975. Australia increasingly became one of ABBA's most successful regions where the group managed to release a total of six number one songs. An ABBA TV show even ran in Australia, drawing more viewers than the first moon landing.

As ABBA continued to rack up hit songs they began to release compilation albums filled with their most popular music. In 1976, ABBA released *Greatest Hits* and *The Best of ABBA*. These two albums contributed to the group's worldwide fame and helped them to achieve a number one rating in the U.S. with "Dancing Queen" in 1977 (which would be the only song ever reaching a

[i] "Mamma Mia" the song is separate from the musical "Mamma Mia!"

number one place on the U.S. charts). At one time during the late 1970s, only the automaker Volvo surpassed ABBA as Sweden's top export.

In late 1976, ABBA released its fourth album, *Arrival.* This was followed by concert tours in Europe the next year. The tour completely sold out and was consequently brought to Australia where the group decided to begin working on a film entitled "ABBA—The Movie."

In 1978 the group came to the United States on a promotional tour that preceded the release of their sixth album, *Voulez-Vous.* However, earlier in the year, Björn and Agnetha had announced their divorce. While the group remained determined to continue their work as ABBA, the news started rumors of the group's breakup.

In late 1979, the group released a second compilation album, *Greatest Hits Vol. 2* that coincided with a major tour of Canada, the United States, and Europe.

In March 1980, ABBA took their tour to Japan for what turned out to be one of their last live concerts. For the rest of the year, the group recorded the album *Super Trouper.*

In February 1981 Benny and Frida also announced their divorce. Many fans considered this the breakup of the group. Yet, the event did not stop the foursome from working together. At the end of the year, ABBA released their eighth album, *The Visitors.*[7]

"CHESS"

At the end of 1982, the group decided to take a break. Benny and Björn had tired of ABBA and were looking to branch out into musical theater. At the same time, Tim Rice was looking for someone to write the score for his musical, "Chess."

Working as a lyricist/producer, Rice reached fame by collaborating with producer Andrew Lloyd Webber in "Joseph and the Amazing Technicolor Dreamcoat" and "Jesus Christ Superstar," and was considered to be a musical pioneer in theater. As Rice pointed out:

> Doing shows on record first and without a book[ii] may have been things that Andrew [Lloyd Webber] and I pioneered, but we really did it by mistake. The only reason we recorded "Jesus Christ Superstar" first was because we couldn't get a theater deal. It had no book because we didn't know anyone who could write one. Geography had a lot to do with our success. Had we been in America, we would have been subject to the Broadway tradition. But because we were so far away we felt there was no need to follow any rules. After the Beatles, anybody with ambitions to write songs went into records and performing. But since we weren't performers and since Andrew loved theater so much, we took all our favorite rock things and used them in our scores. As with the Beatles, it finally wasn't brilliant thinking so much as luck that made us so successful. We happened to be in the right place at the right time.[8]

Rice's reputation, and the work that he was doing (he has since been a major part of productions such as "Evita," "Aladdin," "Beauty and the Beast," "The Lion King," and "Aida") turned out to be an instant draw for Benny and Björn. They immediately signed on to the project.

Using the world of international chess as a metaphor, Tim Rice conceived to write a musical about how the Cold War affected the lives of all those it touched. The story follows an international chess match from Bangkok to Budapest. The plot revolves around Florence, a Hungarian-born woman who works as an assistant for the upstart American challenger, Freddie. Freddie is jointly modeled after Bobby Fischer and the tennis star John McEnroe. In the middle of the match with the Russian champion, Anatoly, the American precipitates a dispute. As the match seems about to fall apart, Florence, attempting to intercede, meets and falls in love with the Russian, who promptly decides to defect to the West. When the Russians pressure Anatoly to change his mind, he becomes the focus of an international tug of war.

Rice originally approached Andrew Lloyd Webber to write the score, but his former partner was already committed to other projects. Then, in 1981, producer Richard Vos introduced Rice to Benny Andersson and Björn Ulvaeus. The team immediately set about creating a concept album. Two numbers did well in the charts. "One Night in Bangkok" first appeared on the U.K. charts on November 10, 1984, and stayed there for 13 weeks, at one point reaching #12. In the U.S., it jumped to #9 in April of 1985 and topped the charts in France, Australia, Belgium, Austria, South Africa, Denmark, Israel, West Germany, Switzerland, Holland, and Sweden. Another single, "I Know Him So Well" followed, eventually reaching #1 on the U.K. charts during its 16 week run. With "Chess" already a worldwide phenomenon before it had even opened, expectations were high. The London production team of Tim Rice, Judy Craymer, Andersson, and Ulvaeus brought the show to

[ii]A "book" is the baseline story behind the production and is similar to a screenplay for a movie.

the West End[iii] on May 14, 1986, where it ran for three years. However, the high tech spectacle never garnered a lot of interest from London's theatergoers and failed to make back its initial investment. The production team, still believing in the project, decided to bring the show to Broadway.

The show was drastically altered before moving to Broadway. Instead of having the performance completely sung-through[iv] as it had been in London, director Trevor Nunn chose to bring in playwright Richard Nelson to write a book. Rice also added several new songs including "Someone Else's Story."

The Broadway production opened at the Imperial Theater on April 28, 1988, with an entirely new cast. With a poor review from *The New York Times* leading to a series of unfavorable criticisms, the show proved even less of a commercial success than its predecessor, losing $6 million and closing after only 68 performances. A later concert, however, which featured the Broadway cast at Carnegie Hall, was a huge hit.[9]

The concert was a bittersweet end to the "Chess" story for Björn Ulvaeus:

> We weren't surprised, in one sense that "Chess" failed because the bad review in *The New York Times* came right after our run in the West End and we were already losing steam. The songs were hits four years earlier and their popularity was not recent enough to carry us through [the bad review]. But we were very proud of it—the music and lyrics and everything.[10]

Where the "Chess" episode did succeed, however, was in bringing Ulvaeus and Andersson into the world of theater, offering the duo a unique platform for continuing their love of composing while also offering them a fresh start.

LONDON THEATER

London Theater falls into three broad and sometimes overlapping categories—West End, National Repertory Companies, and Off-West End/Fringe—terms analogous to Broadway, Regional Theater, and Off-Broadway in the United States.

Geographically, the West End encompasses a two square mile section of London in the vicinity of Leicester Square, Piccadilly, and Covent Garden, where more than 40 "picture frame" theaters, most dating from the Victorian and Edwardian eras, are clustered. These are commercial theaters in which producers present shows with the expectation of making a profit.

The most prestigious groups of British theater are the two national repertory companies that enjoy the support of government subsidies through the Arts Council, as well as through their huge ticket sales.

The Royal National Theater, located in a three-stage complex on the South Bank, and the Royal Shakespeare Company (RSC), with stages in London at the Barbican Center and in Stratford-upon-Avon, are large companies of actors, directors, and technicians who produce a formidable number of plays in repertory throughout the year.

On these stages, audiences see performances of the highest quality, made possible by conditions not often met in commercial theater: longer rehearsal periods, freedom to commit to new work and innovative approaches, support from expert voice coaches, the security of a firmly scheduled run, and, most significantly, the devotion of seasoned British actors who return to these companies throughout their careers. In these venues, as well, audiences discover emerging actors, directors, and designers who are about to become the leading figures of British theater, film, and television.

At any one time, there are around 70 small, so-called Fringe theaters operating in pubs, warehouses, and a few purpose-built theaters in and around London. They constitute the breeding ground from which the rising generation of British actors, directors, playwrights, and designers emerge and to which seasoned theater artists occasionally return in order to be able to see and do cutting-edge work.

Cross-fertilization from the subsidized companies and the varied Off-West End and Fringe theaters to the commercial West End accounts for the high productivity of the entire British theater. Major productions from the National or the RSC are sometimes picked up by a commercial producer for long runs in the West End. The repertory company benefits from extended royalties, sometimes many years' worth, as in the case of the RSC's "Les Miserables." That show opened at the Barbican Theater in 1985 and soon transferred under commercial sponsorship to the Palace, where it continued to run through May 2003. The West End producer benefits from getting a production that has already demonstrated it "has legs" and will go on attracting audiences when its limited repertory run is over.

The work of the Off-West End and Fringe sector is an important aspect of British theater. These companies

[iii] London's version of Broadway.

[iv] All dialogue and character lines in musical verse.

cultivate audiences for a wide range of new work and new talent. As a result, in London, a high number of very young directors and writers get opportunities for significant careers. Productions from these theaters sometimes transfer to the commercial West End, as in the case of the 1992 production "Medea," which went on to a long run in the West End and then played on Broadway.

Judy Craymer

With a pedigree in London theater including working for the likes of Tim Rice, Cameron Mackintosh, and Andrew Lloyd Webber on productions of "Cats," "Les Miserables," "Phantom of the Opera," and "Miss Saigon," Craymer was well known throughout the theater production world. This reputation suffered with her work on "Chess" but ultimately allowed her to continue on her quest to produce an ABBA musical.

From the time "Chess" closed down in 1988, Craymer worked to make her idea of an all-ABBA musical a reality. She was convinced that there was a theatrical performance behind the songs of ABBA and would toil for 10 years on the project, selling her house and eventually squatting in her office in order to keep the project alive.[11]

It was her determination and passion that persuaded ABBA's Benny Andersson and Björn Ulvaeus to "take a chance" and let her hire writer Catherine Johnson and director Phyllida Lloyd and create "Mamma Mia!" Johnson remarked:

> Benny and Björn didn't think it was such a great idea at first, because they had really moved away from ABBA, but Judy pursued this concept with them for 10 years. Finally Björn told Judy that if she found a writer who could come up with a story everyone is keen on, then she could go ahead with the project.[12]

Catherine Johnson

In 1997, after finally getting the go-ahead from Benny and Björn to create a story, Craymer found Catherine Johnson, a single, nearly broke, mother of two. The two women worked on a script from opposite ends of England, each taking the train half way to save money in order to conduct meetings with each other. There was a lot of collaboration and work on the book as it was the key to getting ABBA's consent on the whole project. As Johnson pointed out:

> Judy Craymer conceived the original idea in 1988 when she was working on "Chess" with Björn and Benny, but it took her ever so long to come up with a writer. I came on board when she was working with a director that I once worked with. She told him about the project and he suggested me. It was very fortunate because I hadn't heard of it and it certainly wouldn't have been something I would have thought of doing.[13]

For Ulvaeus and Andersson, the story was what would either make or break the project. They had told Craymer that they wanted the plot to be the first and foremost priority, with the music coming in afterward to help the narrative. As Ulvaeus pointed out:

> I said to Catherine, "We have a catalog of 95 to 100 ABBA songs, and you can choose whatever you like, not just the hits." I told her, "The story is more important than the songs." I saw this as a challenge and an experiment, and was ready to call it off at any point. In the end what I saw was a seamless story, not something that would make you say, "They've shoe-horned the songs in."[14]

Johnson's story follows a 20-year-old, Sophie, on the eve of her wedding. Sophie has been raised by her mother, Donna, on a Greek island without ever knowing her father. Eager to have him walk her down the aisle, Sophie tracks down the three probable candidates based on her mother's youthful indiscretions and secretly invites each of them to the wedding. She confronts her potential dads but none of them seems to be the right one. As the plot moves along, complications arise among the characters, most notably with her mother, who is forced to confront her past. There are many other secondary characters that add to the stereotypes and humorous situations that come about. All of the action is carried along and highlighted by 22 ABBA songs mixed throughout the performance.

Phyllida Lloyd

Once the story was completed, Craymer and Ulvaeus brought director Phyllida Lloyd onto the project. Renowned for her work at England's Royal National Theater and on international opera productions, Lloyd helped the project gather further momentum. She was behind the assembly of the creative team of Mark Thompson (design), Howard Harrison (lighting), Andrew Bruce and Bobby Aitken (sound), Martin Koch (musical supervisor), and Anthony Van Laast (choreography) who were credited with making the show as successful as it was. As Lloyd told the actors involved in an early workshop: "'Mamma Mia!' is the musical Benny and Bjorn wrote years ago. They just decided to release the songs first."[15]

THE ROAD SHOW

Traditionally, Broadway had been the proving ground for most large-scale theatrical productions known as equity productions, with the "equity" referring to the large amounts of money needed to produce fancy, glamorous shows. These performances are a large draw for audiences.

During the 1998–99 season more than 11.6 million people attended a show on Broadway. This amounted to over $588 million in gross ticket sales. Of those shows, the ones that realized success then sent touring companies on the road. During the same season, these touring companies brought shows to over 100 U.S. cities and sold tickets to 14.6 million people, yielding $707 million in "road grossed"[16] receipts. That represents nearly 55 percent of the industry's combined $1.3 billion take in New York and on the road.

As such, road shows today are big business and have a rather involved process. Every road show starts with the producer who then hires a booking agent, whose job it is to contact presenters at theaters across the country and "book" the production into their theaters for specific weeks during the season. Presenters range from entrepreneurs who rent theaters, to performing arts organizations and municipalities who own and operate their own locales and venues.

In many cases, production companies search for shows that they are interested in booking. For the popular musicals it is not uncommon for bidding wars to take place among production companies looking to take the show on the road. Sometimes the original Broadway producers even take their own shows on the road themselves.

Once the decision to take a performance on the road has been made, the booking agent, in concert with the producer or production company, decides where to take it and how long to stay at certain locations. For the large productions, surveys and marketing data are collected and analyzed to aid in this process of deciding the best travel destinations. In some cases, the size of the venue or city determines how long a run the show will have.[17]

From there, producers negotiate guarantees[v] with presenters. This amount, coupled with the show's capitalization and weekly expenditure requirements, ultimately determines how many weeks the production must be on the road for. Of course, the producers always also get a percentage of the box office receipts above and beyond the guarantee.[vi]

[v]A "guarantee" is the weekly figure the presenter promises to pay the producer no matter what the box office intake happens to be.

[vi]This percentage is typically around 40%.

Originally, road shows were non-equity or bus-and-truck[vii] versions of the Broadway originals, and were dramatically scaled down productions with fewer, less known actors and simpler sets. This trend changed however in the late 1970s. Some credit English producer Cameron Mackintosh with these changes. Mackintosh produced "Miss Saigon," "Cats," "Les Miserables," and "Phantom of the Opera." When he started, the "road" was primarily made up of the bus-and-truck variety. However, Mackintosh did not want to do that with "Les Miserables":

> When I first put "Les Miz" out I was not going to cut corners in any way. I wanted to give audiences the same show that they would see on Broadway. And the combination of my four big shows completely changed the standards of the road.[18]

These productions sent box-office receipts soaring and resulted in theaters upgrading their facilities and cities even building state-of-the-art performing arts centers to take advantage of the blockbusters. In order to be profitable, these productions required multi-week stays at a minimum. However, in the absence of blockbuster productions, and proportionally scaled down ticket prices, few patrons ended up filling the seats.[19] As such, the manner in which road shows are produced has tended to change as the popularity of theater has cycled.

TAKING "MAMMA MIA!" ON THE ROAD

In total, Craymer was able to fund the first production of "Mamma Mia!" with $4.8 million.[20] In 1999, "Mamma Mia!" debuted in London's Prince Edward Theater and was met by rave reviews from fans. Once the show opened, it took fewer than 27 weeks for Craymer to make back the initial investment. The show has continued to have advance ticket sales of more than $6.5 million through 2003.

Very little advertising was done as Craymer relied on word-of-mouth advertising for nearly two years. As the show proved capable of delivering a return for investors, the decision for Craymer was not whether to take the act to North America, but rather how. The costs for a large-scale production were immense, particularly if the group was going to tour through Canada and the U.S. However, a scaled down production could result in poor ticket sales and reviews, and could stop a tour before it was able to gain any momentum. Craymer was able to put this decision off, at least for a few months.

[vii]The term "bus-and-truck" comes from the way in which sets, actors, musicians, etc., were carted around the country. Typically, these shows have runs at theaters for no more than a week or two.

In May of 2000, the group brought the show to Toronto's Princess of Wales Theater where it planned a 6-month stay before going on the road across the U.S. A full-scale production, Craymer believed, would draw audiences and positive reviews while the extended stay would serve as insurance if the production failed to live up to expectations. In short, future road shows in the U.S. could be cancelled without incurring the large up-front costs of a full-scale tour. While Craymer believed the strategy was sound, she ultimately altered the plans to take advantage of the situation:

> Our strategy was to see if it worked in London, and it did. Then we had the opportunity to go to Toronto for six months, and the bookings were so positive that they suggested we stay in Toronto and create a new touring company in the United States.[21]

In fact, two touring companies were created and "Mamma Mia!" brought productions to Buffalo, Atlanta, Cincinnati, Columbus, Charlotte, Louisville, Norfolk, Pittsburgh, Providence, Memphis, Miami, Nashville, Rochester, and Tampa.[22]

As the touring companies performed across the U.S. and the Toronto and London productions continued to sell out, Craymer and the production team slowly edged closer to bringing the show to Broadway. Hype for the musical was built slowly by word-of-mouth and the producers continued to use little advertising. Craymer explained:

> After the first London preview, the audience came out of the theater, got on their cell phones and called their friends, saying, "You've just got to come see this." That's the effect we wanted to create before we came to Broadway.[23]

"Mamma Mia!" proved popular enough to sustain multi-week runs on the road without the usual publicity of a successful Broadway run. In its first 18 months, "Mamma Mia!" had proved a hit at every major theatrical level except Broadway.

With the four "Mamma Mia!" productions performing at once, three of which were in North America, Benny, Björn, and Craymer decided to finally take the plunge, and return ABBA to the world of Broadway.

BROADWAY

As soon as Ulvaeus and Andersson gave her the go-ahead, Judy Craymer began planning for the "Mamma Mia!" Broadway debut. It proved to be a long, hard fought battle. Craymer recalls:

> The whole thing started 12 years before we would bring the show to New York. I used to go home and listen to ABBA records, dreaming of songs as part of a Broadway musical. When we finally got the show together there was no way that Benny and Björn would let it go straight to Broadway because of "Chess."[24]

Because of Benny and Björn's stance, Craymer began devising alternative ways to bring the show to the U.S:

> London and Europe were never going to be problems; everyone knew ABBA. It was getting the show to The States that I worried about. We couldn't bring it right to Broadway and when I came up with the strategy of building interest through a tour, people told me that it would never be successful unless it was a Broadway-branded production. Either way, the stakes were quite high; I just kind of followed my heart and instincts.[25]

As skeptics quickly discovered, the tour was a huge success and the word-of-mouth strategy had proved successful as each new tour location routinely sold out prior to opening night. The financial returns were further magnified by the reduced need for advertising. Moreover, to the delight of Craymer and Ulvaeus, as "Mamma Mia!" got closer and closer to Broadway, advance sales began racking up. Officially, "Mamma Mia!" sold over $27 million worth of tickets before opening night. The production team could not have been happier; they had achieved all of their goals and had the momentum to roll over any poor review.

This momentum, however, came to a violent stop a little over a month before opening night, when the World Trade Center was attacked. At first there was little thought about her own problem as Craymer worried for the actors who were rehearsing in studios close to ground zero. As a few days passed and when it was determined that everyone involved was safe, Ulvaeus and Craymer asked themselves, "Can we really go on with this?"[26] They questioned whether or not it would be appropriate to stage such an exuberant show amidst the intense mourning of an entire city. Very quickly they made the decision to carry on. Ulvaeus pointed out:

> At first I did not know what to do. I did not know if our feel-good music and text would strike the right chord. But then what was said by many people and by Mayor Giuliani especially made sense to me: [NewYorkers] needed to see people coming here from the outside and doing things, moving ahead. This is how you fight back; this is how you don't give in. I thought: May be we're meant to be here to do this show for people, now of all times.[27]

Judy Craymer agreed:

> Many of the cast had seen it happen, because the rehearsal rooms are downtown. I was just off to the dentist when I saw it on television. But to have withdrawn would have been a huge psychological blow to New York. Having seen a preview performance, I think the show had come at exactly the right time. The audience was on its feet dancing at the end.[28]

The recession and loss of tourists from September 11th cost most shows millions of dollars, closed a myriad of productions, and threatened a number more. "Mamma Mia!" however, proved to be somewhat immune. The Broadway version cost $10 million to produce and was able to recoup its entire investment in just six months. The show played to near sell-outs for the first two years breaking all kinds of box-office records along the way. The show not only gave a boost to Broadway but also to the community, and in addition raised nearly $500,000 for the attack victims' families.

"MAMMA MIA!" THE CORPORATION

The success on Broadway helped the production company expand its reach around the world. Before Broadway there were productions of "Mamma Mia!" running in London, Toronto, and touring the United States. A second U.S. tour opened in Providence, R.I., in February of 2001, playing shorter runs in many cities. A third production was opened in Melbourne, Australia.

With six productions of the show performing concurrently worldwide, Craymer began licensing the show to production companies in other countries, where it was translated into different languages. The first foreign show to start was a German version in Hamburg, in November 2002. A second production in Japanese began in December 2002. A third and fourth opened shortly thereafter in Moscow and Madrid. According to Craymer, "'Mamma Mia!' has become a corporation in a sense; it had turned into a sizable organization running shows all over the world.[29]

By the end of 2002, the globalwide phenomenon had grossed more than $400 million with a one-day box office record in London of $831,000 in ticket sales. While the numbers suggest a well thought out business plan combined with experienced market-savvy, Craymer calls the success "A sheer fluke," and Ulvaeus agreed:

> I thought when we split up in 1981, that it was the end of it. I thought I would hardly hear ABBA again. I have no idea why all this is happening and why the music is so much [more present now].[30]

While Craymer's realization of an ABBA inspired musical had exceeded her dreams, she and Ulvaeus were still not certain as to why the results of "Chess" and "Mamma Mia!" had differed to such a great extent. Unlike "Chess," "Mamma Mia!" had started with a loose concept and ended up a worldwide sensation. Along the way it had overcome skeptics, poor reviews which had similarly sunk "Mamma Mia"'s predecessor, and even September 11th. They wondered how their original, simple business plan had morphed into a 9-production sensation employing over 700 people.

THE BUSINESS OF "MAMMA MIA!"

Critics from both inside and outside performing arts circles have heavily debated the run of "Mamma Mia!" While a great deal of criticism subsided when the show became an unabashed success, some still continue to question whether the production team's accolades are warranted, since nothing "new" has really been created with the exception of a story-line around some old hit songs.

The question ultimately centers on how theater, and its broader category of the performing arts, is classified by business analysts and the world around them. Are plays, musicals, and productions merely another avenue through which to make money, or are other metrics such as creative expression the true return-on-investment? Are these types of ventures managed like "traditional businesses," with a projected profit motive, or is performance quality emphasized above all else? Perhaps it's a combination of the two approaches that matters to producers, directors and choreographers alike. . . .

Additionally, where does "Mamma Mia!" stand when compared with Broadway classics like "Les Miserables," "Miss Saigon," and "Cats"? Can those who come up with something new in theater be considered entrepreneurs? What about people like Craymer, who simply bring existing material into a new arena? Is she an entrepreneur? Is the success of "Mamma Mia!" attributable to skill and business acumen, or was it a "fluke"?

In the end, does it really matter to Craymer, her critics, and the many fans?

END NOTES

1. www.micromash.net.
2. www.cpazone.org.
3. www.picpa.org.
4. Beijing Sammies is the name of the entire company, while "a Sammies" is a particular café.
5. Marcus Tustin, www.abbamail.com/mamma_bwy_variety.htm (accessed July 2003).
6. Ibid.
7. www.abbasite.com (accessed July 2003).
8. Stephen Holden, "'Chess' Seeks to Shed Its Checkered Past," *The New York Times* (April 24, 1998).
9. www.abbasite.com, op. cit.
10. Roy Proctor, "ABBA Cadabra It's 'Mamma Mia!'" *Richmond Times Dispatch* (February 9, 2003).
11. John Moore, "Viva ABBA! Three Women's Dream Changes Face of Theater," *Denver Post* (November 24, 2002).
12. Ibid.
13. Ibid.
14. Proctor, op. cit.
15. www.playbill.com (accessed July 2003).
16. Steven Winn, "Paying Big Bucks and Getting Shortchanged," *San Francisco Chronicle* (January 23, 2000).
17. Bruce Lazarus, "Getting Your Act Together and Taking It on the Road," *Producer's Corner* (accessed July 2003).
18. "Looking Out on a Different Broadway" (October 26, 2002), www.ctnow.com.
19. Ibid.
20. Tustin, op. cit.
21. Moore, op. cit.
22. Tom Buckhan, "'Mamma Mia!' Proves a Record Crowd Pleaser," *Buffalo News* (January 18, 2003).
23. Frank Rizzo, "Mamma Mia!" *Hartford Courant* (November 3, 2003).
24. Miriam Souccar, "Dancing Queen; 'Mamma Mia!' Charms in Broadway Slump," *Crain's NY Business* (December 17, 2001).
25. Ibid.
26. Janet Maslin, "Trying to Make ABBA's Oldies Young Again," *The New York Times* (October 14, 2001).
27. Ibid.
28. Ibid.
29. "Mamma Mia!" *Associated Press* (October 28, 2002).
30. www.playbill.com, op. cit.

CREATING AND STARTING THE VENTURE

5

CREATIVITY, THE BUSINESS IDEA, AND OPPORTUNITY ANALYSIS

LEARNING OBJECTIVES

1
To identify various sources of ideas for new ventures.

2
To discuss methods available for generating new venture ideas.

3
To discuss creativity and the techniques for creative problem solving.

4
To discuss the importance of innovation.

5
To understand an opportunity analysis plan.

6
To discuss the aspects of the product planning and development process.

7
To discuss aspects of e-commerce and starting an e-commerce business.

OPENING PROFILE

FREDERICK W. SMITH

www.fedex.com

Who would think that an entrepreneur with a $10 million inheritance would need more capital to get his company off the ground? The business world is filled with stories of companies, large and small, that started in a garage with an initial investment of a few hundred dollars. But none of those companies needed a nationwide distribution system in place, complete with a fleet of airplanes and trucks, before accepting its first order. And none of those garage start-ups grew to be Federal Express.

Frederick W. Smith, a Memphis native whose father made his fortune in founding a bus company, conceived of the idea for his air-cargo company while studying economics at Yale University in the 1960s. The professor of one of Smith's classes was a staunch supporter of the current system of air freight handling in which a cargo package literally hitched a ride in any unused space on a passenger flight. Fred Smith saw things differently and, in a paper, described the concept of a freight-only airline that would fly all packages to one central point, where they would then be distributed and flown out again to their destinations. This operation could take place at night when the airports were less crowded, and, with proper logistics control, the packages could be delivered the next day. Whether it was the novelty of the idea, the fact that it went against the professor's theories, or the fact that it was written in one night and was turned in late, the first public display of Smith's grand idea earned him a C.

Smith's idea constituted far more than a concept for a creative term paper, however. He had seen how the technological base of the country was changing. More companies were becoming involved in the production and use of small, expensive items such as computers, and Smith was convinced that businesses could use his air-cargo idea to control their inventory costs. Overnight delivery from a single distribution center to anywhere in the country could satisfy customers' needs without a company needing a duplicate investment in inventory to be stored in regional warehouses. Smith even thought of the Federal Reserve Banks as a potential customer with the vast quantities of checks that had to be delivered to all parts of the country every day. But the Vietnam War and a family history of patriotic service intervened. Smith joined the Marine Corps and was sent to Vietnam, first as a platoon leader and then as a pilot.

After nearly four years of service and 200 ground support missions as a pilot, he left Vietnam, ready to start building something. He went to work with his stepfather, first managing and subsequently purchasing a controlling interest in Arkansas Aviation Sales, a struggling aircraft modification and overhaul shop. Difficulty in getting parts to the shop in Little Rock, Arkansas, revived his interest in the air-cargo concept. He commissioned two feasibility studies, both of which returned favorable results based on a high initial investment. The key to this company would be its ability to serve a large segment of the business community from the very beginning, and the key to the required level of service was cash. Full of optimism, Smith went to Chicago and New York, confident that he would be returning with basket loads of investment checks. Progress turned out to be slower than Smith had anticipated, but through his boundless energy, belief in his idea, and technical knowledge of the air freight field, he was finally able to get enthusiastic backing (around $5 million in capital) from New Court Securities, a Manhattan-based, Rothschild-backed venture-capital investment bank. This commitment from New Court spurred substantial additional financing. Five other institutions, including General Dynamics and Citicorp Venture Capital, Ltd., got involved, and Smith went back to Memphis with $72 million. This was the largest venture-capital start-up deal in the history of American business.

Federal Express took to the skies on March 12, 1973, to test its service. Servicing an11-city network (extending from Dallas to Cincinnati), it initially shipped only six packages. On the night of April 17, the official start-up of Federal Express, the network had been expanded to include 25 cities (from Rochester, New York, to Miami, Florida), shipping a total of 186 packages. Volume picked up rapidly and service was expanded; it looked as though Federal Express was a true overnight success. Smith's understanding of a market need had been accurate, but he had not counted on OPEC causing a massive inflation of fuel costs just as his company was getting started. By mid-1974, the company was losing more than $1 million a month. His investors were not willing to keep the company going, and his relatives were suing him for mismanaging the family fortune (nearly $10 million of Smith money was invested). But Smith never lost faith in his idea and finally won enough converts in the investment community to keep the doors open long enough to straighten out the pricing problems caused by OPEC.

After losing $27 million in the first two years, Federal Express turned a profit of $3.6 million in 1976. The development and growth of Federal Express were tightly regulated. Due to old laws designed to protect the early pioneers of the passenger airline industry, Smith was required to obtain approval for operating any aircraft with a payload in excess of 7,500 pounds. Since the major airlines—at the time, the giants of the industry—were not ready to share the cargo market, he was not able to obtain this needed approval and had to operate a fleet of small Falcon jets instead. While this situation worked well at start-up, by 1977 his operation had reached the capacity of these smaller planes. Since the company was already flying several planes on the most active routes, it did not make sense to buy more Falcons. Smith took his salesmanship to Washington and, with the help of a grassroots Federal Express employee effort, was able to obtain legislation creating a new class of all-cargo carriers. This gave Smith the operating latitude he needed.

Although Smith had the approval to operate large jets, he needed to find a way to purchase them. The corporate balance sheet of the company was still a mess from early losses, and the long-suffering early investors needed some reward. Smith took his company public on April 12, 1978, raising enough money to purchase used Boeing 727s from ailing passenger airlines. The investors were indeed richly rewarded, with General Dynamics watching its $5 million grow to more than $40 million by the time Federal Express was first traded on the New York Stock Exchange in December 1978. The company has continued to perform well since its public offering, combining technical innovation and an obsession with customer orientation (Federal Express was the first company to win the Malcolm Baldrige National Quality Award in the service category, and in 1994 it became the first global express transportation company to receive simultaneous worldwide ISO 9001 certification) to ensure exceptional growth.

Since 2002, with sales revenue of $20.6 billion and the company's first-in-its-history cash dividend, FedEx has continued to grow. By the end of 2005, the company had grown into a $31 billion network of companies, offering just the right mix of transportation, e-commerce, and business solutions. FedEx is composed of Federal Express, FedEx Ground, FedEx Freight, FedEx Kinko's Office and Print Services, FedEx Customer Critical, FedEx Trade Networks, FedEx Supply Chain Services, and FedEx Services. In 2005, FedEx averaged: (1) more than 6 million shipments for express, ground, freight, and expedited delivery services a day; (2) more than 260,000 employees and contractors worldwide; and (3) more than 220 countries and territories, including every address in the United States.

The company has over 15 million visitors monthly and processes more than 3 million tracking requests daily. There are more than 15 million packages shipped via FedEx Ship Manager monthly and 677 aircraft serving more than 375 airports worldwide. FedEx has: more than 70,000 motorized vehicles for express, ground, freight, and expedited delivery service; 715 FedEx World Service Centers; 1,281 FedEx Kinko's Office and Print Centers; 7,524 FedEx Authorized ShipCenters®; and 41,643 FedEx Drop Boxes (including 4,990 U.S. Postal Service locations). The firm's stock price is about $98 per share—up from $45 per share in the past five years.

At the heart of Frederick Smith's success story is the creativity and uniqueness of the initial business concept. This part of the new venture creation process is perhaps the most difficult to actualize. What specific features does the new product or service need? A wide variety of techniques can be used to obtain the new product idea. Smith expressed his original idea in a paper he wrote to complete a college course. For others—such as Bob Reis of Final Technology, Inc., and Frank Perdue of Perdue Chickens—the idea came from work experience. No matter how it occurs, a sound unique idea for a new product (or service), properly evaluated, is essential to successfully launching a new venture. Throughout this evaluation, or opportunity analysis, the entrepreneur must remember that most ideas do *not* provide the basis for a new venture; rather, it is important to sift through and identify those ideas that *can* provide such a basis, so that they can be the entrepreneur's focus.

SOURCES OF NEW IDEAS

Some of the more frequently used sources of ideas for entrepreneurs include: consumers, existing products and services, distribution channels, the federal government, and research and development.

Consumers

Potential entrepreneurs should continually pay close attention to potential customers. This attention can take the form of informally monitoring potential ideas and needs or formally arranging for consumers to have an opportunity to express their opinions. Care needs to be taken to ensure that the idea or need represents a large enough market to support a new venture.

Existing Products and Services

Potential entrepreneurs should also establish a formal method for monitoring and evaluating competitive products and services on the market. Frequently, this analysis uncovers ways to improve on these offerings that may result in a new product or service that has more market appeal and better sales and profit potential.

Distribution Channels

Members of the distribution channels are also excellent sources for new ideas because of their familiarity with the needs of the market. Not only do channel members frequently have suggestions for completely new products, but they can also help in marketing the entrepreneur's newly developed products. One entrepreneur found out from a salesclerk in a large department store that the reason his hosiery was not selling well was its color. By heeding the suggestion and making the appropriate color changes, his company became one of the leading suppliers of nonbrand hosiery in that region of the United States.

Federal Government

The federal government can be a source of new product ideas in two ways. First, the files of the Patent Office contain numerous new product possibilities. Although the patents themselves may not be feasible, they can frequently suggest other more marketable product ideas. Several government agencies and publications are helpful in monitoring patent applications. The *Official Gazette,* published weekly by the U.S. Patent Office, summarizes each patent granted and lists all patents available for license or sale. Also, the Government Patents Board publishes lists of abstracts of thousands of government-owned patents; a good resource of such information is the *Government-Owned Inventories Available for License.* Other government agencies, such as the Office of Technical Services, assist entrepreneurs in obtaining specific product information.

Second, new product ideas can come in response to government regulations. For example, the Occupational Safety and Health Act (OSHA) mandated that first-aid kits be available in business establishments employing more than three people. The kits had to contain specific items that varied according to the company and the industry. The weatherproofed first-aid kit needed for a construction company had to be different from the one needed by a company manufacturing facial cream or a company in retail trade. In response to OSHA, both established and newly formed ventures marketed a wide variety

AS SEEN IN *ENTREPRENEUR* MAGAZINE

PROVIDE ADVICE TO AN ENTREPRENEUR ABOUT BECOMING MORE CREATIVE

You have decided to build a creatively agile company based on a firm belief that creativity will help you and your company thrive . . . or you're a skeptic who, nonetheless, is willing to give it a try. In either case, experience is the best teacher. Begin by experimenting.

Learning how to be more creative is like learning any skill: You gain expertise over time. Starting small can help deal with skepticism among the staff and your own uncertainty. Begin by trying some techniques by yourself or with a few colleagues. By practicing creative techniques and attitudes, you'll gain the confidence and skill to build a company that includes everyone in its creative practice. Remember the goal is always to find a way to tap the creativity of everyone in your company.

I've used the following exercise many times because it's simple yet evocative. Making a collage from magazine images is a great prompt for new ideas. It's nonthreatening because everyone can tear pictures out of magazines and arrange them—and it's fun because you get to make a mess. Decide on the issue or problem that needs some fresh thinking or new solutions. It should be clearly defined before beginning to let the collage spark ideas and associations. If you identify the most fundamental issue before you begin, the ideas that emerge will be more useful. You can pose the question or problem before or after you have collected the images. Experiment with what works best for you.

Give yourself or your group five minutes to look through the magazines and tear out images that speak to you. They don't have to be related to the problem you're trying to solve. Arrange your images by pasting them on a background or just on the surface in front of you. If you're doing this with others, share your thoughts and associations. Have a discussion about the meaning of the collage as a whole and also the relationship of the individual images within the collage. Why, for example, is one image in the center and another on the edge? Are the images active or reflective? Do the images show nature or cityscapes? The choice of images will help you identify what has meaning for you as well as spark new thinking about the issue under consideration. This simple exercise will surprise you with the depth and amount of ideas it can generate.

ADVICE TO AN ENTREPRENEUR

An inventor has read the above article and comes to you for advice:

> I want to spur creativity and innovation in my organization, but I fear that if I bring in magazines and suggest we start ripping out pictures, they will think that I have gone nuts.

1. Does thinking outside the box always feel a little uncomfortable?
2. How can I get others to take it seriously?
3. What other creativity techniques would you recommend?

Source: Reprinted with permission of Entrepreneur Media, Inc., "Food for Thought. Creativity Is an Acquired Taste, So Start Your Company Off with Small Bites," by Juanita Weaver, March 2003, *Entrepreneur* magazine: www.entrepeneur.com.

of first-aid kits. One newly formed company, R&H Safety Sales Company, was successful in developing and selling first-aid kits that allowed companies to comply with the standards of the act.

Research and Development

The largest source of new ideas is the entrepreneur's own "research and development" efforts, which may be a formal endeavor connected with one's current employment or an informal lab in a basement or garage. One research scientist in a Fortune 500 company developed a new plastic resin that became the basis of a new product, a plastic molded modular cup pallet, as well as a new venture—the Arnolite Pallet Company, Inc.—when the Fortune 500 company was not interested in developing the idea.

METHODS OF GENERATING IDEAS

Even with such a wide variety of sources of ideas available, coming up with an idea to serve as the basis for a new venture can still pose a problem. The entrepreneur can use several methods to help generate and test new ideas, such as: focus groups, brainstorming, and problem inventory analysis.

Focus Groups

focus groups Groups of individuals providing information in a structured format

Focus groups have been used for a variety of purposes since the 1950s. A moderator leads a group of people through an open, in-depth discussion rather than simply asking questions to solicit participant response. For a new product area, the moderator focuses the discussion of the group in either a directive or a nondirective manner. The group of 8 to 14 participants is stimulated by comments from other group members in creatively conceptualizing and developing a new product idea to fill a market need. One company interested in the women's slipper market received its new product concept for a "warm and comfortable slipper that fits like an old shoe" from a focus group of 12 women from various socioeconomic backgrounds in the Boston area. The concept was developed into a new women's slipper that was a market success. Even the theme of the advertising message came from comments of focus group members.

In addition to generating new ideas, the focus group is an excellent method for initially screening ideas and concepts. With the use of one of several procedures available, the results can be analyzed more quantitatively, making the focus group a useful method for generating new product ideas.[1]

Brainstorming

brainstorming A group method for obtaining new ideas and solutions

The *brainstorming* method allows people to be stimulated to greater creativity by meeting with others and participating in organized group experiences. Although most of the ideas generated from the group have no basis for further development, sometimes a good idea emerges. This has a greater frequency of occurrence when the brainstorming effort focuses on a specific product or market area. When using brainstorming, these four rules should be followed:

1. No criticism is allowed by anyone in the group—no negative comments.
2. Freewheeling is encouraged—the wilder the idea, the better.
3. Quantity of ideas is desired—the greater the number of ideas, the greater the likelihood of the emergence of useful ideas.
4. Combinations and improvements of ideas are encouraged; ideas of others can be used to produce still another new idea.

The brainstorming session should be fun, with no one dominating or inhibiting the discussion.

A large commercial bank successfully used brainstorming to develop a journal that would provide quality information to its industrial clients. The brainstorming among financial executives focused on the characteristics of the market, the information content, the frequency of issue, and the promotional value of the journal for the bank. Once a general format and issue frequency were determined, focus groups of vice presidents of finance of Fortune 1000 companies were held in three cities—Boston, Chicago, and Dallas—to discuss the new journal format and its relevancy and value to them. The results of these focus groups served as the basis for a new financial journal that was well received by the market.

Problem Inventory Analysis

problem inventory analysis A method for obtaining new ideas and solutions by focusing on problems

Problem inventory analysis uses individuals in a manner that is analogous to focus groups to generate new product ideas. However, instead of generating new ideas themselves, consumers are provided with a list of problems in a general product category. They are then asked to identify and discuss products in this category that have the particular problem. This method is often effective since it is easier to relate known products to suggested problems and arrive at a new product idea than to generate an entirely new product idea by itself. Problem inventory analysis can also be used to test a new product idea.

An example of this approach in the food industry is illustrated in Table 5.1. One of the most difficult problems in this example was in developing an exhaustive list of problems, such as weight, taste, appearance, and cost. Once a complete list of problems is developed, individuals can usually associate products with the problem.

Results from product inventory analysis must be carefully evaluated as they may not actually reflect a new business opportunity. For example, General Foods's introduction of a compact cereal box in response to the problem that the available boxes did not fit well on the shelf was not successful, as the problem of package size had little effect on actual purchasing behavior. To ensure the best results, problem inventory analysis should be used primarily to identify product ideas for further evaluation.

TABLE 5.1 Problem Inventory Analysis

Psychological	Sensory	Activities	Buying Usage	Psychological/Social
A. Weight • Fattening • Empty calories B. Hunger • Filling • Still hungry after eating C. Thirst • Does not quench • Makes one thirsty D. Health • Indigestion • Bad for teeth • Keeps one awake • Acidity	A. Taste • Bitter • Bland • Salty B. Appearance • Color • Unappetizing • Shape C. Consistency/ texture • Tough • Dry • Greasy	A. Meal planning • Forget • Get tired of it B. Storage • Run out • Package would not fit C. Preparation • Too much trouble • Too many pots and pans • Never turns out D. Cooking • Burns • Sticks E. Cleaning • Makes a mess in oven • Smells in refrigerator	A. Portability • Eat away from home • Take lunch B. Portions • Not enough in package • Creates leftovers C. Availability • Out of season • Not in supermarket D. Spoilage • Gets moldy • Goes sour E. Cost • Expensive • Takes expensive ingredients	A. Serve to company • Would not serve to guests • Too much last-minute preparation B. Eating alone • Too much effort to cook for oneself • Depressing when prepared for just one C. Self-image • Made by a lazy cook • Not served by a good mother

Source: From *Journal of Marketing* by Edward M. Tauber. Copyright © 1975 by American Marketing Association (AMA-Chicago). Reproduced with permission of American Marketing Association via Copyright Clearance Center.

TABLE 5.2 Creative Problem-Solving Techniques

• Brainstorming	• Forced relationships
• Reverse brainstorming	• Collective notebook method
• Brainwriting	• Attribute listing method
• Gordon method	• Big-dream approach
• Checklist method	• Parameter analysis
• Free association	

CREATIVE PROBLEM SOLVING

Creativity is an important attribute of a successful entrepreneur. Unfortunately, creativity tends to decline with age, education, lack of use, and bureaucracy. Creativity generally declines in stages, beginning when a person starts school. It continues to deteriorate through the teens and continues to progressively lessen through ages 30, 40, and 50. Also, the latent creative potential of an individual can be stifled by perceptual, cultural, emotional, and organizational factors. Creativity can be unlocked and creative ideas and innovations generated by using any of the *creative problem-solving* techniques indicated in Table 5.2.[2]

creative problem solving A method for obtaining new ideas focusing on the parameters

Brainstorming

The first technique, brainstorming, is probably the most well known and widely used for both creative problem solving and idea generation. In creative problem solving, brainstorming can generate ideas about a problem within a limited time frame through the spontaneous contributions of participants. A good brainstorming session starts with a problem statement that is neither too broad (which would diversify ideas too greatly so that nothing specific would emerge) nor too narrow (which would tend to confine responses).[3] Once the problem statement is prepared, 6 to 12 individuals are selected to participate. To avoid inhibiting responses, no group member should be a recognized expert in the field of the problem. All ideas, no matter how illogical, must be recorded, with participants prohibited from criticizing or evaluating during the brainstorming session.

Reverse Brainstorming

reverse brainstorming A group method for obtaining new ideas focusing on the negative

Reverse brainstorming is similar to brainstorming, except that criticism is allowed. In fact, the technique is based on finding fault by asking the question, "In how many ways can this idea fail?" Since the focus is on the negative aspects of a product, service, or idea, care must be taken to maintain the group's morale. Reverse brainstorming can be effectively used before other creative techniques to stimulate innovative thinking.[4] The process usually involves the identification of everything wrong with an idea, followed by a discussion of ways to overcome these problems. Reverse brainstorming almost always produces some worthwhile results as it is easier for an individual to be critical about an idea than to come up with a new idea.

Brainwriting

Brainwriting is a form of written brainstorming. It was created by Bernard Rohrbach at the end of the 1960s under the name Method 635 and differs from classical brainstorming by giving participants more time to think than in brainstorming sessions, where the ideas are

AS SEEN IN *ENTREPRENEUR* MAGAZINE

TRY THIS TECHNIQUE FOR CREATIVE SOLUTIONS

You've heard the stories about how chance, an accident, or a mistake led to valuable inventions—penicillin, Velcro, and Post-it Notes are just a few. But you don't have to rely on fate to provide inspiration. You can create conditions that spark new ideas any time by using creativity techniques such as the novel prompt. Once you've clarified the ideas you're looking for—say, a spinoff of a highly successful product or ideas for a new ad campaign—introduce a novel and unlikely prompt as a catalyst for the free association of ideas. After you generate lots of ideas, sort and refine them into practical and innovative actions.

A novel prompt can be anything: a word, an object, a fantasy, a color. The theory behind this technique is that by using something unusual to launch your thinking, you'll generate ideas you wouldn't otherwise. Many people find objects are the most evocative prompts. You can use one or more objects for this exercise. The following example uses three.

Place a mask, a bell, and a moveable child's toy (or any objects you like) on the table in clear view. Notice everything you can about each object: its function, color, shape, texture. Focus on only one object or each in turn, or the objects in relation to each other. List the qualities of the objects and then see what they suggest to you, or think about the function of the object and see what that generates. For example, if you're trying to generate new marketing strategies, the mask might suggest what people don't know about your product or service; the bell may evoke ideas about the reach and clarity of your message. The child's toy may be green, which reminds you of spring, and that prompts the idea of doing a special promotion. Let your ideas flow freely.

Don't stop until you come up with at least 10 ideas. When you first begin to free-associate, it may seem difficult to come up with that many, but keep going. This forces you to move past your limiting judgments about what is appropriate or possible. You never know what will work or what will spark another idea that might work. Remember, in this generating stage, the ideas that come to you don't have to be realistic. You want to go for volume. Quality control comes later. By using the novel prompt technique, inspiration no longer has to depend on chance.

TRY THIS!

Choose a topic, use this technique, and come up with 10 ideas.

Source: Reprinted with permission of Entrepreneur Media, Inc., "Ideas on Demand. You Don't Have to Wait for Inspiration," by Juanita Weaver, April 2003, *Entrepreneur* magazine: www.entrepreneur.com.

expressed spontaneously. Brainwriting is silent, written generation of ideas by a group of people. The participants write their ideas on special forms or cards that circulate within the group, which usually consists of six members. Each group member generates and writes down three ideas during a five-minute period. The form is passed on to the adjacent person, who writes down three new ideas, and so on, until each form has passed all participants. A leader monitors the time intervals and can reduce or lengthen the time given to participants according to the needs of the group. In a variation of this idea-generation method, the participants are located at their own workplaces and the sheets are rotated by e-mail; in this case, the time interval can be longer.[5]

Gordon Method

Gordon method Method for developing new ideas when the individuals are unaware of the problem

The *Gordon method,* unlike many other creative problem-solving techniques, begins with group members not knowing the exact nature of the problem. This ensures that the solution is not clouded by preconceived ideas and behavioral patterns.[6] The entrepreneur starts by mentioning a general concept associated with the problem. The group responds by expressing a number of ideas. Then a concept is developed, followed by related concepts, through guidance by the entrepreneur. The actual problem is then revealed, enabling the group to make suggestions for implementation or refinement of the final solution.

Checklist Method

checklist method Developing a new idea through a list of related issues

In the *checklist method,* a new idea is developed through a list of related issues or suggestions. The entrepreneur can use the list of questions or statements to guide the direction of developing entirely new ideas or concentrating on specific "idea" areas. The checklist may take any form and be of any length. One general checklist is as follows:[7]

- Put to other uses? New ways to use as-is? Other uses if modified?
- Adapt? What else is like this? What other ideas does this suggest? Does past offer parallel? What could I copy? Whom could I emulate?
- Modify? New twist? Change meaning, color, motion, odor, form, shape? Other changes?
- Magnify? What to add? More time? Greater frequency? Stronger? Larger? Thicker? Extra value? Plus ingredient? Duplicate? Multiply? Exaggerate?
- Minify? What substitute? Smaller? Condensed? Miniature? Lower? Shorter? Lighter? Omit? Streamline? Split up? Understated?
- Substitute? Who else instead? What else instead? Other ingredient? Other material? Other process? Other power? Other place? Other approach? Other tone of voice?
- Rearrange? Interchange components? Other pattern? Other layout? Other sequence? Transpose cause and effect? Change track? Change schedule?
- Reverse? Transpose positive and negative? How about opposites? Turn it backward? Turn it upside down? Reverse roles? Change shoes? Turn tables? Turn other cheek?
- Combine? How about a blend, an alloy, an assortment, an ensemble? Combine units? Combine purposes? Combine appeals? Combine ideas?

Free Association

free association Developing a new idea through a chain of word associations

One of the simplest yet most effective methods that entrepreneurs can use to generate new ideas is *free association.* This technique is helpful in developing an entirely new slant to a problem. First, a word or phrase related to the problem is written down, then another and another, with each new word attempting to add something new to the ongoing thought processes, thereby creating a chain of ideas ending with a new product idea emerging.

Forced Relationships

forced relationships Developing a new idea by looking at product combinations

Forced relationships, as the name implies, is the process of forcing relationships among some product combinations. It is a technique that asks questions about objects or ideas in an effort to develop a new idea. The new combination and eventual concept is developed through a five-step process:[8]

1. Isolate the elements of the problem.
2. Find the relationships between these elements.
3. Record the relationships in an orderly form.
4. Analyze the resulting relationships to find ideas or patterns.
5. Develop new ideas from these patterns.

Table 5.3 illustrates the use of this technique with paper and soap.

TABLE 5.3 Illustration of Forced Relationship Technique

Elements: Paper and Soap		
Forms	**Relationship/Combination**	**Idea/Pattern**
Adjective	Papery soap	Flakes
	Soapy paper	Wash and dry travel aid
Noun	Paper soaps	Tough paper impregnated with soap and usable for washing surfaces
Verb-correlates	Soaped papers	Booklets of soap leaves
	Soap "wets" paper	In coating and impregnation processes
	Soap "cleans" paper	Suggests wallpaper cleaner

Source: William E. Souder and Robert W. Ziegler, "A Review of Creativity and Problem Solving Techniques," *Research Management* (July 1975), p. 37.

Collective Notebook Method

collective notebook method Developing a new idea by group members regularly recording ideas

In the *collective notebook method,* a small notebook that easily fits in a pocket—containing a statement of the problem, blank pages, and any pertinent background data—is distributed. Participants consider the problem and its possible solutions, recording ideas at least once, but preferably three times, a day. At the end of a week, a list of the best ideas is developed, along with any suggestions.[9] This technique can also be used with a group of individuals who record their ideas, giving their notebooks to a central coordinator who summarizes all the material and lists the ideas in order of frequency of mention. The summary becomes the topic of a final creative focus group discussion by the group participants.

Attribute Listing

attribute listing Developing a new idea by looking at the positives and negatives

Attribute listing is an idea-finding technique that requires the entrepreneur to list the attributes of an item or problem and then look at each from a variety of viewpoints. Through this process, originally unrelated objects can be brought together to form a new combination and possible new uses that better satisfy a need.[10]

Big-Dream Approach

big-dream approach Developing a new idea by thinking without constraints

The *big-dream approach* to coming up with a new idea requires that the entrepreneur dream about the problem and its solution—in other words, think big. Every possibility should be recorded and investigated without regard to all the negatives involved or the resources required. Ideas should be conceptualized without any constraints until an idea is developed into a workable form.[11]

parameter analysis Developing a new idea by focusing on parameter identification and creative synthesis

Parameter Analysis

A final method for developing a new idea—*parameter analysis*—involves two aspects: parameter identification and creative synthesis.[12] As indicated in Figure 5.1, step one

FIGURE 5.1 Illustration of Parameter Analysis

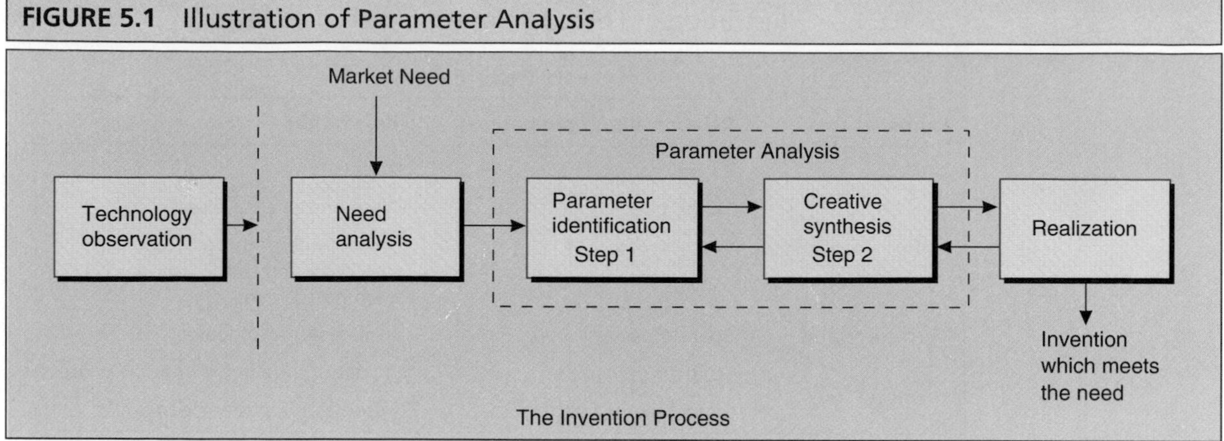

(parameter identification) involves analyzing variables in the situation to determine their relative importance. These variables become the focus of the investigation, with other variables being set aside. After the primary issues have been identified, the relationships between parameters that describe the underlying issues are examined. Through an evaluation of the parameters and relationships, one or more solutions are developed; this solution development is called creative synthesis.

INNOVATION

Innovation is the key to the economic development of any company, region of a country, or country itself. As technologies change, old products decrease in sales and old industries dwindle. Inventions and innovations are the building blocks of the future of any economic unit. Thomas Edison reportedly said that innovative genius is 1 percent inspiration and 99 percent perspiration.

Types of Innovation

There are various levels of innovation based on the uniqueness of the idea. As indicated in Figure 5.2, there are three major types of innovation, in decreasing order of uniqueness: breakthrough innovation, technological innovation, and ordinary innovation. As you would expect, the fewest innovations are of the breakthrough type. These extremely unique innovations often establish the platform on which future innovations in an area are developed. Given that they are often the basis for further innovation in an area, these innovations should be protected as much as possible by strong patents, trade secrets, and/or copyrights (see Chapter 6). Breakthrough innovations include such ideas as: penicillin, the steam engine, the computer, the airplane, the automobile, the Internet, and nanotechnology. One person in the field of nanotechnology who invents elegant solutions to engineering problems is Chung-Chiun Liu, a professor and director of the Center for Micro and Nano Processing at Case Western Reserve University. Dr. Liu is a world expert on sensor technology and invents and builds nano sensor systems for automotive, biomedical, commercial, and industrial applications. Despite publishing a majority of his inventions, Dr. Liu still holds 12 patents in electrochemical and sensor technology, many of which have been licensed. One of his inventions is the technology for an electrochemical sensor system that can transmit findings to a nearby receiver. One of these nano devices can analyze the

FIGURE 5.2 Innovation Chart

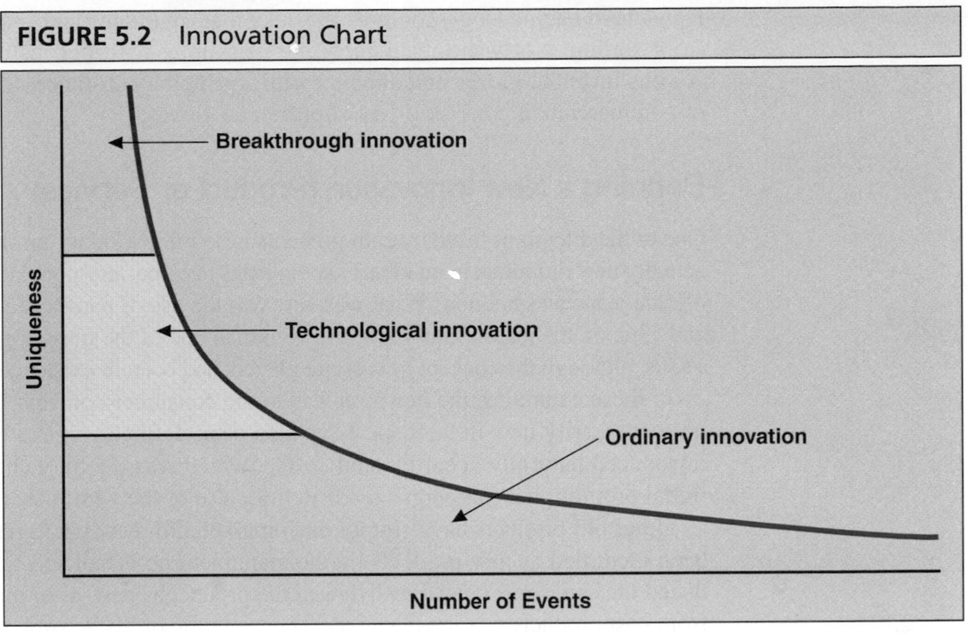

condition of motor oil from inside an engine. Another nano device can measure blood glucose levels. One of his latest nano inventions can detect black mold in homes, hidden bombs, illegal drugs, and termites; this technology is presently being commercialized through a licensing agreement with Development Corporation.

The next type of innovation—technological innovation—occurs more frequently than breakthrough innovation and in general is not at the same level of scientific discovery and advancement. Nonetheless, these are very meaningful innovations, as they do offer advancements in the product/market area. As such, they usually need to be protected. Such innovations as the personal computer, the flip watch for containing pictures, voice and text messaging, and the jet airplane are examples of technological innovations.

Analiza, Inc., a seven-year-old bioscience company, invented, developed, and sells a system that allows drug manufactures to quickly screen chemical compounds for the ones most suitable for new drugs. This automated discovery workstation simultaneously tests many different drug compounds, identifying the compounds most suitable for a new drug based on how the human body is likely to react to the compound. The company is further exploring other technological innovations such as: an advanced blood test product for diagnosing cancer; a product for extending the shelf life of blood platelets; and a pregnancy test for cows.

The final type of innovation—ordinary innovation—is the one that occurs most frequently. These more numerous innovations usually extend a technological innovation into a better product or service or one that has a different—usually better—market appeal. These innovations usually come from market analysis and pull not technology push. In other words, the market has a stronger effect on the innovation (market pull) than the technology (technology push). One ordinary innovation was developed by Sara Blakely, who wanted to get rid of unsightly panty lines. To do this, she cut off the feet of her control-top pantyhose to produce a footless pantyhose. Investing her total money available ($5,000), Sara Blakely started Spanx, an Atlanta-based company, which in five years had annual earnings of $20 million.

Similarly, Martha Aarons, the second flutist of the Cleveland Symphony, practices a 5,000-year-old Hindu system of physical and spiritual exercise. One of the exercises—the

Downward Facing Dog—requires a "sticky mat" in order to prevent the gloves and slippers from sliding. Not wanting to carry the mat along with her instrument on trips, Martha Aarons invented gloves and slippers with a gripping substance. She is now in the process of commercializing her skid-free slippers and gloves.

Defining a New Innovation (Product or Service)

One of the dilemmas faced by entrepreneurs is defining a "new" product or identifying what is actually new or unique in an idea. Fashion jeans became very popular even though the concept of blue jeans was not new. What was new was the use of names such as Sassoon, Vanderbilt, and Chic on the jeans. Sony made the Walkman one of the most popular new products of the 1980s, although the concept of cassette players had been in existence for many years.

In these examples, the newness was in the consumer concept. Other types of products, not necessarily new in concept, have also been defined as new. When coffee companies introduced naturally decaffeinated coffee, which was the only change in the product, the initial promotional campaigns made definite use of the word *new* in the copy.

Other old products have simply been marketed in new packages or containers but have been identified as new products by the manufacturer. When soft drink manufactures introduced the can, some consumers viewed the product as new, even though the only difference from past products was the container. The invention of the aerosol can is another example of a change in the package or container that added an element of newness to old, established products, such as whipped cream, deodorant, and hair spray. Flip-top cans, plastic bottles, aseptic packaging, and the pump have also contributed to a perceived image of newness in old products. Some firms, such as detergent manufactures, have merely changed the colors of their packages and then added the word *new* to the package and their promotional copy.

Pantyhose is another product that has undergone significant marketing strategy changes. L'eggs (a division of Hanes Corporation) was the first to take advantage of supermarket merchandising, packaging, lower prices, and a new display.

In the industrial market, firms may call their products "new" when only slight changes or modifications have been made in the appearance of the product. For example, improvements in metallurgical techniques have modified the precision and strength of many raw materials that are used in industrial products, such as machinery. These improved characteristics have led firms to market products containing the new and improved metals as "new." Similarly, each new version of Microsoft Word usually includes only minor improvements.

In the process of expanding their sales volume, many companies add products to their product line that are already marketed by other companies. For example, a drug company that added a cold tablet to its product line and a longtime manufacturer of soap pads that entered the dishwasher detergent market both advertised their products as new. In both cases the product was new to the manufacturer but not new to the consumer. With the increased emphasis on diversification in the world economy, this type of situation is quite common today. Firms are constantly looking for new markets to exploit in order to increase profits and make more effective use of their resources. Other firms are simply changing one or more of the marketing mix elements to give old products a new image.

Classification of New Products

New products may be classified from the viewpoint of either the consumer or the firm. Both points of view should be analyzed by the entrepreneur since both the ability to establish and attain product objectives and consumer perception of these objectives can determine the success or failure of any new product.

FIGURE 5.3 Continuum for Classifying New Products

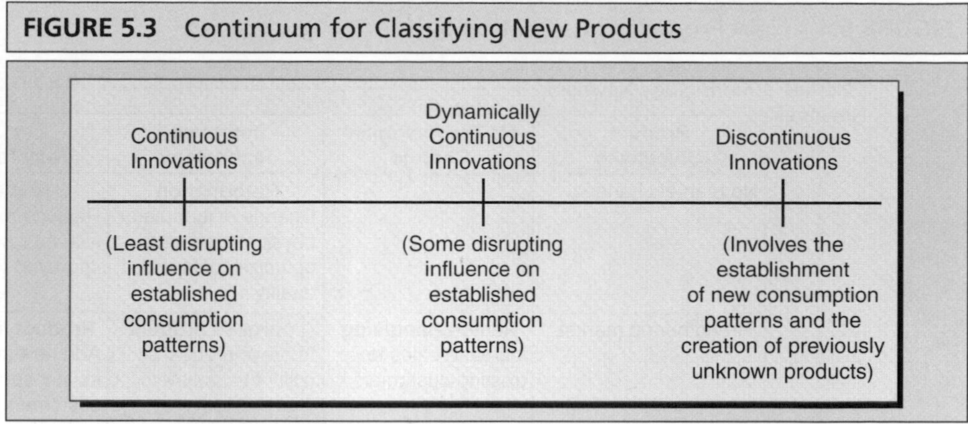

Source: Adapted from Thomas Robertson, "The Process of Innovation and the Diffusion of Innovation," *Journal of Marketing* (January 1967), pp. 14–19.

From a Consumer's Viewpoint There is a broad interpretation of what may be labeled a new product from the consumer's viewpoint. One attempt to identify new products classifies the degree of newness according to how much behavioral change or new learning is required by the consumer in order to use the product. This technique looks at newness in terms of its effect on the consumer rather than whether the product is new to a company, is packaged differently, has changed physical form, or is an improved version of an old or existing product.

The continuum proposed by Thomas Robertson and shown in Figure 5.3 contains three categories based on the disrupting influence that use of the product has on established consumption patterns. Most new products tend to fall at the "continuous innovations" end of the continuum. Examples are annual automobile style changes, fashion style changes, package changes, or product size or color changes. Products such as compact disks, Sony Walkmans, and the iPod tend toward the "dynamically continuous" portion of the continuum. The truly new products, called "discontinuous innovations," are rare and require a great deal of new learning by the consumer because these products perform either a previously unfulfilled function or an existing function in a new way. The Internet is one example of a discontinuous innovation that has radically altered our society's lifestyle. The basis for identifying new products according to their effect on consumer consumption patterns is consistent with the marketing philosophy that "satisfaction of consumer needs" is fundamental to a venture's existence.

From a Firm's Viewpoint The innovative entrepreneurial firm, in addition to recognizing the consumer's perception of newness, may also find it necessary to classify its new products on some similar dimensions. One way of classifying the objectives of new products is shown in Figure 5.4. In this figure, an important distinction is made between new products and new markets (i.e., market development). New products are defined in terms of the amount of improved technology, whereas market development is based on the degree of new segmentation.

The situation in which there is new technology *and* a new market is the most complicated and difficult—and it has the highest degree of risk. Since the new product involves new technology and customers that are not now being served, the firm will need a new and carefully planned marketing strategy. Replacements, extensions, product improvements,

FIGURE 5.4 New Product Classification System

Market Newness ↓ / Technology Newness →

Product Objectives	No Technological Change	Improved Technology	New Technology
No market change		**Reformation** Change in formula or physical product to optimize costs and quality	**Replacement** Replace existing product with new one based on improved technology
Strengthened market	**Remerchandising** Increase sales to existing customers	**Improved product** Improve product's utility to customers	**Product life extension** Add new similar products to line; serve more customers based on new technology
New market	**New use** Add new segments that can use present products	**Market extension** Add new segments modifying present products	**Diversification** Add new markets with new products developed from new technology

reformulations, and remerchandising involve product and market development strategies that range in difficulty depending on whether the firm has had prior experience with a similar product or with the same target market.

OPPORTUNITY RECOGNITION

Some entrepreneurs have the ability to recognize a business opportunity which is fundamental to the entrepreneurial process as well as growing a business. A business opportunity represents a possibility for the entrepreneur to successfully fill a large enough unsatisfied need that enough sales and profits result. There has been significant research done on the opportunity recognition process and several models developed.[13] One model that clearly identifies the aspects of this opportunity recognition process is indicated in Figure 5.5.

As is indicated, recognizing an opportunity often results from the knowledge and experience of the individual entrepreneur and, where appropriate, the entrepreneurial business. This prior knowledge is a result of a combination of education and experience, and the relevant experience could be work related or could result from a variety of personal experiences or events. The entrepreneur needs to be aware of this knowledge and experience and have the desire to understand and make use of it. The other important factors in this process are entrepreneurial alertness and entrepreneurial networks. There is an interaction effect between entrepreneurial alertness and the entrepreneur's prior knowledge of markets and customer problems. Those entrepreneurs who have the ability to recognize meaningful business opportunities are in a strategic position to successfully complete the product planning and development process and successfully launch new ventures.

OPPORTUNITY ANALYSIS PLAN

Each and every innovative idea and opportunity should be carefully assessed by the global entrepreneur. One good way to do this is to develop an opportunity analysis plan. An opportunity analysis plan is *not* a business plan, as it focuses on the idea and the market (the opportunity) for the idea—not on the venture. It also is shorter than a business plan and does not contain any

FIGURE 5.5 A Model of the Opportunity Recognition Process

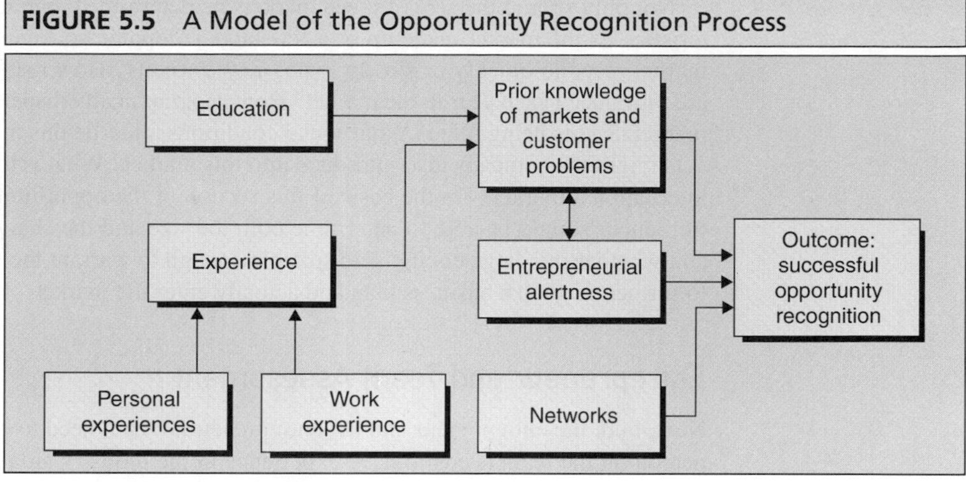

Source: From Alexander Ardichivili and Richard N. Cardozo, "A Model of the Entrepreneurial Opportunity Recognition Process," *Journal of Enterprising Culture* 8, no. 2 (June 2000). Reprinted with permission of World Scientific Publishing Co, Inc.

formal financial statements of the business venture. The opportunity analysis plan is developed to serve as the basis for the decision to either act on the opportunity or wait until another (hopefully better) opportunity comes along. A typical opportunity analysis plan has four sections: (1) a description of the idea and its competition; (2) an assessment of the domestic and international market for the idea; (3) an assessment of the entrepreneur and the team; and (4) a discussion of the steps needed to make the idea the basis for a viable business venture.

The Idea and Its Competition

One of the major sections of the opportunity analysis plan, this section focuses on the idea itself and the competition. The product or service needs to be described in as much detail as possible. A prototype or schematic of the product is helpful in fully understanding all its aspects and features. All competitive products and competitive companies in the product (service) market space need to be identified and listed. The new product/service idea should be compared with at least three competitive products/services that are most similar in filling the identified market need. This analysis will result in a description of how the product/service is different and unique and will indicate its unique selling propositions (USP). If the idea does not have at least 3–5 unique selling propositions versus competitive products/services on the market, the entrepreneur will need to even more carefully examine whether or not the idea is really unique enough to compete and be successful in the market.

The Market and the Opportunity

The second section of the opportunity analysis plan addresses the size and the characteristics of the market. Market data should be collected for at least three years so that a trend is apparent for the overall industry, the overall market, the market segment, and the target market. This can be done through gathering as much secondary (published) data as possible. For example, if you had an idea for a motorized wheelchair for small children that was shaped like a car, you would get market statistics on the health care industry (overall industry), wheelchairs (overall market), motorized wheelchairs (market segment), and children needing wheelchairs (target market). This funnel approach indicates the overall, industry market size as well as the size of the specific target market.

Not only should the size of these markets be determined, but also each of their characteristics. Is the market made up of a few large companies or many small ones? Does the market respond quickly or slowly to any new entrants? How many (if any) new products are introduced each year in the market? How geographically dispersed is the market? What market need is being filled? What social conditions underlie this market? What other products might the company also introduce into this market? What is the nature and size of the international market? On the basis of this section of the opportunity analysis plan, the entrepreneur should be able to determine both the size and the characteristics of the market and whether it is large enough and suitable enough to warrant the time and effort required to further develop a business plan and actually enter the market.

Entrepreneur and Team Assessment

Next, both the entrepreneur and the entrepreneurial team need to be assessed. At least one person on the team needs to have experience in the industry area of the new idea. This is one characteristic that correlates to the probability of success of the venture. Several questions need to be answered, such as: Why does this idea and opportunity excite you? Will this idea and opportunity sustain you once the initial excitement has worn off? How does the idea and opportunity fit your personal background and experience? How does it fit your entrepreneurial team? This section of the opportunity analysis plan is usually smaller than the previous two sections and allows the entrepreneur to determine if indeed he is really suited to successfully move his idea into the market.

The Next Steps

This final section of the opportunity analysis plan delineates the critical steps that need to be taken to make the idea a reality in the marketplace. The steps need to be identified and put in sequential order, and the time and the money needed for each step needs to be determined. If the idea cannot be self-financed, then sources of capital need to be identified. The entrepreneur should always keep in mind that most entrepreneurs tend to underestimate both the costs and the time it will take by about 30 percent.

PRODUCT PLANNING AND DEVELOPMENT PROCESS

Once ideas emerge from idea sources or creative problem solving, they need further development and refinement. This refining process—the product planning and development process—is divided into five major stages: idea stage, concept stage, product development stage, test marketing stage, and commercialization; it results in the start of the *product life cycle* (see Figure 5.6).[14]

product life cycle The stages each product goes through from introduction to decline

Establishing Evaluation Criteria

product planning and development process The stages in developing a new product

At each stage of the *product planning and development process,* criteria for evaluation need to be established. These criteria should be all-inclusive and quantitative enough to screen the product carefully in the particular stage of development. Criteria should be established to evaluate the new idea in terms of market opportunity, competition, the marketing system, financial factors, and production factors.

A market opportunity in the form of a new or current need for the product idea must exist. The determination of market demand is by far the most important criterion of a proposed new

FIGURE 5.6 The Product Planning and Development Process

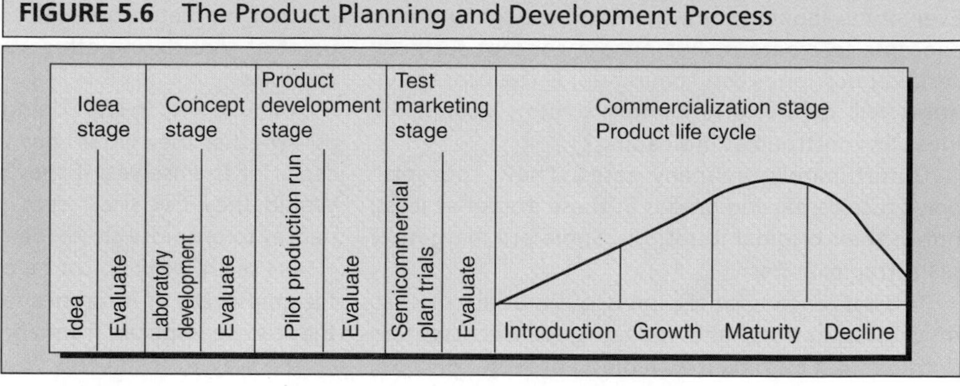

Source: From *Marketing Decisions for New and Mature Products,* 2nd edition, by Robert D. Hisrich and Michael P. Peters, 1991. Reprinted by permission of Pearson Education, Inc., Upper Saddle River, NJ.

product idea. Assessment of the market opportunity and size needs to consider: the characteristics and attitudes of consumers or industries that may buy the product, the size of this potential market in dollars and units, the nature of the market with respect to its stage in the life cycle (growing or declining), and the share of the market the product could reasonably capture.

Current competing producers, prices, and marketing efforts should also be evaluated, particularly in terms of their impact on the market share of the proposed idea. The new idea should be able to compete successfully with products/services already on the market by having features that will meet or overcome current and anticipated competition. The new idea should have some unique differential advantage based on an evaluation of all competitive product/services filling the same consumer needs.

The new idea should have synergy with existing management capabilities and marketing strategies. The firm should be able to use its marketing experience and other expertise in this new product effort. For example, General Electric would have a far less difficult time adding a new lighting device to its line than Procter & Gamble. Several factors should be considered in evaluating the degree of fit: the degree to which the ability and time of the present sales force can be transferred to the new product; the ability to sell the new product through the company's established channels of distribution; and the ability to "piggyback" the advertising and promotion required to introduce the new product.

The proposed product/service idea should be able to be supported by and contribute to the company's financial well-being. The manufacturing cost per unit, the marketing expense, and the amount of capital need to be determined along with the break-even point and the long-term profit outlook for the product.

The compatibility of the new product's production requirements with existing plant, machinery, and personnel should also be evaluated. If the new product idea cannot be integrated into existing manufacturing processes, more costs such as plant and equipment are involved which need to be taken into account. All required materials for the production of the product need to be available and accessible in sufficient quantity.

When dealing with competition and competitive situations, concerns regarding ethics and ethical behavior frequently arise, as indicated in the Ethics box.

Entrepreneurs need to be concerned with formally evaluating an idea throughout its evolution. Care must be taken to be sure the product can be the basis for a new venture. This can be done through careful evaluation that results in a go or no-go decision at each of the stages of the product planning and development process: the idea stage, the concept stage, the product development stage, and the test marketing stage.

ETHICS

Everyone is looking for a competitive edge and new concepts to create it. But once a concept surfaces, certain questions keep coming up: Is the concept viable? Will it survive regulatory scrutiny? Could the ideas be construed as misleading?

Unfortunately, in many cases, "new concepts" don't receive passing grades in these areas—at least, not in their original iterations. Some are marginally mainstream, at best.

This is a concern for the industry, especially since so much time, effort, and money goes into creating *products* that become the lifeblood of these concepts, and since distributors put so much time, effort, and money into trying to sell those products and concepts.

Some recent court cases make the problems all too clear. In one, involving a Section 419 plan, the court examined special life insurance products that were intended to take advantage of perceived tax loopholes in Section 419. The court suggested that, in order to gain the benefits of Section 419, the marketers essentially turned the life products inside out so they would have the characteristics to qualify for Section 419. For instance, the term product was heavily loaded, creating very high premiums—so high, the product could never sell outside of the 419 arena.

Here is a special area of concern: Most troublesome insurance products and concepts involve taxpayers taking deductions—deductions that may be eventually thrown out by the courts, with the possibility of underpayment penalties and interest. Knowing that, marketers are well advised to make a special point of considering ethical aspects when designing products.

A simple way to start doing this is for executives to ask whether they would buy these products and concepts for themselves, if they were at risk personally. Would they risk their own peace of mind and finances to promote these ideas?

As I see it, *ethics* must be owned by the rank-and-file employees of insurance firms. It is not something that can be imposed from above.

The way to instill this "ownership" is to ask employees what kinds of situations can lead to ethics problems. Where products are concerned, ask employees what they think about a cutting-edge design or concept before even developing it or putting it on the street. Also, be sure to measure the product or concept not only against the IMSA standards of fair play and market conduct, but also against the firm's own code of conduct and ethics.

Having employees at the ground level describe the problems they see can transform those problems into corporate ethics policies. This should help avert the rollout of bad products and concepts. It should also help make a firm's ethical policies become real for its employees, not some abstract idea that is being forced down their throats by supervisors.

Source: This material was adapted from Douglas I. Friedman, "Ethics Need to Be Part of the Cutting Edge," *National Underwriter/Life & Health Financial Services* 104, no. 49 (2001), pp. 14–18.

Idea Stage

idea stage First stage in product development process

Promising new product/service ideas should be identified and impractical ones eliminated in the *idea stage,* allowing maximum use of the company's resources. One evaluation method successfully used in this stage is the systematic market evaluation checklist, where each new idea is expressed in terms of its chief values, merits, and benefits. Consumers are presented with clusters of new product/service values to determine which, if any, new product/service alternatives should be pursued and which should be discarded. A company can test many new idea alternatives with this evaluation method; promising ideas can be further developed and resources not wasted on ideas that are incompatible with the market's values.

It is also important to determine the need for the new idea as well as its value to the company. If there is no need for the suggested product, its development should not be continued. Similarly, the new product/service idea should not be developed if it does not have any benefit or value to the firm. In order to accurately determine the need for a new idea, it is helpful to define the potential needs of the market in terms of timing, satisfaction, alternatives, benefits and risks, future expectations, price-versus-product performance features, market structure and size, and economic conditions. A form for helping in this need determination process is indicated in Table 5.4. The factors in this table should be evaluated not

TABLE 5.4 Determining the Need for a New Product/Service Idea

Factor	Aspects	Competitive Capabilities	New Product Idea Capability
Type of Need			
Continuing need			
Declining need			
Emerging need			
Future need			
Timing of Need			
Duration of need			
Frequency of need			
Demand cycle			
Position in life cycle			
Competing Ways to Satisfy Need			
Doing without			
Using present way			
Modifying present way			
Perceived Benefits/Risks			
Utility to customer			
Appeal characteristics			
Customer tastes and preferences			
Buying motives			
Consumption habits			
Price versus Performance Features			
Price-quantity relationship			
Demand elasticity			
Stability of price			
Stability of market			
Market Size and Potential			
Market growth			
Market trends			
Market development requirements			
Threats to market			
Availability of Customer Funds			
General economic conditions			
Economic trends			
Customer income			
Financing opportunities			

Source: From *Marketing Decisions for New and Mature Products*, 2nd edition, by Robert D. Hisrich and Michael P. Peters, 1991. Reprinted by permission of Pearson Education, Inc., Upper Saddle River, NJ.

only in terms of the characteristics of the potential new product/service but also in terms of the new product/service's competitive strength relative to each factor. This comparison with competitive products/services will indicate the proposed idea's strengths and weaknesses.

The need determination should focus on the type of need, its timing, the users involved with trying the product/service, the importance of controllable marketing variables, the overall market structure, and the characteristics of the market. Each of these factors should be evaluated in terms of the characteristics of the new idea being considered and the aspects and capabilities of present methods for satisfying the particular need. This analysis will indicate the extent of the opportunity available.

In the determination of the value of the new product/service to the firm, financial scheduling—such as cash outflow, cash inflow, contribution to profit, and return on investment—needs to be evaluated in terms of other product/service ideas as well as investment alternatives. With the use of the form indicated in Table 5.5, the dollar amount of each of the considerations important to the new idea should be determined as accurately as possible so that a quantitative evaluation can be made. These figures can then be revised as better information becomes available and the product/service continues to be developed.

Concept Stage

concept stage Second stage in product development process

After a new product/service idea has passed evaluation in the idea stage, it should be further developed and refined through interaction with consumers. In the *concept stage,* the refined idea is tested to determine consumer acceptance. Initial reactions to the concept are obtained from potential customers or members of the distribution channel when appropriate. One method of measuring consumer acceptance is the conversational interview in which selected respondents are exposed to statements that reflect the physical characteristics and attributes of the product/service idea. Where competing products (or services) exist, these statements can also compare their primary features. Favorable as well as unfavorable product features can be discovered by analyzing consumers' responses, with the favorable features then being incorporated into the new product/service.

Features, price, and promotion should be evaluated for both the concept being studied and any major competing products by asking the following questions:

How does the new concept compare with competitive products/services in terms of quality and reliability?

Is the concept superior or deficient compared with products/services currently available in the market?

Is this a good market opportunity for the firm?

Similar evaluations should be done for all the aspects of the marketing strategy.

Product Development Stage

product development stage Third stage in product development process

In the *product development stage,* consumer reaction to the physical product/service is determined. One tool frequently used in this stage is the consumer panel, in which a group of potential consumers are given product samples. Participants keep a record of their use of the product and comment on its virtues and deficiencies. This technique is more applicable for product ideas and works for only some service ideas.

The panel of potential customers can also be given a sample of the product and one or more competitive products simultaneously. Then one of several methods—such as multiple brand comparisons, risk analysis, level of repeat purchases, or intensity of preference analysis—can be used to determine consumer preference.

TABLE 5.5 Determining the Value of a New Product/Service Idea

Value Consideration	Cost (in $)
Cash Outflow	
R&D costs	
Marketing costs	
Capital equipment costs	
Other costs	
Cash Inflow	
Sales of new product	
Effect on additional sales of existing products	
Salvageable value	
Net Cash Flow	
Maximum exposure	
Time to maximum exposure	
Duration of exposure	
Total investment	
Maximum net cash in a single year	
Profit	
Profit from new product	
Profit affecting additional sales of existing products	
Fraction of total company profit	
Relative Return	
Return on shareholders' equity (ROE)	
Return on investment (ROI)	
Cost of capital	
Present value (PV)	
Discounted cash flow (DCF)	
Return on assets employed (ROA)	
Return on sales	
Compared to Other Investments	
Compared to other product opportunities	
Compared to other investment opportunities	

Source: From *Marketing Decisions for New and Mature Products*, 2nd edition, by Robert D. Hisrich and Michael P. Peters, 1991. Reprinted by permission of Pearson Education, Inc., Upper Saddle River, NJ.

Test Marketing Stage

test marketing stage Final stage before commercialization in product development process

Although the results of the product development stage provide the basis of the final marketing plan, a market test can be done to increase the certainty of successful commercialization. This last step in the evaluation process, the *test marketing stage,* provides actual sales results, which indicate the acceptance level of consumers. Positive test results indicate the degree of probability of a successful product launch and company formation.

E-COMMERCE AND BUSINESS START-UP

Throughout the evaluation process of a potential new idea as well as in the development of marketing strategy, the role of e-commerce needs to be continually assessed. E-commerce offers the entrepreneur the opportunity to be very creative and innovative. Its increasing importance is indicated in the continually increasing amount of both business-to-business and business-to-consumer e-commerce sales. E-commerce (Internet spending) continues to increase on an annual basis. According to *comScore Networks,* total Internet spending (including travel) reached $143.2 billion in 2005, an increase of 22 percent over the total spending of $117.2 billion in 2004. The $143.2 billion was composed of $82.3 billion nontravel spending and $60.9 billion travel spending. Apparel and accessories together constituted one of the fastest-growing categories, with $13.2 billion in sales, a 36 percent increase over 2004.

Other categories that experienced a significant increase in 2005 sales over 2004 sales included: computer software—excluding PC games (36 percent); home and garden (32 percent); toys and hobbies (32 percent); jewelry and watches (27 percent); event tickets (26 percent); furniture (24 percent); and flowers, greeting cards, and gifts (23 percent). Travel also increased to $60.9 billion in 2005—up from $50.7 billion in 2004.

Factors that facilitated the high growth of electronic commerce on a business-to-consumer or business-to-business basis are still in existence today: widespread use of personal computers, the adoption of intranets in companies, the acceptance of the Internet as a business communications platform, and faster and more secure systems. Numerous benefits—such as access to a broader customer base, lower information dissemination costs, lower transaction costs, and the interactive nature of the Internet—will continue to expand the volume of e-commerce.

Using E-Commerce Creatively

Electronic commerce is increasingly used by existing corporations to extend their marketing and sales channels, as well as being the basis for some new ventures. The Internet is especially important for small and medium-sized companies, as it enables them to minimize marketing costs while reaching broader markets. An entrepreneur starting an Internet commerce venture needs to address the same strategic and tactical questions as any other entrepreneur. Additionally, some specific issues of doing business online need to be addressed due to the new and perpetually evolving technology used in Internet commerce. An entrepreneur has to decide whether he or she will run the Internet operations within the company or outsource these operations to Internet specialists. In the case of in-house operations, computer servers, routers, and other hardware and software as well as support services such as Web site information have to be maintained. Alternatively, there are numerous possibilities for outsourcing the Internet business. The entrepreneur can hire Web developers to design the company's Web pages and then upload them on the server maintained by the Internet service provider. In this case, the entrepreneur's main task is to regularly update the information on the Web pages. Another option is to use the packages for e-commerce available from different software companies. The correct decision for in-house operations or outsourcing depends on the size of the Internet-related business, particularly where Internet operations are the company's primary business, and the relative costs of each alternative.

The two major components of Internet commerce are front-end and back-end operations. Front-end operations are encompassed in the Web site's functionality. Search capabilities, shopping cart, and secure payment are only a few examples. The biggest mistake of many companies on the Internet is believing that an attractive, interactive Web site will secure success; this leads to underestimating the importance of back-end operations. Seamless integration of customer orders should be developed, with distribution channels and manufacturing capabilities that are flexible enough to handle any specific customer's desire. The integration of front-end and back-end operations represents the greatest challenge for doing Internet business and at the same time provides the opportunity for developing a sustained competitive advantage.

Web Sites

The use of Web sites by entrepreneurial firms has been increasing at a significant rate. About 90 percent of small businesses today have operating Web sites. However, the majority of small businesses and entrepreneurs feel that they do not have the technical capability to build and operate quality Web sites.

One of the keys to a good Web site is ease of use. In a ranking by Citigroup of 44 retail Web sites according to ease of use, Amazon was ranked number one, followed by American Eagle Outfitters, Banana Republic, Talbots, Cosco, and Comp USA.

In developing a Web site, an entrepreneur needs to remember that a Web site is a communication vehicle and should address the following questions: Who is the audience? What are the objectives for the site? What do you want the consumers to do upon visiting the site? Is the Web site an integral part of the venture's total communication program? In addressing these questions, the entrepreneur needs to structure the Web site and organize the information to effectively engage the target market. This requires that the material be fresh, with new material added on a regular basis. The material should be interactive to engage the individual. And, of course the Web site needs to be known and as visible as possible.

One of the most important features of every Web site is search capability. It should be easy to find information about the products and services that a company offers over the Internet. This function can be accomplished through an advanced search tool, site map, or subject browsing. Other functions that should be available on every e-commerce Web site are shopping cart, secure server connection, credit card payment, and a customer feedback feature. Shopping cart is software that accepts product orders and automatically calculates and totals customers' orders based on the product availability information. Orders and other sensitive customer information should be transferred only through secure servers. Another important feature of the Web site is an e-mail response system that allows customers to send their feedback to the company.

There are three characteristics of successful Web sites: speed, speed, and speed. Additionally, a Web site should be easy to use, customized for specific market target groups, and compatible with different browsers. It should also take into consideration the international nature of the Internet. Ease of use goes hand in hand with speed; if visitors find Web pages easy to navigate, then they will be able to quickly find products, services, or information. One of the greatest advantages of the Internet is the simplicity of customization of the Web site content for different market segments. An entrepreneur should also keep in mind any nontargeted segments. For example, if a company is not planning to sell products beyond the U.S. border, then it should clearly indicate on its Web site that it is shipping its products only within the United States. If, on the other hand, the company is targeting international markets as well, then issues of translation and cultural adaptation need to be considered. As for the technical aspects, the designer should ensure that the Web site works properly in different browsers and platforms that are used by Internet visitors. Once the Web site is operational, it is important that it appear in all marketing materials, including business cards, company letterhead, and of course company advertising.

A good example of Web site development and operation is Transition Networks Inc. (www.transition.com). The Minneapolis-based company is in the high-technology business of marketing local area network (LAN) hardware. The company had these goals for its Web site: help control collateral costs, provide a mechanism for easily accessible product and technology training for resellers, provide a mechanism for getting to know resellers better, and provide company exposure to end users of the company's products. To meet these goals, Transition Networks designed a Web site that is multilayered. The site is interactive in the test procedure with the participant getting immediate feedback concerning responses given. The site is coordinated in both content and graphics with other marketing communications of the company, with the front page of the site updated weekly to draw people and give them a reason to revisit. The content of the site is updated every two weeks with at least one new item.

Tracking Customer Information

Electronic databases support the strategy of personalized one-to-one marketing. The database can not only track activity of the industry, segment, and company but also support personal marketing targeted at individual clients. The motivation for tracking customer information is to capture customer attention with customized one-to-one marketing. Care must be taken in doing this to follow the laws protecting the privacy of individuals.

Doing E-Commerce as an Entrepreneurial Company

The decision to go online for the first time and develop an e-commerce site for your business needs to be a strategic one and should be based on several factors. First, the products should be able to be delivered economically and conveniently. Fresh fruits and vegetables for individual consumers are not very appropriate for online sales and long-distance deliveries. Second, the product has to be interesting for a large number of people and the company must be ready to ship the product outside its own geographical location. Third, online operations have to bring significant cost reductions compared with the present brick-and-mortar operations. The fourth factor reflects the company's ability to economically draw customers to its Web site.

Conflict between traditional and online marketing channels (channel conflict) arises because of disagreements between manufacturers and retailers, which eventually lead into a hostile, competing position of once partnering companies. Partners in supply chains have to focus on their core competencies and outsource the noncore activities. When introducing the competing distribution channels, companies have to weigh the costs and benefits of that decision while taking into account the loss of existing business.

IN REVIEW

SUMMARY

The starting point for any successful new venture is the basic product or service to be offered. This idea can be generated internally or externally through various techniques.

The possible sources of new ideas range from the comments of consumers to changes in government regulations. Monitoring the comments of acquaintances, evaluating the new products offered by competitors, becoming familiar with the ideas contained in previously granted patents, and becoming actively involved in research and development are techniques for coming up with a good product idea. In addition, there are specific techniques entrepreneurs can use to generate ideas. For example, a better understanding of the consumer's true opinions can be gained from using a focus group. Another consumer-oriented approach is problem inventory analysis, through which consumers associate particular problems with specific products and then develop a new product that does not contain the identified faults.

Brainstorming, a technique useful in both idea generation and problem solving, stimulates creativity by allowing a small group of people to work together in an open, nonstructured environment. Other techniques useful in enhancing the creative process are checklists of related questions, free association, idea notebooks, and the "big-dream" approach. Some techniques are very structured, while others are designed to be more free form. Each entrepreneur should know the techniques available.

Once the idea or group of ideas is generated, the planning and development process begins. If a large number of potential ideas have been uncovered, they must be screened and evaluated to determine their appropriateness for further development. Ideas showing the most potential are then moved through the concept stage, the product development stage, the test marketing stage, and finally into commercialization. The entrepreneur should constantly evaluate the idea throughout this process in order to be able to successfully launch the venture.

RESEARCH TASKS

1. Choose a product or technology. Interview five consumers who buy that product and ask them what major problems they have with the product (or what major things they dislike about it). Then ask them to describe the attributes of the "perfect product" that would satisfy all their needs and replace the existing product. Next, interview the representatives of five companies that offer the product and ask them what they believe are the major problems customers experience with their product. Come up with some futuristic solutions.
2. Obtain a patent of a technology (e.g., go to the patent office Web site) and come up with 10 creative uses of the technology.
3. Choose three different products that you might be interested in purchasing and that are sold on the Internet. For each product, visit three Web sites and go through the process as if you were going to actually purchase the product. Which Web site was the best? Why? Which was the worst? Why? If you could create the perfect Web site, what features would it have?

CLASS DISCUSSION

1. Take the following problem statement and brainstorm solutions. Be prepared to present your three most "creative" solutions. Problem statement: "Customers too frequently use an airline and fly to a destination only to find out that their luggage has not arrived."
2. Choose a product and use the checklist method to develop new ideas. Be prepared to discuss your product and the three most creative ideas generated.
3. Do you think that the Internet can be a source of advantage for one firm over other firms or do you think that it is a necessity just to be able to compete? Be prepared to justify your answer.

SELECTED READINGS

Amabile, Teresa M. (September–October 1998). How to Kill Creativity. *Harvard Business Review*, pp. 77–87.

This article explains what kinds of management practices foster creativity and which practices inhibit creativity in organizations. Creativity needs to be understood in light of its three individual-level components: creative thinking skills, expertise, and motivation. Managerial practices that affect creativity fall into six general categories: challenge, freedom, resources, work-group features, supervisory encouragement, and organizational support.

Åmo, Bjørn Willy; and Lars Kolvereid. (March 2005). Organizational Strategy, Individual Personality and Innovation Behavior. *Journal of Enterprising Culture*, vol. 13, no. 1, pp. 7–19.

This article discusses two competing models of innovation behavior in organizations. The first model is derived from the corporate entrepreneurship literature, suggesting that the extent to which the organization has a deliberate entrepreneurship strategy determines employees' involvement in innovation and change. The competing model is derived from the intrapreneurship literature, where the emphasis is on the employee's individual personality.

Di Gregorio, Dante; and Scott Shane. (February 2003). Why Do Some Universities Generate More Start-Ups than Others? *Research Policy*, vol. 32, no. 2, p. 209.

This paper discusses why some universities generate more new companies to exploit their intellectual property than do others. The paper compares four different explanations for cross-institutional variation in new firm formation rates from university technology licensing offices—the availability of venture capital in the university area; the commercial orientation of university research and development; intellectual eminence; and university policies.

Ernst, Holger; Peter Witt; and German Brachtendorf. (June 2005). Corporate Venture Capital as a Strategy for External Innovation: An Exploratory Empirical Study. *R & D Management*, vol. 35, no. 3, pp. 233–42.

This paper proposes that by creating corporate venture capital (CVC) units, large corporations predominantly pursue strategic objectives, especially the realization of external innovations. The paper analyzes a sample of 21 corporate venture units in Germany and whether the respective CVC programs pursue the strategic objective to leverage external innovation and whether these programs are managed accordingly.

Fassin, Yves. (September 2000). Innovation and Ethics: Ethical Considerations in the Innovation Business. *Journal of Business Ethics*, vol. 27, no. 1/2, pp.193–203.

This paper describes the growth process of a company and the valuation of an innovation project. It offers an overview of a number of ethical issues at different stages in the innovation business and in the lifetime of a start-up company, such as the problems of intellectual property, the confidentiality of information, the negotiation process between the entrepreneur and the financier, the marketing of raising funds and of an IPO, and finally information and insider trading. The paper concludes with a plea for increased ethical behavior and the need for rules of best practice for all parties: the inventor, the entrepreneur, the financial investor, and other stakeholders.

Ferrary. (2003). Managing the Disruptive Technologies Life Cycle by Externalizing the Research: Social Network and Corporate Venturing in the Silicon Valley. *International Journal of Technology Management*, vol. 25, no. 1/2, p.165.

This paper argues that the capability to generate and develop disruptive technologies drives the market in the high-tech sector. The Silicon Valley example points out that the most successful high-tech companies such as Cisco Systems, Intel, and Sun externalize their research by doing corporate venturing. These companies manage their portfolio of technologies by acquiring small businesses that have developed disruptive technologies.

Fillis, Ian. (2002). An Andalusian Dog or a Rising Star? Creativity and the Marketing/Entrepreneurship Interface. *Journal of Marketing Management*, vol. 18, pp. 379–395.

This paper discusses the origins of the study of creativity, from social psychology to the business discipline. Creativity is then viewed as a key competency at the Marketing/Entrepreneurship Interface, linked with related issues such as innovation, leadership, vision, and motivation. A model of creativity as competitive advantage is developed and recommendations are made, focusing on the need to challenge convention in order to move ideas, products, and services into the new century.

Goldenberg, Jacob; Roni Horowitz; Amnon Levav; and David Mazursky. (March 2003). Finding Your Innovation Sweet Spot. *Harvard Business Review*, pp. 120–29.

Most ideas for new products are either uninspired or impractical. This article introduces a systematic process based on five innovation patterns that can generate ideas that are both ingenious and viable.

Gundry, Lisa; Jill Kickul; Harold P. Welsch; and Margaret Posig. (November 2003). Technological Innovation in Women-Owned Firms: Influence of Entrepreneurial Motivation and Strategic Intention. *International Journal of Entrepreneurship & Innovation*, vol. 4, no. 4, pp. 265–74.

This article seeks to determine the influence of the underlying factors that facilitate the growth and implementation of new technologies within women-owned businesses. Implications for research and practice related to ways in which entrepreneurs' strategic focus can enable technological innovations are discussed.

Huang, Xueli; Geoffrey N. Soutar; and Alan Brown. (2002). New Product Development Process in Small and Medium-Sized Enterprises: Some Australian Evidence. *Journal of Small Business Management*, vol. 40, no. 1, pp. 27–42.

This article examines the new product development process in 267 Australian small and medium-sized innovative firms. The findings suggest that marketing-related activities were undertaken less frequently and were less well executed than technical activities in developing new products. However, the existence of the new product strategy seemed to have a significant positive impact on the quality of new product development activities.

Keh, Hean Tat; Maw Der Foo; and Boon Chong Lim. (Winter 2002). Opportunity Evaluation under Risky Conditions: The Cognitive Processes of Entrepreneurs. *Entrepreneurship Theory and Practice*, pp. 125–48.

This article describes a study that uses a cognitive approach to examine opportunity evaluation, as the perception of opportunity is essentially a cognitive phenomenon. The findings indicate that illusion of control and belief in the law of small numbers are related to how entrepreneurs evaluate opportunities. Results also indicate that risk perception mediates opportunity evaluation.

Lahdesmaki, M. (October 2005). When Ethics Matters—Interpreting the Ethical Discourse of Small Nature-Based Entrepreneurs. *Journal of Business Ethics*, vol. 61, no. 1, pp. 55–68.

This article examines the unique ethical concerns faced by small nature-based entrepreneurs in their everyday business operations. This article also shows that the variety of ethical arguments used and the important role of customers and employees in influencing the ethical views of the entrepreneurs are typical for the decision making of the small nature-based entrepreneurs in an ethical sense.

Park, John S. (July 2005). Opportunity Recognition and Product Innovation in Entrepreneurial Hi-Tech Start-Ups: A New Perspective and Supporting Case Study. *Technovation*, vol. 25, no.7, pp. 739–52.

This paper seeks to synthesize the available literature into a more complete and integrative model of opportunity recognition in high-tech start-ups. The paper proposes that opportunity recognition is a complex, interactive process involving three main components: the founding entrepreneur, the knowledge and experience of the firm, and technology. It is argued that more widespread use of the qualitative research can reveal new insights into the complex and interactive process of opportunity recognition in the high-tech start-up.

Tidd, Joe; and Kirsten Bodley. (2002). The Influence of Project Novelty on the New Product Development Process. *R&D Management*, vol. 32, no. 2, pp. 127–38.

This paper reviews the range of formal tools and techniques available to support the new product development process and examines the use and usefulness of these by means of a survey of 50 projects in 25 firms. Cross-functional development teams are commonplace for all types of projects, but they are significantly more effective for the high-novelty cases.

Tsai, Kuen-Hung; and Jiann-Chyuan Wang. (2004). The Innovation Policy and Performance of Innovation in Taiwan's Technology-Intensive Industries. *Problems & Perspectives in Management,* no. 1 (2004), pp. 62–75.

This paper shows that much greater emphasis is now being placed upon innovation following the recognition that it plays an increasingly important role in enhancing industrial technology. Thus the governments of many countries are currently adopting specific strategies aimed at stimulating innovation within firms. Taiwan is no exception; however, since the industrial structure of Taiwan comprises predominantly small and medium-sized enterprises (SME), their willingness to engage in innovative activities is rather low.

Venkataraman, Sankaran. (January 2004). Regional Transformation through Technological Entrepreneurship. *Journal of Business Venturing*, vol. 19, no. 1, p.153.

This paper discusses that if risk capital is expected to produce extraordinary wealth, it must be accompanied by seven other intangibles, including: access to novel ideas, role models, informal forums, region-specific opportunities, safety nets, access to large markets, and executive leadership.

Werker, C. (April 2003). Innovation, Market Performance, and Competition: Lessons from a Product Life Cycle Model. *Technovation,* vol. 23, no. 4 (April 2003), p. 281.

This paper explains how innovation, market performance, and competition are intertwined and serve as a basis for the decisions of firms and policy makers. To model the market evolution and the resulting changes, Dosi's concept of technological paradigms and Winter's concept of technological regimes are integrated into a product life cycle model. The results of the simulation runs show a much more differentiated picture than economic intuition suggests and therefore give useful hints for firms' strategies and innovation policies.

END NOTES

1. For an in-depth presentation on focus group interviews in general and quantitative applications, see "Conference Focuses on Focus Groups: Guidelines, Reports, and 'the Magic Plaque,'" *Marketing News* (May 21, 1976), p. 8; Keith K. Cox, James B. Higginbotham, and John Burton, "Application of Focus Group Interviews in Marketing," *Journal of Marketing* 40, no. 1 (January 1976), pp. 77–80; and Robert D. Hisrich and Michael P. Peters, "Focus Groups: An Innovative Marketing

Research Technique," *Hospital and Health Service Administration* 27, no. 4 (July–August 1982), pp. 8–21.

2. A discussion of each of these techniques can be found in Robert D. Hisrich and Michael P. Peters, *Marketing Decisions for New and Mature Products* (Columbus, OH: Charles E. Merrill, 1984), pp. 131–46; and Robert D. Hisrich, "Entrepreneurship and Intrapreneurship: Methods for Creating New Companies That Have an Impact on the Economic Renaissance of an Area." In *Entrepreneurship, Intrapreneurship, and Venture Capital* (Lexington, MA: Lexington Books, 1986), pp. 77–104.
3. For a discussion of this aspect, see Charles H. Clark, *Idea Management: How to Motivate Creativity and Innovation* (New York: ANA Com., 1980), p. 47.
4. For a discussion of this technique, see J. Geoffrey Rawlinson, *Creative Thinking and Brainstorming* (New York: John Wiley & Sons, 1981), pp. 124, 126; and W. E. Souder and R. W. Ziegler, "A Review of Creativity and Problem-Solving Techniques," *Research Management* 20 (July 1977), p. 35.
5. Knut Holt, "Brainstorming—From Classics to Electronics," *Journal of Engineering Design* 6, no. 1 (1996), pp. 77–84.
6. This method is discussed in J. W. Haefele, *Creativity and Innovation* (New York: Van Nostrand Reinhold, 1962), pp. 145–47; Sidney J. Parnes and Harold F. Harding, *A Source Book for Creative Thinking* (New York: Charles Scribner's Sons, 1962), pp. 307–23; and Souder and Ziegler, "A Review of Creativity and Problem-Solving Techniques," pp. 34–42.
7. Alex F. Osborn, *Applied Imagination* (New York: Scribner Book Companies, 1957), p. 318.
8. Rawlinson, *Creative Thinking,* pp. 52–59.
9. For a thorough discussion of the collective notebook method, see J. W. Haefele, *Creativity and Innovation,* p. 152.
10. S. J. Parnes and H. F. Harding, eds., *A Source Book for Creative Thinking* (New York: Charles Scribner's Sons, 1962), p. 308.
11. For a discussion of this approach, see M. O. Edwards, "Solving Problems Creatively," *Journal of Systems Management* 17, no. 1 (January–February 1966), pp. 16–24.
12. The procedure for parameter analysis is thoroughly discussed in Yao Tzu Li, David G. Jansson, and Ernest G. Cravalho, *Technological Innovation in Education and Industry* (New York: Reinhold, 1980), pp. 26–49, 277–86.
13. For some examples of this research and models, see Lenny Herron and Harry J. Sapienza, "The Entrepreneur and the Initiation of New Venture Launch Activities," *Entrepreneurship Theory and Practice* (Fall 1992), pp. 49–55; C. M. Gaglio and R. P. Taub, "Entrepreneur and Opportunity Recognition," *Babson Research Conference* (May 1992), pp. 136–47; L. Buzenitz, "Research on Entrepreneurial Alertness," *Journal of Small Business Management* 34, no. 4 (1996), pp. 35–44; S. Shane, "Prior Knowledge and Discovery of Entrepreneurial Opportunities," *Organizational Science* 11, no. 4 (2000), pp. 448–69; Hean Tat Key, Mow Der Foo, and Boon Chong Lim, "Opportunity Evaluation under Risky Conditions: The Cognitive Process of Entrepreneurs," *Entrepreneurship Theory and Practice* (Winter 2002), pp. 125–48; and Noel J. Lindsay and Justin Craig, "A Framework for Understanding Opportunity Recognition," *Journal of Private Equity* (Winter 2002), pp. 13–25.
14. For a detailed description of this process, see Robert D. Hisrich and Michael P. Peters, *Marketing Decisions for New and Mature Products* (Columbus, OH: Charles E. Merrill, 1991), pp. 157–78.

6

INTELLECTUAL PROPERTY AND OTHER LEGAL ISSUES FOR THE ENTREPRENEUR

LEARNING OBJECTIVES

1
To identify and distinguish intellectual property assets of a new venture including software and Web sites.

2
To understand the nature of patents, the rights they provide, and the filing process.

3
To understand the purpose of a trademark and the procedure for filing.

4
To learn the purpose of a copyright and how to file for one.

5
To identify procedures that can protect a venture's trade secrets.

6
To understand the value of licensing to either expand a business or start a new venture.

7
To recognize the implications of new legislation that affects the board of directors and internal auditing processes for public companies.

8
To illustrate important issues related to contracts, insurance, and product safety and liability.

OPENING PROFILE

STEVE LIPSCOMB

One of the hottest media concepts today is television poker. As this market continues to gain popularity and spin dozens of new innovations for entrepreneurs, it represents one of the most difficult business models for which to provide any intellectual property protection. Steve Lipscomb has emerged as one of the most aggressive and innovative entrepreneurs amongst those trying to compete in this media market. His World Poker Tour broadcast on the cable television Travel channel became an instant hit show in 2003, as evidenced by its audience size or television rating points. With this success, however, new competitors evolved, making the strategy of protecting his investment even more challenging.

www.worldpokertour.com

Steve Lipscomb grew up in Nashville, Tennessee, and came from a long line of Baptist ministers. His first entrepreneurial effort, after becoming an attorney, was to launch an attorney referral venture. However, even after early entrepreneurial success, his career made some dramatic changes, primarily because of discrimination issues experienced by his mother after she had chosen to enter the Baptist Church seminary. His anger over this experience led him to make a documentary film so that the world would be made more aware of some of these discriminatory issues. He then sold his attorney referral business, taught himself filmmaking, and proceeded to make *Battle of the Minds,* which won acclaim and numerous awards after appearing on PBS television. This success resulted in a friendship with producer Norman Lear and a film project to provide audiences with an inside look at the World Series of Poker.

Although poker was not a foreign concept to Lipscomb, having once entered a $100 satellite tournament, he felt that ESPN's televising of the World Series of Poker was poorly presented. After his film project, Lipscomb had the strong vision that not only could poker be made to be more interesting but that it would be possible to create a major league of poker that would allow for entrepreneurial expansion into merchandise, foreign licensing, Internet competition, and other business opportunities. With the help of two friends with television and licensing experience, Lipscomb established a league of poker players that could enter tournaments as they pleased for prize money raised from sponsors. His business model was to establish a league of poker players similar to golf's PGA Tour. Thus, anyone with $10,000 could enter one of the World Poker Tour events with a chance to win a large prize of $1 million or more.

Lipscomb's strategy was to produce a show before getting television to buy it. With the support of Lakes Entertainment, a developer of casino gaming, and an investment of $3.5 million, the World Poker Tour and WPT Enterprises was born, including listing on NASDAQ (WPTE). With this investment Lipscomb subsequently had to give up 70 percent control of his business, but he was able to retain 16.5 percent for himself. Armed with this infusion of venture capital Lipscomb hit the road to try to persuade the many popular casinos to support these poker tournaments. His format included two unique concepts to make the televising of poker more interesting to the viewer. One of these was a small camera under the table that allowed the viewers to see the two cards that were dealt face down. Viewers could then play along with the tournament players. In addition, he added unique graphics that presented on-screen icons of each player's cards. Odds of winning were included at each stage of the betting process, making this programming unique and more interesting to the television audience.

These unique additions are regarded by Lipscomb as intellectual property, but this has created controversy with some of the competition. ESPN has duplicated Lipscomb's camera and graphics in its presentation of another league, the World Series of Poker Circuit. Lipscomb argues that the camera and graphics are proprietary with applications for patents pending. Although ESPN argues it has done nothing wrong, the future of WPT may be seriously affected by such a power player in the cable television business. Lawsuits may be inevitable.

As of the end of 2005, the World Poker Tour has increased the number of casinos hosting tournaments to 10. In addition Lipscomb has continued to meet his objectives by signing an international syndication of a new televised poker franchise, the Professional Poker Tour. Unlike the World Poker Tour, this program will include only professional poker players.

Now in its third season, tournament prize money for the World Poker Tour has surpassed $10 million. Although the company is struggling financially in 2005, there have been some positive trends. From 2003 to 2004, the company grew to $17.6 million in revenue, with a profit of $752,000. However, in 2005 revenue is running equal to that of 2004 and there have been higher selling and administrative costs, resulting in a loss through the third quarter of 2005 of about $3.5 million. Lipscomb is confident that with international syndication, and the continued aggressive marketing of poker equipment, apparel, publishing, giftware, and Internet game playing, the future outlook should be very favorable. Establishing the on-screen graphics and small cameras as proprietary may also prove a strong barrier to competition in this potentially large global market.[1]

WHAT IS INTELLECTUAL PROPERTY?

intellectual property
Any patents, trademarks, copyrights, or trade secrets held by the entrepreneur

Intellectual property—which includes patents, trademarks, copyrights, and trade secrets—represents important assets to the entrepreneur and should be understood even before engaging the services of an attorney. Too often entrepreneurs, because of their lack of understanding of intellectual property, ignore important steps that they should have taken to protect these assets. This chapter will describe all the important types of intellectual property, including software and Web sites, that have become unique problems to the Patent and Trademark Office.[2]

NEED FOR A LAWYER

Since all business is regulated by law, the entrepreneur needs to be aware of any regulations that may affect his or her new venture. At different stages of the start-up, the entrepreneur will need legal advice. It is also likely that the legal expertise required will vary based on such factors as whether the new venture is a franchise, an independent start-up, or a buy-out; whether it produces a consumer versus an industrial product; whether it is nonprofit; and whether it involves some aspect of computer software, exporting, or importing.

The chapter begins with a discussion of how to select a lawyer. Since most lawyers have developed special expertise, the entrepreneur should carefully evaluate his or her needs before hiring one. By being aware of when and what legal advice is required, the entrepreneur can save much time and money. Many of the areas in which the entrepreneur will need legal assistance are discussed in this chapter.

HOW TO SELECT A LAWYER

Lawyers, like many other professionals, are specialists not just in the law but in specific areas of the law. The entrepreneur does not usually have the expertise or know-how to handle possible risks associated with the many difficult laws and regulations. A competent attorney is in a better position to understand all possible circumstances and outcomes related to any legal action.

In today's environment, lawyers are much more up-front about their fees. In fact, in some cases these fees, if for standard services, may even be advertised. In general, the lawyer may work on a retainer basis (stated amount per month or year) by which he or she provides office and consulting time. This does not include court time or other legal fees related to the action. This gives the entrepreneur the opportunity to call an attorney as the need arises without incurring high hourly visit fees.

In some instances the lawyer may be hired for a one-time fee. For example, a patent attorney may be hired as a specialist to help the entrepreneur obtain a patent. Once the patent is obtained, this lawyer would not be needed, except perhaps if there was any litigation regarding the patent. Other specialists for setting up the organization or for purchase of real estate may also be paid on a service-performed basis. Whatever the fee basis, the entrepreneur should confront the cost issue initially so that no questions arise in the future.

Choosing a lawyer is like hiring an employee. The lawyer with whom you work should be someone you can relate to personally. In a large law firm, it is possible that an associate or junior partner would be assigned to the new venture. The entrepreneur should ask to meet with this person to ensure that there is compatibility.

A good working relationship with a lawyer will ease some of the risk in starting a new business and will give the entrepreneur necessary confidence. When resources are very limited, the entrepreneur may consider offering the lawyer stock in exchange for his or her services. The lawyer then will have a vested interest in the business and will likely provide more personalized services. However, in making such a major decision, the entrepreneur must consider any possible loss of control of the business.

LEGAL ISSUES IN SETTING UP THE ORGANIZATION

The form of organization as well as franchise agreements are discussed in Chapters 9 and 16 and will not be addressed in detail here. Since there are many options that an entrepreneur can choose in setting up an organization (see Chapter 9), it will be necessary to understand all the advantages and disadvantages of each, regarding such issues as liability, taxes, continuity, transferability of interest, costs of setting up, and attractiveness for raising capital. Legal advice for these agreements is necessary to ensure that the most appropriate decisions have been made.

PATENTS

patent Grants holder protection from others making, using, or selling similar idea

A *patent* is a contract between the government and an inventor. In exchange for disclosure of the invention, the government grants the inventor exclusivity regarding the invention for a specified amount of time. At the end of this time, the government publishes the invention and it becomes part of the public domain. As part of the public domain, however, there is the assumption that the disclosure will stimulate ideas and perhaps even the development of an even better product that could replace the original.

Basically, the patent gives the owners a negative right because it prevents anyone else from making, using, or selling the defined invention. Moreover, even if an inventor has been granted a patent, in the process of producing or marketing the invention he or she may find that it infringes on the patent rights of others. The inventor should recognize the distinction between utility and design patents and some of the differences in international patents that are discussed later in this chapter.

- *Utility patents.* When speaking about patents, most people are referring to utility patents. A utility patent has a term of 20 years, beginning on the date of filing with the Patent and Trademark Office (PTO). Any invention requiring FDA approval has also been amended to extend the term of the patent by the amount of time it takes the FDA to review the invention. Filing fees for a utility patent equal $790. Additional fees exist depending on the number of claims made in the patent application.

  A utility patent basically grants the owner protection from anyone else making, using, and/or selling the identified invention and generally reflects protection of new, useful, and unobvious processes such as film developing, machines such as photocopiers, compositions of matter such as chemical compounds or mixtures of ingredients, and articles of manufacture such as the toothpaste pump.
- *Design patents.* Covering new, original, ornamental, and unobvious designs for articles of manufacture, a design patent reflects the appearance of an object. These patents are granted for a 14-year term and, like the utility patent, provide the inventor with a negative right excluding others from making, using, or selling an article having the ornamental appearance given in the drawings included in the patent. The initial filing fee for each design application is $200. There are also issuance fees, depending on the size of the item. These fees are much lower than for a utility patent.

  Traditionally, design patents were thought to be useless because it was so easy to design around the patent. However, there is renewed interest in these patents. Examples are shoe companies such as Reebok and Nike that have become more interested

AS SEEN IN *ENTREPRENEUR* MAGAZINE

PROVIDE ADVICE TO AN ENTREPRENEUR ABOUT INTELLECTUAL PROPERTY PROTECTION

Locked doors and a security system protect your equipment, inventory, and payroll. But what protects your business's most valuable possessions? Intellectual property laws can protect your trade secrets, trademarks, and product design, provided you take the proper steps. Chicago attorney Kara E. F. Cenar of Welsh & Katz, an intellectual property firm, contends that businesses should start thinking about these issues earlier than most do. "Small businesses tend to delay securing intellectual property protection because of the expense," Cenar says. "They tend not to see the value of intellectual property until a competitor infringes." But a business that hasn't applied for copyrights or patents and actively defended them will likely have trouble making its case in court.

One reason many business owners don't protect their intellectual property is that they don't recognize the value of the intangibles they own. Cenar advises business owners to take their business plans to an experienced intellectual property attorney and discuss how to deal with these issues. Spending money up front for legal help can save a great deal later by giving you strong copyright or trademark rights, which can deter competitors from infringing and avoid litigation later.

Once you've figured out what's worth protecting, you have to decide how to protect it. That isn't always obvious. Traditionally, patents prohibit others from copying new devices and processes, while copyrights do the same for creative endeavors such as books, music, and software. In many cases, though, the categories overlap. Likewise, trademark law now extends to such distinctive elements as a product's color and shape. Trade dress law concerns how the product is packaged and advertised. You might be able to choose what kind of protection to seek.

For instance, one of Welsh & Katz's clients is Ty Inc., maker of plush toys. Before launching the Beanie Baby line, Cenar explains, the owners brought in business and marketing plans to discuss intellectual property issues. The plan was for a limited number of toys in a variety of styles, and no advertising except word-of-mouth. Getting a patent on a plush toy might have been impossible and would have taken several years, too long for easily copied toys. Trademark and trade dress protection wouldn't help much, because the company planned a variety of styles. But copyrights are available for sculptural art, and they're inexpensive and easy to obtain. The company chose to register copyrights and defend them vigorously. Cenar's firm has fended off numerous knockoffs.

That's the next step: monitoring the marketplace for knockoffs and trademark infringement, and taking increasingly firm steps to enforce your rights. Efforts typically begin with a letter of warning and could end with a court-ordered cease-and-desist order or even an award of damages. "If you don't take the time to enforce [your trademark], it becomes a very weak mark," Cenar says. "But a strong mark deters infringement, wins lawsuits and gets people to settle early." Sleep on your rights, and you'll lose them. Be proactive, and you'll protect them—and save money in the long run.

ADVICE TO AN ENTREPRENEUR

An inventor with a newly invented technology comes to you for advice on the following matters.

1. In running this new venture, I need to invest all available resources in producing the products and attracting customers. How important is it for me to divert money from those efforts to protect my intellectual property?
2. I have sufficient resources to obtain intellectual property protection, but how effective is that protection without a large stock of resources to invest in going after those that infringe on my rights? If I do not have the resources to defend a patent, is it worth obtaining one in the first place?
3. Are there circumstances when it is better for me not to be an innovator but rather produce "knockoffs" of others' innovations? What do I need to watch out for when imitating the products of others?

in obtaining design patents as a means of protecting their ornamental designs. These types of patents are also valuable for businesses that need to protect molded plastic parts, extrusions, and product and container configurations.

- *Plant patents.* These are issued under the same provisions as utility patents and are for new varieties of plants. These patents represent a limited area of interest, and thus very few of these types of patents are issued.

Patents are issued by the PTO. In addition to patents, this office administers other programs. One of these is the Disclosure Document Program, whereby the inventor files disclosure of the invention, giving recognition that he or she was the first to develop or invent the idea. In most cases, the inventor will subsequently patent the idea. A second program is the Defensive Publication Program. This gives the inventor the opportunity to protect an idea for which he or she does not wish to obtain a patent. It prevents anyone else from patenting this idea, but gives the public access to the invention. As of July 1, 2005, applicants may file for utility patents online. Software for filing is also available for download at the PTO Web site.

International Patents

With the World Trade Organization (WTO) and its predecessor, the General Agreement on Tariffs and Trade (GATT), more global free trade has been encouraged. However, although international trade has increased at the rate of about 6 percent per year since GATT was created in 1948, until recently there still was a need for an international patent law to protect firms from imitations and knockoffs. Another mechanism also was needed to provide firms some protection in global markets.[3]

In response, the Patent Cooperation Treaty (PCT)—with over 100 participants—was established to facilitate patent filings in multiple countries in one office rather than filing in each separate country. Administered by the World Intellectual Property Organization (WIPO) in Geneva, Switzerland, it provides a preliminary search that assesses whether the filing firm will face any possible infringements in any country.[4] The company can then decide whether to proceed with the required filing of the patent in each country. It has a 20-month time frame to file for these in-country patents. Even though the PCT allows for simultaneous filing of a patent in all member countries, there may be significant differences in patent laws in each of these countries. For example, patent laws in the U.S. allow computer software to receive both patent and copyright protection. On the other hand, in the European Union, patent protection is not extended to software.[5]

The Disclosure Document

disclosure document Statement to U.S. Patent and Trademark Office by inventor disclosing intent to patent idea

It is recommended that the entrepreneur first file a *disclosure document* to establish a date of conception of the invention. This document can be important when two entrepreneurs are filing for patents on similar inventions. This filing date is now also relevant when there is a foreign company involved. In that instance, the entrepreneur who can show that he or she was the first one to conceive of the invention will be given the rights to the patent.

To file a disclosure document, the entrepreneur must prepare a clear and concise description of the invention. In addition to the written material, photographs may be included. A cover letter and a duplicate are included with the description of the invention. Upon receipt of the information, the PTO will stamp and return the duplicate copy of the letter to the entrepreneur, thus establishing evidence of conception. The disclosure document is retained for two years and then destroyed unless a patent application is filed within this time. There is also a fee for this filing, which can be determined by contacting the PTO.

The disclosure document is not a patent application. Before actually applying for the patent it is advisable to retain a patent attorney to conduct a patent search. After the attorney completes the search, a decision can be made as to the patentability of the invention.

The Patent Application

The patent application must contain a complete history and description of the invention as well as claims for its usefulness. The actual form can be downloaded from the Patent and Trademark Office Web site. In general, the application will be divided into the following sections:

- *Introduction.* This section should contain the background and advantages of the invention and the nature of problems that it overcomes. It should clearly state how the invention differs from existing offerings.
- *Description of invention.* Next the application should contain a brief description of the drawings that accompany it. These drawings must comply with PTO requirements. Following this would be a detailed description of the invention, which may include engineering specifications, materials, components, and so on, that are vital to the actual making of the invention.
- *Claims.* This is probably the most difficult section of the application to prepare since claims are the criteria by which any infringements will be determined. They serve to specify what the entrepreneur is trying to patent. Essential parts of the invention should be described in broad terms so as to prevent others from getting around the patent. At the same time, the claims must not be so general that they hide the invention's uniqueness and advantages. This balance is difficult and should be discussed and debated with the patent attorney.

In addition to the above sections, the application should contain a declaration or oath that is signed by the inventor or inventors. This form will be supplied by an attorney. The completed application is then ready to be sent to the PTO, at which time the status of the invention becomes patent pending. This status is important to the entrepreneur because it now provides complete confidential protection until the application is approved. At that time, the patent is published and thus becomes accessible to the public for review.

A carefully written patent should provide protection and prevent competitors from working around it. However, once granted, it is also an invitation to sue or be sued if there is any infringement.

The fees for filing an application will vary, depending on the patent search and on claims made in the application. Attorney fees are also a factor in completing the patent application. Filing fees are mentioned earlier in the chapter. There are also maintenance fees that are paid at intervals during the life of a patent.

Patent Infringement

To this point, we have discussed the importance of and the procedures for filing a patent. It is also important for the entrepreneur to be sensitive about whether he or she is infringing on someone else's patent. The fact that someone else already has a patent does not mean the end of any illusions of starting a business. Many businesses, inventions, or innovations are the result of improvements on, or modifications of, existing products. Copying and improving on a product may be perfectly legal (no patent infringement) and actually good business strategy. If it is impossible to copy and improve the product to avoid patent infringement,

FIGURE 6.1 Options to Avoid Infringement

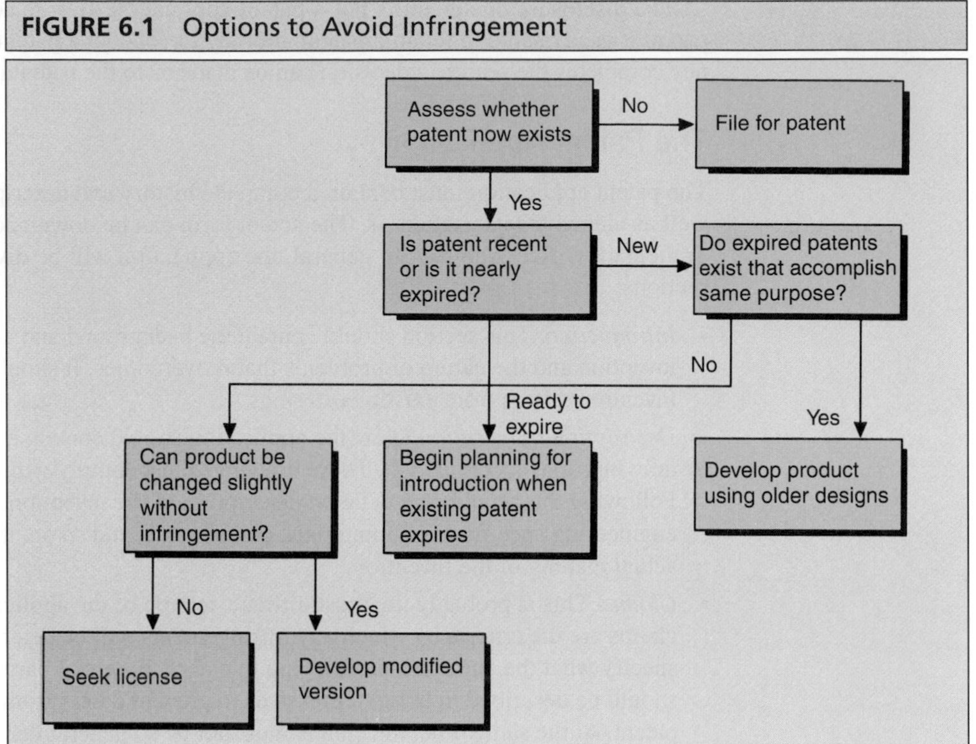

Source: Adapted from H. D. Coleman and J. D. Vandenberg, "How to Follow the Leader," *Inc.* (July 1988), pp. 81–82.

the entrepreneur may try to license the product from the patent holder. Figure 6.1 illustrates the steps that an entrepreneur should follow as he or she considers marketing a product that may infringe on an existing patent. The entrepreneur can now make use of the Internet to identify Web sites and services that can assist in the search process. If there is an existing patent that might involve infringement by the entrepreneur, licensing may be considered. If there is any doubt as to this issue, the entrepreneur should hire a patent attorney to ensure that there will not be any possibility of patent infringement. Table 6.1 provides a simple checklist that should be followed by an entrepreneur to minimize any patent risks.

BUSINESS METHOD PATENTS

With the growth of Internet use and software development has emerged the use of business method patents. For example, Amazon.com owns a business method patent for the single clicking feature used by a buyer on its Web site to order products. EBay was recently sued by Tom Woolston and his company MercExchange claiming a violation of a patent he owned that covered many fundamental aspects of eBay's operations, such as the buying and selling of products through a reverse auction process. Priceline.com claims that it holds a patent related to its service where a buyer can submit a price bid for a particular service. Expedia was forced to pay royalties to Priceline.com after being sued for patent infringement by Priceline.com. Many firms that hold these types of patents have used them to assault competitors and subsequently provide a steady stream of income from royalties or licensing fees. Whether these types of patents will hold up over a long period of time is still being debated.[6]

TABLE 6.1 Checklist for Minimizing Patent Risks

- Seek a patent attorney who has expertise in your product line.
- The entrepreneur should consider a design patent to protect the product design or product look.
- Before making an external disclosure of an invention at a conference or to the media, or before setting up a beta site, the entrepreneur should seek legal counsel since this external disclosure may negate a subsequent patent application.
- Evaluate competitor patents to gain insight into what they may be developing.
- If you think your product infringes on the patent of another firm, seek legal counsel.
- Verify that all employment contracts with individuals who may contribute new products have clauses assigning those inventions or new products to the venture.
- Be sure to properly mark all products granted a patent. Not having products marked could result in loss or damages in a patent suit.
- Consider licensing your patents. This can enhance the investment in a patent by creating new market opportunities and can increase long-term revenue.

Recently, technology entrepreneurs Mark Pincus and Reid Hoffman spent $700,000 for a patent on Web social networking. Both entrepreneurs had recently launched their own companies. Pincus had launched Tribe, offering online classifieds, and Hoffman had launched Linkedin, offering business leads. Both Pincus and Hoffman went through the effort of applying for their patent primarily after they had invested in Friendster, a Web site founded by former Netscape engineer Jonathon Abrams. Friendster offers online dating and has far exceeded the memberships of either Tribe or Linkedin. Pincus and Hoffman want the three Web sites to work together and insist they do not want to take down Friendster. However, the issue remains that, with Abrams's control of this business method patent, how much power do Pincus and Hoffman hold over the future of Friendster?[7]

START-UP WITHOUT A PATENT

Not all start-ups will have a product or concept that is patentable. In this case the entrepreneur should understand the competitive environment (see Chapters 7 and 8) to ascertain any advantages that may exist or to identify a unique positioning strategy (see Chapter 8). With a unique marketing plan, the entrepreneur may find that striking early in the market provides a significant advantage over any competitors. Maintaining this differential advantage will be a challenge but represents an important means of achieving long-term success.

TRADEMARKS

trademark A distinguishing word, name, or symbol used to identify a product

A *trademark* may be a word, symbol, design, or some combination of such, or it could be a slogan or even a particular sound that identifies the source or sponsorship of certain goods or services. Unlike the patent, a trademark can last indefinitely, as long as the mark continues to perform its indicated function. For all registrations filed after November 16, 1989, the trademark is given an initial 10-year registration with 10-year renewable terms. In the fifth to sixth year, the registrant is required to file an affidavit with the PTO indicating that the mark is currently in commercial use. If no affidavit is filed, the registration is canceled. Between the ninth and tenth year after registration, and every 10 years thereafter, the owner must file an application for renewal of the trademark. Otherwise, the registration is canceled. (There is a six-month grace period.)

Trademark law allows the filing of a trademark solely on the intent to use the trademark in interstate or foreign commerce. The filing date then becomes the first date use of the mark. This does not imply that the entrepreneur cannot file after the mark has already been in use. If this is the case, the entrepreneur may file a sworn statement that the mark is in commercial use, listing the date of first use. A properly worded declaration is included in the PTO application form.

It is also possible to file for a trademark if you intend to use this mark in the future. You are allowed to file in good faith along with a sworn statement in the application that there is intent to use the trademark. Actual use of the trademark must occur before the PTO will register the mark.[8]

The protection awarded is dependent on the character of the mark itself. There are four categories of trademarks: (1) coined marks denote no relationship between the mark and the goods or services (e.g., Mercedes, Kodak) and afford the possibility of expansion to a wide range of products; (2) an arbitrary mark is one that has another meaning in our language (e.g., Apple) and is applied to a product or service; (3) a suggestive mark is used to suggest certain features, qualities, ingredients, or characteristics of a product or service (i.e., Halo shampoo). It differs from an arbitrary mark in that it tends to suggest some describable attribute of the product or service. Finally, (4) a descriptive mark must have become distinctive over a significant period of time and gained consumer recognition before it can be registered. The mark then is considered to have secondary meaning; that is, it is descriptive of a particular product or service (e.g., Rubberoid as applied to roofing materials that contain rubber).[9]

Registering a trademark can offer significant advantages or benefits to the entrepreneur. Table 6.2 summarizes some of these benefits.

Registering the Trademark

As indicated earlier, the PTO is responsible for the federal registration of trademarks. To file an application, the entrepreneur must complete a simple form that can be downloaded and either submitted by mail or filed electronically using the Trademark Electronic Application System (TEAS) available on the PTO Web site.

TABLE 6.2 Benefits of a Registered Trademark

- It provides notice to everyone that you have exclusive rights to the use of the mark throughout the territorial limits of the United States.
- It entitles you to sue in federal court for trademark infringement, which can result in recovery of profits, damages, and costs.
- It establishes incontestable rights regarding the commercial use of the mark.
- It establishes the right to deposit registration with customs to prevent importation of goods with a similar mark.
- It entitles you to use the notice of registration.®
- It provides a basis for filing trademark application in foreign countries.

Filing of the trademark registration must meet four requirements: (1) completion of the written form, (2) a drawing of the mark, (3) five specimens showing actual use of the mark, and (4) the fee. Each trademark must be applied for separately. Upon receipt of this information, the PTO assigns a serial number to the application and sends a filing receipt to the applicant.

The next step in the registering process is a determination by the examining attorney at the PTO as to whether the mark is suitable for registration. Within about three months, an initial determination is made as to its suitability. Any objections by the entrepreneur must be raised within six months, or the application is considered abandoned. If the trademark is refused, the entrepreneur still has the right to appeal to the PTO.

Once accepted, the trademark is published in the *Trademark Official Gazette* to allow any party 30 days to oppose or request an extension to oppose. If no opposition is filed, the registration is issued. This entire procedure usually takes about 13 months from the initial filing.

COPYRIGHTS

copyright Right given to prevent others from printing, copying, or publishing any original works of authorship

A *copyright* protects original works of authorship. The protection in a copyright does not protect the idea itself, and thus it allows someone else to use the idea or concept in a different manner.

The copyright law has become especially relevant because of the tremendous growth of the use of the Internet, especially to download music, literary work, pictures, and videos, to name a few. Although software was added to copyright law in 1980, the issues surrounding access to material on the Internet have led to major legal battles for the entertainment industry.

When Napster made its entrance in 1999, Internet users were able to exchange music files at will. The music industry scrambled and fought against this use since its sales of CDs were significantly impacted. After three years the music industry was able to win its battle with Napster. However, recently the Supreme Court heard arguments that peer-to-peer (P2P) file-sharing software used specifically by StreamCast Networks and Grokster were infringing on copyrights held by entertainment companies. The case was based on the argument that StreamCast and Grokster should be accountable for secondary liability; in other words, they should be responsible for the illegal activities of their users. StreamCast and Grokster argued that technology campanies should not be restricted according to the use of their technology by customers because this could be a threat to technology innovation.[10]

However, in June 2005 the Supreme Court ruled that StreamCast and Grokster showed a clear intent to facilitate illegal file-sharing amongst their users. As a result of this ruling, Grokster has shut down its Web site and, along with other P2P firms, is looking for a more legitimate download service method, such as the popular Apple iTunes. The ruling may actually create a new impetus for the entertainment industry to negotiate agreements with these P2P firms in order to enhance their venture into online music distribution.[11]

Copyright protection related to the Internet will continue to be a concern and a gray area until precedents and regulations are made clear. Although these issues seem complicated, the registering procedure for copyright protection is fairly simple.

Copyrights are registered with the Library of Congress and will not usually require an attorney. To register a work, the applicant can send a completed application (available online at www.copyright.gov), two copies of the work, and the required filing fees (the initial filing fee is $30 but other fees may apply based on the number of works included). The term of the copyright is the life of the author plus 70 years.

AS SEEN IN *ENTREPRENEUR* MAGAZINE

PROVIDE ADVICE TO AN ENTREPRENEUR ABOUT INTERNATIONAL TRADEMARK PROTECTION

Your trademark is a valuable asset because that's how customers recognize your product or service. But in many countries, trademark protection belongs to the first company to register a trademark, not the first to use it. "Companies that have been using a mark for a long time sometimes don't bother with a search until there's a problem," says attorney Kara Cenar of the intellectual property firm Welsh & Katz in Chicago. But that approach could lead to trouble. "You [might] find that some other company has rushed to the trademark office and registered your mark," she says. The company might be trying to extract payment for the legal rights to your own mark, or it may want to hitch a ride on your reputation.

Just as it is in the United States, it's important to conduct a trademark search in other countries by hiring a firm that specializes in it, then to register your mark and defend it. There's no way to search all countries simultaneously. You have to do one at a time. A U.S.-only trademark search costs $400 to $500. It comes back in a thick bound report, telling which businesses have used your trade name for which products or services, and who has trademarks similar to yours. But you'd do well to have an experienced intellectual property lawyer formulate the search in the first place, to make sure you're not missing crucial elements, and then examine the results with an expert eye. Even if a given company lets its rights to your trade name lapse, it might still have common law rights to the name in a given state. You don't want to have to stay away from that state or operate there under a different name. The lawyer's time for all this typically costs $500 to $1,500—or even more.

Now multiply that by the world's 190 jurisdictions, and imagine the cost. That's why Cenar recommends a strategic approach to global trademarks. First, she says, consider which trademarks are most important. You might have several trademarks, but you only plan to use one of them overseas in the near future. Then decide where you want trademark protection first. Because the NAFTA treaty (North American Free Trade Agreement) makes North America one single market, first international registrations should be in Canada and Mexico. Then you'll want a Community Trademark, which covers the 15 countries of the European Union. After that, you may expand to other countries a few at a time, depending on your marketing plans. If the firm that handles your intellectual property has a relationship with a firm in that country, a few calls may be all that's needed.

Registering your business's trademark in another country doesn't necessarily give you all the rights you enjoy here at home. How your trademark is regulated depends on the laws of that country. But intellectual property law is broadly similar around the world, Cenar says. So with some strategic planning and investment in legal services, before long you can use your trademarks worldwide without unpleasant surprises.

ADVICE TO AN ENTREPRENEUR

An entrepreneur who wants to expand internationally over the next few years has read the above article and comes to you for advice:

1. Here we go again, more money for intellectual property protection. Are the lawyers just being overly conservative and not taking into sufficient consideration the cost of diverting resources away from growing my business and into funding these searches and registrations?
2. Should I even bother going through the process of registering my trademark in countries that don't seem to respect intellectual property protection?
3. I don't plan on entering into China, Thailand, and Malaysia for another four years. When do you suggest that I register for trademarks in these countries?

Source: Reprinted with permission of Entrepreneur Media, Inc., "Imperial Guard. If You Want a Global Empire,You'll Have to Tackle International Trademerk Protection," by Steven C. Bahls and Jane Easter Bahls, February 2003, *Entrepreneur* magazine: www.entrepreneur.com.

HOW MUCH RESPONSIBILITY SHOULD OUR YOUTH HAVE FOR ILLEGAL DOWNLOADING?

The lines have been drawn between the file-sharing companies (P2P) that provide software for free downloading of music and movies and the entertainment industry. The Supreme Court has ruled that these P2P companies do in fact facilitate the illegal downloading and sharing of entertainment. However, in spite of the fact that there has been so much publicity surrounding the legality of such initiatives, the youth of our nation continue to illegally download material that has been given copyright protection. This includes college students as well, recently evidenced by the fact that the Recording Industry Association of America (RIAA) filed copyright infringement lawsuits against 405 students at 18 different colleges. This list of colleges included Columbia, Harvard, and Princeton. According to the lawsuit, these students were allegedly using a new file-sharing application called i2hub to download songs and movies at lightning speeds. The RIAA also has evidence that this high-speed network is also being used at another 140 schools in 41 states.

In addition to these college and university incidents, a recent Harris Interactive poll found that kids and teens, ranging in age from 8 to 18, continue to download and share files that are copyright protected—in spite of the fact that nearly 90 percent know it is illegal. What is alarming in this study is the fact that 80 percent of the participants understand the meaning of a copyright, yet they continue to perform illegal functions. This finding illustrates a challenging ethical dilemma that persists in our society. The participants were more concerned with downloading a virus or spyware than they were with getting in trouble with the law. It is apparent from this research that young people consider stealing software a victimless crime, which would seem to underline the need for more ethics education at home and at school.

Sources: Robert Sebastian, "Infringing Copyrights at March 5," *PC Magazine* (June 7, 2005), p. 24, and "Majority of Youth Understand 'Copyright,' but Many Continue to Download Illegally," *PR Newswire* (May 18, 2004) pp. 1–3.

Besides computer software, copyrights are desirable for such things as books, scripts, articles, poems, songs, sculptures, models, maps, blueprints, collages, printed material on board games, data, and music. In some instances, several forms of protection may be available. For example, the name of a board game may be protected by trademark, the game itself protected by a utility patent, the printed matter or the board protected by a copyright, and the playing pieces covered by a design patent.

TRADE SECRETS

trade secret Protection against others revealing or disclosing information that could be damaging to business

In certain instances, the entrepreneur may prefer to maintain an idea or process as confidential and to sell or license it as a *trade secret*. The trade secret will have a life as long as the idea or process remains a secret.

A trade secret is not covered by any federal law but is recognized under a governing body of common laws in each state. Employees involved in working with an idea or process may be asked to first sign a confidential information agreement that will protect against their giving out the trade secret either while an employee or after leaving the organization. A simple example of a trade secret nondisclosure agreement is illustrated in Table 6.3. The entrepreneur should hire an attorney to help draw up any such agreement. The holder of the trade secret has the right to sue any signee who breaches such an agreement.

What or how much information to give to employees is difficult to judge and is often determined by the entrepreneur's judgment. Historically, entrepreneurs tended to protect

TABLE 6.3 A Simple Trade Secret Nondisclosure Agreement

WHEREAS, New Venture Corporation (NVC), Anywhere Street, Anyplace, U.S.A., is the Owner of information relating to; and

WHEREAS, NVC is desirous of disclosing said information to the undersigned (hereinafter referred to as "Recipient") for the purposes of using, evaluating, or entering into further agreements using such trade secrets as an employee, consultant, or agent of NVC; and

WHEREAS, NVC wishes to maintain in confidence said information as trade secret; and

WHEREAS, the undersigned Recipient recognizes the necessity of maintaining the strictest confidence with respect to any trade secrets of NVC.

Recipient hereby agrees as follows:

1. Recipient shall observe the strictest secrecy with respect to all information presented by NVC and Recipient's evaluation thereof and shall disclose such information only to persons authorized to receive same by NVC. Recipient shall be responsible for any damage resulting from any breach of this Agreement by Recipient.
2. Recipient shall neither make use of nor disclose to any third party during the period of this Agreement and thereafter any such trade secrets or evaluation thereof unless prior consent in writing is given by NVC.
3. Restriction on disclosure does not apply to information previously known to Recipient or otherwise in the public domain. Any prior knowledge of trade secrets by the Recipient shall be disclosed in writing within (30) days.
4. At the completion of the services performed by the Recipient, Recipient shall within (30) days return all original materials provided by NVC and any copies, notes, or other documents that are in the Recipient's possession pertaining thereto.
5. Any trade secrets made public through publication or product announcements are excluded from this agreement.
6. This agreement is executed and delivered within the State of _____ and it shall be construed, interpreted, and applied in accordance with the laws of that State.
7. This agreement, including the provision hereof, shall not be modified or changed in any manner except only in writing signed by all parties hereto.

Effective this ______________ day of ____________ 20 ____

RECIPIENT: ______________________________

NEW VENTURE CORPORATION:

By: ____________________

Title: ____________________

Date: ____________________

sensitive or confidential company information from anyone else by simply not making them privy to this information. Today, there is a tendency to take the opposite view, that the more information entrusted to employees, the more effective and creative employees can be. The argument is that employees cannot be creative unless they have a complete understanding of what is going on in the business.

Most entrepreneurs have limited resources, so they choose not to find means to protect their ideas, products, or services. This could become a serious problem in the future, since extolling competitive information legally is so easy to accomplish, unless the entrepreneur takes the proper precautions. For example, it is often easy to learn competitive information through such means as trade shows, transient employees, media interviews or announcements, and even Web sites. In all instances, overzealous employees are the problem. To try to control this problem, entrepreneurs should consider some of the ideas listed below.

- Train employees to refer sensitive questions to one person.
- Provide escorts for all office visitors.
- Avoid discussing business in public places.
- Keep important travel plans secret.
- Control information that might be presented by employees at conferences or published in journals.
- Use simple security such as locked file cabinets, passwords on computers, and shredders where necessary.
- Have employees and consultants sign nondisclosure agreements.
- Debrief departing employees on any confidential information.
- Avoid faxing any sensitive information.
- Mark documents confidential when needed.

Unfortunately, protection against the leaking of trade secrets is difficult to enforce. More important, legal action can be taken only after the secret has been revealed. It is not necessary for the entrepreneur to worry extensively about every document or piece of information. As long as minimal precautions are taken, most problems can be avoided, primarily because leaks usually occur inadvertently.

LICENSING

licensing Contractual agreement giving rights to others to use intellectual property in return for a royalty or fee

Licensing may be defined as an arrangement between two parties, where one party has proprietary rights over some information, process, or technology protected by a patent, trademark, or copyright. This arrangement, specified in a contract (discussed later in this chapter), requires the licensee to pay a royalty or some other specified sum to the holder of the proprietary rights (licensor) in return for permission to copy the patent, trademark, or copyright.

Thus, licensing has significant value as a marketing strategy to holders of patents, trademarks, or copyrights to grow their business in new markets when they lack resources or experience in those markets. It is also an important marketing strategy for entrepreneurs who wish to start a new venture but need permission to copy or incorporate the patent, trademark, or copyright with their ideas.

A patent license agreement specifies how the licensee would have access to the patent. For example, the licensor may still manufacture the product but give the licensee the rights to market it under their label in a noncompetitive market (i.e., foreign market). In other instances, the licensee may actually manufacture and market the patented product under its own label. This agreement must be carefully worded and should involve a lawyer, to ensure the protection of all parties.

Licensing a trademark generally involves a franchising agreement. The entrepreneur operates a business using the trademark and agrees to pay a fixed sum for use of the trademark, pay a royalty based on sales volume, buy supplies from the franchisor (examples would be Shell, Dunkin' Donuts, Pepsi Cola or Coca Cola bottlers, or Midas Muffler shops), or some combination of these. Franchising is discussed later in the text as an option for the entrepreneur as a way to start a new business or as a means of financing growth.

Copyrights are another popular licensed property. They involve rights to use or copy books, software, music, photographs, and plays, to name a few. In the late 1970s, computer games were designed using licenses from arcade games and movies. Television shows have also licensed their names for board games or computer games. Celebrities will often license the right to use their name, likeness, or image in a product (i.e., Andre Agassi tennis clothing, Elvis Presley memorabilia, or Mickey Mouse lunch boxes). This is actually analogous to a trademark license.

Licensing has become a revenue boom for many Fortune 500 companies. These firms spend billions of dollars each year on the research and development of new technologies that they will never bring to market. As a result, they will often license patents, trademarks, and other intellectual property to small companies that can profit from them. Microsoft Corporation, with its IP Ventures Division, is a great example of a firm that has offered technologies for biometric identity authentication, counterfeit-resistant labels, face detection and tracking, and other intellectual property that it does not know how to market or has no intent to market.[12] These agreements have generated millions of dollars in revenue for Microsoft. IBM has benefited from licensing agreements to the tune of more than $1 billion in 2004. Texas Instruments and Hewlett-Packard, also significant players in licensing, also have amassed billions from these deals.[13]

Through 2005, domestic technology firms in the U.S. market amassed more than $45 billion. Worldwide licensing revenue for these technology firms was about $100 billion. Indications are that these licensing agreements will continue to grow and be a major revenue generator for technology firms.[14]

Although technology is one of the largest generators of licensing revenue, there are other significant players in this market. The entertainment industry, particularly motion picture studios such as Disney, DreamWorks, Fox, Sony, and Warner Brothers, generates millions of dollars for its bottom line with licensing agreements for clothing, toys, games, and other related items. Although Disney recently ended its licensing agreement with McDonald's, it has inked huge deals with clothing retailers to market its line of distressed T-shirts and sportswear featuring Disney characters.[15] McDonald's, on the other hand, has moved on and signed licensing agreements with other motion picture studios such as DreamWorks, Animation SKG, and Pixar Animation Studios.[16]

Licensing is also popular around special sporting events, such as the Olympics, marathons, bowl games, and tournaments. Licenses to sell T-shirts, clothing, and other accessories require written permission in the form of a license agreement before sales are allowed.

Although licensing opportunities are often plentiful, they must be carefully considered as part of the venture's total business model. One licensing approach actually proved to be the salvation of a company headed for financial disaster. Ampex Corporation, once one of the premier innovators in the recording industry (Ampex invented the commercial video recorder in 1956 and the first U.S. tape recorder in 1948), had incurred five straight years of losses, had its listing on the American Stock Exchange removed, and found its stock price had dropped below $1. The company, however, found that patents that it held on digital imaging had been infringed upon by many large companies such as Sony, Canon, Sanyo, and Kodak. Ampex's strategy was to negotiate licensing agreements with these companies to allow their use of the technology held in Ampex patents, instead of trying to bring lawsuits for infringement. Sony alone agreed to pay $40 million for the rights to use the digital technology that was protected by one of these patents. An even larger claim exists against Kodak, but as of this date, it has refused to cut a deal.

With its new source of revenue, the company has shown a 2004 profit of $47.1 million on revenue of $101.5 million, mostly resulting from these licensing agreements. It also may soon be listed on NASDAQ. The only question that remains in regard to this new-found source of revenue for Ampex is whether the lack of disclosure on some of these deals has violated SEC rules. However, the company is making efforts toward broader disclosure and has even presented some of its future plans for obtaining licensing agreements with companies that market cell phones, camcorders, and other devices in those cases where Ampex may have some legal right to royalties based on its digital imaging patents.[17]

Before entering into a licensing agreement, the entrepreneur should ask the following questions:

- Will the customer recognize the licensed property?
- How well does the licensed property complement my products or services?
- How much experience do I have with the licensed property?
- What is the long-term outlook for the licensed property? (For example, the loss of popularity of a celebrity can also result in an end to a business involving that celebrity's name.)
- What kind of protection does the licensing agreement provide?
- What commitment do I have in terms of payment of royalties, sales quotas, and so on?
- Are renewal options possible and under what terms?

Licensing is an excellent option for the entrepreneur to increase revenue, without the risk and costly start-up investment. To be able to license requires the entrepreneur to have something to license, which is why it is so important to seek protection for any product, information, name, and so on, with a patent, trademark, or copyright. On the other hand, licensing can also be a way to start a new venture when the idea may infringe on someone else's patent, trademark, or copyright. In this instance, the entrepreneur has nothing to lose by trying to seek a license agreement from the holder of the property.

Licensing continues to be a powerful marketing tool. With the advice of a lawyer, entrepreneurs may find that licensing opportunities are a way to minimize risk, expand a business, or complement an existing product line.

PRODUCT SAFETY AND LIABILITY

product safety and liability Responsibility of a company to meet any legal specifications regarding a new product covered by the Consumer Product Safety Act

It is very important for the entrepreneur to assess whether any product that is to be marketed in the new venture is subject to any regulations under the Consumer Product Safety Act. The act, which was passed in 1972, created a five-member commission that has the power to prescribe safety standards for more than 15,000 types of consumer products.

In addition to setting standards for products, the commission also has a great deal of responsibility and power to identify what it considers to be substantial hazards and bar products it considers unsafe. It is especially active in recognizing whether possible product defects may be hazardous to consumers. When this is the case, the commission will request the manufacturer, in writing, to take corrective action.

The act was amended and signed into law in 1990. The amended law establishes stricter guidelines for reporting product defects and any injury or death resulting from such defects. The cost of not reporting a hazard can result in large fines (millions of dollars), as evidenced by the recent fine of $950,000 levied against Bowflex fitness machines for delaying reports of injuries from its customers. In addition, a manufacturer of infant carriers, strollers, and high chairs recently agreed to pay a record $4 million in penalties for failing to report defects in its products. It is clear that the Consumer Products Safety Commission is continuing its enforcement efforts. Examples such as these illustrate the importance of the timely reporting of any hazard issues.[18]

Any new product that is responsible for the entrepreneur's entry into a business should be assessed to ascertain whether it falls under the Consumer Product Safety Act. If it does, the entrepreneur will have to follow the appropriate procedures to ensure that he or she has met all the necessary requirements.

Product liability problems are complex and continue to be an important consideration for entrepreneurs. Changes in the legislation, thus far unsuccessful, are proposed by some who feel reform is necessary to address many longtime concerns of businesses such as the amount of punitive damages allowed in certain cases and the application of the product liability laws to durable goods that have been in use for more than 15 years. Changes in the global market have also contributed to the need for reform. Risk managers claim that without new reform legislation start-up companies that do not have a product liability track record may have difficulty finding this type of coverage.

Claims regarding product liability usually fall under one of the following categories:

1. *Negligence.* Extends to all parts of the production and marketing process. It involves being negligent in the way a product is presented to a client, such as using deficient labels, false advertising, and so on.
2. *Warranty.* Consumers may sue if advertising or information overstates the benefits of a product, or if the product does not perform as stated.
3. *Strict liability.* In this action, a consumer is suing because the product in question was defective before its receipt.
4. *Misrepresentation.* This occurs when advertising, labels, or other information misrepresents material facts concerning the character or quality of the product.

The best protection against product liability is to produce safe products and to warn consumers of any potential hazards. It is impossible to expect zero defects, so entrepreneurs should be sensitive to what kinds of product liability problems may occur.

INSURANCE

Some of the problems relating to product liability were discussed in the previous section. Besides being cautious, it is also in the best interests of the entrepreneur to purchase insurance in the event that problems do occur. Service-related businesses such as day-care centers, amusement parks, shopping centers, and so on, have had significant increases in the number of lawsuits.

In general, most firms should consider coverage for those situations described in Table 6.4. Each of these types of insurance provides a means of managing risk in the new business. The main problem is that the entrepreneur usually has limited resources in the beginning. Thus, it is important to first determine whether any of these types of insurance are needed. Note that some insurance, such as disability and vehicle coverage, is required by law and cannot be avoided. Other insurance, such as life insurance of key employees, is not required but may be necessary to protect the financial net worth of the venture. Once the entrepreneur determines what types of insurance are needed, then a decision can be made as to how much insurance and from what company. It is wise to get quotes from more than one insurance firm since rates and options can also vary. The total insurance cost represents an important financial planning factor, and the entrepreneur needs to consider increasing premiums in cost projections.

Skyrocketing medical costs have probably had the most significant impact on insurance premiums. This is especially true for workers' compensation premiums, which for some

TABLE 6.4 Types of Insurance and Possible Coverage

Types of Insurance	Coverage Possible
Property	• Fire insurance to cover losses to goods and premises resulting from fire and lightning. Can extend coverage to include risks associated with explosion, riot, vehicle damage, windstorm hail, and smoke.
	• Burglary and robbery to cover small losses for stolen property in cases of forced entry (burglary) or if force or threat of violence was involved (robbery).
	• Business interruption will pay net profits and expenses when a business is shut down because of fire or other insured cause.
Casualty	• General liability covers the costs of defense and judgments obtained against the company resulting from bodily injury or property damage. This coverage can also be extended to cover product liability.
	• Automobile liability is needed when employees use their own cars for company business.
Life	• Life insurance protects the continuity of the business (especially a partnership). It can also provide financial protection for survivors of a sole proprietorship or for loss of a key corporate executive.
Workers' compensation	• May be mandatory in some states. Provides benefits to employees in case of work-related injury.
Bonding	• This shifts responsibility to the employee for performance of a job. It protects company in case of employee theft of funds or protects contractor if subcontractor fails to complete a job within an agreed-upon time frame.

entrepreneurs have doubled or tripled in the last few years. Insurance companies calculate the premium for workers' compensation as a percentage of payroll, the type of business, and the number of prior claims. Given the problems with fraudulent or suspicious claims, some states are beginning to undertake reforms in the coverage. Even before reforms are enacted, the entrepreneur can take some action to control the premiums by paying attention to details, such as promoting safety through comprehensive guidelines that are communicated to every staff member. Being personally involved with safety can, in the long run, significantly control workers' compensation premiums.

Entrepreneurs also have to consider health care coverage. This is an important benefit to employees and will require the venture to cover a significant portion of this expense for the employee. Rates to the company will vary significantly depending on the plan and its various options. Health insurance premiums are less expensive if there is a large group of insured participants. This is, of course, difficult for a start-up venture but can be resolved by joining a group such as a professional association that offers such coverage.

However, if you are a self-employed entrepreneur, the options are limited. If you are leaving a corporate position, consider extending your health care benefits with a COBRA. This usually allows you to continue on the same health care policy you were on for about three years. However, you will have to now pay the entire premium on the policy. If your

COBRA has expired or one is not available, you can consider contacting your state insurance department, which can supply a list of insurance companies that provide individual health care insurance. Policies that have higher deductibles can also be considered because of their lower premiums. For additional assistance in these matters it is recommended that the entrepreneur contact the Association of Health Insurance Agents, the Health Insurance Association of America, or the U.S. Labor Department, all located in Washington, DC.

Most recently there has been some controversy regarding safety for employees in home-based businesses. The government's response has been that the company is responsible for safety or health violations in home-based offices. The best protection for entrepreneurs operating home-based businesses is to write handbooks with stated policies on home office safety.

Seeking advice from an insurance agent is often difficult because the agent is trying to sell insurance. However, there are specialists at universities or the Small Business Administration who can provide this advice at little or no cost.

SARBANES-OXLEY ACT

After a lengthy period of reported corporate misconduct involving companies such as Enron and Arthur Andersen, Congress passed the Sarbanes-Oxley Act in 2002. Although this act has provided a mechanism for greater control over the financial activities of public companies, it also has created some difficulties for start-ups and smaller companies. Arguments are now being put forth that the law was passed too quickly as a result of all of the corporate scandals and that the provisions are too vague and their implementation by CPAs too rigid. In fact it is argued that the cost of compliance is not only prohibitive but that it has led to a decline in the number of start-ups going public.[19]

The act contains a number of provisions and no attempt will be made here to cover them all. Instead an overview of the law's requirements will be discussed. The complete law or relevant sections can be downloaded from the Internet.

The Sarbanes-Oxley Act covers a wide range of corporate governance activities. Under this law, CEOs are required to vouch for financial statements through a series of internal control mechanisms and reports. Directors must meet background, length of service, and responsibilities requirements regarding internal auditing and control. Any attempt to influence the auditor or impede the internal auditing process is considered a criminal act. In addition, the law covers bank fraud; securities fraud; and fraud by wire, radio, or TV.[20]

With the passage of this law there has been some concern as to the interpretation of this law and subsequent directors' liability. For example, will this law discourage qualified individuals from being members of important boards because of their concern for negative publicity that could be initiated by a disgruntled employee or stockholder?

Foreign companies that trade on U.S. stock exchanges are often delisted since there are major conflicts with the provisions of the new law and the laws of that foreign country. For example, independent audit committees, required by the new law, conflict with some foreign countries' rules and customs. This is only one example of the many conflicts that presently exist with foreign laws and customs.[21]

At present, private companies are not included in this act. However, there could be some future controls established to prevent any of these governance issues in private companies. Private companies are also subject to control if they consult with a public company and in any way influence that public company in any wrongdoing established by the Sarbanes-Oxley Act.

The other option, of course, is for the entrepreneur to set up a board of advisors instead of an extended board of directors. Advisors would not be subject to liability since they do not formulate final policy for the venture but only provide recommendations to the actual board of directors, which in this case could consist of the management of the start-up venture. If a venture capitalist or even an angel investor were involved, they would require a board seat, in which case the use of a board of advisors would not likely be acceptable and liability protection would be necessary.

CONTRACTS

contract A legally binding agreement between two parties

The entrepreneur, in starting a new venture, will be involved in a number of negotiations and *contracts* with vendors, landlords, and clients. A contract is a legally enforceable agreement between two or more parties as long as certain conditions are met. Table 6.5 identifies these conditions and the outcomes (breaches of contract) should one party not live up to the terms of the contract. It is very important for the entrepreneur to understand the fundamental issues related to contracts while also recognizing the need for a lawyer in many of these negotiations.

Often business deals are concluded with a handshake. Ordering supplies, lining up financing, reaching an agreement with a partner, and so on, are common situations in which a handshake consummates the deal. Usually, when things are operating smoothly, this procedure is sufficient. However, if there are disagreements, the entrepreneur may find that there is no deal and that he or she may be liable for something never intended. The courts generally provide some guidelines based on precedence of cases. One rule is to never rely on a handshake if the deal cannot be completed within one year. For example, a company that trains salespeople asked another firm to produce videotapes used in the training. The training firm was asked to promise to use the tapes only for its own sales force and not to sell the tapes to others. Some time after the tapes were produced, this firm began to produce and sell the tapes under a newly formed company. The original developer of the tapes brought suit, and the courts ruled that an oral agreement for more than one year is not

TABLE 6.5 Contract Conditions and Results of a Breach of Contract

Contract Conditions

- An offer is made. It can be oral or written but is not binding until voluntary acceptance of offer is given.
- Voluntary acceptance of offer.
- Consideration (something of value) is given by both parties.
- Both parties are competent and/or have the right to negotiate for their firms.
- Contract must be legal. Any illegal activities under a contract are not binding. An example might be gambling.
- Any sales of $500 or more must be in writing.

Results of a Contract Breach

- The party in violation of a contract may be required to live up to the agreement or pay damages.
- If one party fails to live up to its end of a contract, the second party may also agree to drop the matter and thus not live up to the agreement as well. This is referred to as contract restitution.

enforceable. The only way that this could have been prevented was if the copying firm had signed a contract.

In addition to the one-year rule of thumb, the courts insist that a written contract exist for all transactions over $500. Even a quote on a specified number of parts from a manufacturer may not be considered a legal contract. For example, if an entrepreneur asked for and received a quote for 10 items and then ordered only 1 item, the seller would not have to sell that item at the original quoted price unless a written contract existed. If the items totaled over $500, even the quoted price could be changed without a written contract.

Most sellers would not want to try to avoid their obligations in the above example. However, unusual circumstances may arise that force the seller to change his or her mind. Thus, the safest way to conduct business deals is with a written contract, especially if the amount of the deal is over $500 and is likely to extend beyond one year.

Any deal involving real estate must be in writing to be valid. Leases, rentals, and purchases all necessitate some type of written agreement.

Although a lawyer might be necessary in very complicated or large transactions, the entrepreneur cannot always afford one. Therefore, it is helpful for the entrepreneur to understand the four essential items in an agreement to provide the best legal protection.[22]

1. All the parties involved should be named and their specific roles in the transaction specified (e.g., buyer, seller, consultant, client).
2. The transaction should be described in detail (e.g., exact location of land, dates, units, place of delivery, payor for transportation).
3. The exact value of the transaction should be specified (e.g., installment payment with finance charges).
4. The signature(s) of the person(s) involved in the deal should be obtained.

IN REVIEW

SUMMARY

This chapter explores some of the major concerns regarding intellectual property of the entrepreneur, as well as other important legal issues such as product safety, insurance, contracts, and the Sarbanes-Oxley Act. The problems with intellectual property have become more complicated with the growth of the Internet. It is important for the entrepreneur to seek legal advice in making any intellectual property legal decisions such as patents, trademarks, copyrights, and trade secrets. Lawyers have specialties that can provide the entrepreneur with the most appropriate advice under the circumstances. There are also resources identified in the chapter that should be considered before hiring an attorney. Some of this information can save time and money for the entrepreneur.

A patent requires a patent attorney, who assists the entrepreneur in completing an application to the Patent and Trademark Office with the history and description of the invention, as well as claims for its usefulness. An assessment of the existing patent(s) will help to ascertain whether infringement is likely and to evaluate the possibilities of modifying the patented product or licensing the rights from the holder of the patent.

A trademark may be a word, symbol, design, or some combination, or a slogan or sound that identifies the source of certain goods or services. Trademarks give the entrepreneur certain benefits as long as the following four requirements are met: (1) completion of the written application form, (2) submission of a drawing of the mark, (3) submission of five specimens showing actual use of the mark, and (4) payment of the required fees.

Copyrights protect original works of authorship. Copyrights are registered with the Library of Congress and do not usually require an attorney. Copyrights have become relevant to the use of the Internet especially to download music, literary works, pictures, or videos. Copyright protection related to the Internet will continue to be a gray area until regulations are made more clear. Both trademark and copyright applications can be filed electronically.

Licensing is a viable means of starting a business using someone else's product, name, information, and so on. It is also an important strategy that the entrepreneur can use to expand the business without extensive risk or large investments.

The entrepreneur should also be sensitive to possible product safety and liability requirements. Careful scrutiny of possible product problems, as well as insurance, can reduce the risk. Other risks relating to property insurance, life insurance, health insurance, workers' compensation, and bonding should be evaluated to ascertain the most cost-effective program for the entrepreneur.

Contracts are an important part of the transactions that the entrepreneur will make. As a rule of thumb, oral agreements are invalid for deals over one year and over $500. In addition, all real estate transactions must be in writing to be valid. It is important in a written agreement to identify all the parties and their respective roles, to describe the transaction in detail, to specify the value of the deal, and to obtain the signatures of the persons with whom you are doing business.

The Sarbanes-Oxley Act was passed in 2002 and places a great burden on public companies to streamline their financial reporting, modify the role and responsibility of boards of directors, and basically provide more checks and balances to avoid repeating the scandals of WorldCom, Enron, and others. There are a number of provisions of the law and entrepreneurs should be aware of any relevant requirements, particularly if there is intent to take the company public. At this point the law applies only to public companies, but there are possible interactions with private firms as well as likely changes to these laws that will require continued scrutiny by entrepreneurs.

RESEARCH TASKS

1. Using the Internet, obtain copies of three patents that are at least three years old. What are the elements that are common across these patents? What are the differences? Which do you believe will be the greatest success? Can you find any evidence of products that are now on the market that incorporate any of these patented technologies?
2. Search press reports for patent infringement cases. Describe the process and the outcome. Of particular value are examples that list the legal costs of defending patent infringements and the amount awarded for a successful defense.
3. What are some of the world's most famous trademarks? Use data to back up your answer.
4. Provide a real-life example for each of the following different types of product liability: (a) negligence, (b) warranty, (c) strict liability, and (d) misrepresentation. When possible, report both the details and the payouts.
5. How much does it cost to apply for and obtain a patent?

CLASS DISCUSSION

1. Provide three examples of companies that use trade secrets to keep competitors from imitating their products. What activities do they undertake to maintain this secrecy? How effective do you think they are?
2. Should copyrighted music be available on the Internet free of charge, even if it is against the wishes of the artist and the recording company? Consider both sides of the argument to make a more convincing argument.
3. To what extent should the government be involved in creating and enforcing safety laws and to what extent should companies (and industries) be responsible for creating their own standards and self-policing those standards?

SELECTED READINGS

Banham, Russ. (2005). Valuing IP Post Sarbanes-Oxley. *Journal of Accountancy,* vol. 200, no. 5, pp. 72–78.

This article discusses business valuation issues faced by certified public accountants after the passage of the Sarbanes-Oxley Act. The sections of this law that particularly affect public companies and intellectual property are the primary focus of the paper.

Baroncelli, Eugenia; Carsten Fink; and Beata Javorcik. (2005). The Global Distribution of Trademarks: Some Stylised Facts. *World Economy,* vol. 28, no. 6, pp. 765–82.

This paper provides the first empirical analysis of the global distribution of trademarks. The analysis is based on data compiled and published by the World Intellectual Property Organization. It includes an analysis of trademark registrations across countries of different income groups and different sectors of the economy. The results provide implications for changes in intellectual property protection in international trade.

Basnet, Chuda; L. R. Foulds; and Warren Parker. (2006). IP Manager: A Microcomputer Based DSS for Intellectual Property Management. *Decision Support Systems,* vol. 41, no. 2, pp. 532–41.

This paper proposes a decision support system (DSS) for the management of the costs associated with the payment of fees to protect the intellectual property of organizations involved in research and development. The system aids in creating or improving intellectual property (IP) registration and maintenance strategies.

Caballero-Sanz, F.; R. Moner-Colonques; and J. Sempere-Monerris. (2005). Licensing Policies for a New Product. *Economics of Innovation & New Technology,* vol. 14, no. 8, pp. 697–713.

This paper assesses the licensing policies for the developer of a new product. The study argues that the best licensing policy is fixed-fee licensing with an exclusive territory clause. Consumers are felt to be better off with the fixed-fee arrangement but do not prefer the exclusive territory provision.

Cromley, Timothy. (2004). Twenty Steps for Pricing a Patent. *Journal of Accountancy,* vol. 198, no. 5, pp. 31–34.

There are a number of steps that can be followed to assist the accountant in determining an evaluation of a patent. In addition to a discussion of these procedures, this paper also discusses the makeup of a valuation team.

Depoorter, Ben; Francisco Parisi; and Sven Vanneste. (2005). Problems with the Enforcement of Copyright Law: Is There a Social Norm Backlash? *International Journal of the Economics of Business,* vol. 12, no. 3, pp. 361–69.

Copyright norms have developed in opposition to existing copyright laws. This article argues that copyright enforcement efforts may actually induce further copyright disobedience by reinforcing the moral and social beliefs against conventional copyright law.

France, M.; and S. Siwolop. (1996). How to Skin a Copycat. *BusinessWeek* (October 21, 1996), pp. 4–7.

Small businesses are particularly vulnerable to knockoffs because of their limited resources. A number of examples, with effective strategies that can be used to fight knockoffs, are presented.

Goodden, Randall. (2001). Product Liability Prevention—The Next Dimension in Quality. *Total Quality Management,* vol. 12, no. 5, pp. 623–28.

This article focuses on the area of product liability prevention as a revolutionary new dimension in product quality. It argues that manufacturers need to see the connection between product liability and quality by discussing issues of safety, quality, and reliability of products.

Halligan, Mark R.; and Richard F. Weyand. (2005). The Economic Valuation of Trade Secret Assets. *Computer and International Lawyer,* vol. 22, no. 7 (July 2005), pp. 4–7.

This article focuses on a method for valuing a trade secret asset. Depreciated cost, replacement cost, fair market value, and the net present values of future cash flows are all acceptable methods, depending on the situation. The cash flow method works best since it separates economic and legal issues. Value is thus based on the total amount of income that will be derived from keeping the information secret as compared to the expected income over time if the information were in the public domain.

Hundt, Reed. (2006). Patently Obvious. *Forbes,* vol. 177, no. 2 (January 30, 2006), p. 36.

This article provides some interesting arguments as to why the United States needs to create a new patent system. It points to the fight between Blackberry producer Research in Motion (RIM) and NTP—a patent-holding company that claims that RIM has infringed on wireless technology patents that it holds. The article argues that a fast track basis for challenging a patent should be made available to avoid such long-term implications for the possibly infringing firm.

Johnson, Scott. (2003). Using and Protecting Trademarks. *The CPA Journal* (February 2003), pp. 39–41.

This article argues that because a trademark is an appreciating asset with a potentially perpetual life, it is important to choose trademarks carefully and protect them through federal registration and controlled licensing. It discusses issues of trademark clearance, the establishment of trademark rights, the federal trademark registration and application process, and domain names.

Lawrence, William F.; Barry S. White; Thomas J. Kowalski; Susan K. Lehnhardt; and David A. Zwally. (2001). Licensing Intellectual Property. *Journal of Commercial Biotechnology,* vol. 7, no. 3, pp. 208–17.

This paper presents an overview of several issues concerning licensing intellectual property in or from the United States. It addresses (1) circumstances requiring government approval of intellectual property license; (2) licensing of intellectual property created with the help of government grants; and (3) the value of a patent license in litigation settlements.

Leenes, Ronald; and Bert-Jaap Koops. (2005). Code: Privacy's Death or Saviour? *International Review of Law, Computers & Technology,* vol. 19, no. 3 (November 2005), pp. 329–40.

The relationship between code and privacy is a very complex issue. The authors argue that privacy threats on code are usually not implemented on purpose but that privacy erosion is just a side effect of technological development. It is argued that digital rights management systems can actually prevent users from breaching copyrights more effectively than copyright law.

Newiss, Hilary; and Audrey Horton. (2001). Practical and Legal Preparation for Young Companies Seeking Technology Transfer. *Journal of Commercial Biotechnology,* vol. 7, no. 4, pp. 335–42.

This paper looks at the basic law of intellectual property as it applies to a small biotechnology company or start-up. It focuses on the systems and attention to paperwork required so that the company can maximize its intellectual property protection.

Ryan, Kenneth E. (2003). Product Liability Risk Control. *Professional Safety* (February 2003), pp. 20–25.

In the current legal climate, parties injured by the defective product can easily sue not only the manufacturer of the product, but also any commercial supplier in the distribution channel, including the wholesaler and the retailer. The article discusses some of the risks and liabilities that these parties face and some of the product quality guidelines that they can follow in order to limit their liability.

END NOTES

1. See L. Olmstead, "How Steve Lipscomb Reinvented Poker and Built the Hottest Business In America," *Inc.* (May 2005), pp. 80–92; S. Fitch, "Poker's New Suit," *Forbes* (November 1, 2004), p. 62; and "WPT Enterprises, Inc., Announces Third Quarter 2005 Financial Results," *PR Newswire* (November 8, 2005), pp.1–2.
2. Patent and Trademark Office, U.S. Department of Commerce Web Site (www.uspto.gov).
3. "Weighing Up the WTO," *Economist* (November 23, 2002), p. 72.
4. W. B. State, "Filing Strategies under the Patent Cooperation Treaty," *Intellectual Property and Technology Law Journal* (October 2002), pp. 1–6.
5. G. H. Pike, "Global Technology and Local Patents," *Information Today* (May 2005), pp. 41–46.
6. R. C. Scheinfield and J. D. Sullivan, "Lawyers and Technology Internet-Related Patents: Are They Paying Off?" *New York Law Journal* (December 10, 2002), p. 5.
7. V. Murphy, "You're Not My Friendster," *Forbes* (December 8, 2003), p. 59.
8. See www.uspto.gov/main/trademarks.htm.
9. S. W. Halpern, C. A. Nard, and K. L. Post, *Fundamentals of United States Intellectual Property Law* (Boston: Klumer Law International, 1999), pp. 30–34.
10. "Face the Music," *Economist* (April 2, 2005), pp. 57–58.
11. "Calling the Tune," *Economist* (October 8, 2005), p. 75.
12. M. Hendricks, "License to Thrive," *Entrepreneur* (October 2005), p. 22.
13. "Patents: Cuffing Innovation," *Electronics Design* (April 28, 2005), pp. 49–55.
14. "A Market for Ideas," *Economist* (October 22, 2005), pp. 3–6.
15. L. Decarlo, "Americas Most Wanted," *Women's Wear Daily* (July 2005), p. 52.
16. M. Marr and S. Grey, "McDonald's Woos New Partners as Disney Pact Nears End," *The Wall Street Journal Eastern Edition* (June 6, 2005) p. B1–B2.
17. S. E. Ante and J. Hibbard, "How Ampex Squeezed Out Cash," *BusinessWeek* (April 18, 2005), pp. 61–62.

18. G. D. Hailey and J. D. Knowles, "Report Your Defective Products to the CPSC Immediately," *Response* (July 2005), p. 51.
19. I. Mount, "Death of the IPO Dream," *Fortune Small Business* (April 2005), pp. 16–18.
20. G. Weiss, "Tighter Nooses for White Collars," *BusinessWeek* (April 7, 2003), p. 10.
21. S. Bahls and J. E. Bahls, "Witness Protection," *Entrepreneur* (April 3, 2003), pp. 68–70.
22. M. Marley, "Let's Shake on That," *Inc.* (June 1986), pp. 131–32.

7

THE BUSINESS PLAN: CREATING AND STARTING THE VENTURE

LEARNING OBJECTIVES

1
To define what the business plan is, who prepares it, who reads it, and how it is evaluated.

2
To understand the scope and value of the business plan to investors, lenders, employees, suppliers, and customers.

3
To identify information needs and sources for each critical section of the business plan.

4
To enhance awareness of the value of the Internet as an information resource and marketing tool.

5
To present examples and a step-by-step explanation of the business plan.

6
To present helpful questions for the entrepreneur at each stage of the planning process.

7
To understand how to monitor the business plan.

OPENING PROFILE

BELINDA GUADARRAMA

www.gcmicro.com

The business plan, although it is often criticized as being "dreams of glory," is probably the single most important document to the entrepreneur at the start-up stage. Potential investors are not likely to consider investing in a new venture until the business plan has been completed. In addition, the business plan helps the entrepreneur maintain perspective as to what needs to be accomplished.

The development and preparation of a business plan can entail many obstacles and takes a strong commitment by an entrepreneur before it can actually be completed and then implemented. No one knows this better than Belinda Guadarrama, the president and CEO of GC Micro Corporation. Her company supplies computer hardware and software to Fortune 1000 companies as well as the defense and aerospace industry.

As the entrepreneur of this now multi-million-dollar company, Belinda has been recognized by two Hispanic organizations—the U.S. Hispanic Chamber of Commerce and the Latin Business Association—as Hispanic Businesswoman of the year 2002. She also was runner-up for National Small Business Person of the year and her firm has been ranked among the 500 largest Hispanic-owned companies.

Although today she is a successful entrepreneur, the journey was a long and arduous process with a number of highs and lows. After graduating from Trinity University and taking a number of graduate courses at the University of Texas at Austin, she began working for the Texas attorney general as the director of personnel and training. She later moved to California during the 1980s technology boom to work for a mail-order software company. Like many others, she arrived at work one day to find a note on the door indicating that the business was closed.

At that point Belinda made the decision to start her own business. She felt it was a great time to take some risk since she had no job and limited prospects. In 1986, with a few former co-workers, she launched GC Micro Corporation. To raise initial capital and money for other expenses while a business plan was being developed, she sold her house and cashed in her retirement money. She made a conscious decision at this point to put everything on the line. Eventually, with business plan in hand, she began knocking on doors to try to raise money for the start-up. It was then that she began to face some of the lows in the entrepreneurial process as she incurred one rejection after another. She could not even get a bank to lend her $5,000 to keep going. Fortunately, she persisted until she came upon the Small Business Administration (SBA) loan program that guarantees a large percentage of a loan through a local participating bank. After submitting her plan through this program, she received her first loan from a local bank.

Raising the start-up capital was only one of the early obstacles that she overcame. Being a woman and a Latina she had to overcome many negative stereotypes. In one meeting with a potential client she was told that as a minority woman she did not have sufficient management qualifications to represent its product line and was hence turned down. However, her hard work and persistence paid off and at the end of the first year of business the company attained revenue of $209,000. With this success, the client that had turned her down changed its mind and she became an authorized dealer for its products.

Other success followed and soon she was pursuing contracts with the U.S. Department of Defense. In researching this market, she discovered that many government contractors are required to include a percentage of minority-owned businesses as subcontractors. She also discovered that there were not enough minority-owned businesses, presenting great opportunities for her venture. However, as she continued to investigate her opportunities she found she was blocked from records to which she had previously had access. She decided to pursue this in court, knowing that this could put her entire business on the line. Subsequently the case *GC Micro Corporation v. the Defense Logistics Agency* reached the courts and then dragged on for several years. During this time her business was in jeopardy since many companies stated they would no longer work with her. Eventually she won her case. Her reputation as someone not afraid to take a stand and with strong leadership skills spread throughout the industry.

The company has become one of the few just-in-time (JIT) system contract suppliers. In 2003 the company received the JIT Supplier Partnership Award. Guadarrama's entrepreneurial skills have also spilled over to civic-minded activities, supporting such programs as the California Latino-Chicano High School Drop-Out Prevention Program, the Canal Community Alliance, the Ochoa Migrant Farm Workers Camp, and the Gilroy YMCA. Belinda's success is a tribute to her strong entrepreneurial character. She was not afraid of the hard work required to plan her business—and she was not afraid to stand up for what she felt was right. Her commitment to the community has made her an inspiration to many other Hispanic business men and women.

GC Micro Corporation now has 14 warehouses across the U.S., representing inventory of more than 280,000 products valued at more than $2 billion. The fruits of Belinda's successful business plan now include authorized dealer partnerships with many Fortune 500 companies such as Apple, Cisco, Gateway, Hewlett-Packard, IBM, Microsoft, Sun Microsystems, and Toshiba.[1]

PLANNING AS PART OF THE BUSINESS OPERATION

Before we begin a discussion of the business plan, it is important for the reader to understand the different types of plans that may be part of any business operation. Planning is a process that never ends for a business. It is extremely important in the early stages of any new venture when the entrepreneur will need to prepare a preliminary business plan. The plan will become finalized as the entrepreneur has a better sense of the market, the product or services to be marketed, the management team, and the financial needs of the venture. As the venture evolves from an early start-up to a mature business, planning will continue as management seeks to meet its short-term or long-term business goals.

For any given organization, it is possible to find financial plans, marketing plans, human resource plans, production plans, and sales plans, to name a few. Plans may be short-term or long-term, or they may be strategic or operational. Plans will also differ in scope depending on the type of business or the anticipated size of the start-up operation. Even though they may serve different functions, all these plans have one important purpose: to provide guidance and structure to management in a rapidly changing market environment.

WHAT IS THE BUSINESS PLAN?

business plan Written document describing all relevant internal and external elements and strategies for starting a new venture

The *business plan* is a written document prepared by the entrepreneur that describes all the relevant external and internal elements involved in starting a new venture. It is often an integration of functional plans such as marketing, finance, manufacturing, and human resources. As in the case of Belinda Guadarrama, it addresses the integration and coordination of effective business objectives and strategies when the venture contains a variety of products and services. It also addresses both short-term and long-term decision making for the first three years of operation. Thus, the business plan—or, as it is sometimes referred to, the game plan or road map—answers the questions Where am I now? Where am I going? How will I get there? Potential investors, suppliers, and even customers will request or require a business plan.

If we think of the business plan as a road map, we might better understand its significance. Let's suppose you were trying to decide whether to drive from Boston to Los Angeles (mission or goal) in a motor home. There are a number of possible routes, each requiring different time frames and costs. Like the entrepreneur, the traveler must make some important decisions and gather information before preparing the plan.

The travel plan would consider external factors such as emergency car repair, weather conditions, road conditions, sights to see, and available campgrounds. These factors are basically uncontrollable by the traveler but must be considered in the plan, just as the entrepreneur would consider external factors such as new regulations, competition, social changes, changes in consumer needs, or new technology.

On the other hand, the traveler does have some idea of how much money is available; how much time he or she has; and the choices of highways, roads, campgrounds, sights, and so forth. Similarly, the entrepreneur has some control over manufacturing, marketing, and personnel in the new venture.

The traveler should consider all these factors in determining what roads to take, what campgrounds to stay in, how much time to spend in selected locations, how much time and money to allow for vehicle maintenance, who will drive, and so on. Thus, the travel plan responds to three questions: Where am I now? Where am I going? How do I get there? Then the traveler in our example—or the entrepreneur, the subject of our book—will be able to determine how much money will be needed from existing sources or new sources to achieve the plan.

We saw in the opening example of this chapter how Belinda Guadarrama used the business plan to address these questions. The functional elements of the business plan are discussed here but are also presented in more detail in the chapters that follow.

WHO SHOULD WRITE THE PLAN?

The business plan should be prepared by the entrepreneur; however, he or she may consult with many other sources in its preparation. Lawyers, accountants, marketing consultants, and engineers are useful in the preparation of the plan. Some of the above sources can be found through services offered by the Small Business Administration (SBA), Service Core of Retired Executives (SCORE), Small Business Development Centers (SBDC), universities, and friends or relatives. The Internet also provides a wealth of information as well as actual sample templates or outlines for business planning. Most of these sources are free of charge or have minimal fees for workshop attendance or to purchase or download any information. In many instances entrepreneurs will actually hire or offer equity (partnership) to another person who might provide the appropriate expertise in preparing the business plan as well as become an important member of the management team.

To help determine whether to hire a consultant or to make use of other resources, the entrepreneur can make an objective assessment of his or her own skills. Table 7.1 is an illustration of a rating to determine what skills are lacking and by how much. For example, a sales engineer recently designed a new machine that allows a user to send a 10-second personalized message in a greeting card. A primary concern was how best to market the machine: as a promotional tool a firm could use for its distributors, suppliers, shareholders, or employees; or as a retail product for end users. This entrepreneur, in assessing his skills, rated himself as excellent in product design and sales, good in organizing, and only fair or poor in the remaining skills. To supplement the defined weaknesses the entrepreneur found a partner who could contribute those skills that were lacking or weak. Through such an assessment, the entrepreneur can identify what skills are needed and where to obtain them.

TABLE 7.1 Skills Assessment

Skills	Excellent	Good	Fair	Poor
Accounting/taxes				
Planning				
Forecasting				
Marketing research				
Sales				
People management				
Product design				
Legal issues				
Organizing				

SCOPE AND VALUE OF THE BUSINESS PLAN—WHO READS THE PLAN?

The business plan may be read by employees, investors, bankers, venture capitalists, suppliers, customers, advisors, and consultants. Who is expected to read the plan can often affect its actual content and focus. Since each of these groups reads the plan for different purposes, the entrepreneur must be prepared to address all their issues and concerns. In some ways, the business plan must try to satisfy the needs of everyone; whereas in the actual marketplace the entrepreneur's product will be trying to meet the needs of selected groups of customers.

However, there are probably three perspectives that should be considered in preparing the plan. First is the perspective of the entrepreneur, who understands better than anyone else the creativity and technology involved in the new venture. The entrepreneur must be able to clearly articulate what the venture is all about. Second is the marketing perspective. Too often, an entrepreneur will consider only the product or technology and not whether someone would buy it. Entrepreneurs must try to view their business through the eyes of their customer. This customer orientation is discussed further in Chapter 8. Third, the entrepreneur should try to view his or her business through the eyes of the investor. Sound financial projections are required; if the entrepreneur does not have the skills to prepare this information, then outside sources can be of assistance.[2]

The depth and detail in the business plan depend on the size and scope of the proposed new venture. An entrepreneur planning to market a new portable computer will need a comprehensive business plan, largely because of the nature of the product and market. An entrepreneur who plans to open a retail video store will not need the comprehensive coverage required by a new computer manufacturer. A new e-commerce business, however, may require a very different focus, particularly on how to market the Web site that will offer the goods and services. Thus, differences in the scope of the business plan may depend on whether the new venture is a service, involves manufacturing, or is a consumer good or industrial product. The size of the market, competition, and potential growth may also affect the scope of the business plan.

The business plan is valuable to the entrepreneur, potential investors, or even new personnel, who are trying to familiarize themselves with the venture, its goals, and objectives. The business plan is important to these people because:

- It helps determine the viability of the venture in a designated market.
- It provides guidance to the entrepreneur in organizing his or her planning activities.
- It serves as an important tool in helping to obtain financing.

Potential investors are very particular about what should be included in the business plan. Even if some of the information is based on assumptions, the thinking process required to complete the plan is a valuable experience for the entrepreneur since it forces him or her to assess such things as cash flow and cash requirements. In addition, the thinking process takes the entrepreneur into the future, leading him or her to consider important issues that could impede the road to success.

The process also provides a self-assessment by the entrepreneur. Usually, he or she feels that the new venture is assured of success. However, the planning process forces the entrepreneur to bring objectivity to the idea and to reflect on such questions as: "Does the idea make sense? Will it work? Who is my customer? Does it satisfy customer needs? What kind of protection can I get against imitation by competitors? Can I manage such a business? Whom will I compete with?" This self-evaluation is similar to role playing, requiring the entrepreneur to think through various scenarios and consider obstacles that might prevent the venture from succeeding. The process allows the entrepreneur to plan ways to avoid such obstacles. It may even be possible that, after preparing the business plan, the entrepreneur will realize the obstacles cannot be avoided or overcome. Hence, the venture may be terminated while still on paper. Although this certainly is not the most desirable conclusion, it would be much better to terminate the business endeavor before investing further time and money.

HOW DO POTENTIAL LENDERS AND INVESTORS EVALUATE THE PLAN?

As stated earlier, there are a number of cookbook or computer-generated software packages or samples on the Internet that are available to assist the entrepreneur in preparing a business plan. These sources, however, should be used only to assist in its preparation, since the business plan should address the needs of all the potential readers or evaluators and should reflect the strengths of management and personnel, the product or service, and available resources. There are many different ways to present a quality business plan and thus any attempt to imitate or fit your strategy and objectives into a cookie-cutter approach could have very negative results. The plan needs to focus on the above-mentioned factors and should ultimately consider its purpose.

It is conceivable that the entrepreneur will prepare a first draft of the business plan from his or her own personal viewpoint without consideration of the constituencies that will ultimately read and evaluate the plan's feasibility. As the entrepreneur becomes aware of who will read the plan, appropriate changes will be necessary. For example, one constituency may be suppliers, who may want to see a business plan before signing a contract to produce either components or finished products or even to supply large quantities of materials on consignment. Customers may also want to review the plan before buying a product that may require significant long-term commitment, such as a high-technology telecommunications system. In both cases the business plan should consider the needs of these constituencies, who may pay more attention to the experience of the entrepreneur(s) and his or her projection of the marketplace.

Another group that may evaluate the plan are the potential suppliers of capital. These lenders or investors will likely vary in terms of their needs and requirements in the business plan. For example, lenders are primarily interested in the ability of the new venture to pay back the debt including interest within a designated period of time. Banks want facts with an objective analysis of the business opportunity and all the potential risks inherent in the new venture. It is also important that, along with a solid business plan, the entrepreneur develop a strong personal relationship with the loan officer of the bank. Brad Barbeau's California-based Monterey Beverage Company needed growth capital for his organic soft drink business. Given the low rates of interest and the community's eagerness to support the growth, he sought a bank loan through the Small Business Administration. The initial business plan needed to be revised a number of times before the capital would be released. In addition, projected expenses, revenue, and sales were carefully monitored by the bank during each year of the five-year loan period. This annual review meant that Brad had to constantly review, assess his business objectives, and revise the plan in order to continue in the loan program. The personal relationship he developed with the loan officer enhanced his ability to keep focused on his business plan objectives. So far the process has resulted in additional working capital and successful sales growth.[3] Typically, lenders focus on the four Cs of credit: character, cash flow, collateral, and equity contribution. Basically, what

PROTECTING YOUR BUSINESS IDEA

One of the serious concerns that entrepreneurs voice relates to how to protect their business ideas, when they are also advised to share their business plans with many friends and associates. Since these plans provide comprehensive discussion of the new venture, the concern is understandable. Most individuals who are asked to comment and review a business plan would act in an ethical and professional manner in providing any advice to entrepreneurs. However, there are also many examples of situations in which a family member, friend, or business associate has been accused of "stealing" an idea.

The best strategy for an entrepreneur, outside of seeking the advice of an attorney, is to ask all readers who are not representing a professional firm (such as a venture capitalist) to sign a noncompete or nondisclosure agreement. An example of such an agreement can be found in Chapter 6. Those representing a professional organization (such as a bank or venture capitalist) need not be asked to complete a nondisclosure form since they would be insulted and would be inclined to reject the venture before they had even read the plan.

this means is that lenders want the business plan to reflect the entrepreneur's credit history, the ability of the entrepreneur to meet debt and interest payments (cash flow), the collateral or tangible assets being secured for the loan, and the amount of personal equity that the entrepreneur has invested.

Investors, particularly venture capitalists, have different needs since they are providing large sums of capital for ownership (equity) and the expected cashing out within five to seven years. Investors often place more emphasis on the entrepreneur's character than lenders do, and often spend much time conducting background checks. This is important not only from a financial perspective but also because the venture capitalist will play an important role in the actual management of the business. Hence, investors want to make sure that the entrepreneur is compliant and willing to accept this involvement. These investors will also demand high rates of return and will thus focus on the market and financial projections during this critical five- to seven-year period.

In preparing the business plan, it is important for entrepreneurs to consider the needs of external sources and not merely provide their own perspective. This will keep the plan from being an internalized document that emphasizes only the technical advantages of a product or market advantages of a service, without consideration of the feasibility of meeting market goals and long-term financial projections.

Entrepreneurs, in sharing their business plan with others, often become paranoid, fearing that their idea will be stolen by one of the external readers. Most external advisors and potential investors are bound by a professional code of ethics, and the entrepreneur should not be deterred from seeking external advice (see Ethics box).

PRESENTING THE PLAN

Often, colleges and universities or locally sponsored business meetings offer an opportunity for selected entrepreneurs to present their business plans in a competitive and structured setting. Typically, each selected entrepreneur is asked to present the highlights of his or her business plan in a defined time frame. The entrepreneur is expected to "sell" his or her business concept in this designated period of time. This implies that the entrepreneur must decide what to say and how to present the information. Typically the entrepreneur will focus on why this is a good opportunity, providing an overview of the marketing program (how the opportunity will convert to reality) and the results of this effort (sales and profits). Concluding remarks might reflect the recognized risks and how the entrepreneur plans to address them.

Audiences at these presentations usually include potential investors who are given an opportunity to ask pointed questions regarding any of the strategies conveyed in the business plan presentation. After the completion of all of the scheduled business plan presentations a winner is usually declared, with a financial reward that can range from $10,000 to $50,000. The benefit of these competitions is not necessarily the financial award since there can be only one winner. However, since the audience is made up of professional investors, there is always the opportunity for any one of the business plans presented to attract the attention of a venture capitalist or private investor. This interest may result in further negotiations and perhaps a future investment in the new venture. The number of schools that sponsor these business plan competitions seems to be growing significantly and often the schools will advertise, requesting that interested entrepreneurs submit an application for participation in the competition.[4]

Some investors describe these presentations as elevator pitches, since they are analogous to an entrepreneur getting on an elevator with one or more investors and trying to persuade them that his or her business concept is a good investment before the elevator reaches its final destination. Even for those who do not win a prize, the opportunity to present a plan and then make adjustments in the plan based on the feedback is a great learning experience.

INFORMATION NEEDS

Before committing time and energy to preparing a business plan, the entrepreneur should do a quick feasibility study of the business concept to see whether there are any possible barriers to success. The information, obtainable from many sources, should focus on marketing, finance, and production. The Internet, discussed below, can be a valuable resource for the entrepreneur. Before beginning the feasibility study, the entrepreneur should clearly define the goals and objectives of the venture. These goals help define what needs to be done and how it will be accomplished. These goals and objectives also provide a framework for the business plan, marketing plan, and financial plan.

Goals and objectives that are too general or that are not feasible make the business plan difficult to control and implement. For example, an entrepreneur starting a sporting goods store that specialized in the off-beat sports (e.g., roller blading, skate boarding, snow boarding, and so on) developed a business plan that called for six stores to be opened by year two of the start-up. A friend and business confidant read the plan and immediately asked the entrepreneur to explain how and where these stores would be located. Not having a clear understanding of the answers to these questions suggested to the entrepreneur that his business objectives needed to be much more reasonable and that they needed to be clarified in the marketing and strategy segments of the plan. The business associate explained to the entrepreneur that a business plan is similar to building a house, in that it is necessary that each step in the process be related to the goals and objectives or outcome of the construction. From this experience the entrepreneur rewrote the business plan to reflect more reasonable goals and objectives.

EarthLink, an Internet service provider, recently experienced a significant decline in subscribers and revenue, from $348 million in 2004 to $325 million in 2005. Managers put their heads together and with some newly gathered information determined that there was a real need to provide wireless broadband service to cities that could not feasibly be wired for this service. It then developed a new strategy based on clearly defined goals and objectives. Its early goals and objectives were to pursue two major cities: Philadelphia and San Francisco. Also part of this plan was to build the network necessary to provide wireless service within the boundaries of any city. To achieve this goal the company sought a partnership with Korea's SK Telecom, a company that could provide some of this needed technology. With the partnership, EarthLink created a new company, SK-EarthLink, which is armed with improved technology, an aggressive business plan, and a clear set of objectives. Success has followed, with awards of contracts in both Philadelphia and San Francisco. Company revenue has grown significantly and SK-EarthLink is optimistic that there are opportunities in 20–40 other metro areas as well as hundreds of smaller cities.[5]

From these two examples we can see the importance of feasible, well-defined goals and objectives in the business plan. Once this solid foundation is in place, strategy decisions can then be established that will allow the company to achieve those goals and objectives.

Market Information

One of the initial pieces of information needed by the entrepreneur is the market potential for the product or service. In order to ascertain the size of the market, it is first necessary for the entrepreneur to define the market. For example, is the product most likely to be purchased by men or women? People of high income or low income? Rural or urban dwellers? Highly educated or less educated people? A well-defined target market will make it easier to project market size and subsequent market goals for the new venture. For example, let's assume that an entrepreneur in the Boston area notes the success of businesses such as Au Bon Pain and Panera Bread Company, and thus is considering launching a food business that offers the convenience of "fast food" but with the taste of a sit-down restaurant. With a huge tourism trade the entrepreneur decides on a mobile (food cart) crepe business that will include a number of carts situated in high-traffic areas.

In order to build a strong marketing plan with reasonable and measurable market goals and objectives the entrepreneur will need to gather information on the industry and market. Most entrepreneurs have difficulty with this stage and do not often know where to begin. The best way to start is to first visualize this process as an inverted pyramid (see Figure 7.1). This means that we start with very broad-based data and information and work down until we can develop a positioning strategy and quantifiable goals and objectives. All this information can then be used in the industry analysis and marketing planning sections of the business plan that are discussed later in this chapter. (Also see Chapter 8.)

As noted in Figure 7.1, we begin the process by evaluating general environmental trends. This would include household income trends, population shifts, food consumption habits and trends, travel, and employment trends. This information can be found in sources such as the U.S. Census Bureau, Bureau of Labor Statistics, Forrester, Reuter Business Insight, and Statistical Abstracts, to name a few. These sources are available in the local college or university library. Some sources such as the U.S. Census Bureau can be found online or in the local community library.

The next step is the assessment of trends in the national food service industry. We would look for data on total food sales and commercial restaurant sales by type of restaurant. This information can be found in *Standard & Poor's Market Investment News: Industry Surveys: Restaurants and the National Restaurant Association.*

Notice that the first two stages in Figure 7.1 focus on the national market, and the next two stages consider trends in the local market where the business will be located. This consists of general local economic trends and an assessment of the local food service industry. The sources may include the same ones mentioned above except data related only to the local market would be considered. In addition, the state of Massachusetts publishes data on tourism (*The Massachusetts Travel Industry Report*) and economic trends (U.S. Census Bureau). Also implicit in this local food service industry analysis is the regulatory

FIGURE 7.1 An Upside-Down Pyramid Approach to Gathering Market Information

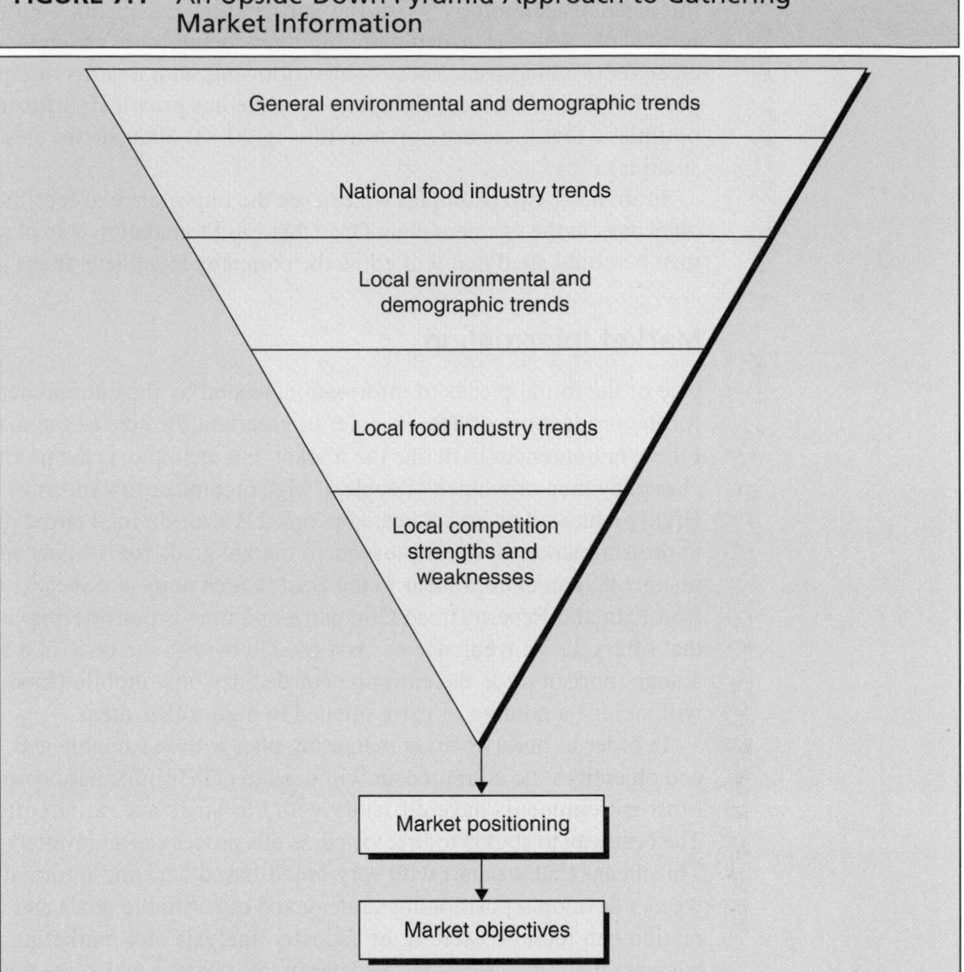

environment. Each state has distinct regulations regarding alcohol and food delivery license requirements. These data can also be found online or in your local library.

The final step is an analysis of the local competitive environment. In this example the entrepreneur would need to identify any restaurants, food stands, or push-cart food services that could be a competitor. This list can be found in the yellow pages, local town hall (food license bureau), or through observation. Each local competitor's strengths and weaknesses should be assessed. This can be judged by using marketing research (discussed in Chapter 8); evaluating the competitors' Web sites, advertising, menus, and locations; and reviewing any published articles that have appeared in the local media. A spreadsheet can then be prepared with the list of competitors in the first column, followed by columns devoted to their strengths and weaknesses.

Once all this analysis has been completed, the entrepreneur is ready to clarify the product or service offering, actual market positioning in the competitive environment, and market objectives. These are part of the marketing plan and are discussed in more detail in Chapter 8. These data, in addition to contributing to the preparation of the marketing plan, lay the groundwork for the financial projections and forecasts discussed in Chapter 10.

AS SEEN IN *ENTREPRENEUR* MAGAZINE

ELEVATOR PITCH FOR DISC MARKETING INC.

A wealthy friend has asked you to keep your eye out for attractive businesses in which she can invest. Your wealthy friend is very busy and you only want to introduce those businesses that are genuinely attractive. After hearing the following pitch, would you introduce Tena to your wealthy friend?

Tena Clark: 50, founder and CEO of Disc Marketing Inc. in Pasadena, California.

Description: Marketing company using music and new media to produce CDs, E-CDs (enhanced CDs), and DVDs.

Start-Up: $500,000 in 1997.

Sales: Projected sales for current year of $20 million.

Musical Medley: Enjoying a successful career creating jingles, scoring movies, and penning songs for major artists, Clark decided to flex her musical muscle in the marketing arena. Says Clark, "I know the media, how to make and sell records for major brands. All my worlds came together."

E-What? Making up 80 percent of Disc Marketing's business, E-CDs are interactive CDs that combine multimedia content like audio, video, and links to online content. Toyota, Target, and Betty Crocker are just a few clients opting in.

Mile-High Club: Disc Marketing not only creates the audio programming for United Airlines Worldwide, it has also piped in tunes for Air Force One and Two since the Clinton administration. Clark was also commissioned to write NASA's Centennial of Flight Anniversary song, "Way Up There."

On Fire: Based in Pasadena's historic, original firehouse, Disc Marketing added Firehouse Recording Studios last summer, a production home to corporate, film, television, and recording industry clients. The recently launched Five Alarm Music Library houses production music for film and TV usage.

Operations Information Needs

The relevance of a feasibility study of the manufacturing operations depends on the nature of the business. Most of the information needed can be obtained through direct contact with the appropriate source. The entrepreneur may need information on the following:

- *Location.* The company's location and its accessibility to customers, suppliers, and distributors need to be determined.
- *Manufacturing operations.* Basic machine and assembly operations need to be identified, as well as whether any of these operations would be subcontracted and to whom.
- *Raw materials.* The raw materials needed and suppliers' names, addresses, and costs should be determined.
- *Equipment.* The equipment needed should be listed, with its cost and whether it will be purchased or leased.
- *Labor skills.* Each unique skill needed, the number of personnel required for each skill, pay rate, and an assessment of where and how these skills will be obtained should be determined.
- *Space.* The total amount of space needed should be determined, including whether the space will be owned or leased.

- *Overhead.* Each item needed to support manufacturing—such as tools, supplies, utilities, and salaries—should be determined.

Most of the above information should be incorporated directly into the business plan. Each item may require some research, but this information is necessary to those who will assess the business plan and consider funding the proposal.

FINANCIAL INFORMATION NEEDS

Before preparing the financial section of the business plan, the entrepreneur will need to prepare a budget that includes a list of all possible expenditures in the first year and a list of all revenue sources, including sales and any external available funds. Thus the budget includes capital expenditures, direct operating expenses, and cash expenditures for nonexpense items. The revenue from sales must be forecast from market data, as discussed above. Forecasting is discussed in more detail in Chapter 8. To prepare the actual budget (see Chapter 10) the entrepreneur will need to identify benchmarks in the industry that can be used in preparing the final pro forma statements in the financial plan. These benchmarks or norms establish reasonable assumptions regarding expenditures based on industry history and trends. This is a very acceptable method to arrive at the necessary projected costs for the new venture.

We return to our crepe business example. In projecting his costs for operating the business, our entrepreneur might choose to consider the many secondary sources that provide percentage norms for such costs. For example, these sources would provide percentage norms in the industry for such costs as food, beverages, equipment, personnel, and licenses. Expenditures such as rent, utilities, insurance, and personnel costs can also be ascertained from newspapers or advertisements, or from phone conversations with real estate agents, insurance agents, equipment suppliers, and the utility companies in the area.

The benchmarks or financial ratios needed to prepare financial statements can be found in such sources as *Financial Studies of the Small Business* (Financial Research Associates), *Industry Norms and Key Business Ratios* (Dun & Bradstreet), *Annual Statement Studies* (Robert Morris Associates), and the *Almanac of Business and Financial Ratios* (Prentice-Hall). It is also possible to find benchmarks by reviewing 10K reports of similar public competitors. Trade associations and trade magazines also may publish valuable data that can supplement the above sources to prepare the financial statements in the business plan. These pro forma statements will need to be prepared monthly in the first year and then either quarterly or annually for the next two years. Some investors require five-year projections, so the entrepreneur may need to clarify exactly what is needed by those who review the business plan.

USING THE INTERNET AS A RESOURCE TOOL

The changing world of technology offers new opportunities for entrepreneurs to be able to access information for many business activities efficiently, expediently, and at very little cost. The Internet can serve as an important source of information in the preparation of the business plan for such segments as the industry analysis, competitor analysis, and measurement of market potential, to name a few. Entrepreneurs will also find the Internet a valuable resource in later-stage planning and decision making. Besides being a business intelligence resource, the Internet also provides opportunities for marketing strategy; through its Web site, a firm can provide information on the company, its products and services, and ordering instructions.

According to Shop.org, the online trade association of the National Retail Federation (NRF), online retail sales are expected to continue to increase by double digits. In a recent report, Forrester indicated that online retail sales should grow to $329 billion by 2010, compared to the $172 billion reported for 2005. The online audience is not only increasing but it is attracting a much broader cross section of consumers. Many online retailers will combine Web-based sales and catalog mailings to reach an even wider audience.[6]

An entrepreneur in the process of writing a business plan can also access one of the popular search engines: Google, Yahoo!, MSN, AOL, or Ask Jeeves. Simply conducting a search of a topic (for example, "online sporting goods") may reveal several Web sites, articles, or sources of information to assist the entrepreneur in writing the business plan. Use of these searches has grown about 20 percent, depending on the search engine.[7]

An entrepreneur should access competitors' Web sites to gain more knowledge about their strategy in the marketplace. Internet service is not costly and is an important vehicle for the entrepreneur to gather information about the market, competition, and customers as well as to distribute, advertise, and sell company products and services.

In addition to Web sites, the entrepreneur can also investigate newsgroups to gather information anonymously from experts and customers on competitors and market needs. There are thousands of newsgroups online that cover a wide range of topics. These newsgroups represent online customers having the same interest in a topic (for example, gourmet food). Using the Usenet, which represents the newsgroups on the Internet, the entrepreneur can use key words to identify the most appropriate newsgroups. These newsgroups represent potential customers who can be asked specific questions on their needs, competitive products, and potential interest in the newventure's products and services. Individuals who are members of the newsgroups will then respond to these questions, providing valuable information to the entrepreneur.

Compared with alternative sources the entrepreneur need only make a small investment in hardware and software to be ready to use these online services. With its continuous improvements and modifications, the Internet will continue to provide invaluable opportunities for the entrepreneur in planning the start-up or the growth of a venture.

WRITING THE BUSINESS PLAN

The business plan could take hundreds of hours to prepare, depending on the experience and knowledge of the entrepreneur as well as the purpose it is intended to serve. It should be comprehensive enough to give any potential investor a complete picture and understanding of the new venture and it should help the entrepreneur clarify his or her thinking about the business.

Many entrepreneurs incorrectly estimate the length of time that an effective plan will take to prepare. Once the process has begun, however, the entrepreneur will realize that it is invaluable in sorting out the business functions of a new venture.

The outline for a business plan is illustrated in Table 7.2. Each of the items in the outline is detailed in the following paragraphs of this chapter. Key questions in each section are also appropriately detailed.

Introductory Page

This is the title or cover page that provides a brief summary of the business plan's contents. The introductory page should contain the following:

The name and address of the company.

The name of the entrepreneur(s), telephone number, fax number, e-mail address, and Web site address if available.

TABLE 7.2 Outline of a Business Plan

I. Introductory Page
   - A. Name and address of business
   - B. Name(s) and address(es) of principal(s)
   - C. Nature of business
   - D. Statement of financing needed
   - E. Statement of confidentiality of report

II. Executive Summary—Two to three pages summarizing the complete business plan

III. Industry Analysis
   - A. Future outlook and trends
   - B. Analysis of competitors
   - C. Market segmentation
   - D. Industry and market forecasts

IV. Description of Venture
   - A. Product(s)
   - B. Service(s)
   - C. Size of business
   - D. Office equipment and personnel
   - E. Background of entrepreneur(s)

V. Production Plan
   - A. Manufacturing process (amount subcontracted)
   - B. Physical plant
   - C. Machinery and equipment
   - D. Names of suppliers of raw materials

VI. Operational Plan
   - A. Description of company's operation
   - B. Flow of orders for goods and/or services
   - C. Technology utilization

VII. Marketing Plan
   - A. Pricing
   - B. Distribution
   - C. Promotion
   - D. Product forecasts
   - E. Controls

VIII. Organizational Plan
   - A. Form of ownership
   - B. Identification of partners or principal shareholders
   - C. Authority of principals
   - D. Management-team background
   - E. Roles and responsibilities of members of organization

IX. Assessment of Risk
   - A. Evaluate weakness(es) of business
   - B. New technologies
   - C. Contingency plans

X. Financial Plan
   - A. Assumptions
   - B. Pro forma income statement
   - C. Cash flow projections
   - D. Pro forma balance sheet
   - E. Break-even analysis
   - F. Sources and applications of funds

XI. Appendix (contains backup material)
   - A. Letters
   - B. Market research data
   - C. Leases or contracts
   - D. Price lists from suppliers

A paragraph describing the company and the nature of the business.

The amount of financing needed. The entrepreneur may offer a package (e.g., stock, debt, and so on). However, many venture capitalists prefer to structure this package in their own way.

A statement of the confidentiality of the report. This is for security purposes and is important for the entrepreneur.

This title page sets out the basic concept that the entrepreneur is attempting to develop. Investors consider it important because they can determine the amount of investment needed without having to read through the entire plan. An illustration of this page can be found in Table 7.3.

Executive Summary

This section of the business plan is prepared after the total plan is written. About two to three pages in length, the executive summary should stimulate the interest of the potential investor. This is a very important section of the business plan and should not be taken lightly by the entrepreneur since the investor uses the summary to determine if the entire business plan is worth reading. Thus, it should highlight in a concise and convincing manner the key points in the business plan.

Generally the executive summary should address a number of issues or questions that anyone picking up the written plan for the first time would want to know. For example:

What is the business concept or model?

How is this business concept or model unique?

Who are the individuals starting this business?

How will they make money and how much?

TABLE 7.3 Sample Introductory Page

KC CLEANING SERVICE
OAK KNOLL ROAD
BOSTON, MA 02167
(617) 969-0010
www.cleaning.com

Co-owners: Kimberly Peters, Christa Peters

Description of Business:

This business will provide cleaning service on a contract basis to small and medium-sized businesses. Services include cleaning of floors, carpets, draperies, and windows, and regular sweeping, dusting, and washing. Contracts will be for one year and will specify the specific services and scheduling for completion of services.

Financing:

Initial financing requested is a $100,000 loan to be paid off over six years. This debt will cover office space, office equipment and supplies, two leased vans, advertising, and selling costs.

This report is confidential and is the property of the co-owners listed above. It is intended for use only by the persons to whom it is transmitted, and any reproduction or divulgence of any of its contents without the prior written consent of the company is prohibited.

If the new venture has a strong growth plan and in five years expects to be positioned for an initial public offering (IPO) then the executive summary should also include an exit strategy. If the venture is not initially expecting this kind of growth, the entrepreneurs should avoid any discussion of an exit strategy in the executive summary.

Any supportive evidence, such as data points from marketing research or legal documents or contracts that might strengthen the case on the above issues, also should be included. Under no circumstances should the entrepreneur try to summarize every section of the plan, especially since the emphasis placed on the above issues depends on who is reading the plan.

It should be remembered that this section is only meant to highlight key factors and motivate the person holding the plan to read it in its entirety. Key factors for some plans might be the people involved. For example, if one of the entrepreneurs has been very successful in other start-ups, then this person and his or her background needs to be emphasized. If the venture has a contract in hand with a large customer, then this would be highlighted in the executive summary. It is similar to the opening statement a lawyer might make in an important court trial or the introductory statements made by a salesperson in a sales call.

Environmental and Industry Analysis

environmental analysis Assessment of external uncontrollable variables that may impact the business plan

It is important to put the new venture in a proper context by first conducting an *environmental analysis* to identify trends and changes occurring on a national and international level that may impact the new venture. This process was described earlier in this chapter. Examples of these environmental factors are:

Economy. The entrepreneur should consider trends in the GNP, unemployment by geographic area, disposable income, and so on.

Culture. An evaluation of cultural changes may consider shifts in the population by demographics, for example, the impact of the baby boomers or the growing elderly population. Shifts in attitudes, such as "Buy American," or trends in safety, health, and nutrition, as well as concern for the environment, may all have an impact on the entrepreneur's business plan.

Technology. Advances in technology are difficult to predict. However, the entrepreneur should consider potential technological developments determined from resources committed by major industries or the U.S. government. Being in a market that is rapidly changing due to technological development will require the entrepreneur to make careful short-term marketing decisions as well as to be prepared with contingency plans given any new technological developments that may affect his or her product or service.

Legal concerns. There are many important legal issues in starting a new venture; these were discussed in Chapter 6. The entrepreneur should be prepared for any future legislation that may affect the product or service, channel of distribution, price, or promotion strategy. The deregulation of prices, restrictions on media advertising (e.g., ban on cigarette ads or requirements for advertising to children), and safety regulations affecting the product or packaging are examples of legal restrictions that can affect any marketing program.

All of the above external factors are generally uncontrollable. However, as indicated, an awareness and assessment of these factors using some of the sources identified can provide strong support for the opportunity and can be invaluable in developing the appropriate marketing strategy.

industry analysis Reviews industry trends and competitive strategies

As stated earlier (see Figure 7.1), this process can be visualized as an upside-down pyramid leading to specific market strategy and objectives. Once an assessment of the environment is complete, the entrepreneur should conduct an *industry analysis* that will focus on specific industry trends. Some examples of these factors are:

Industry demand. Demand as it relates to the industry is often available from published sources. Knowledge of whether the market is growing or declining, the number of new competitors, and possible changes in consumer needs are all important issues in trying to ascertain the potential business that might be achieved by the new venture. The projected demand for the entrepreneur's product or service will require some additional marketing research, which will be discussed in Chapter 8.

Competition. Most entrepreneurs generally face potential threats from larger corporations. The entrepreneur must be prepared for these threats and should be aware of who the competitors are and what their strengths and weaknesses are so that an effective marketing plan can be implemented. Most competitors can be easily identified from experience, trade journal articles, advertisements, Web sites, or even the yellow pages.

There are numerous sources that the entrepreneur can consult to attain general industry and competitive data for inclusion in this part of the business plan. Some of these were mentioned earlier in this chapter, in relation to our discussion of the gathering of market information. Many of these sources can be found in local or university libraries. They include: *Encyclopedia of American Industries, Encyclopedia of Emerging Industries, Standard and Poor's Industry Surveys, MarketLine Business Information Centre, Forrester, Faulkner's Advisory for IT Studies, Investext Plus,* and *Mintel Reports.* Each of these sources focuses on different types of industries or markets and can be easily evaluated as to their benefit either by an online search (such as Google) or by a visit to a local library.

The last part of the business plan's industry analysis section should focus on the specific market, which would include such information as who the customer is and what the business environment is like in the specific market and geographic area where the venture will compete. Thus, any differences in any of the above variables that reflect the specific market area in which the new venture will operate must be considered. This information is particularly significant to the preparation of the marketing plan section of the business plan, which is discussed in Chapter 8.

In addition to the numerous industry sources above, there are also many market databases that can be researched for relevant data to incorporate into this section of the business plan. Market share and size of market often can be assessed from databases such as: *Tablebase and Business and Industry, Market Share Reporter, Economic Census, County Business Patterns, Current Industrial Reports, Service Annual Survey,* and *Monthly Retail and Food Service Sales and Inventories.* More specific data on demographic trends and possible target market numbers can be found in: *Profiles of General Demographic Characteristics 2000 Census/Population, Population Projections, Mediamark Reporter,* and *Lifestyle Market Analyst.* Finally, state-by-state population, demographic, and housing data usually are available from each state's Web site.

A list of some key questions the entrepreneur should consider for this section of the business plan is provided in Table 7.4.

description of the venture Provides complete overview of the product(s), service(s), and operations of new venture

Description of Venture

The *description of the venture* should be detailed in this section of the business plan. This will enable the investor to ascertain the size and scope of the business. This section should begin with the mission statement or company mission of the new venture. This statement

TABLE 7.4 Critical Issues for Environmental and Industry Analysis

1. What are the major economic, technological, legal, and political trends on a national and an international level?
2. What are total industry sales over the past five years?
3. What is anticipated growth in this industry?
4. How many new firms have entered this industry in the past three years?
5. What new products have been recently introduced in this industry?
6. Who are the nearest competitors?
7. How will your business operation be better than this?
8. Are the sales of each of your major competitors growing, declining, or steady?
9. What are the strengths and weaknesses of each of your competitors?
10. What trends are occurring in your specific market area?
11. What is the profile of your customers?
12. How does your customer profile differ from that of your competition?

TABLE 7.5 Describing the Venture

1. What is the mission of the new venture?
2. What are your reasons for going into business?
3. Why will you be successful in this venture?
4. What development work has been completed to date?
5. What is your product(s) and/or service(s)?
6. Describe the product(s) and/or service(s), including patent, copyright, or trademark status.
7. Where will the business be located?
8. Is your building new? old? in need of renovations? (If renovation is needed, state costs.)
9. Is the building leased or owned? (State the terms.)
10. Why is this building and location right for your business?
11. What office equipment will be needed?
12. Will equipment be purchased or leased?
13. What experience do you have and/or will you need to successfully implement the business plan?

basically describes the nature of the business and what the entrepreneur hopes to accomplish with that business. This mission statement or business definition will guide the firm through long-term decision making. After the mission statement, a number of important factors that provide a clear description and understanding of the business venture should be discussed. Key elements are the product(s) or service(s), the location and size of the business, the personnel and office equipment that will be needed, the background of the entrepreneur(s), and the history of the venture. Table 7.5 summarizes some of the important questions the entrepreneur needs to answer when preparing this section of the business plan.

Location of any business may be vital to its success, particularly if the business is retail or involves a service. Thus, the emphasis on location in the business plan is a function of the type of business. In assessing the building or space the business will occupy, the entrepreneur may need to evaluate such factors as parking, access from roadways to facility, and access to customers, suppliers, distributors, delivery rates, and town regulations or zoning laws. An enlarged local map may help give the location some perspective with regard to roads, highways, access, and so forth.

Recently an entrepreneur considered opening a new doughnut shop at a location diagonally across from a small shopping mall on a heavily traveled road. Traffic counts indicated a large potential customer base if people would stop for coffee, and so on, on their way to work. After enlarging a local map, the entrepreneur noted that the morning flow of traffic required drivers to make a left turn into the doughnut shop, crossing the outbound lane. Unfortunately, the roadway was divided by a concrete center strip with no break to allow for a left-hand turn. The only possibility for entry into the shop required the customer to drive down about 400 yards and make a U-turn. It would also be difficult for the customer to get back on the roadway traveling in the right direction. Since the town was unwilling to open the road, the entrepreneur eliminated this site from any further consideration.

This simple assessment of the location, market, and so on, saved the entrepreneur from a potential disaster. Maps that locate customers, competitors, and even alternative locations for a building or site can be helpful in this evaluation. Some of the important questions that might be asked by an entrepreneur are as follows:

How much space is needed?

Should I buy or lease the building?

What is the cost per square foot?

Is the site zoned for commercial use?

What town restrictions exist for signs, parking, and so forth?

Is renovation of the building necessary?

Is the facility accessible to traffic?

Is there adequate parking?

Will the existing facility have room for expansion?

What is the economic and demographic profile of the area?

Is there an adequate labor pool available?

What are local taxes?

Are sewage, electricity, and plumbing adequate?

If the building or site decision involves legal issues, such as a lease, or requires town variances, the entrepreneur should hire a lawyer. Problems relating to regulations and leases can be avoided easily, but under no circumstances should the entrepreneur try to negotiate with the town or a landlord without good legal advice.

Production Plan

production plan Details how the product(s) will be manufactured

If the new venture is a manufacturing operation, a *production plan* is necessary. This plan should describe the complete manufacturing process. If some or all of the manufacturing process is to be subcontracted, the plan should describe the subcontractor(s), including location, reasons for selection, costs, and any contracts that have been completed. If the manufacturing is to be carried out in whole or in part by the entrepreneur, he or she will

AS SEEN IN *ENTREPRENEUR* MAGAZINE

VIRTUAL REALITY—HOT OR NOT?

Do you believe this technology represents an opportunity for entrepreneurs in different industries or do you believe that it is merely a fad that has seen its day?

Virtual reality (VR) isn't just about clunky goggles and bodysuits. Think back a few years, and you may remember the buzz and excitement surrounding VR. Holograms were popping up in unlikely places, movies and TV programs featured VR themes, and forward-thinking people were contemplating how it all might fit into the business world. Though much of the initial excitement has abated, VR hasn't totally dropped off the radar. Take a visit to the VR section of technology services company EDS. It offers everything from training visualization (such as a virtual environment where someone can learn to put together a product) to Web-based visualization (3D online images).

So far, advanced VR is mainly in the realm of large companies like automobile manufacturers that create holographic walk-around 3D virtual models of cars, but the technology also has applications in other design, manufacturing, and product development businesses such as architecture or electronics design. Costs, though, are still on the high end for most entrepreneurs' budgets. Holograms appear occasionally in advertising, but the novelty has largely worn off, and growing businesses can find more effective uses for their marketing budget.

The first place VR trickles down in affordable fashion could be on the Internet. Virtual Reality Modeling Language (VRML) pretty much faded away after some initial excitement, but has recently been given a new life. The Extensible 3D specification is a descendent of VRML and allows for 3D graphics on the Web. It has been submitted for approval to the International Organization for Standardization and could be cleared within two years. Potential e-commerce uses for Web 3D could be found in enhanced user interfaces or product images. Imagine offering retail customers an advanced virtual tour around the product they're interested in. Visit the Web3D Consortium at www.web3d.org to keep up on the latest developments.

Source: Reprinted with permission of Entrepreneur Media, Inc., "Reality Is Quickly Becoming Outdated. Can Virtual Reality Make Your Business Better?" by Amanda C. Kooser, February 2003, *Entrepreneur* magazine: www.entrepreneur.com.

need to describe the physical plant layout; the machinery and equipment needed to perform the manufacturing operations; raw materials and suppliers' names, addresses, and terms; costs of manufacturing; and any future capital equipment needs. In a manufacturing operation, the discussion of these items will be important to any potential investor in assessing financial needs.

Table 7.6 summarizes some of the key questions in this section of the business plan. If the new venture does not include any manufacturing functions, this section should be eliminated from the plan.

OPERATIONS PLAN

All businesses—manufacturing or nonmanufacturing—should include an operations plan as part of the business plan. This section goes beyond the manufacturing process (when the new venture involves manufacturing) and describes the flow of goods and services from production to the customer. It might include inventory or storage of manufactured products, shipping, inventory control procedures, and customer support services. A nonmanufacturer such as a retailer or service provider would also need this section in the business plan in order to explain the chronological steps in completing a business transaction. For example, an Internet retail sports clothing operation would need to describe how and where the products offered would be purchased, how they would be stored, how the inventory would be managed, how products would be shipped and, importantly,

TABLE 7.6 Production Plan

1. Will you be responsible for all or part of the manufacturing operation?
2. If some manufacturing is subcontracted, who will be the subcontractors? (Give names and addresses.)
3. Why were these subcontractors selected?
4. What are the costs of the subcontracted manufacturing? (Include copies of any written contracts.)
5. What will be the layout of the production process? (Illustrate steps if possible.)
6. What equipment will be needed immediately for manufacturing?
7. What raw materials will be needed for manufacturing?
8. Who are the suppliers of new materials and what are the appropriate costs?
9. What are the costs of manufacturing the product?
10. What are the future capital equipment needs of the venture?

If a Retail Operation or Service:

1. From whom will merchandise be purchased?
2. How will the inventory control system operate?
3. What are the storage needs of the venture and how will they be promoted?
4. How will the goods flow to the customer?
5. Chronologically, what are the steps involved in a business transaction?
6. What are the technology utilization requirements to service customers effectively?

how a customer would log on and complete a transaction. In addition, this would be a convenient place for the entrepreneur to discuss the role of technology in the business transaction process. For any Internet retail operation, some explanation of the technology requirements needed to efficiently and profitably complete a successful business transaction should be included in this section.

It is important to note here that the major distinction between services and manufactured goods is services involve intangible performances. This implies that they cannot be touched, seen, tasted, heard, or felt in the same manner as manufactured products. Airlines, hotels, car rental agencies, theaters, and hospitals, to name a few, rely on business delivery or quality of service. For these firms, performance often depends on location, facility layout, and personnel, which can, in turn, affect service quality (including such factors as reliability, responsiveness, and assurance). The process of delivering this service quality is what distinguishes one new service venture from another and thus needs to be the focus of an operations plan. Some key questions or issues for both the manufacturing and nonmanufacturing new venture are summarized in Table 7.6.

Marketing Plan

marketing plan Describes market conditions and strategy related to how the product(s) and service(s) will be distributed, priced, and promoted

The *marketing plan* (discussed in detail in Chapter 8) is an important part of the business plan since it describes how the product(s) or service(s) will be distributed, priced, and promoted. Marketing research evidence to support any of the critical marketing decision strategies as well as for forecasting sales should be described in this section. Specific forecasts for a product(s) or service(s) are indicated in order to project the profitability of the venture. The budget and appropriate controls needed for marketing strategy decisions are also discussed in detail in Chapter 8. Potential investors regard the marketing plan as critical to the success of the new venture. Thus, the entrepreneur should make every effort to prepare as comprehensive and detailed a plan as possible so that investors can be clear as to what the goals of the venture are and what strategies are to be implemented to effectively achieve these goals. Marketing planning will be an annual requirement (with careful monitoring and changes made on a weekly or monthly basis) for the entrepreneur and should be regarded as the road map for short-term decision making.

Organizational Plan

organizational plan Describes form of ownership and lines of authority and responsibility of members of new venture

The *organizational plan* is the part of the business plan that describes the venture's form of ownership—that is, proprietorship, partnership, or corporation. If the venture is a partnership, the terms of the partnership should be included. If the venture is a corporation, it is important to detail the shares of stock authorized and share options, as well as the names, addresses, and resumes of the directors and officers of the corporation. It is also helpful to provide an organization chart indicating the line of authority and the responsibilities of the members of the organization. Table 7.7 summarizes some of the key questions the entrepreneur needs to answer in preparing this section of the business plan. This information provides the potential investor with a clear understanding of who controls the organization and how other members will interact in performing their management functions.

Assessment of Risk

assessment of risk Identifies potential hazards and alternative strategies to meet business plan goals and objectives

Every new venture will be faced with some potential hazards, given its particular industry and competitive environment. It is important that the entrepreneur make an *assessment of risk* in the following manner. First, the entrepreneur should indicate the potential risks to the new venture. Next should be a discussion of what might happen if these risks become reality. Finally, the entrepreneur should discuss the strategy that will be employed to either prevent, minimize, or respond to the risks should they occur. Major risks for a new venture could result from a competitor's reaction; weaknesses in the marketing, production, or management team; and new advances in technology that might render the new product

TABLE 7.7 Organization Structure

1. What is the form of ownership of the organization?
2. If a partnership, who are the partners and what are the terms of agreement?
3. If incorporated, who are the principal shareholders and how much stock do they own?
4. How many shares of voting or nonvoting stock have been issued and what type?
5. Who are the members of the board of directors? (Give names, addresses, and resumes.)
6. Who has check-signing authority or control?
7. Who are the members of the management team and what are their backgrounds?
8. What are the roles and responsibilities of each member of the management team?
9. What are the salaries, bonuses, or other forms of payment for each member of the management team?

obsolete. Even if these factors present no risks to the new venture, the business plan should discuss why that is the case.

Financial Plan

financial plan
Projections of key financial data that determine economic feasibility and necessary financial investment commitment

Like the marketing, production, and organization plans, the *financial plan* is an important part of the business plan. It determines the potential investment commitment needed for the new venture and indicates whether the business plan is economically feasible. (The financial plan is discussed in more detail in Chapter 10.)

Generally, three financial areas are discussed in this section of the business plan. First, the entrepreneur should summarize the forecasted sales and the appropriate expenses for at least the first three years, with the first year's projections provided monthly. The form for displaying this information is illustrated in Chapter 10. It includes the forecasted sales, cost of goods sold, and the general and administrative expenses. Net profit after taxes can then be projected by estimating income taxes.

The second major area of financial information needed is cash flow figures for three years, with the first year's projections provided monthly. Since bills have to be paid at different times of the year, it is important to determine the demands on cash on a monthly basis, especially in the first year. Remember that sales may be irregular, and receipts from customers also may be spread out, thus necessitating the borrowing of short-term capital to meet fixed expenses such as salaries and utilities. A form for projecting the cash flow needs for a 12-month period can be found in Chapter 10.

The last financial item needed in this section of the business plan is the projected balance sheet. This shows the financial condition of the business at a specific time. It summarizes the assets of a business, its liabilities (what is owed), the investment of the entrepreneur and any partners, and retained earnings (or cumulative losses). A form for the balance sheet is included in Chapter 10, along with more detailed explanations of the items included. Any assumptions considered for the balance sheet or any other item in the financial plan should be listed for the benefit of the potential investor.

Appendix

The appendix of the business plan generally contains any backup material that is not necessary in the text of the document. Reference to any of the documents in the appendix should be made in the plan itself.

Letters from customers, distributors, or subcontractors are examples of information that should be included in the appendix. Any documentation of information—that is, secondary data or primary research data used to support plan decisions—should also be included. Leases, contracts, or any other types of agreements that have been initiated also may be included in the appendix. Finally, price lists from suppliers and competitors may be added.

USING AND IMPLEMENTING THE BUSINESS PLAN

The business plan is designed to guide the entrepreneur through the first year of operations. It is important that the implementation of the strategy contain control points to ascertain progress and to initiate contingency plans if necessary. Some of the controls necessary in manufacturing, marketing, financing, and the organization are discussed in subsequent chapters. Most important to the entrepreneur is that the business plan not end up in a drawer somewhere once the financing has been attained and the business launched.

TABLE 7.8 Sources of Information
Small Business Administration
Department of Commerce
Federal information centers
Bureau of Census
State and municipal governments
Banks
Chambers of commerce
Trade associations
Trade journals
Libraries
Universities and community colleges

Source: Richard Siklos, "Oxygen Gets Airborne," *BusinessWeek* (September 28, 1998), p. 52.

There has been a tendency among many entrepreneurs to avoid planning. The reason often given is that planning is dull or boring and is something used only by large companies. This may be an excuse; perhaps the real truth is that some entrepreneurs are afraid to plan.[8] Planning is an important part of any business operation. Without good planning, the entrepreneur is likely to pay an enormous price. All one has to do is consider the planning done by suppliers, customers, competitors, and banks to realize that it is important for the entrepreneur. It is also important to realize that without good planning the employees will not understand the company's goals and how they are expected to perform in their jobs.

Bankers are the first to admit that few business failures result from a lack of cash but, instead, that businesses fail because of the entrepreneur's inability to plan effectively. Intelligent planning is not a difficult or impossible exercise for the inexperienced entrepreneur. With the proper commitment and support from many outside resources, such as those shown in Table 7.8, the entrepreneur can prepare an effective business plan.

In addition, the entrepreneur can enhance effective implementation of the business plan by developing a schedule to measure progress and to institute contingency plans. These frequent readings or control procedures will be discussed further below.

Measuring Plan Progress

During the introductory phases of the start-up, the entrepreneur should determine the points at which decisions should be made as to whether the goals or objectives are on schedule. Typically, the business plan projections will be made on a 12-month schedule. However, the entrepreneur cannot wait 12 months to see whether the plan has been successfully achieved. Instead, on a frequent basis (i.e., the beginning of each month) the entrepreneur should check the profit and loss statement, cash flow projections, and information on inventory, production, quality, sales, collection of accounts receivable, and disbursements for the previous month. Company Web sites should also be assessed as part of this process. This feedback should be simple but should provide key members of the organization with current information in time to correct any major deviations from the goals and objectives outlined. A brief description of each of these control elements is given below:

- *Inventory control.* By controlling inventory, the firm can ensure maximum service to the customer. The faster the firm gets back its investment in raw materials and finished goods, the faster that capital can be reinvested to meet additional customer needs.
- *Production control.* Compare the cost figures estimated in the business plan with day-to-day operation costs. This will help to control machine time, worker hours, process time, delay time, and downtime cost.
- *Quality control.* This will depend on the type of production system but is designed to make sure that the product performs satisfactorily.
- *Sales control.* Information on units, dollars, specific products sold, price of sales, meeting of delivery dates, and credit terms is useful to get a good perspective of the sales of the new venture. In addition, an effective collections system for accounts receivable should be set up to avoid aging of accounts and bad debts.
- *Disbursements.* The new venture should also control the amount of money paid out. All bills should be reviewed to determine how much is being disbursed and for what purpose.
- *Web site control.* With more and more sales being supported or garnered from a company's Web site, it is very important to continually evaluate the Web site to ascertain its effectiveness in meeting the goals and objectives of the plan. There are many services and software packages available to assist the entrepreneur in this process. These service companies and software alternatives are too numerous to mention here but can easily be identified from an Internet search.[9]

Updating the Plan

The most effective business plan can become out-of-date if conditions change. Environmental factors such as the economy, customers, new technology, or competition—and internal factors such as the loss or addition of key employees—can all change the direction of the business plan. Thus, it is important to be sensitive to changes in the company, industry, and market. If these changes are likely to affect the business plan, the entrepreneur should determine what revisions are needed. In this manner, the entrepreneur can maintain reasonable targets and goals and keep the new venture on a course that will increase its probability of success.

WHY SOME BUSINESS PLANS FAIL

Generally a poorly prepared business plan can be blamed on one or more of the following factors:

- Goals set by the entrepreneur are unreasonable.
- Goals are not measurable.
- The entrepreneur has not made a total commitment to the business or to the family.
- The entrepreneur has no experience in the planned business.
- The entrepreneur has no sense of potential threats or weaknesses to the business.
- No customer need was established for the proposed product or service.

Setting goals requires the entrepreneur to be well informed about the type of business and the competitive environment. Goals should be specific and not so mundane as to lack any basis of control. For example, the entrepreneur may target a specific market share, units sold, or revenue. These goals are measurable and can be monitored over time.

In addition, the entrepreneur and his or her family must make a total commitment to the business in order to be able to meet the demands of a new venture. For example, it is difficult to operate a new venture on a part-time basis while still holding onto a full-time position. And it is also difficult to operate a business without an understanding from family members as to the time and resources that will be needed. Lenders or investors will not be favorably inclined toward a venture that does not have full-time commitment. Moreover, lenders or investors may expect the entrepreneur to make a significant financial commitment to the business even if it means a second mortgage or a depletion of savings.

Generally, a lack of experience will result in failure unless the entrepreneur can either attain the necessary knowledge or team up with someone who already has it. For example, an entrepreneur trying to start a new restaurant without any experience or knowledge of the restaurant business would be in a disastrous situation.

The entrepreneur should also document customer needs before preparing the plan. Customer needs can be identified from direct experience, letters from customers, or marketing research. A clear understanding of these needs and how the entrepreneur's business will effectively meet them is vital to the success of the new venture.

IN REVIEW

SUMMARY

This chapter has established the scope and value of the business plan and has outlined the steps in its preparation. The business plan may be read by employees, investors, lenders, suppliers, customers, and consultants. The scope of the plan will depend on who reads it, the size of the venture, and the specific industry for which the venture is intended.

The business plan is essential in launching a new venture. The result of many hours of preparation will be a comprehensive, well-written, and well-organized document that will serve as a guide to the entrepreneur and as an instrument to raise necessary capital and financing.

Before beginning the business plan, the entrepreneur will need information on the market, manufacturing operations, and financial estimations. This process can be viewed as an upside-down pyramid, beginning with a very broad-based analysis down to specific market positioning and the determination of specific goals and objectives. The Internet represents a low-cost service that can provide valuable information on the market, customers and their needs, and competitors. This information should be evaluated based on the goals and objectives of the new venture. These goals and objectives also provide a framework for setting up controls for the business plan.

The chapter presents a comprehensive discussion and outline of a typical business plan. Each key element in the plan is discussed, an information-gathering process is described, and examples are provided. Control decisions are presented to ensure the effective implementation of the business plan. In addition, some insights as to why business plans fail are discussed.

RESEARCH TASKS

1. Approximately how many books have been written on "how to write a business plan"? How many software packages are there that aim to help entrepreneurs to write a business plan? Use data to back up your estimates. Why are there so many?
2. Find five business plans. What are the common topics covered across all five plans? What are the differences? Choose the one that you believe is the best written and then describe why you believe it is better than the others.
3. Speak to five entrepreneurs and find out why they have (or do not have) a business plan. For those that do have a business plan, find out when it was written, the purpose for which it was created, and whether it has been used and/or kept up-to-date.

CLASS DISCUSSION

1. Given the difficulties in accurately predicting the future, is a business plan useful?
2. What makes an excellent business plan?
3. Would the entrepreneur be better off spending more time selling his or her product rather than investing so much time in writing a business plan?
4. If a business plan is to be used to raise capital, then why would the entrepreneur want to advertise the firm's major risks by detailing them in the business plan?
5. What is the purpose of the business plan if the audience is (a) the entrepreneur, (b) an investor, and (c) a key supplier? How might the plan be adapted for these different audiences? Or do you believe that it is better to simply have one business plan that serves all audiences?

SELECTED READINGS

Burmeister, Paul. (March 2003). What to Present to Venture Capitalists. *Strategic Finance*, pp. 36–39.

This article describes some of the key aspects of each section of the business plan that should be presented to venture capitalists. It also emphasizes the importance of the format and the presentation of the business plan.

Chiagouris, Larry; and Brant Wansley. (September/October 2003). Start-Up Marketing. *Marketing Management,* vol. 12, no. 5, pp. 38–43.

This paper reflects on the experience of the authors as consultants and executives and develops insight as to marketing practices that make a difference for a start-up company. They report that the executives of these firms, representing a wide variety of industries, all created formal marketing and business plans to obtain financing for their ventures. Many also regarded monitoring competitor activity and industry trends as essential to success.

Clarke, Geri. (Summer 2005). International Marketing Environment Analysis. *Marketing Review,* pp. 159–73.

This paper proposes a framework for international industry and environmental analysis. The authors argue that international market analysis is lacking and that domestic environmental audits are not sufficient in the more complicated international markets.

Duffy, Bobby; Kate Smith; George Terhanian; and John Bremer. (2005). Comparing Data from Online and Face to Face Surveys. *Journal of Market Research,* vol. 47, no. 6, pp. 615–39.

This paper explores some of the issues surrounding the use of Internet-based methodologies compared to face-to-face data collection. Data from parallel surveys using both data collection techniques are compared. The authors put forth a number of theories as to why differences may exist.

Ernst & Young LLP. (1997). *Outline for a Business Plan.*

This generalized outline for a business plan is simple to follow and provides additional understanding of the information that should be included in a quality business plan.

Grote, Jim. (2002). The Role of the Planner in Start-Ups: Angels, Advisors, Devil's Advocates. *Journal of Financial Planning* (July 2002), pp. 54–61.

Since new businesses both start and stop in significant numbers, this article discusses the issues that financial planners face when they work with small businesses. It provides information on the types of clients in the market for start-up advice, on how advisors should define their role with a start-up, and on the issues that they are likely to face.

Lancioni, Richard A. (February 2005). A Strategic Approach to Industrial Product Pricing: The Pricing Plan. *Industrial Marketing Management,* vol. 34, no. 2, pp. 177–83.

The pricing decision is at the core of every business plan and impacts directly on the critical components of a company's marketing strategy. In this article, the importance of price planning in industrial marketing is discussed, including the major components needed to make an industrial pricing strategy successful.

Mason, Colin; and Matthew Stark. (June 2004). What Do Investors Look For in a Business Plan? A Comparison of the Investment Criteria of Bankers, Venture Capitalists and Business Angels. *International Small Business Journal,* vol. 22, no. 3, pp. 227–48.

This article studies investors' perceptions of the business plan. The business plan is the ticket of admission giving the entrepreneur his first and often only chance to impress prospective sources of finance with the quality of the proposal. The decision by the prospective funder whether to proceed beyond the initial reading of the business plan to consider the proposal in more detail will therefore depend on the quality of the business plan used to support the funding proposal.

Matherne, Brett P. (November 2004). If You Fail to Plan, Do You Plan to Fail? *Academy of Management Executive,* vol. 18, no. 4, pp. 156–57.

This article discusses a study completed by Delmar and Shane regarding the significance of business planning. Their finding supports the argument that planning first, before any action is taken in starting a new venture, reduces the chance of failure. In this article it is argued that not only should planning take place but that the founders of any new venture need to also act immediately, even at the expense of completion of the business plan.

Montgomery, David B.; Marian Moore; and Joel E. Urbany. (Winter 2005). Reasoning about Competitive Reactions: Evidence from Executives. *Marketing Science,* vol. 24, no. 1, pp. 138–49.

Much of the research on competitive reactions has been based on a competitor's past actions, not on the competitor's likely future actions. This is primarily because managers think that any attempt to predict competitor actions has a low return relative to the cost of such an attempt. This paper suggests a need for more research on competitor behavior in order to influence and improve managerial judgment and decision making.

Perry, Stephen C. (2001). The Relationship between Written Business Plans and the Failure of Small Businesses in the U.S. *Journal of Small Business Management,* vol. 39, no. 3, pp. 201–8.

This paper describes a study that investigates the influence of planning on U.S. small business failures. The main conclusion is that very little formal planning goes on in U.S. small businesses; however, non-failed firms do more planning than similar failed firms prior to failure.

Sahlman, William A. (1997). How to Write a Great Business Plan. *Harvard Business Review,* vol. 75, no. 4, pp. 98–108.

This paper proposes that a great business plan is one that focuses on a series of questions relating to four factors critical to the success of every new venture. These factors are: the people, the opportunity, the context, and the possibilities for both risk and reward. The questions related to these four factors are discussed.

Toftoy, Charles N.; and Joydeep Chatterjee. (Fall 2004). Mission Statements and the Small Business. *Business Strategy Review*, vol. 15, no. 3, pp. 41–44.

This article argues that small businesses need a clearly defined strategic plan and an honest, concise, and meaningful mission statement if the rate of business failure is to be reduced. The mission statement answers the question: What business is it in and what is its reason for being? The lack of a well-written mission statement is hypothesized as one of the foremost contributors to business failures.

END NOTES

1. See Katherine A. Diaz, "A Champion for Small Business: GC Micro's Belinda Guadarrama Breaks Barriers," HispanicTrends.com (Spring 2003), pp. 1–6; "On the Move," *The Press Democrat* (November 3, 2002), p. 24; and www.gcmicro.com.
2. Donald F. Kuratko and Arnold Cirtin, "Developing a Business Plan for Your Clients," *The National Public Accountant* (January 1990), pp. 24–27.
3. David Worrell, "Attacking a Loan," *Entrepreneur* (July 2, 2002), pp. 51–52.
4. David E. Gumpert, "A Winning Plan Is Just the Start," *BusinessWeek Online* (November 22, 2005).
5. Brad Smith, "Earthlink Gambles on Wireless Broadband," *Wireless Week* (October 15, 2005), pp. 22–26.
6. "Online Retail Sales to Reach $329 billion by 2010: Forrester," *TWICE: This Week in Consumer Electronics* (October 10, 2005), p. 14.
7. "Volume of Search Queries Jumps 15 Percent in Past Five Months, Driven by 'Big Three' Search Engines, according to Nielsen Nettracking," *PR Newswire* (December 13, 2005).
8. Bruce G. Posner, "Real Entrepreneurs Don't Plan," *Inc.* (November 1985), pp. 129–35.
9. John Clyman, Molly K. McLaughlin, Michael J. Steinhart, and Sahil Gambhir, "Manage Your Customers and Contacts," *PC Magazine* (November 30, 2004), pp. 146–47.

APPENDIX A: SAMPLE BUSINESS PLAN—GOPHER IT

The following business plan has been condensed and edited somewhat because of space requirements. However, the areas where editing has taken place are clearly identified and do not in any way detract from the meaningfulness of this example. An average business plan will vary in length depending on the industry, the size of the appendix, and the number of illustrations. The actual text of a business plan would conservatively range between 15 and 25 pages.

Venture Description

Gopher It is a personal shopping service located in the downtown business district of Boston, Massachusetts. It is based on the belief that people's schedules today are more demanding; thus the value of personal leisure time has increased. As we continue the 21st century with more and more dual-career families, personal convenience services are a high-growth market opportunity. The professional white-collar employee in the downtown district, who has high disposable income and a strong motive to increase leisure time, represents the main focus of the venture's marketing efforts.

Running errands before work, during lunch breaks, or after work takes time and is often irritating. People often have to wait in line for services, fight traffic, and skip lunch or an opportunity for a quiet time away from the pressures of the office. Gopher It has established an errand service for professionals in the heart of the downtown business district of Boston. The company will be located at _____ Street, on the first floor, where employees will have direct access to public transportation and customers will be able to stop by and conveniently request any service. Employees will typically be college students, who will perform services on foot, use public transportation, or ride a bicycle to efficiently meet customer needs. The office will contain storage space for pickup and delivery items as well as refrigeration for any specific food products. The entry area where customers will place their service order will be professionally decorated and staffed with trained individuals to answer questions and attend to customer needs. The number of staff will vary, depending on when the office is most busy (early morning, lunchtimes, and at close of business day).

The diverse services that will be offered are categorized as standard or custom. Standard services include dropping and/or picking up laundry, dry cleaning, mail, tickets such as airline or theater, prescriptions; shopping for groceries or gifts; and making bank deposits. Customized or special services, not specifically listed or identified, may also be offered based on the amount of time it takes to complete the errand. An example of a special service would be picking up an automobile that was being repaired. These special services would be priced on an hourly basis and, in the case of an automobile, may also include the expense of parking.

Industry Analysis

The service sector in the United States continues to grow. Entrepreneurs have initiated many new ventures in the service sector in response to greater demand for leisure time, the increasing number of dual-career families, and more disposable income.

Demographic Trends [*This section of the business plan would provide statistical data and discussion of some of the significant demographic trends that would support the needs being addressed by this proposed venture.*]

Competitor Analysis Although there are many indirect competitors to Gopher It, there are none in the Boston market that offer such a broad range of services. Courier services have existed for many years, but other service businesses have been slow in their response to customer needs by offering only pickup and delivery services. Today it is more common to find supermarkets, dry cleaners, restaurants, video stores, and auto repair shops offering pickup and/or delivery for their customers. Typically this service tends to be ad hoc, with little effort made to organize it based on customer needs.

Although there are a number of small businesses in other states that offer pickup and delivery services, none compares with Gopher It in terms of the extent of services offered. Shopping services for professional clients exist in almost every major market. However, Gopher It will not offer this service since it requires a distinctive trained and knowledgeable staff. There are also businesses that will pick up and deliver laundry, and others that will provide grocery shopping services. Most of these businesses are in the specific retail business for which they are providing the service; hence their purpose is to offer pickup and delivery as an incentive to buy their retail goods. Some of the companies that offer pickup and delivery services that would indirectly compete with Gopher It are as follows:

[*Direct and indirect competitors would be listed here with a description of their businesses and the services they provide.*]

Marketing Plan

The marketing strategy was designed on the basis of personal interviews conducted with employers and business professionals in the downtown Boston market, which represents our target market. These interviews indicated that the individuals preferred to have someone else perform many of the time-consuming errands that they were required to do on a weekly or regular basis. The majority of these individuals commented that they had less leisure time than in the past and, as a result, valued this free time more than ever before. They indicated a need for the types of services offered by Gopher It and a willingness to pay for these services.

The errand market is untapped and has a large customer base. The target market for our services would be white-collar, highly educated baby boomers, working in professional jobs and likely members of two-career professional households. The office is located in the downtown business district and near a major transit station where there are many individuals who fit our target market. Recent traffic statistics indicated that more than 13,000 individuals would pass our office to and from their office to their transit stop. This high traffic location lends itself to the convenience services that we can provide for our target market.

Marketing Goals

- To meet the growing needs of a target market defined on the basis of geography, demographics, lifestyle, and buyer intentions.
- To evaluate the competitive environment and continue to establish a differential advantage.
- To establish an effective and profitable marketing mix of service, place, price, and promotion.

Marketing Objectives

- To establish a customer base of 10 percent of the defined target market in the first year.
- To generate $150,000 in sales for the first year.

- To increase sales by 10 percent annually for the first three years.
- To expand to at least two new locations by the end of the first three years.

Size of Market According to our research, there are about 250,000 people in the central business district of the city of Boston. There are approximately 10,300 to 13,200 people (represents the primary market) who pass our office every business day. On the basis of our research and on demographic studies conducted in the city of Boston, about 75 percent of these individuals match our target market. This would consist of individuals between the ages of 28 and 65, male or female, with high disposable income, employed as professional businesspersons or office staff.

There is also the potential to reach an additional 10,000 customers who work on the fringe of this area and may not directly pass our office on a regular basis. This secondary market may be penetrated through advertising, word of mouth, and the distribution of marketing literature.

On the basis of the above information, it is estimated that the potential market is between 17,000 and 20,000 people. Our objective is to reach 10 percent of the primary market and 5 percent of the secondary market. Thus, in our first year the market would consist of about 1,275 customers.

Service The services that will be provided by Gopher It are designed to provide customers with the benefits of convenience and the saving of time. Although the services vary widely, there are standard services offered to the customer. Standard services include lunch delivery, dry cleaning pickup and drop-off, grocery shopping (maximum of 10 items), and gift shopping in the downtown area. Customized services of almost any kind will also be offered on a fee-for-time basis. Examples of these customized services are auto pickup and/or drop-off, pickup of theater tickets, supply pickup, post office visits, and bank deposits. Delivery and pickup will typically involve walking, riding a bicycle, or using the transit. The most efficient and economic solution will be chosen for each situation.

Price Pricing strategy is based on a fee per errand. This strategy was determined from an evaluation of Errands Unlimited, a similar business located in Milwaukee, Wisconsin, as well as a marketing research study of the target market. For the customized services the price will be based on the amount of time necessary to perform the errand, including time in transit. The lowest fee would be $5 for a quick errand that took less than five minutes. Prices for errands taking longer than five minutes would increase accordingly and are indicated below.

Miscellaneous Personal Services

Pick up tickets for theater district shows.

Pick up tickets for sporting events.

Wait in line for a book autograph.

Pick up automobile at repair shop.

Post office visits.

Office supply shopping.

Bank deposits.

Any other personal errands.

Time Spent (in Minutes)	Price
0–5	$10
6–10	$15
11–15	$20
16–20	$25
21–25	$30
26 +	$40

Regular or Standard Services	Price
Express lunch delivery	$7
Dry cleaning drop-off	$7
Dry cleaning pickup	$7
Grocery shopping (maximum of 10 items)	$12
Gift shopping in downtown area	$18

Promotion Gopher It will rely extensively on word-of-mouth advertising. However, it will be important to create an awareness of our services to the target market. To attract attention and to create awareness, signs will display our name and describe our services to the many individuals who actually pass by the office. Pamphlets will also be distributed to office buildings in the target market.

Facilities Plan The location of Gopher It will be in the lobby at _____ Street in the downtown district of Boston. This location is ideal because it provides access to a large base of potential customers who pass the office going to and from work to the transit station or garage as well as those who stroll around the area during lunchtime. Estimates of the daily traffic are between 4,000 and 5,000 individuals passing through the lobby at each rush hour, which projects to between 8,000 and 10,000 passes per day. There are also about 1,000 people who work in this building and another 1,300 to 2,200 individuals who pass through the lobby at non-rush-hour time. Thus, in a typical day there are between 10,300 and 13,200 potential consumers who are likely to pass by our business location. If we also include the Bank of Boston and Shawmut building, both on a connecting street, we have effectively extended our potential market to over 20,000 people. This large base of potential consumers is an excellent target market for our services. Even with limited resources, our store front and location will be an important asset in promoting an awareness of Gopher It's services.

The initial location will be leased. Rent will be based on a $40 per square foot price. With electricity and other charges the rental cost will be $50 per square foot or $10,000 per month.

Certain equipment will also be necessary to operate the business effectively—a multiline phone system; computer and printer; fax machine; storage for hot and cold foods; and storage for garments, gifts, and groceries. Counters will be set up in a small area at the front of the office for conducting business with clients. Little space is needed for the attendant, whose main function will be to take orders from walk-in clients and to answer the phone for call-in orders. The storage space would have food storage on one side, and garment and gift storage on the other.

Organizational Plan

Gopher It will be established as a partnership. There will be three partners: Chris Bentley, Jack Welch, and Laura Shanley. Each will assume an equal ownership in the business. Background and roles of each of the three partners are described below. A partnership agreement is summarized in the Appendix.

Management Team Background Chris Bentley was born in San Diego, California, and graduated from Swarthmore College with an accounting degree. Past employers include numerous restaurants, a specialty retailer, and a large bank (mutual funds). He has significant experience in managing and training people as well as financial management.

Jack Welch was born in Atlanta, Georgia, and has a food science degree from the University of Maryland and an MBA degree from Boston College. He has had extensive experience in food retailing and more recently in sales and marketing with a large consumer food producer.

Laura Shanley was born in Jamaica Plain, Massachusetts, and has a bachelor of science degree in marketing from Boston College. She has extensive experience in a family business, a chain of small retail gift shops. This gift shop experience involved expansion to new locations, buying, promotion, and customer relations. The business has since been sold, and Laura is seeking new endeavors in a start-up venture.

Duties and Responsibilities of the Partners

Laura Shanley—General Administrator and Manager Laura will oversee the daily operations of the business. This includes the hiring and firing of employees as well as training and supervising. Periodic employee evaluations will be completed by the general administrator and manager. She will also handle all purchasing for the office and will be responsible for opening and closing the office each day.

Jack Welch—Marketing and Sales Manager Jack will be responsible for creating promotional activities, monitoring sales, and establishing effective strategies for creating awareness of the business. He will be responsible for the design and distribution of all direct marketing materials.

Chris Bentley—Financial Manager Chris will be responsible for finance, accounting, payroll, billing, taxes, and any other matters related to sales and revenue budgets.

The Financial Plan

Financial statements are presented in the following pages. Explanations of all financial information are also provided. The business is expected to break even in the early part of the second year with the first positive profit achieved in the month of August. Total start-up expenditures will be about $20,000. We are seeking a $40,000 loan that will be paid back over five years at 12 percent.

Risk Assessment

The proposed errand service offered by Gopher It, although free from any direct competition, has a very low barrier to entry. Setup costs and high liquidity will be a significant attraction to competitors, who could subsequently penetrate some of Gopher It's market. Gopher It will need to rely on its quality of service and being first in the market to protect its market share. Our convenient location and flexibility in providing a wide range of services should support the long-term success of Gopher It in this market.

Appendix*

Resumes of Partners

Partnership Agreement

Lease Agreement

Facility Layout

Market Research Survey Results

Marketing Brochure with Price List

*The actual information in the Appendix has not been included because of space. However, the student should be able to infer from the example provided here the scope and content of a complete business plan.

8

THE MARKETING PLAN

LEARNING OBJECTIVES

1
To understand the relevance of industry and competitive analysis to the market planning process.

2
To describe the role of marketing research in determining marketing strategy for the marketing plan.

3
To illustrate an effective and feasible procedure for the entrepreneur to follow in engaging in a market research study.

4
To define the steps in preparing the marketing plan.

5
To explain the marketing system and its key components.

6
To illustrate different creative strategies that may be used to differentiate or position the new venture's products or services.

OPENING PROFILE

WARREN G. JACKSON, CIRCULATION EXPERTÍ, LTD.

Some experts argue that organizing and launching a business is the easiest part of getting started, while sustaining the business is the most difficult and challenging part. As we've seen in earlier chapters, businesses fail at an alarming rate, yet too often we blame lack of finances or poor management for the demise. A closer look often reveals that the real problems relate to marketing issues such as identifying the customer, defining the right product or service to meet customer needs, pricing, distribution, and promotion.

www.experti.com

As technology continues to change, providing easier access to extended international markets, it is significantly more important that today's entrepreneur become more focused on developing a comprehensive and detailed marketing plan. Markets are much more dynamic than ever before, making it necessary to anticipate changes in consumer needs and make the necessary changes in marketing actions. Planning, as discussed in the previous chapter, spans a wide range of activities and is intended to formally detail the business activities, strategies, responsibilities, budgets, and controls to meet specific, designated goals. The marketing plan is a tool that can assist the entrepreneur in monitoring critical short-term goals and objectives and marketing strategies, as well as a tool that can alert the entrepreneur to make necessary changes in those strategies to avoid long-term failure.

One of the most important marketing challenges facing the entrepreneur is to effectively position the venture's products or services in a highly competitive environment. Most markets already contain major players that may dominate the market and have significant resources to defend against any new venture. However, within many of these large markets there are customers who are not completely satisfied with the existing offerings. Effective marketing planning that targets and positions the new venture's products or services can meet the needs of these customers, leading to opportunity and long-term success. Such an approach was taken by Circulation Expertí, Ltd.

This family-run company is a wholly black-owned public relations, advertising, marketing, and consulting firm. It officially began in 1968 as the brainstorm of Warren G. Jackson, who recognized that major newspapers were not effectively reaching the African American community.

Warren Jackson entered the newspaper business at *The New York Times* in 1952, where he eventually became an assistant manager in the circulation department. Later working for the *Amsterdam News,* he was asked by Time, Inc., to assist that firm in the circulation and distribution of a new general market daily afternoon publication. Although it was never published, Warren realized that his newspaper knowledge and expertise could be beneficial to media and major corporations all across the country. With this knowledge and a $12,500 contract from *Tuesday* magazine he then started Circulation Expertí out of his home. Within a year of this beginning, Expertí's contract volume reached $200,000, leading Warren to move out of his home to a new small office in Hartsdale, New York. Although he was not armed with a formal marketing plan, Warren's understanding and recognition of the unmet needs of a significant and growing consumer target market led Expertí to become the largest and most prominent minority-owned public relations agency in the United States.

This successful company is unique—not only in the growth it has experienced over the years but also because the firm has remained a family-owned organization involving Warren's wife, Tena, who came on as CFO in 1972, and their three children, Tenley-Ann, Terrance, and Garrison. Warren and Tena have since given up the reins of the day-to-day activities, with Garrison now assuming the position of president and CEO.

Over the years the company has added an advertising division (1978) and a Hispanic division (1988). Both new divisions have allowed the company to offer one-stop shopping to clients looking for African American and Hispanic marketing. This effort has provided opportunities to add major clients to an already noteworthy list. Some of the clients that the company has serviced include many major Fortune 500 clients such as JPMorgan Chase, Colgate-Palmolive, IBM, Miller Brewing, Seven-Up, Kraft, General Motors, Reebok, Sears, Ryder Systems, Unilever, and ITT Continental Banking, to name a few. Billings have also grown, from around $1 to $2 million in the early years to $20 million in more recent years. The company anticipates significant growth in 2006, with new clients and company-owned initiatives already in the fold.

The Jacksons represent a unique success story dating back to Warren's recognition of a need that he felt he could meet with a marketing plan. This firm's success is not notable for its client base alone but also because of the significant amount of charity and philanthropic work in which all members of the family are actively engaged. For its success in business and related philanthropic endeavors the company has been recognized with numerous awards from *PRWeek, Black Enterprise Magazine, National Association of Market Developers, Public Relations Society of America,* and *Family Digest Magazine,* in addition to receiving numerous awards from major corporations and the New York City Department of Health. Under the direction of Garrison and his brother and sister, and with Warren and Tena always there for support, the firm's outlook is extremely favorable. Today the company plans and sets clear goals and objectives and continues to evaluate market opportunities to sustain successful long-term growth.[1]

As we can see from the example of Circulation Expertí, many opportunities exist in a competitive environment. Warren's efforts in creating the venture began with an understanding and assessment of the needs of a particular segment of the market. Developing an appropriate strategy to meet those needs includes an understanding and assessment of the industry, which is where we will begin our discussion in this chapter.

INDUSTRY ANALYSIS

Prior to the preparation of the marketing plan the entrepreneur will need to complete the industry analysis section of the business plan. The primary focus of the industry analysis is to provide sufficient knowledge of the environment (national and local market) that can affect marketing strategy decision making. In Chapter 7 we described this information-seeking process as an upside-down pyramid (see Figure 7.1). It begins with the broadest-based assessment of environmental and industry trends. Then it proceeds to more local market environmental and industry trends, including competition. The entrepreneur should review this section of Chapter 7 to understand what information is included and how it can be obtained.

Secondary sources can provide much of the information needed on each of these issues. Sample sources along with an appropriate example are also identified in Chapter 7. In addition to the secondary sources the entrepreneur may also decide that a market research initiative is needed to secure more specific information on such variables as customer needs, competitive strengths and weaknesses, price, promotion, distribution, and product or service benefits. This market research project may add important valuable insights that can assist the entrepreneur in determining the most effective market position, setting market goals and objectives, and determining what action programs are necessary to meet those goals and objectives. The steps in the market research process and the avenues available to the entrepreneur for obtaining assistance in this process are discussed later in this chapter.

One of the important benefits of the upside-down-pyramid approach to industry analysis is that the entrepreneur can begin to understand competitors' strengths and weaknesses, which may provide valuable insight into how to position the products or services of the new venture. Techniques for recording and evaluating this information on the competitive environment are discussed below.

Competitor Analysis

The entrepreneur should begin this step by first documenting the current strategy of each primary competitor. This can be organized by using the model in Table 8.1. The information on competitors can be gathered initially by using as much public information as possible and then complementing this with a marketing research project. Newspaper articles, Web sites, catalogs, promotions, interviews with distributors and customers, and any other marketing strategy or company information available should be reviewed. Articles that have been written on the competitors can be found by using a computer search in any university or local library. These articles should be scanned for information on competitor strategies and should identify the names of individuals who were interviewed, referenced, or even mentioned in the article. Any of these individuals as well as the author of the article can then be contacted to obtain further information. All the information can then be summarized

TABLE 8.1 An Assessment of Competitor Marketing Strategies and Strengths and Weaknesses

	Competitor A	Competitor B	Competitor C
Product or service strategies			
Pricing strategies			
Distribution strategies			
Promotion strategies			
Strengths and weaknesses			

in the model provided in Table 8.1. Once the strategy has been summarized, the entrepreneur should begin to identify the strengths and weaknesses of each competitor, as shown in the table.

All the information included in Table 8.1 can then be utilized to formulate the market positioning strategy of the new venture. Will the new venture imitate a particular competitor or will it try to satisfy needs in the market that are not being filled by any other company? This analysis will enlighten the entrepreneur and provide a solid basis for any marketing decision making discussed in the marketing plan. If a more formal data collection process is being considered, the following paragraphs will help explain the steps in gathering primary data as well as some of the secondary sources that can provide data to the entrepreneur.

MARKETING RESEARCH FOR THE NEW VENTURE

Information for developing the marketing plan may necessitate conducting some marketing research. Marketing research involves the gathering of data in order to determine such information as who will buy the product or service, what is the size of the potential market, what price should be charged, what is the most appropriate distribution channel, and what is the most effective promotion strategy to inform and reach potential customers. Since marketing research costs vary significantly, the entrepreneur will need to assess available resources and the information needed. There are also some research techniques that are not costly and can provide, at least initially, significant evidence to support the market potential for the new venture. One of these techniques is the focus group, which is discussed later in this section.

Marketing research may be conducted by the entrepreneur or by an external supplier or consultant. There are also opportunities for entrepreneurs to contact their local colleges or universities to identify faculty who teach marketing and are willing to have external clients for student research projects. Suggestions on how to conduct market research are discussed next.

Market research begins with a definition of objectives or purpose. This is often the most difficult step since many entrepreneurs lack knowledge or experience in marketing and often don't even know what they want to accomplish from a research study. This, however, is the very reason why marketing research can be so meaningful to the entrepreneur.[2]

Step One: Defining the Purpose or Objectives

The most effective way to begin is for the entrepreneur to sit down and make a list of the information that will be needed to prepare the marketing plan. For example, the entrepreneur may think there is a market for his or her product but not be sure who the customers will be or even whether the product is appropriate in its present form. Thus, one objective would be to ask people what they think of the product or service and whether they would buy it, and to collect some background demographics and attitudes of these individuals. This would satisfy the objective or problem that the entrepreneur defined above. Other objectives may be to determine the following:

- How much would potential customers be willing to pay for the product or service?
- Where would potential customers prefer to purchase the product or service?
- Where would the customer expect to hear about or learn about such a product or service?

Step Two: Gathering Data from Secondary Sources

Secondary sources, discussed earlier in this chapter and in Chapter 7, offer a means of gathering information for the industry analysis section of the business plan. There are many other market research secondary sources that may be used to address the specific objectives of the project identified in step one. As mentioned, trade magazines, newspaper articles, libraries, government agencies, and the Internet can provide much information on the industry market and competitors. The Internet can even be used to gather informal primary data through chat groups.

Commercial data may also be available, but the cost may be prohibitive to the entrepreneur. However, business libraries may subscribe to some of these commercial services such as Nielsen Indexes, Audits and Survey's National Market Indexes, Selling Areas Marketing Inc. (SAMI), and Information Resources, Inc.

Before considering either primary sources or commercial sources of information, the entrepreneur should exhaust all free secondary sources. At the federal level, the U.S. Bureau of Census publishes a wide range of census reports, as does the Department of Commerce. Other excellent sources at the state and local levels are the State Department of Commerce, chambers of commerce, local banks, state departments of labor and industry, and local media. Private sources of data, some of which can be found in a good business library, are Dun and Bradstreet's Million Dollar Directory, Gale's Encyclopedias, the Small Business Index, Reuters, Market Share Reporter, Forrester, STAT-USA, TableBase, and a variety of directories and publications available from the Small Business Association (SBA). In addition there are numerous databases available online at such sites as Statistical Resources on the Web, FedStats, MarketResearch.com, USDATA.com, and EconData.Net. A university library can usually provide access to all of these secondary database sources.

Step Three: Gathering Information from Primary Sources

Information that is new is primary data. Gathering primary data involves a data collection procedure—such as observation, networking, interviewing, focus groups, or experimentation—and usually a data collection instrument, such as a questionnaire.

Observation is the simplest approach. The entrepreneur might observe potential customers and record some aspect of their buying behavior. Networking, which is more of an informal method to gather primary data from experts in the field, can also be a valuable low-cost method to learn about the marketplace. One study of new ventures found that the

TABLE 8.2 A Comparison of Survey Methods

	Characteristics of Methods				
Method	**Costs**	**Flexibility**	**Response Rate**	**Speed**	**Depth**
Telephone	Can be inexpensive, depending on telephone distance and length of interview.	Some flexibility; possible to clarify or explain questions.	Good response rate possible (possible 80%) depending on not-at-homes or refusals.	Fastest method of obtaining information. Can contact many respondents in a short period.	Least detailed because of 8- to 10-minute time limitation.
Mail	Can be inexpensive, depending on number of units mailed and weight.	No flexibility since questionnaire is self-administered. Instrument needs to be self-explanatory.	Poorest response rate since respondent has choice of whether to complete questionnaire.	Slowest method because of time required to mail and wait for respondents to complete and return questionnaire.	Some depth possible since respondent completes questionnaire at his or her leisure.
Personal	Most expensive technique. Requires face-to-face contact.	Most flexible of all methods because of face-to-face contact.	The most effective response rate because of face-to-face contact.	Somewhat slow because of dead time needed for travel.	Most detailed because of open-ended questions.
Internet	Inexpensive.	No flexibility since self-administered.	Good response rate with incentives, but still relatively new method.	Very fast method since questionnaire is sent electronically.	Some depth possible since respondent completes questionnaire at his or her leisure.

most successful ventures (based on growth rate) were focused on information about competitors, the customer, and the industry, using networking, trade associations, and recent publications. Less successful ventures were more focused on gathering information on general economic and demographic trends and hence had less of a sense of what was happening in their specific target market.[3]

Interviewing or surveying is the most common approach used to gather market information. It is more expensive than observation but is more likely to generate more meaningful information. Interviews may be conducted in person, by telephone, through the mail, or online, an approach growing in popularity, particularly for firms with an existing customer base. Each of these methods offers advantages and disadvantages to the entrepreneur and should be evaluated accordingly.[4] Table 8.2 provides comparisons of each of these three methods of data collection.

The questionnaire, or data collection instrument, used by the entrepreneur should include questions specifically designed to fulfill one or more of the objectives the entrepreneur listed earlier. Questions should be designed so they are clear and concise, do not bias the respondent, and are easy to answer. Table 8.3 illustrates a sample questionnaire employed by an entrepreneur trying to assess the need for a personal errand service, such as the venture Gopher It, whose business plan is used as an example in Chapter 7. The questions are designed to satisfy the objectives of the entrepreneur, which are to ascertain

TABLE 8.3 Sample Questionnaire for Personal Errand Service

1. Of the following, please check the three most frequent errands that you are likely to carry out during the workweek.
   - _____ Dry cleaners
   - _____ Drugstore
   - _____ Shopping for clothing items
   - _____ Buying a gift
   - _____ Other ___________ Please specify
   - _____ Post office
   - _____ Bank
   - _____ Shopping for nonclothing and nongrocery items
   - _____ Automotive service or repair
   - _____ Other ___________ Please specify
2. Of the following, please indicate which items you would be willing to pay for someone to carry out for you.
   - _____ Dry cleaners
   - _____ Drugstore
   - _____ Shopping for clothing items
   - _____ Buying a gift
   - _____ Other ___________ Please specify
   - _____ Post office
   - _____ Bank
   - _____ Shopping for nonclothing and nongrocery items
   - _____ Automotive service or repair
   - _____ Other ___________ Please specify
3. What do you consider the two most important reasons for having someone else complete an errand? (Check only two).
   - _____ Waiting in lines
   - _____ Inconvenient location
   - _____ Imposes on my relaxation time
   - _____ Difficult work schedule
   - _____ Traffic
   - _____ Other ___________ Please specify
   - _____ Other ___________ Please specify
4. If an errand service was conveniently available to you, how much would you be willing to pay for a standard errand such as delivering or picking up dry cleaning, going to the post office, or picking up a prescription?
   - _____ $3.00
   - _____ $6.00
   - _____ $9.00
   - _____ $4.00
   - _____ $7.00
   - _____ $10.00
   - _____ $5.00
   - _____ $8.00
   - _____ More than $10.00
5. Please indicate by rank ordering (1 being highest rank, 2 being second highest rank, and so on) your preference for the most convenient location for a personal errand service.
   - _____ In my building
   - _____ Near my office
   - _____ Near the train station
   - _____ Prefer to have item(s) delivered to my office
6. The following information is needed for categorizing the results of the survey. Please check the appropriate box.

   Sex: _____ Male _____ Female

   Marital/household status:
   - _____ Bachelor
   - _____ Single parent
   - _____ Married, both spouses working
   - _____ Married, one spouse working

   Age:
   - _____ Under 25
   - _____ 25–34
   - _____ 35–44
   - _____ 45–54
   - _____ 55 and over

   Household income:
   - _____Under $40,000
   - _____$40,000–$54,000
   - _____$55,000–$69,000
   - _____$70,000–$84,000
   - _____$85,000–$99,000
   - _____$100,000 and above

the need, location, and determination of the most important services to offer and price. Support in the design of questionnaires can often be attained through small business development centers, members of the Senior Core of Retired Executives (SCORE), or students in marketing research classes at a local college or university. Since the instrument is important in the research process, it is recommended that entrepreneurs seek assistance if they have no experience in designing questionnaires.

Focus groups are a more informal method for gathering in-depth information. A focus group is a sample of 10 to 12 potential customers who are invited to participate in a discussion relating to the entrepreneur's research objectives. The focus group discusses issues in an informal, open format, enabling the entrepreneur to ascertain certain information.

For example, two entrepreneurs were considering a chain of hair salons that would specialize in hair styling and hair care services for African Americans. In order to understand the hair care needs and most effective marketing strategy for this market, focus groups of a cross section of African American women were organized. The focus groups were designed to ascertain what services should be offered, the demand for these services, pricing strategy, and the most effective advertising/promotion strategy. The information gathered was then used in the preparation of the marketing plan.

Focus groups should be led by an experienced monitor or by someone other than the entrepreneur. Often this is a good project for students at a college or university in a marketing research class.

Step Four: Analyzing and Interpreting the Results

Depending on the size of the sample, the entrepreneur can hand-tabulate the results or enter them on a computer. In either case, the results should be evaluated and interpreted in response to the research objectives that were specified in the first step of the research process. Often, summarizing the answers to questions will give some preliminary insights. Then data can be cross-tabulated in order to provide more focused results. For example, the entrepreneur may want to compare the results to questions by different age groups, sex, occupation, location, and so on. Continuing this fine-tuning can provide valuable insights, particularly regarding the segmentation of the market, which is discussed later in this chapter.

UNDERSTANDING THE MARKETING PLAN

Once the entrepreneur has gathered all the necessary information, he or she can sit down to prepare the marketing plan. The marketing plan represents a significant element in the business plan for a new venture. It serves a number of important functions or purposes. Primarily the marketing plan establishes how the entrepreneur will effectively compete and operate in the marketplace and thus meet the business goals and objectives of the new venture. Once the strategies of how the business will operate have been established, the entrepreneur can assign costs to these strategies, which then serves the important purpose of establishing budgets and making financial projections. The marketing plan, like any other type of plan, may be compared to a road map used to guide a traveler. It is designed to provide answers to three basic questions:[5]

1. Where have we been? When used as a stand-alone document (operational plan), this would imply some background on the company, its strengths and weaknesses, some background on the competition, and a discussion of the opportunities and threats in the marketplace. When the marketing plan is integrated as part of the business plan, this segment would focus on some history of the marketplace, marketing strengths and weaknesses of the firm, and market opportunities and threats.

TABLE 8.4 Outline for a Marketing Plan

Situation analysis
Background of venture
Strengths and weaknesses of venture
Market opportunities and threats
Competitor analysis
Marketing objectives and goals
Marketing strategy and action programs
Budgets
Controls

2. Where do we want to go (in the short term)? This question primarily addresses the marketing objectives and goals of the new venture in the next 12 months. In the initial business plan, the objectives and goals often go beyond the first year because of the need to project profits and cash needs for the first three years.
3. How do we get there? This question discusses the specific marketing strategy that will be implemented, when it will occur, and who will be responsible for the monitoring of activities. The answers to these questions are generally determined from the marketing research carried out before the planning process is begun. Budgets will also be determined and used in the income and cash flow projections.

Management should understand that the marketing plan is a guide for implementing marketing decision making and not a generalized, superficial document. The mere organization of the thinking process involved in preparing a marketing plan can be helpful to the entrepreneur because in order to develop the plan, it is necessary to formally document and describe as many marketing details as possible that will be part of the decision process during the next year. This process will enable the entrepreneur not only to understand and recognize the critical issues but also to be prepared in the event that any change in the environment occurs.

Each year the entrepreneur should prepare an annual marketing plan before any decisions are made regarding production or manufacturing, personnel changes, or financial resources needed. This annual plan becomes the basis for planning other aspects of the business and for developing budgets for the year. Table 8.4 provides a suggested outline for the marketing plan. Variations of this outline will depend on the market and nature of the product or service, as well as the general company mission. The remainder of this chapter focuses on the short-term aspects of the marketing plan, while not ignoring the fact that the entrepreneur will also need to provide market projections for years 2 and 3 as part of the business plan.

CHARACTERISTICS OF A MARKETING PLAN

The marketing plan should be designed to meet certain criteria. Some important characteristics that must be incorporated in an effective marketing plan are as follows:

- It should provide a strategy for accomplishing the company mission or goal.
- It should be based on facts and valid assumptions. Some of the facts needed are illustrated in Table 8.5. It must provide for the use of existing resources. Allocation of all equipment, financial resources, and human resources must be described.

TABLE 8.5 Facts Needed for Market Planning

- Who are the users, where are they located, how much do they buy, from whom do they buy, and why?
- How have promotion and advertising been employed and which approach has been most effective?
- What are the pricing changes in the market, who has initiated these changes, and why?
- What are the market's attitudes concerning competitive products?
- What channels of distribution supply consumers, and how do they function?
- Who are the competitors, where are they located, and what advantages/disadvantages do they have?
- What marketing techniques are used by the most successful competitors? By the least successful?
- What are the overall objectives of the company for the next year and five years hence?
- What are the company's strengths? Weaknesses?
- What are one's production capabilities by product?

- An appropriate organization must be described to implement the marketing plan.
- It should provide for continuity so that each annual marketing plan can build on it, successfully meeting longer-term goals and objectives.
- It should be simple and short. A voluminous plan will be placed in a desk drawer and likely never used. However, the plan should not be so short that details on how to accomplish a goal are excluded.
- The success of the plan may depend on its flexibility. Changes, if necessary, should be incorporated by including "what if" scenarios and appropriate responding strategies.
- It should specify performance criteria that will be monitored and controlled. For example, the entrepreneur may establish an annual performance criterion of 10 percent of market share in a designated geographic area. To attain this goal, certain expectations should be made at given time periods (e.g., at the end of three months we should have a 5 percent share of market). If not attained, then new strategy or performance standards may be established.

It is clear from the preceding discussion that the market plan is not intended to be written and then put aside. It is intended to be a valuable document that is referred to often and a guideline for the entrepreneur during the next time period.

marketing plan Written statement of marketing objectives, strategies, and activities to be followed in business plan

marketing system Interacting internal and external factors that affect venture's ability to provide goods and services to meet customer needs

Since the term *marketing plan* denotes the significance of marketing, it is important to understand the *marketing system*. The marketing system identifies the major interacting components, both internal and external to the firm, that enable the firm to successfully provide products and/or services to the marketplace. Figure 8.1 provides a summary of the components that constitute the marketing system.[6]

As can be seen from Figure 8.1, the environment (external and internal) plays a very important role in developing the market plan. These factors should be identified and discussed in the Industry Analysis section of the business plan discussed earlier in this chapter. It should also be noted that these factors are typically uncontrollable but need to be recognized as part of the marketing plan.

In addition to the external environmental factors, there are internal environmental factors which, although more controllable by the entrepreneur, can also affect the preparation of the marketing plan and implementation of an effective marketing strategy. Some of the major internal variables are as follows:

FIGURE 8.1 The Marketing System

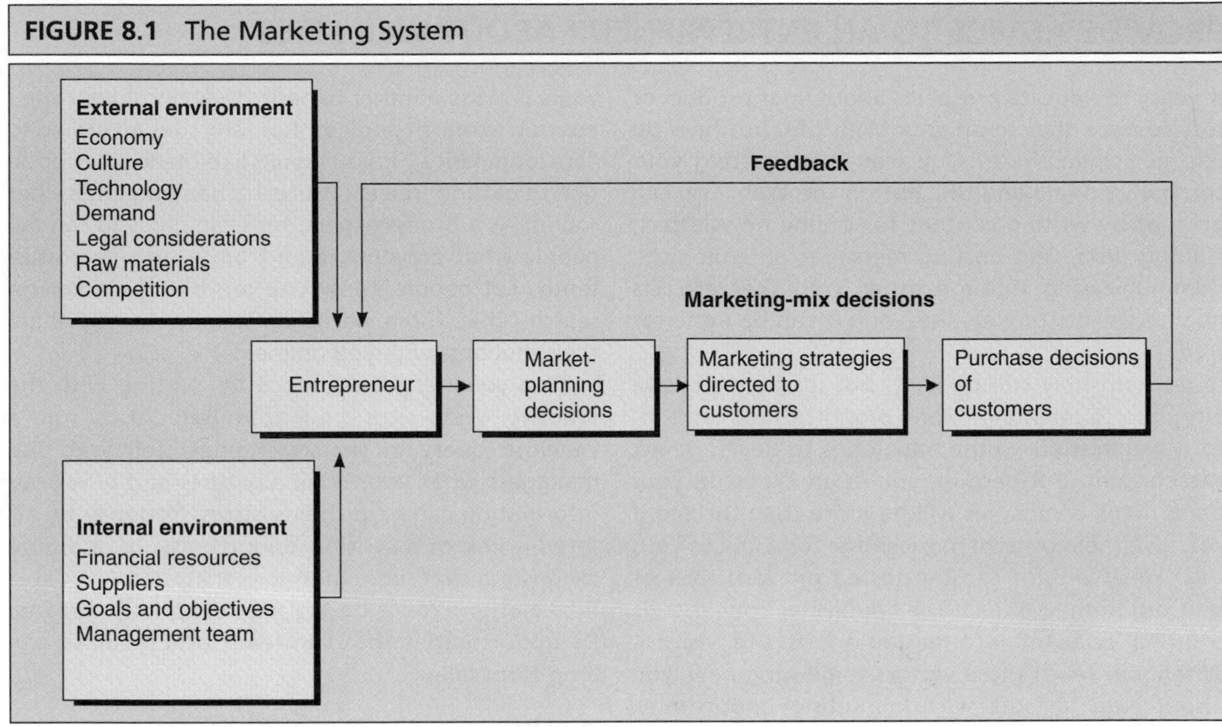

- *Financial resources*. The financial plan, discussed in Chapter 10, should outline the financial needs for the new venture. Any marketing plan or strategy should consider the availability of financial resources as well as the amount of funds needed to meet the goals and objectives stated in the plan.
- *Management team*. It is extremely important in any organization to make appropriate assignments of responsibility for the implementation of the marketing plan. In some cases the availability of a certain expertise may be uncontrollable (e.g., a shortage of certain types of technical managers). In any event, the entrepreneur must build an effective management team and assign the responsibilities to implement the marketing plan.
- *Suppliers*. The suppliers used are generally based on a number of factors such as price, delivery time, quality, and management assistance. In some cases, where raw materials are scarce or there are only a few suppliers of a particular raw material or part, the entrepreneur has little control over the decision. Since the price of supplies, delivery time, and so on, are likely to impact many marketing decisions, it is important to incorporate these factors into the marketing plan.
- *Company mission*. As indicated in Chapter 5, every new venture should define the nature of its business. This statement helps to define the company's mission and basically describes the nature of the business and what the entrepreneur hopes to accomplish with that business. This mission statement or business definition will guide the firm through long-term decision making.

THE MARKETING MIX

The above environmental variables will provide much important information in deciding what will be the most effective marketing strategy to be outlined in the marketing plan. The actual short-term marketing decisions in the marketing plan will consist of four important

AS SEEN IN *ENTREPRENEUR* MAGAZINE

PROVIDE ADVICE TO AN ENTREPRENEUR ABOUT WEB SITES

It's easy to educate prospects about your product or service once they're on your Web site, but how do you get them there? One way is by getting your company's name and URL out on the Web. You can do that by writing content for online newsletters, trading links, and posting messages on chat sites. Communicating through other Web sites attracts quality visitors to your site—and it can be done for free.

Content may still be king, but it's an expensive kingdom to maintain. Many organizations can't afford webmasters whose only job is to develop new site content. But because you're an expert in your field, many companies will be more than thrilled if you give them content in exchange for a link to your site. Your content can be posted on Web sites or sent out in their e-mail. The "publisher" benefits by offering relevant information to its site visitors. When you teach these visitors something new, you also create a "soft sell" marketing opportunity. Don't pitch your business. Rather, share some educational information to establish trust and brand awareness.

Just what is "educational information"? It's content that addresses your prospects' problems. For example, if your company sells exercise equipment, you can provide tips, case studies, or statistics about fitness. Your readers will want to know how you, the fitness expert, can help them achieve their goals. With a simple click on your URL, prospects can travel to your site and discover your company's line of fitness products.

Of course, you aren't limited to providing articles to Web sites. Try asking for a link to your site or a link trade. Just don't put someone else's link on your home page—that encourages people to leave your site as soon as they arrive! Links from sites related to yours provide another benefit: They boost your site's position in search engines that rank sites according to "link popularity." If you would like feedback in addition to getting free exposure, try hanging out in chat rooms. As a fitness expert, for example, you can ask people what prevents them from exercising consistently. Let people know you are doing market research. Chat room participants may happily share their thoughts with you online.

Find your target audience by starting with the industry Web sites you frequent. Also, run a keyword query in search engines. Tell Web site managers what your company does and how your information can help their visitors. You may be offered a link or a writing opportunity. In addition, try posting chat room messages that reveal valuable information. You'll be greatly rewarded with free PR opportunities that can lead to immediate and long-term sales.

ADVICE TO AN ENTREPRENEUR

An entrepreneur who has a Web site for his business has read the above article and comes to you for advice:

1. Seems like a lot of work in writing articles and spending time in chat rooms. Although it might be a way of getting people to my Web site with only a small expense, do you think that this approach is worth the investment of time?
2. What are the other benefits of this approach over and above simply a cost saving?
3. Are there particular businesses and products more suitable for this approach?

Source: Reprinted with permission of Entrepreneur Media, Inc., "Attention, Please. Yell Out 'Look at Me!' for Free by Using Other Websites to Your Advantage," by Catherine Seda, March 2003, *Entrepreneur* magazine: www.entrepreneur.com.

marketing mix Combination of product, price, promotion, and distribution and other marketing activities needed to meet marketing objectives

marketing variables: product or service, pricing, distribution, and promotion. These four factors are referred to as the *marketing mix*. Each variable will be described in detail in the strategy or action plan section of the marketing plan discussed later in this chapter. Although flexibility may be an important consideration, the entrepreneur needs a strong base to provide direction for the day-to-day marketing decisions. Some of the critical decisions in each area are described in Table 8.6.

TABLE 8.6 Critical Decisions for Marketing Mix

Marketing Mix Variable	Critical Decisions
Product	Quality of components or materials, style, features, options, brand name, packaging, sizes, service availability, and warranties
Price	Quality image, list price, quantity, discounts, allowances for quick payment, credit terms, and payment period
Channels of distribution	Use of wholesalers and/or retailers, type of wholesalers or retailers, how many, length of channel, geographic coverage, inventory, and transportation
Promotion	Media alternatives, message, media budget, role of personal selling, sales promotion (displays, coupons, etc.), and media interest in publicity

STEPS IN PREPARING THE MARKETING PLAN

Figure 8.2 illustrates the various stages involved in preparing the marketing plan. Each of these stages, when completed, will provide the necessary information to formally prepare the marketing plan. Each of the steps is outlined and discussed, using examples to assist the reader in fully understanding the necessary information and procedure for preparing the marketing plan.[7]

Defining the Business Situation

situation analysis Describes past and present business achievements of new venture

The *situation analysis* is a review of where we have been. It responds to the first of the three questions mentioned earlier in this chapter. It also considers many of the factors that were defined in both the Environmental Analysis section of the business plan (see Chapter 7) and the Industry Analysis section discussed earlier in this chapter.

To fully respond to this question, the entrepreneur should provide a review of past performance of the product and the company. If this is a new venture, the background will be more personal, describing how the product or service was developed and why it was developed (e.g., to satisfy consumer needs). If the plan is being written after the new venture has started up, it would contain information on present market conditions and performance of the company's goods and services. Any future opportunities or prospects should also be included in this section of the plan.

The industry and competitive environment has already been discussed in an earlier section of the business plan. Thus, at this point the entrepreneur should simply review some of the key elements of this section to help provide a context for the marketing segmentation and actions that will be stated in this section of the business plan.

Defining the Target Market/Opportunities and Threats

target market Specific group of potential customers toward which venture aims its marketing plan

Either from the industry analysis or from the marketing research done earlier, the entrepreneur should have a good idea of who the customer or *target market* will be. Knowledge of the target market provides a basis for determining the appropriate marketing action strategy that will effectively meet its needs. The defined target market will usually represent one or more segments of the entire market. Thus, it is important even before beginning the research to understand what market segmentation is before determining the appropriate target market.

FIGURE 8.2 Sample Flowchart of a Marketing Plan

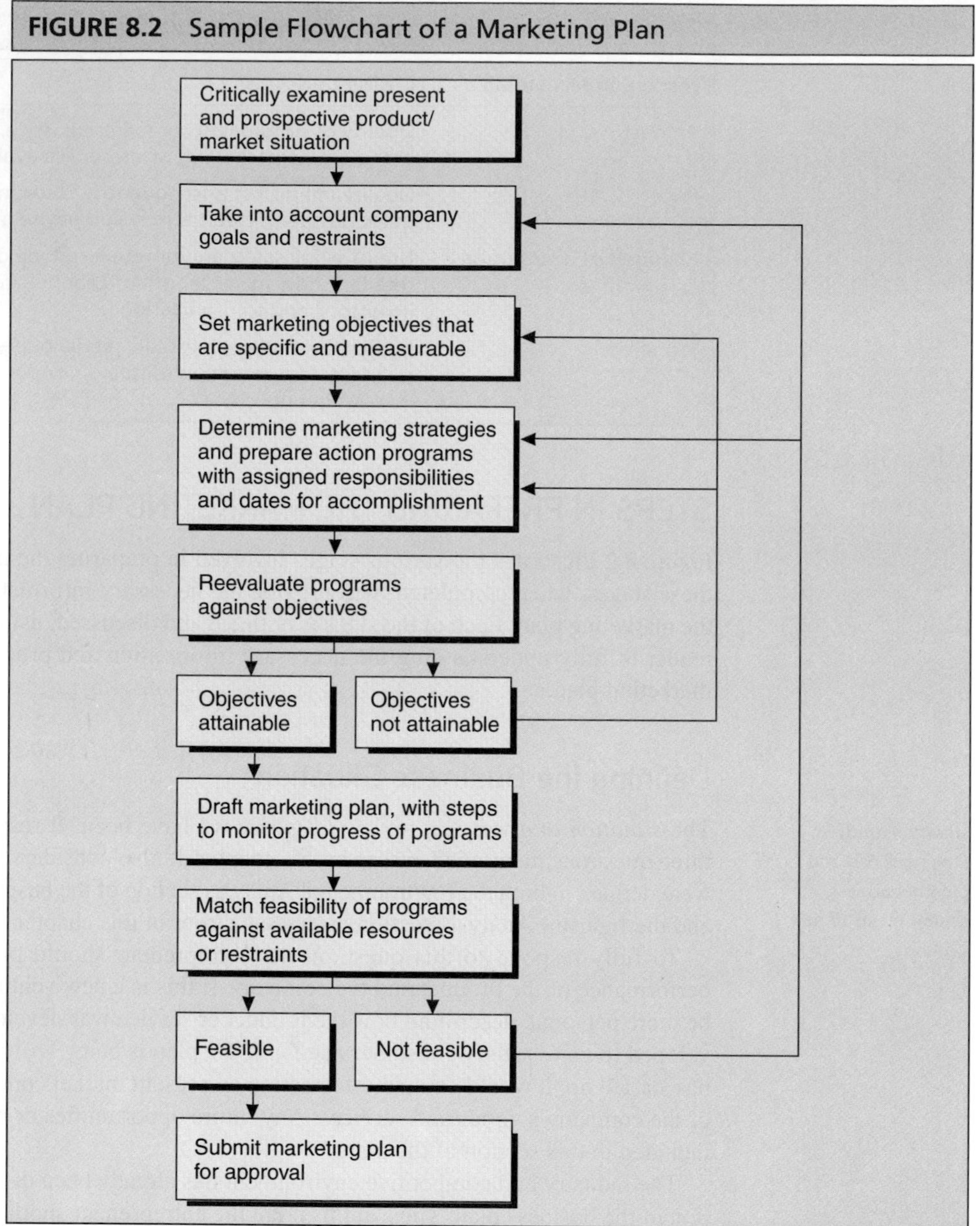

Source: Adapted from David S. Hopkins, *The Marketing Plan* (New York: The Conference Board, 1981), p. 17.

market segmentation Process of dividing a market into definable and measurable groups for purposes of targeting marketing strategy

Market segmentation is the process of dividing the market into small homogeneous groups. Market segmentation allows the entrepreneur to more effectively respond to the needs of more homogeneous consumers. Otherwise the entrepreneur would have to identify a product or service that would meet the needs of everyone in the marketplace.

Henry Ford's vision was to manufacture a single product (one color, one style, one size, etc.) for the mass market. His Model T was produced in large numbers on assembly lines, enabling the firm to reduce costs through specialization of labor and materials. Although his strategy was unique, any successful mass-market strategy employed today would be unlikely.

In 1986, Paul Firestone of Reebok discovered that many consumers who bought running shoes were not athletes. They bought the shoes for comfort and style. Firestone then developed a marketing plan that was targeted directly to this segment.

The process of segmenting and targeting customers by the entrepreneur should proceed as follows:[8]

I. Decide what general market or industry you wish to pursue.
II. Divide the market into smaller groups based on characteristics of the customer or buying situations.
   A. Characteristics of the customer
      1. Geographic (e.g., state, country, city, region)
      2. Demographic (e.g., age, sex, occupation, education, income, and race)
      3. Psychographic (e.g., personality and lifestyle)
   B. Buying situation
      1. Desired benefits (e.g., product features)
      2. Usage (e.g., rate of use)
      3. Buying conditions (e.g., time available and product purpose)
      4. Awareness of buying intention (e.g., familiarity of product and willingness to buy)
III. Select segment or segments to target.
IV. Develop a marketing plan integrating product, price, distribution, and promotion.

Let's assume that an entrepreneur is considering offering an after-school student shuttle service in a local community in the suburbs of Boston. The service will be marketed to households that have high income, both spouses working (most likely professionals), and young children typically between 10 and 15 years old. The shuttle service is designed to taxi children (10–15 years old) using a minivan or similar vehicle to medical or other related appointments and after-school activities. These activities would be non-school-related activities since schools would most likely offer bus service for their students.

The first decision to be made, since we know the target market, is to identify candidate communities that would match the user profile. Town census research and any other available secondary sources are a logical starting place and will reveal demographic data on income, ages of children, and employment. Once this step is complete and a few towns have been identified, the entrepreneur can then conduct marketing research in the identified towns that seem to match the target market profile. This would help the entrepreneur understand the needs and buying intentions of any potential target market. The analysis from this research would then assist the entrepreneur in selecting the community in which to launch the service.

The buying situation is dependent on the venture's establishing credibility in the community. Even if specific households can be targeted, the marketing strategy (particularly sales strategy) will need to concentrate on first establishing credibility and community trust. This can be accomplished in a number of ways but will likely begin with an effort to gain the support of the key townspeople, such as school administrators, PTA members, or other local agencies. In addition, marketing actions will need to focus on getting the target market's attention and creating an awareness of the benefits that this service can provide. For example, the venture might choose to sponsor school events and activities, appoint local respected community members to its board, place advertisements in local newspapers, or send company information through direct mail.

The major issues initially involve careful targeting, using the approach mentioned above, as well as understanding the needs of this target market. With a clear understanding of who the customer is and a combined sales effort and marketing program, the entrepreneur can be more assured of sales growth and increased revenue. A continued presence in the community may also allow the entrepreneur to expand this shuttle service to include other segments of the market, such as senior citizens. Once credibility has been established in one community, it will be easier to expand to other communities.

Considering Strengths and Weaknesses

It is important for the entrepreneur to consider strengths and weaknesses in the target market. For example, to refer back to the student shuttle service venture, its primary strengths in its market are: there is no existing competition, the company has the support of local schools, and its usage base in the selected community is an excellent match for the projected target market. In addition, the experience gained from initiating this service in one community will be a major factor in soliciting new business in other communities.

Weaknesses could relate to the venture's inability to gain complete credibility in the town—given such widespread concern regarding the abduction and molestation of children. Credibility could be easily—and negatively—affected by any bad publicity. Also the success of the venture will depend heavily on the reliability of its drivers, who may not be sensitive to consumer needs. Thus, it will be important to carefully select and train all drivers.

Establishing Goals and Objectives

marketing goals and objectives Statements of level of performance desired by new venture

Before any marketing strategy decisions can be outlined, the entrepreneur must establish realistic and specific goals and objectives. These *marketing goals and objectives* respond to the question: "Where do we want to go?" and should specify things such as market share, profits, sales (by territory and region), market penetration, number of distributors, awareness level, new product launching, pricing policy, sales promotion, and advertising support.

For example, the entrepreneur of a new frozen diet product may determine the following objectives for the first year: 10 percent market penetration, 60 percent of market sampled, distribution in 75 percent of the market. All these goals must be considered reasonable and feasible given the business situation described earlier.

All the above goals are quantifiable and can be measured for control purposes. However, not all goals and objectives must be quantified. It is possible for a firm to establish such goals or objectives as: research customer attitudes toward a product, set up a sales training program, improve packaging, change name of product, or find new distributor. It is a good idea to limit the number of goals or objectives to between six and eight. Too many goals make control and monitoring difficult. Obviously, these goals should represent key areas to ensure marketing success.

Defining Marketing Strategy and Action Programs

marketing strategy and action plan Specific activities outlined to meet the venture's business plan goals and objectives

Once the marketing goals and objectives have been established, the entrepreneur can begin to develop the *marketing strategy and action plan* to achieve them. These strategy and action decisions respond to the question: "How do we get there?" As indicated earlier, these decisions reflect on the marketing mix variables. Some possible decisions that might be made for each variable are discussed below.

Product or Service This element of the marketing mix indicates a description of the product or service to be marketed in the new venture. This product or service definition may consider more than the physical characteristics. For example, Dell Computer's product is computers, which is not distinctive from many other existing competitors. What makes the products distinctive is the fact that they are assembled from off-the-shelf components and are marketed with direct-marketing and Internet techniques promising quick delivery and low prices. Dell also provides extensive customer service with e-mail and telephone available to the customer to ask technical or nontechnical questions. Thus, the product is more than its physical components. It involves packaging, the brand name, price, warranty, image, service, delivery time, features, style, and even the Web site that will be seen by most customers. When considering market strategy, the entrepreneur will need to consider all or some of these issues, keeping in mind the goal of satisfying customer needs.

Pricing Prior to setting the price, the entrepreneur, in the majority of situations, will need to consider three important elements: costs, margins or markups, and competition. There are some exceptions and these are discussed at the end of this section on pricing. Also explained below is the interaction of these elements in the pricing process. Appropriate examples involving the use of each element are also discussed in the next few paragraphs.

Costs. One of the important initial considerations in any pricing decision is to ascertain the costs directly related to the product or service. For a manufacturer this would involve determining the material and labor costs inherent in the production of the product. For a nonmanufacturer, such as a clothing retailer, this would involve determining the cost of the goods from the suppliers. For a service venture such as our student shuttle service there are no manufacturing costs or costs of goods such as those that exist for a clothing retailer. Instead, the service venture's costs relate entirely to labor and overhead expenses.

Whether a manufacturer, retailer, or service venture, the entrepreneur would need to ascertain the approximate costs for overhead (some examples would be utilities, rent, promotion, insurance, and salaries). Let's assume a manufacturer of a special oxygen-based rug cleaner incurs a materials and labor cost of $2.20 per unit (24 ounces). Estimated sales are 500,000 units, with overhead at this level of sales at $1 million or $2.00 per unit. Total costs would add to $4.20 and a unit profit of 30 percent of cost or $1.26 would mean a final price of $5.46.

For a retail example of pricing let's consider a clothing store that sells T-shirts. Let's assume the company buys the T-shirts for $5.00 (cost of goods) from a supplier. Overhead costs are estimated to be $10,000 and the entrepreneur expects to sell 5,000 units for a unit overhead cost of $2.00 per shirt. An additional $2.00 is added for profit, resulting in a final price of $9.00.

For our shuttle service example, the entrepreneur estimates that the cost per mile is approximately $6.00. This includes the depreciation of the vehicle, insurance, driver salary, utilities, advertising, and all other operating costs. Each vehicle is expected to travel about 60 miles per day and service about 30 students. Thus total cost per day would be $360, or $12 per student. Adding a profit of $3.00 would set the final price for this service at $15.00 per student or ride.

In each of these examples the entrepreneur may find it necessary to consider the role of competition and markups (discussed below) as well as an overall positioning strategy before finalizing price.

Markups or margins. In many industries, such as jewelry, beauty supplies, furniture, and clothing, the retailers of the products use a standard markup to price goods in their stores. For example, a standard markup for beauty supplies is 100 percent on cost. Thus, if the retailer buys nail polish for $1.50 per unit, the markup would be $1.50 and

DEVIL'S ADVOCATE

Do your sales reps know how far is too far when it comes to landing that sale? Ethics in sales may not be the quickest route to success—cutting corners is almost always a more expeditious, if short-lived, route to riches. But, in addition to the morality of adhering to ethical business practices, entrepreneurs know that selling with a conscience makes good balance-sheet sense over time. Here are a few reasons to encourage your sales force to behave honorably in a frequently shameful world:

- Reputation rules. Every business owner understands that an impaired reputation is death to trade. Selling ethically translates into treating customers, suppliers, and employees with integrity.
- Reps are your brand's emissaries. If a salesperson crosses the ethical line—whether by lowballing a price or by making unrealizable promises—the client will not trust your product or service in the future.
- Cynicism is nipped in the bud. Having been burned by companies ranging from telecommunications to financial services, consumers are warier than ever. Working with clients in an aboveboard way helps you surpass less trustworthy competitors and make your company a safe place to do business.
- Repeat customers are a bargain. Smart entrepreneurs know that honorable and ethical business practices not only boost your reputation, but also act as affordable advertising vehicles.
- A culture that rewards doing the right thing is good for business. Dell Computer, for instance, encourages its employees to report integrity issues. It thus sets high standards for employee conduct and gives employees a forum for reporting unethical behavior.
- In establishing your ethics parameters, be clear about which behaviors are acceptable and which cross the line, and then hold your employees accountable. There will be times when an employee will need to be disciplined or even fired.
- You must practice what you preach. Keep tabs on employees by investigating credible ethics violations claims from co-workers and customers. The problem may be easily corrected by a sit-down with the employee and by taking time to reiterate company ethics policies.

By requiring your reps to sell with class, you'll prove to your staff you do more than just lip-sync empty dogmas about values.

Source: Adapted from Kimberly L. McCall, "Devil's Advocate," *Entrepreneur* (May 3, 2003), p. 75.

the final price to the consumer would be $3.00. Given that the retailer maintains costs equivalent to the industry standards, this markup would be expected to cover overhead costs and some profit. Standard markups can be ascertained from trade publications or by asking suppliers. A retailer may look at the $3.00 price and decide that, since competition offers the same product for $2.99, he or she would like to offer the item at $2.89. The lower markup and hence lower profit accepted by the entrepreneur in this case is a strategy used to increase demand in the short term (market penetration strategy) but could influence the competition to also lower its price, thus eventually reducing the profit margins for everyone.

Competition. Often, when products cannot be easily differentiated (see T-shirt example on page 249), the entrepreneur is forced to charge the same price as the competition. For the oxygen-based rug cleaner, the entrepreneur may find it possible to justify a higher price (say $6.50) than the competition's price of $5.75 because the product has unique benefits (oxygen and other ingredients). The clothing retailer may be able to charge more than $9.00 for the T-shirt if it is unique enough. If competitors' T-shirts are $9.00 but the quality of our clothing retailer's shirts is graphically superior, then a higher than $9.00 price may be charged. Otherwise, if consumers are unable to discern any difference, the price will need to be equivalent to that of the competition. In our student shuttle example, it is more difficult to compare prices with competitors since the competition is more indirect. Here we might compare taxi cab prices or bus prices. However, this service is more likely to be considered a convenience by the target market, and as such, price may not be a concern. The target market is also in the upper income category, and therefore convenience may be more important than the cost of the service.

A higher price may also be supported by market research data. Innovations such as technology products (LCD and plasma televisions) or new drug products may warrant a higher price or skimming strategy in order for the new venture to recover some of its high development costs. In a nondifferentiated product market (such as clothing or a portable radio), marketing research may reveal that consumers are willing to pay more if you offer service benefits such as free home delivery, guarantees on the life of the item, or free long-term repair. Although these services would increase the costs to the entrepreneur, they would establish a distinctive image for the product in a nondifferentiated product category, allowing a higher price and, potentially, a higher quality image than that of the competition.

Generally in a nondifferentiated product market there is little room for price variations from the competition. Any attempt to increase profits in this situation would have to come from reduced costs. For those situations where the product or service is unique in the marketplace, the entrepreneur has more flexibility and should have a clear understanding of the inherent costs. The important thing to remember is that there is a total cost and profit margin to get to the final price. Changing one of these items will impact the other two factors in some manner.

Distribution This factor provides utility to the consumer; that is, it makes a product convenient to purchase when it is needed. This variable must also be consistent with other marketing mix variables. Thus, a high-quality product will not only carry a high price but should also be distributed in outlets that have a quality image.

Channel of distribution strategy considerations are summarized in Table 8.7. If the market for a new venture is highly concentrated, such as a major metropolitan area, the entrepreneur may consider direct sales to the customer or to a retailer rather than using a wholesaler. If the market is dispersed across a wide geographic area, the cost of direct sales may be prohibitive and the use of a longer channel with wholesalers and retailers may be necessary.

Attributes of the product also affect the channel decision. If the product is very expensive, perishable, or bulky, a more direct channel would make sense because the costs of handling and shipping would drive the costs up to a prohibitive level.

Middlemen such as wholesalers and retailers can add important value to the product. Their costs for providing these benefits are much lower than the costs for a small, single-product start-up because they operate with economies of scale by representing many other businesses. They can provide functions such as storage, delivery, a sales staff, promotion or advertising, and maintenance that would not be feasible for a start-up venture. Middlemen also have important experience in the marketplace that can support and assist the entrepreneur in his or her marketing strategy.

Environmental issues may also be important in channel strategy. Special considerations and regulations regarding such products as chemicals or food and drug products, to name a few, are too costly for a small start-up to absorb. Competitor strategy is also important to consider since alternative choices may help to differentiate the product. For example, Dell Computer chose to use direct mail and the Internet to distribute its products, creating a major differentiation from its direct competitors.

A new venture may also consider brokers' or manufacturers' representatives to reach retailers or end users. Manufacturers' representatives do not take title or physical possession

TABLE 8.7 Major Considerations in Channel Selection

Degree of Directness of Channel

- Market conditions—Concerned whether end users are concentrated (direct) or dispersed (indirect) in market.
- Product attributes—Concerned with whether product is large (direct) or small (indirect), bulky (direct), perishable (direct), hazardous (direct), expensive (direct).
- Cost benefits—Considers the cost benefits in selection of channel members; many benefits (indirect) minimal or no benefit (direct).
- Venture attributes—Considers financial strength, size, channel experience, and marketing strategy of venture.

Number of Channel Members

- Intensive—Selection of as many retailers and/or wholesalers as possible.
- Selective—Choose only small number of channel members based on some set of criteria or requirements.
- Exclusive—Select only one wholesaler and/or retailer.

Criteria in Selection of Channel Members

- Reputation
- Services provided

Number of Channels

- One channel for one target market or multiple target markets.
- Multiple channels for one target market or multiple target markets.

of any products. Their role is to act on behalf of a number of noncompeting companies that will share the cost of their services. In our oxygen-based rug cleaner example, the entrepreneur may consider contracting with manufacturers' representatives that sell commercial products (such as cleaning supplies, furniture, or carpeting) that would add the rug cleaner as a complement to their other products. They would be paid a commission only when a product was sold (usually 6 to 8 percent depending on the product). Manufacturers' representatives could also be used to market to the consumer or household market. In this case the entrepreneur may look for those representatives that are presently marketing household cleaners or other similar products to retail outlets. Orders then would be sent directly to the new venture and would be shipped from there to the end user. This saves on the costs of a sales staff, storage, and multiple shipping points. Brokers are similar to manufacturers' representatives and are common in food or dry goods businesses.

In selecting the channel the entrepreneur should look at all of the above factors. In some instances it may be necessary to use more than one channel in order to service customers more efficiently as well as increase sales potential. Clothing retailers such as Sports Authority, L. L. Bean, Macy's, Wal-Mart, and Target, to name a few, all sell their products using multiple channels such as retail stores, Web sites, catalogs, and newspapers. Each of these may require a different communications channel to enable the customer to buy the desired products. Channel decisions will also change over time. As the venture grows the entrepreneur may find that hiring its own sales force is more efficient and is no longer cost prohibitive.

Promotion It is usually necessary for the entrepreneur to inform potential consumers about the product's availability or to educate the consumer, using advertising media such as print, radio, or television. Usually television is too expensive unless the entrepreneur considers cable television a viable outlet. A local service or retail company such as a pet store may find that using community cable stations is the most cost-effective method to reach customers. Larger markets can be reached using the Internet, direct mail, trade magazines, or newspapers. The entrepreneur should carefully evaluate each alternative medium, considering not just costs but the effectiveness of the medium in meeting the market objectives mentioned earlier in the marketing plan. As stated earlier, a Web site may also be valuable to create awareness and to promote the products and services of the new venture.

Sometimes the entrepreneur has to be creative with the existing budget and costs of buying major media space or time. Recently, Becky Lerdal and May Swenson did just that by getting *Teen Magazine* to agree to attach their word magnets to the magazine cover. This idea came about when the entrepreneurs decided to send out press releases about their venture along with product samples to teen magazines. *Teen Magazine* liked the idea and agreed to a partnership for only the cost of the magnets. The move proved to be very successful as visitors to the venture's Web site increased tenfold and sales passed the $2 million mark.

Press releases about the venture or its products or services are often of interest to media. Local newspapers, television, radio, or trade magazines are always looking for interesting stories about new ventures or entrepreneurs. It is good strategy to send out professionally written news releases on a regular basis to these media to take advantage of any coverage that could result in free advertising.[9]

Marketing Strategy: Consumer versus Business-to-Business Markets

Marketing strategy decisions for a consumer product may be very different from the decisions for a business-to-business product. In business-to-business markets the entrepreneur sells the product or service to another business that uses the product or service as part of its operations. Dell Computer markets its products to both consumers and businesses. In marketing to consumers the company uses direct mail and the Internet, and to businesses it uses its own sales force. This sales force calls on businesses with the intent of selling a large volume of PCs or accessories in one transaction. The consumer marketing effort, however, does support the business marketing effort since the advertising and promotions will be seen or read by both markets. Consumer markets involve sales to households for personal consumption. Food, beverages, household products, furniture, and computers would be a few examples.

Usually business-to-business marketing strategy involves a more direct channel of distribution because of the volume of each transaction and the need to relate product knowledge to the business buyers. Advertising and promotion for the business-to-business market involve more trade magazine advertising, direct sales, and trade shows. For a start-up venture the attendance at a trade show can be one of the most effective means to reach many potential buyers in one location. At trade shows it is important to distribute material on the venture's products and service and to keep a log of all interested visitors to the trade show booth. Have visitors sign in or leave their business cards. From the log or business cards a list can then be prepared and used as a prospect list for sales reps. It is also important that, right after the trade show, a follow-up letter be sent to all visitors thanking them for their interest and explaining how they might be contacted.

Overall the marketing mix for the consumer or business markets is the same. However, the techniques and strategies within the mix of these factors will often vary significantly.

All of these marketing mix variables will be described in detail in the marketing strategy or action plan section of the marketing plan. As indicated earlier, it is important that the marketing strategy and action programs be specific and detailed enough to guide the entrepreneur through the next year.

AS SEEN IN *ENTREPRENEUR* MAGAZINE

ANALYSIS AND ADVICE ON SIMPLE IMAGES

BEFORE

Founded in 1990 by Richard Squire, Breckenridge Brewery began with the goal of making great beer in a Colorado town better known for skiing than anything else. Originally producing just 3,000 barrels per year, it now operates seven pubs and restaurants and produces almost 30,000 barrels. Though the brewery was nabbing top honors at microbrewery competitions in the late 1990s, competitors were entering not only its core markets, but also its hometown of Denver—"the Napa Valley of microbreweries," according to marketing director Steve Kurowski.

DURING

Teaming up with design firm Barnhart/CMI, the brewery poured out its computer-generated logo and created one as handcrafted as its beer, eliminating complicated elements that were difficult to translate into packaging and merchandising, such as the drop-shadow effect on the mountain. A more colloquial voice was adopted for ads, with taglines such as "Brewed the way it is because we drink most of it." The new visuals debuted on materials for the brewery's SummerBright Ale.

AFTER

Today, Breckenridge is ready to uncap the new packaging of its flagship brand, Avalanche Amber Ale, and its new Hefeweizen. SummerBright sales overflowed expectations by 25 percent. And for the first time, consumers can buy promotional items such as pint glasses and T-shirts. Sometimes, the best way to show great taste is with simplicity rather than flash.

ADVICE TO AN ENTREPRENEUR

1. A cheaper way of advertising that is more effective at attracting customers—is this too good to be true? Why has the "simpler is better" approach worked for Breckenridge Brewery?
2. Assume that the CEO asked you about pricing its pint glasses and T-shirts: "Should I price the pint glasses and T-shirts to maximize profit from these items, or should I have a lower price to increase volume and benefit from the promotional impact that the purchase of these items has on the sales of my beer?"
3. Would you advise this approach to an entrepreneur whose primary products are highly technological? What about an entrepreneur whose products are sold to industrial buyers?

Source: Reprinted with permission of Entrepreneur Media, Inc., "Attention, Please. Yell Out 'Look at Me!' for Free by Using Other Websites to Your Advantage," by Catherine Seda, March 2003, *Entrepreneur* magazine: www.entrepreneur.com.

Budgeting the Marketing Strategy

Effective planning decisions must also consider the costs involved in the implementation of these decisions. If the entrepreneur has followed the procedure of detailing the strategy and action programs to meet the desired goals and objectives, costs should be reasonably clear. If assumptions are necessary, they should be clearly stated so that anyone else who reviews the written marketing plan (e.g., a venture-capital firm) will understand these implications.

This budgeting of marketing action and strategy decisions will also be useful in preparing the financial plan. Details of how to develop a financial plan are discussed in Chapter 10.

Implementation of the Market Plan

The marketing plan is meant to be a commitment by the entrepreneur to a specific strategy. It is not a formality that serves as a superficial document to outside financial supporters or suppliers. It is meant to be a formal vehicle for answering the three questions posed earlier in this chapter and a commitment to make adjustments as needed or dictated by market conditions. Someone in the venture should be assigned the responsibility of coordinating and implementing the plan.

Monitoring the Progress of Marketing Actions

Generally, monitoring of the plan involves tracking specific results of the marketing effort. Sales data by product, territory, sales rep, and outlet are a few of the specific results that should be monitored. What is monitored is dependent on the specific goals and objectives outlined earlier in the marketing plan. Any "weak" signals from the monitoring process will provide the entrepreneur with the opportunity to redirect or modify the existing marketing effort to allow the firm to achieve its initial goals and objectives.

In addition to monitoring the progress of the existing plan the entrepreneur should also be prepared for contingencies. For example, reliance on a single supplier in a geographic area that is vulnerable to hurricanes could be disastrous if that supplier were to be shut down as a result of a hurricane. Adjustments in marketing actions are usually minor if the plan has been effectively developed and implemented. If the entrepreneur is constantly faced with significant changes in the marketing strategy, then it is likely that the plan was not prepared properly. Weaknesses in market planning are usually the result of poor analysis of the market and competitive strategy, unrealistic goals and objectives, or poor implementation of the outlined plan actions. There are also acts of God—such as weather or war—that can affect a marketing plan. These are usually difficult to predict but may be considered in a contingency plan.

IN REVIEW

SUMMARY

Before beginning the marketing plan section of the business plan, the entrepreneur should provide a comprehensive review and assessment of the industry and market trends at the national and local levels. In addition, a comprehensive assessment of competitor strategies and their strengths and weaknesses should be documented. From this analysis the entrepreneur can begin to formulate the marketing plan section of the business plan. The marketing plan designates the response to three questions: Where have we been? Where are we going? and How do we get there?

To be able to respond effectively to these questions, it is generally necessary for the entrepreneur to conduct some marketing research. This research may involve secondary sources or a primary data collection process. Information from the research will be very important in determining the marketing mix factors or the marketing strategy to be implemented in the marketing plan.

The marketing plan entails a number of major steps. First, it is important to conduct a situation analysis to assess the question "Where have we been?" Market segments must be defined and opportunities identified. This will help the entrepreneur determine a profile of the customer. Goals and objectives must be established. These goals and objectives must be realistic and detailed (quantified if possible). Next, the marketing strategy and action programs must be defined. Again, these should be detailed so that the entrepreneur clearly understands how the venture is going to get where it wants to go.

The marketing strategy section or action plan describes how to achieve the goals and objectives already defined. There may be alternative marketing approaches that could be used to achieve these defined goals. The use of creative strategies such as Internet marketing may give the entrepreneur a more effective entry into the market.

The action programs should also be assigned to someone to ensure their implementation. If the plan has been detailed, the entrepreneur should be able to assign some costs and budgets for implementing the marketing plan. During the year, the marketing plan will be monitored in order to discern the success of the action programs. Any "weak" signals will provide the entrepreneur with the opportunity to modify the plan and/or develop a contingency plan.

Careful scrutiny of the marketing plan can enhance its success. However, many plans fail, not because of poor management or a poor product but because the plan was not specific or had an inadequate situation analysis, unrealistic goals, or did not anticipate competitive moves, product deficiencies, and acts of God.

RESEARCH TASKS

1. Participate in an online focus group. Then conduct research on the advantages and disadvantages of conducting a focus group online versus a "face-to-face" focus group.
2. Choose an industry and then use the library or the Internet to find data from secondary sources that will be highly useful in developing a marketing plan.
3. Find five examples of product advertising (e.g., advertisements cut out of a magazine or recorded on videotape). Bring them to class and be prepared to explain how they fit in with the rest of the marketing mix and which group of customers is being targeted.
4. Find a marketing strategy that is being used now that you believe will be ineffective. Be prepared to justify your answer.

CLASS DISCUSSION

1. What are the three most effective advertisements on television? Why are they effective? What are the three least effective advertisements on television? Why are they ineffective? Are they really ineffective if you have been able to recall them?
2. Define a customer group and then invent a product and come up with a price, promotion, and distribution strategy. Have some fun in coming up with a particularly creative marketing mix.
3. Segment the class into groups, label those groups, and determine a specific demand that is unique to each group. You may be asked to reveal your market (class) segmentation to the rest of the class and people will have a chance to respond to your classification.
4. Is market segmentation just a nice way of using "stereotypes" to sell your products? Can people really be classified so easily into groups that share common needs, wants, and demands?

SELECTED READINGS

Cooper, Marjorie J.; Nancy Upton; and Samuel Seaman. (July 2005). Customer Relationship Management: A Comparative Analysis of Family and Nonfamily Business Practices. *Journal of Small Business Management*, vol. 43, no. 3, pp. 242–56.

The importance of customer relationship management implementation amongst family and nonfamily businesses is analyzed. Results indicate that both types of organizations show similar attitudes toward the implementation of customer relationship management. However, the study found that actual implementation strategies differ significantly between these two types of firms.

Dias, Sam; David Pihlens; and Lorena Ricci. (2002). Understanding the Drivers of Customer Value: The Fusion of Macro and Micromodeling. *Journal of Targeting, Measurement and Analysis for Marketing,* vol. 10, no. 3, pp. 269–81.

This paper proposes that consideration of both macro and micro levels of analysis reveals deep insights into the impact of marketing activity on customer profitability. It contends that brand drivers, such as pricing and advertising, have a different impact on customer segments, and that understanding these differences will enable marketers to optimize their marketing strategy in a way that maximizes valuable customer behavior.

Dibb, Sally. (2002). Marketing Planning Best Practice. *The Marketing Review 2002,* vol. 2, pp. 441–59.

This paper explains the role that marketing planning plays and shows how it is used by organizations. Each stage of the marketing planning process is described in detail and the role and format of the Marketing Plan document are explored. The marketing planning process is then illustrated using a detailed case example from the construction equipment industry, and guidance on best marketing planning practice is offered.

Fam, Kim-Shyan; and Zhilin Yang. (February 2006). Primary Influences of Environmental Uncertainty on Promotions Budget Allocation and Performance: A Cross Country Study of Retail Advertisers. *Journal of Business Research,* vol. 59, no. 2, pp. 259–67.

Planning is not something that is a regular activity of many small retailers. This study examines whether small retailers undertake planning when faced with an uncertain environment. In particular the study focuses on whether small retailers switch from in-store promotion to outdoor advertising during this uncertain period.

Kara, Ali; John E. Spillane; and Oscar W. DeShields, Jr. (April 2005). The Effect of a Marketing Orientation on Business Performance: A Study of Small-Sized Service Retailers Using MARKOR Scale. *Journal of Small Business Management,* vol. 43, no. 2, pp. 105–18.

Using the MARKOR scale to measure market orientation, the authors evaluate the relationship of market orientation to the performance of small retail firms. The results indicate a significant link between market orientation and performance.

Lehman, Donald R.; and Russell S. Winer. (2005). *Analysis for Marketing Planning,* 6th ed. (Burr Ridge, IL: McGraw-Hill/Irwin).

This paperback book focuses on the process of developing a marketing plan. In particular it discusses the analysis of information pertaining to a product or service's environment, customers, and competitors. The first chapter is particularly relevant to an entrepreneur as it provides a good overview of an operating marketing plan.

Nour, Mohamed A.; and Adam Fadlalla. (Spring 2000). A Framework for Web Marketing Strategies. *Information Systems Management,* pp. 41–50.

Although the Web has the potential to level the playing field for all competitors, those companies that effectively market themselves on the Web have a distinct advantage. This article presents strategies for gaining that advantage.

Pilmar, John. (July 2005). Small Business? Small Budget? How to Measure for Success. *Public Relations Tactics,* vol. 12, no. 7, p. 23.

This article suggests that public relations is one of the most effective means that small businesses can use to gain a strong foothold in their industry and also become more competitive with much larger firms. It describes the public relations process of research, planning, implementation, and measurement.

Robins, Fred. (2000). The Marketing E-Mix. *The Marketing Review,* vol. 1, pp. 249–74.

This paper examines some of the changes that are occurring in marketing practice as a result of the rapid development of electronic commerce. An examination of contemporary online business reveals the emergence of a subtle new e-marketing mix. The paper concludes with some observations about how managers might best respond.

Saban, Kenneth; and Stephen E. Rau. (June 2005). The Functionality of Websites as Export Marketing Channels for Small and Medium Enterprises. *Electronic Markets,* vol. 15, no. 2, pp. 128–35.

The e-commerce literature suggests that the Internet levels the playing field for small ventures trying to market their goods and services worldwide. As a marketing channel, the study found that small businesses may use the Internet as an export marketing channel but because of limited resources they are constrained by the sophistication of these transactions.

Song, Jaeki; and Mariam Fatemeh. (2006). Internet Market Strategies: Antecedents and Implications. *Information & Management,* vol. 43, no. 2, pp. 222–38.

In this paper the authors differentiate between the Internet and traditional market channels and define two fundamental strategies for operating on the Internet. They develop a conceptual model for selection of the appropriate channel.

Taylor, Steven A.; Stephen Goodwin; and Kevin Celuch. (2005). An Exploratory Investigation into the Question of Direct Selling via the Internet in Industrial Equipment Markets. *Journal of Business to Business Marketing,* vol. 12, no. 2, pp. 37–70.

This study seeks to provide exploratory insight into considerations of Internet-based direct marketing strategies aimed at industrial consumers. The research provides managerial and research implications regarding the use of the Internet in industrial markets.

Williams, David. (2001). Writing a Marketing Report. *The Marketing Review,* vol. 1, pp. 363–72.

This article looks at the process of constructing a basic marketing report, an area where there has hitherto been very little written guidance. Although often taken for granted, constructing the marketing report can consume a substantial amount of the marketer's time and effort.

END NOTES

1. "Making It," *Black Enterprise* (July 1975), p. 6; Wendy Beech, "Keeping It in the Family," *Black Enterprise* (November 1998), pp. 98–104: *Agency Profile, Circulation Expertí, Ltd.* (2005), pp. 1–16; and www.experti.com. Discussions with Garrison Jackson, president and CEO, also contributed to this profile.
2. Carl McDaniel and Roger Gates, *Marketing Research,* 6th ed. (Hoboken, NJ: John Wiley & Sons, Inc., 2005), pp. 50–60.
3. M. P. Peters and C. Brush, "Market Information Scanning Activities and Growth in New Ventures: A Comparison of Service and Manufacturing Businesses," *Journal of Business Research* (May 1996), pp. 81–89.
4. McDaniel and Gates, *Marketing Research,* pp. 144–73.
5. R. D. Hisrich and M. P. Peters, *Marketing Decisions for New and Mature Products,* 2nd ed. (Upper Saddle River, NJ: Prentice-Hall, Inc., 1991), pp. 63–78.
6. E. Berkowitz, R. Kerin, S. Hartley, and W. Rudelius, *Marketing,* 8th ed. (Burr Ridge, IL:McGraw-Hill/Irwin, 2006), pp. 7–24.
7. D. R. Lehmann and R. S. Winer, *Analysis for Marketing Planning,* 6th ed. (Burr Ridge, IL: McGraw-Hill/Irwin, 2005), pp. 9–10.
8. Berkowitz et al., *Marketing,* pp. 255–73.
9. April Pennington, "Cover Girls," *Entrepreneur* (October 1, 2001), p. 106.

APPENDIX A: MARKETING PLAN OUTLINES

Exhibit 1. Marketing Plan for a Consumer Products Company.

Exhibit 2. Marketing Plan for a Business-to-Business Company.

Exhibit 3. Marketing Plan for a Service Company.

EXHIBIT 1 Marketing Plan for a Consumer Products Company

I. ANALYZE AND DEFINE THE BUSINESS SITUATION—past, present, and future
An analysis of where we are, perhaps how we got there. Data and trend lines should go back three to five years.
Suggested items to cover:
  A. The scope of the market (class of trade)
  B. Sales history by products, by class of trade, by regions
  C. Market potential, major trends anticipated
  D. Distribution channels
    1. Identification of principal channels (dealer or class of trade), sales history through each type
    2. Buying habits and attitudes of these channels
    3. Our selling policies and practices
  E. The customer or end user
    1. Identification of customers making the buying decision, classified by age, income level, occupation, geographical location, etc.
    2. Customer attitudes on product or services, quality, price, etc. Purchase or use habits that contribute to attitudes
    3. Advertising history: expenditures, media and copy strategy, measurements of effectiveness
    4. Publicity and other educational influences
  F. The product or services:
    1. Story of the product line, quality development, delivery and service
    2. Comparison with other approaches to serve the customers' needs
    3. Product research; product improvements planned

II. IDENTIFY PROBLEMS AND OPPORTUNITIES
  A. In view of the facts cited in (I) above, what are the major problems that are restricting or impeding our growth?
  B. What opportunities do we have for
    —Overcoming the above problems?
    —Modifying or improving the product line or adding new products?
    —Serving the needs of more customers in our market or developing new markets?
    —Improving the efficiency of our operation?

III. DEFINE SPECIFIC AND REALISTIC BUSINESS OBJECTIVES
  A. Assumptions regarding future conditions
    —Level of economic activity
    —Level of industry activity
    —Changes in customer needs
    —Changes in distribution channels
    —Changes beyond our control, increased costs, etc.
  B. Primary marketing objectives (the establishment of aim points and goals). Consider where you are going and how you will get there. Objectives are the necessary base of any plan since a plan must have precise direction.
  C. Overall strategy for achievement of primary objectives. The division's overall strategy to accomplish its primary objective—sample: shifting of sales emphasis, products, or classes of trade; changes for improvement of sales coverage, etc.
  D. Functional (departmental) objectives. (In this section "explode" your primary objectives into subobjectives, or goals, for each department. Show the interrelation vertically, by marketing project. Show time schedule on objectives below.)
    1. Advertising and promotion objectives
    2. Customer service objectives
    3. Product modification objectives
    4. New product objectives
    5. Expense control objectives
    6. Workforce objectives
    7. Personnel training objectives
    8. Market research objectives

IV. DEFINE MARKETING STRATEGY AND ACTION PROGRAMS—to accomplish the objectives
  A. Here, *detail the action steps,* priorities, and schedules relating to each of the functional objectives above. If, for example, one of your estimates was "an increase in sales of product X from 10,000 to 20,000 units," now is the time to pinpoint specific customers. In order to explain who must do what, and when, you can show the interaction of the departments listed above (III-D) and how their objectives serve to meet this increased demand.
  B. If one of your objectives was to introduce a new product by "x" date, now show the details and deadlines, production schedule, market introduction plans, advertising and merchandising support, sales and service training needed, etc. Define responsibility and dates for each step.
  C. Alternatives—In the event of a delay in a project or program, what alternative plans are available?

V. CONTROL AND REVIEW PROCEDURES
How will the execution of the plan be monitored?
  A. What kinds of "feedback" information will be needed?
  B. When and how will reviews be scheduled (departments, regions, etc.)?
  C. Date for full-scale review of progress vs. plan.

Source: David S. Hopkins, *The Marketing Plan*, The Conference Board, 1981. Reprinted with permission of The Conference Board.

EXHIBIT 2 Marketing Plan for a Business-to-Business Company

Marketing Plan Outline

For each major product/product category: Time Period—One, Three, and Five-Plus Years

I. MANAGEMENT SUMMARY
What is our marketing plan for this product in brief?

This is a one-page summary of the basic factors involving the marketing of the product in the plan period, along with the results expected from implementing the plan. It is intended as a brief guide for management.

II. ECONOMIC OUTLOOK
What factors in the overall economy and industry will affect the marketing of the product in the plan period, and how?

This section will contain a summary of the specific economic and industry factors that will affect the marketing of this product during the plan period.

III. THE MARKET—qualitative
Who or what kinds of market segments constitute the major prospects for this product?

This section will define the qualitative nature of our market segments. It will include definitive descriptions and profiles of major distributors, specifiers, users, and/or consumers of the product.

IV. THE MARKET—quantitative
What is the potential market for this product?

This section will apply specific quantitative measures to this product. Here we want to include numbers of potential customers, dollar volume of business, our current share of the market—any specific measures that will outline our total target for the product and where we stand competitively now.

V. TREND ANALYSIS
Based on the history of this product, where do we appear to be headed?

This section is a review of the past history of this product. Ideally, we should include annual figures for the last five years showing dollar volume, accounts opened, accounts closed, share of market, and all other applicable historical data.

VI. COMPETITION
Who are our competitors for this product, and how do we stand competitively?

This section should define our current competition. It should be a thoughtful analysis outlining who our competitors are, how successful they are, and what actions they might be expected to take regarding this product during the coming year.

VII. PROBLEMS AND OPPORTUNITIES
Internally and externally, are there problems inhibiting the marketing of this product, or are there opportunities we have not taken advantage of?

This section will include a frank commentary on both inhibiting problems and unrealized opportunities. It should include a discussion of the internal and external problems we can control, for example, by changes in policies or operational programs. It should also point to areas of opportunity regarding this product that we are not now exploring.

VIII. OBJECTIVES AND GOALS
Where do we want to go with this product?

This section will outline the immediate short- and long-range objectives for this product. Short-range goals should be specific and will apply to next year. Intermediate to long-range goals will necessarily be less specific and should project for the next three to five years and beyond. Objectives should be stated in two forms.

(1) Qualitative—reasoning behind the offering of this product and what modification or other changes we expect to make.

(2) Quantitative—number of accounts, dollar volume, share of market, and profit goals.

IX. `ACTION PROGRAMS
Given past history, the economy, the market, competition, etc., what must we do to reach the goals we have set for this product or service?

This section will be a description of the specific actions we plan to take during the coming plan period to ensure reaching the objectives we have set for the product in VIII. These would include the full range of factors comprising our marketing mix. The discussion should cover what is to be done, schedules for completion, methods of evaluation, and assignment of accountability for executing the program and measuring results.

Source: David S. Hopkins, *The Marketing Plan*, The Conference Board, 1981. Reprinted with permission of The Conference Board.

EXHIBIT 3 Marketing Plan for a Service Company

Marketing Plan Outline

For each major bank service:

I. MANAGEMENT SUMMARY
What is our marketing plan for this service in brief?

This is a one-page summary of the basic factors involving the marketing of the service next year along with the results expected from implementing the plan. It is intended as a brief guide for management.

II. ECONOMIC PROJECTIONS
What factors in the overall economy will affect the marketing of this service next year, and how?

This section will include a summary of the specific economic factors that will affect the marketing of this service during the coming year. These might include employment, personal income, business expectations, inflationary (or deflationary) pressures, etc.

III. THE MARKET—quantitative
Who or what kinds of organizations could conceivably be considered prospects for this service?

This section will define the qualitative nature of our market. It will include demographic information, industrial profiles, business profiles, and so on, for all people or organizations that could be customers for this service.

IV. THE MARKET—quantitative
What is the potential market for this service?

This section will apply specific quantitative measures to this bank service. Here we want to include numbers of potential customers, dollar volume of business, our current share of the market—any specific measures that will outline our total target for the service and where we stand competitively now.

V. TREND ANALYSIS
Based on the history of this service, where do we appear to be headed?

This section is a review of the past history of this service. Ideally, we should include quarterly figures for the last five years showing dollar volume, accounts opened, accounts closed, share of market, and all other applicable historical data.

VI. COMPETITION
Who are our competitors for this service, and how do we stand competitively?

This section should define our current competition, both bank and nonbank. It should be a thoughtful analysis outlining who our competitors are, how successful they are, why they have (or have not) been successful, and what actions they might be expected to take regarding this service during the coming year.

VII. PROBLEMS AND OPPORTUNITIES
Internally and externally, are there problems inhibiting the marketing of this service, or are there opportunities we have not taken advantage of?

This section will contain a frank commentary on both inhibiting problems and unrealized opportunities. It should include a discussion of the internal and external problems we can control, for example, changes in policies or operational procedures. It should also point to areas of opportunity regarding this service that we are not now exploiting.

VIII. OBJECTIVES AND GOALS
Where do we want to go with this service?

This section will outline the immediate short- and long-range objectives for this service. Short-range goals should be specific and will apply to next year. Long-range goals will necessarily be less specific and should project for the next five years. Objectives should be stated in two forms:

(1) Qualitative—reasoning behind the offering of this service and what modifications or other changes we expect to make.

(2) Quantitative—number of accounts, dollar volume, share of market, profit goals.

IX. ACTION PROGRAMS
Given past history, the economy, the market, competition, and so on, what must we do to reach the goals we have set for this service?

This section will be a description of the specific actions we plan to take during the coming year to ensure reaching the objectives we have set for the service in VIII. These would include advertising and promotion, direct mail, and brochure development. It would also include programs to be designed and implemented by line officers. The discussion should cover what is to be done, schedules for completion, methods of evaluation, and officers in charge of executing the program and measuring results.

Source: David S. Hopkins, *The Marketing Plan*, The Conference Board, 1981. Reprinted with permission of The Conference Board.

9

THE ORGANIZATIONAL PLAN

LEARNING OBJECTIVES

1
To understand the importance of the management team in launching a new venture.

2
To understand the advantages and disadvantages of the alternative legal forms for organizing a new venture.

3
To explain and compare the S corporation and limited liability company as alternative forms of incorporation.

4
To learn the importance of both the formal and the informal organization.

5
To illustrate how the board of directors or board of advisors can be used to support the management of a new venture.

OPENING PROFILE

JIM SINEGAL, COSTCO

Building a strong and lasting organization requires careful planning and strategy. No one knows this better than Jim Sinegal, the founder and CEO of Costco Wholesale Corporation, a successful warehouse chain store. Jim's philosophy is that a successful organization depends heavily on its employees and that happy employees are loyal and stable and can help generate successful sales and revenue growth.

www.costco.com

Jim Sinegal has had a long history with the warehouse concept. It began appropriately when he was a student at San Diego State University. In 1954 a classmate and good friend asked him if he would be willing to help unload mattresses for the day at a newly opened discount store called Fed-Mart. Jim didn't realize at that time how significant this would be as an introduction to the more modern warehouse concept. He not only went to work for Fed-Mart but he made it a career, rising eventually to executive vice president. More importantly, as part of this career at Fed-Mart, Jim was able to learn a great deal about this business from Fed-Mart's chairman, Sol Price, who is credited with being the inventor of the concept of high-volume warehouse stores.

After many successful years working at Fed-Mart Jim left the company in 1975 when Sol Price was fired, having sold Fed-Mart to a German retailer. Both he and Sol then teamed up to start a new warehouse company, Price Club. The success of Price Club attracted competition from Wal-Mart, which launched Sam's Club, and Zayre's, which started BJ's Wholesale Club. Noting the potential for these warehouse stores, Jim left Price Club and with the help of a Seattle entrepreneur launched Costco. Sol Price and Jim Sinegal became partners again in 1993 when Costco and Price Club merged to form the largest membership chain in the United States.

In 1995 Sol Price and Jim Sinegal again parted ways, mainly because they could not agree on a strategy for building the business. Sol maintained some of the real estate and concentrated his efforts on licensing PriceSmart warehouse stores in foreign markets. Jim retained control of all of the warehouse stores in the United States and has since built the business to be the fifth largest retailer in the country.

Jim Sinegal would emphatically summarize the successful strategy of Costco in two simple statements. First, build a strong organization with loyal, hard-working employees by paying them above-average salaries, providing excellent benefits, and giving them the feeling that you care about their welfare. Second, maintain the business model of a warehouse store by limiting the product offerings, allowing fledging companies to supply inventory, and maintaining low prices.

Wages start at $10/hour but more than half of the employees earn $18.32/hour. The company covers 94 percent of the health care costs of full- and part-time employees. It also contributes between 3 percent and 9 percent of each employee's pay to a 401(k). With this policy Jim brags about the astoundingly low first-year employee turnover rate of 5.5 percent.

Wall Street, however, has been very critical of Costco's industry-high labor cost of 70 percent of total cost of operations. Analysts argue that Costco treats its employees and cardholders better than its stockholders. Sinegal's response is clear and undaunted. He argues that one of the most important aspects of a successful organization is its people. It's important to hire the best people you can and then keep them long term so they in turn will have some job security. He states, "It's not altruism. In the final analysis, it's good business."

Even with its high labor costs and low revenue-to-sales ratio (in 2004 this figure was 1.7 cents for every sales dollar, compared to 3.3 cents for Wal-Mart), Costco surpassed Sam's Club in sales and its stock was up 34 percent while Wal-Mart was about even for the year. For the year 2005 Costco continued to achieve greater sales than Sam's Club ($48.1 billion compared to $37.1 billion). In 2005 Costco's profits rose over 20 percent to $1.06 billion on sales of $52.9 billion. This growth was consistent with the growth from 2003–2004. Beginning with the single store in 1983, Costco now has more than 450 stores mostly in the U.S. but with some in Canada, the U.K., South Korea, Taiwan, and Japan. Sales per store average $121 million, compared to $70 million for Sam's Club.

It's impossible to argue with the huge success that Jim Sinegal has achieved. His combination of a quality, loyal labor force and his relentless attention to maintaining the warehouse store concept by offering a bare bones cement floor retail space, charging a membership fee for the right to shop, and maintaining a limited product offering at low prices with high inventory turnover has proven to be a successful business model.

Jim Sinegal takes only a modest salary, spends a lot of time traveling to many stores, and works with a lot of fledging supplier enterprises, giving them an opportunity that would not be likely with other giant retailers. Beginning in 2005 he initiated a new six-year plan to increase profit margins by 3 to 4 percent. On the basis of the performance of the company thus far, Costco has already begun to meet these growth objectives. However, Sinegal states that this increase in profitability will not be at the expense of its workers.[1]

DEVELOPING THE MANAGEMENT TEAM

We can see from the Costco example the importance of employees and their loyalty and commitment to the organization. Also significant to potential investors is the management team and its ability and commitment to the new venture.

Investors will usually demand that the management team not attempt to operate the business as a sideline or part-time venture while employed full time elsewhere. It is assumed that the management team is prepared to operate the business full time and at a modest salary. It is unacceptable for the entrepreneurs to try to draw a large salary out of the new venture, and investors may perceive any attempt to do so as a lack of psychological commitment to the business. Later in this chapter the roles of various team members are discussed, particularly as the firm evolves to a legitimate ongoing concern. In addition the entrepreneur should consider the role of the board of directors and/or a board of advisors in supporting the management of the new venture. At this point, however, the entrepreneur needs to consider the alternatives regarding the legal form of the organization. Each of these forms has important implications for taxes, liability, continuity, and financing the new venture.

LEGAL FORMS OF BUSINESS

There are three basic legal forms of business formation and one new form that is gaining acceptance. The three basic legal forms are (1) proprietorship, (2) partnership, and (3) corporation, with variations particularly in partnerships and corporations. The newest form of business formation is the limited liability company (LLC), which is now possible in all 50 states and the District of Columbia. The typical corporation form is known as a *C corporation.* Table 9.1 describes the legal factors involved in each of these forms with the differences in the limited liability partnership (LLP) and S corporation noted where appropriate. These three basic legal forms are compared with regard to ownership, liability, start-up costs, continuity, transferability of interest, capital requirements, management control, distribution of profits, and attractiveness for raising capital. Later in the chapter the S corporation and the LLC are compared and discussed as alternatives forms of business, especially for the new venture.

C corporation Most common form of corporation, regulated by statute and treated as a separate legal entity for liability and tax purposes

It is very important that the entrepreneur carefully evaluate the pros and cons of the various legal forms of organizing the new venture. This decision must be made before the submission of a business plan and request for venture capital.

The evaluation process requires the entrepreneur to determine the priority of each of the factors mentioned in Table 9.1, as well as tax factors discussed later in this chapter. These factors will vary in importance, depending on the type of new business.

In addition to these factors, it is also necessary to consider some intangibles. Various types of organizational structures reflect an image to suppliers, existing clients, and prospective customers. For example, suppliers may prefer to deal with profit-making organizations rather than nonprofit companies. This attitude may be reflected in the perceived impressions that nonprofit firms are slow in paying their bills. Customers may sometimes prefer to do business with a corporation. Because of their continuity and ownership advantages, they are sometimes viewed as a more stable type of business. For a customer, it may be desirable to have assurance that the firm will be in business for a long time.

The variations of organizational structure as well as the advantages and disadvantages are numerous and can be quite confusing to the entrepreneur. In the next section of this chapter, some of these differences are clarified to assist the entrepreneur in making the best decision regarding organizational structure.

proprietorship Form of business with single owner who has unlimited liability, controls all decisions, and receives all profits

partnership Two or more individuals having unlimited liability who have pooled resources to own a business

Ownership

In the *proprietorship,* the owner is the individual who starts the business. He or she has full responsibility for the operations. In a *partnership,* there may be some general partnership owners and some limited partnership owners. There are also limited liability partnerships

TABLE 9.1 Factor's Three Forms of Business Formation

Factors	Proprietorship	Partnership	Corporation
Ownership	Individual.	No limitation on number of partners.	No limitation on number of stockholders.
Liability of owners	Individual liable for business liabilities.	In general partnership, all individuals liable for business liabilities. Limited partners are liable for amount of capital contribution. In limited liability partnership (LLP), there is no liability except when negligence exists.	Amount of capital contribution is limit of shareholder liability.
Costs of starting business	None other than filing fees for trade name.	Partnership agreement, legal costs, and minor filing fees for trade name.	Created only by statute. Articles of incorporation, filing fees, taxes, and fees for states in which corporation registers to do business.
Continuity of business	Death dissolves the business.	Death or withdrawal of one partner terminates partnership unless partnership agreement stipulates otherwise. Death or withdrawal of one of limited partners has no effect on continuity.	Greatest form of continuity. Death or withdrawal of owner(s) will not affect legal existence of business.
Transferability of interest	Complete freedom to sell or transfer any part of business.	General partner can transfer his/her interest only with consent of all other general partners. Limited partner can sell interest without consent of general partners. No transfer of interest in an LLP.	Most flexible. Stockholders can sell or buy stock at will. Some stock transfers may be restricted by agreement. In S corporation, stock may be transferred only to an individual.
Capital requirements	Capital raised only by loan or increased contribution by proprietor.	Loans or new contributions by partners require a change in partnership agreement. In LLP partnership, entity raises money.	New capital raised by sale of stock or bonds or by borrowing (debt) in name of corporation. In S corporation, only one class of stock and limited to 100 shareholders.
Management control	Proprietor makes all decisions and can act immediately.	All general partners have equal control and majority rules. Limited partners have limited control. Can vary in an LLP.	Majority stockholder(s) have most control from legal point of view. Day-to-day control in hands of management who may or may not be major stockholders.
Distribution of profits and losses	Proprietor responsible and receives all profits and losses.	Depends on partnership agreement and investment by partners.	Shareholders can share in profits by receipt of dividends.
Attractiveness for raising capital	Depends on capability of proprietor and success of business.	Depends on capability of partners and success of business.	With limited liability for owners, more attractive as an investment opportunity.

corporation Separate legal entity that is run by stockholders having limited liability

(LLP) in which the partnership is treated as a legal entity. In the *corporation,* ownership is reflected by ownership of shares of stock. Unlike the S corporation, where the maximum number of shareholders is 100, there is no limit as to the number of shareholders who may own stock in a corporation.

AS SEEN IN *ENTREPRENEUR* MAGAZINE

PROVIDE ADVICE TO AN ENTREPRENEUR ABOUT SOME LEGAL ASPECTS OF STARTING A BUSINESS

You just started your business—who has time to think about an exit strategy? If you're putting off making such plans, you've committed a very common legal mistake, says Alan S. Kopit, partner at Hahn Loeser & Parks LLP in Cleveland and advisor to Lawyers.com. "Now is the time to decide those issues—not after a problem develops," he says. Here, Kopit runs down a few more common legal blunders to avoid:

1. *Failing to get good advice*. Don't ever go it alone. Instead, Kopit suggests entrepreneurs enlist the services and counsel of a good lawyer, an accountant, and an insurance agent at the very beginning of their start-up ventures. "Younger [entrepreneurs] particularly need people to bounce their ideas off of," he says.
2. *Neglecting important employment considerations*. Hiring issues are a major legal consideration for start-ups. Consider whether you need a written non-compete contract with employees, whether you'll use independent contractors, and so on.
3. *Selecting the wrong business structure*. Should you classify your business as a sole proprietorship, an LLC, an LLP, or a corporation? "There are tax implications that go along with [each choice]," cautions Kopit. Be sure to weigh each option with the help of your advisors to determine which form will best serve your business plan.

ADVICE TO AN ENTREPRENEUR

An entrepreneur who is looking to create a new business has read the above article and comes to you for advice:

1. It is not surprising that a lawyer should say that an entrepreneur needs a lawyer to start a business. I certainly do not have money to burn on unnecessary legal fees. Which things do I need a lawyer for now, which things need a lawyer but can be delayed, and finally which things can I do myself?
2. Other than the costs, are there any disadvantages to "bouncing ideas" off a lawyer?
3. I certainly don't want to pay more taxes than I must. What are the tax implications of the different legal structures for the business?

Source: Reprinted with permission of Entrepreneur Media, Inc., "Laying Down the Law. Don't Be Legally Blind—Watch for These Common Start-Up Blunders," by Nichole L. Torres, March 2003, *Entrepreneur* magazine: www.entrepreneur.com.

Liability of Owners

Liability is one of the most critical reasons for establishing a corporation rather than any other form of business. The proprietor and general partners are liable for all aspects of the business. Since the corporation is an entity or legal "person," which is taxable and absorbs liability, the owners are liable only for the amount of their investment. In the case of a proprietorship or regular partnership, no distinction is made between the business entity and the owner(s). Then, to satisfy any outstanding debts of the business, creditors may seize any assets the owners have outside the business.

In a partnership, the general partners usually share the amount of personal liability equally, regardless of their capital contributions, unless there is a specific agreement to the contrary. The only protection for the partners is insurance against liability suits and each partner putting his or her assets in someone else's name. The government may disallow the latter action if it feels this was done to defraud creditors.

In a general partnership there also may be limited partners. These limited partners are liable for only what they contribute to the partnership. This amount, by law, must be registered at a local courthouse, thus making this information public. The limited liability partnership (LLP) has become very popular amongst larger law firms and accounting CPA firms. The LLP is actually a form of a limited liability company (LLC), where the firm elects this status when filing its entity classification with the IRS on Form 8832. Thus the advantages of the LLP are the same as the LLC, allowing the partners to protect their personal assets from liability risk. The LLP will be distinguished from the general partnership as appropriate in our comparison of the various forms of an organization that follows.[2]

Costs of Starting a Business

The more complex the organization, the more expensive it is to start. The least expensive is the proprietorship, where the only costs incurred may be for filing for a business or trade name. In a partnership, in addition to filing a trade name, a partnership agreement is needed. This agreement requires legal advice and should explicitly convey all the responsibilities, rights, and duties of the parties involved. A limited partnership may be somewhat more complex than a general partnership because it must comply strictly with statutory requirements.

The corporation can be created only by statute. This generally means that before the corporation may be legally formed, the owners are required to (1) register the name and articles of incorporation and (2) meet the state statutory requirements (some states are more lenient than others). In complying with these requirements, the corporation will likely incur filing fees, an organization tax, and fees for doing business in each state. Legal advice is necessary to meet all the statutory requirements.

Continuity of Business

One of the main concerns of a new venture is what happens if one of the entrepreneurs (or the only entrepreneur) dies or withdraws from the business. Continuity differs significantly for each of the forms of business. In a sole proprietorship, the death of the owner results in the termination of the business. Sole proprietorships are thus not perpetual, and there is no time limit on how long they may exist.

The partnership varies, depending on whether it is a general partnership or a limited liability partnership (LLP). In a general partnership, the death or withdrawal of one of the partners results in termination of the partnership unless the partnership agreement stipulates otherwise. Thus, the partnership agreement may contain stipulations that allow for a buyout of the deceased or withdrawn partner's share, based on some mechanism or predetermined value. It also may be possible to have a member of the deceased partner's family take over as a partner and share in the profits accordingly. Life insurance owned by the partnership can be valuable protection for the partnership, often providing the funds necessary to buy out the deceased partner's share.

If there are limited liability partners in a general partnership, their death or withdrawal has no effect on the continuity of the business. A limited partner also may be replaced depending on the partnership agreement.

In a limited liability partnership (LLP), the death or withdrawal of a partner has no effect on the partnership. The deceased or withdrawn partner may be replaced much like any employee of a corporation.

The corporation has the most continuity of all the forms of business. Death or withdrawal has no impact on the continuation of the business. Only in a closely held corporation, where all the shares are held by a few people, may there be some problems trying to find a market for the shares. Usually, the corporate charter requires that the corporation or the remaining shareholders purchase the shares. In a public corporation this, of course, would not be an issue.

Transferability of Interest

There can be mixed feelings as to whether the transfer of interest in a business is desirable. In some cases the entrepreneur(s) may prefer to evaluate and assess any new owners before giving them a share of the business. On the other hand, it is also desirable to be able to sell one's interest whenever one wishes. This may be of particular significance when there is the need to consider a succession plan or strategy. This is discussed in more detail in Chapter 17. Each form of business offers different advantages as to the transferability of interest.

In the sole proprietorship, the entrepreneur has the right to sell or transfer any assets in the business. Limited partners, if existing in a general partnership organization, have more flexibility and may typically sell their interest at any time without consent of the general partners. The new limited partner's rights will remain the same as those of the prior partner. However, this may vary depending on the partnership agreement. General partners usually cannot sell their interest without first refusal from the remaining general partners, even if the partnership agreement allows for the transfer of interest.

In an LLP, the transfer of interest of one limited partner is typically not allowable. As stated previously, the LLP has become popular among law and CPA firms. Limited partners also may vary in distinction (e.g., there may be associate partners or junior partners), in which case they also may not share the same profit percentages as full partners. Full partners in law or CPA firms may elect to sell the business but such a decision usually requires the approval of all or a majority.

The corporation has the most freedom in terms of selling one's interest in the business. Shareholders may transfer their shares at any time without consent from the other shareholders. The disadvantage of the right is that it can affect the ownership control of a corporation through election of a board of directors. Shareholders' agreements may provide some limitations on the ease of transferring interest, usually by giving the existing shareholders or corporation the option of purchasing the stock at a specific price or at the agreed-on price. Thus, they sometimes can have the right of first refusal. In the S corporation, the transfer of interest can occur only as long as the buyer is an individual.

Capital Requirements

The need for capital during the early months of the new venture can become one of the most critical factors in keeping a new venture alive. The opportunities and ability of the new venture to raise capital will vary, depending on the form of business.

For a proprietorship, any new capital can come only from loans by any number of sources or by additional personal contributions by the entrepreneur. In borrowing money from a bank, the entrepreneur in this form of business may need collateral to support the loan. Often, an entrepreneur will take a second mortgage on his or her home as a source of capital. Any borrowing from an outside investor may require giving up some of the equity in the proprietorship. Whatever the source, the responsibility for payment is in the hands of the entrepreneur, and failure to make payments can result in foreclosure and liquidation of the business. However, even with these risks the proprietorship is not likely to need large sums of money, as might be the case for a partnership or corporation.

In the partnership, loans may be obtained from banks but will likely require a change in the partnership agreement. Additional funds contributed by each of the partners will also require a new partnership agreement. As in the proprietorship, the entrepreneurs are liable for payment of any new bank loans.

In the corporation, new capital can be raised in a number of ways. The alternatives are greater than in any of the other legal forms of business. Stock may be sold as either voting or nonvoting. Nonvoting stock will of course protect the power of the existing major stockholders. Bonds also may be sold by the corporation. This alternative would be more difficult for the new venture since a high bond rating will likely occur only after the business has been successful over time. Money also may be borrowed in the name of the corporation. As stated earlier, this protects the personal liability of the entrepreneur(s).

Management Control

In any new venture, the entrepreneur(s) will want to retain as much control as possible over the business. Each of the forms of business offers different opportunities and problems as to control and responsibility for making business decisions.

In the proprietorship, the entrepreneur has the most control and flexibility in making business decisions. Since the entrepreneur is the single owner of the venture, he or she will be responsible for and have sole authority over all business decisions.

The partnership can present problems over control of business decisions if the partnership agreement is not concise regarding this issue. Usually in a partnership, the majority rules unless the partnership agreement states otherwise. It is quite important that the partners be friendly toward one another and that delicate or sensitive decision areas of the business be spelled out in the partnership agreement.

The existence of limited partners in a general partnership offers a compromise between the partnership and the corporation. In this type of organization, we can see some of the separation of ownership and control. The limited partners in the venture have no control over business decisions. As soon as the limited partner is given some control over business decisions, he or she then assumes personal liability and can no longer be considered a limited partner. In the LLP, the rights of all partners are clearly defined in the partnership agreement. As mentioned earlier, these types of organizations use titles such as junior partner, associate partner, and so on as a means of designating management responsibilities.

Control of day-to-day business in a corporation is in the hands of management, who may or may not be major stockholders. Control over major long-term decisions, however, may require a vote of the major stockholders. Thus, control is separated based on the types of business decisions. In a new venture, there is a strong likelihood that the entrepreneurs who are major stockholders will be managing the day-to-day activities of the business. As the corporation increases in size, the separation of management and control becomes more probable.

Stockholders in the corporation can indirectly affect the operation of the business by electing someone to the board of directors who reflects their personal business philosophies. These board members, through appointment of top management, then affect the operation and control of the day-to-day management of the business.

Distribution of Profits and Losses

Proprietors receive all distributions of profits from the business. As discussed earlier, they are also personally responsible for all losses. Some of the profits may be used to pay back the entrepreneur for any personal capital contributions that are made to keep the business operating.

In the partnership, the distribution of profits and losses depends on the partnership agreement. It is likely that the sharing of profits and losses will be a function of the partners' investments. However, this can vary depending on the agreement. As in the proprietorship, the partners may assume liability. Limited partners in a general partnership or the formation of an LLP are alternatives that protect those limited partners against personal liability but that may also reduce their share in any profits.

Corporations distribute profits through dividends to stockholders. These distributions are not likely to absorb all the profits that may be retained by the corporation for future investment or capital needs of the business. Losses by the corporation will often result in no dividends. These losses will then be covered by retained earnings or through other financial means discussed earlier.

Attractiveness for Raising Capital

In both the proprietorship and the partnership, the ability of the entrepreneurs to raise capital depends on the success of the business and the personal capability of the entrepreneur. These two forms are the least attractive for raising capital, primarily because of the problem of personal liability. Any large amounts of capital needed in these forms of business should be given serious consideration.

The corporation, because of its advantages regarding personal liability, is the most attractive form of business for raising capital. Shares of stock, bonds, and/or debt are all opportunities for raising capital with limited liability. The more attractive the corporation, the easier it will be to raise capital.

TAX ATTRIBUTES OF FORMS OF BUSINESS

The tax advantages and disadvantages of each of the forms of business differ significantly. Some of the major differences are discussed next. There are many minor differences that, in total, can be important to the entrepreneur. If the entrepreneur has any doubt about these advantages, he or she should get outside advice. Table 9.2 provides a summary of the major tax advantages of these forms of business.

Tax Issues for Proprietorship

For the proprietorship, the IRS treats the business as the individual owner. All income appears on the owner's return as personal income. Thus, the proprietorship is not regarded by the IRS as a separate tax entity. As can be seen in Table 9.2, this treatment of taxes affects the taxable year, distribution of profits to owners, organization costs, capital gains, capital losses, and medical benefits. Each of these is treated as if it were incurred by the individual owner and not the business.

The proprietorship has some tax advantages when compared with the corporation. First, there is no double tax when profits are distributed to the owner. Another advantage is that there is no capital stock tax or penalty for retained earnings in the business. Again, these advantages exist because the proprietorship is not recognized as a separate tax entity; all profits and losses are part of the entrepreneur's tax return.

Tax Issues for Partnership

The partnership's tax advantages and disadvantages are similar to those of the proprietorship, especially regarding income distributions, dividends, and capital gains and losses. Limited partners in a traditional general partnership have the advantage of limited liability (they are liable only for the amount of their investment) but they can share in the profits at a percentage stipulated in the partnership agreement. The LLP is treated the same as the LLC for tax purposes and all profits are distributed through the partners in some designated fashion as personal income.

Both the partnership and proprietorship are organizational forms that serve as non-taxable conduits of income and deductions. These forms of business do have a legal

TABLE 9.2 Tax Attributes of Various Legal Forms of Business

Attributes	Proprietorship	Partnership	Corporation
Taxable year	Usually a calendar year.	Usually calendar year, but other dates may be used.	Any year-end can be used at beginning. Any changes require changes in incorporation.
Distribution of profits to owners	All income appears on owner's return.	Partnership agreement may have special allocation of income. Partners pay tax on their pro rata shares of income on individual return even if income not immediately distributed.	No income is allocated to stockholders.
Organization costs	Not amortizable.	Amortizable over 60 months.	Amortizable over 60 months.
Dividends received	$100 dividend exclusion for single return and $200 on joint return.	Dividend exclusion of partnership passes to partner (conduit).	80% or more of dividend received may be deducted.
Capital gains	Taxed at individual level. A deduction is allowed for long-term capital gains.	Capital gain to partnership will be taxed as a capital gain to the partner (conduit).	Taxed at corporate level.
Capital losses	Carried forward indefinitely.	Capital losses can be used to offset other income. Carried forward indefinitely (conduit).	Carry back three years and carry over five years as short-term capital loss offsetting only capital gains.
Initial organization	Commencement of business results in no additional tax for individual.	Contributions of property to a partnership not taxed.	Acquisition of stock for cash entails no immediate taxes. Transfer of property in exchange for stock may be taxable if stock value greater than contributed property.
Limitations on losses deductible by owners	Amount at risk may be deducted except for real estate activities.	Partnership investment plus share of recourse liability if any. At-risk rules may apply except for real estate partnership.	No losses allowed except on sale of stock or liquidation of corporation. In S corporation, shareholder's investment in corporation is deductible.
Medical benefits	Itemized deductions for medical expenses in excess of percentage of adjusted gross income on individual's return. No deduction for insurance premium.	Cost of partner's benefits not deductible to business as an expense. Possible deduction at partner level.	Cost of employee-shareholder coverage deductible as business expense if designed for benefit of employee.
Retirement benefits	Limitations and restrictions basically same as regular corporation.	Same as for corporations.	Limitations on the benefits that can be derived and on the benefits that can be contributed to a defined contribution plan.

identity distinct from the partners or owners, but this identity is only for accounting reporting.

It is especially important for partnerships to report income since this serves as the basis for determining the share of each partner. The income is distributed based on the partnership agreement. The owners then report their share as personal income and pay taxes based on this amount.

ETHICS

If we ask a business owner to list his or her most important assets, employees often will be at the top of the list. In a small company or new venture, an honest and high-integrity approach in dealing with employees is the most effective strategy for ensuring high performance from these assets. Yet in spite of this, there are still owners who try to take advantage of their employees in order to save money. Two examples involve attempts to cut costs at the expense of an employee.

In the first example, the owner of a fast-growing business hired a new salesman and set his compensation to incentives, thus reducing any fixed expense. The salesman, however, successfully achieved one of the key goals, which was to sell a high-end product to a highly valued customer. This was to trigger a $10,000 bonus. Instead, the owner reduced the bonus to $5,000 and explained to the salesman that more support was required to complete the sales transaction, such as long-distance travel to the prospect's headquarters. Thus, according to the owner, the $10,000 bonus would be reduced to $5,000 instead. The salesman, although still employed at this company, now spends less time seeking high-end sales to high-value customers and much more time searching online for a new job.

In the second situation, the owner of an established small venture decided to replace a highly paid, experienced computer programmer with a less experienced person at half the salary. The departure of the experienced programmer was amicable and was to include 20 weeks of severance pay or two weeks for each of the 10 years that this person had been with the company. Nothing was in writing. Before the programmer's departure, the owner had second thoughts and decided that the package would be cut in half and would include only one week's pay for each year of employment, thus saving the owner approximately $20,000 at the expense of the former employee. The owner stated that the policy had been misunderstood and then proceeded to prepare a new, written severance agreement, which the employee was obliged to sign or receive no severance pay. One of the employee's first stops after leaving the premises was a lawyer's office.

Creative cost cutting at the expense of an employee is not the way to establish the trust and integrity discussed in this chapter. The successful entrepreneurs highlighted in this chapter all point out the importance of their employees to the long-term success of the company. Satisfied employees contribute to the satisfaction of customers, which should be the primary goal of all entrepreneurs.

Source: David E. Gumpert, "No Savings in Unethical Cost-Cutting," *BusinessWeek Online* (December 21, 2004).

Tax Issues for Corporation

Since the corporation is recognized by the IRS as a separate tax entity, it has the advantage of being able to take many deductions and expenses that are not available to the proprietorship or partnership. The disadvantage is that the distribution of dividends is taxed twice, as income of the corporation and as income of the stockholder. This double taxation can be avoided if the income is distributed to the entrepreneur(s) in the form of salary. Bonuses, incentives, profit sharing, and so on, are thus allowable ways to distribute income of the corporation as long as the compensation is reasonable in amount and payment was for services rendered.

The corporate tax may be lower than the individual rate. The entrepreneur is best advised to consider the tax pros and cons and decide on that basis. Projected earnings may be used to calculate the actual taxes under each form of business in order to identify the one that provides the best tax advantage. Remember, tax advantages should be balanced by liability responsibility in the respective form of business.

THE LIMITED LIABILITY COMPANY VERSUS THE S CORPORATION

Although the perception among entrepreneurs is that the C corporation is the desired entity by investors, the actual desired entity by venture capitalists is the limited liability company (LLC), which is similar to the S corporation. The emergence of the LLC as a more popular alternative has resulted from the finalization of new regulation. This new regulation now allows an LLC to be automatically taxed as a partnership, unless the entrepreneur actively makes another choice (taxed as a corporation). This easing of election is one important factor that has enhanced the LLC popularity.

The S corporation (the S refers to Subchapter S of the Internal Revenue Code) had been the most popular choice of organization structure by new ventures and small businesses. However, the growth rate of the formation of S corporations has leveled off in the last few years primarily because of acceptance of the LLC in all states and amendments in several states making the LLC more attractive.[3]

S CORPORATION

S corporation Special type of corporation where profits are distributed to stockholders and taxed as personal income

The *S corporation* combines the tax advantages of the partnership and the corporation. It is designed so that venture income is declared as personal income on a pro rata basis by the shareholders. In fact, the shareholders benefit from all the income and the deductions of the business. Before the passing of the Small Business Protection Act of 1996 the rules governing the S corporation were considered too rigid. The passage of the 1996 law loosened some of the restrictions that existed in regard to number of shareholders, ownership of stock of another corporation, role of trusts as stockholders, classes of stock, and a number of other changes. In 2004, Congress again responded to some of the criticisms of the restrictions on S corporations as compared to LLCs. As a result a number of changes were made, such as an increase in the number of shareholders to 100, allowing family members to be treated as one stockholder, allowing IRAs to own shares in banks that are declared S corporations, as well as some modifications regarding the transfer of stock in a divorce. The intent was to make the S corporation as advantageous as the LLC since it is difficult to change status once a firm has declared itself an S corporation. It is anticipated that Congress may revisit the S corporation again in the future.[4]

One of the issues with the S corporation is that its status must be carefully monitored and maintained. For example, its tax status as a pass-through entity (with its income taxed as personal income of shareholders) still requires an affirmative election of shareholders. If the S corporation status is ever lost, it usually cannot be reelected for five years and with some costs. As stated earlier, the differences between the S corporation and the LLC are generally minimal but should be evaluated on a case-by-case basis because of the existing company and shareholder circumstances.

Advantages of an S Corporation

The S corporation offers the entrepreneur some distinct advantages over the typical corporation, or C corporation. However, there are also disadvantages. In those instances when the disadvantages are great, the entrepreneur should elect the C corporation form. Some of the advantages of the S corporation are as follows:

- Capital gains or losses from the corporation are treated as personal income or losses by the shareholders on a pro rata basis (determined by number of shares of stock held). The corporation is thus not taxed.
- Shareholders retain limited liability protection of C corporation.
- S corporation is not subject to a minimum tax, as is the C corporation.
- Stock may be transferred to low-income-bracket family members (children must be 14 years or older).
- Stock may be voting or nonvoting.

- This form of business may use the cash method of accounting.
- Corporate long-term capital gains and losses are deductible directly by the shareholders to offset other personal capital gains or losses.

Disadvantages of an S Corporation

Although the advantages appear to be favorable for the entrepreneur, this form of business is not appropriate for everyone. The disadvantages of the S corporation are as follows:

- Even with the regulations passed in 1996 and 2004, there are still some restrictions regarding qualification for this form of business.
- Depending on the actual amount of the net income, there may be a tax advantage to the C corporation. This will depend on the company payout ratio, the corporate tax rate, the capital gains tax rate for the investor, and the personal income tax rate of the investor.[5]
- The S corporation may not deduct most fringe benefits for shareholders.
- The S corporation must adopt a calendar year for tax purposes.
- Only one class of stock (common stock) is permitted for this form of business.
- The net loss of the S corporation is limited to the shareholder's stock plus loans to the business.
- S corporations cannot have more than 100 shareholders.

THE LIMITED LIABILITY COMPANY

As stated earlier, the new flexibility offered by LLC status has enhanced its choice by entrepreneurs. The tax rules for an LLC fall under Subchapter K, and this business form is considered a partnership-corporation hybrid with the following characteristics:

- Whereas the corporation has shareholders and partnerships have partners, the LLC has members.
- No shares of stock are issued, and each member owns an interest in the business as designated by the articles of organization, which is similar to the articles of incorporation or certificates of partnership.
- Liability does not extend beyond the member's capital contribution to the business. Thus, there is no unlimited liability, which can be detrimental in a proprietorship or general partnership.
- Members may transfer their interest only with the unanimous written consent of the remaining members.
- The Internal Revenue Service now automatically treats LLCs as partnerships for tax purposes, unless another option is elected. Thus, as mentioned earlier in this chapter, members may elect to designate the firm as a partnership or a corporation.
- The standard acceptable term of an LLC is 30 years. Dissolution is also likely when one of the members dies, the business goes bankrupt, or all members choose to dissolve the business. Some states allow continuity with majority or unanimous consent of the members. One of the important characteristics of the LLC is that the laws governing its formation differ from state to state. Thus, a firm that is operating in more than one state may be subject to different treatment. An analysis of these differences should be considered before choosing this form of organization.

Advantages of an LLC

A number of advantages of an LLC over an S corporation are described below.[6]

- In a highly leveraged enterprise the LLC offers the partnership a distinct advantage over an S corporation in that the partners can add their proportionate shares of the LLC liabilities to their partnership interests.
- With the exception of Texas and Pennsylvania, states do not tax LLCs.
- One or more (without limit) individuals, corporations, partnerships, trusts, or other entities can join to organize or form an LLC. This is not feasible in an S corporation.
- Members are allowed to share income, profit, expense, deduction, loss and credit, and equity of the LLC among themselves. This is the only form of organization that offers all these features.

The one major concern with the LLC is in international business, where the context of unlimited liability is still unclear. Otherwise the LLC offers all the distinct advantages of a C corporation but with a pass-through tax to the members. Owners of an LLC can neither be paid as employees nor participate in certain employee benefits. Instead they are paid in the form of guaranteed payments with no federal or state withholding involved. Thus, members are responsible for filing estimated taxes on a regular basis.[7] The LLC appears to be the favorite choice for venture capitalists since it offers more flexibility based on the advantages discussed above. However, entrepreneurs should compare all the alternative forms of organization before election. This should be done with the advice of a tax attorney, since once a decision is made, it may be difficult to change without some penalty.

DESIGNING THE ORGANIZATION

Generally, the design of the initial organization will be simple. In fact, the entrepreneur may find that he or she performs all the functions of the organization alone. This is a common problem and a significant reason for many failures. The entrepreneur sometimes thinks that he or she can do everything and is unwilling to give up responsibility to others or even include others in the management team. In most cases when this occurs, the entrepreneur will have difficulty making the transition from a start-up to a growing, well-managed business that maintains its success over a long period of time. Regardless of whether one or more individuals are involved in the start-up, as the workload increases, the organizational structure will need to expand to include additional employees with defined roles in the organization. Effective interviewing and hiring procedures will need to be implemented to ensure that new employees will effectively grow and mature with the new venture. All the design decisions involving personnel and their roles and responsibilities reflect the formal structure of the organization. In addition to this formal structure there is an informal structure or organization culture that evolves over time that also needs to be addressed by the entrepreneur. Although we are speaking of an organization culture rather than an organization design, the entrepreneur can have some control over how it evolves. Since issues related to this culture can be just as critical as the formal design of the organization for ensuring a successful and profitable enterprise, they will be discussed in more detail in the next section of this chapter.

For many new ventures, predominantly part-time employees may be hired, raising important issues of commitment and loyalty that Jim Sinegal was able to successfully overcome with some creativity in his organization. However, regardless of the number of actual personnel involved in running the venture, the organization must identify the major activities required to operate it effectively.

The design of the organization will be the entrepreneur's formal and explicit indication to the members of the organization as to what is expected of them. Typically these expectations can be grouped into the following five areas:[8]

- *Organization structure*. This defines members' jobs and the communication and relationship these jobs have with each other. These relationships are depicted in an organization chart.
- *Planning, measurement, and evaluation schemes*. All organization activities should reflect the goals and objectives that underlie the venture's existence. The entrepreneur must spell out how these goals will be achieved (plans), how they will be measured, and how they will be evaluated.
- *Rewards*. Members of an organization will require rewards in the form of promotions, bonuses, praise, and so on. The entrepreneur or other key managers will need to be responsible for these rewards.
- *Selection criteria*. The entrepreneur will need to determine a set of guidelines for selecting individuals for each position.
- *Training*. Training, on or off the job, must be specified. This training may be in the form of formal education or learning skills.

The organization's design can be very simple—that is, one in which the entrepreneur performs all the tasks (usually indicative of a start-up)—or more complex, in which other employees are hired to perform specific tasks. As the organization becomes larger and more complex, the preceding areas of expectation become more relevant and necessary.

Figure 9.1 illustrates two stages of development in an organization. In Stage 1, the new venture is operated by basically one person, the entrepreneur. This organizational chart reflects the activities of the firm in production, marketing/sales, and administration. Initially,

FIGURE 9.1 Stages in Organizational Design

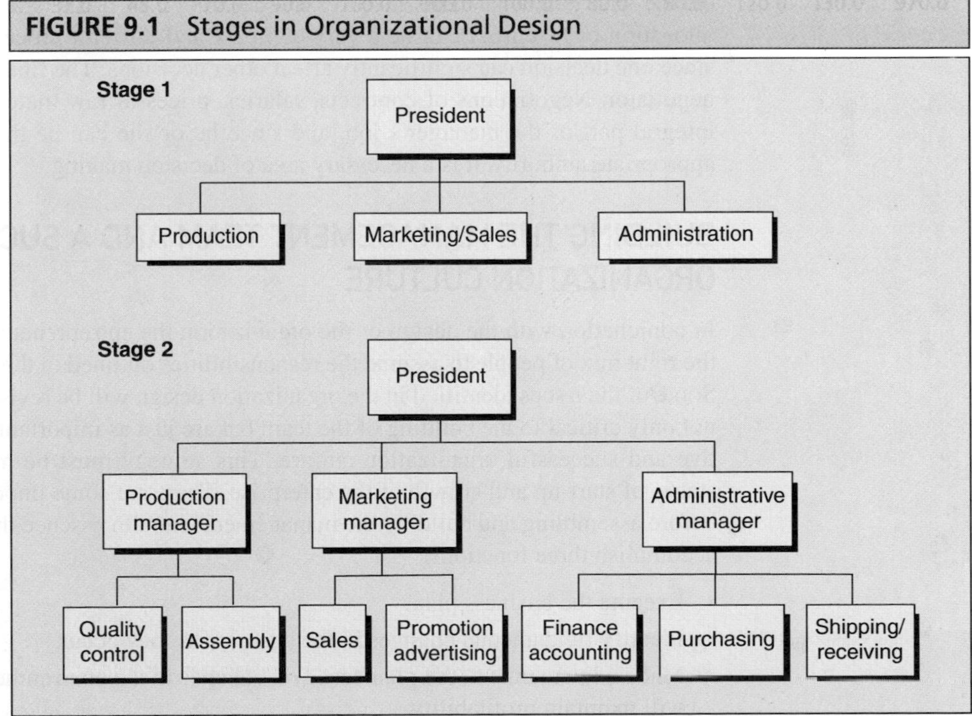

the entrepreneur may manage all these functions. At this stage, there is no need for submanagers; the owner deals with everyone involved in the business and all aspects of the operation. In this example, the president manages production, which may be subcontracted; marketing and sales (possible use of agents or reps); and all administrative tasks such as bookkeeping, purchasing, and shipping. Planning, measurement and evaluation, rewards selection criteria, and training would not yet be critical in the organization.

As the business expands, the organization may be more appropriately described by Stage 2. Here, submanagers are hired to coordinate, organize, and control various aspects of the business. In the example in Figure 9.1, the production manager is responsible for quality control and assembly of the finished product by the subcontractor. The marketing manager develops promotion and advertising strategy and coordinates the efforts of the expanding rep organization. The administrative manager then assumes the responsibility for all administrative tasks in the business operation. Here the elements of measurement, evaluation, reward, selection, and training become apparent.

A third stage may exist when the firm achieves a much larger size (i.e., 1,000 employees). The activities below each manager in Stage 2 would then be represented by a third level of managers (i.e., quality control managers).

As the organization evolves, the manager or entrepreneur's decision roles also become critical for an effective organization. As an entrepreneur, the manager's primary concern is to adapt to changes in the environment and seek new ideas. When a new idea is found, the entrepreneur will need to initiate development either under his or her own supervision (Stage 1 in Figure 9.1) or by delegating the responsibility to someone else in the organization (Stage 2 in Figure 9.1). In addition to the role of adaptor, the manager will also need to respond to pressures such as an unsatisfied customer, a supplier reneging on a contract, or a key employee threatening to quit. Much of the entrepreneur's time in the start-up will be spent "putting out fires."

Another role for the entrepreneur is that of allocator of resources. The manager must decide who gets what. This involves the delegation of budgets and responsibilities. The allocation of resources can be a very complex and difficult process for the entrepreneur since one decision can significantly affect other decisions. The final decision role is that of negotiator. Negotiations of contracts, salaries, prices of raw materials, and so on, are an integral part of the manager's job, and since he or she can be the only person with the appropriate authority, it is a necessary area of decision making.

BUILDING THE MANAGEMENT TEAM AND A SUCCESSFUL ORGANIZATION CULTURE

In conjunction with the design of the organization the entrepreneur will need to assemble the right mix of people to assume the responsibilities outlined in the organization structure. Some of the issues identified in the organization design will be revisited here since they are not only critical to the building of the team but are just as important in establishing a positive and successful organization culture. This strategy must be maintained through the stages of start-up and growth of the enterprise. There are some important issues to address before assembling and building the management team. In essence the team must be able to accomplish three functions:

- Execute the business plan.
- Identify fundamental changes in the business as they occur.
- Make adjustments to the plan based on changes in the environment and market that will maintain profitability.

Although these functions may seem simple and easy to achieve, the people engaged and the culture promoted by the entrepreneur are critical in accomplishing these functions. As we discussed in the organization design section previously, the entrepreneur will first need to assume the responsibility of determining what skills and abilities are needed to meet the goals in the business plan. Not only are the skills and abilities important but also the entrepreneur will need to consider the personality and character of each individual in order to create a viable organization culture. The organization culture will be a blend of attitudes, behaviors, dress, and communication styles that make one business different from another. There is no specific technique for accomplishing this since every organization will be different. However, below we explore some of the important considerations and strategies in recruiting and assembling an effective team and hence in creating an effective and positive organization culture.

First, the entrepreneur's desired culture must match the business strategy outlined in the business plan. For example, Fran Bigelow, founder of Fran's Chocolates in Seattle, has been able to get her team to consider themselves artisans, focus on detail, and strive for perfection. Fran feels that this strategy is effective for her venture because of her premium product line but might result in disaster for someone marketing a high-volume, low-cost manufactured product.[9]

Second, the leader of the organization must create a workplace where communication from the bottom up is encouraged. Tory Johnson, the CEO and founder of the New York–based career fair organizer named Women For Hire, LLC, stresses the importance of employee input either by e-mail, phone, or face to face. Finding the right employees begins in the interviewing process, where she asks prospective employees to describe a situation in which they actually communicated their disagreement either with a co-worker or supervisor. Tory considers it important when interviewees state an occasion of disagreement, as opposed to being demure with their response. Her reasoning behind this fits with her leadership and organization philosophy, which is that an effective business needs to have an environment where employees respect the leadership enough to offer suggestions or criticism.[10]

Third, the entrepreneur should be flexible enough to try different things. This is not always possible in a very small organization but has been the successful strategy in the growth of Google. The leadership of this company has an abundance of talent, and the attitude of management is that this talent needs to be given enough flexibility to make decisions, as long as they do so within the model established by the company. Founders Larry Page and Sergey Brin have chosen a very flat organizational structure which they believe provides more flexibility and in the long run provides the customer with a better product and better service. This organizational strategy has certainly proven to be successful given this firm's very successful IPO in August of 2004 and a stock price that grew to over $400 by the end of 2005.[11] Steven Jobs also believed in this approach. He moved key personnel to a separate building and allowed them to spend all their working hours developing the new-generation computer of that time, the Macintosh.

Fourth, it is necessary to spend extra time in the hiring process. There is sometimes a tendency to want to hurry the process of finding the appropriate skills to fill the organization's needs. As stated earlier, there is more to a person than his or her skills. Character is also an important factor in building an effective organization culture. One thing that can be implemented is a hiring plan that establishes the procedure for screening, interviewing, and assessing all candidates. Job descriptions along with specifications of the type of person who will match the desired culture should be documented for this process.

Next, the entrepreneur needs to remember that it is easier to change a person's behavior than it is to change the person's attitude.[12] Leadership needs to establish core values and provide the appropriate tools so that employees can effectively complete their jobs. An approach such as "We're all in this together, no one is bigger than anyone else, and here are the rules we live by" can lead to greater challenges and job satisfaction. A reward system is part of the tools needed to provide consistent and positive behavior patterns.

Finding the most effective team and creating a positive organization culture is a challenge for the entrepreneur but is just as critical as having an innovative, marketable product. It is an important ingredient in an organization's success.

THE ROLE OF A BOARD OF DIRECTORS

An entrepreneur may find it necessary in his or her organization plan to establish a board of directors or board of advisors. The board of advisors is discussed below. The board of directors may serve a number of functions: (1) reviewing operating and capital budgets, (2) developing longer-term strategic plans for growth and expansion, (3) supporting day-to-day activities, (4) resolving conflicts among owners or shareholders, (5) ensuring the proper use of assets, or (6) developing a network of information sources for the entrepreneurs. These functions may be a formal part of the organization, with responsibilities assigned to the directors depending on the needs of the new venture.

Most important in establishing these responsibilities is the consideration of the impact of the Sarbanes-Oxley Act passed in 2002. Passage of this act resulted because of accounting irregularities, fraud, bankruptcy, insider trading, excessive management compensation, and other illegal or unethical actions that have become newsworthy in the last couple of years (see Chapter 6 for more discussion of the Sarbanes-Oxley Act). Although there is still some concern about the effectiveness of the new law, its intent is to establish a more independent functioning board. This is particularly relevant in public companies where the board members must represent all shareholders and are responsible for "blowing the whistle" on any discrepancies that may be suspected. An entrepreneur considering a public company will need to review all the provisions of this law before selecting board members. In the case of privately held companies, the shareholders (entrepreneurs and investors) may actually represent the board of directors. The law has less impact in this instance because the representation of shareholders is confined to a few individuals such as family members.[13] In either case the purpose of the board of directors is to provide important leadership and direction for the new venture and it should be carefully chosen to meet the requirements of the Sarbanes-Oxley Act and also the following criteria:[14]

- Select individuals who can work with a diverse group and will commit to the venture's mission.
- Select candidates who understand the market environment or can contribute important skills to the new venture's achievement of planning goals.
- Select candidates who will show good judgment in business decision making.

Candidates should be identified using referrals of business associates or from any of the external advisors such as banks, investors, lawyers, accountants, or consultants. Ideally, the board should consist of 7 to 12 members with limited terms to allow for continuous infusion of new ideas from different people.

Board of director performance needs to be regularly evaluated by the entrepreneurs. It is the chair's responsibility to provide an appraisal of each board member. In order to provide this appraisal, the chairperson (and/or founders) should have a written description of the responsibilities and expectations of each member.

AS SEEN IN *ENTREPRENEUR* MAGAZINE

PROVIDE ADVICE TO AN ENTREPRENEUR ABOUT FIRING EMPLOYEES

Firing an employee is a messy business. Just the thought of having to recruit, train, and manage a new sales soul is enough to keep some sales managers from following through with the task. But holding on to a salesperson who's not performing or who's disruptive to the team is guaranteed to exacerbate matters down the road. But how do you know when it's time to say, "You've gotta go"? It's simple, according to Tricia Tamkin: "Lack of production, lack of production, lack of production," says the president of Padigent, a Carol Stream, Illinois, human resources consulting firm for emerging companies.

Dave Anderson, president of Dave Anderson's Learn to Lead, concurs that performance is one criterion for firing. Anderson, whose Los Altos, California, company offers sales, management, and leadership consulting, thinks reps who are "dishonest, selfish, or disrespectful" should face the axe.

You may fear firing a rep will cause a morale dip in the troops. After all, someone's buddy is getting shown the door. But making a tough choice can bolster the spirits of your sales squad. Says Tamkin: "Firing can positively affect morale [because] it sends a message that the company will take strong measures to ensure the success of the organization. Poor performers lower the morale of the team, and they continually break momentum and diminish the credibility of the sales manager."

Before firing, however, steps must be taken to legally protect your business. It's crucial that the employee has been warned in advance in writing. Coaching sessions with failing salespeople will help protect you when it comes time to separate. Tamkin advises that documentation must be developed in advance of the firing, and that when it comes time for the employee to go, the manager should conduct an exit interview. Though firing will never be a savory part of a manager's job description, it's short-term pain for long-term gain. "Managers have to realize that when they keep the wrong person," Anderson says, "there's more damage to the company than just lack of production."

Here are some firing guidelines from William Skip Miller's ProActive Sales Management (AMACOM):

1. *Never in your office:* If it's your office, you can't leave if the employee wants to stay and talk.
2. *Short and sweet:* As you walk in the door, say, "The reason I'm here is to tell you this is your last day of employment with this company." Just get it out.
3. *Never on a Friday:* If fired on a Friday, the employee can't start the process of feeling good. All he or she can do is stew about it over the weekend.
4. *Outside help:* If the employee says he or she has consulted an attorney or other legal counsel, stop the conversation immediately and consult your HR department or attorney, whoever helped you craft your company policy.
5. *No hanging around:* Personal effects can be retrieved, but have the person leave the building.

ADVICE TO AN ENTREPRENEUR

An entrepreneur whose business has stopped growing has read the above article and comes to you for advice:

1. Gee, these managers discussed in the article are a bit rough. Even if one particular person is not producing as expected, doesn't this person still deserve to be treated with respect?
2. It appears that the automatic assumption is that the employee is at fault for not performing and therefore should be fired. But shouldn't the responsibility fall on me as the manager and the system that I have introduced? Maybe the person is performing as well as the situation allows.
3. How am I to build a team spirit within my small company when I single out one person for lack of production and fire him or her?

Source: Reprinted with permission of Entrepreneur Media, Inc., "You're Dismissed. Face It—Part of Your Job Is Relieving Others of Theirs. So How Do You Do It Right?" by Kimberly L. McCall, March 2003, *Entrepreneur* magazine: www.entrepreneur.com.

Compensation for board members can be shares of stock, stock options, or dollar payment. Often the new venture will tie compensation to the performance of the new venture. Compensation is important since it reinforces the obligation of board members. If board members were only volunteers, they would tend to take the role lightly and not provide any value to the entrepreneur.

THE BOARD OF ADVISORS

Compared to a board of directors, a board of advisors would be more loosely tied to the organization and would serve the venture only in an advisory capacity for some of the functions or activities mentioned above. It has no legal status, unlike the board of directors, and hence is not subject to the regulations stipulated in the Sarbanes-Oxley Act. These boards are likely to meet less frequently or depending on the need to discuss important venture decisions. A board of advisors is very useful in a family business where the board of directors may consist entirely of family members.

The selection process for advisors can be similar to the process for selecting a board of directors, including determining desired skills and interviewing potential candidates. Advisors may be compensated on a per-meeting basis or with stock or stock options. Just as in the case of the board of directors, the members should be evaluated as to their contribution to meeting the mission of the new venture.

Boards of advisors can provide an important reality check for the entrepreneur or owner of any noncorporate type of business. Robin Chase, the founder of Zipcar, a self-service car rental business, regularly calls on a group of advisors to help her hash out ideas, provide recommendations for advancing her company, or just get a sanity check.[15] Ocean Resources Inc., a venture engaged in deep water research, exploration, survey, and the recovery operation of valuable shipwrecks, formed its board of advisors last year. Its purpose was to gain additional expertise and wisdom from individuals with extensive backgrounds and education in such areas as maritime operations, finance, and business development.[16] The flexibility in size, background requirements, number of meetings, and compensation makes these boards a very desirable alternative to the more formal boards of directors.

THE ORGANIZATION AND USE OF ADVISORS

The entrepreneur will usually use outside advisors such as accountants, bankers, lawyers, advertising agencies, and market researchers on an as-needed basis. These advisors, who are separate from the more formal board of advisors mentioned above, can also become an important part of the organization and thus will need to be managed just like any other permanent part of the new venture.

The relationship of the entrepreneur and outside advisors can be enhanced by seeking out the best advisors and involving them thoroughly and at an early stage. Advisors should be assessed or interviewed just as if they were being hired for a permanent position. References should be checked and questions asked to ascertain the quality of service as well as compatibility with the management team.

Hiring and managing outside experts can be effectively accomplished by considering these advisors as advice suppliers. Just as no manager would buy raw materials or supplies without knowledge of their cost and quality, the same approval can apply for advisors. Entrepreneurs should ask these advisors about fees, credentials, references, and so on, before hiring them.

Even after the advisors have been hired, the entrepreneur should question their advice. Why is the advice being given? Make sure you understand the decision and its potential implications. There are many good sources of advisors, such as the Small Business Administration, other small businesses, chambers of commerce, universities, friends, and relatives. Careful evaluation of the entrepreneur's needs and the competency of the advisor can make advisors a valuable asset to the organization of a new venture.

IN REVIEW

SUMMARY

One of the most important decisions the entrepreneur(s) must make in the business plan is the legal form of business. The three major legal forms of business are the proprietorship, partnership, and corporation. Each differs significantly and should be evaluated carefully before a decision is made. This chapter provides considerable insight and comparisons regarding these forms of business to assist the entrepreneur in this decision.

The S corporation and the limited liability company are alternative forms of business that are gaining popularity. Each of these allows the entrepreneur to retain the protection from personal liability provided by a corporation as well as the tax advantages provided by a partnership. There are important advantages as well as disadvantages to these forms of business, and entrepreneurs should carefully weigh both before deciding.

The organization plan for the entrepreneur also requires some major decisions that could affect long-term effectiveness and profitability. It is important to begin the new venture with a strong management team that is committed to the goals of the new venture. The management team must be able to work together effectively toward these ends.

The design of the organization requires the entrepreneur to specify the types of skills needed and the roles that must be filled. These would be considered part of the formal organization. In addition to the formal organization the entrepreneur must consider the informal organization or culture that is desired to match the strategy stipulated in the business plan. This organization culture represents the attitudes, behaviors, dress, and communication styles that can differentiate one company from another. Both of these are important in establishing an effective and profitable organization.

A board of directors or board of advisors can provide important management support for an entrepreneur starting and managing a new venture. Boards of directors are now governed by the Sarbanes-Oxley Act, which was passed because of a rash of illegal and unethical behaviors that were newsworthy. The intent of this new law is to make the board of directors more independent and to make its members accountable to the shareholders. The law is particularly relevant to public companies and has less impact on privately held companies. The board of advisors is a good alternative to a board of directors when the stock is held privately or in a family business.

In spite of the new regulations, a board of directors or advisors can still provide excellent support for an organization. Either one can be formed in the initial business planning phase or after the business has been formed and financed. In either case the selection of board members should be made carefully, so that members will take their roles seriously and will be committed to their roles and responsibilities.

Advisors will also be necessary in the new venture. Outside advisors should be evaluated as if they were being hired as permanent members of the organization. Information on their fees and referrals can help determine the best choices.

RESEARCH TASKS

1. In this country, what proportion of all businesses are (a) proprietorships, (b) partnerships, (c) private companies, and (d) public companies? Provide an example of an industry that has a large share of proprietorships. Why is this the case?

Provide an example of an industry that has a large share of partnerships. Why is this the case? Provide an example of an industry that has a large share of private companies. Why is this the case? Provide an example of an industry that has a large share of public companies. Why is this the case?

2. How much does it cost to set up a private company? What are the ongoing costs?
3. Study the local newspaper and choose three good examples and three poor examples of job advertisements. Be prepared to explain your choices.
4. Interview five entrepreneurs about their use of a board of advisors. Ask who is on the board, how the members were selected, how they were encouraged to join the board, how useful the board has been, and so on.

CLASS DISCUSSION

1. Why would entrepreneurs open themselves up to personal financial losses by choosing a proprietorship rather than a company form of organization?
2. Why do suppliers sometimes ask entrepreneurs of small companies to provide personal guarantees for a line of business credit? If an entrepreneur is asked (forced) to provide personal guarantees, then what personal protection does a company as a legal form really provide?
3. Does the old saying "You get what you pay for" apply to a board of directors or a board of advisors?
4. Design a structure for the following organization and detail the changes that you would make (if any) to that structure as the company develops.
   a. *Stage 1.* You are the CEO of a company ("Party On") that specializes in the sale of party merchandise (e.g., paper cups, plates, and streamers). You have a retail store and three employees, and you serve the local area. A differentiation strategy is used. What structure (configuration, prime coordinating mechanisms, and type of decentralization) are you going to implement and why? Which is the key part of the organization?
   b. *Stage 2.* After five years, Party On has expanded to 150 stores throughout the United States. The company is still following a differentiation strategy, selling primarily the same range of products in each store. What structure (configuration, prime coordinating mechanisms, and type of decentralization) are you going to implement and why? Which is the key part of the organization?
   c. *Stage 3.* After a further seven years, Party On has expanded to 225 stores in the United States, 57 stores in the U.K., 30 stores in Sweden, 10 stores in France, 8 stores in Mexico, and 5 stores in Germany. The company's strategy is to sell its range of products through company-owned stores at a premium price. What structure (configuration, prime coordinating mechanisms, and type of decentralization) are you going to implement and why? Which is the key part of the organization?
   d. *Stage 4.* Not long after the new structure has been put in place, a consortium of department stores offers you a very lucrative contract to sell Party On's products in its stores worldwide. Its requirement is that Party On's current retail stores must be closed over a five-year period (it doesn't want to compete with Party On), and it wants to offer the products at lower prices. You accept the terms and conditions of the deal. What structure (configuration, prime coordinating

mechanisms, and type of decentralization) are you going to implement and why? Which is the key part of the organization?

e. *Stage 5*. The contract has been enormously successful. Further, a number of other opportunities have arisen. First, the founder and CEO of your major supplier of party merchandise died and you were able to purchase the company at a very reasonable price. Second, rather than close your outlet stores, which are in excellent positions, you decided to sell sporting collectibles (e.g., baseball cards, signed photographs, and jerseys) at a very nice mark-up indeed. However, while U.S. sporting collectibles are somewhat popular outside the United States, each country is quite different. What structure (configuration, prime coordinating mechanisms, and type of decentralization) are you going to implement and why? Which is the key part of the organization?

SELECTED READINGS

Bunderson, J. Stuart; and Kathleen M. Sutcliffe. (2002). Comparing Alternative Conceptualizations of Functional Diversity in Management Teams: Process and Performance Effects. *Academy of Management Journal*, vol. 45, no. 5, pp. 875–93.

This paper examines the process and performance effects of dominant functional diversity (the diversity of functional experts on a team) and intrapersonal functional diversity (the aggregate functional breadth of team members). In a sample of business unit management teams, dominant functional diversity had a negative effect and intrapersonal functional diversity had a positive effect on information sharing and unit performance.

Cooney, Thomas M. (June 2005). Editorial: What Is an Entrepreneurial Team? *International Small Business Journal*, vol. 23, no. 3, pp. 226–35.

This article focuses on the role of the entrepreneurial team in industrial success. It argues that it is typically a myth to assume that the entrepreneur is a lone hero battling the storms of economic, government, social, and other environmental forces. These individuals play an important role in helping the venture through these external forces.

Denis, David, J.; and Atulya Sarin. (2002). Taxes and the Relative Valuation of S Corporations and C Corporations. *Journal of Applied Finance*, Fall/Winter 2002, pp. 5–14.

This paper analyzes the net tax advantages of S corporations relative to C corporations. The analysis indicates that the net tax advantage is economically important; it varies directly with the company's payout ratio, the marginal corporate tax rate, and the capital gains rate of the marginal investor; and it varies inversely with the personal tax rate of the marginal investor. The analysis predicts that the fair market value of an S corporation will exceed that of an otherwise identical C corporation.

Ellentuck, Albert B. (October 2005). Converting a Sole Proprietorship into an LLC. *Tax Advisor*, vol. 36, no. 10, pp. 648–49.

This article presents a case study on the conversion of a sole proprietorship company to a limited liability company (LLC). It describes the filing information necessary and tax implications in the conversion.

Ewing, Bradley T.; and Phanindra V. Wunnava. (December 2004). The Trade-Off between Supervision Cost and Performance Based Pay: Does Gender Matter? *Small Business Economics*, vol. 23, no. 5, pp. 453–60.

The researchers introduce a model that is empirically tested based on efficiency wage theory, which argues that higher wages resulting from greater efficiencies of internal supervision result in higher efficiencies. The research uses a new measure of the cost of supervising workers to test the theory.

Feltham, Tammi S.; Glenn Feltham; and James J. Barnett. (January 2005). The Dependence of Family Businesses on a Single Decision Maker. *Journal of Small Business Management*, vol. 43, no. 1, pp. 1–15.

This study focuses on the implications of dependence on a single individual in family businesses. The study suggests that family businesses are highly dependent on a single individual and that this dependence decreases with the age of the owner/manager and is significantly greater when the owner/manager's family has voting control. In addition, a number of other factors are noted as related to the degree of dependence on a single individual.

Ferrante, Francesco. (September 2005). Revealing Entrepreneurial Talent. *Small Business Economics*, vol. 25, no. 2, pp. 159–74.

In this paper the researcher offers evidence that the amount of working time spent by small business owners in entrepreneurial activities affects the performance of the business and reveals their entrepreneurial talent. The main finding confirms previous studies that have found that education is an important part of entrepreneurial human capital—which is the main factor in sustaining a small firm's competitiveness in a global economy.

Fiegener, Mark K. (September 2005). Determinants of Board Participation in the Strategic Decisions of Small Corporations. *Entrepreneurship: Theory & Practice*, vol. 29, no. 5, pp. 627–50.

Agency, strategic choice, and cognitive perspectives are used to identify the conditions under which chief executive officers of small private corporations involve the board of directors in strategic decisions. Boards are more likely to participate in strategic decisions when the firm is larger, the board has a critical mass of outside directors, or CEO power is low.

Goold, Michael; and Andrew Campbell. (2002). Do You Have a Well-Designed Organization? *Harvard Business Review*, March 2002, pp. 117–24.

Creating a new organizational structure is one of the toughest—and most politically explosive—challenges that an executive faces. This article provides nine tests of organizational design, which can be used either to evaluate an existing structure or to create a new one. Using this framework will help make the process more rational, shifting it away from issues of personality and toward strategy and effectiveness.

Muse, Lori A.; Matthew W. Rutherford; and Sharon L. Oswald. (March 2005). Commitment to Employees: Does It Help or Hinder Small Business Performance? *Small Business Economics*, vol. 24, no. 2, pp. 97–111.

This study used a sample of 4,637 small businesses to test the relationship between organizational commitment to employees (OCE) and company performance. The results reveal a significant positive relationship between organizational commitment and company performance. This suggests that small businesses may be able to realize some benefits from OCE programs.

Ranft, Annette L; and Hugh M. O'Neil. (2001). Board Composition and High-Flying Founders: Hints of Trouble to Come? *Academy of Management Executive*, vol. 15, no. 1, pp. 126–38.

This paper argues that business success creates personal and organizational forces that lead to a form of cautious conservatism, and perhaps arrogant disdain, in the face of competitive pressures. One protection against this inertia-inducing conservatism is a strong board, which can help founders avoid the traps of success and maintain the entrepreneurial zest that helped to build their companies and their reputations.

Sonnenfeld, Jeffrey A. (2002). What Makes Great Boards Great. *Harvard Business Review*, September 2002, pp. 106–13.

In light of the recent meltdowns of many once-great companies, enormous attention has been focused on the companies' boards. And yet a close examination of those boards reveals no broad pattern of incompetence or corruption. They passed the test that would normally be applied to ascertain whether a board of directors was likely to do a good job. This article argues that it is time for fundamentally new thinking about how corporate boards should operate and be evaluated and that it is important to consider not only how the work of the board is structured but also how the board is managed.

Talaulicar, Till; Jens Grundei; and Axel V. Werder. (July 2005). Strategic Decision Making in Start-Ups: The Effect of Top Management Team Organization and Processes on Speed and Comprehensiveness. *Journal of Business Venturing*, vol. 20, no. 4, pp. 519–41.

This study argues that characteristics of the top management team (TMT) organization as well as TMT processes—namely, debate and trust—significantly influence the comprehensiveness and speed of strategic decision making in start-ups.

END NOTES

1. See S. Greenhouse, "How Costco Became the Anti Wal-Mart," *The New York Times* (July 17, 2005), Section BU, p. 1; Christine Frey, "Costco's Love of Labor: Employees' Well-Being Part and Parcel of Success," *The Seattle Post-Intelligencer* (March 29, 2004), p. C1; Stephanie Clifford, "Because Who Knew a Big Box Chain Could Have a Generous Soul?" *Inc.* (April 2005), p. 88; and "Profits Jump at Costco," *Home Textiles Today* (December 12, 2005), p. 14.
2. Daniel S. Kleinberger, "The Closely Held Business through the Entity-Aggregate Prism," *Wake Forest Law Review* (Fall 2005), pp. 827–81.
3. Alan L. Kinnard, "The Limited Liability Company versus the S Corporation," *Corporate Business Taxation Monthly* (June 2002), pp. 10–17.
4. Zev Landau, "Recent Reform and Simplifications for S Corporations," *CPA Journal* (November 2005), pp. 46–50.
5. David J. Denis and Atulya Sarin, "Taxes and Relative Valuation of S Corporations and C Corporations," *Journal of Applied Finance* (Fall–Winter 2002), pp. 5–15.
6. Kinnard, "The Limited Liability Company versus the S Corporation," pp. 12–14.
7. Robert M. Digiantimmaso, "LLC and LLP Issues for Small Privately Owned Businesses," *Tax Advisor* (January 2005), pp. 24–25.
8. J. W. Lorsch, "Organization Design: A Situational Perspective," in *Perspectives on Behavior in Organizations*, 2nd ed., eds. J. R. Hackman, E. E. Lawler III, and L. W. Porter (Burr Ridge IL: McGraw-Hill/Irwin, 1983), pp. 439–47.
9. Steven T. Barnett, "Culture Is Critical to a Company's Success," *Seattle Post-Intelligencer* (April 14, 2003), p. C1.
10. Mark Henricks, "The Truth? Your Employees Can Handle It, So Just Communicate with Them, Already," *Entrepreneur* (July 2005), pp. 85–86.
11. David LaGesse, "Engine of Fun and Profit," *U.S. News and World Report* (October 31, 2005), p. 26.
12. Rick Berg, "Values Added," *Marketplace* (September 10, 2002), p. 8.
13. James Olan Hutcheson, "Board Silly: A Bad Board of Directors Can Be Worse than No Board at All," *Financial Planning Lexis Nexis* (April 1, 2002), pp. 1–3.
14. Nicole Gull, "Assemble a Board of Directors," *Inc.* (October 2004), p. 102.
15. Stephanie N. Mehta, "Experts for Hire," *Fortune Small Business* (May 1, 2002), p. 67.
16. "Ocean Resources Forms Board of Advisors," *Business Wire* (February 19, 2004).

10

THE FINANCIAL PLAN

LEARNING OBJECTIVES

1
To understand the role of budgets in preparing pro forma statements.

2
To understand why positive profits can still result in a negative cash flow.

3
To learn how to prepare monthly pro forma cash flow, income, balance sheet, and sources and uses of funds statements for the first year of operation.

4
To explain the application and calculation of the break-even point for the new venture.

5
To illustrate the alternative software packages that can be used for preparing financial statements.

OPENING PROFILE

BILL PORTER—E*TRADE AND ISE

Although the Internet has changed the lives of many consumers in the past few years, one entrepreneur in 1982 recognized its future relevance as a tool that would allow individual investors to digitally trade securities. Bill Porter, now in his early 70s, identified an opportunity that has had a significant impact on the brokerage industry. As an individual investor he had been curious as to why it was necessary to pay a broker hundreds of dollars for stock transactions. His vision was that eventually everyone would own a computer and thus would be able to invest online. In 1982 he founded Trade Plus, which provided online quotes and trading services for Fidelity, Charles Schwab, and Quick & Reilly. His first online trade took place on July 11, 1983. Porter soon realized that this would be the wave of the future. It would take years before the marketplace would recognize the significance of computer technology, but his persistence paid off.[1]

www.etrade.com

Bill Porter had been an entrepreneur all his life, although he admits that he really did not understand what entrepreneurship was all about. His early years as president of Treton Shoes, as a management consultant, as founder of Commercial Electronics Inc., as director of research and planning at Textron, and as research manager at General Electric's Electronic Center had given him many opportunities to see the future in online business. During this period he had also developed more than 20 products and obtained 14 patents.

While providing the online services for other brokerage houses, Trade Plus began to develop its own in-house systems to accommodate traders. Trade Plus was thus competing with its own clients for trader services. So in 1992, Porter created E*TRADE Securities Inc. as a subsidiary of Trade Plus that became Compuserve's and later America Online's online trading service. The demand for these services exploded. In 1996 he created www.etrade.com, one of the original Internet stock trading companies offering consumers stock transactions for $14.95 on Dow Jones stocks and $19.95 on NASDAQ stocks. That summer the company went public, and the revolution had begun.

For E*TRADE, as for many other Internet start-ups, it was a number of years before a profit occurred, in the year 2000. At the end of the third quarter of 2005, the company reported net income of $107.5 million based on revenue of $422.8 million—up more than 26 percent from the previous year. At present, E*TRADE has client assets of over $106.4 billion, including a record $19.5 billion in customer cash and deposits. Trades now cost between $6.99 and $9.99.

In the last two years E*TRADE has also acquired Brown Company from JPMorgan Chase and Harrisdirect from the Bank of Montreal. Both of these acquisitions have significantly increased E*TRADE's client base and allowed it to remain competitive with giants Charles Schwab, TD Waterhouse, and Fidelity Investments. In 2006 it continues to announce enhancements in its investment tools and services, particularly regarding research information and education designed to help investors manage their portfolios online.

Right after the IPO, Porter hired Christos Cotsakos to take over as chair and CEO, while he assumed the role of chair emeritus. After a short tenure, Cotsakos resigned and was replaced by Mitchell H. Caplan. Rather than basking in his success, Porter almost immediately continued his entrepreneurial ways by launching in May 2000 the International Securities Exchange (ISE) www.iseoptions.com. It is the first fully electronic U.S. options exchange. Along with partners Marty Averbuch, David Krell, and Gary Katz, Porter sought a solution to the costs and barriers that prevented retail investors from buying and selling options. The new options exchange—the ISE—that evolved from their efforts was funded initially by a consortium of broker-dealers that was willing to purchase memberships.

Bill Porter has not slowed down and has continued to contribute the leadership and drive that he displayed in his younger years. The ISE, a major breakthrough in the financial industry, has experienced significant growth in its five-plus years of existence. Though the ISE was ridiculed by other exchanges when it began operations, its ability to reduce costs and increase efficiency led to its position as market share leader among all of the options exchanges, with more than 32 percent of the market in 2005. Its major competitors, the Chicago Board of Options Exchange, the American Stock Exchange, and the Pacific Exchange, all with double-digit shares, have also introduced electronic exchanges. Not only has this heightened the challenges to ISE, but it also has significantly increased the total number of options trades. In March 2005, ISE celebrated a successful IPO with an offering price of $18 and closed the day at $25.75—a 69 percent increase and the biggest first-day gain of any IPO since 2001. Today, with options trading growth leveling off and competition becoming more intense, the company is aggressively pursuing new market opportunities most likely in overseas markets.[2]

One of the most significant parts of planning for the launch and growth of both E*TRADE and ISE was the financial planning. Since Internet businesses take a number of years to become profitable, Bill Porter needed to focus on his financial projections and pro formas with great diligence.

The financial plan provides the entrepreneur with a complete picture of how much and when funds are coming into the organization, where funds are going, how much cash is available, and the projected financial position of the firm. It provides the short-term basis for budgeting control and helps prevent one of the most common problems for new ventures—lack of cash. We can see from the above example how important it is to understand the role of the financial plan. Without careful financial planning in the early stages, E*TRADE and ISE could have suffered serious cash flow problems. The financial plan must explain to any potential investor how the entrepreneur plans to meet all financial obligations and maintain the venture's liquidity in order to either pay off debt or provide a good return on investment. In general, the financial plan will need three years of projected financial data to satisfy any outside investors. The first year should reflect monthly data.

This chapter discusses each of the major financial items that should be included in the financial plan: pro forma income statements, pro forma cash flow, pro forma balance sheets, and break-even analysis. As we saw in the E*TRADE and ISE examples above, Internet start-ups have some unique financial characteristics, which are included in the discussion that follows.

OPERATING AND CAPITAL BUDGETS

Before developing the pro forma income statement, the entrepreneur should prepare operating and capital budgets. If the entrepreneur is a sole proprietor, then he or she is responsible for the budgeting decisions. In the case of a partnership, or where employees exist, the initial budgeting process may begin with one of these individuals, depending on his or her role in the venture. For example, a sales budget may be prepared by a sales manager, a manufacturing budget by the production manager, and so on. Final determination of these budgets will ultimately rest with the owners or entrepreneurs.

As can be seen below, in the preparation of the pro forma income statement, the entrepreneur must first develop a sales budget that is an estimate of the expected volume of sales by month. Methods of projecting sales are discussed next. From the sales forecasts the entrepreneur will then determine the cost of these sales. In a manufacturing venture the entrepreneur could compare the costs of producing these internally or subcontracting them to another manufacturer. Also included will be the estimated ending inventory needed as a buffer against possible fluctuations in demand and the costs of direct labor and materials.

Table 10.1 illustrates a simple format for a production or manufacturing budget for the first three months of operation. This provides an important basis for projecting cash flows for the cost of goods produced, which includes units in inventory. The important information

TABLE 10.1 A Sample Manufacturing Budget for First Three Months

	Jan.	Feb.	Mar.
Projected sales (units)	5,000	8,000	12,000
Desired ending inventory	100	200	300
Available for sale	5,100	8,200	12,300
Less: beginning inventory	0	100	200
Total production required	5,100	8,100	12,100

from this budget is the actual production required each month and the inventory that is necessary to allow for sudden changes in demand. As can be seen, the production required in the month of January is greater than the projected sales because of the need to retain 100 units in inventory. In February the actual production will take into consideration the inventory from January as well as the desired number of units needed in inventory for that month. This continues for each month, with inventory needs likely increasing as sales increase. Thus, this budget reflects seasonal demand or marketing programs that can increase demand and inventory. The pro forma income statement will only reflect the actual cost of goods sold as a direct expense. Thus, in those ventures in which high levels of inventory are necessary or where demand fluctuates significantly because of seasonality, this budget can be a very valuable tool to assess cash needs.

After completing the sales budget, the entrepreneur can then focus on operating costs. First a list of fixed expenses (incurred regardless of sales volume) such as rent, utilities, salaries, advertising, depreciation, and insurance should be completed. Estimated costs for many of these items can be ascertained from personal experience or industry benchmarks, or through direct contact with real estate brokers, insurance agents, and consultants. Industry benchmarks for preparing financial pro forma statements were discussed in the financial plan section of Chapter 7. Anticipation of the addition of space, new employees, and increased advertising can also be inserted in these projections as deemed appropriate. These variable expenses must be linked to strategy in the business plan. Table 10.2 provides an example of an operating budget. In this example we can see that salaries increase in month three because of the addition of a shipper, advertising increases because the primary season for this product is approaching, and payroll taxes increase because of the additional employee. This budget, along with the manufacturing budget illustrated in Table 10.1, provides the basis for the pro forma statements discussed in this chapter.

Capital budgets are intended to provide a basis for evaluating expenditures that will impact the business for more than one year. For example, a capital budget may project expenditures for new equipment, vehicles, computers, or even a new facility. It may also consider evaluating the costs of make or buy decisions in manufacturing or a comparison of leasing, buying used, or buying new equipment. Because of the complexity of these decisions, which can include the computation of the cost of capital and the anticipated return on the investment using present value methods, it is recommended that the entrepreneur enlist the assistance of an accountant.

TABLE 10.2 A Sample Operating Budget for First Three Months ($000s)

Expense	January	February	March
Salaries	$23.2	$23.2	$26.2
Rent	2	2	2
Utilities	0.9	0.9	0.9
Advertising	13.5	13.5	17
Selling expenses	1	1	1
Insurance	2	2	2
Payroll taxes	2.1	2.1	2.5
Depreciation	1.2	1.2	1.2
Office expenses	1.5	1.5	1.5
Total expenses	$47.4	$47.4	$53.9

PRO FORMA INCOME STATEMENTS

The marketing plan discussed in Chapter 8 provides an estimate of sales for the next 12 months. Since sales are the major source of revenue and since other operational activities and expenses relate to sales volume, it is usually the first item that must be defined.

Table 10.3 summarizes all the profit data during the first year of operations for MPP Plastics. This company makes plastic moldings for such customers as hard goods manufacturers, toy manufacturers, and appliance manufacturers. As can be seen from the *pro forma income* statement in Table 10.3, the company begins to earn a profit in the eleventh month. Cost of goods sold remains consistent at 50 percent of sales revenue.

pro forma income Projected net profit calculated from projected revenue minus projected costs and expenses

In preparation of the pro forma income statement, sales by month must be calculated first. Marketing research, industry sales, and some trial experience might provide the basis for these figures. Forecasting techniques such as survey of buyers' intentions, composite of sales force opinions, expert opinions, or time series may be used to project sales.[3] It may also be possible to find financial data on similar start-ups to assist with these projections. As would be expected, it will take a while for any new venture to build up sales. The costs for achieving these increases can be disproportionately higher in some months, depending on the given situation in any particular period.

Sales revenue for an Internet start-up is often more difficult to project since extensive advertising will be necessary to attract customers to the Web site. For example, a giftware Internet company can anticipate no sales in the first few months until awareness of the Web site has been created. Heavy advertising expenditures (discussed below) also will be incurred

TABLE 10.3 MPP Plastics, Inc., Pro Forma Income Statement, First Year by Month ($000s)

	Jan.	Feb.	Mar.	Apr.	May	June	July	Aug.	Sept.	Oct.	Nov.	Dec.	Totals
Sales	20.0	32.0	48.0	70.0	90.0	100.0	100.0	100.0	80.0	80.0	120.0	130.0	970.0
Less: Cost of goods sold	10.0	16.0	24.0	35.0	45.0	50.0	50.0	50.0	40.0	40.0	60.0	65.0	485.0
Gross profit	10.0	16.0	24.0	35.0	45.0	50.0	50.0	50.0	40.0	40.0	60.0	65.0	485.0
Operating expenses													
Salaries*	23.2	23.2	26.2	26.2	26.2	26.2	26.2	26.2	26.2	26.2	26.2	26.2	308.4
Rent	2.0	2.0	2.0	2.0	2.0	2.0	2.0	2.0	2.0	2.0	2.0	2.0	24.0
Utilities	0.9	0.9	0.9	0.8	0.8	0.8	0.9	0.9	0.9	0.8	0.8	0.9	10.3
Advertising	13.5	13.5	17.0	17.0	17.0	17.0	14.0	14.0	14.0	21.0†	17.0	17.0	192.0
Sales expenses	1.0	1.0	1.0	1.0	1.0	1.0	1.0	1.0	1.0	1.0	1.0	1.0	12.0
Insurance	2.0	2.0	2.0	2.0	2.0	2.0	2.0	2.0	2.0	2.0	2.0	2.0	24.0
Payroll taxes	2.1	2.1	2.5	2.5	2.5	2.5	2.5	2.5	2.5	2.5	2.5	2.5	29.2
Depreciation‡	1.2	1.2	1.2	1.2	1.2	1.2	1.2	1.2	1.2	1.2	1.2	1.2	14.4
Office expenses	1.5	1.5	1.5	1.7	1.8	2.0	2.0	2.0	1.8	1.8	2.2	2.2	22.0
Total operating expenses	47.4	47.4	54.3	54.4	54.5	54.7	51.8	51.8	51.6	58.5	54.9	55.0	636.3
Gross profit	(37.4)	(31.4)	(30.3)	(19.4)	(9.5)	(4.7)	(1.8)	(1.8)	(11.6)	(18.5)	5.1	10.0	(151.3)

* Added shipper in month three

†Trade show

‡Plant and equipment of $72,000 depreciated straight line for five years.

to create this awareness. Some data are now available on the number of "hits" by type of Web site. Thus, a giftware Internet start-up could project the number of average hits expected per day or month based on industry data. From the number of "hits" it is possible to project the number of consumers who will actually buy products from the Web site and the average dollar amount per transaction. Using a reasonable percentage of these "hits" times the average transaction will provide an estimate of sales revenue for the Internet start-up.

The pro forma income statements also provide projections of all operating expenses for each of the months during the first year. As discussed above and illustrated in Table 10.2, each of the expenses should be listed and carefully assessed to make sure that any increases in expenses are added in the appropriate month.[4] For example, selling expenses such as travel, commissions, and entertainment should be expected to increase somewhat as territories are expanded and as new salespeople or representatives are hired by the firm. Selling expenses as a percentage of sales also may be expected to be higher initially since more sales calls will have to be made to generate each sale, particularly when the firm is an unknown. The cost of goods sold expense can be determined either by directly computing the variable cost of producing a unit times the number of units sold or by using an industry standard percentage of sales. For example, for a restaurant, the National Restaurant Association or Food Marketing Institution publishes standard cost of goods percentages of sales. These percentages are determined from members and studies completed on the restaurant industry.

Salaries and wages for the company should reflect the number of personnel employed as well as their role in the organization (see the organization plan in Chapter 9). As new personnel are hired to support the increased business, the costs will need to be included in the pro forma statement. In March, for example, a shipper is added to the staff. Other increases in salaries and wages may also reflect raises in salary.

The entrepreneur should also consider increasing selling expenses as sales increase, adjusting taxes because of the addition of new personnel or raises in salary, increasing office expenses relative to the increase in sales, and modifying the advertising budget as a result of seasonality or simply because in the early months of start-up the budget may need to be higher to increase visibility. These adjustments actually occur in our MPP Plastics example (Table 10.3) and are reflected in the month-by-month pro forma income statement for year 1. Any noteworthy changes that are made in the pro forma income statement are also labeled, with explanations provided.

It is conceivable that an entrepreneur could experience changes in expenses during the first year that would necessitate month-by-month illustration. Likely examples of adjustments, besides those in our MPP Plastics example, might be increased rent because of the addition of new space, increased insurance expense as a result of adding a benefit program for employees, increased utilities expense because of the increase in office space, and depreciation expense if new equipment or furniture is purchased. The entrepreneur needs to consider any possible changes that might result in an increase in individual expenses and therefore need to be reflected in the first year's pro forma income statement.

In addition to the monthly pro forma income statement for the first year, projections should be made for years 2 and 3. Generally, investors prefer to see three years of income projections. Year 1 totals have already been calculated in Table 10.3. Table 10.4 illustrates the yearly totals of income statement items for each of the three years. Calculation of the percent of sales of each of the expense items for year 1 can be used by the entrepreneur as a guide for determining projected sales and expenses for year 2; those percentages then can be considered in making the projections for year 3. In addition, the calculation of percent of sales for each year is useful as a means of financial control so that the entrepreneur can ascertain whether any costs are too high relative to sales revenue. In year 3, the firm expects

TABLE 10.4 MPP Plastics, Inc., Pro Forma Income Statement, Three-Year Summary ($000s)

	Percent	Year 1	Percent	Year 2	Percent	Year 3
Sales	100.0	970.0	100.0	1,264.0	100.0	1,596.0
Less: Cost of goods sold	50.0	485.0	50.0	632.0	50.0	798.0
Gross profit	50.0	485.0	50.0	632.0	50.0	798.0
Operating expenses						
Salaries	31.8	308.4	24.4	308.4	21.8	348.4
Rent	2.5	24.0	1.9	24.0	1.5	24.0
Utilities	1.1	10.3	0.8	10.3	0.7	10.3
Advertising	19.8	192.0	13.5	170.0	11.3	180.0
Sales expenses	1.2	12.0	1.0	12.5	0.8	13.5
Insurance	2.4	24.0	1.9	24.0	1.5	24.0
Payroll & misc. taxes	3.0	29.2	2.3	29.2	2.0	32.0
Depreciation	1.5	14.4	1.1	14.4	0.9	14.4
Office expenses	2.3	22.0	1.8	22.5	1.5	23.5
Total operating expenses	65.6	636.3	48.7	615.3	42.0	670.1
Gross profit (loss)	(15.6)	(151.3)	1.3	16.3*	8.0	127.9*
Taxes	0.0	0.0	0.0	0.0	0.0	0.0
Net profit	(15.6)	(151.3)	1.3	16.3	8.0	127.9

*No taxes are incurred in profitable years two and three because of the carryover of losses in year one.

to significantly increase its profits as compared with the first and second years. In some instances, the entrepreneur may find that the new venture does not begin to earn a profit until sometime in year 2 or 3. This often depends on the nature of the business and start-up costs. For example, a service-oriented business may take less time to reach a profitable stage than a high-technology company or one that requires a large investment in capital goods and equipment, which will take longer to recover.

In the pro forma statements for MPP Plastics (Tables 10.3 and 10.4), we can see that the venture begins to earn a profit in the eleventh month of year 1. In the second year, the company does not need to spend as much money on advertising and, with the sales increase, shows a modest profit of $16,300. However, in year 3 we see that the venture adds an additional employee and also incurs a 26 percent increase in sales, resulting in a net profit of $127,900.

In projecting the operating expenses for years 2 and 3, it is helpful to first look at those expenses that will likely remain stable over time. Items like depreciation, utilities, rent, insurance, and interest can be more easily determined if you know the forecasted sales for years 2 and 3. Some utility expenses such as heat and power can be computed by using industry standard costs per square foot of space that is utilized by the new venture. Selling expenses, advertising, salaries and wages, and taxes may be represented as a percentage of the projected net sales. When calculating the projected operating expenses, it is most important to be conservative for initial planning purposes. A reasonable profit that is earned with conservative estimates lends credibility to the potential success of the new venture.

AS SEEN IN *ENTREPRENEUR* MAGAZINE

PROVIDE ADVICE TO AN ENTREPRENEUR ABOUT NONTRADITIONAL FINANCING

When Lissa D'Aquanni created a gourmet chocolate business in her Albany, New York, basement in 1998, she had not only a passion for candy-making, but also a knack for spurring citizen involvement. The former nonprofit executive had worked for women's advocacy groups, most recently promoting breast cancer awareness. If there was one thing she knew, it was how to rally community support.

Her ability to leverage local resources would be invaluable as she made her business a fixture of her Albany neighborhood. And in no area were those skills as critical as in financing. Last year, when D'Aquanni wanted to move her business, The Chocolate Gecko, to an abandoned building three blocks away, she needed $25,000 in owner's equity for the $260,000 renovation project. So she mailed letters to area residents soliciting financial support for her revitalization plan. "Within a month," she recalls, "we had raised the $25,000." Volunteers also helped renovate the building, cutting project costs from an estimated $300,000.

Check out D'Aquanni's unorthodox and creative financing plan: An economic development group, the Albany Local Development Corp., loaned her $95,000 to buy the building. D'Aquanni obtained a $100,000 government-guaranteed loan from a local credit union to renovate the structure. Facade improvements were funded through a matching grant program to encourage commercial development in Albany. A local community development financial institution used a state program to fund energy-efficient upgrades, including new windows, light fixtures, furnaces, and siding. Says D'Aquanni, "There were lots of different pieces of the puzzle to identify and figure out how to access."

Conventional financing wasn't an option. "I was looking at a business that did about $44,000 in sales doing a $260,000 project, and the traditional funders were apprehensive," explains D'Aquanni, 37. They urged her to rent a storefront rather than buy the rundown building. Undeterred, D'Aquanni met with a neighborhood group to develop her expansion plan. It wasn't the first time the community had helped out. In 1999, the cash-strapped chocolatier needed molds and a temperer for the Christmas rush. Recalling a strategy she had seen in a magazine, she sold discounted gift certificates to raise capital. D'Aquanni offered customers $25 in free chocolates for every $100 in gift certificates purchased. Within two weeks, she had $5,000 for the equipment purchase. "A lot of folks mailed them as gifts to friends, family, and co-workers," D'Aquanni says. "And most of those people ordered chocolates. My customer base exploded."

Indeed, many entrepreneurs successfully launch a business only to encounter funding hardships as they attempt to grow. The ability to think outside the box, experts say, is critical for firms short on funding. "There are pockets of money out there, whether it be municipalities, counties, chambers of commerce," says Bill Brigham, director of the Small Business Development Center in Albany. "Those are the loan programs that no one seems to have information about. A lot of these programs will not require the collateral and cash that is typical of traditional [loans]. They may be a little more lenient as far as credit history goes. That's one of the key roles we can play—what entrepreneur is going to think [he or she] can qualify for HUD money?"

ADVICE TO AN ENTREPRENEUR

An entrepreneur who is looking to expand but has limited access to traditional financing has read the above article and comes to you for advice:

1. I want to find a little pot of gold like Lissa D'Aquanni. Where should I look?
2. I like the gift certificate idea to raise money and build my business. What other types of products do you think that approach will work for?
3. Over the years I have paid a lot of taxes. Should I feel guilty for accessing government-subsidized monies to build my business, or should I feel justified?

Source: Reprinted with permission of Entrepreneur Media, Inc., "Out on a Limb. When the Money Tree Looks Dry, Sometimes You Just Have to Create Your Own Branch," by Crystal Detamore-Rodman, March 2003, *Entrepreneur* magazine: www.entrepreneur.com.

For the Internet start-up, capital budgeting and operating expenses will tend to be consumed by equipment purchasing or leasing, inventory, and advertising expenses. For example, the giftware Internet company introduced earlier would need to purchase or lease an extensive amount of computer equipment to accommodate the potential buyers from the Web site. Inventory costs would be based on the projected sales revenue just as would be the case for any retail store. Advertising costs, however, would need to be extensive to create the awareness for the giftware Web site. These expenses would typically involve a selection of search engines such as Yahoo!, Lycos, and Google; links from the Web sites of magazines such as *Woman's Day, Family Circle,* and *Better Homes and Garden;* and extensive media advertising in magazines, television, radio, and print—all selected because of their link to the target market.

PRO FORMA CASH FLOW

Cash flow is not the same as profit. Profit is the result of subtracting expenses from sales, whereas cash flow results from the difference between actual cash receipts and cash payments. Cash flows only when actual payments are received or made. Sales may not be regarded as cash because a sale may be incurred but payment may not be made for 30 days. In addition, not all bills are paid immediately. On the other hand, cash payments to reduce the principal on a loan do not constitute a business expense but do constitute a reduction of cash. Also, depreciation on capital assets is an expense, which reduces profits, not a cash outlay.

For an Internet start-up such as our giftware company discussed above, the sales transaction would involve the use of a credit card in which a percentage of the sale would be paid as a fee to the credit card company. This is usually between 1 and 3 percent depending on the credit card. Thus, for each sale only 97 to 99 percent of the revenue would be net revenue because of this fee.

As stated earlier, one of the major problems that new ventures face is cash flow. On many occasions, profitable firms fail because of lack of cash. Thus, using profit as a measure of success for a new venture may be deceiving if there is a significant negative cash flow.

For strict accounting purposes there are two standard methods used to project cash flow, the indirect and the direct method. The most popular of these is the indirect method, which is illustrated in Table 10.5. In this method the objective is not to repeat what is in the income statement but to understand there are some adjustments that need to be made to the net income based on the fact that actual cash may or may not have actually been received or disbursed. For example, a sales transaction of $1,000 may be included in net income, but if the amount has not yet been paid, no cash has been received. Thus, for cash flow purposes there is no cash available from the sales transaction. For simplification and internal monitoring of cash flow purposes, many entrepreneurs prefer a simple determination of cash in less cash out. This method provides a fast indication of the cash position of the new venture at a point in time and is sometimes easier to understand.

It is important for the entrepreneur to make monthly projections of cash like the monthly projections made for profits. The numbers in the cash flow projections are constituted from the pro forma income statement with modifications made to account for the expected timing of the changes in cash. If disbursements are greater than receipts in any time period, the entrepreneur must either borrow funds or have cash in a bank account to cover the higher disbursements. Large positive cash flows in any time period may need to be invested in short-term sources or deposited in a bank in order to cover future time periods when disbursements are greater than receipts. Usually the first few months of the start-up will require external cash (debt) in order to cover the cash outlays. As the business succeeds and cash receipts accumulate, the entrepreneur can support negative cash periods.

TABLE 10.5 Statement of Cash Flows: The Indirect Method

Cash Flow from Operating Activities: (+ or − Reflects Addition or Subtraction from Net Income)	
Net income	XXX
Adjustments to net income:	
Noncash nonoperating items:	
+ depreciation and amortization	XXX
Cash provided by changes in current assets or liabilities:	
Increase(+) or decrease(−) in accounts receivable	XXX
Increase(+) or decrease(−) in inventory	XXX
Increase(+) or decrease(−) in prepaid expenses	XXX
Increase(+) or decrease(−) in accounts payable	XXX
Net cash provided by operating activities	XX,XXX
Cash Flow from Other Activities	
Capital expenditures (−)	(XXX)
Payments of debt (−)	(XXX)
Dividends paid (−)	(XXX)
Sale of stock (+)	XXX
Net cash provided by other activities	(XXX)
Increase (Decrease) in Cash	**XXX**

pro forma cash flow Projected cash available calculated from projected cash accumulations minus projected cash disbursements

Table 10.6 illustrates the *pro forma cash flow* over the first 12 months for MPP Plastics. As can be seen, there is a negative cash flow based on receipts less disbursements for the first 11 months of operation. The likelihood of incurring negative cash flows is very high for any new venture, but the amount and length of time before cash flows become positive will vary, depending on the nature of the business. In Chapter 14 we discuss how the entrepreneur can manage cash flow in the early years of a new venture. For this chapter, we will focus on how to project cash flow before the venture is launched.

The most difficult problem with projecting cash flows is determining the exact monthly receipts and disbursements. Some assumptions are necessary and should be conservative so that enough funds can be maintained to cover the negative cash months. In this firm, it is anticipated that 60 percent of each month's sales will be received in cash with the remaining 40 percent paid in the subsequent month. Thus, in February we can see that the cash receipts from sales totaled $27,200. This resulted from cash sales in February of 60 percent of $32,000, or $19,200, plus the 40 percent of sales that occurred in January (.40 × $20,000 = $8,000) but was not paid until February, thus resulting in the total cash received in February of $27,200. This process continues throughout the remaining months in year 1.

Similar assumptions are made for the cost of goods disbursement. It is assumed in our example that 80 percent of the cost of goods is paid in the month that it is incurred, with the remainder paid in the following month. Thus, referring back to Table 10.3, we can note that in February the actual cost of goods was $16,000. However, we actually pay only 80 percent of this in the month incurred—but we also pay 20 percent of the cost of goods sold that is still due from January. Thus, the actual cost of goods cash outflow in February is .8 × $16,000 + .2 × $10,000, or a total of $14,800.

TABLE 10.6 MPP Plastics, Inc., Pro Forma Cash Flow, First Year by Month ($000s)

	Jan.	Feb.	Mar.	Apr.	May	June	July	Aug.	Sept.	Oct.	Nov.	Dec.
Receipts												
Sales	12.0	27.2	41.6	61.2	82.0	96.0	100.0	100.0	88.0	80.0	104.0	126.0
Disbursements												
Equipment purchase	72.0	—	—	—	—	—	—	—	—	—	—	—
Cost of goods	8.0	14.8	22.4	37.6	43.0	49.0	50.0	50.0	42.0	40.0	56.0	60.0
Salaries	23.2	23.2	26.2	26.2	26.2	26.2	26.2	26.2	26.2	26.2	26.2	26.2
Rent	2.0	2.0	2.0	2.0	2.0	2.0	2.0	2.0	2.0	2.0	2.0	2.0
Utilities	0.9	0.9	0.9	0.8	0.8	0.8	0.9	0.9	0.9	0.8	0.8	0.9
Advertising	13.5	13.5	17.0	17.0	17.0	17.0	14.0	14.0	14.0	21.0	17.0	17.0
Sales expense	1.0	1.0	1.0	1.0	1.0	1.0	1.0	1.0	1.0	1.0	1.0	1.0
Insurance	2.0	2.0	2.0	2.0	2.0	2.0	2.0	2.0	2.0	2.0	2.0	2.0
Payroll & misc. taxes	2.1	2.1	2.5	2.5	2.5	2.5	2.5	2.5	2.5	2.5	2.5	2.5
Office expenses	1.5	1.5	1.5	1.7	1.8	2.0	2.0	2.0	1.8	1.8	2.2	2.2
Inventory*	0.2	0.4	0.6	0.6	0.8	0.8	1.0	1.0	1.0	1.0	1.2	1.2
Total disbursements	126.4	61.4	76.1	91.4	97.1	103.3	101.6	101.6	93.4	98.3	110.9	115.0
Cash flow	(114.4)	(34.2)	(34.5)	(30.2)	(15.1)	(7.3)	(1.6)	(1.6)	(5.4)	(18.3)	(6.9)	11.0
Beginning balance†	300.0	185.6	151.4	116.9	86.7	71.6	64.3	62.7	61.1	55.7	37.4	30.5
Ending balance	185.6	151.4	116.9	86.7	71.6	64.3	62.7	61.1	55.7	37.4	30.5	41.5

*Inventory is valued at cost or average of $2.00/unit.

†Three founders put up $100,000 each for working capital through the first three years. After the third year the venture will need debt or equity financing for expansion.

Using conservative estimates, cash flows can be determined for each month. These cash flow projections assist the entrepreneur in determining how much money he or she will need to raise to meet the cash demands of the venture. In our example, the venture starts with a total of $300,000, or $100,000 from each of the three founders. We can see that by the twelfth month the venture begins to turn a positive cash flow from operations, still leaving enough cash available ($41,500) should the projections fall short of expectations. If the entrepreneurs in our example had to use debt for the start up, then they would need to show the interest payments in the income statement as an operating expense and indicate the principal payments to the bank as a cash disbursement, not as an operating expense. This issue often creates cash flow problems for entrepreneurs when they do not realize that debt is a cash disbursement only and that interest is an operating expense.

It is most important for the entrepreneur to remember that the pro forma cash flow, like the income statement, is based on best estimates. As the venture begins, it may be necessary to revise cash flow projections to ensure that their accuracy will protect the firm from any impending disaster. The estimates or projections should include any assumptions so that potential investors will understand how and from where the numbers were generated.[5]

In the case of both the pro forma income statement and the pro forma cash flow, it is sometimes useful to provide several scenarios, each based on different levels of success of the business. These scenarios and projections not only serve the purpose of generating pro forma income and cash flow statements but, more importantly, familiarize the entrepreneur with the factors affecting the operations.

PRO FORMA BALANCE SHEET

The entrepreneur should also prepare a projected balance sheet depicting the condition of the business at the end of the first year. The balance sheet will require the use of the pro forma income and cash flow statements to help justify some of the figures.[6]

pro forma balance sheet Summarizes the projected assets, liabilities, and net worth of the new venture

The *pro forma balance sheet* reflects the position of the business at the end of the first year. It summarizes the assets, liabilities, and net worth of the entrepreneurs.

Every business transaction affects the balance sheet, but because of the time and expense, as well as need, it is common to prepare balance sheets at periodic intervals (i.e., quarterly or annually). Thus, the balance sheet is a picture of the business at a certain moment in time and does not cover a period of time.

Table 10.7 depicts the balance sheet for MPP Plastics. As can be seen, the total assets equal the sum of the liabilities and owners' equity. Each of the categories is explained below:

assets Items that are owned or available to be used in the venture operations

- *Assets*. These represent everything of value that is owned by the business. Value is not necessarily meant to imply the cost of replacement or what its market value would be but is the actual cost or amount expended for the asset. The assets are categorized as current or fixed. Current assets include cash and anything else that is

TABLE 10.7 MPP Plastics, Inc., Pro Forma Balance Sheet, End of First Year ($000s)

Assets		
Current assets		
Cash	$41.5	
Accounts receivable	52.0	
Inventory	1.2	
Total current assets		$ 94.7
Fixed assets		
Equipment	72.0	
Less depreciation	14.4	
Total fixed assets		57.6
Total assets		$152.3
Liabilities and Owners' Equity		
Current liabilities		
Accounts payable	$13.6	
Total liabilities		$ 13.6
Owners' equity		
K. Peters	100.0	
C. Peters	100.0	
J. Welch	100.0	
Retained earnings	(151.3)	
Total owners' equity		148.7
Total liabilities and owners' equity		$152.3

AS SEEN IN *ENTREPRENEUR* MAGAZINE

ELEVATOR PITCH FOR TARYN ROSE INTERNATIONAL INC.

A wealthy friend has asked you to keep your eye out for attractive businesses in which she can invest. Your wealthy friend is very busy and you only want to introduce those businesses that are genuinely attractive. After hearing the following pitch, would you introduce Taryn Rose to your wealthy friend?

Vital Stats: Taryn Rose, 35, founder of Taryn Rose International Inc.

Company: High-end shoes for women and men that boast classic style and handcrafted comfort

Sales: $15 million projected for 2003

Woe My Feet! "I was a resident at USC School of Medicine, on my feet up to 14 hours a day. I had a hard time finding shoes attractive enough to go with my wardrobe, but also comfortable enough to meet my functional needs. Also, I saw a lot of women who needed foot surgery because of tight footwear. I thought, 'I should see if there is something out in the market.'"

Say Again, Doc? "My family was opposed [to my starting a business]. They're a traditional Asian family. They thought I was giving up prestige and a good income to take on a lot of risk. For me, that was exciting. That was how I wanted to live—to have a vision, build on that vision and be proud."

More Talk, Less Ads: "I find editorial is more important than advertising because we want to educate so people understand what we're all about, and you can't do that with an ad."

Sole Searcher: "I targeted a niche, the luxury market, with comfort as a philosophy. My customers are like myself—independent [people] who are in control of their lives. They're not victims anywhere, and they're not going to be fashion victims."

Source: Reprinted with permission of Entrepreneur Media, Inc., "An Orthopedic Surgeon-Turned-Entrepreneur Proves to the World She Can Stand Tall on Her Own," by April Y. Pennington, January 2003, *Entrepreneur* magazine: www.entrepreneur.com.

expected to be converted into cash or consumed in the operation of the business during a period of one year or less. Fixed assets are those that are tangible and will be used over a long period of time. These current assets are often dominated by receivables or money that is owed to the new venture from customers. Management of these receivables is important to the cash flow of the business since the longer it takes for customers to pay their bills, the more stress is placed on the cash needs of the venture. A more detailed discussion of the management of receivables is presented in Chapter 14.

liabilities Money that is owed to creditors

- *Liabilities*. These accounts represent everything owed to creditors. Some of these amounts may be due within a year (current liabilities), and others may be long-term debts. There are no long-term liabilities in our MPP Plastics example because the venture used funds from the founders to start the business. However, should the entrepreneurs need to borrow money from a bank for the future purchase of equipment or for additional growth capital, the balance sheet would show long-term liabilities in the form of a note payable equal to the principal amount borrowed. As stated earlier, any interest on this note would appear as an expense in the income statement and the payment of any principal would be shown in the cash flow statement. Subsequent end-of-year balance sheets would show only the remaining amount of principal due on the note payable. Although prompt payment of what is owed (payables) establishes good credit ratings and a good relationship with suppliers, it is often necessary to delay payments of bills in order to more effectively manage cash flow. Ideally, any business owner wants bills to be paid on time by suppliers so that he or she can pay any bills owed on time. Unfortunately, during recessions, many firms hold back payment of their bills in order to better manage cash flow. The problem with this strategy is that while the entrepreneur may think that slower payment of bills will generate better cash flow, he or she may also find that customers are thinking the same thing, with the result that no one gains any cash advantage. These issues are discussed in more detail in Chapter 14.

owner equity The amount owners have invested and/or retained from the venture operations

- *Owner equity*. This amount represents the excess of all assets over all liabilities. It represents the net worth of the business. The $300,000 that was invested into the business by MPP Plastics's three entrepreneurs is included in the owners' equity or net worth section of the balance sheet. Any profit from the business will also be included in the net worth as retained earnings. In our MPP Plastics example, retained earnings is negative, based on the net loss incurred in year one. Thus, revenue increases assets and owners' equity, and expenses decrease owners' equity and either increase liabilities or decrease assets.

BREAK-EVEN ANALYSIS

In the initial stages of the new venture, it is helpful for the entrepreneur to know when a profit may be achieved. This will provide further insight into the financial potential for the start-up business. Break-even analysis is a useful technique for determining how many units must be sold or how much sales volume must be achieved in order to break even.

We already know from the projections in Table 10.3 that MPP Plastics will begin to earn a profit in the eleventh month. However, this is not the break-even point since the firm has obligations for the remainder of the year that must be met, regardless of the number of units sold. These obligations, or fixed costs, must be covered by sales volume in order for a company to break even. Thus, *breakeven* is that volume of sales at which the business will neither make a profit nor incur a loss.

breakeven Volume of sales where the venture neither makes a profit nor incurs a loss

The break-even sales point indicates to the entrepreneur the volume of sales needed to cover total variable and fixed expenses. Sales in excess of the break-even point will result in a profit as long as the selling price remains above the costs necessary to produce each unit (variable cost).[7]

The break-even formula is derived in Table 10.8 and is given as:

$$B/E(Q) = \frac{TFC}{SP - VC/\text{Unit (marginal contribution)}}$$

As long as the selling price is greater than the variable costs per unit, some contribution can be made to cover fixed costs. Eventually, these contributions will be sufficient to pay all fixed costs, at which point the firm has reached breakeven.

The major weakness in calculating the breakeven lies in determining whether a cost is fixed or variable. For new ventures these determinations will require some judgment. However, it is reasonable to regard costs such as depreciation, salaries and wages, rent, and insurance as fixed. Materials, selling expenses such as commissions, and direct labor are most likely to be variable costs. The variable costs per unit usually can be determined by allocating the direct labor, materials, and other expenses that are incurred with the production of a single unit.

Recall that in our MPP Plastics example the venture produces plastic molded parts for the toy industry and hard goods and appliance manufacturers. Since the company is likely to be selling a large volume of these parts at various prices, it is necessary to make an assumption regarding the average selling price based on production and sales

TABLE 10.8 Determining the Break-Even Formula

By definition, breakeven is where Total Revenue (*TR*)	= Total Costs (*TC*)
Also by definition:	
(*TR*)	= Selling Price (*SP*) × Quantity (*Q*)
and (*TC*)	= Total Fixed Costs (*TFC*)* + Total Variable Costs (*TVC*)†
Thus: $SP \times Q = TFC + TVC$	
Where *TVC*	= Variable Costs/Unit (*VC*/Unit)‡ × Quantity (*Q*)
Thus $SP \times Q = TFC + (VC/\text{Unit} \times Q)$	
$(SP \times Q) - (VC/\text{Unit} \times Q)$	$= TFC$
$Q\,(SP - VC/\text{Unit})$	$= TFC$
Finally, Breakeven(*Q*)	$= \dfrac{TFC}{SP - VC/\text{Unit}}$

* Fixed costs are those costs that, without change in present productive capacity, are not affected by changes in volume of output.

†Variable costs are those that are affected in total by changes in volume of output.

‡The variable costs per unit is all those costs attributable to producing one unit. This cost is constant within defined ranges of production.

revenue. The entrepreneurs determine that the average selling price of all these components is \$4.00/unit. From the pro forma income statement (Table 10.4) we see that fixed costs in year 1 are \$636,300. We also know from our example that cost of goods sold is 50 percent of sales revenue so we can assume a variable cost per unit of \$2.00. Using these calculations we can then determine the venture's break-even point in units as follows:

$$
\begin{aligned}
B/E &= \frac{TFC}{SP - VC/\text{Unit}} \\
&= \frac{\$636{,}300}{\$4.00 - \$2.00} \\
&= \frac{\$636{,}300}{\$2.00} \\
&= 318{,}150 \text{ units}
\end{aligned}
$$

Any units beyond the 318,150 that are sold by the venture will result in a profit of \$2.00 per unit. Sales below this number will result in a loss for the company. In cases where the firm produces more than one product and it is feasible to allocate fixed costs to each product, then it is possible to calculate a break-even point for each product. Fixed costs are determined by weighting the costs as a function of the sales projections for each product. For example, if it is assumed that 40 percent of the sales are for product X, then 40 percent of fixed costs should be allocated to that product.

In our MPP Plastics example, the large number of different products and the size lots of customer purchases prohibit any individual product break-even calculation. In this case we estimate the average selling price of all components for use in our calculations.

One of the unique aspects of breakeven is that it can be graphically displayed, as in Figure 10.1. In addition, the entrepreneur can try different states of nature (e.g., different selling prices, different fixed costs and/or variable costs) to ascertain the impact on breakeven and subsequent profits.

FIGURE 10.1 Graphics Illustration of Breakeven

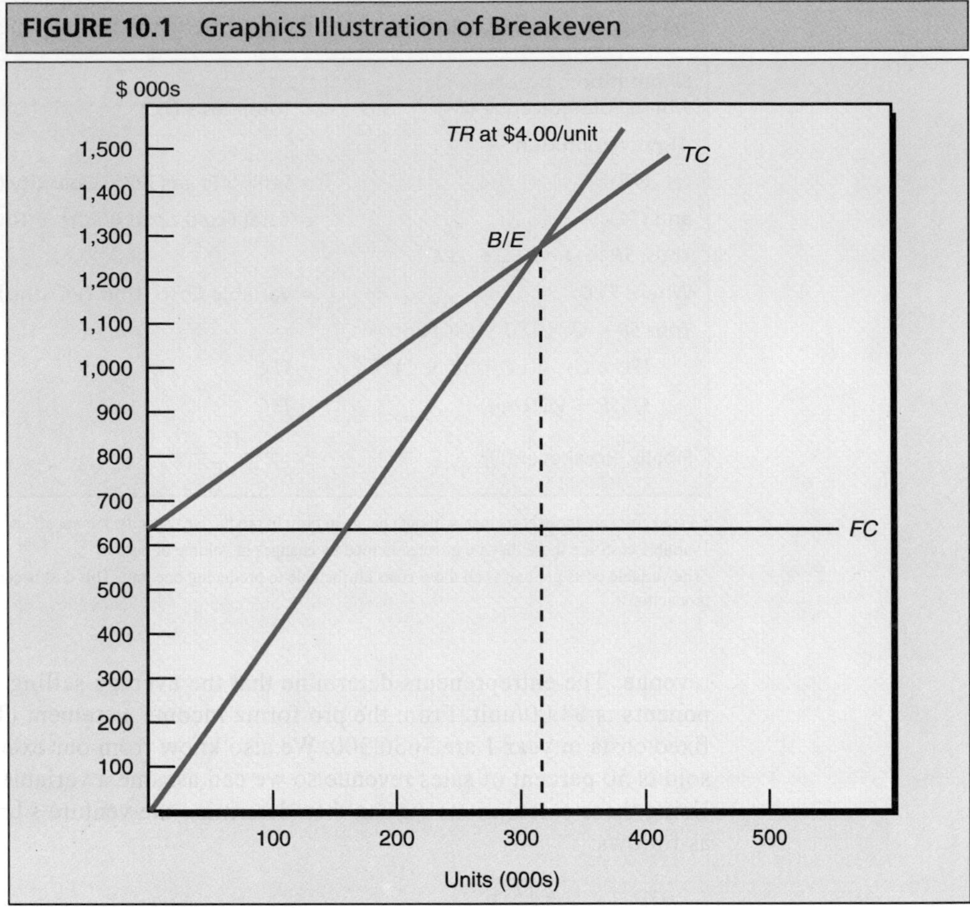

PRO FORMA SOURCES AND APPLICATIONS OF FUNDS

pro forma sources and applications of funds Summarizes all the projected sources of funds available to the venture and how these funds will be disbursed

The *pro forma sources and applications of funds* statement illustrates the disposition of earnings from operations and from other financing. Its purpose is to show how net income and financing were used to increase assets or to pay off debt.

It is often difficult for the entrepreneur to understand how the net income for the year was disposed of and the effect of the movement of cash through the business. Questions often asked are, Where did the cash come from? How was the cash used? What happened to asset items during the period?

Table 10.9 shows the pro forma sources and applications of funds for MPP Plastics, Inc., after the first year of operation. Many of the funds were obtained from personal funds or loans. Since at the end of the first year a profit was earned, it too would be added to the sources of funds. Depreciation is added back because it does not represent an out-of-pocket expense. Thus, typical sources of funds are from operations, new investments, long-term borrowing, and sale of assets. The major uses or applications of funds are to increase assets, retire long-term liabilities, reduce owner or stockholders' equity, and pay dividends. The sources and applications of funds statement emphasizes the interrelationship of these items to working capital. The statement helps the entrepreneur as well as investors to better understand the financial well-being of the company as well as the effectiveness of the financial management policies of the company.

TABLE 10.9 MPP Plastics, Inc., Pro Forma Sources and Applications of Funds, End of First Year

Source of funds		
Personal funds of founders	$ 300,000	
Net income (loss) from operations	(151,300)	
Add depreciation	14,400	
Total funds provided		$163,100
Application of funds		
Purchase of equipment	$ 72,000	
Inventory	1,200	
Total funds expended		73,200
Net increase in working capital		89,900
		$163,100

SOFTWARE PACKAGES

There are a number of financial software packages available for the entrepreneur that can track financial data and generate any important financial statement. For purposes of completing the pro forma statements, at least in the business planning stage, it is probably easiest to use a spreadsheet program, since numbers may change often as the entrepreneur begins to develop budgets for the pro forma statements. Microsoft Excel is the most widely used spreadsheet software and is available in Macintosh and PC formats.

The value of using a spreadsheet in the start-up phase for financial projections is simply being able to present different scenarios and assess their impact on the pro forma statements. It helps answer such questions as, What would be the effect of a price decrease of 10 percent on my pro forma income statement? What would be the impact of an increase of 10 percent in operating expenses? How would the lease versus purchase of equipment affect my cash flow? This type of analysis, using the computer spreadsheet software, will provide a quick assessment of the likely financial projections given different scenarios.

It is recommended in the start-up stage, where the venture is very small and limited in time and resources, that the software selected be very simple and easy to use. The entrepreneur will need software to maintain the books and to generate financial statements. Most of these software packages allow for check writing, payroll, invoicing, inventory management, bill paying, credit management, and taxes.

The software packages vary in price and complexity. The simplest to use and least expensive ($99–$299) software products are QuickBooks (Intuit Inc.), Peachtree (Best Software), and packages offered by Medlin Accounting and Checkmark Software Inc. These packages offer basic payroll and general ledger accounting software for the start-up venture. They typically offer tutorials and support geared toward the successful implementation of these packages, particularly for new users. Best software also offers more comprehensive accounting software, as do many other companies. Prices for these packages can range from $199 to $999 (and up) depending on the comprehensiveness of the software. Some of the more popular of these comprehensive software packages

CRIMES AGAINST THE INFORMATION AGE

In this era, the price of bad data can be disaster. When a company lies or inflates its numbers, everyone suffers: Investors, the financial markets, and even competitors.

Here's a simple observation: Many of the leading figures in today's corporate scandals, such as Kenneth Lay and Jeffrey Skilling of Enron, Bernard Ebbers of WorldCom, and Gary Winnick of Global Crossing, may never be convicted of a single crime. They got approval from their boards of directors and accountants for most of their actions. And while their financing and accounting techniques were aggressive to an extreme, they may not rise to the level needed to put the executives in jail.

But that's no solace to investors, who discovered all too late that those companies and a slew of others were far weaker than they believed: Debt levels were higher, true revenues were lower, and prospects for future growth far less optimistic than the executives had made them seem at the time.

Misrepresentations by top executives can jeopardize the efficiency of the financial markets. In particular, the accounting misrepresentations at companies such as WorldCom and Qwest Communications kept far too much capital flowing for too long into the telecom sector—perhaps as much as $30 billion, much of that in bonds which will never be paid back. That's money that could have been used much more profitably and productively elsewhere.

The financial markets are not the only ones to suffer when a company provides bad information. Competitors in the same industry are hurt, too. They're keenly aware of how their rivals are doing, especially in a sector with rapid technological change. If one company seems to be faring exceptionally well, everyone else tries to figure out why and copy it. That's how innovations diffuse through an economy.

That process doesn't work right if one company is lying about its performance. When Enron Corp. reported revenue growth of 70 percent annually from 1997 to 2000, and operating profit growth of 35 percent a year, that drew other electric and gas utility companies into energy trading. The fact that Enron achieved much of its gains by moving debt off the books and using other accounting tricks was not obvious at the time. Similarly, in 1999 and 2000 WorldCom Inc. reported operating profits equal to 21.4 percent of sales, compared to 15.4 percent at Sprint and 11.8 percent at AT&T, its two main competitors. If WorldCom's profits were in part bogus, that meant Sprint and AT&T were getting the wrong signals: They weren't doing as badly compared to WorldCom as it appeared.

Finally, companies that provide bad information to outsiders end up hurting themselves. Internal financial reports are supposed to help executives determine which parts of their company need improvement. But the accounting at companies like Enron and WorldCom hid rather than illuminated, and these troubled companies didn't make the changes they needed to survive. The result: two major bankruptcies, leading to economywide disruptions.

Nobody would seriously consider instituting a new class of felony consisting of "crimes against the economy." But the damage that these executives have done is measured in billions—and we are all going to pay.

Source: Adapted from Michael J. Mandel, "Crimes against the Information Age," *BusinessWeek* (August 19, 2002), pp. 80–81.

(besides Peachtree) are Microsoft Office Small Business Accounting, Redwing Software, and Cougar Mountain Software, to name a few. A simple Google Internet search will identify hundreds of accounting software companies. The most basic and most popular comprehensive packages are mentioned above and these usually can be purchased online or at a local computer store. If a more comprehensive package is needed, the entrepreneur should discuss the options with a business associate, friend, or consultant who can assess his or her needs, evaluate the benefits of the most appropriate options, and assist the entrepreneur in selecting the package that will best fit the venture's needs.

IN REVIEW

SUMMARY

This chapter introduces several financial projection techniques. A single fictitious example of a new venture (MPP Plastics, Inc.) is used to illustrate how to prepare each pro forma statement. Each of the planning tools is designed to provide the entrepreneur with a clear picture of where funds come from, how they are disbursed, the amount of cash available, and the general financial well-being of the new venture.

The pro forma income statement provides a sales estimate in the first year (monthly basis) and projects operating expenses each month. These estimates are determined from the appropriate budgets, which are based on marketing plan projections and objectives.

Cash flow is not the same as profit. It reflects the difference between cash actually received and cash disbursements. Some cash disbursements are not operating expenses (e.g., repayment of loan principal); likewise, some operating expenses are not a cash disbursement (e.g., depreciation expense). Many new ventures have failed because of a lack of cash, even when the venture is profitable.

The pro forma balance sheet reflects the condition of the business at the end of a particular period. It summarizes the assets, liabilities, and net worth of the firm.

The break-even point can be determined from projected income. This measures the point where total revenue equals total cost.

The pro forma sources and applications of funds statement helps the entrepreneur to understand how the net income for the year was disposed of and the effect of the movement of cash through the business. It emphasizes the interrelationship of assets, liabilities, and stockholders' equity to working capital.

Software packages to assist the entrepreneur in accounting, payroll, inventory, billing, and so on are readily available. The cost of these packages will vary depending on the size and type of business.

RESEARCH TASKS

1. Research the software packages available to help entrepreneurs with the financials for a business plan. Which do you believe is the best? Why?
2. Companies planning to make an initial public offering (IPO) must submit a financial plan as part of their prospectus. From the Internet collect a prospectus from three different companies and analyze their financial plans. What were the major assumptions made in constructing these financial plans? Compare and contrast these financial plans with what we would expect of a financial plan as part of a business plan.
3. Find an initial public offering prospectus for three companies. What items are listed as assets? As liabilities? How much is the owners' equity? For what purpose do they say they are going to use the additional funds raised from the initial public offering?

CLASS DISCUSSION

1. Is it more important for an entrepreneur to track cash or profits? Does it depend on the type of business and/or industry? What troubles will an entrepreneur face if she or he tracks only profits and ignores cash? What troubles will an entrepreneur face if she or he tracks only cash and ignores profits?

2. What volume of sales is required to reach breakeven for the following business: The variable cost of producing one unit of the product is $5, the fixed costs of plant and labor are $500,000, and the selling price of a single product is $50. It is not always easy to classify a cost as fixed or variable. What happens to the breakeven calculated above if some of the fixed costs are reclassified as variable costs? What happens if the reverse is the case—some of the variable costs are reclassified as fixed costs?
3. How useful is a financial plan when it is based on assumptions of the future and we are confident that these assumptions are not going to be 100 percent correct?

SELECTED READINGS

Adelman, Philip J.; and Alan M. Marks. (2004). *Entrepreneurial Finance—Finance for Small Businesses*, 3rd ed. Upper Saddle River, N.J.: Prentice-Hall, Inc.

A practical-oriented text that focuses specifically on the needs of individuals starting their own businesses. Its emphasis is on financial issues for proprietorships, partnerships, limited liability companies, and S corporations.

Barth, Mary E.; Donald P. Cram; and Karen K. Nelson. (2001). Accruals and the Prediction of Future Cash Flows. *The Accounting Review*, vol. 76, no. 1, pp. 27–58.

This study investigates the role of accruals in predicting future cash flows. The model shows that each accrual component reflects different information relating to future cash flows; aggregate earnings mask this information. The cash flow and accrual components of current earnings have substantially more predictive ability for future cash flows than several lags of aggregate earnings.

Bodie, Zvi; Robert S. Kaplan; and Robert C. Merton. (2003). For the Last Time: Stock Options Are an Expense. *Harvard Business Review*, pp. 62–71.

The authors of the article believe that the case for expensing options is overwhelming and examine and dismiss the principal claims put forward by those who continue to oppose it. They demonstrate that stock option grants have real cash flow implications, that the way to quantify these implications is available, that footnote disclosure is not an acceptable substitute for reporting, and that full recognition of option costs need not emasculate the incentives of entrepreneurial ventures.

Carter, Richard B.; and Howard Van Auken. (2005). Bootstrap Financing and Owners' Perceptions of Their Business Constraints and Opportunities. *Entrepreneurship and Regional Development*, vol. 17, no. 2, pp. 129–44.

The results of a regional survey of small business entrepreneurs are presented. These entrepreneurs were queried regarding their use of and their motivation to use bootstrap financing. Extending the work of Winborg and Landstrom, these results indicate that perceived risk is highly associated with the owners' assessment of the importance of bootstrap financing techniques. The results should be helpful to consultants and agencies that assist small firms with funding alternatives.

Gahagan, Jim. (2004). Reaching for Financial Success. *Strategic Finance*, vol. 20, no. 7, pp. 12–13.

This article discusses the importance of reaching financial success for a business enterprise. As market conditions change dramatically within a single planning period, budgeting and planning forecasts and the financial plans they produce are critical to the business owner.

Gramlich, Jeffrey D.; Mary Lea McNally; and Jacob Thomas. (2001). Balance Sheet Management: Case of Short-Term Obligations Reclassified as Long-Term Debt. *Journal of Accounting Research*, vol. 39, no. 2, pp. 283–95.

This paper investigates the potential management of balance sheet ratios by a sample of firms that reclassify short-term obligations as long-term debt and subsequently declassify that debt (return it to the current liability section). The results suggest that firms reclassify and declassify to smooth reported liquidity and leverage relative to the prior year and to industry benchmarks.

Hope, Jeremy; and Robin Fraser. (2000). Beyond Budgeting. *Financial Management*, October 2000, pp. 30–35.

This article argues that the traditional performance management model is too rigid to reflect today's fast-moving economy. Only by overcoming the constraints of the traditional budgeting approach can managers build a business model that operates at high speed; is self-questioning, self-renewing, and self-controlling; and rewards innovation and learning.

Hope, Jeremy; and Robin Fraser. (2001). Figures of Hate. *Financial Management*, February 2001, pp. 22–25.

This article argues that traditional budgets hold companies back, restrict staff creativity, and prevent them from responding to customers. The authors describe a new method called "Beyond Budgeting" that consists of 12 principles of effective organization and behavior and effective performance management. In essence, the new approach entails a shift from a numbers-based performance emphasis to one based on people.

Jordan, Charles E.; and Marilyn A. Waldron. (2001). Predicting Cash Flow from Operations: Evidence on the Comparative Abilities for a Continuum of Measures. *Journal of Applied Business Research*, vol. 17, no. 3, pp. 87–94.

Prior studies have attempted to confirm or reject the assertion that accrual accounting measures provide better information for predicting cash flows than do cash basis measures. However, their results have proved largely inconclusive and contradictory. This study identifies research constructs that may have driven these inconsistent findings and makes adjustments to mitigate their effects.

Rappaport, Alfred. (2005). The Economics of Short-Term Performance. *Financial Analysts Journal*, vol. 61, no. 3, pp. 65–79.

This article focuses on a three-pronged program for reducing short-term corporate performance obsession. The author argues that short-term performance is particularly important to young companies. However, it is important to recognize that because there is such flexibility in estimating the timing of accruals, these short-term performance predictions may not accurately picture the cash flow forecasts.

Rezaee, Zabihollah. (2003). High Quality Financial Reporting. The Six-Legged Stool. *Strategic Finance*, February 2003, pp. 26–30.

This article argues that quality financial reports can be achieved when there is a well-balanced, functioning system of corporate governance. For good corporate governance, companies should develop a "six-legged stool" model that supports responsible and reliable reports. The model is based on the active participation of all parties, which are: the board of directors, the audit committee, the top management team, internal auditors, external auditors, and governing bodies.

Ruback, Richard S. (2002). Capital Cash Flows: A Simple Approach to Valuing Risky Cash Flows. *Financial Management*, Summer 2002, pp. 85–103.

This paper presents the capital cash flow (CCF) method of valuing risky cash flows and shows that the CCF method is equivalent to discounting free cash flows (FCF) by the weighted average cost of capital. The CCF approach is easier to apply whenever debt is forecasted in levels instead of as a percent of total enterprise value.

Strischek, Dev. (2001). A Banker's Perspective on Working Capital and Cash Flow Management. *Strategic Finance*, October 2001, pp. 38–45.

This article argues that when bankers consider providing a loan, they look at working capital and cash flow management skills, which impact the cost of capital. Lenders have a vested interest in three key areas: sound collection practices, inventory controls, and trade credit discipline.

Tarantino, David. (2001). Understanding Financial Statements. *The Physician Executive*, September/October 2001, pp. 72–76.

This article describes the critical "financials" that can make or break a business. It explains each financial statement, how it differs from other financial statements, and what useful information about the business can be obtained from each statement.

END NOTES

1. See L. Lee, "Tricks of E*TRADE," *BusinessWeek E Biz* (February 7, 2000), pp. 18–31; Christopher Wang, "E*TRADE to Buy JPMorgan's BrownCo for $1.6 Billion," *Lexis Nexis Online* (September 29, 2005); "E*TRADE Accelerates Delivery of Advanced Research, Investment Tools, and Services," *PR Newswire* (January 10, 2006); and E*TRADE's Web site, www.etrade.com.
2. See Justin Hibbard and Adrienne Carter, "Options Trading Grows Up," *BusinessWeek* (May 30, 2005), p. 87; Suzanne McGee, "Is the ISE Age Over?" *Institutional Investor* (June 2005), pp. 132–38; and ISE's Web site, www.iseoptions.com.
3. E. Berkowitz, R. Kerin, S. Hartley, and W. Rudelius, *Marketing*, 8th ed. (Burr Ridge, IL: McGraw-Hill/Irwin, 2006), pp. 252–53.
4. E. A. Helfert, *Techniques of Financial Analysis*, 11th ed. (Burr Ridge, IL: McGraw-Hill/Irwin, 2003), pp. 152–78.
5. Norman Brodsky, "Learning from Mistakes," *Inc.* (June 2003), pp. 55–57.
6. Clyde P. Stickney, Paul Brown, and James Whalen, *Financial Reporting and Statement Analysis: A Strategic Approach*, 5th ed. (Mason, OH: South-Western Publishing, 2004), pp. 450–88.
7. Berkowitz et al., *Marketing*, pp. 351–55.

CASES FOR PART 2

CASE 2A
BIZLAND, INC.

BizLand, Inc., was founded by Ravi Agarwal in 1997 as a provider of online resources for small businesses and was his second start-up in only six months. His first venture, an online Web site selling movie videos, was shut down shortly before its planned debut. "While we were in the process of launching the site and doing competitive research," Ravi explained, "we found out that reel.com had just been funded, and they were offering our potential distribution partner 'big bucks' to sign an agreement with them instead."

Despite the video site's short-lived existence as a bona fide company, the development process had yielded many dividends for Ravi. It had provided him with an opportunity to experience the power of e-commerce first-hand, and more importantly had taught him what types of electronic "attractions" genuinely appealed to online customers. "When I founded my next start-up, BizLand, Inc.," Ravi said, "I knew I had read the market correctly this time. The Internet site really took off, and almost immediately began attracting tons of [useful] online traffic. The customers loved it."

Like many nascent businesses, BizLand, Inc. (known as BizLand.com through the end of 2000) encountered some potentially fatal incidents in its first few months of operation. Ravi categorized them in the areas of profitability, customer relations, staffing, and growth:

Source: Boston College Professor Gregory Stoller prepared this case as the basis for class discussion rather than to illustrate either effective or ineffective handling of an administrative situation.

> We originally launched the company as a credit card processing business. It was re-launched in January 1999, when we added free Web-hosting services," he said. "Through Web hosting we could acquire customers at a cheaper cost, and use the site as a feeder for our higher margin credit card business. However, we later discovered many of these services, while popular with our customers, were inherently unprofitable to us. They were also a constant drain on cash. My economic decision to eliminate them cost me a great deal of credibility with our newly formed client base.
>
> While the site's revenue was enough to cover our rent and operating expenses, after 1 1/2 years, my co-founder left to take "a real job." He said he needed to receive a dependable salary. I was afraid about the effect on the rest of the staff. They were mostly being "paid" in stock, and had no guarantee that they could ever cash out.
>
> Even though I knew I had discovered a successful business model, I also wasn't quite sure what I needed to do to move the company forward. Growth would be crucial if we wanted to remain in business. The only thing I *was* certain about was that we had great people working for us. It would be their contributions, not the technology, that would ultimately bring us to the next level.

In January 1999, five people strong, BizLand, Inc., was beginning to gain some financial strength and market share. They quickly outgrew their office space, and would be forced to move a third time in the next six months in order to keep everyone in the same building. Concurrently, in an ongoing attempt to stem the company's "burn rate" of cash, Ravi also began making presentations to angel investors.

On June 1, 1999, Ravi achieved his funding objective. The investors liked what they saw and committed first round financing of $1.3 million. BizLand, Inc., could now survive for at least another six to nine months. (Refer to Gregory Stoller's case entitled *BizLand, Inc.: Navigating through the Land of E-Business,* for an in-depth discussion of the company's continued changes to its business strategy, competitive threats, and its plans to become profitable, available from Boston College.)

One month later, BizLand, Inc., went through yet another strategic shift. Ravi explained:

> We had matured beyond our Web hosting roots. By working with small business customers directly, I realized they had many more needs than simply Web hosting and credit card processing. They wanted help with the other aspects of their businesses, and we decided to tailor our site's offering to their market. The [small business] segment was the fastest growing sector of the U.S. economy, and we thought it offered a lot of potential.

BizLand, Inc., condensed its business into two main service lines: (1) Marketing advice for small businesses and (2) a co-operative market, offering products such as payroll and telephone at wholesale prices. In addition to those listed in Exhibit 1, BizLand, Inc., also sold books and computers.

BUILDING THE TEAM

With the infusion of first-round funding completed, Ravi could once again focus on strategy and business development. A key success factor in both of these areas was executive staffing. While he was confident in his abilities to continue growing BizLand, Inc., on his own, he was also aware of the potential opportunity costs associated with the status quo. As Ravi explained,

> I wasn't under any particular pressure from the Board of Directors to hire a CEO, but I knew it was in the best interests of the company. Competition was becoming more intense in the market from well-funded ventures—companies like AllBusiness and BigStep had come out of nowhere—and I realized that if we wanted to reach our strategic goals, and eventually become profitable, I couldn't do it all by myself fast enough to succeed.
>
> The most frustrating part of the decision centered on speed and control. I didn't want to give up control of the venture I had started and run for so long, but knew we couldn't "get there" without some professional management installed.

On the advice of the Board, Ravi retained John Hoagland III, a partner, and head of the North American Technology Practice at Whitehead Mann Pendleton James (formerly Pendleton James Associates). [See Exhibits 2 and 3]. They met several times to discuss BizLand, Inc.'s future, intellectual requirements for the position, and ideal personality traits. As John explained,

> This was not your typical CEO search, since there were only a handful of other people in the company, and it was still operating from its sole round of funding. It was crucial to find someone who was a strong leader, and could move the company forward at a fast, but not uncontrollable rate. People had to like the CEO, and want to follow him. Up to now, all of the staff had done nearly everything on its own. Ravi also had to feel comfortable that he was not giving up control, and potentially throwing away all of his hard work.

FINDING THE PERFECT CANDIDATE

In addition to the traditional attributes one looks for in the perfect CEO, such as business acumen and breadth of experience, John and Ravi decided that a large part of the selection criteria should also focus on the candidate's interpersonal skills. "Soft" qualities would be rated on an equal level with professional accomplishments, given the extremely young age of the business.

After several meetings, they arrived at the following list of "must haves" for the position:

- Extensive direct marketing experience
- Significant knowledge of B-to-B (business-to-business), ideally with a small company focus
- Management experience in a multi-tier distribution channel
- Comfort, and a demonstrated record of accomplishment with equity fund-raising
- In-depth knowledge of "Internet economics" and the emerging "new" business economy
- Experience in high-tech companies, preferably software
- Strong educational background
- Exceptional leadership skills

Ravi and the Board were prepared to offer a competitive financial package. The base salary would be "well into the six figure range," and contain the additional incentive of an almost 30 percent cash bonus based on company and individual performance. The amount of the bonus would be determined by Board review. The CEO would receive slightly over 10 percent of the company's outstanding shares at the time, with a four-year vesting period, and anti-dilution protection.

There would not be an employment contract. Neither Ravi, the Board, nor John, believed this level of

EXHIBIT 1 Menu of BizLand, Inc.'s Original Online Services (as of January 1999)

Product	Description	Launched	Partner
Animated Ad Banners $25	Create online banners	Dec-99	Animation.com
Banner Network	Purchase banner ad impressions on member sites	Dec-00	BizLand
BizBuilder	Web site editing tool	Oct-99	BizLand
BizLand Plus (3 months)	Disable Ads, 30 MB more space, POP accounts	Jan-99	BizLand
Browser Compatibility	Check if browsers are compatible to your Web site	Jul-99	NetMechanic
Counter	Place a counter on your site	Jun-99	BizLand
Dead Links	Find Dead Links on your site	Jul-99	NetMechanic
Dial-up ISP	Internet dial-up service	Sep-00	Laserlink
Direct Mail Quotes	Obtain quotes, find a vendor; offline mail campaign	Apr-00	DMQ
Directed Traffic	Pay for positioning on GoTo.com	Dec-99	GoTo.com
Disk usage	Check how much disk space is left	Jan-99	BizLand
Domain Name Parking	Host a domain name	Jan-99	BizLand
E-Commerce Manager Bundle	Create online catalog and storefront	Jan-00	ShopSite
E-Commerce Pro Bundle	Create online catalog and storefront	Jan-00	ShopSite
E-Mail List Manager	Set up an E-mail List	May-00	BizLand
Email2Friend	Promote site through e-mail from visitors	Jun-99	BizLand
Fax2Friend	Let visitors to Web site fax page to their friends	Apr-00	J2
Faxes for Free	Send faxes for free within U.S.	Jul-99	J2
Freedom Membership	Host a business Web site and more—do-it-yourself	Jan-99	BizLand
Guest Book	Receive feedback from visitors	Jun-99	BizLand
HTML Syntax	Check your HTML for errors	Jul-99	NetMechanic
Lead Generation Service	Get qualified sales leads	Dec-99	Respond.com
Lifetime Email	Free e-mail address (Web-based)	Jul-99	Commtouch
Load Time	Check how long it takes to load your site	Jul-99	NetMechanic
Merchant Account	Account to accept credit cards	Jan-00	Heartland
Meta Tag Generator	Create Meta Tags, optimize search engine success	Mar-00	BizLand
More Space (3 months)	Purchase additional 20 MB of space	Jan-99	BizLand
My BizLand	Customized home page with news, stocks, etc.	Sep-00	iSyndicate
Online Coupon Service	Place coupons on heavily trafficked sites	Jun-00	eCoupons
Online Customer Service	Provide personal, immediate service to site visitors	Nov-00	HumanClick
Online Meeting Center	Hold meetings and share documents	Mar-00	Webex
Optimize Graphics	Speed up your site, optimize graphics	Jul-99	NetMechanic
Payment Gateway	Process credit card transaction	Jan-00	Signio
Poll Taker	Take polls and gather info from users	Feb-00	BizLand
QuickLink	Create navigation links for Web sites	Mar-00	BizLand
Register Domain	Register a new domain or transfer an existing one	Apr-00	Tucows
Search Engine Ranking	Find where your site ranks on search engines	Mar-00	BizLand
Search Engine Submission—Enhanced	1,300 search engines and directories	Dec-00	SiteSolutions
Search Engine Submission—Free	Submit your site to top 8 search engines	Jan-99	BizLand
ShopSite Manager	E-Commerce Package	Jan-00	ShopSite
ShopSite Pro	Pro E-Commerce Package	Jan-00	ShopSite
Spell Check	Check for spelling errors	Jul-99	NetMechanic
Transfer Domain	Register a new domain or transfer an existing one	Jan-99	BizLand
Value Membership	Host a business Web site and more—premium service	Dec-00	BizLand
Visitor Statistics	Check site traffic	Jan-99	Webalizer
Web Site Phone Service	Allows visitors to make free Web phone calls to you	Nov-00	Net2Phone

Source: BizLand, Inc.

EXHIBIT 2 About Whitehead Mann

Whitehead Mann, founded in 1976 and floated on the London Stock Exchange in 1997, is a leading international executive search and HR strategy consultancy operating at the highest levels of business leadership. The quality of our people, our strong team culture, and a continuous process of innovation make us unique in the search market. 75% of our business comes from existing clients.

Drawing upon in-house expertise across a range of sectors and functional disciplines, the *E-Business team* works to identify and recruit functional e-business executives for mainstream businesses using the Internet to develop new channels to market, and also executive teams for "pure play" Internet companies.

Recent work for classic corporates includes a Managing Director Digital for a major media business and a Head of Online Business for a globally renowned personal computer manufacturer looking to aggressively grow its Internet sales channel. We have also worked closely with an international airline on a major e-business recruitment drive, comprehensively mapping the market for Internet-skilled executives and subsequently identifying candidates for a range of senior positions.

Within the "pure play" Internet arena we recruit across all functions including Chief Executive, Human Resources, Chief Technology Officer, Sales, Marketing, and Business Development roles. We have been engaged by two of the biggest names in consumer online services to recruit for their EMEA businesses. Other clients include venture capital–backed businesses, Internet incubators, and e-business start-ups operating in both the business-to-consumer and business-to-business space.

Source: Whitehead Mann.

EXHIBIT 3 Background of John H. Hoagland III

John H. Hoagland III

John joined Pendleton James Associates in 1993 with prior experience in general management, human resources, and sales in the employee benefits and software services industries. John was previously with Versyss Incorporated, a $100 million software and computer services company. He was a General Manager of Versyss-Benchmark Systems in Arlington, Virginia, as well as the company's Atlanta branch. Prior to that, he had served as Vice President, Human Resources and Administration with responsibility for strategic initiatives in manufacturing and end user services, executive and technical recruitment, and training and development.

Before joining Versyss, John worked in sales and marketing in the corporate insurance industry with a focus on employee benefit programs, first with Prudential and then as Group Marketing Executive for Equicor (a CIGNA subsidiary).

John received his B.A. from Principia College. He is an officer and President of the Business Associates Club of Boston. He and his family reside in Dover, MA, where John serves on the Dover-Sherborn Regional School Committee.

Source: Whitehead Mann Pendleton James.

complexity was necessary, given the stage of BizLand, Inc.'s development. Finally, Whitehead Mann would be compensated with a flat fee based on the successful appointment of the candidate.

The following hiring process would be used:

1. John and his company would provide BizLand, Inc., with a universe of potential candidates.
2. John and Ravi would distill this list based on resume quality and years of relevant experience.
3. Candidates passing the resume test would be further screened by John in face-to-face interviews.
4. Recommended candidates would go through a series of interviews with Ravi and individual Board members.
5. The short list would be brought back for final interviews with the entire Board of Directors.

CANDIDATE PROFILES

After the mining of Whitehead Mann Pendleton James's database, the screening of hundreds of resumes, and the completion of several face-to-face interviews, four candidates were presented to Ravi and the Board of Directors. The following background was available on each:

Candidate #1: Michael Speer

- Undergraduate Education: University of Michigan
- Graduate Education: University of Chicago, MBA
- Professional Certifications: CPA
- Current Position: General Manager, G.E. Capital, Small Business Services Initiative

Prior to receiving his MBA, this 37-year-old candidate worked in the audit department of KPMG. Post-MBA, he joined G.E. Capital in the operations department of the company's vendor finance business. His position involved asset-based lending to large and small companies needing to purchase business equipment (i.e., computers, copiers, etc.). He also acted as a liaison with G.E. Capital's Financing Department to assist his clients with financing.

After three years in vendor financing, Mr. Speer was promoted to G.E. Capital's Commercial Direct business division, with responsibility for developing and implementing programs aimed at aggregating small business purchasing requirements. A typical transaction involves the purchase of telecommunications services in bulk, and then resale directly to his small business clients. He has been active in this role for 11 years, with the past three years spent as the General Manager of the entire division.

Candidate #2: Robert Barbers

- Undergraduate Education: Culver-Stockton College (Canton, Missouri)
- Graduate Education: Harvard Business School, MBA
- Professional Certifications: CPA
- Current Position: Senior Vice-President, Excel Software

Prior to receiving his MBA, this 42-year-old candidate worked in both New York and Tokyo as a junior consultant for Boston Consulting Group (BCG). Post-MBA, he re-joined BCG and worked as an associate consultant for two additional years. In his next move, he became a macroeconomic and political consultant for a firm founded by former President Gerald Ford. Parlaying his political consulting experience with his successful bid for Class President at Harvard Business School, he took a leave-of-absence and ran for a congressional seat against the incumbent in his home state of Montana in 1986. Although he won the primary, he lost the general election.

In 1987, he joined Excel Software in a senior position reporting directly to the CEO, and as one of their first one hundred employees. He has remained at Excel for the past 12 years, in a variety of roles ranging from head of strategy to Senior Vice-President of sales. Mr. Barbers was directly responsible for launching the company's international operations, and worked directly with the CEO on the road show that brought Excel public. During Mr. Barbers's tenure, overall sales have increased from $4 million to $150 million.

Candidate #3: Sanjay Gupta

- Undergraduate Education: University of Connecticut
- Graduate Education: Boston College, MBA
- Professional Certifications: CPA
- Current Position: Chief Marketing Officer, egghead.com

Prior to receiving his MBA, this 39-year-old candidate worked in the audit department of Ernst & Young for five years. Post-MBA, he joined Black & Decker as a financial planning and analysis manager. For an additional five years, and as a member of a six-person team, he benchmarked the performance of Black & Decker's products, and made financial and strategy recommendations to senior management. He subsequently joined KPMG, where he worked for another five years as an IT strategy consultant.

His next move placed him back in a financial role, as the controller of a surplus-direct catalog re-seller of computer equipment, called Onsale, Inc. The company's business strategy was to purchase old copies of software and hardware (i.e., Windows 3.1) and then re-sell them via catalog. He increased sales from $12 million to $100 million in three years, and was named President of the company.

In Onsale's efforts to raise capital for expansion, they merged with Egghead Software, and formed a new entity, egghead.com. Egghead was in the process of closing its unprofitable retail locations and needed a new distribution channel for its products. Onsale needed cash for the projected growth of its core business, as well as entry into complementary lines associated with new technology and online auctions. Senior management was reorganized, and executives were hand-selected from both companies to run the new entity. Mr. Gupta was named Chief Marketing Officer, with responsibility for the establishment of direct marketing initiatives and online partnerships. He has been in this role for the past 18 months.

Candidate #4: Daniel Peters

- Undergraduate Education: Middlebury College
- Graduate Education: Columbia University, MBA
- Professional Certifications: None
- Current Position: General Manger, G.E. Capital, Commercial Credit Card Business

Prior to receiving his MBA, this 39-year-old candidate worked on "ski patrol" for two years, and later joined an architectural firm as the head of marketing and public relations. Post-MBA, he joined American Express, as an analyst for their commercial business travel and traveler check divisions.

Seven years later, Mr. Peters joined G.E. Capital as a senior manager in their commercial credit card business, with responsibilities in product management, direct marketing, co-branding, and alliances. Customers ran the gamut from large and small companies to individual business consumers, and joint venture (branding) partnerships. He has been in this role for five years, with the past two spent as General Manager of the entire division. G.E. Capital has also recently tasked him with launching a new Internet initiative for its commercial card business.

NEXT STEPS

By the third quarter of 1999, BizLand, Inc., was continuing its pattern of fast growth. The company had well over 50,000 members, and was growing its database by over 500 per day. The capital markets were also in the midst of their own economic expansion, with the Dow Jones Industrial Average at the 11,000 mark, and the NASDAQ index squarely above its psychologically important value of 2,500.

Online business ideas ranging from vitamins (mothernature.com), to pet supplies (pets.com), were being funded *en masse* by the venture capital community. In order to stay in the game, rival firms were regularly outbidding one another to secure equity in the most promising companies. Non-e-businesses were also in vogue, even in such staid industries as dry cleaning (ZOOTS), and flowers (KaBloom).

At the same time, well-funded competition continued to enter the market, all aimed at servicing small business needs. Ravi knew it would only be a matter of time before some of them became large enough to potentially impact BizLand, Inc.

1 1/2 months had elapsed since the CEO search with John first began. While Ravi certainly didn't want to rush the process, he knew he couldn't keep up his intense work pace forever. Among the different projects he was working on, in addition to running the day-to-day operations of the company:

1. *Senior executive staffing:* Vice-Presidents in Business Development, Marketing, and Member Support had to be hired, in order to truly capitalize on the growth being experienced by BizLand, Inc.
2. *Office space expansion:* The company was beginning to run out of office space, as the employee base had grown to over 10 people. Today alone, there were three phone calls from commercial leasing brokers responding to Ravi's requests.
3. *Equity fund raising:* More equity had to be raised. Based on BizLand, Inc.'s greater-than-anticipated rate of actual expansion, and projected marketing spending, the $1.3 million risked being utilized far more quickly than anyone had originally anticipated.

While Ravi and John were pleased with the quality of the four candidates, many questions still remained in their minds:

1. Had they compiled an exhaustive list of criteria for their "must haves"? Had some important qualities been omitted? Were all of the items really necessary? If he and John did make changes, how would the four candidates measure up to the revised list?
2. Did the four candidates offer any *real* possibilities? Should they invite any of them for an interview with the entire Board of Directors? Or, even though it would further elongate the process, should Ravi and John begin considering other candidates not previously screened or interviewed?
3. If Ravi had to make a decision today, which of the four candidates should he choose, and why?

CASE 2B
THE BEACH CARRIER

Mary Ricci has a new product concept, The Beach Carrier, that she is ready to bring to market. Ricci is creative, optimistic, enthusiastic, flexible, and motivated. She is willing to put substantial time into developing and bringing The Beach Carrier to market. Although she lacks capital, Ricci is unwilling to license or sell the pattern to a manufacturer; she is determined to maintain control and ownership of the product throughout the introduction and market penetration phases. Ricci believes there is a significant amount of money to be made and refuses to sell her product concept for a flat fee.

THE PRODUCT

The Beach Carrier is a bag large enough to carry everything needed for a day at the beach, including a chair. When empty, the bag can be folded down to a 12-inch by 12-inch square for easy storage. The bag's 36-inch by 36-inch size, adjustable padded shoulder strap, and various-sized pockets make it ideal for use in carrying chairs and other items to the beach or other outdoor activities, such as concerts, picnics, and barbecues. The bag can also be used to transport items, such as ski boots, that are difficult to carry. Manufactured in a lightweight, tear-resistant, fade-proof fabric that dries quickly, the bag will be available in a variety of fluorescent as well as conservative colors.

COMPETITION

Currently there are two competitive products sold online that Ricci felt would compete with The Beach Carrier. The first one, found at www.shadeusa.com, is the "Caddy Sack" and is advertised as a backpack-type product that can hold a beach chair, an umbrella, a boogie board, and even a small collapsing table. There is also an outside pocket for a towel, a snorkel, or fins. It is available in three colors and is priced at $16.95. Ricci purchased one of these and felt that it would not hold all the items advertised at one time. The chair had to be very small and room for extra beach accessories was very limited. This item was ideal for someone biking or walking to the beach with gear for only himself or herself.

The second item is called the "Wonder Wheeler" and can be found at www.4thebeach.com. It looks similar to a two-wheel shopping cart that might be used to carry purchased groceries while walking home from the store. This product is advertised as having oversized wheels; it weighs less than 10 pounds and folds up easily. It can hold a significant amount of beach gear, such as multiple chairs, an umbrella, a cooler, beach towels, and toys. It has a list price of $59.99 and Ricci felt that even with the advertised oversized wheels it would be cumbersome to maneuver on the sand. Its high price was also felt to be a negative for many consumers.

MARKETING RESEARCH

Ricci commissioned a consulting company to perform a feasibility study for the product, which included a demographic profile, cost estimates, packaging recommendations, and a patent search. The patent search revealed the above-mentioned products and a chair that could be folded and carried as a small tote bag that could also hold a few small beach items. None of these were felt to be a threat to Ricci's product, and she was optimistic that a patent could be obtained.

A focus group was used to determine potential consumer response. Results of the focus group indicated that several features of the product should be modified. For example, the material was perceived as durable; however, the fluorescent color was see-through and considered "trendy," lessening the perceived quality of the bag. The size also represented an issue, as the bag was perceived as much larger than necessary.

MARKET POTENTIAL

People who use suntan and sunscreen products have been identified as the primary target market for The Beach Carrier. Research indicates that 43.9 percent of the adult U.S. population, or 77,293,000 people, use suntan and sunscreen products. Of these, 57.8 percent are female. Assuming that women are the primary purchasers of beach bags, the potential market is estimated at 44,675,000. Beach bags are replaced every three

EXHIBIT 1

Segment	Percentage of Total Users of Suntan/Sunscreen Products
Ages 18–44	66.9
High school graduate	40.2
Employed full time	60.5
No child in household	54.5
Household income of $30,000+	55.3

EXHIBIT 2

	Population	Sunscreen Users	Replace Bag This Year
Total adults	176,251,000	77,293,000	25,764,333
Females	92,184,000	44,671,000	14,890,333
		Market Share	
	1%	**2%**	**5%**
Total adults	257,643	515,287	1,288,217
Females	148,903	297,807	744,517

EXHIBIT 3A

	Population	Sunscreen Users	Women	Replace Bag This Year
Northeast	37,366,000	17,165,000	9,921,370	3,307,123
Midwest	43,426,000	19,630,000	11,346,140	3,782,047
South	60,402,000	23,980,000	13,860,440	4,620,147
West	35,057,000	16,518,000	9,547,404	3,182,468
Total	176,251,000	77,293,000	44,675,354	14,891,785

years. The primary market for suntan and sunscreen products is described in Exhibit 1. The marketing share objectives for the first year of The Beach Carrier's sales have been determined based on the following assumptions:

- People who use suntan and sunscreen products represent the market for The Beach Carrier.
- Most men do not buy beach bags; consider women only (57.8 percent of population).
- Women buy new beach bags every three years on average; that is, one-third will buy a new bag this year.

Based on these assumptions, the unit sales needed to achieve market share objectives of 1 percent, 2 percent, and 5 percent of the total market during the first year of The Beach Carrier's sales are shown in Exhibit 2. Ricci is targeting 1 percent of this potential market. Regional market share objectives can be developed from the same data as seen in Exhibits 3A and 3B.

EXHIBIT 3B

	Market Share		
	1%	2%	5%
Northeast	33,071	66,142	165,356
Midwest	37,820	75,641	189,102
South	46,201	92,403	231,007
West	31,825	63,649	159,123
Total	148,917	297,835	744,588

STRATEGY

Ricci investigated several methods of marketing The Beach Carrier, including selling it in upscale (i.e., Bloomingdale's) or discount (i.e., Wal-Mart) stores, licensing the product concept to a manufacturer, selling the idea for a flat fee, selling the bag to corporations for use as a promotional item, selling it on the Internet, and setting up a mail-order operation. Ricci believes that the mail-order option, while requiring the most effort, will provide higher margins, lower risk, and the overall best fit with Ricci's strengths and weaknesses, her market penetration objectives, and her limited financial resources. The Internet could also create opportunities but Ricci was unsure of this option.

The mail-order sales strategy will be implemented nationally using a regional rollout and following a seasonal demand pattern. With three-month intervals between rollout phases, national market exposure will be achieved within 12 months. Ricci is also exploring how to set up a Web site with a local university team of student consultants.

PROMOTION

The product initially will be promoted in novelty and general interest mail-order catalogs and special interest magazines that appeal to beachgoers and boat owners.

PRICING

The costs of manufacturing have been estimated at $6.50 per unit for material, zippers, Velcro, and so on. The costs for assembly and packaging have been estimated at $3.50 per unit, bringing the total manufacturing cost to $10.00. After analysis of competitive products and focus group results, a mail-order price in the $12.99 to $14.99 range has been established.

DISTRIBUTION

The product will be manufactured at a local New England factory, drop-shipped to a storage facility, and shipped via UPS to the consumer. Initially, inventory can be carried at no cost in Ricci's house or garage. This same process could also be used if the Web site is developed.

FINANCING

A $30,000 small business loan is the minimum amount Ricci needs to fund her fixed costs for the first phase of the rollout for the mail-order program. Marketing the product through traditional retail channels would require approximately $250,000 for advertising and other selling costs associated with a new product introduction.

BREAK-EVEN ANALYSIS

Break-even analysis was performed at three mail-order prices, as seen in Exhibit 4. On the basis of this analysis, Ricci must meet only one-fourth of her target sales goal, or one-quarter of 1 percent of the total market, in order to break even in the first year.

EXHIBIT 4

	Unit Variable	Cost per Unit	Price Contribution
Materials	$6.50	$12.99	$2.99
Assembly	3.00	$13.99	$3.99
Packaging	0.50	$14.99	$4.99
Total unit VC	$10.00		

Fixed Costs

	Northeast	Midwest	South	West	Total
Advertising	$25,000	$25,000	$25,000	$25,000	$100,000
Warehousing	266	305	372	256	1,199
General S&A	2,500	2,500	2,500	2,500	10,000
Total fixed costs	$27,766	$27,805	$27,872	$27,756	$111,199

Break-Even Units

$12.99	9,286	9,299	9,322	9,283	37,190
Percent of total market	0.28	0.25	0.20	0.29	0.25
$13.99	6,959	6,969	6,985	6,956	27,869
Percent of total market	0.21	0.18	0.15	0.22	0.19
$14.99	5,564	5,572	5,586	5,562	22,284
Percent of total market	0.17	0.15	0.12	0.17	0.15

CASE 2C
GOURMET TO GO

INTRODUCTION

Today, many households have two incomes. At the end of the day the questions arise, "Who will cook?" or "What do I cook?" Time is limited. After a long day at work, few people want to face the lines at the grocery store. Often the choice is to eat out. But the expense of dining out or the boredom of fast food soon becomes unappealing. Pizza or fast-food delivery solves the problem of going out but does not always satisfy the need for nutritious, high-quality meals. Some people prefer a home-cooked meal, especially without the hassle of grocery shopping, menu planning, and time-consuming preparation.

Jan Jones is one of those people. She is a hard-working professional who would like to come home to a home-cooked meal. She would not mind fixing it herself but, once at home, making an extra trip to the store is a major hassle. Jones thought it would be great to have the meal planned and all the ingredients at her fingertips. She thought of other people in her situation and realized there might be a market need for this kind of service. After thinking about the types of meals that could be marketed, Jones discussed the plan with her colleagues at work. The enthusiastic response led her to believe she had a good idea. After months of marketing research, menu planning, and financial projections, Jones was ready to launch her new business. The following is the business plan for Gourmet to Go.

EXECUTIVE SUMMARY

Gourmet to Go is a new concept in grocery marketing. The product is a combination of menu planning and grocery delivery; a complete package of groceries and recipes for a week's meals is delivered to a customer's door. The target market consists of young urban professionals living in two-income households in which individuals have limited leisure time, high disposable income, and a willingness to pay for services.

The objective is to develop a customer base of 400 households by the end of the third year after start-up.

This level of operation will produce a new income of about $120,000 per year and provide a solid base for market penetration in the future.

The objective will be achieved by creating an awareness of the product through an intense promotional campaign at start-up and by providing customers with first-class service and premium-quality goods.

The capital required to achieve objectives is $258,000. Jones will invest $183,000 and will manage and own the business. The remainder of the capital will be financed through bank loans.

PRODUCT

The product consists of meal-planning and grocery-shopping services. It offers a limited selection of preplanned five-dinner packages delivered directly to the customer.

The criteria for the meal packages will be balanced nutrition, easy preparation, and premium quality. To ensure the nutritional requirements, Gourmet to Go will hire a nutritionist as a consultant. Nutritional information will be included with each order. The most efficient method for preparing the overall meal will be presented. Meals will be limited to recipes requiring no more than 20 minutes to prepare. Premium-quality ingredients will be a selling feature. The customer should feel that he or she is getting better-quality ingredients than could be obtained from the grocery store.

MANUFACTURING AND PACKAGING

Since the customer will not be shopping on the premises, Gourmet to Go will require only a warehouse-type space for the groceries. The store location or decor will be unimportant in attracting business. There will be fewer inventory expenses since the customer will not be choosing among various brands. Only premium brands will be offered.

It will be important to establish a reliable connection with a distributor for high-quality produce and to maintain freshness for delivery to the customer.

As orders are processed, the dinners will be assembled. Meats will be wrapped and ready for the home freezer. All ingredients will be labeled according to the dinner to which they belong. The groceries will be sorted and bagged according to storage requirements: freezer, refrigerator, and shelf. Everything possible will be done to minimize the customer's task. Included in the packaging will be the nutritional information and preparation instructions.

Customers will be given the option of selecting their own meals from the monthly menu list or opting for a weekly selection from the company.

FUTURE GROWTH

Various options will be explored in order to expand the business. Some customers may prefer a three- or four-meal plan if they eat out more often or travel frequently. Another possibility might be the "last-minute gourmet"; that is, they can call any evening for one meal only.

Increasing the customer base will increase future sales. Expansion of Gourmet to Go can include branches in other locations or even future franchising in other cities. With expansion and success, Gourmet to Go might be a prime target for a larger food company to buy out.

INDUSTRY

The Gourmet to Go concept is a new idea with its own market niche. The closest competitors would be grocery stores and restaurants with delivery services.

Of the 660 grocery stores in the Tulsa/Tulsa County region, only two offer delivery service. They are higher-priced stores and will deliver for $4, regardless of order size. However, they offer no assistance in meal planning.

A number of pizza chains will deliver pizza as well as fried chicken. There is also a new service that will pick up and deliver orders from various restaurants. However, Gourmet to Go would not be in direct competition with these services because the meals available from them are either of a fast-food type or far more expensive than a Gourmet to Go meal.

SALES PREDICTION

The market segment will be households with an income of at least $65,000 per year. In Tulsa/Tulsa County, this will cover an area including over 16,600 households that meet the target requirements of income with an age range of 24 to 50 years. By the end of the third year, a customer base of 400 households will be developed (2.3 percent of the target market). At a growth rate of 2.73 percent a year, the target market of households should increase over three years to 18,000.

FINANCIAL

Various financial statements are included in Exhibits 1 through 8.

MARKETING

Distribution

The product will be delivered directly to the customer.

Sales Strategy

Advertising will include newspaper ads, radio spots, an Internet Web page, and direct-mail brochures. All four will be used during normal operations, but an intense campaign will precede start-up. A series of "teaser" newspaper ads will be run prior to start-up, announcing a revolution in grocery shopping. At start-up, the newspaper ads will have evolved into actually introducing the product, and radio spots will begin as well. A heavy

EXHIBIT 1 Start-Up Expenses

Ad campaign		
Ad agency*	$3,000	
Brochures[†]	7,000	
Radio spots[‡]	8,000	
Newspaper ads[§]	7,000	
Total		$25,000
Pre-start-up salaries**		16,000
Nutritionist consulting		6,000
Miscellaneous consulting (legal, etc.)		1,500
Pre-start-up rent and deposits		4,000
Pre-start-up utilities and miscellaneous supplies		2,000
		$54,600

*40 hrs. @ $75/hr.

[†]20,000 brochures; printing, development, etc. @ $0.35/ea.

[‡]4 weeks intense campaign: 20 spots/week (30 seconds); $100/spot.

[§]50 ads at an average of $100/ad.

**Jan Jones @ 3 months; clerks, two @ 2 weeks.

EXHIBIT 2 Capital Equipment List

Computers:		
Apple, Macintosh Office System		
3 Mac systems	$3,000	
Laser printer HP2300 series	1,000	
Networking	2,000	
Software	3,000	
Total		$ 9,000
Delivery vans, Chevrolet Astro		66,000
Food lockers and freezers		15,000
Phone system (AT&T)		1,500
Furniture and fixtures		3,500
		$95,000

EXHIBIT 3 Pro Forma Income Statement

	Year 1											
	Mo. 1	Mo. 2	Mo. 3	Mo. 4	Mo. 5	Mo. 6	Mo. 7	Mo. 8	Mo. 9	Mo. 10	Mo. 11	Mo. 12
Sales[1]	2,600	3,900	6,500	13,000	19,500	23,400	26,000	28,600	31,200	33,800	36,400	39,000
Less: Cost of goods sold[2]	1,700	2,550	4,250	8,500	12,750	15,300	17,000	18,700	20,400	22,100	23,800	25,500
Gross profit	900	1,350	2,250	4,500	6,750	8,100	9,000	9,900	10,800	11,700	12,600	13,500
Less: Operating expenses												
Salaries and wages[3]	7,400	7,400	7,400	7,400	7,400	7,400	9,800	9,800	9,800	9,800	9,800	9,800
Operating supplies	300	300	300	300	300	300	300	300	300	300	300	300
Repairs and maintenance	250	250	250	250	250	250	250	250	250	250	250	250
Advertising and promotion[4]	130	195	325	650	975	1,170	1,300	1,430	1,560	1,690	1,820	1,950
Bad debts	100	100	100	100	100	100	100	100	100	100	100	100
Rent[5]	1,667	1,667	1,667	1,667	1,667	1,667	1,667	1,667	1,667	1,667	1,667	1,667
Utilities	1,000	1,000	1,000	1,000	1,000	1,000	1,000	1,000	1,000	1,000	1,000	1,000
Insurance	600	600	600	600	600	600	600	600	600	600	600	600
General office	150	150	150	150	150	150	150	150	150	150	150	150
Licenses	200	0	0	0	0	0	0	0	0	0	0	0
Interest[6]	310	310	310	310	310	310	530	530	530	530	530	530
Depreciation[7]	1,271	1,271	1,271	1,271	1,271	1,271	1,271	1,271	1,271	1,271	1,271	1,271
Total operating expenses	13,378	13,243	13,373	13,698	14,023	14,218	16,968	17,098	17,228	17,358	17,488	17,618
Profit (loss) before taxes	(12,478)	(11,893)	(11,123)	(9,198)	(7,273)	(6,118)	(7,968)	(7,198)	(6,428)	(5,658)	(4,888)	(4,118)
Less: Taxes	0	0	0	0	0	0	0	0	0	0	0	0
Net profit (loss)	(12,478)	(11,893)	(11,123)	(9,198)	(7,273)	(6,118)	(7,968)	(7,198)	(6,428)	(5,658)	(4,888)	(4,118)

(1)Average unit sale for groceries is about $43,00, plus $10.00 per week for delivery (Exhibit 1), making the monthly unit sales per household (2 people) about $212,00.

(2)Cost of goods sold—80% of retail grocery price, or $40.00 per household per week ($170.00/month household). (80% an average margin on groceries.)

(3)Salaries and wages—Ms. Jones's salary will be $5,000/month. Order clerks will be paid $1,300/month, and delivery clerks will be paid $1,100/month. One additional order clerk and delivery clerk each will be added once sales reach 100 households, and again at 200 households. Salaries will escalate at 6%/year.

(4)Advertising and promotion—The grocery industry standard is 1% of sales. However, Gourmet to Go being a new business will require more than that level; 5% of sales is used in this plan. (Special pre-start-up advertising is covered with other start-up expenses.)

(5)Rent—2,000/ft.^{2} @ $10.00/ft.^{2}; $1,667/month; escalate at 6%/year.

(6)Interest—Loans on computer ($9,000) and delivery vehicles ($22,000 ea.) at 12.0%/year. (Delivery vehicles will be added with delivery clerks.) (Debt service—based on three-year amortization of loans with payments of ⅓ at the end of each of three years.)

(7)Depreciation—All equipment will be depreciated per ACRS schedules: vehicles and computers—3 years; furniture and fixtures—10 years.

EXHIBIT 4 Pro Forma Income Statement

	Year 2				Year 3			
	Q1	Q2	Q3	Q4	Q1	Q2	Q3	Q4
Sales[1]	136,500	156,000	194,698	234,000	253,500	273,000	292,500	312,000
Less: Cost of goods sold[2]	89,250	102,000	127,302	153,000	165,750	178,500	191,250	204,000
Gross profit	47,250	54,000	67,395	81,000	87,750	94,500	101,250	108,000
Less: Operating expenses								
Salaries and wages[3]	31,164	38,796	38,796	38,796	41,124	41,124	41,124	41,124
Operating supplies	900	900	900	900	900	900	900	900
Repairs and maintenance	750	750	750	750	750	750	750	750
Advertising and promotion[4]	6,825	7,800	9,735	11,700	12,675	13,650	14,625	15,600
Bad debts	300	300	300	300	300	300	300	300
Rent[5]	5,301	5,301	5,301	5,301	5,619	5,619	5,619	5,619
Utilities	3,000	3,000	3,000	3,000	3,000	3,000	3,000	3,000
Insurance	1,800	1,800	1,800	1,800	1,800	1,800	1,800	1,800
General office	450	450	450	450	450	450	450	450
Interest[6]	1,280	1,940	1,720	1,720	1,410	1,190	970	970
Depreciation[7]	6,910	6,910	6,910	6,910	7,493	7,493	7,493	7,493
Total operating expenses	58,680	67,947	69,662	71,627	75,520	76,275	77,030	78,005
Profit (loss) before taxes	(11,430)	(13,947)	(2,267)	9,373	12,230	18,225	24,220	29,995
Less: Taxes	0							
Net profit (loss)	(11,430)	(13,947)	(2,267)	9,373	12,230	18,225	24,220	29,995

(1) Average unit sale for groceries is about $43,00, plus $10.00 per week for delivery (Exhibit 1), making the monthly unit sales per household (2 people) about $212,00.

(2)Cost of goods sold—80% of retail grocery price, or $32.00 per household per week ($138.00/month household). (80% an average margin on groceries—*Progressive Grocer;* April 1984; p. 94.)

(3)Salaries and wages—Ms. Jones's salary will be $4,500/month. Order clerks will be paid $1,000/month, and delivery clerks will be paid $900/month. One additional order clerk and delivery clerk each will be added once sales reach 100 households, and again at 200 households. Salaries will escalate at 6%/year.

(4)Advertising and promotion—The grocery industry standard is 1% of sales. However, Gourmet to Go being a new business will require more than that level; 5% of sales is used in this plan. (Special pre-start-up advertising is covered with other start-up expenses.)

(5)Rent—2,000/ft.^{2} @ $8.00/ft.^{2}; 1,333 $1/month; escalate at 6%/year.

(6)Interest—Loans on computer ($10,000) and delivery vehicles ($12,000 ea.) at 12.5% year. (Delivery vehicles will be added with delivery clerks.) (Debt service—based on three-year amortization of loans with payments of ⅓ at the end of each of three years.)

(7)Depreciation—All equipment will be depreciated per ACRS schedules: vehicles and computers—3 years; furniture and fixtures—10 years.

EXHIBIT 5 Pro Forma Cash Flow Statement

	Year 1												
	Mo. 1	Mo. 2	Mo. 3	Mo. 4	Mo. 5	Mo. 6	Mo. 7	Mo. 8	Mo. 9	Mo. 10	Mo. 11	Mo. 12	Total
Cash receipts													
Sales	2,600	3,900	6,500	13,000	19,500	23,400	26,000	28,600	31,200	33,800	36,400	39,000	263,900
Other													
Total cash receipts	2,600	3,900	6,500	13,000	19,500	23,400	26,000	28,600	31,200	33,800	36,400	39,000	263,900
Cash disbursements													
Cost of goods sold	1,700	2,550	4,250	8,500	12,750	15,300	17,000	18,700	20,400	22,100	23,800	25,500	172,550
Salaries and wages	7,400	7,400	7,400	7,400	7,400	7,400	9,800	9,800	9,800	9,800	9,800	9,800	103,200
Operating supplies	300	300	300	300	300	300	300	300	300	300	300	300	3,600
Repairs and maintenance	250	250	250	250	250	250	250	250	250	250	250	250	3,000
Advertising and promotion	130	195	325	650	975	1,170	1,300	1,430	1,560	1,690	1,820	1,950	13,195
Bad debts	100	100	100	100	100	100	100	100	100	100	100	100	1,200
Rent	1,667	1,667	1,667	1,667	1,667	1,667	1,667	1,667	1,667	1,667	1,667	1,667	20,004
Utilities	1,000	1,000	1,000	1,000	1,000	1,000	1,000	1,000	1,000	1,000	1,000	1,000	12,000
Insurance	600	600	600	600	600	600	600	600	600	600	600	600	7,200
General office	150	150	150	150	150	150	150	150	150	150	150	150	1,800
Licenses	200	0	0	0	0	0	0	0	0	0	0	0	200
Interest	310	310	310	310	310	310	530	530	530	530	530	530	5,040
Debt service (principal)												10,333	10,333
Total cash disbursements	13,807	14,522	16,352	20,927	25,502	28,247	32,697	34,527	36,357	38,187	40,017	52,180	353,322
Net cash flow	(11,207)	(10,622)	(9,852)	(7,927)	(6,002)	(4,847)	(6,697)	(5,927)	(5,157)	(4,387)	(3,617)	(13,180)	(89,422)

EXHIBIT 6 Pro Forma Cash Flow Statement

	Year 2				Year 3			
	Q1	Q2	Q3	Q4	Q1	Q2	Q3	Q4
Cash receipts								
Sales	136,500	156,000	194,698	234,000	253,500	273,000	292,500	312,000
Other								
Total cash receipts	136,500	156,000	194,698	234,000	253,500	273,000	292,500	312,000
Cash disbursements								
Cost of goods sold	89,250	102,000	127,302	153,000	165,750	178,500	191,250	204,000
Salaries and wages	31,164	38,796	38,796	38,796	41,124	41,124	41,124	41,124
Operating supplies	900	900	900	900	900	900	900	900
Repairs and maintenance	750	750	750	750	750	750	750	750
Advertising and promotion	6,825	7,800	9,735	11,700	12,675	13,650	14,625	15,600
Bad debts	300	300	300	300	300	300	300	300
Rent	5,301	5,301	5,301	5,301	5,619	5,619	5,619	5,619
Utilities	3,000	3,000	3,000	3,000	3,000	3,000	3,000	3,000
Insurance	1,800	1,800	1,800	1,800	1,800	1,800	1,800	1,800
General office	450	450	450	450	450	450	450	450
Licenses	0	0	0	0	0	0	0	0
Interest	1,280	1,940	1,720	1,720	1,410	1,190	970	970
Debt service (principal)		7,333		10,333	7,333	7,333		10,333
Total cash disbursements	141,020	170,370	190,054	228,050	241,111	254,616	260,788	284,846
Net cash flow	(4,520)	(14,370)	4,643	5,950	12,389	18,384	31,712	27,154

EXHIBIT 7 Pro Forma Balance Sheets

End of:	Year 1	Year 2	Year 3		Year 1	Year 2	Year 3
Assets				**Liabilities**			
Current assets				Accounts payable	12,750	21,217	31,875
Cash	3,000	5,000	7,000	Notes payable	0	0	0
Accounts receivable	19,500	32,450	48,750	Total current liabilities	12,750	21,217	31,875
Inventory	12,750	21,217	31,875	Long-term liabilities			
Supplies	300	300	300	Bank loans payable	42,667	47,000	22,000
Prepaid expenses	1,667	1,767	1,873	Personal loans payable	0	0	0
Total current assets	37,217	60,734	89,798	Total long-term liabilities	42,667	47,000	22,000
Fixed assets				Total liabilities	55,417	68,217	53,875
Furniture and fixtures	18,000	16,000	14,000	Owner's equity			
Vehicles	33,000	32,780	8,140	Paid-in capital	133,889	62,897	28,068
Equipment	6,750	3,330	0	Retained earnings	(94,339)	(18,271)	29,995
Total fixed assets	57,750	52,110	22,140	Total owner's equity	39,550	44,627	58,063
Total assets	94,967	112,844	111,938	Total liabilities and equity	94,967	112,844	111,938

EXHIBIT 8 Sources and Uses of Funds

Sources of Funds	
Jan Jones (personal funds)	$182,913
Bank loans for computer and vehicles	75,000
Total sources	$257,913
Uses of Funds	
Computer, peripherals, and software	$9,000
Food lockers and freezers	15,000
Delivery vehicles*	66,000
Phone system	1,500
Miscellaneous furniture and fixtures	3,500
Start-up expenses	54,600
Working capital†	108,313
Total uses‡	$257,913

*See detail, following.

†To cover negative cash flow over first 1½ years of operation. (See pro forma cash flow statements.)

‡Total for initial 3-year period. Computer and one delivery van will be acquired prior to start-up, one delivery van will be added 6 months after start-up, and another will be added 15 months after start-up. Financing will be handled simultaneously with procurement.

advertising schedule will be used during the first four weeks of business. After start-up, a direct mailing will detail the description of the service and a menu plan.

Newspaper ads aimed at the target markets will be placed in entertainment and business sections. Radio spots will be geared to stations most appealing to the target market. Since the product is new, it may be possible to do interviews with newspapers and obtain free publicity.

Sales promotions will offer large discounts to first-time customers. These promotions will continue for the first six months of operations.

The service will be priced at $10 per week for delivery and planning, with the groceries priced at full retail level. According to the phone survey, most people who were interested in the service would be willing to pay the weekly service charge.

MANAGEMENT

The management will consist of the owner/manager. Other employees will be delivery clerks and order clerks. It is anticipated that after the business grows, an operations manager might be added to supervise the employees.

CASE 2D
INTERVELA D.O.O. KOPER—VICTORY SAILMAKERS

Zvonko and Zeljko stepped through the glass door of the sail loft they started a decade ago and paused on the blue iron stairs. Their glances drifted out to the sea, shimmering in the evening sunshine. The ships in the Bay of Koper were set on a southerly course. The sailboats in the marina were quietly moored as if patiently waiting for the helmsmen and crews to finally untie them and unfurl their sails. Grey clouds coming in from the southwest did not disturb their thoughts; they were already thinking past dinner to the next day, when time limits would again be pressuring them. Their most successful business year was now behind them and several new options were emerging.

SAILING

Zvonko Bezic and Zeljko Perovic, both born in 1962, met each other in the early 1970s when they both started sailing with the Galeb Sailing Club in Rijeka, Croatia. As students, they sailed together in the Flying Dutchman Class. At that time they were already modifying their racing sails, primarily of foreign make, adjusting them to their weight and style of sailing. They finished their university studies in the late 1980s (Zvonko Bezic with a degree in pedagogy and Zeljko Perovic in maritime traffic engineering).

In 1988, they were both employed, Zvonko Bezic as a journalist and editor for the Rijeka region with the Trade Union paper "Radnicke novine," and Zeljko Perovic (who usually goes by his sailing nickname, Huck) as a sailing coach in Galeb. Zeljko Perovic occasionally worked with Mr. Grego, who was making sails. It was here that Zeljko learned how to make sails for large sailboats; this involved knowing how much curve is needed for each horizontal panel and how to make the sail's final cut. In addition, he read English books dealing with this topic, which he found extremely interesting. In

Source: The case was written by Bostjan Antoncic, Faculty of Management at the University of Primorska.

The case is intended as a basis for class discussion rather than to illustrate either effective or ineffective handling of management situations.

1988, Zvonko Bezic and Zeljko Perovic started making sails on their own, at first only for the smallest optimist-class sailboats. They made their first design for these sails by taking apart a sail produced by Green, the most renowned sail manufacturer among sailors and coaches in the optimist class at that time. The same sail was also usable for larger sailboats, which was particularly important. The first set of sails for the sailing school in Rijeka was a direct copy of such a sail.

THE AFFABLE ESTABLISHMENT OF A COMPANY

At that time a friend from Rijeka, who himself was already a well-established and experienced tradesman, persuaded Zvonko Bezic to start his own business. He even suggested the type of business (chemicals) and a partner, but in the end they did not go into that field. Instead, together with Zeljko Perovic, they decided to establish a sail loft business. The above-mentioned friend offered them a loan of SFR 2,000 under the following conditions: should their enterprise survive for two years, they would not have to pay back the loan, but should they go bankrupt and not be successful, they would have to repay the loan together with accrued interest. They accepted the offer. Their friend also provided them with business cards and promotional material.

In 1989, the two started manufacturing regatta sails for the youth Optimist Class. They adapted the basic design and cut of the panels from the disassembled Green sail to the needs of lighter sails. Zeljko Perovic said that "they began to play with the form of sails." They simultaneously started to manufacture sails for larger sailboats and yachts. The sails were cut in the school gym they rented on weekends; on weekdays the sails were sewed at home together with Zeljko Perovic's grandmother. He remembers: ". . . we occupied a part of her house, first a small room and then an entire floor and even the garage." In the manufacturing of sails for larger sailboats the know-how and information acquired from Mr. Grego helped them extensively.

In 1990, the two decided to go into the sail business full time. They studied books and magazines and gathered a great deal of information on: (1) the materials used for sailmaking, (2) the manufacturing process itself, its history and developmental trends, and (3) other sail manufacturers. They learned about computer-aided sail cutting, and were also able to obtain information directly from sail manufacturers, particularly those from Slovenia and northern Italy. In the then relatively large factory for the mass production of sails in Forli, Italy, where the pair offered to sell the Italian firm's sails in the former Yugoslavia, they learned how the factory organized sail production and what equipment they used. "They employed an expert from New Zealand and used a computer program. In Forli we primarily tried to learn what they do and how they do it," relates Zeljko Perovic. They also learned a great deal during their visit to the newly opened sail loft of the largest global manufacturer, North, in Monfalcone, Italy, accompanying Dusan Puh who was then ordering sails for "Elan Team," of which Zvonko Bezic was a member, and for the Elan sailboat then called "Packa." They got useful information about the equipment they used and about where it could be ordered. While looking for a sail loft on Sardegna to have his torn sails repaired, Zeljko Perovic by chance found himself in a sail loft manufacturing Fois sails. He saw how simply they finish some details on the sail (e.g. edges and reinforcements) and how they have adapted their machines for this process.

The two decided to purchase a computer program for cutting the sails. For half a year they gathered data on which program to buy and tested five different demo programs. At the end of 1990, they bought a personal computer and Sailmaker Software (SMSW) from Autometrix, USA. While they knew that renowned sail manufacturers were also using plotters and cutters in addition to computers, they could not afford them. They also had difficulties financing production and covering fixed costs, since they had rented manufacturing facilities in Rijeka.

STANDSTILL AND A NEW START

In 1991 they accepted positions as hired sailors in Italy in order to raise some money. Concurrently, the market for sails in Croatia and Slovenia shrank that year, resulting in their not manufacturing sails but only maintaining some resale business. As there was practically no market in Croatia, they started looking for a new location for their sail loft—somewhere closer to Italy. They were about to decide on either Portorose, Slovenia, or Ravenna, Italy, when Mr. J. Kosmina offered them the opportunity to take over the sail repair service during the Match Race in Koper, Slovenia. They decided to stay in Koper and rented premises in the Koper Marina to start making sails again. At the beginning of 1992 they used their savings to buy a second-hand Autometrix plotter. "We were among the first in the local market (i.e., Slovenia, Croatia, and northern Italy) to start applying computer technology in the manufacturing of sails; in the whole of Italy, only the leading manufacturer—North—availed itself of computer technology," explains Zeljko Perovic.

In 1992, while they were making sails in Koper, they launched an additional activity—making advertising signs. As they started to plot the letters, they learned from other sign makers what programs to use, how they read the sketches and transfer them to the plotter (in terms of size and form). They used this know-how also in the computer aided design of reinforcements. The company was becoming known in this local market and could more easily establish contacts and exchange information with other local sailmakers. At the end of 1992, the company moved into larger premises in the marina and modernized their manufacturing process with the purchase of additional new sewing machines.

MARKETING STRATEGY

In 1993, sales increased and the company was obtaining customers from Italy, Germany, and Austria. At that time, the main local competitors of Intervela (their company) were: Olimpic Trieste, Italy (with sales of about USD 900,000 in 1993), Ulmer Kolius Lignano, Italy (USD 600,000), North Monfalcone, Italy (USD 180,000), Seaway Portorose, Slovenia (USD 180,000), and Zadro Trieste, Italy (USD 90,000). At the end of that year a sailor from Koper who had the status of junior researcher at the Faculty of Economics of the University of Ljubljana, Slovenia, prepared, in cooperation with both proprietors, a marketing plan for Intervela, which had hitherto only haphazardly planned a marketing strategy. Based on an analysis of the current demand and the competition, an increase in sales of 58 percent over the next three years (1994–1996) was established as the main goal, along with: a gradual increase in market share, the promotion of the company and its products to potential customers, and an improvement in the internal efficiency of the company and the quality of its products. The strengths (price and quality, including the finishing of sails and a two-year warranty), weaknesses (marketing communication, standardization, design), opportunities (selling larger series to companies, manufacturing sails for larger yachts), and threats (market contraction, poor advertising for sails, essential technological changes) were also established for sails—the key product of the company.

Development and market penetration were the primary focus of the company's business plan. The marketing strategy was formulated: product (standardization, design improvements, the transfer of improvements from racing sails to other sails, following trends closely, the introduction and improvement of after-sale services—i.e., the tuning of sails and instructing customers); price (competitive prices with regard to individual customers); place (the extension of the distribution network); and promotion (promotion by means of a first-class sailboat—*Gaia Cube*—in races, personal contacts, the distribution of promotional material to sailboat owners, and advertising in the Slovenian nautical magazine "Val"). They focused on the promotion of the Victory sail trademark.

In 1993, Intervala was the first to introduce a novelty in the production of larger sails: double batten pockets. This concept had previously only been applied to smaller Olympic sailboats and mentioned in professional journals. Some local rivals soon copied this idea.

Despite the shrinkage of the Italian market, the company consistently enjoyed increasing sales throughout 1994. The quality of their sails and the good publicity gained when the *Gaia Cube* sailboat won races contributed much to the sales results. In that year, Mr. Vencato, a rival from Trieste and the manufacturer of Ullman sails, proposed cooperation in part to learn what computer program and plotter they were using and how they worked. Soon afterwards, Mr. Vencato bought an improved version of the same software and plotter that at the same time worked as a cutter.

A DECISION ON THE CUTTER AND THE SITUATION IN 1995

In 1995, after another successful business year (a further increase in sales to USD 128,300—see Exhibit 1), the owner-managers of Intervela decided, among other new investments, to purchase a new plotter-cutter to cut sailcloth material. They also visited Mr. DeMartisu of the Olimpic sail loft in Trieste, who had purchased a new plotter-cutter that year. In 1995 more competitors visited Intervela than in the year before.

Intervela d.o.o. Koper is a relatively small limited liability company wholly owned by Zvonko Bezic and Zeljko Perovic. In 1995, the company primarily manufactured sails for racing sailboats and keelboats.[1] Sales under the brand name Victory accounted for 90 percent of total sales in 1995 (of which 65 percent were regatta sails), while sail repairs, advertising-sign making, and the manufacture of canvas covers, bags, and trapezes for sailboats accounted for the remaining 10 percent.

EXHIBIT 1 The Growth of Intervela d.o.o.

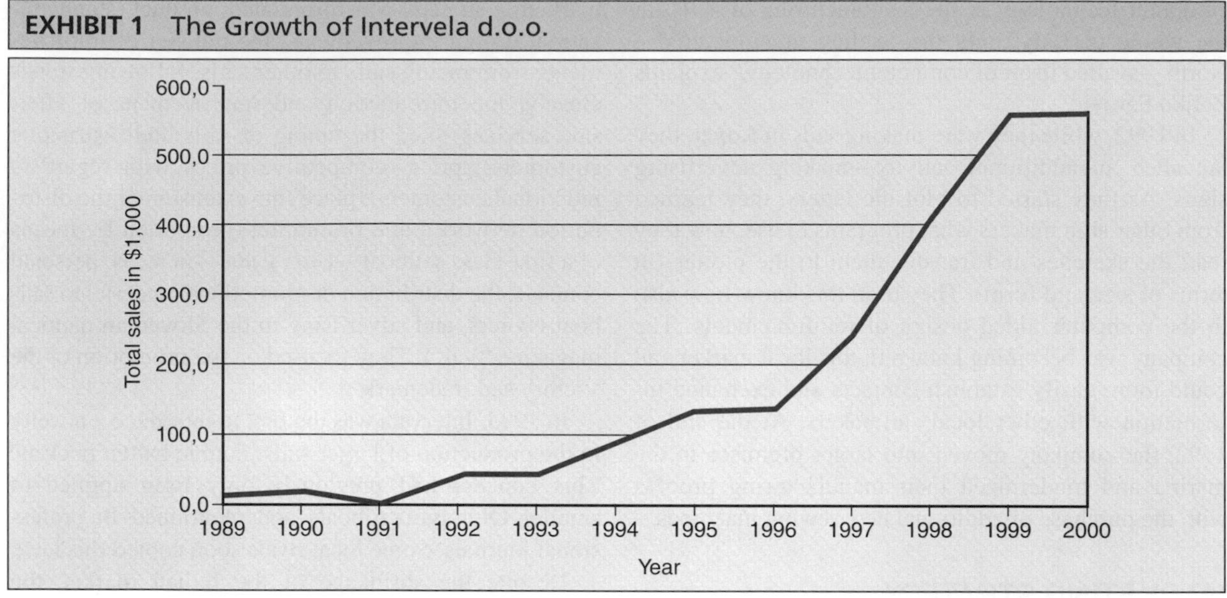

Source: Data from the company and the annual accounts of Intervela d.o.o.

Intervala in 1994 had USD 86,300 in sales revenue and six full-time staff (including owners) and USD 128,300 in sales revenue with five full-time employees in 1995. Zvonko Bezic is primarily responsible for marketing, while Zeljko Perovic is in charge of production.

THE PURCHASE OF A CUTTER

In 1995, Intervela purchased a sailcloth material cutter and two software packages for planning and designing sails, resulting in the use of three different software packages: SMSW, ProSail, and Crain. The American ProSail software program is, as one of the sail loft owners says, rather easy to use particularly for the designs for the cruising sails. The American SMSW and the French Crain software packages are more complex and require more time to design sails and are appropriate for the more demanding sails used in racing. The company started using SMSW in the first half of the nineties.

THE ACQUISITION OF THE KUTIN SAIL LOFT WORKSHOP

Due to the rapidly increasing demand for Victory sails, the two partners looked for additional workspace and staff in 1996. When the Kutin sail loft in Rijeka declared bankruptcy, the company acquired the workshop and moved their old plotter to Rijeka. The new location in Croatia began operations in May 2000.

ELAN

Prior to the bankruptcy, Kutin made sails for Elan, the biggest producer of sailboats in Slovenia. The Kutin-Elan relationship had difficulties due to quality problems and customer complaints. One of the Intervela owners explained that about 60 percent of the complaints received by Elan at that time concerned sails produced by Kutin, causing Elan to look for a new supplier.

Elan desired to have an inland supplier. Elan tried to have Rado Pelajic manufacture sails for small Zeta class sailboats, but that cooperation did not last. Elan then contacted Intervela and Zvonko and Zeljko prepared a contract. Because Victory sails were of higher quality than those produced by Kutin, a higher price was quoted, above Kutin's delivery price to Elan. Through negotiations a slightly lower price was agreed to in the final contract.

Zvonko and Zeljko thought that "this would be some business to fill in the gaps—in winter time when the market is flat." It involved the rather simple mass production of sails. A regular customer would also "provide a certain degree of security." However, in dealing with such a big customer as Elan, payment difficulties occurred. In spite of the agreed 60-day payment term, payment was received after 120 days or later. In 1998 a sailboat was received in compensation for unpaid invoices. In 2000 that sailboat, an Elan 36, captained by Franci Stres, sunk in a storm along the Croatian coast. In a second compensation deal in 1999, an Elan 333 Cruising boat was received as payment. In that year, Elan "faced bankruptcy."

Elan sent to Intervela a proposal for writing off such receivable claims, but Zvonko and Zeljko did not agree to it. Negotiations on the allocation of bankruptcy assets dragged on into mid-2001. "Since we were among the more important suppliers, they retained us as suppliers and did not write off our receivables," stated Zvonko Bezic. In 2001, Intervela continued to do business with Elan, but required pre-payment for the sails supplied. Orders from Elan increased. From 60 sailboats per year, sales of Elan sailboats (and Victory sails) increased to about 110 sailboats in the year 2000 and a planned 150 sailboats in 2001. Sales to Elan accounted for about one-fourth (about USD 137,500) of the total sales (about USD 550,000) of Intervela in 2000.

THE *GAIA CUBE* PROJECT

Intervela made their first sails for the racing boat *Gaia Cube* (subsequently the *Gaia Legend*) Consortium in 1995. In the period 1995–1997 they were also members of the crew and won races at the famous sailing event Barcolana in the bay of Trieste. Later, in 1998, the Kosmina family, which played the leading role in the consortium, decided to use sails made by the Trieste-based Olimpic. Olimpic, being the strongest local company at that time, offered some very low prices. The company made money by selling sails for smaller sailboats, which made it important to enter into this project regardless of the low price.

PENETRATING THE GLOBAL MARKET WITH FINN CLASS SAILS

At the end of 1997 and at the beginning of 1998 Intervela started to manufacture sails for the Olympic one-man Finn sailboat. Karlo Kuret, a renowned Croatian sailor in the class, asked them to make him a sail, because in his Olympic program the cost of sails was very high. He proposed they make him a copy of the Sobstadt sail, but Zvonko and Zeljko decided to develop a completely new sail. This new sail was a great international success. Using the Victory sail, Kuret won the Olympic Week race in Athens in February 1998.

Olympic champion Mateusz Kusnierewicz from Poland wanted to test the new sail at the pre-Olympic regatta in Medemblik, Netherlands. The sail was sown by Intervela overnight. The next day Kusnierewicz was racing with his sail. At the next pre-Olympic regatta, in Kiel, Germany, Kuznierewicz won seven out of nine races. From 1999 to 2001, using the Victory sail, he was the number one sailor in the world—his worst result was second place in the World and European championships (World Champion 1999 in Greece and 2000 in England); he took fourth place at the Olympic Games in Sydney.

When Intervela started to produce the Finn class sails, they also started to cooperate with the University of Zagreb, Croatia, where the first analyses of sailcloth were done. A comparison of various materials was made by analyzing 26 parameters. This analysis helps the company determine the quality of materials and the appropriateness of a material for their products.

Zvonko and Zeljko believe that, in addition to the development of a new product, the securing of top sailors in the Finn class having good results, and the application of new materials, the following three factors were important in their penetration into the Finn sails market:

- *Development of sails.* Victory sail representatives visit regattas, watch the races, and collect information and comments; Intervela has composed a team of top-level sailors (four of them were among the top ten in the world ranking in 2000 as well as as of mid-2001) and offers them special conditions such as adjusting the sails to their specific needs.
- *Novelty in sail design technology.* Intervela used sophisticated computer software in designing and constructing the sails for "one-design" types of sailboats, such as the Finn.
- *Analysis of sail quality.* The company tests sails by attaching sensors to the sail and a camera to the top of the mast to record sail performance during sailing; they then improve the sails based on an analysis of their performance.

Intervela was growing into a globally renowned company with the Victory brand name. At the Olympics in Sydney, 18 of the 25 sailors in the Finn class used Victory sails. The sails are now being sold all over the world: Canada, USA, Brazil, Australia, New Zealand, Republic of South Africa, China, Japan, Sweden, Denmark, Poland, Russia, Belarus, Ukraine, Lithuania, Germany, Great Britain, Belgium, France, Spain, Italy,

Ireland, Austria, Croatia, Slovenia, Hungary, Greece, and Turkey.

EUROPE CLASS

The company also succeeded in penetrating the European Dinghy class market. In 1999 the company's sails dominated the Slovene, Croatian, and Italian market and realized some sales even in Poland and Belarus. At the 2000 Olympics, female representatives of the USA, Italy, Belarus, and Poland raced with Victory sails.

THE OPTIMIST CLASS

In 2001, Intervela started developing a sail for the Optimist youth dinghy. In February and March 2001 the new sail was completed. They employed Karel Kuret, a top-sailor and an authority among Croatian sailors, who helped them with the development of the sail.

The company entered into an agreement with Sime Fantella, the 2000 World Champion, and with his father who was also his coach, that he would test their sail during the preparation stage (from February to April 2001), even though he had been racing with sails made by Olimpic of Trieste. Sime and his father were satisfied with the sail and soon other members of the Croatian team started to use Victory sails in races. In April 2001, Fantella won the South American Championship. The second Croatian competitor took third place; and in the women's competition, first place was won by a Croatian sailor. The Croatian team also won the team competition. In spite of the fact that in mid-2001 Olimpic enjoyed a market share of 50 percent, followed by North, Denmark and Toni Tio from Spain, the company established an objective of having 50 percent of the Croatian market within two years.

Even before manufacturing sails for the Optimist class, the company had encountered some competitive problems. After making a sail for an Italian, who finished very high in a regatta, an Olimpic representative gave the Italian one of their sails as a gift. Similarly, when the company tried to cooperate with Milan Morgan, who makes Optimist dinghies in Portorose, Slovenia, Intervela gave him some promotional sails. Milan used these sails as the basis for negotiating with Olimpic. Because of these and other unpleasant experiences, Intervela decided to proceed in a different way in Croatia. "Our first goal is the Croatian market—and we will not give up; we will attain this goal by September (2001). If you do not control your domestic market, you cannot control foreign ones," stated Zvonko Bezic. In 2001, there were already too many potential sales agents in Croatia and the company was receiving calls from agents from Peru, Brazil, Sweden, England, and the United States.

CLASS 470

Another goal established was to make it to the top in the 470 Olympic class. They started to develop the sails in cooperation with the coach of Russia's female sailors. In Slovenia they started to cooperate with the Olympian Vesna Dekleva, and in Croatia with Bulaja, who had participated in the Olympic Games in Sidney.

SAILS FOR CRUISING & RACING YACHTS

In addition to sails for smaller one-design dinghies, such as the Finn, Europe, Optimist and 470, which in mid-2001 accounted for around 30 percent of Intervela's sales, and sails produced for Elan, which accounted for about 30 percent of sales revenue, the company was continually evaluating new market opportunities. The entrepreneurs were always evaluating their rivals' products and how they were producing sails. At the end of the twentieth century, independent computer aided development and design of sails became important. The main markets for their sails were Slovenia and Croatia, and to a lesser extent Italy.

PROMOTION AND MARKETING IN 2000 AND 2001

At the beginning Intervela relied primarily on word of mouth advertising (satisfied owners of sails told other sailors about their experiences). The company did more formalized promotion and advertising in 2000 and 2001. They participated in nautical fairs in Slovenia and Croatia. They advertised in specialized nautical journals, such as "Val" and "Navtika" in Slovenia and "More" in Croatia, as well as in the specialized magazines of international sailing classes such as Finnfare and Optimist Dinghy. They also promoted their sails in newspaper articles which they wrote themselves or were written by journalists. Articles on sailors' preparations and their cooperation with Intervela, the success of Victory sails and the Intervela company appeared particularly in the Slovene newspapers "Primorske novice" and "Slovenske novice," in the Croatian "Novi list," and in the Italian journals "Fare Vela" and "Giornale della vela."

In 1998 the Web site of the company was designed. They increased the number of "hits" or visits by publishing news from regattas and by reporting the results online. At the same time, sailing clubs, organizers of races, and sailing associations started using the Internet for the real-time online reporting of race results.

The company made the sail covers and packaging (particularly the sail bags) uniform. They enlarged the Victory logo and decided on a red-white combination for the brand and background, because red made the logo very visible.

The company also created a clearer identity for the Victory brand name by using special material. They contracted with one of the factories to have a special sailcloth made exclusively for Victory sails. The material is Kevlar and the usual black thread in the cloth was exchanged for a red one. In this way, with no additional costs, easier and clearer recognition of their sails occurred. When they first introduced this novelty in the Finn class, many sailors believed that it was a completely new type of sail, not just a new material.

The two started doing more lectures and presentations in sailing clubs and during sailing races. In sailing clubs, they discussed, in particular, how sails operate and are trimmed. After having returned from the United States in the fall 2000, they presented to the organizer of the Europe class regatta the material used during that day's racing. Digital photos were shown and their presentation focused on sails and technical advice on trimming the mast. After establishing the cooperation with Karel Kuret Intervela decided to organize training camps for the best coaches and sailors in the class.

VISIT TO THE USA IN AUTUMN 2000

In the fall 2000, Zvonko Bezic and Zeljko Perovic went to visit some of the most important factories producing sailcloth material on the East Coast of the United States. "When we started, we could not even talk to or visit such factories or talk to sailcloth material sales representatives. . . . Today sales representatives visit us at least every three months," explained Zvonko Bezic.

When they arrived at the biggest sailcloth producer in the world, Bainbridge International, the general manager spent the entire day with them. A Power Point presentation, containing a section on cooperation between Bainbridge International and Intervela, and a "slide" showing the logos of both brand names and a link between them demonstrating future cooperation between the two companies occurred. They were guests of Bainbridge International for three days and it was there they got the idea to start using sales presentations to promote their sails.

MAIN CHANGES IN THE MARKET

In ten years of existence, Intervela has grown and become an important factor in the sail market. They have grown faster than their competition and reached and surpassed most. In 2001 the nautical market was still growing. "There is no recession, many people are buying yachts, sails. . . . The market is growing. . . . And Intervela is growing even faster," Zvonko Bezic commented.

STAFF, OUTSOURCING, AND REORGANIZATION

By mid-2001, Intervela had 15 regularly employed individuals working on contracts in Slovenia and 5 individuals in Croatia. Since the company did not have sufficient production space, they started to outsource the manufacturing of some parts, such as bags and reinforcements, to suppliers in Koper. A subcontractor was given two sewing machines and started sewing for Intervela in his garage.

The company introduced the special position of plotter operator, in order to use their facilities more efficiently. This person's job was to operate the computer or some other operation of the plotter. "We are looking for new people all the time. We also employ through the Employment Agency of Slovenia. But the number employed through the Agency is actually very low," commented Zvonko Bezic.

The friend who first helped Zvonko Bezic and Zeljko Perovic in the start-up of their company, decided—after the bankruptcy of his relatively large company in Croatia—to help establish production standards and improve the organization of the workshop. He analyzed how much a worker can do per hour, how much time is needed for each element of the production process, and the capabilities of workers. Zvonko Bezic said: "an experienced entrepreneur entered our workshop and found a hundred mistakes. . . . We are burdened with complicated issues. . . . Regarding simpler issues, such as the proper laying of material, however, improvements can also be found in the details, which add up to a lot in the end."

INTERNATIONAL PRODUCTION

Having taken over the workshop in Rijeka, Croatia, the company began production there as well. From this production facility the company covered the Croatian market and also produced Optimist sails. Two main possibilities are available for establishing production facilities in Italy.

The company first considered a location in Gorizia—in the International Business Center (a business incubator in Trieste with a branch office in Gorizia). The incubator offered assistance such as: sales staff with 50 percent of the pay subsidized, Internet services at minimum rates, assistance in getting loans and other forms of financing, and lower rent for business premises.

In 2001 the company considered purchasing the company of a local Italian sailor who had machines and workers but was not successful and had no desire to continue in the business. With the intention to expand their activities in Italy, they began training an Italian in their sail loft in Koper so he could then manage the work in Italy.

OTHER PLANS FOR THE FUTURE AND OPTIONS

In 2001, Intervela was planning to expand their 450 square meter facilities in Croatia. "Particularly for cruising sails . . . charter business is on the increase: 120 percent more tourists, 300 percent more than in 1999. . . . We shall have to invest here too," Zvonko Bezic reasoned. They began to search for a new location with about 1,000 square meters of space.

The company was also considering the possibility of using the brand name Victory on garments (jackets, T-shirts, etc.). This would promote the brand name on the one hand and bring in additional income. They started to look for partners who manufacture sportswear who would be willing and able to carry out such a project. In 1999, the company negotiated with a potential partner, but the potential partner withdrew from the project. In 2001, Intervela was still opposed to pushing the project forward without finding a good partner who was very interested.

At this same time, the company had contact with some major sailmakers, mainly in the United States. They started discussing a possible merger or at least joining an already established group. The two main conditions needed were money and less operational work. Right now Zvonko Bezic and Zeljko Perovic are in a dilemma regarding the following three alternatives:

- Develop a foreign trade name and work as a member of a group;
- Merge with a foreign company; or
- Sell the company—find a potential partner with money who would acquire a part or the entire company.

CASE 2E
THE GRIL-KLEEN CORPORATION

"Well, where do I begin?" Warren Ryan wondered as he surveyed the chaos before him. Boxes and bottles were piled all over the place, invoices and order forms cluttered the desk top and filled the drawers, and he couldn't seem to locate anything resembling an orderly set of books.

It was spring of 2001, and just a few days earlier Ryan had quit his job with a large management consulting firm to assume the presidency of Gril-Kleen Corporation and help get the young company off the ground.

The company's efforts to market its innovative product, a liquid restaurant grill cleaner, had been extremely successful. Ryan felt that with a professional marketing approach, the product could capture a sizable share of a national market.

The product, a chemical solution which could be applied directly to a working grill and would clean off bumt-on food and accumulated grease in a matter of minutes, represented a significant departure from the existing methods of cleaning restaurant grills. It appeared to have several major advantages over competing products, and initially it had generated such enthusiastic response from users that the product had practically sold itself.

PRODUCT EVOLUTION

Gril-Kleen had been developed for their own use by two brothers who owned a small, busy restaurant in Eastern Massachusetts. The restaurant's grill needed cleaning several times a day, especially during busy periods, and the brothers were disturbed by the amount of time and effort it took to clean the grill. They were also bothered by the orders they lost while the grill was being cleaned.

Most grill-cleaning products then available could not be used on a hot grill, and the time required to cool, clean, and then reheat the grill varied from about 20 minutes to almost an hour, depending on the method being used and the condition of the grill.

Two of the most popular methods of cleaning grills used a carborundum "stone" or a wire mesh screen to scrub the grill clean. Though inexpensive, they required a great deal of physical labor and both products tended to wear, with some danger of stone chips or metal particles ending up in food cooked on the grill.

Spray foam oven-cleaner type products, similar to those sold for home use, were easier to use but considerably more expensive. Most had critical effective temperatures of around 160°–200° Fahrenheit, compared to normal grill operating temperatures of around 350°, and often had objectionable odors, which restricted their use in small or poorly ventilated restaurants.

Dissatisfied with the products then on the market, the two brothers decided to develop their own grill cleaner. They sought the advice of one of their customers in the chemical business, and from him they learned of some chemicals and began to experiment with different combinations in various proportions.

The cleaner they sought would clean grills quickly, easily, and at normal operating temperature. It had to be economical, easy to mix, and have no discernible odor or taste, and it would have to pass safety requirements (i.e., be both nontoxic for use on food preparation surfaces and noncaustic to the user's skin). In addition, it had to leave the grill "seasoned" so that food wouldn't stick to the grill after it had been cleaned.

After experimenting and modifying the solution for a couple of years, the brothers finally arrived at a mixture having all the desired properties. It would work on both hot and cold grills, and the grill operator could clean a grill in less than five minutes by simply pouring the solution on, allowing it to dry, and then rinsing the grill with water. After a light seasoning with cooking oil, the grill was ready for use again.

Soon, friends in the restaurant business heard about the product and began asking for samples, then coming back for more. As demand increased, the brothers started to sell the product by the gallon, charging whatever they felt the market would bear.

THE GRIL-KLEEN CORPORATION

The product appeared to be so successful that the brothers began to think about marketing it on a larger scale. One of the restaurant's customers, a line foreman for the Boston Edison Company, was impressed by the demand for the product, and urged the brothers to consider manufacturing and selling it on a regular basis. In early 1997, the three of them formed the Gril-Kleen Corporation.

Working out of the basement of the restaurant, the three new partners bottled and sold Gril-Kleen in their spare time and on their days off. The chemicals were mixed in a large plastic tub with a spigot, then transferred to gallon-size plastic bottles labeled "Gril-Kleen."

On Tuesdays, when the restaurant was closed, the two brothers made sales calls to other restaurants, leaving behind samples of the product. Even with this minimal sales effort, orders began to increase to the point where larger facilities were needed to bottle and store the product. Less than a year after its incorporation, the Gril-Kleen Corporation moved to a new and larger headquarters in a nearby Industrial Park.

The new plant was a 1,500-square-foot cinderblock building, and the equipment consisted of a large stainless steel tub, formerly used for pasteurizing milk and capable of producing 450 gallons of Gril-Kleen per day. The company hired one part-time employee to mix the chemicals and fill the bottles.

After one unfortunate experience with a traveling salesman who offered to sell the product and instead, sold several phony "exclusive distributorships" for Gril-Kleen throughout New England before he disappeared, the company established relationships with half a dozen bona fide distributors of restaurant and cleaning supplies in New England.

As sales volume grew, the need for a full-time manager became increasingly apparent. Orders and invoices were piling up, billing was haphazard, records were disorganized and incomplete. With no regular system of record-keeping, orders often went unfilled, or customers were never billed for orders that had been shipped.

Recognizing that the company had grown too large to continue operating on a one-day-per-week basis, the owners hired a local politically ambitious individual to run the company, and offered him a 25 percent interest in the business. The new partner was well known locally, had a number of important connections, and the company owners felt that his name would lend some prestige to the operation.

As it turned out, he devoted little of his time and attention to running the business and most of it to campaigning for re-election, even charging some of his campaign expenses to the company. After more than a year, with company sales declining, the other three partners bought him out, paid his bills, and returned to running the business on their days off.

WARREN RYAN

At this point, Warren Ryan, a management consultant working on an assignment nearby, began patronizing the restaurant and became friendly with the owners. When he learned of the situation at Gril-Kleen, he suggested that the company hire his consulting firm to do a market study and map out an operating and marketing plan for the company. He also recommended that they utilize his firm's Executive Search service to find a new president for Gril-Kleen.

Reluctant to deal with a large consulting firm or to hire anyone they didn't know to run the company, the brothers asked Ryan if he would take over the job himself. Ryan, an MBA with extensive experience in marketing, advertising, and industrial management, was intrigued by the idea. He had grown up in a household with a small, family-owned business, and had long been interested in applying his management and marketing skills to running a company. He agreed to consider the offer, and then began to research the product and its market. From library sources, he estimated the national restaurant cleaning market at about $80 million a year, and learned that no single company held a dominant share of the market.

From experience with the product and interviews with current users of Gril-Kleen, he became convinced of Gril-Kleen's performance superiority over competing products. Moreover, he was impressed by the apparent success of the company despite the lack of good planning, and concluded that the product could be developed successfully. After serious consideration and considerable research, he decided to accept the offer, and in April of 2001, became the new president of the Gril-Kleen Corporation.

THE SITUATION IN EARLY 2001

When Ryan took over, he found the product being manufactured in the small, one-story cinderblock plant in Hingham. The company's one part-time employee could mix and bottle up to 200 gallons a day to meet orders, and plant capacity could easily be increased by buying a larger mixing tank and hiring more labor. It was also possible to rent additional floor space if necessary. The product was packaged in cases of four (4) one-gallon-size plastic containers. It was sold for $28 a case retail, $18 a case wholesale, F.O.B. the wholesaler's warehouse. Included with each case was a 16-ounce squeeze-type plastic applicator bottle.

Sales volume at the time was approximately $35,000 a year. The average usage rate was approximately one case per month. The company's primary customers were six wholesale distributors in Massachusetts: the Gantlin Company, a supplier of chemicals to restaurants and institutions; the Downer Company, a paper products distributor; the Bay State Restaurant Equipment and Supply Company; Alden Sales Corporation, which supplies cleaning products to small restaurants; the Janitor Supply Company, selling to hotels and motels; and Theatres, Inc., a distributor of food products and supplies to theatres and drive-ins.

Ryan found few records, little financial data, and no regular flow of paperwork within the company. Prices were based on those charged for a competitive product, with no regard for or knowledge of actual costs or profit margins.

To apply for a working capital loan, Ryan had to develop a marketing plan for the next 12 months and projected cash flow statements for the next three years and then present his marketing plan and cash requirements to a bank.

ADDITIONAL PRODUCT USES

Before he could develop a marketing plan, Ryan had to decide which markets to approach and determine realistic market-share goals for Gril-Kleen. There was considerable evidence that the product could do much more than just clean restaurant grills. Preliminary tests had indicated that the product was effective in cleaning stainless steel, ceramic tile, formica, vinyl, plastic, chrome, machine tools, clothing, and fiberglass. The last use suggested a possible application in cleaning boat hulls, a market which strongly appealed to the owners of Gril-Kleen (See Exhibit 3). The product also appeared to be effective as a rust remover and preventative, suggesting a wide variety of possible industrial uses.

Ryan had to determine which markets to develop, which product lines to offer, and what degree of market penetration could be achieved in each market segment before he could set profit targets and schedules. The restaurant, marine, and industrial markets required different selling methods and different channels of distribution and posed different pricing, packaging, promotion, and selling requirements.

Before deciding which markets to pursue, Ryan needed additional information on the requirements of each market segment and the dollar and volume potential for each. Within each market, he had to decide whether to segment the market by uses, type of customer, or geographical territory.

Ryan wondered whether market testing would be useful in analyzing market need, product potential, and the habit patterns of users in the various markets, and if so, whether market testing should be accomplished by field product testing, field interviews, or mail or telephone surveys.

It was felt by Warren Ryan that Gril-Kleen could significantly increase its share in this market. Current sales of $35,000 a year represented a little less than half of 1 percent of the potential market for restaurant cleaning products in the New England area alone. However, the product appeared to fill a particular need in this market, while there was considerable competition from similar products in the other markets under consideration (marine, industrial, consumer).

PRICING

To help determine standard costs, break-even volumes over a range of possible product prices, and profit margins, Ryan collected the cost data in Exhibit 1.

Ryan needed to determine a pricing strategy, set profit targets, determine the volume necessary to meet those targets, and establish a policy on trade discounts, allowances, and credit terms. He also needed further information on price elasticity (one dealer had tripled his sales from 4 to 13 cases a month by lowering the retail price from $28 a case to $24).

EXHIBIT 1 Cost Data for Gril-Kleen

Materials:

1 ounce = $.0028

1 batch = 32 cases = 1,120 lbs. = $45.32 (83 percent water)

Bottles (cost per thousand):

	Number of Units (dollar amount is cost per 1,000)			
Size	**1,000**	**5,000**	**10,000**	**25,000**
16 oz.	$ 90	$ 85	$ 78	$ 60.75
32 oz.	155	135	125	97.30
64 oz.	220	195	154.75	147.25
128 oz.*	245	202.75	184.75	178.95
Caps				
28 mm	$ 12			$ 10
33 mm	15			12
38 mm	20			15
Printing				
16 oz.	$ 17.50	$ 15	$ 12.50	$ 12.50
32 oz.	20	17.50	15	15
64 oz.	25	20	20	20
128 oz.	30	30	30	30

Sprayer: (bought separately by customer)

for 28 mm cap $.48 ea. $.43 ea. $.39 ea. $.38 ea. for 15,000 or more

* = 1 gallon

Shipping Costs: $6.00 per hundredweight, or about $1.50 per case

Approximate Fixed Costs (per month)		**Labor**
Rent	$1,000	32 oz.: $.046 per bottle 128 oz.: .057 per bottle
Travel	400	
Telephone	80	
Gas heat	450	Sales costs estimated at 400 percent of labor, G & A at 250 percent of labor.
Insurance	200	
Accounting	300	
Depreciation	300	
Office	500	

Checking the reorder rates, Ryan calculated the rate of usage of the product to be approximately one case every month in a small, one-grill restaurant. Approximately 97 percent of end-users who had tried Gril-Kleen continued to order it.

DISTRIBUTION

Among the distribution decisions to be made were whether to (1) hire a sales force (and if so, how large), (2) use manufacturer's representatives (and if so, how many and with what commissions) (3) sell exclusively to wholesalers; (4) sell directly to restaurants and large chain operations; and (5) grant exclusive privileges to any dealers, distributors, or representatives (and if so, what demands to make upon the holders of such exclusive rights).

Other decisions related to distribution included questions on consignment sales, volume discounts, and shipping costs. Ryan also had to decide whether to expand his distribution network geographically or to concentrate on getting a larger share of the New England market.

PROMOTION

To successfully promote the product, Ryan had to determine which media to employ, how much to spend on advertising, and how to push or pull the product through to the ultimate user. In addition, he had to design some catalog sheets and fact sheets for Gril-Kleen similar to those in Exhibits 2 and 3. In designing these, he had to decide which product features to stress: price, convenience, effectiveness, safety, etc.

PATENT AND TRADEMARK

Ryan also wondered whether he should try to patent the product. He didn't know if it was patentable, if it infringed upon any existing patents, or if he could obtain a trademark on the name Gril-Kleen and/or on the product logo he planned to design.

He wasn't sure that a patent would be valuable to the company, or even necessary, or whether it was worth all the trouble and expense required for a patent application. Legal costs alone, whether the patent were granted or not, could amount to about $4,000 or more and would afford doubtful protection from imitators. The company would have the right to sue if it discovered anyone else using its formula, but patent litigation would be too time-consuming and expensive for a company of Gril-Kleen's size.

COMPETITION

The most common grill cleaning products then in use, especially in smaller restaurants, were the "stone" and the "screen." The stone is a block of carborundum (hard soapstone) about the size of a brick, which was used to scrub the grill and remove grease and food residue. The screen was a wire mesh screen placed in a device similar to a sandpaper holder which was used to scour the grill much like home scouring pads. Both were inexpensive but required a great deal of effort to use, took about an hour to clean a fairly dirty grill, and could not be used on a hot grill. In addition, the stone especially tended to wear and chip, with some danger that stone chips might end up in food cooked on the grill.

There were also several chemical liquid and spray foam over-cleaner-type products on the market that could be used to clean grills. Most of these were fairly expensive and had critical effective temperatures of around 160–200°. These competitive products were generally marketed by fairly large companies, with large advertising budgets and wide distribution networks. Among these were Swell, DuBois, Easy-Off, and Jifoam. Colgate-Palmolive and Lever Brothers also had plans to introduce new chemical oven cleaner products.

DuBois liquid oven cleaner (see Exhibit 2) was sold in four-gallon cases for $28.00 a case retail and employed its own sales force to sell directly to retailers. Swell was marketed via wholesale distributors for $7.00 a gallon or $26.50 a case retail and used its own sales force to sell to wholesalers.

DEVELOPING A MARKETING PLAN

To develop a sound marketing plan, it was necessary to determine the size of the potential market in units and dollars, estimate the market share that Gril-Kleen could expect to attain, and then develop sales projections over a 12-month period.

They needed to find out who and where the distributors of restaurant cleaning products in New England were and determine the best means of selling to them. They also had to calculate potential sales volumes at various prices and price the product to maximize profits (or volume). They would need to construct volume discount schedules and determine the effects of any increase or decrease in price on demand and on profits.

EXHIBIT 2 Sample Catalog Sheet

TECHNICAL DATA FOR OVEN CLEANER AND DEGREASER

General Description—DUBOIS OVEN CLEANER and DEGREASER is a light tan alkaline liquid which is highly effective for the removal of baked-on fats, greases, and carbon deposits normally found in baking ovens. Also recommended for grills, deep fryers, and undersides of range hoods or canopies, where grease and carbon accumulate. OVEN CLEANER is nonflammable and USDA acceptable in meat and poultry plants.

PROPERTIES—Chemical Composition .... Caustic, soil suspending agents and foam boosting surfactants.

Biodegradable .... Yes, all surfactants

Caustic .... Present

pll 1% Solution 11.7

Metal Safety .... Safe on iron, steel, stainless steel, nickel, porcelain, and glass. May be used on enamel and paint (when diluted). It may etch aluminum and will tarnish copper, brass, zinc, and tin, and galvanize on long contact.

USING PROCEDURE—Oven & Equipment—For first-time cleaning of heavy carbon and grease, use UNDILUTED. Thereafter, use 1:1 to 1:3 with water.

For best results, use on a warm oven (160°–200°). Spray on with Trigger Spray Unit, direct from gallon bottle of solution. Foaming action allows product to cling to walls and top side of oven: thus, cleaner works harder. Allow cleaner to penetrate for five minutes. For heavy carbon, use oven brush, or Scotch Bright brand applicator on a handle. Rinse with wet sponge, to remove all grease and carbon residue. Can be applied with good results on cold oven when cleaner is allowed to set 15 to 20 minutes. Heavily encrusted ovens may require a second application. One application will be adequate for periodically cleaned ovens.

Grills—use 1:1 to 1:3 with water.

Hoods—use 1:4 with water

Fryers—use 1:15 with water

Steak Platter—use 1:1 with water.

PACKAGING—Four 1 gal. plastic bottles per case (35# net weight)

6 gal. cans (53# net weight)

30 gal. drums (264# net weight)

CAUTION—ALKALINE. Do not take internally. Do not get in eyes or on skin. In case of contact, flush skin with plenty of water; for eyes, flush with plenty of water for at least 15 minutes and get medical attention. If swallowed drink a large quantity of water, followed by whites of eggs or mineral oil, and call physician.

DUBOIS CHEMICALS DIVISION W. R. GRACE & COMPANY

DuBois Technical Representatives are located throughout the U.S., Canada, the United Kingdom, Latin America, Germany, France, Japan, and Africa.

They should consider whether any market or product testing is necessary, and if so, what type and how much. These decisions would form the basis for Gril-Kleen's marketing plan, from which Warren Ryan could develop projected cash flow statements and estimate his working capital needs over the next 12 months.

EXHIBIT 3 Sample Fact Sheet

FANTASTIK BOAT CLEANER—MARINE WHOLESALE FACT SHEET

PRODUCT: Fantastik Boat Cleaner

MANUFACTURER: Texize Chemicals, Inc., P.O. Box 368, Greenville, SC 29602

PACKS:	32 oz. Spray Gun	64 oz. Refill
Code	#298	#299
Case pack	12	6
Case weight	31 lbs.	30 lbs.
UNIT RETAIL:	$ 2.59	$ 3.29
CASE RETAIL:	$ 31.08	$ 19.74
WHOLESALE DISCOUNT:	50%–10%	
WHOLESALE COST:	$ 13.99	$ 8.88
TERMS:	2%/10 Days	Net 30 Days

WHOLESALE INTRODUCTORY OFFER:

Texize Offers One Case Free with Each Five Cases Purchased on All Orders

BILLING: Free Goods to Be Invoiced at No Charge

SALESMAN INCENTIVE OFFER:

Texize to Pay $1.00 per Case to Salesman for Each Case Sold to Retail Outlets
PAYMENT: Payment to Be Made on a Count and Recount Basis by Texize Representative
Monies to Be Paid Directly to Individual Salesman at the Close of Each Month

WHOLESALE EXCLUSIVE:

Fantastik Boat Cleaner Will Be Offered for Sale Only through Bonified Wholesale Distributors

Shipments Will Not Be Made Directly to Any Exclusively Retail Accounts

SALES GUARANTEE:

Texize Guarantees the Sale of This Product When Adequately Displayed at Retail Sales Point

ADVERTISING:

Fantastik Boat Cleaner Will Be Advertised with Full and Half-Page Spreads in the Following Publications: BOATING, MOTOR BOATING, RUDDER, YACHTING, LAKELAND BOATING, BOAT BUYER'S GUIDE, BOATING INDUSTRY, MARINE PRODUCTS, and MARINE MERCHANDISING.

(Plus: The Bonus of a Multi-Million Dollar Campaign That Is Making the Fantastik Name a Household By-Word)

SHIPPING POINTS: Texize Plant or Warehouse

PRODUCT LIABILITY INSURANCE: Yes

END NOTE

1. Keelboats are medium-sized and larger sailing boats that now prevail in all marinas in the world. They shall be distinguished from smaller dinghies that, in most cases, are single-type sport sailboats made according to strictly defined international rules in order to avoid, as much as possible, any differences within the same class (e.g., class: 470, Finn, Laser, Europe, Optimist, etc.).

FINANCING THE NEW VENTURE

CHAPTER 11
Sources of Capital

CHAPTER 12
Informal Risk Capital, Venture Capital, and Going Public

CASES FOR PART 3

11

SOURCES OF CAPITAL

LEARNING OBJECTIVES

1
To identify the types of financing available.

2
To understand the role of commercial banks in financing new ventures, the types of loans available, and bank lending decisions.

3
To discuss Small Business Administration (SBA) loans.

4
To understand the aspects of research and development limited partnerships.

5
To discuss government grants, particularly small business innovation research grants.

6
To understand the role of private placement as a source of funds.

OPENING PROFILE

SCOTT WALKER

Some entrepreneurs are born and others are created through focus, energy, and desire. Scott Walker is the latter style, developing his own lifelong learning curriculum in creating opportunities and taking risks.

www.BillMatrix.com

Walker was born an Air Force brat; his family was posted at stations across the country throughout his childhood. This training, including six different grade schools and three high schools in three different states, gave him the ability to get along anywhere, to be comfortable with different types of people, and to be self-sufficient. Walker brought these capabilities to a series of start-up companies, including one very successful financial technology firm.

After receiving a BA from Utah State University in 1977, Walker selected a graduate school that would initiate his career as an entrepreneur. Thunderbird, The Garvin School of International Management, provided an environment for learning how an interesting idea can become a business—as well as exposure to the broader world as represented by students and faculty from around the globe. Walker graduated in 1981 with an MBA.

The banking world and its activity in mergers and acquisitions was the first professional stop for Walker. Based in Dallas, he centered much of his effort on the oil and gas industry, including working with T. Boone Pickens, the notorious corporate raider of the 1980s, and his Mesa Petroleum Co. Pickens prided himself on being able to see undervalued assets and subsequently make a profit when outside parties and the market recognized that value. That lesson was not lost on Walker. Nor was the idea that businesses need to be responsive to their shareholders and stakeholders, even if they have to be dragged to that realization—as Pickens did to staid management teams with his hostile takeover bids.

After a number of years in banking with such firms as Lloyd's Bank and GE Capital, Walker noticed that many of the people he respected in this industry were leaving to work on riskier, more nontraditional and stimulating ventures. This appealed to Walker, playing to his strengths and providing a new channel for his energy. However, he did not feel that he understood all the details of how to successfully build a new venture, so he searched for an established entrepreneur who could show him the basics. That person was William Conley, a friend and successful serial business builder, who was starting an Internet backbone infrastructure company to provide Internet points of presence, or POPs. Walker was the second employee and CFO of the fledgling technology firm in 1995. After one year of hard work with few paychecks, the firm was sold to GTE. It remains a portion of the Internet backbone today.

While that first taste of risk taking was exhilarating, Walker returned to the corporate world as CFO of Precept Business Services, a $200 million company. He gathered useful experience in the process of taking a company public, as he was instrumental in achieving that status for Precept through an S-4 registration, where securities are issued in a business combination transaction.

When Conley again touched base with Walker in 1998, he was ready for a new challenge. This opportunity was [the establishment of] a not-for-profit [educational assistance] company. This company, one2one Learning Foundation, provided individualized curriculum programs for children not enrolled in traditional public or private institutions. While serving as CFO of the foundation, Walker was approached by Clint Norton, another friend, to assist with the sale of a small company Norton's father had invested in three years earlier.

After a short time, it became clear to Walker that the ongoing talks were not going to lead to a transaction with the buyer and he requested a 30-day leave from his current responsibilities to clean up the company and find someone else to buy it. Once inside, he discovered that there was a great concept hiding inside this poorly managed company, which was called TelePay. The firm provided large recurring billers with a way to have their consumers pay their bills using an automated telephone service known as interactive voice response, or IVR (the "press 1 for . . ." technology). A wide range of payment choices, including credit cards, ATM debit cards, and ACH or electronic checks, was offered to provide not only speed but also great flexibility for the consumer. The revenue model for TelePay reflected the "many small slices" nature of the transaction industry—the consumers paid a small incremental fee above the amount owed for the convenience of not writing a check or visiting an office. The biller did not pay for the setup or ongoing maintenance of the service.

Walker recognized the potential and joined it as president and CEO in early 1999, when there were only four employees. This was the chance to put all that he had learned as an apprentice into his own company. He saw that TelePay had very loyal clients despite a number of nagging technical glitches, so his first decision was to completely rebuild the system on a single software platform. The key to success was to ensure that the resulting architecture would scale up from 1,000 transactions to 10 million transactions. His second act was to bring on a senior sales executive who could leverage the loyalty of the existing customers into references for new prospects. This expensive investment required trusting that the person could deliver new clients quickly. On advice from Conley, Walker hired the right person. Both early decisions proved correct; the company's infrastructure has readily grown with the client base and two of its initial four employees, as well as the sales executive, remain with the company today.

After renaming the company BillMatrix Corporation, the team started to develop a stellar client list. Walker built out the senior executive staff, adding a COO, CFO, and both client and consumer support personnel. The company has been cash flow positive since the first month of his tenure and revenue has grown over 100 percent year after year, every year. Because of its cash flow, the company has not required venture capital for growth, thereby keeping the majority control of the company and all of the decision-making processes in the hands of the senior executives. Walker's ability to make skillful choices, based upon what is good for the business and good for the clients (but not necessarily those with the least risk), has created a strong organization.

The company has been at the forefront in applying new technology to electronic bill payments since its restart by Walker in 1999. Internet-based payments were added to the telephone service as use of that channel is now expected by consumers. Multiple technologies are used for real-time connectivity to client systems for data verification and immediate posting of payments. A self-service client information portal delivers real-time payment data to client personnel. The company continually looks to add other innovations to its service as they become available.

BillMatrix serves a diverse client base of over 125 companies today, including those in the utilities, telecom, insurance, and consumer finance industries. Walker's organization has over 175 employees and a strong reputation for operational excellence and exceptional client service in the electronic payments industry. His mantra to the employees is: "We handle two of the most important things for our clients—their money and their customers. We must always act with the highest ethics and integrity."

In 2005, the electronic payments industry was considered a hot area and the time was ripe for maximizing the value of an acquisition. Walker led the company in a buyout process with a large number of interested parties. The resulting transaction was an acquisition of BillMatrix by Fiserv, Inc. (NASDAQ: FISV) of Brookfield, Wisconsin, for $350 million in August 2005. This was the second largest acquisition in dollar value for Fiserv, which has built itself primarily by acquisition into a $3.4 billion company with over 16,000 clients worldwide and 22,000 employees. BillMatrix is serving as the cornerstone of Fiserv's greater role in the overall payment business, a growth engine for its core business of financial technology and services.

For all his success, Walker is dedicated to being an entrepreneurship philanthropist. While he is a generous monetary donor to his alma mater—Thunderbird—he also provides the more important gift of time with students who are looking for the same knowledge he needed early in his career. His goal is to help the next generation get a quicker start on their ventures by sharing his knowledge about how to build a strong business around a good idea.

AN OVERVIEW

One of the most difficult problems in the new venture creation process is obtaining financing. For the entrepreneur, available financing needs to be considered from the perspective of debt versus equity and using internal versus external funds.

Debt or Equity Financing

debt financing Obtaining borrowed funds for the company

Two types of financing need to be considered: debt financing and equity financing. *Debt financing* is a financing method involving an interest-bearing instrument, usually a loan, the payment of which is only indirectly related to the sales and profits of the venture. Typically, debt financing (also called asset-based financing) requires that some asset (such as a car, house, plant, machine, or land) be used as collateral.

Debt financing requires the entrepreneur to pay back the amount of funds borrowed as well as a fee expressed in terms of the interest rate. There can also be an additional fee, sometimes referred to as points, for using or being able to borrow the money. If the financing is short term (less than one year), the money is usually used to provide working capital to finance inventory, accounts receivable, or the operation of the business. The funds are typically repaid from the resulting sales and profits during the year. Long-term debt (lasting more than one year) is frequently used to purchase some asset such as a piece of machinery, land, or a building, with part of the value of the asset (usually from 50 to 80 percent of the total value) being used as collateral for the long-term loan. Particularly when interest rates are low, debt (as opposed to equity) financing allows the entrepreneur to retain a larger ownership portion in the venture and have a greater return on the equity. The entrepreneur needs to be careful that the debt is not so large that regular interest payments become difficult if not impossible to make, a situation that will inhibit growth and development and possibly end in bankruptcy.

equity financing Obtaining funds for the company in exchange for ownership

Equity financing does not require collateral and offers the investor some form of ownership position in the venture. The investor shares in the profits of the venture, as well as any disposition of its assets on a pro rata basis based on the percentage of the business owned. Key factors favoring the use of one type of financing over another are the availability of funds, the assets of the venture, and the prevailing interest rates. Usually, an entrepreneur meets financial needs by employing a combination of debt and equity financing.

All ventures will have some equity, as all ventures are owned by some person or institution. Although the owner may sometimes not be directly involved in the day-to-day management of the venture, there is always equity funding involved that is provided by the owner. The amount of equity involved will of course vary by the nature and size of the venture. In some cases, the equity may be entirely provided by the owner, such as in a small ice cream stand or pushcart in the mall or at a sporting event. Larger ventures may require multiple owners, including private investors and venture capitalists. This equity funding provides the basis for debt funding, which together make up the capital structure of the venture.

Internal or External Funds

Financing is also available from both internal and external funds. The funds most frequently employed are internally generated funds. Internally generated funds can come from several sources within the company: profits, sale of assets, reduction in working capital, extended payment terms, and accounts receivable. In every new venture, the start-up years involve putting all the profits back into the venture; even outside equity investors do not expect any payback in these early years. The needed funds can sometimes be obtained by selling little-used assets. Assets, whenever possible, should be on a rental basis (preferably on a lease with an option to buy), not an ownership basis, as long as there is not a high level of inflation and the rental terms are favorable. This will help the entrepreneur conserve cash, a practice that is particularly critical during the start-up phase of the company's operation.

A short-term, internal source of funds can be obtained by reducing short-term assets: inventory, cash, and other working-capital items. Sometimes an entrepreneur can generate the needed cash for a period of 30 to 60 days through extended payment terms from suppliers. Although care must be taken to ensure good supplier relations and continuous sources of supply, taking a few extra days in paying can generate needed short-term funds. A final method of internally generating funds is collecting bills (accounts receivable) more quickly. Key account holders should not be irritated by implementation of this practice, as certain customers have established payment practices. Mass merchandisers, for example, pay their bills to supplying companies in 60 to 90 days, regardless of a supplying company's accounts receivable policy, the size of the company, or the discount offered for prompt payment. If a company wants this mass merchandiser to carry its product, it will have to abide by this payment schedule.

One entrepreneur who is very successful at leveraging the discounts from vendors is home product distributor Jeff Schreiber. At a Dallas trade show in January, he negotiated a deal with the manufacturer to purchase $40,000 in ceiling fans, giving him a 3 percent discount if payment was received by May 1 and an extra 3/4 percent for payment received each month earlier. He would receive no discount if payment was received after May 1, and he had until July as the absolute payment deadline. Schreiber received the fans earlier, as well as $1,800 in savings by paying in February. Schreiber always tries to take advantage of any discounts for prompt payments, and he obtained over $15,000 in early payment savings in 2002 alone.[1]

The other general source of funds is external to the venture. Alternative sources of external financing need to be evaluated on three bases: the length of time the funds are available, the costs involved, and the amount of company control lost. In selecting the best source of funds, each of the sources indicated in Table 11.1 needs to be evaluated along these three dimensions. The more frequently used sources of funds (self, family and

TABLE 11.1 Alternative Sources of Financing

	Length of Time		Cost			Control		
Source of Financing	Short Term	Long Term	Fixed Rate Debt	Floating Rate Debt	Percent of Profits	Equity	Covenants	Voting Rights
Self		×				×	×	×
Family and friends	×	×	×	×		×	×	×
Suppliers and trade credit	×				×			
Commercial banks	×		×	×			×	
Government loan programs	×	×	×	×			×	
R&D limited partnerships		×			×	×	×	
Private investors (angels)		×	×			×	×	×
Venture capital		×	×			×	×	×
Private equity placements						×	×	×
Public equity offerings					×	×		×
Other government programs		×						

ETHICS

It was not the first time he discovered fraud committed by his boss—also the owner of the company. A year after he joined the firm, as the head of accounting, he came across several loans that were financed not once but two and three times. The owner claimed the loans were obtained "inadvertently" and, further, "it was no big deal and won't happen again." A year later, the accountant discovered it did happen again. This time his boss said, "Don't worry," and promised, "I'll take care of it." Over the next few years, more signs of trouble surfaced: serious cash flow difficulties, officers' loan accounts exceeding net worth, doctored financial transactions, and extravagant spending by the principals. Then, some seven years after he first came to the company, the firm pled guilty to check kiting and received the maximum penalty under the law.

Why would the accountant stay under these circumstances? Clearly, the company was in deep financial trouble and a principal had resorted to fraud and other forms of misconduct in the past, and, therefore, was quite capable of doing it again. Why not get out? The accountant eventually did leave, but only after he and other inside accountants had discovered hard evidence of fraud amounting to more than $40 million—and that was for only one year. On leaving, the accountant did not reveal what he knew to the authorities. Nor did the other accountants, who continued to work for the company. A year after he resigned, a massive fraud was uncovered—19 financial institutions had been swindled out of more than $220 million during a 10-year period. Could the fraud have been prevented? Why didn't the accountant and many others, who either knew or strongly suspected the fraud, take action?

Signs of trouble are typically present, but simply missed by the persons involved. How do you know a fraud is being committed by a client, customer, or someone within your own organization?

- Insufficient working capital or credit.
- Extremely high debt with rigid restrictions imposed by creditors.
- Dependence on few products, services, or customers.
- Unfavorable and declining industry or business conditions.
- Management of the organization or department dominated by one or a few individuals.
- Understaffed or inexperienced financial and accounting functions.
- Weak internal control system.
- Rapid turnover in key financial positions and/or frequent change in auditors.
- Numerous unexplained and undocumented transactions.
- Apparent tolerance by management of unethical and even illegal conduct.

Source: This material was adapted from Bob Gandoss and Rosabeth Moss Kanter, "'See No Evil, Hear No Evil, Speak No Evil'—Leaders Must Respond to Employee Concerns about Wrongdoing," *Business and Society Review* 107, no. 4 (2001), pp. 415–22.

friends, commercial banks, R&D limited partnerships, government loan programs and grants, venture capital, and private placement) indicated in the table are discussed at length below. The firms in the *Entrepreneur* 2003 Hot 100 list got start-up capital from savings (61 percent), private investors (31 percent), friends and family (18 percent), home equity lines of credit (17 percent), bank loans (16 percent), credit cards (10 percent), the sale of another business (1 percent), SBA loans (1 percent), and other sources (2 percent).

Whenever an entrepreneur deals with items external to the firm, particularly with people and institutions that could become stakeholders, ethical dilemmas can sometimes occur. An ethical problem involving the owner of a company is indicated in the Ethics box.

PERSONAL FUNDS

Few, if any, new ventures are started without the personal funds of the entrepreneur. Not only are these the least expensive funds in terms of cost and control, but they are absolutely essential in attracting outside funding, particularly from banks, private investors, and venture capitalists. The typical sources of personal funds include savings, life insurance, or mortgage on a house or car. These outside providers of capital feel that the entrepreneur may not be sufficiently committed to the venture if he or she does not have money invested. As one venture capitalist succinctly said, "I want the entrepreneurs so financially committed that when the going gets tough, they will work through the problems and not throw the keys to the company on my desk."

This level of commitment is reflected in the percentage of total assets available that the entrepreneur has committed, not necessarily in the amount of money committed. An outside investor wants an entrepreneur to have committed all available assets, an indication that he or she truly believes in the venture and will work all the hours necessary to ensure success. Whether this is $1,000, $100,000, or $250,000 depends on the assets available. The entrepreneur should always remember that it is not the amount but rather the fact that all monies available are committed that makes outside investors feel comfortable with their commitment level and therefore more willing to invest.

FAMILY AND FRIENDS

After the entrepreneur, family and friends are a common source of capital for a new venture. They are most likely to invest due to their relationship with the entrepreneur. This helps overcome one portion of uncertainty felt by impersonal investors—knowledge of the entrepreneur. Family and friends provide a small amount of equity funding for new ventures, reflecting in part the small amount of capital needed for most new ventures. Although it is relatively easy to obtain money from family and friends, like all sources of capital, there are positive and negative aspects. Although the amount of money provided may be small, if it is in the form of equity financing, the family members or friends then have an ownership position in the venture and all rights and privileges of that position. This may make them feel they have a direct input into the operations of the venture, which may have a negative effect on employees, facilities, or sales and profits. Although this possibility must be guarded against as much as possible, frequently family and friends are not problem investors and in fact are more patient than other investors in desiring a return on their investment.

In order to avoid problems in the future, the entrepreneur must present the positive and negative aspects and the nature of the risks of the investment opportunity to try to minimize the negative impact on the relationships with family and friends should problems occur. One thing that helps to minimize possible difficulties is to keep the business arrangements strictly business. Any loans or investments from family or friends should be treated in the same businesslike manner as if the financing were from an impersonal investor. Any loan should specify the rate of interest and the proposed repayment schedule of interest and principal. The timing of any future dividends must be disclosed in terms of an equity investment. If the family or friend is treated the same as any investor, potential future conflicts can be avoided. It is also beneficial to the entrepreneur to settle everything up front and in writing. It is amazing how short memories become when money is involved. All the details of the financing must be agreed upon before the money is put into the venture. Such things as the amount of money involved, the terms of the money, the rights and responsibilities of the investor, and what happens if the business fails must all be agreed upon and written down. A formal agreement with all these items helps avoid future problems.

Finally, the entrepreneur should carefully consider the impact of the investment on the family member or friend before it is accepted. Particular concern should be paid to any

AS SEEN IN *ENTREPRENEUR* MAGAZINE

ELEVATOR PITCH FOR JACK BLACK

A wealthy friend has asked you to keep your eye out for attractive businesses in which she can invest. Your friend is very busy and you only want to introduce those businesses that are genuinely attractive. After hearing the following pitch, would you introduce Emily and Curran to your wealthy friend?

Entrepreneurs Emily Dalton (37) and Curran Dandurand (43), co-founders of Jack Black in Addison, Texas.
Description High-end men's grooming products
Start-Up $400,000 in 2000
Sales Projected sales for current year of $5 million
Crossing Gender Lines Dalton and Dandurand spent years in branding and marketing for makeup and skin-care giants and met while working at Mary Kay. They looked at the world of men's personal care and saw promise. "We knew there was a huge opportunity with men. A lot of big companies had tried to [launch] a line but failed to break through. [It had to be] a start-up company with fresh thinking," reasons Dandurand.
Tall, Dark and Simple The partners did massive research to get inside the minds of men. Targeting "the guy's guy," Dalton reports: "He cares about how he looks. But he's not going to do a five-step skin-care regimen." To fulfill men's desire for simplicity, the entire Jack Black line is multifunctional, like the All-Over Wash for face, hair and body. Inspired by the package design of premium liquor and cigars, they created packaging that's distinctively masculine and alluringly familiar.
Delivered Male Besides selling in Nordstrom and Saks Fifth Avenue and at GetJackBlack.com, the co-founders get innovative by distributing to private country clubs, resorts, and professional sports teams' locker rooms. Says Dalton, "We've been able to connect with guys in a way no brand has been able to do."

Source: Reprinted with permission of Entrepreneur Media, Inc., "Emily Dalton and Curran Dandurand," by April Y. Pennington, March 2003, *Entrepreneur* magazine: www.entrepreneur.com.

hardships that might result should the business fail. Each family member or friend should be investing in the venture because they think it is a good investment, not because they feel obligated.

COMMERCIAL BANKS

Commercial banks are by far the source of short-term funds most frequently used by the entrepreneur when collateral is available. The funds provided are in the form of debt financing and, as such, require some tangible guaranty or collateral—some asset with value. This collateral can be in the form of business assets (land, equipment, or the building of the venture), personal assets (the entrepreneur's house, car, land, stock, or bonds), or the assets of the cosigner of the note.

Types of Bank Loans

There are several types of bank loans available. To ensure repayment, these loans are based on the assets or the cash flow of the venture. The *asset base for loans* is usually accounts receivable, inventory, equipment, or real estate.

asset base for loans
Tangible collateral valued at more than the amount of money borrowed

Accounts Receivable Loans Accounts receivable provide a good basis for a loan, especially if the customer base is well known and creditworthy. For those creditworthy customers, a bank may finance up to 80 percent of the value of their accounts receivable. When customers such as the government are involved, an entrepreneur can develop a factoring arrangement whereby the factor (the bank) actually "buys" the accounts receivable at a value below the face value of the sale and collects the money directly from the account. In this case, if any of the receivables is not collectible, the factor (the bank) sustains the loss, not the business. The cost of factoring the accounts receivable is of course higher than the cost of securing a loan against the accounts receivable without factoring being involved, since the bank has more risk when factoring. The costs of factoring involve the interest charge on the amount of money advanced until the time the accounts receivable are collected, the commission covering the actual collection, and protection against possible uncollectible accounts.

Inventory Loans Inventory is another of the firm's assets that is often a basis for a loan, particularly when the inventory is liquid and can be easily sold. Usually, the finished goods inventory can be financed for up to 50 percent of its value. Trust receipts are a unique type of inventory loan used to finance floor plans of retailers, such as automobile and appliance dealers. In trust receipts, the bank advances a large percentage of the invoice price of the goods and is paid on a pro rata basis as the inventory is sold.

Equipment Loans Equipment can be used to secure longer-term financing, usually on a 3- to 10-year basis. Equipment financing can fall into any of several categories: financing the purchase of new equipment, financing used equipment already owned by the company, sale-leaseback financing, or lease financing. When new equipment is being purchased or presently owned equipment is used as collateral, usually 50 to 80 percent of the value of the equipment can be financed depending on its salability. Given the entrepreneur's tendency to rent rather than own, sale-leaseback or lease financing of equipment is widely used. In the sale-leaseback arrangement, the entrepreneur "sells" the equipment to a lender and then leases it back for the life of the equipment to ensure its continued use. In lease financing, the company acquires the use of the equipment through a small down payment and a guarantee to make a specified number of payments over a period of time. The total amount paid is the selling price plus the finance charges.

Real Estate Loans Real estate is also frequently used in asset-based financing. This mortgage financing is usually easily obtained to finance a company's land, plant, or another building, often up to 75 percent of its value.

Cash Flow Financing

conventional bank loan Standard way banks lend money to companies

The other type of debt financing frequently provided by commercial banks and other financial institutions is cash flow financing. These *conventional bank loans* include lines of credit, installment loans, straight commercial loans, long-term loans, and character loans. Lines of credit financing is perhaps the form of cash flow financing most frequently used by entrepreneurs. In arranging for a line of credit to be used as needed, the company pays a "commitment fee" to ensure that the commercial bank will make the loan when requested and then pays interest on any outstanding funds borrowed from the bank. Frequently, the loan must be repaid or reduced to a certain agreed-upon level on a periodic basis.

Installment Loans Installment loans can also be obtained by a venture with a track record of sales and profits. These short-term funds are frequently used to cover working capital needs for a period of time, such as when seasonal financing is needed. These loans are usually for 30 to 40 days.

Straight Commercial Loans A hybrid of the installment loan is the straight commercial loan, by which funds are advanced to the company for 30 to 90 days. These self-liquidating loans are frequently used for seasonal financing and for building up inventories.

Long-Term Loans When a longer time period for use of the money is required, long-term loans are used. These loans (usually available only to strong, mature companies) can make funds available for up to 10 years. The debt incurred is usually repaid according to a fixed interest and principal schedule. The principal, however, can sometimes start being repaid in the second or third year of the loan, with only interest paid the first year.

Character Loans When the business itself does not have the assets to support a loan, the entrepreneur may need a character (personal) loan. These loans frequently must have the assets of the entrepreneur or other individual pledged as collateral or the loan cosigned by another individual. Assets that are frequently pledged include cars, homes, land, and securities. One entrepreneur's father pledged a $50,000 certificate of deposit as collateral for his son's $40,000 loan. In extremely rare instances, the entrepreneur can obtain money on an unsecured basis for a short time when a high credit standing has been established.

Bank Lending Decisions

One problem for the entrepreneur is determining how to successfully secure a loan from the bank. Banks are generally cautious in lending money, particularly to new ventures, since they do not want to incur bad loans. Regardless of geographic location, commercial loan decisions are made only after the loan officer and loan committee do a careful review of the borrower and the financial track record of the business. These decisions are based on both quantifiable information and subjective judgments.[2]

The bank-lending decisions are made according to the five Cs of lending: character, capacity, capital, collateral, and conditions. Past financial statements (balance sheets and income statements) are reviewed in terms of key profitability and credit ratios, inventory turnover, aging of accounts receivable, the entrepreneur's capital invested, and commitment to the business. Future projections on market size, sales, and profitability are also evaluated to determine the ability to repay the loan. Several questions are usually raised regarding this ability. Does the entrepreneur expect to be carried by the loan for an extended period of time? If problems occur, is the entrepreneur committed enough to spend the effort necessary to make the business a success? Does the business have a unique differential advantage in a growth market? What are the downside risks? Is there protection (such as life insurance on key personnel and insurance on the plant and equipment) against disasters?

Although the answers to these questions and the analysis of the company's records allow the loan officer to assess the quantitative aspects of the loan decision, the intuitive factors, particularly the first two Cs—character and capacity—are also taken into account. This part of the loan decision—the gut feeling—is the most difficult part to assess. The entrepreneur must present his or her capabilities and the prospects for the company in a way that elicits a positive response from the lender. This intuitive part of the loan decision becomes even more important when there is little or no track record, limited experience in financial management, a nonproprietary product or service (one not protected by a patent or license), or few assets available.

Some of the concerns of the loan officer and the loan committee can be reduced by providing a good loan application. While the specific loan application format of each bank differs to some extent, generally the application format is a "mini" business plan that consists of an executive summary, business description, owner/manager profiles, business projections, financial statements, amount and use of the loan, and repayment schedule. This information provides the loan officer and loan committee with insight into the creditworthiness of the individual and the venture as well as the ability of the venture to make enough sales and profit to repay the loan and the interest. The entrepreneur should evaluate several alternative banks, select the one that has had positive loan experience in the particular business area, call for an appointment, and then carefully present the case for the loan to the loan officer. Presenting a positive business image and following the established protocol are necessary to obtain a loan from a commercial bank.

Generally, the entrepreneur should borrow the maximum amount that can possibly be repaid as long as the prevailing interest rates and the terms, conditions, and restrictions of the loan are satisfactory. It is essential that the venture generate enough cash flow to repay the interest and principal on the loan in a timely manner. The entrepreneur should evaluate the track record and lending procedures of several banks in order to secure the money needed on the most favorable terms available. This "bank shopping procedure" will provide the needed funds at the most favorable rates.

ROLE OF SBA IN SMALL BUSINESS FINANCING

Frequently, an entrepreneur is missing the necessary track record, assets, or some other ingredient to obtain a commercial bank loan. When the entrepreneur is unable to secure a regular commercial bank loan, an alternative is a guarantee from the Small Business Administration (SBA). The SBA offers numerous loan programs to assist small businesses. In each of these, the SBA is primarily a guarantor of loans made by private and other institutions. The basis 7(a) Loan Guaranty is the SBA's primary business loan program. This program helps qualified small businesses obtain financing when they cannot obtain business loans through regular lending channels. The proceeds from such a loan can be used for a variety of business purposes, such as working capital; machinery and equipment; furniture and fixtures; land and building; leasehold improvements; and even, under some conditions, debt refinancing.

In order to get a 7(a) loan, the small business person or entrepreneur must be eligible. While repayment ability from the cash flow of the business is of course essential, other criteria include good character, management capability, collateral, and owner's equity contribution. Eligibility factors for all 7(a) loans include size, type of business, use of proceeds, and the availability of funds from other sources. All owners of 20 percent or more are required to personally guarantee SBA loans.

The SBA 7(a) loan program has a maximum loan amount of $2 million with the SBA's maximum exposure of $1 million. In the case of a $2 million loan, the maximum guarantee to the lender by the SBA will be $1 million or 50 percent. Though the interest rates on the loan are negotiated between the borrower and the lender, they are subject to SBA maximums, which are pegged to the prime rate and may be fixed or variable. For example, a fixed rate loan of $50,000 or more must not exceed prime plus 2.25 percent if the maturity is less than seven years.

Most of the loans have the same guarantee features. The SBA can guarantee 85 percent of loans of $150,000 or less and 75 percent of loans above $150,000 to a maximum of $1 million. Some differences occur in SBA Express loans (maximum guarantee of 50 percent) and export working capital loans (maximum guarantee of 90 percent). To help offset the costs of the SBA loan programs, lenders are charged a guaranty and servicing fee for each approved loan. These fees can be passed on to the borrower and vary depending on the amount of the loan.

In addition to the 7(a) loan program, the SBA has several other programs. The 504 loan program provides fixed-rate financing to enable small businesses to acquire machinery, equipment, or even real estate in order to expand or modernize. The maximum of the program is usually $1 million, and the loan can take a variety of forms, including a loan from a Community Development Company (CDC) backed by a 100 percent SBA-guaranteed debenture.

Another more recent SBA loan program that many entrepreneurs have used is the SBA Microloan, a 7(m) loan program. This program provides short-term loans of up to $35,000 to small businesses for working capital or the purchase of inventory, supplies, furniture, fixtures, machinery, or equipment. The loan cannot be used to pay existing debts. The small business receives the loan from a bank or other organization, with the loan being guaranteed by the SBA. The SBA also provides such loans as Home and Personal Property Disaster Loans, Physical Disaster Business Losses Loans, and Military Reservist Economic Injury Disaster Loans. The entrepreneur should check with the SBA to see whether a loan program is available, if a loan cannot be obtained without the SBA guarantee.

RESEARCH AND DEVELOPMENT LIMITED PARTNERSHIPS

research and development limited partnerships Money given to a firm for developing a technology that involves a tax shelter

Research and development limited partnerships are another possible source of funds for entrepreneurs in high-technology areas. This method of financing provides funds from investors looking for tax shelters. A typical R&D partnership arrangement involves a sponsoring company developing the technology with funds being provided by a limited partnership of individual investors. R&D limited partnerships are particularly good when the project involves a high degree of risk and significant expense in doing the basic research and development, since the risks, as well as the ensuing rewards, are shared.

Major Elements

The three major components of any R&D limited partnership are the contract, the sponsoring company, and the limited partnership. The contract specifies the agreement between the sponsoring company and the limited partnership, whereby the sponsoring company agrees to use the funds provided to conduct the proposed research and development that hopefully will result in a marketable technology for the partnership. The sponsoring company does not guarantee results but rather performs the work on a best-effort basis, being compensated by the partnership on either a fixed-fee or a cost-plus arrangement. The typical contract has several key features. The first is that the liability for any loss incurred is borne by the limited partners. Second, there are some tax advantages to both the limited partnership and the sponsoring company.

limited partner A party in a partnership agreement that usually supplies money and has a few responsibilities

The second component involved in this contract is the limited partners. Similar to the stockholders of a corporation, the *limited partners* have limited liability but are not a total taxable entity. Consequently, any tax benefits of the losses in the early stages of the R&D limited partnership are passed directly to the limited partners, offsetting other income and reducing the partners' total taxable incomes. When the technology is successfully developed in later years, the partners share in the profits. In some instances, these profits for tax purposes are at the lower capital gains tax rate as opposed to the ordinary income rate.

general partner The overall coordinating party in a partnership agreement

The final component, the sponsoring company, acts as the *general partner* developing the technology. The sponsoring company usually has the base technology but needs funds to further develop and modify it for commercial success. It is this base technology that the company is offering to the partnership in exchange for money. The sponsoring company usually retains the rights to use this base technology to develop other products and the right to use the developed technology in the future for a license fee. Sometimes, a cross-licensing agreement is established whereby the partnership allows the company to use the technology for developing other products.

Procedure

An R&D limited partnership generally progresses through three stages: the funding stage, the development stage, and the exit stage. In the funding stage, a contract is established between the sponsoring company and limited partners, and the money is invested for the proposed research and development effort. All the terms and conditions of ownership, as well as the scope of the research, are carefully documented.

In the development stage, the sponsoring company performs the actual research, using the funds from the limited partners. If the technology is subsequently successfully developed, the exit stage commences, in which the sponsoring company and the limited partners commercially reap the benefits of the effort. There are three basic types of arrangements for doing this: equity partnerships, royalty partnerships, and joint ventures.

In the typical equity partnership arrangement, the sponsoring company and the limited partners form a new, jointly owned corporation. On the basis of the formula established in the original agreement, the limited partners' interest can be transferred to equity in the new corporation on a tax-free basis. An alternative is to incorporate the R&D limited partnership itself and then either merge it into the sponsoring company or continue as a new entity.

Another possible exit to the equity partnership arrangement is a royalty partnership. In this situation, a royalty based on the sale of the products developed from the technology is paid by the sponsoring company to the R&D limited partnership. The royalty rates typically range from 6 to 10 percent of gross sales and often decrease at certain established sales levels. Frequently, an upper limit, or cap, is placed on the cumulative royalties paid.

A final exit arrangement is through a joint venture. Here the sponsoring company and the partners form a joint venture to manufacture and market the products developed from the technology. Usually, the agreement allows the company to buy out the partnership interest in the joint venture at a specified time or when a specified volume of sales and profit has been reached.

Benefits and Costs

As with any financing arrangement, the entrepreneur must carefully assess the appropriateness of establishing an R&D limited partnership in terms of the benefits and costs involved. Among the several benefits is that an R&D limited partnership provides the funds needed with a minimum amount of equity dilution while reducing the risks involved. In addition, the sponsoring company's financial statements are strengthened through the attraction of outside capital.

There are some costs involved in this financial arrangement. Typically, it is more expensive to establish than conventional financing. First, time and money are expended. An R&D limited partnership frequently takes a minimum of six months to establish and $50,000 in professional fees. These can increase to a year and $400,000 in costs for a major effort. And the track record is not as good, as most R&D limited partnerships are unsuccessful. Second, the restrictions placed on the technology can be substantial. To give up the technology developed as a by-product of the primary effort may be too high a price to pay for the funds. Third, the exit from the partnership may be too complex and involve too much fiduciary responsibility. These costs and benefits need to be evaluated in light of other financial alternatives available before a research and development limited partnership is chosen as the funding vehicle.

Examples

In spite of the many costs involved, there are numerous examples of successful R&D limited partnerships. Syntex Corporation raised $23.5 million in an R&D limited partnership to develop five medical diagnostic products. Genentech was so successful in developing human growth hormone and gamma Interferon products from its first $55 million R&D limited partnership that it raised $32 million through a second partnership six months later to develop a tissue-type plasminogen activator. Trilogy Limited raised $55 million to develop a high-performance computer. And the list goes on. Indeed, R&D limited partnerships offer one financial alternative to fund the development of a venture's technology.

GOVERNMENT GRANTS

The entrepreneur can sometimes obtain federal grant money to develop and launch an innovative idea. The Small Business Innovation Research (SBIR) program, designed for the small business, was created as part of the Small Business Innovation Development Act. The act requires that all federal agencies with R&D budgets in excess of $100 million award a portion of their R&D funds to small businesses through the *SBIR grants program*. This act not only provides an opportunity for small businesses to obtain research and development money but also offers a uniform method by which each participating agency solicits, evaluates, and selects the research proposals for funding.

SBIR grants program Grants from the U.S. government to small technology-based businesses

Ten federal agencies are involved in the program (see Table 11.2). Each agency develops topics and publishes solicitations describing the R&D topic it will fund. Small businesses submit proposals directly to each agency using the required format, which is somewhat standardized, regardless of the agency. Each agency, using its established evaluation

TABLE 11.2 Federal Agencies Participating in Small Business Innovation Research Program

- Department of Defense (DOD)
- National Aeronautics and Space Administration (NASA)
- Department of Energy (DOE)
- Department of Health and Human Services (DHHS)
- National Science Foundation (NSF)
- U.S. Department of Agriculture (USDA)
- Department of Transportation (DOT)
- Nuclear Regulatory Commission (NRC)
- Environmental Protection Agency (EPA)
- Department of Education (DOED)
- Department of Commerce (DOC)

criteria, evaluates each proposal on a competitive basis and makes awards through a contract, grant, or cooperative agreement.

The SBIR grant program has three phases. Phase I awards are up to $100,000 for six months of feasibility-related experimental or theoretical research. The objective here is to determine the technical feasibility of the research effort and assess the quality of the company's performance through a relatively small monetary commitment. Successful projects are then considered for further federal funding support in Phase II.

Phase II is the principal R&D effort for those projects showing the most promise at the end of Phase I. Phase II awards are up to $750,000 for 24 months of further research and development. The money is to be used to develop prototype products or services. A small business receiving a Phase II award has demonstrated good research results in Phase I, developed a proposal of sound scientific and technical merit, and obtained a commitment for follow-on private-sector financing in Phase III for commercialization.

Phase III does not involve any direct funding from the SBIR program. Funds from the private sector or regular government procurement contracts are needed to commercialize the developed technologies in Phase III.

Procedure

Applying for an SBIR grant is a straightforward process. The government agencies participating (indicated in Table 11.2) publish solicitations describing the areas of research they will fund. Each of these annual solicitations contains documentation on the agency's R&D objectives, proposal format, due dates, deadlines, and selection and evaluation criteria. The second step involves the submission of the proposal by a company or individual. The proposal, which is 25 pages maximum, follows the standard proposal format. Each agency screens the proposals it receives. Knowledgeable scientists or engineers then evaluate those that pass the screening on a technological basis. Finally, awards are granted to those projects that have the best potential for commercialization. Any patent rights, research data, technical data, and software generated in the research are owned by the company or individual, not by the government.

The SBIR grant program is one viable method of obtaining funds for a technology-based entrepreneurial company that is independently owned and operated, employs 500 or fewer individuals, and has any organizational structure (corporation, partnership, sole proprietorship).

Another grant program available to the entrepreneur is the Small Business Technology Transfer (STTR) program, which was established by the Small Business Technology Transfer Act of 1992. Federal agencies with budgets over $1 billion are required to set aside 0.3 percent for small businesses. Five agencies participate in the STTR program—the Department of Defense (DOD), the Department of Energy (DOE), the Department of Health and Human Services (DHHS), the National Aeronautics and Space Administration (NASA), and the National Science Foundation (NSF). All these, except DHHS, also participate in the SBIR program. While a comparison of the SBIR and STTR programs is found in Table 11.3, the two programs differ in two major ways. First, while in the SBIR program, the principal investigator must have his/her primary employment with the small business concern receiving the award. In contrast, for the duration of the project, there is no employment stipulation in the STTR program. Second, the STTR program requires research partners at universities or other nonprofit institutions, with at least 40 percent of the research conducted by the small business concern and at least 30 percent conducted by the partnering nonprofit institution. The SBIR program has a maximum of 33% [Phase I] and 50% [Phase II] in consulting costs. The procedure for obtaining a STTR award is the same as for the SBIR award.

TABLE 11.3 Comparison of SBIR and STTR Programs

Requirements	SBIR	STTR
Applicant organization	Small Business Concern (SBC)	Small Business Concern (SBC)
Award period	Phase I—6 months, normally Phase II—2 years, normally	Phase I—1 year, normally Phase II—2 years, normally
Award dollar guidelines	Phase I—$100,000 normally Phase II—$750,000 normally	Phase I—$100,000 normally Phase II—$750,000 normally
Principal investigator	Employed by company more than 50% of her or his time *during* award. Minimum level of effort on the project not stipulated.	Employment not stipulated. The PI must spend a minimum of 10% effort on the project and have a formal appointment with or commitment to the SBC.
Subcontract/consultant costs	Phase I—Total amount of contractual and consultant costs normally may not exceed 33% of total amount requested. Phase II—Total amount of contractual and consultant costs normally may not exceed 50% of total amount requested.	Phase I and Phase II—SBC must perform at least 40% of work, and the single, partnering U.S. nonprofit research institution (RI) must perform at least 30% of the work.
Performance site	Must be entirely in United States. Part of research must take place in company-controlled research space.	Must be entirely in United States. Part of research must take place in company-controlled research space and part in that of partnering U.S. research institution.

PRIVATE PLACEMENT

Another source of funds for the entrepreneur is private investors, also called angels, who may be family and friends or wealthy individuals. Individuals who handle their own sizable investments frequently use advisors such as accountants, technical experts, financial planners, or lawyers in making their investment decisions. Business angels are discussed in more detail in Chapter 12.

Types of Investors

An investor usually takes an equity position in the company, can influence the nature and direction of the business to some extent, and may even be involved to some degree in the business operation. The degree of involvement in the day-to-day operations of the venture is an important point for the entrepreneur to consider in selecting an investor. Some investors want to be actively involved in the business; others desire at least an advisory role in the direction and operation of the venture. Still others are more passive in nature, desiring no active involvement in the venture at all. Each investor is primarily interested in recovering his or her investment plus a good rate of return.

Private Offerings

private offering A formalized method for obtaining funds from private investors

A formalized approach for obtaining funds from private investors is through a *private offering*. A private offering is different from a public offering or going public (the focus of Chapter 16) in several ways. Public offerings involve a great deal of time and expense, in large part due to the numerous regulations and requirements involved. The process of registering the securities with the Securities and Exchange Commission (SEC) is an arduous task requiring a significant number of reporting procedures once the firm has gone public. Since this process was established primarily to protect unsophisticated investors, a private offering is faster and less costly when a limited number of sophisticated investors are involved who have the necessary business acumen and ability to absorb risk. These sophisticated investors still need access to material information about the company and its management. What constitutes material information? Who is a sophisticated investor? How many is a limited number? Answers to these questions are provided in Regulation D.

Regulation D

Regulation D Laws governing a private offering

Regulation D contains (1) broad provisions designed to simplify private offerings, (2) general definitions of what constitutes a private offering, and (3) specific operating rules—Rule 504, Rule 505, and Rule 506. Regulation D requires the issuer of a private offering to file five copies of Form D with the Securities and Exchange Commission (SEC) 15 days after the first sale, every 6 months thereafter, and 30 days after the final sale. It also provides rules governing the notices of sale and the payment of any commissions involved.

The entrepreneur issuing the private offering carries the burden of proving that the exemptions granted have been met. This involves completing the necessary documentation on the degree of sophistication of each potential investor. Each offering memorandum presented to an investor needs to be numbered and must contain instructions that the document should not be reproduced or disclosed to any other individual. The date that the investor (or the designated representative) reviews the company's information—that is, its books and records—as well as the date(s) of any discussion between the company and the investor need to be recorded. At the close of the offering, the offering company needs to verify and note that no persons other than those recorded were contacted regarding the offering. The book documenting all the specifics of the offering needs to be placed in the company's permanent file. The general procedures of Regulation D are further broadened by the three rules—504, 505, and 506. Rule 504 provides the first exemption to a company seeking to raise a small amount of capital from numerous investors. Under Rule 504, a company can sell up to $500,000 of securities to any number of investors, regardless of their sophistication, in any 12-month period. While there is no specific form of disclosure required, the issuing company cannot engage in any general solicitation or advertising. Some states do not allow investors to resell their shares unless the security is registered.

Rule 505 changes both the investors and the dollar amount of the offering. This rule permits the sale of $5 million of unregistered securities in the private offering in any 12-month period. These securities can be sold to any 35 investors and to an unlimited number of accredited investors. This eliminates the need for the sophistication test and disclosure requirements called for by Rule 504. What constitutes an "accredited investor"? Accredited investors include (1) institutional investors, like banks, insurance companies, investment companies, employee benefit plans containing over $5 million in assets, tax-exempt organizations with endowment funds of over $25 million, and private business development companies; (2) investors who purchase over $150,000 of the issuer's securities; (3) investors whose net worth is $1 million or more at the time of sale; (4) investors with incomes in excess of $200,000 in each of the last two years; and (5) directors, executive officers, and general partners of the issuing company.

AS SEEN IN *ENTREPRENEUR* MAGAZINE

PROVIDE ADVICE TO AN ENTREPRENEUR ABOUT SMALL BUSINESS INVESTMENT COMPANIES

It started out as a straightforward consulting project for Mahendra Vora and research partner Sundar Kadayam. They were analyzing software trends and perusing market research studies to assess the size of various software markets. But after spending 40 hours looking for information that should have taken 10 minutes to access, the pair concluded that more advanced tools were needed to search the Internet and databases of public information. Within months, they launched Intelliseek Inc., providing software to capture, track, and analyze information for use in strategic planning, market research, product development, and brand marketing. Vora, 39, was no stranger to start-ups. By the time he co-founded Intelliseek in 1997, he already had three business launches under his belt. He sold all three to Fortune 500 firms, providing capital for Intelliseek. His initial investment of a few million dollars supported operations the first couple of years and two major product launches.

By 1999, the Cincinnati company was laying the groundwork for its first round of venture capital. Vora had had two years to contemplate his dream investor. Foremost, size did matter: The venture capitalist should have the wherewithal for ongoing financing, but not be so large that it shunned all but elaborate business models. Finding an investor with a broad network of investing partners also was important to the $10 million company. "If you become wildly successful and plan to raise $50 million someday, then [the investor] should have access to the big investors. The network is also important because it can [introduce] you to customers," says Vora, whose clients include CBS, Ford Motor Co., and Nokia. Finally, Vora was looking for operational experience. "A lot of VCs are phenomenal in advising you about what to do, but they've never done it themselves," he observes. Vora ultimately found his venture match in Cincinnati-based River Cities Capital Funds, a Small Business Investment Company. While River Cities was not large, it was well-connected and managed by industry veterans with extensive professional experience.

STARTING SMALL

Licensed and regulated by the SBA, SBICs are generally organized and operated like any other venture capital fund. But unlike traditional funds, SBICs use their own capital, plus funds borrowed from the federal government, to provide equity capital and long-term loans to small companies. On the whole, SBICs tend to be more risk-tolerant than banks or traditional venture capitalists. . . . Intelliseek's SBIC backer removed barriers to reaching larger, mainstream investors. Led by River Cities Capital Funds, the initial $6 million investment included capital from the venture arm of Nokia; later investors included Ford Motor Co. and General Atlantic Partners LLC. "Once you get a VC like River Cities, it is much easier to get access to bigger VCs," says Vora. "They can go to VCs and say 'One of our companies is doing so well, we're going to put in more money, and you guys should come in.'"

DOWN BUT NOT OUT

SBICs invested roughly $2.8 billion in about 2,100 companies in the 12-month period ending September 30, 2002, down from $4.6 billion invested in 2,254

Like Rule 504, Rule 505 permits no general advertising or solicitation through public media. When only accredited investors are involved, no disclosure is required under Rule 505 (similar to the issuance under Rule 504). However, if the issuance involves any unaccredited investors, additional information must be disclosed. Regardless of the amount of the offering, two-year financial statements for the two most recent years must be available unless such a disclosure requires "undue effort and expense." When this occurs for any issuing company other than a limited partnership, a balance sheet as of 120 days before the offering can be used instead. All companies selling private-placement securities to both accredited and unaccredited investors must furnish appropriate company information to both and allow any questions to be asked before the sale. Rule 506 goes one step further than Rule 505 by allowing an issuing company to sell an unlimited number of securities to 35 investors and an unlimited number of accredited investors and

companies in the same period one year earlier. Like mainstream investors, they have had to adjust to deteriorating economic conditions. "Valuations have come down on deals, and due diligence periods have increased," says Patrick Hamner, vice president of Capital Southwest Corp., a Dallas-based SBIC. "People are being far more discriminating in how they invest their capital. . . . The bar has been raised even more for small businesses trying to get capital," he continues. "As opposed to the overall venture industry, which has had a very marked decline in financing activity, SBICs are down but still active."

Nor has quality been an overriding concern, even as SBICs engage in riskier deals than their mainstream counterparts. "Part of what has happened with the bursting of the bubble is that the ideas being proposed are based on more substantive models," says Edwin Robinson, managing director of River Cities Capital Funds. "A lot of the excess is being wrung out of the system." While the venture shakeup has impacted conventional investors more profoundly, it also has changed the way some SBICs operate. "During the bubble years, there was probably more of an inclination to overfund," says NASBIC's Mercer. "I don't mean in the sense that money might not be justified, but to make the unconditional investment. I suspect that what you're seeing now is a lot more investing on a milestone basis." For instance, a company that requires $3 million over three years is likely to receive $1 million upfront, getting the rest after meeting revenue and growth targets.

Fewer venture dollars, coupled with the banking industry's reticence to lend to small businesses, has contributed to an overall capital shortage, adds Mercer. "Banks that had been out doing subordinated debt financing had gotten out a little bit further on the risk curve than they probably normally do," he says. "The banks' own proclivity and the regulators kind of forced a pullback, so there has been a tremendous pullback in bank credit available even for small businesses that have had longtime banking relationships."

The SBIC program, meanwhile, is attracting mainstream investors having difficulty raising capital for venture-backed investments. The increased interest bodes well for the small firms that SBICs target: companies with a net worth of less than $18 million and average after-tax earnings of less than $6 million for the past two years.

ADVICE TO AN ENTREPRENEUR

An entrepreneur who is an owner/manager of a small business and looking to raise $400,000 has read the above article and comes to you for advice:

1. What are the advantages of going to an SBIC over and above a business angel or a venture capitalist?
2. What are the disadvantages and how can they be minimized?

Source: Reprinted with permission of Entrepreneur Media, Inc., "Solid Backing. Even SBICs Feel This Economy, but They May Have the Resources to Make Your Deal Work," by Crystal Detamore-Rodman, February 2003, *Entrepreneur* magazine: www.entrepreneur.com.

relatives of issuers. Still, no general advertising or solicitation through public media can be involved.

In securing any outside funding, the entrepreneur must take great care to disclose all information as accurately as possible. Investors generally have no problem with the company as long as its operations continue successfully and this success is reflected in the valuation. But if the business turns sour, both investors and regulators scrutinize the company's disclosures in minute detail to determine if any technical or securities law violations occurred. When any violation of securities law is discovered, management and sometimes the company's principal equity holders can be held liable as a corporation and as individuals. When this occurs, the individual is no longer shielded by the corporation and is open to significant liability and potential lawsuits. Lawsuits under securities law by damaged investors have almost no statute of limitations, as the time does not begin until the person harmed discovers or should reasonably be expected to discover the improper disclosure. The suit may be brought in federal court in any jurisdiction in which the defendant is found or lives or transacts business. An individual can file suit as a single plaintiff or as a class action on behalf of all persons similarly affected. Courts have awarded large attorney's fees as well as settlements when any security law violation occurs. Given the number of lawsuits and the litigious nature of U.S. society, the entrepreneur needs to be extremely careful to make sure that any and all disclosures are accurate. If this is not enough of an incentive, it should be kept in mind that the SEC can take administrative, civil, or criminal action as well, without any individual lawsuit involved. This action can result in fines, imprisonment, or the restoration of the monies involved.

BOOTSTRAP FINANCING

One alternative to acquiring outside capital that should be considered is bootstrap financing.[3] This approach is particularly important at start-up and in the early years of the venture when capital from debt financing (i.e., in terms of higher interest rates) or from equity financing (i.e., in terms of loss of ownership) is more expensive.

In addition to the monetary costs, outside capital has other costs as well. First, it usually takes between three and six months to raise outside capital or to find out that there is no outside capital available. During this time, the entrepreneur may not be paying enough attention to the important areas of marketing, sales, product development, and operating costs. A business usually needs capital when it can least afford the time to raise it. One company's CEO spent so much time raising capital that sales and marketing were neglected to such an extent that the forecasted sales and profit figures on the pro forma income statements were not met for the first three years after the capital infusion. This led to investor concern and irritation that, in turn, required more of the CEO's time.

Second, outside capital often decreases a firm's drive for sales and profits. One successful manager would never hire a person as one of his commission salespeople if he or she "looked too prosperous." He felt that if a person was not hungry, he or she would not push hard to sell. The same concept could apply to outside funded companies that may have the tendency to substitute outside capital for income.

Third, the availability of capital increases the impulse to spend. It can cause a company to hire more staff before they are needed and to move into more costly facilities. A company can easily forget the basic axiom of venture creation: staying lean and mean.

Fourth, outside capital can decrease the company's flexibility. This can hamper the direction, drive, and creativity of the entrepreneur. Unsophisticated investors are particularly a problem as they often object to a company's moving away from the focus and direction outlined in the business plan that attracted their investment. This attitude can encumber a company to such an extent that the needed change cannot be implemented or else is implemented very slowly after a great deal of time and effort have been spent in consensus building. This can substantially demoralize the entrepreneur who likes the freedom of not working for someone else.

Finally, outside capital may cause disruption and problems in the venture. Capital is not provided without the expectation of a return, sometimes before the business should be giving one. Also, particularly if certain equity investors are involved, the entrepreneur is under pressure to continuously grow the company so that an initial public offering can occur as soon as possible. This emphasis on short-term performance can be at the expense of the long-term success of the company.

Bootstrap financing involves using any possible method for conserving cash. While some entrepreneurs can take advantage of any supplier discounts available, entrepreneurs with restricted cash flow need to take as long as possible to pay without incurring interest or late payment fees or being cut off from any future items from the supplier. The entrepreneur should always ask about discounts for volume, frequent customer discounts, promotional discounts for featuring the vendor's product, and even "obsolescence money," which allows for upgrading to an enhanced product at no additional cost.

Savings can also be obtained by asking for bulk packaging instead of paying more for individually wrapped items as well as using co-op advertising with a channel member so that the cost of the advertisement is shared.

Consignment financing can also be used to help conserve cash. Some vendors allow entrepreneurs to place a standing order for the entire amount of goods to be used over a period of time but take shipment and make payment only as needed, therefore securing the lower price of a larger order without having to carry the cost of the inventory. These are just some examples. The only possible limitation in bootstrap financing is the imagination of the entrepreneur.

In spite of these potential problems, an entrepreneur at times needs some capital to finance growth, which would be too slow or nonexistent if internal sources of funds were used. Outside capital should be sought only after all possible internal sources of funds have been explored. And when outside funds are needed and obtained, the entrepreneur should not forget to stay intimately involved with the basics of the business.

IN REVIEW

SUMMARY

All business ventures require capital. While capital is needed throughout the life of a business, the new entrepreneur faces significant difficulties in acquiring capital at start-up. Before seeking outside financing, an entrepreneur should first explore all methods of internal financing, such as using profits, selling unused assets, reducing working capital, obtaining credit from suppliers, and collecting accounts receivable promptly. After all internal sources have been exhausted, the entrepreneur may find it necessary to seek additional funds through external financing. External financing can be in the form of debt or equity. When considering external financing, the entrepreneur needs to consider the length of time, cost, and amount of control of each alternative financial arrangement.

Commercial bank loans are the most frequently used source of short-term external debt financing. This source of funding requires collateral, which may be asset-based or may take the form of cash flow financing. In either case, banks tend to be cautious about lending and carefully weigh the five Cs: character, capacity, capital, collateral, and condition. Not every entrepreneur will qualify under the bank's careful scrutiny. When this occurs, an alternative for an entrepreneur is the Small Business Administration Guaranty Loan. The SBA guarantees 80 percent of the loan, allowing banks to lend money to businesses that might otherwise be refused.

A special method of raising capital for high-technology firms is a research and development (R&D) limited partnership. A contract is formed between a sponsoring company and a limited partnership. The partnership bears the risk of the research, receiving some tax advantages and sharing in future profits, including a fee to use the research in developing any future products. The entrepreneur has the advantage of acquiring needed funds for a minimum amount of equity dilution while reducing his or her own risk in the venture. However, setting up an R&D limited partnership is expensive, and the time factor (at least six months) may be too long for some ventures. Restrictions placed on the technology as well as the complexities of exiting the partnership need careful evaluation.

Government grants are another alternative available to small businesses through the SBIR program. Businesses can apply for grants from 11 agencies. Phase I awards carry a stipend of up to $50,000 for six months of initial research. The most promising Phase I projects may qualify for Phase II support of up to $500,000 for 24 months of research.

Finally, the entrepreneur can seek private funding. Individual investors frequently require an equity position in the company and some degree of control. A less expensive and less complicated alternative to a public offering of stock is a private offering. By following the procedures of Regulation D and three of its specific rules—504, 505, and 506—an entrepreneur can sell private securities. When making a private offering, the entrepreneur must exercise care in accurately disclosing information and adhering precisely to the requirements of the SEC. Securities violations can lead to lawsuits against individuals as well as the corporation.

The entrepreneur needs to consider all possible sources of capital and select the one that will provide the needed funds with minimal cost and loss of control. Usually, different sources of funds are used at various stages in the growth and development of the venture, as occurred in the case of Scott Walker, a successful entrepreneur indeed.

RESEARCH TASKS

1. Interview a business loan officer at a bank to determine the bank's lending criteria for small businesses and new businesses. Does it use the five Cs? Which of the five Cs appears to be the most important?
2. Obtain a loan application from the local bank and categorize each question in terms of which of the five Cs it is attempting to assess.
3. Choose a type of business you would like to run. Then search the Internet for government grants that might be applicable for you and your business.
4. Interview three small business owners about things they do (or have done) to bootstrap the financing of their business. How effective were these techniques? Be prepared to present this list to the class and describe how the techniques work.

CLASS DISCUSSION

1. What is the cheapest source of funds? When all other sources turn down your request for funding, what source is most likely to say yes? Why is this the case? Is the entrepreneur exploiting a personal relationship with this potential source of capital? What are the consequences of using this source of capital if the business goes bankrupt?

2. Should the government provide grants for entrepreneurs starting new businesses? Should the government guarantee loans for small businesses that are missing the necessary track record, assets, or other ingredients to obtain a commercial bank loan? What benefit do we, as a nation of taxpayers, receive from such grants and loan guarantees?
3. Why don't all firms use bootstrap financing? Are there any dangers with this approach? What are the benefits of having some financial slack (e.g., some extra cash in reserve)? What are the costs of that financial slack?

SELECTED READINGS

Åstebro, Thomas; and Irwin Bernhardt. (July 2003). Start-Up Financing, Owner Characteristics, and Survival. *Journal of Economics & Business,* vol. 55, no. 4, p. 303.

This article investigates the relationship between the survival of new small businesses and bank loans. This is done using a model that includes other loan sources, human capital variables, and company and industry descriptors. The authors find that there is a negative correlation between having a bank loan and business survival, and a positive correlation between having a nonbank loan and survival. However, having a bank loan is a ceteris paribus *positive predictor of the survival of start-up companies. These findings enable some inferences about the process of loan source selection by start-up business owners and banks' loan-granting process.*

Basu, Anuradha; and Simon C. Parker. (2001). Family Finance and New Business Start-Ups. *Oxford Bulletin of Economics and Statistics,* vol. 63, no. 3, pp. 333–58.

It is widely recognized that a key determinant of successful start-ups is adequate financing. Since in most countries the largest source of funds is self-finance, provided by the entrepreneur's own savings or assets, this paper presents a theoretical model of family finance and conducts an empirical analysis to identify its determinants.

Carlson, Jr., Donald A. (Winter 2004). Access to Capital—A Growing Concern. *Frontiers of Health Services Management*, vol. 21, no. 2, pp. 15–30.

Access to capital over the next 10 years will be one of the biggest challenges health care organizations will face as they strive to remain competitive and serve their communities. Meeting the growing needs for capital will require a disciplined and honest assessment of the capital sources available and the best ways of positioning an organization to maximize their uses. It is incumbent on chief executive officers and other senior leaders to create a disciplined process for allocating capital and conveying how that process will be linked to the organization's strategic plan. All of the credit constituencies "buying" health care need to fully understand how the organization is positioning itself for future growth and success, and detailed bond marketing plans need to be implemented well before the actual sale of a new bond issue. Large and small health care providers will have sufficient access to capital in the future if investors believe that senior hospital executives have a credible plan and are disciplined enough to execute it.

Coleman, Susan. (July 2000). Access to Capital and Terms of Credit: A Comparison of Men- and Women-Owned Small Businesses. *Journal of Small Business Management*, pp. 37–52.

This article compares access to capital for men- and women-owned small businesses. Findings reveal that women-owned firms are less likely to use external financing as a source of capital. It does not appear, however, that lenders discriminate against women on the basis of gender. A second part of the study reveals that women-owned firms paid higher interest for their most recent loans and women-owned service firms were more likely to put up collateral.

Collingwood, Harris. (March 2003). The Private-Capital Survival Guide. *Inc.*, pp. 100–109.

Even with both the economy and the stock market sputtering, private capital deals are more appealing than ever because many private investors still have financing resources for which they cannot get a fair return in the stock or bond markets. This guide gives advice on how to find and attract private investors and how to structure a fair deal and maintain a relationship with investors, using them as a valuable resource.

Dushnitsky, Gary; and Michael J. Lenox. (October 2005). When Do Firms Undertake R&D by Investing in New Ventures? *Strategic Management Journal*, vol. 26, no. 10, pp. 947–65.

This article explores the conditions under which firms are likely to pursue equity investment in new ventures as a way to source innovative ideas. The authors find that firms invest more in new ventures—commonly referred to as "corporate venture capital"—in industries with weak intellectual property protection and, to some extent, in industries with high technological ferment and where complementary distribution capability is important. Furthermore, they find that the greater a firm's cash flow and absorptive capacity, the more likely it is to invest. These results suggest that in Schumpeterian environments incumbents may supplement their innovative efforts by tapping into the knowledge generated by new ventures.

Harrison, Richard T.; Colin M. Mason; and Paul Girling. (July 2004). Financial Bootstrapping and Venture Development in the Software Industry. *Entrepreneurship & Regional Development*, vol. 16, no. 4, pp. 307–33.

Access to finance has been identified as a significant constraint on the development of technology-based businesses. Although important, institutional venture capital and business angel finance are used by only a small proportion of new and growing ventures. The role of bootstrapping—defined here as access to resources not owned or controlled by the entrepreneur—has been largely overlooked in studies of small firm financing. This paper redresses this omission by analyzing the role and importance of bootstrapping in product development and business development in the independently owned software industry. Results from two regions of the U.K.—Northern Ireland and South East England—are compared with equivalent data from the U.S. (Massachusetts). Overall, bootstrapping techniques are less extensively used in the Northern Ireland industry than in South East England, and in both regions bootstrapping is less common than in Massachusetts. This may account for the smaller employment size, growth profile, and stronger service/consulting orientation of these firms. Moreover, there appear to be considerable variations in the use of bootstrapping. Larger firms tend to make more use of bootstrapping for product development and consider it more important than do smaller firms, which more highly value business development-related bootstrapping. Small firms are also more likely to use and value cost-reducing bootstrapping techniques, whereas larger firms make more use of the exploitation of value-chain-based relationships.

Kutsuna, Kenji; and Nobuyuki Harada. (October–December 2004). Small Business Owner-Managers as Latent Informal Investors in Japan: Evidence from a Country with a Bank-Based Financial System. *Venture Capital*, vol. 6, no. 4, pp. 283–311.

Start-up support by small business owner-managers looks extremely promising for the formation of a pool of latent informal investors in countries like Japan with a bank-based financial system and small-scale informal investing. First, small business owner-managers have superior potential in regard to the hands-on capacity to provide management know-how. Second, there are a large number of small businesses in Japan. Third, small businesses exist not only in financial centers and new venture clustering areas, but also in all regional areas. This paper demonstrates the activities of small business owner-managers acting as financial and nonfinancial supporters of business start-ups in Japan, by using two data sets (both surveyed in 1999 by the National Life Finance Corporation). The empirical results show that owner-managers who are younger, from larger small businesses, or who have received support when their own businesses were starting tend to provide start-up support. It is shown that there is a clear tendency to provide financial support to business types "different" from the managers' own businesses. One way of increasing the pool of informal investors would be to attract managers in various positions to make informal investments and expand their businesses and entrepreneurial skills.

Lefton, Ray B. (Winter 2004). Capital Access—A Key to Survival. *Frontiers of Health Services Management*, vol. 21, no. 2, pp. 37–41.

This article focuses on capital access by organizations in health care. Cash flow from operations, philanthropy, tax-exempt borrowing, off-balance sheet financing, and monetization of assets are the five primary sources of capital available for tax-exempt organizations. Access to capital is highly dependent on an organization's credit rating and overall creditworthiness, which is a function of many factors such as market position, profitability, liquidity, and debt burden. Highly credited hospitals are able to raise affordable capital. Health care organization should focus on operating margins generating sufficient cash to support planned increases in capital spending.

Marlow, Susan; and Dean Patton. (November 2005). All Credit to Men? Entrepreneurship, Finance, and Gender. *Entrepreneurship: Theory & Practice*, vol. 29, no. 6, pp. 717–35.

This article contends that availability of, and access to, finance is a critical element to the start-up and consequent performance of any enterprise. It discusses findings that have been somewhat inconsistent. For example, the authors offer support for the notion that women entrepreneurs entering self-employment are disadvantaged by their gender.

Modigliani, Franco; and Enrico Perotti. (2002). Security Markets versus Bank Finance: Legal Enforcement and Investors' Protection. *International Review of Finance*, vol. 1, no. 2, pp. 81–96.

This article reports supporting evidence for a few countries showing that when minority investors' rights are poorly protected, the ability of firms to raise capital is impaired, leading to fewer firms being financed with outside equity. The article argues that, as a result, provision of funding shifts from capital to debt, and to a predominance of intermediated over market financing.

Morris, Michael H.; John W. Watling; and Minet Schindehutte. (July 2000). Venture Capitalist Involvement in Portfolio Companies: Insights from South Africa. *Journal of Small Business Management*, pp. 68–77.

The research described in this paper explores the following issues in the context of South Africa, where a formal venture capital community is emerging: (1) the extent to which venture capitalists actually fulfill their other roles of management consultants, advisors, networkers, and board members; (2) the considerations that lead them to get more involved with a given venture; and (3) the effectiveness or impact of their involvement.

Steier, Lloyd; and Royston Greenwood. (2000). Entrepreneurship and the Evolution of Angle Financial Networks. *Organizational Studies,* vol. 21, no. 1, pp. 163–92.

The success of a new venture often depends on an entrepreneur's ability to establish a network of supportive relationships, especially with informal or "angel" investors, who represent a significant source of venture capital. This paper reports the findings of a longitudinal study of the development and evolution of an angel financial network within a newly created firm and refines how theories of social capital and structural holes might be applied.

Van Auken, Howard. (August 2004). The Use of Bootstrap Financing among Small Technology-Based Firms. *Journal of Developmental Entrepreneurship,* vol. 9, no. 2, pp. 145–59.

This study examines the use of 28 bootstrap financing methods among a sample of 44 small technology-based firms. The results indicate that, in general, the owners of these firms did not view bootstrap financing as an important source of capital. The use of bootstrap financing was directly related to the risk of the firm, but inversely related to the size of the firms' market and whether the owner had searched for capital during the past year. The results can be used by owners of small technology-based firms, consultants, and support agencies that provide assistance to technology-based firms in areas of financial planning and capital acquisition. Understanding the use and availability of all sources of capital can help owners develop comprehensive financial strategies. Agencies that provide support services can use the information to better assist small technology-based firms in developing financial strategies. This information could be incorporated into training programs for owners and managers of small technology-based firms.

Van Auken, Howard E. (July 2001). Financing Small Technology-Based Companies: The Relationship between Familiarity with Capital and Ability to Price and Negotiate Investment. *Journal of Small Business Management,* vol. 39, no. 3, pp. 240–58.

This study examines the financing of small technology-based firms. Specifically, the study investigates the familiarity of owners of small technology-based firms with alternative forms of capital by stage of development and in comparison with their ability to price and negotiate external equity and debt investment. The results indicate that owners are most familiar with traditional sources of capital, somewhat less familiar with capital commonly used to fund growth, and least familiar with government funding initiatives. Owners believe that they are better able to negotiate than to price equity and debt. The perceived ability to negotiate and price externally funded investments increases as the firm matures through the various stages of development.

White, Steven; Jian Gao; and Wei Zhang. (August 2005). Financing New Ventures in China: System Antecedents and Institutionalization. *Research Policy,* vol. 34, no. 6, pp. 894–913.

China's system for funding new ventures is a relatively recent phenomenon emerging from decades of government-led technology policy and a still-transitioning business system. This paper first proposes a general framework in which this financing system is defined as the country-specific configuration of actors, rules, and practices by which investment funds are pooled, investment targets identified, funds invested and monitored, and returns appropriated. The paper uses this framework to link the centralized government system of the 1980s to today's nascent venture capital industry. The analysis leads to policy and managerial implications, as well as a research agenda for further studies in the Chinese context and across different venture financing systems.

END NOTES

1. Crystal Detramone-Rodman, "Cash In, Cash Out," *Entrepreneur* (June 2003), pp. 53–54.
2. For a discussion of bank-lending decisions, see A. D. Jankowicz and R. D. Hisrich, "Institution in Small Business Lending Decisions," *Journal of Small Business Management* (July 1987), pp. 45–52; N. C. Churchill and V. L. Lewis, "Bank Lending to New and Growing Enterprises," *Journal of Business Venturing* (Spring 1986), pp. 193–206; R. T. Justis, "Starting a Small Business: An Investigation of the Borrowing Procedure," *Journal of Small Business Management* (October 1982), pp. 22–32; and L. Fertuck, "Survey of Small Business Lending Practices," *Journal of Small Business Management* (October 1982), pp. 42–48.
3. Bootstrap financing is discussed in Anne Murphy, "Capital Punishment," *Inc.* (November 1993), pp. 38–42; and Michael P. Cronin, "Paradise Lost," *Inc.* (November 1993), pp. 48–53.

12

INFORMAL RISK CAPITAL, VENTURE CAPITAL, AND GOING PUBLIC

LEARNING OBJECTIVES

1
To explain the basic stages of venture funding.

2
To discuss the informal risk-capital market.

3
To discuss the nature of the venture-capital industry and the venture-capital decision process.

4
To explain all aspects of valuing a company.

5
To identify several valuation approaches.

6
To explain the proccess of going public.

OPENING PROFILE

TOM KITCHIN

www.jamesoninns.com

Thomas Kitchin was born in 1941 in Kansas City, Missouri, to parents who survived the Great Depression. Witnesses to the endemic unemployment that characterized the Depression, Kitchin's parents strongly instilled in him the importance of having a job. His mother in particular taught Kitchin the value of employment by encouraging him to obtain work during vacations from his Catholic school. He performed a wide variety of jobs that included stocking shelves, bagging groceries, selling shoes, unloading grain cars at a railroad company, and working on an assembly line in an automobile factory. Kitchin's mother further promoted his pursuits by throwing parties to celebrate each new job. Although his parents' support gave Kitchin pride in his efforts, the greatest benefit he enjoyed was having money to spend on dates, entertainment, and clothing, and, eventually, to buy and maintain his own car.

Kitchin studied business courses in college, a decision that set him on the path to becoming the first businessman in his family. His first position following graduation was in the area of finance and required the completion of an intensive management-training program in addition to night classes. This in turn led Kitchin into a commercial banking position as a commercial lender. By the age of 36, Kitchin had cultivated an expertise in banking and finance and was president and chief operating officer of a bank. Although he was very challenged by his work, Kitchin could not quiet his desire to start his own business.

In March 1977, Kitchin finally struck out on his own, leaving the security of his banking career to begin an oil and gas company. The new venture enjoyed early success that Kitchin attributes to his hiring of extremely competent professional geologists and engineers. A mere three years following its inception, the company had a solid track record and a sufficiently strong growth plan to accomplish an initial public offering of common stock. The company went on to raise over $100 million from Wall Street to finance its exploration and acquisition projects.

Kitchin decided in December 1986 to sell his controlling interest in the company and—in 1987, in an effort to expand his professional interests—began searching for the right business to acquire. Kitchin soon found a new business to explore in his purchase of a small hotel in Georgia. Kitchin had been doing research in the hotel business and learned that the general public, especially the business traveler, clearly desired travel lodging that was consistent and predictable. He also determined that most of the hotel industry consists of franchise owners whose management practices vary from excellent to terrible. This discontinuity in service left customers confused when trying to choose a hotel. Kitchin's due diligence in researching the hotel industry led him to the conclusion that the public was ready for a new and consistent hotel brand that would offer limited service with clean, safe, and affordable rooms in small industrialized markets.

The newly designed Jameson Inn opened for business in November 1988. Eventually, Kitchin commenced expansion of Jameson Inns according to the following guidelines: building properties consistent in appearance, expanding in a contiguous fashion to existing properties and states to ensure brand awareness, and providing service to a growing customer base. In 1994, Jameson Inns completed an initial public offering of common stock that generated capital for growth. Jameson Inns's desire to expand is exemplified by its utilization of this capital to finance its expansion across the United States as well as by its May 7, 1999, merger with Signature Inns. Jameson Inns was left the sole surviving entity of this merger after the company absorbed the 26 hotels owned by Signature Inns, located in the midwestern United States.

In 2003, the company owned 120 hotels in 14 states, with over 8,000 hotel rooms. Jameson Inns's workforce had increased exponentially from 3 employees in 1987 to over 2,000. Lease revenue was $37,616,000 in 2004. The company changed its organizational structure from a real estate investment trust (REIT) to a regular C corporation and lodging revenue increased to $84,510,000 in 2004 and $90,577,000 in 2005.

During this three-year period (2003–2005), the occupancy rate of Jameson Inns increased from 54.5 percent to 55.6 percent to 59.3 percent and its RevPAR (revenue per available room) increased from $31.77 to $33.50 to $37.82, reflecting the increase in Jameson's occupancy and room rate.

Unlike Tom Kitchin, many entrepreneurs find it difficult to both manage and expand the venture they have created. In order to start and grow the venture, an entrepreneur must understand venture financing and obtain the necessary funding from a variety of sources.

FINANCING THE BUSINESS

In evaluating the appropriateness of financing alternatives, particularly angel versus venture capital financing, an entrepreneur must determine the amount and the timing of the funds required, as well as the projected company sales and growth. Conventional small businesses and privately held middle-market companies tend to have a difficult time obtaining

TABLE 12.1 Stages of Business Development Funding

Early-Stage Financing	
• Seed capital	Relatively small amounts to prove concepts and finance feasibility studies
• Start-up	Product development and initial marketing, but with no commercial sales yet; funding to actually get company operations started
Expansion or Development Financing	
• Second stage	Working capital for initial growth phase, but no clear profitability or cash flow yet
• Third stage	Major expansion for company with rapid sales growth; company is at breakeven or positive profit levels but is still private
• Fourth stage	Bridge financing to prepare company for public offering
Acquisition and Leveraged Buyout Financing	
• Traditional acquisitions	Assuming ownership and control of another company
• Leveraged buyouts (LBOs)	Management of a company acquiring company control by buying out the present owners
• Going private	Some of the owners/managers of a company buying all the outstanding stock, making the company privately held again

external equity capital, especially from the venture-capital industry. Most venture capitalists like to invest in software, biotechnology, or high-potential ventures like Frederick W. Smith's Federal Express. The three types of funding as the business develops are indicated in Table 12.1. The funding problems, as well as the cost of the funds, differ for each type. *Early-stage financing* is usually the most difficult and costly to obtain. Two types of financing are available during this stage: seed capital and start-up capital. Seed capital, the most difficult financing to obtain through outside funds, is usually a relatively small amount of funds needed to prove concepts and finance feasibility studies. Since venture capitalists usually have a minimum funding level of above $500,000, they are rarely involved in this type of funding, except in the case of high-technology ventures of entrepreneurs who have a successful track record and need a significant amount of capital. The second type of funding is start-up financing. As the name implies, start-up financing is involved in developing and selling some initial products to determine if commercial sales are feasible. These funds are also difficult to obtain. Angel investors are active in these two types of financing.

early-stage financing One of the first financings obtained by a company

Expansion or *development financing* (the second basic financing type) is easier to obtain than early-stage financing. Venture capitalists play an active role in providing funds here. As the firm develops in each stage, the funds for expansion are less costly. Generally, funds in the second stage are used as working capital to support initial growth. In the third stage, the company is at breakeven or a positive profit level and uses the funds for major sales expansion. Funds in the fourth stage are usually used as bridge financing in the interim period as the company prepares to go public.

development financing Financing to rapidly expand the business *acquisition financing* Financing to buy another company

risk-capital markets Markets providing debt and equity to nonsecure financing situations

informal risk-capital market Area of risk-capital markets consisting mainly of individuals

venture-capital market One of the risk-capital markets consisting of formal firms

public-equity market One of the risk-capital markets consisting of publicly owned stocks of companies

business angels A name for individuals in the informal risk-capital market

Acquisition financing or leveraged buyout financing (the third type) is more specific in nature. It is issued for such activities as traditional acquisitions, leveraged buyouts (management buying out the present owners), and going private (a publicly held firm buying out existing stockholders, thereby becoming a private company).

There are three *risk-capital markets* that can be involved in financing a firm's growth: the *informal risk-capital market,* the *venture-capital market*, and the *public-equity market.* Although all three risk-capital markets can be a source of funds for stage-one financing, the public-equity market is available only for high-potential ventures, particularly when high technology is involved. Recently, some biotechnology companies raised their first-stage financing through the public-equity market since investors were excited about the potential prospects and returns in this high-interest area. This also occurred in the areas of oceanography and fuel alternatives when there was a high level of interest. Although venture-capital firms also provide some first-stage funding, the venture must require the minimum level of capital ($500,000). A venture-capital company establishes this minimum level of investment due to the high costs in evaluating and monitoring a deal. By far the best source of funds for first-stage financing is the informal risk-capital market—the third type of risk-capital market.

INFORMAL RISK-CAPITAL MARKET

The informal risk-capital market is the most misunderstood type of risk capital. It consists of a virtually invisible group of wealthy investors, often called *business angels,* who are looking for equity-type investment opportunities in a wide variety of entrepreneurial ventures. Typically investing anywhere from $10,000 to $500,000, these angels provide the funds needed in all stages of financing, but particularly in start-up (first-stage) financing. Firms funded from the informal risk-capital market frequently raise second- and third-round financing from professional venture-capital firms or the public-equity market.

Despite being misunderstood by, and virtually inaccessible to, many entrepreneurs, the informal investment market contains the largest pool of risk capital in the United States. Although there is no verification of the size of this pool or the total amount of financing provided by these business angels, related statistics provide some indication. A 1980 survey of a sample of issuers of private placements by corporations, reported to the Securities and Exchange Commission under Rule 146, found that 87 percent of those buying these issues were individual investors or personal trusts, investing an average of $74,000.[1] Private placements filed under Rule 145 average over $1 billion per year. Another indication becomes apparent on examination of the filings under Regulation D—the regulation exempting certain private and limited offerings from the registration requirements of the Securities Act of 1933, discussed in Chapter 11. In its first year, over 7,200 filings, worth $15.5 billion, were made under Regulation D. Corporations accounted for 43 percent of the value ($6.7 billion), or 32 percent of the total number of offerings (2,304). Corporations filing limited offerings (under $500,000) raised $220 million, an average of $200,000 per firm. The typical corporate issuers tended to be small, with fewer than 10 stockholders, revenues and assets less than $500,000, stockholders' equity of $50,000 or less, and five or fewer employees.[2]

Similar results were found in an examination of the funds raised by small technology-based firms prior to their initial public offerings. The study revealed that unaffiliated

AS SEEN IN *ENTREPRENEUR* MAGAZINE

ELEVATOR PITCH FOR ALEXANDER GLOBAL PROMOTION

A wealthy friend has asked you to keep your eye out for attractive businesses in which she can invest. Your wealthy friend is very busy and you only want to introduce those businesses that are genuinely attractive. After hearing the following pitch, would you introduce Malcolm to your wealthy friend?

Entrepreneur Malcolm Alexander (44), founder of Alexander Global Promotions in Bellevue, Washington.

Description Promotional products company; created Bobble Dobbles bobbleheads.

Start-Up $15,000 in 1996.

Sales Projected sales for current year of $35 million.

Grand-Slam Giveaway In 1999, when the San Francisco Giants asked Alexander if he could make bobbleheads for a promotional game day, he said, "Absolutely." In reality, he had no idea what bobbleheads were. After seven months of R&D, Alexander presented 35,000 Willie Mays bobbleheads to a sold-out game. The Giants team has remained a customer ever since, along with a long list of other professional sports teams.

Doll Play "Characters" sit for several seconds while a 3-D laser digitally maps their faces, resulting in close replications on their handpainted Bobble Dobble faces. In addition to sports figures, Alexander already has licenses for Disney, KISS, and the Rolling Stones.

Soldier of Fortune Australian-born Alexander was once a special-forces officer in charge of the country's marine counter-terrorist unit. "The Australian military teaches innovation and adaptability," says Alexander. "Many of these lessons have been applicable to business."

Change-Up Bobble Dobbles now account for 80 to 85 percent of sales. With a library of 3,000-plus facial images, Alexander is working on bendable characters and a line of superhero figurines with athletes' faces.

Source: Reprinted with permission of Entrepreneur Media, Inc., "Malcolm Alexander," by April Y. Pennington, May 2003, *Entrepreneur* magazine: www.entrepreneur.com.

individuals (the informal investment market) accounted for 15 percent of these funds, while venture capitalists accounted for only 12 to 15 percent. During the start-up year, unaffiliated individuals provided 17 percent of the external capital.[3]

A study of angels in New England again yielded similar results. The 133 individual investors studied reported risk-capital investments totaling over $16 million in 320 ventures between 1976 and 1980. These investors averaged one deal every two years, with an average size of $50,000. Although 36 percent of these investments averaged less than $10,000, 24 percent averaged over $50,000. While 40 percent of these investments were start-ups, 80 percent involved ventures less than five years old.[4]

The size and number of these investors have increased dramatically, due in part to the rapid accumulation of wealth in various sectors of the economy. One study of consumer finances found that the net worth of 1.3 million U.S. families was over $1 million.[5] These families, representing about 2 percent of the population, accumulated most of their wealth from earnings, not inheritance, and invested over $151 billion in nonpublic businesses in which they have no management interest. Each year, over 100,000 individual investors finance between 30,000 and 50,000 firms, with a total dollar investment of between $7 billion and $10 billion. Given their investment capability, it is important to know the characteristics of these angels.

One article determined that the angel money available for investment each year was about $20 billion.[6] This amount was confirmed by another study indicating that there are about 250,000 angel investors who invest an amount of $10 billion to $20 billion annually in about 30,000 firms.[7] A recent study found that only about 20 percent of the angel investors surveyed tended to specialize in a particular industry, with the typical investment in the first round being between $29,000 to over $100,000.[8]

The characteristics of these informal investors, or angels, are indicated in Table 12.2. They tend to be well educated; many have graduate degrees. Although they will finance

TABLE 12.2 Characteristics of Informal Investors

Demographic Patterns and Relationships

- Well educated, with many having graduate degrees.
- Will finance firms anywhere, particularly in the United States.
- Most firms financed within one day's travel.
- Majority expect to play an active role in ventures financed.
- Many belong to angel clubs.

Investment Record

- Range of investment: $10,000–$500,000
- Average investment: $175,000
- One to two deals each year

Venture Preference

- Most financings in start-ups or ventures less than 5 years old
- Most interest in financing:
  - Manufacturing—industrial/commercial products
  - Manufacturing—consumer products
  - Energy/natural resources
  - Services
  - Software

Risk/Reward Expectations

- Median 5-year capital gain of 10 times for start-ups
- Median 5-year capital gain of 6 times for firms under 1 year old
- Median 5-year capital gain of 5 times for firms 1–5 years old
- Median 5-year capital gain of 3 times for established firms over 5 years old

Reasons for Rejecting Proposals

- Risk/return ratio not adequate
- Inadequate management team
- Not interested in proposed business area
- Unable to agree on price
- Principals not sufficiently committed
- Unfamiliar with area of business

firms anywhere in the United States (and a few in other parts of the world), most of the firms that receive funding are within one day's travel. Business angels will make one to two deals each year, with individual firm investments ranging from $10,000 to $500,000 and the average being $175,000. If the opportunity is right, angels might invest from $500,000 to $1 million. In some cases, angels will join with other angels, usually from a common circle of friends, to finance larger deals.

Is there a preference in the type of ventures in which they invest? While angels invest in every type of investment opportunity, from small retail stores to large oil exploration operations, some prefer manufacturing of both industrial and consumer products, energy, service, and the retail/wholesale trade. The returns expected decrease as the number of years the firm has been in business increases, from a median five-year capital gain of 10 times for start-ups to 3 times for established firms over five years old. These investing angels are more patient in their investment horizons and do not have a problem waiting for a period of 7 to 10 years before cashing out. This is in contrast to the more predominant five-year time horizon in the formal venture-capital industry. Investment opportunities are rejected when there is an inadequate risk/return ratio, a subpar management team, a lack of interest in the business area, or insufficient commitment to the venture from the principals.

The angel investor market has declined from $30 billion in 2001 to $15.7 billion in 2002, according to the Center for Venture Research. Along with the 50 percent decrease in total dollars invested, the number of entrepreneurial ventures receiving funding similarly decreased by 25 percent, to 36,000 in 2002. The number of active investors is about 200,000 individuals, with five or six investors typically being involved in an investment. There are approximately 150 organized angel investor groups throughout the United States.

Where do these angel investors generally find their deals? Deals are found through referrals by business associates, friends, active personal research, investment bankers, and business brokers. However, even though these *referral sources* provide some deals, most angel investors are not satisfied with the number and type of investment referrals. Fifty-one percent of the investors surveyed were either partially or totally dissatisfied with their referral systems and indicated that at least moderate improvement is needed.

referral sources Ways individual investors find out about potential deals

VENTURE CAPITAL

The important and little understood area of venture capital will be discussed in terms of its nature, the venture-capital industry in the United States, and the venture-capital process.

Nature of Venture Capital

Venture capital is one of the least understood areas in entrepreneurship. Some think that venture capitalists do the early-stage financing of relatively small, rapidly growing technology companies. It is more accurate to view venture capital broadly as a professionally managed pool of equity capital. Frequently, the *equity pool* is formed from the resources of wealthy limited partners. Other principal investors in venture-capital limited partnerships are pension funds, endowment funds, and other institutions, including foreign investors. The pool is managed by a general partner—that is, the venture-capital firm—in exchange for a percentage of the gain realized on the investment and a fee. The investments are in early-stage deals as well as second- and third-stage deals and leveraged buyouts. In fact, venture capital can best be characterized as a long-term investment discipline, usually occurring over a five-year period, that is found in the creation of early-stage companies, the expansion and revitalization of existing businesses, and the financing of leveraged buyouts of existing divisions of major corporations or privately owned

equity pool Money raised by venture capitalists to invest

AS SEEN IN *ENTREPRENEUR* MAGAZINE

ANGELS

John Garcia was in the right place at the right time. It was 1982 when he sold his surgical supply company to Baxter Healthcare and started looking for investment opportunities. It wasn't long before he found several small, private companies looking for financial help—including a little-known retail concept called Mail Boxes Etc. Garcia's investments eventually returned several times his money, catapulting him into angel investing. Now, at 45, he makes a full-time job of connecting businesses with angel capital.

Garcia, founder of Angel Strategies in Tustin, California, has seen the nature of angel investing change. "There was a time when we all believed in 100 times returns. But most angels today would be happy with 10 times—and they'll settle for 3 to 5 times." Tarby Bryant, founder of The Gathering of Angels in Santa Fe, New Mexico, concurs. "Today, angels are looking for 40 to 50 percent internal rate of return." That translates to about 4 times their investment over three years.

CHANGING EXPECTATIONS

It's no mystery why angels have lowered their expectations. During the heyday of the public markets, angel investors were able to cash out when a company went public. The public was paying big bucks for small-company stock, and that unlocked huge gains for angel investors. But today's successful small business is more often acquired by a larger company—at a price that is sometimes below average because of overall economic conditions. The decline of the IPO market has brought another significant change to angel investing. Rather than count on any kind of investment liquidity, many of today's angels are looking for something almost unheard of in the past: dividends. "Angels may be willing to forgo higher return if they can get some part of the revenue stream on the back end," according to Garcia.

Today's savvy investor simply has more conservative expectations. Unfortunately for the entrepreneur, lower expected returns are accompanied by lower initial valuations. Just as all boats rose with the IPO tide, all boats fall as that tide recedes. In fact, valuations of private companies have fallen right along with those of public companies. Entrepreneurs won't get top dollar for their private stock, as Garcia points out, when public stocks like Microsoft and Oracle are trading at 30 to 50 percent below their highs.

TIGHTENING THE BELT

Falling public exchanges have a double impact on companies seeking financing—not only devaluing private stock but also wiping out vast amounts of angel capital. Garcia estimates Angel Strategies investors lost an average of 50 to 60 percent of their net worth during the declines of 2001 and 2002. When private investors see their portfolios shrink, they become more conservative. These days, money that might have gone into early-stage, private investments is headed to safer harbors like real estate, CDs, and mutual funds.

As investors lick their wounds, offer them less risk and more reward. "The new ideal," says Garcia, "is to be profitable in year one—and by year two, to have excess profits for reinvestment." Businesses that can

equity participation Taking an ownership position

businesses. In each investment, the venture capitalist takes an *equity participation* through stock, warrants, and/or convertible securities and has an active involvement in the monitoring of each portfolio company, bringing investment, financing planning, and business skills to the firm.[9]

Overview of the Venture-Capital Industry

Although the role of venture capital was instrumental throughout the industrialization of the United States, it did not become institutionalized until after World War II. Before World War II, venture-capital investment activity was a monopoly led by wealthy individuals, investment banking syndicates, and a few family organizations with a professional manager. The first step toward institutionalizing the venture-capital industry took place in 1946 with the formation of the American Research and Development Corporation

show strong sales growth, share profits, or offer creative exit strategies will have better chances with angel investors. Today, entrepreneurs who ignore investors' demands for strong sales and profits do so at their own peril.

THE GOOD NEWS

Despite being somewhat pickier in their deal-making, angels are giving entrepreneurs reason to hope. As venture-capital investments decline, many angels are aggressively seeking to fill the gap. "Fewer VC dollars means better deals for angels," explains Bryant, who sees more and more individual investors stepping up to the plate.

The level of activity is also on the rise within Garcia's Angel Strategies group. In 2002, the group closed more deals than in the previous two years combined. The success of such groups as The Gathering of Angels and Angel Strategies, which bring individual investors together to find, evaluate, and nurture growing companies, is an encouraging sign. Similar groups are popping up in almost every city. If your banker or lawyer can't point you toward one, contact a local VC or SBA office. Entrepreneurs have a better chance of finding interested angels when they're presenting to one of these groups. Further, when a deal is done, companies also stand to benefit from the collective expertise that such organizations offer.

DEVIL'S IN THE DETAILS

Any business that is looking for financing these days should not overlook the huge opportunity that angel investors present. Whether individually or in groups, angels are an important source of funds for entrepreneurs—perhaps even more so now that VCs have pulled in their horns. Be prepared, however, for an angel to take a long, hard look at your business and financial plans. Few investors will be fooled by a promise of a quick IPO, and many might prefer a reasonable, steady return on their capital. That, plus a realistic valuation and a reasonable assurance of return, will go a long way toward attracting today's individual investor.

ADVICE TO AN ENTREPRENEUR

An entrepreneur who raised money in 1995 is looking to raise a further $450,000 to grow his business. He comes to you for advice and asks:

1. How has the informal risk capital market changed since 1995? Given these changes, what is the best approach for me to raise the capital that I need?
2. I have looked for business angels, but they are not easy to find. What do you think of these "dating" type registries that match entrepreneurs with business angels?
3. Are there any downsides to going through one of these services, or things that I should be careful about in using them?

Source: Reprinted with permission of Entrepreneur Media, Inc., "Our Little Angels. Angel Investors Haven't Left Us; They're Just Scaling Back Their Operations," by David Worrell, January 2003, *Entrepreneur* magazine: www.entrepreneur.com.

(ARD) in Boston. The ARD was a small pool of capital from individuals and institutions put together by General Georges Doriot to make active investments in selected emerging businesses.

The next major development, the Small Business Investment Company Act of 1958, married private capital with government funds to be used by professionally managed small business investment companies (*SBIC firms*) to infuse capital into start-ups and growing small businesses. With their tax advantages, government funds for leverage, and status as a private capital company, SBICs were the start of the now formal venture-capital industry. The 1960s saw a significant expansion of SBICs with the approval of approximately 585 SBIC licenses that involved more than $205 million in private capital. Many of these early SBICs failed due to inexperienced portfolio managers, unreasonable expectations, a focus on short-term profitability, and an excess of government regulations. These early failures caused the SBIC program to be restructured, which in

SBIC firms Small companies with some government money that invest in other companies

turn eliminated some of the unnecessary government regulations and increased the amount of capitalization needed. There are approximately 360 SBICs operating today, of which 130 are minority small business investment companies (MESBICs) funding minority enterprises.

private venture-capital firms A type of venture-capital firm having general and limited partners

During the late 1960s, small *private venture-capital firms* emerged.[10] These were usually formed as limited partnerships, with the venture-capital company acting as the general partner that received a management fee and a percentage of the profits earned on a deal. The limited partners, who supplied the funding, were frequently institutional investors such as insurance companies, endowment funds, bank trust departments, pension funds, and wealthy individuals and families. There are about 980 venture-capital establishments in the United States today.

Another type of venture-capital firm was also developed during this time: the venture-capital division of major corporations. These firms, of which there are approximately 100, are usually associated with banks and insurance companies, although companies such as 3M, Monsanto, and Xerox house such firms as well. Corporate venture-capital firms are more prone to invest in windows on technology or new market acquisitions than private venture-capital firms or SBICs. Some of these corporate venture-capital firms have not had strong results.

state-sponsored venture-capital fund A fund containing state government money that invests primarily in companies in the state

In response to the need for economic development, a fourth type of venture-capital firm has emerged in the form of the *state-sponsored venture-capital fund*. These state-sponsored funds have a variety of formats. While the size and investment focus and industry orientation vary from state to state, each fund typically is required to invest a certain percentage of its capital in the particular state. Generally, the funds that are professionally managed by the private sector, outside the state's bureaucracy and political processes, have performed better.

An overview of the types of venture-capital firms is indicated in Figure 12.1. Besides the four types previously discussed, there are now emerging university-sponsored venture-capital funds. These funds, usually managed as separate entities, invest in the technology of the particular university. Often, particularly at schools such as Stanford, Columbia, and Case Western Reserve University, students assist professors and other students in creating business plans for funding as well as assisting the fund manager in his or her due diligence, thereby learning more about the venture-funding process.

FIGURE 12.1 Types of Venture-Capital Firms

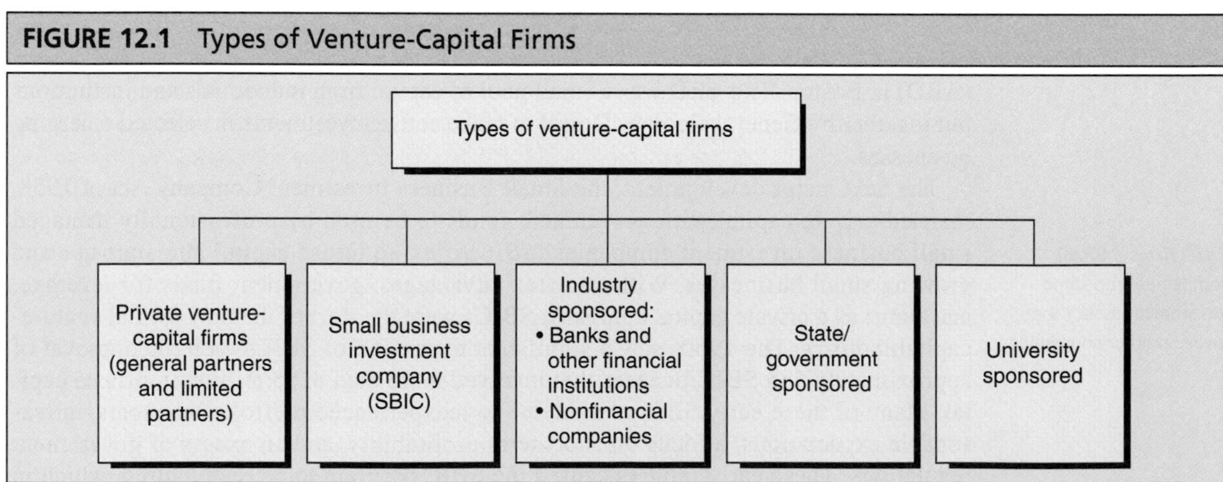

TABLE 12.3 Total Venture Dollars Invested and Number of Deals

Year	Total	# of Deals
1995	$ 7,879,331,900	1,773
1996	11,014,332,900	2,471
1997	14,612,026,900	3,084
1998	20,810,583,100	3,553
1999	53,475,711,500	5,396
2000	104,700,717,300	7,809
2001	40,703,455,300	4,456
2002	21,697,809,100	3,057
2003	19,585,475,700	2,865
2004	21,635,323,900	2,966
2005	21,679,998,500	2,939

Source: PricewaterhouseCoopers/Thomson Venture Economics/National Venture Capital Association Money Tree™ Survey.

The venture-capital industry has not returned to the highest level of dollars invested in 1999, 2000, and 2001. While the total amount of venture-capital dollars invested increased steadily from $7.8 billion in 1995 to a high of $104.7 billion in 2000 (as indicated in column 2 of Table 12.3),[11] the total dollars invested declined to $40.7 billion in 2001, $21.7 billion in 2002, and $19.6 billion in 2003. There was a slight increase to $21.6 billion in 2004 and $21.7 billion in 2005.

The total amount of venture-capital dollars invested, disseminated across the number of deals, is indicated in column 3 of Table 12.3. The number of venture-capital deals went from 1,773 in 1995 to a high of 7,809 in 2000. In 2003, 2004, and 2005, the number of deals stayed fairly steady, at 2,865, 2,966, and 2,939, respectively.

These deals concentrated in two primary areas in 2005: software—$1,180 billion (22 percent), and biotechnology—$611 billion (12 percent). This investment has significantly impacted the growth and development of these two industry sectors. As indicated in Figure 12.2, other industry areas receiving venture-capital investment include: financial services (9.1 percent), telecommunications (7.8 percent), medical devices and equipment (7.9 percent), media and entertainment (7.3 percent), industrial/energy (5.2 percent), and IT services (5.2 percent).

At what stage of the business development is this money invested? The percentage of venture-capital money raised by stage of the venture is indicated in Figure 12.3. A somewhat different pattern emerged in 2005. The largest amount of money raised was for early-stage investments (42 percent), followed by expansion (32 percent), later stage (13 percent), and start-up/seed stage (13 percent). Traditionally the largest amount of money raised is for expansion, followed by early-stage investment. In 2002, for example, 57 percent of the venture money raised was for expansion, followed by early stage (23 percent), later stage (18 percent), and start-up (2 percent).

The money invested by stage and year from 1995 to 2005 is broken down in Table 12.4. Venture-capital money invested at the start-up stage (for seed capital) went from $1,313 million in 1995 to a high of $3,275 million in 1995, before declining to a low of $356 million in 2003. The amount invested in this area increased to $406 million in 2004 and again to $735 million in 2005. Venture capitalists in 2005 showed a

FIGURE 12.2 Percentage of Venture Dollars Invested in 2005 by Industry Sector

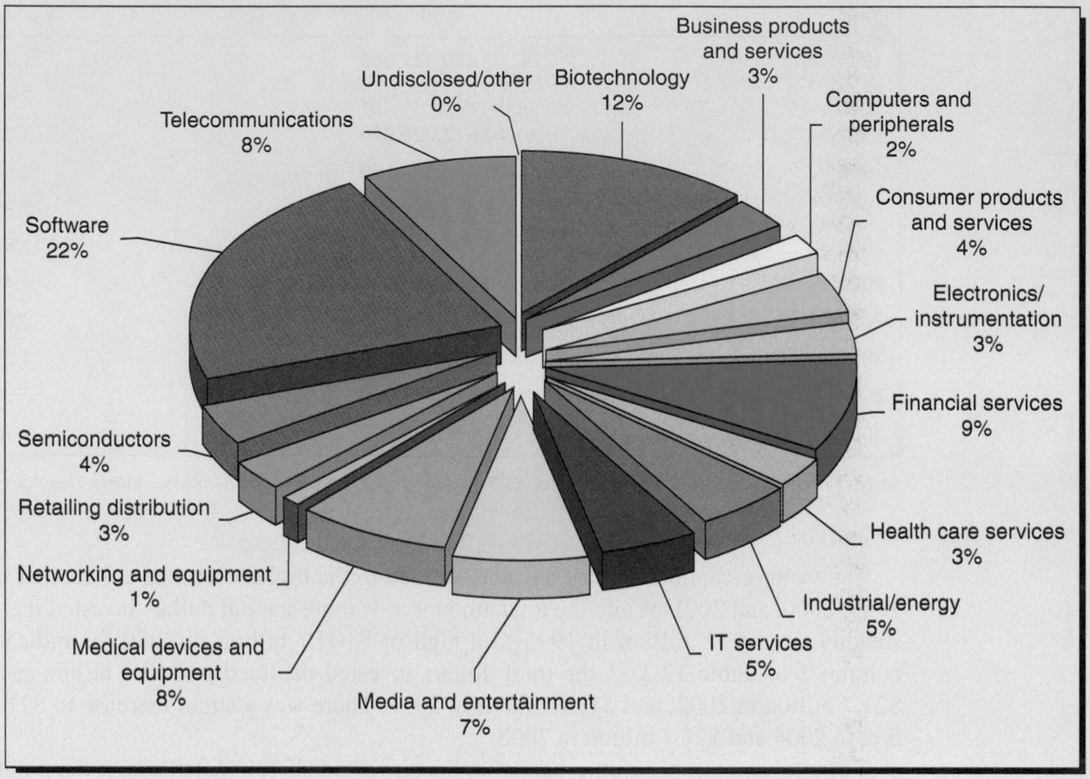

Numbers rounded to the nearest whole percent.
Source: PricewaterhouseCoopers/Thomson Venture Economics/National Venture Capital Association Money Tree™ Survey.

significant interest in funding start-up/seed capital situations, as opposed to funding early-stage deals.

Where do these deals take place? Table 12.5 shows the amount of money invested in 2005 ($21.6 billion) by region of the country. It should come as no surprise that the areas receiving the largest amount of venture capital were the Silicon Valley—$7.6 billion (35 percent) in 895 deals (31 percent), and New England—$2.6 billion (12 percent) in 385 deals (13 percent). Other leading areas receiving funding were: New York metro—$1.7 billion (7.8 percent) in 164 deals (6 percent); Los Angeles/Orange County—$1.5 billion (69 percent) in 176 deals (6 percent); and the Southeast—$1.2 billion (5.6 percent) in 202 deals (7 percent).

Venture-Capital Process

venture-capital process
The decision procedure of a venture-capital firm

To be in a position to secure the funds needed, an entrepreneur must understand the philosophy and objectives of a venture-capital firm, as well as the *venture-capital process*. The objective of a venture-capital firm is to generate long-term capital appreciation through debt and equity investments. To achieve this objective, the venture capitalist is willing to make any changes or modifications necessary in the business investment. Since the objective of the entrepreneur is the survival of the business, the objectives of the two are frequently at odds, particularly when problems occur.

FIGURE 12.3 Percentage of Venture Dollars Raised by Stage in 2005

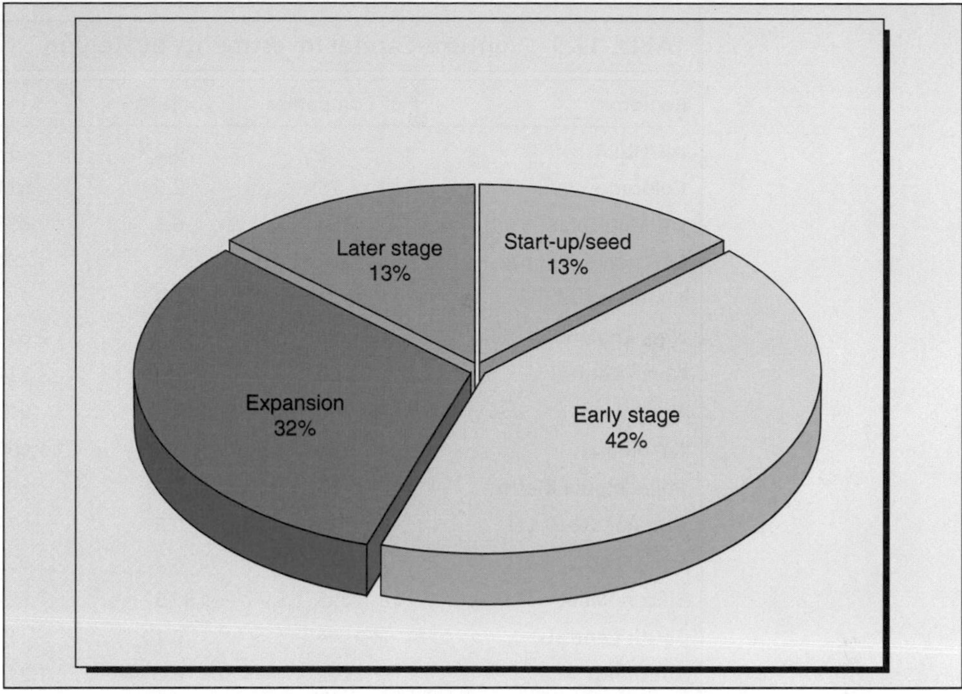

Source: PricewaterhouseCoopers/Thomson Venture Economics/National Venture Capital Association Money Tree™ Survey.

TABLE 12.4 Venture Investment Stages

	Stage					
Year	Start-Up/Seed	Early Stage	Expansion	Later Stage	Undisclosed/ Other	Total
1995	$1,313,003,200 16.66%	$ 1,683,669,900 21.37%	$ 3,681,412,900 46.72%	$ 1,198,496,900 15.21%	$2,749,000 0.03%	$ 7,879,331,900 100.00%
1996	$1,491,929,600 13.55%	$ 2,744,424,100 24.92%	$ 5,143,362,400 46.70%	$ 1,632,308,800 14.82%	$2,308,000 0.02%	$ 11,014,332,900 100.00%
1997	$1,310,211,300 8.97%	$ 3,450,280,200 23.61%	$ 7,592,260,300 51.96%	$ 2,259,175,100 15.46%	$ 100,000 0.00%	$ 14,612,026,900 100.00%
1998	$1,751,147,700 8.41%	$ 5,421,221,800 26.05%	$10,434,249,900 50.14%	$ 3,194,201,700 15.35%	$9,762,000 0.05%	$ 20,810,583,100 100.00%
1999	$3,275,102,900 6.12%	$11,700,579,100 21.88%	$29,848,031,900 55.82%	$ 8,651,897,600 16.18%	$ 100,000 0.00%	$ 53,475,711,500 100.00%
2000	$3,093,872,800 2.95%	$25,573,393,600 24.43%	$59,978,976,800 57.29%	$16,054,335,100 15.33%	$ 139,000 0.00%	$104,700,717,300 100.00%
2001	$ 729,536,900 1.79%	$ 8,960,880,200 22.02%	$23,024,298,000 56.57%	$ 7,988,740,200 19.63%	$— 0.00%	$ 40,703,455,300 100.00%
2002	$ 289,981,200 1.34%	$ 3,927,463,300 18.10%	$12,320,043,800 56.78%	$ 5,160,320,800 23.78%	$— 0.00%	$ 21,697,809,100 100.00%
2003	$ 356,692,900 1.82%	$ 3,454,022,800 17.64%	$10,100,409,700 51.57%	$ 5,674,100,300 28.97%	$ 250,000 0.00%	$ 19,585,475,700 100.00%
2004	$ 406,634,900 1.88%	$ 3,986,741,200 18.43%	$ 9,256,962,600 42.79%	$ 7,984,985,200 36.91%	$— 0.00%	$ 21,635,323,900 100.00%
2005	$ 735,850,000 3.39%	$ 3,396,162,100 15.66%	$ 7,820,983,600 36.07%	$ 9,727,002,800 44.87%	$— 0.00%	$21,679,998,500 100.00%

Source: PricewaterhouseCoopers/Thomson Venture Economics/National Venture Capital Association Money Tree™ Survey.

TABLE 12.5 Venture-Capital Investments by Region

Region	# of Companies	%	$ Invested	%
AK/HI/PR	5	0.2%	$ 17,044,900	0.08%
Colorado	75	2.6	611,693,100	2.82
DC/Metroplex	184	6.3	885,249,900	4.08
LA/Orange County	176	6.0	1,484,049,200	6.85
Midwest	144	4.9	773,533,100	3.57
New England	385	13.1	2,618,443,600	12.08
North Central	60	2.0	314,005,100	1.45
Northwest	150	5.1	913,811,700	4.21
NY Metro	164	5.6	1,690,372,600	7.80
Philadelphia Metro	91	3.1	687,841,800	3.17
Sacramento/N.Cal	15	0.5	79,897,000	0.37
San Diego	122	4.2	1,032,772,300	4.76
Silicon Valley	895	30.5	7,622,771,400	35.16
South Central	4	0.1	15,104,000	0.07
Southeast	202	6.9	1,215,323,200	5.61
Southwest	79	2.7	590,303,100	2.72
Texas	158	5.4	1,068,924,200	4.93
Upstate NY	30	1.0	58,858,300	0.27
Other US	—	0.0	—	0.00
Grand Total	2,939	100.0%	$21,679,998,500	100.0%

Source: PricewaterhouseCoopers/Thomson Venture Economics/National Venture Capital Association Money Tree™ Survey.

A typical portfolio objective of venture-capital firms in terms of return criteria and risk involved is shown in Figure 12.4. Since there is more risk involved in financing a business earlier in its development, more return is expected from early-stage financing (50 percent ROI) than from acquisitions or leveraged buyouts (30 percent ROI), which are later stages of development. The significant risk involved and the pressure that venture-capital firms feel from their investors (limited partners) to make safer investments with higher rates of return have caused these firms to invest even greater amounts of their funds in later stages of financing. In these late-stage investments, there are lower risks, faster returns, less managerial assistance needed, and fewer deals to be evaluated.

The venture capitalist does not necessarily seek control of a company, but would rather have the firm and the entrepreneur at the most risk. The venture capitalist will want at least one seat on the board of directors. Once the decision to invest is made, the venture capitalist will do anything necessary to support the management team so that the business and the investment prosper. Whereas the venture capitalist expects to provide guidance as a member of the board of directors, the management team is expected to direct and run the daily operations of the company. A venture capitalist will support the management team with investment dollars, financial skills, planning, and expertise in any area needed.

Since the venture capitalist provides long-term investment (typically five years or more), it is important that there be mutual trust and understanding between the

FIGURE 12.4 Venture-Capital Financing: Risk and Return Criteria

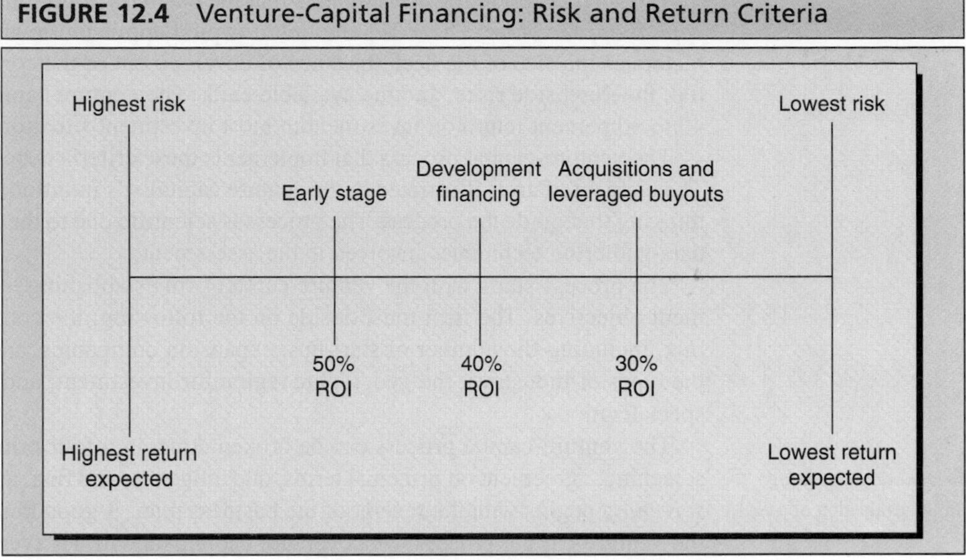

Source: © 1992, American Economic Development Council (AEDC). All rights reserved. Reprinted from the *Economic Development Review*, vol. 10, no. 2, Spring 1992, p. 44, with the permission of AEDC.

entrepreneur and the venture capitalist. There should be no surprises in the firm's performance. Both good and bad news should be shared, with the objective of taking the necessary action to allow the company to grow and develop in the long run. The venture capitalist should be available to the entrepreneur to discuss problems and develop strategic plans.

The venture capitalist expects a company to satisfy three general criteria before he or she will commit to the venture. First, the company must have a strong management team that consists of individuals with solid experience and backgrounds, a strong commitment to the company, capabilities in their specific areas of expertise, the ability to meet challenges, and the flexibility to scramble wherever necessary. A venture capitalist would rather invest in a first-rate management team and a second-rate product than the reverse. The management team's commitment should be reflected in dollars invested in the company. Although the amount of the investment is important, more telling is the size of this investment relative to the management team's ability to invest. The commitment of the management team should be backed by the support of the family, particularly the spouse, of each key team player. A positive family environment and spousal support allow team members to spend the 60 to 70 hours per week necessary to start and grow the company. One successful venture capitalist makes it a point to have dinner with the entrepreneur and spouse, and even to visit the entrepreneur's home, before making an investment decision. According to the venture capitalist, "I find it difficult to believe an entrepreneur can successfully run and manage a business and put in the necessary time when the home environment is out of control."

The second criterion is that the product and/or market opportunity must be unique, having a differential advantage in a growing market. Securing a unique market niche is essential since the product or service must be able to compete and grow during the investment period. This uniqueness needs to be carefully spelled out in the marketing portion of the business plan and is even better when it is protected by a patent or a trade secret.

The final criterion for investment is that the business opportunity must have *significant capital appreciation*. The exact amount of capital appreciation varies, depending on such factors as the size of the deal, the stage of development of the company, the upside potential, the downside risks, and the available exits. The venture capitalist typically expects a 40 to 60 percent return on investment in most investment situations.

The venture-capital process that implements these criteria is both an art and a science.[12] The element of art is illustrated in the venture capitalist's intuition, gut feeling, and creative thinking that guide the process. The process is scientific due to the systematic approach and data-gathering techniques involved in the assessment.

The process starts with the venture-capital firm establishing its philosophy and investment objectives. The firm must decide on the following: the composition of its portfolio mix, including the number of start-ups, expansion companies, and management buyouts; the types of industries; the geographic region for investment; and any product or industry specializations.

preliminary screening Initial evaluation of a deal

The venture-capital process can be broken down into four primary stages: preliminary screening, agreement on principal terms, due diligence, and final approval. The *preliminary screening* begins with the receipt of the business plan. A good business plan is essential in the venture-capital process. Most venture capitalists will not even talk to an entrepreneur who doesn't have one. As the starting point, the business plan must have a clear-cut mission and clearly stated objectives that are supported by an in-depth industry and market analysis and pro forma income statements. The executive summary is an important part of this business plan, as it is used for initial screening in this preliminary evaluation. Many business plans are never evaluated beyond the executive summary. When evaluating the business, the venture capitalist first determines if the deal or similar deals have been seen previously. The investor then determines if the proposal fits his or her long-term policy and short-term needs in developing a portfolio balance. In this preliminary screening, the venture capitalist investigates the economy of the industry and evaluates whether he or she has the appropriate knowledge and ability to invest in that industry. The investor reviews the numbers presented to determine whether the business can reasonably deliver the ROI required. In addition, the credentials and capability of the management team are evaluated to determine if they can carry out the plan presented.

The second stage is the agreement on principal terms between the entrepreneur and the venture capitalist. The venture capitalist wants a basic understanding of the principal terms of the deal at this stage of the process before making the major commitment of time and effort involved in the formal due diligence process.

due diligence The process of deal evaluation

The third stage, detailed review and *due diligence,* is the longest stage, involving anywhere from one to three months. There is a detailed review of the company's history, the business plan, the resumes of the individuals, their financial history, and target market customers. The upside potential and downside risk are assessed, and there is a thorough evaluation of the markets, industry, finances, suppliers, customers, and management.

final approval A document showing the final terms of the deal

In the last stage, *final approval,* a comprehensive, internal investment memorandum is prepared. This document reviews the venture capitalist's findings and details the investment terms and conditions of the investment transaction. This information is used to prepare the formal legal documents that both the entrepreneur and venture capitalist will sign to finalize the deal.[13]

Locating Venture Capitalists

One of the most important decisions for the entrepreneur lies in selecting which venture-capital firm to approach. Since venture capitalists tend to specialize either geographically by industry (manufacturing industrial products or consumer products, high technology, or service) or by size and type of investment, the entrepreneur should approach only those that may have an interest in the investment opportunity. Where do you find this venture capitalist?

Although venture capitalists are located throughout the United States, the traditional areas of concentration are found in Los Angeles, New York, Chicago, Boston, and San Francisco.[14] An entrepreneur should carefully research the names and addresses of prospective venture-capital firms that might have an interest in the particular investment opportunity. There are also regional and national venture-capital associations. For a nominal fee or none at all, these associations will frequently send the entrepreneur a directory that lists their members, the types of businesses their members invest in, and any investment restrictions. Whenever possible, the entrepreneur should be introduced to the venture capitalist. Bankers, accountants, lawyers, and professors are good sources for introductions.

Approaching a Venture Capitalist

The entrepreneur should approach a venture capitalist in a professional business manner. Since venture capitalists receive hundreds of inquiries and are frequently out of the office working with portfolio companies or investigating potential investment opportunities, it is important to begin the relationship positively. The entrepreneur should call any potential venture capitalist to ensure that the business is in an area of investment interest. Then the business plan should be sent, accompanied by a short professional letter.

Since venture capitalists receive many more plans than they are capable of funding, many plans are screened out as soon as possible. Venture capitalists tend to focus and put more time and effort on those plans that are referred. In fact, one venture-capital group said that 80 percent of its investments over the last five years were in referred companies. Consequently, it is well worth the entrepreneur's time to seek out an introduction to the venture capitalist. Typically this can be obtained from an executive of a portfolio company, an accountant, a lawyer, a banker, or a business school professor.

The entrepreneur should be aware of some basic rules of thumb before implementing the actual approach and should follow the detailed guidelines presented in Table 12.6. First, great care should be taken in selecting the right venture capitalist to approach. Venture capitalists tend to specialize in certain industries and will rarely invest in a business outside those areas, regardless of the merits of the business proposal and plan. Second, recognize that venture capitalists know each other, particularly in a specific region of the country. When a large amount of money is involved, they will invest in the deal together, with one venture-capital firm taking the lead. Since this degree of familiarity is present, a venture-capital firm will probably find out if others have seen your business plan. Do not shop among venture capitalists, as even a good business plan can quickly become "shopworn." Third, when meeting the venture capitalist, particularly for the first time, bring only one or two key members of the management team. A venture capitalist is investing in you and your management team and its track record, not in outside consultants and experts. Any experts can be called in as needed.

Finally, be sure to develop a succinct, well-thought-out oral presentation. This should cover the company's business, the uniqueness of the product or service, the prospects for growth, the major factors behind achieving the sales and profits indicated, the backgrounds and track records of the key managers, the amount of financing required, and the returns anticipated. This first presentation is critical, as is indicated in the comment of one venture capitalist: "I need to sense a competency, a capability, a chemistry within the first half hour of our initial meeting. The entrepreneur needs to look me in the eye and present his story clearly and logically. If a chemistry does not start to develop, I start looking for reasons not to do the deal."

TABLE 12.6 Guidelines for Dealing with Venture Capitalists

- Carefully determine the venture capitalist to approach for funding the particular type of deal. Screen and target the approach. Venture capitalists do not like deals that have been excessively "shopped."
- Once a discussion is started with a venture capitalist, do not discuss the deal with other venture capitalists. Working several deals in parallel can create problems unless the venture capitalists are working together. Time and resource limitations may require a cautious simultaneous approach to several funding sources.
- It is better to approach a venture capitalist through an intermediary who is respected and has a preexisting relationship with the venture capitalist. Limit and carefully define the role and compensation of the intermediary.
- The entrepreneur or manager, not an intermediary, should lead the discussions with the venture capitalist. Do not bring a lawyer, accountant, or other advisors to the first meeting. Since there are no negotiations during this first meeting, it is a chance for the venture capitalist to get to know the entrepreneur without interference from others.
- Be very careful about what is projected or promised. The entrepreneur will probably be held accountable for these projections in the pricing, deal structure, or compensation.
- Disclose any significant problems or negative situations in this initial meeting. Trust is a fundamental part of the long-term relationship with the venture capitalist; subsequent discovery by the venture capitalist of an undisclosed problem will cause a loss of confidence and probably prevent a deal.
- Reach a flexible, reasonable understanding with the venture capitalist regarding the timing of a response to the proposal and the accomplishment of the various steps in the financing transaction. Patience is needed, as the process is complex and time-consuming. Too much pressure for a rapid decision can cause problems with the venture capitalist.
- Do not sell the project on the basis that other venture capitalists have committed themselves. Most venture capitalists are independent and take pride in their own decision making.
- Be careful about glib statements such as, "There is no competition for this product" or "There is nothing like this technology available today." These statements can reveal a failure to do one's homework or can indicate that a perfect product has been designed for a nonexistent market.
- Do not indicate an inordinate concern for salary, benefits, or other forms of current compensation. Dollars are precious in a new venture. The venture capitalist wants the entrepreneur committed to an equity appreciation similar to that of the venture capitalist.
- Eliminate to the extent possible any use of new dollars to take care of past problems, such as payment of past debts or deferred salaries of management. New dollars of the venture capitalist are for growth, to move the business forward.

Following a favorable initial meeting, the venture capitalist will do some preliminary investigation of the plan. If favorable, another meeting between the management team and the venture capitalist will be scheduled so that both parties can assess the other and determine if a good working relationship can be established and if a feeling of trust and confidence is evolving. During this mutual evaluation, the entrepreneur should be careful not to be too inflexible about the amount of company equity he or she is willing to share. If the entrepreneur is too inflexible, the venture capitalist might end negotiations. During this meeting, initial agreement of terms is established. If you are turned down by one venture capitalist, do not become discouraged. Instead, select another venture-capitalist candidate and repeat the procedure. A significant number of companies denied funding by one venture capitalist are able to obtain funds from other outside sources, including other venture capitalists.[15]

We may have gotten a small foretaste last week of the endgame of the Internet Investment boom. The hallmark of any boom is unbridled confidence, which conceals and condones practices that—in a less giddy climate—would seem sloppy, unethical, or illegal. The Internet has been so profitable for so many that people instinctively confuse economic success with more infallibility. This can't last forever, if only because human nature isn't perfect—even the human nature of the people behind the Internet and computer booms.

What happened last week provided a cautionary tale. Early Monday, MicroStrategy—a prominent software company—announced that it was revising its 1999 financial results. Sales would drop roughly 25 percent, from $205 million to about $150 million. Profits would change from a reported 15 cents a share to a loss of between 43 cents and 51 cents. The reaction was swift. On Monday, MicroStrategy's stock plunged 62 percent, from $226.75 to $86.75.

Bombarded by shareholder suits, MicroStrategy will have ample opportunity to explain its actions. No one can yet say whether it committed fraud—or was the victim of overly conservative accounting rules. "I don't think we made a mistake," says MicroStrategy chairman Michael Saylor. "The technology has outstripped accounting guidelines." He says the company merely booked revenue it had in hand and that auditors insisted be spread over the life of software contracts. However the episode ends, it suggests that the high-tech frenzy has created an ethical quagmire.

There are huge pressures to project optimism—and prop up stock prices. The line between what people genuinely believe and what serves their economic interests has blurred. Perhaps some people can no longer see the line. Stretching accounting rules (if that is what MicroStrategy did) is a flagrant trespass. But others are more subtle, ambiguous, and, possibly, pervasive. Questions abound about underwriting practices, the independence of stock "research," and the use of stock options.

Capitalism is about risk and reward. If there's risk, some people will lose. Companies fall. Business plans flop. The dot-com phenomenon won't (and shouldn't) be any different. That is not the issue. But to work, capitalism requires reasonably reliable information. If it's skewed, then the risk-reward equation becomes skewed.

In good times, people often do things that—with hindsight—look less than upstanding. The MicroStrategy case may be misleading. Or it might portend a larger reckoning.

Source: Adapted from Robert J. Samuelson, "A High-Tech Accounting?" *Newsweek*, 04/03/2000, Volume 135, Issue 14, p. 37.

VALUING YOUR COMPANY

A problem confronting the entrepreneur in obtaining outside equity funds, whether from the informal investor market (the angels) or from the formal venture-capital industry, is determining the value of the company. This valuation is at the core of determining how much ownership an investor is entitled to for funding the venture. This is determined by considering the *factors in valuation*. This, as well as other aspects of securing funding, has a potential for ethical conflict that must be carefully handled.

factors in valuation Nonmonetary aspects that affect the fund valuation of a company

Factors in Valuation

There are eight factors that, although they vary by situation, the entrepreneur should consider when valuing the venture. The first factor, and the starting point in any valuation, is the nature and history of the business. The characteristics of the venture and the industry in which it operates are fundamental to every evaluation process. The history of the company from its inception provides information on the strength and diversity of the company's operations, the risks involved, and the company's ability to withstand any adverse conditions.

The valuation process must also consider the outlook of the economy in general as well as the outlook for the particular industry. This, the second factor, involves an examination of the financial data of the venture compared with that of other companies in the industry.

Management's capability now and in the future is assessed, as well as the future market for the company's products. Will these markets grow, decline, or stabilize, and in what economic conditions?

The third factor is the book value (net value) of the stock of the company and the overall financial condition of the business. The book value (often called owner's equity) is the acquisition cost (less accumulated depreciation) minus liabilities. Frequently, the book value is not a good indication of fair market value, as balance sheet items are almost always carried at cost, not market value. The value of plant and equipment, for example, carried on the books at cost less depreciation may be low due to the use of an accelerated depreciation method or other market factors, making the assets more valuable than indicated in the book value figures. Land, particularly, is usually reflected lower than fair market value. For valuation, the balance sheet must be adjusted to reflect the higher values of the assets, particularly land, so that a more realistic company worth is determined. A good valuation should also value operating and nonoperating assets separately and then combine the two into the total fair market value. A thorough valuation involves comparing balance sheets and profit and loss statements for the past three years when available.

While book value develops the benchmark, the future earning capacity of the company, the fourth factor, is the most important factor in valuation. Previous years' earnings are generally not simply averaged but weighted, with the most recent earnings receiving the highest weighting. Income by product line should be analyzed to judge future profitability and value. Special attention should be paid to depreciation, nonrecurring expense, officers' salaries, rental expense, and historical trends.

The fifth valuation factor is the dividend-paying capacity of the venture. Since the entrepreneur in a new venture typically pays little if any in dividends, it is the future capacity to pay dividends rather than actual dividend payments made that is important. The dividend-paying capacity should be capitalized.

An assessment of goodwill and other intangibles of the venture is the sixth valuation factor. These intangible assets usually cannot be valued without reference to the tangible assets of the venture.

The seventh factor in valuation involves assessing any previous sale of stock. Previous stock sales accurately represent future sales if the stock sales are recent. Motives regarding the new sale (if other than arriving at a fair price) and any change in economic or financial conditions during the intermittent period should be considered.

The final valuation factor is the market price of the stocks of companies engaged in the same or similar lines of business. This factor is used in the specific valuation method discussed later in this section. The critical issue is the degree of similarity between the publicly traded company and the company being valued.

Ratio Analysis

Financial ratios
Control mechanisms to test the financial strength of the new venture

Calculations of *financial ratios* can also be extremely valuable as an analytical and control mechanism to test the financial well-being of a new venture during its early stages. These ratios serve as a measure of the financial strengths and weaknesses of the venture, but should be used with caution since they are only one control measure for interpreting the financial success of the venture. There is no single set of ratios that must be used, nor are there standard definitions for all ratios. However, there are industry rules of thumb that the entrepreneur can use to interpret the financial data. Ratio analysis is typically used on actual financial results but can also provide the entrepreneur with some sense of where problems exist in the pro forma statements as well. Throughout this section we will use information taken from the financial statements of MPP Plastics (Chapter 10) to illustrate.

Liquidity Ratios

Current Ratio This ratio is commonly used to measure the short-term solvency of the venture or its ability to meet its short-term debts. The current liabilities must be covered from cash or its equivalent; otherwise the entrepreneur will need to borrow money to meet these obligations. The formula and calculation of this ratio when current assets are $108,050 and current liabilities are $40,500 is:

$$\frac{\text{Current assets}}{\text{Current liabilities}} = \frac{108{,}050}{40{,}500} = 2.67 \text{ times}$$

While a ratio of 2:1 is generally considered favorable, the entrepreneur should also compare this ratio with any industry standards. One interpretation of this result is that for every dollar of current debt, the company has $2.67 of current assets to cover it. This ratio indicates that MPP Plastics is liquid and can likely meet any of its obligations even if there were a sudden emergency that would drain existing cash.

Acid Test Ratio This is a more rigorous test of the short-term liquidity of the venture because it eliminates inventory, which is the least liquid current asset. The formula given the same current assets and liabilities and inventory of $10,450 is:

$$\frac{\text{Current assets} - \text{Inventory}}{\text{Current liabilities}} = \frac{108{,}050 - 10{,}450}{40{,}500} = 2.40 \text{ times}$$

The result from this ratio suggests that the venture is very liquid since it has assets convertible to cash of $2.40 for every dollar of short-term obligations. Usually a 1:1 ratio would be considered favorable in most industries.

Activity Ratios

Average Collection Period This ratio indicates the average number of days it takes to convert accounts receivable into cash. This ratio helps the entrepreneur to gauge the liquidity of accounts receivable or the ability of the venture to collect from its customers. Using the formula with accounts receivable of $46,400 and sales of $995,000 results in:

$$\frac{\text{Accounts receivable}}{\text{Average daily sales}} = \frac{46{,}000}{995{,}000/360} = 17 \text{ days}$$

This particular result needs to be compared with industry standards since collection will vary considerably. However, if the invoices indicate a 20-day payment required, then one could conclude that most customers pay on time.

Inventory Turnover This ratio measures the efficiency of the venture in managing and selling its inventory. A high turnover is a favorable sign indicating that the venture is able to sell its inventory quickly. There could be a danger with a very high turnover that the venture is understocked, which could result in lost orders. Managing inventory is very important to the cash flow and profitability of a new venture. The calculations of this ratio when the cost of goods sold is $645,000 and the inventory is $10,450 is:

$$\frac{\text{Cost of goods sold}}{\text{Inventory}} = \frac{645{,}000}{10{,}450} = 61.7 \text{ times}$$

This would appear to be an excellent turnover as long as the entrepreneur feels that he or she is not losing sales because of understocking inventory.

Leverage Ratios

Debt Ratio Many new ventures will incur debt as a means of financing the start-up. The debt ratio helps the entrepreneur to assess the firm's ability to meet all its obligations (short and long term). It is also a measure of risk because debt also consists of a fixed commitment in the form of interest and principal repayments. With total liabilities of $249,700 and total assets of $308,450, the debt ratio is calculated below:

$$\frac{\text{Total liabilities}}{\text{Total assets}} = \frac{249{,}700}{308{,}450} = 81\%$$

This result indicates that the venture has financed about 81 percent of its assets with debt. On paper this looks very reasonable but it would also need to be compared with industry data.

Debt to Equity This ratio assesses the firm's capital structure. It provides a measure of risk to creditors by considering the funds invested by creditors (debt) and investors (equity). The higher the percentage of debt, the greater the degree of risk to any of the creditors. The calculation of this ratio using the same total liabilities, with stockholder's equity being $58,750, is:

$$\frac{\text{Total liabilities}}{\text{Stockholder's equity}} = \frac{249{,}700}{58{,}750} = 4.25 \text{ times}$$

This result indicates that this venture has been financed mostly from debt. The actual investment of the entrepreneurs or the equity base is about one-fourth of what is owed. Thus, the equity portion represents a cushion to the creditors. For MPP Plastics this is not a serious problem because of its short-term cash position.

Profitability Ratios

Net Profit Margin This ratio represents the venture's ability to translate sales into profits. You can also use gross profit instead of net profit to provide another measure of profitability. In either case it is important to know what is reasonable in your industry as well as to measure these ratios over time. The ratio and calculation when net profit is $8,750 and net sales are $995,000 is:

$$\frac{\text{Net profit}}{\text{Net sales}} = \frac{8{,}750}{995{,}000} = 0.88\%$$

The net profit margin for MPP Plastics, although low for an established firm, would not be of great concern for a new venture. Many new ventures do not incur profits until the second or third year. In this case we have a favorable profit situation.

Return on Investment The return on investment measures the ability of the venture to manage its total investment in assets. You can also calculate a return on equity, which substitutes stockholders' equity for total assets in the formula below and indicates the ability of the venture in generating a return to the stockholders. The formula and calculation of the return on investment when total assets are $200,400 and net profit is $8,750 is:

$$\frac{\text{Net profit}}{\text{Total assets}} = \frac{8{,}750}{200{,}400} = 4.4\%$$

The result of this calculation will also need to be compared with industry data. However, the positive conclusion is that the firm has earned a profit in its first year and has returned 4.4 percent on its asset investment.

There are many other ratios that could also be calculated. However, for a start-up these would probably suffice for an entrepreneur in assessing the venture's financial strengths and weaknesses. As the firm grows, it will be important to use these ratios in conjunction with all other financial statements to provide an understanding of how the firm is performing financially.

General Valuation Approaches

general valuation approaches Methods for determining the worth of a company

There are several *general valuation approaches* that can be used in valuing the venture. One of the most widely used approaches assesses comparable publicly held companies and the prices of these companies' securities. This search for a similar company is both an art and a science. First, the company must be classified in a certain industry, since companies in the same industry share similar markets, problems, economies, and potential of sales and earnings. The review of all publicly traded companies in this industry classification should evaluate size, amount of diversity, dividends, leverage, and growth potential until the most similar company is identified. This method is inaccurate when a truly comparable company is not found.

present value of future cash flow Valuing a company based on its future sales and profits

A second widely used valuation approach is the *present value of future cash flow*. This method adjusts the value of the cash flow of the business for the time value of money and the business and economic risks. Since only cash (or cash equivalents) can be used in reinvestment, this valuation approach generally gives more accurate results than profits. With this method, the sales and earnings are projected back to the time of the valuation decision when shares of the company are offered for sale. The period between the valuation and sale dates is determined, and the potential dividend payout and expected price/earnings ratio or liquidation value at the end of the period are calculated. Finally, a rate of return desired by investors is established, less a discount rate for failure to meet those expectations.

replacement value The cost of replacing all assets of a company

Another valuation method, used only for insurance purposes or in very unique circumstances, is known as *replacement value*. This method is used when, for example, there is a unique asset involved that the buyer really wants. The valuation of the venture is based on the amount of money it would take to replace (or reproduce) that asset or another important asset or system of the venture.

book value The indicated worth of the assets of a company

The *book value* approach uses the adjusted book value, or net tangible asset value, to determine the firm's worth. Adjusted book value is obtained by making the necessary adjustments to the stated book value by taking into account any depreciation (or appreciation) of plant and equipment and real estate, as well as necessary inventory adjustments that result from the accounting methods employed. The following basic procedure can be used:

Book value	$________
Add (or subtract) any adjustments such as appreciation or depreciation to arrive at figure on next line—the fair market value	$________
Fair market value (the sale value of the company's assets)	$________
Subtract all intangibles that cannot be sold, such as goodwill	$________
Adjusted book value	$________

Since the book valuation approach involves simple calculations, its use is particularly good in relatively new businesses, in businesses where the sole owner has died or is disabled, and in businesses with speculative or highly unstable earnings.

earnings approach Determining the worth of a company by looking at its present and future earnings

The *earnings approach* is the most widely used method of valuing a company since it provides the potential investor with the best estimate of the probable return on investment. The potential earnings are calculated by weighting the most recent operating year's earnings after they have been adjusted for any extraordinary expenses that would not have normally occurred in the operations of a publicly traded company. An appropriate price-earnings multiple is then selected based on norms of the industry and the investment risk. A higher multiple will be used for a high-risk business and a lower multiple for a low-risk business. For example, a low-risk business in an industry with a seven-times-earnings multiple would be valued at $4.2 million if the weighted average earnings over the past three years were $0.6 million (7 × $0.6 million).

factor approach Using the major aspects of a company to determine its worth

An extension of this method is the *factor approach,* wherein the following three major factors are used to determine value: earnings, dividend-paying capacity, and book value. Appropriate weights for the particular company being valued are developed and multiplied by the capitalized value, resulting in an overall weighted valuation. An example is indicated below:

Approach (in 000s)	Capitalized Value	Weight	Weighted Value
Earnings: $40 × 10	$400	0.4	$160
Dividends: $15 × 20	$300	0.4	$120
Book value: $600 × 0.4	$240	0.2	$ 48
Average $328			
10% discount $33			
Per share value $295			

liquidation value Worth of a company if everything was sold today

A final valuation approach that gives the lowest value of the business is *liquidation value*. Liquidation value is often difficult to obtain, particularly when costs and losses must be estimated for selling the inventory, terminating employees, collecting accounts receivable, selling assets, and performing other closing-down activities. Nevertheless, it is also good for an investor to obtain a downside risk value in appraising a company.

General Valuation Method

One approach an entrepreneur can use to determine how much of the company a venture capitalist will want for a given amount of investment is indicated below:

$$\text{Venture capitalist ownership (\%)} = \frac{\text{VC \$ investment} \times \text{VC investment multiple desired}}{\text{Company's projected profits in year 5} \times \text{Price earnings multiple of comparable company}}$$

Consider the following example:

A company needs $500,000 of venture-capital money.
The company is anticipating profits of $650,000.
The venture capitalist wants an investment multiple of 5 times.
The price-earnings multiple of a similar company is 12.

According to the calculations below, the company would have to give up 32 percent ownership to obtain the needed funds:

$$\frac{\$500{,}000 \times 5}{\$650{,}000 \times 12} = 32\%$$

TABLE 12.7 Steps in Valuing Your Business and Determining Investors' Share

1. Estimate the earnings after taxes based on sales in the fifth year.
2. Determine an appropriate earnings multiple based on what similar companies are selling for in terms of their current earnings.
3. Determine the required rate of return.
4. Determine the funding needed.
5. Calculate, using the following formulas:

$$\text{Present value} = \frac{\text{Future valuation}}{(1 + i)^n}$$

where:

$$\text{Future valuation} = \text{Total estimated value of company in 5 years}$$
$$i = \text{Required rate of return}$$
$$n = \text{Number of years}$$
$$\text{Investors' share} = \frac{\text{Initial funding}}{\text{Present value}}$$

A more accurate method for determining this percentage is given in Table 12.7. The step-by-step approach takes into account the time value of money in determining the appropriate investor's share. The following hypothetical example uses this step-by-step procedure. H&B Associates, a start-up manufacturing company, estimates it will earn \$1 million after taxes on sales of \$10 million. The company needs \$800,000 now to reach that goal in five years. A similar company in the same industry is selling at 15 times earnings. A venture-capital firm, Davis Venture Partners, is interested in investing in the deal and requires a 50 percent compound rate of return on investment. What percentage of the company will have to be given up to obtain the needed capital?

$$\text{Present value} = \frac{\$1{,}000{,}000 \times 15 \text{ times earning multiple}}{(1 + 0.50)^5}$$
$$= \$1{,}975{,}000$$

$$\frac{\$800{,}000}{\$1{,}975{,}000} = 41\% \text{ will have to be given up}$$

Evaluation of an Internet Company

The valuation process for early-stage Internet companies is quite different from the traditional valuation process.[16] Traditionally, private-equity companies would examine historical financials and operations as part of a very quantitative process using such things as discounted cash flow (DCF), comparables, and/or multiples of EBITDA (earnings before interest, taxes, depreciation, and amortization). Following this, the culture and management are examined in a more qualitative way. When institutional investors focus on earlier-stage companies—in particular Internet companies that have little or no history, no historical financials, and no comparables—a different approach has to be taken in the valuation process.

For these companies, the qualitative portion of due diligence carries much more weight than in other evaluations. The focus is more on the market itself. How big is it? How is it segmented? Who are the players? How will it evolve? Once these questions are resolved, the potential entrepreneurial company's financial projections are compared with the future market in terms of fit, realism, and opportunity. After getting comfortable with the market size and potential revenue of a company, the investor examines the management team. Is this a management team that will take the company "all the way"? Who will they need to bring in? How much should be set aside for an employee stock ownership plan (ESOP)? The more complete the management team is, the higher the valuation. If the management team is still thin, then a substantial portion of the company's assets needs to be set aside to attract and retain good employees. It is difficult to generalize in terms of the product or service as different industries demand different valuations. For example, an infrastructure business is viewed very differently from a business-to-business firm.

After going through the process of deriving a value, the investor looks at all the opportunities available in the investor market. In today's market, there is a lot of money chasing high-quality deals, which is then guided by basic economic supply and demand. With more firms going after a deal, the price of a good deal gets bid up in favor of the entrepreneur. Overall, the value in early-stage technology companies is driven by a combination of market structure and management team maturity, modified by the supply and demand forces that exist in a market that is highly competitive for good, solid companies.

An entrepreneur seeking financing should keep in mind that this is a revolution quite similar to the industrial revolution 100 years ago and the biotechnology industry funding between 1978 and 1992. Markets are changing, and traditional systems are being turned upside down. Investors and entrepreneurs who have a sense of how this is going to occur and can predict the impact new technologies will have on traditional and newly formed markets are the ones who will be highly rewarded by the market.

DEAL STRUCTURE

deal structure The form of the transaction when money is obtained by a company

In addition to valuing the company and determining the percentage of the company that may have to be given up to obtain funding, a critical concern for the entrepreneur is the *deal structure,* or the terms of the transaction between the entrepreneur and the funding source.[17] In order to make the venture look as attractive as possible to potential sources of funds, the entrepreneur must understand the needs of the investors as well as his or her own needs. The needs of the funding sources include the rate of return required, the timing and form of return, the amount of control desired, and the perception of the risks involved in the particular funding opportunity. Whereas certain investors are willing to bear a significant amount of risk to obtain a significant rate of return, others want less risk and less return. Still, other investors are more concerned about their amount of influence and control once the investment has been made.

The entrepreneur's needs revolve around similar concerns, such as the degree and mechanisms of control, the amount of financing needed, and the goals for the particular firm. Before negotiating the terms and the structure of the deal with the venture capitalist, the entrepreneur should assess the relative importance of these concerns in order to negotiate where needed. Both the venture capitalist and the entrepreneur should feel comfortable with the final deal structure, and a good working relationship needs to be established to deal with any future problems.

GOING PUBLIC

going public Selling some part of the company by registering with the SEC

Going public occurs when the entrepreneur and other equity owners of the venture offer and sell some part of the company to the public through a registration statement filed with the Securities and Exchange Commission (SEC) pursuant to the Securities Act of 1933. The resulting capital infusion to the company from the increased number of stockholders and outstanding shares of stock provides the company with financial resources and generally with a relatively liquid investment vehicle. Consequently, the company will have

TABLE 12.8 Advantages and Disadvantages of Going Public

Advantages	Disadvantages
• Ability to obtain equity capital. • Enhanced ability to borrow. • Enhanced ability to raise equity. • Liquidity and valuation. • Prestige. • Personal wealth.	• Increased risk of liability. • Expense. • Regulation of corporate governance policies and procedures. • Disclosure of information. • Pressures to maintain growth pattern. • Loss of control.

greater access to capital markets in the future and a more objective picture of the public's perception of the value of the business. However, given the reporting requirements, the increased number of stockholders, and the costs involved, the entrepreneur must carefully evaluate the advantages and disadvantages of going public before initiating the process. A list of these advantages and disadvantages is given in Table 12.8.

Advantages

The three primary advantages of going public are: obtaining new equity capital, realizing an enhanced valuation due to the greater liquidity of an equity investment in the company, and enhancing the company's ability to obtain future funds. Whether it is first-stage, second-stage, or third-stage financing that is desired, a venture is in constant need of capital. The new capital provides the needed working capital, plant and equipment, or inventories and supplies necessary for the venture's growth and survival. Going public is often the best way to obtain capital on the best possible terms.

Going public generally results in a public trading market and provides a mechanism for valuing the company and allowing this value to be easily transferred among parties. Many family-owned or other privately held companies may need to go public so that the value of the company can be disseminated among the second and third generations. Venture capitalists view going public as one of the most beneficial ways to attain the liquidity necessary to exit a company with the best possible return on their earlier-stage funding. Other investors benefit as well due to easier liquidation of their investment when the company's stock takes on value and transferability. Because of this liquidity, the value of a publicly traded security is sometimes higher than shares of one that is not publicly traded. In addition, publicly traded companies often find it easier to acquire other companies by using their securities in the transactions.

As noted above, the third primary advantage is that publicly traded companies usually find it easier to raise additional capital, particularly debt. Money can often be borrowed more easily and on more favorable terms, the company's balance sheet is strengthened by the new equity capital, and the company has better prospects for raising future equity capital.

Disadvantages

initial public offering (IPO) The first public registration and sale of a company's stock

Although the advantages of going public are significant for a new venture, they must be carefully weighed against the numerous disadvantages. Some entrepreneurs want to keep their companies private, even in times of a hot stock market. Why do entrepreneurs avoid the supposed gold rush of an *initial public offering (IPO)?*

Two major reasons are public exposure and the potential loss of control that can occur in a publicly traded company. To stay on the cutting edge of technology, companies frequently need to sacrifice short-term profits for long-term innovation. This can require reinvesting in technology that in itself may not produce any bottom-line results, particularly in the short run. Making long-term decisions can be difficult in publicly traded companies where sales and profit evaluations indicate the capability of management via stock values. When enough shares are sold to the public, the company can lose control of decision making, which can even result in the venture's being acquired through an unfriendly tender offer.

Some of the most troublesome aspects of being public are the resulting loss of flexibility as well as increased duties to public stockholders and administrative burdens. The company must make decisions with respect to the fiduciary duties owed to the public shareholder, and it is obliged to disclose to the public all material information regarding the company, its operations, and its management. One publicly traded company had to retain a more expensive investment banker than would have been required by a privately held company in order to obtain an "appropriate" fairness opinion in a desired merger. The investment banker increased the expenses of the merger by $150,000, in addition to causing a three-month delay in the merger proceedings. Management of a publicly traded company also spends a significant amount of additional time and expense addressing queries from shareholders, press, and financial analysts and assuring compliance with the complicated accessing, reporting, and securities trading regulations.

With the enactment of the Sarbanes-Oxley Act in 2002, corporate governance and disclosure requirements of public companies and the practices and conduct of accountants and lawyers engaged by public companies became subject to significantly greater regulation enforcement by the Securities and Exchange Commission and the stock exchanges. As a result, the expense and administrative responsibilities of being a public company, as well as the liability risks of officers and directors, are greater than ever. Among the other consequences of the new regulation, the recruitment of qualified independent directors has become a much more difficult challenge for most public companies.

If all these disadvantages have not caused the entrepreneur to look for alternative financing rather than an IPO, the expenses involved may. The major expenses of going public include accounting fees, legal fees, underwriter's fees, registration and blue-sky filing fees, and printing costs. The accounting fees involved in going public vary greatly, depending in part on the size of the company, the availability of previously audited financial statements, and the complexity of the company's operations. Generally, the costs of going public average $500,000, although they can be much greater when significant complexities are involved. Additional reporting, accounting, legal, and printing expenses can run anywhere from $50,000 to $250,000 per year, depending on the company's past practices in the areas of accounting and shareholder communications. In addition to the SEC reports that must be filed, a proxy statement and other materials must be submitted to the SEC for review before distribution to the stockholders. These materials contain certain disclosures concerning management, its compensation, and transactions with the company, as well as the items to be voted on at the meeting. Public companies must also submit an annual report to the shareholders containing the audited financial information for the prior fiscal year and a discussion of any business developments. The preparation and distribution of the proxy materials and annual report are some of the more significant items of additional expense incurred by a company after it is public.

Accounting fees for an initial public offering fluctuate widely but typically average $150,000. Fees are at the lower end of this range if the accounting firm has regularly audited the company over the past several years. They are at the higher end of the range if the company has no prior audits or if it engages a new accounting firm. The accounting fee covers the preparation of financial statements, the response to SEC queries, and the preparation of "cold comfort" letters for the underwriters described later in this chapter.

Legal fees will vary significantly, typically ranging from $150,000 to $350,000. These fees generally cover preparation of corporate documents, preparation and clearing of the registration statement, negotiation of the final underwriting agreement, and closing of the sale of the securities to these underwriters. Additional legal fees may also be assessed and can be extensive, particularly if a major organization is involved. A public company also pays legal fees for the work involved with the National Association of Securities Dealers, Inc. (NASD) and state blue-sky filings. The legal fees for NASD and state blue-sky filings range from $8,000 to $30,000, depending on the size of the offering and the number of states in which the securities will be offered.

In most of the more significant public offerings, the company technically sells the shares to the underwriters, who then resell the shares to the public investors. The difference in the per share price at which the underwriters purchase the shares from the company and the price at which they sell them to the public is the underwriters' discount, which usually ranges from 7 to 10 percent of the public offering price of the new issue. In some IPOs, the underwriters can also require additional compensation, such as warrants to purchase stock, reimbursement for expenses, and the right of first refusal on any future offerings. The NASD regulates the maximum amount of the underwriters' compensation and reviews the actual amount for fairness before the offering can take place.

There are other expenses in the form of SEC, NASD, and state blue-sky registration fees. Of these, the SEC registration fee is quite small: one-fiftieth of 1 percent of the maximum aggregate public offering price of the security. For example, the SEC fee would be $4,000 on a $20 million offering. The minimum fee is $100. The SEC fee must be paid by certified or cashier's check. The NASD filing fee is also small in relation to the size of the offering: $100 plus one-hundredth of 1 percent of the maximum public offering price. In the above example of a $20 million offering, this would be $2,100. The NASD fee is $5,100.

The final major expense, printing costs, typically ranges from $50,000 to $200,000. The registration statement and prospectus discussed later in this chapter account for the largest portion of these expenses. The exact amount of expenses varies, depending on the length of the prospectus, the use of color or black and white photographs, the number of proofs and corrections, and the number printed. It is important for the company to use a good printer because accuracy and speed are required in the printing of the prospectus and other offering documents.

Some help in stemming these rapidly increasing costs could come from more significant use of the Internet in the publication and distribution of prospectuses, as well as from other stockholder communications such as proxy statements and annual reports. However, use of this medium is still somewhat in its infancy state. The SEC is continually refining its rules in this regard in an effort to allow companies to take advantage of this technology while maintaining the disclosure principles originally developed in the 1930s.

Not only can going public be a costly event, but the process leading up to it can be exasperating as well. Just ask Bing Yeh, who went through some trying circumstances starting when he decided to go public in July 1995 and ending when his company, Silicon Storage Technology (SST), issued its IPO on November 22.[18] While the exact process varies with each company, the goal is the same as it was for SST—make over the company so that it is seen in the best possible light and is well received by Wall Street. The many changes in a company that occur usually take place over a six-month to one-year period of time, not the 100 days it took for SST. For some companies, getting ready to go public can involve eliminating members of the management team and board, dumping marginal products,

AS SEEN IN *ENTREPRENEUR* MAGAZINE

PROVIDE ADVICE TO AN ENTREPRENEUR ABOUT THE "INITIAL PUBLIC OFFERING" MARKET

Ah, 1999. The days when companies were going public like raindrops, and stock prices were soaring through the roof before the sound of the opening bell had even faded. The days when young companies counted the minutes to their IPOs and then reaped the multimillion-dollar benefits. "An IPO was a cheap and easy way to raise money," says Nick Hanauer, a founding partner of Seattle-based VC firm Second Avenue Partners and an early investor in Amazon.com. "The markets were frothy and irrational."

Skip ahead to spring 2001. Those heady days of 1999 now seem like a distant memory. Of the 717 IPO filings in 2000, according to business Web site Hoover's Online, 201 never saw an opening bell. In fact, by fall 2000, more companies were filing to withdraw their IPOs than were filing to go public. This year hasn't fared much better: More than 50 companies withdrew their offerings before March alone. While only a short time ago there was a mad scramble to pick up new offers, even if they were overvalued, burned investors now run from anything that smacks of an IPO. AltaVista is just one high-profile name to pull its offering in recent months as a result.

THOSE WHO DARED

Companies going public in this climate are finding that things certainly aren't what they used to be. Take Loudcloud Inc., the Silicon Valley tech company founded by Marc Andreessen of Netscape fame, which went public in March only to have its shares immediately fall below the IPO price of $6 per share. The company's market value was estimated at $450 million, a far cry from the $1.3 billion Andreessen wanted. "The market is awful," says Mitch Mumma, a general partner with VC firm Intersouth Partners in Durham, North Carolina. "Companies that were considering going public a year ago aren't considering it now." For companies that are holding back, it's a waiting game.

The recent boom years were good while they lasted. Making money was easy: Just strap your fortune to the overall economy, and ride the rocket to riches. And just because Alan Greenspan took the punchbowl away, that doesn't mean the party has to end for entrepreneurs. "The opportunity for fast growth, profits and accumulation of wealth is still possible," says Nina McLemore, chair of the National Foundation for Women Business Owners and president of Regent Capital Partners LP in New York City.

However, you shouldn't expect to grow your business in overfarmed fields. Yes, some of you will still be able to find venture capital, but you are the exotic breeds. If entrepreneurs want to achieve 20 to 30 percent annual growth, most of them will have to find a new way. The old business model relied on large capital inputs to offset high fixed costs, says Elizabeth Gatewood, the Jack M. Gill chair of entrepreneurship at Indiana University, Bloomington's Kelly School of Business. "If the VC spigot is turned off," she notes, "you've got to look to a different model: lower fixed costs, higher variable costs."

If that approach sounds vaguely familiar, it's because businesses worked this way before, oh, 1995. Back to the basics is the new mantra. And one cornerstone of the old-time strategy for building a business is the alliance. But before you go pulling out your college economics textbooks for a refresher course on running a business, recognize that the Internet revolution made drastic changes in all our familiar business concepts—including the partnership.

ADVICE TO AN ENTREPRENEUR

An entrepreneur who is looking to raise 2.5 million to grow his business has read the above article and comes to you for advice:

1. Should I even bother waiting until the IPO market gets hot again?
2. I know the IPO market is pretty tough on dot-coms but what types of businesses are most attractive to the investors—that is, what are the key business attributes that can still lead to a successful IPO today? What other options are available to me?
3. Is a "hot" IPO market really an unambiguous blessing? The advantages of such a market are pretty obvious, but what are the disadvantages for the entrepreneurs and venture capitalists? What are the advantages of a slow IPO market?

Source: Reprinted with permission of Entrepreneur Media, Inc., "Take My IPO . . . Please!" by Chris Penttila, June 2001, and "What Now?" by Chris Sandlund, June 2001, *Entrepreneur* magazine: www.entrepreneur.com.

eliminating treasured perks such as the corporate jet, hiring a new accounting firm, subduing some personality traits, dressing up the senior management, or hiring new members of the management team. For Bing Yeh and SST, the makeover centered around four primary tasks: (1) hiring a chief financial officer, (2) reorganizing the financials, (3) writing a company biography, and (4) preparing for the road show.

Regardless of how much reading is done, like Bing Yeh, almost every entrepreneur is unprepared and wants to halt the preparations at some point in the makeover process. Yet for a successful IPO, each entrepreneur must follow Yeh's example by listening to the advice being given and then making the recommended changes swiftly.

TIMING OF GOING PUBLIC AND UNDERWRITER SELECTION

Probably the two most critical issues in a successful public offering are the timing of the offering and the underwriting team. An entrepreneur should seek advice from several financial advisors as well as other entrepreneurs who are familiar with the process in making decisions in these two areas.

Timing

Am I ready to go public? This is the critical question that entrepreneurs must ask themselves before launching this effort. Some criteria to evaluate in making this decision are indicated below.

First, is the company large enough? While it is not possible to establish rigid minimum-size standards that must be met before an entrepreneur can go public, New York investment banking firms prefer at least a 100,000 share offering at a minimum of $20 per share. This means that the company would have to have a post offering value of at least $50 million in order to support this $20 million offering, given that the company is willing to sell shares representing not more than 40 percent of the total number of shares outstanding after the offering is completed. This size of offering will occur only with past significant sales and earnings performance or a solid prospect for future growth and earnings.

Second, what is the amount of the company's earnings, and how strong is its financial performance? Not only is this performance the basis of the company valuation, but it also determines if a company can successfully go public and the type of firm willing to underwrite the offering. While the exact criteria vary from year to year, thereby reflecting market conditions, generally a company must have at least one year of good earnings and sales before its stock offering will be acceptable to the market. Larger underwriting firms have more stringent criteria, such as sales as high as $15 million to $20 million, a $1 million or more net income, and a 30 to 50 percent annual growth rate.

Third, are the market conditions favorable for an initial public offering? Underlying the sales and earnings, as well as the size of the offering, is the prevailing general market condition. Market conditions affect both the initial price that the entrepreneur will receive for the stock and the aftermarket, or the price performance of the stock after its initial sale. Some market conditions are more favorable for IPOs than others. Unless the need for money is so urgent that delay is impossible, the entrepreneur should attempt to take his or her company public in the most favorable market conditions.

Fourth, how urgently is the money needed? The entrepreneur must carefully appraise both the urgency of the need for new money and the availability of outside capital from other sources. Since the sale of common stock decreases the ownership position of the entrepreneur and other equity owners, the longer the time before going public, given that profits and sales growth occur, the less percentage of equity the entrepreneur will have to give up per dollar invested.

Finally, what are the needs and desires of the present owners? Sometimes the present owners lack confidence in the future viability and growth prospects of the business, or they have a need for liquidity. Going public is frequently the only method by which present stockholders may obtain the cash needed.

Underwriter Selection

managing underwriter Lead financial firm in selling stock to the public

underwriting syndicate Group of firms involved in selling stock to the public

Once the entrepreneur has determined that the timing for going public is favorable, he or she must carefully select a *managing underwriter* that will then take the lead in forming the *underwriting syndicate*. The underwriter is of critical importance in establishing the initial price for the stock of the company, supporting the stock in the aftermarket, and creating a strong following among security analysts.

Although most public offerings are conducted by a syndicate of underwriter, the entrepreneur needs to select the lead or managing underwriter(s). The managing underwriter will then develop the syndicate of underwriters for the initial public offering. An entrepreneur should ideally develop a relationship with several potential managing underwriters (investment bankers) at least one year before going public. Frequently, this occurs during the first- or second-round financing, when the advice of an investment banker helps structure the initial financial arrangements to position the company to go public later.

Since selecting the investment banker is a major factor in the success of the public offering, the entrepreneur should approach one through a mutual contact. Commercial banks, attorneys specializing in securities work, major accounting firms, providers of the initial financing, or prominent members of the company's board of directors can usually provide the needed suggestions and introductions. Also, because the relationship will be ongoing and will not end with the completion of the offering, the entrepreneur should employ several criteria in the selection process, such as reputation, distribution capability, advisory services, experience, and cost.

Since an initial public offering rarely involves a well-known company, the managing underwriter needs a good reputation to develop a strong syndicate team and provide confidence to potential investors. This reputation helps sell the public offering and supports the stock in the aftermarket. The ethics of the potential underwriter is an aspect that must be carefully evaluated.

The success of the offering also depends on the underwriter's distribution capability. An entrepreneur wants the stock of his or her company distributed to as wide and varied a base as possible. Since each investment banking firm has a different client base, the entrepreneur should compare client bases of possible managing underwriters. Is the client base strongly institutional or is it composed of individual investors? Or is it balanced between the two? Is the base more internationally or domestically oriented? Are the investors long term or speculators? What is the geographic distribution—local, regional, or nationwide? A strong managing underwriter and syndicate with a quality client base will help the stock sell and perform well in the aftermarket.

Some underwriters are better able than others to provide financial advisory services. Although this factor is not as important as the previous two in selecting an underwriter, financial counsel is frequently needed before and after the IPO. An entrepreneur should pose such questions as the following: Can the underwriter provide sound financial advice? Has the underwriter given good financial counsel to previous clients? Can the underwriter render assistance in obtaining future public or private financing? The answers to these questions will indicate the degree of ability among prospective underwriters.

As reflected in the previous questions, the experience of the investment banking firm is important. The firm should have experience in underwriting issues of companies in the same or at least similar industries. This experience will give the managing underwriter credibility, the capability to explain the company to the investing public, and the ability to price the IPO accurately.

The final factor to be considered in the choice of a managing underwriter is cost. Going public is a very costly proposition, and costs can vary significantly among underwriters. Costs associated with various possible managing underwriters must be carefully weighed against the other four factors. The key is to obtain the best possible underwriter and not try to cut corners, given the stakes involved in a successful initial public offering.

REGISTRATION STATEMENT AND TIMETABLE

Once the managing underwriter has been selected, a planning meeting should be held among those company officials responsible for preparing the registration statement, the company's independent accountants and lawyers, and the underwriters and their counsel. At this important meeting, frequently called the "all hands" meeting, a timetable is prepared that indicates dates for each step in the registration process. This timetable establishes the effective date of the registration, which determines the date of the final financial statements to be included. The timetable should indicate the individual responsible for preparing the various parts of the registration and offering statement. Problems may arise in an initial public offering due to the timetable not being carefully developed and agreed to by all parties involved.

After the completion of the preliminary preparation, the first public offering normally requires six to eight weeks to prepare, print, and file the registration statement with the SEC. Once the registration statement has been filed, the SEC generally takes 6 to 12 weeks to declare the registration effective. Delays frequently occur in this process, especially (1) during the heavy periods of market activity; (2) during peak seasons such as March, when the SEC is reviewing a large number of proxy statements; (3) when the company's attorney is not familiar with federal or state regulations; (4) when issues arise over requirements of the SEC resulting from its review of the filing; or (5) when the managing underwriter is inexperienced.

full and fair disclosure The nature of all material submitted to the SEC for approval

In reviewing the registration statement, the SEC attempts to ensure that the document makes a *full and fair disclosure* of the material reported. The SEC has no authority to withhold approval of or require any changes in the terms of an offering that it deems unfair or inequitable, so long as all material information concerning the company and the offering is fully disclosed. The National Association of Securities Dealers (NASD) will review each offering, principally to determine the fairness of the underwriting compensation and its compliance with NASD bylaw requirements.

prospectus Document for distribution to prospective buyers of a public offering

registration statement Materials submitted to the SEC for approval to sell stock to the public

Form S-1 Form for registration for most initial public offerings of stock

The registration statement itself consists primarily of two parts: the *prospectus* (a legal offering document normally prepared as a brochure or booklet for distribution to prospective buyers) and the *registration statement* (supplemental information to the prospectus, which is available for public inspection at the office of the SEC and EDGAR). Both parts of the registration statement are governed principally by the Securities and Exchange Act of 1933 (the "1933 Act"), a federal statute requiring the registration of securities to be offered to the public. This act also requires that the prospectus be furnished to the purchaser at or before the making of any written offer or the actual confirmation of a sale. Specific SEC forms set forth the informational requirements for a registration. Most initial public offerings will use a *Form S-1* registration statement. Smaller offerings may be able to use the shorter forms SB-1 or SB-2.

The Prospectus

The prospectus portion of the registration statement is almost always written in a highly stylized narrative form, since it is the selling document of the company. While the exact format is decided by the company, the information must be presented in an organized, logical sequence and in an easy-to-read, understandable manner in order to obtain SEC approval. Some of the most common sections of a prospectus include the cover page; prospectus summary; description of the company; risk factors; use of proceeds; dividend policy; capitalization; dilution; selected financial data; the business, management, and owners; type of stock; underwriter information; and the actual financial statements.

The cover page includes such information as company name, type and number of shares to be sold, a distribution table, date of prospectus, managing underwriter(s), and syndicate of underwriters involved. There is a preliminary prospectus and then a final prospectus once it has been approved by the SEC. The preliminary prospectus is used by the underwriters to solicit investor interest in the offering while the registration is pending. The final prospectus contains all of the changes and additions required by the SEC and the information concerning the price at which the securities will be sold. The final prospectus must be delivered with or prior to the written confirmation of purchase orders from investors participating in the offering.

The prospectus starts with a table of contents and summary. The prospectus summary highlights the important features of the offering, similar to the executive summary of a business plan that was discussed previously.

A brief introduction of the company follows, which describes the nature of the business, the company's history, major products, and location.

Then a discussion of the risk factors involved is presented. Such issues as a history of operating losses, a short track record, the importance of certain key individuals, dependence on certain customers, significant level of competition, or market uncertainty are the typical risk factors revealed to ensure that the purchaser is aware of the speculative nature of the offering and the degree of risk involved in purchasing.

The next section, use of proceeds, needs to be carefully prepared since the actual use of the proceeds must be reported to the SEC after the offering. This section is of great interest to potential purchasers as it indicates the reason(s) the company is going public and its future direction.

The dividend policy section details the company's dividend history and any restrictions on future dividends. Most entrepreneurial companies have not paid any dividends but have retained their earnings to finance future growth.

The capitalization section indicates the overall capital structure of the company both before and after the public offering.

Whenever there is significant disparity between the offering price of the shares and the price paid for shares by officers, directors, or founding stockholders, a dilution section is necessary in the prospectus. This section describes the dilution, or difference between the share price paid by the public investors and the weighted average price at which all shares have been issued, including the pre-IPO shares sold to officers, directors, and founding stakeholders.

Form S-1 requires that the prospectus contain selected financial data for each of the last five years of company operation to highlight significant trends in the company's financial condition. There must also be a discussion of management's analysis of the company's financial condition and results of operations. This analysis should cover at least the last three years of operation.

The next section, the business, is the largest part of the prospectus. It provides information on the company, its industry, and its products, and includes the following: the historical development of the company; principal products, markets, and distribution methods; new products being developed; sources and availability of raw materials; backlog orders; export sales; number of employees; and nature of any patents, trademarks, licenses, franchises, and physical property owned; competition; and effects of governmental regulations.

Following the business section is a discussion of management and security holders. This section covers background information, ages, business experience, total remuneration, and stock holdings of directors, nominated directors, and executive officers. Also, any stockholder (not in the above categories) who beneficially owns more than 5 percent of the company must be indicated.

The description of the capital stock section, as the name implies, indicates the par and stated value of the stock being offered, dividend rights, voting rights, liquidity, and transferability if more than one class of stock exists.

Following this, the underwriter information section explains the plans for distributing the securities, such as the amount of securities to be purchased by each underwriting participant involved.

The prospectus part of the registration statement concludes with the actual financial statements. Form S-1 normally requires audited balance sheets for the last two fiscal years, audited income statements and statements of retained earnings for the last three fiscal years, and unaudited interim financial statements as of 135 days prior to the date when the registration statement becomes effective. It is this requirement that makes it so important to pick a date for going public in light of year-end operations and to develop a good timetable. This will help avoid the time and costs of preparing additional interim statements.

Part II

This section of Form S-1 contains certain information regarding the offering, the past unregistered securities offering of the company, and any other undertakings by the company. Part II also includes exhibits such as the articles of incorporation, the underwriting agreement, company bylaws, stock option and pension plans, and initial contracts.

Procedure

red herring Preliminary prospectus of a potential public offering

comment letter A letter from the SEC to a company indicating corrections that need to be made in the submitted prospectus

pricing amendment Additional information on price and distribution submitted to the SEC to develop the final prospectus

Once the preliminary prospectus is filed as a part of the registration statement, it can be distributed to the underwriting group. This preliminary prospectus is called a *red herring,* because a statement printed in red ink appears on the front cover. The registration statement is then reviewed by the SEC to determine the adequacy of the disclosure. Some deficiencies are almost always found and are communicated to the company via either telephone or a *comment letter*. This preliminary prospectus contains all the information that will appear in the final prospectus except that which is not known until shortly before the effective date: offering price, underwriters' commission, and amount of proceeds. These items are filed through a *pricing amendment* and appear in the final prospectus. The time between the initial filing of the registration statement and its effective date, usually around 2 to 10 months, is called the waiting period. During this time the underwriting syndicate is formed and briefed. Any company publicity regarding the proposed offering is very restrictive during this period.

LEGAL ISSUES AND BLUE-SKY QUALIFICATIONS

Legal Issues

quiet period 90-day period in going public when no new company information can be released

In addition to all the legal issues surrounding the actual preparation and filing of the prospectus, there are several other important legal concerns. Perhaps the one that is of the most concern to the entrepreneur is the *quiet period,* the period of time from when the decision to go public is made to 90 days following the date the prospectus becomes effective. Care must be taken during this period regarding any new information about the company or key personnel. Any publicity effort creating a favorable attitude about the securities to be offered is illegal. The guidelines established by the SEC regarding the information that can and cannot be released should be understood not only by the entrepreneur but by everyone else in the company as well. All press releases and other printed material should be cleared with the attorneys involved as well as the underwriter. The entrepreneur and key personnel must curtail speaking engagements and television appearances to avoid any possible problematic response to interviewer or audience questions. One entrepreneur whose company was in the process of going public had to postpone a TV guest appearance on *The Today Show,* where she was to discuss women entrepreneurs, not her company.

Blue-Sky Qualifications

blue-sky laws Laws of each state regulating public sale of stock

The securities of certain smaller companies going public must also be qualified under the *blue-sky laws* of each state in which the securities will be offered. This is true unless the state has an exemption from the qualification requirements. These blue-sky laws may cause additional delays and costs to the company going public. Offerings of securities that will be traded on the more prominent stock exchanges or listed on the NASDAQ National Market have been preempted from most state registration requirements by the National Securities Markets Improvements Act of 1996. Many states allow their state securities administrators to prevent an offering from being sold in their state on such substantive grounds as past stock issuances, too much dilution, or too much compensation to the underwriter, even though all required disclosures have been met and clearance has been granted by the SEC.

AFTER GOING PUBLIC

aftermarket support Actions of underwriters to help support the price of stock following the public offering

After the initial public offering has been sold, there are still some areas of concern to the entrepreneur. These include *aftermarket support,* relationship with the financial community, and reporting requirements.

Aftermarket Support

Once issued, the price of the stock is typically monitored, particularly in the initial weeks after its offering. Usually the managing underwriting firm will be the principal market maker in the company's stock and will be ready to purchase or sell stock in the interdealer market. To stabilize the market, and prevent the price from going below the initial public offering price, the underwriter will usually enter bids to buy the stock in the early stages after the offers, therefore giving aftermarket support. This support is important in allowing the stock not to be adversely affected by an initial drop in price.

Relationship with the Financial Community

Once a company has gone public, the financial community usually takes a greater interest. An entrepreneur will need an increasing portion of time to develop a good relationship with this community. The relationship established has a significant effect on the market interest and the price of the company's stock. Since many investors rely on analysts and brokers for investment advice, the entrepreneur should attempt to meet as many of these individuals as possible. Regular appearances before societies of security analysts should be a part of establishing this relationship, as well as public disclosures through formal press releases. Frequently, it is best to designate one person in the company to be the information officer, ensuring that the press, public, and security analysts are dealt with in a friendly, efficient manner. There is nothing worse than a company not responding in a timely manner to information requests.

Reporting Requirements

The company must file annual reports on Form 10-K, quarterly reports on Form 10-Q, and specific transaction or event reports on Form 8-K. The information in Form 10-K on the business, management, and company assets is similar to that in Form S-1 of the registration statement. Of course, audited financial statements are required.

The quarterly report on Form 10-Q primarily contains the unaudited financial information for the most recently completed fiscal quarter. No Form 10-Q is required for the fourth fiscal quarter.

A Form 8-K report must be filed within two to five days of such events as the acquisition or disposition of significant assets by the company outside the ordinary course of the business, the resignation or dismissal of the company's independent public accountants, or a change in control of the company.

Under the Sarbanes-Oxley Act, the due dates for reports have been accelerated. In addition, by adopting its Regulation FD, the Securities and Exchange Commission has tried to minimize selective disclosures of important corporate developments and information. Under this regulation, public companies are required to make immediate and broad public disclosures of important information at the same time they release the information to anyone outside the company.

The company must follow the proxy solicitation requirements in connection with holding a meeting or obtaining the written consent of security holders. The timing and type of materials involved are detailed in Regulation 14A under the Securities Exchange Act of 1934. These are but a few of the reporting requirements of public companies. All the requirements must be carefully observed, since even inadvertent mistakes can have negative consequences for the company. The reports required must be filed on time.

IN REVIEW

SUMMARY

In financing a business, the entrepreneur determines the amount and timing of funds needed. Seed or start-up capital is the most difficult to obtain, with the most likely source being the informal risk-capital market (angels). These investors, who are wealthy individuals, average one or two deals per year, ranging from $10,000 to $500,000, and generally find their deals through referrals.

Although venture capital may be used in the first stage, it is primarily used in the second or third stage to provide working capital for growth or expansion. Venture capital is broadly defined as a professionally managed pool of equity capital. Since 1958, small business investment companies (SBICs) have combined private capital and government funds to finance the growth and start-up of small businesses. Private venture-capital firms have developed since the 1960s, with limited partners supplying the funding. At the same time, venture-capital divisions operating within major corporations began appearing. States also sponsor venture-capital funds to foster economic development.

In order to achieve the venture capitalist's primary goal of generating long-term capital appreciation through investments in business, three criteria are used: The company must have strong management; the product/market opportunity must be unique; and the capital appreciation must be significant, offering a 40 to 60 percent return on investment. The process of obtaining venture capital includes a preliminary screening, agreement on principal terms, due diligence, and final approval. Entrepreneurs need to approach a potential venture capitalist with a professional business plan and a good oral presentation. After a successful initial presentation, the entrepreneur and investor agree on principal terms before the due diligence process is begun. Due diligence involves a detailed analysis of the markets, industry, and finances and can take up to three months. The final stage requires comprehensive documentation of the details of the transaction.

Valuing the company is of concern to the entrepreneur. Eight factors can be used as a basis for valuation: the nature and history of the business, the economic outlook, book value, future earnings, dividend-paying capacity, intangible assets, sales of stock, and the market price of stocks of similar companies. Numerous valuation approaches can be used and include an assessment of comparable publicly held companies, present value of future cash flow, replacement value, book value, earnings approach, factor approach, and liquidation value.

In the end, the entrepreneur and investor must agree on the terms of the transaction, known as the deal. When care is taken in structuring the deal, the entrepreneur and the investor will maintain a good relationship while achieving their goals through the growth and profitability of the business.

Going public—transforming a closely held corporation into one in which the general public has proprietary interest—is indeed arduous. An entrepreneur must carefully assess whether the company is ready to go public as well as whether the advantages outweigh the disadvantages of doing so.

Once the decision is made to proceed, a managing investment banking firm must be selected and the registration statement prepared. The expertise of the investment banker is a major factor in the success of the public offering. In selecting an investment banker, the entrepreneur should consider reputation, distribution capability, advisory services, experience, and cost. To prepare for the registration date, the entrepreneur must organize an "all hands" meeting of company officials, the company's independent accountants and lawyers, and the underwriters and their counsel. A timetable must be established for the effective date of registration and for the preparation of necessary financial documents, including the preliminary and final prospectuses. After registration and review by the SEC, the entrepreneur must carefully observe the 90-day quiet period and, in the case of certain smaller companies, qualify under the blue-sky laws of each state in which the securities will be offered. After the initial public offering, the entrepreneur should strive to maintain a good relationship with the financial community and adhere strictly to the reporting requirements of public companies.

RESEARCH TASKS

1. Go to a directory of venture capitalists and ascertain what percentage of funds for a typical venture-capital firm are invested in seed, start-up, expansion or development, and acquisitions or leveraged buyouts. What criteria do venture capitalists report using in their initial screening of business proposals?
2. Obtain an initial public offering prospectus for three companies. Use at least two different approaches for valuing each company.
3. Search the Internet for services that provide access to business angels or informal investors. How do these sites work? If you were an entrepreneur looking for funding, how much would it cost to use this service? How many business angels are registered on the typical database? How many entrepreneurs are registered on the typical database? How effective do you believe these services are? (Use data where possible to back up your answer.)
4. How many companies went public per year over the last 10-year period? How do you explain this variation in the "popularity" of going public?
5. Analyze the prospectuses of 10 companies that went public in 2005. In your opinion, which companies are likely to do well in the public offering, and which are less likely to do well? Conduct the following calculation to test your propositions: Stock price after 1 week − Offering price ÷ Offering price. Compare this price with the original IPO price.
6. Analyze the prospectus of five companies going public. What are the reasons they state for going public? How are they going to use the proceeds? What are the major risk factors presented?

CLASS DISCUSSION

1. An investor provides an entrepreneurial firm with the capital that it needs to grow. Over and above the capital, in what other ways can the investor add value to the firm? What are the possible downsides of having a venture capitalist as an investor in the business?
2. Assume that you have been very lucky and have been given a considerable fortune. You want to become a business angel (straight after graduation). How would you go about setting up and running your "business angel" business? Be specific about generating deal flow, selection criteria, the desired level of control and involvement in the investee, etc.
3. What drives the market for IPOs? Why is it so volatile?
4. If you were an entrepreneur in a "hot" market, would you invest the substantial amount of time, energy, and other resources necessary to try and go public before the bubble bursts? Or would you prefer to utilize those resources to build your business and create value for customers?

SELECTED READINGS

Birnir, Jóhanna Kristín. (October 2005). Public Venture Capital and Party Institutionalization. *Comparative Political Studies*, vol. 38, no. 8, pp. 915–38.

This article analyzes the effect of money on new systems of government and the role of public funding. Two hypotheses are formulated about the expected effects of the introduction of and marginal increases in public funding on the institutionalization of the party system. The hypotheses are then tested in a statistical study of all new democracies in Eastern Europe, the Baltics, and other former Soviet Republics.

Boubakri, Narjess; Maher Kooli; and Jean-François L'Her. (Summer 2005). Is There Any Life After Going Public? Evidence from the Canadian Market. *Journal of Private Equity*, vol. 8, no. 3, pp. 30–40.

This article examines the survival profile of Canadian initial public offerings (IPOs). More specifically, the authors develop multinomial logit models based on the information contained in the prospectus and attempt to determine what factors influence the post-issue transition of the IPO firms into survivors, nonsurvivors, or targets. The authors also estimate an accelerated-failure-time model as a robustness test and find that the survival time for IPOs increases with the level of underpricing and decreases during hot issue periods.

Bradley, Daniel J.; and Bradford D. Jordan. (2002). Partial Adjustment to Public Information and IPO Underpricing. *Journal of Financial and Quantitative Analysis*, vol. 37, no. 4, pp. 595–616.

This paper examines the extent to which offer prices reflect public information for 3,325 IPOs over the period 1990–99, focusing primarily on four variables: share overhang, file range amendments, venture capital backing, and previous issue underpricing. The paper shows that 35–50 percent of the variation in IPO underpricing can be predicted using public information.

Brau, James C.; and Jerome S. Osteryoung. (2001). The Determinants of Successful Micro-IPOs: An Analysis of Issues Made under the Small Corporate Offering Registration (SCOR) Procedure. *Journal of Small Business Management*, vol. 39, no. 3, pp. 209–27.

This article extends the existing IPO literature to the case of micro-IPOs. It identifies variables that should impact the probability of success or failure in a Small Corporate Registration (SCOR) offering and then empirically tests them.

Certo, S. Trevis; Catherine M. Daily; and Dan R. Dalton. (Winter 2001). Signaling Firm Value through Board Structure: An Investigation of Initial Public Offerings. *Entrepreneurship Theory and Practice*, pp. 35–50.

This paper investigates the relationship between board structure and IPO underpricing, a performance indicator unique to the IPO context, among a sample of IPOs during the 1990s. The findings indicate that the board size and board reputation are negatively associated with IPO underpricing, but board composition and board leadership structure are not negatively associated with IPO underpricing.

Champion, David. (February 2001). Too Soon to IPO? *Harvard Business Review*, pp. 35–46.

This article is a Harvard Business Review *case study demonstrating a decision facing a company in the high-tech area concerning whether to go public now or wait until the situation is more favorable. The issues discussed involve company valuation over the long term, real cash that the IPO can bring, and the feasibility of the market and technology.*

Corwin, Shane A.; and Jeffrey H. Harris. (Spring 2001). The Initial Listing Decisions of Firms That Go Public. *Financial Management*, pp. 35–55.

This paper analyzes the initial listing decisions of IPOs that qualify for NYSE listing and describes findings that IPOs are more likely to list on the exchange where their industry peers are listed. Although direct issue costs are higher on the NYSE than on NASDAQ, total issue costs do not differ across exchanges and are unlikely to affect the listing decision.

Cumming, Douglas J. (September 2005). Agency Costs, Institutions, Learning, and Taxation in Venture Capital Contracting. *Journal of Business Venturing*, vol. 20, no. 5, pp. 573–622.

This paper introduces a data set on forms of finance used in 12,363 Canadian and U.S. venture capital (VC) and private equity financings of Canadian entrepreneurial firms from 1991 to 2003. The data comprise different types of venture-capital institutions, including corporate, limited partnership, government, and labor-sponsored funds, as well as U.S. funds that invest in Canadian entrepreneurial firms.

Cumming, Douglas; Grant Fleming; and Jo-Ann Suchard. (February 2005). Venture Capitalist Value-Added Activities, Fundraising and Drawdowns. *Journal of Banking & Finance*, vol. 29, no. 2, pp. 295–331.

This paper is the first to introduce an analysis of the effect of different types of venture capitalist value-added activities (financial, administrative, marketing, strategic/management) on fund-raising. In addition, the authors include an analysis of the functional difference between committed funds and drawdowns from capital commitments vis-à-vis pension funds and venture-capital funds.

De Clercq, Dirk; and Harry J. Sapienza. (July 2005). When Do Venture Capital Firms Learn from Their Portfolio Companies? *Entrepreneurship: Theory & Practice*, vol. 29, no. 4, pp. 517–35.

This article examines situations wherein venture-capital firms (VCFs) learn from their portfolio companies (PFCs). Relying primarily on learning and behavioral theories, the authors develop hypotheses regarding the effects of prior experience, knowledge overlap, trust, and PFC performance on learning by VCFs. The article discusses the limitations and implications of the findings and also suggests avenues for future research.

Farag, Hady; Ulrich Hommel; Peter Witt; and Mike Wright. (October–December 2004). Contracting, Monitoring, and Exiting Venture Investments in Transitioning Economies: A Comparative Analysis of Eastern European and German Markets. *Venture Capital*, vol. 6, no. 4, pp. 257–82.

This paper analyzes investment practices in the private equity markets of transitioning economies in Central and Eastern Europe. Using a proprietary set of survey data and nonparametric tests, the study compares findings for the Czech Republic, Hungary, and Poland with those for the more established German private equity market. The analysis also highlights the specificities of early-stage and later-stage investors in truly emerging venture-capital markets.

Florin, Juan. (January 2005). Is Venture Capital Worth It? Effects on Firm Performance and Founder Returns. *Journal of Business Venturing*, vol. 20, no. 1, pp. 113–35.

This paper extends research on venture capital finance by studying its effects on a venture's performance and on its founders' returns beyond an initial public offering (IPO). A "founder performance" construct, defined as a founder's financial and nonfinancial returns, is proposed and used to measure and compare returns to founders with returns to investors and firm performance.

Fraser-Sampson, Guy. (September 2005). How European Venture Capital Functions as an Asset Class for Pensions. *Pensions*, vol. 10, no. 4, pp. 290–93.

This article presents information on the British pension industry. The author discusses: the fact that the average corporate plan is 99 percent funded and the average local authority plan is 90 percent funded; information on the unprecedented funding crisis in the industry; and the case of British pension trustees who have made consistently wrong asset allocation decisions.

Green, Jason. (2004). Venture Capital at a New Crossroads: Lessons from the Bubble. *Journal of Management Development*, vol. 23, no. 10, pp. 972–76.

This paper asserts that the venture-capital industry is an essential source of capital for new enterprises and a major engine of growth in the U.S. economy. The author's conclusions are based on an assessment of the prospects of the enterprises venture capital decides to support, their products and markets, and the facilities they will need.

Harding, Rebecca. (January 2002). Plugging the Knowledge Gap: An International Comparison of the Role for Policy in the Venture Capital Market. *Venture Capital*, vol. 4, no. 1, pp. 59–76.

This paper examines the role of policy in creating venture-capital structures that support innovative, high-growth companies. It compares the policy challenges and the emerging structures and measures in the U.S., Germany, Singapore, France, Ireland, the Netherlands, and the U.K. The paper provides evidence to demonstrate that the equity gap is actually the measurable outcome of this information asymmetry, or "knowledge gap," and that policy has been most effective in countries that have approached the development of a venture-capital market through demand rather than supply-side measures.

Jungwirth, Carola; and Petra Moog. (April–September 2004). Selection and Support Strategies in Venture Capital Financing: High-Tech or Low-Tech, Hands-Off or Hands-On? *Venture Capital*, vol. 6, no. 2/3, pp. 105–23.

This article argues that specialization in venture-capital financing makes the presence of generalist investors perplexing. In order to understand their function, the authors investigate the knowledge resource bases of both generalist and specialist venture-capital funds, the types of enterprises they select, and their corresponding support strategies. Arguing that differences in strategy can be attributed to differences in knowledge, the authors hypothesize that specialists select high-tech projects; generalists, on the other hand, select low-tech projects.

Klonowski, Darek. (September 2005). The Evolution of the Venture Capital Industry in Transition Economies: The Case of Poland. *Post-Communist Economies*, vol. 17, no. 3, pp. 331–48.

This article focuses on the evolution of the venture-capital industry in emerging markets by examining the Polish experience between 1990 and 2003. Evidence is provided to demonstrate that the venture-capital industry developed in three distinct phases (development, expansion, and correction) and broadly followed a normal Western-type venture-capital cycle.

Knyphausen-Aufseß, Dodo zu. (January–March 2005). Corporate Venture Capital: Who Adds Value? *Venture Capital*, vol. 7, no. 1, pp. 23–49.

This paper argues that different corporate venture-capital firms rely on different resource bases. Thus, different "types" of corporate venture-capital providers can be distinguished. A number of propositions are derived in order to determine which of these corporate venture-capital investors may be best suited to add different kinds of value to the start-up firms. The derived propositions may lead empirical research in the future.

Mäkelä, Markus M.; and Markku V. J. Maula. (July 2005). Cross-Border Venture Capital and New Venture Internationalization: An Isomorphism Perspective. *Venture Capital*, vol. 7, no. 3, pp. 227–57.

This paper discusses how the fastest growing global ventures are backed by cross-border venture capitalists. The paper suggests that foreign venture capitalists located in a venture's target market of internationalization can be valuable for the venture by legitimizing the unknown new venture in that market. However, foreign investors tend to drive portfolio companies toward their home markets, and the benefits may turn into disadvantages if the target market differs from the home markets of the foreign investors.

Marshall, Jeffrey; and Ellen M. Heffes. (November 2004). Tips for Evaluating Business Credit Risk. *Financial Executive*, vol. 20, no. 8, pp.11–13.

This article presents tips for evaluating business credit risk. For one, credit managers should evaluate how the firm is capitalized and if it has reliable access to future capital and determine sources of capital and how the capital is structured. Also, credit managers should find out if complex hedging strategies are in place that may not be actual hedges, and they should determine if derivatives used are liquid and if there are naked positions. They should also check to see if big write-offs are coming.

Maula, Markku; Erkko Autio; and Gordon Murray. (January–March 2005). Corporate Venture Capitalists and Independent Venture Capitalists: What Do They Know, Who Do They Know and Should Entrepreneurs Care? *Venture Capital*, vol. 7, no. 1, pp. 3–21.

This article compares the social capital–based and knowledge-based forms of value-added provided by independent and corporate venture capitalists to their portfolio firms. Primary data from U.S. technology-based new firms that received both corporate venture-capital and independent venture-capital funding are analyzed. This study demonstrates that the value-adding contributions of corporate venture capital and independent venture-capital investors are different both in their origins and in their consequences.

Millman, Gregory J. (September 2005). Venture Capital Forecast HOT with a Chance of STORMS. *Financial Executive*, vol. 21, no. 7, pp. 28–31.

This article examines the condition of the venture-capital market in the U.S. in 2005. Interest in venture-capital investing is so strong that some complain that the supply of funds is far greater than what the industry can economically invest. But despite the flood of capital looking for venture opportunities, it is harder than ever for start-ups to raise money. Most venture capitalists look for some proof of concept in a track record and prefer later-stage investments.

Neus, Werner; and Uwe Walz. (April 2005). Exit Timing of Venture Capitalists in the Course of an Initial Public Offering. *Journal of Financial Intermediation*, vol. 14, no. 2, pp. 253–77.

This article analyzes the disinvestment decisions of venture capitalists in the course of an IPO of their portfolio firms. The capital market learns of the project quality only in the period following the IPO. Venture capitalists with high-quality firms must choose between immediately selling their stake in the venture at a price below the true value and waiting until the true value is revealed. The article explains the phenomenon of "hot-issue market behavior" involving early disinvestments and a high degree of price uncertainty.

Pratch, Leslie. (Summer 2005). Value-Added Investing: A Framework for Early Stage Venture Capital Firms. *Journal of Private Equity*, vol. 8, no. 3, pp. 13–29.

This article presents a framework that describes how one early-stage venture-capital firm makes its expertise and contacts available to an often inexperienced management team in order to move a portfolio company further and faster along the process leading to an IPO or sale.

Singh, Shashank; Shailendra J Singh; and Ashok Dylan Jadeja. (Fall 2005). Venture Investing in India? Think Twice. *Journal of Private Equity*, vol. 8, no. 4, pp. 35–40.

This article examines the condition of the venture-capital industry in India. Factors that must be considered by U.S. venture capitalists in pursuing direct investments in India include: the potential effect of high investment interest rates on the country's venture capital activities; and strategies for investors to develop proprietary deal flow and encourage entrepreneurship in the country.

Tan, Justin; and David Tan. (March 2004). Entry, Growth, and Exit Strategies of Chinese Technology Start-Ups: Choosing between Short-Term Gain or Long-Term Potential. *Journal of Management Inquiry*, vol. 13, no. 1, pp. 49–54.

This article presents information on Chinese business enterprises. Although knowledge of entrepreneurial strategies in market economies lags behind other areas of research, an understanding of entrepreneurial growth in transitional economies such as China is even more limited. Given the role entrepreneurs play in economic growth, especially in transitional economies, an improved understanding of entrepreneurial strategies will have profound implications in theory and in practice.

Wang, Clement K.; and Valerie Y. L. Sim. (October 2001). Exit Strategies of Venture Capital–Backed Companies in Singapore. *Venture Capital*, vol. 3, no. 4, pp. 337–58.

This article shows that the exit of venture capital (VC) is essential for the growth of the VC industry. An empirical study is conducted on the VC exit mechanism in Singapore using survey and interview data. This study presents empirical evidence of the various determinants which affect Singapore venture capitalists' exit choices, and it explores the local VC investment/exit process. Based on the study, the article concludes with a discussion of the immaturity of Asia's capital markets compared with those of the West.

END NOTES

1. *Report of the Use of the Rule 146 Exemption in Capital Formation* (Washington, DC: Directorate of Economic Policy Analysis, Securities and Exchange Commission, 1983).
2. *An Analysis of Regulation D* (Washington, DC: Directorate of Economic Policy Analysis, Securities and Exchange Commission, 1984).
3. Charles River Associates, Inc., *An Analysis of Capital Market Imperfections* (Washington, DC: National Bureau of Standards, February 1976).
4. W. E. Wetzel, Jr., "Entrepreneurs, Angels, and Economic Renaissance." In *Entrepreneurship, Intrapreneurship, and Venture Capital,* ed. R. D. Hisrich, (Lexington, MA: Lexington Books, 1986), pp. 119–40. Other information on angels and their investments can be found in W. E. Wetzel, Jr., "Angels and Informal Risk Capital," *Sloan Management Review* 24 (Summer 1983), pp. 23–24; and W. E. Wetzel, Jr., "The Informal Venture Capital Market: Aspects of Scale and Market Efficiency," *Journal of Business Venturing* (Fall 1987), pp. 299–314.
5. R. B. Avery and G. E. Elliehausen, "Financial Characteristics of High Income Families," *Federal Reserve Bulletin,* Washington, DC (March 1986).
6. M. Gannon, "Financing Purgatory: An Emerging Class of Investors Is Beginning to Fill the Nether Regions of Start-Up Financing—the Murky World between the Angels and the Venture Capitalists," *Venture Capital Journal* (May 1999), pp. 40–42.
7. S. Prowse, "Angel Investors and the Market for Angel Investments," *Journal of Banking and Finance* 23 (1998), pp. 785–92.
8. Joseph Bell, Kenneth Huggins, and Christine McClatchey, "Profiling the Angel Investor," *Proceedings, Small Business Institute Directors Association 2002 Conference,* February 7–9, 2002, San Diego, CA, pp. 1–3.
9. Aspects of venture capital are discussed in J. Timmons and W. D. Bygrave, "Venture Capital's Role in Financing Innovation for Economic Growth," *Journal of Business Venturing* 1 (Spring 1986), pp. 161–76; R. B. Robinson, Jr., "Emerging Strategies in the Venture Capital Industry," *Journal of Business Venturing* 2 (Winter 1987), pp. 53–78; and H. H. Stevenson, D. F. Muzyka, and J. A. Timmons, "Venture Capital in Transition: A Monte Carlo Simulation of Changes in Investment Patterns," *Journal of Business Venturing* 2 (Winter 1987), pp. 103–22.
10. For the role of SBICs, see Farrell K. Slower, "Growth Looms for SBICs," *Venture* (October 1985), pp. 46–47; and M. H. Fleischer, "The SBIC 100—More Deals for the Bucks," *Venture* (October 1985), pp. 50–54.
11. Most of the information on the venture-capital industry in this section as well as other information can be found in the PricewaterhouseCoopers/Thomson Venture Economics/National Venture Capital Association Money Tree™ Survey.
12. For a thorough discussion of the venture-capital process, see B. Davis, "Role of Venture Capital in the Economic Renaissance of an Area." In *Entrepreneurship, Intrapreneurship, and Venture Capital,* ed. R. D. Hisrich, (Lexington, MA:

Lexington Books, 1986), pp. 107–18; Robert D. Hisrich and A. D. Jankowicz, "Intuition in Venture Capital Decisions: An Exploratory Study Using a New Technique," *Journal of Business Venturing* 5 (January 1990), pp. 49–63; Robert D. Hisrich and Vance H. Fried, "The Role of the Venture Capitalist in the Management of Entrepreneurial Enterprises," *Journal of International Business and Entrepreneurship* 1, no. 1 (June 1992), pp. 75–106; Vance H. Fried, Robert D. Hisrich, and Amy Polonchek, "Research Note: Venture Capitalists' Investment Criteria: A Replication," *Journal of Small Business Finance* 3, no. 1 (Fall 1993), pp. 37–42; and Vance H. Fried and Robert D. Hisrich, "The Venture Capitalist: A Relationship Investor," *California Management Review* 37, no. 2 (Winter 1995), pp. 101–13.

13. A discussion of some of the important sectors in this decision process can be found in I. MacMillan, L. Zemann, and Subba Narasimba, "Criteria Distinguishing Successful from Unsuccessful Ventures in the Venture Screening Process," *Journal of Business Venturing* 2 (Spring 1987), pp. 123–38; Robert D. Hisrich and Vance H. Fried, "Towards a Model of Venture Capital Investment Decision-Making," *Financial Management* 23, no. 3 (Fall 1994), pp. 28–37; and Vance H. Fried, B. Elonso, and Robert D. Hisrich, "How Venture Capital Firms Differ," *Journal of Business Venturing* 10, no. 2 (March 1995), pp. 157–79.
14. A complete listing of venture-capitalist firms in the United States and throughout the world can be found in *Venture's Guide to International Venture Capital* (New York: Simon and Schuster, 1985); and E. S. Pratt, *Guide to Venture Capital Sources* (Wellesley, MA: Capital Publishing, 1995).
15. A. V. Bruno and T. T. Tyebjee, "The One That Got Away: A Study of Ventures Rejected by Venture Capitalists," *Proceedings*, 1983 Babson Research Conference, 1983, Wellesley, MA, pp. 289–306.
16. The material in this section is adapted from material provided by John R. Farrall, associate, Crystal Internet Venture Funds.
17. For a discussion of some problems with venture-capital deals, see "Why Smart Companies Are Saying No to Venture Capitalists," *Inc.* (August 1984), pp. 65–75.
18. For the full details of this story, see John Kerr, "The 100-Day Makeover," *Inc.* (May 1996), pp. 54–63.

CASES FOR PART 3

CASE 3A
THE WINSLOW CLOCK COMPANY

For the third time, Dr. Winslow sat up in bed, flipped on the light, and reached for The Winslow Clock Company business plan. Maybe reading through it again would calm his growing fears. As he flipped through the pages, he recalled again all the years of thinking, tinkering, and discovery that had gone into the development of his alarm clock. How could something he spent so much time and energy on be wrong? It was such a good idea, this "throwable" alarm clock: Millions of Americans would want to get this kind of revenge on their daily call to the rat race. And, in its final design, it contained all kinds of computer-age technology. Surely, the investors tomorrow will love it!

What had happened to his confidence? He had been sure enough to invest all his savings in the clock's development. What a time to get second thoughts! Didn't he use the best technical help available to design the clock and plan the production and marketing? Maybe that was his problem—too much dependence on "experts." Being a practicing psychiatrist, he considered himself a good judge of character and motivation, but maybe his obsession with his clock had clouded his perception. Should he take more time to personally study the different production and marketing scenarios? He didn't have any more time, if he wanted to get production started in time to hit the Christmas season. Should he wait another year, or risk going to market at a slow time of year, or …?

The more he thought, the more the doubts and worries grew. He had to put a stop to this pointless mental exercise. The business plan he held in his hands was what he had to sell tomorrow at the meeting, so he'd better have confidence in it. If things went badly, then he could think about changes. For now, he would read over the business plan for The Winslow Clock Company (which follows) just once more, concentrating on the favorable arguments his business "experts" had made.

SUMMARY

The attached five-year business plan for The Winslow Clock Company is based primarily on the estimated potential of the company's first product, an alarm clock designed and patented by Dr. Michael Winslow, a psychiatrist by profession. He expected the sales and profits generated by this product to reach $8.5 million and $1.5 million, respectively, within three years, which would provide sufficient resources to enable the company to expand its line into related products now under consideration.

History of the Product

Under development for 10 years, the concept for the clock stems from Dr. Winslow's thought that it would be fun to have the liberty to "get back at" the alarm that so readily awakens everyone each morning. The "fun" part—and what makes the alarm unique—is that you throw it to turn it off.

Development of the microchip and related technology in recent years has made the design of such a clock possible at a reasonable cost. The technical assistance on the clock was provided by students at the MIT Innovation Center under the guidance of its director. The business and marketing planning for the clock was done with the help of Boston College MBA candidates at the Small Business Development Center under the direction of its faculty associate.

In addition, Dr. Winslow has contracted with a number of professional consultants in the areas of product design, product engineering, marketing and advertising, production, legal matters, and accounting.

Market Acceptance

Early reaction from such major retailers as Bloomingdale's and Hammacher Schlemmer in New York has been very positive, thus supporting the belief that the targeted levels of sales are achievable.

Thus, in what might otherwise be considered a mature market, new design and technology are eagerly sought by retailers and customers anxious to provide or find a refreshing selection of alternatives. The company's projected level of sales in its first year represents less than 1 percent of this growing segment of the U.S. clock market.

Competition

Although several major manufacturers account for most clock sales (with Japanese manufacturers dominating the sale of quartz movements), there is nevertheless a significant annual volume attributable to smaller specialty designers, most of whom purchase the clock movements on an OEM (original equipment manufacturer) basis from the larger producers and concentrate on unique housing designs.

Seiko, the company supplying the movement for Dr. Winslow's clock, has made impressive strides in the United States in the last four years by increasing its annual OEM business from 400,000 to 2 million units. Besides selling its own Seiko and Picco brands, it is developing a reputable supplier business. This strategy allows Seiko to enjoy some of the profit opportunity created by an expanded market without all the marketing costs and risks.

In addition, a number of large retailers contract with the major manufacturers for private-label production. This somewhat fragmented structure has created profitable opportunities for products designed for niches within the large clock market.

The question arises, If the product is attractive enough to create a niche in the market, how soon will it have competition? The concept of a "throwable" alarm and several components designed specifically for the product are patented. In addition, it would require some time and expense for potential competitors to develop the impact switch and the microchip used in Dr. Winslow's clock.

Financial Projections: Opportunities and Risks

Financial projections for the first five years of the company are summarized below. (Sales are based on only the first product, to be introduced in 2004.)

	Year 1	Year 2	Year 3	Year 4	Year 5
Unit sales (000s)	50	150	200	150	125
Selling price	$42.50	$42.50	$42.50	$40.00	$40.00
Net sales (000s)	$2,125	$6,375	$8,500	$6,000	$5,000
Net profit (000s)	$333	$823*	$1,503	$781	$496
Profit ratio	16.0%	13.0%	17.7%	13.0%	10.0%

*Assuming $650,000 term loan (plus interest) paid back in December.

Since components and subassemblies would be purchased rather than manufactured by the company, and then assembled and shipped by an outside contractor, the capital investment required is minimal, estimated at less than $50,000, the majority of which would be for tooling. Another $50,000 for start-up expenses, prototypes, and preproduction operating expenses would also be required in the first two months of 2004.

By March, however, the commitment increases. Because of the company's lack of credit history, all indications suggest that suppliers will require letters of credit to accompany the $814,000 in parts orders placed between March and September of 2004, when shipments are expected to begin. In addition, operating expenses between March and October are forecasted at $176,000.

Given the projected level of sales in the first two years, the company is seeking equity capital of $600,000 as early as possible in 2004. An additional term loan of approximately $650,000 would be needed by June to carry financing and operating costs through year's end.

It should be emphasized that although this combined cash injection of $1.2 million is at apparent risk for at least the six to eight months prior to the beginning of shipments (and, of course, beyond), two factors diminish this risk. First, the initial selling effort in the spring of 2004 to secure orders for the Christmas season should provide a clear indication of market acceptance by the end of April. The long lead time required to order components then becomes a positive factor. Orders for 40,000 of the first season's production of 50,000 units could be canceled without penalty a month in advance on standard items such as the clock movement. This alone would save almost $730,000. In addition, many operating expenses could be curtailed accordingly and alternative marketing plans put into place. (Direct mail-order marketing, for example, is an approach that will be explored from the beginning anyway and, in a down-side case, certainly would be a viable alternative.)

The second factor that diminishes the risk is that low fixed costs allow the break-even point to be projected at 16,000 units, which should be achieved in October, the second month of actual shipments.

According to its projected cash flow, the company should be able to repay its term loan in full within 18 months. From that point on, it can fund its continuing operations from the generated working capital.

The returns on investment are calculated at 19, 33, and 37 percent in the first three years, respectively, with returns on net worth at 34, 46, and 45 percent. Net present value for the original investors would be $1.7 million, based on five years of net cash flow and not including the salable value of the firm or its continuing earning power after that time. Payback is expected in one year, based on the forecast of sales and profits. Specific financial details are found in Exhibits 1 through 7.

INDUSTRY INFORMATION

The clock market in the United States has been growing at a rate of between 8 and 10 percent per year, with significantly higher growth (three times the industry average) recorded in the segments where innovative design or a technological change has been offered. The recent introduction of battery-operated quartz mechanisms combined with sleek styling to create lightweight, portable, wireless clocks has led to at least a 25 percent annual growth rate for decorative or kitchen wall clocks and to almost a 29 percent increase for alarm clocks.

Clocks are in most households and constitute an enduring and important retail gift category. As with many items that are so inherently useful that they might be considered a household necessity, the greater the opportunity to differentiate the product, the greater the ability to segment the market by appealing to consumers through unique designs that are fashioned to suit a wide variety of tastes and income levels.

A handful of major competitors serve as the dominant force in the industry and often not only sell their

EXHIBIT 1

THE WINSLOW CLOCK COMPANY
Pro Forma Income Statements
Five-Year Projection

	Year 1	Year 2	Year 3	Year 4	Year 5
Unit sales	50,000	150,000	200,000	150,000	125,000
Price	$42.50	$42.50	$42.50	$40.00	$40.00
Net sales (000s)	$2,125	$6,375	$8,500	$6,000	$5,000
Bad debt allowance (2%)	43	128	170	120	100
Adjusted net sales	2,082	6,247	8,330	5,880	4,900
Cost of goods sold	1,093	3,253	4,630	3,655	3,267
Gross margin	989	2,994	3,700	2,225	1,633
Operating costs	323	552	695	663	642
E.B.I.T.	666	2,442	3,005	1,562	991
Taxes (50%)	333	1,221	1,502	781	495
Net income	$ 333	$1,221	$1,503	$ 781	$ 496

own brands but also make private-label brands for large retailers as well. (Seiko, for example, produces the private-label quartz alarm clocks for both JCPenney and Sears.) As a result, clock movements are inexpensive and readily available, which in turn spawns a significant opportunity for a number of smaller companies to specialize in unique designs that range from the very inexpensive to one-of-a-kind collector's items.

Clocks are sold through a variety of retail outlets that include mass merchandisers, department and specialty stores, furniture and interior design stores, jewelry stores, shops that deal exclusively in clocks, and museum gift stores.

Catalog sales are also an important means of reaching the clock consumer. Furthermore, within a department store, clocks can be found in various departments that include gifts, luggage, electronics, fine collectibles, furniture, jewelry, and occasionally even in their own clock department.

This diversity of product as well as placement makes the clock market a natural arena in which independent sales representatives may operate. This fact simplifies, to some extent, the problems that the smaller producers face in trying to get their product to the national marketplace without incurring a disproportionate expense for the hiring, training, and support of a sales force.

It is apparent, then, that the market for clocks has ample room for product differentiation. Dr. Winslow's clock, we believe, presents an exciting opportunity to capitalize on a segment of this significant market.

EXHIBIT 2

THE WINSLOW CLOCK COMPANY
Pro Forma Balance Sheet
As of December 31 ($000s)

	Year 1	Year 2	Year 3	Year 4	Year 5	Year 6
Assets						
Cash	5	203	256	1,019	2,722	3,539
Accounts receivable	—	1,345	2,044	2,726	1,924	1,283
Inventory						
Finished goods	—	73	44	48	53	58
Work-in-process	—	106	—	78	—	—
Raw materials	55	—	141	155	171	188
Net fixed assets	40	36	32	29	26	24
Total assets	100	1,763	2,517	4,055	4,896	5,092
Liabilities						
Accounts payable	40	50	141	155	171	181
Accrued liabilities	—	—	560	581	626	309
Est'd tax liability	—	70	—	—	—	—
Short-term debt	—	650	—	—	—	—
Long-term debt	—	—	—	—	—	—
Common stock	—	600	600	600	600	600
Paid-in capital						
(M. Winslow)	60	60	60	60	60	60
Retained earnings	—	333	1,156	2,659	3,439	3,935
Total liabilities	100	1,763	2,517	4,055	4,896	5,092

EXHIBIT 3

THE WINSLOW CLOCK COMPANY
Statement of Sources and Uses of Funds*
Year Ended December 31 ($000s)

	Year 1	Year 2	Year 3	Year 4	Year 5
Sources					
Funds provided by operations					
Net income after taxes	333	823	1,503	780	496
Plus depreciation	4	4	3	3	2
Inc.—accounts payable	10	91	14	16	17
Inc.—accrued liabilities	—	560	21	45	—
Inc.—taxes payable	70	—	—	—	—
Inc.—common stock	600	—	—	—	—
Inc.—short-term debt	650				
Dec.—accounts receivable	—	—	—	802	641
Dec.—inventories	—	—	—	57	—
Total sources	1,667	1,478	1,541	1,703	1,156
Uses					
Inc.—cash	198	53	763	1,703	817
Inc.—accounts receivable	1,345	699	682	—	—
Inc.—inventories	124	6	96	—	22
Dec.—accrued liabilities	—	—	—	—	317
Dec.—taxes payable	—	70	—	—	—
Dec.—short-term debt	—	640	—	—	—
Total uses	1,667	1,478	1,541	1,703	1,156

*Based on pro forma balance sheets and income statements.

EXHIBIT 4 Break-Even Quantity Calculation

1. Contribution margin per unit is estimated to be $20.81 in 2004 and 2005. (See unit sales, cost, margin analysis in Exhibit 5.)
2. Fixed costs for unit sales in the first year of 50,000 units are estimated to be $332,910, including $10,200 paid for prototype development in 2003. Break-even quantity would be $332,910/20.81 = 16,000 units.
3. Based on the expected seasonality of sales in the first year of selling, the break-even point should be reached in mid-October 2004, in the second full month of product shipments.

EXHIBIT 5 Financial Data Backup

Unit sales, cost, margin analysis	
Retail suggested list	$85.00
Dealer margin	42.50
Mfr. selling price (dealer cost)	42.50
Cost of goods sold*	14.60
Gross margin	$27.90
Other variable costs*	
Warranty	.05
Quality control allowance	.29
Shipping & handling contribution	.20
Co-op advertising allowance	2.13
Selling commissions	4.25
Designer/developer fee	.17
Subtotal variable costs	7.09
Net margin	$20.81
Note: Total cost of goods	$21.69

*Backup detail provided.

EXHIBIT 6 Financial Data Backup

Cost of goods sold analysis		
Item		
Movement*	$2.77	$ 3.87
(and circuit board)	$1.10	
Chip (production model)		.79
Capacitors (3)		.30
Impact switch		1.03
Battery holder		.20
Photo transistor		.30
Ball		.87
Molded sphere		.20
Velcro®		.07
Molded cube (housing)		2.00
Batteries		.95
Face, crystal, hands, etc.		.60
Board		.40
Board assembly		1.00
Feet		.05
Speaker, lamp, socket		1.08
Assembly		.50
Product subtotal		$14.21
Package (inc. inside corrugated)		.24
Printed inserts		.05
Portion (1/6) master carton		.10
Package subtotal		$14.60

*Add $0.30 premium per unit for air shipments.

Note: Tooling not amortized in these calculations because first production run estimated to be 10K units; all other costs listed here based on runs of 100K. Tooling at this point treated as a capital expenditure and listed under fixed costs.

THE PRODUCT: PRESENT AND FUTURE

The product will first be described and then discussed in terms of its future potential.

Product Description

The battery-operated quartz alarm clock consists of two basic parts, the first of which is a lightweight black foam ball, approximately 4 inches in diameter, that contains the "brains" of the clock—a microchip, circuit board, impact switch, small batteries, and the audio device for the alarm. These are held inside a plastic capsule that is secured by a Velcro enclosure within the larger foam ball. The second part of the clock is the quartz movement that is housed in a handsomely styled cube of molded plastic.

What makes the clock functionally unique is that throwing the ball turns off the alarm. Great care was taken to use materials that have virtually no chance of damaging the wall or any other object. The specifically designed impact switch is sensitive enough that even a light impact will stop the alarm. On the other hand, a throw of considerable force will not disturb the contents of the inner capsule. Two insurance companies specializing in product liability testing have been consulted. They both feel that the product is safe and free enough from liability risk that they have quoted The Winslow Clock Company the minimum premium for liability insurance.

Several achievements have made the clock technologically possible. There is no need for an electrical connection between the clock base and the ball because an ultrasound device signals the alarm to go off. A receiver in the inner capsule "reads" the signal and triggers the humorous crescendo of the alarm; upon "advice" from the impact switch, a satisfying tone of demise is produced when the alarm hits the wall. In addition, a timing device has been built into the circuitry that automatically shuts off the alarm after one minute if the ball is not thrown.

EXHIBIT 7 Critical Risks and Problems

Listed below are those areas of particular concern and importance to the management.

1. *Timing* will play a critical role in the success of this venture. The key variables are:
   - Product readiness
   - Financing
   - Approach to the marketplace
   - Production, from delivery of components to assembly, inventory, and shipping procedures
2. *Projections* used are "best" estimates, and all financial needs and operating costs have been based on what is considered to be the most likely volume of sales achievable. Because selling activities will begin early in 2004, reaction from the marketplace should be clear by late spring. Decisions can still be made to cut back—or to gear up—for the 2004 season.

   The first commitment to Seiko for 10,000 units (cost of $4.17 each) will have been made by mid-March, and estimates for the entire year will be in their production plan by then. While cutbacks can be made as late as a month in advance, increased production might be a problem since it would bump into Seiko's heaviest production season.
3. *Financing* would be another major consideration if sales were much in excess of expectations, particularly because we must assume that early orders are going to require an accompanying letter of credit. For this and other reasons, the marketing plan is meant to guard against some of these problems and is specifically geared to reach upscale stores and catalogs that will commit early to carry the "limited production" of the first year.
4. *Ironing out production* and assembly problems will be of major importance in June and July. Although the process is not complex, it will be totally new, and the production rate is currently scheduled at 5,000 units in July and 10,000 in August in order to meet anticipated shipping requirements in September and to build minimal inventory requirements. For these reasons, selection of an experienced production manager will be critical.

The overall design and finish of the clock are clean and sophisticated in order to eliminate any sense of gimmickry that might lessen the perceived value of the clock. This elegant styling and the sophisticated electronics, combined with both the psychological satisfaction and the sense of fun and playfulness inherent in being able to throw one's alarm clock, should appeal to a significant cross section of consumers, from executives to athletes. The product has a strong appeal to retailers as well, who, in the words of a Bloomingdale's executive, look for "something refreshing and new to pull people into the stores."

Technical specifications of the product are as follows:

Dimension: Base—4½″ × 4½″ × 4½″ Ball—4½″ diameter

Color: Model A—white clock housing with black face, charcoal ball, white, yellow, and red hands

Model B—black housing with other colors in Model A

Accuracy of movement: +/− 20 seconds per month

Hands: Luminescent minute and hour hands

Foam ball: 35 ppi Crest Foam

Future Potential

The new technologic innovations that have emerged during the development of this first product have significance for the future of the company as well. First, extensions of the basic concept are possible in a variety of clocks with other features. Obvious examples are clock radios and snooze alarms. In addition, as production quantities increase, specialty designs for the premium market become possible at reasonable cost.

A family of related products such as posters, a wall-mountable target, and other clocks—all dealing with the frustration people feel with time, alarm clocks, and schedules—are natural offshoots of the throwable alarm, and their development is currently being explored.

MARKETING PLAN AND STRATEGY

Given the clock's unique function, design, and appeal, the first year's marketing plan will focus on placing the clock in upscale department stores, clock specialty stores, and catalogs that reach upper-middle-income and upper-income executives and families. The early strategy is to keep the clock out of the mass market and discounters' trade, instead making it readily available to consumers more interested in its characteristics and uniqueness than its suggested list price of $85. The sales, cost, and margin analysis is based on the assumption that the suggested list price of $85 and dealer price of $42.50 will be held constant for three years. The goal is to introduce the product with a large enough margin for the dealer in the higher-end retail and catalog business to make an adequate return and to allow the company to recapture its fixed costs as quickly as possible.

While the suggested list and dealer prices at this time are expected to remain the same in the second and third years, part of the strategy will be to refine the production and assembly costs, negotiate volume discounts with suppliers, and devise other cost-saving measures in order to offer more marketing support to the expanded dealer base without sacrificing profitability. If necessary, cost-saving measures will be adopted that will make it possible to lower the price dramatically as a means of defense against competitors in years 3 and 4 of the product's life.

Sales Tactics

The principals of the firm will contact potential buyers directly at first, beginning in early 2004 when there are still budgets available for merchandise for the 2004 Christmas season. Sales in 2004 are planned at 50,000 units, on a first-come, first-served basis, unless a retailer will commit for a guaranteed order prior to June 1. A sales rep organization will also be retained to continue these early sales efforts and to expand distribution after the first season. A commission averaging 10 percent of the dealer price per unit has been incorporated into the cost of sales to cover the activities of these sales reps.

In addition, an experienced, full-time, in-house sales manager will coordinate the selling and promotional activities of the independent rep organization. Other responsibilities of the sales manager will include (1) making direct contact with buyers, (2) making direct contact with sales reps and evaluating their performance, (3) coordinating the marketing support and promotional activities of the sales rep force, and (4) developing other possible avenues for marketing the company's products. The direct marketing approach referred to earlier is an obvious example of this.

Advertising and Publicity

A publicity campaign aimed at generating interest in the clock's development, its state-of-the-art technology, and its founder's concept of "functional fun" will be launched in early fall 2004. This publicity and accompanying new product announcements will target the "executive toy" purchaser.

In addition, a print ad campaign slated for the 2004 Christmas retail market and a cooperative advertising plan to help participating dealers are expected to aid sell-through in the clock's first major season on the market.

Expanded advertising marketing support for the second season will include the following: attendance at trade shows (notably the Consumer Electronics Show, the National Hardwares Show, and at least one of the major gift shows); an in-store promotion plan highlighted by a 90-second video spot designed and produced by a Clio-award-winning studio based in Cambridge, Massachusetts; continuation of the co-op advertising plan; and an overall advertising budget slated at 5 percent of anticipated sales for the year.

OPERATIONS MANAGEMENT

Since all assembly and subassembly operations will be handled by independent contractors, with final shipment emanating from the final point of assembly, the need for an office, a production staff, and overhead would be kept to a minimum.

Although Dr. Winslow will oversee all operations, his regular staff will supervise the critical functions of marketing and business development, administration (including office management, billing, accounts receivable and payable), and production management (the control of all facets of outside assembly and vendor supplies and relations).

Marketing and business development (including sales in the initial stages) would be managed by Ms. Kristen Jones, who has 15 years of experience in marketing and finance in both domestic and international operations for Polaroid Corporation. She has an MBA from Boston College and a BA from Brown University.

The production management area (including product engineering) is currently handled in an advisory capacity by several consultants, including Mr. Steve Canon (see profile below). As the company approaches actual production (now slated for June–July 2004 start-up), a full-time production manager will be hired. Several candidates are presently being considered for this position.

Strong relationships with highly responsible subcontractors have already been established. These include Seiko, for the precision quartz movement and related technology; Rogers Foam in Somerville, Massachusetts, for the ball; Aerodyne Control Corporation in Farmingdale, New York, for the switch; and Santin Engineering in Beverly, Massachusetts, for the plastic molding.

An outside contractor in the Boston area will handle the assembly operation, which includes packaging and shipment to fulfill sales orders. Several companies are being considered and will be submitting quotes on the specifications early in 2004. A decision is expected to be made by the beginning of February. The possibility of an assembly operation outside the United States will be investigated as a cost-saving measure once production is being handled efficiently here.

The administrative position will have the responsibility of handling all office functions, including billing, receivables, credit, and payables. Two candidates are now being considered. It will be important to fill this function as soon as possible, even if it is on a part-time basis for the first few months. The candidates are available for such a schedule, if necessary.

Other critical areas that are now, and will continue to be, handled by consultants are advertising (including sales promotion and publicity)—Bill Barlow—and product design—John Edwards.

MANAGEMENT

Dr. Michael Winslow is the inventor of the clock and founder and president of the company. His profession is psychiatric medicine, and he is currently practicing at the Boston Evening Medical Center in Boston, Massachusetts, as well as at the Matthew Thornton Health Plan in Nashua, New Hampshire. He also maintains his own private practice. Dr. Winslow earned his undergraduate BS degree at the University of Michigan and his medical degree at Boston University Medical School.

It was while he was a resident in psychiatry that he conceived of the idea for the clock. He first pursued the concept as a hobby, trying to find a way to throw the clock without damaging either it or the surface it hit. Within the last two years, as it became apparent that it would be possible to create and produce such a clock at a reasonable cost, further development of the idea became another full-time occupation for Dr. Winslow.

Though he is a man of great energy, part of Dr. Winslow's success in bringing the product from the initial concept to the prototype stage lies in his effectiveness in finding and utilizing the outside resources he has needed. He has also had enough confidence in, and received enough encouragement about, the ultimate marketability of the product that he has invested his own savings in development costs, a sum of approximately $60,000 to date.

Because his profession is very important to him, Dr. Winslow intends to continue his private medical practice. But he will also serve as president of The Winslow Clock Company, hiring professional managers to run the day-to-day operations for him and using consultants in those aspects of the business where a particular expertise is needed.

Kristen Jones—following a year at the Museum of Fine Arts, Boston, as an assistant to the head of research—joined Polaroid Corporation, Cambridge, Massachusetts, where her experience and responsibilities grew over a broad range of marketing and finance assignments.

During the years in which Polaroid's International Division grew from $30 million to $350 million in annual sales, Jones was responsible for sales planning and forecasting for all its amateur photographic products. Later, as a financial analyst, her job was to assess the company's 130 distributor markets around the world for potential as profitable wholly owned subsidiaries, as well as to carry out new product profitability analyses.

She then joined the domestic marketing division, where her assignments ranged from sales administration to marketing manager in charge of a test program to assess the potential of selling the company's instant movie system on a direct basis. In her last position as national merchandising manager, she created and managed the merchandising programs to support the national sales efforts for all consumer products.

In February 1992, she took advantage of the company's voluntary severance program to complete work on her master's degree in business administration at Boston College. Ms. Jones earned her BA degree at Brown University in Providence, Rhode Island.

Steve Canon is a consultant, teacher, and businessman whose broad range of experience covers many aspects of new product design, development, and marketing. He presently has over 35 products of his own on the market and also teaches marketing and business law at the Rhode Island School of Design. In addition, he published a book in the spring of 1996 that deals with invention, product development, and marketing.

Among his numerous accomplishments, he has taught product design at Harvard, Yale, Princeton, and the Rhode Island School of Design. He has won awards for his contributions to the field, including two from Ford Motor Company for innovative product development. Canon has appeared on television talk shows, as both guest and host, discussing product marketing.

Although his primary contributions to The Winslow Clock Company are in the fields of product development and manufacturing/production, his knowledge of new product introductions has been very helpful in a number of other areas as well.

Bill Barlow has been president and creative director of Bill Barlow Advertising since 1998. Prior to establishing his own company, Barlow was director of advertising for Bosc Corporation in Framingham, Massachusetts, a national sales promotion manager and creative director at Polaroid Corporation, and a creative supervisor for New York Telephone in New York City.

In his five years as an entrepreneur, Barlow has built an impressive list of clients and has won numerous awards and honors for excellence in advertising. His current list of clients includes Polaroid Corporation, Hewlett-Packard, Data General, Bose, and Anaconda-Ericsson Telecommunications.

He will be responsible for advertising, promotional support materials, and publicity for The Winslow Clock Company.

John Edwards is the founder of Edwards Design Associates, Inc., a firm that specializes in industrial design, product development, and graphic design. For the past seven years, this company has provided an integrated approach to the design of both products and the packaging and collateral materials to support the products.

Among his clients, primarily in the fields of consumer products and finance, are Polaroid, Bose, Revlon, Chaps, Helena Rubinstein, Avco, Putnam Funds, and Hallmark.

Edwards has a BS degree in mechanical engineering from Worcester Polytechnic Institute and an MS degree in industrial design from the Illinois Institute of Technology.

In addition to designing Dr. Winslow's product, Edwards has also provided invaluable help in finding sources for the manufacture of several components, for injection molding and for packaging.

CASE 3B
NEOMED TECHNOLOGIES

Marc Umeno, president and founder of NeoMed Technologies, and George Coleman, chief operating officer and vice president of business development and marketing, arrived back at NeoMed headquarters after a frustrating and disheartening meeting with venture capital investors. Now late into August of 2002, after months of revising the company strategy, continuously improving the technology and product design, and meeting with investors still not willing to commit their capital, the company had finally run out of cash. Such brutal reality made Marc and George wonder what they could possibly be doing wrong. There was no doubt in their mind[s] that NeoMed had the right people and an outstanding technology. They were convinced that NeoMed's device had the potential for helping people in a way that other alternatives could not. This dedication has sustained the company to this point. However, despite the great commercial opportunity of its innovation, the company had walked a tight rope between technical development and business and financing issues. Though each team member is convinced that the capital that the company needs to prove the technology is available, the existing financing environment had investors becoming cautious and risk averse. In light of the present situation, NeoMed was at a decision point as to what actions to take to finally close a deal with investors and avoid dissolving the company.

COMPANY HISTORY AND FOUNDERS

Marc Umeno, one of the founders of NeoMed Technologies, developed the initial concept for NeoMed during graduate work in the Physics Entrepreneurship

Source: This case study was prepared by Amanda Holland, Nadya Tolshchikova, Jeff Glass, and Robert Hisrich, with the intention of providing a basis for class discussion.

Program, a partnership between the Physics Department and the Weatherhead School of Management at Case Western Reserve University (CWRU) in Cleveland, Ohio. Before starting the program, Marc, in collaboration with a radiologist from West Virginia University, created patents for a technology that had been introduced to him earlier that year by a scientist looking to commercialize his ideas. Marc conducted preliminary research and evaluated the market opportunities for the technology while participating in the program at CWRU. As a result, in spring of 2001, NeoMed was officially formed with the purpose of commercializing a novel radionuclide imaging technology for cardiac testing, developed based on research conducted over the past three decades in experimental particle physics detector technology at the Department of Energy National Laboratories and in nuclear cardiology imaging at UCLA. It was decided to locate the new company in Cleveland, Ohio, a region that supported world-class research in the area of medical imaging. This allowed NeoMed to have access to top-notch engineering services, software partners, and industry suppliers. Major players in the diagnostic imaging market, such as GE Medical and Philips, have also been historically located in this region. From the very beginning NeoMed was thought to have a bright future due to the very promising commercial potential of the market for cardiac testing. This was based on the fact that in the United States, as well as other industrialized nations, CAD[1] is a leading cause of fatalities, with the first symptom of this disease often being death. Given this sobering reality, it is not surprising that NeoMed's vision is as follows:

> NeoMed Technologies is committed to establishing its technology as the standard of care for initial diagnosis of coronary artery disease and will be instrumental in saving millions of lives.

Marc Umeno, Stan Majewski, and Harry Bishop were the three original founders of NeoMed. After searching for recommendations for someone with industry experience who would work well in the start-up environment, Marc was introduced to George Coleman. George joined the company as COO shortly thereafter, and Walt Bieganski joined subsequently as the chief financial officer (Exhibit 1). As a part of the company formation process, the Board of Directors was initiated early on in NeoMed's existence, and from the very beginning, played a significant role in the company's strategic positioning. By 2002, the carefully selected Board consisted of five members (Exhibit 1).

CORONARY ARTERY DISEASE (CAD)

CAD is the leading cause of death in the U.S. and throughout the world. It caused more than 1 out of every 5 deaths in the United States in 2000 claiming the lives of 681,000 people. In 2003 an estimated 650,000 people in the U.S. alone will have a first coronary attack and 450,000 a recurring attack.[2] For example, in the U.S. approximately every 29 seconds a person will suffer a coronary event and nearly every minute someone will die from it. Nearly 47 percent of coronary events are fatal, of which 250,000 occur without previous symptoms of the disease. Coronary artery disease takes place when one or more of the coronary arteries are narrowed down or blocked resulting in decreased blood supply to the heart, which can be fatal. It is believed that the addition of this plaque to the heart blood vessels is a detectible process that can be estimated indirectly through the measurement of coronary circulation.

In 1997 there were about 700,000 outpatient surgical procedures performed on the cardiovascular system, 1,200,000 inpatient cardiac catheterizations, and 607,000 coronary bypass surgeries. This level of surgical intervention not only presents high risk for both patients and physicians, but uses a very large share of the nation's health care resources. For example, the average cost of coronary artery surgery in 1995 was $44,820. In 1996, for anyone under the age of 65, the average cost of a coronary event from admission to discharge was $22,720, with the average length of stay 4.3 days.[3] Furthermore, in 1998, Medicare paid $10.6 billion to its beneficiaries for hospital expenses due to coronary heart disease (CHD)[4] ($10,428 per discharge for acute myocardial infarction (MI);[5] $11,399 per discharge for coronary atherosclerosis; and $3,617 per discharge for other CHDs).[6] Moreover, the problem of an aging population is more likely to escalate these costs as a result of increased incidence of coronary artery disease in older people. According to the U.S. Census, there will be 40 million Americans age 65 and older in 2010. In addition, an increase in the prevalence of obesity and type 2 diabetes also amplifies the risk of heart disease. Given the costs and increase in scope of this health problem, early identification and nonsurgical treatment and prevention of CAD are becoming as important as ever.

EXHIBIT 1 Principals/Management Team Board of Directors*

Management Team

Marc Umeno, PhD, President and Founder‡

Dr. Umeno is currently developing NeoMed full-time. He received his BS in Physics at Harvey Mudd College and his PhD in Physics at American University while doing Neuroscience research at the National Institutes of Health. Dr. Umeno has served as a Nuclear Medical Science Officer in the U.S. Army, where he led a multi-agency team of experts to develop critical nuclear weapons standards, was the U.S. representative for three NATO committees, chaired three Department of Defense–wide groups, and was involved in FDA approval of a military pharmaceutical. Prior to his work with NeoMed, Dr. Umeno was a project manager at Veridian, where he managed multiple projects with over $2 million annual budget and led the commercialization of a medical software tool.

George Coleman, Chief Operating Officer and Vice President of Business Development and Marketing

Mr. Coleman is a full-time member of the NeoMed team. He has over 25 years of experience in the medical, biotechnology, and specialty chemical industries. He has start-up experience as General Manager and V.P. of Sales and Marketing for an innovative medical engineering firm that produced image processing and micro-endoscope systems, surgical instruments, and MEMS components. Mr. Coleman also has experience as managing director at Federal Process, new business development manager of biotechnology at British Petroleum, and sales, sales management and marketing management for a division of Merck, where he was awarded Merck's highest management award for performance.

Walt Bieganski, Chief Financial Officer and General Counsel

Mr. Bieganski is a full-time member of the NeoMed team. He has 16 years of financial and tax advisory experience with Ernst & Young LLP, including 9 years of experience building and managing a multi-million-dollar specialty practice where he serviced clients in various industries, including financial services, distribution, manufacturing, natural resources, and power generation. He also spent two years as a co-leader of the firm's e-business initiatives in the region. Mr. Bieganski is a CPA and has an MBA in Finance from Cleveland State University and a JD from Ohio State University.

Stan Majewski, PhD, Chief Scientific Officer and Founder

Dr. Majewski is head of the detector group at the Thomas Jefferson National Accelerator Facility. He received his educational degrees in Experimental Particle and High Energy Physics from the University of Warsaw in Poland. Dr. Majewski's career has included significant work under two Nobel Prize winners at the European Center for Particle Research (CERN) and the Fermi National Accelerator Laboratory. Dr. Majewski has developed many similar devices involving breast cancer detection, surgical probes, and small animal imaging, and has consulted for NIH, NASA, and UCLA. He also has start-up company experience with a device that successfully gained FDA approval and has launched a small technology start-up. At Jefferson Lab, Dr. Majewski led the development of novel biomedical imagers, co-authored over 100 publications, and invented or co-invented eight patents.

Harry Bishop, MD, Medical Advisor and Founder

Dr. Bishop, inventor of the NeoMed cardiac screening test, is an adjunct associate professor of radiology at West Virginia University. He serves as a medical advisor to the company. He has over 40 years of medical experience, specializing in radiology and nuclear medicine. Dr. Bishop received his BA in Physics from UC Berkeley and his MD from UC San Francisco. He was the first physician in the U.S. to perform coronary angiography and was awarded the Picker Fellowship to study cardiac physiology. Dr. Bishop is also an expert in nuclear cardiology and PET for breast cancer imaging. He is a Fellow of the American College of Radiology and has numerous publications.

(*Continued*)

CAD DIAGNOSTIC PROCEDURES

Normally, patients are screened for CAD during routine office visits, even if the patient doesn't have any symptoms of CAD disease. Frequently detection occurs when the patient arrives to the emergency room with a myocardial infarction (heart attack). Typically though, CAD detection starts with a thorough physical exam and careful documentation of family, personal history, lifestyle habits, and other factors. Blood cholesterol tests and blood pressure measurements are also used to screen for CAD. Recently, the U.S. government recommended new guidelines of CAD testing that increase the likelihood of disease detection with the following test methods actively used to screen patients.

Chest X-Ray produces images of the heart and the surrounding areas showing the size and shape of the coronary system. This technology enables detection

EXHIBIT 1 Principals/Management Team Board of Directors* (Continued)

Allen Goode, MS

Mr. Goode has committed his availability to coordinate clinical trials and to participate in software development as a consultant. Mr. Goode is coordinator for five multicenter cardiovascular-related trials in the Division of Nuclear Cardiology at the University of Virginia. Mr. Goode is also board certified as a nuclear medicine technologist.

Norm Yager

Mr. Yager is currently assisting NeoMed with the FDA approval process. He has written 11 successful FDA 510(k) applications as a regulatory manager for Picker International (now Marconi Medical, a subsidiary of Philips) and was previously at Johnson & Johnson.

Board of Directors

Paul Amazeen, PhD‡

Dr. Amazeen has been a senior executive developing medical imaging products for more than 20 years, including Raytheon, General Electric, Rohe Scientific Corporation, and Sound Imaging. Dr. Amazeen received his BSEE from the University of New Hampshire and his MS and PhD from Worchester Polytechnic Institute. He has received the Ford Foundation Faculty Fellowship at MIT and has a patent for a real-time ultrasonic image display.

Robert D. Hisrich, PhD‡

Dr. Hisrich is Professor of Entrepreneurial Studies at Case Western Reserve University's Weatherhead School of Management. He has had extensive experience in starting and growing companies and is presently on the Board of Directors of two publicly traded companies. Dr. Hisrich has been an entrepreneurship professor at the University of Tulsa and MIT and also has held Fulbright Professorships in Hungary and Ireland. He received his BA from DePauw University, and his MBA and PhD degrees from the University of Cincinnati.

Mark Lowdermilk, MBA‡

Mr. Lowdermilk is currently CEO of a network infrastructure start-up company. He has 28 years of management experience, including 10 years with medical device components and nuclear medicine. Mr. Lowdermilk was formerly with Saint-Gobain Crystals and Detectors serving as Business Manager of Nuclear Medicine. He received his BS in Business Administration from Kent State University and his MBA from the Weatherhead School of Management at Case Western Reserve University.

Alan Markowitz, MD‡

Dr. Markowitz is currently Chief of Cardiothoracic Surgery at University Hospitals of Cleveland. He received his MD from the Albany Medical School of Union College. Along with his distinguished clinical record, Dr. Markowitz has been a consultant for many companies such as Medtronic and Johnson & Johnson, involved in clinical trials for their cardiac products.

*NeoMed Business Plan, March 2002.

of misshaped or enlarged hearts as well as abnormal calcification in the main blood vessels.

Electrocardiogram (ECG or EKG) is a graphical record of the electrical activity of the heart. Typically, a normal ECG rules out the presence of heart disease while an abnormal ECG has been relatively good at indicating the existence of the disease.

Stress Test involves taking ECG before, during, and after the exercise on the treadmill. Although widely accepted by health care professionals and reimbursement organizations due to its low cost, ease of use, and 50–80 percent accuracy, it has some major drawbacks such as relatively low accuracy, ineligibility of some patients due to the high risk of heart attack during the performance of the test, and insurance reimbursement problems for asymptomatic patients.

A preliminary test using *Fast/Multi-Slice CT Scan* with ECG is a relatively new noninvasive method of heart and coronary artery imaging. It is often used as an alternative for invasive catheterization to determine calcium deposits in the coronaries and stenoses (narrowing of arteries) that can eventually lead to a heart attack.

EBCT,[7] when it was first introduced to the market, attracted attention in the medical community due to its ability to screen asymptomatic patients for CAD. Although it was proven that a negative EBCT scan is highly accurate at excluding CAD, it is not certain whether the levels of coronary calcification that EBCT detects can be translated into high CAD risk.

NUCLEAR DIAGNOSTIC IMAGING

Nuclear medicine uses radioactive material that is injected into the patient to diagnose disease or assess a patient's condition. Nuclear imaging is different from regular imaging in several important ways: (1) the source of rays is internal to the patient versus external, (2) the radioactivity is attached to biochemically active agents injected into the patient's body so that an organ's functionality is observed rather than simply viewing the image of an organ.

Equipment for nuclear imaging typically contains several common components. One of these components is the sodium iodide detector, which consists of a crystal that scintillates with blue light, a photomultiplier to convert the light into a proportional electrical signal, and support electronics to intensify and shape the electric signal into a readable form.

Early nuclear imaging devices used scanning procedures to record information from the patient. More recent devices are the gamma cameras that are simultaneously sensitive to the entire radioactivity within a large field of view and do not require scanning. These cameras are advantageous because they can measure changes in the radioactive distribution as a function of time. In general, nuclear images have a fundamental resolution that is about 1 percent of the image dimension, and the images are fairly simple to investigate quantitatively.[8]

NEOMED NUCLEAR DIAGNOSTIC IMAGING

During the initial research, NeoMed considered several applications for its proprietary technology. Founders recognized that it could be used for the in vivo analysis of animals in drug studies, allowing researchers to conduct long-term drug experiments on animals and analyze the results without sacrificing the animals' lives, thus significantly reducing laboratory costs. In addition, NeoMed could apply its technology to screening drug candidates, drug delivery applications, or perhaps even to detecting cancer. Furthermore, Marc and his team were convinced that the core set of technologies could be applied in Homeland Defense for detection of nuclear weapons or "dirty bombs."

However, despite the numerous possible applications for the technology, it was decided to focus on cardiac testing for several reasons. Primary among these was the ability of this technology to fill the largest market need and address a very real problem in society. It was estimated that based on a high cholesterol level, 36 million people in the U.S. are at risk of CAD, of which 11.3 million visit cardiologists each year. If each CAD diagnostic test is estimated to be between $200 and $400 a test, the overall market potential is projected to be between $7.2 and $14.4 billion.

Taking into consideration the above reasoning, NeoMed has developed a device to monitor coronary artery function that combines 75 years of expertise in the fields of detector physics and nuclear cardiology and is unique in its sensors, data acquisition electronics, and analytical software. Recent developments in scintillation technology make the NeoMed device possible, allowing for small, compact, and inexpensive gamma detectors that can measure high rates of activity while still maintaining excellent resolution. In addition, NeoMed's proprietary state-of-the-art software allows detailed analysis of the CTI measurements. This powerful functional package is based on proven technology applied in a new way, thereby avoiding technological risks and supplier challenges inherent in a less mature technology.

NeoMed's diagnostic system provides medical personnel with the ability to detect coronary artery disease (CAD) with a quick and painless noninvasive test. In the process of testing, the patient while at rest is injected with a radioactive tracer, the passage of which is dynamically measured as it flows through the heart. As a result, Coronary Transit Index (CTI) is generated, which allows determination of the performance of the heart system. The radiation dose used in this test is much lower than in standard diagnostic imaging procedures involving CT, fluoroscopy, or traditional nuclear cardiology. Furthermore, the NeoMed test has a much higher degree of accuracy than conventional

EXHIBIT 2 Accuracy of CAD Diagnostic Procedures

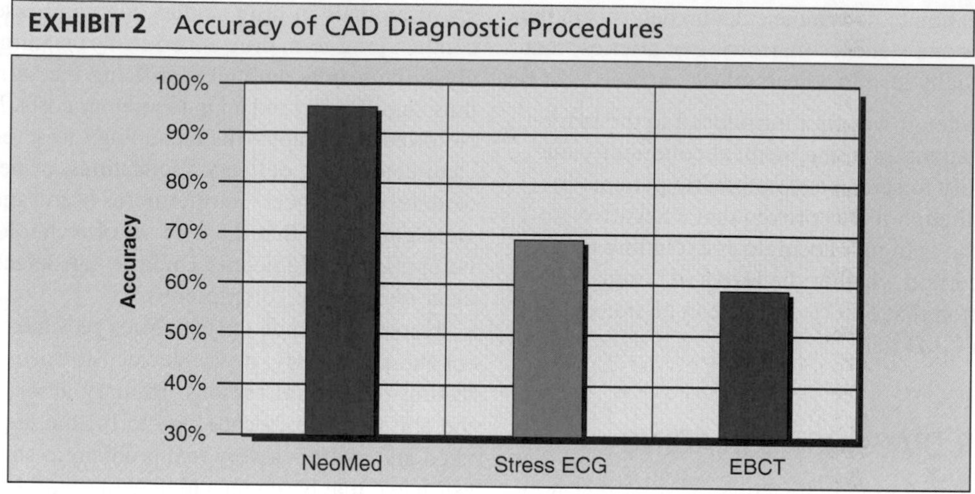

Source: NeoMed Business Plan, March 2002.

methods of detection, as illustrated in Exhibit 2. The NeoMed test is expected to be less expensive, will last less than five minutes, and the results will be obtainable immediately after the completion of the test. NeoMed's objectives for its state-of-the-art technology are to provide quick and accurate cardiac testing of patients at risk for CAD and to monitor patients who have had an acute myocardial infarction or stent surgery.

COMPETITION

The main competition for any new nuclear diagnostic imaging equipment is most likely to come from the alternative methods rather than in the form of direct competition from other manufacturers. NeoMed decided early on to focus on functional testing, which acts as a preliminary "gate" test for more detailed and expensive diagnostic procedures such as nuclear profusion, electron beam tests, and angiography, which are used at later stages of the diagnostic process. Although not all CAD diagnostic methods directly compete with NeoMed's technology, overcoming ECG Stress Test's and EBCT's popularity in the current health care system presents a significant barrier to entry for NeoMed.

ECG stress test is a current industry standard that has been on the market for a few decades and is well received and accepted by both medical professionals and Medicare reimbursement agents. Although the technological shortcomings of this test are well known, the ease of use, low cost, and although not necessarily high, but consistent, predictive accuracy rate of 50–80 percent have established the ECG stress test as an industry standard. Some of the drawbacks of this test, where NeoMed saw an opportunity for its technology, were absence of ECG test Medicare Reimbursement for patients with no symptoms, and a risk of performing the test on certain patients with severe symptoms of CAD. One in 10,000 people will die, and 2–3 in 10,000 will have a major myocardial infarction while performing a physical exercise as a part of this test.[9]

Another major competitor to the NeoMed technology is the EBCT test. However, NeoMed feels that the controversy around the effectiveness of this technology in its ability to detect noncalcium plaques in coronary arteries and its high cost could limit long term and widespread use of this technology in the future. According to the recent statistic, the cost of the device is about $2 million and the cost of the test ranges from $420 to $500.[10] There are many smaller companies specializing in EBCT screening tests. One of them is HeartCheck, a national marketing firm with 7 locations in California, Illinois, and Pennsylvania that targets smaller regional markets with low penetration of EBCT systems. Currently there are around 100 hospitals and outpatient imaging centers that provide EBCT tests to patients, and despite the cost and technology shortcoming, their number is expected to rapidly increase.

NEOMED BUSINESS MODEL

According to NeoMed's current business model, revenue will be generated through license arrangements with outpatient imaging centers, cardiology groups, and hospitals. When the test is administered by the diagnostics provider, a $233 reimbursement fee will be collected from insurance companies, of which NeoMed will receive $133. This arrangement allows for a 20 percent profit margin for the service providers and a 70 percent gross margin for NeoMed. The price of the NeoMed test will be set at $400, taking into consideration the pricing for compatible CAD screening tests ranging from $300 to $700.

Distribution

The first facilities licensed to perform the NeoMed procedure commercially are expected to be the sites used to conduct the clinical trials. Using the contacts at these facilities, NeoMed can further expand its customer base. Another possible distribution channel is through mobile nuclear medicine firms who service rural areas. Also, the international market holds considerable potential for NeoMed technology and could possibly be tapped through strategic partnerships. Using these existing sales and distribution channels would allow NeoMed to establish a broad market presence more rapidly than building its own.

Strategic Partnerships

Due to its geographic positioning in an area with the strong presence of two renowned medical centers (University Hospitals and Cleveland Clinic), NeoMed was able to take advantage of strategic partnerships with these institutions that enabled in-kind clinical trials, pilot projects, and animal studies. It also provided NeoMed founders with exposure to the world class medical professionals in the field of cardiology and an opportunity to test ideas for the product during multiple stages of prototype design, market assessment, and effectiveness trials.

Sales and Marketing Plan

NeoMed expects for its technology to be adopted in the early stages of the market introduction by Cardiologists, whom NeoMed chose to target as a primary audience. After an extensive analysis of various market segments, the company decided to focus its entry strategy on two niche markets that have no current solutions:

- Patients who cannot be stressed (3.5 million patients per year)
- Monitoring CAD treatment progress (1.5 million patients per year)

Traditional exercise ECG stress tests cannot be administered to 1/3 of patients due to their physical disability, heart attack risk, or other physical factors. Also, a large percentage of patients that have undergone surgical treatments for CAD experience a reversal of their treatment. For instance, approximately 20 percent of coronary artery stents will undergo rejection within two months and 80 percent within 5 years. These patients have no reliable noninvasive means of detecting recurring problems. Therefore, NeoMed expects that its diagnostic method will serve both of these market segments, which together represent a market potential of $1.2 billion (Exhibit 3). However, when it comes to marketing the product, as with most pharmaceutical products and medical device systems, NeoMed must primarily market its technology not to the patients, but instead to the cardiologists who are the main decision makers in the choice of the diagnostic testing procedures. NeoMed estimated that there were close to 19,623 cardiologists in the United States, including 4,500 nuclear cardiologists.

NeoMed is planning on penetrating the market through initially targeting cardiologist opinion leaders and establishing positive working relationships with such organizations as the American Heart Association, American College of Cardiology, and others, hoping to receive their endorsements when the product is ready to be launched. NeoMed expects to create product awareness among the rest of the nation's cardiologists through active participation in trade shows, publications in professional journals, and through sales representatives.

The company anticipates its revenue to increase over 5 years reaching $182 million in 2007. To achieve these sales, NeoMed's technology will need to capture 4 percent of the U.S. target market. This revenue is projected based on the assumption that out of 49 patients a cardiologist sees each week, 15 are nonstress patients.[11] If taking an average of 5 cardiologists per facility working an average of 50 weeks per year, one facility is estimated to perform 3,750 tests per year, which amounts to 75 percent capacity utilization of a single NeoMed unit. The table that follows shows the projected sales volume for years 2003 through 2007.

EXHIBIT 3 Market Potential for NeoMed

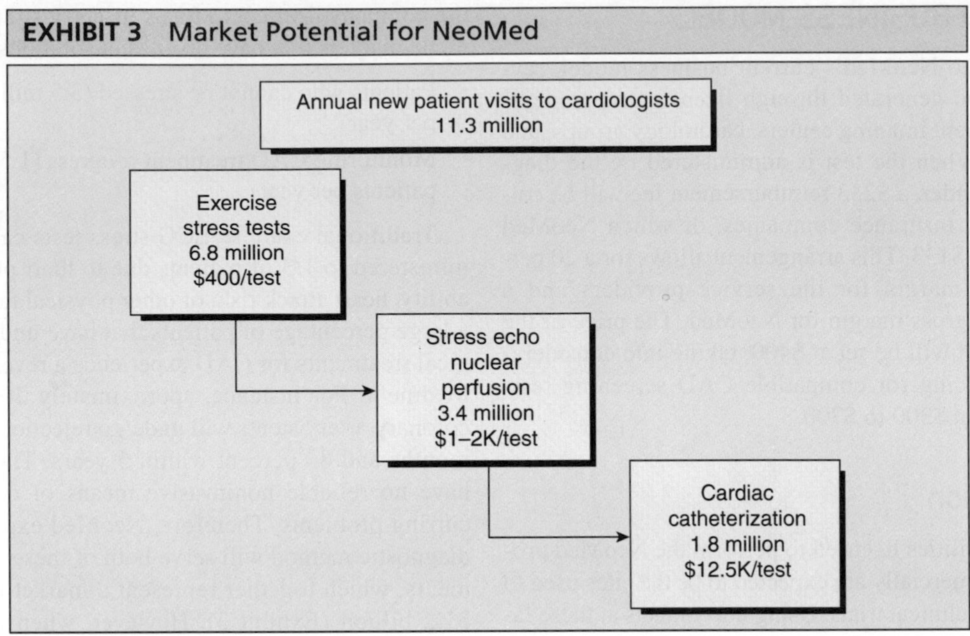

Source: NeoMed Business Plan, March 2002.

Projected Sales Volume

Year	2003	2004	2005	2006	2007
Revenue (millions)	**$4.7**	**$22.0**	**$47.1**	**$90.6**	**$182**
Gross margin (millions)	$1.7	$12.6	$29.2	$58.0	$119
Gross margin %	36%	57%	62%	64%	65%
Net income (millions)	**($1.1)**	**$3.6**	**$8.6**	**$18.6**	**$41.0**
Net Income %	−27%	19%	21%	24%	26%
Centers	4	6	8	10	12
Licenses	21	61	121	242	484
# of Tests—Centers	10,000	21,000	28,000	35,000	50,000
# of Tests—Licensees	29,000	156,000	342,000	700,000	1,415,000

COMPANY SITUATION

As of August 2002, NeoMed has built an initial prototype of its nuclear imaging device suitable for use in research-level patient testing. It has also been approved for use in preclinical trials at West Virginia University. In addition, NeoMed was invited to participate in clinical trials at University Hospitals in Cleveland, Ohio. Further, an advanced prototype was constructed to be used for clinical testing, FDA approval, and product development. In January 2002, animal studies were performed at the University of Virginia, resulting in strong evidence supporting the CTI procedure. Pilot clinical studies are planned and will be directed by Dr. George Beller, a leading nuclear cardiologist at the university, as soon as the additional financing is obtained. For the complete outline of NeoMed milestones refer to Exhibit 4.

There are numerous challenges that the management team at NeoMed is facing. First of all, the company seriously lacks the financing that is needed to keep

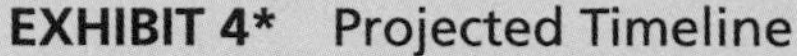

EXHIBIT 4* Projected Timeline

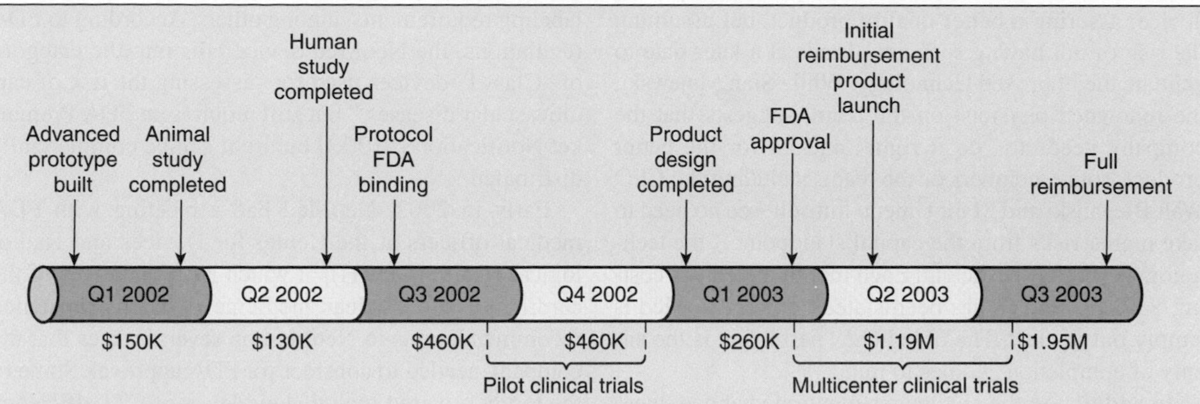

Description of Milestones for the Timeline Graph:

1. Animal Study. This study will confirm the physiological basis of the NeoMed technology and clinical application.
2. Human Study. 5–10 subject human study to further establish the link between coronary vascular blood flow and the NeoMed exam.
3. Protocol/FDA Binding.
4. Pilot Clinical Trials. A pilot clinical trial involving 80–120 patients is planned to compare the NeoMed technology with coronary catheterization. Positive results from the clinical trials will be leveraged to assure market adoption of the NeoMed technology.
5. Product Development. The commercial design and development of the product will be finalized based on feedback from clinical trials and in-house assessments at NeoMed.
6. FDA Approval.
7. Multicenter Clinical Trials. Multicenter clinical trials are planned involving examination of 400–500 patients to verify the results from the pilot clinical trial.
8. Product Launch. Establishing operations at targeted hospitals and geographic locations through use of personal relationships with clinicians involved with the trials.
9. Reimbursement. Widespread reimbursement approval from the Center for Medicare and Medicaid Services and the private insurance industry as a result of leveraging successful outcomes from the clinical trials.

*The costs detailed [here] include allocations of general and administrative expenses.

the company solvent and to continue the process of validating the technology. This requires that clinical studies be performed, and due to external factors such as the struggling economy and weak venture capital environment, NeoMed has had a difficult time securing the funds to conduct these trials. While seemingly close to proving that their technology will beat the competition, frustration has been mounting within the ranks of NeoMed, and Marc and his team have had to constantly keep the people around them motivated and focused on the long-term vision of the company. While always maintaining a belief in their technology, Marc and his colleagues have been forced to reanalyze their business strategy to determine the reasons for not getting the financing they need.

NeoMed has also been faced with an ongoing issue of "how good is good enough," an issue faced by many companies in product development situations. While the NeoMed technology is better than many competing alternatives, and its accuracy has been proven in animal studies, the possibility exists that the device can be further improved to make it easier for technicians to operate, and thus increase the likelihood of an accurate reading. The company is faced with two options: (1) keep the technology as it is and proceed with clinical trials, with the likelihood of overall trial success, but at a lower degree of accuracy, or (2) take four to five months and the remaining capital to make improvements in the device, assuring a better quality product, but assuming the risk of not having sufficient funds at a later date to validate the improved technology. While Stan Majewski, the renowned physicist on the team, suggests that the company needs to "do it right" and go for the better product, some members of the team, including the CFO Walt Bieganski and Marc Umeno himself, see no need to take higher risks from the capital standpoint if the technology is already sufficient. Each month of delay is costing $30,000, and as has been stated before, NeoMed is simply out of cash. The old cliché "perfection is the enemy of completion" comes to mind.

In addition to the challenges mentioned above, there are two main contingencies that affect the success of NeoMed's diagnostic system: FDA approval and insurance reimbursement.

FDA Approval

NeoMed, as any medical equipment manufacturer and distributor, faces an FDA approval process. FDA's Center for Devices and Radiological Health (CDRH) is responsible for regulating firms who manufacture, repackage, relabel, and/or import medical devices sold in the United States. In addition, CDRH regulates radiation-emitting electronic products (medical and nonmedical) such as lasers, x-ray systems, ultrasound equipment, and many household electronic items. Medical devices usually fall into Class I, II, or III category under FDA classification, with regulatory control significantly increasing from Class I to Class III. The device classification regulation defines the level of regulatory requirements and the stage of market introduction at which device approval or notification becomes necessary. Most Class I devices are exempt from Premarket Notification 510(k); most Class II devices require Premarket Notification 510(k); and most Class III devices require Premarket Approval. If the device requires the submission of a Premarket Notification 510(k), the manufacturer cannot commercially distribute the device until the "letter of substantial equivalence" from FDA is received. This letter states that the device is substantially equivalent to the device that received authorization to be legally commercialized in the United States or to the device that has already been determined by FDA to be substantially equivalent.

In addition to the Premarket Notifications, there are basic regulatory requirements that manufacturers of medical devices distributed in the U.S. must fulfill, such as establishment registration, medical device listing, and labeling requirements, among others. According to FDA regulations, the NeoMed device falls into the category of "Class I" devices used for "assessing the risk of cardiovascular diseases," but still requires an FDA Premarket Notification [510(k)] before it can be commercially distributed.

Early in 2002, NeoMed had a meeting with FDA medical officers at the Center for Devices and Radiological Health (CDRH), at which representatives of the cardiology and nuclear medicine divisions presented recommendations to NeoMed on several issues that the company needed to consider for FDA approval. Some of the topics covered included evidence of CTI efficiency in diagnosing CAD, explanation of the physiology underlying the CTI procedure using previous clinical data and animal studies, and estimation of correct patient population size.

NeoMed was planning to submit an FDA application by the end of 2002, which would allow the company to obtain 510(k) approval for its CAD diagnostic probe system in early 2003, since the approval process typically takes 3–6 months from the date of submission of the application. However, given the financial situation the company is currently facing, it is difficult for Marc and his team to predict if NeoMed will be able to stick to its original timeline with an FDA approval process and submit the application in the next three to four months.

Insurance Reimbursement

In order to get insurance reimbursement from any company in the health care field, the given procedure must receive an approval from the American Medical Association (AMA). In the initial stages of this process, most companies typically hire consultants who help them to determine whether their procedure falls under one of the AMA's reimbursement Current Procedure Terminology (CPT) codes. If existing codes are identified, the company files the description of the procedure with the AMA, along with a Physicians Procedure Report explaining how the test will be administered. Once the approval, which typically takes two to three months, is granted, the procedure can be reimbursed by Medicare and Medicaid. This is perceived as an important step in the product commercialization, since it opens up a likelihood of procedure reimbursement by private insurance companies.

NeoMed is currently in the process of investigating insurance reimbursement issues and application procedures to prepare the company for the initial CPT code reviews.

FINANCING

Obtaining adequate financing has been NeoMed's major area of concern. Despite the fact that the company has demonstrated a great commercial opportunity of its nuclear diagnostic technology, it is facing the challenges of balancing technical development with business and financing objectives of the new venture.

During the initial stages of the fundraising process that started in early 2001, NeoMed was able to generate $85,000 in financing through various sources. In February 2001 the company received a $20,000 grant from the National Collegiate Inventors and Innovators Alliance (NCIIA). Since one of the founders, Marc Umeno, was in the process of completing his graduate degree at Case Western Reserve University in Cleveland, the company was able to participate in the Case Western Reserve University Business Launch Competition in May of 2001, winning an additional $35,000. Another $30,000 came from the company's founders. Using this capital, NeoMed was able to construct the initial prototype and begin preclinical tests. However, the company continued to actively seek additional capital. The efforts paid off in October of 2001 when NeoMed was able to secure an additional $200,000 in private equity, which was used to build an advanced prototype, conduct animal studies, and file additional patent applications.

The next step for the company is to raise further capital to conduct a human clinical study of 5–10 subjects and develop the clinical protocol for FDA approval. The founders estimated that they would need around $130,000. Simultaneously, NeoMed is planning two future rounds of equity financing. In the Series A round, the company will be seeking $2 million to perform clinical testing using the advanced prototype, complete product development, and obtain FDA approval. In the Series B round, the company is expecting to obtain $10 million to begin the development of the commercially applicable device and its market introduction. This would involve approval of insurance reimbursement from Medicare and Medicaid, as well as private insurance companies, and also active product endorsement strategies involving the American Heart Association and American College of Cardiology. Exhibit 5 illustrates the sources and uses of the Series A plus the preseed and seed investments. Unfortunately, the venture capital industry climate and overall financing environment have affected NeoMed's ability to obtain financing, in ways Marc and his partners could not have foreseen when they started the company less than two years ago.

EXHIBIT 5 Sources and Uses of Funds*

Sources of Funds	
Entrepreneurs	$ 85,000
Seed investors	330,000
Series A investors	2,000,000
Total	$2,415,000
Application of Funds	
Legal/IP/planning	$ 135,000
Clinical studies	640,000
FDA approval	570,000
Product development	640,000
Reserve for contingencies	430,000
Total	$2,415,000

*[This] table . . . summarizes the sources and uses of the Series A plus the preseed and seed investments.

VENTURE CAPITAL FINANCING

The economic downturn, equity market decline, and increased overall political and national uncertainty in 2002 took its toll on venture capital (VC) investments. After an unprecedented rise in 2000, VC investment continued to decline and by the third quarter of 2002, the VC investment in entrepreneurial firms amounted to only $4.5 billion invested over 671 companies. In 2002 the total venture capital investment was a modest $21.2 billion compared to $43.1 billion invested in 2001. Many believed this downturn was simply a return to normalcy after the bubble of the late 90s, but either way, it severely affected the prospects for NeoMed.

Venture Capital Firms

As many expected, venture capital funds experienced a significant decline in 2002 due to fewer high quality

EXHIBIT 6 Funds Raised by VC Firms, 2000–2002

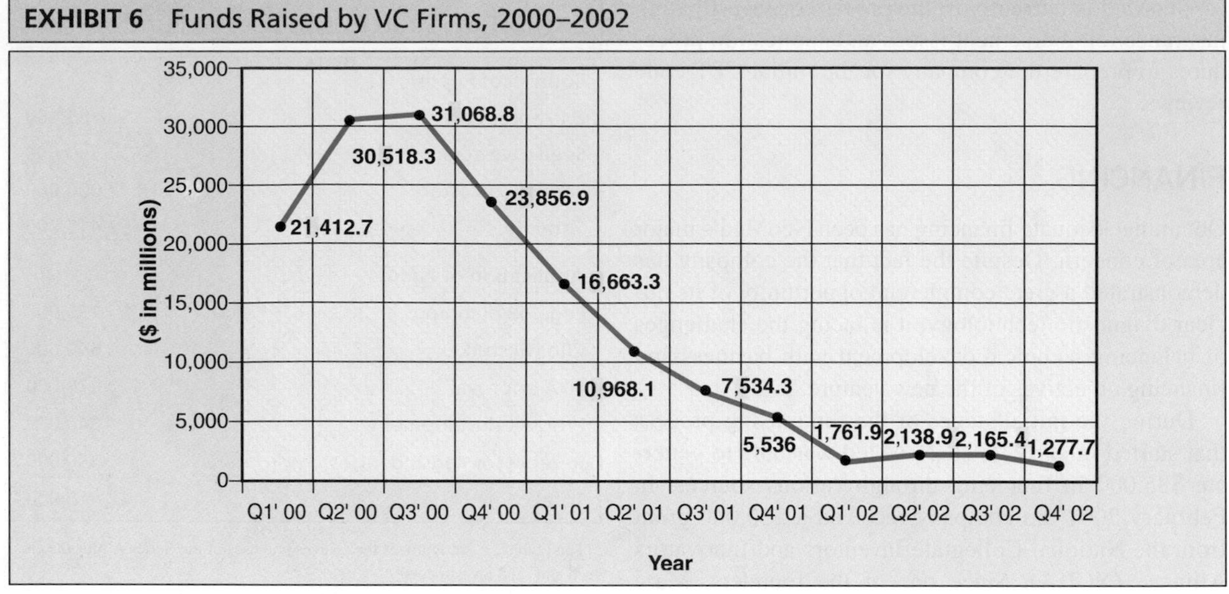

Source: PricewaterhouseCoopers/Thomson Venture Economics/National Venture Capital Association MoneyTree™ Survey; http://www.pwcmoneytree.com/moneytree/index.jsp.

investment opportunities, lower private company valuations, and increased economic uncertainty. An additional factor that contributed to the situation was the high level of capital already committed to venture capital funds, but not yet invested. Such surplus of investment capital coupled with the shortage of feasible investment opportunities created an unprecedented situation in the entire venture capital industry. As a result, in 2002, 108 venture funds raised only $6.9 billion, compared to 331 funds in 2001 raising $40.7 billion. The situation did not seem to be improving. A breakdown of number of funds and amounts raised in 2002 further illustrates this downward trend[12] (Exhibit 6).

There are several factors that could explain this situation. First, many large funds were not raising any additional capital. Instead, they were returning substantial amounts to the investors who contributed to the funds in earlier high growth years. Second, as mentioned earlier, there still existed a large amount of noninvested capital. It was estimated that, as of the second half of 2002, there was $80 billion committed capital that had not yet been invested. This is an indicator of the fact that many venture capital firms were not raising additional funds, due to availability of resources to cover the then-current and near-future investment opportunities, the overall number of which had also significantly decreased over the last two years. Third, company valuations dropped considerably since the downturn in the economy. In addition, there was a clear shift in investment opportunities from previous industry sectors, to those more aligned with the industrial sectors of growing national priority such as homeland security, military applications, and protection from various biological and chemical threats. For example, in 2002, there were funds in the country that raised capital exclusively for investments in these areas.

These external factors, coupled with internal opportunities and threats, forced many venture capital firms to significantly alter their investment strategies in 2002. Previously, over the last few years, it was a standard practice to close a fund within a few months while, by the end of 2002 the process could last as long as a few quarters. Furthermore, increased budgetary constraints, prolonged due diligence, and a willingness to invest only in established firms with a proven track record, contributed to the changes in the fundraising process.[13]

Private Investors

Angel investors are individuals who are willing to invest in businesses where they can get a higher return than if

EXHIBIT 7 Venture Capital Investments by State in 2002 (Number of Deals)

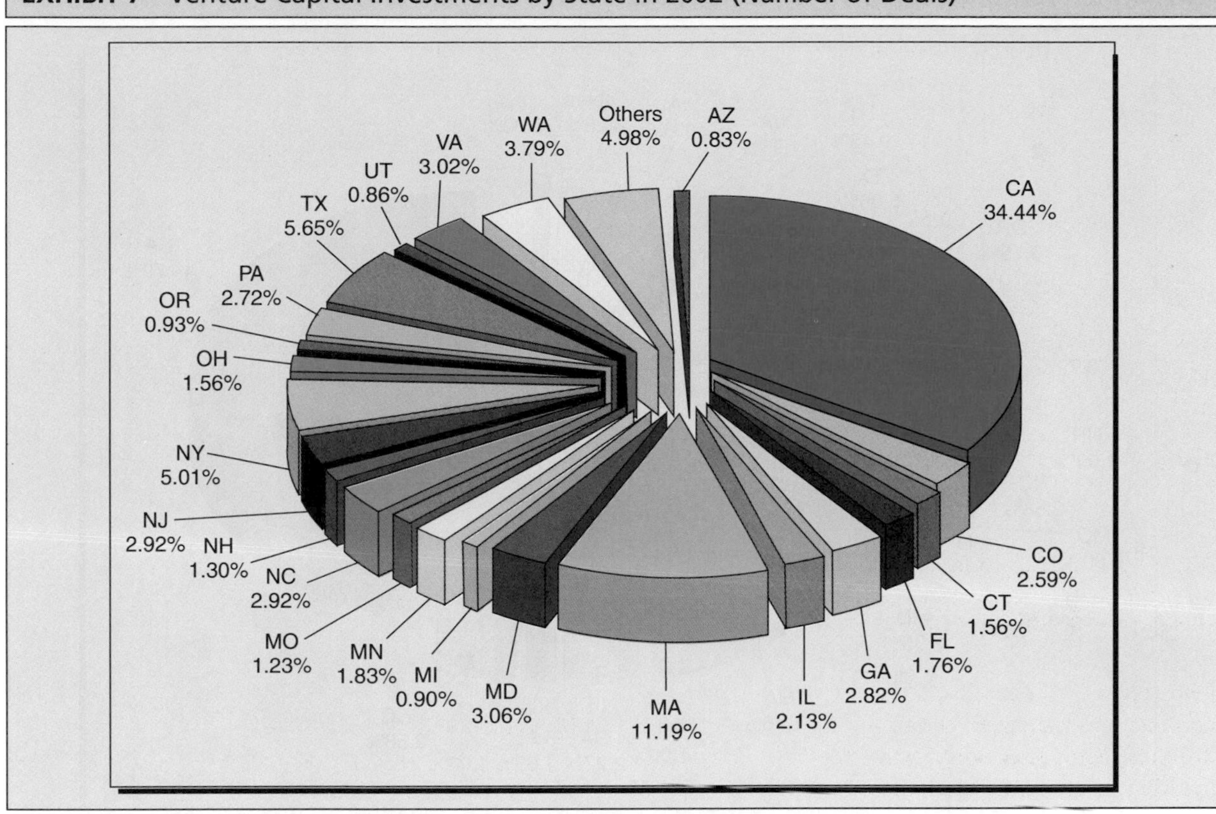

Source: PricewaterhouseCoopers/Thomson Venture Economics/National Venture Capital Association. MoneyTree™ Survey 2002 by State and by Quarter, http://www.pwcmoneytree.com/moneytree/index.jsp.

investing into traditional ventures. Many of these people are entrepreneurs themselves, who have started successful businesses and would like to help other entrepreneurs succeed. Although, due to the privacy of information, it is difficult to approximate how much angels invest, it is estimated by the Small Business Administration that there are about 250,000 angel investors active in the United States, funding about 30,000 ventures each year with amounts ranging from $150,000 to $1.5 million. It is estimated that the total angel investment is anywhere from $20 to $50 billion a year, compared to the $3 to $5 billion a year that a formal venture capital community invests. See Chapter 12 for a description of a typical angel investor.

Most angel investors have clear expectations for the businesses in which they choose to invest. Although each investor has his or her own criteria, most of them expect a board seat or at least a consulting position, and anywhere from a 5 to 25 percent stake in the business, an internal rate of return of five times the investment in a period of five years, and the right of first refusal in the next round of financing.[14]

Venture Capital and Private Investors in Ohio

The fact that NeoMed chose to start its business in Ohio presents the company with certain challenges. Typically this part of the country has not provided companies with an abundance of financing opportunities. As Exhibits 7 and 8 indicate, historically, venture capital investments in Ohio have not represented more than 2 percent of venture capital investments in the country. The current overall venture capital creates even greater financing difficulties for companies in Ohio as they are dealing with a certain level of conservatism of

EXHIBIT 8 Venture Capital Investments by State in 2002 ($ Amount)

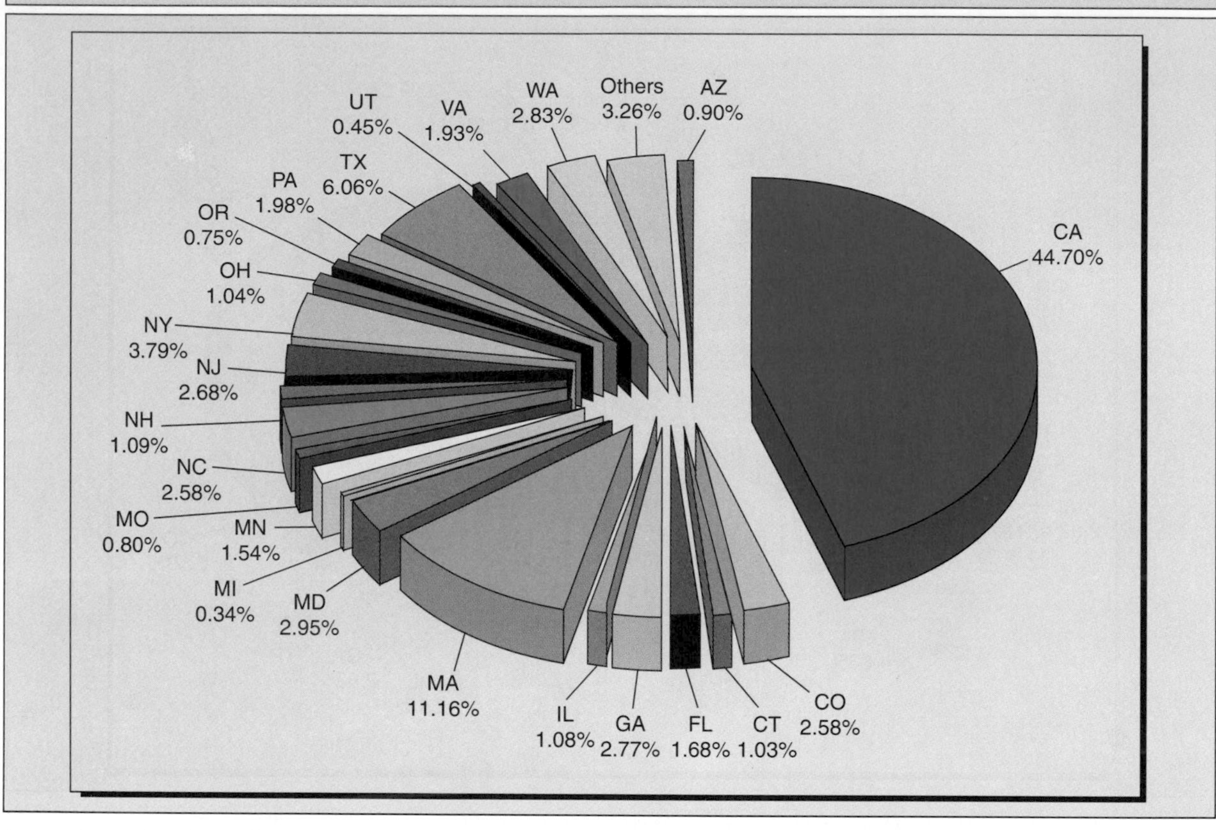

Source: PricewaterhouseCoopers/Thomson Venture Economics/National Venture Capital Association. MoneyTree™ Survey 2002 by State and by Quarter, http://www.pwcmoneytree.com/moneytree/index.jsp.

Ohio investors in addition to the naturally low level of available funding.

Although, as Exhibit 9 indicates, financing in the biotechnology arena has been affected less than many other industries, start-up/seed investments, which were already low compared to other stages of financing, have declined greatly, starting in 2000 (Exhibit 10). Ohio was not an exception in this respect, with a steady decline in start-up/seed capital financing over the last two years. These factors made obtaining financing for NeoMed extremely difficult. After many months of VC presentations to various Ohio-based VC firms and follow-up meetings with discouraging results, NeoMed's founders wondered what was keeping them from obtaining capital. As 2002 progressed, NeoMed was quickly running out of cash. While the level of frustration and disappointment increased with every venture capital meeting, Marc and his team wondered if their company would ever make it to the next important strategic milestone of clinical trials—a stage that Marc saw as a true chance to test the technology that he was convinced could save the lives of many people.

CONCLUSION

Now that the situation is more critical then ever, NeoMed must re-analyze what steps to take in order to obtain the desperately needed financing. It is clear to the team that investors are not yet comfortable with investing in NeoMed. While every meeting with venture capitalists seemed encouraging, the follow-up consisted of multiple requests to make certain changes to the concept, product, positioning strategy, or some other aspect of NeoMed's business concept. As the team brainstormed possible strategic solutions, a number of ideas were brought up, among which were to

EXHIBIT 9 Investments by Industry in the 4th Quarter 2002

	Total $ Invested	Average $ Per Deal	Deals
	$4,081,008,000	$5,923,088	689
Industries Defined	**Amount in $ millions**	**% of Total**	**Deals**
Software	869	21	183
Telecommunications	502	12	78
Medical devices and equipment	486	12	57
Biotechnology	474	12	61
Networking and equipment	457	11	47
Semiconductors	243	6	28
IT services	218	5	33
Media and entertainment	142	3	32
Industrial/energy	140	3	37
Computers and peripherals	134	3	26
Health care services	98	2	17
Business products and services	94	2	29
Consumer products and services	68	2	18
Electronics/instrumentation	53	1	11
Financial services	54	1	17
Retailing/distribution	49	1	14
Other	2	0	1

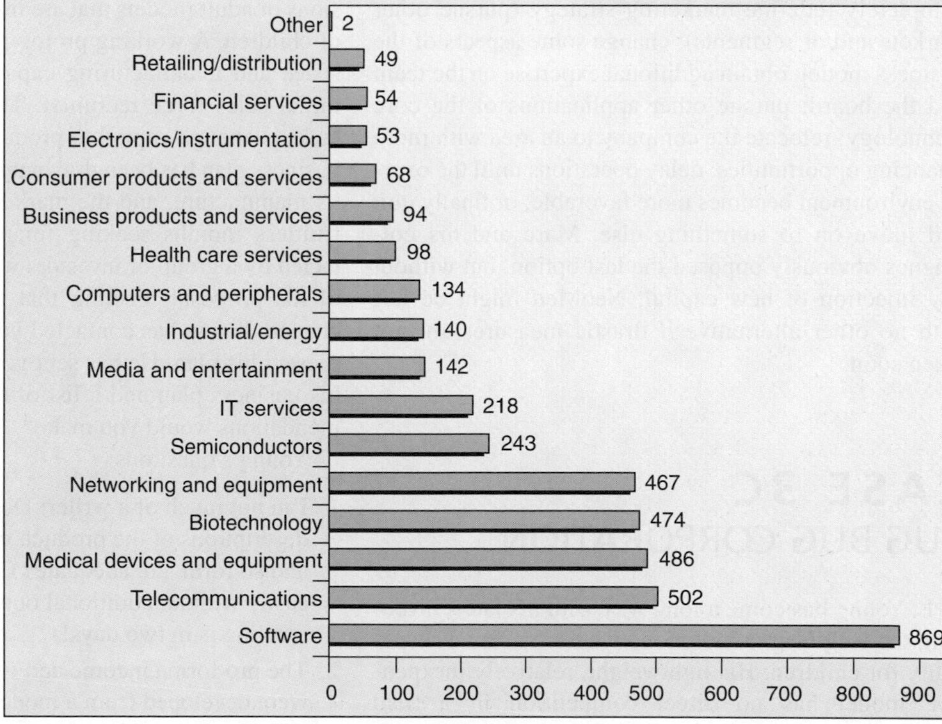

Source: PricewaterhouseCoopers/Thomson Venture Economics/National Venture Capital Association MoneyTree™ Survey 2002.

EXHIBIT 10 PricewaterhouseCoopers/Thomson Venture Economics/National Venture Capital Association MoneyTree™ Survey

	Start-Up/Seed Stage		Early Stage		Expansion Stage		Later Stage	
Year–Qtr	($ in millions)	Deals	($ in millions)	Deals	($ in millions)	Deals	($ in millions)	Deals
1995–1	20,418,000	2	10,349,000	5	8,841,000	5	300,000	1
1995–2	1,491,000	2	7,076,000	5	6,525,000	4	1,266,000	1
1995–3	147,000	1	3,886,000	2	2,300,000	1	0	1
1996–1	6,157,000	3	5,206,000	3	3,173,000	5	750,000	1
1996–2	10,262,000	6	3,250,000	2	6,193,000	3	6,000,000	1
1997–1	2,514,000	2	8,953,000	1	11,846,000	5	18,953,000	2
1997–2	6,395,000	3	22,103,000	2	53,250,000	6	10,900,000	2
1997–4	15,000,000	1	12,132,000	5	22,719,000	9	200,000	1
1998–1	4,550,000	3	11,500,000	1	50,223,000	17	3,700,000	3
1998–2	6,500,000	2	26,700,000	5	21,891,000	7	3,282,000	3
1998–3	3,750,000	2	46,724,000	3	63,815,000	6	1,299,000	1
1999–2	3,825,000	2	27,125,000	5	13,374,000	6	6,500,000	1
2000–2	1,000,000	1	20,532,000	6	231,637,000	15	2,700,000	1
2002–3	3,000,000	1	11,500,000	3	7,300,000	4	365,000	1

Source: PricewaterhouseCoopers/Thomson Venture Economics/National Venture Capital Association MoneyTree™ Survey 2002.

completely redefine marketing strategy (pursue other markets and/or segments); change some aspects of the business model; obtain additional expertise on the team and the board; pursue other applications of the core technology; relocate the company to an area with more financing opportunities; delay operations until the overall environment becomes more favorable; or finally quit and move on to something else. Marc and his colleagues obviously opposed the last option, but without any injection of new capital, NeoMed might be left with no other alternative if drastic measures are not taken soon.

CASE 3C
RUG BUG CORPORATION

A. L. Young has come a long way with his latest invention, the Rug Bug, a motorized wheelchair made especially for children. His lightweight, relatively inexpensive model has no direct competition in a field dominated by companies that produce scaled-down versions of adult models that are inappropriate to the needs of children. A working prototype has been built, office space and manufacturing capacity contracted, and an initial sales force recruited. The only element Young lacks is enough capital to produce the first 200 units. A business plan has been drawn up describing the product, its manufacture, and the marketing plan. After several fruitless months seeking financing, Young was contacted by a group of investors who had seen a summary of his proposal. Feeling that this might be his only chance, Young has contacted you for advice on how to present his plan. He has sent you the following copy of his business plan and a list of questions. What recommendations would you make?

Young's questions:

1. I'm not much of a writer: Do you think my descriptions of the product, competition, marketing, and so forth, are adequate? Could it be improved easily without additional outside information (my meeting is in two days!)?
2. The pro forma income and cash flow statements were developed from a model I found in a book. Did I leave anything out?

3. I think $150,000 is a good amount to ask for—big enough to show we are serious about creating a growing business but not large enough to scare them away. Are they going to want to know what I plan to do with every penny? What should I do if they are only willing to invest less?
4. I really don't know what to expect from these investors. I have my own idea of how much of the company I want to give up for the $150,000, but I don't know what they would consider reasonable. Can you give me any suggestions?

Mr. and Mrs. A. L. Young established the Rug Bug Corporation as a Delaware corporation. The sole purpose is to manufacture and distribute a revolutionary motorized wheelchair, designed for children under the age of 10. The Rug Bug motorized wheelchair will retail for approximately one-half the cost of any other motorized wheelchair for this age group. It will weigh almost 50 percent less than the standard motorized wheelchair. The unique design of the Rug Bug accounts for the differences in the retail cost and weight of the chair. In addition, the Rug Bug has numerous safety features that are not found on other available motorized wheelchairs. These three features of cost, weight, and safety allow the Rug Bug to fill a special niche in the market. It is an appropriate time to introduce this product in light of the current trend in the medical field to recommend the use of motorized wheelchairs for children. This recommendation of medical professionals arises from their determination that the spatial relations and sense of movement offered by a motorized chair provide a handicapped child with sensory experiences normal for young children. The target market for this product will be greatly increased due to this philosophical change. In order to establish the company, the Rug Bug Corporation will need $150,000. This will finance the production of the molds for various parts, the manufacture of 200 units (of which 190 will be sold), and initial marketing efforts. In addition, the company will use the funds for product liability insurance, legal fees, and continued research and development.

DESCRIPTION OF THE BUSINESS

The Rug Bug Corporation is primarily a manufacturing and distribution company in the start-up phase of operation. The inventor's initial research led to the development of a prototype. Marketing research shows the Rug Bug to be the only vacuum-molded, plastic, motorized wheelchair with unique safety features currently available. The owners of the Rug Bug Corporation believe the company will be successful because of low production costs, reasonable retail costs, safety factors, low weight, and visual appeal. The use of motorized chairs by the target age group has been limited primarily for two reasons. First, the current cost of motorized wheelchairs ranges from $3,000 to $20,000. It has been difficult to justify such an investment for a chair since a child's growth is typically rapid, therefore limiting the time the chair can be utilized. The Rug Bug will retail for $1,850. This is a significant price differential, especially for a chair that offers additional features such as safety control. The second limitation was the medical community's view that muscle use was of primary concern in a handicapped child's development. They have recently shifted away from that stance, with many professionals now emphasizing the development of spatial skills, spatial relations, and sense of movement—all areas that the motorized chair can help strengthen.

DESCRIPTION OF THE PRODUCT

The Rug Bug is a vacuum-molded, plastic-body wheelchair powered by a rechargeable battery. The 25-pound chair has the following safety features as standard equipment:

1. A pressure-sensitive bumper strip surrounding the vehicle allows the unit to move away from any obstruction it might encounter.
2. Dual front antennae extend upward to prevent the chair from moving under low objects, such as a coffee table.
3. In the case of a confrontation with an uneven surface, an electric eye located under the front of the chair will deactivate power in that direction. The power remains operative in other directions, allowing the occupant to move away from the potential hazard.
4. A handheld remote control unit enables an adult to take over control of the chair from the occupant.
5. A variable speed control is built into the unit which is beyond reach of the occupant. As the ability of the occupant to maneuver the chair increases, so may the speed.
6. Though built with a very low center of gravity, the chair is designed with a roll bar.

The computerized control panel defines the Rug Bug as a technical machine; however, in appearance, the Rug Bug is more similar to a currently popular battery-operated riding toy. The visual appeal immediately distinguishes the Rug Bug from any other motorized wheelchair on the market today.

MARKETING COMPONENT

1. *Market and competition*. According to *The New York Times*, the U.S. market for home medical equipment has exceeded $2.5 billion in the late nineties, growing at a rate of about 10 percent per year. Wheelchairs account for 38 percent of the market (*The Wheeled Mobility Market Report*). According to the *Medical and Healthcare Marketplace Guide*, worldwide wheelchair revenue exceeded $1 billion in 1995. U.S. market accounts for roughly half of these sales.

   The wheelchair market is composed of standard, lightweight, ultralight, powered, and scooter segments. There are approximately 1.3 million wheelchair users in the United States, and the number is increasing at a rate of 3 percent per year (*Medical and Healthcare Marketplace Guide*). Motorized and ultralight wheelchairs are the most dynamic segment of the market of mobility aids.

   According to the *U.S. Census Bureau*, there are more than 4.5 million children under the age of 15 with disabilities in this country. In the 6–14 age group alone there are more than 70,000 children who use wheelchairs. This figure does not reflect any other potential users in this age bracket, such as the muscular dystrophy population.

   The market has changed significantly for the last two decades. Specific federal regulations and the introduction of para-Olympics have focused attention on the improvements in wheelchairs and the needs of disabled people. Other market trends include the use of two or more wheelchairs by patients, and a steady demand for new designs, interest in a range of colors and styles to choose from, and design improvements based on new materials (*Medical and Healthcare Marketplace Guide*).

   There are several major players on the wheeled mobility market. A dominant participant is Sunrise. Others include Orthokinetics, Everest & Jennings, Guardian, Theradyne, and Invacare. Sunrise has pioneered new marketing strategy reaching customers directly. Competitive dimensions include new technologies, use of new materials, wheelchair weight, and maneuverability parameters. The current level of prices for motorized wheelchairs is in the range from $3,000 to $20,000 per unit with average weight of about 20–30 pounds.

2. *Distribution*. Since there are distinct and different methods for purchasing wheelchairs, Rug Bug will establish two different distribution systems. A direct system, initially employing individuals connected with the company, will call on hospitals, the Veterans Administration, Shriners, and other organizations connected with the care and development of handicapped children. Of the initial 200 products, 190 will be sold in these outlets in order to generate sales without paying retail markups. This will also give the product good exposure. Manufacturers' representatives will make direct sales for subsequent production runs. A 15 percent commission on the selling price will be paid on all direct sales. After the initial 190 units have been sold (with 10 units being kept for demonstration purposes), the company will add a retail distribution system. Several retail outlets will be used in each of the major markets, including drugstores, bicycle shops, and medical supply stores. Drugstores account for a significant share of wheelchair sales and are an important outlet for the company. Bicycle shops, while not usually a source for the purchase of wheelchairs, are an important outlet, as they will provide any service needed in addition to sales. Company-authorized service outlets will be established in each market for ease of repair, an aspect the consumer should appreciate. Retail margins will be 30 percent off the established retail selling price of $1,850.

3. *Price*. The company will sell the product to the retailer for $1,290; the retailer will mark up the product 30 percent, resulting in a selling price of $1,850 for the wheelchair. This price will position the product favorably against competition and allow for significant growth in market share as well as profit.

4. *Promotion*. Quality brochures describing the product and its characteristics will be developed and distributed as point-of-purchase sale materials in the retail outlets as well as in all hospitals,

clinics, and other organizations working with handicapped children. In addition, sales material, including a price list indicating markups and return per square foot of selling space required, will be developed for use in the company's direct sales effort.

LOCATION OF THE BUSINESS

The office section of the Rug Bug will be located at Barn Bicycle on East 61st Street, Tulsa, Oklahoma. The molded plastic body will be manufactured, and the product assembled, at the Inter-Ocean Oil Company, located at 2630 Mohawk Boulevard, Tulsa, Oklahoma. The Rug Bug Corporation will not be charged for usage of either facility, although it will pay for utilities and telephones at both.

MANAGEMENT/OPERATIONS

Inventor Al Young will serve as the president of Rug Bug Corporation. In addition, Young will concentrate on the research and development section of operations. Mr. Young's past experience with electronics and computers fits well with the needs of the company. His ability to transform a concept into a viable product is shown through the prototype that Rug Bug currently has in existence.

Wayne Dunn and Dwaine Farrill will continue to operate in the marketing component of the company. Their extensive knowledge of and profound belief in the product make both Dunn and Farrill ideal people to initially market it on a commissioned basis.

Linda Bryant will initially serve as the unpaid controller of the company. Ms. Bryant will serve as single signatory on the banking account and prepare and monitor monthly financial reports. She has served as a cash management officer at The Fourth National Bank of Tulsa for over two years and is currently its director of business development.

FINANCIAL INFORMATION

To ramp up, the Rug Bug Corporation needs $150,000. The funds will be used to develop the molds for various parts, manufacture 200 units (of which 190 will be sold), start the initial marketing effort, and pay employee salaries, product liability insurance, legal fees, and other expenses of the organization (see Exhibit 1). The company will achieve significant sales and profits starting in the first year, as indicated in the various pro forma income statements (see Exhibits 1 to 3). The pro forma income cash flow statements (Exhibits 4 to 6) and balance sheets (Exhibits 7 to 9) further indicate the tremendous growth and profit potential.

EXHIBIT 1

THE RUG BUG CORPORATION
Pro Forma Income Statement
First Year, by Month

	Mo. 1	Mo. 2	Mo. 3	Mo. 4	Mo. 5	Mo. 6	Mo. 7	Mo. 8	Mo. 9	Mo. 10	Mo. 11	Mo. 12	Total
Sales	0	0	0	$37,000	$55,500	$55,500	$74,000	$74,000	$74,000	$74,000	$92,500	$92,500	$629,000
Less: Cost of goods sold	0	0	0	8,720	13,080	13,080	17,440	17,440	17,440	17,440	21,800	21,800	148,240
Commission	0	0	0	5,550	8,325	8,325	11,100	11,100	11,100	11,100	13,875	13,875	94,350
Gross profit	0	0	0	$22,730	$34,095	$34,095	$45,460	$45,460	$45,460	$45,460	$56,825	$56,825	$386,410
Operating expenses													
President salary	$ 2,000	$ 2,000	$ 2,000	$ 2,000	$ 2,000	$ 2,000	$ 2,000	$ 2,000	$ 2,000	$ 2,000	$ 2,000	$ 2,000	$24,000
Secretary salary	0	0	0	0	0	1,167	1,167	1,167	1,167	1,167	1,167	1,167	8,169
Employee insurance	42	42	42	42	42	42	42	42	42	42	42	42	500
Product liability insurance				370	555	555	740	740	740	740	925	925	6,290
Research and development				1,850	2,775	2,775	3,700	3,700	3,700	3,700	4,625	4,625	31,450
Advertising/printing	417	417	417	417	417	417	417	417	417	417	417	417	5,000
Travel expenses	625	625	625	625	625	625	625	625	625	625	625	625	7,500
Organization expenses	850	850	850	850	850	850	850	850	850	850	850	850	10,200
Total operating expenses	$ 3,933	$ 3,933	$ 3,933	$ 6,153	$ 7,263	$ 8,430	$ 9,540	$ 9,540	$ 9,540	$ 9,540	$10,650	$10,650	$ 93,109
Profit (loss) before tax	(3,933)	(3,933)	(3,933)	16,577	26,832	25,665	35,920	35,920	35,920	35,920	46,175	46,175	293,301
Taxes	0	0	0	6,631	10,733	10,266	14,368	14,368	14,368	14,368	18,470	18,470	122,040
Net profit (loss)	$(3,933)	$(3,933)	$(3,933)	$ 9,946	$16,099	$15,399	$21,552	$21,552	$21,552	$21,552	$27,705	$27,705	$171,261
Quantity sold	0	0	0	20	30	30	40	40	40	40	50	50	340
Price	1,850	1,850	1,850	1,850	1,850	1,850	1,850	1,850	1,850	1,850	1,850	1,850	
DL-DM-MAGF cost	436	436	436	436	436	436	436	436	436	436	436	436	
Commission percent	15	15	15	15	15	15	15	15	15	15	15	15	
Tax rate	40	40	40	40	40	40	40	40	40	40	40	40	

(1) President salary at $24,000 per year.
(2) Secretary salary begins on the 6th month.
(3) Product liability is proportionate to quantity sold.
(4) Organization expenses (registration fee, legal fee, etc.) are amortized over the first year.

EXHIBIT 2

THE RUG BUG CORPORATION
Pro Forma Income Statement
Second Year, by Quarter

	Qtr 1	Qtr 2	Qtr 3	Qtr 4	Total
Sales—Direct	$555,000	$1,110,000	$2,220,000	$3,330,000	$7,215,000
Sales—Retail	194,250	388,500	582,750	777,000	1,942,500
Total sales	$749,250	$1,498,500	$2,802,750	$4,107,000	$9,157,500
Less: Cost of good sold—Direct	130,800	261,600	523,200	784,800	1,700,400
Cost of goods sold—Retail	65,400	130,800	196,200	261,600	654,000
Commission—Direct	83,250	166,500	333,000	499,500	1,082,250
Commission—Retail	29,138	58,275	87,413	116,550	291,375
Gross profit	$440,663	$ 881,325	$1,662,938	$2,444,550	$5,429,475
Operating expenses					
President salary	$ 7,200	$ 7,200	$ 7,200	$ 7,200	$ 28,800
Secretary salary	3,500	3,500	3,500	3,500	14,000
VP—Finance salary			12,500	12,500	25,000
Employee insurance	125	125	125	125	500
Product liability insurance	7,493	14,985	28,028	41,070	91,575
Research and development	37,463	74,925	140,138	205,350	457,875
Advertising/printing	2,500	2,500	2,500	2,500	10,000
Travel expenses	1,875	1,875	1,875	1,875	7,500
Accounting services	2,500	2,500	2,500	2,500	10,000
Depreciation—Computer system	250	250	250	250	1,000
Bad debt expense	5,828	11,655	17,483	23,310	58,275
Total operating expenses	$ 68,733	$ 119,515	$ 216,098	$ 300,180	$ 704,525
Profit (loss) before tax	371,930	761,810	1,446,840	2,144,370	4,724,950
Taxes	148,772	304,724	578,736	857,748	1,889,980
Net profit (loss)	$223,158	$ 457,086	$ 868,104	$1,286,622	$2,834,970
Quantity sold—Direct	300	600	1,200	1,800	3,900
Quantity sold—Retail	150	300	450	600	1,500
Price—Direct	1,850	1,850	1,850	1,850	
Price—Retail	1,295	1,295	1,295	1,295	
Manufacturing cost	436	436	436	436	
Commission percent	15	15	15	15	
Tax rate	40	40	40	40	

(1) Product liability insurance = 1% of sales, R + D − 5% of sales.
(2) Computer system depreciated at straight line over a 5-year life with no salvage value.
(3) Bad debt expense provision at 3% of retail sales.
(4) Taxes (federal and state) provided at 40%.

EXHIBIT 3

THE RUG BUG CORPORATION
Pro Forma Income Statement
Third Year, by Quarter
2006/2007

	Qtr 1	Qtr 2	Qtr 3	Qtr 4	Total
Sales—Direct	$3,700,000	$5,550,000	$ 7,400,000	$ 9,250,000	$25,900,000
Sales—Retail	1,554,000	2,331,000	3,108,000	3,885,000	10,878,000
Total sales	$5,254,000	$7,881,000	$10,508,000	$13,135,000	$36,778,000
Less					
Cost of goods sold—Direct	$ 872,000	$1,308,000	$ 1,744,000	$ 2,180,000	$ 6,104,000
Cost of goods sold—Retail	523,200	784,800	1,046,400	1,308,000	3,662,400
Commission—Direct	555,000	832,500	1,110,000	1,387,500	3,885,000
Commission—Retail	233,100	349,650	466,200	582,750	1,631,700
Gross profit	$3,070,700	$4,606,050	$ 6,141,400	$ 7,676,750	$21,494,900
Operating expenses					
President salary	$ 8,640	$ 8,640	$ 8,640	$ 8,640	$ 34,560
Secretary salary	3,500	3,500	3,500	3,500	14,000
VP—Finance salary	15,000	15,000	15,000	15,000	60,000
Employee insurance	125	125	125	125	500
Product liability insurance	52,540	78,810	105,080	131,350	367,780
Research and development	262,700	394,050	525,400	656,750	1,838,900
Advertising/printing	3,125	3,125	3,125	3,125	12,500
Travel expenses	1,875	1,875	1,875	1,875	7,500
Accounting services	2,500	2,500	2,500	2,500	10,000
Depreciation—Computer system	250	250	250	250	1,000
Bad debt expense	46,620	69,930	93,240	116,550	326,340
Total operating expenses	$ 386,875	$ 577,805	$ 758,735	$ 939,665	$ 2,673,080
Profit (loss) before tax	2,673,825	4,023,245	5,382,665	6,737,085	18,821,820
Taxes	1,069,530	1,611,298	2,153,066	2,694,834	7,528,728
Net profit (loss)	$1,604,295	$2,416,447	$ 3,229,599	$ 4,042,251	$11,243,042
Quantity sold—Direct	2,000	3,000	4,000	5,000	14,000
Quantity sold—Retail	1,200	1,800	2,400	3,000	8,400
Price—Direct	1,850	1,850	1,850	1,850	
Price—Retail	1,295	1,295	1,295	1,295	
Manufacturing cost	436	436	436	436	
Discount percent	30	30	30	30	
Commission percent	15	15	15	15	
Tax rate	40	40	40	40	

EXHIBIT 4

THE RUG BUG CORPORATION
Pro Forma Cash Flow Statement
First Year, by Month

	Mo. 1	Mo. 2	Mo. 3	Mo. 4	Mo. 5	Mo. 6	Mo. 7	Mo. 8	Mo. 9	Mo. 10	Mo. 11	Mo. 12
Cash receipts												
Sales	0	0	0	$37,000	$55,500	$55,500	$74,000	$74,000	$74,000	$74,000	$92,500	$92,500
Others	$75,000	$75,000		0								
Total cash receipts	$75,000	$75,000	0	$37,000	$55,500	$55,500	$74,000	$74,000	$74,000	$74,000	$92,500	$92,500
Cash disbursements												
Salaries												
President	$ 2,000	$ 2,000	$ 2,000	$ 2,000	$ 2,000	$ 2,000	$ 2,000	$ 2,000	$ 2,000	$ 2,000	$ 2,000	$ 2,000
Secretary	0	0	0	0	0	1,167	1,167	1,167	1,167	1,167	1,167	1,167
Employee insurance	100	150	250									
Product liability insurance	6,290											
Research and development	0	0	0	1,850	2,775	2,775	3,700	3,700	3,700	3,700	4,625	4,625
Advertising	2,500	1,500	1,000									
Travel expense	3,750	2,250	1,500									
Organization fees	5,100	3,060	2,040									
Commissions	0	0	0	5,550	8,325	8,325	11,100	11,100	11,100	11,100	13,875	13,875
Inventory	17,421	26,131	43,552				10,900	10,900	21,800	21,800	65,400	65,400
Total disbursements	$37,161	$35,091	$50,342	$ 9,400	$13,100	$14,267	$28,867	$28,867	$39,767	$39,767	$87,067	$87,067
Net cash flow	37,839	39,909	(50,342)	27,600	42,400	41,233	45,133	45,133	34,233	34,233	5,433	5,433
Cumulative cash flow	37,839	77,748	27,406	55,006	97,406	138,639	183,772	228,905	263,138	297,371	302,804	308,237
Inventory calculation (units produced)	40	60	100				25	25	50	50	150	150

EXHIBIT 5

THE RUG BUG CORPORATION
Pro Forma Cash Flow Statement
Second Year, by Quarter
2005/2006

	Qtr 1	Qtr 2	Qtr 3	Qtr 4	Total
Cash receipts					
Sales	$674,325	$1,423,575	$2,672,325	$3,976,575	$8,746,800
Others					
Total cash receipts	$674,325	$1,423,575	$2,672,325	$3,976,575	$8,746,800
Cash disbursements					
Salaries					
President	$ 7,200	$ 7,200	$ 7,200	$ 7,200	$ 28,800
Secretary	3,500	3,500	3,500	3,500	14,000
VP—Finance	0	0	12,500	12,500	25,000
Employee insurance	125	125	125	125	500
Product liability insurance	91,575				91,575
Research and development	37,463	74,925	140,138	205,350	457,875
Advertising	2,500	2,500	2,500	2,500	10,000
Travel expense	1,875	1,875	1,875	1,875	7,500
Accounting services	2,500	2,500	2,500	2,500	10,000
Commissions	101,149	213,536	400,849	596,486	1,312,020
Inventory	327,000	610,400	937,400	1,308,000	3,182,800
Taxes	122,040				122,040
Computer system	5,000				5,000
Total cash disbursements	$701,927	$ 916,561	$1,508,586	$2,140,036	$5,267,110
Net cash flow	(27,602)	507,014	1,163,739	1,836,539	3,479,690
Cumulative cash flow	(27,602)	479,412	1,643,151	3,479,690	
Units produced	750	1,400	2,150	3,000	7,300
Unit cost	$436	$436	$436	$436	

EXHIBIT 6

THE RUG BUG CORPORATION
Pro Forma Cash Flow Statement
Third Year, by Quarter

	Qtr 1	Qtr 2	Qtr 3	Qtr 4	Total
Cash receipts					
Sales	$5,170,442	$7,618,300	$10,245,300	$12,872,300	$35,906,342
Others					
Total cash receipts	$5,170,442	$7,618,300	$10,245,300	$12,872,300	$35,906,342
Cash disbursements					
Salaries					
President	$ 8,640	$ 8,640	$ 8,640	$ 8,640	$ 34,560
Secretary	3,500	3,500	3,500	3,500	14,000
VP—Finance	15,000	15,000	15,000	15,000	60,000
Employee insurance	125	125	125	125	500
Product liability insurance	52,540	78,810	105,080	131,350	367,780
Research and development	262,700	394,050	525,400	656,750	1,838,900
Advertising	2,500	2,500	2,500	2,500	10,000
Travel expense	1,875	1,875	1,875	1,875	7,500
Accounting services	2,500	2,500	2,500	2,500	10,000
Commissions	775,566	1,142,745	1,536,795	1,930,845	5,385,951
Inventory	1,831,200	2,528,800	3,313,600	3,749,600	11,423,200
Taxes	1,917,690				1,917,690
Total cash disbursements	$4,873,836	$4,178,545	$ 5,515,015	$ 6,502,685	$21,070,081
Net cash flow	296,605	3,439,755	4,730,285	6,369,615	14,836,260
Cumulative cash flow	296,605	3,736,360	8,466,645	14,836,260	
Units produced	4,200	5,800	7,600	8,600	26,200
Unit cost	$436	$436	$436	$436	

EXHIBIT 7

THE RUG BUG CORPORATION
Pro Forma Balance Sheet
As of End of Year 1

Cash	$171,261
Inventory	135,225
Accounts receivable	0
Total assets	$306,486
Commissions payable	0
Taxes payable	122,040
Retained earnings	34,445
Common stock	150,000
	$306,486

EXHIBIT 8

THE RUG BUG CORPORATION Pro Forma Balance Sheet As of End of Year 2	
Cash	$2,876,535
Computer system	4,000
Inventory	1,017,145
Accounts receivable	259,000
Total assets	$4,156,680
Commissions payable	38,850
Taxes payable	1,917,690
Retained earnings	2,088,990
Common stock	150,000
	$4,156,680

EXHIBIT 9

THE RUG BUG CORPORATION Pro Forma Balance Sheet As of End of Year 3	
Cash	$11,495,496
Computer	3,000
Inventory	1,541,938
Accounts receivable	1,259,000
Total assets	$14,299,434
Commissions payable	188,850
Taxes payable	7,663,664
Retained earnings	6,485,770
Contributed capital	150,000
	$14,299,434

CASE 3D
NATURE BROS. LTD.

BACKGROUND

Thanksgiving Day 1993 is the day that Dale Morris remembers as the "public debut" of his creation, a new seasoned salt mix. Although he was a salesman by temperament and career, his hobby was cooking. Having experimented with both traditional home cooking and more exotic gourmet cooking, Morris had developed an appreciation for many herbs and spices. He had also done a lot of reading about the health hazards of the typical American diet. When his mother learned that she had high blood pressure, Morris decided it was time for some action. He created a low-salt seasoning mix, based on a nutritive yeast extract, that could be used to replace salt in most cases. This Thanksgiving dinner, prepared for 25 family members and friends, would be his final testing ground. He used his mix in all the recipes except the pumpkin pie—everything from the turkey and dressing to the vegetables and even the rolls. As the meal progressed, the verdict was unanimously in favor of his secret ingredient, although he had a hard time convincing them that it was his invention and was only 10 percent salt. Everyone wanted a sample to try at home.

Over the next two years, Morris perfected his product. Experiments in new uses led to "tasting parties" for friends and neighbors, and the holiday season found the Morris kitchen transformed into a miniature assembly line producing gift-wrapped bottles of the mix. Morris became something of a celebrity in his small town, but it wasn't until the Ladies' Mission Society at his church approached him with the idea of allowing them to sell his mix as a fund-raiser that he realized the possibilities of his creation. His kitchen-scale operation could support the sales effort of the church women for a short time, but if he wanted to take advantage of a truly marketable product, he would have to make other arrangements.

Morris agreed to "test-market" his product through the church group while he looked for ways to expand and commercialize his operation. The charity sale was a huge success (the best the women had ever experienced), and, based on this success, Morris moved to create his own company. Naming his product "Nature Bros. Old Fashioned Seasoning," he incorporated the company in 1995 as Nature Bros. Ltd. Morris used most of his savings to develop and register the trademarks, for packaging, and for product displays. He researched the cost of manufacturing and bottling his product in large quantities and concluded that he just didn't have the cash to get started. His first attempts to raise money, in the form of a personal bank loan, were unsuccessful, and he was forced to abandon the project.

For several years he concentrated on his career, becoming a regional vice president of the insurance company he worked for. He continued to make "Nature Bros. Seasoning" in small batches, mainly for his mother and business associates. These users eventually enabled Morris to get financial support for his company. To raise $65,000 to lease manufacturing equipment and building space, he sold stock to his mother and to two other regional vice presidents of the insurance company. For their contributions, each became the owner of 15 percent of Nature Bros. Ltd. The process of getting the product to the retail market began in August 2002, and the first grocery store sales started in March 2003. The initial marketing plan was fairly simple—to get the product in the hands of the consumer. Morris personally visited the managers of individual supermarkets, both chains and independents, and convinced many to allow a tasting demonstration booth to be set up in their stores. These demonstrations proved as popular as the first Thanksgiving dinner trial nearly 10 years earlier. Dale Morris's product was a hit, and in a short time he was able to contract with food brokerage firms to place his product in stores in a 10-state region.

PRESENT SITUATION

As indicated in the balance sheet (see Exhibit 1), more capital is needed to support the current markets and expand both markets and products. Two new products are being developed: a salt-free version of the original product and an MSG-based flavor enhancer that will compete with Accent. Morris worked with a business consultant in drawing up a business plan to describe his company, its future growth, and its capital needs.

OVERALL PROJECTIONS

The first section discusses the objectives and sales projections for 2004 and 2005 (Exhibits 2 and 3). The resulting pro forma income statements for 2004 to 2005 are in Exhibits 4 and 5.

2004 OBJECTIVES

The company's objectives for 2004 are to stabilize its existing markets and to achieve a 5 percent market share in the category of seasoned salt, a 10 percent market share in salt substitutes, and a 5 percent market share in MSG products. Although the original product contains less than 10 percent salt, the company has developed a salt-free product to compete with other such products, such as the one shown in the advertisement in Exhibit 6. The dollar volume for the seasoned salt category in the seven markets the company is in will amount to $7,931,889 in 2004. In 2003, sales of the company in the Oklahoma market were 5.5 percent of the total sales for that market for the eight-month period that the company was operational.

EXHIBIT 1

NATURE BROS. LTD.
Balance Sheet
As of September 30, 2003

Unaudited	
Current assets	
110 Cash—American Bank	$ 527.11
112 Cash—Bank of Okla-Pryor	31.86
115 Cash on hand	24.95
120 Accounts receivable	21,512.75
125 Employee advances	327.37
140 Inventory—Shipping	940.43
141 Inventory—Raw materials	1,082.29
142 Inventory—Work-in-progress	803.70
143 Inventory—Packaging	4,548.41
144 Inventory—Promotional	2,114.95
Total current assets	$31,913.82
Fixed assets	
160 Leasehold improvements	$ 2,402.25
165 Fixtures and furniture	1,222.46
167 Equipment	18,768.21
169 Office equipment	.00
170 1986 Lincoln town car	15,000.00
180 Less: Accumulated depreciation	(7,800.01)
181 Less: Amortization	(502.50)
Total fixed assets	$29,090.41
Other assets	
193 Organizational cost	$ 4,083.36
194 Prepaid interest	2,849.69
195 Utility deposits	.00
Total fixed and other assets	$36,023.46
Total assets	$67,937.28
Current liabilities	
205 Accounts payable	$15,239.41
210 Note payable-premium finances	88.26
220 Federal tax withheld	150.00
225 FICA tax withheld	937.92
230 State tax withheld	266.49
231 State and federal employment taxes	230.92
Total current liabilities	$16,913.00
Long-term liabilities	
245 Note payable—All fill	$ 2,734.86
246 Note payable—American Bank	23,740.00
247 Note payable—Sikeston Leasing	15,126.66
Total long-term liabilities	$41,601.52
Total liabilities	$58,514.52
Capital account	
290 Original capital stock	$ 1,000.00
291 Additional paid-in capital	41,580.00
292 Treasury stock	(70.00)
295 Retained earnings	(3,819.71)
298 Net profit or loss	(29,267.53)
Total owner's equity account	$ 9,422.76
Total liabilities and equity	$67,937.28

EXHIBIT 2 2004 Sales Projection

Category	Seasoned Salt	Salt Substitute	MSG
Our Product	**Old Fashioned Seasoning**	**Salt-Free Old Fashioned Seasoning**	**Enhance**
Existing markets #1			
Oklahoma	$1,101,844	$ 715,638	$ 237,778
Nebraska	799,260	605,538	201,916
Springfield, MO	508,620	385,432	128,034
Arkansas	435,960	330,294	109,742
Houston	1,671,180	1,266,128	420,684
Dallas	2,325,120	1,761,570	585,298
Albuquerque	1,089,900	825,736	274,358
	$7,931,884	$5,890,246	$1,957,090
Market share (%)	×5%	×10%	×5%
1st year sales	$ 396,594	$ 589,024	$ 97,854
		396,594	
		589,024	
		97,854	
Total 1st year sales volume		$1,083,472	

Since these sales were accomplished with absolutely no advertising, the company can be even more successful in the future in all seven current markets with a fully developed and funded advertising campaign. The marketing approach will include advertisements in the print media, with ads on "food day" offering cents-off coupons. This program will take place in all seven markets, while stores will continue to use floor displays for demonstrations. Nearly 100 percent warehouse penetration should be achieved in 2004 in these markets.

The goal for the category of salt substitutes for 2004 is 10 percent of the market share. This larger market share can be achieved since there are only a few competitors, Mrs. Dash, AMBI Inc. with Cordia Salt Alternative, and RCN with No Salt. The company's product is superior in all respects and has a retail price advantage of 10 to 20 cents per can. In addition, the company's product is much more versatile than competitors' products. Aggressive marketing and advertising will emphasize the tremendous versatility of usage as well as the great taste and health benefits of the product. The informal consumer surveys at demonstrations indicated that consumers prefer Nature Bros. to competitors' products by a wide margin.

A new product, which is already developed, will be added during this time. Called "Enhance," it too is a dry-mixed, noncooked, low-overhead, high-profit food product. Its category of MSG products has a dollar volume of $1,957,090 in these markets. This category includes only one main competitor, Accent, made by Pet Inc. Accent has not been heavily advertised, and it is a one-line product with little initial name recognition. The company's new product will have a 10 to 20 cent per can retail price advantage to help achieve a 5 percent share of this category. In summary, 2004 will be spent solidifying the company's present market positions.

2005 OBJECTIVES

The company intends to open eight new markets in 2005 that include Los Angeles, Phoenix, Portland, Sacramento, Salt Lake City, San Francisco, Seattle, and Spokane. These new markets make up 17.1 percent of grocery store sales, according to the *Progressive Grocer's Marketing Guidebook*, the industry standard. In the category of

EXHIBIT 3 2005 Sales Projection

Category	Seasoned Salt	Salt Substitute	MSG
Our Product	**Old Fashioned Seasoning**	**Salt-Free Old Fashioned Seasoning**	**Enhance**
Existing markets #1			
Oklahoma	$ 1,156,936	$ 751,418	$ 249,778
Nebraska	978,946	635,816	211,350
Springfield, MO	622,966	404,610	134,496
Arkansas	533,970	346,808	115,282
Houston	2,046,886	1,329,432	441,914
Dallas	2,847,842	1,885,644	614,838
Albuquerque	1,334,926	867,020	288,206
Existing markets total	$ 9,522,472	$ 6,220,748	$2,055,864
Market share	×7.5%	×12.5%	×7.5%
Existing markets $ volume	$ 714,185	$ 775,593	$ 154,189
New markets:			
Los Angeles	$ 5,784,678	$ 3,757,088	$1,248,888
Phoenix	1,245,930	809,218	268,990
Portland	1,157,294	751,418	249,776
Sacramento	1,690,906	1,098,226	365,060
Salt Lake City	1,157,294	751,416	249,776
San Francisco	2,313,870	1,502,838	499,554
Seattle	1,157,294	751,416	249,776
Spokane	711,960	462,412	153,708
New markets total	$15,218,886	$10,064,028	$3,285,528
Market share	×5%	×10%	×5%
New markets $ volume	$760,943	$ 1,006,420	$164,276
New markets $ total	760,943	1,006,420	164,276
Existing markets $ total +	714,185	777,593	154,189
Total volume	$ 1,475,128	$ 1,784,013	$ 318,465
Old Fashioned Seasoning sales			$1,475,128
Salt-Free Old Fashioned Seasoning sales			1,784,013
Enhance sales (a new product)			318,465
Total 2005 sales			$3,557,606

seasoned salt, these markets have a dollar volume of $15,218,886 a year. Salt substitutes sell at a volume of $10,064,028, and the MSG category $3,285,528. With proper advertising, the company's shares forecast in our current markets will also be realized.

A 5 percent penetration of the seasoned salt category is a very conservative projection considering the strong health consciousness of the West Coast. The products will be introduced in shippers, used in store demonstrations, and supported with media advertising to achieve

EXHIBIT 4 2004 Pro Forma Totals

	2004	Percent
Sales	$1,083,472	100
Cost of goods		
Packaging	129,444	11.9
Ingredients	175,668	16.2
Plant labor	35,580	3.2
Freight in	24,036	2.2
Shipping materials	924	.08
Total cost of goods sold	$ 365,004	33.68
Gross profit	718,468	66.31
Operating expenses		
President's salary	43,200	
Sales manager	30,000	
Secretary	14,400	
Employee benefits	2,400	
Insurance	1,992	
Rent	3,000	
Utilities	1,800	
Phone	7,200	
Office supplies	1,200	
Postage	1,200	
Car lease	5,640	
Professional services	3,000	
Travel and entertainment	24,000	
Freight out	59,088	5.4
Advertising	216,684	20.0
Promotion	12,036	1.1
Brokerage	54,168	5.0
Incentives	7,500	.6
Cash discounts	21,660	2.0
Total expenses	$ 510,168	47.0
Cash flow		
Taxes	207,648	19.1
Net profit before debt service	155,736	14.3

at least a 5 percent market share. This would result in sales of $760,943 in that category.

A 10 percent penetration is targeted in the salt-free category. Using aggressive marketing, price advantage at retail, and better packaging, the company will be well positioned against the lower-quality products of our competitors. With the dollar volume of this category at $10,064,028, a conservative estimate of our share would be $1,006,420. In the category of MSG, a 5 percent share will be achieved. The main competitor in this category does very little advertising. Again, attractive packaging, aggressive marketing, high quality, and a

EXHIBIT 5

NATURE BROS. LTD.
Pro Forma Income Statement
2005–2008

	2005	2006	2007	2008
Sales	$3,557,606	$6,136,224	$10,089,863	$18,506,302
Cost of goods				
Packaging	423,355	730,210	1,200,693	2,202,249
Ingredients	572,774	987,932	1,624,467	2,979,514
Plant labor	37,359	48,826	60,867	63,910
Freight in	72,930	125,793	206,842	379,379
Shipping materials	2,960	4,908	8,071	14,805
Total cost of goods sold	$1,106,575	$1,897,618	$ 3,100,240	$ 5,639,858
Percent of sales	31.36%	31.41%	30.90%	30.65%
Gross profit	2,451,031	4,238,606	6,988,923	12,866,444
Operating expenses				
President's salary	43,200	51,840	62,208	74,649
Sales manager	30,000	36,000	39,000	45,000
Sales rep	25,000	30,000	34,000	38,000
Sales rep		25,000	30,000	34,000
Sales rep			26,000	30,000
Sales rep				28,000
Secretary	16,000	18,000	20,000	22,000
Secretary				15,000
Employee benefits	2,400	4,000	10,000	15,000
Insurance	3,000	4,000	5,000	5,000
Rent	3,600	3,600	3,600	3,600
Utilities	2,400	3,000	3,500	4,500
Phone	12,000	14,000	15,000	18,000
Office supplies	2,000	2,500	3,000	5,000
Postage	2,000	2,500	3,000	4,000
Car lease	5,640	5,640	5,640	5,640
Car lease	3,600	3,600	4,000	4,000
Car lease		3,600	3,600	4,000
Car lease			4,000	4,000
Professional services	6,000	8,000	8,000	10,000
Travel and entertainment	48,000	72,000	96,000	120,000
New equipment	4,000	14,000	14,000	24,000
Freight out	197,269	334,424	549,897	1,000,859
Advertising	711,521	1,227,244	2,017,972	3,701,260
Promotion	40,000	68,112	111,997	205,419
Brokerage	177,880	306,811	504,493	925,315
Incentives	24,547	42,399	69,680	205,419
Cash discounts	71,152	122,724	201,792	370,126
Total expenses	$1,431,209	$2,402,994	$ 3,845,192	$ 6,921,787
Cash flow before taxes	1,019,822	1,835,612	3,845,192	6,921,787
Taxes	209,063	458,903	785,932	1,486,164
Net profit before debt service	$ 810,759	$1,376,709	$ 2,357,799	$ 4,458,493
Percent of sales	22.78%	22.43%	23.36%	24.09%

EXHIBIT 6

Sources: *Tulsa World,* June 17, 2003.

retail price advantage of 30 to 40 cents per unit will enable the company to realize a 5 percent market penetration. This share of the West Coast markets will generate sales of $164,276. Total sales of all three products in these eight new markets will be around $1,931,639. The company plans to continue to solidify the markets previously established through the use of coupons, co-op advertising, quality promotions, and word-of-mouth advertising. Market share in these original markets should increase by another 2.5 percent in 2005. The dollar volume of the seasoned salt category in 2005 should be around $9,522,472, and our market share at 7.5 percent would amount to $714,185. The dollar volume for the salt substitute category would be $6,220,748, giving sales at 12.5 percent of $775,593. In the MSG category, a 7.5 percent market share of the $2,055,864 volume would give sales of $154,189. The company's total sales for the existing markets in 2005 will be in excess of $1,643,967. The totals for 2005 sales of Nature Bros. Old Fashioned Seasoning will be $1,475,128. Nature Bros. Salt-Free volume should be $1,784,013. The sales of Enhance, our MSG product, should be $318,465. This will give us a total sales volume of $3,557,606 for all three products in 2005.

FINANCIAL NEEDS AND PROJECTIONS

In this plan, Morris indicated a need for $100,000 equity infusion to expand sales, increase markets, and add new products. The money would be used to secure warehouse stocking space, do cooperative print advertising, give point-of-purchase display allowances, and pay operating expenses.

NEW PRODUCT DEVELOPMENT

The company plans to continue an ongoing research and development program to introduce new and winning products. Four products are already developed that will be highly marketable and easily produced. Personnel are dedicated to building a large and profitable company and attracting quality brokers. The next new product targets a different market segment but can be brought online for about $25,000 by using our existing machinery, types of containers, and display pieces. A highly respected broker felt that the product would be a big success. The broker previously represented the only major producer of a similar product, Pet Inc., which had sales of $4.36 million in 1985.

The company can achieve at least a 5 percent market share with this product in the first year. The company's product will be at least equal in quality and offer a 17 percent price advantage to the consumer, while still making an excellent profit.

Another new product would require slightly different equipment. This product would be initially produced by a private-label manufacturer. The product would be established before any major machinery was purchased. Many large companies use private-label manufacturers, or co-packers, as they are called in the trade. Consumer tests at demonstrations and food shows have indicated that each of these products will be strong.

PLANT AND EQUIPMENT

The company's plant is located in a nearly new metal building in Rose, Oklahoma. The lease on the building limits payments to no more than $300 per month for the next seven years. The new computer-controlled filling equipment will be paid off in two months, and the seaming equipment is leased from the company's container manufacturer for only $1 per year. The company has the capability of producing about 300,000 units a month with an additional $15,000 investment for an automatic conveyer system and a bigger product mixer. This production level would require two additional plant personnel, working one shift with no overtime. The company could double this production if needed with the addition of another shift. One of the main advantages of the company's business is the very small overhead required to produce the products. The company can generate enough product to reach sales of approximately $4 million a year while maintaining a production payroll of only $37,000 a year.

To meet the previously outlined production goals, the company will need to purchase another filling machine in 2005. This machine will be capable of filling two cans at once with an overall speed of 75 cans per minute, which would increase capacity to 720,000 units a month. A higher-speed seaming machine will also need to be purchased. The filling machine would cost approximately $22,000; a rebuilt seamer would cost $25,000, while a new one would cost $50,000. With the addition of these two machines, the company would have a capacity of 1,020,000 units per month on one shift.

By 2006, the company will have to decide whether to continue the lease or buy the property where located and expand the facilities. The property has plenty of land for expansion for the next five years. The company has the flexibility to produce other types of products with the same equipment and can react quickly to changes in customer preferences and modify its production line to meet such demands as needed.

Source: This case was modified by Sergey Anokhin of the Weatherhead School of Management, Case Western Reserve University, as a basis for classroom discussion rather than to illustrate either effective or ineffective handling of an administrative situation.

The name of the company and the names of its officers have been disguised. Support for the development of this case was provided by the Centre for International Business Studies, University of Manitoba, Canada.

*Market size estimates are based on two decades of average growth rate for the human nutrition salt market, with some corrections to reflect the growing share of salt substitutes in total consumption of salt-like substances.

END NOTES

1. Coronary artery disease.
2. Heart Disease and Stroke Statistics—2003 Update, American Heart Association.
3. http://www.nicore.com/economicfacts.htm.
4. Includes heart attack, angina pectoris (chest pain), or both.
5. Myocardial infarction (heart attack).
6. Heart Disease and Stroke Statistics—2003 Update, American Heart Association.
7. http://imaginis.com/heart-disease/cad_screen.asp?mode=1.
8. John G. Webster, *Medical Instrumentation: Application and Design,* 3rd edition, pp. 555–561.
9. "Clinical Exercise Stress Testing—Safety and Performance Guidelines," *MJA The Cardiac Society of Australia and New Zealand,* 164 (1996), pp. 282–84.
10. Robert Roos, "Noninvasive Detection of Coronary Artery Disease. Can the New Imaging Techniques Help?" *The Physician and Sportsmedicine,* vol. 28, no. 1, January 2000.
11. 1998 Socioeconomic Monitoring System survey of nonfederal patient care physicians; cited in "Overview of the Physician Market," American Medical Association.
12. National Venture Capital Association, February 10, 2003.
13. National Venture Capital Association, February 10, 2003.
14. "Angel Investors," Small Business Notes, http://www.smallbusinessnotes.com/financing/angelinvestors.html.

MANAGING, GROWING, AND ENDING THE NEW VENTURE

13

ENTREPRENEURIAL STRATEGY: GENERATING AND EXPLOITING NEW ENTRIES

LEARNING OBJECTIVES

1
To understand that the essential act of entrepreneurship involves new entry.

2
To be able to think about how an entrepreneurial strategy can first generate, and then exploit over time, a new entry.

3
To understand how resources are involved in the generation of opportunities.

4
To be able to assess the attractiveness of a new entry opportunity.

5
To acknowledge that entrepreneurship involves making decisions under conditions of uncertainty.

6
To be able to assess the extent of first-mover advantages and weigh them against first-mover disadvantages.

7
To understand that risk is associated with newness, but there are strategies that the entrepreneur can use to reduce risk.

OPENING PROFILE

JUSTIN PARER

Sorry it had taken so long to get back to you. I think in some way I have been avoiding this because I don't know if I actually know the answers to what you are asking. I think sometimes you justify afterwards why you did something.

www.BSE.net.au

This quote is from Justin Parer, an Australian entrepreneur, in response to my direct questions about the plan he followed for entrepreneurial success. His history indicates a series of steps and missteps that have emerged into a strategy of personal and business success—a strategy that may be more obvious to the objective observer taking a long-run perspective than to the actor who is immersed in the daily details of a pressurized situation, and is making "intuitive" decisions.

Justin's first entrepreneurial venture failed. The story is not pretty. He started up a mobile pizza business when he was 18 years old. "The idea for the van was actually someone else's. I was working in a pizza shop as a delivery driver trying to decide what I wanted to do in my life. I had recently been thrown out of uni [university] for gross failing and was at a loose end. One of the other guys in the shop said, 'Why don't they sell pizzas outside night clubs?' The market at the time was being serviced by a number of very unhygienic hot dog vendors who operated out of questionable mobile huts." Eventually Justin's business failed because, among other things, the local council terminated permits for these types of mobile food businesses.

When asked about the failed business, Justin's first comment was that it was the best learning experience of his life. His second comment was that it was a great motivator. It provided motivation "to avoid that sick feeling that rips at your guts when you know things are not going well and you can't pay your bills," to "face reality," and where necessary to "cut your losses" and get out.

He went on to say: "I am not sure that straight after the failure I was that motivated to get back into it. I knew I enjoyed business and was frustrated that I couldn't make it work, but I felt more like a failure than a 'success waiting to happen.' My confidence was hurt and I was looking for a lot more security. How was I ever [going] to buy a house? Have a family? I had few options and no clear vision, so when the opportunity came along to go back to university, I grabbed it with both hands. With the pizza van failure I knew I could work like a dog and get nowhere. I needed to have an edge. University gave me options."

Justin's second attempt at university had no resemblance to his first attempt. He had become an exceptional student with a passion to learn and a passion to apply that knowledge. He majored in accounting and his first job out of university was with Ernst & Young (an accounting consulting firm). Accounting education and experience provided valuable knowledge about the inner workings of a business (with the auditing department) and the numbers reflecting the entrepreneurial decision-making process (in the business services and tax department). Over and above the opportunity to build important knowledge, Justin also chose accounting as the foundation from which to relaunch his entrepreneurial career because it gave him legitimacy with others in the business community (including potential stakeholders), helped him build a large network with influential people, and would act as an income "insurance policy" if his business failed.

One of Justin's accounting clients was a slipway (ship building and repair) business. From this work he was able to gain considerable industry-specific knowledge and an industry-specific network. This newly formed network provided early information about a business in the industry that might come on the market, and his new industry-specific knowledge meant that he could assess the value of this opportunity. He bought the business and is growing it while simultaneously improving its efficiency. The success of the business has even exceeded his own dreams for it at the time of purchase.

He has recently gone into partnership with his brother Warwick and purchased another business—a metal-working business. This business has considerable potential in its own right but has the added benefit of synergies with the slipway. This business is also on the path to success. When I think of the "ideal" entrepreneur, I think of Justin. Justin is an optimistic and charismatic entrepreneur who attacks his tasks and life with confidence and passion (with the possible exception of answering questions about his success). He has control over the money side of his businesses but also has the flexibility to allow his strategies to emerge.

NEW ENTRY

new entry Offering a new product to an established or new market, offering an established product to a new market, or creating a new organization

One of the essential acts of entrepreneurship is new entry. *New entry* refers to (1) offering a new product to an established or new market, (2) offering an established product to a new market, or (3) creating a new organization (regardless of whether the product or the market is new to competitors or customers).[1] Whether associated with a new product, a new market, and/or a new organization, "newness" is like a double-edged sword. On the one hand, newness represents something rare, which can help differentiate a firm from its competitors. On the other hand, newness creates a number of challenges for entrepreneurs. For example, newness can increase entrepreneurs' uncertainty over the value of a new product and place a greater strain on the resources necessary for successful exploitation.[2]

FIGURE 13.1 Entrepreneurial Strategy: The Generation and Exploitation of New Entry Opportunities

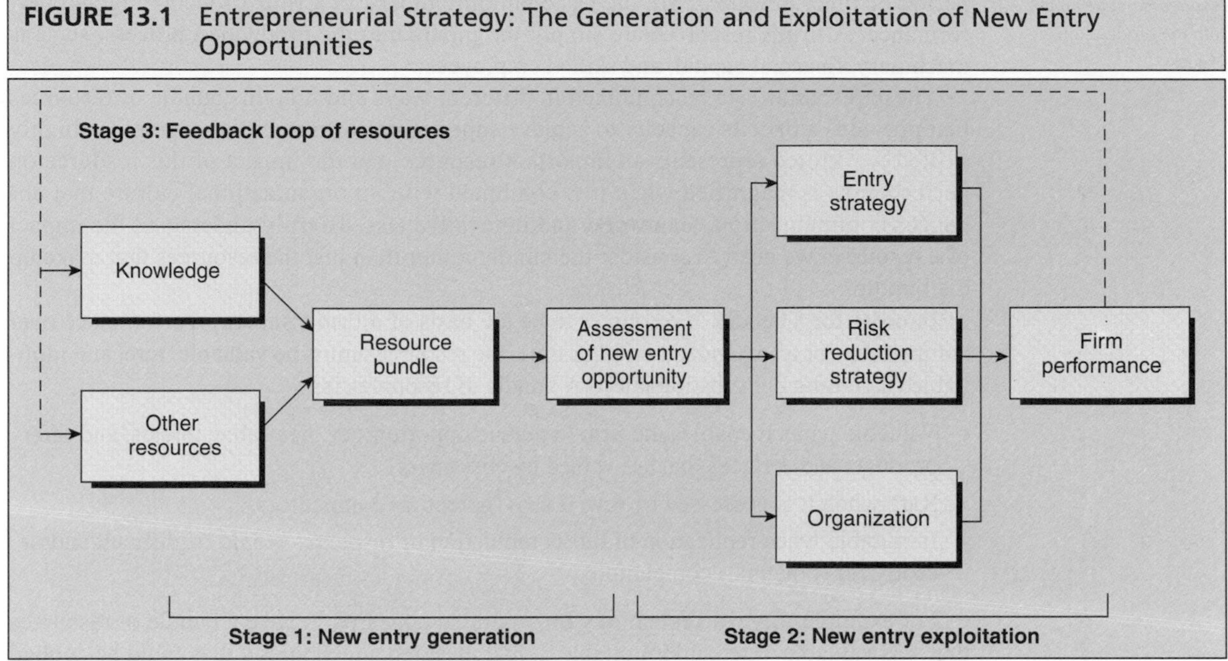

entrepreneurial strategy The set of decisions, actions, and reactions that first generate, and then exploit over time, a new entry

Entrepreneurial strategy represents the set of decisions, actions, and reactions that first generate, and then exploit over time, a new entry in a way that maximizes the benefits of newness and minimizes its costs.

Figure 13.1 illustrates the important elements of an entrepreneurial strategy. An entrepreneurial strategy has three key stages: (1) the generation of a new entry opportunity, (2) the exploitation of a new entry opportunity, and (3) a feedback loop from the culmination of a new entry generation and exploitation back to stage 1. The generation of a new entry is the result of a combination of knowledge and other resources into a bundle that its creators hope will be valuable, rare, and difficult for others to imitate. If the decision is that the new entry is sufficiently attractive that it warrants exploitation, then firm performance is dependent upon the entry strategy; the risk reduction strategy; the way the firm is organized; and the competence of the entrepreneur, management team, and the firm.

Although the remainder of this chapter focuses on stages 1 and 2, we should not underestimate the importance of the feedback loop of stage 3 because an entrepreneur cannot rely on the generation and exploitation of only one new entry; rather, long-run performance is dependent upon the ability to generate and exploit numerous new entries. If the firm does rely on only one new entry, then as the life cycle for the product enters maturity and declines, so goes the life cycle of the organization.

GENERATION OF A NEW ENTRY OPPORTUNITY

Resources as a Source of Competitive Advantage

When a firm engages in a new entry, it is hoped that this new entry will provide the firm with a sustainable competitive advantage. Understanding where a sustainable competitive advantage comes from will provide some insight into how entrepreneurs can generate new entries that are likely to provide the basis for high firm performance over an extended

resources The inputs into the production process

period of time. *Resources* are the basic building blocks to a firm's functioning and performance. A firm's resources are simply the inputs into the production process, such as machinery, financial capital, and skilled employees.

These resources can be combined in different ways and it is this bundle of resources that provides a firm its capacity to achieve superior performance. For example, a highly skilled workforce represents an important resource, but the impact of this resource on performance is magnified when it is combined with an organizational culture that enhances communication, teamwork, and innovativeness. To truly understand the impact of a resource, we need to consider the bundle rather than just the resources that make up the bundle.

In order for a bundle of resources to be the basis of a firm's superior performance over competitors for an extended period of time, the resources must be valuable, rare, and inimitable (including nonsubstitutable).[3] A bundle of resources is:[4]

- Valuable when it enables the firm to pursue opportunities, neutralize threats, and offer products and services that are valued by customers.
- Rare when it is possessed by few, if any, (potential) competitors.
- Inimitable when replication of this combination of resources would be difficult and/or costly for (potential) competitors.

For example, Breeze Technology Incorporated appeared to have a bundle of resources that was valuable, rare, and inimitable. It had invented a technology that could be applied to the ventilation of athletic shoes to reduce foot temperature. A ventilated athletic shoe is likely to be highly valued by customers because people have problems with their current athletic shoes—their feet get hot and sweat, which in turn causes blisters, fungal infections, and odor. (I know my wife would be happy for me to wear shoes that reduced foot odor.) The product was also valuable to the newly formed management team of Breeze Technology because it provided the means of entering into a large and highly lucrative market.

This technology also appeared to be rare and inimitable. It was rare because others had failed to adequately ventilate people's feet. Some had attempted to blow air into the shoe and found that it only increased foot temperature. Current footwear attempted to passively ventilate feet but found that the porous uppers on shoes were relatively ineffective at this task and also made the shoe vulnerable to water intrusion—that is, if you stepped into a puddle, your feet would get wet. Breeze Technology pumped air out of the shoe, which was a novel and unobvious approach to shoe ventilation.

Given that this technology was deemed likely to be valuable to customers, novel, and unobvious, it was provided a patent. The purpose of the patent is to protect the owner of the technology from people imitating the technology. Along with other intellectual property protection such as copyrights and trademarks, Breeze Technology had a new product that could be protected from competition (at least for a period of time). Therefore Breeze Technology had a bundle of resources that was valuable, rare, and inimitable. The important questions are, then: (1) where does this valuable, rare, and difficult-to-imitate bundle of resources come from? and (2) how can it best be exploited?

Creating a Resource Bundle That Is Valuable, Rare, and Inimitable

entrepreneurial resource The ability to obtain, and then recombine, resources into a bundle that is valuable, rare, and inimitable

The ability to obtain, and then recombine, resources into a bundle that is valuable, rare, and inimitable represents an important *entrepreneurial resource*. Knowledge is the basis of this entrepreneurial resource, which in itself is valuable. This type of knowledge is built up over time through experience, and it resides in the mind of the entrepreneur and in the

AS SEEN IN *ENTREPRENEUR* MAGAZINE

ELEVATOR PITCH FOR PROJECT ALABAMA

A wealthy friend has asked you to keep your eye out for attractive businesses in which she can invest. Your wealthy friend is very busy and you only want to introduce those businesses that are genuinely attractive. After hearing the following pitch, would you introduce Natalie and Enrico to your wealthy friend?

Entrepreneurs Natalie Chanin (41) and Enrico Marone-Cinzano (39), co-founders of Project Alabama in Florence, Alabama

Description Clothing company that largely uses recycled materials

Start-Up 2000 for $20,000

Sales Projecting $1.5 million in 2003

Helping Hands Heading to a party one night, Chanin hand-sewed a T-shirt and was hooked. With a costume design and fashion stylist background, Chanin joined forces with co-founder Marone-Cinzano, a businessman with experience in finance and marketing. She was unable to find a manufacturer in New York to do the handwork—her collection's resemblance to quilting inspired Chanin to return to her native Alabama and find "quilting circles" that could lend a hand (she now lives in both New York and Alabama, but spends most of her time in Alabama).

Recycled Goods Project Alabama's growth necessitates branching out to include new materials, but the core of the collection is made from recycled cotton jersey T-shirts. Retailing for $250 to $4,000, their target has always been high-end. "We made a conscious effort to contact those type of stores," explains Chanin. "Luckily, we had some of the world's best stores buy from the beginning, like Barneys New York and Browns in London."

Supplies Needed "Project Alabama consists of two components: the use of recycled materials and the quality of handwork," says Chanin, speaking proudly of the 120 women who subcontract stitchwork. "The kind of pride they have in each and every piece is rare."

Source: Reprinted with permission of Entrepreneur Media, Inc., "Natalie Chanin and Enrico Marone-Cinzano," by April Y. Pennington, February 2003, *Entrepreneur* magazine: www.entrepreneur.com.

collective mind of management and employees. To a large extent such an experience is idiosyncratic—unique to the life of the individual—and therefore can be considered rare. Furthermore, it is typically difficult to communicate this knowledge to others, which makes it all the more difficult for (potential) competitors to replicate such knowledge.

Therefore, knowledge is important for generating a bundle of resources that will lead to the creation of a new venture with a long and prosperous life. Does this mean that only highly experienced managers and/or firms will typically generate these opportunities for new entry? On the contrary, the evidence suggests that it is the outsiders that come up with the most radical innovations. For example, the pioneers of mountain bikes were biking enthusiasts, and it was quite a considerable time before the industry giants, such as Schwinn and Huffy, reacted to the trend.[5]

It appears that the existing manufacturers of bikes had difficulty "thinking outside the box" or they had little incentive to do so. Notice that those who did invent the mountain bike were bike enthusiasts. They had knowledge about current technology and the problems that customers (themselves included) had with the current technology under certain circumstances. This knowledge was unique and based upon personal experience. It was this knowledge that provided the basis for their innovation.

Those wishing to generate an innovation need to look to the unique experiences and knowledge within themselves and their team. This sort of knowledge is unlikely to be learned in a textbook or in class, because then everyone would have it and what would be unique about that? Knowledge that is particularly relevant to the generation of new entries is that which is related to the market and technology.

market knowledge Possession of information, technology, know-how, and skills that provide insight into a market and its customers

Market Knowledge *Market knowledge* refers to the entrepreneur's possession of information, technology, know-how, and skills that provide insight into a market and its customers. Being knowledgeable about the market and customers enables the entrepreneur to gain a deeper understanding of the problems that customers have with the market's existing products. In essence the entrepreneur shares some of the same knowledge that customers have about the use and performance of products. From this shared knowledge, entrepreneurs are able to bring together resources in a way that provides a solution to customers' dissatisfaction.

In this case, the entrepreneur's market knowledge is deeper than the knowledge that could be gained through market research. Market research, such as surveys, has limited effectiveness because it is often difficult for customers to articulate the underlying problems they have with a product or service. Entrepreneurs who lack this intimate knowledge of the market, and of customers' attitudes and behaviors, are less likely to recognize or create attractive opportunities for new products and/or new markets.

The importance of this knowledge to the generation of a new entry is best illustrated by returning to the example of the invention of the mountain bike. These guys were bike enthusiasts and therefore were aware of the problems that they personally encountered, as well as the problems their friends encountered, in using bikes that relied on the current technology. It could be that these individuals were using their bikes in a way that was not anticipated by the bike manufacturers, such as taking them off-road and exploring rough terrain.

Market research would not likely have revealed this information about deficiencies in the current technology. It is difficult for people to articulate the need for something that does not exist. Besides, the manufacturers may have dismissed any information that they received. For example, "Of course the frame broke, this idiot was going 30 miles per hour down a stony hiking track." It was because these bike enthusiasts had an intimate knowledge of the market and customers' attitudes and behaviors that they were able to bring together resources in a way that provided a solution to customers' dissatisfaction—the mountain bike represented a solution and opened up a new market.

technological knowledge Possession of information, technology, know-how, and skills that provide insight into ways to create new knowledge

Technological Knowledge *Technological knowledge* is also a basis for generating new entry opportunities. Technological knowledge refers to the entrepreneur's possession of information, technology, know-how, and skills that provide insight into ways to create new knowledge. This technological knowledge might lead to a technology that is the basis for a new entry, even though its market applicability is unobvious.

For example, the laser was invented over 30 years ago and has led to many new entry opportunities. Those with expertise in laser technology are more able to adapt and improve the technology and in doing so open up a potentially attractive market. Laser technology has been adapted to navigation, precision measurement, music recording, and fiber optics. In surgery, the laser technology has been used to repair detached retinas and reverse blindness. These new entries were derived from the knowledge of laser technology, and market applicability was often of only secondary consideration.[6]

Similarly, the initial reaction to the invention of the computer was that its market was rather limited. If we investigate the application of the computer to one industry we can see the sort of new markets that have arisen from the further development of the computer technology. Computers are used in the aviation industry to conduct aerodynamic research to find efficient aircraft designs; in the automation of the navigation and flying functions of pilots, such as the autopilot; in the radar system used by air traffic control; in flight simulators used by airlines to train pilots on new aircraft; and in the computer network system for ticketing and tracking baggage (although my bags still seem to get lost).[7]

Therefore, technological knowledge has led to technological advancement that in many ways has created new markets rather than generating a technology to satisfy an unmet market need. Often these technologies were created by people wanting to advance knowledge, without concern for commercial applicability. Other times, a technology has been invented for a specific and narrow purpose only to find out later that the technology has broader implications. For example, Tang, freeze-dried coffee, Velcro, and Teflon were all products invented for the space program but were found to have broader applications.

In sum, a resource bundle is the basis for a new entry. This resource bundle is created from the entrepreneur's market knowledge, technological knowledge, and other resources. The new entry has the potential of being a source of sustained superior firm performance if the resource bundle underlying the new entry is valuable, rare, and difficult for others to imitate.

ASSESSING THE ATTRACTIVENESS OF A NEW ENTRY OPPORTUNITY

Having created a new resource combination, the entrepreneur needs to determine whether it is in fact valuable, rare, and inimitable by assessing whether the new product and/or the new market are sufficiently attractive to be worth exploiting and developing. This depends on the level of information on a new entry and the entrepreneur's willingness to make a decision without perfect information.

Information on a New Entry

Prior Knowledge and Information Search The prior market and technological knowledge used to create the potential new entry can also be of benefit in assessing the attractiveness of a particular opportunity. More prior knowledge means that the entrepreneur starts from a position of less ignorance about the assessment task at hand. That is, less information needs to be collected in order to reach a threshold where the entrepreneur feels comfortable making a decision to exploit or not to exploit.

Knowledge can be increased by searching for information that will shed some light on the attractiveness of this new entry opportunity. Interestingly, the more knowledge the entrepreneur has, the more efficient the search process. For example, entrepreneurs who have a large knowledge base in a particular area will know where to look for information and will be able to quickly process this information into knowledge useful for the assessment.

The search process itself represents a dilemma for an entrepreneur. On the one hand, a longer search period allows the entrepreneur time to gain more information about whether this new entry does represent a resource bundle that is valuable, rare, and difficult for others to imitate. The more information the entrepreneur has, the more accurately she or he can assess whether sufficient customer demand for the product can be generated and whether the product can be protected from imitation by competitors.

However, there are costs associated with searching for this information—costs in both money and time. For example, rather than deciding to exploit a new product, an entrepreneur may decide to search for more information in order to make a more accurate assessment of whether this new product is an attractive one for her; but while this entrepreneur continues with her information search, the opportunity may cease to be available.

window of opportunity The period of time when the environment is favorable for entrepreneurs to exploit a particular new entry

Window of Opportunity The dynamic nature of the viability of a particular new entry can be described in terms of a *window of opportunity*. When the window is open, the environment is favorable for entrepreneurs to exploit a particular new product or to enter a new market with an existing product; but the window of opportunity may close, leaving the environment for exploitation unfavorable. An example of a window of opportunity closing is when another entrepreneur has entered the industry and erected substantial barriers to entry and to imitation. While more information is desirable, the time spent in collecting additional information increases the likelihood that the window of opportunity will close.

Comfort with Making a Decision under Uncertainty

The trade-off between more information and the likelihood that the window of opportunity will close provides a dilemma for entrepreneurs. This dilemma involves a choice of which error they prefer to commit: Do they prefer to commit an error of commission over an error of omission, or vice versa?[8] An *error of commission* occurs from the decision to pursue this new entry opportunity only to find out later that the entrepreneur had overestimated his or her ability to create customer demand and/or to protect the technology from imitation by competitors. The costs to the entrepreneur were derived from acting on the perceived opportunity.

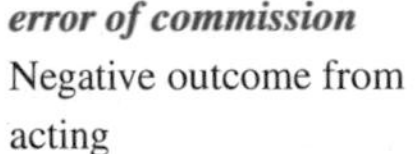

error of commission
Negative outcome from acting

error of omission
Negative outcome from not acting

An *error of omission* occurs from the decision not to act on the new entry opportunity, only to find out later that the entrepreneur had underestimated his or her ability to create customer demand and/or to protect the technology from imitation by competitors. In this case, the entrepreneur must live with the knowledge that he let an attractive opportunity slip through his fingers.

Decision to Exploit or Not to Exploit the New Entry

As illustrated in Figure 13.2, the decision to exploit or not to exploit the new entry opportunity depends on whether the entrepreneur has what she or he believes to be sufficient information to make a decision, and on whether the window is still open for this new entry

FIGURE 13.2 The Decision to Exploit or Not to Exploit the New Entry Opportunity

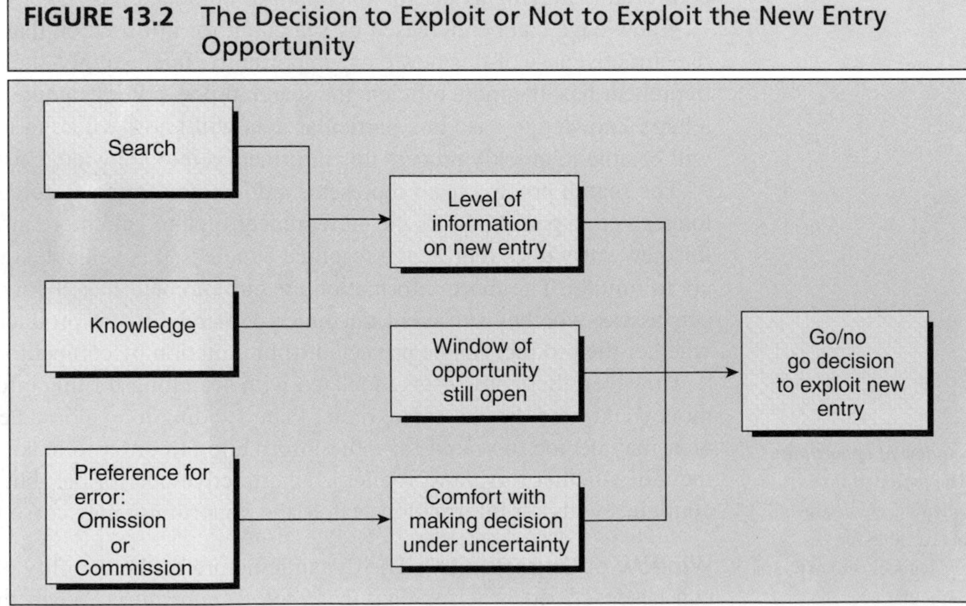

opportunity. A determination by an entrepreneur that she has sufficient information depends on the stock of information (accumulated through search and from prior knowledge) and on the level of comfort that this entrepreneur has with making the decision without perfect information (which depends on a preference of one type of error over another).

assessment of a new entry's attractiveness Determining whether the entrepreneur believes she or he can make the proposed new entry work

It is important to realize that the *assessment of a new entry's attractiveness* is less about whether this opportunity "really" exists or not and more about whether the entrepreneur believes he or she can make it work—that is, create the market demand, efficiently produce the product, build a reputation, and develop customer loyalty and other switching costs. Making it work depends, in part, on entrepreneurial strategies.

ENTRY STRATEGY FOR NEW ENTRY EXPLOITATION

The common catch phrase used by entrepreneurs when asked about their source of competitive advantage is, "Our competitive advantage comes from being first. We are the first movers." Whether they are the first to introduce a new product and/or the first to create a new market, these claims have some merit. Being first can result in a number of advantages that can enhance performance. These include:

- *First movers develop a cost advantage*. Being first to offer and sell a particular product to a specific market means that the first mover can begin movement down the "experience curve." The experience curve captures the idea that as a firm produces a greater volume of a particular product, the cost of producing each unit of that product goes down. Costs are reduced because the firm can spread its fixed costs over a greater number of units (economies of scale) as well as learn by trial and error over time (learning curve) to improve products and processes.[9]
- *First movers face less competitive rivalry*. Although first movers might initially have only a few customers, if they have correctly assessed the opportunity, the market will grow rapidly. Even though competitors will enter this growing market, the market share lost to new competitors will be more than compensated for by market growth. In fact, in the growth stage of the market, firms are more concerned with keeping up with demand than they are with taking actions, such as price cutting, to take market share from others.
- *First movers can secure important channels*. First movers have the opportunity to select and develop strong relationships with the most important suppliers and distribution channels. This may represent a barrier to those considering entry and may force those who do eventually enter to use inferior suppliers and distribution outlets.
- *First movers are better positioned to satisfy customers*. First movers have the chance to (1) select and secure the most attractive segments of a market, and (2) position themselves at the center of the market, providing an increased ability to recognize, and adapt to, changes in the market. In some cases, they may even (3) establish their product as the industry standard.
- *First movers gain expertise through participation*. First movers have the opportunity to (1) learn from the first generation of products and improve, for example, product design, manufacturing, and marketing; (2) monitor changes in the market that might be difficult or impossible to detect for those firms not participating in the market; and (3) build up their networks, which can provide early information about attractive opportunities. These learning opportunities may be available only to those participating in the market. In this case, knowledge is gained through learning-by-doing rather than through observing the practices of others (vicarous learning).

AS SEEN IN *ENTREPRENEUR* MAGAZINE

PROVIDE ADVICE TO AN ENTREPRENEUR ABOUT BEING MORE INNOVATIVE

When Neil Franklin began offering round-the-clock telephone customer service in 1998, customers loved it. The offering fit the strategic direction Franklin had in mind for Dataworkforce, his Dallas-based telecommunications-engineer staffing agency, so he invested in a phone system to route after-hours calls to his 10 employees' home and mobile phones. Today, Franklin, 38, has nearly 50 employees and continues to explore ways to improve Dataworkforce's service. Twenty-four-hour phone service has stayed, but other trials have not. One failure was developing individual Web sites for each customer. "We took it too far and spent $30,000, then abandoned it," Franklin recalls. A try at globally extending the brand by advertising in major world cities was also dropped. "It worked pretty well," Franklin says, "until you added up the cost."

Franklin's efforts are similar to an approach called a "portfolio of initiatives" strategy. The idea, according to Lowell Bryan, a principal in McKinsey & Co., the New York City consulting firm that developed it, is to always have a number of efforts under way to offer new products and services and attack new markets or otherwise implement strategies, and to actively manage these experiments so you don't miss an opportunity or overcommit to an unproven idea.

The portfolio of initiatives approach addresses a weakness of conventional business plans—that they make assumptions about uncertain future developments, such as market and technological trends, customer responses, sales, and competitor reactions. Bryan compares the portfolio of initiatives strategy to the ship convoys used in World War II to get supplies across oceans. By assembling groups of military and transport vessels and sending them in a mutually supportive group, planners could rely on at least some reaching their destination. In the same way, entrepreneurs with a portfolio of initiatives can expect some of them to pan out.

MAKING A PLAN

Three steps define the portfolio of initiatives approach. First, you search for initiatives in which you have or can readily acquire a familiarity advantage—meaning you know more than competitors about a business. You can gain familiarity advantage using low-cost pilot programs and experiments, or by partnering with more knowledgeable allies. Avoid businesses in which you can't acquire a familiarity advantage, Bryan says.

After you identify familiarity-advantaged initiatives, begin investing in them using a disciplined, dynamic management approach. Pay attention to how initiatives relate to each other. They should be diverse enough that the failure of one won't endanger the others, but should also all fit into your overall strategic direction. Investments, represented by product development efforts, pilot programs, market tests, and the like, should start small and increase only as they prove themselves. Avoid overinvesting before initiatives have proved themselves. The third step is to pull the plug on initiatives that aren't working out, and step up investment in others. A portfolio of initiatives will work in any size company. Franklin pursues 20 to 30 at any time, knowing 90 percent won't pan out. "The main idea is to keep those initiatives running," he says. "If you don't, you're slowing down."

ADVICE TO AN ENTREPRENEUR

An entrepreneur who wants his firm to be more innovative has read the above article and comes to you for advice:

1. This whole idea of experimentation seems to make sense, but all these little failures can add up, and if there are enough of them, then this could lead to one big failure—the business going down the drain. How can I best get the advantages of experimentation in terms of innovation while also reducing the costs so that I don't run the risk of losing my business?
2. My employees, buyers, and suppliers like working for my company because we have a lot of wins. I am not sure how they will take it when our company begins to have a lot more failures (even if those failures are small)—it is a psychological thing. How can I handle this trade-off?
3. Even if everyone else accepts it, I am not sure how I will cope. When projects fail it hits me pretty hard emotionally. Is it just that I am not cut out for this type of approach?

Source: Reprinted with permission of Entrepreneur Media, Inc., "Worth a Try. Who Knows What's Going to Work? So Put as Many Ideas as You Can to the Test," by Mark Hendricks, February 2003, *Entrepreneur* magazine: www.entrepreneur.com.

FIGURE 13.3 Factors That Influence the Decision to Enter the Market Now or to Delay Entry

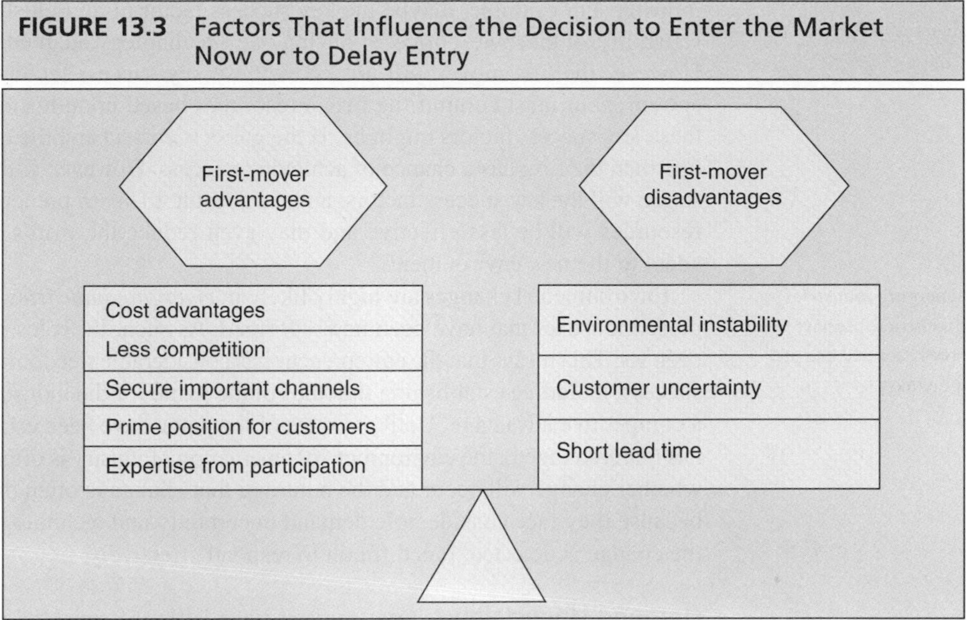

First movers do not always prosper. Many first movers with new products in new markets have been surpassed by firms that entered later. For example, in the market for video recorders the first movers were Ampex and Sony, yet they were surpassed by JVC and Matsushita. Similarly, in the ballpoint pen market the first movers (Reynolds and Eversharp) disappeared, whereas later entrants (Parker and Bic) have been highly successful.

As illustrated by the scales in Figure 13.3, there are forces pushing toward first-mover advantages, but there are also environmental conditions that can push a first mover toward performance disadvantages. When considering whether to be one of the first to enter with a new product and/or into a new market, entrepreneurs must determine whether the first-mover advantages outweigh the first-mover disadvantages. Such an assessment depends on (1) the stability of the environment surrounding the entry, (2) the ability of the entrepreneur to educate customers, and (3) the ability of the entrepreneur to erect barriers to entry and imitation in order to extend the firm's lead time. We now explore each of these influences.

Environmental Instability and First-Mover (Dis)Advantages

The performance of a firm depends on the fit between its bundle of resources and the external environment. If there is a good fit between its resources and the external environment, then the firm will be rewarded with superior performance; however, if the fit is poor, then performance will also be poor. For example, if the entrepreneur offers a new product that has attributes that the market does not value, then there is a poor fit between the firm's current product offerings and the external environment and performance will be poor.

key success factors The requirements that any firm must meet in order to successfully compete in a particular industry

To obtain a good fit with the external environment, the entrepreneur must first determine the key success factors of the industry being targeted for entry. *Key success factors* are the requirements that any firm must meet in order to successfully compete in a particular industry. For example, maybe the key success factor of an industry is superior service, or reliability, or the lowest price, or having one's technology adapted as the industry standard. However the first mover will not know these key success factors in advance; rather, the entrepreneur must commit the firm's resources based upon his or her best guess of what these key success factors might be. If the guess is correct and the environment remains stable, then the firm has a chance of achieving success. However, if the environment changes, so too will the key success factors, and, as a result, the entrepreneur's prior commitment of resources will be less effective and may even reduce the firm's ability to recognize and adapt to the new environment.

emerging industries
Industries that have been newly formed and are growing

Environmental changes are highly likely in *emerging industries*. Emerging industries are those industries that have been newly formed. As such, the rules of the game have not yet been set. This means that the entrepreneur has considerable freedom in how he or she achieves success, including establishing the rules of the game for the industry such that the firm is at a competitive advantage. Until the rules of the game have been established and the industry has matured (aged), the environment of an emerging industry is often changing. Determining whether change will occur and the nature of that change is often difficult for entrepreneurs because they face considerable demand uncertainty and technological uncertainty. Even if the change is detected, it is difficult to respond effectively.

demand uncertainty
Considerable difficulty in accurately estimating the potential size of the market, how fast it will grow, and the key dimensions along which it will grow

Demand Uncertainty First movers have little information upon which to estimate the potential size of the market and how fast it will grow. Such *demand uncertainty* makes it difficult to estimate future demand, which has important implications for new venture performance as both overestimating and underestimating demand can negatively impact performance. By overestimating demand, the entrepreneur will suffer the costs associated with overcapacity (there was no need to build such a large factory, for instance) and will find that the market may be so small that it cannot sustain the entrepreneur's business. By underestimating market demand, the entrepreneur will suffer the costs of undercapacity, such as not being able to satisfy existing and new customers and losing them to competitors, or will face the additional costs of incrementally adding capacity.

Demand uncertainty also makes it difficult to predict the key dimensions along which the market will grow. For example, customers' needs and tastes may change as the market matures. If the entrepreneur is unaware of these changes (or is incapable of adapting to them), then there is an opportunity for competitors to provide superior value to the customers. For example, as the personal computer industry matured, the key success factors changed from reputation for quality to being the low-cost provider. Dell was able to create a business model that enabled it to sell personal computers at a low price. Those that were late to adapt to the change in customer demand and continued to rely primarily on their reputation for quality were surpassed by Dell.

Entrepreneurs that delay entry have the opportunity to learn from the actions of first movers without the need of incurring the same costs. For example, Toyota delayed entry into the small-car market of the United States and was able to reduce demand uncertainty by surveying customers of the market leader (Volkswagen) and using this information to produce a product that better satisfied customers.[10] Therefore, followers have the advantage of more information about market demand. They also have more information over long-run customer preferences because the additional time before entry means that the market is more mature and customer preferences are more stable. Therefore, when demand is unstable and unpredictable, first-mover advantages may be outweighed by first-mover disadvantages and the entrepreneur should consider delaying entry.

Technological Uncertainty First movers often must make a commitment to a new technology. There are a number of uncertainties surrounding a new technology, such as whether the technology will perform as expected and whether an alternate technology will be introduced that leapfrogs the current technology. If the technology does not perform as expected, the entrepreneur will incur a number of costs that will negatively impact performance, for example, damage to the entrepreneur's (and his or her firm's) reputation and also the additional R&D and production costs incurred by making necessary changes to the technology.

Even if the technology works as expected, there is the possibility that a superior technology might be introduced that provides later entrants a competitive advantage. For example, Docutel provided almost all the automatic teller machines in 1974. However, when technology became available that allowed customers to electronically transfer funds, companies such as Honeywell, IBM, and Burroughs were in a position to adopt the new technology and better satisfy customer demands. As a result, Docutel's market share dropped to 10 percent in just four years.[11]

technological uncertainty Considerable difficulty in accurately assessing whether the technology will perform and whether alternate technologies will emerge and leapfrog over current technologies

Delayed entry provides entrepreneurs with the opportunity to reduce *technological uncertainty*. For example, they can reduce technological uncertainty by learning from the first mover's R&D program. This could involve activities such as reverse engineering the first mover's products. This provides a source of technological knowledge that can be used to imitate the first mover's product (unless there is intellectual property protection) or to improve upon the technology. Delayed entry also provides the opportunity to observe and learn from the actions (and mistakes) of the first mover. For example, a first mover may enter a particular market segment only to find out that there is insufficient demand to sustain the business. The later entrant can learn from this failure and can avoid market segments that have proved themselves to be unattractive. Therefore, when technological uncertainty is high, first-mover advantages may be outweighed by first-mover disadvantages and the entrepreneur should consider delaying entry.

Adaptation Changes in market demand and technology do not necessarily mean that first movers cannot prosper. They do mean that the entrepreneur must adapt to the new environmental conditions. Such changes are difficult. The entrepreneur will likely find it difficult to move away from the people and systems that brought initial success and toward new configurations requiring changes to employees' roles and responsibilities as well as changes to systems. In other words, the organization has an inertia that represents a force for continuation that resists change. For example, Medtronics was the market leader in heart pacemakers but lost its position after it was slow to change from its existing technology to a new lithium-based technology. A new entrant, unconstrained by organizational inertia, was able to exploit and penalize Medtronics for its tardiness.[12]

In addition, the entrepreneurial attributes of persistence and determination, which are so beneficial when the new venture is on the "right course," can inhibit the ability of the entrepreneur to detect, and implement, change. For example, there is a tendency for entrepreneurs to escalate commitment; that is, when faced with a new technology, the entrepreneur commits more resources to his or her current technology and reinforces the initial strategic direction, rather than adopting the new technology and changing strategic direction,[13] which has the effect of accelerating the firm's demise. Therefore, adaptation to changes in the external environment is important for all firms (especially first movers), but is often a very difficult task to conduct in practice.

Customers' Uncertainty and First-Mover (Dis)Advantages

uncertainty for customers Customers may have considerable difficulty in accurately assessing whether the new product or service provides value for them

Whether introducing a new product into an established market or an established product into a new market, the entry involves an element of newness. Embedded in this newness is *uncertainty for customers*. They may be uncertain about how to use the product and whether it will perform as expected. Even if it does perform, they may wonder to what extent its performance provides benefits over and above the products that are currently being used. Customers, like most people, are uncertainty averse, which means that even if the potential benefits of the new product are superior to existing products, customers may still not switch from the old to the new because of the uncertainties described above. Therefore, offering a superior product is not sufficient to enable a first mover to make sales; the entrepreneur must also reduce customer uncertainties.

To do this, the entrepreneur can offer informational advertising that, for example, provides customers with information about how the product performs and articulates the product's benefits. The entrepreneur may even use comparison marketing to highlight how the product's benefits outweigh those of substitute products. If this approach works, customers will be more likely to switch to the firm's product. The "home shopping" channels on television provide numerous examples of this informational advertising. For example, an adverstisement describes a set of plastic bags into which clothes (or other things), may be inserted, and the air within the bags evacuated (using a vacuum cleaner), which substantially reduces the volume of the clothes and allows more to be packed into a suitcase (so much so that the weight of the case exceeds one's ability to lift it, as I learned by experience).

However, providing customers with information on the performance of a new product does not always work. When the new product is highly innovative, as are the products that create a new market, the customers may lack a frame of reference for processing this information.[14] For example, products developed for the purpose of national defense and for other high-technology government purposes may provide an opportunity for new entry but require that customers be given a context for understanding their application. Teflon, developed for use in construction of the space shuttle, required customers to develop a new frame of reference before they could understand how it performed as a nonstick surface in frying pans and the benefits to them from this surface.[15] Therefore, entrepreneurs may be faced with the challenging task of creating a frame of reference within the potential customers before providing informational advertising.

Potential customers' uncertainty may also stem from the broader context in which the product is to be used. For example, even if the potential customers understand how the product performs, they are unlikely to purchase a product until they are convinced that the product is consistent with enabling products, systems, and knowledge. For example, a customer may know that a new software package provides more powerful spreadsheet functions and at a lower price but will remain reluctant to purchase the new product until she or he knows how long it will take to learn how to use the new software. In this circumstance, the entrepreneur can educate customers through demonstration and documentation on how to use the product. This could include an extensive tutorial as part of the software package as well as a free "help line."

Those that decide to enter later face a market that is more mature and one in which customers' uncertainties have already been substantially reduced by those who pioneered the market. In essence, by delaying entry into a market that requires considerable education, the entrepreneur may be able to receive a free ride on the investments made by the first movers.

However, it still may pay to be a first mover in this type of market if the educational effort can be used for the firm's advantage rather than to the advantage of the industry as a whole. For example, education may direct customer preferences in ways that will give the firm an advantage over potential customers (e.g., it may create an industry standard around the firm's products); it might enable the entrepreneur to build a reputation as "founder," encouraging customer loyalty; and it could benefit the company through the erection of other barriers to entry and imitation. We now explore the role of barriers to entry and imitation in influencing the performance of an entrepreneur's entry strategy.

Lead Time and First-Mover (Dis)Advantages

Being first to market might provide some initial advantages, but unless the entrepreneur can stop or retard potential competitors from entering the industry and offering similar products, the initial advantage will be quickly eroded, diminishing firm performance. Entry barriers provide the first mover (and nobody else) with the opportunity to operate in the industry for a grace period under conditions of limited competition (although the firm must still battle for customers with firms that offer substitute products). This grace period represents the first mover's lead time.

lead time The grace period in which the first mover operates in the industry under conditions of limited competition

The *lead time* gives the entrepreneur a period of limited competition to best prepare the firm for when competition does increase. This preparation could involve a concerted effort to influence the direction in which the market develops to the advantage of the first mover. For example, during the lead time the entrepreneur can use marketing to define quality in the minds of existing and potential customers—a definition of quality that is highly consistent with the entrepreneur's products.

Lead time can be extended if the first mover can erect barriers to entry. Important barriers to entry are derived from relationships with key stakeholders, which may dissuade entry by (potential) competitors. This can be done by:

Building customer loyalties. First movers need to establish their firms and their products in the minds of their customers and thus build customer loyalty. Such customer loyalty will make it more difficult and more costly for competitors to enter the market and take the first mover's customers. Loyalty is sometimes established when customers associate the industry with the first mover. For example, Japanese beer drinkers associated "super-dry beer" with the pioneer of a new form of beer, Asahi. This customer loyalty made it more difficult for others, including the dominant beer producer (Kirin), to enter the super-dry market and gain market share.

switching costs The costs that must be borne by customers if they are to stop purchasing from the current supplier and begin purchasing from another

Building switching costs. First movers need to develop *switching costs* in an effort to lock in existing customers. This is a mechanism by which customer loyalty is enhanced. Reward programs, such as frequent flyer points with a particular airline, establish for the customer a financial and/or emotional attachment to the first mover, which makes it costly for the customer to switch to a competitor.

Protecting product uniqueness. If the uniqueness of the product is a source of advantage over potential competitors, then first movers need to take actions to maintain that uniqueness. Intellectual property protection can take the form of patents, copyrights, trademarks, and trade secrets (detailed in Chapter 6).

Securing access to important sources of supply and distribution. First movers that are able to develop exclusive relationships with key sources of supply and/or key distribution channels will force potential entrants to use less attractive alternatives or even to develop their own. For example, Commercial Marine Products was the

DO THE RIGHT THING

Smart Entrepreneurs Are Doing Well by Doing Good: Charlie Wilson is trying to run an ethical business. He's made social responsibility part of the mission statement at his $1.6 million Houston-based salvage company, SeaRail International Inc. And he's made "self-actualization"—not wealth—his ultimate goal as an entrepreneur.

But don't mistake Wilson for some moralistic stick-in-the-mud. It's all about success. "Ethics is what's spearheading our growth," says Wilson. "It creates an element of trust, familiarity and predictability in the business. We're in an industry where a lot of people cut corners. I just don't think that's good for business. You don't get a good reputation doing things that way. And eventually, customers don't want to do business with you."

For years, ethics and business had a rocky marriage. Ask entrepreneurs to talk about ethics, and the responses ranged from scorn to ridicule. Here are folks who—by definition—like breaking the rules. Suggesting that entrepreneurs should follow a predefined set of edicts was about as popular as asking them to swear off electricity.

But this may be changing. Whether people are hung over from the freewheeling '80s or reflective about the coming millennium, talk about values, integrity, and responsibility is not only becoming acceptable in the business community, it's almost required.

"This looks just like the quality movement of 20 years ago," says Frank Walker, chairman of Indianapolis-based Walker Information Inc., a research and consulting company that tracks customer satisfaction and business ethics. "Customers need a way to differentiate one firm from another." For years, the dominant point of differentiation has been quality. Now, says Walker, "Everyone can deliver quality, [so businesses] need to step up to a higher plane."

Are the nation's entrepreneurs ready to ascend to new heights of ethical literacy and compliance? Well, sort of. Although most entrepreneurs still aren't trying to unseat the likes of Socrates and Plato, many are giving considerable thought to improving their ethics, with hopes that doing good business will be good for business as well.

Source: Reprinted with permission of Entrepreneur Media, Inc., "Do the Right Thing," by Gayle Sato Stodder, August 1998, *Entrepreneur* magazine: www.entrepreneur.com.

first to find an infestation of a special kind of seaweed in Tasmania, Australia. This seaweed is called *wakame* and is a staple food for Japanese and Koreans. Commerical Marine Products was able to obtain an exclusive license to manage and harvest this area of the Tasmanian coast, the only known location in Australia (and possibly the Southern Hemisphere) where wakame was growing. Being first meant that Commercial Marine Products was able to secure the only source of supply.

These barriers to entry can reduce the amount of competition faced by the first mover. Because competition typically puts downward pressure on prices and may increase marketing costs, it usually results in reduced profit margins and a drop in overall profitability. However, competition is not always bad; sometimes it can enhance the firm's performance. Competition within an industry can have a positive effect on industry growth. For example, competition among firms encourages them to become efficient and innovative in order to create even more value in their products for customers. Increases in customer value (whether from increases in product quality, lower prices, or both) will mean that more customers will enter the new market. New customers might be added by entering international markets.

Therefore first movers need to keep in mind that they might win the battle by lowering the level of potential competition within an industry through the creation of barriers to entry but lose the war because insufficient customers are willing to substitute into the new industry. Under these conditions the first mover should consider allowing a number of competitors into the industry in order to share the pioneering costs and then working together to erect barriers to subsequent entry by potential competitors.

RISK REDUCTION STRATEGIES FOR NEW ENTRY EXPLOITATION

risk The probability of, and magnitude of, downside loss

A new entry involves considerable risk for the entrepreneur and his or her firm. *Risk* here refers to the probability, and magnitude, of downside loss,[16] which could result in bankruptcy. The risk of downside loss is partly derived from the entrepreneur's uncertainties over market demand, technological development, and the actions of competitors. Strategies can be used to reduce some or all of these uncertainties and thereby reduce the risk of downside loss. Two such strategies are market scope and imitation.

Market Scope Strategies

scope A choice about which customer groups to serve and how to serve them

Scope is a choice by the entrepreneur about which customer groups to serve and how to serve them.[17] The choice of market scope ranges from a narrow- to a broad-scope strategy and depends on the type of risk the entrepreneur believes is more important to reduce.

Narrow-Scope Strategy A narrow-scope strategy offers a small product range to a small number of customer groups in order to satisfy a particular need. The narrow scope can reduce the risk that the firm will face competition with larger, more established firms in a number of ways.

- A narrow-scope strategy focuses the firm on producing customized products, localized business operations, and high levels of craftsmanship. Such outcomes provide the basis for differentiating the firm from larger competitors who are oriented more toward mass production and the advantages that are derived from that volume. A narrow-scope strategy of product differentiation reduces competition with the larger established firms and allows the entrepreneur to charge premium prices.
- By focusing on a specific group of customers, the entrepreneur can build up specialized expertise and knowledge that provide an advantage over companies that are competing more broadly. For instance, the entrepreneur pursuing a narrow-scope strategy is in the best position to offer superior product quality, given his or her intimate knowledge of the product attributes customers desire most.
- The high end of the market typically represents a highly profitable niche that is well suited to those firms that can produce customized products, localized business operations, and high levels of craftsmanship. From the first point listed above, we know that firms pursuing a narrow-scope strategy are more likely to offer products and services with these attributes than are larger firms that are more interested in volume.

However, a narrow-scope strategy does not always provide protection against competition. For example, the firm may offer a product that the entrepreneur believes is of superior quality, yet customers may not value the so-called product improvements or, if they do perceive those improvements, they may be unwilling to pay a premium price for them, preferring to stick with the products currently being offered by the larger firms.

That is, the boundary between the market segment being targeted by the entrepreneur is not sufficiently clear from that of the mass market and thus provides little protection against competition.

Furthermore, if the market niche is attractive there is an incentive for the larger and more established firms (and all firms) to develop products and operations targeted at this niche. For example, a larger, more mass market–oriented firm might create a subsidiary to compete in this attractive market segment.

Although a narrow-scope strategy can sometimes reduce the risks associated with competition, this scope strategy is vulnerable to another type of risk: the risk that market demand does not materialize as expected and/or changes over time. For example, a narrow-scope strategy focuses on a single customer group (or a small number of customer groups), but if the market changes and decreases substantially the size and attractiveness of that market segment, then the firm runs a considerable risk of downside loss. Having a narrow-scope strategy is like putting all your eggs in one basket. If that basket is fundamentally flawed, then all the eggs will be dropped and broken. A broad-scope strategy, on the other hand, provides a way of managing demand uncertainty and thereby reducing an aspect of the entrepreneur's risk.

Broad-Scope Strategy A broad-scope strategy can be thought of as taking a "portfolio" approach to dealing with uncertainties about the attractiveness of different market segments. By offering a range of products across many different market segments, the entrepreneur can gain an understanding of the whole market by determining which products are the most profitable. Unsuccessful products (and market segments) can then be dropped and resources concentrated on those product markets that show the greatest promise. In essence, the entrepreneur can cope with market uncertainty by using a broad-scope strategy to learn about the market through a process of trial and error.[18]

The entrepreneur's ultimate strategy will emerge as a result of the information provided by this learning process. In contrast, a narrow-scope strategy requires the entrepreneur to have sufficient certainty about the market that he is willing to focus his resources on a small piece of the market, with few options to fall back on if the initial assessment about the product proves incorrect. Offering a range of products across a range of market segments means that a broad-scope strategy is opening the firm up to many different "fronts" of competition. The entrepreneur may need to compete with the more specialized firms within narrow market niches and simultaneously with volume producers in the mass market.

Therefore, a narrow-scope strategy offers a way of reducing some competition-related risks but increases the risks associated with market uncertainties. In contrast, a broad-scope strategy offers a way of reducing risks associated with market uncertainties but faces increased exposure to competition. The entrepreneur needs to choose the scope strategy that reduces the risk of greatest concern. For example, if the new entry is into an established market then competitors are well entrenched and ready to defend their market shares. Also the market demand is more stable and market research can inform the entrepreneur on the attractiveness of the new product with a particular group of customers. In this situation, where the risk of competition is great and market uncertainties are minimal, a narrow-scope strategy is more effective at risk reduction.

However, if new entry involves the creation of a new market or entry into an emerging market then competitors are more concerned with satisfying new customers entering the market than on stealing market share from others or retaliating against new entrants. Also there is typically considerable market uncertainty about which products are going to be winners and which are going to be losers. In this situation, a broad-scope strategy reduces the major risk, namely, risks associated with uncertainties over customer preferences.

Imitation Strategies

Why Do It? Imitation is another strategy for minimizing the risk of downside loss associated with new entry. Imitation involves copying the practices of other firms, whether those other firms are in the industry being entered or from related industries. This idea of using *imitation strategies* to improve firm performance at first appears inconsistent with the argument at the start of the chapter that superior performance arises from the qualities of being valuable, rare, and inimitable. An imitation strategy cannot be rare or inimitable.

imitation strategies
Copying the practices of other firms

Although this may be true, an imitation strategy can still enhance firm performance because a successful new entry does not need to be valuable, rare, and inimitable in terms of every aspect of the firm's operations. Rather, imitation of others' practices that are peripheral to the competitive advantage of the firm offers a number of advantages.

Entrepreneurs may simply find it easier to imitate the practices of a successful firm than to go through the process of a systematic and expensive search that still requires a decision based on imperfect information.[19] In essence, imitation represents a substitute for individual learning and is well illustrated by the following quote from the president of Rexhaul Industries (a firm that sells cheaper recreational vehicles than its competitors): "In this industry, we call it R&C: research and copy."[20]

Imitating some of the practices of established successful firms can help the entrepreneur develop the skills necessary to be successful in the industry, rather than attempting to work out which skills are required and develop these skills from scratch. This use of imitation allows the entrepreneur to quickly acquire the skills that will be rewarded by the industry without necessarily having to go through the process of first determining what those key success factors actually are. It is a mechanism that allows the entrepreneur to skip a step in the stages of solving a puzzle (or at least to delay the need, and the importance, of solving that particular step).

Imitation also provides organizational legitimacy. If the entrepreneur acts like a well-established firm, it is likely to be perceived by customers as well established. Imitation is a means of gaining status and prestige. Customers feel more comfortable doing business with firms that they perceive to be established and prestigious. This is particularly the case for service firms. For example, a new consulting firm will need to go out of its way to look like an established prestigious firm, even though some of its trappings (e.g., a prime location office, leather chairs and couches, and a well-tailored suit) put a strain on resources and are only incidental to the quality of the service.

Types of Imitation Strategies Franchising is an example of a new entry that focuses on imitation to reduce the risk of downside loss for the franchisee. A franchisee acquires the use of a "proven formula" for new entry from a franchisor. For example, an entrepreneur might enter the fast food industry by franchising a McDonald's store in a new geographic location. This entrepreneur is imitating the business practices of other McDonald's stores (in fact, imitation is mandatory) and benefits from an established market demand; an intellectual property–protected name and products; and access to knowledge of financial, marketing, and managerial issues.

This new entry is unique because it is the only McDonald's store in a dedicated geographical area (although it must compete with Burger King, KFC, etc). More broadly, this

McDonald's store is differentiated from potential competitors in the same geographic space. Much of the risk of new entry for the entrepreneur has been reduced through this imitation strategy (Chapter 16 discusses franchising in more detail).

Franchising is not the only imitation strategy. Some entrepreneurs will attempt to copy successful businesses. For example, new entry can involve copying products that already exist and attempting to build an advantage through minor variations. This form of imitation is often referred to as a *"me-too" strategy*. In other words, the successful firm occupies a prime position in the minds of customers, and now the imitator is there too and hopes to be considered by the customers. Variation often takes the form of making minor changes to the launch product being offered, taking an existing product or service (which is unprotected by intellectual property rights) to a new market not currently served, or delivering the product to customers in a different way.

"me-too" strategy Copying products that already exist and attempting to build an advantage through minor variations

Ice cream shops are an example of a "me-too" imitation strategy, where new entrants have imitated successful stores but have also been able to differentiate themselves from those already in the industry by offering some form of variation. We have seen competing ice cream shops imitate each other by offering similar shop layouts and locations (e.g., inside malls), the same choice of flavors and cones (e.g., waffle cones), and similar promotional strategies (such as "Taste before you buy"). Often the point of variation is simply the location of the store.

In the ice cream retail industry we have noticed that new entrants are increasingly relying on even greater levels of imitation to provide the necessary competitive advantage—more and more new entrants are entering into a franchise agreement with Baskin and Robbins, Häagen Dazs, or other international franchisors. These franchisors have introduced a national or global brand name and reputation (previously only regional), standardized operating procedures, interstore communication, and economies of scale in marketing.[21]

However, a "me-too" imitation strategy might be more difficult to successfully implement than first expected. The success of the firm being copied may depend on its underlying organizational knowledge and corporate culture. Peripheral activities may not produce the desired outcomes when used in a different organizational context. Furthermore, entrepreneurs are often legally prevented from other avenues of imitation, such as the use of registered trademarks and brand names.

Overall, an imitation strategy can potentially reduce the entrepreneur's costs associated with research and development, reduce customer uncertainty over the firm, and make the new entry look legitimate from day one. In pursuing an imitation strategy for new entry, the entrepreneur should focus on imitating those elements of the business that are not central to the firm's competitive advantage. These central aspects of advantage must be valuable, rare, and inimitable for the firm to achieve high performance over an extended period of time.

Managing Newness

New entry can occur through the creation of a new organization. The creation of a new organization offers some challenges not faced by entrepreneurs who manage established firms. These *liabilities of newness* arise from the following unique conditions.

liabilities of newness Negative implications arising from an organization's newness

- New organizations face costs in learning new tasks. It may take some time and training to customize employees' skills to the new tasks they are asked to perform.
- As people are assigned to the roles of the new organization, there will be some overlap or gaps in responsibilities. This will often cause conflict until the boundaries around particular roles are more formally set (once management has gained sufficient

knowledge to do so) and/or until they have been informally negotiated by the parties to the conflict.

- Communication within the organization occurs through both formal and informal channels. A new organization has not yet had the opportunity to develop informal structures, such as friendships and organizational culture. It takes time for a new firm to establish these informal structures.

Managing a new firm requires special attention to educating and training employees so that their knowledge and skills will develop quickly to meet the needs of their tasks, to facilitate conflicts over roles, and to foster social activities that will in turn quickly foster informal relationships and a functional corporate culture. If these liabilities of newness can be overcome, then the entrepreneur can benefit from some *assets of newness*. These assets acknowledge the advantages that a new organization has over a mature one, particularly in environments that are changing.

assets of newness Positive implications arising from an organization's newness

Although mature organizations have established routines, systems, and processes that increase the efficiency of their operations, these routines, systems, and processes can be a liability when there is a need for those firms to adapt to changes in their environment. Previous practices create a momentum along the same path, and redirection is difficult. Mature firms also find it difficult to attain new knowledge because their thoughts are narrowed by what has been done in the past and what they are good at rather than by the external environment and what is needed.

In contrast, new firms find that their lack of established routines, systems, and processes means that they have a clean slate, which gives them learning advantages over older firms.[22] They do not need to unlearn old knowledge and old habits in order to learn new knowledge and create thc new routines, systems, and processes that are more attuned with the changed environment.

A heightened ability to learn new knowledge represents an important source of competitive advantage that needs to be fostered by the entrepreneur. It is particularly advantageous in a continuously changing environment because the firm needs to incrementally build its strategy as it learns information while acting. Previous strategic planning will not be successful in such environments because the development of such an environment is not knowable in advance (unless the entrepreneur is extremely lucky).

Therefore, although entrepreneurs must be aware of, and manage, liabilities of newness, it is not all doom and gloom. Rather, new ventures have an important strategic advantage over their mature competitors, particularly in dynamic, changing environments. Entrepreneurs need to capitalize on these assets of newness by creating a learning organization that is flexible and able to accommodate this new knowledge in its future actions. This shifts the emphasis in understanding firm performance from a heavy reliance on strategic plans to greater emphasis on the strategic learning and flexibility of the entrepreneur and his or her management team.

IN REVIEW

SUMMARY

One of the essential acts of entrepreneurship is new entry—entry based on a new product, a new market, and/or a new organization. Entrepreneurial strategies represent the set of decisions, actions, and reactions that first generate, and then exploit over time, a new entry in a way that maximizes the benefits of newness and minimizes its costs. The creation of resource bundles is the basis for new entry opportunities. A resource bundle is created from the entrepreneur's market knowledge, technological knowledge, and other resources. The new entry has the potential of being a source of sustained superior firm performance if the resource bundle underlying the new entry is valuable, rare, and difficult for others to imitate. Therefore, those wishing to generate an innovation need to look to the unique experiences and knowledge within themselves and their team.

Having created a new resource combination, the entrepreneur needs to determine whether it is in fact valuable, rare, and inimitable by assessing whether this new product and/or new market is sufficiently attractive to be worth exploiting and then acting on that decision. The decision to exploit or not to exploit the new entry opportunity depends on whether the entrepreneur has what she or he believes to be sufficient information to make a decision and on whether the window is still open for this new entry opportunity. The entrepreneur's determination of sufficient information depends on the stock of information and the entrepreneur's level of comfort in making such a decision without perfect information.

Successful new entry requires that the entrepreneur's firm have an advantage over competitors. Entrepreneurs often claim that their competitive advantage arises from being first to market. Being first can result in a number of advantages that can enhance performance, such as cost advantages, reduced competition, securing important sources of supply and distribution, obtaining a prime position in the market, and gaining expertise through early participation. But first movers do not always prosper, and in fact there are conditions that can push a first mover toward performance disadvantages, such as high instability of the environment surrounding the entry, a lack of ability among the management team to educate customers, and a lack of ability among the management team to erect barriers to entry and imitation in order to extend the firm's lead time.

A new entry involves considerable risk for the entrepreneur and his or her firm. This risk of downside loss is partly derived from the entrepreneur's uncertainties over market demand, technological development, and the actions of competitors. Strategies can be used to reduce some or all of these uncertainties and thereby reduce the risk of downside loss. Two such strategies are market scope and imitation. Scope is a choice by the entrepreneur about which customer groups to serve and how to serve them—for example, the choice between a narrow and a broad scope. Imitation involves copying the practices of other firms, whether those other firms are in the industry being entered or in related industries; for instance, "me too" and franchising are both imitation strategies.

Entrepreneurship also can involve the creation of a new organization. The creation of a new organization offers some challenges for entrepreneurs that are not faced by those who manage established firms. These challenges, referred to as liabilities of newness, reflect a new organization's higher costs of learning new tasks, increased conflict over newly created roles and responsibilities, and the lack of a well-developed informal communication network. However, new organizations also may have some assets of newness, the most important of which is an increased ability to learn new knowledge, which can provide an important strategic advantage over mature competitors, particularly in dynamic, changing environments.

RESEARCH TASKS

1. Choose three major inventions that have led to successful products. Who were the inventors? How did they invent the technology? Why do you believe they were the first to invent this technology?

2. Find three examples of firms that pioneered a new product in a new market and were able to achieve long-run success based on that entry. Find three examples of firms that were not the pioneers but entered later to eventually overtake the pioneer as market leader. In your opinion, why were the successful pioneers successful, and why were the unsuccessful ones unsuccessful?
3. What is the failure rate of all new businesses? What is the failure rate of all new franchises? What inferences can you make from these numbers?

CLASS DISCUSSION

1. Come up with five examples of firms that have used imitation as a way of reducing the risk of entry. What aspects of risk was imitation meant to reduce? Was it successful? What aspects of the firm were not generated by imitation, made the firm unique, and were a potential source of advantage over competitors?
2. Provide two examples of firms with a broad scope, two with a narrow scope, and two that started narrow and became broader over time.
3. Is it a waste of time to detail the firm's strategy in the business plan when the audience for that plan (e.g., venture capitalists) knows that things are not going to turn out as expected and, as a result, places considerable importance on the quality of the management team? Why not submit only the resumes of those in the management team? If you were a venture capitalist, would you want to see the business plan? How would you assess the quality of one management team relative to another?

SELECTED READINGS

Ardichvili, Alexander; Richard Cardozo; and Sourav Ray. (2003). A Theory of Entrepreneurial Opportunity Identification and Development. *Journal of Business Venturing*, vol. 18, no. 1, pp. 105–24.

This paper proposes a theory of the opportunity identification process. It identifies the entrepreneur's personality traits, social networks, and prior knowledge as antecedents of entrepreneurial alertness to business opportunities. Entrepreneurial alertness, in its turn, is a necessary condition for the success of the opportunity identification triad: recognition, development, and evaluation. A theoretical model, laws of interaction, a set of propositions, and suggestions for further research are provided.

Barney, Jay B. (2001). Resource-Based "Theories" of Competitive Advantage: A Ten-Year Retrospective on the Resource-Based View. *Journal of Management*, vol. 27, no. 6, pp. 643–751.

The resource-based view is discussed in terms of its positioning relative to three theoretical traditions: SCP-based theories of industry determinants of firm performance, neoclassical microeconomics, and evolutionary economics. It also discusses some of the empirical implications of each of these different resource-based theories.

Bruton, Gary D.; and Yuri Rubanik. (2002). Resources of the Firm, Russian High-Technology Startups, and Firm Growth. *Journal of Business Venturing*, vol. 17, no. 6, pp. 553–77.

This study investigates the extent to which founding factors in Russia help high-technology firms to prosper. It was found that the team establishing the business mitigated the liability of newness. However, in contrast to the culture of the United States, the culture of Russia does not produce negative results if the founding team grows very large. Additionally, it was shown that firms that pursued more technological products and entered the market later performed best.

Erikson, Truls. (2002). Entrepreneurial Capital: The Emerging Venture's Most Important Asset and Competitive Advantage. *Journal of Business Venturing*, vol. 17, no. 3, pp. 275–91.

This study presents a parsimonious model of entrepreneurial capital, defined as a multiplicative function of entrepreneurial competence and entrepreneurial commitment. The presence of both entrepreneurial competence and commitment lays the foundation for enterprise generation and performance. Inherent in this view on competence is the capacity to identify opportunities.

Fiol, C. Marlene; and Edward J. O'Connor. (2003). Waking Up! Mindfulness in the Face of Bandwagons. *Academy of Management Review*, vol. 28, no. 1, pp. 54–71.

This article models the interactions between mindfulness as a decision-maker characteristic and the decision-making context, and shows the impact of those interactions on managers' ability to discriminate in the face of bandwagons. The authors illustrate the framework by applying it to recent integration and disintegration bandwagon behaviors in the U.S. health care market.

Keh, Hean T.; Maw Der Foo; and Boon C. Lim. (2002). Opportunity Evaluation under Risky Conditions: The Cognitive Processes of Entrepreneurs. *Entrepreneurship: Theory & Practice*, vol. 27, no. 2, pp. 125–49.

This study uses a cognitive approach to examine opportunity evaluation. It finds that illusion of control and belief in the law of small numbers are related to how entrepreneurs evaluate opportunities. The results also indicate that risk perception mediates opportunity evaluation.

Lévesque, Moren; and Dean A. Shepherd. (2004). Entrepreneurs' Choice of Entry Strategy in Emerging and Developed Markets. *Journal of Business Venturing*, vol. 19, no. 1, pp. 29–45.

From speculations over the differences between emerging and developed economies, the model offers a systematic way to determine the optimal entry strategy in terms of entry timing and level of mimicry. An implication of the model is that the cost/benefit ratio of using a high-mimicry entry strategy is lower for companies entering emerging economies than it is for companies entering developed economies.

Lichtenstein, Benyamin; G. Thomas Lumpkin; and Rodney Shrader. (2003). A Theory of Entrepreneurial Action." In J. Katz and D. A. Shepherd, eds., *Advances in Entrepreneurship: Firm Emergence and Growth* (vol. 6). Greenwich, CT: JAI Press.

This chapter categorizes the organizational learning literature into behavioral, cognitive, and action learning and suggests a number of ways in which new ventures could be more successful at learning than larger and older organizations. It also explores three entrepreneurial contexts in which learning might be particularly important and matches them to the categories of learning.

Lieberman, Marvin B.; and David B. Montgomery. (1998). First-Mover (Dis)advantages: Retrospective and Link with the Resource-Based View. *Strategic Management Journal*, vol. 19, no. 12, pp. 1111–26.

This article suggests that the resource-based view and first-mover advantage are related conceptual strategic planning frameworks that can benefit from closer linkage. It presents an evolution of the literature based on these concepts.

McEvily, Susan K.; and Bala Chakravarthy. (2002). The Persistence of Knowledge-Based Advantage: An Empirical Test for Product Performance and Technological Knowledge. *Strategic Management Journal*, vol. 23, no. 4, pp. 285–306.

The authors find that the complexity and tacitness of technological knowledge are useful for defending a firm's major product improvements from imitation, but not for protecting its minor improvements. The design specificity of technological knowledge delayed imitation of minor improvements in this study.

McMullen, Jeffery S.; and Dean A. Shepherd. (2003). A Theory of Entrepreneurial Action. In J. Katz and D. A. Shepherd, eds., *Advances in Entrepreneurship, Firm Emergence and Growth* (vol. 6). Greenwich, CT: JAI Press, pp. 203–48.

This chapter proposes that the decision to pursue opportunity requires concomitant consideration of belief (uncertainty) and desire (motivation). When the proposed framework is applied to the better-known economic theories of the entrepreneur, it demonstrates that these theories rely upon one construct or the other.

Robinson, William T.; and Sungwook Min. (2002). Is the First to Market the First to Fail? Empirical Evidence for Industrial Goods Businesses. *Journal of Marketing Research*, vol. 39, no. 1, pp. 120–29.

The main conclusion of this study is that the pioneer's temporary monopoly over the early followers plus its first-mover advantages typically offset the survival risks associated with market and technological uncertainties. These results are consistent with previous research in the sense that first-mover advantages that increase a pioneer's market share also help protect the pioneer from outright failure.

Teplensky Jill D.; John R. Kimberly; Alan L. Hillman; and J. Stanford Schwartz. (1993). Scope, Timing and Strategic Adjustment in Emerging Markets: Manufacturer Strategies and the Case of MRI. *Strategic Management Journal*, vol. 14, pp. 505–27.

This study examines the realized strategies of domestic manufacturers in a growing, high-technological industrial market in the United States. It offers a typology of entry strategies focusing on issues of timing and scope and on the impact that these entry strategies have on a firm's performance.

Ucbasaran, Deniz; Mike Wright; Paul Westhead; and Lowell W. Busenitz. (2003). The Impact of Entrepreneurial Experience on Opportunity Identification and Exploitation: Habitual and Novice Entrepreneurs. In J. Katz and D. A. Shepherd, eds., *Advances in Entrepreneurship, Firm Emergence and Growth* (vol. 6). Greenwich, CT: JAI Press.

This paper synthesizes human capital and cognitive perspectives to highlight behavioral differences between habitual and novice entrepreneurs. Issues related to opportunity identification and information search as well as opportunity exploitation and learning are discussed.

Watson, Warren; Wayne Stewart, Jr.; and Anat BarNir. (2003). The Effects of Human Capital, Organizational Demography, and Interpersonal Processes on Venture Partner Perceptions of Firm Profit and Growth. *Journal of Business Venturing*, vol. 18, no. 2, pp. 145–65.

This study examines the effects of human capital, organizational demography, and interpersonal processes on partner evaluations of venture performance, defined as the presence of profit and growth. The results support this approach in analyzing venture teams, and it is proposed that this perspective be included in future venture viability assessment and used for intervention to enhance venture success.

Zahra, Shaker A.; Donald O. Neubaum; and Galal M. El–Hagrassey. (2002). Competitive Analysis and New Venture Performance: Understanding the Impact of Strategic Uncertainty and Venture Origin. *Entrepreneurship: Theory & Practice*, vol. 27, no. 1, pp. 1–29.

Using survey data from 228 new ventures, this study concludes that the formality, comprehensiveness, and user orientation of competitor analysis activities are positively associated with new venture performance. Strategic uncertainty and venture origin also significantly moderate the relationship between competitive analysis and new venture performance.

END NOTES

1. G. Lumpkin and G. G. Dess, "Clarifying the Entrepreneurial Orientation Construct and Linking It to Performance," *Academy of Management Review* 21, no. 1 (1996), 135–72.
2. F. H. Knight, *Risk, Uncertainty and Profit* (New York: Houghton Mifflin, 1921); E. M. Olson, O. C. Walker, Jr., and R. W. Ruekert, "Organizing for Effective New Product Development: The Moderating Role of Product Innovativeness," *Journal of Marketing* 59 (January 1995), pp. 48–62; H. J. Sapienza and A. K. Gupta, "Impact of Agency Risks and Task Uncertainty on Venture Capitalist-Entrepreneur Relations," *Academy of Management Journal* 37 (1994), pp. 1618–32.
3. J. B. Barney, "Firm Resources and Sustained Competitive Advantage," *Journal of Management* 17, pp. 99–120.
4. This list is adapted from M. A. Hitt, R. D. Ireland, and R. E. Hoskisson, *Strategic Management: Competitiveness and Globalization,* 3rd ed. (London: South-Western Publishing Co., 1999).
5. S. P. Schnaars, *Managing Imitation Strategies: How Later Entrants Seize Markets from Pioneers* (New York: Free Press, 1994).
6. Nathan Rosenberg, "Trying to Predict the Impact of Tomorrow's Inventions," *USA Today* 123 (May 1995), pp. 88ff.
7. Ibid.
8. J. McMullen and D. A. Shepherd, "A Theory of Entrepreneurial Action," in J. Katz and D. A. Shepherd, eds., *Advances in Entrepreneurship, Firm Emergence and Growth,* vol. 6 (Greenwich, CT: JAI Press, 2003), pp. 203–48.
9. Dean A. Shepherd and M. Shanley, *New Venture Strategy: Timing, Environmental Uncertainty and Performance* (Newburg Park, CA: The Sage Series in Entrepreneurship and the Management of Enterprises, 1998).
10. M. B. Lieberman and D. B. Montgomery, "First Mover Advantages," *Strategic Management Journal* 9 (1988), pp. 127–140.
11. D. F. Abell, "Strategic Windows," *Journal of Marketing* 42, no. 3 (1978), pp. 21–26.
12. D. A. Aaker and G. S. Day, "The Perils of High Growth Markets," *Strategic Management Journal* 7 (1986), pp. 409–21; Shepherd and Shanley, *New Venture Strategy.*
13. Shepherd and Shanley, *New Venture Strategy.*
14. S. F. Slater, "Competing in High Velocity Markets," *Industrial Marketing Management* 24, no. 4 (1993), pp. 255–68.
15. Shepherd and Shanley, *New Venture Strategy.*
16. T. W. Ruefli, J. M. Collins, and J. R. LaCugna, "Risk Measures in Strategic Management Research: Auld Lang Syne?" *Strategic Management Journal* 20 (1999), pp. 167–94.

17. J. D. Teplensky, J. R. Kimberly, A. L. Hillman, and J. S. Schwartz, "Scope, Timing and Strategic Adjustment in Emerging Markets: Manufacturer Strategies and the Case of MRI," *Strategic Management Journal* 14 (1993), pp. 505–27.
18. Shepherd and Shanley, *New Venture Strategy*.
19. Ibid.
20. Schnaars, *Managing Imitation Strategies*.
21. Shepherd and Shanley, *New Venture Strategy*.
22. B. B. Lichtenstein, G. T. Lumpkin, and R. Shrader, "A Theory of Entrepreneurial Action," in J. Katz and D. A. Shepherd, eds., *Advances in Entrepreneurship, Firm Emergence and Growth* 6 (Greenwich, CT: JAI Press, 2003).

14

STRATEGIES FOR GROWTH AND MANAGING THE IMPLICATIONS OF GROWTH

LEARNING OBJECTIVES

1
To know where to look for (or how to create) possible growth opportunities.

2
To understand the implications of business growth for a national economy.

3
To understand the primary challenges for managing business growth and to be prepared to effectively manage those challenges.

4
To recognize that people differ and to understand how these differences impact their intentions to grow a business.

OPENING PROFILE

BRIAN AND JENNIFER MAXWELL

olympics.powerbar.com

Brian Maxwell, an internationally ranked marathon runner and coach at the University of California, Berkeley, was leading a marathon race in England when at the 21-mile mark he began to experience dizziness and tunnel vision, which forced him to quit the race. His consumption of energy drinks on the day of the race had failed and motivated him to find a solution for a better energy source. He teamed up with Jennifer Biddulph, a student studying nutrition and food science (now a PhD chemist), and they began the quest for an energy bar that would taste good, be healthy and nutritious, and provide the appropriate ingredients to optimize performance. With $50,000 gathered from savings they were determined to find a solution.[1]

During their three years of research, experts indicated to them that it would be impossible to produce a healthy product because of the large amounts of saturated fats necessary for lubricating machinery in the food bar manufacturing process. However, after many failures they found the solution. They understood that their efforts required developing a food bar manufacturing process that would not require adding fats for lubrication of machinery and would produce a product that would meet the above desired attributes. The product needed to provide a balance of simple carbohydrates for quick energy, complex carbohydrates for longer lasting energy, and low fat for easy digestion. Hundreds of recipes were tested with athletes until the most effective and best-tasting product was found. Continued requests among these athletes to have more of those "power bars" led to the final brand name, and in 1986 they officially formed the company, PowerBar Inc.

Initially the company was operated from Brian and Jennifer's basement. The first products, which went on sale in 1987, were the Malt-Nut and Chocolate flavors. After their marriage in 1988 they moved to a new facility and began hiring employees to meet the growing demand.

Their vision of finding a solution to a serious runner's energy source wasn't the only factor in forming this new venture. Both Brian and Jennifer were determined to create a work environment where employees would feel important and have a strong sense of pride in the company. They wanted a company that did not have all the things that they hated about jobs they had held previously. Thus, they created a work environment where employees are called team members, the dress is casual, and the atmosphere is on sports. To Brian and Jennifer it was important that their employees enjoyed the workplace and developed an important loyalty and commitment to the company's mission.

In the early part of the 1990s sales for the new venture increased by 50 to 60 percent. In 1997 sales began to slow and increased by only 23 percent. In 1995 Brian and Jennifer turned down an opportunity to purchase Balance Bar, a producer of an energy bar that targeted the more casual athlete and those who were looking for a nutritious snack. They had believed that their company did not need to add any new products and could continue to grow with the one product. In retrospect, they realized this was a mistake in strategy and that the venture could not survive on the one product, especially when they saw sales begin to stall in 1995. At that time there were many new competitors who recognized the opportunities in a larger market by introducing energy bars for casual exercisers and snackers. So in 1997 Brian and Jennifer began efforts to find new products. In 1998 they launched PowerBar Harvest, a crunchy, textured energy bar available in a number of flavors that would target casual athletes and consumers looking for a nutritious snack. In 1999 a new creamy bar called Essentials and a new line of sports drinks were launched.

Today PowerBar is still the leader in the serious athlete market, and Harvest has just passed Clif bar to become the number 3 brand in this category. Sales in 1999 reached $135 million. The company also opened a state-of-the-art manufacturing facility in Idaho and two distribution centers in Idaho and North Carolina. It also established two subsidiaries in Canada and Germany as opportunities for sales growth in international markets occurred.

Brian still runs 40 to 50 miles per week. Jennifer was recently recognized in the first annual Working Women Entrepreneurial Excellence Awards competition by winning for Harvest in the Best Innovation category. In 2000, PowerBar was purchased by Nestlé USA, which intends to grow and expand it globally. Brian Maxwell will continue to play an integral role in the company.

In this chapter, important management decision areas are reviewed and discussed. Building a solid management team and a loyal employee base, recognized by entrepreneurs like Brian and Jennifer Maxwell as being very important during the early years, is discussed in detail, along with financial and marketing control decisions.

GROWTH STRATEGIES: WHERE TO LOOK FOR GROWTH OPPORTUNITIES

In the previous chapter we discussed new entry as an essential act of entrepreneurship. A successful new entry provides the opportunity for the entrepreneur to grow his or her business. For example, introducing a new product into an existing market provides the opportunity to take market share from competitors; entry into a new market provides the opportunity to service a new group of customers; and a new organization has a chance to make, and build upon, its first sales. Although it is difficult to provide direct guidance to entrepreneurs on a step-by-step process for generating a highly attractive opportunity, in this chapter we provide a model that offers suggestions on where to look for growth opportunities in which the firm may already have a basis for a sustainable competitive advantage. We then investigate the implications of that growth for an economy, for the firm, and for the entrepreneur, as well as the possible need to negotiate for resources from external sources to sustain firm growth.

We know from the previous chapter that opportunities for new entry are generated by the knowledge of the entrepreneur and from organizational knowledge. We use this as a basis for deciding on the best place to look for opportunities to grow the business. From a simple perspective we can assume that the entrepreneur and the firm have knowledge about the product that they are currently producing and selling (the existing product) and have knowledge about the group of customers to which they are currently selling that product (the existing market).

Different combinations of different levels of these types of knowledge are represented in Figure 14.1 and provide a model of different growth strategies.[2] Most of these growth strategies can lead to a competitive advantage because they capitalize on some aspect of the entrepreneur's, and the firm's, knowledge base. These growth strategies are: (1) penetration strategies, (2) market development strategies, (3) product development strategies, and (4) diversification strategies.

Penetration Strategies

penetration strategy
A strategy to grow by encouraging existing customers to buy more of the firm's current products

A *penetration strategy* focuses on the firm's existing product in its existing market. The entrepreneur attempts to penetrate this product or market further by encouraging existing customers to buy more of the firm's current products. Marketing can be effective in encouraging more frequent repeat purchases. For example, a pizza company engages in an extensive marketing campaign to encourage its existing customer base of university students to eat its pizza three nights a week rather than only twice a week. This growth strategy does not involve anything new for the firm and relies on taking market share from

FIGURE 14.1 Growth Strategies Based upon Knowledge of Product and/or Market

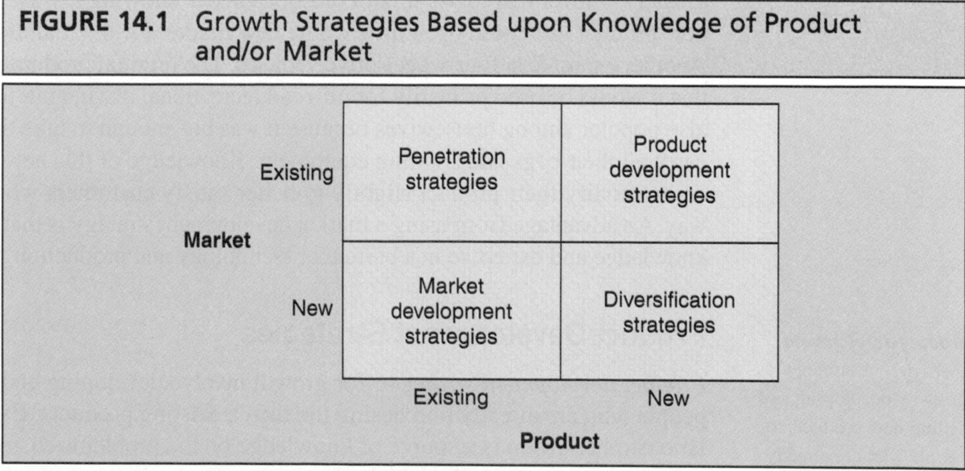

Source: H. I. Ansoff, *Corporate Strategy: An Analytical Approach to Business Policy for Growth and Expansion* (New York: McGraw-Hill, 1965).

competitors and/or expanding the size of the existing market. Therefore, this growth strategy attempts to better exploit its original entry.

Market Development Strategies

market development strategy Strategy to grow by selling the firm's existing products to new groups of customers

Growth also can occur through market development strategies. *Market development strategies* involve selling the firm's existing products to new groups of customers. New groups of customers can be categorized in terms of geographics or demographics and/or on the basis of new product use.

New Geographical Market This simply refers to selling the existing product in new locations. For example, a firm selling its products in Singapore could start selling its products in Malaysia, Thailand, and Indonesia. This has the potential of increasing sales by offering products to customers who have not previously had the chance to purchase them. The entrepreneur must be aware of possible regional differences in customer preferences, language, and legal requirements that may necessitate a slight change in the product (or packaging).

New Demographic Market Demographics are used to characterize (potential) customers based upon their income; where they live; their education, age, and sex; and so on. For an entrepreneur that is currently selling the firm's existing product to a specific demographic group, the business could grow by offering the same product to a different demographic group. For example, a studio currently produces and sells computer games (specializing in games on baseball and soccer) to males between the ages of 13 and 17. However, there is an opportunity for this company to expand its sales by also targeting males between the ages of 24 and 32 who are university educated, have high disposable incomes, and would likely enjoy the escapism of these computer game products.

New Product Use An entrepreneurial firm might find out that people use its product in a way that was not intended or expected. This new knowledge of product use provides insight into how the product may be valuable to new groups of buyers. For example, when I moved from Australia to Chicago, I bought a baseball bat. I did not use the bat to play baseball; rather I kept it beside my bed for security against anyone who might break into my apartment. Fortunately, I never had to use it but I did sleep better knowing it was there. Recognition of this new product use could open up a whole new market for the manufacturers of baseball bats. Another example is four-wheel-drive vehicles. The original producers of this product thought that it would be used primarily for off-road recreational driving but found that the vehicle was also popular among housewives because it was big enough to take the children to school and carry all their bags and sporting equipment. Knowledge of this new use allowed the producers to modify their product slightly to better satisfy customers who use the product in this way. An advantage from using a market development strategy is that it capitalizes on existing knowledge and expertise in a particular technology and production process.

Product Development Strategies

product development strategy A strategy to grow by developing and selling new products to people who are already purchasing the firm's existing products

Product development strategies for growth involve developing and selling new products to people who are already purchasing the firm's existing products. Experience with a particular customer group is a source of knowledge on the problems customers have with existing technology and ways in which customers can be better served. This knowledge is an important resource in coming up with a new product. For example, Disney Corporation built on its existing customer base of Disney movie viewers and developed merchandising products specifically aimed at this audience. A further advantage of using a product development strategy is the chance to capitalize on existing distribution systems and on the corporate reputation the firm has with these customers.

Diversification Strategies

diversification strategy
A strategy to grow by selling a new product to a new market

Diversification strategies involve selling a new product to a new market. Even though both knowledge bases appear to be new, some diversification strategies are related to the entrepreneur's (and the firm's) knowledge. In fact there are three types of related diversification that are best explained through a discussion of the value-added chain.

As illustrated in Figure 14.2, a value-added chain captures the steps it takes to develop raw materials into a product and get it into the hands of the customers. Value is added at every stage of the chain. For the value added, each firm makes some profit. If we focus on the manufacturer, opportunities for growth arise from backward integration, forward integration, and horizontal integration. *Backward integration* refers to taking a step back (up) on the value-added chain toward the raw materials, which in this case means that the manufacturer also becomes a raw materials wholesaler. In essence the firm becomes its own supplier. *Forward integration* is taking a step forward (down) on the value-added chain toward the customers, which in this case means that the firm also becomes a finished goods wholesaler. In essence the firm becomes its own buyer.

backward integration
A step back (up) in the value-added chain toward the raw materials

forward integration
A step forward (down) on the value-added chain toward the customers

Backward or forward integration provides an entrepreneur with a potentially attractive opportunity to grow his or her business. First, these growth opportunities are related to the

FIGURE 14.2 Example of a Value-Added Chain and Types of Related Diversification

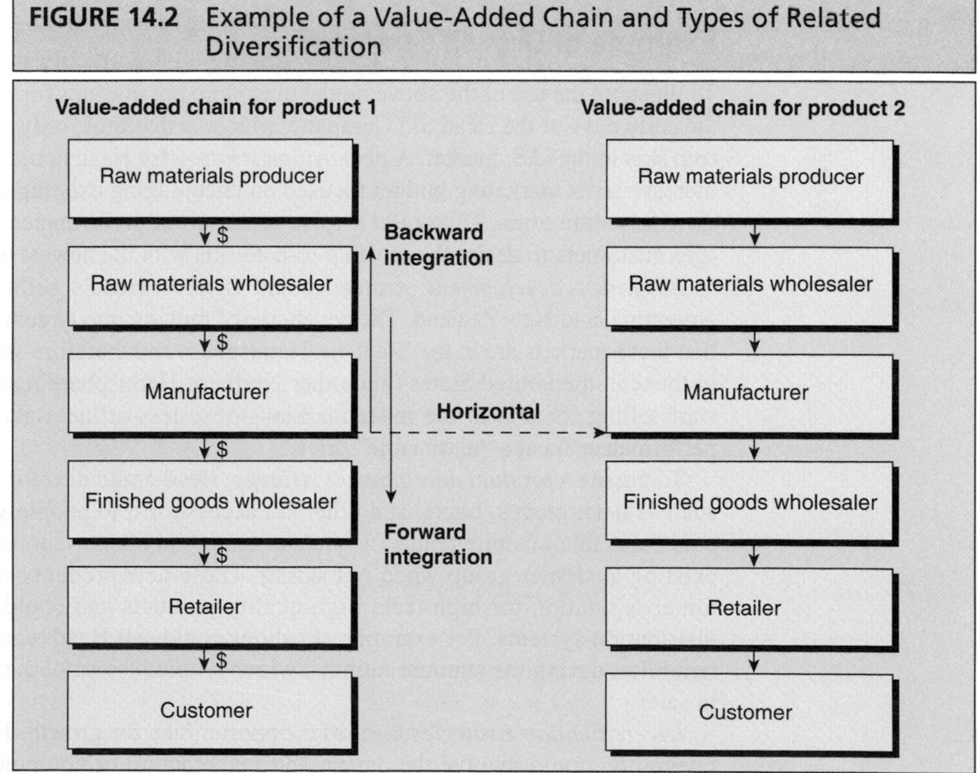

firm's existing knowledge base, and the entrepreneur could therefore have some advantage over others with no such experience or knowledge. Second, being one's own supplier and/or buyer provides synergistic opportunities to conduct these transactions more efficiently than they are conducted with independent firms fulfilling these roles. Third, operating as a supplier and/or a buyer of the original business provides learning opportunities that could lead to new processes and/or new product improvements that would not have been available if this integration had not taken place.

horizontal integration Occurs at the same level of the value-added chain but simply involves a different, but complementary, value-added chain

A third type of related diversification is *horizontal integration*. The growth opportunity occurs at the same level of the value-added chain but simply involves a different, but complementary, value-added chain. For example, a firm that manufactures washing machines may go into the manufacture of detergent. These products are complementary in that they need each other to work. Again the relatedness of the new product to the firm's existing product means that the firm will likely have some competencies in this new product and may provide learning opportunities. Further, horizontal integration provides the opportunity to increase sales of the existing product. For example, the existing product and the new product may be bundled and sold together, which may provide increased value to customers and increase sales. Examples of bundled products include computer hardware and software, televisions and video recorders, and telephones and answering machines.

What about introducing a new product into a new market that is not related to the existing business (i.e., not forward, backward, or horizontal integration)? The short answer is, "Don't do it." If it is not related to the current business, then what possible advantage can this firm have over competitors? Ego and the mistaken belief in the benefits of a firm's diversifying its risk lead some entrepreneurs to pursue unrelated diversification to their own peril.

Example of Growth Strategies

To illustrate the use of the above model to explore possibilities for firm growth we consider the early days of the Head Ski Company, which, at that time, only produced and sold high-tech skis in the U.S. market. A *penetration strategy* for Head could be achieved through an increase in its marketing budget focused on encouraging existing customers to "upgrade" their skis more often. This could involve some sort of performance imperative that encourages customers to desire the most up-to-date skis with the newest technological features.

A *market development strategy* could involve Head's selling its skis in Europe, Argentina, and New Zealand. The advantage of moving into Argentina and New Zealand is that these markets are in the Southern Hemisphere and therefore sales are counterseasonal to those in the United States (and other Northern Hemisphere markets). Head could also start selling its skis to the mass market—those less affluent skiers who want a good-performance ski at a "reasonable" price.

To pursue a *product development strategy*, Head could develop and sell new products, such as hats, gloves, boots, and other ski accessories, to people who buy its skis. Head could also manufacture tennis racquets or mountain bikes—equipment that is used by its existing customer group when not skiing. These new products would build on its customer reputation for high-tech, high-quality products and could capitalize on existing distribution systems. For example, ski shops could sell Head tennis racquets and mountain bikes during the summer months, which would also smooth out seasonal variability in sales.

Diversification strategies also offer opportunities for growth. For example, backward integration could involve the design and manufacture of equipment used to make skis,

AS SEEN IN *ENTREPRENEUR* MAGAZINE

PROVIDE ADVICE TO AN ENTREPRENEUR ABOUT GROWING INTO NEW MARKETS USING THE INTERNET

Dot-com mania may have ended, but selling products and services online has scarcely begun. In fact, estimates from a variety of sources have total online retail sales increasing approximately 30 percent in 2002. And after years of similarly rapid growth, the absolute numbers aren't tiny either: Projections based on the U.S. Department of Commerce's conservative data reports indicate that online sales of goods and services topped $42 billion in 2002. And the Department of Commerce doesn't include online travel sales, which typically account for 40 percent or more of online revenue.

One thing driving online sales growth is the still-increasing number of people going online. Market trackers at Jupiter Media Metrix forecast the number of online Americans will double in five years to 132 million. Because about half of Internet users buy something online during any particular year, that translates to solid growth for online commerce.

The online market isn't just growing; it's also changing. To begin with, the shoppers themselves are transforming. Once mostly men, they're now mostly women. Though the Net is seen as a youthful medium, seniors are the fastest-growing age group. And though ethnic groups have lagged behind the mainstream in embracing online, they are catching up fast. "While the general market is tending to flatten out a little bit, the ethnic market continues to have rapid growth," says Derene Allen, vice president of The Santiago Solutions Group, a San Francisco multicultural marketing consulting firm.

These groups all have their own reasons for shopping online, their own styles, and their own favored purchases. They're buying a broader range of products and services as well. Once, goods were divided into those suitable for sale on the Internet and those not suitable. Supposedly, items such as furniture were not online-ready, for instance. But increasingly, nearly everything is being sold online. Furniture makes up most of the volume at PoshTots, a 16-person Glen Allen, Virginia, online seller of high-end children's products. "Our customers are buying cribs and beds," says Karen Booth Adams, 33-year-old co-founder, "and we sell a lot of playhouses."

Continuing growth of the online market calls for evolving business strategies as well. The frenzy to achieve the first-mover advantage that characterized the early years of online retail has subsided. Today, selling online is less about having the latest technology and more about having the best insight into customers. "It's back to tried-and-true principles of marketing," says Keith Tudor, professor of marketing at Kennesaw State University in Kennesaw, Georgia. "Look at your customers' wants, needs, and motivations."

ADVICE TO AN ENTREPRENEUR

An entrepreneur who runs a "bricks and mortar" retail business comes to you for advice:

1. With all the failures associated with dot-com businesses, do you think it is safe now for me to start advertising and selling my products online?
2. If I can't enter this market and rely on first-mover advantages or on a technological advantage, then how can I develop a competitive advantage in the proposed online division of my retail business? Do I need to enter just to keep up with my competitors and maintain market share?
3. If it reverts back to the basic principles of marketing, then how do you target your product at a particular audience when everyone is using the Internet?

Source: Reprinted with permission of Entrepreneur Media, Inc., "Net Meeting. Let Us Introduce You to the Most Important People on the Internet. If You Think You Know E-Commerce Consumers, This Might Surprise You," by Mark Hendricks, February 2003, *Entrepreneur* magazine: www.entrepreneur.com.

forward integration could involve control of a chain of retail ski shops, and horizontal integration could involve ownership of ski mountains (lifts, lodges, etc.).

As this example demonstrates, the model offers a tool for entrepreneurs, to force them to think and look in different directions for growth opportunities where the firm may already have a basis for a sustainable competitive advantage. The pursuit and achievement of growth have an impact on the economy, the firm, and the entrepreneur.

ECONOMIC IMPLICATIONS OF GROWTH

In 1996 *Inc.* magazine conducted a study of its 500 fastest-growing ventures in 1984 to ascertain what happens to those ventures that are entering a growth phase.[3] In 1984 these 500 fastest-growing ventures had aggregate sales of $7.4 billion and 64,000 full-time employees and were all experiencing the beginning of the rapid growth described above. By 1995, among the original 500 ventures, there had been 95 failures or shutdowns and 135 had been sold to new owners. The 233 companies that were willing to report earnings, however, more than made up for the failures in jobs created and revenue generated. These 233 companies had reached sales of $29 billion and employed 127,000 people full time. Thus, these 233 firms represented revenue and total numbers of employees that were significantly larger than the original list of 500 ventures.

Figure 14.3 compares the 1984 results with the reported 1994 revenue and number of full-time employees. You can see how significant the growth has been when you compare the 1994 sales and numbers of employees of the 233 companies that participated with the 1984 sales and numbers of employees of the same 233 companies.

In addition to the sales and employees, it was reported that 48 percent were still privately held under the same ownership and only 6 percent had actually gone public. The fact that there were so few ventures that had gone public probably defies conventional thinking in entrepreneurship that becoming a big business requires you to go public to finance the growth. A comparison of the ventures that did go public, however, revealed that they had achieved much larger growth than those that did not go public. These 32 companies from the 1984 list grew by $18.9 billion in revenue, which was an average growth rate of 32 percent. As a group these 32 firms included some of the top entrepreneurial performers in the United States, such as Microsoft, Merisel, and Tech Data. Many of these companies had also retained the original founder of the company as CEO.

The sample of *Inc.* magazine ventures does not capture those businesses that grow more modestly, especially small businesses. However, modest levels of growth by small businesses can still have a dramatic impact on an economy. For example, the majority of new jobs in most industrialized economies are created by small business.[4] This does not necessarily mean that most small firms do grow; rather the population of small firms is so large that even when a small percentage of them do grow the impact on an economy is still significant and important.[5]

The sample of *Inc.* magazine ventures does capture some businesses that were at one stage growing rapidly but later failed. We should not consider business failure a negative outcome for an economy. On the contrary, entrepreneurs that pursue growth opportunities, even if such pursuit increases the potential for failure, generate knowledge that stimulates improvements in technologies and increases economic resilience.[6]

For example, an entrepreneur that "goes for it" and develops a new technology could hit the jackpot, which obviously provides benefits to the economy in terms of tax revenue, employment, reduction of the trade deficit, and so on. But what if the new technology does not work as expected and the business is bankrupted? How does this improve the economy? A failed attempt provides information for that entrepreneur and other entrepreneurs. Although the new technology itself did not work, another entrepreneur may have learned from the attempt, which may have provided an important piece of the puzzle and, ultimately, success (and the associated economic benefits).

An economy made up of entrepreneurs that do not fail is likely a poorly performing economy. Such an economy does not have entrepreneurs willing to pursue high-risk–high-potential-growth opportunities and therefore does not benefit from the rewards of technologies that "hit" and does not learn from those that are pursued but fail. Next we address the implications of firm growth for the firm and then for the entrepreneur.

FIGURE 14.3 A Follow-Up of *Inc.* Magazine's 1984 Fastest-Growing Ventures

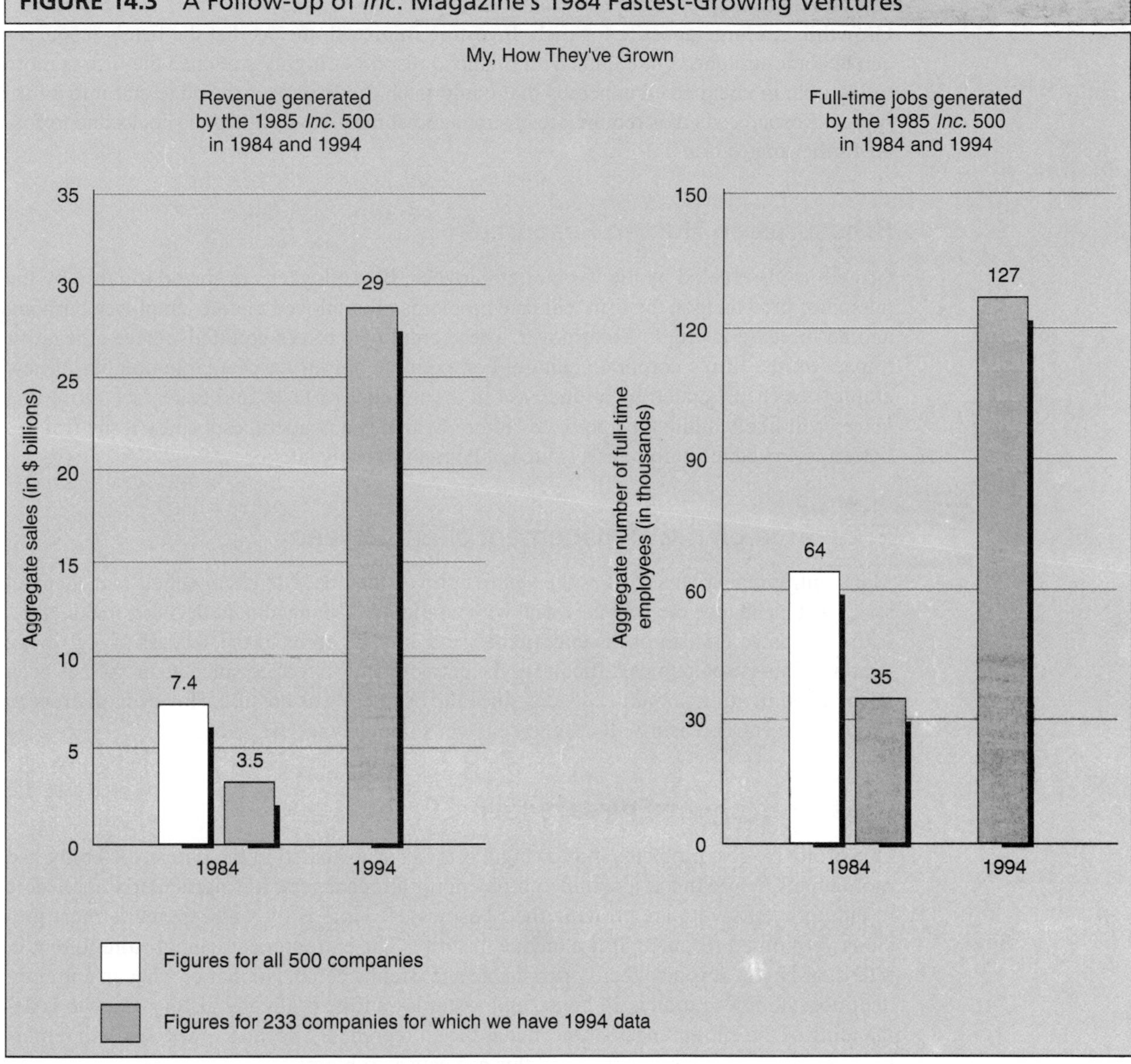

Source: Martha E. Mangelsdorf, "The Startling, Truth about Growth Companies," *Inc.* (May 21, 1996), p. 85. Copyright © 1996 by Mansueto Ventures LLC. Reproduced with permission of Mansueto Ventures LLC via Copyright Clearance Center.

IMPLICATIONS OF GROWTH FOR THE FIRM

Because growth makes a firm bigger, the firm begins to benefit from the advantages of size. For example, higher volume increases production efficiency, makes the firm more attractive to suppliers, and therefore increases its bargaining power. Size also enhances the legitimacy of the firm, because firms that are larger are often perceived by customers, financiers, and other stakeholders as being more stable and prestigious. Therefore, the growing of a business can provide the entrepreneur more power to influence firm performance. But as the firm grows, it changes. These changes introduce a number of managerial challenges. These challenges arise from the following pressures.

Pressures on Existing Financial Resources

Growth has a large appetite for cash. Investing in growth means that the firm's resources can become stretched quite thin. With financial resources highly stretched the firm is more vulnerable to unexpected expenses that could push the firm over the edge and into bankruptcy. Resource slack is required to ensure against most environmental shocks and to foster further innovation.

Pressures on Human Resources

Growth is also fueled by the work of employees. If employees are spread too thin by the pursuit of growth, then the firm will face problems of employee morale, employee burnout, and an increase in employee turnover. These employee issues could also have a negative impact on the firm's corporate culture. For example, an influx of a large number of new employees (necessitated by an increase in the number of tasks and to replace those that leave) will likely dilute the corporate culture, which is a concern, especially if the firm relies on its corporate culture as a source of competitive advantage.

Pressures on the Management of Employees

Many entrepreneurs find that as the venture grows, they need to change their management style, that is, change the way they deal with employees. Management decision making that is the exclusive domain of the entrepreneur can be dangerous to the success of a growing venture. This is sometimes difficult for the entrepreneur to realize since he or she has been so involved in all important decisions since the business was created. However, in order to survive, the entrepreneur will need to consider some managerial changes.

Pressures on the Entrepreneur's Time

One of the biggest problems in growing a firm is encapsulated in the phrase "If I only had more time." While this is a common problem for all managers, it is particularly applicable to entrepreneurs who are growing their businesses. Time is the entrepreneur's most precious yet limited resource. It is a unique quantity: The entrepreneur cannot store it, rent it, hire it, or buy it. It is also totally perishable and irreplaceable. No matter what an entrepreneur does, today's ration is 24 hours, and yesterday's time is already history. Growth is demanding of the entrepreneur's time, but as the entrepreneur allocates time to growth it must be diverted from other activities and this can cause problems.

There are actions the entrepreneur can take to better manage these issues and more effectively grow his or her business. We will now discuss some of these actions.

OVERCOMING PRESSURES ON EXISTING FINANCIAL RESOURCES

To overcome pressures on existing financial resources, the entrepreneur could acquire new resources. The acquisition of new resources is expensive, whether in terms of the equity sold or the interest payments from debt. The need or the magnitude of the new resources required can be reduced through better management of existing resources. Such important management activities include applying effective financial control, managing inventory, and maintaining good records.

FINANCIAL CONTROL

The financial plan, as an inherent part of the business plan, was discussed in Chapter 10. Just as we outlined how to prepare pro forma income and cash flow statements for the first three years, the entrepreneur will need some knowledge of how to provide appropriate controls to ensure that projections and goals are met. Some financial skills are thus necessary for the entrepreneur to manage the venture during these early years. Cash flows, the income statement, and the balance sheet are the key financial areas that will need careful management and control. Since Chapter 10 explains how to prepare these pro forma statements, the focus in this section will be controls and the management of these elements to alleviate financial "growing" pains.

Managing Cash Flow

Since cash outflow may exceed cash inflow when growing a business, the entrepreneur should try to have an up-to-date assessment of his or her cash position. This can be accomplished by preparing monthly cash flow statements, such as that found in Table 14.1, and comparing the budgeted or pro forma statements with the actual results. The July budgeted amounts are taken from the pro forma cash flow statement of MPP Plastics. The entrepreneur can indicate the actual amounts next to the budgeted amounts. This will be useful for adjusting the pro forma for the remaining months, as well as for providing some indication as to where cash flow problems may exist.

Table 14.1 shows a few potential problem areas. First, sales receipts were less than anticipated. Management needs to assess whether this was due to nonpayment by some

TABLE 14.1 MPP Plastics Inc. (Statement of Cash Flow) July, Year 1 (000s)

	July	
	Budgeted	**Actual**
Receipts		
Sales	$ 24.0	$ 22.0
Disbursements		
Equipment	100.0	100.0
Cost of goods	20.8	22.5
Selling expenses	1.5	2.5
Salaries	6.5	6.5
Advertising	1.5	1.5
Office supplies	0.3	0.3
Rent	2.0	2.0
Utilities	0.3	0.5
Insurance	0.8	0.8
Taxes	0.8	0.8
Loan principal and interest	2.6	2.6
Total disbursements	$137.0	$140.0
Cash flow	(113.1)	(118.0)
Beginning balance	275.0	275.0
Ending balance	161.9	157.0

customers or to an increase in credit sales. If the lower amount is due to nonpayment by customers, the entrepreneur may need to try enforcing faster payment by sending reminder letters or making telephone calls to delinquent customers. Bounced checks from customers can also affect cash flow since the entrepreneur has likely credited the amount to the account and assumed that the cash is readily available. If the lower receipts are resulting from higher credit sales, the entrepreneur may need to either consider short-term financing from a bank or try to extend the terms of payment to his or her suppliers.[7]

Cash disbursements for some items were greater than budgeted and may indicate a need for tighter cost controls. For example, cost of goods was $22,500, which was $1,700 more than budgeted. The entrepreneur may find that suppliers increased their prices, which may require a search for alternative sources or even raising the prices of the products/services offered by the new venture. If the higher cost of goods resulted from the purchase of more supplies, then the entrepreneur should assess the inventory costs from the income statement. It is possible that the increased cost of goods resulted from the purchase of more supplies because sales were higher than expected. However, if these additional sales resulted in more credit sales, the entrepreneur may need to plan to borrow money to meet short-term cash needs. Conclusions can be made once the credit sales and inventory costs are evaluated.

The higher selling expenses also may need to be assessed. If the additional selling expenses were incurred in order to support increased sales (even if they were credit sales), then there is no immediate concern. However, if no additional sales were generated, the entrepreneur may need to review all of these expenses and perhaps institute tighter controls.

Projecting cash flow in the early stages can also benefit by conducting sensitivity analysis. For each monthly expected cash flow the entrepreneur can use 1 plus and minus 5 for an optimistic and pessimistic cash estimate, respectively. Thus, our MPP Plastics example (Table 14.1) might have projected in the prior month sales receipts of $24,000 and, using the 1 plus and minus 5 percent, would have a column indicating a pessimistic amount of $22,800 and an optimistic amount of $25,200. This sensitivity analysis would then be computed for all disbursements as well. In this manner the entrepreneur would be able to ascertain the maximum cash needs given a pessimistic outcome and could prepare for any cash needs.

For the very new venture it may be necessary to prepare a daily cash sheet. This might be particularly beneficial to a retail store, restaurant, or service business. Table 14.2 provides an illustration of the cash available at the beginning of the day with additions and deletions of cash recorded as indicated. This would provide an effective indication of any daily shortfall and give a clear sense of where problems exist or where errors have occurred.

Comparison of budgeted or expected cash flows with actual cash flows can provide the entrepreneur with an important assessment of potential immediate cash needs and indicate possible problems in the management of assets or control of costs. These items are discussed further in the next sections.

Managing Inventory

During the growth of a new venture the management of inventory is an important task. Too much inventory can be a drain on cash flow since manufacturing, transportation, and storage costs must be borne by the venture. On the other hand, too little inventory to meet customer demands can also cost the venture in lost sales, or it can create unhappy customers who may choose another firm if their needs are not met in a timely manner.

Growing ventures typically tie up more cash in their inventory than in any other part of the business. Skolnik Industries, a $10 million manufacturer of steel containers for storage and disposal of hazardous materials, recently developed an inventory control system that allows it to ship products to its customers within 24 to 48 hours. This was accomplished

TABLE 14.2 Daily Cash Activity (Date)

Beginning day's cash balance:	$XXX	
Add:		
Day's cash sales (cash, charges, checks)	$XXX	
Collection of receivables	$XXX	
Total		$XXX
Less:		
Charge account sales (from day's cash sales)		$XXX
Total cash collected		$XXX
Cash disbursed:		
Cash refunds	$XXX	
Cash returns	$XXX	
Petty cash expenses (such as postage, travel, supplies, or repairs)	$XXX	
Total cash disbursed (subtract from total cash collected)		$XXX
Amount of cash that should be on hand		$XXX
Actual count of cash on hand		$XXX
Difference between what should be on hand and actual		$XXX

Note: If the final number is negative or positive, then an error has occurred in collections or payments.

with a very lean inventory, thanks to the installation of a computerized inventory-control system that allows the firm to maintain records of inventory on a product-by-product basis. In addition to this capability, the system allows the company to monitor gross margin return on investment, inventory turnover, percentage of orders shipped on time, length of time to fill back orders, and percentage of customer complaints to shipped orders. Software to accomplish these goals is readily available and in many cases can even be modified to meet the exact needs of the business. The reports from this system are generated every two to four weeks in normal sales periods and weekly in heavy sales periods. This system not only provides Skolnik with an early warning system but also frees up cash normally invested in inventory and improves the overall profitability of the firm.[8]

From an accounting point of view, the entrepreneur will need to determine the value of inventory and how it affects the cost of goods sold (income statement). For example, assume that an entrepreneur made three purchases of inventory for manufacturing a finished product. Each purchase of inventory involved a different price. The issue will be what to use as a cost of goods sold. Generally, either a *FIFO* (first-in, first-out) or *LIFO* (last-in, first-out) method will be used. Most firms use a FIFO system since it reflects truer inventory and cost of goods sold values. However, there are good arguments for using the LIFO method in times of inflation, as will be seen later in this section.

FIFO Inventory costing method whereby first items into inventory are first items out

LIFO Inventory costing method whereby last items into inventory are first items out

The differences between using FIFO or LIFO are shown below. We can see how inventory affects cost of goods sold. Using either FIFO or LIFO, the first 800 units sold would be valued at $1. The next 600 units sold under FIFO would result in a cost of goods sold of $640: 200 units sold at $1, and 400 units sold at $1.10. Under the LIFO method, the 600 units would have a cost of goods sold of $650. This is determined by 500 units at $1.10 and 100 units at $1. The next 950 units sold under FIFO would have a cost of goods sold of $1,037.50, or 100 units at $1.10 and 850 units at $1.15. For LIFO, cost of goods sold would be $1,092.50, which results from 950 units costed at $1.15.

Cost of Goods Inventory	Units Sold	FIFO	LIFO
1,000 units @ $1.00	800	$ 800.00	$ 800.00
500 units @ $1.10	800	640.00	650.00
1,000 units @ $1.15	950	1037.50	1092.50

As stated above, there are occasions on which the entrepreneur might find that the LIFO method can actually increase cash flow. A case in point was the Dacor Corporation, a manufacturer of scuba diving equipment. In the early 1980s, the venture switched from FIFO to LIFO and incurred average annual increases in cash flow of 10 percent, until the early 1990s, when inflation increased so much that the company showed an increase of 25 percent in its cash flow. This decision was timely for Dacor and was implemented in the following manner.

First, it was necessary to decide if inventory was to be grouped into categories or to cost each item individually. These costs must also be pinpointed at the beginning of the year, at the end, or must be based on an annual average. For a very large inventory, the entrepreneur should categorize or pool the inventory. For those ventures with limited product lines, each item or product can be costed individually. Because of the wide variety of products sold, Dacor chose to categorize or pool its inventory for costing purposes. These options in stage 1 should be assessed carefully, because once the decision is made, it is very difficult to change back without incurring penalties from the IRS.

In stage 2, all inventory must be costed by searching through historical records. The amount of effort required for a venture will depend again on the breadth of the product line.

Once the inventory cost has been ascertained for each category or product, an average inventory cost must be calculated. For a new venture with only one or a few products, this would be relatively easy. For Dacor, with a wide product line, this required the assistance of an accounting firm. After all the calculations are made, management must notify the IRS (Form 970) that it is converting to the LIFO method.

The decision to convert from a FIFO to a LIFO system is not simple; thus it is important for the entrepreneur to carefully evaluate his or her goals before making any commitment. Conversion to LIFO can typically be beneficial if the following conditions exist.[9]

1. Rising labor, materials, and other production costs are anticipated.
2. The business and inventory are growing.
3. The business has some computer-assisted inventory control method capability.
4. The business is profitable. (If the start-up is losing money, there is no point in converting methods.)

Regardless of the inventory costing method used, it is important for the entrepreneur to keep careful records of inventory. Perpetual inventory systems can be structured using computers or a manual system. As items are sold, inventory should be reduced. To check the inventory balance, it may be necessary to physically count inventory periodically.

Efficient electronic data interchanges (EDI) among producers, wholesalers, and retailers can enable these firms to communicate with one another. Linking the needs of a retailer with the wholesaler and producer allows for a fast order entry and response. These systems also allow the firm to track shipments internationally.[10] The linking of firms in a computerized system has also been developed by the grocery and pharmaceutical industries using a software system called efficient consumer response (ECR). Supply chain members work together in this system to manage demand, distribution, and marketing such that minimum inventory levels are necessary to meet consumer demands. Computerized checkout machines are usually part of these systems so that linked members are able to anticipate inventory needs before stock-outs occur.[11]

Transport mode selection can also be important in inventory management. Some transportation modes, such as air transport, are very expensive. Rail and truck are the most often used methods of transportation when a next-day delivery for a customer is not necessary. Careful management of inventory through a computerized system and by working with customers and other channel members can minimize transportation costs. Anticipating customer needs can avoid stock-outs and the unexpected cost of having to meet a customer's immediate need by shipping a product by next-day air. These mistakes can be costly and are likely to significantly reduce the margins on any transaction.

Managing Fixed Assets

Fixed assets generally involve long-term commitments and large investments for the new venture. These fixed assets, such as the equipment appearing in Table 14.3, will have certain costs related to them. Equipment will require servicing and insurance and will affect utility costs. The equipment also will be depreciated over time, which will be reflected in the value of the asset over time.

If the entrepreneur cannot afford to buy equipment or fixed assets, leasing could be considered as an alternative. Leasing may be a good alternative to buying depending on the terms of the lease, the type of asset to be leased, and the usage demand on the asset. For example, leases for automobiles may contain a large down payment and possible usage or mileage fees that can make the lease much more expensive than a purchase. On the other

TABLE 14.3 MPP Plastics Inc., Income Statement, First Quarter Year 1 (000s)

		Actual (%)	Standard (%)
Net sales	$150.0	100.0	100.0
Less cost of goods sold	100.0	66.7	60.0
Gross margin	(50.0)	32.3	40.0
Operating expenses			
Selling expenses	11.7	7.8	8.0
Salaries	19.8	13.2	12.0
Advertising	5.2	3.5	4.0
Office supplies	1.9	1.3	1.0
Rent	6.0	4.0	3.0
Utilities	1.3	0.9	1.0
Insurance	0.6	0.4	0.5
Taxes	3.4	2.3	2.0
Interest	3.6	2.4	2.0
Depreciation	9.9	6.6	5.0
Miscellaneous	0.3	0.2	0.2
Total operating expenses	$ 66.3	42.6	38.7
Net profit (loss)	(13.3)	(9.3)	1.3

hand, lease payments represent an expense to the venture and can be used as a tax deduction. Leases are also valuable for equipment that becomes obsolete quickly. The entrepreneur can take a lease for short periods, reducing the long-term obligation to any specific asset. As with any other make or buy decision, the entrepreneur should consider all costs associated with the decision as well as its impact on cash flows.

Managing Costs and Profits

Although the cash flow analysis discussed earlier in the chapter can assist the entrepreneur in assessing and controlling costs, it is also useful to compute the net income for interim periods during the year. The most effective use of the interim income statement is to establish cost standards and compare the actual with the budgeted amount for that time period. Costs are budgeted based on percentages of net sales. These percentages can then be compared with actual percentages and can be assessed over time to ascertain where tighter cost controls may be necessary.

Table 14.3 compares actual and expected (standard) percentages on MPP Plastic's income statement for its first quarter of operation. This analysis gives the entrepreneur the opportunity to manage and control costs before it is too late. Table 14.4 shows that cost of goods sold is higher than standard. Part of this may result from the initial small purchases of inventory, which did not provide any quantity discounts. If this is not the case, the entrepreneur should consider finding other sources or raising prices.

Most of the expenses appear to be reasonably close to standard or expected percentages. The entrepreneur should assess each item to determine whether these costs can be reduced or whether it will be necessary to raise prices to ensure future positive profits. As the venture begins to evolve into the second and third years of operation, the entrepreneur should also compare current actual costs with prior incurred costs. For example, in the second year of operation, the entrepreneur may find it useful to look back at the selling expenses incurred in the first year of operation. Such comparisons can be done on a month-to-month basis (i.e., January, year 1, to January, year 2) or even quarterly or yearly, depending on the volatility of the costs in the particular business.

Where expenses or costs have been much higher than budgeted, it may be necessary for the entrepreneur to carefully analyze the account to determine what the exact cause of the overrun is. For example, utilities represent a single expense account yet may include a number of specific payments for such things as heat, electricity, gas, hot water, and so on. Thus, the entrepreneur should retain a running balance of all these payments to ascertain the cause of an unusually large utility expense. In Table 14.1 we see that the utility expense was $500, which was $200 over the budgeted amount, or a 67 percent increase. What caused the increase? Was any particular utility responsible for the overrun, or was it a result of higher oil costs, which affected all the utility expenses? These questions need to be resolved before the entrepreneur accepts the results and makes any needed adjustments for the next period.

Comparisons of the actual and budgeted expenses in the income statement can be misleading for those new ventures where there are multiple products or services. For financial reporting purposes to shareholders, bankers, or other investors, the income statement would summarize expenses across all products and services. This information, although helpful to get an overview of the success of the venture, does not indicate the marketing cost for each product, the performance of particular managers in controlling costs, or the most profitable product(s). For example, selling expenses for MPP Plastics Inc. (Table 14.3) were $11,700. These selling expenses may apply to more than one product, in which case the entrepreneur would need to ascertain the amount of

TABLE 14.4 MPP Plastics Inc., Balance Sheet, First Quarter Year 1

Assets		
Current assets		
Cash	$ 13,350	
Accounts receivable (40% of $60,000 in sales the previous month)	24,000	
Merchandise inventory	12,850	
Supplies	2,100	
Total fixed assets		$ 51,300
Fixed assets	$240,000	
Equipment		
Less depreciation	9,900	
Total fixed assets		$230,100
Total assets		281,400
Liabilities and Owners' Equity		
Current liabilities		
Accounts payable (20% of 40 CGS)	$ 8,000	
Current portion of L-T debt	13,600	
Total current liabilities		$ 21,600
Long-term liabilities		
Notes payable		223,200
Total liabilities		244,800
Owners' equity		
C. Peter's capital	$ 25,000	
K. Peter's capital	25,000	
Retained earnings	(13,400)	
Total owners' equity		$ 36,600
Total liabilities and owners' equity		$281,400

selling expense for each product. He or she may be tempted to prorate the expense across each product, which would not provide a realistic picture of the relative success of each product. Thus, if MPP Plastics Inc. produced three different products, the selling expense for each might be assumed to be $3,900 per product, when the actual selling expenses could be much more or less.

Some products may require more advertising, insurance, administrative time, transportation, storage, and so on, which could be misleading if the entrepreneur chooses to allocate these expenses equally across all products. In response to this problem, it is recommended that the entrepreneur allocate expenses as effectively as possible, by product. Not only is it important to evaluate these costs across each product, but also it is important to evaluate them by region, customer, distribution channel, department, and so on. Arbitrary allocation of costs should be avoided in order to get a real profit perspective of every product marketed by the new venture.

Taxes

Don't forget the tax agent! The entrepreneur will be required to withhold federal and state taxes for his or her employees. Each month or quarter (depending on the size of the payroll), deposits or payments will need to be made to the appropriate agency for funds withheld from wages. Generally, federal taxes, state taxes, Social Security, and Medicare are withheld from employees' salaries and are deposited later. The entrepreneur should be careful not to use these funds since, if payments are late, there will be high interest and penalties assessed. In addition to withholding taxes, the new venture may be required to pay a number of taxes, such as state and federal unemployment taxes, a matching FICA and Medicare tax, and other business taxes. These taxes will need to be part of any budget since they will affect cash flow and profits. To determine the exact amount, dates due, and procedures, the unemployment agency for the federal government and the appropriate state or the tax department can be contacted.

The federal and state governments will also require the entrepreneur to file end-of-year returns of the business. If the venture is incorporated, there may be state corporation taxes to be paid regardless of whether the venture earned a profit. The filing periods and tax responsibilities will vary for other types of organizations. Chapter 10 provides some insights into the tax responsibilities of proprietorships, partnerships, and corporations. As stated earlier, use of a tax accountant should also be considered to avoid any errors and provide advice in handling these expenses. The accountant can also assist the entrepreneur in planning or budgeting appropriate funds to meet any of these expenses.

Record Keeping

In order to support this effort toward financial control, it is helpful to consider using a software package to enhance the flow of this type of information. With a growing venture it may also be necessary to enlist the support and services of an accountant or a consultant to support record keeping and financial control. These external service firms can also help train employees using the latest and most appropriate technology to meet the needs of the venture.

A system for storing and using customer information becomes vitally important for a growing firm. Growth typically involves marketing to new customers, and a large influx of new customers can overwhelm more primitive systems. For example, previously customer information may have been stored in the memory of the different salespeople. However, as the sheer number of customers increases, the memory capacity of a salesperson may be exceeded and important information (and new and existing sales) could be lost.

Not only will a database increase the capacity to hold and process information, it begins to accumulate bits of knowledge contained within different individuals into an organizational knowledge that is accessible to everyone within the firm. By building organizational knowledge the entrepreneur is less dependent upon any one individual. For example, if the top salesperson were to die or otherwise leave the organization, then a considerable amount of important information could be lost to the firm. Specifically, customer information should be retained in a database that includes information on a contact person (including telephone number and address), as well as important data on the amount of units and dollars of business transacted by each account. New accounts should also be designated for follow-up, such as welcoming customers and providing them with important information about the company and its products and services.

AS SEEN IN *ENTREPRENEUR* MAGAZINE

ELEVATOR PITCH FOR eVEST

A wealthy friend has asked you to keep your eye out for attractive businesses in which she can invest. Your wealthy friend is very busy and you only want to introduce those businesses that are genuinely attractive. After hearing the following pitch, would you introduce Scott to your wealthy friend?

Entrepreneur Scott Jordan, 38, founder and CEO of Scott eVest LLC

Company Clothing and licensing company featuring a line of vests/jackets with 16 to 22 pockets that discreetly hold tech gadgets

Sales Projections for the Current Year $5 million

Weighed Down "I was practicing law and commuting back and forth, carrying the things that most businesspeople carry with them nowadays—PDA, cell phone, an expandable keyboard. Working in a business casual environment, I would wear sports jackets just to have the extra pockets to put my stuff in. I started asking around and found the need for more pockets was common."

(Un) orderly Fashion Now selling through www.scottevest.com, Jordan was initially wary of e-commerce when he started the company in 2001. "On the day [the site] went live, a Web site referred to it, and I got 50,000 hits and more than 100 orders. I didn't even have a manufacturer lined up. I had six samples. I had to juggle between sending them to retailers, catalog companies, and Asia for production pricing. Each one was like gold to me."

Apparel Appeal On exhibit at Disneyland's Tomorrowland, the Scott eVest has appeared on *ER* and HBO's *The Wire*. "Every other day, I get a call from a branch of the military, CIA, Secret Service, INS. I'm told the president got one with the presidential seal on it."

Source: Reprinted with permission of Entrepreneur Media, Inc., "This Entrepreneur Will Never Find His Pockets Empty—No Matter How Many of Them He Has," by April Y. Pennington, February 2003, *Entrepreneur* magazine: www.entrepreneur.com.

OVERCOMING PRESSURES ON EXISTING HUMAN RESOURCES

Generally the new venture does not have the luxury of a human resource department that can interview, hire, and evaluate employees. Most of these decisions will be the responsibility of the entrepreneur and perhaps one or two other key employees. The process of human resource management should not be any different from what was previously discussed in Chapter 9, where we outline some of the important procedures for preparing job descriptions and specifications for new employees.

Some entrepreneurs are using professional employer organizations (PEOs). One such company is TriNet Employer Group Inc., which came to the rescue of Robert Teal, cofounder of a Silicon Valley start-up, Quinta Corporation. Robert had found it time consuming and costly to hire and retain employees. His banker suggested he consider TriNet. After an assessment of TriNet's services, he hired it to assume most of the human resource tasks of the new venture. This involved such things as recruiting, hiring, setting up benefit programs, payroll, and even firing decisions. This has given Robert more time to devote to other aspects of his growing venture.[12]

In growing the workforce, entrepreneurs face the decision of what proportion of the workforce should be permanent and what proportion should be part time, and this decision involves a number of trade-offs. On the one hand, a greater percentage of part-time workers represents a lower fixed cost, which provides the firm greater flexibility in dealing with changes in the external environment. On the other hand, personnel instability is more likely with part-time workers because turnover is typically higher[13] and part-time workers are less committed to the firm because they have less of a personal stake in its performance. Therefore building a functional organizational culture is more difficult when the workforce has a greater proportion of part-time workers.

Regardless of the composition of the firm's workforce, mistakes will be made in the selection and hiring of some people. This leads to one of the most difficult decisions for an entrepreneur to make—the firing of incompetent employees. Having a fair employee evaluation process is essential in justifying the firing of an employee. Employees should be given feedback on a regular basis, and any problems should be identified with a proposed solution agreeable to the employee and the entrepreneur. In this manner, continued problems with the employee that necessitate a firing decision will be well documented.

An integral part of the firm's human resource strategy for effectively growing the business must take into consideration how to maintain the corporate culture despite the influx of new employees. New employees can be inculcated through early training sessions that perpetuate the stories and rituals that form the basis of the culture. But the majority of this responsibility falls on the shoulders of the entrepreneur. The entrepreneur must be the walking, talking embodiment of the culture, although in cases of rapid growth the work of the entrepreneur can be complemented by the work of a cultural ambassador. For example, as IKEA expanded internationally Ingvar Kamprad took a number of steps to ensure that the corporate culture would still have an impact in foreign stores. For example, he documented the "IKEA way" and used cultural ambassadors and training sessions to inculcate new employees of new stores in foreign locations.

OVERCOMING PRESSURES ON THE MANAGEMENT OF EMPLOYEES

participative style of management The manager involves others in the decision-making process

As the venture grows, it changes. Managing change is often a complex task, one that is better undertaken with a participative style of management. A *participative style of management* is one in which the entrepreneur involves others in the decision-making process. There are a number of advantages to using a participative management style when a firm is growing. First, the complexity of growing a business and managing change increases the information-processing demands on the entrepreneur. Involving others in the decision-making process is a way of reducing these demands. Second, highly qualified managers and employees are an important resource for coming up with new ways to tackle current problems. Third, if employees are involved in the decision-making process, they are more prepared and more motivated to implement the decided course of action. Finally, in most cultures employees enjoy the added responsibility of making decisions and taking initiatives. In such a case, a participative management style will enhance job satisfaction. The following captures some of the activities the entrepreneur can do to institute a more participative style of management and successfully grow the business.

Establish a Team Spirit A team spirit involves the belief by everyone in the organization that they are "in this thing together" and by working together great things can be achieved. Small but important actions by the entrepreneur can create this team spirit. For example, the entrepreneur should establish a "we" spirit—not a "me" spirit—in meetings and memoranda to employees as well as to other stakeholders.

Communicate with Employees Open and frequent communication with employees builds trust and diminishes fear. Often the fear of change associated with firm growth is worse

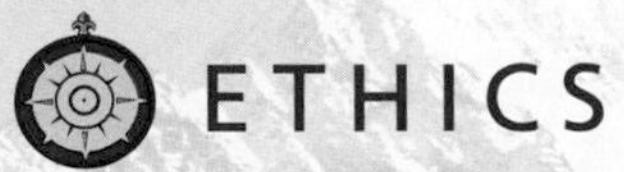

LESSONS FROM ENRON

Even the Smallest Business Can Learn What *Not* to Do from This Giant Company

Q: What can a business owner learn from the mistakes of Enron?

A: So you wanted to own a multibillion-dollar corporation and fly around the world in the latest Lear jet. Then along comes Enron, the seventh largest company in the United States, a firm most folks probably never even heard of, and it ruins your dreams. And perhaps your 401(k), too. The excesses that caused this disintegration will be thoroughly examined by lawmakers and regulators. When their work is completed, even the innocent will find new government-mandated rules and regulations to make doing business more difficult. Well, don't despair—"mistakes were made," but lessons can be learned.

And don't think for a minute the Enron problem is something that only giant corporations face. Although the magnitude of its collapse won't be matched by the local print shop or pizza parlor, the collapse of even the smallest of businesses impacts many people. The failure of your business will greatly and negatively impact you, your partners, your employees, customers, and vendors as well as the families of each of those groups. As business owners, we have a duty to operate in a prudent, lawful, and ethical manner.

So what can we do? Every good business has a solid business plan and a realistic design for implementing that plan. While Enron is fresh in our minds, we think the first thing to do is to examine our business plan from the perspective of its fidelity to the prudence, legality, and ethics mentioned above, and then compare the business plan to the reality. Have business "necessities" caused us to step over the line? How will the deviations from the plan come back to bite us and those who depend on us? Try to recall your first day in business—it wasn't about bending the rules, it wasn't about living high on the hog (or as they say today, living large), and it had nothing to do with cheating others—that first day was all about launching a dream and bringing others along. It's time to relight the flame.

As we said, on a local scale, the collapse of a small business will match the collapse of an Enron for those involved. If we get caught playing the business game dirty, we won't see ourselves on national TV, but our next-door neighbor will know that side of our character we've tried to hide. So will our families and close friends.

Let's think about the things we may be doing now, things that were never in our plan and were never a part of our dreams. And let's purge them from our business practices. A few of the common legal and ethical missteps some business owners take, which must be ended today, are:

- Paying personal expenses out of business funds and writing them off
- Not reporting all cash receipts
- Cheating customers on price, quality, delivery, or warranty
- Using misleading advertising
- Failing to pay our business bills on time
- Lying to employees, customers, and vendors

Some may think these lapses pale in comparison to the allegations against Enron. They don't. If you act illegally or unethically in your business, given the opportunity, you'd do so if your canvas were larger. Take a good look at the list above and ask yourself, "What is the penalty if I get caught?" Then ask yourself a more important question: "Is this who I really am?" Finally, fix it.

We may yet get to fly in that Lear jet, but we'll only deserve to if we're honest, hard-working business owners.

Source: Reprinted with permission of Entrepreneur Media, Inc., "Even the Smallest Business Can Learn What *Not* to Do from This Giant Company," by Rod Walsh and Dan Carrison, February 2002, *Entrepreneur* magazine: www.entrepreneur.com.

than the reality of change and communication will alleviate some of that anxiety. Open and frequent communication is a two-way street. The entrepreneur must listen to what is on the minds of his or her employees. The entrepreneur should solicit suggestions on how a department or the firm as a whole can more effectively manage growth and improve its performance.

Provide Feedback The entrepreneur should frequently provide feedback to employees. Feedback needs to be constructive such that it enables the employee to improve the quality of a particular task but does not attack the person and create a fear of failure. The entrepreneur should also seek feedback from others. For this feedback to be valuable it must be honest, which requires a culture that values open and honest communication. An entrepreneur confident in his or her own abilities, and with a desire to effectively grow the business, should be open to, and should encourage, this type of feedback.

Delegate Some Responsibility to Others With an increasing number of tasks for the entrepreneur, he or she cannot be available to make every management decision. Key employees must be given the flexibility to take the initiative and make decisions without the fear of failure. This requires the entrepreneur to create a culture that values and rewards employees for taking initiative and sees failure as a positive attempt rather than a negative outcome.

Provide Continuous Training for Employees By training employees, the entrepreneur increases employees' ability and capacity to improve their own performance at a particular task and, as a result, improves the chance of successfully growing the firm. Training should reflect the new management style by involving employees in deciding upon training session topics.

OVERCOMING PRESSURES ON ENTREPRENEURS' TIME

Entrepreneurs can always make better use of their time, and the more they strive to do so, the more it will enrich their venture as well as their personal lives. How does one more effectively manage time? *Time management* is the process of improving an individual's productivity through more efficient use of time. The entrepreneur reaps numerous benefits from effectively managing his or her time, some of which follow.

time management The process of improving an individual's productivity through more efficient use of time

Increased Productivity Time management helps the entrepreneur determine the tasks of greatest importance and focuses his or her attention on successfully completing those tasks. This means that there will always be sufficient time to accomplish the most important things.

Increased Job Satisfaction Increased productivity means that more of the important tasks are successfully completed, which in turn enhances the entrepreneur's job satisfaction. The entrepreneur is less likely to feel "swamped" and overwhelmed by the increasing number of tasks generated from firm growth. Getting more important things done and being more successful in growing and developing the venture will give the entrepreneur more job satisfaction.

Improved Interpersonal Relationships Although the total time an entrepreneur spends with other individuals in the company may in fact decrease through better time management, the time spent will be of a higher quality (quality time), allowing him or her to improve relationships with others inside and outside the firm (including family). Furthermore, as others in the company experience less time pressure, better results, and greater job satisfaction, relationships within the firm become more harmonious and the firm can build an *espirit de corps*.

Reduced Time Anxiety and Tension Worry, guilt, and other emotions tend to reduce the entrepreneur's information-processing capacity, which can lead to less effective assessments and decisions. Effective time management reduces concerns and anxieties, which "frees up" information processing and improves the quality of the entrepreneur's decisions.

Better Health By reducing anxiety and tension and improving productivity, job satisfaction, and relationships with others, there is less psychological and physiological strain on the mind and body, resulting in improved health. Time management can also include scheduling time to eat well and exercise. Good health, and the energy that it brings, is vital for an entrepreneur growing his or her business.

Basic Principles of Time Management

Time management provides a process by which the entrepreneur can become a time saver, not a time server. This efficient use of time enables the entrepreneur to expand and grow the venture properly, increase personal and firm productivity, and lessen the encroachment of the business into his or her private life. An entrepreneur develops good time management by adhering to six basic principles, as follows.

principle of desire A recognition of the need to change personal attitudes and habits regarding the allocation of time

Principle of Desire The *principle of desire* requires that the entrepreneur recognize that he or she is a time waster, that time is an important resource, and that there is a need to change personal attitudes and habits regarding the allocation of time. Therefore, effective time management depends on the entrepreneur's willpower, self-discipline, and motivation to optimize his or her time.

principle of effectiveness A focus on the most important issues

Principle of Effectiveness The *principle of effectiveness* requires the entrepreneur to focus on the most important issues, even when under pressure. Whenever possible, an entrepreneur should try to complete each task in a single session, which requires that enough time be set aside to accomplish that task. This eliminates time wasted in catching up to where one left off. Although quality is of course important, perfectionism is not and often leads only to procrastination. The entrepreneur must not spend excessive time on trying to make a small improvement in one area when time would be better spent in another area.

principle of analysis Understanding how time is currently being allocated, and where it is being inefficiently invested

Principle of Analysis The *principle of analysis* provides information to the entrepreneur about how time is currently being allocated, which will also highlight inefficient or inappropriate investments of time. The entrepreneur should track his or her time over a two-week period, using a time sheet with 15-minute intervals, and then analyze how time has been spent, where time has been wasted, and how these "time traps" can be avoided in the future (using the other principles). For example, the entrepreneur should not "reinvent the wheel" in solving similar problems; rather, standardized forms and procedures should be developed for all recurring events and operations.

principle of teamwork Acknowledgment that only a small amount of time is actually under one's control and that most of one's time is taken up by others

Principle of Teamwork Analysis of time will likely reveal to the entrepreneur that only a small amount of time is actually under his or her control—most of his or her time is taken up by others. The *principle of teamwork* acknowledges the increasing importance of delegation for an entrepreneur of a growing firm; that is, the entrepreneur must require others to take responsibility for the completion of tasks previously undertaken by the entrepreneur. The entrepreneur must also help members of the management team become more sensitive to the time management concept when dealing with others in the company, especially in dealing with the entrepreneur. Note that managing one's time does not mean that the entrepreneur must make himself or herself inaccessible to others; rather, accessibility is increased because the time that is spent with others can now be fully focused on them.

principle of prioritized planning Categorization of tasks by their degree of importance and then the allocation of time to tasks based on this categorization

Principle of Prioritized Planning The *principle of prioritized planning* requires the entrepreneur to categorize his or her tasks by their degree of importance and then to allocate time to tasks based on this categorization. For example, each day, an entrepreneur should list all tasks to be accomplished and indicate their degree of importance using a scale from 1 to 3, with 1 being most important, 2 somewhat important, and 3 moderately important. The entrepreneur can then focus on those tasks of most importance (those with a number 1). Furthermore, the entrepreneur can prioritize his or her time. For example, some entrepreneurs are most efficient in the morning, some during the afternoon, and some at night. The most efficient period of the day should be used to address the most important issues.

principle of reanalysis Periodic review of one's time management process

Principle of Reanalysis The *principle of reanalysis* requires the entrepreneur to periodically review his or her time management process. In this reanalysis, entrepreneurs can often improve their time management by investigating more systemic (systemwide) issues and revisiting potential opportunities for delegation. For example, the clerical staff and close assistants should be well trained and encouraged to take the initiative, including sorting correspondence and returning phone calls based on importance, dealing with issues of low importance to the entrepreneur, and instituting routines such as standard letters for the entrepreneur to sign, a daily diary, reminder lists, operations board, and an efficient "pending" file. All meetings should be analyzed to ensure that they are being run effectively. If not, the person who runs the meeting should be trained to do so. The purpose of all committees should also be reanalyzed to ensure that they still provide value.

IMPLICATIONS OF FIRM GROWTH FOR THE ENTREPRENEUR

Firm growth introduces a number of managerial challenges for the entrepreneur; challenges with which they may be unfamiliar and ill equipped to deal with. Above we have offered a number of tools that entrepreneurs can develop to more effectively cope with, and manage, the growth process. Some entrepreneurs lack the ability to make the transition to this more professional management approach. Another group of entrepreneurs may be able but unwilling to focus their attention on achieving those tasks necessary to successfully achieve firm growth.

For example, Pearce Jones, founder and president of Design Edge, controlled growth by putting a halt on all growth for one full year. The company realized that if it did not get control over growth, serious problems were likely. At this point in 1998, the company had quadrupled its number of employees and had invested in a new building. Even though each new employee was contributing an increase of $150,000 in sales, the margins were small. The additional debt from the new facility and the additional costs for employees led to this abrupt decision to cease hiring, deactivate marketing and sales, refuse any new business, and basically focus only on existing customers. Although Pearce admits this decision was emotionally painful, it led to dramatic changes as profits actually doubled and no employee turnover was experienced.[14]

Another example of a reluctance to grow is illustrated by this quote from the founder and CEO of Southwest Airlines in 1993, Herb Kelleher: "Southwest has had more opportunities for growth than it has airplanes. Yet, unlike other airlines, it has avoided the trap of growing beyond its means. . . . Employees just don't seem to be enamored of the idea that bigger is better."[15] Growth may not be pursued because there is a belief that in doing so firm profitability and/or the firm's chances of survival will be sacrificed.

Even if there is a belief that the pursuit of growth will improve firm performance and enhance personal wealth, some entrepreneurs will still avoid growing their business. These entrepreneurs are not necessarily motivated by economics. Consider an individual who chooses to start a business because she or he is tired of being controlled by others—this person wants the independence that comes from being one's own boss. Growth may not be an attractive option for this entrepreneur, because acquiring the necessary resources for growth will mean selling equity (for example, to a venture capitalist) or raising debt capital (for example, from a bank). Both sources of resources place limits on the entrepreneur's ability to make strategic decisions for the firm. In this case the entrepreneur may prefer to have full ownership, be debt-free, and remain small.

Evan Douglas is a professor of entrepreneurship at the Brisbane Graduate School of Business in Australia. His dream is to create and manage a business that rents a small number of yachts to tourists. The office (preferably a shack) would be on the beach somewhere on the Great Barrier Reef. When he achieves this dream, the last thing that he wants to do is to grow the business such that his task moves to one of professional manager and away from the task of "beach bum." His dream business is an example of a lifestyle business. Growth can be perceived by such lifestyle entrepreneurs as threatening the very reason for becoming an entrepreneur in the first place.

A Categorization of Entrepreneurs and Their Firms' Growth

Based on the arguments above, Figure 14.4 categorizes entrepreneurs in terms of two dimensions: the first dimension represents an entrepreneur's abilities to successfully make the transition to more professional management practices, and the second dimension represents an entrepreneur's growth aspirations. Depending on the entrepreneur's position along these two dimensions, four types of firm growth outcomes are identified.

Actual Growth of the Firm Entrepreneurs in the upper-right quadrant possess both the necessary abilities to make the transition to a more professional management approach and the aspiration to grow their businesses. These are the entrepreneurs who are the most likely to achieve firm growth.

Unused Potential for Growth Entrepreneurs in the upper-left quadrant possess the necessary abilities for transition *but* do not aspire to do so. These are the entrepreneurs of firms

FIGURE 14.4 Four Types of Entrepreneurs* and Firm Growth

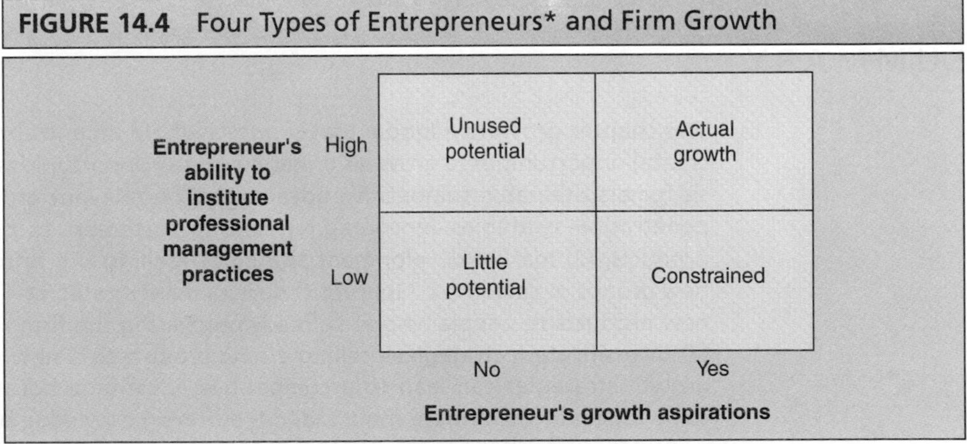

*Based on ability to make a transition to professional management and aspiration.

Source: Adapted from J. Wiklund and D. A. Shepherd, "Aspiring for and Achieving Growth: The Moderating Role of Resources and Opportunities," *Journal of Management Studies* (2003), vol. 40, no. 8, pp. 1919–42.

that have unused potential. A relatively large proportion of all lifestyle firms are represented by this classification.

Constrained Growth Entrepreneurs in the lower-right quadrant aspire to grow their businesses *but* do not possess sufficient abilities to successfully satisfy this aspiration. These entrepreneurs are most likely to be frustrated by the firm's lack of growth and are in the most danger of failure because the firm may be pushed toward the pursuit of growth opportunities and beyond the entrepreneur's ability to cope. However, the entrepreneur might replace himself or herself as the CEO with a professional manager. This will allow the aspiration to be fulfilled (move to the upper-right quadrant). This does not necessarily mean that the entrepreneur will leave the business, rather the entrepreneur might manage R&D, new products, and/or new markets where his or her strengths are highly valued and enhance rather than constrain the growth of the firm.

Little Potential for Firm Growth Entrepreneurs in the lower-left quadrant possess neither the necessary abilities to make the transition to a more professional management approach *nor* the aspirations to grow their businesses. These businesses have little potential for growth but due to the limited abilities of the entrepreneur to manage growth, these firms may actually perform better if they remain at a smaller scale.

Although the abilities of the entrepreneur and the existing resources of the firm can limit the effective pursuit of growth opportunities, the resources necessary for growth can be acquired externally—we refer to these sources as external growth mechanisms. These external mechanisms for growth, which include joint ventures, acquisitions, mergers, and so on, each offer a number of different advantages and disadvantages in providing the resources for effective growth but all require the entrepreneur to negotiate a new relationship. For example, negotiation is a critical element to forming a joint venture.

Chapter 16 introduces the basic concepts and skills required for an entrepreneur to negotiate the best agreement with these potential growth partners—an agreement that maximizes the entrepreneur's interests. It then describes each external growth mechanism and its advantages and disadvantages.

IN REVIEW

SUMMARY

This chapter provides a model that suggests where an entrepreneur can look for (or create) opportunities to grow his or her business—opportunities that can provide a basis for a sustainable competitive advantage. The relevant growth strategies are: (1) penetration strategies—encouraging existing customers to buy more of the firm's products, (2) market development strategies—selling the firm's existing products to new groups of customers, (3) product development strategies—developing and selling new products to people who are already purchasing the firm's existing products, and (4) diversification strategies—selling a new product to a new market. Most of these growth strategies can lead to a competitive advantage because they capitalize on some aspect of the entrepreneur's, and the firm's, knowledge base.

Business growth has important implications for the economy, the firm, and the entrepreneur. High-growth businesses can stimulate an economy, improve its international competitiveness, and reduce unemployment. Even modest levels of growth by small businesses can have a dramatic impact on an economy because the population of small firms is so large. It is also important to acknowledge that growth strategies often involve the entrepreneur's taking some risk, which means that sometimes they will not succeed. A failed attempt provides information for that entrepreneur and other entrepreneurs, and learning from failure has an important positive impact on an economy.

Because growth makes a firm bigger, the firm begins to benefit from the advantages of size but also introduces a number of managerial challenges. It puts pressure on existing financial resources, human resources, the management of employees, and the entrepreneur's time. There are actions the entrepreneur can take to better manage these pressures and more effectively grow his or her business.

To overcome pressures on existing financial resources the entrepreneur should apply more effective financial control, record keeping, and inventory management techniques. To overcome pressures on existing human resources the entrepreneur must address the question of what proportion of the workforce should be permanent and what proportion should be part time, should be prepared to fire incompetent employees, and, at the same time, should build and maintain a functional organizational culture. It is important that the entrepreneur interact with employees, so as to establish a team spirit; effect open and frequent communication to build trust and provide constructive feedback; provide key employees with the flexibility to take the initiative and make decisions without the fear of failure; and provide continuous training for employees.

Entrepreneurs can always make better use of their time, and the more they strive to do so, the more it will enrich their venture as well as their personal lives. Better use of time can lead to increased productivity, increased job satisfaction, improved interpersonal relationships with people inside and outside the business, reduced anxiety and tension, and possibly even better health. Efficient use of time enables the entrepreneur to expand and grow the venture properly, increase personal and firm productivity, and lessen the encroachment of the business into his or her private life. Effective time management requires adherence to six basic principles: desire, effectiveness, analysis, teamwork, prioritized planning, and reanalysis.

Some entrepreneurs lack the ability to make the transition to this more professional management approach, while others may be unwilling to do so. Entrepreneurs who possess both the necessary abilities and the aspiration are most likely to achieve firm growth. Entrepreneurs who possess the necessary abilities but do not aspire to do so will manage firms that have unused potential and/or lifestyle firms. Entrepreneurs who aspire to grow their business but do not possess sufficient abilities are most likely to be frustrated by the firm's lack of growth and are in the most danger of business failure unless the entrepreneur replaces himself or herself. Finally, entrepreneurs who possess neither the necessary abilities nor the aspirations to grow their businesses may run businesses that provide a sufficient income if the businesses remain at a smaller scale.

RESEARCH TASKS

1. What different software packages are available to help entrepreneurs with their different record-keeping and control activities? How effective do you believe software can be for each of these tasks?
2. Assume you have started a new bricks-and-mortar retail business but want to create a Web site to advertise and provide information about your business. What are the attributes of a good Web site for this purpose? How much will it cost?

3. How costly is it to put an advertisement in the local paper, in the business telephone directory, on the radio, on television, and in a magazine? What types of products would benefit from each advertising outlet mentioned above? Why?
4. Which are the three fastest-growing companies in the country? What opportunities have they pursued to achieve this level of growth? What growth mechanism have they used (internal, joint venture, acquisitions, franchising, etc.)?
5. Use research to come up with three examples of founding entrepreneurs who stepped aside once their firms had grown to a certain size and brought in "professional managers." In each case, what relationship did the entrepreneur continue to have with the firm after the transition? Provide an example of a founding entrepreneur being forced out of the position of CEO to be replaced by a professional manager.

CLASS DISCUSSION

1. To what extent does the use of software help and hinder the entrepreneur's ability to perform the important tasks of record keeping and financial control?
2. The firm needs to make sales. What is the best way to motivate salespeople to make more sales and improve the performance of the firm? How would you effectively monitor their performance under the proposed motivation system? What are the pros and cons of your motivation and monitoring system?
3. Categorize those people in the class who you believe would be well suited for starting a business and managing initial growth but would be less effective at conducting the professional management tasks when the firm became larger. What can they do to improve their ability to successfully make the transition with the firm? Categorize those people in your class who you believe would be well suited to the role of professionally managing a larger (more established) firm but less effective at starting a firm and managing early growth. What can they do to improve their ability to manage a firm earlier in its development? Is there anybody in the class (except maybe yourself) who you believe would be equally effective at both tasks?
4. Think of a company that produces one product and sells it to one group of customers (or make one up). Advise the entrepreneur of the many opportunities there are for growth—opportunities for penetration strategies, market development strategies, product development strategies, and diversification strategies.
5. Are you a time waster or a time server? What time management techniques do you use? How can you better manage your time?

SELECTED READINGS

Baum, J. Robert; Edwin A. Locke; and Ken G. Smith. (2001). A Multidimensional Model of Venture Growth. *Academy of Management Journal,* vol. 44, no. 2, pp. 292–304.

The authors formed an integrated model of venture growth. CEOs' specific competencies and motivations and firm competitive strategies were found to be direct predictors of venture growth. CEOs' traits and general competencies and the environment had significant indirect effects.

Chrisman, James; Ed McMullan; and Jeremy Hall. (2005). The Influence of Guided Preparation on the Long-Term Performance of New Ventures. *Journal of Business Venturing,* vol. 20, no. 6, pp. 769–91.

In this article the authors further develop a theory of guided preparation and new venture performance and test its fundamental relationships on a sample of 159 new ventures that had received outsider assistance 5–9 years earlier and had been in business for 3–8 years. The results suggest that the long-term growth of the ventures since start-up is significantly related to guided preparation. However, a curvilinear model, rather than a linear model, was found to best capture the relationships of interest.

Danneels, Erwin. (2002). The Dynamics of Product Innovation and Firm Competences. *Strategic Management Journal,* vol. 23, no. 12, pp. 1095–122.

This study examines how product innovation contributes to the renewal of the firm through its dynamic and reciprocal relation with the firm's competences.

Davidsson, Per; Bruce Kirchhoff; Abdulnasser Hatemi; and Helena Gustavsson. (2002). Empirical Analysis of Business Growth Factors Using Swedish Data. *Journal of Small Business Management,* vol. 40, no. 4, pp. 332–50.

Although business growth differs among industrial sectors, youth, ownership independence, and small size are found to be major factors that underlie growth across all industries.

Delmar, Frédéric; Per Davidsson; and William B. Gartner. (2003). Arriving at the High-Growth Firm. *Journal of Business Venturing,* vol. 18, no. 2, pp. 189–217.

Using 19 different measures of firm growth (such as relative and absolute sales growth, relative and absolute employee growth, organic growth versus acquisition growth, and the regularity and volatility of growth rates over the 10-year period), the authors identified seven different types of firm growth patterns. These patterns were related to firm age and size as well as industry affiliation. Implications for research and practice are offered.

Gongming Qian. (2002). Multinationality, Product Diversification, and Profitability of Emerging U.S. Small- and Medium-Sized Enterprises. *Journal of Business Venturing,* vol. 17, no. 6, pp. 611–34.

This paper examines empirically individual and joint effects of multinationality and product diversification on profit performance for a sample of emerging small- and medium-sized enterprises (SMEs). The results suggest a curvilinear relationship between them: that is, they are positively related up to a point, after which a further increase in multinationality and product diversification was associated with declining performance.

Park, Choelsoon. (2003). Prior Performance Characteristics of Related and Unrelated Acquirers. *Strategic Management Journal,* vol. 24, no. 5, pp. 471–81.

This paper focuses on a single event of a large acquisition, which enables the authors to better identify the sequential relationships between prior firm profitability, prior industry profitability, and subsequent acquisition strategies. By doing so, this paper makes clearer the causal relationships between firm profitability, industry profitability, and acquisition strategies.

Penrose, Edith. (1959). *The Theory of the Growth of the Business.* Oxford: Oxford University Press.

Pettus, Michael L. (2001). The Resource-Based View as a Developmental Growth Process: Evidence from the Deregulated Trucking Industry. *Academy of Management Journal,* vol. 44, no. 4, pp. 878–97.

This paper develops a resource-based perspective for predicting the sequencing of a firm's resources that best provides for firm growth. The sequencing that generated the highest firm growth combines a Penrosian (1959) perspective with the more recent resource-based literature.

Rebecca Reuber, A.; and Eileen Fischer. (2002). Foreign Sales and Small Firm Growth: The Moderating Role of the Management Team. *Entrepreneurship: Theory & Practice*, vol. 27, no. 1, pp. 29–46.

The premise of this article is that the management team of a small firm plays a key role in internationalization outcomes. Findings indicate that the behavioral integration of the management team moderates the relationship between foreign sales growth and overall firm growth.

Rugman, Alan M.; and Alan Verbeke. (2002). Edith Penrose's Contribution to the Resource-Based View of Strategic Management. *Strategic Management Journal*, vol. 28, no. 8, pp. 769–81.

Edith Penrose's 1959 book, The Theory of the Growth of the Firm, *is considered by many scholars in the strategy field to be the seminal work that provided the intellectual foundations for the modern, resource-based theory of the firm. However, the present paper suggests that Penrose's direct or intended contribution to resource-based thinking has been misinterpreted.*

Schulze, William S., Michael H. Lubatkin; and Richard N. Dino. (2003). A Social Capital Model of High-Growth Ventures. *Academy of Management Journal*, vol. 46, no. 3, pp. 374–85.

In this article the authors use social capital theory to explain how human and social capital affect a venture's ability to accumulate financial capital during its growth stages and its performance during the two-year period after going public. They found indications that social capital leverages the productivity of a venture's resource base and provides the venture with a durable source of competitive advantage.

Wiklund, Johan; and Dean A. Shepherd. (2003). Aspiring for, and Achieving Growth: The Moderating Role of Resources and Opportunities. *Journal of Management Studies*, vol. 40, no. 8, pp. 1919–42.

In this article, the authors find that small business managers' aspirations to expand their business activities are positively related to actual growth. However, the relationship between aspirations and growth appears more complex than stated. Education, experience, and environmental dynamism magnify the effect of growth aspirations on the realization of growth.

Wiklund, Johan; Per Davidsson; and Frédéric Delmar. (2003). What Do They Think and Feel about Growth? An Expectancy-Value Approach to Small Business Managers' Attitudes toward Growth. *Entrepreneurship: Theory & Practice*, vol. 27, no. 3, pp. 247–71.

This study focuses on small business managers' motivation to expand their firms. The results suggest that concern for employee well-being comes out strongly in determining the overall attitude toward growth. The authors interpret this as reflecting a concern that the positive atmosphere of the small organization may be lost in growth, which might cause recurrent conflict for small business managers when deciding about the future route for their firms.

Zimmerman, Monica A.; and Gerald Z. Zeitz. (2002). Beyond Survival: Achieving New Venture Growth by Building Legitimacy. *Academy of Management Review*, vol. 27, no. 3, pp. 414–32.

In this article the authors argue that (1) legitimacy is an important resource for gaining other resources, (2) such resources are crucial for new venture growth, and (3) legitimacy can be enhanced by the strategic actions of new ventures. They review the impact of legitimacy on new ventures as well as sources of legitimacy for new ventures, present strategies for new ventures to acquire legitimacy, explore the process of building legitimacy in the new venture, and examine the concept of the legitimacy threshold.

END NOTES

1. See, "PowerBar Reaps Bounty with New Harvest Bar; Crunched for Time, Americans Devour Energy Bars," *Business Wire* (August 4, 1998), p. 1; C. Adams, "A Lesson from PowerBar's Slow Start to Diversity," *The Wall Street Journal* (June 14, 1999), p. 4; and "The PowerBar Story," Company Web site www.powerbar.com.
2. H. I. Ansoff, *Corporate Strategy: An Analytical Approach to Business Policy for Growth and Expansion* (New York: McGraw-Hill, 1965).
3. Martha E. Mangelsdorf, "Growth Companies," *Inc.* (May 21, 1996), pp. 85–92.
4. P. Davidsson, L. Lindmark, and C. Olofsson, *Dynamiken i svenskt näringsliv (Business Dynamics in Sweden).* (Lund, Sweden: Studentlitteratur, 1994).
5. J. Wiklund, *Small Firm Growth and Performance: Entrepreneurship and Beyond,* Doctoral Dissertation (Jönköping: Jönköping International Business School, 1998).
6. R. McGrath, "Falling Forward: Real Options Reasoning and Entrepreneurial Failure," *Academy of Management Review* 24 (1994), pp. 13–30; F. A. Hayek, "The Use of Knowledge in Society," *American Economic Review* 5 (1945), pp. 519–30.
7. E. Pofeldt, "Collect Calls," *Success* (March 1998), pp. 22–23.
8. J. Fraser, "Hidden Cash," *Inc.* (February 1991), pp. 81–82.
9. J. Fraser, "Taking Stock," *Inc.* (November 1989), pp. 161–62.
10. Ivan T. Hoffman,"Current Trends in Small Package Shipping," *International Business* (March 1994), p. 33.
11. "Unlocking the Secrets of ECR," *Progressive Grocer* (January 1994), p. 3.
12. "You Do the Work, They Do the Paperwork," *BusinessWeek* (November 17, 1997), p. 54.
13. K. Carley, "Organizational Learning and Personnel Turnover," *Organization Science* 3, no. 1 (1992), pp. 20–47.
14. I. Mochari, "Too Much, Too Soon," *Inc.* (November 1999), p. 119.
15. M. A. Hitt, R. D. Ireland, and R. E. Hoskisson, *Strategic Management: Competitiveness and Globalization,* 3rd ed. (London: South-Western College Publishing, 1999).

15

GOING GLOBAL

LEARNING OBJECTIVES

1
To identify the options for entering international markets.

2
To learn the problems of going global.

3
To understand the role of international intermediaries.

4
To understand the best strategy for entering and growing a business in another country.

OPENING PROFILE

SAM WALTON

Sam Walton, the Wal-Mart magnate, was frequently identified as one of the richest men in America. Although he was well known for his marketing strategy of introducing discount stores to the smaller cities and towns ignored by other chains, this was not the foundation for his success. In large part, the growth of his company and the concurrent growth of his personal wealth can be directly attributed to his judicious use of the equity markets and entry into new markets.

www.wal-mart.com

Walton got his start in retailing in 1940 as a salesman and management trainee at JCPenney. He was one of the best shirt salesmen in the organization, but he knew that it was just a training ground for his real calling as a store owner. In 1945, along with his brother Bud, he began operating a Ben Franklin five-and-dime store in Newport, Arkansas. After five successful years, they moved to a store in Bentonville, Arkansas, where Sam would live until his death. The Walton brothers began expanding by buying other variety stores in the area. Utilizing his knowledge about sales, Sam set up his own buying office and applied the advertising and other marketing principles to his group of stores that others thought were applicable only to bigger ventures. In the 1960s, the Waltons owned enough stores to be the most successful Ben Franklin franchisee in the country.

A new concept was developing in the retail business in the early 1960s: discounting. When Gibson's, a Texas-based discounter, opened a store in Fayetteville, where the Waltons had a variety store, Sam decided to try an experiment. Starting with a single department, his discounting attempt soon enveloped a complete store. Despite Walton's success with this experiment, and the growing threat of discounting to the local variety stores, the Ben Franklin executives were not receptive to changing the positioning of their chain and Sam decided to strike out on his own. After a brief tour around the country in search of new ideas, he developed a plan to begin operating his own discount stores in towns with populations of less than 25,000. The first Wal-Mart was opened in Rogers, Arkansas, in 1962. Sam's profits dictated the growth rate of his business. This make-do-with-what-you-have philosophy carried over to the new Wal-Mart stores. To open the first store, Sam and Bud pooled all their available resources and planned the size and the location of the store based on that amount of capital. There was no room in the tight budget for fancy displays or large offices if they were to offer quality merchandise at competitive prices in small towns. Evidently, the pipe-rack displays and bare floors were only a minor inconvenience to the shoppers, because Wal-Mart was a success from the start.

Early in the development of the Wal-Mart concept, Sam realized the vital role of distribution in determining profitability. He knew he needed the same low-cost, efficient delivery methods used by his larger counterparts. Rather than build warehousing to serve existing outlets, he clustered his expansion outlets around existing distribution points. In 1970, after eight years in the discount store business, there were about 30 Wal-Mart Discount City stores. It became apparent to Walton that he needed his own warehouse system to be able to buy merchandise in the volume necessary to support new openings. Yet he did not feel that the company could afford to incur the heavy debt burden required. In the midst of a boom in new issues and on the strength of his impressive growth record, Walton sold a small part of his business to the public for $3.3 million. This cash helped pay for a $5 million distribution center that was big enough to serve 80 to 100 stores.

With his distribution center in place, Sam was ready to grow. Two years later, with 512 stores and $678 million in sales, Wal-Mart was listed on the New York Stock Exchange. The single share purchased by original investors in 1970 for $16.50 has seen 11 splits, resulting in 2,048 shares trading at $57 per share in July 2003, for a total value of $116,736—or a total return of 707,300 percent on the initial investment. Sam tapped the public equity market several additional times when he needed to expand or upgrade his system, managing to keep his overall capital costs well below those of his competitors with his careful planning and tight budgeting. This helped sales, earnings, and dividends to continue to grow. In 1987, sales were $15,879 million with earnings of $.28 billion and a dividend of $.03. This has increased in a progressive fashion, with 1996 sales of over $93.6 billion, earnings of $1.19 billion, and dividends of $.20 per share posted. And the growth has continued through the end of the 20th century. The year 2000 set records, with sales of over $165 billion, up 20 percent, or $27 billion, from 1999. Earnings per share increased by 21 percent, return on assets remained a high 9.5 percent, and the company paid dividends of almost $900 million to shareholders.

Of course, one of the more recent significant challenges to the company has been filling Sam Walton's shoes after his death. The successor, Wal-Mart president and CEO David Glass, has had to provide clear direction and leadership as the company wrestles with the problems of compounded annual growth, changing market demographics, advances in communication and technology, merchandise selection and sourcing flexibility, and a movement toward a more impersonal, bureaucratic organization due to its large size and increasing diversity.

The venture has grown from the initial store in Rogers, Arkansas, to Wal-Mart Stores, Inc., the world's largest retailer, with $218 billion in sales in the fiscal year ending January 31, 2002. The company employs more than 1.3 million associates worldwide through more than 3,200 facilities in the United States and more than 1,100 abroad. Its four retail divisions—Wal-Mart Supercenters, Discount Stores, Neighborhood Markets, and SAM'S CLUB warehouses—are visited by more than 100 million customers per week.

The company has continued this growth rate over the last years as well. As of January 31, 2006, Wal-Mart had 1,209 Wal-Mart stores, 1,980 Supercenters, 567 SAM'S CLUBs, and 101 Neighborhood Markets in the United States. Internationally, the company operates units in Argentina (11), Brazil (156), Canada (278), Central America (139), China (56), Germany (88), Japan (442), Mexico (786), Puerto Rico (54), South Korea (16), and the United Kingdom (315). Today, Wal-Mart is a global company with nearly 5,000 stores and wholesale clubs across 15 countries. Wal-Mart is regarded as the "most admired retailer" according to *Fortune* magazine. At year-end (January 31, 2006), the company had: $312.43 billion in revenue; an 8.967 percent return on assets; a 21.9 percent return on equity; and a stock price of $45.5 per share.

Indeed, Sam Walton and his predecessors have judiciously decided when to expand both domestically and internationally. Before expanding—particularly internationally—each entrepreneur must carefully address several issues, in much the same way Sam Walton and his predecessors have. These include considering the strategic effects of going global and the strategic issues involved, selecting the foreign market, developing the correct entry strategy, and, possibly, partnering with a foreign entrepreneur.

INTRODUCTION

To be a global entrepreneur it is necessary to establish an international vision. Your level of international skills and knowledge, as well as that of any associates you may have in your company, will help determine the international strategy you implement. If you have not had any international experience, you may want to avoid starting out initially with a plan that needs significant overseas market involvement, using instead a foreign sales office or an R&D alliance. Your success in global business will ultimately reflect how well you identify and leverage your core competencies and those of your venture. This chapter will address going global by looking at motivations for going global, the strategic effects of going global, strategic issues involved, environmental analysis, entry strategies, and the process of developing and executing an international business plan. The chapter concludes with a discussion of an important aspect of going global—entrepreneurial partnering.

MOTIVATIONS TO GO GLOBAL

Unless they are born global, most entrepreneurs will pursue international activities only when stimulated to do so. As indicated in Table 15.1, a variety of proactive and reactive motivations can cause an entrepreneur to become involved in international business. Profits, of course, are one of the most significant reasons for going global. Usually, the expected profitability of going global is not reflected in the actual profits obtained. The profitability is adversely affected by the costs of getting ready to go global, an underestimation of the costs involved, and losses resulting from mistakes. The difference between the planned and actual results may be particularly large in the entrepreneur's first attempt to go global. Anything that the entrepreneur thinks won't happen probably will—even to the extent of having significant shifts in foreign exchange rates.

TABLE 15.1 Motivations for Going Global

- Profits
- Competitive pressures
- Unique product(s) or service(s)
- Excess production capacity
- Declining home country sales
- Unique market opportunity
- Economies of scale
- Technological advantage
- Tax benefits

The allure of profits is reflected in the motive to sell to other markets. For a U.S.–based entrepreneurial firm, the 95 percent of the world's population living outside the United States offers a very large market opportunity. These sales may even be necessary to cover any significant research and development and start-up manufacturing costs that have been incurred in the domestic market. Without sales to international markets, these excessive costs have to be spread over domestic sales alone, resulting in less sales and profits. This can be a problem, particularly in price-sensitive markets.

Sales to other markets also may reflect another reason for going global—the home domestic market may be leveling out or may even be declining in sales or sales potential. This is occurring in several markets in the United States due to aging demographics.

Sometimes an entrepreneur moves into international markets to avoid increased regulations or governmental or societal concerns about the firm's products or services. Cigarette companies such as Philip Morris, confronted with increased government regulations and antismoking attitudes among consumers and the government, have aggressively pursued sales outside the United States, particularly in developing economies. Sometimes this has taken the form of purchasing existing companies in these foreign markets, which is what occurred in Russia.

When the entrepreneur's technology becomes obsolete in the domestic market and/or the product or service is near the end of its life cycle, there may be sales opportunities in foreign markets. One entrepreneur found new sales life in the European Union for the company's gas permeable hard contact lenses and solutions when the domestic market in the United States was negatively affected by highly competitive soft lenses. Volkswagen continued to sell its original VW Beetles in Latin and South America for years after stopping its sales in the United States.

Entrepreneurs often go global to take advantage of lower costs in foreign countries in labor, manufacturing overhead, and raw materials. The "Flip Watch" of newly started Hour-Power could never be marketed at its price point in Things Remembered and JC Penney stores were it not produced in China. Waterford is producing some products in Prague to help offset the higher labor costs in Ireland. This cost advantage may become obsolete as the Czech Republic develops as a member of the European Union. There are often some cost advantages of having at least a distribution and sales office in a foreign market. Graphi Soft, a Hungarian software company, found that its sales significantly increased in the United States when it opened a sales office in Los Angeles, California.

Several more esoteric motivations, beyond the traditional ones of sales and profits, also can motivate an entrepreneur to go global. One of the more predominant motivations is the desire to establish and exploit a global presence. When an entrepreneur truly goes global, many company operations can be internationalized and leveraged. For example, when going global, an entrepreneur will establish a global distribution system and an integrated manufacturing capability. Establishing these gives the entrepreneurial company a competitive advantage as they not only facilitate the firm's successful production and distribution of present products, but help keep out competitive products as well. By going global, an entrepreneur can offer a variety of different products at better price points.

STRATEGIC EFFECTS OF GOING GLOBAL

While going global presents a wide variety of new environments and new ways of doing business, it is also accompanied by an entirely new set of wide-ranging problems. Carrying out business internationally involves a variety of new documents, such as commercial invoices, bills of lading, inspection certificates, and shipper's export declarations, as well as the need to comply with an entirely new set of domestic and international regulations.

One major effect of going global centers around the concept of proximity to the firm's customers and ports. Physical and psychological closeness to the international market significantly affects some global entrepreneurs. Geographic closeness to the foreign market may not necessarily provide a perceived closeness to the foreign customer. Sometimes cultural variables, language, and legal factors can make a foreign market that is geographically close seem psychologically distant. For example, some U.S. entrepreneurs perceive Canada, Ireland, and the U.K. as being much closer psychologically due to similarities in culture and language.

Three issues are involved in this psychological distance. First, the distance envisioned by the entrepreneur may be based more on perception than reality. Some Canadian and even Australian entrepreneurs focus too much on the similarities they share with the United States market, losing sight of the vast differences. These differences, which exist in every international market to some extent, need to be taken into account to avoid costly mistakes. Second, closer psychological proximity does make it easier for an entrepreneurial firm to enter a market. It may be advantageous for the entrepreneur to start going global by selecting a market that is closer psychologically in order to gain some experience before entering markets that are more psychologically distant. Finally, the entrepreneur should also keep in mind that there are more similarities than differences between individual entrepreneurs regardless of the country. Each has gone through the entrepreneurial process, taken on the risks, and struggled for success, and each one passionately loves the business idea.

STRATEGIC ISSUES

Four strategic issues are of paramount importance to an entrepreneur going international: (1) the allocation of responsibility between the U.S. and foreign operations; (2) the nature of the planning, reporting, and control systems to be used throughout the international operations; (3) the appropriate organized structure for conducting international operations; and (4) the degree of standardization possible.

- *Stage 1.* When making his or her first movements into international business, an entrepreneur typically follows a highly centralized decision-making process. Since the entrepreneur generally has access to a limited number of individuals with international experience, a centralized decision-making network is usually used.
- *Stage 2.* When the business is successful, the entrepreneur no longer finds it possible to use a completely centralized decision-making process. The multiplicity of environments becomes far too complex to handle from a central headquarters. In response, the

AS SEEN IN *ENTREPRENEUR* MAGAZINE

GENERALIZING FROM ONE COUNTRY TO ANOTHER

Mashti Malone's Ice Cream shop in Hollywood, California, never advertised—co-owners Mashti and Mehdi Shirvani were happy with word-of-mouth. But when the Food Network got a whiff of their exotic delights, it changed the way the brothers did business.

Mashti, 52, and Mehdi, 38, both raised in Iran, offer the ice cream flavors they grew up with, like rosewater, orange blossom, and ginger. Media interest led to an April 2002 Food Network segment, and following their TV appearance, there was no need to persuade—calls came from across the country begging for a taste of their 30-plus aromatic offerings.

Soon, the shop's Web site (www.mashti.com) began shipping orders nationally. Last summer, the Shirvanis opened an ice cream plant in Garden Grove, California, to keep up with demand. With 2003 sales projected at more than $2 million and plans to open more locations in southern California, the brothers couldn't be happier. "The great thing about America," Mehdi muses, "is if something is good, it is welcome here."

ANALYSIS OF THE BUSINESS OPPORTUNITY

1. Do you agree with Mehdi's sentiment that if something is popular in another country then it has a good chance of being successful in the U.S.?
2. What are some examples of products that are popular in another country and, though not yet sold in this country, could be successful if introduced here?
3. What are some examples of products that are popular in another country but, though not yet sold in this country, would be unlikely to be popular if sold here?
4. To what extent does the success of Mashti Malone's Ice Cream shop in Hollywood depend on the political relationship between the United States and Iran?

Source: Reprinted with permission of Entrepreneur Media, Inc., "Ice and Easy. With TV Publicity, This Treat Wasn't Hard to Sell," by April Y. Pennington, January 2003, *Entrepreneur* magazine: www.entrepreneur.com.

entrepreneur often decentralizes the entire international operation. The philosophy at this point can be summed up as follows: "There's no way I am ever going to be able to understand the differences between all of those markets. Let them make their own decisions."

- *Stage 3*. The process of decentralization carried out in Stage 2 becomes intolerable once further success is attained. Business operations in the different countries end up in conflict with each other. The U.S. headquarters is often the last to receive information about problems. When this occurs, limited amounts of power, authority, and responsibility are pulled back to the U.S. base of operations. A balance is usually achieved, with the U.S. headquarters having reasonably tight control over major strategic marketing decisions and the in-country operating unit having responsibility for the tactical implementation of corporate strategy. Planning, reporting, and control systems become very important aspects of international success at this stage.

IMPORTANT CONSIDERATIONS

To understand what is required for effective planning, reporting, and control in international operations, the entrepreneur should consider the following questions:

Environmental Analysis

1. What are the unique characteristics of each national market? What characteristics does each market have in common with other national markets?

2. Can any national markets be clustered together for operating and/or planning purposes? What dimensions of markets should be used to cluster markets?

Strategic Planning

3. Who should be involved in marketing decisions?
4. What are the major assumptions about target markets? Are these valid?
5. What needs are satisfied by the company's products in the target markets?
6. What customer benefits are provided by the products in the target markets?
7. What are the conditions under which the products are used in the target markets?
8. How great is the ability to buy the company's products in the target markets?
9. What are the company's major strengths and weaknesses relative to existing and potential competition in the target markets?
10. Should the company extend, adapt, or invent products, prices, advertising, and promotion programs for target markets?
11. What are the balance-of-payments and currency situations in the target markets? Will the company be able to remit earnings? Is the political climate acceptable?
12. What are the company's objectives, given the alternatives available and the assessment of opportunity, risk, and company capability?

Structure

13. How should the organization be structured to optimally achieve the established objectives, given the company's skills and resources? What is the responsibility of each organizational level?

Operational Planning

14. Given the objectives, structure, and assessment of the market environment, how can an effective operational marketing plan be implemented? What products should be marketed, at what prices, through what channels, with what communications, and to which target markets?

Controlling the Marketing Program

15. How does the company measure and monitor the plan's performance? What steps should be taken to ensure that marketing objectives are met?[1]

One key to successful strategic planning is an appreciation of the market. While questions 1 and 2 of the preceding list of 15 questions focus on this dimension of the planning process, the first step in identifying markets and clustering countries is to analyze data on each country in the following six areas:

1. Market characteristics
   a. Size of market; rate of growth
   b. Stage of development
   c. Stage of product life cycle; saturation levels
   d. Buyer behavior characteristics
   e. Social/cultural factors
   f. Physical environment
2. Marketing institutions
   a. Distribution systems
   b. Communication media
   c. Marketing services (advertising and research)

3. Industry conditions
   a. Competitive size and practices
   b. Technical development
4. Legal environment (laws, regulations, codes, tariffs, and taxes)
5. Resources
   a. Personnel (availability, skill, potential, and cost)
   b. Money (availability and cost)
6. Political environment
   a. Current government policies and attitudes
   b. Long-range political environment

FOREIGN MARKET SELECTION

With so many prospective countries available, critical issues for the global entrepreneur are foreign market selection and entry strategies. Should you enter the top prospective country or should you employ a more regional focus? Should you choose the largest market possible or one that is easier to understand and navigate? Is a foreign market that is more developed preferable to one that is developing?

These are just some of the questions confronting the global entrepreneur in deciding which market to enter. The market selection decision should be based on both past sales and competitive positioning as well as an assessment of each foreign market alternative. Data needs to be collected on a systematic basis on both a regional/and a country basis. A region can be a collection of countries, such as the European Union, or an area within a country, such as the southeastern part of China.

A systematic process is needed so that a ranking of the foreign markets being considered can be established. Why is ranking markets so important? Ranking helps avoid the mistake of so many entrepreneurs—doing a very poor job of establishing a rigorous market selection process and relying too much on assumptions and gut feel. As discussed in Chapter 4, there are significant differences between global and domestic markets. These differences and the entire global decision process require that the market selection process consist of a series of steps, with informed decisions made at each step based on as much information as possible. These data should be for at least three years so that trends appear. The global entrepreneur must always remember that a single data point does not make a trend, so data based on less than three periods need to be interpreted cautiously. The data collected and analyzed for market selection also will be used in developing the appropriate entry strategy and marketing plan.

While there are several market selection models available, one good method employs a five-step approach: (1) develop appropriate indicators; (2) collect data and convert into comparable indicators; (3) establish an appropriate weight for each indicator; (4) analyze the data; and (5) select the appropriate market from the market rankings.

In step 1, appropriate indicators need to be developed based on past sales, competitive research, experience, and discussions with other global entrepreneurs. Specific indicators for the company need to be developed in three general areas: overall market size indicators, market growth indicators, and product indicators. Market size indicators generally center around: (1) population, (2) per capita income, (3) the market for the specific product (for consumer products), and (4) the types of companies and their sales and profits of particular products (for industrial products). In terms of market growth, the overall country growth (GDP) should be determined as well as the growth rate for the particular market of the venture. Finally, appropriate product indicators such as export of the specific product category to the market and the number of sales leads and level of interest should be established.

INCREASING INTEREST IN SMALL BUSINESS ETHICS

Small business ethics has received extremely limited attention. Nevertheless, there have been some early indications that assumptions about competition as "combat" between small businesses in the same sector may be an inaccurate view.

Conventional (large firm) wisdom maintains that firms need to remain independent of their competitors in order to retain certain trading advantages. There are circumstances, however, under which firms may join forces with a competitor in a loose or tight collaborative situation. Cooperation may range from lending plant or machinery for a particular job to developing alliances that result in new organizations and opportunities. This tends to be influenced by the particular industrial sector, and small firms in areas such as pharmaceuticals and information technology have been found to be more likely to cooperate with competitors than others.

Some of the benefits of cooperation have been identified as (1) cost savings and risk reduction, (2) better control of market uncertainties, and (3) access to external knowledge sources. Rothwell cites cost sharing, access to scientific resources, and other economies of scale as advantages for the small firm participating in a collaboration. In turn, small enterprises offer the advantage of flexibility, dynamism, and effective internal communication. Others have pointed out the extent to which small firms participate in informal knowledge exchange networks. Saxenian notes that the tendency toward "flexible specialization" in small, highly innovative firms makes external networking essential to their survival. Lawton Smith et al. identify equitable sharing of benefits, good communication, and mutual priorities as critical factors in the success of interfirm cooperation.

Dangers of cooperation include the potential risk of takeover (which is less if collaborating with other small rather than large firms), loss of both technical and market knowledge, and regulation of the sharing of outcomes. Self-protection becomes a question of utilizing both formal and informal methods of control, including legal contracts and technical specifications, as well as interpersonal trust and personal discretion. In short, this means developing good stakeholder relations with collaborating competitors.

"Competitor-as-stakeholder" relationship development is likely to be conscious and strategic. In new relationships, trust has to be built between the actual participants and may develop into a stronger bond if the relationship is tested through shared difficulties. Sako distinguishes three types of trust: contractual, competence, and goodwill. Contractual trust exists such that each partner adheres to agreements and keeps promises. Competence trust concerns the expectation that a trading partner will perform his or her role competently. Goodwill trust occurs when "someone . . . is dependable and can be endowed with high discretion, as he can be entrusted to take initiative while refraining from unfair advantage taking." This represents a higher level of trust than the other two forms, although they [contractual and competence trust] can form the basis of goodwill trust.

Source: Excerpt from Laura J. Spence, Ann-Marie Coles, and Lisa Harris, "The Forgotten Stakeholder? Ethics and Social Responsibility in Relation to Competitors," *Business & Society Review* 106, no. 4 (2001). Reprinted with permission of Blackwell Publishing.

Step 2 involves collecting data for each of these indicators and converting the data so that comparisons can be made. Both primary data (original information collected for the particular requirement) and secondary data (published data already existing) need to be collected. Typically, secondary data are collected first to establish what information still needs to be collected through primary research. When collecting international secondary data, there are several problems which vary to some extent based on the stage of economic development of the country. These problems include: (1) comparability (the data for one country will not be the same as the data of another); (2) availability (some countries have much more country data than others, depending upon the stage of economic development); (3) accuracy (sometimes the data have not been collected using vigorous standards or are even biased due to the interests of the government of the country; the latter is particularly a problem in non-market-oriented economies); and (4) cost (only the United States has the

Freedom of Information Act, which makes all government-collected data—with the exception of data related to security and defense—available to all). One global entrepreneur was interested in setting up the first western health club in Moscow. He was going to charge two rates: a higher hard currency rate to foreigners and a lower ruble rate to Russians and other citizens of countries in the former Soviet Union. In determining the best location, he was interested in identifying areas of the city where most foreigners lived. After significant searching to no avail and a high degree of frustration, he finally was able to buy the data needed from the former KGB (Soviet Union Security branch).

When researching foreign markets, the entrepreneur will usually want economic and demographic data such as population, GDP, per capita income, inflation, literacy rate, unemployment, and education levels. There are many sources for this and other foreign information in government agencies, Web sites, and embassies. One important source of data is STAT-USA and its National Trade Data Bank (NTDB), which is managed by the U.S. Department of Commerce. The STAT-USA database has good information due in part to the large number of government agencies contributing information. This results in a large number of international reports such as Country Reports, Country Analysis Briefs (CABs), Country Commercial Guides (CCG), Food Market Reports, International Reports and Reviews, Department of State Background Notes, and Import/Export Reports.

Another good source of data is trade associations and U.S. and foreign embassies. While trade associations are a good source of domestic and international data, sometimes more specific information can be obtained by contacting the U.S. Department of Commerce industry desk officer or the economic attaché in the appropriate U.S. or foreign embassy.

The collected data for each selected indicator then need to be converted to a point score so that each indicator of each country can be numerically ranked against the other countries. Various methods can be used to achieve this, each of which involves some judgment on the part of the global entrepreneur. Another method is to compare country data for each indicator against global standards.

The third step is to establish appropriate weights for the indicators to reflect the importance of a particular indicator in predicting foreign market potential. For one company manufacturing hospital beds, the number and types of hospitals, the age of the hospitals and their beds, and the government's expenditure on health care and its socialized system were the best country indicators in selecting a foreign market. This procedure results in each indicator receiving a weight that reflects the relative importance of the indicator. The assignment of points and weights as well as the selection of indicators varies greatly from one global entrepreneur to another and indeed is somewhat arbitrary. Regardless, this requires intensive thinking and internal discussion and results in far better market selection decisions being made.

Step 4 involves analyzing the results. When looking at the data, the global entrepreneur should carefully scrutinize and question the results. He or she should also look for errors, as mistakes can be easily made. Also, a what-if analysis should be conducted by changing some of the weights and seeing how the results vary.

The final step—step 5—involves selecting a market to enter as well as follow-up markets so that an appropriate entry strategy can be selected and a market plan developed.

ENTREPRENEURIAL ENTRY STRATEGIES

There are various ways an entrepreneur can market products internationally. The method of entry into a market and the mode of operating overseas are dependent on the goals of the entrepreneur and the company's strengths and weaknesses. The modes of entering or engaging in international business can be divided into three categories: exporting, nonequity arrangements, and direct foreign investment. (See Table 15.2.)

TABLE 15.2 Various Entry Modes

Entry Mode	Advantage	Disadvantage
Exporting	Ability to realize location and experience curve economies	• High transport costs • Trade barriers • Problems with local marketing agents
Turn-key contracts	Ability to earn returns from process technology skills in countries where FDI is restricted	• Creation of efficient competitors • Lack of long-term market presence
Licensing	Low development costs and risks	• Lack of control over technology • Inability to realize location and experience curve economies • Inability to engage in global strategic coordination
Franchising	Low development costs and risks	• Lack of control over quality • Inability to engage in global strategic coordination
Joint ventures	• Access to local partner's knowledge • Shared development costs and risks • Politically acceptable	• Lack of control over technology • Inability to engage in global strategic coordination • Inability to realize location and experience curve economies
Wholly owned subsidiaries	• Protection of technology • Ability to engage in global strategic coordination • Ability to realize location and experience curve economies	• High costs and risks

Exporting

exporting The sale and shipping of products manufactured in one country to a customer located in another country

indirect exporting In international business, involves having a foreign purchaser in the local market or using an export management firm

Usually, an entrepreneur starts doing international business through exporting. *Exporting* normally involves the sale and shipping of products manufactured in one country to a customer located in another country. There are two general classifications of exporting: direct and indirect.

Indirect Exporting *Indirect exporting* involves having a foreign purchaser in the local market or using an export management firm. For certain commodities and manufactured goods, foreign buyers actively seek out sources of supply and have purchasing offices in markets throughout the world. An entrepreneur wanting to sell into one of these overseas markets can deal with one of these buyers. In this case, the entire transaction is handled as though it were a domestic transaction, even though the goods will be shipped out of the country. This method of exporting involves the least amount of knowledge and risk for the entrepreneur.

Export management firms, another avenue of indirect exporting, are located in most commercial centers. For a fee, these firms will provide representation in foreign markets. Typically, they represent a group of noncompeting manufacturers from the same country who have no interest in becoming directly involved in exporting. The export management firm handles all of the selling, marketing, and delivery, in addition to any technical problems involved in the export process.

Direct Exporting If the entrepreneur wants more involvement without any financial commitment, *direct exporting* through independent distributors or the company's own overseas sales office is a way to get involved in international business. Independent foreign distributors usually handle products for firms seeking relatively rapid entry into a large number of foreign markets. This independent distributor directly contacts foreign customers and potential customers and takes care of all the technicalities of arranging for export documentation, financing, and delivery for an established rate of commission.

direct exporting Involves the use of independent distributors or the company's own overseas sales office in conducting international business

Entrepreneurs also can open their own overseas sales offices and hire their own salespeople to provide market representation. In starting out, the entrepreneur may send a U.S. or domestic salesperson to be a representative in the foreign market. As more business is done in the overseas sales office, warehouses are usually opened, followed by a local assembly process when sales reach a level high enough to warrant the investment. The assembly operation can eventually evolve into the establishment of manufacturing operations in the foreign market. Entrepreneurs can then export the output from these manufacturing operations to other international markets.

Nonequity Arrangements

When market and financial conditions warrant the change, an entrepreneur can enter into international business by one of three types of *nonequity arrangements:* licensing, turn-key projects, and management contracts. Each of these allows the entrepreneur to enter a market and obtain sales and profits without direct equity investment in the foreign market.

nonequity arrangement A method by which an entrepreneur can enter a market and obtain sales and profits without direct equity investment in the foreign market

licensing Involves giving a foreign manufacturer the right to use a patent, technology, production process, or product in return for the payment of a royalty

turn-key project A method of doing international business whereby a foreign entrepreneur supplies the manufacturing technology or infrastructure for a business and then turns it over to local owners

Licensing *Licensing* involves an entrepreneur who is a manufacturer (licensee) giving a foreign manufacturer (licensor) the right to use a patent, trademark, technology, production process, or product in return for the payment of a royalty. The licensing arrangement is most appropriate when the entrepreneur has no intention of entering a particular market through exporting or direct investment. Since the process is low risk, yet provides a way to generate incremental income, a licensing agreement can be a good method for the entrepreneur to engage in international business. Unfortunately, some entrepreneurs have entered into these arrangements without careful analysis and have later found that they have licensed their largest competitor into business or that they are investing large sums of time and money in helping the licensor adopt the technology or know-how being licensed.

Wolverine World Wide, Inc., opened a Hush Puppies store in Sofia, Bulgaria, through a licensing agreement with Pikin, a combine. Similar arrangements were made a year later in the former U.S.S.R. with Kirov, a shoe combine, with most stores still doing well.[2]

Turn-Key Projects Another method by which the entrepreneur can do international business without much risk is through *turn-key projects*. The underdeveloped or lesser-developed countries of the world have recognized their need for manufacturing technology and infrastructure and yet do not want to turn over substantial portions of their economy to foreign ownership. One solution to this dilemma has been to have a foreign entrepreneur build a factory or other facility, train the workers, train the management, and then turn it over to local owners once the operation is going—hence the name turn-key operation.

Entrepreneurs have found turn-key projects to be an attractive alternative. Initial profits can be made from this method, and follow-up export sales can also result. Financing is provided by the local company or the government, with periodic payments being made over the life of the project.

management contract A nonequity method of international business in which an entrepreneur contracts his or her management techniques and skills to a (foreign) purchasing company

Management Contracts A final nonequity method the entrepreneur can use in international business is the *management contract*. Several entrepreneurs have successfully entered international business by contracting their management techniques and skills. The management contract allows the purchasing country to gain foreign expertise without giving ownership of its resources to a foreigner. For the entrepreneur, the management contract is another way of entering a foreign market without a large equity investment.

Direct Foreign Investment

The wholly owned foreign subsidiary has been a preferred mode of ownership for entrepreneurs using direct foreign investment for doing business in international markets. Joint ventures and minority and majority equity positions are also methods for making direct foreign investments. The percentage of ownership obtained in the foreign venture by the entrepreneur is related to the amount of money invested, the nature of the industry, and the rules of the host government.

minority interest A form of direct foreign investment in which the investing entrepreneur holds a minority ownership position in the foreign venture

Minority Interests Japanese companies have been frequent users of the minority equity position in direct foreign investment. A *minority interest* can provide a firm with a source of raw materials or a relatively captive market for its products. Entrepreneurs have used minority positions to gain a foothold or acquire experience in a market before making a major commitment. When the minority shareholder has something of strong value, the ability to influence the decision-making process is often far in excess of the amount of ownership.

joint venture The joining of two firms in order to form a third company in which the equity is shared

Joint Ventures Another direct foreign investment method used by entrepreneurs to enter foreign markets is the *joint venture*. Although a joint venture can take on many forms, in its most traditional form, two firms (for example, one U.S. firm and one German firm) get together and form a third company in which they share the equity.

Joint ventures have been used by entrepreneurs most often in two situations: (1) when the entrepreneur wants to purchase local knowledge as well as an already established marketing or manufacturing facility, and (2) when rapid entry into a market is needed. Sometimes joint ventures are dissolved and the entrepreneur takes 100 percent ownership.

Even though using a joint venture to enter a foreign market is a key strategic decision, the keys to its success are not well understood, and the reasons for forming a joint venture today are different from those of the past. Previously, joint ventures were viewed as partnerships and often involved firms whose stock was owned by several other firms.

Joint ventures in the United States were first used by mining concerns and railroads as early as 1850. The use of joint ventures, mostly vertical joint ventures, started increasing significantly during the 1950s. Through the vertical joint venture, two firms could absorb the large volume of output when neither could afford the diseconomies associated with a smaller plant.

What has caused this significant increase in the use of joint ventures, particularly when many have not worked? Studies examining the success and failure of joint ventures have found many different reasons for their formation. One of the most frequent reasons an entrepreneur forms a joint venture is to share the costs and risks of a project. Projects where costly technology is involved frequently need resource sharing. This can be particularly important when an entrepreneur does not have the financial resources necessary to engage in capital-intensive activities.

synergy In a joint venture, the qualitative impact on the acquiring firm brought about by complementary factors inherent in the firm being acquired

Synergy between firms is another reason that an entrepreneur may form a joint venture. Synergy is the qualitative impact on the acquiring firm brought about by complementary factors inherent in the firm being acquired. Synergy in the form of people, customers, inventory, plant, or equipment provides leverage for the joint venture. The degree of the synergy determines how beneficial the joint venture will be for the companies involved.

Another reason for forming a joint venture is to obtain a competitive advantage. A joint venture can preempt competitors, allowing an entrepreneur to access new customers and expand the market base.

Joint ventures are frequently used by entrepreneurs to enter markets and economies that pose entrance difficulties or to compensate for a company's lack of foreign experience. This has been the case for the transition economies of Eastern and Central Europe and the former U.S.S.R. It is not surprising that it is easier to establish a joint venture in Hungary because of its fewer registration requirements than it is to start your own company there.

majority interest The purchase of over 50 percent of the equity in a foreign business

Majority Interest Another equity method by which the entrepreneur can enter international markets is through the purchase of a majority interest in a foreign business. In a technical sense, anything over 50 percent of the equity in a firm is *majority interest.* The majority interest allows the entrepreneur to obtain managerial control while maintaining the acquired firm's local identity. When entering a volatile international market, some entrepreneurs take a smaller position, which they increase up to 100 percent as sales and profits occur.

Mergers An entrepreneur can obtain 100 percent ownership to ensure complete control. Many U.S. entrepreneurs desire complete ownership and control in cases of foreign investments. If the entrepreneur has the capital, technology, and marketing skills required for successful entry into a market, there may be no reason to share ownership.

Mergers and acquisitions have been used significantly in international business as well as within the United States. During periods of intense merger activity, entrepreneurs may spend significant time searching for a firm to acquire and then finalizing the transaction. While any merger should reflect the basic principles of any capital investment decision and make a net contribution to shareholders' wealth, the merits of a particular merger are often difficult to assess. Not only do the benefits and costs of a merger need to be determined, but special accounting, legal, and tax issues must be addressed. The entrepreneur therefore must have a general understanding of the benefits and problems of mergers as a strategic option as well as an understanding of the complexity of integrating an entire company into present operations.

horizontal merger A type of merger combining two firms that produce one or more of the same or closely related products in the same geographic area

vertical merger A type of merger combining two or more firms in successive stages of production

product extention merger A type of merger in which acquiring and acquired companies have related production and/or distribution activities but do not have products that compete directly with each other

There are five basic types of mergers: horizontal, vertical, product extension, market extension, and diversified activity. A *horizontal merger* is the combination of two firms that produce one or more of the same or closely related products in the same geographic area. The merger is motivated by economies of scale in marketing, production, or sales. An example of a horizontal merger is the acquisition of convenience food store chain Southland Stores by 7-Eleven Convenience Stores.

A *vertical merger* is the combination of two or more firms in successive stages of production that often involve a buyer–seller relationship. This form of merger stabilizes supply and production and offers more control of these critical areas. Examples are McDonald's acquiring its store franchises and Phillips Petroleum acquiring its gas station franchises. In each case, these outlets become company-owned stores.

A *product extension merger* occurs when acquiring and acquired companies have related production and/or distribution activities but do not have products that compete directly with each other. Examples are the acquisitions of Miller Brewing (beer) by Philip Morris (cigarettes), and Western Publishing (children's books) by Mattel (toys).

market extension merger A type of merger combing two firms that produce the same products but sell them in different geographic markets

A *market extension merger* is a combination of two firms producing the same products but selling them in different geographic markets. The motivation is that the acquiring firm can economically combine its management skills, production, and marketing with that of the acquired firm. An example of this type of merger is the acquisition of Diamond Chain (a West Coast retailer) by Dayton Hudson (a Minneapolis retailer).

diversified activity merger A conglomerate merger involving the consolidation of two essentially unrelated firms

The final type of merger is a *diversified activity merger*. This is a conglomerate merger involving the consolidation of two essentially unrelated firms. Usually, the acquiring firm is not interested in either using its cash resources to expand shareholder wealth or actively running and managing the acquired company. An example of a diversified activity merger is Hillenbrand Industries (a caskets and hospital furniture manufacturer) acquiring American Tourister (a luggage manufacturer).

Mergers are a sound strategic option for an entrepreneur when synergy is present. Several factors cause synergy to occur and make two firms worth more together than apart. The first factor, economies of scale, is probably the most prevalent reason for mergers. Economies of scale can occur in production, coordination and administration, and in the sharing of central services such as office management and accounting, financial control, and upper-level management. Economies of scale increase operating, financial, and management efficiency, thereby resulting in better earnings.

The second factor is taxation or, more specifically, unused tax credits. Sometimes a firm has had a loss in previous years but not enough profits to take advantage of the tax-loss carryover. Corporate income tax regulations allow the net operating losses of one company to reduce the taxable income of another when they are combined. By combining a firm with a loss with a firm with a profit, the tax-loss carryover can be used.

The final important factor for mergers refers to the benefits received in combining complementary resources. Many entrepreneurs will merge with other firms to ensure a source of supply for key ingredients, to obtain a new technology, or to keep the other firm's product from being a competitive threat. It is often quicker and easier for a firm to merge with another that already has a new technology developed—combining the innovation with the acquiring firm's engineering and sales talent—than it is to develop the technology from scratch.

Regardless of the entry mode, a successful entry strategy and growth in a global market often require the development of a global business plan. The global business plan varies somewhat from the domestic business plan discussed in Chapter 7. An outline of a typical global business plan is presented in Appendix 15A, at the end of this chapter.

ENTREPRENEURIAL PARTNERING

One of the best methods for an entrepreneur to enter an international market is to partner with an entrepreneur in that country. These foreign entrepreneurs know the country and culture and therefore can facilitate business transactions while keeping the entrepreneur current on business, economic, and political conditions. This partnering is facilitated by understanding the nature of entrepreneurship in the country.

There are several characteristics of a good partner. A good partner can help the entrepreneur achieve his or her goals such as market access, cost sharing, or core competency obtainment. Good partners also share the entrepreneur's vision and are unlikely to try to opportunistically exploit the partnership for their own benefit.

How does the entrepreneur go about selecting a good partner? First, he or she needs to collect as much information as possible on the industry and potential partners in the country. This information can be obtained from embassy officials, members of the country's chamber of commerce, firms doing business in that country, and customers of the potential partner. The entrepreneur also will need to attend any appropriate trade shows. References for each potential partner should be checked and each reference should be asked for other references. Finally, it is most important that the entrepreneur meet several times with a potential partner to get to know the individual and the company as well as possible before any commitment is made.

IN REVIEW

SUMMARY

Going global is becoming increasingly important to more and more entrepreneurs and to their countries' economies. International entrepreneurship—the conducting of business activities by an entrepreneur across national boundaries—is occurring much earlier in the growth of new ventures as opportunities open up in the hypercompetitive global arena.

The following four strategic issues are important for an entrepreneur to consider before going international: the allocation of responsibility between the U.S. and foreign operations; the type of planning, reporting, and control system to be used; the appropriate organizational structure; and the degree of standardization possible.

Once an entrepreneur decides to be involved in international business, three general modes of market entry need to be considered: exporting, nonequity arrangements, and equity arrangements. Each mode includes several alternatives that provide varying degrees of risk, control, and ownership.

Entrepreneurs in the United States can find their counterparts in a wide variety of economies. Entrepreneurship is thriving from Dublin to Hong Kong, providing new products, new jobs, and new opportunities for partnering.

RESEARCH TASK

1. Choose a specific industry in a specific country. Which mode of entry has been used the most by foreign firms entering this industry in this country? Explain why, using examples of successful entry and examples of unsuccessful entry.

CLASS DISCUSSION

1. Is going international something that only large and established firms should pursue after they have achieved success in their domestic market? Or should entrepreneurs think about international markets "right off the bat"? Which sorts of products are more amenable to "going international" by small and new firms?

SELECTED READINGS

Alon, Ilan. (Winter 2004). International Market Selection for a Small Enterprise: A Case Study in International Entrepreneurship. *SAM Advanced Management Journal,* vol. 69, no. 1 (1984), pp. 25–33.

This article is about the effect of the participation of small enterprises in international business. The recent growth in exports has been fueled by smaller enterprises that tend to have fewer resources and, as a result, have less flexibility in choosing appropriate markets and modes of entry.

Altinay, Levent. (2004). Implementing International Franchising: The Role of Intrapreneurship. *International Journal of Service Industry Management,* vol. 15, no. 5, pp. 426–43.

This paper fills a gap in the research undertaken on the role of intrapreneurs in the international franchise process of an organization. The paper suggests that human factors play an important role in the expansion process and, in a culturally diverse context, franchising is very much the concern of the development directors who provide the attributes of intrapreneurs externally in the market.

Andersson, Svante. (November 2004). Internationalization in Different Industrial Contexts. *Journal of Business Venturing,* vol. 19, no. 6, pp. 851–75.

This article argues that the appropriateness of the theories depends on the industrial context to which they are applied. Whether a theory is appropriate depends on the firm's degree of internationalization and whether the industry is mature or growing.

Antoncic, Bostjian; and Robert D. Hisrich. (1999). An Integrative Conceptual Model. In Leo Paul Dana, ed., *International Entrepreneurship: An Anthology*. Singapore: NTU-Entrepreneurship Development Centre, pp. 15–32.

Two mainstreams in international entrepreneurship research (SME internationalization and international start-ups) are integrated into a conceptual model. Central to this model is the concept of internationalization that consists of internationalization properties (time and mode) and internationalization performance. Other elements of the model are internationalization antecedents (environmental conditions and organizational characteristics) and internationalization consequences (organizational performance).

Burpitt, William J.; and Dennis A. Rondinelli. (2000). Small Firms' Motivations for Exporting: To Earn and Learn? *Journal of Small Business Management,* October 2000, pp. 1–14.

This paper describes a study of 138 small firms with exporting experience. The findings indicate that although financial success is a crucial factor, financial gains alone do not fully explain the propensity of small companies to continue exporting. Firms that strongly value learning from international experience are more likely to continue exporting even when initial financial returns are disappointing.

Calori, Roland; Leif Melin; Tugrul Atamer; and Peter Gustavsson. (2000). Innovative International Strategies. *Journal of World Business,* vol. 35, no. 4, pp. 333–54.

This paper describes four industry case studies that suggest an empirical classification of innovative international strategies based on four main dimensions: nature of the firm's competitive advantage, process of internationalization, segment scope, and level of coordination across borders. From these dimensions the authors derive six types of innovative international strategies that change the rules of competition.

Crick, Dave; and Martine Spence. (April 2005). The Internationalization of "High Performing" U.K. High-Tech SMEs: A Study of Planned and Unplanned Strategies. *International Business Review,* vol. 14, no. 2, pp. 167–85.

This paper discusses the findings from an investigation into the internationalization strategies of "high performing" U.K. high-tech small and medium-sized enterprises. The paper suggests that while support for certain existing theories (namely, the resource-based view, networking, and contingency factors) was evident, no single theory could fully explain entrepreneurial decisions.

Dimitratos, Pavlos; Spyros Lioukas; and Sara Carter. (February 2003). The Relationship between Entrepreneurship and International Performance: The Importance of Domestic Environment. *International Business Review,* vol. 13, no. 1, pp. 19–41.

This article investigates the effect of environmental conditions on the association between entrepreneurship and international performance. The article presents evidence related to mainly contingency and configurational effects of international and domestic environments. The article suggests that the alignment of entrepreneurship with domestic environmental conditions enhances international performance and also suggests that domestic country risk reduction policies may not be implemented since these can lower performance abroad for entrepreneurial activities.

Geursen, Gus M.; and Leo Paul Dana. (September 2001). International Entrepreneurship: The Concept of Intellectual Internationalization. *Journal of Enterprising Culture,* vol. 9, no. 3, pp. 331–52.

This article is about an exploratory study to stimulate future research that examines what has changed in business contexts, structures, and markets, and to place intellectual entrepreneurship at the core of the internationalization discussion.

Kumar, Sameer; and Dan Liu. (2005). Impact of Globalization on Entrepreneurial Enterprises in the World Markets. *International Journal of Management & Enterprise Development,* vol. 2, no. 1, pp. 1–11.

This article summarizes that globalization has made a significant impact on entrepreneurial enterprises. The changing international environment in finance, human resources, technology, politics, economics, and social conditions has created opportunities for entrepreneurial enterprises to expand their international businesses at a much faster pace.

Rialp, Alex; Josep Rialp; and Gary A. Knight. (April 2005). The Phenomenon of Early Internationalizing Firms: What Do We Know after a Decade (1993–2003) of Scientific Inquiry? *International Business Review,* vol. 14, no. 2, pp. 147–66.

This article summarizes studies from the last decade that deal with international new ventures, global start-ups, and born-global firms. The article gives some suggestions, and implications are provided in the form of a new research model and future research directions.

END NOTES

1. W. J. Keegan, "A Conceptual Framework for Multinational Marketing," *Journal of World Business* (November-December 1972), p. 75.
2. J. A. Cohen, "Footwear and the Jet Set," *Management Review* (March 1990), pp. 42–45.

APPENDIX 15A: EXAMPLE OUTLINE OF AN INTERNATIONAL BUSINESS PLAN

I. EXECUTIVE SUMMARY

One-page description of the project.

II. INTRODUCTION

The type of business proposed, followed by a brief description of the major product and/or service involved. A brief description of the country proposed for trade, the rationale for selecting the country, identification of existing trade barriers, and identification of sources of information (research resources and interviews).

III. ANALYSIS OF THE INTERNATIONAL BUSINESS SITUATION

A. Economic, Political, and Legal Analysis of the Trading Country

1. Describe the trading country's economic system, economic information important to your proposed product and/or service, and the level of foreign investment in that country.

2. Describe the trading country's governmental structure and stability, and how the government controls trade and private business.
3. Describe laws and/or governmental agencies that affect your product and/or service (i.e., labor laws, trade laws, etc.).

B. Trade Area and Cultural Analysis

1. Geographic and demographic information, important customs and traditions, other pertinent cultural information, and competitive advantages and disadvantages of the proposed business opportunity.

IV. PLANNED OPERATION OF THE PROPOSED BUSINESS

A. Proposed Organization

Type of ownership and rationale; start-up steps to form the business; planned personnel (or functional) needs; proposed staffing to handle managerial, financial, marketing, legal, and production functions; proposed organization chart; and brief job descriptions, if necessary.

B. Proposed Product/Service

1. Product and/or service details include potential suppliers, manufacturing plans, and inventory policies, if applicable. Include necessary supplies if a service is provided.
2. Transportation information includes costs, benefits, risks of the transportation method, and documents needed to transport the product.

C. Proposed Strategies

1. Pricing policies include what currency will be used, costs, mark-ups, markdowns, relation to competition, and factors that could affect the price of the product (e.g., competition, political conditions, taxes, tariffs, and transportation costs).
2. Promotional program details include promotional activities, media availability, costs, one-year promotional plan outline, and local customs related to business readiness.

V. PLANNED FINANCING

A. Projected Income and Expenses

1. Projected income statements for first year's operation.
2. Balance sheet for the end of the first year.
3. A brief narrative description of the planned growth of the business, including financial resources, needs, and a brief three-year plan projection.

VI. BIBLIOGRAPHY

VII. APPENDIX

16

ACCESSING RESOURCES FOR GROWTH FROM EXTERNAL SOURCES

LEARNING OBJECTIVES

1
To understand franchising from the perspective of both the entrepreneur looking to reduce the risk of new entry and the entrepreneur looking for a way to grow his or her business.

2
To understand how joint ventures can help an entrepreneur grow his or her business and acknowledge the challenges of finding, and maintaining, an effective joint venture relationship.

3
To be aware of the pros and cons of using acquisitions to grow a business and to know what to look for in an acquisition candidate.

4
To understand the possibilities of achieving growth through mergers and leveraged buyouts and the challenges associated with each.

5
To understand the tasks of negotiation and develop the skills to more effectively conduct these tasks.

OPENING PROFILE

BILL GROSS

How does a start-up company take advantage of the seemingly endless opportunities of the Internet by using the creative talents of one person and then letting other selected entrepreneurs take over the responsibility of running these businesses? It sounds like a repeat of history when Thomas Edison made invention a business. But the new kid on the block is Bill Gross, whose vision is to grow his Idealab by nurturing and monitoring other Internet businesses that have resulted because of his ingenuity. He refers to Idealab as Internet start-ups in a box. Basically the concept is simple. Bill comes up with an idea for an Internet start-up. He locates someone, either a former executive or even an engineering student who he thinks is right for the job. That person is then given the reins to start this venture all under the roof of an incubator-like operation, where Bill provides the structure and services necessary to make these start-ups rapidly grow into successful enterprises.

www.idealab.com

Bill describes Idealab as a combination of incubator, venture capitalist, and creative think tank. Like an incubator it provides shared space and administrative services, it offers seed financing for a minority equity position (up to 49 percent), and it uses everyone to brainstorm on the most opportune technology applications. Started in 1996 in Pasadena, California, to date the company has created 30 Internet ventures, all at various stages of development. Each idea came from Gross or one of his Idealab staff managers. For each firm a CEO was found and hired using Bill's networking skills in the Internet industry and at Caltech, his alma mater. Then the core expert staff becomes involved to get these ventures up and running as quickly as possible. This involves developing the technology, conducting marketing research, preparing a business plan, hiring management, launching the venture, and finally either going public or selling the business. The seed financing that Idealab provides to these start-ups does not exceed $250,000. Bill believes that Internet start-ups do not need large amounts of capital to get started but, more importantly, need knowledge, intelligence, and speed. Knowledge and intelligence are provided by Bill and the Idealab's staff experts, and speed focuses on the ability to quickly grow a start-up, but with few mistakes. According to Bill, these two elements are much more important in the successful launch and growth of an Internet company than money.

Bill Gross personifies the real meaning of an entrepreneur. He probably holds the unique distinction in the field of entrepreneurship of not only starting many businesses but also turning all of them into successful enterprises. As an enterprising 12-year-old he noticed that the corner drugstore was selling candy at 9 cents and at the Sav-On nearby it was selling for 7 cents. He quickly figured out that with no overhead he could make an easy profit on the price spread. Bill then moved on to his next successful enterprise by placing ads in *Popular Mechanics,* where he sold $25,000 worth of solar devices and plans. The proceeds from this effort were used to finance his freshman year's tuition at Caltech. While at Caltech he proceeded to launch GNP Inc., a stereo equipment maker. This enterprise not only was very successful but was recognized as one of *Inc.* magazine's top 500 growth ventures in 1982 and 1985. His next enterprise was created when Bill and his brother found a way to make Lotus 1-2-3 obey simple commands. Mitch Kapor, the founder of Lotus, was impressed with their software and purchased their business for $10 million.

The success streak continued with the launch of Knowledge Adventure in 1991. This venture developed and marketed educational software and was considered to be his most successful venture to date. He sold the business in 1997 for $100 million. Idealab actually was created in 1996 when Bill was stepping down from Knowledge Adventure and negotiating the sale.

A sample of some of the companies launched by Idealab includes CitySearch, which competes with Microsoft and provides online services for urban communities; EntertainNet, an Internet broadcaster that provides news and related information; and Answer.com, a Web site that will answer any question you might have and which has already been acquired by another company. Last year Bill expanded his operations into Silicon Valley. He wanted to be close to the action and take advantage of Idealab's ability to quickly transform some of these Internet opportunities into successful ventures.

Growing these start-ups is a challenge to Bill Gross, and although there is high risk in the Internet industry, Bill feels that Idealab will continue to stay focused on its mission.[1]

USING EXTERNAL PARTIES TO HELP GROW A BUSINESS

In Chapter 13, we introduced franchising as a means of new entry that can reduce the risk of downside loss for the franchisee. Franchising is also an alternative means by which an entrepreneur may expand his or her business by having others pay for the use of the name, process, product, service, and so on. Using franchising as a growth mechanism is the primary focus of this chapter. Given the importance of franchising for both new entry and growth, the first section explores franchising from the perspective of the entrepreneur looking to franchising to reduce the risks of new entry and from the perspective of the entrepreneur looking to use franchising as a way to grow his or her business. The second section explores other external mechanisms for growing a business, namely, joint ventures, acquisitions, and mergers. Finally, this chapter provides some useful advice for those entrepreneurs who need to negotiate to obtain the human and financial resources necessary to fuel business growth.

FRANCHISING

Franchising is an arrangement whereby a franchisor gives exclusive rights of local distribution to a franchisee in return for their payment of royalties and conformance to standardized operating procedures.

Franchising is as "an arrangement whereby the manufacturer or sole distributor of a trademarked product or service gives exclusive rights of local distribution to independent retailers in return for their payment of royalties and conformance to standardized operating procedures."[2] The person offering the franchise is known as the *franchisor.* The *franchisee* is the person who purchases the franchise and is given the opportunity to enter a new business with a better chance to succeed than if he or she were to start a new business from scratch.

Advantages of Franchising—to the Franchisee

One of the most important advantages of buying a franchise is that the entrepreneur does not have to incur all the risks associated with creating a new business. Table 16.1 summarizes the important advantages of a franchise. Typically, the areas that entrepreneurs have problems with in starting a new venture are product acceptance, management expertise, meeting capital requirements, knowledge of the market, and operating and structural controls. In franchising, the risks associated with each are minimized through the franchise relationship, as discussed below.

Product Acceptance The franchisee usually enters into a business that has an accepted name, product, or service. In the case of Subway, any person buying a franchise will be using the Subway name, which is well known and established throughout the United States. The franchisee does not have to spend resources trying to establish the credibility of the business. That credibility already exists based on the years the franchise has existed. Subway has also spent millions of dollars in advertising, thus building a favorable image of the products and services offered. An entrepreneur who tries to start a sandwich shop would be unknown to the potential customers and would require significant effort and resources to build credibility and a reputation in the market.

Management Expertise Another important advantage to the franchisee is the managerial assistance provided by the franchisor. Each new franchisee is often required to take a training program on all aspects of operating the franchise. This training could

TABLE 16.1 What You May Buy in a Franchise

1. A product or service with an established market and favorable image.
2. A patented formula or design.
3. Trade names or trademarks.
4. A financial management system for controlling the financial revenue.
5. Managerial advice from experts in the field.
6. Economies of scale for advertising and purchasing.
7. Head office services.
8. A tested business concept.

include classes in accounting, personnel management, marketing, and production. McDonald's, for example, requires all its franchisees to spend time at its school, where everyone takes classes in these areas. In addition, some franchisors require their new franchisees to actually work with an existing franchise owner or at a company-owned store or facility to get on-the-job training. Once the franchise has been started, most franchisors will offer managerial assistance on the basis of need. Toll-free numbers are also available so that the franchisee can ask questions anytime. Local offices for the larger franchises continually visit the local franchisees to offer advice and keep owners informed of new developments.

The training and education offered is actually an important criterion that the entrepreneur should consider in evaluating any franchise opportunity. If the assistance in start-up is not good, the entrepreneur should probably look elsewhere for opportunities unless he or she already has extensive experience in the field.

Capital Requirements As we've seen in previous chapters, starting a new venture can be costly in terms of both time and money. The franchise offers an opportunity to start a new venture with up-front support that could save the entrepreneur significant time and possibly capital. Some franchisors conduct location analysis and market research of the area that might include an assessment of traffic, demographics, business conditions, and competition. In some cases, the franchisor will also finance the initial investment to start the franchise operation. The initial capital required to purchase a franchise generally reflects a fee for the franchise, construction costs, and the purchase of equipment.

The layout of the facility, control of stock and inventory, and the potential buying power of the entire franchise operation can save the entrepreneur significant funds. The size of the parent company can be advantageous in the purchase of health care and business insurance, since the entrepreneur would be considered a participant in the entire franchise organization. Savings in start-up are also reflected in the pooling of monies by individual franchisees for advertising and sales promotion. The contribution by each franchisee is usually a function of the volume and the number of franchises owned. This allows advertising on both a local and a national scale to enhance the image and credibility of the business, something that would be impossible for a single operation.

Knowledge of the Market Any established franchise business offers the entrepreneur years of experience in the business and knowledge of the market. This knowledge is usually reflected in a plan offered to the franchisee that details the profile of the target customer and the strategies that should be implemented once the operation has begun. This is particularly important because of regional and local differences in markets. Competition, media effectiveness, and tastes can vary widely from one market to another. Given their experience, franchisors can provide advice and assistance in accommodating any of these differences.

Most franchisors will be constantly evaluating market conditions and determining the most effective strategies to be communicated to the franchisees. Newsletters and other publications that reflect new ideas and developments in the overall market are continually sent to franchisees.

Operating and Structural Controls Two problems that many entrepreneurs have in starting a new venture are maintaining quality control of products and services and establishing effective managerial controls. The franchisor, particularly in the food business, will identify suppliers that meet the quality standards established. In some instances, the supplies are actually provided by the franchisor. Standardization in the supplies, products, and services provided helps ensure that the entrepreneur will maintain quality standards that are so important. Standardization also supports a consistent image on which the franchise business depends for expansion.

Administrative controls usually involve financial decisions relating to costs, inventory, and cash flow, and personnel issues such as criteria for hiring/firing, scheduling, and training to ensure consistent service to the customer. These controls will usually be outlined in a manual supplied to the franchisee upon completion of the franchise deal.

Although all the above are advantages to the franchisee, they also represent important strategic considerations for an entrepreneur who is considering growing the business by selling franchises. Since there are so many franchise options for an entrepreneur, the franchisor will need to offer all of the above services in order to succeed in the sale of franchises. One of the reasons for the success of such franchises as McDonald's, Burger King, KFC, Boston Market, Subway, Midas, Jiffy Lube, Holiday Inn, Mail Boxes Etc., and Merry Maids is that all these firms have established an excellent franchise system that effectively provides the necessary services to the franchisee.

Advantages of Franchising—to the Franchisor

The advantages a franchisor gains through franchising are related to expansion risk, capital requirements, and cost advantages that result from extensive buying power. Consider the success of the Subway chain. Clearly, Fred DeLuca would not have been able to achieve the size and scope of his business without franchising it. In order to use franchising as an expansion method, the franchisor must have established value and credibility that someone else is willing to buy.

Expansion Risk The most obvious advantage of franchising for an entrepreneur is that it allows the venture to expand quickly using little capital. This advantage is significant when we reflect on the problems and issues that an entrepreneur faces in trying to manage and grow a new venture (see Chapter 14). A franchisor can expand a business nationally and even internationally by authorizing and selling franchises in selected locations. The capital necessary for this expansion is much less than it would be without franchising. Just think of the capital that DeLuca would require to build 8,300 Subway sandwich shops.

The value of the franchise depends on the to-date track record of the franchisor and on the services offered to the entrepreneur or franchisee. Subway's low franchise fee has enhanced expansion opportunities, as more people can afford it.

Operating a franchised business requires fewer employees than a nonfranchised business. Headquarters and regional offices can be lightly staffed, primarily to support the needs of the franchisees. This allows the franchisor to maintain low payrolls and minimizes personnel issues and problems.

Cost Advantages The mere size of a franchised company offers many advantages to the franchisees. The franchisor can purchase supplies in large quantities, thus achieving economies of scale that would not have been possible otherwise. Many franchise businesses produce parts, accessories, packaging, and raw materials in large quantities, then in turn sell these to the franchisees. Franchisees are usually required to purchase these items as part of the franchise agreement, and they usually benefit from lower prices.

One of the biggest cost advantages of franchising a business is the ability to commit larger sums of money to advertising. Each franchisee contributes a percentage of sales (1 to 2 percent) to an advertising pool. This pooling of resources allows the franchisor to conduct advertising in major media across a wide geographic area. If the business were not franchised, the company would have to provide funds for the entire advertising budget.

Disadvantages of Franchising

Franchising is not always the best option for an entrepreneur. Anyone investing in a franchise should investigate the opportunity thoroughly. Problems between the franchisor and the franchisee are common and have recently begun to receive more attention from the government and trade associations.

The disadvantages to the franchisee usually center on the inability of the franchisor to provide services, advertising, and location. When promises made in the franchise agreement are not kept, the franchisee may be left without any support in important areas. For example, Curtis Bean bought a dozen franchises in Checkers of America Inc., a firm that provides auto inspection services. After losing $200,000, Bean and other franchisees filed a lawsuit claiming that the franchisor had misrepresented advertising costs and had made false claims—including that no experience was necessary to own a franchise.[3]

The franchisee may also face the problem of a franchisor's failing or being bought out by another company. No one knows this better than Vincent Niagra, an owner of three Window Works franchises. Niagra had invested about $1 million in these franchises when the franchise was sold in 1988 to Apogee Enterprises and then resold in 1992 to a group of investors. This caused many franchises to fail, leaving a total of 50. The failure of these franchises has made it difficult for Niagra to continue because customers are apprehensive about doing business with him for fear that he will go out of business. None of the support services that had been promised were available.[4]

The franchisor also incurs certain risks and disadvantages in choosing this expansion alternative. In some cases, the franchisor may find it very difficult to find quality franchisees. Poor management, in spite of all the training and controls, can still cause individual franchise failures and, therefore, can reflect negatively on the entire franchise system. As the number of franchises increases, the ability to maintain tight controls becomes more difficult.

Types of Franchises

There are three available types of franchises.[5] The first type is the dealership, a form commonly found in the automobile industry. Here, manufacturers use franchises to distribute their product lines. These dealerships act as the retail stores for the manufacturer. In some instances, they are required to meet quotas established by the manufacturers, but as is the case for any franchise, they benefit from the advertising and management support provided by the franchisor.

The most common type of franchise is the type that offers a name, image, and method of doing business, such as McDonald's, Subway, KFC, Midas, Dunkin' Donuts, and Holiday Inn. There are many of these types of franchises, and their listings, with pertinent information, can be found in various sources.[6]

A third type of franchise offers services. These include personnel agencies, income tax preparation companies, and real estate agencies. These franchises have established names and reputations and methods of doing business. In some instances, such as real estate, the franchisee has actually been operating a business and then applies to become a member of the franchise.

Franchising opportunities have often evolved from changes in the environment as well as important social trends. Several of these are discussed below.[7]

- *Good health.* Today people are eating healthier food and spending more time keeping fit. Many franchises have developed in response to this trend. For example, Bassett's

Original Turkey was created in 1983 in response to consumer interest in eating foods lower in cholesterol. Frozen yogurt franchises, such as TCBY in New England and Nibble-Lo's in Florida, also responded to the same trend. In Los Angeles, a unique restaurant, The Health Express, offers its customers a 100 percent vegetarian menu.

- *Time saving or convenience.* More and more consumers prefer to have things delivered to them as opposed to going out of their way to buy them. In fact, many food stores now offer home delivery services. In 1990, Auto Critic of America Inc. was started as a mobile car inspection service. About the same time, Ronald Tosh started Tubs To Go, a company that delivers Jacuzzis to almost any location for an average of $100 to $200 per night.
- *Environmental consciousness.* Radon-testing service franchises have grown as a response to consumers' need to protect themselves and their families from dangerous radon gas. In 1987, Ecology House, a gift store, began to add consumer products such as water-saving devices, rechargeable batteries, and energy-saving light fixtures.
- *The second baby boom.* Today's baby boomers have had babies themselves, which has resulted in the need for a number of child-related service franchises. Child care franchises such as Kinder Care and Living and Learning are thriving. In 1989, two attorneys, David Pickus and Lee Sandoloski, opened Jungle Jim's Playland. This is an indoor amusement park with small-scale rides in a 20,000- to 27,000-square-foot facility. One franchise, Computertots, teaches classes on computers to preschoolers. This franchise has spread to 25 locations in 15 states.

INVESTING IN A FRANCHISE

Franchising involves many risks to an entrepreneur. Although we read about the success of McDonald's or Burger King, for every one of these successes there are many failures. Franchising, like any other venture, is not for the passive person. It requires effort and long hours, as any business does, since duties such as hiring, scheduling, buying, accounting, and so on, are still the franchisee's responsibility.

Not every franchise is right for every entrepreneur. He or she must evaluate the franchise alternatives to decide which one is most appropriate. A number of factors should be assessed before making the final decision.

1. *Unproven versus proven franchise.* There are some trade-offs in investing in a proven or unproven franchise business. Whereas an unproven franchise will be a less expensive investment, the lower investment is offset by more risk. In an unproven franchise, the franchisor is likely to make mistakes as the business grows. These mistakes could inevitably lead to failure. Constant reorganization of a new franchise can result in confusion and mismanagement. Yet, a new and unproven franchise can offer more excitement and challenge and can lead to significant opportunities for large profits should the business grow rapidly. A proven franchise offers lower risk but requires more financial investment.
2. *Financial stability of franchise.* The purchase of a franchise should entail an assessment of the financial stability of the franchisor. A potential franchisee should seek answers to the following questions:
   - How many franchises are in the organization?
   - How successful is each of the members of the franchise organization?
   - Are most of the profits of the franchise a function of fees from the sale of franchises or from royalties based on profits of franchisees?
   - Does the franchisor have management expertise in production, finance, and marketing?

Some of the above information can be obtained from the profit-and-loss statements of the franchise organization. Face-to-face contact with the franchisor can also indicate the success of the organization. It is also worthwhile to contact some of the franchisees directly to determine their success and to identify any problems that have occurred. If financial information of the franchisor is unavailable, the entrepreneur may purchase a financial rating from a source such as Dun & Bradstreet. Generally, the following are good external sources of information:

- Franchise association
- Other franchisees
- Government
- Accountants and lawyers
- Libraries
- Franchise directories and journals
- Business exhibitions

3. *Potential market for the new franchise*. It is important for the entrepreneur to evaluate the market that the franchise will attract. A starting point is evaluating the traffic flow and demographics of the residents from a map of the area. Traffic flow information may be observed by visiting the area. Direction of traffic flow, ease of entry to the business, and the amount of traffic (pedestrian and automobile) can be estimated by observation. The demographics of the area can be determined from census data, which can be obtained from local libraries or the town hall. It can also be advantageous to locate competitors on the map to determine their potential effect on the franchise business. Marketing research in the market area is helpful. Attitudes about and interest in the new business can be assessed in the market research. In some instances, the franchisor will conduct a market study as a selling point to the franchisee.
4. *Profit potential for a new franchise*. As in any start-up business, it is important to develop pro forma income and cash flow statements. The franchisor should provide projections in order to calculate the needed information.

In general, most of the above information should be provided in the disclosure statement or the prospectus. The Federal Trade Commission's Franchise Rule requires franchisors to make full presale disclosure in a document that provides information about 20 separate aspects of a franchise offering.[8] The information required in this disclosure is summarized in Table 16.2. Some of the information will be comprehensive and some will be sketchy. There are always weaknesses that must be evaluated before making a commitment. The disclosure statement represents a good resource, but it is also important to evaluate the other services mentioned earlier in this chapter.

Front-end procedure fees, royalty payments, expenses, and other information should be compared with those of franchises in the same field, as well as in different business areas. If a franchise looks good as an investment, the entrepreneur may request a franchise package from the franchisor, which usually contains a draft franchise agreement or contract. Generally, this package will require a deposit of $300 to $500, which should be fully refundable.

The contract or franchise agreement is the final step in establishing a franchise arrangement. Here a lawyer experienced in franchising should be used. The franchise agreement contains all the specific requirements and obligations of the franchisee. Things such as the exclusivity of territory coverage will protect against the franchisor's granting another franchise within a certain radius of the business. The renewable terms will indicate the length

TABLE 16.2 Information Required in Disclosure Statement

1. Identification of the franchisor and its affiliates and their business experience.
2. The business experience of each of the franchisor's officers, directors, and management personnel responsible for franchise services, training, and other aspects of the franchise programs.
3. The lawsuits in which the franchisor and its officers, directors, and management personnel have been involved.
4. Any previous bankruptcies in which the franchisor and its officers, directors, and management personnel have been involved.
5. The initial franchise fee and other initial payments that are required to obtain the franchise.
6. The continuing payments that franchisees are required to make after the franchise opens.
7. Any restrictions on the quality of goods and services used in the franchise and where they may be purchased, including restrictions requiring purchases from the franchisor or its affiliates.
8. Any assistance available from the franchisor or its affiliates in financing the purchase of the franchise.
9. Restrictions on the goods or services franchises are permitted to sell.
10. Any restrictions on the customers with whom franchises may deal.
11. Any territorial protection that will be granted to the franchisee.
12. The conditions under which the franchise may be repurchased or refused renewal by the franchisor, transferred to a third party by the franchisee, and terminated or modified by either party.
13. The training programs provided to franchisees.
14. The involvement of any celebrities or public figures in the franchise.
15. Any assistance in selecting a site for the franchise that will be provided by the franchisor.
16. Statistical information about the present number of franchises; the number of franchises projected for the future; and the number of franchises terminated, the number the franchisor has decided not to renew, and the number repurchased in the past.
17. The financial statements of the franchisor.
18. The extent to which the franchisees must personally participate in the operation of the franchise.
19. A complete statement of the basis of any earnings claims made to the franchisee, including the percentage of existing franchises that have actually achieved the results that are claimed.
20. A list of the names and addresses of other franchises.

of the contract and the requirements. Financial requirements will stipulate the initial price for the franchise, the schedule of payments, and the royalties to be paid. Termination of franchise requirements should indicate what will happen if the franchisee becomes disabled or dies and what provisions are made for the family. Terminating a franchise generally results in more lawsuits than any other issue in franchising. These terms should also allow the franchisee to obtain fair market value should the franchise be sold. Even though the agreement may be standard, the franchisee should try to negotiate important items to reduce the investment risk.

AS SEEN IN *ENTREPRENEUR* MAGAZINE

PROVIDE ADVICE TO AN ENTREPRENEUR ABOUT FRANCHISING

TOP 10 FASTEST-GROWING FRANCHISES FOR 2003

1. Curves for Women
2. Subway
3. 7-Eleven Inc.
4. Taco Bell Corp.
5. Jani-King
6. McDonald's
7. Jan-Pro Franchising Int'l. Inc.
8. Baskin-Robbins USA Co.
9. The Quiznos Franchise Co.
10. KFC Corp.

Curves for Women Women-only fitness center

Company Background Year began: 1992. Franchising since: 1995. At the age of 20, premed student Gary Heavin had taken over a failing fitness center in Houston, turning the business around and, within five years, opened six more centers. After 10 years and 17 centers, Heavin's business went under. Not wanting to give up, Heavin took lessons from the strengths and weaknesses of his first chain and decided to open a second. In 1992, Heavin opened Curves for Women, a women-only fitness center, in Harlingen, Texas. The company began franchising in 1995.

Where Seeking Franchisees Nationwide; Outside the U.S.: Australia/New Zealand, Canada, Central America, Japan, Mexico, South America, Western Europe. Exclusive territories available.

Costs & Fees Total investment: $25,600–31,100; Franchise fee: $19,900; and Ongoing royalty fee: $395/month

Qualifications Net worth requirement: $20,000; Cash liquidity requirement: $10K

ADVICE TO A POTENTIAL ENTREPRENEUR

A friend who is looking to go into business has heard about franchising and the success of Curves for Women and has a couple of questions for you:

1. Are the risks of losing money really less if I go into a franchise rather than setting up the business myself?
2. To what extent can I copy the formula that has been developed by the franchise and get the benefits of the proven approach without having to pay the full price?
3. What do you think about this Curves for Women franchise? It is obviously a good one but do you think that I have missed the boat—maybe all the good locations have already been taken?

Source: Reprinted with permission of Entrepreneur Media, Inc., "Think Fast. Don't Blink, or Else the 100 Fastest-Growing Franchises for 2003 Might Pass You By," May 2003, *Entrepreneur* magazine: www.entrepreneur.com.

Franchise Growth for Curves for Women

Year	U.S. Franchises	Canadian Franchises	Foreign Franchises	Company Owned
2006	7,879	730	859	0
2005	7,748	713	667	0
2004	7,044	641	324	0
2003	5,205	498	130	0
2002	3,130	295	21	0

JOINT VENTURES

With the increase in business risks, hypercompetition, and failures, joint ventures have occurred with increased regularity and often involve a wide variety of players.[9] Joint ventures are not a new concept, but rather have been used as a means of expansion by entrepreneurial firms for a long time.

joint venture Two or more companies forming a new company

What is a joint venture? A *joint venture* is a separate entity that involves a partnership between two or more active participants. Sometimes called strategic alliances, joint ventures involve a wide variety of partners that include universities, not-for-profit organizations, businesses, and the public sector.[10] Joint ventures have occurred between such rivals as General Motors and Toyota as well as General Electric and Westinghouse. They have occurred between the United States and foreign concerns in order to penetrate an international market, and they have been a good conduit by which an entrepreneur can enter an international market.

Whenever close relationships between two companies are being developed, concerns about the ethics and ethical behavior of the potential partner arise.

Types of Joint Ventures

Although there are many different types of joint venture arrangements, the most common is still between two or more private-sector companies. For example, Boeing/Mitsubishi/Fuji/Kawasaki entered into a joint venture for the production of small aircraft in order to share technology and cut costs. To cut costs, agreements were made between Ford and Mesasurex in the area of factory automation and between General Motors and Toyota in the area of automobile production. Other private-sector joint ventures have had different objectives, such as entering new markets (Corning and Ciba-Geigy as well as Kodak and Cetus), entering foreign markets (AT&T and Olivetti), and raising capital and expanding markets (U.S. Steel and Phong Iron and Steel).

Some joint ventures are formed to do cooperative research. Probably the best known of these is the Microelectronics and Computer Technology Corporation (MCC) formed in 1983 in Austin, Texas. Supported by 13 major U.S. companies, this for-profit venture does long-range research with scientists who are loaned to MCC for up to four years before returning to their competing companies to apply the results of their research activities. MCC retains title to all the resulting knowledge and patents, making them available for license to the companies participating in the program. Another type of joint venture for research development is the Semi-Conductor Research Corporation, located in Triangle Park, North Carolina. A not-for-profit research organization, it began with the participation of 11 U.S. chip manufacturers and computer companies. The number has grown to over 35 since its inception in 1981. The goal of the corporation is to sponsor basic research and train professional scientists and engineers to be future industry leaders.

Industry–university agreements created for the purpose of doing research are another type of joint venture that has seen increasing usage. However, two major problems have kept these types of joint ventures from proliferating even faster. A profit corporation has the objective of obtaining tangible results, such as a patent, from its research investment and wants all proprietary rights. Universities want to share in the possible financial returns from the patent, but the university researchers want to make the knowledge available through research papers. In spite of these problems, numerous industry–university teams have been established. In one joint venture agreement in robotics, for example, Westinghouse retains patent rights while Carnegie-Mellon receives a percentage of any license royalties. The university also has the right to publish the research results as long as it withholds from publication any critical information that might adversely affect the patent.

The joint venture agreement between Celanese Corporation and Yale University, created for researching the composition and synthesis of enzymes, took a somewhat different form—cost sharing. Although Celanese assumes the expense of any needed supplies and equipment for the research, as well as the salaries of the postdoctoral researchers, Yale pays the salaries of the professors involved. The research results can be published only after a 45-day waiting period.

International joint ventures, discussed in Chapters 4 and 15, are rapidly increasing in number due to their relative advantages. Not only can both companies share in the earnings and growth, but the joint venture can have a low cash requirement if the knowledge or patents are capitalized as a contribution to the venture. Also, the joint venture provides ready access to new international markets that otherwise may not be easily attained. Finally, since talent and financing come from all parties involved, an international joint venture causes less drain on a company's managerial and financial resources than a wholly owned subsidiary.

There are several drawbacks to establishing an international joint venture. First, the business objectives of the joint venture partners can be quite different, which can result in problems in the direction and growth of the new entity. In addition, cultural differences in each company can create managerial difficulties in the new joint venture. Finally, government policies can sometimes have a negative impact on the direction and operation of the international joint venture.

In spite of these problems, the benefits usually outweigh the drawbacks, as evidenced by the frequency rate of establishing international joint ventures. For example, an international joint venture between General Motors and Fanuc Ltd., a Japanese firm, was established to develop the 20,000 robots needed by GM to automate its plants. In this 50–50 joint venture partnership, GM supplies the initial design and Fanuc supplies the engineering and technology needed to develop and produce the car-painting robots.

Another type of international joint venture was established between Dow Chemical (United States) and Asaki Chemicals (Japan) to develop and market chemicals on an international basis. While Asaki provided the raw materials and was a sole distributor, Dow provided the technology and obtained distribution in the Japanese market. The arrangement eventually dissolved because of the concerns of the Japanese government and the fundamental difference in motives between the two partners: Dow was primarily concerned with the profits of the joint venture, whereas Asaki was primarily concerned with having a purchaser for its basic petrochemicals.

Factors in Joint Venture Success

Clearly, not all joint ventures succeed. An entrepreneur needs to assess this method of growth carefully and understand the factors that help ensure success as well as the problems involved before using it. The most critical factors for success are:

1. The accurate assessment of the parties involved in order to best manage the new entity in light of the ensuing relationships. The joint venture will be more effective if the managers can work well together. Without this chemistry, the joint venture has a low likelihood of success and may even fail.
2. The degree of symmetry between the partners. This symmetry goes beyond chemistry to objectives and resource capabilities. When one partner feels that he or she is bringing more to the table, or when one partner wants profits and the other desires product outlet (as in the case of the Asaki-Dow international joint venture), problems arise. For a joint venture to be successful, the managers in each parent company, as well as those

in the new entity, must concur on the objectives of the joint venture and the level of resources that will be provided. Good relationships must be nurtured between the managers in the joint venture and those in each parent company.

3. The expectations of the results of the joint venture must be reasonable. Far too often, at least one of the partners feels that a joint venture will be the cure-all for other corporate problems. Expectations of a joint venture must be realistic.
4. The timing must be right. With environments constantly changing, industrial conditions being modified, and markets evolving, a particular joint venture could be a success one year and a failure the next. Intense competition leads to a hostile environment and increases the risks of establishing a joint venture. Some environments are just not conducive to success. An entrepreneur must determine whether the joint venture will offer opportunities for growth or will penalize the company, for example, by preventing it from entering certain markets.

A joint venture is not a panacea for expanding the entrepreneurial venture. Rather, it should be considered one of many options for supplementing the resources of the firm and responding more quickly to competitive challenges and market opportunities. The effective use of joint ventures as a strategy for expansion requires the entrepreneur to carefully appraise the situation and the potential partner(s). Other strategic alternatives to the joint venture—such as acquisitions, mergers, and leveraged buyouts—should also be considered.

ACQUISITIONS

acquisition Purchasing all or part of a company

Another way the entrepreneur can expand the venture is by acquiring an existing business. Acquisitions provide an excellent means of expanding a business by entering new markets or new product areas. One entrepreneur acquired a chemical manufacturing company after becoming familiar with its problems and operations as a supplier of the entrepreneur's company. An *acquisition* is the purchase of an entire company, or part of a company; by definition, the company is completely absorbed and no longer exists independently. An acquisition can take many forms, depending on the goals and position of the parties involved in the transaction, the amount of money involved, and the type of company.

Although one of the key issues in buying a business is agreeing on a price, successful acquisition of a business actually involves much, much more. In fact, often the structure of the deal can be more important to the resultant success of the transaction than the actual price. One radio station was successful after being acquired by a company primarily because the previous owner loaned the money and took no principal payment (only interest) on the loan until the third year of operation.

From a strategic viewpoint, a prime concern of the entrepreneurial firm is maintaining the focus of the new venture as a whole. Whether the acquisition will become the core of the new business or rather represents a needed capability—such as a distribution outlet, sales force, or production facility—the entrepreneur must ensure that it fits into the overall direction and structure of the strategic plan of the present venture.

Advantages of an Acquisition

For an entrepreneur, there are many advantages to acquiring an existing business, as indicated below:

1. *Established business.* The most significant advantage is that the acquired firm has an established image and track record. If the firm has been profitable, the entrepreneur need only continue its current strategy to be successful with the existing customer base.

2. *Location.* New customers are already familiar with the location.
3. *Established marketing structure.* An acquired firm has its existing channel and sales structure. Known suppliers, wholesalers, retailers, and manufacturers' reps are important assets to an entrepreneur. With this structure already in place, the entrepreneur can concentrate on improving or expanding the acquired business.
4. *Cost.* The actual cost of acquiring a business can be lower than other methods of expansion.
5. *Existing employees.* The employees of an existing business can be an important asset to the acquisition process. They know how to run the business and can help ensure that the business will continue in its successful mode. They already have established relationships with customers, suppliers, and channel members and can reassure these groups when a new owner takes over the business.
6. *More opportunity to be creative.* Since the entrepreneur does not have to be concerned with finding suppliers, channel members, hiring new employees, or creating customer awareness, more time can be spent assessing opportunities to expand or strengthen the existing business and tapping into potential synergies between the businesses.

Disadvantages of an Acquisition

Although we can see that there are many advantages to acquiring an existing business, there are also disadvantages. The importance of each of the advantages and disadvantages should be weighed carefully with other expansion options.

1. *Marginal success record.* Most ventures that are for sale have an erratic, marginally successful, or even unprofitable track record. It is important to review the records and meet with important constituents to assess that record in terms of the business's future potential. For example, if the store layout is poor, this factor can be rectified; but if the location is poor, the entrepreneur might do better using some other expansion method.
2. *Overconfidence in ability.* Sometimes an entrepreneur may assume that he or she can succeed where others have failed. This is why a self-evaluation is so important before entering into any purchase agreement. Even though the entrepreneur brings new ideas and management qualities, the venture may never be successful for reasons that are not possible to correct. Often managers are overconfident in their ability to overcome cultural differences between their current business and the one being acquired.
3. *Key employee loss.* Often, when a business changes hands, key employees also leave. Key employee loss can be devastating to an entrepreneur who is acquiring a business since the value of the business is often a reflection of the efforts of the employees. This is particularly evident in a service business, where it is difficult to separate the actual service from the person who performs it. In the acquisition negotiations, it is helpful for the entrepreneur to speak to all employees individually to get some assurance of their intentions as well as to inform them of how important they will be to the future of the business. Incentives can sometimes be used to ensure that key employees will remain with the business.
4. *Overvaluation.* It is possible that the actual purchase price is inflated due to the established image, customer base, channel members, or suppliers. If the entrepreneur has to pay too much for a business, it is possible that the return on investment will be unacceptable. It is important to look at the investment required in purchasing a business and at the potential profit and establish a reasonable payback to justify the investment.

After balancing the pros and cons of the acquisition, the entrepreneur needs to determine a fair price for the business.

Synergy

The concept that "the whole is greater than the sum of its parts" applies to the integration of an acquisition into the entrepreneur's venture. The synergy should occur in both the business concept, with the acquisition functioning as a vehicle to move toward overall goals, and the financial performance. The acquisition should positively impact the bottom line, affecting both long-term gains and future growth. Lack of synergy is one of the most frequent causes of an acquisition's failure to meet its objectives.

Structuring the Deal

Once the entrepreneur has identified a good candidate for acquisition, an appropriate deal must be structured. Many techniques are available for acquiring a firm, each having a distinct set of advantages to both the buyer and seller. The deal structure involves the parties, the assets, the payment form, and the timing of the payment. For example, all or part of the assets of one firm can be acquired by another for some combination of cash, notes, stock, and/or employment contract. This payment can be made at the time of acquisition, throughout the first year, or extended over several years.

The two most common means of acquisition are the entrepreneur's direct purchase of the firm's entire stock or assets or the bootstrap purchase of these assets. In the direct purchase of the firm, the entrepreneur often obtains funds from an outside lender or the seller of the company being purchased. The money is repaid over time from the cash flow generated from the operations. Although this is a relatively simple and clear transaction, it usually results in a long-term capital gain to the seller and double taxation on the funds used to repay the money borrowed to acquire the company.

In order to avoid these problems, the entrepreneur can make a bootstrap purchase, acquiring a small amount of the firm, such as 20 to 30 percent, for cash. He or she then purchases the remainder of the company with a long-term note that is paid off over time out of the acquired company's earnings. This type of deal often results in more favorable tax advantages to both the buyer and the seller.

Locating Acquisition Candidates

brokers People who sell companies

If an entrepreneur is seriously planning to buy a business, there are some sources of assistance. There are professional business *brokers* that operate in a fashion similar to a real estate broker. They represent the seller and will sometimes aggressively find buyers through either referrals, advertising, or direct sales. Since these brokers are paid a commission on the sale, they often expend more effort on their best deals.

Accountants, attorneys, bankers, business associates, and consultants may also know of good acquisition candidates. Many of these professionals have a good working knowledge of the business, which can be helpful in the negotiations.

It is also possible to find business opportunities in the classified sections of the newspaper or in a trade magazine. Since these listings are usually completely unknown, they may involve more risk but can be purchased at a lower price.

Determining the best option for an entrepreneur involves significant time and effort. The entrepreneur should gather as much information as possible, read it carefully, consult with advisors and experts, consider his or her own situation, and then make a constructive decision.

MERGERS

merger Joining two or more companies

A *merger*—or a transaction involving two, or possibly more, companies in which only one company survives—is another method of expanding a venture. Acquisitions are so similar to mergers that at times the two terms are used interchangeably. A key concern in any merger (or acquisition) is the legality of the purchase. The Department of Justice frequently issues guidelines for horizontal, vertical, and conglomerate mergers which further define the interpretation that will be made in enforcing the Sherman Act and Clayton Act. Since the guidelines are extensive and technical, the entrepreneur should secure adequate legal advice when any issues arise.

Why should an entrepreneur merge? There are both defensive and offensive strategies for a merger, as indicated in Figure 16.1. Merger motivations range from survival to protection to diversification to growth. When some technical obsolescence, market or raw material loss, or deterioration of the capital structure has occurred in the entrepreneur's venture, a merger may be the only means for survival. The merger can also protect against market encroachment, product innovation, or an unwarranted takeover. A merger can provide a great deal of diversification as well as growth in market, technology, and financial and managerial strength.

How does a merger take place? It requires sound planning by the entrepreneur. The merger objectives, particularly those dealing with earnings, must be spelled out with the resulting gains for the owners of both companies delineated. Also, the entrepreneur must carefully evaluate the other company's management to ensure that, if retained, it would be competent in developing the growth and future of the combined entity. The value and appropriateness of the existing resources should also be determined. In essence, this involves a careful analysis of both companies to ensure that the weaknesses of one do not compound those of the other. Finally, the entrepreneur should work toward establishing a climate of mutual trust to help minimize any possible management threat or turbulence.

The same methods for valuing an acquisition candidate can be used to determine the value of a merger candidate. The process involves the entrepreneur looking at the synergistic product/market position, the new domestic or international market position, any undervalued financial strength, whether or not the company is skilled in a related industry,

FIGURE 16.1 Merger Motivations

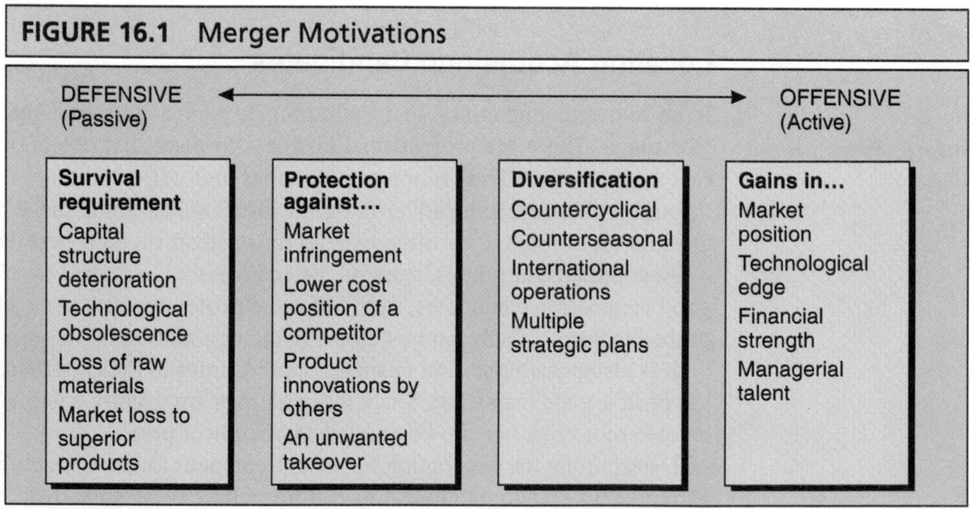

Source: F. T. Haner, *Business Policy, Planning, and Strategy* (Cambridge, MA: Winthrop, 1976), p. 399.

and any underexploited company asset. A common procedure for determining value is to estimate the present value of discounted cash flows and the expected after-tax earnings attributable to the merger. This should be done on optimistic, pessimistic, and probable scenarios of cash flows and earnings using various acceptable rates of return.

LEVERAGED BUYOUTS

leveraged buyout (LBO) Purchasing an existing venture by any employee group

A *leveraged buyout (LBO)* occurs when an entrepreneur (or any employee group) uses borrowed funds to purchase an existing venture for cash. Most LBOs occur because the entrepreneur purchasing the venture believes that he or she could run the company more efficiently than the current owners. The current owner is frequently an entrepreneur or other owner who wants to retire. The owner may also be a large corporation desiring to divest itself of a subsidiary that is too small or that does not fit its long-term strategic plans.

The purchaser needs a great amount of external funding since the personal financial resources needed to acquire the firm directly are frequently limited. Since the issuance of additional equity as a means of funding is usually not possible, capital is acquired in the form of long-term debt financing (five years or more), and the assets of the firm being acquired serve as collateral. Who usually provides this long-term debt financing? Banks, venture capitalists, and insurance companies have been the most active providers of the debt needed in LBOs.

The actual financial package used in an LBO reflects the lender's risk-reward profile. Whereas banks tend to use senior-debt issues, venture capitalists usually use subordinated debt issues with warrants or options. Regardless of the instrument used, the repayment plan established must be in line with the pro forma cash flows that the company expects to be generated. The interest rates are usually variable and are consistent with the current yields of comparable risk investment.

In most LBOs, the debt capital usually exceeds the equity by a ratio of 5 to 1, with some ratios as high as 10 to 1. This is significantly more debt relative to equity than in a typical firm's capital structure. Although this makes the financial risk great, the key to a successful LBO is not the relative debt-equity ratio but rather the ability of the entrepreneur taking over to cover the principal and interest payments through increased sales and profits. The ability depends on the skills of the entrepreneur and the strength and stability of the firm.

How does the entrepreneur determine whether a specific company is a good candidate for an LBO? This determination can be made through the following evaluation procedure:

1. The entrepreneur must determine whether the present owner's asking price is reasonable. Many subjective and quantitative techniques can be used in this determination. Subjective evaluations need to be made of the following: the competitiveness of the industry and the competitive position of the firm in that industry; the uniqueness of the offering of the firm and its stage in the product life cycle; and the abilities of management and other key personnel remaining with the firm. Quantitative techniques are used to evaluate the fairness of the asking price. The price-earnings ratio of the LBO prospect should be calculated and compared with those of comparable companies, as well as the present value of future earnings of the prospect and its book value.
2. The entrepreneur must assess the firm's debt capacity. This is particularly critical since the entrepreneur wants to raise as much of the capital needed as possible in the form of long-term debt. The amount of long-term debt a prospective LBO can carry depends

on the prospect's business risk and the stability of its future cash flows. The cash flow must cover the long-term debt required to finance the LBO. Any financial amount that cannot be secured by long-term debt, due to the inadequacy of the cash flow, will need to be in the form of equity from the entrepreneur or other investors.

3. The entrepreneur must develop the appropriate financial package. The financial package must meet the needs and objectives of the providers of the funds as well as the company's and the entrepreneur's situation. Although each LBO financial package is tailored to the specific situation, there are usually some restrictions, such as no payment of dividends. Frequently, an LBO agreement with venture capitalists has warrants that are convertible into common stock at a later date. A sinking fund repayment of the long-term debt is frequently required.

There are many instances of both successful and unsuccessful LBOs. One of the most publicized involved R. H. Macy and Co., a well-known department store chain. Macy's was not in bad condition in terms of the traditional measures of sales per square foot, profitability, and return on assets. However, it had experienced a significant drop in profits and was losing talented middle executives. The LBO was accomplished by some 345 executives participating and sharing a 20 percent ownership in the $4.7 billion retailer. Ultimately, the LBO provided the following benefits: a new entrepreneurial spirit in management that fostered more loyalty in the employees; increased motivation among employees, with middle managers actually selling and earning sales floor bonuses during slack time; and a long-term planning direction for the board of directors that meets five times a year instead of once a month.

OVERCOMING CONSTRAINTS BY NEGOTIATING FOR MORE RESOURCES

distribution task Negotiating how the benefits of the relationship will be allocated between the parties

integration task Exploring possible mutual benefits from the relationship so that the "size of the pie" can be increased

There are two primary tasks for an entrepreneur negotiating with another party for access to an external growth mechanism. The *distribution task* is the first—how the benefits of the relationship are distributed between the parties. That is, given a certain sized pie, the parties work out who gets what proportion of that pie. Second is the *integration task,* in which mutual benefits from the relationship are explored. This requires a collaborative mind-set so that the "size of the pie" can be increased.

Often people focus on the first task and ignore the second. However, making the pie bigger before distribution provides the opportunity to generate greater benefits for both parties and increases the likelihood of an agreement being reached. Besides, the collaborative and creative aspects of working together to find ways to increase the size of the pie are more enjoyable and more beneficial than a conflict resolution approach, which involves simply allocating outcomes under a purely distributive approach.

To negotiate in a way that maximizes benefits requires the entrepreneur to use information about one's own preferences and those of the other party to create an outcome that is mutually beneficial. This requires an initial assessment of oneself and the other party and the use of strategies to elicit more information during the negotiation interactions to better inform those initial assessments. Based on the work of Max Bazerman and Margaret Neale, two leading experts on negotiation, there are a number of assessments that an entrepreneur should make when negotiating with a growth partner.[11]

reservation price The price (the bundle of resources from the agreement) at which the entrepreneur is indifferent about whether to accept the agreement or choose the alternative

Assessment 1: What Will You Do If an Agreement Is Not Reached? The answer to such a question provides an important basis for any negotiation strategy. The answer represents the entrepreneur's "best alternative to a negotiated agreement." This best alternative helps to determine a reservation price for the negotiation. The *reservation price* is the price (the bundle of

FAIR ENOUGH

To Be a Better Negotiator, Learn to Tell the Difference between a Lie and a *Lie*

No one really likes to think about how much lying goes on at the bargaining table. Of course not—it's troubling. On the one hand, we aspire to principled negotiation, win-win solutions, and civility with our opponents. On the other, our whole notion of negotiation is built on ethical quicksand: To succeed, you must deceive.

I'm not talking about the obvious cases, such as the bald lie. Those we all condemn, and in fact, our courts provide remedies for them—albeit slow, aggravating, inconsistent, and expensive ones. To me, it's the little lies, the omissions and evasions, that are more curious.

In negotiation, exaggerating benefits, ignoring flaws, or saying "I don't know" when in reality you do is not considered lying. Rather, it's sales ability. Declaring your bottom line to be non-negotiable (even when you're posturing) is not lying. It's a show of strength. Pretending to bend over backward to make meaningless concessions is not lying. It's applied psychology. Savvy businesspeople accept these rituals without undue introspection. Of course, the pathologically honest among us find them disturbing. But we have a place for those people . . . in the back room, far away from any bargaining table.

Still, some evasiveness and deception we consider out of bounds. Following are some tips for staying in bounds without getting clobbered.

On defense, vigilant skepticism is a tremendous asset. Reflect on everything you hear. Reflect on everything you don't. If you're suspicious, ask questions, especially ones that require more than just a simple yes or no answer. Keep probing until you're satisfied. J. P. Morgan used to say, "A man always has two reasons for the things he does—a good one and the real one." So after you get the good ones, ask for the real ones by saying, "And why else?" Also, get important promises in writing, and scrutinize their wording with and without your lawyer. To discourage dishonesty, tell your opponent you will independently verify the important stuff. If you can, do it. By the way, experts say it's easier to detect lying on the phone than in person. The voice all by itself (without distracting visual cues) is more of a giveaway.

To the terminally honest, I say: Negotiation is not group therapy. Generally, if you bare your soul, you will be fleeced. Respect the rules—or have someone else do your bargaining for you. If you're a liar (and you know who you are), I hope you get nailed big time. And if you're morally sturdy and find yourself unsure of what to say or omit, just keep Richard Nixon's comments about Watergate in mind: "I was not lying. I said things that later on seemed to be untrue."

Source: Reprinted with permission of Entrepreneur Media, Inc., "To Be a Better Negotiator, Learn to Tell the Difference between a Lie and a *Lie*," by Marc Diener, January 2002, *Entrepreneur* magazine: www.entrepreneur.com.

resources from the agreement) at which the entrepreneur is indifferent about whether to accept the agreement or choose the alternative. For example, the best alternative to a negotiated agreement with a joint venture partner would be the benefits from pursuing growth at a slower rate using existing resources (knowledge, money, network, etc.). Recognizing that there is an alternative to this joint venture relationship, albeit a slower route, provides a minimum acceptable level of benefits that the negotiated outcome must reach.

Assessment 2: What Will the Other Party to the Negotiation Do If an Agreement Is Not Reached? It can be difficult for the entrepreneur to assess his or her own reservation prices, and it is even more difficult to assess those of the negotiation partner. If these prices can be determined, the entrepreneur has a good idea of the *bargaining zone,* or the range of outcomes between the entrepreneur's reservation price and the reservation price of the other party. Consideration of the bargaining zone encourages the entrepreneur not to focus prematurely on a settlement price but rather to consider the range of possible outcomes within the bargaining zone. If the bargaining zone can be determined by the entrepreneur while

bargaining zone The range of outcomes between the entrepreneur's reservation price and the reservation price of the other party

AS SEEN IN *ENTREPRENEUR* MAGAZINE

PROVIDE ADVICE TO AN ENTREPRENEUR ABOUT ENTERING INTO AGREEMENTS

Entrepreneurs James Tiscione, 49, and Anthony Tiscione, 79, founders of ACM Enterprises in Tucson, Arizona

Product Description The Auto Card Manager (ACM), a thin metal case that holds a driver's license and up to five credit cards. When users push one of the six buttons on the case, the selected credit card is dispensed.

Start-Up $50,000 in 2000 and 2001, to pay for the first production run of 25,000 units

Sales $1.8 million in 2002

The Challenge Bringing a new product to market with a limited marketing budget

James Tiscione didn't have a lot of money when he launched his business, but that didn't stop him from finding a way to bring his unusual product to market. Here are the steps he followed:

1. *Obtain a patent.* Tiscione started by visiting www.uspto.gov, the official Web site of the U.S. Patent and Trademark Office, to look for similar patents. "I looked at over 1,000 patents and found only two that were even remotely similar to mine," he says. "Only after completing the search did I go to a patent attorney." Doing some research on his own did more than just save Tiscione money: "I was trying to hedge my bets before investing dollars in attorney fees, engineering design, and prototypes. I also wanted to see what other ideas were out there. I was surprised no one else ever had the idea." Before long, Tiscione applied for a provisional patent, which doesn't give inventors patent protection, but does allow them to show their ideas to people. "It is an inexpensive way of protection that allows inventors one year for research and development," Tiscione says. In 2001, he applied for his utility patent.
2. *Decide what help you need.* Because Tiscione had never developed a product before, he felt he lacked the experience he needed to launch the idea. He asked his father, Anthony, an inventor, for help in finalizing his product design. Tiscione also approached Steve Pagac, a marketing whiz who owned a real estate and investment firm. Says Tiscione, "Steve invested sweat equity in our venture, and he is responsible for lining up all our customers."
3. *Make a prototype.* Tiscione knew people wouldn't understand the ACM without trying it, so he made a prototype. Tiscione ended up choosing a prototype supplier in California. Once he began using the prototype, people started asking where they could buy one. The positive feedback played a major role in moving the business ahead.
4. *Locate a production source.* Tiscione's first stop was the Hong Kong Chamber of Commerce, which has an office in San Francisco. "They sent me a list of companies I e-mailed," he says. He narrowed it down to one—but only signed the final agreement after visiting the company several times and viewing a few trial production pieces.
5. *Explore all possibilities to find distribution outlets.* Tiscione and Pagac weren't sure which retailers would want to buy their product, so they started by approaching catalogs and stores such as

keeping his or her reservation price hidden from the other party, then the entrepreneur is in a position to negotiate an outcome that is largely beneficial to the entrepreneur and only marginally beneficial to the other party (i.e., just above the other party's reservation price). Of course, such an approach focuses on the distribution stage and not the integrative stage.

Assessment 3: What Are the Underlying Issues of This Negotiation? How Important Is Each Issue to You? Answers to these questions focus the negotiation toward achieving aspects of the relationship that are most desirable for the entrepreneur by trading off aspects of less importance for those of greater importance. For example, an entrepreneur might be more concerned about having control over a joint venture than about his or her share of the profits generated by the joint venture. Recognizing the relative

Brookstone, The Sharper Image, and Things Remembered. "While the stores didn't bite, one promotional company did—AMG of Plymouth, Wisconsin," Tiscione says. "AMG signed an exclusive agreement with us for the promotional products market in 2001." Tiscione and Pagac also approached SkyMall, a specialty retailer that produces a cost-sharing catalog targeting in-flight airline passengers. "After two quarters ending in September," says Tiscione, "SkyMall reported that the ACM was the No. 1–selling product in [the catalog], and they agreed to carry the product through March." Tiscione and Pagac also contacted MJ Media, a TV marketer in Phoenix that signed a nonexclusive agreement to sell the ACM through TV ads. "We revamped our original agreement with MJ Media to include a broader base of distribution," Tiscione says. "Originally, the contract was for TV advertising only. Since then, MJ Media has expanded into Internet sales and master distribution to small distributors." Now, Tiscione has a broad range of customers selling his products. As a bonus, Taylor Gifts, a major consumer catalog, picked up the ACM for the 2002 Christmas season.

6. *Sign deals that maximize marketing exposure but limit financial risk.* Advertising and marketing expenses can kill a product—but Tiscione avoided these expenses by signing contracts with limited risk. Both AMG and MJ Media signed agreements to purchase the product from ACM and promote it themselves. Also, Tiscione's deal with SkyMall was cooperative. Tiscione paid nothing to be listed in SkyMall, but all the sales went to SkyMall up to a certain sales level. Once that level was reached, sales were split equally between SkyMall and ACM. At press time, ACM switched to a standard contract, which requires them to pay for the ad but allows them to retain all sales.

ADVICE TO AN ENTREPRENEUR

An inventor has read the above article and comes to you for advice. "This is exactly what I want to do," he says, "I don't have the expertise or the money to manufacture the product myself or to market and sell it. What I need is for someone else to do that for me. Here are my questions:"

1. Is it really that simple to find and then establish a relationship with someone to produce my product? Should the producer have a manufacturing license or should I enter into a joint venture?
2. Same sorts of issues on the marketing end, but I also want to know how much control I can maintain over how the product is marketed and sold. Or should I not worry about that and let the experts do their thing?
3. One dilemma for me is how much money I should invest in the prototypes. The more money I invest, the better the prototype looks, but I don't want to waste money either.

Source: Reprinted with permission of Entrepreneur Media, Inc., "Play Your Cards Right. Presenting a Case Study in Striking the Best Deals to Launch Your Own Great Product on a Limited Budget," by Don Debelak, March 2003, *Entrepreneur* magazine: www.entrepreneur.com.

importance of these aspects of the relationship allows the entrepreneur to "sacrifice" equity (maybe through nonvoting shares) but obtain control (e.g., to have 51 percent of the stock and/or one more seat on the board of directors and the position of chairman of the board).

Assessment 4: What Are the Underlying Issues of This Negotiation? How Important Is Each Issue to the Other Party? By understanding more about the other party, the entrepreneur has a greater opportunity to achieve integration—make the size of the pie bigger. This information provides the opportunity for the entrepreneur to sacrifice aspects that are of less importance to him or her but of high importance to the other party. Similarly, the entrepreneur can obtain from the other party aspects of high importance to him or her but of low importance to the other party. If this information is known to both parties, then it is likely that the outcome will be mutually beneficial (because the size of the pie has been increased).

Being aware of the assessments that need to be made is an important step toward a successful negotiation but requires strategies for eliciting information from the other party that can benefit the distributive and/or integrative elements of a negotiation. Again based on the work of Bazerman and Neale (1992),[12] we offer a number of these strategies. These strategies should be thought of as tools. No one tool is perfect for every job. Some jobs require that a number of different tools be used simultaneously, while other jobs require that the tools be used sequentially. The entrepreneur needs to make his or her own decision as to which strategies should be used and when. This may not be known in advance and the entrepreneur might experiment with different strategies to get an idea of which ones will work best for the current negotiation.

Strategy 1: Build Trust and Share Information As discussed above, the best negotiated outcome likely arises from integration, where the parties find mutually beneficial trade-offs. To find them requires both parties to have information about each other's underlying issues and the relative importance of those issues. Although providing information is beneficial to integration, it can be detrimental to the entrepreneur in distributing benefits if the other party has kept hidden his or her own preferences (e.g., the other party is aware of the entrepreneur's reservation price but the entrepreneur is unaware of the other party's reservation price). Therefore, releasing information requires trust—a belief that the other party will not act opportunistically to the detriment of the entrepreneur.

Building trust is an important aspect of negotiation and is important for the ongoing relationship if an agreement is reached. One way to start this process is to share some information with the other party, such as the relative importance of a particular issue (not one's reservation price). The other party may reciprocate by also sharing information, as part of an incremental process of building trust. If possible, the entrepreneur should assess the other party's trustworthiness (maybe by investigating the other party's previous relationships). If the other party appears to be untrustworthy, then the worst outcome for the entrepreneur would be that an agreement is reached, because a relationship with an untrustworthy partner can be detrimental to the long-run performance of the firm.

Strategy 2: Ask Lots of Questions Asking questions provides an opportunity to learn more about the preferences of the other party, because this information is the foundation for finding the trade-offs necessary for integrative agreements. Even if the other party does not answer certain questions, the nonanswer itself might provide some information. For example, an entrepreneur negotiating an exclusive license agreement could ask the potential licensee, "How much would it cost you to get out of your current contract with firm YY to free yourself up to license our technology?"

Strategy 3: Make Multiple Offers Simultaneously Relationships are rarely defined by one dimension, and therefore there can be numerous possible offers based on combinations of different levels on different dimensions. Recognizing this, the entrepreneur can simultaneously make multiple offers. By determining which offer is the closest to being acceptable, the entrepreneur can infer which issues are of greatest importance to the other party. This information is valuable in reaching an integrative agreement. It also sends a signal to the other party that the entrepreneur is flexible.

Strategy 4: Use Differences to Create Trade-Offs That Are a Source of Mutually Beneficial Outcomes Differences between the entrepreneur and the other party in expectations, risk preferences, and time preferences all provide opportunities to reach an integrative agreement. We can investigate these differences in the context of an entrepreneur negotiating a license agreement. One difference could be in expectation—the entrepreneur expects the introduction of the licensed technology into the other party's product to increase sales more substantially than the other party expects. This difference in expectation could be the basis for an integrative agreement. For example, both parties would prefer to have a lower "up-front" fee for the technology and a greater royalty percentage. Both parties perceive that they do better based on their expectations of sales.

A similar license agreement would be mutually beneficial when the entrepreneur has less risk aversion than the other party—that is, when the entrepreneur is more willing to give up a certain gain from the up-front fee for a greater, but uncertain, stream of revenue from an increased royalty payment. Alternatively, differences in time preference could lead to the above negotiated license agreement. The entrepreneur prefers to accept less now for more later, whereas the licensee is prepared to pay more later, when the income from the license is generated.

IN REVIEW

SUMMARY

In this chapter we explored alternate means by which an entrepreneur can grow his or her business. Franchising was discussed as a means of new entry that can reduce the risk of downside loss for the franchisee and also as a way that an entrepreneur can expand his or her business by having others pay for the use of the business formula. For the franchisee, the advantages of franchising are that he or she enters into a business with an accepted name, product, or service; has access to managerial assistance provided by the franchisor; receives up-front support that could save the entrepreneur significant time and possibly capital; has access to extensive information about the market; and has other operating and structural controls to assist in the effective management of the business. However, there are a number of potential disadvantages, which usually center on the inability of the franchisor to provide the services, advertising, and location that were promised.

For the franchisor, the primary advantage of franchising is that he or she can expand the business quickly, using little personal capital. But the franchisor also incurs certain risks in choosing this expansion alternative. In some cases, the franchisor may find it very difficult to locate quality franchisees. Poor management, in spite of all the training and controls, can still cause individual franchise failures, and these can reflect negatively on the entire franchise system. As the number of franchises increases, the ability to maintain tight controls becomes more difficult.

Entrepreneurs can also achieve growth through joint ventures. The effective use of joint ventures as a strategy for expansion requires the entrepreneur to carefully appraise the situation and the potential partner(s). First, the entrepreneur needs an accurate assessment of the other party in order to best manage the new entity in light of the ensuing relationship. Second, there needs to be symmetry between the two (or more) firms in terms of "chemistry" and the combination of their resources. Third, expectations of the results of the joint venture must be reasonable. Far too often, at least one of the partners feels that a joint venture will be the cure-all for other corporate problems. Expectations of a joint venture must be realistic. Finally, the timing must be right.

Another way the entrepreneur can expand the venture is by acquiring an existing business. For an entrepreneur, there are many advantages to acquiring an existing business, such as gaining access to an established image and track record, familiar location, established distribution and resource channels, and knowledgeable and skilled employees. Besides, the cost of an acquisition can be cheaper than other mechanisms for growth. However, history suggests that acquisitions have only a marginal success record. Entrepreneurs seem to be overly confident about their ability to achieve envisioned synergies, integrate organizational cultures, and retain key employees. After balancing the pros and cons of the acquisition, the entrepreneur needs to determine a fair price for the business.

Mergers and leveraged buyouts are other ways that entrepreneurs can grow their businesses. An essential skill for all these alternatives is the ability of the entrepreneur to negotiate. Good negotiation involves two tasks. The first task involves determining how the benefits of the relationship are going to be distributed between the parties. The second task is exploring the mutual benefits that can be gained from the relationship. To negotiate in a way that maximizes benefits requires the entrepreneur to use information about one's own preferences and those of the other party to create an outcome that is mutually beneficial. This requires an initial assessment of oneself and the other party and the use of strategies to elicit more information during the negotiation interactions to better inform those initial assessments. To these ends, this chapter offered four important assessments an entrepreneur should make and four strategies that can be used to achieve a successful negotiation.

RESEARCH TASKS

1. Find information about three joint ventures that were failures, and be prepared to discuss the underlying reasons for the failure in each case.
2. Search on the Internet for franchises for sale. Choose three. What commonalities are there across the businesses and the information provided? What differences are there? For one of these businesses, obtain all franchise information. For this business, what are the benefits of being a franchisee rather than setting up an independent business? What are all the associated costs of being a franchisee for this business?
3. Interview three franchisees to better understand their relationship with the franchisor.
4. Find three types of business license agreements (only one of these should be a software license agreement). In what ways are these license agreements the same and in what ways are they different? Why have these companies decided to license their product or technology rather than simply sell it?
5. Find three reports of acquisitions that were unsuccessful. Why were these acquisitions deemed unsuccessful?

CLASS DISCUSSION

1. Being a franchisor seems to be a mechanism for growth, but what are the growth prospects for entrepreneurs that are franchisees? Isn't the entrepreneur limited in his or her ability to pursue all the different types of growth strategies? Is being a franchisee simply substituting one type of employment for another type of employment? How can a franchisee grow his or her business(es)?
2. Recently the Chinese government has been encouraging foreign firms to enter into joint venture relationships with local (Chinese) firms. What are the benefits to the Chinese economy from these joint venture relationships? What are the benefits to the local Chinese firm? What are the benefits to the foreign firm? What is the impact of the joint venture on the foreign firm's domestic economy?

3. Identify a local franchise in your area, and determine where the competitors are located and where other franchises from the same organization are located. Evaluate the existing potential for the franchise.
4. Why are there so many different techniques for determining the worth of a firm? In any given situation, is there one "right answer" for a company's value? What effects do your answers to these questions have on the entrepreneur making an acquisition?

SELECTED READINGS

Bazerman, Max H.; and Jared R. Curhan. (2000). Negotiation. *Annual Review of Psychology,* vol. 51, no. 1, pp. 279–315.

Focuses on the psychological study of negotiation, including the history of the negotiation game; the development of mental models on negotiation; the definition of negotiation rules based on concerns of ethics, fairness, and values; the impact of the selection of communication medium on the negotiation game; and the impact of cross-cultural issues on perception and of behavior on negotiation.

Chang, Sea Jin. (2004). Venture Capital Financing, Strategic Alliances, and the Initial Public Offerings of Internet Startups. *Journal of Business Venturing,* vol. 19, no. 5, pp. 721-41.

In this study the author examines how Internet start-ups' venture-capital financing and strategic alliances affect these start-ups' ability to acquire the resources necessary for growth. Using the initial public offering (IPO) event as an early-stage measure for Internet start-ups' performance and controlling for the IPO market environment, this study found that three factors positively influence a start-up's time to IPO: (1) the reputations of participating venture-capital firms and strategic alliance partners, (2) the amount of money the start-up raised, and (3) the size of the start-up's network of strategic alliances.

Dietmeyer, Brian J.; and Max H. Bazerman. (2001). Value Negotiation. *Executive Excellence,* vol. 18, no. 4, p. 7.

This article advises executives on value negotiation, including developing wise trades in value creation; building trust and sharing information in an open and truthful manner; asking questions; making multiple offers simultaneously; and searching for postsettlement settlements.

George, Gerard; Shaker A. Zahra; and Robley D. Wood. (2002). The Effects of Business–University Alliances on Innovative Output and Financial Performance: A Study of Publicly Traded Biotechnology Companies. *Journal of Business Venturing,* vol. 17, no. 6, pp. 557–90.

Analysis of 2,457 alliances undertaken by 147 biotechnology firms shows that companies with university linkages have lower R&D expenses and higher levels of innovative output. However, the results do not support the proposition that companies with university linkages achieve higher financial performance than similar firms without such linkages.

Gulati, Ranjay; and Monica C. Higgins. (2003). Which Ties Matter When? The Contingent Effects of Interorganizational Partnerships on IPO Success. *Strategic Management Journal,* vol. 24, no. 2, pp. 127–45.

This paper investigates the contingent value of interorganizational relationships at the time of a young firm's initial public offering (IPO). Results show that ties to prominent venture-capital firms are particularly beneficial to IPO success during cold markets, while ties to prominent investment banks are particularly beneficial to IPO success during hot markets; a firm's strategic alliances with major pharmaceutical and health care firms did not have such contingent effects.

Holmberg, Stevan R.; and Kathryn B. Morgan. (2003). Franchise Turnover and Failure: New Research and Perspectives. *Journal of Business Venturing,* vol. 18, no. 3, pp. 403–19.

This paper's new franchise failure concept reconciles many prior, seemingly inconsistent study results based largely on franchisors' surveys. Overall franchisee turnover rates are significant and appear to have increased over time.

Kelley, Donna J.; and Mark P. Rice. (2002). Advantage beyond Founding the Strategic Use of Technologies. *Journal of Business Venturing,* vol. 17, no. 1, pp. 41–58.

Explores the interrelationship between efforts to build technology portfolios and to form alliances, and the link between technology-based strategic actions and product innovation rates in start-up firms.

Kenis, Patrick; and David Knoke. (2002). How Organizational Field Networks Shape Interorganizational Tie-Formation Rates. *Academy of Management Review,* vol. 27, no. 2, pp. 275–94.

The authors investigate the impact of communication in field-level networks on rates of formation of interorganizational collaborative ties, such as strategic alliances and joint ventures.

Marino, Louis; Karen Strandholm; Kevin H. Steensma; and Mark K. Weaver. (2002). The Moderating Effect of National Culture on the Relationship between Entrepreneurial Orientation and Strategic Alliance Portfolio Extensiveness. *Entrepreneurship: Theory & Practice,* vol. 26, no. 4, pp. 145–61.

This article examines the moderating effect of national culture on the relationship between entrepreneurial orientation and strategic alliance portfolio extensiveness.

Michael, Steven C. (2003). First Mover Advantage through Franchising. *Journal of Business Venturing,* vol. 18, no. 1, pp. 61–81.

Franchising has been argued to be a technique used by entrepreneurs in service industries to assemble resources in order to rapidly create large chains and gain first-mover advantage. Whether and how such first-mover advantage is created is the subject of this paper. A structural equations model is specified, and empirical results from the restaurant industry support the model's predictions that the first-mover advantage initially takes the form of a lead in the number of retail outlets, followed by a market share lead and, finally, superior profitability.

Michael, Steven C. (2000). Investment to Create Bargaining Power: The Case of Franchising. *Strategic Management Journal,* vol. 21, no. 4, pp. 497–517.

In this article the author argues that the franchisor can make investments in activities to increase its bargaining power and decrease conflict and litigation in a franchise system. Includes tapered integration, ownership of some units with franchisement of others, selection of inexperienced franchisees, and employment of a long training program.

Nicholls-Nixon, Charlene L.; and Arnold C. Cooper. (2000). Strategic Experimentation: Understanding Change and Performance in New Ventures. *Journal of Business Venturing,* vol. 15, no. 5/6, pp. 493–524.

The authors discuss the concept of strategic experimentation as the organizing framework for the study of change in joint ventures, covering the relationship between perceived environmental hostility and experimentation efforts, reasons for engaging in strategic experimentation, and the importance of perceived environmental hostility in strategic experimentation.

Park, Seung H.; Roger R. Chen; and Scott Gallagher. (2002). Firm Resources as Moderators of the Relationship between Market Growth and Strategic Alliances in Semiconductor Start-Ups. *Academy of Management Journal,* vol. 45, no. 3, pp. 527–46.

The results of this study indicate that, in volatile markets, resource-rich firms access external resources through alliances whereas resource-poor firms are less likely to do so. However, in relatively stable markets, this relationship reverses, and resource-poor firms become more active in alliance formation.

Pearce II, John A.; and Louise Hatfield. (2002). Performance Effects of Alternative Joint Venture Resource Responsibility Structures. *Journal of Business Venturing,* vol. 17, no. 4, pp. 343–65.

The authors examine the relationship between the acquirers of a joint venture's (JV's) resources and the JV's performance in achieving its partners' goals in the United States. Topics covered include the impact of alternative resource responsibility structures on JV performance, variation in resources received by JVs, and implications for business theory development and practicing managers.

Sarkar, M.B.; R. A. J. Echambadi; and Jeffrey S. Harrison. (2001). Alliance Entrepreneurship and Firm Market Performance. *Strategic Management Journal,* vol. 22, no. 6/7, pp. 701–12.

This article extends entrepreneurship into the domain of alliances and examines the effect of alliance proactiveness on market-based firm performance, including the higher performance of firms that are proactive in forming alliances, and the moderating influences of firm size and environmental uncertainty on the relationship between alliance proactiveness and performance.

END NOTES

1. See J. Useem, "The Start-up Factory," *Inc.* (February 9, 1997), pp. 40–52; E. Matson, "He Turns Ideas into Companies—at Net Speed," *Fast Company* (December 1996), p. 34; and Idealab Web site www.idealab.com.
2. D. D. Seltz, *The Complete Handbook of Franchising* (Reading, MA: Addison-Wesley Publishing Co., 1982), p. 1.
3. L. Bongiorno, "Franchise Fracas," *BusinessWeek* (March 22, 1993), pp. 68–71.
4. F. Huffman, "Under New Ownership," *Entrepreneur* (January 1993), pp. 101–105.
5. W. Siegel, *Franchising* (New York: John Wiley & Sons, 1983), p. 9.
6. *Directory of Franchising Organizations* (Babylon, NY: Pilot Industries, 1985).
7. K. Rosenburg, "Franchising, American Style," *Entrepreneur* (January 1991), pp. 86–93.
8. D. J. Kaufmann and D. E. Robbins, "Now Read This," *Entrepreneur* (January 1991), pp. 100–105.
9. For some different perspectives on joint ventures, see R. D. Hisrich, "Joint Ventures: Research Base and Use in International Methods." In *The State of the Art of Entrepreneurship* (Boston: PWS-Kent Publishing Co.), pp. 520–79; and J. McConnell and T. J. Nantell, "Corporate Combinations and Common Stock Returns: The Case of Joint Ventures," *Journal of Finance* 40 (June 1985), pp. 519–36.
10. For a discussion of some different types of joint ventures, see R. M. Cyert, "Establishing University–Industry Joint Ventures," *Research Management* 28 (January–February 1985), pp. 27–28; F. K. Berlew, "The Joint Venturer—A Way into Foreign Markets," *Harvard Business Review* (July–August 1984), pp. 48–49 and 54; and Kathryn Rudie Harrigan, *Strategies for Joint Ventures* (Lexington, MA: Lexington Books, 1985).
11. Max H. Bazerman and Margaret A. Neale, *Negotiating Rationally* (New York: Free Press, 1992).
12. Ibid.

17

ENDING THE VENTURE

LEARNING OBJECTIVES

1
To illustrate differences in alternative types of bankruptcy under the Bankruptcy Act of 1978 (amended in 1984 and again in 2004).

2
To illustrate the rights of creditors and entrepreneurs in different cases of bankruptcy.

3
To provide the entrepreneur with an understanding of the typical warning signs of bankruptcy.

4
To illustrate how some entrepreneurs can turn bankruptcy into a successful business.

5
To examine the options in providing for an exit strategy, focusing primarily on the succession of a business to family or nonfamily members and the sale of the business to employees (ESOP) or to an external source.

OPENING PROFILE

TERESA CASCIOLI

It is not often that a bankrupt small business is able to successfully recover from bankruptcy. However, one such case involves Teresa Cascioli, the first woman in Canada to become president of a major brewery. Teresa not only led Lakeport Brewing out of bankruptcy but launched the venture into one of the more successful Canadian microbreweries.

www.lakeportbrewing.ca

In 1999 Teresa was getting ready to enter law school. She had spent 12 years with the city of Hamilton in Ontario, Canada, as finance manager and another two years with Phillip Services Corporation. Born of immigrant Italian parents, she had spent her entire life in the city. Before she reached law school a group of private investors approached her to see if she could help out at an ailing company for the summer. The company, Lakeport Brewing, was in trouble. The beer market is extremely competitive and had seen companies like Amstel come and go during this period. Lakeport was now in bankruptcy with little chance of being revitalized unless it could find a new marketing niche in a very competitive market. Teresa was a bit concerned that her only knowledge of beer was being able to tell a good brew from a bad one. However, she not only took on the challenge but six months later actually took control of Lakeport after Alphacorp Holdings invested $3.1 million in equity and working capital.

Teresa describes the first years of managing the bankrupt brewery as "hell." She had many ups and downs during those first few years that took a great deal of energy, tenacity, and a vision of success that would not be deterred. She had to work without senior managers and often was in the plant seven days a week trying to learn the business. At one point she actually spent time at night inside the bottling plant learning the business from employees who had been working there for 20 years or more. In the early years she dedicated Lakeport's excess capacity to contract manufacturing of beer, near beer, and coolers for brand names and private labels. This was the beginning of the turnaround and kept the company in a positive cash flow until a major relaunch strategy could be devised.

In the summer of 2002, Teresa Cascioli was beginning to develop this new strategy for the relaunch of Lakeport's beer products. It was time to find a profitable niche for the Ontario-based brewery. She became aware of how many of her competitors were constantly saturating newspapers with ads of $5.00 off. Her response to these ads was always, "$5.00 off what?" As far as she was concerned, none of the beer ads had a clear message. It seemed that they were all trying to do the same thing—outprice one another with heavy advertising. Her response to this was a simple genius marketing strategy in her ads: A case of 24 for $24.00. At the time, this strategy amounted to a $5 to $10 savings from what her competitors were charging. More importantly, it provided a clear message to the customer.

This low-priced strategy was successful because the company had extended serious time and effort redesigning and restructuring its infrastructure to allow for more effective cost controls. As a result, the low prices still allowed the company enough margin to earn a profit. This strategy made Lakeport a significant player in the Ontario market. Market share of the take-home beer market, one of the company's primary targets, grew from a .5 percent share to more than a 6 percent share by the end of 2004.

Teresa now has complete control of the company. With financing from Vengrowth Capital Partners and National Bank, she has been able to purchase 100 percent of the 200-employee company. Her effort has been rewarded not only by the success of the company but also by the recognition of her peers. She has been ranked eighth in the annual list of the top 100 successful women business owners in Canada, and she was a finalist for the Ernst & Young turnaround entrepreneur of the year, as well as being named entrepreneur of the year by the same company. In addition to its successful labels such as Brava, Steeler Lager, and Lakeport Honey Lager, the company also has kept its production lines busy by aggressively seeking deals to pack products such as hard lemonade and ready-to-drink mixes for other makers. Lakeport is now the third largest supplier of beer to Ontario's take-home market and the fourth largest brewery in the province.

In June of 2005 Lakeport went public on the Toronto Stock Exchange. The result was a successful IPO as investors responded favorably to the company and Teresa's leadership. The company's gross revenue after the IPO continued to grow and at the end of the third quarter of 2005 reached $39.2 million, up 86 percent from the previous year. Market share of the take-home market at the end of 2005 surpassed 10 percent. Lakeport Brewing's success has drawn a lot of attention in the entrepreneurial literature thanks to Teresa Cascioli's impressive leadership. The company continues to grow and be a leader in the value category that Teresa actually pioneered. All of this was achieved by a company brought back from near death by a person who was willing to be innovative, take risks, and hold on to a vision of success.[1]

BANKRUPTCY—AN OVERVIEW

Failure is not uncommon in many new ventures, especially in light of the dot-com demise and the disasters caused by war and terrorism that have strangled many economies all over the world. According to the Small Business Administration, about half of all new start-ups fail in their first years. The failures are personally painful for the entrepreneur

FIGURE 17.1 Business and Nonbusiness U.S. Bankruptcy Filings, 1984–2004

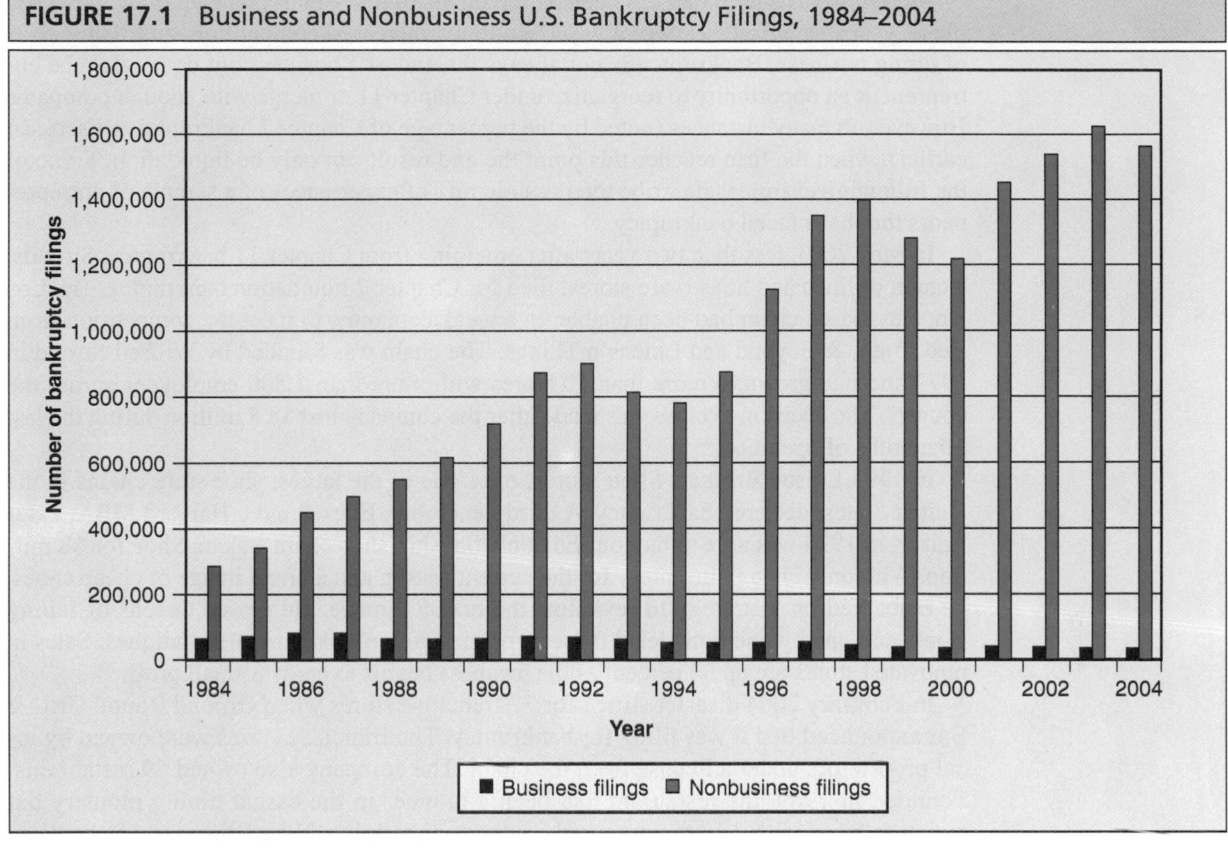

Source: American Bankruptcy Institute, www.abiworld.org.

and too often could have been prevented by paying more attention to certain critical factors in the business operation. Figure 17.1 compares business and nonbusiness bankruptcy filings from 1984 to 2004. Both business and nonbusiness bankruptcy filings are divided by chapter filings that will be explained in more detail later. It can be seen from Figure 17.1 that the combination of business and nonbusiness filings was the highest in 2003 compared with all other years included. The majority of these filings—about 98 percent of the total number filed—are nonbusiness or personal bankruptcies. However, it is not clear how many of these resulted from failed proprietorships or home businesses.

The most common type of bankruptcy (business or nonbusiness) is Chapter 7 or liquidation, which accounted for about 70 percent of the total. Chapter 13 bankruptcies, which allow creditors to be repaid in installments (usually nonbusiness types), represented about 29 percent of the total. The remaining bankruptcies (about 1 percent) are Chapter 11 filings, which result in reorganization and possibly a turnaround. The actual number of business filings for bankruptcy has declined each year since 2001. The highest number of business filings (82,446) was recorded in 1987. However, the issue has not been the number of filings but the size and type of bankruptcies. For example, in 2001 there were 22 Fortune 1000 firms and 10 Fortune 500 firms that filed for bankruptcy. Factors such as executive negligence, fraud, a poor economy, and expensive executive buyouts have caused many of these bankruptcy filings.[2]

In April 2005 Congress passed new laws effective October 17, 2005, relating to personal bankruptcies. These new regulations are expected to make it harder and more expensive for individuals to erase or restructure their debts.[3]

Bankruptcy is a term that has been on the minds of many entrepreneurs in the past couple of years, as businesses face a weak economy, increased competition, and rising costs of doing business. Bankruptcy is not always the end of a business but does offer the entrepreneur an opportunity to reorganize under Chapter 11 or merge with another company. However, in many instances (noted by the percentage of Chapter 7 bankruptcies discussed earlier), when the firm reaches this point the end result can only be liquidation. Some of the following examples describe the possible mix of experiences of a sample of entrepreneurs that have faced bankruptcy.

In May 2003, less than two years after emerging from Chapter 11 bankruptcy, Strouds, a chain of linen and houseware stores, filed for Chapter 7 liquidation bankruptcy. The Los Angeles–based chain had been unable, in a weak economy, to meet the competition from Bed, Bath, & Beyond and Linens'n Things. The chain was founded by Wilfred Stroud in 1979 and had grown to more than 70 stores with more than 1,500 employees across the country. The decision to close was made after the company lost $8.8 million during the last 10 months of operation.[4]

In 1995 Edison Brothers Shoe Stores, once one of the largest shoe store chains in the United States, declared bankruptcy. A third-generation Edison and a Harvard MBA, Peter Edison in 1999 was able to buy out Edison's flagship shoe chain Bakers Shoe for $8 million. With only enough inventory for the current season and a brand image of cheap shoes, he embarked on a strategy to revitalize the brand's image. He closed dozens of failing stores and one by one remodeled those remaining to look like upscale boutiques. Sales in renovated stores are up 50 percent as the business begins to enjoy a small profit.[5]

In February 2004 disaster struck for 72 franchise stores when Ground Round Grill & Bar announced that it was filing for bankruptcy. The franchise stores were owned by local proprietors under a license from the chain. The company also owned 59 restaurants. Founded in 1969, the restaurant had been a pioneer in the casual dining industry but now was faced with debt to unsecured creditors of between $10 million and $50 million. Sell-offs of a number of the restaurants had provided some funds but any ability to survive the bankruptcy hit a snag when financing was delayed and the company defaulted on its loan payments. The franchisees, however, made some quick and innovative decisions and decided to organize themselves into a cooperative. With this new organization they were able to raise some internal and external funds to buy the brand from the bankruptcy court. Systemwide sales have now reached $125 million, which is equal to what the business was achieving prior to the bankruptcy. The new business model of a cooperative seems to be working as a number of the original franchise owners have now opened new restaurants.[6]

Bankrate is one of a few Internet stocks that were able to survive the dot-com bubble burst. After an IPO at $13 per share in May 1999, the stock reached a low of $1 per share in August 2002. Since that low point the company has made a complete turnaround, primarily due to the leadership of Elizabeth DeMarse. The company Web site lists comparative rate tables and fee information on 100 financial products such as mortgages, credit cards, auto loans, and money markets. Most of its revenue, however, is accumulated from advertising on the site. With a more aggressive marketing effort, DeMarse has been able to achieve earnings of 60 cents a share in 2004 after losses in 2001 and 2002.[7]

Some lessons that can be learned from those who have experienced bankruptcy are as follows:

- Many entrepreneurs spend too much time and effort trying to diversify in markets where they lack knowledge. They should focus only on known markets.

AS SEEN IN *ENTREPRENEUR* MAGAZINE

PROVIDE ADVICE TO AN ENTREPRENEUR ABOUT FACING BUSINESS FAILURE

Chris Staros and Brett Warnock were in dire straits. Their Marietta, Georgia, comic book publishing company, Top Shelf Productions Inc., was going to have to cease publication entirely in April 2002 when their distributor went bankrupt. Because they had been expecting a hefty $100,000 payment from the doomed distributor when it went under, Staros, 39, and Warnock, 36, needed a big cash infusion—fast. Their solution was to send an e-mail to their friends and customers detailing the situation and asking anyone interested in purchasing comic books to do so (and quickly). "It was sort of an act of desperation," says Staros. "[We wanted] to tell them honestly what happened."

The response was overwhelming. Customers forwarded the e-mail to other comic book lovers, and 24 hours later, Top Shelf was working overtime to fill the 1,000 orders received. Says Staros, "Everybody rallied behind our cause."

Though the situation ended well, could this sort of begging approach be a turnoff to a company's customers? "In more cases than not, [this type of plea has come off as] more positive than negative," says Gary C. Glenn, a business consultant with NewsWire One Inc. But in order for the begging strategy to work, Glenn notes, a company needs to know its clients very well. "Be strategic about what you're asking," he says. "And don't cry wolf—don't use [this method] as an easy way out." Staros and Warnock didn't have to be told that—they sent an e-mail that evening spreading the good news to the tight-knit comic book community. Says Staros, "We didn't milk it."

ADVICE TO AN ENTREPRENEUR

An entrepreneur who is close to bankruptcy comes to you for advice:

1. The "begging" approach seemed to work with these comic book guys. What is the downside of trying it?
2. If I decide to proceed with "begging," what are the steps that I should take to increase the likelihood of its being successful?
3. Do you think this approach will be enhanced or hindered by first entering into a Chapter 11 bankruptcy?

Source: Reprinted with permission of Entrepreneur Media, Inc., "Beggar's Market. This Business Got Some Fast Cash the Old-Fashioned Way: The Owners Begged for It," by Nichole L. Torres, February 2003, *Entrepreneur* magazine: www.entrepreneur.com.

- Bankruptcy protects entrepreneurs only from the creditors, not from competitors.
- It's difficult to separate the entrepreneur from the business. Entrepreneurs put everything into the company, including worrying about the future of their employees.
- Many entrepreneurs do not think their businesses are going to fail until it's too late. They should file early.
- Bankruptcy is emotionally painful. Going into hiding after bankruptcy is a big mistake. Bankruptcy needs to be shared with employees and everybody else involved.

Chapter 11 bankruptcy Provides the opportunity to reorganize and make the venture more solvent

Chapter 13 bankruptcy Voluntarily allows individuals with regular income the opportunity to make extended time payments

Chapter 7 bankruptcy Requires the venture to liquidate, either voluntarily or involuntarily

As the above examples indicate, bankruptcy is serious business and requires some important understanding of its applications. The Bankruptcy Act of 1978 (with amendments added in 1984 and 2005) was designed to ensure a fair distribution of assets to creditors, to protect debtors from unfair depletion of assets, and to protect debtors from unfair demands by creditors. The Bankruptcy Act provides three alternative provisions for a firm near or at a position of insolvency. The three alternative positions are (1) reorganization, or *Chapter 11 bankruptcy;* (2) extended time payment, or *Chapter 13 bankruptcy;* and (3) liquidation, or *Chapter 7 bankruptcy*. All attempt to protect the troubled entrepreneur as well as provide a reasonable way to organize payments to debtors or to end the venture.

CHAPTER 11—REORGANIZATION

This is the least severe alternative to bankruptcy. In this situation the courts try to give the venture "breathing room" to pay its debts. Usually, this situation results when a venture has cash flow problems, and creditors begin to pressure the firm with lawsuits. The entrepreneur feels that, with some time, the business can become more solvent and liquid in order to meet its debt requirements.

A major creditor, any party who has an interest, or a group of creditors will usually present the case to the court. Then a plan for reorganization will be prepared to indicate how the business will be turned around. The plan will divide the debt and ownership interests into two groups: Those who will be affected by the plan and those who will not. It will then specify whose interests will be affected and how payments will be made.

Once the plan is completed, it must be approved by the court. All bankruptcies are now handled by the U.S. Bankruptcy Court, whose powers were restructured under the Bankruptcy Amendments Act of 1984. Approval of the plan also requires that all creditors and owners agree to comply with the reorganization plan as presented to the courts. The decisions made in the reorganization plan generally reflect one or a combination of the following:[8]

1. *Extension.* This occurs when two or more of the largest creditors agree to postpone any claims. This acts as a stimulus for smaller creditors to also agree to the plan.
2. *Substitution.* If the future potential of the venture looks promising enough, it may be possible to exchange stock or something else for the existing debt.
3. *Composition settlement.* The debt is prorated to the creditors as a settlement for any debt.

Even though only 20 to 25 percent of those firms that file for Chapter 11 bankruptcy will make it through the process, it does present an opportunity to find a cure for any business problems. Some of these problems are resolvable, and without the Chapter 11 protection even these 20 to 25 percent that file would never have the opportunity to succeed.

It is generally believed by experts that one of the primary reasons companies do not successfully come out of Chapter 11 bankruptcy is that they wait too long before filing for protection. In May 2005, Heather Antonelli filed for Chapter 7 bankruptcy. She and her mother JoAnn had opened a furniture wholesaling business, Eminence Style, in 1996 and had achieved steady growth in sales, reaching $3 million in 2000. Then in 2001 a buyer from Sears ordered $2 million worth of tables. The production of this large order necessitated financing, which Heather secured from the SBA, the Bank of America, and friends and family. She found a manufacturer in Hungary and made the one-third deposit and budgeted the rest of the money for the final payment. Unfortunately, the value of the dollar took a dive and her cost increased by one-third. Only a minimal profit was made and then the buyer at Sears was replaced by someone who had no interest in reordering. Competitors found cheaper manufacturing in China and Antonelli found she could no longer compete on price. Customers then switched to the lower price competitors and, as sales declined, the Bank of America demanded payment of the full amount of the debt. All during this period Heather still felt compelled to avoid bankruptcy and get things back on track. However, after much deliberation and with advice from a business consultant she finally decided to shut down the company and file for Chapter 7 bankruptcy. She now agrees that she waited too long but, on a positive note, feels she learned some important lessons that will help her to make better decisions in the future.[9]

As in Heather's case, entrepreneurs have a tendency to ignore the warning signs of bankruptcy and hold on until there is an emergency, such as running out of cash. Recognizing the signals may give an entrepreneur the opportunity to develop a strategy or plan.

Surviving Bankruptcy

The most obvious way to survive bankruptcy is to avoid it altogether. However, since bankruptcy is becoming such a common occurrence, it may be helpful for the entrepreneur to have a plan should he or she find it necessary to declare bankruptcy. Some suggestions for survival are listed below.

- Bankruptcy can be used as a bargaining chip to allow the entrepreneur to voluntarily restructure and reorganize the venture.
- File before the venture runs out of cash or has no incoming revenue so that expenses not protected by bankruptcy can be paid.
- Don't file for Chapter 11 protection unless the venture has a legitimate chance of recovery.
- Be prepared to have creditors examine all financial transactions for the last 12 months, seeking possible debtor fraud.
- Maintain good records.
- Understand completely how the protection against creditors works and what is necessary to keep it in place.
- If there is any litigation in existence, transfer it to the bankruptcy court, which may be a more favorable forum for the entrepreneur.
- Focus efforts on preparing a realistic financial reorganization plan.

Following some of the above suggestions and being prepared should bankruptcy be necessary is the best advice that anyone could give to an entrepreneur. Preparation will prevent unfavorable conditions and could increase the likelihood of successfully coming out of bankruptcy.

CHAPTER 13—EXTENDED TIME PAYMENT PLANS

As of October 17, 2005, the ability of an entrepreneur to file for a Chapter 7 bankruptcy is now more difficult. The reforms in the Bankruptcy Code that were signed into law in April 2005 are based on the argument that a person should be obligated to repay some of his or her debt (Chapter 13 bankruptcy); therefore these reforms make it more difficult to walk away from all debt by filing for Chapter 7 bankruptcy. Under this new law individuals are required to obtain credit counseling within six months of filing and to take a means test to ascertain if they are eligible for either Chapter 7 or Chapter 13 bankruptcy. The means test states that individuals may not file for Chapter 7 bankruptcy if their income is at or above the state income median.

Under Chapter 13 bankruptcy the individual creates a five-year repayment plan under court supervision. In each case, a court-appointed trustee receives money from the debtor and then is responsible for making scheduled payments to all creditors. This reform is more favorable to creditors than the old law. The only problem is that, according to the Bankruptcy Institute, about two of every three Chapter 13 filers ultimately fail to meet their planned obligations, thus resulting in a Chapter 7 filing.

The future effects of these reforms are still unknown. There are some who argue that this new law will stifle entrepreneurial activity. On the other hand, creditors have long been the

ETHICS

Who should be made aware when a venture is in trouble? How much responsibility does the entrepreneur have to his or her employees? How much should you tell your banker? Should clients be made aware of your problems? These are all legitimate yet difficult questions that an entrepreneur may struggle with when the business is on the verge of bankruptcy.

Some may feel that their only responsibility is to their family and themselves. Trying to get out of the dilemma with the least effect on your personal reputation and financial well-being could in fact make matters worse. Ethically and morally the entrepreneur is the leader of the organization, and trying to avoid responsibility will not rectify the situation.

In fact, there is evidence to indicate that involving your employees, banker, or other business associates can actually improve matters. Employees may take pay cuts or stock options to stay on with the company and try to turn the business around. Bankers can be your financial best friend and can recommend ways to save money and generate more cash flow. Your clients and suppliers can also support turnaround efforts by helping to provide needed cash during the crisis. One example was an entrepreneur who ran out of cash to produce a product being sold by a large supermarket chain. A meeting with the important client that revealed the situation (brought on by a competitor's lawsuit that was settled) led to a simple solution. The supermarket appreciated the honesty of the entrepreneur and agreed to prepay for all orders so that there would be sufficient cash to produce the product.

The entrepreneur needs to consider the past efforts of employees who made him or her successful in the first place. Thus, the best solution is participation. Get help rather than taking the selfish and perhaps immoral alternative. Honesty is the best strategy.

loser under the old law since it was so easy for individuals to file a Chapter 7 bankruptcy and eliminate all their debt.[10]

CHAPTER 7—LIQUIDATION

The most extreme case of bankruptcy requires the entrepreneur to liquidate, either voluntarily or involuntarily, all nonexempt assets of the business.

voluntary bankruptcy Entrepreneur's decision to file for bankruptcy

involuntary bankruptcy Petition of bankruptcy filed by creditors without consent of entrepreneur

If the entrepreneur files a *voluntary bankruptcy* petition under Chapter 7, it constitutes a determination that his or her venture is bankrupt. Usually, the courts will also require a current income and expense statement.

Table 17.1 summarizes some of the key issues and requirements under the *involuntary bankruptcy* petition. As the table indicates, an involuntary bankruptcy can be very complicated and can take a long time to resolve. However, liquidation is in the best interests of the entrepreneur if there is no hope of recovering from the situation.

STRATEGY DURING REORGANIZATION

Normally, reorganization under Chapter 11 or an extended payment plan under Chapter 13 takes a significant amount of time. During this period, the entrepreneur can speed up the process by taking the initiative in preparing a plan, selling the plan to secured creditors, communicating with groups of creditors, and not writing checks that cannot be covered.

The key to enhancing the bankruptcy process is keeping creditors abreast of how the business is doing and stressing the significance of their support during the process. Improving the entrepreneur's credibility with creditors will help the venture emerge from financial difficulties without the stigma of failure. But trying to meet with groups of creditors usually results in turmoil and ill will, so these meetings should be avoided.

Bankruptcy should be a last resort for the entrepreneur. Every effort should be made to avoid it and keep the business operating.

TABLE 17.1 Liquidation under Chapter 7 Involuntary Bankruptcy

Requirements	Number and Claims of Creditors	Rights and Duties of Entrepreneur	Trustee
Debts are not being paid as they become due.	If 12 or more creditors, at least 3 with unsecured claims totaling $5,000 must sign petition.	Damages may be recovered if creditor files in bad faith.	Elected by creditors. Interim trustee appointed by court.
Custodian appointed within 120 days of filing petition.	If fewer than 12 creditors, 1 creditor whose unsecured claim is at least $5,000 must sign the petition.	If involuntary petition is dismissed by court, costs, fees, or damages may be awarded.	Becomes by law owner of all property considered nonexempt for liquidation.
Considered insolvent when fair value of all assets is less than debts. Called a balance sheet test.	A proof of claim must be filed within 90 days of first meeting of creditors.	Must file a list of creditors with courts. Must file a current income and expense statement.	Can set aside petitions; transfer of property to a creditor under certain conditions.

TABLE 17.2 Requirements for Keeping a New Venture Afloat

- Avoid excess optimism when business appears to be successful.
- Always prepare good marketing plans with clear objectives.
- Make good cash projections and avoid capitalization.
- Keep abreast of the marketplace.
- Identify stress points that can put the business in jeopardy.

KEEPING THE VENTURE GOING

We've already noted in this chapter's opening profile that not all bankruptcies have unfavorable endings. Teresa Cascioli, CEO of Lakeport Brewing, has led the emergence of her company from Chapter 11 bankruptcy to its current position as a formidable player in the Canadian beer market.

Any entrepreneur who starts a business should pay attention to, as well as learn from, the mistakes of others. There are certain requirements that can help keep a new venture going and reduce the risk of failure. We can never guarantee success, but we can learn how to avoid failure.

Table 17.2 summarizes some of the key factors that can reduce the risk of business failure. The entrepreneur should be sensitive to each of these issues regardless of the size or type of business.

Many entrepreneurs have confidence in their abilities, which is necessary for them to be successful in their field. This confidence allows them to meet changing market conditions by implementing new strategies and directions for their firms in order to achieve future success. Sometimes these changes can involve getting back to the core business of the company and disengaging from unsuccessful endeavors. Two examples of this approach are Balaji Krishnamurthy and Frank Weise. Balaji Krishnamurthy was hired in September 1999 by Planar Systems, a maker of electronic displays for military trucks and tanks and for gas station pumps. This business had been stagnant and offered little opportunity for growth. Krishnamurthy recognized that the future was in flat-panel PC displays. Upon further analysis of the company's strengths he discovered that it actually had a supply chain superior to the chains of others in the market. In October 2000 Planar entered the consumer market with candy-colored flat-panel displays that quickly became the company's trademark.[11] More recently, the company has experienced great success in manufacturing flat-panel hardware and software for hospitals, shopping malls, and banks, as well as for original equipment manufacturers (OEMs) that utilize the Planar products in their own branded systems. The company has shown extensive growth in revenue and profits in the last two years. In 2006, Planar Systems Reported that its last quarter earnings of $.10 per share significantly exceeded the expected earnings of $.02 per share.[12]

Frank Weise took a somewhat different approach. After nearly 30 years as an executive with Procter & Gamble Co. and Campbell Soup Co., he decided to try something else. After a stint at Confab, a producer of feminine hygiene products, he took over Cott Corporation, a Toronto-based soft drink supplier of in-house labels for major food merchandisers in the United States, Canada, and the United Kingdom. Shares listed on both the Toronto exchange and the New York Stock Exchange were at all-time lows, as the company had struggled with attempts to expand into a variety of private-label products. With these low stock prices and stagnating sales, Weise made some dramatic changes in the company's strategy. His first task was to refocus on Cott's core business, producing the in-house labels. He also jettisoned any unprofitable businesses and strengthened relationships with key clients.[13] As a result of these strategies the company continues to achieve double-digit revenue growth.

Both entrepreneurs in the examples above recognized important changes and trends in the environment. They not only had to refocus their companies' products and services but also had to modify critical business activities, particularly marketing and sales. We saw in Chapter 8 of this textbook the importance of market planning to help prepare for contingencies such as those described above.

Preparing an effective marketing plan for a 12-month period is essential for the entrepreneur. The marketing plan helps the entrepreneur prepare for contingencies and control his or her day-to-day activities. This is now an important part of both Planar Systems and Cott Corporation.

Good cash projections are also a serious consideration for the entrepreneur. Cash flow is one of the major causes for an entrepreneur to have to declare bankruptcy. Thus, in preparing cash projections, entrepreneurs should seek assistance from accountants, lawyers, or a federal agency such as the Small Business Administration. This may prevent the situation from reaching the point where it is too late for any hope of recovery.

Many entrepreneurs avoid gathering sufficient information about the market (see Chapter 7 of this textbook). Information is an important asset to any entrepreneur, especially regarding future market potential and forecasting the size of the immediate attainable market. Entrepreneurs will often try to guess what is happening in the market and ignore the changing marketplace. This could spell disaster, especially if competitors are reacting more positively to the market changes.

In the early stages of a new venture, it is helpful for the entrepreneur to be aware of stress points, that is, those points when the venture is changing in size, requiring new survival strategies. Early rapid rises in sales can be interpreted incorrectly so that the venture finds itself adding plant capacity, signing new contracts with suppliers, or increasing inventories, resulting in shrinking margins and being overleveraged. To offset this situation, prices are increased or quality weakened, leading to lower sales. This becomes a vicious circle that can lead to bankruptcy.

Stress points can be identified based on the amount of sales. For example, it may be possible to recognize that sales of $1 million, $5 million, and $25 million may represent key

TABLE 17.3 Warning Signs of Bankruptcy

- Management of finances becomes lax, so that no one can explain how money is being spent.
- Directors cannot document or explain major transactions.
- Customers are given large discounts to enhance payments because of poor cash flow.
- Contracts are accepted below standard amounts to generate cash.
- Bank requests subordination of its loans.
- Key personnel leave the company.
- Materials to meet orders are lacking.
- Payroll taxes are not paid.
- Suppliers demand payment in cash.
- Customers' complaints regarding service and product quality increase.

decision marks in terms of major capital investment and operational expenses such as hiring new key personnel. Entrepreneurs should be aware of the burden of sales levels on capital investment and operational expenses.

WARNING SIGNS OF BANKRUPTCY

Entrepreneurs should be sensitive to signals in the business and the environment that may be early warning signs of trouble. Often, the entrepreneur is not aware of what is going on or is not willing to accept the inevitable. Table 17.3 lists some of the key early warning signs of bankruptcy. Generally, they are interrelated, and one can often lead to another.

For example, when management of the financial affairs becomes lax, there is a tendency to do anything to generate cash, such as reducing prices, cutting back on supplies to meet orders, or releasing important personnel such as sales representatives. A new office furniture business catering to small or medium-sized businesses illustrates how this can happen. Top management of the firm decided that moving merchandise was its top priority. Sales representatives earned standard commission on each sale and were free to reduce prices where necessary to make the sale. Hence, without any cost or break-even awareness, sales representatives often reduced prices below direct costs. They still received their commissions when the price charged was below cost. Thus, the venture eventually lost substantial amounts of money and had to declare bankruptcy.

When an entrepreneur sees any of the warning signs in Table 17.3, he or she should immediately seek the advice of a CPA or an attorney. It may be possible to prevent bankruptcy by making immediate changes in the operation in order to improve the cash flow and profitability of the business. Turnaround strategies are discussed later in this chapter.

STARTING OVER

Bankruptcy and liquidation do not have to be the end for the entrepreneur. History is full of examples of entrepreneurs who have failed many times before finally succeeding.

Gail Borden's tombstone reads, "I tried and failed, and I tried again and succeeded." One of his first inventions was the Terraqueous Wagon, which was designed to travel on land or water. The invention sank on its first try. Borden also had three other inventions that failed to get patents. A fourth invention was patented but eventually wiped him out because of lack of capital and poor sales. However, Borden was persistent and convinced that his vacuum condensation process, giving milk a long shelf life, would be successful. At 56, Borden had his first success with condensed milk.

Over the years, other famous entrepreneurs have also endured many failures before finally achieving success. Rowland Hussey Macy (of Macy's retail stores), Ron Berger (of National Video), and Thomas Edison are other examples of struggling entrepreneurs who lived through many failures.

The characteristics of entrepreneurs were discussed in Chapter 3. From that chapter we know that entrepreneurs are likely to continue starting new ventures even after failing. There is evidence that they learn from their mistakes, and investors often look favorably on someone who has failed previously, assuming that he or she will not make the same mistake again.[14]

Generally, entrepreneurs who have failed in their endeavors tend to have a better understanding and appreciation for the need for market research, more initial capitalization, and stronger business skills. Unfortunately, not all entrepreneurs learn these skills from their experiences; many tend to fail over and over again.

However, business failure does not have to be a stigma when it comes time to seek venture capital. Past records will be revealed during subsequent start-ups, but the careful entrepreneur can explain why the failure occurred and how he or she will prevent it in the future, restoring investors' confidence. As discussed in Chapter 7, the business plan will help sell the business concept to investors. It is in the business plan that the entrepreneur, even after many failures, can illustrate how *this* venture will be successful.

THE REALITY OF FAILURE

Unfortunately, failure does happen, but it isn't necessarily the end. Many entrepreneurs are able to successfully turn failure into success. It is one of the important historical characteristics of entrepreneurs that we have continually identified throughout this text. Since failure can happen, there are also some important considerations that should be mentioned if it should occur.

First and foremost, the entrepreneur should consult with his or her family. As difficult as it is for the entrepreneur to deal with bankruptcy, it is even more so for spouses. Problems occur because the spouse usually has no control over the venture's operations unless it is a family-operated business. As a result, he or she may not even be aware of any bankruptcy threats. Thus, the first thing the entrepreneur should do is sit down with his or her spouse and explain what is happening. This discussion will also help alleviate some of the stress of dealing with bankruptcy.

Second, the entrepreneur should seek outside assistance from professionals, friends, and business associates. Although not all of these people may be sympathetic, it is usually not difficult to find individuals among these groups who will be supportive. Professional support is also available from the Small Business Administration (SBA), universities, the Senior Core of Retired Executives (SCORE), and Small Business Development Centers.

Third, it is important to not try to hang on to a venture that will continually drain resources if the end is inevitable. It is better to consider the time spent trying to save a dying business as an opportunity cost. The time spent could be more effectively and profitably used to either start over or do something else. If a turnaround is considered possible (see discussion below), it is wise to set a time frame and, if it is not accomplished in that time frame, to simply end the venture.

AS SEEN IN *ENTREPRENEUR* MAGAZINE

ELEVATOR PITCH FOR DOUGHMAKERS

A wealthy friend has asked you to keep your eye out for attractive businesses in which she can invest. Your wealthy friend is very busy and you only want to introduce those businesses that are genuinely attractive. After hearing the following pitch, would you introduce Bette and Diane to your wealthy friend?

Entrepreneurs Bette LaPlante (49) and Diane Cuvelier (43), co-founders of Doughmakers LLC in Terre Haute, Indiana

Description Manufacturer of solid aluminum bakeware with a patented pebble pattern

Start-Up $1,000 in 1997

Sales Projected sales for current year of more than $5 million

Bake Sale As den mother for her son's Cub Scout group in 1990, LaPlante was looking for a good fund-raiser. Her husband suggested making and selling cookie sheets, with help from his aluminum-die-cutting business. "I thought it was the silliest idea," says LaPlante. "What boys want to sell cookie sheets?" But she changed her tune when each came back with fistfuls of cash, needing more sheets.

Back-Burner Biz While their children and her husband's business took precedence, LaPlante continued to experiment with different textures and aluminum thicknesses, finding a combination that would yield perfectly baked cookies. With her sister in 1997, LaPlante began attending shows for organizations like Little League and the PTA, offering a fund-raising program that would split the profit.

Labor of Love Doughmakers expanded the line in 2001 to include bakeware such as pizza and jellyroll pans, now sold in more than 2,000 stores, including Macy's. Making the sheets by hand, however, led to carpal tunnel syndrome for LaPlante and Cuvelier. The sisters now have machines to make the sheets, but baking is still hands-on for the family. Says LaPlante, "It's something we can all work on [while having] good conversations."

Source: Reprinted with permission of Entrepreneur Media, Inc., "Bette LaPlante and Diane Cuvelier," by April Y. Pennington, April 2003, *Entrepreneur* magazine: www.entrepreneur.com.

BUSINESS TURNAROUNDS

We have discussed a number of turnaround examples throughout this chapter, such as the opening profile on Lakeport Brewing, Bankrate, Planar Systems, and Cott Corporation. All were faced with declining sales and earnings that either resulted in bankruptcy or threatened bankruptcy. What we have learned from successful examples of turnarounds is summarized and discussed in the next few paragraphs.[15]

During a business's life cycle it is likely that an entrepreneur will face adversity, perhaps because of external factors (the economy; competition; changes in consumer needs; technology; or unpredictable acts such as war, terrorism, or weather); or the adversity may be self-inflicted (that is, due to poor management). The severity of the adversity can result in bankruptcy or in a need to refocus the business and strive for a turnaround. The process of turnaround can take many directions, but there are some basic principles and support that can be considered to help the entrepreneur.

First and foremost it is important for the entrepreneur to recognize the warning signs of bankruptcy discussed earlier and listed in Table 17.3. However, recognition of the warning signs does not solve the problem; instead, it is the point at which the principles discussed below should be considered. If the entrepreneur feels inadequate in dealing with any of these warning signs, then it is recommended that he or she consult with a CPA or an attorney. There are also a number of turnaround management consulting firms that support businesses of all sizes. They can be identified with a simple search on the Internet. The Business Finance Turnaround Association can also provide support in this situation.

The first principle in any successful turnaround (reflected in all our earlier examples) is aggressive hands-on management. Leadership in all these cases focused initial efforts on getting out among, meeting, and communicating with all employees. This high-visibility strategy is significant in order to identify the roots of any issues that are contributing to the threat of bankruptcy or to the need to successfully resurface from bankruptcy. The entrepreneur needs to keep all the employees energized and focused on bringing the company back to a position of market and financial stability and then, it is hoped, moving it toward managed growth. The entrepreneur needs to be honest and up-front with all the employees regarding the situation, in order to get them involved in identifying the issues that need to be addressed. Historically, at this stage neither an absentee management nor a bunker mentality in which management works long hours is sufficient.

The second principle is that management must have a plan. We've discussed many times in this text that there are three questions that need to be addressed in any planning process (see Chapter 8). The same questions are applicable here as part of a turnaround plan. Step 1 in this plan is getting out into the business and trying to understand the problem, as described in the above paragraph. This addresses the situation analysis, or the question "Where are we now?" The second question in any plan is "Where are we going?" This is when the plan becomes important, since goals and objectives will need to be developed to get the company turned around. Again it is important to get everyone in the organization involved in looking for opportunities to improve the company's existing market and financial position by cutting costs, increasing efficiencies, and improving customer service and loyalty, as well as by pursuing strategies to increase sales.

The third and last step, or principle, in the turnaround process is action. This relates to the third question in the planning process, which is "How do we get there?" The plan should involve aggressive corrective action. Time is of the essence here, either to avoid bankruptcy or to prove to the creditors or the bankruptcy court that you can get the company back on track. At this point, a turnaround consultant may be called in to support these actions if the entrepreneur feels inadequate.

EXIT STRATEGY

Every entrepreneur who starts a new venture should think about an exit strategy. A number of possible exit strategies will be discussed in the following paragraphs. Exit strategies include an initial public offering (IPO), private sale of stock, succession by a family member or a nonfamily member, merger with another company, or liquidation of the company. The sale of the company could be to employees (an ESOP) or to an external source (a person or persons, or a company). The IPO, private sale of stock, and merger options are discussed elsewhere in this book (see Chapters 12 and 16).

Each of these exit strategies has its advantages and disadvantages, which are discussed below and in the chapters noted above. The most important issue is that the entrepreneurs have an exit strategy or plan in place at the start-up stage, instead of waiting until it may be too late to effectively implement a desirable option.

TABLE 17.4 Succession Planning Tips

- Allow sufficient time for the process by starting early.
- Estimate the firm's value or hire a consultant to do it for you.
- Evaluate potential successors on their merit—not on whether they remind you of yourself.
- If family members are being considered, make sure they have the skills and motivation necessary to carry on the business.
- Provide a transition period so that the successor can learn the business.
- Consider options such as employee stock option plans (ESOPs) for a management succession.
- Set a date for completion of the transition and stick to it.

SUCCESSION OF BUSINESS

As of 2005, approximately 12 million Americans own small businesses. It is expected that about 40 percent of these businesses will change hands over the next five years. Surveys also show that about 68 percent of these owners do not have a succession or transfer plan in place.[16] In the next sections we will focus on important issues that can help the entrepreneur plan for the succession of the business to either a family member, an employee, or an external party. Table 17.4 provides a summary of important tips that should be considered in any succession plan.

If there is no one in the family interested in the business, it is important for the entrepreneur to either sell the business or train someone within the organization to take over. Each of these transfer possibilities is discussed below.

Transfer to Family Members

Successfully passing the business down to a family member faces tough odds. Experts estimate that half such attempts fail in the transition from first- to second-generation ownership. Only about 14 percent make it to the third generation. In addition, a 2002 survey of 800 family-owned businesses by the Family Firm Institute found that the leading causes of failure were insufficient estate planning, failure to plan for the transition, and lack of funds to pay estate taxes.[17] The solution to minimize the emotional and financial turmoil that can often be created during a transfer to family members is a good succession plan.

An effective succession plan needs to consider the following critical factors:

- The role of the owner in the transition stage: Will he or she continue to work full time? Part time? Or will the owner retire?
- Family dynamics: Are some family members unable to work together?
- Income for working family members and shareholders.
- The current business environment during the transition.
- Treatment of loyal employees.
- Tax consequences.

The transfer of a business to a family member can also create internal problems with employees. This often results when a son or daughter is handed the responsibility of running the business without sufficient training. A young family member's chances of success in taking over the business are improved if he or she assumes various operational responsibilities early on. It is beneficial for the family member to rotate to different areas of the business in order to get a good perspective on the total operation. Other employees in these departments or areas will be able to assist in the training and get to know their future leader.

It is also helpful if the entrepreneur stays around for a while to act as an advisor to the successor. As stated in Table 17.4, however, there should be a set date for when this transition will end. Acting as an advisor during the transition stage can be helpful to the successor in making business decisions. Of course, it is also possible that this can result in major conflicts if the personalities involved are not compatible. In addition, employees who have been with the firm since start-up may resent the younger family member's assuming control of the venture. However, while working in the organization during this transition period, the successor can prove his or her abilities, justifying assumption of the future role.

Transfer to Nonfamily Members

Often a member of the family is not interested in assuming responsibility for the business. When this occurs, the entrepreneur has three choices: Train a key employee and retain some equity, retain control and hire a manager, or sell the business outright.

Passing the business on to an employee ensures that the new principal is familiar with the business and the market. The experience of the employee minimizes transitional problems. In addition, the entrepreneur can take some time to make the transition smoother.

The key issue in passing the business on to an employee is ownership. If the entrepreneur plans to retain some ownership, the question of how much becomes an important area of negotiation. The new principal may prefer to have control, with the original entrepreneur remaining as a minority owner, stockholder, or consultant. The financial capacity and managerial ability of the employee will be important factors in deciding how much ownership is transferred. In many cases the transfer or succession of a venture can take many years to meet all the requirements of the parties involved. Since evidence indicates that most entrepreneurs wait until it is too late, it is important to begin the process long before there is a need to sell or transfer the ownership of the business. The U. S. Commerce Department indicates that about 70 percent of successful ventures never make it to the second generation of ownership.

Ron Norelli was one of the exceptions because he realized the importance of a succession plan and hired a search firm to help him find a successor. Unfortunately, even though he was able to hire someone who was to be groomed as his successor, the individual decided that he did not want to take the risk. Norelli had to start the process all over again and this time conducted the search personally by using his network of trusted business associates. After a number of candidates were evaluated and interviewed by the staff, they settled on a successor who would, over a number of years, buy Norelli out. Norelli went even further by promoting one of his staff to vice president with the intent that this individual would be a good candidate to succeed his successor. The entire process took about five years, and since he began the process early enough, it gave him the opportunity to leave the business gradually with the confidence that it would successfully continue in the future.[18]

If the business has been in the family for some time and the succession to a family member may become more likely in the future, the entrepreneur may hire a manager to run the business. However, finding someone to manage the business in the same manner and with the same expertise as the entrepreneur may be difficult. If someone is found to manage the business, the likely problems are compatibility with the owners and willingness of this person to manage for any length of time without a promise of equity in the business. Executive search firms can help in the search process. It will be necessary to have a well-defined job description to assist in identifying the right person.

In nonfamily business situations, succession planning may take on a slightly different approach. In these businesses a key senior manager or group of managers may be stepping down or leaving the company. Since there are no family members involved, there may be a need to consider replacements from either external or internal sources. For a partnership the process may be clearly outlined in the partnership agreement and could simply involve a predetermined choice. However, there could also be a need to go outside the partnership and find a successor for the partnership. In this instance, as well as in an S corporation or an LLC, where there may be only a small number of shareholders, the succession plan should consider the following important issues:[19]

- Senior management of the company must be committed to any succession plan. The strategy must be one that everyone shares.
- It is important to have well-defined job descriptions and a clear designation of skills necessary to fulfill any and all positions.
- The process needs to be an open one. All employees should be invited to participate so that they will feel comfortable with the transition and thus minimize the possibility of their leaving the company.

The last option is to sell the business outright to either an employee or an outsider. The major considerations in this option are financial, which will likely necessitate the help of an accountant and/or lawyer. This alternative also requires that the value of the business be determined (see Chapter 12).

OPTIONS FOR SELLING THE BUSINESS

There are a number of alternatives available to the entrepreneur in selling the venture. Some of these are straightforward, and others involve more complex financial strategy. Each of these methods should be carefully considered and one selected, depending on the goals of the entrepreneur.

Direct Sale

This is probably the most common method for selling the venture. The entrepreneur may decide to sell the business because he or she wants to move on to some new endeavor or he or she may simply decide that it is time to retire. If the entrepreneur has decided to sell the business and it is not necessary to sell immediately, there are a number of strategies that should be considered early in the process.[20]

- A business can be more valuable if it is focused on a narrow, well-defined segment. In other words, a larger share in a small market niche can be more valuable than a smaller share in a large market.
- The entrepreneur should concentrate on keeping costs under control and focus on higher margins and profits.
- Get all financial statements in order, including budgets and cash flow projections.
- Prepare a management documentation of the business explaining how the business is organized and how it operates.

- Assess the condition of capital equipment. Up-to-date or state-of-the-art equipment can enhance the value of a company.
- Get tax advice, since the sale of a corporation will involve different tax considerations than those for a partnership, LLC, or S corporation.
- Get nondisclosures from key employees.
- Try to maintain a good management team, allowing them to have day-to-day contact with key customers to lessen the firm's dependence on owner–customer relations.
- There is no substitute for advance preparation and planning.

One of the important considerations of any business sale is the type of payment the buyer will use. Often, buyers will purchase a business using notes based on future profits. If the new owners fail in the business, the seller may receive no cash payment and possibly find himself or herself taking back the company that is struggling to survive.

Business brokers in some instances may be helpful since trying to actually sell a business will take time away from running it. Brokers can be discreet about a sale and may have an established network to get the word around. Brokers earn a commission from the sale of a business. Generally these commissions are based on a sliding scale starting at about 10 percent for the first $200,000. The best way to communicate the business to potential buyers is through the business plan. A five-year comprehensive plan can provide buyers of the business with a future perspective and accountability of the value of the company (see Chapters 7 and 8).

Once the business is either sold or passed on to a family member or employee, the entrepreneur's role may depend on the sale agreement or contract with the new owner(s). Many buyers will want the seller to stay on for a short time to provide a smooth transition. Under these circumstances the seller (entrepreneur) should negotiate an employment contract that specifies time, salary, and responsibility. If the entrepreneur is not needed in the business, it is likely that the new owner(s) will request that the entrepreneur sign an agreement not to engage in the same business for a specified number of years. These agreements vary in scope and may require a lawyer to clarify details.

An entrepreneur may also plan to retain a business for only a specified period of time, with the intent to sell it to the employees. This may entail all employees through an employee stock option plan (ESOP) or through a management buyout, which allows the sale to occur to only certain managers of the venture.

Employee Stock Option Plan

employee stock option plan (ESOP) A two- to three-year plan to sell the business to employees

Under an *employee stock option plan (ESOP),* the business is sold to employees over a period of time. The ESOP establishes a new legal entity, called an employee stock ownership trust, that borrows the money against future profits. The borrowed money then buys the owner's shares and allocates them to individual employees' retirement accounts as the loan is paid off. The ESOP has the obligation to repay the loan plus interest out of the cash flow of the business. Typically, these ESOPs are a way to reward employees and clarify the succession process. In addition, ESOPs result in significant stock values for employees, providing that the company continues to succeed.

Presently there are about 11,000 ESOP companies in the United States, of which 2,000 are wholly owned by the ESOP. ESOPs account for about 50 percent of the nation's 10 million employees. In addition, about 800 (or 7 percent) are publicly traded companies.[21]

The ESOP has a number of advantages. First, it offers a unique incentive to employees that can enhance their motivation to put in extra time or effort. Employees recognize that they are working for themselves and hence will focus their efforts on innovations that contribute to the long-term success of the venture. Second, it provides a mechanism to pay back those employees who have been loyal to the venture, particularly during more difficult times. Third, it allows the transfer of the business under a carefully planned written agreement. Finally, the company can reap the advantage of deducting the contributions to the ESOP or any dividends paid on the stock.

ESOPs, due to a new law passed in 1996, are now possible for S corporations. However, there are some important differences in the tax treatment between the C corporation and the S corporation because of the pass-through feature of the S corporation (see Chapter 9). Because of the new tax law, the S corporation pays no income tax on the portion of the stock owned by the ESOP.

However, in spite of its favorable attributes, the ESOP has some disadvantages. This type of stock option plan is usually quite complex to establish. It requires a complete valuation of the venture in order to establish the amount of the ESOP package. In addition, it raises issues such as taxes, payout ratios, amount of equity to be transferred per year, and the amount actually invested by the employees. The agreement also must specify if the employees can buy or sell additional shares of stock once the plan has been completed. Clearly, due to the complexity of this type of plan, the entrepreneur will need the advice of experts if this type of plan is selected. A simpler method may be a more direct buyout by key employees of the venture.

Management Buyout

It is conceivable that the entrepreneur only wants to sell or transfer the venture to loyal, key employees. Since the ESOP described above can be rather complicated and expensive, the entrepreneur may find that a direct sale would be simpler to accomplish.

Management buyouts usually involve a direct sale of the venture for some predetermined price. This would be similar to selling one's house. To establish a price, the entrepreneur would have an appraisal of all the assets and then determine the goodwill value established from past revenue.

Sale of a venture to key employees can be for cash, or it can be financed in any number of ways. A cash sale is unlikely if the value of the business is substantial. Financing the sale of the venture can be accomplished through a bank, or the entrepreneur could also agree to carry the note. This may be desirable to the entrepreneur in that the stream of income from the sale would be spread out over a determined period of time, enhancing cash flow and lessening the tax impact. Another method of selling the venture would be to use stock as the method of transfer. The managers buying the business may sell nonvoting or voting stock to other investors. These funds would then be used as a full or partial payment for the venture. The reason that other investors would be interested in buying stock or that a bank would lend the managers money is that the business is continuing with the same management team and with its established track record.

Other methods of transferring or selling a business are through a public offering or even a merger with another business. These topics are discussed in Chapter 16. Before determining the appropriate selling strategy, the entrepreneur should seek the advice of outsiders. Every circumstance is different, and the actual decision will depend on the entrepreneur's goals. Case histories of each of the above methods can also be reviewed to be able to effectively determine which option is best for the given circumstances.

IN REVIEW

SUMMARY

This chapter of the textbook deals with the decisions, problems, and issues involved in ending the venture. Even though the intent of all entrepreneurs is to establish a business for a long time, many problems can cause these plans to fail. Since about one-half of all new ventures fail in their first four years of business, it is important for the entrepreneur to understand the options for either ending or salvaging a venture.

Bankruptcy offers three options for the entrepreneur. Under Chapter 11 of the Bankruptcy Act of 1978 (amended in 1984 and again in 2004), the venture will be reorganized under a plan approved by the courts. With this plan the entrepreneur strives to revitalize the financial condition of the venture and return to the market with new strategies.

Chapter 13 of the Bankruptcy Act provides for an extended time payment plan to cover outstanding debts. The 2004 amendment to the Bankruptcy Act has made this particular choice a more likely first option—and an option that must be exhausted before the entrepreneur is allowed to file for Chapter 7 liquidation. The courts feel that individuals should be required to pay back some of their debt and therefore this amendment makes it more difficult to file for Chapter 7 liquidation. If the individual is unable to make extended payments, then liquidation, either voluntarily or involuntarily, is the final option.

Keeping the business going is the primary intent of all entrepreneurs. Avoiding excessive optimism, preparing good marketing plans, making good cash projections, keeping familiar with the market, and being sensitive to stress points in the business can help keep the business operating.

Entrepreneurs can also be sensitive to key warning signs of potential problems. Lax management of finances, discounting to generate cash, loss of key personnel, lack of raw materials, nonpayment of payroll taxes, demands of suppliers to be paid in cash, and increased customer complaints about service and product quality are some of the key warning signs that a firm is headed for bankruptcy. If the business does fail, however, the entrepreneur should always consider starting over. Failure can be a learning process, as evidenced by the many famous inventors who succeeded after many failures.

One of the other venture-ending decisions that an entrepreneur may face is succession of the business. If the business is family owned, the entrepreneur would likely seek a family member to succeed. Other options, if no family member is available or interested, include transferring some or all of the business to an employee or outsider, or hiring an outsider to manage the business. Direct sale of the business, employee stock option plans, and management buyouts are alternatives for the entrepreneur in selling the venture. These are all exit strategy options for the entrepreneur.

RESEARCH TASKS

1. Find three accounts by entrepreneurs in which they describe their experience with poorly performing firms and the process of going through bankruptcy. In what ways were their experiences similar? In what ways were they different? Did emotions play a role? Did the entrepreneurs learn from the experience?

2. Interview a member of a family business and gain a deeper understanding of the issues surrounding the management of such a business, especially those related to succession.
3. Write an account of the emotions that you felt when someone or something close to you was lost forever (you will not be required to present this to the class). How did these emotions impact your ability to perform other tasks? How did you overcome these negative emotions? To what extent do you believe that entrepreneurs go through a similar process when their businesses fail?

CLASS DISCUSSION

1. If your family had a highly successful business, would succession to the next generation (you and/or your siblings) likely be smooth, or would there be the potential for conflict and hurt feelings? What would be a "fair" way to set up succession?
2. Do you believe the laws should be changed to make it easier for entrepreneurs to go into, and recover from, bankruptcy? What are the implications of your answer for the entrepreneur, creditors, and the national economy?
3. What are the issues facing an entrepreneur in deciding whether or not the business needs to be put into bankruptcy today?
4. The following role-plays require you to think and act as if you were the person being described in each situation.
   a. *Role-play 1.* One student prepares and presents a speech as if she or he is an entrepreneur informing employees that her or his business has failed and will not be operating from tomorrow on. The rest of the class can respond and ask questions as if they are devoted employees upset about losing their jobs.
   b. *Role-play 2.* In small groups, role-play the interchange between an entrepreneur of a failed business expressing his or her negative emotions and a friend providing advice on how to best cope with the situation.

SELECTED READINGS

Avila, Stephen M; Ramon A. Avila; and Douglas W. Naffziger. (May 2003). A Comparison of Family-Owned Businesses: Succession Planners and Nonplanners. *Journal of Financial Service Professionals,* vol. 57, no. 3, pp. 85–92.

This study compares family-owned businesses that had a business succession plan with those that did not have a plan. Survey results indicate that a succession plan can affect business transition, tax planning, and the ownership structure.

Baird, Douglas G.; and Edward R. Morrison. (December 2005). Serial Entrepreneurs and Small Business Bankruptcies. *Columbia Law Review,* vol. 105, no. 8, pp. 2310–68.

Chapter 11 is thought to preserve the going-concern surplus of a financially distressed business. However, the typical Chapter 11 debtor is a small business whose assets are rarely enough to pay tax claims. This article discusses the implications of Chapter 11 bankruptcy to those entrepreneurs who do not wish to stay with their business but instead are more interested in other opportunities.

Brodzinski, Carrie. (June 13, 2005). ESOP's Fables Can Make Coverage Risky. *National Underwriter/Property Casualty Risks & Benefits Management,* vol. 109, no. 23, pp. 16, 44.

This article focuses on employee stock ownership plans (ESOPs) that invest solely in employer stock. These plans can be risky for employers and employees and are often misunderstood. Important issues related to these plans are discussed.

Buckley, William M. (July 2, 2003). Dot-Com Hope: Akamai, Others Discover New Life. *The Wall Street Journal, Eastern Edition,* vol. 242, no. 2, pp. B1–B2.

This article reports on the dot-com companies that survived the technology bubble and are actually beginning to thrive as going concerns. It focuses on the history of Akamai Technologies Inc., WebMD Corporation, and Monster Worldwide Inc.

Davis, James. (May 2003). Staking Your Life on a Betting Future. *Accountancy,* vol. 131, no. 1317, pp. 54–56.

The author in this article provides a discussion of the factors that need to be considered before implementing a management buyout. The article includes a discussion of the role of the board of directors, management presentations, and due diligence.

Girard, Bryan. (May 2002). Is There an ESOP in Our Company's Future? *Strategic Finance,* vol. 83, no. 11, pp. 48–51.

This article focuses on the employee stock ownership plans (ESOPs) of various companies in the United States. It provides a good description of the ESOP and the procedures involved in setting one up.

Jackson, Kirk. (July 2005). Case Study of a Succession Plan. *Journal of Financial Planning,* vol. 18, no. 7, pp. 39–42.

This article relates the experiences of the author in succession planning. It is a case study of the author's family business and how various conflict situations led to decisions for succession of the business.

Maddy, Monique. (2000). Dream Deferred: The Story of a High-Tech Entrepreneur in a Low-Tech World. *Harvard Business Review,* vol. 78, no. 3, pp. 56–69.

Monique Maddy discusses the important lessons that the failure of her start-up Ademesi taught her about starting a business in an emerging-market country.

Novack, Janet. (June 6, 2005). Protection Time. *Forbes,* vol. 175, no. 12, pp. 146–50.

The author examines the impact of the new bankruptcy legislation enacted in October 2005. The article provides a clear discussion of how this new legislation will affect many who previously were able to file for a Chapter 7 liquidation without payment of any debt. In addition, the impact of these new laws on 401(k) plans is discussed.

Phillips, Edward A. (Winter 2006). Bankruptcy Law: Changes in Protection Make Planning Critical. *CPA Journal,* vol. 76, no. 4, pp. 1–4.

This paper provides in-depth discussion and analysis of the impact of the new bankruptcy laws on accounting issues. The author discusses the importance of planning in the process. Each area that needs to be considered in this plan is discussed.

Pompe, Paul M.; and Jan Bilderbeek. (November 2005). The Prediction of Bankruptcy of Small and Medium Sized Firms. *The Journal of Business Venturing,* vol. 20, no. 6, pp. 847–68.

Using large amounts of data from small and medium-sized firms, this study examines several aspects of bankruptcy prediction. Ratio categories were applied prior to bankruptcy to test their predictive power of bankruptcy. Virtually every ratio investigated had some predictive power of bankruptcy.

Shepherd, Dean A.; Evan J. Douglas; and Mark Shanley. (2000). New Venture Survival: Ignorance, External Shocks, and Risk Reduction Strategies. *Journal of Business Venturing,* vol. 15, no. 5–6, pp. 393–410.

The authors develop a model to explain new venture failure. The theoretical model argues that risk of failure is largely dependent on the degree of novelty (ignorance) associated with a new venture—novelty to the market, novelty to the technology of production, and novelty (experience) to management.

Shepherd, Dean A.; and Andrew Zackarakis. (2000). Structuring Family Business Succession. An Analysis of the Future Leader's Decision Making. *Entrepreneurship Theory & Practice,* vol. 24, no 4., pp. 25–39.

This article examines the perception of potential family business leaders from a behavioral economics theory perspective. The authors argue that founders should structure succession so that the future leader incurs both financial and behavioral sunk costs as well as hold the future leader to stringent performance requirements prior to the succession.

END NOTES

1. See Chris Daniels, "Small-Town Beer, Big Impact," *Marketing Magazine* (December 19, 2005), pp. 22–24; Charles McGregor, "She Is Canadian; and She Makes Beer," *The Toronto Sun* (March 13, 2005), p. HS10; Jennifer Morrison, "Lakeport's Lady Boss Has That Steel City Drive," *Hamilton Spectator* (October 4, 2004), p. AO1; and "Lakeport Brewing Financial Results," *LexisNexis Canadian News Wire* (November 10, 2005).
2. See American Bankruptcy Institute's Web site, www.abiworld.org.
3. Amy Borrus and Anne Tergesen, "Not Necessarily a Fresh Start," *BusinessWeek* (July 11, 2005), pp. 84–85.
4. M. Chandler, "Embattled LA Based Linen, Housewares Retailer Plans to Close Stores," *San Jose Mercury* (May 23, 2003), p. 1.
5. Cate Corcoran, "Bakers Hones Mix," *Womens Wear Daily* 189, no. 105, (May 18, 2005), p. 10.
6. Carlye Adler, "The Grand Rebound," *FSB: Fortune Small Business* (February 2005), pp. 56–60.
7. www.bankrate.com.
8. David Twomey and Marianne Jennings, *Anderson's Business Law and Legal Environment, Standard,* 19th ed. (Mason, OH: West Legal Studies, 2005), pp. 758–79.
9. Nadine Heintz, "Anatomy of a Business Decision: A Case Study," *Inc.* (December 2005), pp. 59–60.
10. Lawrence S. Clark, Randall Hanson, and James K. Smith, "Bankruptcy Reform Is Here," *Journal of Accountancy* 200, no. 5, (November 2005), pp. 51–59.
11. O. Malik, "Adjusting the Picture," *Business 2.0* (July 2003), pp. 56–57.
12. Associated Press, "Planar Systems Stock Up on Raised Outlook," *Lexus-Nexus.com* (January 26, 2006).
13. S. Chakravarty, "Making a Name for Itself," *Institutional Investor* (July 2003), pp. 18–19.
14. L. M. Lament, "What Entrepreneurs Learn from Experience," *Journal of Small Business Management* (1972), p. 36.
15. See W. P. Schuppe, "Leading a Turnaround," *The Secured Lender* (January 2003), pp. 8–14; and W. H. Fetterman, "The Team Approach to Turnarounds," *Journal of Private Equity* (Summer 2003), pp. 9–10.

16. Jack Sharry, "Who's Minding the Store?" *On Wall Street* (November 2005), pp. 77–78.
17. www.ffi.org.
18. C. Dannhauser, "Will My Beloved Survive Me?" *BusinessWeek Frontier* (January 21, 1999), www.businessweek.com.
19. M. Kindley, "Grooming Your Successor," *Network World* (July 22, 2002), p. 7.
20. Clyde E. Witt, "Plan Ahead Stay Ahead," *Material Handling Management* (January 2006), pp. 33–35.
21. www.esopassociation.org.

CASES FOR PART 4

CASE 4A
OKLAHOMA NATIONAL BANK

"The bank that makes dreams come true."

INTRO

It's January 1, 2002, and the momentum is high among the top executive leaders of Oklahoma National Bank. The bank has just been named the fastest growing new bank in its economic region of the country and the future is looking very bright. After opening its doors in January of 2000 with $11 million in capital, the bank has grown to over $127 million in assets. The major growth over the past two years has been fueled by the strong organizational culture and the bank's ability to maintain high asset quality. To look ahead, the major concern is finding other sources of income and building and managing a sustainable growth strategy for the future.

THE U.S. BANKING INDUSTRY

There were 9,613 FDIC-insured banking institutions at the end of 2001. Of these, 8,080 were commercial banks; 1,533 were savings institutions. Total assets at FDIC-insured commercial banks are $6.569 trillion; savings institutions hold $1.299 trillion. Out of 9,613 banks, 5,062 hold less than $100 million in assets. Thus, the majority of banks are small, community banks that hold just 3 percent of the industry's total assets.

In the last decade, the world of commercial banking has undergone significant changes, but the pace of consolidation and mergers has finally slowed. In 2001, mergers absorbed 422 banks and savings institutions. This contrasts with 2000, when 499 institutions merged. In 1999, there were 513 mergers and in 1998, there were 680 mergers. Also in 2001, 146 new banks and/or savings institutions had been chartered, while 208 new banks and savings institutions were chartered during 2000.

Compared to 2000, 56.7 percent of all U.S. commercial banks reported higher annual earnings in 2001. Full year 2001 earnings of $74.3 billion outperformed the previous record of $71.7 billion set in 1999. Key factors in the improvement in industry earnings included sharply lowering funding costs (Federal Reserve's cut in interest rates) and higher gains on sales of securities and other assets. Through much of 2001, lower interest rates continued to boost the values of banks' fixed-rate securities. Rising provisions for loan losses and a lack of growth in noninterest revenues limited this increase in profits. Noninterest income was only $368 million (0.9 percent) higher than the fourth quarter of 2000.

For the year, asset growth slowed to 5.2 percent, the lowest annual rate since 1992. Loans increased by only 2.0 percent in 2001, after growing by 9.4 percent in 2000. Most major banks have been experiencing trouble maintaining the quality of their assets. Declining asset quality has been a trend over the past two years and the level of problems and the pace of deterioration continue to be significantly greater at large banks. Increases in charge-offs were reported on commercial and industrial loans, credit card loans, commercial real estate loans, home equity loans, and residential mortgage loans.

ISSUES AFFECTING THE BANKING INDUSTRY

The first trend, an area of concern, is household and business debt levels. Spending by households and businesses is growing faster than cash income, resulting in debt rapidly increasing. Further, recent growth in business

Source: This case study was prepared by Dana Glover with the intention of providing at basis for class discussion.

indebtedness raises concerns about commercial credit quality. After expanding at the fastest growth rate in more than a decade during 1998, the commercial and industrial (C&I) loan portfolios at insured depository institutions continued to grow rapidly in 1999. Evidence of weakening corporate credit quality began to appear during 1999, and the federal banking regulators have publicly expressed their concerns about the quantity and quality of commercial credit risk in the system. Despite starting from very low levels, net C&I loan charge-offs for all insured institutions totaled \$3.6 billion during 1999—a 51 percent increase over 1998. Moreover, results from the annual interagency review of large commercial credits—the Shared National Credit (SNC) Program—noted a sharp rise in criticized loans. At the same time, corporate bond defaults and negative credit rating revisions during 1999 reached levels not seen since the early 1990s. This deterioration in commercial credit quality occurred during a particularly strong economic environment, leading to questions about how much further credit quality might deteriorate in the event of a moderate to severe recession.

Second, intense competition in banking is driving business strategies. Evidence also suggests that, to maintain loan growth and meet funding needs, institutions are pursuing asset-liability structures with higher levels of interest rate risk. Innovations and cost-cutting initiatives used by insured institutions to counter competitive pressures may introduce new risks associated with complex accounting valuations, weakening internal controls, and the need for more intensive loan servicing.

Third, the economy and the banking system are vulnerable to sudden shocks from financial market instability. The 1990s were marked by recurring, and perhaps more frequent, episodes of financial market turbulence and the banking industry asset growth has outstripped growth in deposits, creating greater reliance on more expensive and less stable market-based sources of funding. These funding trends present challenges for community institutions.

TRENDS SHAPING THE FUTURE OF THE INDUSTRY

Consolidation

While most financial services companies spent most of the past five years scrambling to become bigger so that they could be all things to all people, community banks emerged to fill the gap left by the ongoing consolidation in the banking industry. Many consumers and businesses were left with fewer choices among financial institutions. This created an opportunity for community banks such as Oklahoma National Bank to develop a profitable niche by providing personalized service to local residents and businesses in their communities.

Slow Economic Growth

Rising problem loans and compressed profit margins, combined with slow economic growth over the past two years, have created a much more challenging environment for banks and securities firms. This has caused management teams to focus on nurturing high performing units, cutting costs, and eliminating nonperforming units.

Falling Low Cost Consumer Deposits

Profits derived from the net interest margin achieved by making business and consumer loans funded by relatively low cost consumer deposits make up the bulk of traditional bank earnings. As competition from investment banks and mutual fund companies gets more intense, consumers are leaving less and less low cost money in their checking and savings accounts. Banks have had to bid up their pricing on certificates of deposit in order to attract adequate funding for their loans. As a result, net interest margins have declined.

Non-Interest Income

Non-interest refers to income that is derived from activity other than the interest spread received from loans: service charges, overdraft fees, trust fees, servicing fees on sold loans, and selling insurance and brokerage services. In recent years, banks have increased their focus on non-interest income as a way to increase their profitability. Non-interest income can be more stable than traditional lending and this revenue does not adhere to the typical loan growth cycle. This income also provides an offset to declining net interest margins.

THE OKLAHOMA BANKING INDUSTRY

Despite a nationwide earnings decline in 2001, the Oklahoma banking industry is growing faster than the national industry. In its Quarterly Banking Profile, the Federal Deposit Insurance Corporation reported that Oklahoma banks posted a net income of \$487 million as of December 31, 2001.

Following are details from the FDIC report for Oklahoma:

- Total loans and leases outstanding from Oklahoma banks stood at $27.5 billion as of December 31, 2001, compared to $26.0 billion a year earlier; a 5.8 percent increase.
- Oklahoma bank assets totaled $45.9 billion at the end of the year, up 6.2 percent from the same point in 2000.
- The average return on assets for the state industry was 1.09 percent, up from 1.07 percent a year earlier. Return on equity averaged 11.77 percent across the state.
- Total Oklahoma bank deposits grew by 5.1 percent, from $33.4 billion in 2000 to $35.1 billion in 2001.
- The net interest margin for Oklahoma banks averaged 4.11 percent, compared to 4.18 percent in the same period of 2000.
- The ratio of non-interest income to average earning assets grew from 1.40 percent in 2000 to 1.46 percent in 2001.
- The ratio of net loans and leases to total bank assets was 59.13 percent, down slightly from 59.43 in 2000.
- The percent of unprofitable banks decreased from 5.94 percent in 2000 to 3.55 percent in 2001. However, the number of banks with earning gains decreased from 62.24 percent to 58.16 percent.
- The ratio of noncurrent loans and leases to total loans and leases remained steady at 1.1 percent while the ratio of nonperforming assets to total assets increased slightly.
- The ratio of net loan charge-offs (losses) to total loans increased in 2001 to .44 percent from .32 percent in 2000 and 2001.
- The FDIC reported that Oklahoma had 282 commercial banks as of December 31, 2001, down from 286 in 2000. The number of bank employees in the state grew by more than 400, to 17,701.

HISTORY OF OKLAHOMA NATIONAL BANK

After retiring from 26 years in the banking business and serving as president of Stillwater National Bank in Tulsa, Tom Bennett, Jr., Oklahoma National Bank (ONB) Chairman and Chief Executive Officer, got the idea for a start-up bank from his son, Tom III, during a family ski trip. His first call was to an old friend from college, Garry Groom, who had been CFO at two other Oklahoma banks. In response to Bennett's invitation to create a new bank in a way they had always dreamed that a bank should be run, he became ONB's CFO. A short time later, Bennett was introduced to Michael Bezanson through one of his potential investors. Bezanson had been president and CEO of Security National Bank of Sapulpa and had also been thinking about starting a bank. Bezanson quickly became Oklahoma National Bank's president, and the process of creating a dream to turn into reality began around the Bennetts' kitchen table with three banking veterans (Bennett, Bezanson, & Groom) and one rookie (Tom Bennett III).

Bennett pulled together a group of investors and board members that reflected the bank's interests in small businesses, entrepreneurs, and local professionals. Among the board members are B. J. Dumond, chairman and chief executive officer of Simple Simons Pizza; Dr. Ben Johnson, president of Tulsa Dental Products; and home builder Stephen Murphy of Murphy Resources Inc. It has been said that the bank's investors and board members read like the *Who's Who of Business in Tulsa.*

The bank's employees include a mix of veteran bankers and industry newcomers. Among them are Bennett's wife, Sue, who serves as director of marketing and investor relations, and their son, Tom, who is currently a vice president with the bank. The average banking experience of the 12 senior officers is 22 years and the average banking experience of the 33-person staff is 15 years.

OKLAHOMA NATIONAL BANK OPERATIONS

Products

Oklahoma National Bank offers a variety of deposit products including regular checking, business checking, savings accounts, and tiered rate money market accounts and CDs with the most competitive rates in Tulsa. One depository product that is unique is their personal checking account that pays a CD rate of interest as long as the customer maintains a minimum balance of $5,000. They've developed the NetTeller online banking system to offer customers the opportunity to visit their Oklahoma National Bank account from any Internet connection and they offer to reimburse their customers for ATM access fees charged by other banks when ONB customers use other banks' ATMs to access ONB accounts.

Oklahoma National Bank also makes mortgage loans and consumer loans and specializes in small- to medium-sized business loans, SBA loans, and loans to professionals. They believe that their success at growing a high volume of high quality, well-priced loans has been their ability to understand their customers' financial needs and their willingness to propose creative loan solutions that tailor repayment programs to each customer's unique ability to repay, and to make prompt commitments followed by fast loan closings.

Financial Performance

Like most other start-ups, Oklahoma National Bank was expected to lose money during early operations and not to turn a profit until [its] third year of operations. However, in 2001 Oklahoma National Bank made a net profit of $65,237 for the year; $359,237 ahead of the original plan given to investors. The net profit of $65,237 was after allocating $708,000 to the reserve for loan losses. This represented $809,676 in pre-reserve earnings for 2001, a figure that also outperformed the 2001 budget.

Loan performance also fueled the growth of Oklahoma National Bank during the 2001 operating year as the loan portfolio grew from $42.1 million to $110.8 million. More importantly, even during slow economic growth, Oklahoma National Bank was able to maintain stellar asset quality. As of September of 2001, the bank had no loans that were over 30 days past due and no net charge-offs for the year. The performance of ONB is indicated in Exhibits 1 through 4.

CULTURE

> We like to think that the story of the bank is a story about relationships. The first relationship would be between the founders and God. One unusual aspect of our company is that we open all meetings with a prayer. We see this adventure as a blessing from God, and we earnestly seek to be good stewards.
>
> Certainly there is an element of relationships between our 112 investors, our 37 staff members, and our rapidly increasing number of customers. We say that we are "the bank that makes dreams come true." That begins with listening to each other's dreams, then trying to help each other pursue them. So far, it has been a lot of fun."
>
> Thomas E. Bennett, Jr.
> Chairman & CEO

How many banks announce to their customer that they will be glad to make arrangements to meet with you at any time or a place that is more convenient to you? How many banks promise you will always speak to a "live" person when you give them a call? How many banks start each meeting with a prayer? The unique corporate culture at Oklahoma National Bank has provided an opportunity for the bank to develop a competitive advantage centered on customer service. One of Oklahoma National Bank's major corporate values includes the building of a fun organization with excellent relationships. Tom Bennett feels it is important to know the customer, big or small, and build long-lasting relationships that meet their needs. Employee and customer surveys have revealed that the bank has one of the best reputations in the community.

The bank's founders describe Oklahoma National Bank's business model as a marriage of sound banking principles and dedication to building strong relationships. This model has allowed the bank to effectively manage lending risks while serving the needs of the customers and community. Relationship building is one of the key ingredients in Oklahoma National Bank's risk mitigation strategy.

MARKET DYNAMICS

Oklahoma National Bank has chosen one of the most successful economic regions in Oklahoma as its home. Tulsa, Oklahoma, accounts for 32 percent of all the gross domestic product in the state, but only 23.4 percent of the population. The value of the goods and services produced in the Tulsa area is growing faster than in most cities nationwide. Business expansions and increases in productivity have pushed the gross domestic product in the area to a record $30.7 billion in 2001, up 3.9 percent from 2000. The gross domestic product is expected to increase at a faster rate in Tulsa than in the state and the nation. In 2002, the GDP in Tulsa is expected to increase to $31.7 billion (up 3.3 percent), compared to a 1.1 percent statewide and a 3 percent nationwide increase. In 2005, it is expected to increase 21.6 percent, compared to a 14.5 percent statewide and 22.9 percent nationwide increase.

MAJOR COMPETITORS

Bank of America

Bank of America reported operating earnings of $8.04 billion, or $4.95 per share (diluted), which excludes the charges incurred to exit the auto leasing and sub prime real estate lending businesses. A year earlier, the company reported operating earnings of $7.86 billion, or $4.72 per share. Net income for 2001 was $6.79 billion, or $4.18 per share, compared to net income of $7.52 billion, or $4.52 per share a year ago. Bank of America currently operates 49 full service banking centers in the state of Oklahoma.

Bank of Oklahoma

Bank of Oklahoma (BOK) is a multi-bank holding company based in Tulsa, Oklahoma. The assets of the organization exceed $11 billion and Bank of Oklahoma enjoys market leadership throughout the state of Oklahoma. During the past five years, the organization has sought acquisitions in high-growth markets in contiguous states to Oklahoma. BOK Financial operates four principal lines of business under its Bank of Oklahoma franchise: corporate banking, consumer banking, mortgage banking, and trust services. Bank of Oklahoma's operating philosophy embraces a "community atmosphere" with local boards of directors with local decision making and marketing efforts.

Stillwater National Bank and Trust Company

Stillwater National offers commercial and consumer lending and deposit services from offices in Stillwater, Tulsa, Oklahoma City, and Chickasha, Oklahoma. A substantial portion of current business and focus for the future are services for local businesses, their primary employees, and other managers and professionals living and working in its Oklahoma market areas. At December 31, 2001, Stillwater had total assets of $1.2 billion, deposits of $905 million, and shareholders' equity of $85.1 million. Stillwater's philosophy is to provide a high level of quality customer service, a wide range of financial services, and products responsive to customer needs.

THE FUTURE

The bank plans to add three new branches in the Tulsa area within the next year, but Tom Bennett and his management team know that if they remain fixed on Tulsa it will be very hard to grow. They hope to grow to $170 million in total assets by the year end 2002, and to $250 million by [the] bank's 5th year anniversary in 2005, but where should growth come from? New products? Acquisitions? Market expansion? How can Oklahoma National Bank expand profitability while maintaining its unique culture and unwavering dedication to customer satisfaction? Is it possible to grow without sacrificing service and relationships?

EXHIBIT 1 State of the Bank Report, April 19, 2002

I Introduction

I am pleased to report that the state of your banking company, both Twenty First Century Financial Services Company and Oklahoma National Bank & Trust Company, is excellent! No, now that I think about it, it's better than excellent, it's amazing! I have been an optimist all of my life, and even I am surprised at our extraordinary growth, more rapid than expected profitability, and excellent asset quality. I am also very pleased with the high quality staff that we have continued to assemble and the continued growth in our many wonderful relationships with customers and friends. For ONB, these are the best of times.

II Perspective

Last year our big announcements were:

1. Our first month of profitability in March 2001, our 14th full month of doing business.
2. That in our first 15 months we had exceeded all of our 24 month goals.
3. That we had successfully recruited Oklahoma's #1 Radio Personality, John Erling, to be our spokesman.
4. That we were the fastest growing new bank in the region.
5. That we were about to finish our drive-in at 91st & Yale.
6. That we had just finished our first Habitat for Humanity House.
7. That we had moved from the 17th largest bank in Tulsa to #12 and we rightfully celebrated these achievements!

(continued)

EXHIBIT 1 (Continued)

III The Last 12 Months & Where We Stand Today

Let me tell you now, about the road we have traveled in the last 12 months and where we stand today.

1. Last year we went from being profitable in March, to being profitable for the entire year. In 2001, the Bank earned a net profit of $65,000, which was $241,000 ahead of the original pro forma loss of $176,000 for the year 2001 in your initial private placement memorandum. This resulted in the Holding Company having a net profit of $37,000 for the year, with the major difference being the interest paid by the Holding Company on a bank stock loan that was used to inject capital into the Bank. Overall, our company is $602,000 ahead of our original pro forma losses in our first two years, which I think is pretty amazing!
2. This week, our bank exceeded $155 million in total assets, which is a $5 million increase over our 3/31/02 quarter end. In reaching $155 million in assets, we are two and one-half times the size that we thought we would be at year end 2002 and nearly twice the size that we thought we would be at year end 2003. Now, some of you might think we were bragging in our initial pro formas. The fact is that out of the 22 new banks that were started in 2000 in our region of the country, including banks in Dallas, Houston, Kansas City, and St. Louis, the average size at year end 2001 was $44 million. Our original pro forma showed us at $44 million at year end 2001. So, achieving our pro forma growth would have made us average. While we thought we might be a little better than the average, we never imagined we would be nearly 300 percent of the average which is what we have in fact achieved. To me, this too is amazing!
3. We will never top the [coup] of recruiting John Erling as our spokesman; but we have pulled an equally great, different kind of [coup] in the new Advisory Board members we have recruited from Sapulpa. I will let Mike introduce them all later. But, I have to say that I never believed we could open our first branch in a new town and get the Mayor, the President of the Rotary Club, and a Who's Who of Local Business People to join our cause. Those of you who are members of our Sapulpa Advisory Board—you are amazing!
4. We are still the fastest growing new bank in this region of the country. In addition, we are in the top 10 percent in the country of new banks in growth, earnings, and asset quality! We are in the top 10 in all three categories all at the same time.

   Comparing ONB to the average start-up bank in our region from the year 2000, at year end 2001:

   - They reached $44 million in assets; we reached $124.7 [million].
   - They had experienced an average loss of 5.7 percent on equity; we had a .7 percent profit.
   - They had loan losses of .11 percent of their loans; we had 0.00 percent loan losses.
   - They had .21 percent of their loans over 30 days past due; we had .01 percent.

   To me, all of this is amazing!
5. Last year, we finished our drive-in at 91st & Yale; this year we opened our first full-service branch in Sapulpa on April 10, 2002 (and it has a drive-in), we opened a Loan Production Office in Owasso in February; and we have just been approved by our bank regulators to open our new branch at 21st & Lewis this fall. At our last Board meeting, we approved a budget of $1.5 million to renovate the first floor, build a four-lane drive-in, and provide bank only parking on the north side of the building at 21st Street. I've heard that all the other Banks in town think that is amazing!
6. Last year we finished our first Habitat for Humanity House. This year we have asked our Sapulpa Advisory Board to help us identify a similar type of project to do in Sapulpa . . . it too may be a Habitat for Humanity House, but I'm not sure. I know many members of our staff, and many of you as investors, have been involved in a wide range of philanthropic projects in this last year. It's hard to put it all in perspective following the events of September 11th. However, it is clear that we have much to do in our community, our state, our nation, and throughout the world. My prayer for all of us is that we will find God's activity and listen to His calling, and go to join Him wherever that might be. For some, it will be our local Red Cross or the local bowl-a-thon for Big Brothers & Sisters in which ONB Club is sponsoring eight teams this weekend, for others it will be serving the orphans of Russia or Vietnam. One thing I am sure about is that the challenge for all of us is almost overwhelming. However, I believe that as we follow God's leadership, somehow it will all work out for good, and the fact that we may be a part of that goodness . . . that is amazing!
7. Last year we had moved from the 17th largest bank headquartered in Tulsa when we started #12 on 3/31/01. This year we became the 7th largest bank headquartered in Tulsa on 3-31-02 . . . and I believe in the last three weeks, we are now actually #6. At year end 2001, we became the 64th largest bank in Oklahoma. Probably we are now about 50th out of 290 . . . in two years, two months, and twelve days. Now that's amazing!

EXHIBIT 1 (Continued)

IV Looking Forward

I think in the future, our focus will not be on bigness . . . rather it will be on quality.

1. Our #1 Priority must be quality relationships:
   - With you as our investors, we want to behave like partners.
   - With the members of our staff, we want to be, in the best sense, like family.
   - With our customers, we want to be known as bankers who really have a heart for service.
   - With our regulators, we want to be known as the epitomy of compliance and integrity.
   - With those thousands of people who are not yet our customers who live in our community, we want to be the bank they are comparing their bank to—and considering moving their business to.

   Overall, we really do want to build and maintain quality relationships. So, help us meet your family, friends, neighbors, and associates. And, if you hear about or see, or experience our messing up, please let me know. We want to apologize for our errors and begin again immediately.

   I believe that a focus on quality relationships will move us forward more happily and successfully than anything else that we might do.

   In this regard, we are looking to recruit a few more quality bankers to our staff. If you know good bankers at other banks that we ought to call and recruit, please let me know.
2. We also want to excel at quality service and quality facilities.
   - Tell your friends that ONB is not just another bank . . . we are a better bank.
   - Tell them ONB offers the highest rates in Oklahoma on personal checking accounts and CDs, totally free ATM access at any ATM owned by any bank in Oklahoma, and prompt personalized responses to loan proposals. In all these areas, we really are a better bank than our competitor.
   - And, I hope you are as proud of our facilities as we are. Special thanks to Ward Seibert, and all those involved in this area of our work.
3. We must continue to grow a high volume of quality loans. The #1 thing that can go wrong in a bank is bad loans. I want to compliment Mike, Tom, and all our lenders for the great job they are doing in maintaining the quality of our loan portfolio.

   If you know good people who have borrowing needs, ask them to give your bank a shot at the business. It's the #1 way we make money, so we really need your help in this area.

   Also, if you hear of bad things going on in our local economy, let us know so that we can take efforts to avoid loan problems associated with economic difficulties.
4. We are also going to try to expand the range of our products and services by associating our company with our quality service providers and allowing them to cross sell our customers their products and split the fees with the bank. Mike will tell you about our new venture with Family Business Partners later. We also offer trust services through The Trust Company of Oklahoma, and we are exploring other opportunities that may increase our earnings in the future.
5. We are also looking at branch sites in Owasso and Broken Arrow for 2002, and keeping our eye on Oklahoma City in 2003. We are committed to doing all of those things in a quality manner, to build a company that is both profitable—and a company you can be proud to own.

V Summary and Conclusion

1. Our last year was an amazing year! While we would like to stop and celebrate our successes, they have yielded us many new opportunities . . . so we are pressing on into 2002 in what we hope will be a year known for its quality in all that we do.
2. So far we're off to a very fast start . . . and we are just getting started in Sapulpa, and we are excited about the prospects of Midtown.

EXHIBIT 2 Oklahoma National Bank Financial Performance, 2000–2001

Dollar Figures in Thousands		
Assets and Liabilities	**31-Dec-2000**	**31-Dec-2001**
Total employees (full-time equivalent)	25	34
Total Assets	**64,487**	**127,437**
Cash due from depository institutions	963	3,279
Interest-bearing balances	22	21
Securities	5,479	0
Federal funds sold & reverse repurchase agreements	12,613	3,052
Net loans & leases	42,078	110,799
Loan loss allowance	390	1,097
Trading account assets	0	0
Bank premises and fixed assets	2,300	6,705
All other assets	1,054	3,602
Total liabilities and capital	64,487	127,437
Total Liabilities	**56,929**	**115,763**
Total deposits	50,483	95,545
Interest-bearing deposits	45,032	83,833
Deposits held in domestic offices	50,483	95,545
% insured (estimated)	89.85%	82.60%
Other borrowed funds	6,260	20,000
All other liabilities	186	218
Equity capital	7,558	11,674
Common stock	1,063	1,063
Surplus	7,437	11,511
Undivided profits	−942	−900
Memoranda		
Noncurrent loans and leases	0	15
Income earned, not collected on loans	348	618
Earning assets	60,192	113,872
Long-term assets (5+ years)	740	3,415
Average assets, year-to-date	43,900	96,290
Average assets, quarterly	58,086	120,643
Volatile liabilities	15,503	40,982
Insider loans	2,376	1,400
FHLB advances	N/A	20,000
Loans and leases held for sale	102	1,767
Unused loan commitments	19,788	24,170
Total unused commitments	19,788	24,170

EXHIBIT 3 Income and Expense Statement

	Dollar Figures in Thousands	
Income and Expense	**31-Dec-2000**	**31-Dec-2001**
Number of institutions reporting	1	1
Total interest income	2,883	7,350
Total interest expense	1,576	4,034
Net interest income	1,307	3,316
Provision for loan and lease losses	390	708
Total noninterest income	49	332
Fiduciary activities	N/A	1
Service charges on deposit accounts	37	139
Trading account gains & fees	N/A	0
Additional noninterest income	12	192
Total noninterest expense	2,072	2,912
Salaries and employee benefits	1,195	1,934
Premises and equipment expense	201	19
All other noninterest expense	676	959
Pre-tax net operating income	−1,106	28
Securities gains (losses)	0	74
Applicable income taxes	−385	37
Income before extraordinary items	−721	65
Extraordinary gains—net	0	0
Net Income	**−721**	**65**
Net charge-offs	0	1
Cash dividends	0	0
Sale, conversion, retirement of capital stock, net	8,255	N/A
Net operating income	−721	18

EXHIBIT 4 Performance Ratios

Performance and Condition Ratios	31-Dec-2000	31-Dec-2001
Yield on earning assets	7.23%	8.51%
Cost of funding earning assets	3.95%	4.67%
Net interest margin	3.28%	3.84%
Noninterest income to earning assets	0.12%	0.38%
Noninterest expense to earning assets	5.20%	3.37%
Net operating income to assets	−1.64%	0.02%
Return on assets (ROA)	−1.64%	0.07%
Return on equity (ROE)	−9.25%	0.70%
Retained earnings to average equity (YTD only)	−9.25%	0.70%
Net charge-offs to loans	0	0.00%
Credit loss provision to net charge-offs	N/A	70800.00%
Earnings coverage of net loan charge-offs (x)	N/A	736
Efficiency ratio	152.80%	79.82%
Assets per employee ($ millions)	2.58	3.75
Condition Ratios (%)		
Loss allowance to loans	0.92%	0.98%
Noncurrent loans to loans	0	0.01%
Net loans and leases to deposits	83.35%	115.97%
Net loans and leases to core deposits	120.29%	159.28%
Equity capital to assets	11.72%	9.16%
Core capital (leverage) ratio	12.79%	9.62%
Tier 1 risk-based capital ratio	14.18%	10.39%
Total risk-based capital ratio	14.97%	11.36%

CASE 4B
DATAVANTAGE CORPORATION

. . . CONTINUING THE ENTREPRENEURIAL SPIRIT

> Christopher Columbus set the foundation for the entrepreneurial spirit in America, by pursuing at great risk his vision of a different world. This spirit has evolved from that early point in American history to become the cornerstone of today's business innovation and growth. Those embodying the spirit look beyond current business practices and processes to question their most fundamental beliefs and corporate structures. They seek not merely to satisfy market demands, but to anticipate and create markets that have not yet been conceived. They invent a vibrant corporate culture and elicit the dynamic leadership needed to bring it into action. They rewrite the rules and take on seemingly impossible tasks. And, they invest in a future so bold it redefines not only an organization, but an entire industry.[1]

Source: This case study was prepared by Michael Harriston, Nadya Tolshchikova, Michael Walsh, and Sean Wenger of the Weatherhead School of Management, Case Western Reserve University, with the intention of providing a basis for class discussion.

It was a brisk fall day outside in Cleveland, Ohio, where Chaz Napoli, president of Datavantage, and Marvin Lader, CEO of Datavantage, were having lunch at a new restaurant that had just opened near their office. As the anxious restaurant owner came by to check on their meal, the restauranteur's concern for his business immediately reminded them of their concern regarding the looming decisions they were faced with regarding their own organization. During Chaz and Marvin's discussion of the situation at hand, they remarked how much their business had evolved.

After having initially started out in 1988 as a reseller of third-party software to small distribution businesses and corporate systems for retail home offices, Datavantage made a conscious strategic decision in 1994 to better control its own destiny and internally develop its own Point of Sale software products. Even though Datavantage's financial performance was healthy at that time as a distributor of third-party software, the two owners knew that the transition to become a developer would be best for the long-term success of the company. Now, they were faced with another decision that could potentially change the company—they were in the final stages of negotiation to acquire XBR Track, which was a small loss prevention software company based in Boston, Massachusetts. Chaz and Marvin discussed many related issues regarding the XBR acquisition—was loss prevention going to become a viable new market for the retail industry to justify the price of XBR? What would be the internal implications of this new product line on the company's culture, financial and organizational structure, as well as sales and marketing capabilities? Would it be complimentary to Datavantage's current business model? As the two finished their meal, they began to discuss the options that lay ahead.

DATAVANTAGE—BACKGROUND

Datavantage was founded in 1988 by Marvin Lader, an IBM veteran and a serial entrepreneur from Cleveland, Ohio. Marvin's background in sales and application software/system engineering, gained after many years at IBM, allowed him to collect extensive knowledge of business applications that ranged from sales to feeder distributors to large retail chain applications. Exposure to the retail industry, coupled with the experience of starting two other companies prior to Datavantage, one of which went public, allowed him by 1993 to grow Datavantage to 16 employees and $1.5 million in sales with only $50,000 of external financing. The company was a reseller of business application software to small distribution businesses and corporate systems for the retailers' home offices as well as a provider of legacy Cobol Systems for Distributors (SFD). Only a few programs were written internally and, by 1993, Datavantage was slowly transforming itself into a consulting company. Despite relative success, it wasn't exactly what Marvin envisioned to be an exciting entrepreneurial opportunity and [he] was ready to get out of the business. A radical change was needed in order for Marvin to consider staying and growing the company.

The opportunity arrived in 1994 when Datavantage acquired the retail services division of LDI that was up for sale at an affordable price. LDI was a reseller of products for store systems and provided a complementary foundation for Datavantage's further development. LDI's business was centered on [the] niche, specialty retail market segment, providing Datavantage with a base for future company growth. This acquisition dramatically changed Marvin's perception of Datavantage's overall future potential.

Soon after the acquisition was complete, Chaz, who originally started at LDI and stayed with the company after Datavantage took over, decided to completely redefine the company's product strategy under Marvin's guidance. Chaz's knowledge of the industry came from his background in retail marketing and extensive consulting experience with retail stores. The blend of Marvin's technical background and entrepreneurial skills with Chaz's retail experience resulted in a shift of Datavantage's strategic direction. Not surprisingly, both Marvin and Chaz see this period as the real beginning of Datavantage. (The balance sheet and statement of operations for the company are indicated in Exhibits 2 and 3.)

DATAVANTAGE SOLUTIONS

As a part of the new strategy, Datavantage moved from a pure reseller to a software developer and point-of-sale solution provider. Both Marvin and Chaz felt that this would build the value of the company and allow it to control its own destiny. Furthermore, it was decided not to outsource the product development for two main reasons: (1) it was very rare that companies outsourced product development at that time, making Datavantage somewhat uncertain about the benefits of the yet unproven strategy, and (2) Datavantage had limited time and resources to get the initial product to market. Under these circumstances Chaz and Marvin felt that the development should be kept in-house, which would allow Datavantage to better deal with the pressures of new product introduction. Therefore, the next step was to execute the strategy by defining the market, developing the product, and creating a feasible business model supported by a strong organizational infrastructure.

Target Market

Looking back on that period of time, Chaz and Marvin realize that they did not consciously identify the market segment that Datavantage decided to target; instead, it happened by default. Since LDI had already built substantial expertise and credibility in the niche specialty retail segment, Datavantage decided to initially target this particular area of the retail industry. Specialty retailers concentrate on a single product category niche such as apparel, sporting goods, jewelry, and others. Although grocery stores, mass-merchandising (Wal-Mart), food service and hospitality (hotels, cruise ships), and [convenience] stores (BP, Shell) were also potentially large and profitable segments, specialty retail seemed to be the most attractive retail category. Despite the slow growth in the overall retail industry, the specialty retail segment was experiencing significant expansion with many new start-up retailers opening their stores all over the country.

INDUSTRY/COMPETITION

Point-of-sale software is a relatively young fragmented part of the software industry that in the last few years has started undergoing rapid consolidation. A wave of mergers and acquisitions has transformed the industry, such that it is now dominated by a few large players. This shift has been supported by the fast advances in technology, changing point-of-sale systems from being glorified calculators to sophisticated POS software solutions. Such technology/product shift occurs about every 10 years, bringing new innovations to existing systems. In light of these industry transformations, the Datavantage founders knew that there would emerge only a few highly successful companies in this industry and (they) were determined to have Datavantage be one of this elite group.

Store 21

Having evaluated various point-of-sale packages that were on the market at that time, Datavantage founders were not able to identify a single product that they felt had a true competitive advantage. Therefore, they saw a real market opportunity and decided to launch the development of their own product that could run on Windows technology, a relatively new operating system at the time. This was a very critical decision since at the time POS systems still ran on the DOS platforms. The goal was to develop one product and one user interface that could run all store operations such as register, inventory management, production, internal fraud, employee scheduling, and others. Based on clients' requests, consultants' input, and Chaz's and Marvin's personal industry experiences, the two major requirements for the new product were functionality and simplicity.

When Store 21 was developed and introduced to the market in 1996, it was a complete store management system based on full transaction point-of-sale (POS) applications software that ran on Windows. The system combined point of service features, such as deal pricing and item location, with several back office functions including labor management and scheduling, inventory shipping/receiving, productivity goals, and clientelling.[2]

The software also performed as a state-of-the-art connectivity package that linked individual stores with the home office via secure Internet/Intranet communications. This feature was called the "chatterbox" module, which gave the retailer real-time access to centralized intelligence or enterprise sales reporting. The centralized communication capability allowed for faster credit, debit, and check authorizations which significantly increased productivity of store transaction data streams.

RETAIL INDUSTRY'S CURRENT NEEDS

Despite the presence of the state-of-the-art POS software in many retail stores, most retailers were still struggling to reduce store shrinkage problems. Retailers in the U.S. were losing an average of 2 percent of sales due to retail theft or shrinkage each year. The losses due to shrinkage directly affected the bottom line of the retailer in the form of a pure profit loss. It was estimated that retail employees account for 55 percent to 75 percent of lost revenue because of various fraudulent transactions. Transaction fraud ranged from improper cash refunds and price overrides, to employee discount abuse and fraudulent credit card activity, amounting to $13.2 billion in retail losses annually.

On the basis of a preliminary market study to identify where inventory shrinkage occurs, Datavantage determined that employee theft and shoplifting combined accounted for the largest source of property crime committed annually in the United States[3] with the following classifications:

- Employee Theft 44.5 percent
  - Average financial loss caused by the typical dishonest employee theft is $1,023.
  - A dishonest employee typically works for his or her employer an average of nine months.
- Shoplifting 32.7 percent
  - The average value of merchandise taken by the typical shoplifter is $128.
- Administrative Error 17.5 percent
- Vendor Fraud 5.1 percent

Additionally, the following retail segments were determined to have higher than average shrink rates as a percent of sales:

- Gifts 2.91%
- Toys & Hobbies 2.81%
- Optical 2.59%
- Discount Stores 2.01%
- Sporting Goods 1.91%
- Department Stores 1.89%

Retailers were looking for new technology and techniques to help them become more proactive in identifying problem cashiers or employees at their stores, as well as providing real-time validation that certain employees were in fact committing crimes. Historically, retailers' loss prevention technology had been ineffective due to its highly manual characteristics. Retailers were also hampered by a lack of technical resources available for loss prevention initiatives.

The techniques that existed to specifically link an employee to a theft were not user friendly to a company's loss prevention manager. Transaction logs (t-logs) had to be manually sorted to provide concrete evidence of a specific employee theft. Employees' schedules also needed to be verified with the dates and times of the transactions to make a stronger case to the court system.

The volume of data generated by point-of-sale (POS) key t-logs made it difficult, if not impossible, to sort through transaction activity looking for trends that would identify employee theft. A secondary drawback to existing loss prevention software was the length of time, typically several days, required to alert a retailer of a suspicious transaction. The lack of timeliness in identifying shrinkage limited the effectiveness of an investigation, confrontation, and the ultimate resolution of a theft.

XBR LOSS PREVENTION SOFTWARE

The XBR Loss Prevention software application that Datavantage is considering acquiring is based on "by-exception" reporting methods that are determined by the specialty retail store. The main reason for Datavantage's interest in this software is the groundbreaking solution it can bring to the retail stores. Just as Store 21 is considered to be "best in class" point-of-sale application software, Marvin and Chaz know that XBR has the same potential in the loss prevention segment of the technical solution market for the retail industry. The system is designed to quickly identify, track, and manage potentially fraudulent transactions. An exception history for an associate or store is developed by establishing control points that sift through transactions to identify and analyze trends. The control point feature of XBR also allows for comparisons to other employees and stores in the same risk transaction areas.

In addition, the software has the capability to perform digital register surveillance, which is used to "mark" high risk transactions. A loss prevention officer is then able to retrieve the digital video clip of a specific transaction to verify and resolve employee theft.

The XBR Track software has the potential to substantially reduce employee fraud if it could be optimized to search t-logs for defined exceptions. While Store 21 can give the home office real-time POS transaction data and employee scheduling, it was not designed to scan for fraud. Chaz considers that the combination of the two applications would increase a store's productivity and reduce shrinkage, while creating value for both customers and Datavantage. A number of Datavantage's customers have already successfully integrated XBR Track with Store 21, which allows them to be proactive in dealing with employee fraud through predetermined "by exception" features.

In addition to the technical benefits, Datavantage expects to use XBR as the main instrument to initiate relationships with new customers. Chaz calls it "get into the castle" strategy, which ultimately means establishing a relationship with a customer through a relatively low-cost project that would create the necessary level of trust to commit to larger projects in the future. To Datavantage, XBR is just that instrument due to its relatively low cost and almost guaranteed return on investment. Moreover, the concept of XBR is fairly straightforward compared to the other complex solutions Datavantage is developing, which would make it easier for the sales people to sell XBR to the new Datavantage customers. Finally, both Chaz and Marvin are convinced that if they do not purchase XBR, someone else will, creating a potential to significantly change competitive dynamics, not in Datavantage's favor.

EXHIBIT 1 Datavantage's Largest Customers in 1997

Sunglass Hut	Things Remembered
S&K Menswear	Piercing Pagoda Jewelers
Casual Male	Genesco
Footaction	Lids
The Athlete's Foot	Tradehome Shoes
The Finish Line	

DATAVANTAGE—CUSTOMERS

Early in its existence Datavantage set a goal to differentiate itself by keeping its products and services simple, continuously improving through innovation, excelling at the delivery of the highest quality products and services, and developing stable technology and an unmatched level of customer care.

The Company experienced multiple challenges when going through a rapid growth stage. By 1997 it was able to obtain 5 percent market share in the U.S. specialty retail market, which was a significant accomplishment in the fragmented market that retail systems data management represented at that time. Despite extensive product development beginning in 1994, Datavantage did not launch Store 21 until 1996. At that time, the software was introduced to its then two largest customers, Lids and The Finish Line, which [composed] a significant portion of the company's total revenue.

Although, during the early stages of the company's development, having a few customers account for a substantial portion of annual revenue was an acceptable arrangement, Datavantage recognized that it had to quickly grow its customer base in order to minimize the risk of dependence on a few larger customers. A stated goal was not to allow a single customer to comprise more than a few percent of the revenue base. By 1997, Datavantage had each customer representing between 10 and 20 percent of the total company revenue, with the largest customer varying from year to year.

Further, Chaz and Marvin realized that they had to target only certain types of customers in order to maximize profitability. Accordingly, Datavantage used the following customer selection criteria:

- The client had to be a relatively large retailer operating a minimum of 30 stores; or
- The client's minimum revenue had to be at least $200 million.

Datavantage mainly concentrated on niche retailers that had stores at shopping malls and outlet shopping centers, operated on average from 400 to 1,000 stores, or earned gross revenue anywhere between $200 million and $1 billion.

As of 1997, Datavantage had about 20 customers, many of which were large nationwide retail chains. See Exhibit 1 for the list of Datavantage's largest retail customers in 1997.

Along with growing its client base, Datavantage sought to provide additional solutions to customers. Even though the majority of Datavantage's revenue was driven by Store 21, both Marvin and Chaz understood that the acquisition of XBR Track could provide further growth of already successful Store 21 product, which had been on the market for a year. Although XBR Track was projected to account for only about 15 percent of Datavantage's revenue, it would further strengthen its business by providing Datavantage's customers with the ability to control shrinkage through an integrated suite of applications. Additionally, it would provide customers with remarkable savings of about 2 percent of revenue, which was currently being lost on internal and external shrinkage. The combined benefits of Store 21 and XBR would result in a potentially significant financial savings to the customer, and consequently, a quick return on their investment in the XBR Track product.

DATAVANTAGE—SALES AND MARKETING

The primary methods utilized by Datavantage to sell its products and services are direct marketing, trade shows, and existing client testimonials. After developing Store 21, Chaz and Marvin realized that the existing reseller sales and marketing staff were not capable of selling the new product. The necessary level of knowledge and motivation was simply not there. This resulted in nearly an entire turnover of the sales and marketing staff.

Following this complete turnover, Datavantage was able to create a strong sales and marketing team that followed a very precise and thorough marketing strategy. Instead of using a traditional marketing campaign targeting retailers in general, the company concentrates heavily on what Chaz refers to as "personal marketing and referential selling." This involves using existing client testimonials and case studies (with Datavantage products at the center of the solution) which are featured in the company's publications and regularly mailed to targeted new and prospective customers. However, this approach has its own drawbacks, which includes an increase in the sales cycle period that consequently requires a higher level of persistence and customer relationship building on the part of the sales people.

The company also actively participates in the major retail trade shows and leverages its strong sales force to gain contacts that are often converted into valuable customer relationships. As one Datavantage customer mentioned:

> One of the company's strengths is its very well thought through marketing strategy. They always try to be in the right place at the right time.

Another important strategy that the company incorporated into its standard selling and marketing practice is the "Annual User Conference" organized each year in Cleveland, Ohio, where all Datavantage clients are invited to attend. It is a three-day event full of presentations on new products or updates, Q&A sessions, and entertainment activities. Customers are able to interact in an informal setting with other Datavantage customers, as well as employees, and share their experiences.

In order to support its active sales and marketing efforts, Datavantage implemented an extensive hiring and training program for its sales representatives. This program focuses on good work ethics, honesty, integrity, and the development of close relationships with existing and potential clients. As a result, Datavantage sales people are able to close over 90 percent of sales during the final product presentation round during which customers travel to Cleveland to Datavantage headquarters. When asked for the reason of such success, Chaz responded:

> We hire people with the same grass roots who are concerned with good work.

Convinced that proper sales and marketing techniques significantly contribute to the company's success, Chaz continually encourages the sales people to sell the *benefits* rather than features of Datavantage's products. This strategy is based on the company's "Guiding Principles," which are as follows:

1. Invest in Products "Best in Class."
2. Invest in Infrastructure and Operations.
3. Superior Sales & Marketing: Position Itself as a Retail Company Selling Technology vs. Technology Company Selling Retail Systems.
4. Product, Service and Sales Are Three Key Areas of Main Focus.

HELPDESK/CALL CENTER

Business application software for the retail industry, such as Datavantage's, requires real-time customer support through a call center or help desk, which was established early in the development of Store 21. Although one of the company's goals was to provide the best level of service to its customers, things did not always go as anticipated. The company's strategy to quickly acquire new customers led to an unintentional decrease in the level of service provided to existing long-term customers.

While not losing a single customer due to these shortcomings, Datavantage nevertheless recognized it as a major issue to be addressed. Over time the improvement in the Helpdesk area allowed Datavantage to handle most of the problems over the phone with major problems being solved by sending a specialist on site. Due to its responsiveness and strong drive for customer satisfaction, Datavantage soon was able to build a reputation of being one of the top vendors among clients' large pool of suppliers. Surveyed clients attributed their high level of satisfaction to the dedication of Datavantage personnel, their honesty and openness about issues, customer driven internal culture, and continuous drive for improvement.

As stated by one of the clients, "With Datavantage I never feel that my problems are being put on the corporate agenda when it takes a while to solve a problem. Datavantage always accepts responsibility and if something can't be done right away because of lack of resources or for any other reason, admits it." According to another customer: "They have passion for what they do and get done what needs to get done." Yet one more customer confessed: "They make me feel that they really care about my business."

Chaz and Marvin think the reason for such a high level of customer satisfaction is the very candid way in which the company operates. In fact, Chaz constantly reminds his employees that they are a direct extension of the client's staff, to the extent that their paychecks should not have the Datavantage name on them because the checks entirely come from the client's business.

With Datavantage personnel being carefully selected and capable of providing a high level of service, reflecting on the turnover in sales and marketing personnel related to Store 21, Chaz and Marvin wondered whether the acquisition of XBR would put the company through another hiring and firing turmoil that could threaten the company's strong position with its customers.

DATAVANTAGE—BUSINESS MODEL

Chaz and Marvin continued to develop Datavantage away from a reseller of third-party software, into a business applications technology company that develops its own proprietary business-to-business software for specialty retailers. The company developed a revenue model that incorporated *both* product and service revenue streams that were generated from the following five distinct and standalone profit centers.

The first profit center, Software Licenses & Royalties, generated product-related revenue that accounted for 17 percent of the total sales revenue in 1997, and was forecasted to further increase as a percentage of sales. This profit center was comprised of the Store 21 product line. When XBR is in fact acquired, the associated revenue would be part of this classification.

The second profit center, Hardware & Equipment, generated product-related revenue that accounted for 50 percent of the total sales revenue in 1997, and was forecasted to decrease as a percentage of sales.

The third profit center, Professional Services, generated service-related revenue that accounted for 19 percent of the total sales revenue in 1997, and was forecasted to increase as a percentage of sales. This service component of the company's business model included Datacomm Services, Handling/Restocking, Staging Fees, Professional Services Training, and Consulting.

The fourth profit center, Software Maintenance & Development, generated service-related revenue that accounted for 11 percent of the total sales revenue in 1997, and was forecasted to increase as a percentage of sales. This service component of the company's business model included SMA[4] Fees, Chatterbox, and Custom Software Modifications.

The final profit center of Datavantage was its Help Desk/Call Center Operations.

The strategy behind using these five specific profit centers was to match revenue to key similar functional areas, and allow associated categories of revenue to be pooled together. For example, anything related to hardware procurement had its own revenue category, all the software licensing revenue was grouped in a category, anything to do with a nonprogramming professional service, such as consulting, training, staging systems, technical support, etc., had a revenue category, anything having to do with computer programming, both ongoing software maintenance fees and any custom programming, was in a separate category, and finally the call center services were also in a standalone revenue category.

This categorization allowed for accountability of the company's main services by keeping clean lines of ownership in the profit centers, so that appropriate business plans and goals could be established and monitored on a moving forward basis.

DATAVANTAGE—FINANCING

The company financed its entire operations and growth primarily through Retained Earnings, as a result of solid cash management. A critical success factor in its cash management has been Datavantage's ability to aggressively control its accounts receivable, an especially difficult task in the Retail Industry. This strong cash position allowed the company to consider all possibilities in negotiating the purchase price for XBR. The issue still remained, though, how best to finance the transaction. Should the company purchase the software outright and pay all cash, structure the purchase as an all royalty deal, or come up with some combination of cash and royalties? An all cash purchase would significantly increase the consequences of a situation where the Loss Prevention market did not develop as hoped. If Datavantage incorporates a royalty scenario, and the Loss Prevention market is successful, Datavantage may not realize as much return on its investment as would otherwise be possible from an all cash deal. As a result, Datavantage wondered what would be the best way to structure the XBR Track deal, so as to provide protection against downside risk as well as maximize the upside potential.

Both Chaz and Marvin agreed that the combination of cash and royalties seemed to be the best acquisition financing option. Datavantage planned to structure the deal with an initial $300,000 payment for the right to use the product and royalties of 5 percent of gross revenue resulting from the product sales. A buyout clause was expected to be incorporated into the agreement, which would allow Datavantage to buy out the remaining royalty payments. This option was perceived as a relatively low risk and low upfront cash deal that would provide high expected return on investment.

The company's strong cash position allowed for sustained growth that did not require any equity financing. As a result, Datavantage management and employees maintained 100 percent equity ownership of the company. However, taking into account the trade-offs of external equity financing, Chaz and Marvin wondered if outside financing should be considered to purchase XBR Track, or to possibly pursue future opportunities.

DATAVANTAGE—MANAGEMENT CULTURE

Datavantage has experienced constant evolution over the life of the organization. In early 1994, when the company consisted of 25–30 employees with Marvin and Chaz as the only senior level managers, the two founders made the majority of critical decisions, including sales presentations to new customers. Chaz still feels that in a small company start-up environment this type of top-down organizational structure was necessary to keep control over the company's limited resources and carefully protect the company's emerging image because every strategic decision had a potential of significantly affecting the future success of the organization.

By the time Datavantage reached about $10 million in revenue, Chaz realized that the company needed a well-defined infrastructure and a capable management team. Consequently, Datavantage significantly decentralized its decision making by creating a more distributive culture where each manager had authority to make critical decisions in their area of responsibility. As a direct result of the decision to create an empowered environment, members of the senior management team received authority to contribute input toward the strategic direction of the company. This shift allowed Chaz and Marvin to move away from initiating and following through with each strategic move. Now they mostly review the proposals brought to them by the team of executive managers in the organization.

However, as Datavantage became less centralized, the founders wondered what affect it would have on the entrepreneurial small-company environment that dominated the company internally from the very beginning and significantly contributed to its success. As a result, Chaz and Marvin identified main aspects of the entrepreneurial culture and put strong emphasis on instilling these into Datavantage's rapidly evolving internal organizational structure.

Major elements of entrepreneurial culture:

- Stability of the management team
- Commitment to empowerment
- Limited bureaucracy
- Clearly defined reward and compensation system that involves bonuses and equity
- Clean lines of responsibility
- Working management culture—"hands on" management style

In addition to its entrepreneurial culture, the key characteristic of Datavantage's success is its ability to take calculated risks. While not a risk averse organization, Datavantage put mechanisms in place to help mitigate it. Every important decision, such as an acquisition or new product launch, is first explored in a formal business plan. Team leaders have control over the development of business plans and are expected to execute the plans they create.

Therefore, Chaz and Marvin were able to form an empowered organization measured with a set of controls to oversee the performance of each decision-maker within the organization. Chaz calls this approach "management by exception" and Datavantage's overall organizational culture "decentralized and empowered culture with right controls."

Effective communication, as another key to the success of any small organization going through an active growth and transformation period, was embodied in Datavantage's daily operations. In fact, from the early years of organizational growth, Datavantage made it a rule not to penalize employees for making mistakes as long as a mistake or a shortcoming is immediately reported before it turns into a major problem. To emphasize the importance of communication, twice a year Chaz presents the "*State of the Company*" address to all the employees and senior management. The major objective of this communication tool is to highlight the progress of each department, identify key goals and objectives for the upcoming year, and also restate Datavantage's guiding principles that ensure the company's success.

Similarly to many successful start-ups, Datavantage shared equity with its key managers in order to maintain employees' existing level of commitment to the organization and its future. It did not only allow the company to maintain its successful approach to business, but kept employees from making decisions that sacrificed future growth for immediate results. However, Marvin and Chaz realized that there is significant risk associated with this strategy because giving someone equity does not mean that they would align their performance and the vision for the company with their status. Therefore, since equity stake in business is the most expensive and therefore valuable compensation that the company can offer to an employee, both Marvin and Chaz created a culture where people see the value of this compensation and are willing to perform accordingly by aligning their actions with the organizational goals and objectives.

MERGING OF TWO CULTURES

After deciding to acquire XBR, Marvin and Chaz had to create a strategy to merge the two different organizations. Both founders recall the acquisition of LDI where most of the LDI employees had to be let go. Although this was less likely to be the case with XBR, both Chaz and Marvin knew that the growth and long-term success of the company was directly correlated to the level of its employees' competency. Reflecting on the LDI acquisition, Chaz thought:

> As we grew into a tier one company, we put increasingly high efforts on continuously upgrading our staff.

The acquisition had several factors for the entrepreneurs to consider. The most important issue was integration of the two cultures into one. Marvin and Chaz wondered whether the XBR acquisition would affect Datavantage's well-organized internal structure, which fosters the company's present entrepreneurial environment. Would XBR management buy into Datavantage's rules and principles of internal organization and relationships with external partners? Although XBR had only 12 employees, Datavantage believed that the company had a strong management team in place. Therefore, when considering making a decision regarding the fate of these employees, Chaz believed the two companies had a good chance of success:

> One of the keys to our enthusiasm for their management team is the similarity in cultures. Both cultures are hard working and very customer service oriented.

Location was another issue. Since XBR was headquartered in Boston, several hundred miles away from Cleveland, Datavantage had to decide whether relocation and physical integration of the two companies in Datavantage's headquarters in Cleveland, Ohio, was a feasible option. An alternative would be to have XBR remain in Boston and operate as a standalone division of Datavantage.

The success of this acquisition could bring significant competitive advantage to Datavantage. However, if some of the important factors discussed above are not taken into consideration, the acquisition and postacquisition integration could negatively affect the very factors that allowed Datavantage's success in the first place, inhibiting long-term company performance.

EXHIBIT 2 Datavantage Corporation Balance Sheets

	December 31		
	1995 (Unaudited)	**1996 (Unaudited)**	**1997 (Unaudited)**
Assets			
Current assets:			
Cash and cash equivalents	$ 501,875	$ 362,286	$ 319,885
Accounts receivable	970,836	842,234	1,675,554
Prepaid expenses	97,716	44,961	94,541
Refundable income taxes	—	—	—
Deferred tax asset	—	—	—
Inventory	860,769	84,163	—
Total current assets	2,431,196	1,333,644	2,089,980
Fixed assets:			
Computers and office equipment	458,357	606,613	688,045
Furniture and fixtures	161,776	245,373	241,590
Leasehold improvements	29,787	97,867	106,284
Other	39,480	6,732	34,122
	689,400	956,585	1,070,041
Less allowance for depreciation	(370,280)	(521,293)	(423,215)
	319,120	435,292	646,826
Purchased and licensed software, net	—	—	359,512
Deferred loan costs, net			
Software development costs, net	—	—	—
	—	—	359,512
Deferred tax asset	—	—	—
Other assets	11,233	17,519	12,456
Total assets	$2,761,549	$1,786,455	$3,108,774
Liabilities and Shareholders' Equity			
Current liabilities:			
Bank term loan	$ —	$ —	$ 166,667
Supplier note payable	—	—	—
Notes payable to employees	—	—	—
Current portion of obligation under capital leases	—	—	16,883
Deferred revenue	1,218,086	332,512	1,087,103
Accrued expenses	336,475	426,924	759,291
Income/Franchise tax payable	—	—	—
Salaries, wages, taxes and commissions payable	87,000	6,950	231,032
Accounts payable	355,768	278,487	426,796
Total current liabilities	1,997,329	1,044,873	2,687,772
Long-term obligations:			
Bank term loan & line of credit	—	—	291,667
Subordinated notes payable	—	—	—
Supplier note payable	—	—	—
Obligations under capital leases	—	—	9,802
Total long-term obligations	—	—	301,469
Shareholders' equity:			
Common stock	7,620	7,800	5,578
Treasury stock	—	—	(1,145,043)
Additional capital	115,151	132,971	207,847
Retained earnings	641,449	600,811	1,051,151
Total shareholders' equity	764,220	741,582	119,533
Total liabilities and shareholders' equity	$2,761,549	$1,786,455	$3,108,774

EXHIBIT 3 Datavantage Corporation Statements of Operations

	Actual for the Years Ended December 31					
	1995 (Unaudited)	%	1996 (Unaudited)	%	1997 (Unaudited)	%
Revenue						
Point-of-sale equipment	$5,058,561	64%	$4,887,461	54%	$6,333,718	50%
Software licenses	432,778	5%	489,352	5%	2,180,104	17%
Professional services	1,522,417	19%	2,301,031	25%	2,444,015	19%
Software maintenance & development	840,033	11%	1,181,135	13%	1,379,602	11%
Operating system software	—	0%	69,566	1%	48,084	0%
Other	103,437	1%	155,756	2%	326,867	3%
Total revenue	7,957,226	100%	9,084,301	100%	12,712,390	100%
Operating Costs and Expenses						
Cost of equipment sold	3,851,672	48%	3,689,238	41%	4,967,024	39%
Salaries, wages, and benefits	1,870,324	24%	2,613,105	29%	3,923,645	31%
Professional fees	428,885	5%	712,991	8%	628,093	5%
Selling, general, and administrative	359,346	5%	367,759	4%	437,808	3%
Research and development	339,384	4%	389,777	4%	820,920	6%
Cost of system software sold	—	0%	55,653	1%	35,033	0%
Travel	99,191	1%	137,203	2%	241,173	2%
Depreciation and amortization	137,511	2%	146,788	2%	104,630	1%
Telephone	127,059	2%	287,168	3%	289,346	2%
Purchase of stock option rights	—	0%	—	0%	—	0%
Total operating expenses	7,213,372	91%	8,399,682	92%	11,447,672	90%
Income from operations	743,854	9%	684,619	8%	1,264,718	10%
Other Income (Expense)						
Interest income	33,935	0%	18,603	0%	6,441	0%
Interest expense	—	0%	—	0%	(20,008)	0%
Total other income (expense)	33,935	0%	18,603	0%	(13,567)	0%
Income taxes	—	0%	—	0%	—	0%
Net income	$ 777,789	10%	$ 703,222	8%	$1,251,151	10%
EBITDA	$ 881,365	11%	$ 850,010	9%	$1,375,789	11%

CASE 4C
DUAL PANE COMPANY

John Grayson had been in the housing restoration business for 15 years when, in 2001, he designed a machine that could remove old windows from their frames without destroying the wooden panes known as muntins and mullions that surround the glass (see Exhibit 1). One of the big advantages of the tool is that it was built around a routing drill piece that moved on a three-dimensional plane. This allowed Grayson to replace windows that up until then could not be serviced. Once the small panes were removed, they would be replaced by one large pane of double glass. The muntins and mullions would be inserted over the window to give it the same look as before.

Grayson applied for a patent as soon as he realized his machine was unique, and the patent was granted in August 2002. He has been operating the business since that time under the name of Dual Pane Company. He and his wife, Elizabeth, are the sole owners and employees of the company. She oversees the advertising and promotional aspects, and John does the actual installing. They both engage in the selling process, particularly in the colder months when the actual installation business is slower. Their current geographic market is the Boston area, although they have done business outside it. They

EXHIBIT 1

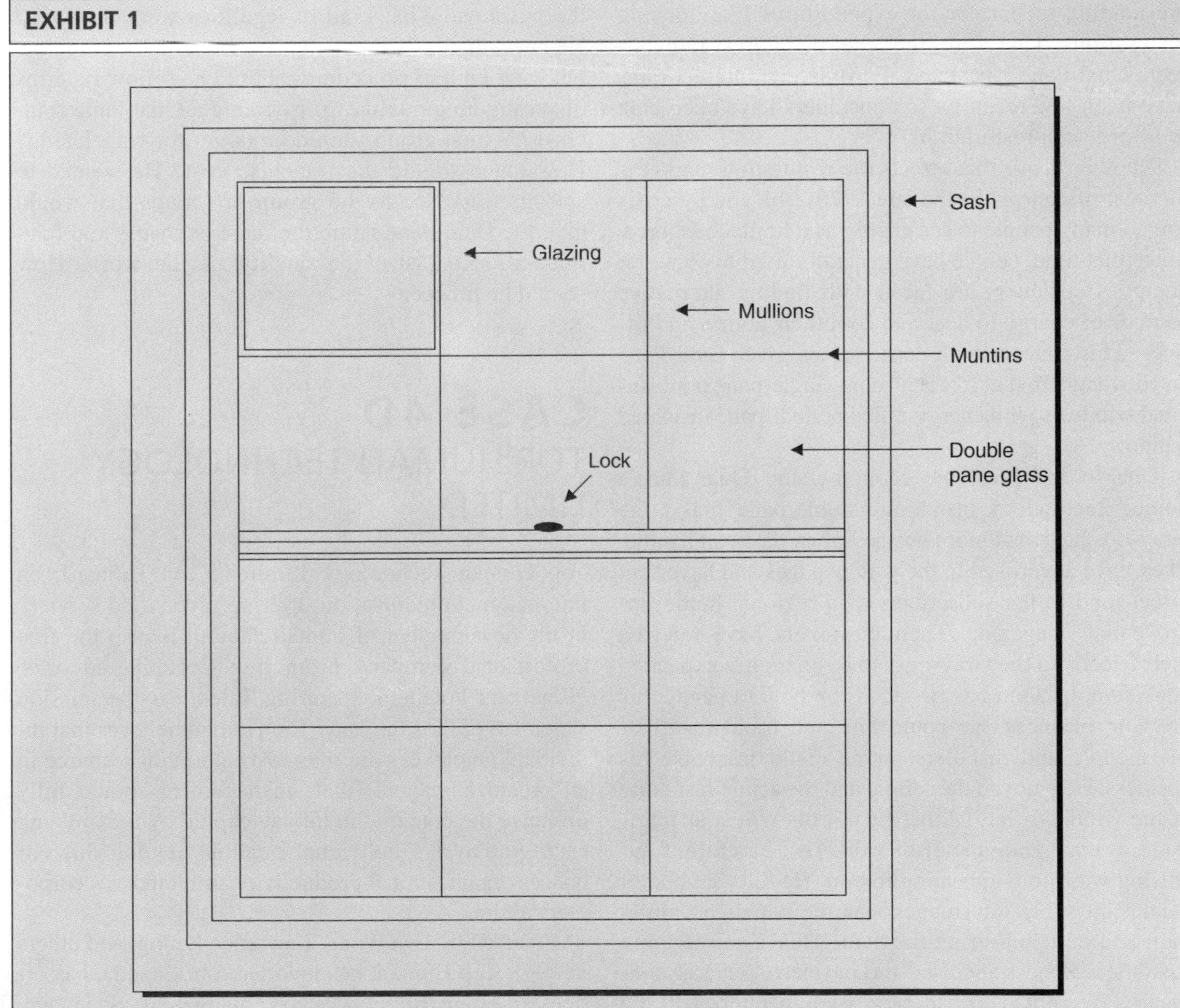

generally have concentrated on the residential market, but have periodically completed commercial jobs.

The restoration market is affected by several factors that include the state of the overall economy, local employment levels, and the amount of a consumer's disposable income. Since the company began operations, the economy has been favorable. The GNP has been increasing, real disposable income has risen moderately, and there has been a decrease in unemployment in the Boston area. The restoration of windows is a relatively large expense, costing between $3,000 and $7,000, depending on the number of windows installed in a house. Home owners are more likely to invest in this type of restoration when their level of net disposable income is greater and when the economy is good. Today, there is a trend toward less saving on the part of many Americans, and consumers are tending to borrow for expenditures like housing restorations. Therefore, the level of interest rates affects Dual Pane's business. Fortunately, interest rates have been low recently, so consumers have been able to afford such restorations.

Another factor that affects the restoration market is the cost of energy. In the late 1970s, the energy crisis forced many people to see energy as a limited resource. Since that time, people have generally tried to conserve energy. Consumers are faced with finding alternative sources of energy to heat and cool their homes and offices. This concern with conservation gives Dual Pane an advantage in that it is replacing single-pane noninsulated windows with energy-efficient dual-pane insulated windows.

Due to the favorable economy and Dual Pane's unique method of installing double-pane glass, the Graysons have had more business than they can handle. They have advertised in the yellow pages and have sent direct mail to the subscribers of a regional home improvement magazine. Their customers have referred their friends to the Graysons, so business has expanded considerably. John has two ideas on how to handle his growing business. He could hire and train a staff of salespeople and installers, or he could franchise his business. He enjoyed the selling and the actual installing of the windows, but neither he nor his wife was interested in managing a staff of workers. Therefore, franchising was more appealing to him. He felt that one of Dual Pane's big advantages was the patented cutting tool, and he could bring the name Dual Pane to more customers if he franchised the business. Several contractors he contacted had expressed an interest in the Dual Pane machine and wondered if he was interested in franchising.

John decided that his goal was to franchise the business. There were three groups of people he could contact regarding franchising. First, he could sell the rights of the product to contractors who were in the business of restoring residential homes or commercial offices. He felt that their reach with consumers could help to broaden the exposure of the Dual Pane name. He also thought that glass companies in the Boston area might be interested in a Dual Pane franchise. Since his tool could cut odd-shaped glass, it had an advantage over existing methods, which glass companies would benefit from. Elizabeth mentioned that individuals who wanted to get into the restoration business might also be potential targets for franchising.

John needed to know how to go about franchising the business. What kind of legalities were involved? He knew that he had patent protection on the machine, but what kind of procedures should he follow in terms of setting up guidelines for owning a Dual Pane franchise? Which group should he target for franchising? How much should the franchise cost? He wanted to sell his franchise to the group or groups that would give the Dual Pane name the most exposure and continue to emphasize the quality of the work. How should he proceed?

CASE 4D
TOP HUMAN TECHNOLOGY LIMITED

Top Human Technology Limited (Top Human), an international organization offering diversified services in the development of human capital, is also the first professional company promoting Coaching in Asia. "Realizing Potential, Inspiring Talent" is the mission statement of the company. Top Human believes that individual employees are the most important resource in an organization and (that) management should fully optimize the potential in human capital by maximizing each employee's individual qualities. Doing this enhances organizational productivity and improves corporate culture.

Founded by Eva Wong, Lawrence Leung, and others in 1995, Top Human, headquartered in Canada, has offices in Hong Kong, Macau, Guangzhou, Shenzhen,

Shanghai, and Beijing. A pioneer of corporate coaching in Asia, Top Human created a unique business model based on "Training plus Coaching" and successfully expanded in various parts of China.

CORPORATE COACHING

Origin

Coaching originally was a methodology used to train sports talent. Corporate Coaching uses various tools and techniques to transfer the concept of sport coaching to the field of corporate management. In the 1970s, retired U.S. Navy veteran Tim Gallway developed an idea from playing tennis—the Art of Focus. He announced that he needed only 20 minutes to teach anyone who could not play tennis to be able to play a basic game. In a test in a televised demonstration, he taught a heavyweight woman, who had never played tennis before, to focus her attention on the tennis ball and when the ball bounced up, shout "hit" and just wave the racket. Surprisingly, in 20 minutes, this heavyweight woman could hit the ball with ease. Tim Gallway explained he did not teach her anything about the techniques in tennis but rather, he helped her overcome her existing attitude of: "I cannot play." AT&T invited Tim Gallway to lecture its managers, which brought his concept of tennis coaching to the field of corporate management. Coaching was born. With the use of Coaching by such companies as Coca-Cola, ExxonMobil, IBM, Ford, BP, and Honda, Coaching occurred throughout Europe and America. One study indicated that while training alone increased productivity by 22.4 percent, training plus coaching increased productivity by 88 percent.

What Is Corporate Coaching?

According to Top Human, "Corporate Coaching is a management skill that facilitates the realization of an individual's full potential and enhances performance via improving mental models." Mental models refer to the set of beliefs and assumptions that influence the way people perceive the surrounding world and the actions they take. These beliefs and assumptions are often embedded deep in the minds of people; it can be invisible, be a subtle awareness, or be one's beliefs and principles in life. Regardless of whether people are conscious of their mental models, the mental models are like mirrors: people intake information to conform with their mental models. They overlook or simply ignore other information, or use various means to deny or distort it. As such, mental models heavily influence an individual's cognition and behavior as well as his/her organizational environment and corporate culture. Furthermore, the concept of mental models plays a very important role in the theory of Learning Organizations, as is indicated in Exhibit 1.

Distinction of Coaching versus Other Forms of Training

The main distinction between Coaching and other forms of training is that training mainly deals with the improvement of the ability of an individual or a group on a technical basis, such as personal skills training or management skills training. Coaching covers both the individual and organizational ability on a macro-societal level. Often the technical factors, which reflect the individual's ability and are the basis of organizational competitiveness, are not a match for the societal factors in the surrounding environment.

The essence of Corporate Coaching is to expand the corporation through respecting the individual's choice and facilitating the individual's development, similar to the concept of motivation. The traditional concept of motivation assumes that the goals of the corporation and its members are not the same, requiring that various management methods be used to help the members support the goals of the corporation. The traditional concept of motivation differentiates between the main subject and the objective targets, with the main subject being the investors or shareholders and the objects being the employees of the corporation. In Corporate Coaching, the main subject and the objects are the same. Corporate Coaching is committed to helping every single member align his or her personal goals with those of the corporation, and through this process the corporation develops. Employees are no longer "worker bees" directed by management; they are "corporate citizens" with rights and opportunities.

Coaching Tools and Techniques and Experiential Learning

In recent years, the coaching tools and techniques developed by Top Human have increased and now include: Enneagram, Core Values, 360° Feedback, Cultural Differences, Body Consciousness and Tai Chi, Emotional Intelligence, and Meditation. Top Human uses the "4 Step Coaching"© process (clarifying goals, reflecting truth,

EXHIBIT 1 Mental Models and Their Relationship with the Other Four Essential Factors

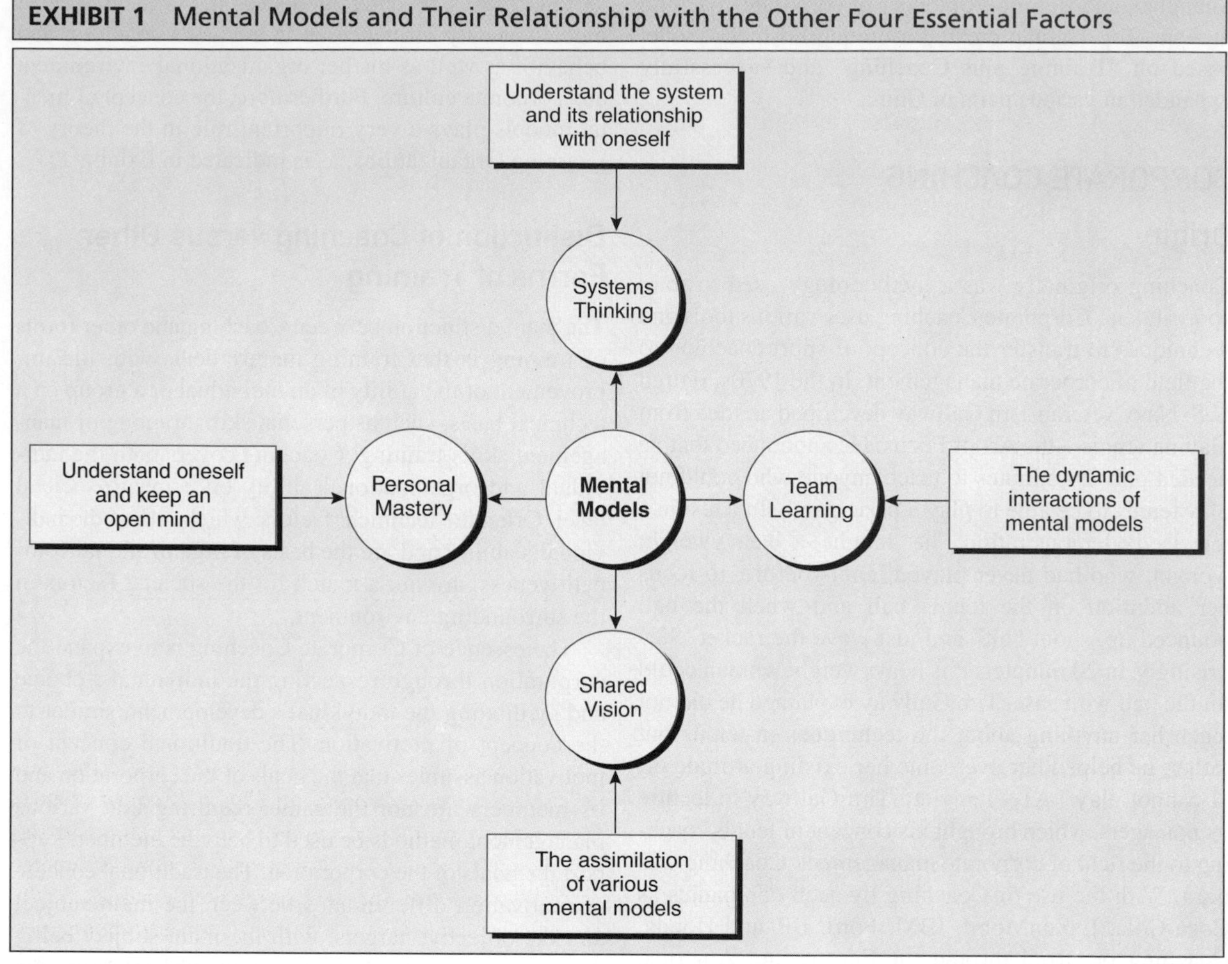

shifting paradigms, and planning actions) and the "4 Coaching Abilities"© (profound listening, precise questioning, perceptive distinction, and powerful feedback). Insight into body language, emotions, and language is also included.

As indicated in Exhibit 2, Top Human uses pre-training counseling, interactive and experiential learning in its training, and post-training follow-up and empowerment to achieve the final objective of behavioral change and enhancement of corporate performance; this is different from traditional training.

The emergence of Corporate Coaching reflects modern society shifting toward the development of human beings and the continual evolvement of organizations; it seeks to cover the socio-cultural factors that technical skills training fails to cover. Coaching Technology,© based on mental models as an entry point, facilitates the realization of one's potential and builds a corporate environment conducive for learning. Training plus Coaching are complementary and their synthesis helps harmonize the technical and societal factors in both individual and corporate ability.

THE DOMESTIC CHINESE MARKET FOR COACHING TECHNOLOGY

The reform of China and the opening of its economy allowed the creation of a large number of private enterprises. By the end of the 20th century, these enterprises were responsible for a substantial portion of the country's economic output. In the early days of the developing economy, many small and medium-sized enterprise owners relied on their spirit of risk-taking and hard work. The initial success of their companies was achieved through their personal perseverance and work; when their companies reached a certain size, problems started to occur.

EXHIBIT 2 Top Human Process of Coaching Technology Training

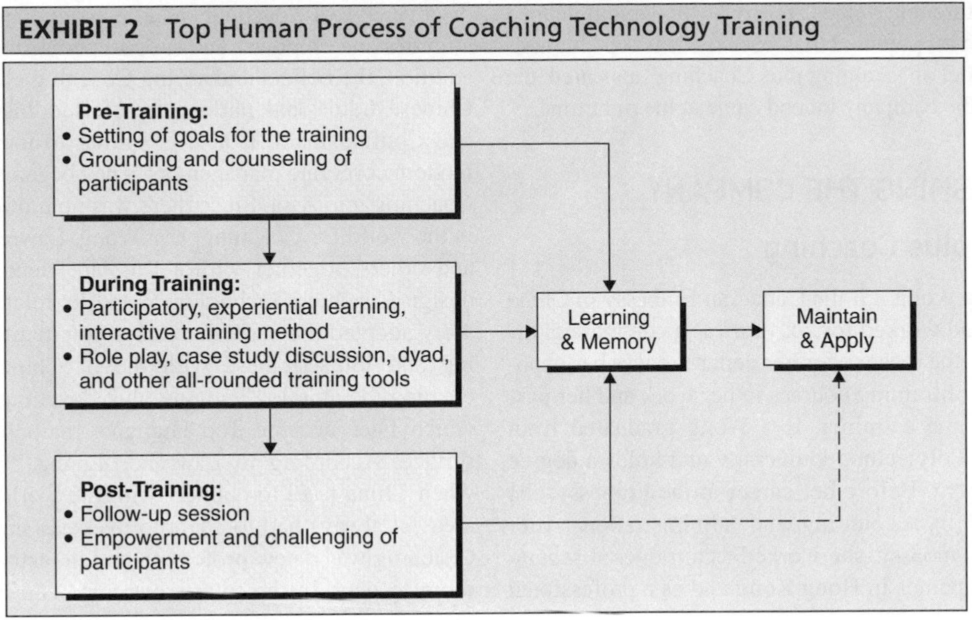

At start-up, the entrepreneurs recruited their own relatives or friends. There was little staff and the team knew each other well so it was easy to coordinate and manage. As the number of employees grew, the company had to recruit and employ individuals beyond its personal relationship network; after 50 employees a company is beyond the ability of a single person. Doing everything oneself or refusing (or not knowing how) to delegate authority exhausts the entrepreneur and creates minimal return. As one entrepreneur stated: "In my corporation, I am the only, and also the most powerful, worker as I have to solve everything myself. The bigger my company becomes, the more tired I get. It is not that I am content with my present assets, but there is no point dying of exhaustion." Another entrepreneur stated: "In the corporation, my management style is to scold; I expect a lot from the staff but they always make mistakes. After attending Top Human training, I realize that the mediocre performance of my staff is largely my responsibility because the caliber of my staff is a reflection of my own caliber." One of Top Human's first clients, the owner of a handicraft company in Zhejiang, said, "I don't consider my company a small one as making several millions annually is very easy. I am the top entrepreneur in my district but all along I have been very fatigued, I do not know what I want to do after earning the money, I have no clue at all."

White-Collar Stratum

The white-collar stratum, which started about the same time as private enterprises in China, is sensitive to its own surroundings and conditions. The rules and regulations in China's society are not at the level of people's expectations, yet the developmental changes in the Chinese society more often than not exceed their expectations. At the same time, each individual's development is also changing, making it difficult to maintain a balance in one's attitude; the uncertainty in change and choices usually leaves people in a state of feeling lost and helpless. The dramatic change in one's material life with a contrastingly blank spiritual life has brought about confusion and maladjustment.

Strangely, for such a large market with such vast potential, no entity filled the void. In the early 1990s in China, the training and consultancy organizations did not provide training that focused on shifting employees' attitudes. During the mid-1990s, the training inside China centered on knowledge and skills. Before the arrival of the 21st century, most of these training and consultancy organizations were one-person organizations. There were few large training and consultancy organizations. The entry of American and European consultancy and training firms into China significantly impacted the individual one-person organizations; these new entrants still needed a period of time to adjust to the domestic needs and the

Chinese culture and values. This was the large untapped market with vast potential that existed when Top Human's business model of "Training plus Coaching" appeared; the entrance of the company indeed came at the right time.

ESTABLISHING THE COMPANY

Training plus Coaching

In 1991, Eva Wong left the Canadian Embassy in China where she had worked for six years as a commercial officer. One of the reasons for her departure was her exposure to a lot of training courses in her work and her passion to become a trainer. Eva Wong graduated from Hong Kong Polytechnic University and holds a degree in management. Before her career at the Embassy, she had worked in accounting and administration. After leaving the Embassy, she worked as a trainer at several training companies in Hong Kong and as a professional trainer in the United States. After facilitating training in Hong Kong for several years, she found that there were some problems in the training content and organizational management of the companies. Eva Wong began to think about solving these problems by starting her own company.

For a newly created training company to succeed, develop, and grow, it needs to have a unique training product. In the initial period, Eva Wong and her then-boyfriend and present husband, Lawrence Leung, and other like-minded friends met frequently to brainstorm various aspects of the training industry and discuss various options for establishing a company. This process of thorough planning and joint contributions, exploring all the possibilities and developing a strategy before taking actions, has become the practice in Top Human. This working style is closely related to the personality of Eva and Lawrence. Eva Wong has an open and straightforward personality and is willing to communicate and share her ideas with others. Her strength lies in her sound listening skills and being able to express her ideas clearly. Lawrence Leung is one who prefers to keep a low profile and is humorous and direct and has keen insight. He is able to inspire others and is a very approachable person. Both Eva Wong and Lawrence Leung have worked for a long time in Hong Kong—the junction of Eastern and Western cultures—and both have a broad international view. They also understand Chinese culture and manners and the domestic market.

It was at this time Eva Wong and the others came into contact with Coaching on the international scene. They discovered that Coaching can effectively adjust people's attitudes and empower and support people to success. In addition, the beliefs underlying Coaching closely fit the Chinese traditional philosophy of Buddhism, Taoism, and Confucianism. It also is similar to the content of modern corporate management. They began to introduce Coaching into Asia. Since there was no unified standard in the world for Coaching, Eva Wong, Lawrence Leung, and others, together with a Russian friend, started to design Coaching Technology© and its related training. They adopted the basic theories of international Coaching and infused these with the of Chinese culture, creating the unique "Training plus Coaching" approach which later became Top Human's main product and service. According to Lawrence Leung, "In the past when China tried to connect with the world in various areas, it always had to adapt to overseas standards, but Coaching was a new profession and industry; there was room to play. In the future, everyone can be on equal footing and define the rules of the game together."

At the heart of the unique Coaching Technology,© principally created by Eva Wong and Lawrence Leung, is building an environment—a special atmosphere where participants can see themselves clearly and their links with their surroundings, and in the process uncover their own potential. For example, during a rope-course challenge training, there are individuals who discover their weaknesses in the process of climbing the pole while others discover their strengths. To individuals who succeed through personal endeavors, the team events at the Outdoor Challenge Center allow them to realize that teamwork can achieve things that are not attainable by individual endeavors. "It is not about teaching them what to do, but rather they discovering and deciding for themselves what to do. Coaching only enables them [to] see a clear reflection of themselves." In the entire course of training, Eva Wong regards herself as a mirror. She feels that modern corporations need more mirrors and that managers need to let their subordinates see their weaknesses and their potential.

The Establishment

In July 1995, Eva Wong, Lawrence Leung, and two other partners jointly invested HKD 750,000 to set up Top Human Technology Limited, with headquarters in Vancouver, Canada. The vision of Top Human was to re-engineer the talent of people and enhance the quality of life through "Training plus Coaching."

When Top Human started in Hong Kong, there was only Eva Wong, a girl who handled the odd jobs, and other friends who frequently came to help Top Human on a voluntary basis. Due to personal interests, one of the partners withdrew from the company. The initial development of the company in Hong Kong was smooth and at the end of 1995, the company had three employees; there were seven employees at the end of 1996 and the company's revenue was more than HKD 7 million. By mid-1997, the company staff reached 12 and that year, the revenue reached HKD 11.5 million, mainly from Hong Kong. Top Human still had the goal to develop the China Mainland market. Although there is a large population in China, the market positioning of Top Human was based on the breadth of the training market as well as Eva Wong's personal experience and understanding of China. While Eva Wong considered herself as a Hongkonger, after many experiences, she realized that she was actually a Chinese. Following her deep understanding of China, she felt a fervent sense of responsibility to the land where she belonged and hoped to contribute something back to the country.

First Site—Guangzhou

In March 1996, Top Human started in the Chinese market in Guangzhou. Guangzhou is not far from Hong Kong and is a large city with most of the people speaking Cantonese, not Mandarin. In addition, a member of the Top Human team, Catherine Ng, who used to be the operating manager for an American shipping company in the province of Guangdong, knew many people in Guangzhou.

Top Human priced its Performance Technology courses in Guangzhou in line with the prices charged in Hong Kong (about RMB 20,000). In the beginning, not many people in Guangzhou understood Top Human's Coaching Technology.© Finally, Top Human had its first course in Guangzhou with only one of the participants being local Chinese. The presence of Hong Kong's participants in these Guangzhou courses played a vital role in the development of the market in Guangzhou. One of Top Human's sales strategies was to find successful people who are usually more comfortable with risk-taking and have a higher probability of having development problems. These successful people were usually at the heart of some network and their sharing of their experience helped Top Human create a market. For example, after one person from the advertising industry became Top Human's client, many in the industry followed. In addition, people who came in contact with these advertising individuals were generally from the management of their company, which further increased the development. This greatly shortened the market development time. By mid-1998, Top Human had four full-time staff in Guangzhou; at the end of 1998, this increased to six.

Some companies, such as Robust Group and TCL Computers, became clients and a few incorporated Coaching into the management of their companies. For example, Fu Jie of Guangzhou Jiu Yi Advertising Ltd. applied Corporate Coaching in leading his team to create a television commercial themed, "The world is but a little place, after all" for China Mobile. This advertisement won a First Place Mobius Statuette in the Television Commercial Category in the 30th Mobius Advertising Awards held in Chicago.

Expansion to Shenzhen

Top Human's business in Guangzhou continued to expand and people from around the vicinity came to Guangzhou for training. There were some Guangzhou-trained participants who volunteered to attract other participants and arranged training venues in places around Guangzhou such as Shenzhen. To adapt to Shenzhen, where Mandarin is the main language, Top Human requested all its staff learn Mandarin and changed the language used in training to Mandarin. Top Human soon discovered not only was Shenzhen a substantial market for Coaching, it also had influence throughout China. Shenzhen has new industry, more high technology, companies, and most companies having a short history and rapid development. The population is young, highly educated, with contemporary ideas and a strong learning ability.

The development of business in Shenzhen shifted the emphasis of the company from Hong Kong to Shenzhen. To handle the business development in Shenzhen, Top Human transferred some key personnel to Shenzhen. In mid-1999, Top Human staff in Shenzhen reached six people, [the] same as Guangzhou. At the end of 1999, the staff was 12, exceeding the 8 people in Guangzhou. Top Human's number of employees in Shenzhen and Guangzhou (20 people) exceeded the number in the Hong Kong Office (19 people). In mid-2001, half the company manpower was located in Shenzhen as was the management for the entire company. Hong Kong stayed the company's technical development base and Guangzhou became a local market office.

Moving into Shanghai

In Shenzhen, Top Human wanted to develop a market with a vast area of geographical coverage. The early market exploration outside Shenzhen and Guangzhou was initiated by the clients. Top Human tried to start a Coaching service in Kunming and Taiyuan, but the result was not good because the standard of economic development in the mid-western region was too low.

The coastal economic development zones consist of the Pearl River Delta, the Yangtze River Delta, and the Bohai Bay area. The interior of the Pearl River Delta region is closely linked, is accessible, and has a similar culture; the Shenzhen and Guangzhou branch offices can cover that entire region. Top Human began to consider entering Shanghai—the hub of the Yangtze River Delta region. To Zhejiang and others along the Yangtze River, Shanghai had a strong growing influence. Some people in Top Human felt that the company was not familiar with the culture of Eastern China and should stay and build its present base to avoid spreading the manpower and resources too thin. Eva Wong and Lawrence Leung thought that the sooner they entered Shanghai, the better able Top Human would be to become a nationwide brand name. Eva Wong also had personal ties with Shanghai. Top Human entered Shanghai in the beginning of 2001. "Since I was young under the influence of my mother, I've always had an indescribable yearning for my hometown Shanghai," Eva Wong stated. Eva finds the people in Shanghai more diplomatic, more careful, and take a long time to build trust.

The first step that Top Human took when it went into Shanghai was to employ six local people and send them to Shenzhen for comprehensive Coaching training and to assimilate into the company's culture. Second, the company modified its existing Coaching case studies as the Coaching examples that appeal to the people in Southern China would not be of interest to people in Shanghai. Third, when Top Human applied for a business license in Shanghai, it found that the business scope of human capital development had no precedence in the past. After going through a lot of effort, Top Human finally got the first foreign enterprise business license for human capital development in Shanghai.

The brand name of Top Human, very well known in Southern China, did not enjoy the same degree of recognition in Eastern China. To propel Top Human into a brand name in China, the company organized the Inaugural Coaching Forum in China. Top Human also got involved with various forums and seminars, such as the seminar "The Winning Way" jointly organized with Yang Cheng Wan Bao "Jobs Classified" in June 2000. After the Shanghai Forum, organizing large forums became a new area of company business.

Establishing the Corporate Technology Department and Its Restructuring

In 1998, the Hong Kong telecommunication industry did not have favorable sales and China Motion was forced to adjust employees' salaries to cut costs; simultaneously the company introduced the "CM Concept" to meet the growing popularity of mobile phones. China Motion wanted to expand its retail arm, from simply retailing pagers to selling an entire series of telecommunication products. The company was afraid that the change from a system of fixed salary to an adjustable salary would decrease the company morale and result in a major loss of staff. China Motion decided to use training to increase staff morale and help in the repositioning.

Even though there were many domestic and overseas training companies taking part in the bidding, China Motion selected Top Human. Top Human conducted a workshop, "Service from the Heart," for China Motion employees and sent three coaches to coach China Motion's over 20 retail supervisors, with the support of two other senior coaches. Top Human senior coaches interacted with the senior management of China Motion every month. Top Human coaches also held meetings with China Motion staff on a regular basis. The close-knit cooperation between the two parties resulted in the successful repositioning of China Motion and the "CM Concept" has been introduced in many cities inside China. The managing director for China Motion then, Mr. Xiao Weidan, said: "The sales figures have increased twofold in a short period of three months. At the same time, our company supervisors have shown considerable improvement in their leadership ability and the warmth displayed by our customer relations officers towards the clients has also greatly improved. . . ."

The use of Coaching for customized corporate training in the case of China Motion was a huge success, and Top Human set up a Corporate Technology Department that was independent of the Performance Technology Department. Manpower was arranged in Hong Kong, Guangzhou, and Shenzhen to develop the business in corporate management. However there was limited success in the Corporate Technology Department. By

March 2000, the staff in the department went from eight to six people.

In the same year, Top Human restructured the Corporate Technology Department and put a full-time professional in charge. Second, the company had the department run the newly constructed Outdoor Challenge Center. Third, the staff in the department was increased to 20 people. Finally the department would actively coordinate with the Performance Technology Department to make full use of the client network to develop its market. In a short period of time, the Top Human Corporate Technology Department had a big improvement and increased its customized workshop topics, including such new ones as: Team Dynamics, Leadership Skills, Communication Skills, Sales Mastery, Creativity, and Innovation.

THE COMPANY CULTURE

A lot of people who come into contact with Top Human are very surprised that the company has been progressing rapidly and aggressively through exploring new activities and has not yet met any major hurdles. Why is it that with such a heavy workload, Top Human employees still maintain their high morale and commit to their job with passion?

Top Human's steady and rapid development and soaring morale are largely due to its use of Coaching in its own company management. At the same time that Top Human is helping other companies become learning organizations through Coaching, it is striving to ensure that Top Human itself has in place the various mechanisms needed to become a real learning organization (shared vision, equal partners, insightful discussion, and the ability to focus inwards).

Shared Vision

Vision is the collective manifestation of the cultural values, interests, and ambitions of the members in the organization. Top Human uses vision in hiring its company employees. However, Top Human's vision is neither the vision of its top management nor one formed from a strategy. Rather through Top Human associates expressing their dreams and listening to other people's dreams, the vision is the result of the true opinions and knowledge and the belief that faith generates from this exchange process. Eva Wong and Lawrence Leung are willing to communicate their thoughts and ideas with the staff, and seek their understanding and support while listening and absorbing their views.

Not only is Top Human good at using vision to enroll and empower its employees, it also places emphasis on breaking the vision down into qualitative goals and measurable targets to guide the effectiveness of the company's operations. The feedback mechanism linking such a corporate vision, quantification of goals, and actual means of operations allows the fine-tuning process to continuously occur.

The Atmosphere for Learning

The core of Top Human's Coaching Technology is to create an atmosphere where the participants can develop their own mental models to equip themselves and to adjust their attitudes. Top Human has been consciously developing an environment for learning inside its own organization. It expects every department manager to be able to take up the role of a coach and adjust the attitude of his or her department staff, to allow everyone to face their work with the correct attitude and to see the opportunities in their daily work where they can improve their own qualities and abilities. One of the primary roles of a manager is to be a coach for subordinates, with the responsibility of using coaching tools and techniques to help others improve their effectiveness, making the role of Top Human management more of a supporter than a controller. Correspondingly, the role of staff members has also switched from one of taking orders to taking responsibility.

Apart from focusing its attention on forming some integral mechanisms, Top Human took other measures to strengthen this relationship of equal partners. For example, people address each other by their English names, even top management. For instance, Eva Wong is "Eva" and Lawrence Leung is "Lawrence." The office layout of Top Human is based on an open concept. Eva Wong and Lawrence Leung did not give themselves extremely luxurious offices but rather go around to interact with other staff. To eliminate the boss-related complex and culture that are present in most companies, Eva Wong and Lawrence Leung started early to convert the ownership of Top Human into a shareholders' system, and to lower themselves from the position of "bosses" to the position of company shareholders and management. Important decisions are decided through the board of directors. The employees of Top Human have the opportunity to become company shareholders and this greatly strengthens their sense of belonging. In company meetings, Eva Wong and Lawrence Leung seldom persist with their ideas or defend their position, but carefully regulate the atmosphere of discussion, ensuring that the discussions end in more fruitful results.

Focusing Inward

Shared vision, equal partners, insightful discussion, and other such components of a Learning Organization established a solid groundwork where members of the organization have the ability and attitude to focus inwards, self-reflect, and self-improve. The management of Top Human, who are really concerned for the members in their organization, let the employees realize the difficulties encountered, actively ponder and find a solution, and make a difficult situation an opportunity for the employees to self-reflect, develop their abilities, and achieve personal growth. In a newly developed market, Eva Wong will personally interview prospective employees. During the interview, she looks for their ability to be molded, to express and to be distinct, their sense of mission towards their career, and their academic qualifications. Eva Wong also frequently uses her own experience to coach the staff in overcoming their own limitations. After her divorce, Eva Wong spent one year by herself traveling across Europe and the Middle East; the trip allowed her to see the world outside her original narrow social circle as a traditional career woman. She went through a very difficult adjustment process. Leaving behind her comfortable job as a commercial officer at the Canadian Embassy and stepping into the training line, Eva Wong similarly experienced a long period of adjustment and exploration in her mind before she successfully established and developed Top Human.

Common Societal Model

Top Human's shared vision, equal partners, insightful discussions, and the use of other such mechanisms is not just restricted to its employees. Top Human extends the use of such mechanisms to its clients and other relevant bodies such as its franchise partners.

One unique feature in Top Human is its associate coaches, who are essential to the entire operations of Top Human. Top Human's associate coaches are all clients who have taken part in Top Human's training; the associate coaches dedicate their service and support to help new participants get into form faster. In this way, associate coaches can apply and practice their newly learned coaching techniques and tools and improve the core of their coaching ability—the ability to enroll and convince.

Top Human is also very concerned about the maintenance of the network among clients. For example, Top Human specially opened up chat rooms on the company's Web site to promote communication between the company and the participants and among the participants themselves. Top Human diligently monitors the progress of the client's development and continuously seeks to expand the number of case studies from the successful individuals among its clients. Publicizing these successful figures and their success stories through various forms of media is a living testament to the effects of Coaching Technology.

Ever since Top Human entered the China market, it has not done any advertising to promote its business. Eva Wong thinks that Coaching is a concept that can only be understood through personal experience, making it hard to accurately portray the essence of Coaching through advertisements. The dissemination by word-of-mouth from loyal, satisfied participants has become the main method of advertising for Top Human.

Organizational Design

The organizational development of Top Human has gone through three stages. The first stage was before the expansion of business in Shenzhen, where Top Human's organizational structure centered around the development of the training business and the structure of the company was like a training department. The second stage was after Top Human set up its subsidiary company in Shenzhen and the company started to build a corporate management structure and the corresponding departments (see Exhibit 3). The third stage followed the company's expansion to various regions. Top Human implemented a series of adjustments which resulted in the organizational structure indicated in Exhibit 4.

Establishing the Knowledge Management Department

Along with the gradual acceptance of the new concept of Coaching Technology by the market, some past participants started to enter the corporate coaching market. Two coaching companies emerged in Guangzhou.

EXHIBIT 3 Top Human Organizational Structure (June 2001)

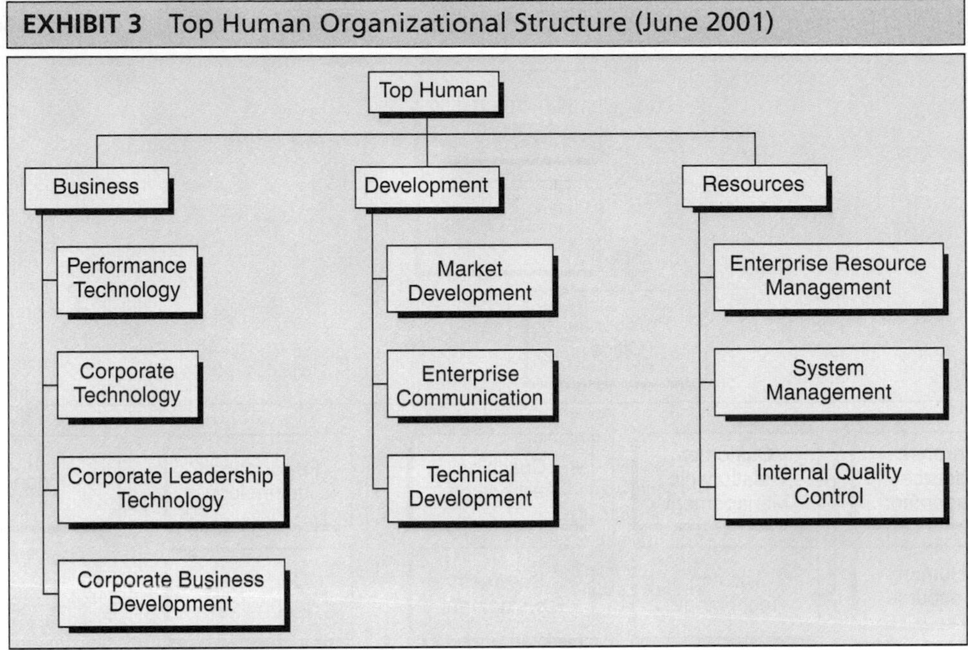

Top Human was concerned that these competitors might not be able to provide a high quality of service, which would affect the image of Coaching and negatively impact the healthy development of the Coaching industry.

Top Human felt that a fundamental strategy to ensure the company's competitive edge and to establish a good reputation for the Coaching industry was to constantly innovate, making it difficult for competitors to copy. Top Human set up a knowledge management and product development department in Hong Kong and started planning for the establishment of the Coaching Technology Research Institute. The main objective of this technical development department was to innovate in the training content, to manage the flow of internal knowledge, and to develop new services for the company. The department was also responsible for training company employees to ensure that the standards of the company trainers were the highest in the industry. New services were developed, tested, and adjusted in the mature market of Hong Kong before being introduced in the mainland market.

The company also wants to establish the Coaching Technology Research Institute, the first one in the world, by partnering with reputable institutions in the country. The Institute would sponsor relevant scholastic research and nurture masters- and doctorate-level researchers.

Establishing Specialized Departments

To increase the image and business of Top Human, the company established an Enterprise Communication Department. The mission of Top Human's Enterprise Communication Department is to promote Top Human's image and make Coaching Technology better known through such things as: organizing the international forum related to Coaching Technology; having "The Human Resource Journey" exhibition; and publishing Coaching-related books.

Although the coaching business is still in the growth stage, Top Human will need to have new services and businesses if the company wants to grow in the future. To accomplish this, Top Human established the Strategic Market Development Department to develop the company's overall strategy and find new areas of business for the company.

Top Human also established the Enterprise Resource Management Department to control the use of funds and resources. Investment plans are carefully formulated before being presented to the board of directors and the

EXHIBIT 4 Top Human Organizational Structure (January 2002) (excluding regional framework)

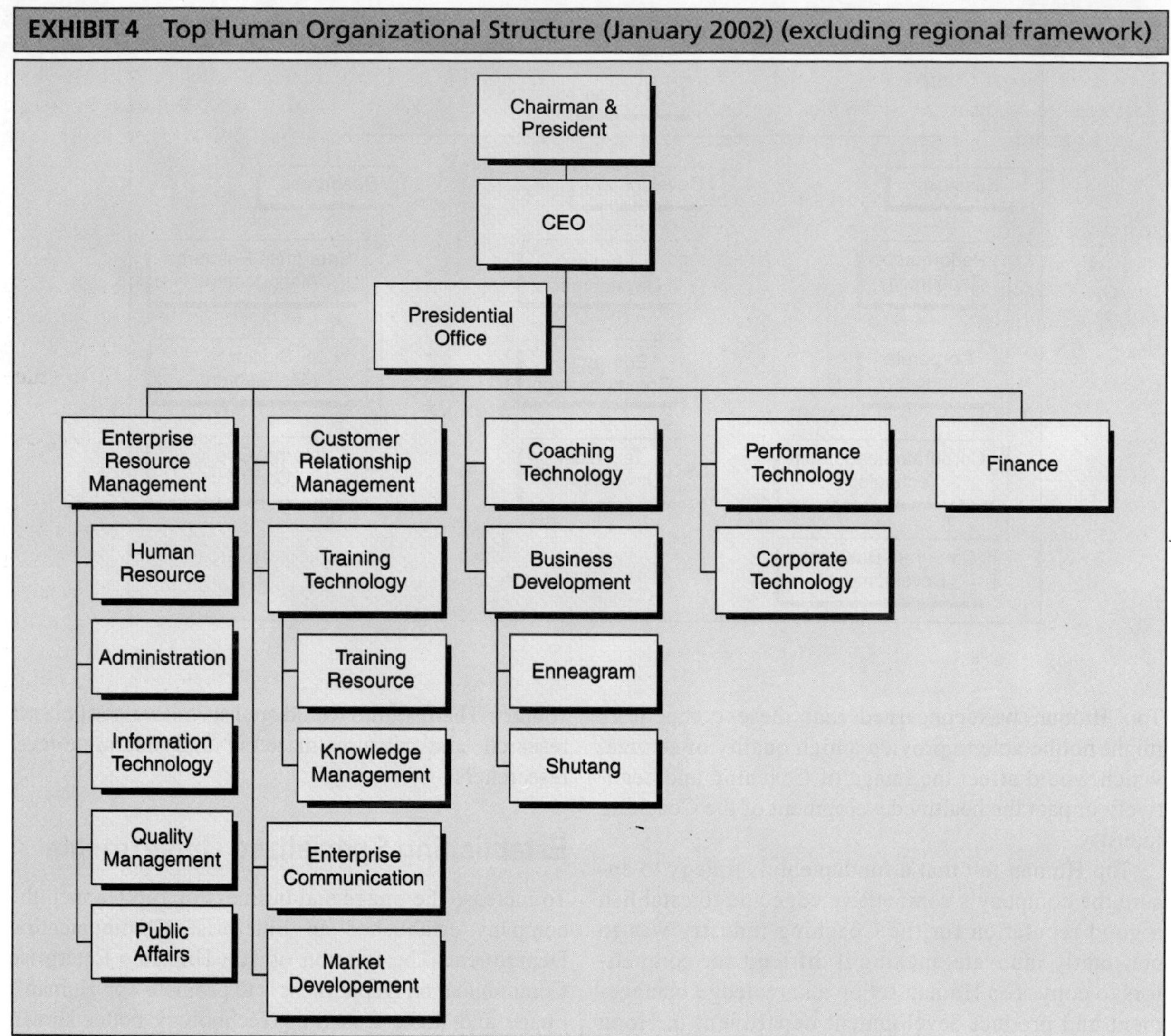

company is planning to become listed on a stock exchange, perhaps in the United States.

The Presidential Office

Eva Wong and Lawrence Leung are coaches as well as company managers, and the growth of the company has significantly increased their workload. The initial objective of setting up the Presidential Office was to lighten this workload and enhance the communication inside and outside the company. However, the Presidential Office has become an incubator for training and new business development. Eva Wong and Lawrence Leung started to train some staff in the Presidential Office and share their management ideals and development goals.

DEVELOPMENT OF THE BRAND AND IMAGE

The brand name of Top Human has been developed through: the Enterprise Communication Department, the choice of office locations, through the organization of various charitable activities, and by doing community work. Top Human continually establishes the "Coaching Brand" and portrays the company as the pioneer and the industry leader for corporate coaching in Asia. In March 2001, Top Human and the Zhongshan University MBA Centre signed a memorandum of understanding to train the university's MBAs and introduce Coaching Technology into the university system in China.

The company also introduced the Coaching Competency Certification Program (CCCP) to train corporate coaches. At the start of 1998, Top Human's board of directors decided to start the implementation of the ISO 9002 Quality Management System to improve its service quality to make the company's operations more systematic and scientific.

In February 2000, Top Human opened its newly constructed Outdoor Challenge Center at Shenzhen Xili Lake Holiday Resort, the first in the country that conformed to international standards. The obstacles at the challenge center include the Pamper Pole, Dangle Duo, Climbing Wall, and Cat Walk among the 10 high elements, and its 17 low element activities include TP Shuffle, Amazon River, Electric Fence, and Initiative Wall. At present, the center is one of the largest outdoor challenge centers in China with comprehensive facilities.

Outdoor challenge training allows the participants to participate in a series of interesting and challenging low and high elements in the outdoor environment, in order to gain a deeper self-understanding, discover one's potential, break through one's existing thinking model, and learn to deal with fear. Outdoor challenge training is a form of experiential learning through interaction.

Sales and Employees

Top Human has steadily grown since 2001. In 2004 Top Human had turnover at HKD 66 million with an additional HKD 12 million coming from franchisees. While the turnover was about the same for 2005, the revenue from franchisees increased to HKD 15 million (see Table 1). The number of employees increased from 3 people in 1995 to 91 employees by 2001 (see Table 2).

As is indicated in Table 3, in a short span of five years, Top Human has trained tens of thousands of people from such companies as: Guangzhou Materials Group, Konka Group, Robust Group, China Motion Concept Limited, Legend Computers, TCL Computer Technology Co. Ltd., Cathay Pacific Airways, Shenzhen Party School of the Chinese Communist Party, Guangzhou Zhongshan University MBA Centre, American International Assurance Company, Conlia Limited, and Sun Microsystems.

TABLE 1 Top Human Annual Income (000 RMB)

			Branches		
RMB' 000	**2001**	**2002**	**2003**	**2004**	**2005**
Coaching Technology 1	¥17,577	¥10,445	¥13,397	¥25,150	¥21,858
Coaching Technology 2	¥13,528	¥ 8,581	¥11,106	¥17,867	¥14,810
Technology in Action	¥ 4,404	¥ 2,480	¥ 4,314	¥ 7,727	¥ 7,989
Coaching Principal	¥ 3,949	¥ 4,960	¥ 5,309	¥11,031	¥12,453
Corporate Technology			¥ 5,190	¥ 4,529	¥ 9,373
Total	**¥39,457**	**¥26,465**	**¥39,316**	**¥66,305**	**¥66,483**
			Franchisees		
RMB' 000	**2001**	**2002**	**2003**	**2004**	**2005**
Coaching Technology 1				¥ 4,405	¥ 5,314
Coaching Technology 2				¥ 3,528	¥ 4,025
Technology in Action				¥ 1,608	¥ 2,104
Coaching Principal				¥ 2,373	¥ 3,807
Total				**¥11,914**	**¥15,250**

TABLE 2 Top Human Employee Distribution by Geographical Region

	Total	Hong Kong	%	Guangzhou	%	Shenzhen	%	Shanghai	%	Beijing	%
Dec 1995	3	3	100.0%	0	0.0%	0	0.0%	0	0.0%		
Jun 1996	5	5	100.0%	0	0.0%	0	0.0%	0	0.0%		
Dec 1996	7	7	100.0%	0	0.0%	0	0.0%	0	0.0%		
Jun 1997	12	12	100.0%	0	0.0%	0	0.0%	0	0.0%		
Dec 1997	13	13	100.0%	0	0.0%	0	0.0%	0	0.0%		
Jun 1998	21	17	81.0%	4	19.0%	0	0.0%	0	0.0%		
Dec 1998	20	14	70.0%	6	30.0%	0	0.0%	0	0.0%		
Jun 1999	28	16	57.1%	6	21.4%	6	21.4%	0	0.0%		
Dec 1999	39	19	48.7%	8	20.5%	12	30.8%	0	0.0%		
Jun 2000	62	26	41.9%	14	22.6%	22	35.5%	0	0.0%		
Dec 2000	83	27	32.5%	15	18.1%	35	42.2%	6	7.2%		
Jun 2001	91	16	17.6%	19	20.9%	48	52.7%	9	9.9%		
Dec 2001	109	14	12.8%	20	18.3%	56	51.4%	19	17.4%		
Jun 2002	107	16	15.0%	21	19.6%	48	44.9%	22	20.6%		
Dec 2002	115	20	17.4%	21	18.3%	45	39.1%	29	25.2%		
Jun 2003	133	21	15.8%	20	15.0%	59	44.4%	33	24.8%		
Dec 2003	147	3	2.0%	20	13.6%	78	53.1%	35	23.8%	11	7.5%
Jun 2004	172	2	1.2%	19	11.0%	82	47.7%	49	28.5%	20	11.6%
Dec 2004	212	2	0.9%	30	14.2%	88	41.5%	63	29.7%	29	13.7%
Jun 2005	282	2	0.7%	29	10.3%	121	42.9%	88	31.2%	42	14.9%
Nov 2005	285	2	0.7%	33	11.6%	121	42.5%	85	29.8%	44	15.4%

TABLE 3 Number of People Attending Top Human Training

Main Branches	**2001**	**2002**	**2003**	**2004**	**2005**
Coaching Technology 1	3,988	3,452	3,233	5,461	4,747
Coaching Technology 2	1,628	1,499	1,423	2,131	1,764
Technology in Action	1,099	951	889	1,337	1,258
Coaching Principal	512	816	726	1,389	1,473
Corporate Technology					
Total	**7,227**	**6,718**	**6,271**	**10,318**	**9,242**
Satellite Offices	**2001**	**2002**	**2003**	**2004**	**2005**
Coaching Technology 1				1,127	1,217
Coaching Technology 2				459	516
Technology in Action				329	348
Corporate Technology				338	481
Total				**2,253**	**2,562**

END NOTES

1. Modified from the Web site of Legacy Consulting.
2. Clientelling is the process of gathering data about an individual customer's buying habits and preferences during interactions in the store, typically applied in high-end or luxury retail stores.
3. 2000 National Retail Security Survey.
4. SMA stands for software maintenance, which is a recurring annual fee that virtually all clients pay for that provides the right to any bug corrections at no additional charge, as well as the right to receive upgrades to the software as new and improved versions are released. The typical fee is 15 percent of all license fees and customization fees paid to Datavantage; therefore, this amount can increase as the client purchases more licenses or pays for more customization.

INDEX

Page numbers followed by n indicate notes.

C

E

M

O

P

T

U

V

W

X

Y

Z